Learning Resources
Centre

D0301319

THE CAMBRIDGE HISTORY OF Greek and Roman Political Thought

THE CAMBRIDGE HISTORY OF Greek and Roman Political Thought

*

Edited by

CHRISTOPHER ROWE
PROFESSOR OF GREEK
UNIVERSITY OF DURHAM

and

MALCOLM SCHOFIELD
PROFESSOR OF ANCIENT PHILOSOPHY
UNIVERSITY OF CAMBRIDGE

in association with

SIMON HARRISON
FELLOW OF ST JOHN'S COLLEGE
CAMBRIDGE

and

MELISSA LANE
UNIVERSITY LECTURER IN HISTORY
UNIVERSITY OF CAMBRIDGE

CAMBRIDGE
UNIVERSITY PRESS

PUBLISHED BY THE PRESS SYNDICATE OF THE UNIVERSITY OF CAMBRIDGE
The Pitt Building, Trumpington Street, Cambridge, United Kingdom

CAMBRIDGE UNIVERSITY PRESS
The Edinburgh Building, Cambridge CB2 2RU, UK http://www.cup.cam.ac.uk
40 West 20th Street, New York, NY 10011-4211, USA http://www.cup.org
10 Stamford Road, Oakleigh, Melbourne 3166, Australia

First published 2000

Printed in the United Kingdom at the University Press, Cambridge

Typeface TEFF Renard 9.5/12.75 pt *System* QuarkXPress® [SE]

A catalogue record for this book is available from the British Library

Library of Congress cataloguing in publication data
The Cambridge History of Greek and Roman Political Thought / edited by
Christopher Rowe and Malcolm Schofield.
p. cm.
Includes bibliographical references and index.
ISBN 0 521 48136 8
1. Political science – Greece – History. 2. Political science –
Rome – History. I. Rowe, Christopher. II. Schofield, Malcolm.
JC51.C294 2000 320′.0938–dc21 99-28162 CIP

ISBN 0 521 48136 8 hardback

Contents

SOCRATES AND PLATO

Maps

Preface

The Editors take this opportunity of thanking all who have helped to make this volume a reality. First among them are the contributing authors, who mostly delivered copy in good order on time – and where not, without too great a delay. Many gave up the time to discuss each others' drafts and to attempt to agree a common house style at an enjoyable workshop held in Corpus Christi College, Oxford, in September 1995. Apologies are accordingly due for editorial delays in preparing their work for the printer. Secondly, with the contributors we salute our successive Associate Editors, Melissa Lane and Simon Harrison, whose energy, enthusiasm and efficiency have been indispensable to the success of the project. Finally, we express our gratitude to all at the Press who have been involved in the production of the book, and above all to Pauline Hire, who has simultaneously nagged and encouraged us until we finished.

CJR · MS
January 1999

Abbreviations

Acronyms are used for modern series or collections of texts as follows:

C *Code* [of Justinian] = *Corpus iuris civilis*, vol. II (Berlin)
CCSL *Corpus Christianorum*, Series Latina (Turnholt)
CIL *Corpus Inscriptionum Latinarum*
CPF *Corpus dei Papyri Filosofici Greci e Latini*: Testi e lessico nei papiri di cultura greca e latina, Accademica Toscana di Scienze e Lettere "La Colombaria" (Florence 1989–)
CSEL *Corpus Scriptorum Ecclesiasticorum Latinorum* (Vienna and Leipzig)
D *Digest* = *Corpus iuris civilis*, vol. I (Berlin)
DK H. Diels and W. Kranz, *Die Fragmente der Vorsokratiker*, 2 vols., sixth edition (Berlin 1951–2)
GCS *Die griechischen christlichen Schriftsteller*, Berlin Academy (Berlin)
GP B. Gentili and C. Prato, *Poetarum elegiacorum testimonia et fragmenta*, vol. I (Leipzig 1988)
IG *Inscriptiones Graecae* (Berlin 1873–)
KRS G. S. Kirk, J. E. Raven, and M. Schofield, *The Presocratic Philosophers* (Cambridge, 2nd edn. 1983)
Migne, PG/PL J.-P. Migne, *Patrologiae cursus completus*, Series Graecus/Latinus (Paris)
ML R. Meiggs and D. Lewis, *A Selection of Greek Historical Inscriptions to the End of the Fifth Century* BC (Oxford, rev. edn. 1988)
NPNF *Nicene and Post-Nicene Fathers* (Grand Rapids MI 1975–)
P D. L. Page, *Poetae Melici Graeci* (Oxford 1962)
SC *Sources Chrétiennes* (Paris)
SVF J. von Arnim, *Stoicorum Veterum Fragmenta*, 3 vols. (Leipzig 1903–5)
W M. L. West, *Iambi et elegi Graeci ante Alexandrum cantati*, 2 vols. (Oxford, 2nd edn. 1992)

Abbreviations of the names and writings of Greek and Latin authors generally follow standard forms, usually but not invariably those adopted in *A Greek–English Lexicon*, by H. G. Liddell and R. Scott, revised by H. S. Jones (Oxford, 9th edn. 1925–40) [= LSJ] and in *A Latin Dictionary*, by C. T. Lewis and C. Short (Oxford 1879). Many of those used in this book are immediately intelligible from the context. Others which may not be are:

Aelian *Ver.Hist.*	Aelian	*Vera Historia*
Arist. *An.Pr.*	Aristotle	*Analytica Priora*

Ath. Pol.		*Athēnaiōn Politeia*
Cael.		*de Caelo*
Cat.		*Categories*
de An.		*de Anima*
EE		*Eudemian Ethics*
EN		*Nicomachean Ethics*
GA		*de Generatione Animalium*
GC		*de Generatione et Corruptione*
HA		*Historia Animalium*
Metaph.		*Metaphysics*
Meteor.		*Meteorology*
MM		*Magna Moralia*
PA		*de Partibus Animalium*
Phys.		*Physics*
Pol.		*Politics*
Rhet.		*Rhetoric*
Somn.		*de Somno*
Top.		*Topics*
Athen. *Deipn.*	Athenaeus	*Deipnosophistae*
August. *CD*	Augustine	*de Civitate Dei* (*City of God*)
C. Iul.		*Contra Julianum*
Retract.		*Retractationes*
Caesar *Civ.*	Julius Caesar	*de Bello Civili*
Cic. *Acad.*	Cicero	*Academica*
ad Brut.		*Letters to Brutus*
Agr.		*de Lege Agraria*
Amic.		*de Amicitia*
Att.		*Letters to Atticus*
Balb.		*pro Balbo*
Brut.		*Brutus*
Clu.		*pro Cluentio*
de Orat.		*de Oratore*
Div.		*de Divinatione*
Fam.		*Letters to his friends*
Fin.		*de Finibus*
Inv.		*de Inventione*
Leg.		*de Legibus*
Lig.		*pro Ligario*
Man.		*pro Lege Manilia*
ND		*de Natura Deorum*
Off.		*de Officiis*
Orat.		*Orator*
Phil.		*Philippics*
Planc.		*pro Plancio*
Q.Fr.		*Letters to his brother Quintus*
Rab.Post.		*pro Rabirio Postumo*

Rep.		*de Re Publica*
Sest.		*pro Sestio*
Tim.		*Timaeus*
Tusc.		*Tusculan Disputations*
Clem. *Strom.*	Clement	*Stromateis* (*Miscellanies*)
D.Chr. *Or.*	Dio Chrysostom	*Orationes*
D.L.	Diogenes Laertius	
Dem.	Demosthenes	
Demetr. *de Eloc.*	Demetrius	*de Elocutione* (*On Style*)
Epict. *Diss.*	Epictetus	*Dissertationes* (*Discourses*)
Ench.		*Encheiridion* (*Handbook*)
Epicurus *KD*	Epicurus	*Kuriai Doxai* (*Key Doctrines*)
Sent.Vat.		*Vatican Sentences*
Epiphan. *Adv.Haer.*	Epiphanius	*Against Heresies*
Eusebius *Hist.Eccl.*	Eusebius	*Church History*
Fronto *ad M.Caes.*	Fronto	*Letters to the Emperor Marcus*
Hdt.	Herodotus	
[Heraclit.] *Ep.*		*Letters* ascribed to Heraclitus
Iambl. *VPyth.*	Iamblichus	*On the Pythagorean Life*
Isid. *Etym.*	Isidore	*Etymologiae*
Isoc.	Isocrates	
Julian *Ep. Them.*	Julian	*Letter to Themistius*
Ep. Theodor.		*Letter to Theodorus*
Frag. Ep.		*Fragments of his Correspondence*
Or.		*Orations*
Lact. *Inst.*	Lactantius	*Divine Institutes*
Liv.	Livy	
Macrobius *Sat.*	Macrobius	*Saturnalia*
Somn.		*The Dream of Scipio*
Nepos *Att.*	Nepos	*Life of Atticus*
Olymp. *Prol.*	Olympiodorus	*Prolegomena to Platonic Philosophy*
Orig. *Cels.*	Origen	*Against Celsus*
Ph. *Abr.*	Philo	*On Abraham*
Cher.		*On the Cherubim*
Deter.		*Quod deterius potiori insidiari soleat*
Fug.		*de Fuga et Inventione*
Immut.		*Quod Deus est immutabilis*
Jos.		*On Joseph*
Leg.		*Legum allegoriae*
Legat.		*Legatio ad Gaium*
Migr.		*de Migratione Abrahamae*
Mos.		*On the Life of Moses*
Opif.		*de Opificio Mundi*
Poster.		*de Posteritate Caini*
Quaest.Ex.		*Questions and Solutions on Exodus*
Quaest.Gen.		*Questions and Solutions on Genesis*

Somn.		*de Somniis*
Spec.		*de Specialibus Legibus*
Virt.		*On the Virtues*
Phld. *Ind.Acad.*	Philodemus	*Index of the Academy*
Piet.		*On Piety*
Stoic.		*On the Stoics*
Phot. *Bibl.*	Photius	*Bibliotheca*
Pl. *Ap.*	Plato	*Apology*
Chrm.		*Charmides*
Cr.		*Crito*
Crat.		*Cratylus*
Ep.		*Letters*
Euthd.		*Euthydemus*
Euthphr.		*Euthyphro*
Gorg.		*Gorgias*
Hi.Mi.		*Hippias Minor*
La.		*Laches*
Lys.		*Lysias*
Menex.		*Menexenus*
Phd.		*Phaedo*
Phdr.		*Phaedrus*
Plt.		*Politicus (Statesman)*
Prm.		*Parmenides*
Prot.		*Protagoras*
Rep.		*Republic*
Smp.		*Symposium*
Sph.		*Sophist*
Tht.		*Theaetetus*
Tim.		*Timaeus*
Plb.	Polybius	
Pliny *Nat.*	Pliny the elder	*Natural History*
Pliny *Ep.*	Pliny the younger	*Letters*
Pan.		*Panegyricus*
Plu. *ad Princ.*	Plutarch	*To an uneducated ruler*
Alex.		*Life of Alexander*
Alex.Fort.		*The luck or virtue of Alexander*
Amat.		*Amatorius (Erōtikos)*
An Recte		*An recte dictum sit latenter est vivendum*
An Seni		*Should the elderly engage in politics?*
Arist.		*Life of Aristides*
Cat.Mai.		*Life of Cato the elder*
Cic.		*Life of Cicero*
Col.		*Against Colotes*
Comm.Not.		*de Communibus Notitiis*
de Frat.Amor.		*de Fraterno Amore*

de Is. et Or.		*On Isis and Osiris*
de Sera		*de Sera Numinis Vindicta*
de Unius		*de Unius in Re Publica Dominatione*
de Virt.Mor.		*de Virtute Morali*
Demetr.		*Life of Demetrius*
Fragm. de Libid. et Aegr.		*Fragments on pleasure and illness*
Lyc.		*Life of Lycurgus*
Max. cum Princ.		*Why the philosopher should especially converse with rulers*
Num.		*Life of Numa*
Phoc.		*Life of Phocion*
Praec.		*Advice on Politics*
Quaest.Conv.		*Quaestiones Conviviales*
Rom.		*Life of Romulus*
Stoic.Rep.		*de Stoicis Repugnantiis*
Tranq.An.		*de Tranquillitate Animi*
Porph. *Abst.*	Porphyry	*On Abstinence*
Marc.		*To Marcella*
Ps.Xen. *Ath.Pol.*	Pseudo-Xenophon	*Constitution of Athens*
Quint. *Inst.*	Quintilian	*Institutiones*
Sal. *Cat.*	Sallust	*Catiline*
Jug.		*Bellum Jugurthinum*
Sen. *Suas.*	Seneca the elder	*Suasoriae*
Sen. *Apoc.*	Seneca the younger	*Apocolocyntosis*
Ben.		*de Beneficiis*
Brev.Vit.		*de Brevitate Vitae*
Clem.		*de Clementia*
Cons.Marc.		*Consolatio ad Marciam*
Const.Sap.		*de Constantia Sapientis*
Ep.		*Letters*
Tranq.An.		*de Tranquillitate Animi*
Sextus *M*	Sextus Empiricus	*adversus Mathematicos*
PH		*Outlines of Pyrrhonism*
SHA	*Scriptores Historiae Augustae*	
Stob.	Stobaeus (John of Stobi)	
Tac. *Ann.*	Tacitus	*Annales*
Hist.		*Historiae*
Theod. *Cur.*	Theodoret	*Graecarum Affectionum Curatio*
Thuc.	Thucydides	
V. Max.	Valerius Maximus	
Vell.	Velleius Paterculus	

Introduction

CHRISTOPHER ROWE

The purpose of this volume is to provide a fresh, critical account of Greek and Roman political thought from its beginnings to the point at which *The Cambridge History of Medieval Political Thought* takes up the story, i.e. c. AD 350. The choice of this date is obviously to some extent arbitrary: there is no implication that 'Greek and Roman' political thinking then suddenly stops short, to be replaced by some entirely new way of thinking about political issues (the 'medieval'). The latter sections of the volume, and the Epilogue, make clear the continuities, as well as the discontinuities, in political thought between the 'ancient' and the 'medieval' periods. Indeed, as the readers of the present *History* may discover, it is a moot question whether the discontinuities here are more significant than, for example, those between Greek and Roman 'periods', or better[1] the 'Classical' and the 'Hellenistic' (beginning with the death of Alexander in the last quarter of the fourth century BC). The political triumph of Christianity over the Greco-Roman world – when for the first time an official, monotheistic, religion came to occupy centre-stage – was certainly momentous. But the changes in the political environment after the fourth century BC were themselves massive. What is striking in both cases is the extent to which political theorizing, if not political thought in the wider sense, remains comparatively, and remarkably, conservative, working as much by selection, adaptation and modification as by downright innovation.

The distinction between 'political thought' and 'political theory' is an important one. 'Political thought', the broader of the two categories, forms the subject of this volume. 'Political theory' represents direct, systematic reflection on things political; but it is of course possible to think politically – to reflect on political actions, or institutions – without doing so systematically or philosophically,[2] and such thinking may be

[1] See below.

[2] Philosophical thinking about politics is likely to include, among other things, some second-order reflection about what it is to think politically, and about the nature and possibility of political knowledge; it will also tend to work at a more general level than practical thinking that responds to actual situations and events.

expressed, as it was in the Greco-Roman context, in literature of all sorts. The writing of political theory is, in that context, an invention of the fifth century BC (in its fully-fledged form, an invention of Plato's), but such writing did not exist in a vacuum; it emerged against the background of the evolution of complex systems of organization – beginning with that highly distinctive form of community, the Greek polis – which to a greater or lesser extent institutionalized debate as a means of managing political conflict. The question, then, which is addressed in the essays that follow is how Greeks and Romans (prior to AD 350)[3] thought, and theorized, about politics. Other cultures and civilizations are considered only insofar as they may have contributed to, or – as in the case of parts of the Jewish intellectual tradition – insofar as they may have become enmeshed with, the Greek and the Roman, in an intellectual context that becomes so cosmopolitan as to render demarcations by national, cultural or linguistic grouping for the most part unhelpful. It accords with this latter point that the main division in the volume is not between Greek and Roman at all, but rather between 'Archaic and Classical' and 'Hellenistic and Roman'; if 'Archaic and Classical' means primarily Greek, to separate out the specifically Roman in 'Hellenistic and Roman', at least at the level of theory, is in part a matter of unravelling a complex web of appropriation and modification which was itself sometimes carried out by Greeks within a Roman context.

The volume adopts a predominantly author-based (rather than a topic-based) approach, for various reasons. We may of course talk loosely of what 'the Greeks' or 'the Romans' thought on this or that subject at this or that time, and there is perhaps no harm in our talking in this fashion, as a way of picking out certain (apparently) widely-shared ideas or patterns of thinking. Both 'thought' and 'theory', however, require individuals to do the thinking. At the level of theory, our concern must inevitably be with the specific theses and arguments advanced by particular individuals, which are in principle as likely to cut across as to support contemporary thought and practice; and the reflections of other writers – poets, historians and others – whom we may class as 'non-philosophical' (though the boundaries between categories here are notoriously permeable) are often themselves highly distinctive and individual. Again, different genres may offer different opportunities for, and invite different modes of, reflection: the thought of a poet like Hesiod, or Sophocles, is quite different in quality and feel from that of a Herodotus or a

[3] 'Greek and Roman' thus corresponds to what writers in English have commonly, and parochially, called 'ancient' (as opposed to 'medieval' and 'modern').

Thucydides. In order to bring out the individuality of such diverse writers, the editors have encouraged contributors where possible to include direct quotation from the original texts.

At an early stage of the project, many of the contributors met to discuss both initial drafts of individual chapters and general issues of policy. One of the benefits of the discussion was to initiate conversations between the contributors which continued until the submission of final versions of the chapters, and this process has ensured (so the editors believe) a degree of coherence in the volume as a whole which might otherwise have been lacking. From the beginning, however, there have inevitably been points of mild disagreement, or difference of emphasis, between editors and contributors, and between the contributors themselves. The editors have not sought to impose any final resolution of such disagreements, since any resulting tensions accurately reflect real, and defensible, differences of approach to a highly complex subject-matter. One such tension that may be apparent is between those contributors who prefer a more historical approach, and those whose interests are primarily philosophical, and who write with closer attention to the connections of the ancient material with modern (or perennial) concerns.[4] Clearly different sorts of material may require different handling; but there must also often be room for discussion of the same material not only in its original context – within a particular text, within the oeuvre of the author, or within the framework of the society and culture in which that author was writing[5] – but also in the larger context of political philosophy as a whole, whether that is seen as an attempt at the impartial resolution of relatively distinct issues, undetermined (unless perhaps accidentally) by any history, or indeed as itself an outcome of historical processes. The productive interaction between historical and philosophical approaches, of whatever sort, is probably one of the chief distinguishing features of current work on Greek and Roman thought in general.

In principle, then, the volume aims to be catholic and comprehensive in its coverage, including differing types of treatment of political thought in

[4] The volume nevertheless avoids affiliation to any specific critical agenda among those on offer (whether Marxist, 'Straussian', communitarian, or any other); if such a stance is itself held to involve an agenda of a kind, however labelled, the editors will not mind. That certain methodological assumptions are in play is not in doubt: see e.g. the following note.

[5] Implied here will be some version of the 'contextualist' thesis associated particularly with Quentin Skinner, which claims – among other things – that the understanding of texts 'presupposes the grasp both of what they were intended to mean, and how this meaning was intended to be taken' (Skinner 1969: 48). No one will deny the particular difficulty of establishing the intentions (in Skinner's sense) of ancient authors or texts; but most will accept both the propriety and the necessity of the task.

the widest sense. It must be acknowledged, however, that once Plato (and Socrates) and Aristotle have made their appearance in the volume, it is political theory which is privileged over other sorts of political thinking. Plato and Aristotle themselves receive a treatment which is necessarily[6] both broader and deeper than that accorded to any other thinker; and much of the 'Hellenistic and Roman' section follows the fate of Platonic and/or Aristotelian ideas[7] in later thinkers, who are either philosophers, or writers drawing on philosophical sources. It is here, as it were, that the main action is taken to be situated. A consequence, however, given the limits on available space, is that other authors (i.e., broadly, those writing in non-theoretical mode) in the later periods are handled rather more selectively than in the earlier. In this sense, the volume may appear somewhat lopsided (why, for example, should the Roman poets be less deserving of mention than the Greek?), but – in the view of the editors – not disturbingly so.

Differences of approach between contributors, of the sort described, inevitably lead to variations in the degree of historical information supplied by individual essays. However, suitable use of the index and bibliographies provided at the end of the volume should be sufficient for the basic repair of gaps in any reader's knowledge of the periods covered. This *History* is not intended in any case as an encyclopaedia or dictionary. The contributors are all actively working in the areas on which they have written. Their brief was to address their particular topic or theme in a way appropriate for any intelligent reader, reflecting what seemed to them the best available scholarship, while at the same time offering new thoughts and suggesting future lines of investigation. Where there is controversy, this is marked, at least by means of references to rival views; the aim is to advance discussion, not to close it off. The bibliography includes those items which contributors regard as essential for anyone wishing to pursue an individual topic in greater detail.

Probably the most important subject of discussion at the preliminary meeting of contributors, and subsequently, was the meaning of 'the political'. Just what is to count as 'political' thought? In Greece down to the Hellenistic period, the answer to the question is simple enough: 'the political' covers any and every aspect of the polis, the 'city-state', or the 'citizen-state', as the fundamental unit into which society is organized.[8] When we apply the term 'political' here, it functions essentially as the

[6] Necessarily, that is, because of the extent, complexity and importance (both historical and philosophical) of their political writing. [7] See below.

[8] To give any precise date in Greek history for the emergence of the polis as a distinct form of organization is probably in principle impossible, but its origins surely lie in the Archaic period. Cf. Raaflaub in Ch. 2 below.

equivalent of the Greek *politikos* ('appertaining to the polis'); when Plato talks of *politikē* (*technē*), 'the art/science of politics', he has in mind a body of expertise that at least includes[9] something resembling our 'political theory', except that the theory in this case is restricted to the polis. That other forms of 'political' organization exist is recognized, but they are not treated as viable alternatives. This way of thinking is encapsulated in Aristotle's formula, according to which human beings are by nature 'political animals', i.e. creatures designed – as it were – for life in a polis. But in that case 'things political' (*ta politika*) will not only include, but actually turn on, the central ethical question about the best life for human beings, insofar as that life must not only be lived in the polis, but will be shaped by it. How is the community, and how are individuals who constitute that community, to live justly and happily, and in general to achieve their proper goals? Ethics is thus a part of 'politics', the whole being conceived of as 'the philosophy of things human' (Aristotle, *Nicomachean Ethics* 1181b15).

Given all of this, the decline of the polis from the later fourth century BC onwards, together with the rise of the Hellenistic monarchies, might have been expected to lead to a sea-change in the conception and function of political theory; and just such a change might be seen as signalled by the apparent reversal of the Aristotelian perspective by the Hellenistic schools, for whom politics was a part of ethical philosophy. On the other hand, from a wider perspective, this is no more than a minor, and essentially technical, shift of emphasis.[10] In the Greco-Roman period as a whole, political and ethical philosophy are for the most part irrevocably intertwined, and differences in the size and nature of the units into which society happens to be, or might be, organized simply add to the complexity of the demands on the study of political theory. 'Classical', Platonic and Aristotelian, *politikē* and its Hellenistic counterpart now turn out to be no more than (partly) different applications of the same type of reflective activity, and the difference between the latter and the former no more than 'an enlargement of the pool of concepts in which political thinking can be done'.[11]

There will, then, clearly be ways in which, to a greater or lesser degree, the conception of 'the political' reflected in large parts of this volume is likely to seem, and actually is, foreign. The modern conception refers to the institutional (and economic) management of society without restriction to any particular form of communal organization,

[9] The qualification is necessary because, for Plato, the expertise is to be acquired primarily to be exercised. [10] For a slightly different, but overlapping, analysis see Griffin 1996.
[11] Griffin 1996: 282.

and tends to banish ethical concerns to the sphere of the private.[12] The overlap, however, between this and the ancient notion or notions is so great that, so long as the differences are borne in mind, it is possible to move between them with little sense of strain; and indeed if it were not, the very project of a history of Greek and Roman 'political thought' would make little sense.

It might be claimed, in fact, that the tight ancient connection between politics and ethics is itself largely the invention of the philosophers. Insofar as we can construct an ancient Greek, or Roman, notion of the political independently of philosophical theorizing,[13] it seems to have rather little to do with what we should call the moral aspects of the citizens' life that so preoccupy a Plato, an Aristotle, or a Cicero, and much more to do with what are to us more recognizably political issues such as equality, autonomy, the distribution of power, and the obligations of the citizen as citizen. Thus when Plato claims, in the *Gorgias*, that Socrates – someone who on Plato's account took no part in practical politics – was in fact the only true *politikos* ('politician' or 'statesman'), because he was the only person who did what a statesman should (tell the straight truth on ethical questions), that would have been as paradoxical[14] to a contemporary Athenian as to us, and for similar if not quite identical reasons. For us, Plato's Socrates is simply non-political, to the extent that he eschews political institutions to achieve his ends; to the Athenians, not only could he not be a politician (who is someone who speaks in the assembly), but he might even be thought to be failing in his role as citizen or *politēs*, just by virtue of his preferring not to participate in the institution of communal debate. The distance between theory and practical reality illustrated by this (extreme) example may lessen in succeeding centuries, but never disappears; it is itself one of the most striking features of Greco-Roman political thinking.[15]

[12] For the contrast with modern notions of politics and the political, and for a more detailed and subtle account of ancient ones, see Cartledge in Ch. 1 below.

[13] That is, by way of reference to what politicians, or historians, would refer to as 'public affairs': *ta politika* in Thucydides' sense, or *res civiles* in Tacitus'.

[14] It is, of course, *intended* as a paradox; the underlying claim is that *politikoi* should use their power to do what Socrates tries to do (change people's attitudes and behaviour) by non-institutional means.

[15] Cf. the exchange between Julian and Themistius, discussed in section 1 of the 'Epilogue' below. The issues there partly relate to the choice between the philosophical and the political life: Socrates' commitment to practice, Julian insists, had nothing to do with politics, and everything to do with philosophy. It is philosophy, and philosophers, that have the power to transform us; by comparison the benefits conferred by those who wield political power pale into insignificance. Socrates would have applauded the general sentiment. But as Julian recognizes, and must (since he has just entered a position of power second only to that of emperor), the practical problems of day-to-day politics will not simply go away.

PART I

ARCHAIC AND CLASSICAL GREECE

*

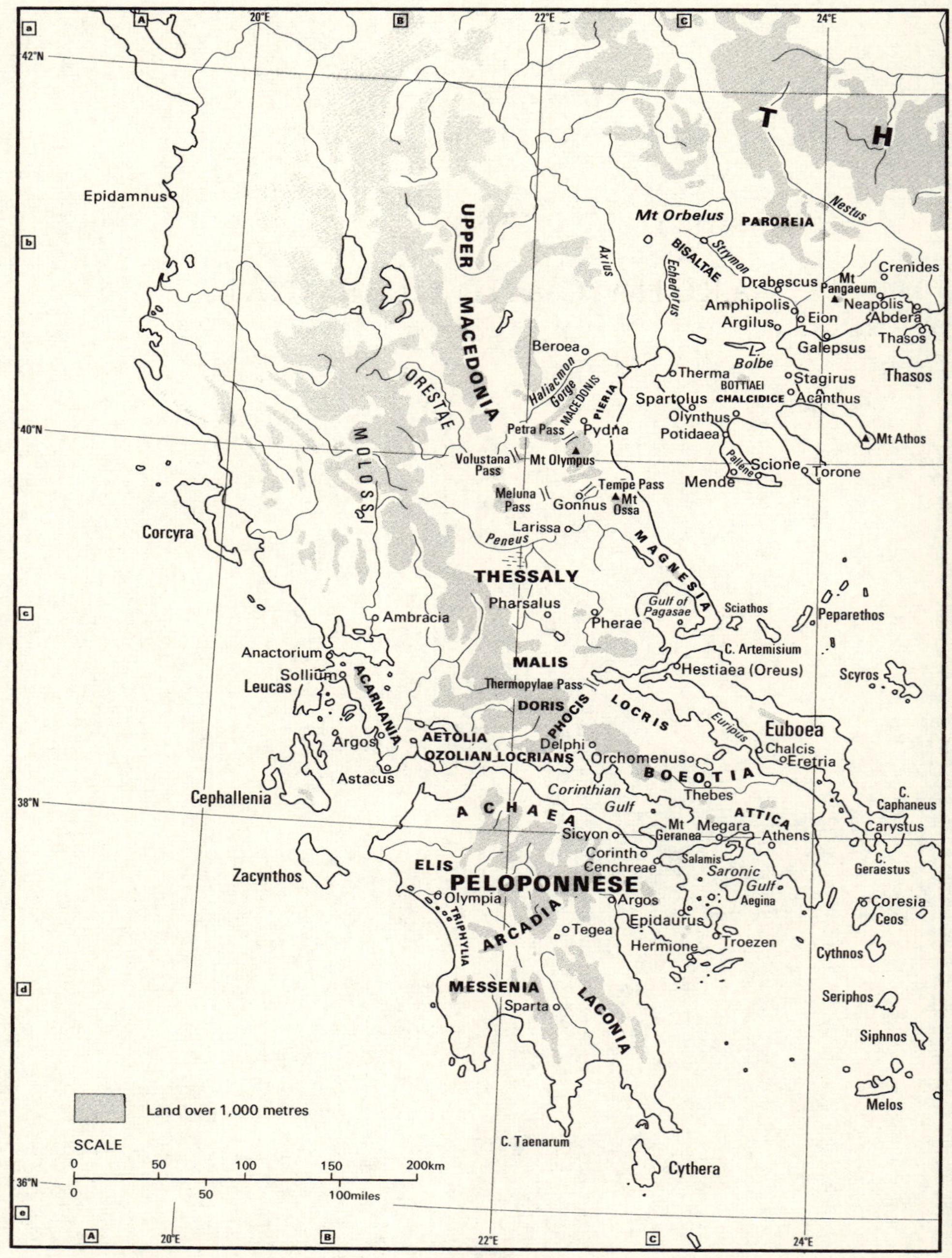

Map 1. Greece in the fifth century BC.

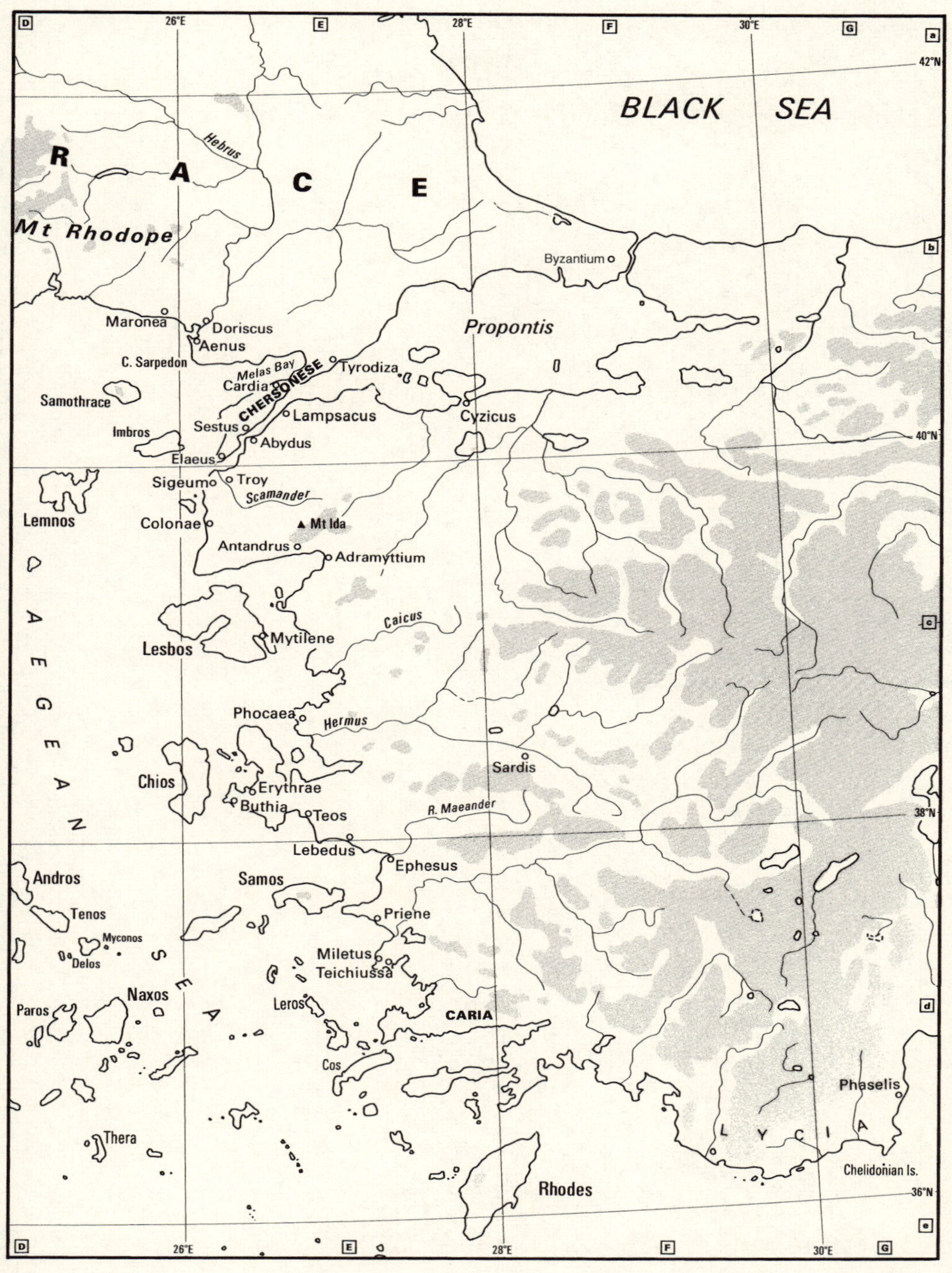

BLACK SEA
R
A
C
E
Hebrus
Mt Rhodope
Byzantium
Propontis
Maronea
Doriscus
Aenus
C. Sarpedon
Melas Bay
Cardia
Tyrodiza
CHERSONESE
Samothrace
Lampsacus
Cyzicus
Sestus
Imbros
Abydus
Elaeus
Sigeum
Troy
Scamander
Lemnos
Colonae
Mt Ida
Antandrus
Adramyttium
Caicus
Mytilene
Lesbos
A
E
G
E
A
N
Phocaea
Hermus
Chios
Erythrae
Sardis
Buthia
Teos
R. Maeander
Lebedus
Ephesus
Andros
Samos
Tenos
Priene
Myconos
Delos
Miletus
Teichiussa
S
E
A
Naxos
Paros
Leros
CARIA
Cos
Phaselis
L
Y
C
I
A
Thera
Chelidonian Is.
Rhodes
26°E
28°E
30°E
42°N
40°N
38°N
36°N

I

Greek political thought: the historical context

PAUL CARTLEDGE

1 Terminology

Much of our political terminology is Greek in etymology: aristocracy, democracy, monarchy, oligarchy, plutocracy, tyranny, to take just the most obvious examples, besides politics itself and its derivatives. Most of the remainder – citizen, constitution, dictatorship, people, republic and state – have an alternative ancient derivation, from the Latin. It is the ancient Greeks, though, who more typically function as 'our' ancestors in the political sphere, ideologically, mythologically and symbolically. It is they, above all, who are soberly credited with having 'discovered' or 'invented' not only city-republican forms but also politics in the strong sense: that is, communal decision-making effected in public after substantive discussion by or before voters deemed relevantly equal, and on issues of principle as well as purely technical, operational matters.[1]

Yet whether it was in fact the Greeks – rather than the Phoenicians, say, or Etruscans[2] – who first discovered or invented politics in this sense, it is unarguable that their politics and ours differ sharply from each other, both theoretically and practically. This is partly, but not only nor primarily, because they mainly operated within the framework of the polis, with a radically different conception of the nature of the citizen, and on a very much smaller and more intimately personal scale (the average polis of the Classical period is thought to have numbered no more than 500 to 2,000 adult male citizens; fifth-century Athens' figure of 40,000 or more was hugely exceptional).[3] The chief source of difference, however, is that for both practical and theoretical reasons they enriched or supplemented politics with practical ethics (as we might put it).

For the Greeks, moreover, the 'civic space' of the political was located

[1] Meier 1980 (1990), Finley 1983, Farrar 1988; cf. Ampolo 1981. For Rome see Part II, especially Ch. 20. [2] Raaflaub 1993; see also Ch. 2 below.

[3] Nixon and Price 1990. Gawantka 1985, an attempt to dismiss the polis as largely a nineteenth-century invention, has not found critical favour. A variety of perspectives: Hansen 1993b.

centrally. Public affairs were placed *es meson* or *en mesōi* ('towards' or 'in the middle'), both literally and metaphorically at the heart of the community, as a prize to be contested. The community in turn was construed concretely as a strongly inclusive political corporation of actively participating and competing citizens.[4] By comparison, or contrast, the 'politics' studied by modern western political theory, to say nothing of modern political science, is an utterly different animal. It is characteristically seen as a merely instrumental affair, to be evaluated in terms of more fundamental ideas and values. Popular usage often reduces it to amoral manipulation of power, or confines it to the force exercised on a national scale by agencies of the state.[5]

2 The 'political'

The point of opening with this comparison and contrast is to emphasize the gulf between ancient Greek and modern (western) politics and political thought. Scholars differ considerably, though, over how precisely to identify 'the political' in ancient Greece, a difference of opinion that is itself political. One school of thought holds to the formalist, almost Platonic view, that it should be defined strictly as the non-utilitarian.[6] Others, more realistically and accurately, deny any absolute separation of politics and economics and see the relationship between them rather in terms of primacy or priority. For the Greeks, to paraphrase and invert Brecht's dictum, politics (including *die Moral*) came first; then and only then came the 'guzzling' (*das Fressen*).[7] Further enlightenment on the particular nature of the political in Greece may be derived from considering the semantics of the public/private distinction.

First, compare, or rather contrast, Greece and Rome. The Romans set the *res publica*, literally 'the People's matter' hence the republic, in opposition to *res privata*. However, the Greek equivalent of *res publica* was not *to dēmosion* (the sphere of the Demos, the People's or public sphere), but *ta pragmata*, literally 'things' or 'deeds' hence (public or common) 'affairs', 'business'. It was for control of *ta pragmata* that revolutionaries in ancient

[4] Vernant 1985: 238–60; cf. Lévêque and Vidal-Naquet 1964 (1983): 13–24, Nenci 1979.

[5] Ancient politico-moral philosophy: Loizou and Lesser 1990, Euben, Wallach and Ober 1994, Gill 1995: esp. ch. 4. Modern political philosophy/science: Waldron 1989, Goodin and Pettit 1993. However, Richter 1980 and Held 1991 are premised on wider and more apt conceptions; see also Dunn 1992, 1993, 1996. Political culture: Pye 1993.

[6] Arendt 1958, Meier 1980/1990.

[7] Rahe 1992, Schmitt-Pantel 1990; cf. Heller 1991. Note also Springborg 1990, a critique of Rahe.

Greece struggled, and the Greek equivalent of 'revolution' was *neōtera pragmata*, literally 'newer affairs'.[8] Moreover, for the antithesis of *to idion* (their equivalent of *res privata*, but susceptible also of a pejorative construal), the Greeks as readily used *to koinon* ('the commonwealth') as *to dēmosion*.[9] In short, the private/public distinction occupied overlapping but markedly different semantic spaces in Greece and Rome. The Romans' construction of the distinction was closer to ours, but in Greece there could be no straightforward opposition of the public = the political to the private = the personal or domestic.[10]

Hence, whereas for us 'The personal is the political' is a counter-cultural, radical, even revolutionary slogan, for the Greeks it would have been just a banal statement of the obvious, for two main reasons. First, lacking the State (in a sense to be specified in the next section), they lacked also our notions of bureaucratic impersonality and facelessness, and therefore required individual citizens to place their persons on the line both officially and unofficially in the cause of the public good. Secondly, society, not the individual, was for them the primary point of political reference, and individualism did not constitute a serious, let alone a normal, alternative pole of attraction. In fact, there was no ancient Greek word for 'individual' in our anti-social, indeed antipolitical, sense.[11]

Gender introduces a further dimension of comparison and contrast.[12] In no Greek city were women of the citizen estate – that is, the mothers, wives and daughters of (adult male) citizens – accorded full public political status equal to that of the citizens themselves, and the societies of Classical Greece were both largely sex-segregated and fundamentally gendered. War, for example, one of the most basic Greek political activities, was considered a uniquely masculine prerogative, and the peculiar virtue of pugnacious courage that it was deemed to require was tellingly labelled *andreia*, 'manliness' (the Greek equivalent of Roman *virtus*).[13] From a mainly economic and cultural point of view, the private domain of the *oikos* (household) might perhaps be represented as more a feminine than a masculine space, and understood as opposed to the polis, rather than simply its basic component. Yet for most important political purposes *oikos*

[8] Vernant, 'The class struggle' (1965) in Vernant 1980: 1–18; Godelier, 'Politics as a relation of production. Dialogue with Edouard Will' in Godelier 1986: 208–24.

[9] These and other Greek/Roman contrasts: Steinmetz 1969, Nicolet 1975, Müller 1987.

[10] Humphreys 1993c, Sourvinou-Inwood 1995.

[11] Strasburger 1954 (1976). The semantic passage from Greek *idiōtēs*, a citizen viewed in an unofficial capacity, to English 'idiot' begins with the Greeks' privileging of the public space: Rubinstein 1998. See further however Goldhill in Ch. 3, pp. 13–16.

[12] Comparatively: Scott 1986, 1991; cf. Okin 1991.

[13] War: Havelock 1972. *Andreia*: Cartledge 1993a: 70–1.

and polis are better viewed as inextricably interwoven and complementary.[14] Two illustrations must suffice.

Firstly, the Greek city's ability to flourish depended crucially on mortals maintaining the right relationships with the divine, and that was thought to require the public religious participation of women, even as high priests, no less than of the male citizens; the religious calendar of all Greek cities included the festival of the Thesmophoria in honour of Demeter, and that was strictly women-only.[15] Secondly, marriage was in itself a purely private arrangement between two *oikoi*, or rather their male heads, and its rituals and ceremonies, however publicly visible, were legally speaking quite unofficial. Yet on the issue of marriages between citizen households depended the propagation and continuity of the citizen estate. So the law stepped in to prescribe and help police the boundaries of legitimacy of both offspring and inheritance. The Periclean citizenship law of 451/0 in democratic Athens, reimposed in 403 and vigorously enforced thereafter, is but the best-known example of this general Greek rule. Among other consequences, it effectively outlawed the interstate marriages that had been a traditional strategy for elite Athenians.[16]

Both the above illustrations of the essential political interconnectedness of polis and *oikos* involve religion. Here is a further major difference between ancient and modern (western) politics. The Greek city was a city of gods as well as a city of humankind; to an ancient Greek, as Thales is said to have remarked, everything was 'full of gods'.[17] Greek religion, moreover, like Roman, was a system ideologically committed to the public, not the private, sphere.[18] Spatially, the civic *agora*, the human 'place of gathering', and the *akropolis*, the 'high city' where the gods typically had their abode, were the twin, symbiotic nodes of ancient Greek political networking. Nicole Loraux's study of Athens' patron goddess Athena and the Athenian acropolis in the context of the Athenian 'civic imaginary' is thus an exemplary demonstration of the necessary imbrication of religion and the political in an ancient Greek polis.[19]

The polis, however, was no theocracy. Worshipping the gods was for the Greeks *nomizein tous theous*, recognizing them duly by thought, word and deed in fulfilment of *nomos* – convention, custom and practice. Yet it was men who chose which gods to worship, and where, when and

[14] Humphreys 1993b; cf. Musti 1985, Swanson 1992.

[15] Bruit 1992.

[16] Harrison 1968, Just 1989, Bruit and Schmitt Pantel 1992: 67–72, Oakley and Sinos 1993.

[17] Bruit and Schmitt Pantel 1992.

[18] Fustel de Coulanges 1864, Burkert 1985; cf. Beard 1994: 732.

[19] Loraux 1984 (1993).

how, availing themselves of the fantastic variety of options on offer under a system of almost limitless polytheism; and they did so without benefit of clergy, dogma or sacred scripture. In its other main sense, which corroborates the significantly man-made character of Greek religious belief and practice, *nomos* meant law, as exemplified by the positive Athenian law against impiety of which Socrates fell foul for 'not duly recognizing the gods which the city recognizes'.[20]

In all the explicit Greek political thought or theory we possess, and in a good deal of other informal political literature besides, the rule of the *nomoi* or of plain *Nomos* in the abstract was a given within the framework of the polis. After positive laws began to be written down in imperishable or lasting media (stone, bronze) in the seventh century BC, a distinction came to be drawn between the unchangeable and universal 'unwritten' laws – chiefly religious in import, and all the more binding for not being written down – and the laws that were 'written', that is, locally variable and open to alteration. Yet although it was men or rather citizens who made the positive, written laws, they too were in principle considered somehow above and beyond the reach of their quotidian interpreters.[21]

The etymological root of *nomos* would seem to be a verb meaning 'to distribute'. What was on offer for distribution within the civic space of the polis was *timē*, status, prestige or honour, both abstractly in the form of the entitlement and encouragement to participate, and concretely in the form of political offices (*timai*). Differing social backgrounds and experiences, and different innate abilities, meant that in practice *timē* and *timai* were of course distributed among the citizens unequally – almost by definition so under a regime of aristocracy or oligarchy. But even in formally as well as substantively inegalitarian regimes there is perceptible an underlying, almost subconscious assumption of equality in some, not in every, respect. The polis in this sense may fairly be described as an inherently egalitarian political community. By 500 BC this broadly egalitarian ideal had engendered the concept of *isonomia*: an exactly, mathematically equal distribution of *timē* for those deemed relevantly equal (*isoi*), a precise equality of treatment for all citizens under the current positive laws (*nomoi*). The earliest known appearance of the term is in an elite social context, whereas its characteristic appropriation after 500 was democratic.

[20] Socrates' trial in religio-political context: Garland 1992: 136–51, Vlastos 1994.

[21] *Nomos*: Ostwald 1969. A polis's *nomoi* might be ascribed en bloc to the initiative of one superwise 'lawgiver' (*nomothetēs*), appeal to whose supposed intentions could serve as a conservative force: Hölkeskamp 1992b [1995]; cf. Ch. 2 below.

This is a measure of the essentially contested nature of the concept of equality in the polis, a feature by no means peculiar to ancient Greece, but given extra force by the Greeks' agonistic mentality and competitive social and political systems.[22]

Scarcely less fundamental to the Greeks' idea of the political than gender, household, religion and *nomos* was the value of freedom. Freedom and equality, indeed, were the prime political sentiments or slogans of the ancient Greeks, as they are our own.[23] But ancient Greek political freedom was arguably a value of a very different kind, embedded as it was in societies whose political, social and economic arrangements were irreducibly alien to modern western ones.[24] Aristotle, for example, advocated a strong form of political freedom for citizens, but simultaneously made a doctrine of natural slavery central to his entire sociopolitical project of description, analysis and amelioration. Although the doctrine may have been peculiarly Aristotelian in crucial respects, a wide range of texts, literary, historical and medical as well as philosophical, makes it perfectly clear that the Greeks' very notion of freedom depended essentially on the antinomy of slavery. For a Greek, being free meant precisely not being, and not behaving in the allegedly typical manner of, a slave. It was probably the accessibility and availability of oriental 'barbarians', living under what the Greeks could easily construe as despotic, anti-political regimes, that most decisively influenced the particular ethnocentric construction and emphasis they placed on their own essentially politicized liberty.[25]

The peculiarity of Greek liberty may also be grasped comparatively, through following the lead given by Benjamin Constant, a pioneer liberal thinker and activist, in a famous speech ('The Liberty of the Ancients compared with that of the Moderns', 1819). If the Greeks did indeed 'discover' liberty, the liberty they discovered was for Constant a peculiarly ancient form – political and civic, public, subjecting the individual completely to the authority of the community, and anyhow available only for male full citizens. The liberty of the moderns, Constant insisted, was incommensurably different. It was social rather than political, for women as well as men, and involved private rights (including those of free speech, choice of occupation, and property-disposal) more importantly than public duties. In short, it was little more than freedom *from* politics as the Greeks understood it.[26]

[22] Equality, ancient: Cartledge 1996a; cf. Vlastos, below, n. 35. Equality, modern: Beitz 1991. Contest-system: below, n. 39.
[23] Raaflaub 1983, 1985, 1990–1, Patterson 1991, Davis 1995.
[24] Garlan 1988; cf. Patterson 1982.
[25] Cartledge 1993a: 118–51, 1993b.
[26] Constant 1819 (1988); cf. Thom 1995: 89–118.

3 The polis

The typical ancient polis was a republic, not a monarchy, nor *a fortiori* an extra- or anti-constitutional tyranny or dictatorship. Republicanism almost definitionally aims to promote what it is pleased to call the public good, but that can mean very different things and may be promoted in very different ways.[27] For example, the paradoxical claim that today 'Most governments try to suppress politics. . . .'[28] exemplifies a peculiarly modern phenomenon, equally applicable to all modern varieties of republican states. An ancient Greek republican would have been puzzled or appalled by this seeming contradiction between theory and practice. The short explanation of this disjunction is that modern governments are part and parcel of the State (capital S), whereas the polis may for all important purposes be classified as a more or less fully stateless political community.[29]

The differences between the politics (including political culture no less than formal political institutions) of the polis and that of modern State-based and State-centred polities may be considered in both positive and negative terms. Positively, and substantively, the chief difference is the direct, unmediated, participatory character of political action in Greece. The citizens were the polis; and there was no distinction or opposition between 'Us', the ordinary citizens, and 'Them', the government or official bureaucracy. Indeed, for Aristotle – whose preferred, actively participatory definition of the citizen was (as he confessed) more aptly suited to the citizen of a democracy than of an oligarchy – the essential difference between the polis and pre-polis or non-polis societies was that the polis was a strong community of adult male citizens with defined honours and obligations. Correspondingly, the category of those who were counted as citizens, and thereby entitled so to participate, was restricted narrowly to free adult males of a certain defined parentage. Their wives and other female relatives were, at best, second-class citizens. Resident foreigners, even if Greek, might qualify at most for inferior metic status. The unfree were by definition deprived of all political and almost all social honour.[30]

Negatively, the (relative) statelessness of the polis reveals itself by a series of absences striking by comparison with the condition of the

[27] Nippel 1994; cf. 1988, Rahe 1992. [28] Crick 1992: 168.

[29] 'State', comparatively: Hall 1986, Skinner 1989. Greek polis as 'stateless': esp. Berent 1994; but not 'acephalous': Rhodes 1995. Ehrenberg 1969 did not address the issue.

[30] Aristotle's citizen: *Pol.* 1274b31–1278b5, esp. 1275b19–20; cf. Cartledge 1993a: 107–11; further section 4, below.

modern, especially the modern liberal, state-community. There was in Greece no Hegelian civil society distinct from a government and its agents; and no formally instituted separation of powers: whoever ruled in a Greek polis (whether one, some or all) did so legislatively and judicially as well as executively.[31] Sovereignty, on the other hand, despite modern legalistic attempts to identify a notion of the 'sovereignty' of Law (or the laws) that would supply the motive force for civil obedience, remained blurred, in so far indeed as it was an issue.[32] There were no political parties in the modern sense, and so no concept of a loyal opposition, no legitimacy of opposition for its own sake. There was no properly constituted police force to maintain public order, or at most a very limited one, as in the case of the publicly owned Scythian slave archers at Athens. Self-help was therefore a necessity, not merely desirable.[33] There was no concept of official public toleration of civil dissent and so (as the trial of Socrates most famously illustrates) no conscientious objectors to appeal to such a concept. Finally, there were no individual, natural rights to life and liberty (as in the French eighteenth-century Rights of Man and Citizen), not even as a metaphor, let alone in the sense of legally entrenched prerogatives (as in the United States Bill of Rights).[34] At most, there might exist an implied assumption of or implicit claim to political entitlement, as in the concept of *isonomia* or equality of status and privilege under the citizen-made laws.[35]

None of these differences between republics ancient and modern was purely a function of unavoidable material or technological factors. Rather, that Greek political theory laid such conspicuous stress on the imperative of self-control was a matter largely of ethical choice. Provided that citizens could control themselves, they were enabled and entitled to rule others (their own wives and children and other disfranchised residents, no less than outsiders in a physical sense). Failure of self-control, on the other hand, would lead to transgression of the communally defined limits of appropriate behaviour, a deviation that when accompanied by violence was informally castigated and formally punished as *hubris* – the ultimate civic crime.[36]

It was from the statelessness of the Greek polis, too, that there stemmed in important measure the material prevalence of and theoretical

[31] Rule/participation: Eder 1991. Hansen 1983 offers an alleged but unpersuasive exception.
[32] Ostwald 1986.
[33] Legitimacy: Finley 1982; cf. MacIntyre 1973–4. Policing: Hunter 1994; cf. Nippel 1995. Self-help: Lintott 1982: 15–17, 21–4, 26–8, Finley 1983: 107 and n. 9.
[34] Ostwald 1969: 113 n. 1; cited by Raaflaub 1983: 539 n. 24. See also Schofield 1995–6.
[35] Vlastos 1953, 1964. [36] Fisher 1992; cf. 1990.

preoccupation with the phenomenon known as *stasis:* civil discord, or outright civil war.[37] *Stasis* had several other contributory sources and causes. A major one was the contradiction between the notional egalitarianism of the citizen estate, expressed by the term *isonomia*, and the existence of exceptionally charismatic individuals denied (so they believed) their due portion of status and honour (*timē*).[38] Politics in the sense of political infighting was typically construed by the Greeks as a zero-sum game of agonistic competition with as its goal the maximization of personal honour. Democratic Athens was quite exceptional in successfully suppressing, or channelling in socially fruitful directions, the public struggle among the elite for political honour over an extended period.[39]

A second and yet more major cause of *stasis*, economic stratification, operated at the deeper level of social structure. The poor were always with the Greeks, whose normative definition of poverty was noticeably broad. Everyone was deemed to be 'poor', except the seriously rich at one end of the scale and the destitute at the other. The criterion of distinction between the rich and the rest was leisure: what counted was whether or not one was obliged to work at all for one's living. Characteristically, the relationship of rich to poor citizens was conceived, by thinkers and activists alike, as one of permanent antagonism, prone to assume an actively political form as 'class struggle on the political plane'.[40] Logically, however, *stasis* was but the most extreme expression of the division that potentially threatened any Greek citizen body when it came together to make decisions competitively *es meson*.

Here indeed lay the paradox of *stasis*, a phenomenon both execrable and yet, given the framework of the Greek city, somehow inevitable and even supportable.[41] It was because of this inherent danger of the division of a split vote turning into the division of civil war that the governing political ideal on both main sides of the political divide was always *homonoia*: not merely consensus, or passive acquiescence in the will or power of the minority or majority, but literally 'same-mindedness', absolute unanimity among the publicly active and politically decisive citizenry. Alternatively, and more theoretically, if not wishfully, Greek political thinkers from at least Thucydides (VIII.97.2) onwards proclaimed the

[37] Lintott 1982, Fuks 1984, Gehrke 1985, Berger 1992, Molyneux 1993.

[38] *Isonomia*: above, n. 35. Charismatic individuals: Finley 'Leaders and followers', in Finley 1985: 3–37.

[39] Zero-sum game: Gouldner 1965; cf. Cartledge 1990. Honour as political goal: Arist. *EN* 1095b19–31; cf. Ste. Croix 1981: 80, 531 n.30. Athens as exception: Cartledge, Millett and von Reden 1998.

[40] Ste. Croix 1981: 278–326; cf. 69–80. Also Fuks 1984, Ober 1989.

[41] Loraux 1987, 1991.

merits of a 'mixed' constitution, one that would ideally offer something substantial to all the contending groups and personalities.[42] If, however, *homonoia* and the mixed constitution proved unachievable, the Greek citizen was expected, and might even be legally required, to fight it out literally to the death with his fellow-citizens.[43]

The contradiction between ancient Greek and early modern (and subsequent) western political thinking on the question of faction is revealingly sharp. From Hobbes to Madison, faction was construed wholly negatively, in line with the general early modern abhorrence of direct popular participation in politics, as a horrible antique bogey to be exorcized utterly from modern, 'progressive' political life. During the nineteenth century, with the rise of an organized working class to political prominence in the industrialized countries, that hostile tradition could not but be honed and polished – or rebutted in the name of revolutionary politics of different sorts. Conversely, the peculiarly modern ideals of pluralism and liberalism, usually represented now under the guise of liberal democracy but increasingly challenged by varieties of communitarianism, presuppose or require the existence of the strong, centralizing and structurally differentiated state.[44]

4 Political theory

The modern political theorist would surely find it odd that the discussion of strictly constitutional questions has been so long delayed. But Greek political theory was never in any case solely about constitutional power. The ancient Greek word that we translate constitution, *politeia*, was used to mean citizenship as well; and it had besides a wider, moral frame of reference than either our 'citizenship' or 'constitution'. Conversely, not some abstraction but men – citizen men – were the polis. *Politeia* thus came to denote both actively participatory citizenship, not just the passive possession of the formal 'rights' of a citizen, and the polis's very life and soul (both metaphors were applied in antiquity).[45] Congruently, whereas modern political theory characteristically employs the imagery of machinery or building-construction, ancient political theory typically thought in organic terms, preferring to speak of sharing (*methexis*) and rule (*archē*) rather than sovereignty or power (*bia*, *kratos*, *anankē*).[46]

[42] Von Fritz 1954, Nippel 1980, 1994. Post-ancient idealization: cf. Blythe 1992.
[43] Raaflaub 1992: 41 and n. 99.
[44] Rawls 1992. This is just one of the reasons why Havelock 1957 is misguided: Brunt 1993: 389–94; so too Hansen 1989.
[45] *Politeia*: Bordes 1982.
[46] Meier 1980 (1990); cf., comparatively, Nippel 1993.

All ancient Greek culture was inherently performative and competitive, and Greek intellectuals reflected the competitiveness of politics in both the manner and the matter of their own internal disputes.[47] Although there is still plenty of room for modern controversy over how long it took for political theory proper to replace mere political thinking, the discovery of constitutional political theory was made in Greece at least a century before Aristotle sat as a pupil of Plato's Academy; it is first unambiguously visible in Herodotus' 'Persian Debate' (III.80–2). By then, some Greek or Greeks had had the stunningly simple intuition that all constitutionally ordered polities must be species subsumable in principle under one of just three genera: rule by one, rule by some, or rule by all. This is a beautiful hypothesis distinguished by its combination of scope and economy, but moving qualitatively beyond the level of political debate visible in Homer in terms of both abstraction and sophistication. In Herodotus, too, we find already the germ of a more complex classification of 'rule', whereby each genus has both a 'good' specification and its corresponding corrupt deviation. Thus rule by one might be the legitimate, hereditary constitutional monarchy of a wise pastor – or the illegitimate despotism of a wicked tyrant; and likewise with the other two genera and their species.[48]

Of the two great fourth-century political theorists, however, Plato seems to have had little interest in the comparative sociological taxonomy of political formations. That was a major preoccupation of his pupil Aristotle's *Politics*, a study based on research into more than 150 of the over 1,000 separate and jealously independent Greek polities situated 'like frogs or ants round a pond' (Plato, *Phaedo* 109b) on the Black Sea and along much of the Mediterranean coastline.[49] In Aristotle's day, the third quarter of the fourth century, democracy and oligarchy were the two most widespread forms of constitution among the Greeks.[50] But before about 500 BC there had been no democracy, anywhere (not only not in the Greek world); and conceivably it was the invention of democracy at Athens that gave the necessary context and impetus for the discovery of political theory – as opposed to mere thinking about politics, which can be traced back in extant Greek literature as far as the second book of Homer's *Iliad*.[51]

Political theory of any sort, properly so called, would have been impossible without politics in the strong sense defined at the start of this

[47] Lloyd 1987: ch. 2.

[48] Among many treatments of the Debate, see e.g. Lloyd 1979: 244–5. [49] Huxley 1979.

[50] *Pol.* 1269a22–3; Aristotle typically claimed to have identified four species of each (oligarchy: 1292a40–1292b; democracy: 1291b31–1292a39).

[51] Finley 1986: 115, Brock 1991; cf. Euben 1986, Raaflaub 1989.

chapter, and there would have been no such politics without the polis. It is generally agreed that this institution, not certainly unique to Greece but certainly given a peculiarly Greek spin, emerged in the course of the eighth century BC. Almost everyone would also accept that there is an unbridgeable divide, politically, between the world of the Bronze Age Mycenaean palace (c.1500–1100 BC) and the world of the historic Greek polis. But there is no such general agreement as to how and why, precisely, the polis emerged when and where it did, although the principal causal variables were probably land-ownership, warfare and religion.[52]

Contemporary sources for this momentous development are mainly archaeological; the literary sources are largely confined to the poetry of Homer and Hesiod. Controversy over the use of Homer for political reconstruction has centred on whether the epics presuppose, imply or at any rate betray the existence of the polis.[53] The significance of Hesiod's testimony is rather that his is the first extended articulation of the idea of the just city.[54] It took rather longer for the Greek polis to become also, ideally, a city of reason.[55] One crucial step was the dispersal of political power downwards, through the tempering of the might of Hesiod's aristocrats by the empowerment of a hoplite 'middle class', who could afford heavy infantry equipment and had the necessary leisure to make profitable use of it in defence both of their polis and of their own new status within it. They were the backbone of the republican Greece that in the Persian Wars triumphantly repulsed the threat of oriental despotism, and the chief weapon with which radical political change and its accompanying revolution in political theory could be effected.[56]

A contemporary of those Wars, the praise-poet Simonides, observed unselfconsciously and accurately that 'the polis teaches a man' – how, that is, to be a citizen.[57] The dominant tradition of ancient Greek political theory, as opposed to mere political thinking or thought, that took its rise round about the same time was dedicated to the proposition that the Simonidean formula was a necessary but not a sufficient condition of political virtue and excellence.[58]

[52] Runciman 1982, Whitley 1991, Funke 1993.

[53] Scully 1990, e.g., is confident that the polis exists in Homer, whereas what seems to me most signally lacking is the concept of citizenship and so of the 'citizen-state' (Runciman 1990).

[54] Snodgrass 1980: ch. 3. [55] Murray 1990a, 1991a.

[56] Cartledge 1977 (1986): esp. 23–4, Hanson 1995.

[57] Simonides *ap.* Plu. *An seni sit gerenda res.* 1 = eleg. 15, ed. D. A. Campbell (*Greek Lyric* III, Loeb Classical Library, Cambridge, MA 1991).

[58] I am indebted to Giulio Einaudi editore s.p.a., and particularly Signor Paolo Stefenelli, for graciously allowing me to draw upon the English originals of my two chapters in the multi-volume work *I Greci* (Turin), ed. S. Settis: Cartledge 1996a and 1996b.

2

Poets, lawgivers, and the beginnings of political reflection in Archaic Greece

KURT A. RAAFLAUB

πόλις ἄνδρα διδάσκει
'The polis teaches a man'
(SIMONIDES 90 (WEST))

1 Polis and political thinking

A few statements, from Simonides back to Homer, will illuminate the social and political setting that was crucial for the development of Greek political thinking.[1] Simonides (556–468) declares: A man who is not evil 'nor too reckless suffices for me, one who has a sound mind and knows the justice that is useful to the polis' (542.33–6P). Xenophanes of Colophon (570–475) polemicizes against the custom of honouring victorious athletes at public expense; for the athlete's skill, unlike the poet's good expertise (*sophiē*), does not contribute to putting the polis in good order (*eunomiē*) nor 'enrich the polis's treasury' (2W). Phocylides of Miletus (sixth century) thinks, 'A small polis on a high cliff that is well run is better than foolish Nineveh' (4GP). Earlier in the sixth century, Theognis of Megara and Solon of Athens, seeing the injustice committed by morally depraved aristocrats, worry about impending social conflicts and tyranny:

> Kyrnos, this polis is pregnant, and I fear that it will give birth to a man who will be a straightener of our base *hubris* . . . (Theognis 39–40, cf. 41–52, tr. Nagy)

> Our polis will never perish by decree of Zeus
> or whim of the immortals . . .
> But by thoughtless devotion to money, the citizens are willing
> to destroy our great polis . . . (Solon 4.1–6W, tr. Mulroy)

[1] All dates are BC, all biographical dates approximate. Editions cited: DK: Diels and Kranz 1951–2; GP: Gentili and Prato 1988; KRS: Kirk, Raven and Schofield 1983; ML: Meiggs and Lewis 1988; P: Page 1962; W: West 1989/92. Translations used (often modified): Athanassakis 1983, Fagles 1990, Fränkel 1973, Freeman 1948, Lattimore 1951, 1960, 1965, Mulroy 1992, Nagy 1985. Due to space restrictions I refer, wherever possible, to recent publications with good bibliographies.

Like Xenophanes, in mid seventh-century Sparta Tyrtaeus rejects commonly praised individual qualities in favour of those that benefit the polis: fierce courage in the thick of battle is

> mankind's finest possession, that is
> the noblest prize that a young man can endeavor to win,
> and it is a good thing his polis and all the people share with him . . .
> (12.13–15W, tr. Lattimore)

Another half-century earlier, Hesiod links individual justice and communal well-being:

> Those who give straight verdicts and follow justice . . .
> live in a polis that blossoms, a polis that prospers . . . [But]
> many times one man's wickedness ruins a whole polis,
> if such a man breaks the law and turns his mind to recklessness.
> (*Works and Days* 225–7, 240–1, tr. Athanassakis)

In the *Iliad* (XII.243) Hector says simply, 'One bird-omen is best, to fight defending the fatherland.'[2]

With varying emphasis, all these testimonia, spanning three centuries and many parts of Archaic Greece, illustrate the centrality of the polis in the thoughts and concerns of Archaic poets. Briefly, the polis was a community of persons or citizens, of place or territory, of cults, customs and laws, and a community that, whether independent or not, was able to administer itself (fully or partly). Usually translated as 'city-state', it should properly be labelled 'citizen-state'. In the Classical period the polis normally had an urban centre. But if we use the term 'city' to describe that centre, we should not conflate city with polis. The city as urban centre presupposed the polis and was part of it, on equal terms with the surrounding countryside. Although large parts of the Greek world were organized not in poleis but 'tribal states' (*ethnē*), during the Archaic and Classical periods the polis was politically and culturally the leading form of state.[3]

Already the 'Homeric world' is a world of poleis.[4] These communities, though reflecting an early, far from fully developed and integrated form of

[2] That is, Troy, conceptualized as a polis: below at nn 4–6.

[3] 'Citizen-state': Runciman 1990: 348, Hansen 1993a. Polis: Ehrenberg 1969: 88–102, Finley 1982a: 3–23, Sakellariou 1989: pt I, Hansen 1998; for the definition presented here, see Raaflaub 1993: 43–4. Ethnos: Snodgrass 1980: 42–7, Morgan 1991, Funke 1993. For hesitations about the applicability of the concept of 'state' to the polis, see Ch. 1 above.

[4] 'Homer' stands for the poet(s) who composed the extant monumental epics, most probably in the second half of the eighth century: Janko 1982: 188–200, 228–31, Kirk 1985: 1–4, Latacz 1996: 56–9; *contra* (early seventh century): West 1995; see also Raaflaub 1998: 187–8 with more bibliography.

the polis, show all its essential characteristics.[5] In the poet's imagination the Trojan War – despite its epic, Panhellenic and trans-Aegean dimensions – resembles a war between two poleis on opposite sides of a large plain. Throughout Greek history, such neighbourhood rivalries often caused long and bitter wars; they are attested for the first time precisely in Homer's time.[6]

More importantly, the poet consciously conceptualizes the polis. Odysseus, approaching the land of the Cyclopes, sets foot on an uninhabited island. A contemporary of the first widespread Greek 'colonization', that is establishment of new settlements throughout the Mediterranean world (section 7 below), the poet notes the island's potential for a polis: it has fertile land for crops and fruits, well-watered meadows, and an easy harbour with a good spring (*Odyssey* IX.131–41). The Cyclopes, however, have not taken advantage of this opportunity. They live in golden age abundance and 'all grows for them without seed planting, without cultivation' (107–11, tr. Lattimore); they have no ships and do not visit the cities of other people (125–9). Although blessed by the gods, they are outrageous and lawless (106) and despise the gods (273–8); they

> have no shared laws (*themistes*), no meetings for counsels (*boulēphoroi agorai*);
> rather they make their habitations in caverns hollowed
> among the peaks of the high mountains, and each one sets the law
> for his own wives and children, and cares nothing about the others.
> (112–15)

The Cyclops society thus does not know the polis and its essential structures; it consists of completely autonomous households (*oikoi*); in every respect it is the extreme opposite of normal human society.

In stark contrast, the Phaeacians, who originally lived near the Cyclopes but were harassed by them until they emigrated and founded their new city on Scheria (*Od.* VI.4–10), represent an ideal polis: they respect the gods, are hospitable and generous to strangers, and have mastered the art of sailing beyond imagination.[7] The contrast is deliberate: there the self-centred monsters who lack a community and violate every norm, here a people who do everything right and fully share their communal experience. In the epics, the polis represents civilization, communica-

[5] Raaflaub 1991: 239–47; 1993: 46–59; cf. Morris 1987: ch. 10, Scully 1990, van Wees 1992: ch. 2. *Contra*: Finley 1977: 33–4, 155–6, Ehrenberg 1937: 155 = 1965: 93, Starr 1986: 35–6, Cartledge in Ch. 1 above.

[6] Raaflaub 1991: 222–5, 1997a: 51–2.

[7] *Od.* Bks. VI–VIII, XIII.1–95; cf. Raaflaub 1993: 48–9.

tion, community and justice; not to live in a polis means primitiveness, isolation, lack of community and lawlessness.[8]

2 Archaic poetry and political thinking

Politics and the political sphere were not conceptualized explicitly before the late fifth and fourth centuries; political treatises and specialized political thinkers appeared only then. Yet in an informal sense, as the preceding section has shown, political reflection, focusing on the polis and relationships within it, existed much earlier. In tracing such thinking, we should consider not only specifically political ideas but a much broader range of aspects. For in Greek self-perception, the polis was more than a political unit. It was a social entity in a very comprehensive sense: its wellbeing depended on many factors, not only on political institutions or decisions.

At first sight, the nature of the extant sources seems to pose great difficulties to using them as evidence for early political thinking. In particular, because the Homeric epics stand in a long tradition of oral poetry, scholars often dismiss the society they depict as an artificial amalgam of many periods and traditions and of poetic imagination.[9] Hesiod's didactic poems, focusing on the divine and private spheres, appear apolitical, while 'lyric poetry' usually is interpreted as individualistic and local. Why, then, should we expect such poetry to offer reliable insight into the political concerns and thoughts of the poets' contemporaries?

Upon closer inspection, things look differently. To oral epic, the interaction between singer and audience was essential; fantasy and archaisms were balanced by the listeners' need to identify with the human drama and ethical dilemmas described by the singer. In each performance, the poet combined heroically elevated actions by extraordinary individuals with material reflecting social, economic and political conditions, values and relationships that were familiar to the audience. M. I. Finley and others have found a high degree of consistency in numerous aspects of 'Homeric society'. For various reasons, this society probably was near-contemporary rather than fully contemporary with the poet's own. Since epic poetry enjoyed Panhellenic acceptance, it must have been widely attractive and meaningful, despite local differences. The 'Homeric world' thus should be assumed to reflect conditions, relationships and concerns

[8] Scully 1981: 5–9.

[9] E.g., Long 1970, Snodgrass 1974, Kirk 1975: 820–50. *Contra*: Adkins 1971, Qviller 1981: esp. 114, Morris 1986: esp. 102–20, and the bibliography in n.10.

existing in wide parts of Hellas in roughly the late ninth and eighth centuries.[10]

Most post-Homeric poets seem firmly anchored in one place, and present themselves as individuals with a distinct personality and biography. For example, Hesiod, a small farmer in a Boeotian village, was involved in an inheritance struggle with his brother and suffered from unjust decisions by corrupt aristocratic judges. Archilochus was a mercenary from Paros who fought with the colonists of Abdera against Thracian natives, enjoyed life, despised traditional values, and hated the aristocracy. Although such biographical details, usually taken literally, may be historically authentic, it is also possible that they are elements of an artfully created persona attributed to the (real or fictitious) 'founding hero' of a poetic genre by the 'guild' of singers performing in that genre. In this view, Hesiod is the archetypal didactic poet performing in dactylic hexameters, Archilochus that of iambic blame poetry. Content and meaning of such poetry, in whatever genre, certainly transcend locality or region, have the same Panhellenic appeal as heroic epic, and thus must reflect concerns shared by the poets' contemporaries in many parts of Hellas.[11]

In ancient Greece, a poet was entertainer, artist, craftsman – and much more: a teacher and educator of his people (see n. 25 below). Poleis usually were small, face-to-face societies, intensely alive and full of conflicts, in which individual actions, especially by powerful leaders, easily affected the community as a whole. Those who were used to expressing their thoughts publicly, not least the poets and singers, could not but think, speak, or sing also about public issues. Hence we are justified in expecting that even non-political poetry often deals with political issues; but, being poetry, it does not necessarily do so openly and directly. The audiences of such poetry, of course, must have been used to picking up political allusions and 'messages' woven into mythological and other narrative; hence what we perceive is likely to be only part of the whole.

3 Homer

The Bronze Age civilization of second millennium Greece was based on state formations centred in large palaces (e.g. Cnossos, Mycenae, Pylos)

[10] Consistency: Finley 1977 and e.g., Adkins 1971, Donlan 1981/2: 172, Herman 1987: xi. Homeric society: recently, Morris 1986, Ulf 1990, Patzek 1992, van Wees 1992, Raaflaub 1997b, 1998 with more bibliography.

[11] Nagy 1979 (Homer, Archilochus); 1982 (Hesiod); 1985 (Theognis); generally: 1990a: ch. 3, 1990b: chs.2–3.

that had its closest analogues in Mesopotamia. In the late twelfth century, these palaces and the economic, social, and political structures connected with them were destroyed.[12] By the mid-eleventh century most traces of the 'Mycenaean' civilization had disappeared and Greece was left in much diminished circumstances (the 'Dark Ages'). With few exceptions, a massively reduced population lived in simple conditions and relative isolation in small and scattered villages surrounded by farms and pastures. Although the question of continuity and rupture is intensely debated, in many essential respects the 'Protogeometric Period' (1050–900) represents a new beginning. In the 'Geometric Period' (900–750), conditions gradually improved, the population increased, contacts with other people broadened, and the economy was transformed. In the eighth century a period of rapid change and development set in.[13] In the course of this process poleis emerged in many areas and land became precious, provoking conflicts both within each polis and between poleis. New forms of communal military and political organization thus became necessary, eventually resulting in a citizen army of heavily armed infantry (the 'hoplite phalanx'), a differentiated apparatus of offices and government, and regulated procedures of decision making, lawgiving, resolution of conflicts and jurisdiction.[14]

Hence, whatever the Greeks of this period may have inherited from their Mycenaean ancestors or learned from their Near Eastern and Egyptian neighbours (section 9), the polis and its culture have their determinant roots in the 'Dark Ages'. The communal structures typical of the polis emerged from smallest beginnings under the influence of factors that were specific to the Aegean world – although comparable developments occurred elsewhere.[15] The beginnings of political reflection, too, just like the development of political institutions, concepts, and terminology, must have been closely connected with the evolution, experiences, and concerns of the early polis and its society.

Inscriptions and other evidence illustrate these developments from about the mid-seventh century. For an earlier stage, Homer and Hesiod

[12] Vermeule 1964, Chadwick 1976, Finley 1982a: ch. 12, Dickinson 1994. Destruction: Desborough 1975, Musti 1991, Deger-Jalkotzy 1991, Ward and Joukowsky 1992, Patzek 1992: pt.2, Drews 1993.

[13] Dark Ages: Snodgrass 1971, 1987: ch. 6, Donlan 1985, 1989, Morris 1997, forthcoming. Geometric and Archaic Greece: Coldstream 1977, Snodgrass 1980, Patzek 1992: 104–35, Morris 1998.

[14] Polis: Snodgrass 1993a, Raaflaub 1993, de Polignac 1995, and the bibliography cited in n.5. Army: n.17. Offices, lawgiving: section 7.

[15] So too e.g., Murray 1993: 8; *contra*: S. Morris 1992: 124. A detailed comparison, especially with 'city-states' in Italy and Phoenicia, remains a *desideratum*; see Davies 1997.

are our only guides. Socially and economically, the Homeric polis is dominated by a group of noble families among whose heads (*basileis*) the paramount leader (also called *basileus*) holds a precarious position of pre-eminence (*Od.* VIII.390–1). These leaders meet in council, debate issues of communal importance in the assembly, lead their followers and fellow citizens in battle, serve as judges and, through guest friendships (*xenia*) and embassies, maintain contacts with other communities. Nurturing a highly competitive ideology of excellence ('always to be the best and to excel above the others,' *Il.* VI.208), this elite projects an image of high status, great refinement, wealth and complete control in the community – an impression that is enhanced further by the epics' focus on a small group of leaders elevated to superhuman ('heroic') status. The masses of non-elite men receive little attention and seem negligible.[16]

Closer examination reveals, however, that these men, presumably independent farmers, play a significant and communally indispensable role. The battles are fought and decided by mass armies. Although lacking initiative and vote, the assembly witnesses and legitimizes decisions and actions that are important to the community and shares the responsibility for them. Leaders who ignore the assembly's opinion do so at their own risk; failure may jeopardize their position.[17] Both in military and political organization, direct lines of development lead from the structures described in Homer to those attested later in Archaic Greek poleis. The poetic and 'ideological' distortion presented by the epics therefore needs to be corrected. The polis was built from the beginning on a foundation of considerable equality: the farmers who fought in the communal army to defend the polis also sat in the assembly to participate in communal decisions.[18]

The status of Homeric *basileis* is determined by their accomplishments and the power they can muster through their *oikos*, but the community acknowledges and legitimizes such status only if their deeds and power serve the interests of the community. As one leader says to his companion,

Why is it you and I are honoured before others
with pride of place, the choice meats and the filled wine cups . . .
and all men look on us as if we were immortals,
and we are appointed a great piece of land . . .

[16] Overall on 'Homeric society': Finley 1977, Ulf 1990, van Wees 1992, Murray 1993: ch. 3, Raaflaub 1997b, and other chapters in Morris and Powell 1997.

[17] As Agamemnon's example demonstrates. Assembly: Havelock 1978: ch. 7, Gschnitzer 1991, Hölkeskamp 1997, Raaflaub 1997c. Army: Snodgrass 1993b, van Wees 1994. Cartledge 1996c offers a different view.

[18] Raaflaub 1996a, 1997a; Morris 1996; also Starr 1977: ch. 6.

good land, orchard and vineyard, and ploughland for the planting of wheat?
Therefore it is our duty in the forefront . . .
to take our stand, and bear our part of the blazing of battle.
(Il. XII.310–16, tr. Lattimore)

The leaders are bound by a 'code' which obliges them, in exchange for honours and privileges, to devote all their efforts to the safety of the community. The tension, built into this value system, between individual aspirations and communal obligations inevitably results in conflicts.[19]

This tension appears already in the proem of the *Iliad* (I.1–7), where the singer promises a song on the wrath of Achilles and his quarrel with Agamemnon – the cause of countless deaths for the Achaeans. In the poet's conception, the Achaean camp represents a makeshift polis, the army the community of citizens; the political concerns the poet formulates thus are those of a polis.[20] The conflict between the two leaders erupts (I.1–303) because Achilles reveals as the cause of a plague sent by Apollo a selfish action by Agamemnon, the overall leader, who has failed to respect the god's priest. Forced to give up his most prestigious war booty, the priest's daughter, Agamemnon directs his frustration at his rival, whom he accuses of conspiracy. He compensates for his loss by taking away Achilles' favourite slave woman, 'that you may learn well how much greater I am than you, and another man may shrink back from likening himself to me and contending against me' (I.185–7, cf. 287–91). Violence is barely avoided, and Achilles withdraws from the fighting.

Achilles is the greatest warrior and the son of a goddess but has to subordinate himself to Agamemnon who is more powerful because he commands the greater number of men: a difficult situation that requires tact and mutual respect, qualities both men are lacking. Achilles is justified in criticizing the leader, but his criticism is unbearable to Agamemnon who feels threatened by the rival and tries desperately to save face. This is a realistic scene, probably familiar to many of the poet's audiences. Its political significance lies in the fact that any quarrel between two leaders of such stature will inevitably affect the entire community. Achilles knows this:

Some day longing for Achilles will come to the sons of the Achaeans . . .
when in their numbers before man-slaughtering Hector
they drop and die. And then you will eat out the heart within you
in sorrow, that you did no honor to the best of the Achaeans. (I.240–4)

19 Redfield 1975: esp. ch. 3. See also the Meleager story (*Il.* IX.527–99).
20 Raaflaub 1993: 47–8.

Yet the primary fault lies with Agamemnon. He knows the 'code': 'I myself desire that my people be safe, not perish' (I.117). By dishonouring his most important ally, he has freed Achilles to withdraw from his obligation and, by thus exposing the Achaeans to mortal danger, he has violated his duty toward the community.

Accordingly, Agamemnon bears the brunt of popular dissatisfaction, as it is described vividly in an assembly scene in Book II (83–398). Accepting his 'invitation' to return home, meant as a test of their morale, the masses rush to the ships, leaving no doubt that they have lost confidence in his leadership. Odysseus finally succeeds in re-establishing order, but one Thersites keeps complaining. He has no authority and power, but what he says echoes Achilles' words and clearly expresses the sentiments of the entire army: 'It is not right for you, their leader, to lead in sorrow the sons of the Achaeans!' (II.233–4). Thersites' appeal to the assembly to desert Agamemnon (236–8) is unsuccessful, but that the words are spoken at all and Odysseus needs to refute 'leadership by many' (203–4) reveals the depth of the crisis Agamemnon has caused.[21]

The leader's responsibility for the common welfare is emphasized on the Trojan side as well. Hector, whose name means 'holder' or 'protector', is respected by his people because his efforts are single-mindedly focused on saving his city.[22] His son, Skamandrios, they call Astyanax ('lord of the city') 'because Hector alone saved Ilion' (VI.402–3). Most of the time, he meets his responsibility admirably, but he too provokes defeat and eventually his own demise by not listening to the voice of reason (his prophetic brother, Poulydamas), and ignoring the opinions of his soldiers (XII.210–50; XVIII.243–313). In the end, he confronts Achilles and refuses to withdraw behind the city walls precisely because he fears that the people will blame him for having caused the Trojan defeat (XXII.99–110).

Hector's brother, Paris, fares much worse. Having abducted Helen, the wife of the Spartan *basileus*, and stolen many valuables from his house, he is responsible for the miseries the war has brought upon the Trojans. He is not alone, though: long before the war, the Achaeans sent an embassy to reclaim queen and goods. The ambassadors spoke in an assembly which, persuaded by a man who was bribed by Paris, rejected their request (III.205–24; XI.123–5, 138–42). All Trojans thus share the responsibility for Paris' deed and for the consequences of the war. That their cause is unjust becomes even more evident when Pandarus violates a sworn truce,

[21] On the Thersites scene: Gschnitzer 1976, Rose 1988; on Thersites: Kirk 1985: 138–9.
[22] Nagy 1979: 146.

wounding Menelaus with an arrow shot – and the Trojan assembly again fails to support a motion to return the contested woman and treasures (IV.69–182; VII.344–411). As Diomedes puts it, even a fool can now see that 'the terms of death hang over the Trojans' (VII.399–402). No wonder this war is unpopular among them, despite their assembly's involvement, and Paris is 'hated among them all as dark death is hated' (III.454, cf. VII.390). Hector, too, bitterly chastises his brother: 'The Trojans are cowards in truth, else long before this you would have been stoned to death for the wrong you did us' (III.56–7).

Without a determined leader the people lack power and no member of the elite is ready to revolt openly against the paramount *basileus*. Hence on neither side is dissatisfaction with the leaders followed by action, and the masses appear easy to control. Yet these men who fight in the war and sit in the assembly represent at least a potential power factor. Otherwise it would be futile for Achilles, Hector, and Thersites to decry the people's passiveness. This tension is brought out even more sharply in the *Odyssey*.

Odysseus' son, Telemachus, whose property is being ravaged by the unruly suitors of his mother, Penelope, tries to put pressure on them by winning the support of the assembly. Problems of an *oikos*, even the leader's, are matters of private, not public concern and thus no business of the assembly (*Od.* II.25–45). Accordingly, Telemachus emphasizes the damage done to the community's reputation by the suitors' misbehaviour, and the danger of divine retribution which will equally hurt the entire community (62–7). He thus appeals to the solidarity of the people and stresses ethical and religious concerns. The people, though overcome by compassion, keep silent (81–3) and, despite an omen and the seer's prediction of impending disaster (161–9), the suitors refuse to drop their competition for queen and kingship.

Wise Mentor then uses a different approach. Odysseus was a good and just *basileus* (230–4, cf. V.8–12). The community thus is obliged to him and his family. By ignoring such obligations, it violates traditional norms and sets a negative example: in the future, since there is no incentive or reward for good leadership, no *basileus* will want to put the interests of the community above his own. While the suitors cannot really be blamed for their violent actions because by injuring the house of Odysseus they risk their own lives (II.235–8, cf. 281–4: a remarkable assessment of excessive aristocratic competition for power and rank), 'It is the rest of you I am indignant with, to see how you all sit dumbly there instead of rebuking them and restraining them; you are many; the suitors are few' (239–41, tr. Shewring). Criticism of the people's inactivity is here turned into a direct appeal and voiced by a respected member of the community: the people themselves are responsible for the common welfare. But Mentor holds no power of his own and, as in the *Iliad*, popular sentiment fails to express itself in action. Yet the people's reactions are watched carefully: in the right circumstances they might suddenly play a much more significant role. Indeed, later in the epic, having failed in an attempt to ambush Telemachus, the suitors fear that he may now be able to rouse the people against them (XVI.361–82).

In contrast to Telemachus, Mentor argues strictly on the political level: what appears to be a private affair is in fact important to the entire community because it affects its safety and influences future relations between leader and community and hence the wellbeing of all. To take a stand is therefore indispensable. The noble leader's obligation to care for the wellbeing of the community, which is rewarded by high status and honours, requires as a corollary the people's willingness to get involved.

One of the scenes on the magnificently decorated shield of Achilles depicts a trial (*Il.* XVIII.497–508) held on the meeting place (*agora*), in front of seated noble judges and a large crowd. This scene is important for our understanding of the evolution of jurisdiction.[23] Its procedural details are much debated but two aspects should be stressed. First, the *basileis* who address the public, in whatever capacity, hold a staff or sceptre (*Il.* I.86, 279; *Od.* II.37–8). The history of Agamemnon's staff is recounted in detail: Hephaestus made it for Zeus; Agamemnon eventually inherited it from his ancestors (*Il.* II.100–8). 'Now the sons of the Achaeans carry it in their hands, the judges, when they administer the norms from Zeus' (I.237–9). The staff, the leader's charisma, and the function as judge: all that comes from Zeus; the words and actions of the speaker who holds the staff claim to be legitimized by Zeus. Unlike in the ancient Near East, however, the leader is neither identified with the highest god nor seen as his human agent (section 9). Hence the *basileus* himself is subject to the norms he administers; these norms provide a platform from which his performance can be assessed, criticized and, eventually, controlled. Second, communal events or actions – such as trials, distribution of booty and political decisions – take place in an assembly. Typically, each phase of the quarrel between Agamemnon and Achilles is placed in an assembly: from its outbreak (I.11–32, 54–305) to the formal reconciliation of the leaders (XIX.54–276). By repairing the damage he has done, properly and generously, Agamemnon acquires higher prestige and

[23] Gagarin 1986: 26–33, Edwards 1991: 213–18, Westbrook 1992.

becomes 'more just', 'for there is no fault when even one who is a *basileus* appeases a man, when the *basileus* was the first one to be angry' (XIX.181–3). Nobody is safe from making errors (83–144); hence it is crucial to pave the way for insight, reparation and reconciliation. The community that depends on the power of its leaders but is threatened by their quarrels develops effective mechanisms to overcome such rifts and reward conciliatory behaviour.

Finally, the *Odyssey* also emphasizes the relations between unequals: upper and lower classes, rich and poor, powerful and weak. Much attention is paid to the misery of the socially underprivileged. Their plight is connected with the vicissitudes of human fate that can turn a *basileus* into a beggar, refugee or slave: Odysseus and Eumaeus are obvious cases (*Od.* XIII.429ff.; XIV.191ff.; XV.404ff.). Such outsiders are protected by the highest god, Zeus. They are treated in an exemplary way by the Phaeacians and the members of Odysseus' *oikos*, whereas the suitors, the elite of noble youth, consciously violate the norms of socially acceptable behaviour. Their disaster therefore represents deserved punishment brought about by the gods and just men.[24]

The epics thus attribute remarkable prominence to basic problems of life and relationships in a community. The poet uses traditional mythical narrative to reflect upon and dramatize ethical and political problems that are important to the audience. By creating positive and negative models of social behaviour, by illuminating the causes and consequences of certain actions and relating these to the wellbeing of the community, he raises the level of awareness among his listeners, he forces them to think, he educates them.[25]

4 Hesiod

Hesiod, usually dated in the early seventh century, also sees the wellbeing of the community threatened by irresponsible actions of its *basileis*. He concentrates not on the power struggles among the nobles and the military side of their leadership but on their role as judges (*Theogony* 80–93; *Works and Days* 27–39, 219–64).[26] Observing their corruption and ten-

[24] Havelock 1978: ch. 9.

[25] Herington 1985: 67–71; more bibliography on the poet as educator in Raaflaub 1991: 249–50 n.144. On political thinking in Homer, see also the bibliography cited in Raaflaub 1988: 266, 1989: 8 n.12; Nicolai 1993, Spahn 1993; Hammer 1998, and forthcoming.

[26] Different assessments of the 'autobiographical' background (section 2) in Gagarin 1974, Erler 1987, Nagy 1982, 1990a: ch. 3. Further: Spahn 1980, Millett 1984. More bibliography in Raaflaub 1993: 59–64.

dency to pass 'crooked sentences', Hesiod reflects on the relationship between justice and prosperity of individual and community. In a series of powerful images and myths, he describes the all-important function of Zeus, the protector of justice, who blesses the just and punishes the unjust: Dike, the goddess of Justice and daughter of Zeus,

> howls when she is dragged about by bribe-devouring men
> whose verdicts are crooked when they sit in judgment...
> She rushes to sit at the feet of Zeus Kronion
> and she denounces the designs of men who are not just,
> so that the people pay for the reckless deeds and evil plans
> of *basileis* whose slanted words twist her straight path.
>
> (*WD* 220–1, 259–62; tr. Athanassakis)

One man's corruption and injustice causes evil for the entire polis, which suffers from famine, plague, infertility of fields, animals and women, and the ravages of war (238–47, cf. *Il.* XVI.384–92). Conversely, 'when men issue straight decisions . . . and do not step at all off the road of rightness, their city flourishes' (235–7, cf. *Od.* XIX.109–14). As the myth of Prometheus, the champion of humankind, explains, man himself is responsible for the origin and predominance of evil in this world (*Th.* 521–616; *WD* 47–106), and by continuing to commit injustice, he continues to harm himself, his community and his descendants. Logically, then, the human race itself is responsible also for improving the miserable conditions on earth by understanding their causes and consequences and acting accordingly.

Here lies the primary obligation of the *basileis*. But the lowly and weak members of the community, although unable to change the distribution of power (*WD* 202–12), share this responsibility. They can draw the appropriate consequences for their own lives, be just, work hard, and realize a 'good order' in their own small world. They can share the truth they have recognized (10) with all those who have chosen the path of injustice (27–36, 106–7, 213–18, 274–97, 298ff.) or suffer under it. Most of all, they can instruct those in power and appeal to them to act justly and responsibly (202–19, 219–69).

This Hesiod does with great insistence. The first part of his *Works and Days* is an 'instruction to princes', devoted to promoting the notion of communal responsibility through justice and proper procedures.[27] While this poem depicts an imperfect world full of injustice and failures on the part of high and low alike, the *Theogony* presents the emergence of an ideal

[27] West 1978: 3–30, Martin 1984; *doubts*: Heath 1985; also Havelock 1978: ch. 11.

world among the gods and of the just leadership of Zeus, the model for any *basileus*. Combining cosmogony and theogony, the poem explains the long and complex evolution of the divine and spiritual world of the present. Within this framework, Hesiod uses genealogy and personification to conceptualize, connect, and organize important social and political factors and values. If, for example, one of Zeus's wives, Themis, gives birth to three daughters, Eunomia, Dike and Eirene (*Th*. 901–3), we are to understand that *themis*, respect for traditional norms of justice, is a major characteristic of Zeus's regime, which promotes good order (*eunomia*), justice (*dikē*), and peace (*eirēnē*).

The *Theogony*'s political component is visible from the proem, a hymn to the Muses, the poet's sponsors. Their song is dedicated especially to praising Zeus who 'surpasses the other gods in rank and might' (49), and has 'made a fair settlement for the gods and given each his domain' (73–4). Hence especially the *basileus* stands under his and the Muses' protection, when 'with straight justice he gives his verdict and with unerring firmness and wisdom brings some great strife to a swift end', rights wrong with gentle persuasion, and therefore is revered like a god by the people (81–93). Zeus's rule among the gods, too, is generally respected because it is based not only on military prowess, might and success (629–716, 820–68), but on a series of wise and politically exemplary measures. He corrects injuries committed by his predecessors and proves a generous leader whose friendliness generates loyalty (651–63, 390–400). He secures the support of the gods for his rule by distributing privileges justly (881–5). And he builds his regime on a broad base of positive values, represented by his wives and offspring (886–917, see above). A political reading of the *Theogony* thus reveals a rich picture, embedded traditionally in actions, myths, and genealogies, but amounting to a full conceptualization of the values and behaviour patterns that are essential for the wellbeing of the community.[28]

Interestingly, Hesiod does not utilize the other approach illustrated by Homer: the direct appeal to the assembly. This is in part because he distrusts the city and the agora with its quarrels and politics (27–32), and partly because the small farmer has to work hard to avoid debt and misery (*WD* 298–316, 361–4, 393–413), and cannot afford to get involved in communal politics. In fact, Hesiod advises his fellow citizens to stay away even from the blacksmith's shop where the lazy crowds gather in cold winter (493–4); rather, he encourages them to focus on their work, family,

[28] Solmsen 1949: 3–75, Brown 1953: 7–50, Raaflaub 1988: 216–20 (218 on the difference between Zeus's rule and that of his ancestors).

farm, and good relations with their neighbours (243–51). This recommendation, urging withdrawal from the public sphere, was soon to be rejected by Solon (section 6).

5 Tyrtaeus to Theognis

Most songs of the Archaic poets are preserved only in small fragments. Even these show that the poets were intensely aware of the social and political issues that troubled their communities, thus allowing us to perceive trends and tensions that influenced the development of early political thinking.

Around 650 Sparta faced a revolt of the enslaved Messenians. In this critical situation Tyrtaeus wrote a series of elegies, intending to bolster the morale of the Spartan army. Whatever the circumstances of their performance, these poems document impressively the ideals of polis solidarity and of the citizen-soldier who proves his excellence (*aretē*) in helping to save his polis. 'It is a beautiful thing when a good man falls and dies fighting for his country' (10.1–2W; cf. 12W (section 1)). The explicit extension of such civic *aretē* to all citizens, including the commoners, goes far beyond the implicit acknowledgment of their contribution in the *Iliad*; it underscores the nature of the polis as an essentially egalitarian 'citizen-state' (section 3). Under the exceptional conditions prevailing in Sparta, this fact was publicly recognized and had institutional consequences earlier than elsewhere (section 7). Tyrtaeus' appeal to all citizens to assume responsibility for the wellbeing of the polis was naturally confined to their military function in the phalanx (11.31–4W).[29] Solon soon tried to enhance such solidarity also in the socio-political sphere (section 6).

The stance of Archilochus, who also dates to the mid-seventh century, is emphatically individualistic, contemptuous of traditional values, and critical of the elite. The Homeric warrior ideal valued death in honourable fight over shameful flight and a long life, and the Spartan mother encouraged her son to come back 'with the shield or on the shield'; Archilochus cheerfully admits that he threw his shield away to run faster: 'but I escaped, so what does it matter? Let the shield go; I can buy another one equally good' (5W, tr. Lattimore). The Homeric hero was supposed to be tall, handsome and elegant; centuries later, these qualities still mattered greatly to the elite (Xenophanes 3W); not to Archilochus:

[29] Bowra 1938: 37–70, Jaeger 1960: 315–37 = 1966: 103–42, Podlecki 1984: 92–105. On the performance context: West 1974: 9–18, Bowie 1986, 1990, Murray 1991b.

I don't like the towering captain with the spraddly length of leg,
one who swaggers in his lovelocks and cleanshaves beneath the chin.
Give me a man short and squarely set upon his legs, a man
full of heart, not to be shaken from the place he plants his feet. (114W)

To the elite, wealth and power were indispensable; Archilochus again disagrees (19W). Rather, projecting the persona of a mercenary (section 2), the poet relies only on his own resources: 'By spear is kneaded the bread I eat, by spear my Ismaric wine is won, which I drink, leaning on my spear' (2W; cf. Hybrias, *Scol. anon.* 909P).[30] Such independence was essential for the emancipation of political thinking from prevailing traditions and social constraints.

The late seventh and sixth centuries were a period of crisis and rapid change. In many poleis social tensions and intense rivalries among the elite resulted in the usurpation of sole power by 'tyrants' (an 'umbrella term' covering many forms of sole rule).[31] Elite abuses of power met with resistance. Successful non-elite members of the community demanded a share in government. The aristocracy lost much of their solidarity, power and authority. Under such pressure, they were forced to reconsider their values and defend what they had taken for granted before. Gradually, there emerged a system of aristocratic ethics.[32] The struggles and debates surrounding these issues are reflected in the *Theognidea*, a collection of short elegies of various authorship and date, the core of which, located in Megara and addressed to young Kyrnos, dates to the sixth century.[33]

Theognis realized that the aristocracy were doomed unless they avoided attitudes and actions that were likely to prompt civil strife (*stasis*) and tyranny (39–52). Social mobility posed another threat: non-elite upstarts made their influence felt (drastically formulated in 53–8), and impoverished elite families were unable to play their traditional public role (173–8, 667–70). To Theognis' horror, some of the latter tried to salvage themselves through marriage alliances with wealthy non-elite families (183–96, 1109–14). All this explains Theognis' insistence on aristocratic exclusiveness and a superiority which was based on centuries of

[30] Rankin 1977, Burnett 1983: 15–104, Podlecki 1984: 30–52. Shield: Schwertfeger 1982. Also Nagy 1976, 1979: 243–52.

[31] Berve 1967, Pleket 1969, Kinzl 1979, Stahl 1987, McGlew 1993, Stein-Hölkeskamp 1996; also Rösler 1980.

[32] Arnheim 1977, Donlan 1980: chs.2–3, Stein-Hölkeskamp 1989, Nagy 1996; also Greenhalgh 1972, Donlan 1973.

[33] Oost 1973, Legon 1981: 106–19. But see section 2 on the Panhellenic validity and appeal of such poetry: Nagy 1985 and, generally, Figueira and Nagy 1985, Donlan 1980: ch. 3, Stein-Hölkeskamp 1989: ch. 3.2. Similar aristocratic values are emphasized in the poetry of Pindar (first half fifth century): Bowra 1964, Donlan 1980: ch. 3, Kurke 1991.

accomplishment and leadership and on the claim that the corresponding qualities were inborn, transmitted by nature (*phusis*), and therefore could not be acquired or learned: 'It is easier to beget and raise a person than to give him a noble mind. Nobody has yet found out how to make a fool wise and a good man out of a bad . . . By teaching one will never make the bad man good' (429–38, tr. Fränkel). In the old and primarily social distinction between noble (*agathos/esthlos*) and non-noble (*kakos*), moral connotations (good/bad) now became predominant. A typology was developed that attributed all positive qualities to the aristocracy (e.g., 145–50, 315–22, 611–14, 635–6), who thus claimed to be alone capable of governing the polis, and all negative qualities to the *kakoi*, who were thus *a priori* supposed to be disqualified from leadership: where they assumed power, disaster was inevitable (667–80). This terminology and the prejudices underlying it had a long-lasting impact on political and constitutional thinking.[34]

Not surprisingly, therefore, Theognis' instructions to Kyrnos begin as follows:

> Reason well: do not encompass achievements (*aretai*), honour or riches through an unworthy act, or by infringement of right. This then comes first; but next: never mingle with bad men (*kakoi*); banish them far from your side, staying with good men (*agathoi*) alone. Always eat and drink in their company: sit with them always; make it your task to please those who have might (*dynamis*) in the land. You will learn good from the good; but once you mingle with bad men, even the wits that you had speedily vanish away. (29–36)

Attempts to establish the aristocracy as a strictly separated 'caste' were unsuccessful. But relationships based on friendship (*philia*) and mutual obligations within the elite were strengthened and institutionally fixed: aristocratic 'clubs' (*hetaireiai*), the symposium, and pederasty, though long existent, assumed increased social, cultural and political significance.[35]

6 Solon

Solon the Athenian is well known as lawgiver and one of the 'Seven Sages' (section 7). The Athens of his time was hit especially hard by economic and social crisis and stood on the brink of violent civil strife. Apparently,

[34] E.g., Hdt. III.81; Ps. Xen. *Ath. Pol.* 1.3–9; Donlan 1980: ch. 4.

[35] *Philia*: Konstan 1997: ch. 1. *Hetaireiai*: Calhoun 1913, Sartori 1957, Rösler 1980. Symposium: Murray 1990c, Slater 1991, Schmitt Pantel 1992. Pederasty: Dover 1978.

two main 'factions' were opposed to each other: the wealthy and powerful and the *dēmos* (Sol. 5W.1–4; 37W.1–5). Solon was elected chief official (archon) in 594 and given full power to resolve the conflict. As it turned out, both sides eventually were dissatisfied with his measures; in particular, some of the '*dēmos*-party' had hoped that, once in power, he would distribute much of the land of the rich to the poor (34W; 37W.7–10; cf. 36W.20–7).[36]

One of Solon's programmatic statements survives (4W).[37] It begins by emphasizing human responsibility for human affairs: the gods do not want to harm the polis – quite the contrary; rather, 'the citizens themselves in their ruthlessness are bent on destruction of their great city' (1–6; cf. *Od.* 1.28–43). Most of all, the blame falls on the injustice, greed and *hubris* of the aristocracy (7–14), whom Solon criticizes much more harshly than earlier authors (cf. 4a/cW; Theogn. 39–52). Accordingly, he draws more radical and specific consequences than they did: Dike, the goddess of Justice, whose 'solemn commitments' have been ignored (14),

> knows well, though silent, what happens and what has been happening,
> and in her time she certainly (*pantōs*) returns to extract her revenge;
> for it comes upon the entire polis as a wound that cannot be avoided . . .
> (15–17, tr. Fränkel)

As a result, the polis will be worn out by slavery, domestic strife and tyranny (19–25).

In Hesiod, Dike is the daughter of Zeus who complains to her father when she is (quite literally) mistreated by the corrupt judges (*WD* 259–60, section 4). Here she stands on her own as divine Justice, and her punishment comes with certainty (*pantōs*, 16, 28; cf. 13.8, 28, 31). The misery caused by her retribution is 'inescapable' and hits the entire community and every community (*pasa polis*). Hesiod has to rely on his trust in Zeus's justice ('I do not believe yet that Zeus's wisdom will allow this,' *WD* 273). Why does Solon *know* where Hesiod believed? Because his thinking is empirical and political. Hesiod's typological picture of the polis that suffers the consequences of one man's wickedness is entirely informed by epic and Near Eastern traditions and, despite an allusion to war, focuses on physical, not political aspects.[38] For Solon such consequences are

[36] Sources: Arist. *Ath.Pol.* 5–13 with comments by Rhodes 1981 and Chambers 1990; Plu. *Solon* with Manfredini and Piccirilli 1977. Generally, Andrewes 1982, Manville 1990: ch. 6, Welwei 1992: 150–206, Murray 1993: ch. 11, Raaflaub 1996b with bibliography.

[37] Jaeger 1960: 315–37 = 1966: 75–99, Vlastos 1946, Stahl 1992; in a wider context: Meier 1990: 40–52.

[38] Walcot 1966: esp. 72–3, West 1978: 213, Erler 1987: 14–21.

entirely social and political: they were experienced by many poleis in and before his time, and alarmingly were becoming part of Athens' experience as well. An empirically proven and generally known chain of cause and effect thus links sociopolitical abuse on the part of the citizens with sociopolitical harm suffered by the community. Solon illustrates the certainty and predictability of this link as follows: 'Out of the cloud comes the heavy snow and the hailstorm; hard on the lightning's flash follows the thunder's report. So through great men is a polis destroyed, and through their foolishness the people are enslaved by a sole ruler. He whom one lifts too high is not pulled down again lightly' (9W). The perception of such political laws, comparable to laws of nature, gives Solon the confidence, in assessing social and political causality, to substitute certainty for belief: *pantōs*.

The programmatic poem continues:

> Thus the public ruin invades the house of each citizen,
> and the courtyard doors no longer have strength to keep it away,
> but it overleaps the lofty wall, and though a man runs in
> and tries to hide in chamber or closet, it ferrets him out. (4W.26–9)

Every citizen is affected. Hence Hesiod's recommendation to focus on the private sphere, hard work, and good relations with neighbours is not viable: the public crisis requires every citizen to be involved in public life. Moreover, Solon's empirical political analysis proves that the aristocracy, despite their resources and power, can no longer afford to act unjustly, because the consequences of their evil acts will destroy them as well. Hence Solon's 'teaching' (30) presents the citizens with a clear alternative: the 'bad order' (*dusnomia*), source of much evil for the polis, the causes of which they know and under which they suffer, or *eunomia*, the 'good order' which they can restore if they all assume responsibility for the common good (30–9 (section 7)).

Unlike Hesiod, Solon had the power to introduce measures that would help realize his ideas. In a later poem he boasts two major accomplishments. One is the 'liberation of the earth' from the markers indicating an encumbrance of the land, and the liberation of the debt bondsmen (36.1–15W), connected with the general abolition of debt bondage (Arist. *Ath.Pol.* 6; Plu. *Solon* 15): 'these things I accomplished by the power of my office, fitting together force and law in true harmony, and I carried out my promise' (15–17). Henceforth personal freedom was an inalienable right of the Athenian citizen. The other accomplishment is his laws: 'I wrote laws for the lowborn and noble alike, fitting out straight justice for each person' (18–20). This legislation was comprehensive in all areas of concern to the early lawgivers. By enacting these laws and reforms, the polis under Solon's leadership brought about deep changes in traditional social and economic structures and relations. The polis forged its own instruments to redress a crisis and assumed an unprecedented amount of power over its citizens (section 7).[39]

Solon's political reforms included the introduction (or refinement) of property classes which determined the level of political participation available to the citizens and replaced birth by wealth as criterion for political power (Arist. *Ath.Pol.* 7.3–4; Plu. *Solon* 18.1–2). The creation of a new council, elected and with limited tenure, which prepared and deliberated the assembly's agenda (*Ath.Pol.* 8.4; Plu. *Solon* 19.1–2), if authentic, must have increased the latter's authority and balanced the power of the traditional aristocratic 'Areopagus Council'; hence it is likely that Solon also formalized, at least minimally, the meetings and powers of the assembly.[40] The citizens' communal responsibility was enhanced by the law that anyone who wished (*ho boulomenos*) could take action on behalf of a person who had been wronged (*Ath.Pol.* 9.1; Plu. *Solon* 18.6–7), and by the creation of a new court of appeal (*hēliaia*, *Ath.Pol.* 9.1; Plu. *Solon* 18.2–3). All in all, Solon's policy, demonstrating deep insight into the nature of the problems he faced, was integrative, trying to strike a delicate balance: he recognized the need to give the *dēmos* a share in power and responsibility without impairing aristocratic leadership (fr. 5–6W).[41]

7 Archaic lawgivers

In other poleis, too, citizens chose to resolve their conflicts by entrusting their polis to the wisdom of a lawgiver with unlimited power (e.g., Hdt. v.28–30.1; Arist. *Pol.* III.1285a30–b3). This approach presupposes confidence in the possibility of fair mediation, and the availability both of persons with experience and authority and of political or institutional instruments suitable to change existing conditions. This in turn presupposes that politics and institutions were sufficiently developed and that the 'constitution' of a polis (in the widest sense of the word) was seen, not as ordained by divine sanction or fixed by tradition, but as changeable by human insight and decision.

[39] Collection of the fragments: Ruschenbusch 1966. See Vlastos 1946, Havelock 1978: ch. 14, Eder 1986, Gagarin 1986: ch. 3.

[40] Cf. ML 8, Fornara 1983: no.19, on the *bolē dēmosiē* of Chios. Areopagus: Wallace 1989.

[41] See the works cited in n. 36 *ad locc.*; more bibliography in Raaflaub 1996b: 1062–7. Wallace 1997 offers a more democratic assessment.

We can only speculate about why the Greeks adopted this method of conflict resolution through political mediation. The role of prophets and lawgivers, and the possibility of written legislation, were probably known to them from Near Eastern sources (section 9). The coexistence of a multitude of poleis, each with its own history, traditions, customs and rules, made it easy to see that polis constitutions and institutions could vary almost infinitely, though within certain limits, and to observe what worked and what did not. Furthermore, in the 'age of colonization' many new poleis were founded around the Mediterranean and Black Seas. Although these tended to imitate the institutions of their metropolis, adjustments and innovations must have been frequent, especially since the colonizers often came from several places. Apollo was the divine sponsor of colonizing ventures; his oracle in Delphi was consulted regularly before the settlers departed. It is possible, therefore, though not universally agreed, that the oracle also served as a kind of depository, clearing house, and advisory centre for political issues.[42]

Not surprisingly, therefore, later tradition knew of many strong personalities who had served as lawgivers and reformers. Several of them were counted among the 'Seven Sages' (a late and fictitious grouping that variously combined more than seven eminent persons) whom tradition connected with Delphi. They stood above the conflicts of the period, occupying, as C. Meier puts it, a 'third position', and became an influential intellectual and political force.[43] For example, according to Herodotus (1.170), Thales of Miletus (section 8) advised the Ionians, who in the mid-sixth century were threatened by the Persian empire, 'to set up a common centre of government and administration (*bouleutērion*) on Teos [north of Ephesus], because it occupied a central position in Ionia; the other cities, though continuing no less to be inhabited, would be considered comparable to demes [districts]'. This proposal would have transformed Ionia into one unified and centralized polis.

Fourth-century political theory believed that 'codification of law' was widespread in Archaic Greece, and modern historians have mostly accepted this view. As K.-J. Hölkeskamp now demonstrates, however, large-scale codification of law was exceptional, documented only in Athens and Gortyn; in most cases legislation was limited to single laws or clusters of laws, dealing with a specific set of problems that had seriously threatened domestic peace. Even so, the enactment of written legislation as a means to resolve potentially harmful conflicts was an important step:

[42] Barker 1918: 3–6, 48–9, Forrest 1957, Kiechle 1958, Malkin 1987: ch. 1, 1989, Meier 1990: 40–52. [43] Meier 1990: 42, 44. Seven Sages: Snell 1938, Gärtner 1975, Fehling 1985.

it reduced the officials' freedom of decision and, by implication, the power of the leading families from among whom these officials were chosen; it also restricted self-help and extended the power of the polis over the citizens' freedom of action. By creating a common obligation to the polis and offering shared protection by the polis, such laws enhanced the emerging concepts of citizenship and community. The increasing certainty of law and elimination of arbitrariness on the part of judges and officials both improved the situation of the non-elite citizens and served the interests of the elite, because it reduced the potential of conflict and thus lowered the risk of their collective loss of power to a tyrant.[44]

The homicide law of Draco the Athenian offers a good example. It was probably enacted in 622 in reaction to the repercussions of the 'Cylonian affair' in 636 (a failed attempt at tyranny, ending in a massacre, despite guarantees of safety). The event left deep scars on the community: the prominent Alcmeonid family was held responsible and forced into exile; there may have been a series of vendettas among the elite; and a religious authority, Epimenides of Crete, was engaged to purify the city.[45] The law on homicide therefore introduced procedures for settling conflicts that were particularly sensitive and potentially harmful to the polis. It distinguished between premeditated and involuntary killing, made self-help (the traditional means of redress) dependent on a court decision, instituted a special jury (the *ephetai*) for this purpose, and, in the case of involuntary murder, granted safe exile to the killer and facilitated his reconciliation with the victim's family.[46]

As Solon's example shows (section 6), on the political side, too, legislation and institutional innovation served to resolve problems and stabilize the community. An early law from Dreros on Crete (650–600) declares: 'This has been decided by the polis: when a man has been *kosmos*, the same man shall not be *kosmos* again for ten years. If he does act as *kosmos*, whatever judgments he gives, he shall owe double, and he shall lose his rights to office, as long as he lives, and whatever he does as *kosmos* shall be nothing.' The *kosmoi* were the chief magistrates. The prohibition of repeated tenure of this office at short intervals must have been prompted by negative experiences; presumably, the intention was to break the holder's immunity

[44] Codification: Bonner and Smith 1930: ch. 3, Gagarin 1986: chs.3–4, Camassa 1988, 1996. (Another example is the Roman Twelve Tables.) *Contra*: Hölkeskamp 1992a, 1992b, and 1999. Significance: Ruschenbusch 1960: 149–52, 1983, Eder 1986, Gehrke 1993, Sealey 1994: ch. 2. Citizenship: Manville 1990: 79–82, Walter 1993: 190–2.

[45] Lang 1967, Welwei 1992: 133–7.

[46] *IG* I^3 104, ML 86, Fornara 1983b: no.15. Ruschenbusch 1960, Stroud 1968, Gagarin 1981, Humphreys 1991, Welwei 1992: 138–46.

and to prevent him from accumulating excessive power for himself and his family.[47] Each regulation of this kind offers limited insight, but their sum gives a good impression of the range of possibilities and the amount of thought that lies behind Archaic legislation.[48]

In a few cases we know more about the range and circumstances of political legislation. For example, in the eighth century, the Spartans concluded the conquest of Laconia, appropriated the best land for themselves, established a system of dependent poleis (called *perioikoi*), and enslaved Messenia. Half a century later, a defeat by Argos and a revolt of the Messenian slaves (helots) prompted a serious crisis and the demand for redistribution of land. As a consequence, the Spartan citizens (Spartiates) transformed themselves into an elite of professional warriors whose community-oriented lifestyle was supported by the products of their state-assigned farms and the labour of the helots. Social and economic differences were not eliminated, but in their public function as citizens and soldiers the Spartiates saw themselves increasingly as peers or 'similars' (*homoioi*). Although the peculiar Spartan social and educational system evolved slowly and essential components were introduced much later, ideology eventually attributed it all to a legendary early lawgiver, Lycurgus. Modern scholarship has demythologized this tradition, but at least three elements can plausibly be dated to the seventh century: the professionalization of the citizen soldiers and their economic support system; the definition of a concept of citizenship resulting from the sharp distinction between helots, *perioikoi*, and Spartiates, and the latter's privileges and obligations; and the formalization of political institutions by law (the 'Great Rhetra').[49]

Cited by Plutarch (*Lycurgus* 6), the Rhetra is also reflected in Tyrtaeus 4W, which ties it to the 'Messenian Revolt' (c. 650). It included a new division of the community into territorial units and a reorganization of the institutions. The council (*gerousia*) comprised thirty life-time members (over sixty years old, hence *gerontes*), certainly fewer than the number of elite families; membership was therefore no longer an automatic prerogative of all these families. The two *basileis* were part of the *gerousia*; while preserving hereditary succession and other privileges, they were now fully integrated into the collective leadership of the polis. The assembly was to

[47] ML 2 with tr., comm. and bibl., Fornara 1983b: no.11, Ehrenberg 1943.

[48] See now the collections of Koerner 1993, van Effenterre and Ruzé 1994, Hölkeskamp 1999.

[49] Oliva 1971, Cartledge 1979, 1980, Mossé 1983, Hodkinson 1983, 1997 (among many articles); Christ 1986 (with a survey of scholarship (1–72) and bibliography (471–503)); Murray 1993: ch. 10, Kennell 1995, Thommen 1996.

meet regularly in connection with the festival of Apollo at a designated place. The assembled *damos* had the power to decide. But this power was restricted by the right of *basileis* and *gerontes* to introduce proposals, control the discussion, and perhaps even refuse to accept 'crooked choices'.[50] Although the *damos* was endowed with supreme power (*kratos*), the system thus was remarkably balanced. Compared to an earlier, more informal one which is reflected in the Homeric epics (section 3), it represents a decisive advance: leadership, council, and assembly are minimally but effectively formalized, their relationship and powers defined. A big step has been made toward establishing in the polis a 'political sphere', conceptualizing the polis as a civic community, and enhancing the citizens' participation in it and responsibility for it.

Correspondingly, Tyrtaeus insists on the quality of the polis as a shared community that supersedes the claims of the individual (section 5). One of his elegies, later called '*Eunomia*' and perhaps mentioning this term, included a summary of the Rhetra, which thus was identified with the ideal of *eunomia* and presented as a solution to the crisis described in the same poem (4W). The same ideal is emphasized by other authors: Solon's poem (4W) offers a striking analogy (section 6); Hesiod introduces Eunomia as daughter of Zeus and Themis and sister of Dike and Eirene (section 4); Alcman, another Spartan poet, praises her as sister of Persuasion (Peitho) and daughter of Foresight (Promathea, 64P). Spartan tradition maintained that an early state of *stasis* and disorder (*kakonomia*) had been transformed into one of *eunomia* which secured lasting stability (Hdt. 1.65–6; Thuc. 1.18). The ideal of *eunomia* thus stands not only for a good social order, but for the political resolution of crisis and *stasis* and for the integration of the polis; it represents the aim of the Archaic lawgivers and encapsulates the main concern of early Greek political thinking.[51]

Solon emphasized the contrast between *eunomia* and *dusnomia*, in which this 'good order' was disturbed and bad order prevailed (4W. 30–9). The absence of good order could also be described as *anomia* or *kakonomia*, and later *eunomia* was modified by equality (*isonomia*, below). Archaic constitutional terminology was thus based on a traditional ideal, *eunomia*, and built on the notion of 'order'.[52] Variations were described by comparing them with the 'good order' par excellence, the aristocratically governed traditional community.

[50] Oliva 1971: 71–102, Cartledge 1979: 131–5, Murray 1993: 165–71, Ruzé 1991.

[51] On *eunomia*: Andrewes 1938, Ehrenberg 1965: 139–58, Meier 1970: 15–25. Through the classical period it remained a powerful concept that encapsulated the essence of the traditional aristocratic order: e.g., Ps. Xen. *Ath. Pol.* 1.8–9.

[52] Ostwald 1969: esp. 62–95, Meier 1970: 15–25.

The combination of 'equality' with this traditional concept was momentous. In their struggle against tyrants the aristocrats discovered the political value of something they previously had taken for granted: their share in power and government, their political equality (*isonomia*, sometimes modified as *isēgoria*, 'equality of speech'). In principle, *isonomia* could mean both 'equality before the law' and 'equality by law, equal shares, equal participation', especially in politics. The physician Alcmaeon of Croton (probably late sixth or early fifth century) illustrates a practical use of this concept: 'The bond of health is the "equal rights" (*isonomia*) of the powers (*dunameis*), moist and dry, cold and hot, bitter and sweet, and the rest, while the *monarchia* of one of them is the cause of disease; for the monarchy of either is destructive . . . Health is the proportionate admixture of the qualities' (DK 24 B4, tr. KRS no. 310). Applying *isonomia* to medicine, Alcmaeon confirms that the meaning of 'equal shares' and 'political equality' was prevalent. The probable allusion to *isonomia* in Anaximander's sole fragment (section 8) makes it likely that the term existed by the middle of the sixth century.[53]

Now equality is a flexible notion, defined by the size and composition of the group to which it is applied. *Isonomia*, the 'order of political equality', though initially confined to the aristocracy, was later expanded to include all those citizens – mostly non-aristocratic farmers – who qualified for service in the hoplite phalanx. In Sparta the political rights of these citizen-soldiers were enhanced and formalized by the Rhetra, in Athens at the end of the sixth century by the reforms of another visionary leader, Cleisthenes. Reflecting important differences, the Spartan citizens eventually became *homoioi*, the Athenians *isoi* ('equals').[54]

Cleisthenes' system was also intended to resolve a serious crisis. Several decades after Solon's reforms, continuing rivalries among leading families enabled Peisistratus to establish a tyranny. His regime was quite popular, succeeded in pacifying and further integrating the community, and improved economic conditions. The rule of his sons, however, soon turned oppressive.[55] The tyrant family was expelled in 510, but the liberated aristocracy immediately resumed their traditional infighting. This led to *stasis* and foreign intervention until the Athenian *dēmos* rose up in arms, expelled one of the faction leaders and his foreign supporters, and

[53] *Isonomia*: Vlastos 1953, 1964, Ostwald 1969: 96–160, Pleket 1972, Raaflaub 1985: 113–17. Alcmaeon: Vlastos 1953: 344–7, 363–5, Guthrie 1962: 341–59, Triebel-Schubert 1984.

[54] Cleisthenes and *isonomia*: Raaflaub 1995: 49–51. Spartan *homoioi*: Cartledge 1996a. Eventually, in full democracy, equality was extended to all citizens; hence *isonomia* could be almost equivalent to *dēmokratia* (e.g. Hdt. III.80.6).

[55] Berve 1967: I.41–77, Andrewes 1982b, Lewis 1988, Eder 1992.

enabled Cleisthenes to realize a set of far-reaching reforms which he had proposed earlier and which evidently were widely acceptable (508/7). The large territory of Attica was divided into more than one hundred 'demes' ('districts', consisting mostly of villages and parts of towns) which were assigned important functions in cult and self-administration; these were combined into 'thirds' (*trittues*) and 'tribes' (*phulai*) so that each tribe united citizens from various areas. Members of the same tribe served in important communal functions (especially in the polis army, in cults and festivals, and in the new Council of Five Hundred, into which every deme delegated elected members according to its population). The system of representation devised for this purpose was highly sophisticated. Its purpose apparently was to encourage familiarity and collaboration among the citizens, to connect the outlying demes with the political centre where council and assembly met to make communal decisions, to get the citizens involved in communal responsibility on the local and polis levels, and to create a thoroughly integrated community. In this, Cleisthenes was successful: Athens' rise to 'world power' and the evolution of full democracy in the first half of the fifth century were rooted in and unthinkable without the political and mental changes brought about by these reforms.[56]

8 Early philosophers

Most of the eminent thinkers of the sixth century came from Ionia. Until the disastrous end of their revolt against Persia (494), Miletus and other Ionian poleis were among the most prominent in the Hellenic world, connected by colonization and trade with the western Mediterranean, the Black Sea region, the Levant and Egypt. Anaximander and Hecataeus who drew the first world maps were Milesians. Herodotus, the explorer and historian of both east and west, was born in Doric Halicarnassus. Hence in this area knowledge and influences came together from many parts of the world, not least, via Anatolia and the Levant, from Mesopotamia (section 9). The conditions for scientific and speculative thought thus were especially favourable there, although we do not know what caused the qualitative leap from empirical observation and practical science to pure speculation and philosophy. Thales of Miletus, for example, was interested in mathematics and astronomy (Hdt. 1.74), and famous for resolving difficult practical problems (75) and giving good

[56] Ostwald 1988, Meier 1990: 53–81, Ober 1993, Raaflaub 1995 (with bibliography); Loraux 1996, and the chapters by Ober and Raaflaub in Morris and Raaflaub 1997.

political advice (170, section 7), but none of this explains why he began to search for the first principle of all things and defined it as water.[57]

Little is reliably known about the lives of these early thinkers, and their works are preserved only in scattered citations by later authors. They were primarily interested not in human society and political phenomena, but in the world and nature (*phusis*) as a whole. Physics, ethics, politics, and religion were not yet separated into special disciplines. Man was part of nature, subject to its laws; conversely, natural processes could be understood and explained by applying relations and rules observed in human society. Alcmaeon of Croton (section 7) offers one example, Anaximander of Miletus (610–540) another. One sentence of his work on *phusis* is preserved: '. . . some other *apeiron* nature, from which come into being all the heavens and the worlds in them. And the source of coming-to-be for existing things is that into which destruction, too, happens, "according to necessity; for they pay penalty (*dikē*) and retribution (*tisis*) to each other for their injustice (*adikia*) according to the assessment of Time"' (DK 12 B1, tr. KRS no.110). The cosmos is here conceptualized as a system that is subject to the laws and relations of justice. In the unlimited *apeiron* all potential being exists in a perfect mixture and dynamic balance. The things that exist emerge from it in a balance of opposites. Such balance represents justice, the domination of one over the other(s) injustice which must be compensated for in the course of time. This view of the cosmos presupposes an analogous concept of social and political order: it functions only on the basis of justice and the balance of power among equals (that is, *isonomia*, section 7).[58]

Xenophanes of Colophon (570–475) was cited above (section 1) for his emphasis on the good of the polis and his critical stance toward the elite; otherwise, he is remarkable for his criticism of Homer's and Hesiod's anthropomorphic concept of the gods (DK 21 B11–16), and for his radical and abstract concept of monotheism (B23–6).[59] Pythagoras of Samos (570/60–480) emigrated to southern Italy around 530, supposedly to escape the tyranny of Polycrates, and founded in Croton a religious and politically active 'order'. Already Xenophanes (fr. 7W) attests to his belief in reincarnation; later members of his 'school' were influential teachers and provoked strong reactions, for example, on the part of Plato, but he left no written statements and his own career and teaching soon became

[57] KRS 76–99, Guthrie 1962: 45–72, Barnes 1979: 5–16. Generally: Emlyn-Jones 1980, Hussey 1995.

[58] KRS 100–42, Guthrie 1962: 72–115, Barnes 1979: 19–37, Vlastos 1947, Vernant 1965: 185–206.

[59] KRS 163–80, Guthrie 1962: 360–402, Barnes 1979: 82–99, Lesher 1992, Schäfer 1996.

so completely enveloped in legend that we have no possibility of retrieving his political thinking.[60]

Heraclitus of Ephesus (550–480) is the most puzzling of the early philosophers. What remains of his book on *phusis* are brief and disconnected aphorisms that can be combined in many ways without indicating any coherent whole. His 'theory of nature' was based on fire as the principle of all things, on the dialectical unity of opposites ('they would not know the name of *dikē* if these things [i.e. injustice] did not exist', DK 22 B23, tr. Freeman), and on the idea of constant change ('In the same river, we both step and do not step, we are and we are not', B49a; hence the statement attributed to Heraclitus, 'all is in flux', *panta rhei*). Like Anaximander, he postulated a correspondence between the structures and relationships in nature or cosmos and human societies.[61] In both spheres, justice, balance and retaliation were the essential factors; hence great importance was attributed to the middle (*meson*) and 'right measure' (*metrion*): even 'the sun will not transgress his measures; otherwise the Furies, ministers of Justice, will find him out' (B94). Trade (B90) and war (B53) served as other metaphors to understand relations in nature: 'One should know that war is togetherness (*xunon*) and *dikē* is strife, and everything comes about by way of strife and necessity' (B80). In his political statements, Heraclitus urged respect for law and the common good: 'If we speak with intelligence (*xun nōi*), we must base our strength on that which is common (*xunon*) to all, as the city on the law (*nomos*), and even more strongly. For all human laws are nourished by one, which is divine' (B114, cf. B2); 'the people should fight for the *nomos* as if for their city-wall' (B44). But Heraclitus' elitist perspective and contempt for the *dēmos* are obvious throughout (B29, 104, 121), and Plato must have approved of his willingness to submit to the authority of one man, 'if he is the best' (B49, cf. B33). In this thinker, who attacked all social powers in existence (tyrants, *dēmos*, customs, religion, popular views, poets, philosophers, and his own city), intellectual independence and critical distance from traditional values reached an early climax.[62]

9 Near Eastern antecedents and influences

In recent years the question of Near Eastern (Mesopotamian, Hittite, Phoenician) and Egyptian influences on Archaic Greek culture has

[60] KRS 214–38, Guthrie 1962: ch. 4, Barnes 1979: 100–20, von Fritz 1940, Burkert 1962, Zhmud 1997; see also Centrone, in Ch. 27 below.

[61] *Kosmos* was used in Doric poleis also for 'state' and 'government'; Plato later added to these dimensions of macrocosm and *kosmos* a third one, governed by the same principles, the microcosm of the human body and soul.

[62] KRS 181–212, Guthrie 1962: 402–92, Barnes 1979: 57–81, 127–35; Kahn 1979.

been discussed with renewed intensity, resulting in much improved understanding – notwithstanding occasional exaggerated claims and conclusions, based in part on questionable evidence and dubious methodologies.[63] For the purposes of this chapter, the question has great importance. After all, Hesiod and, to a lesser degree, Homer integrated into their poems many ideas that originated in Near Eastern myths, theogonies, cosmogonies and wisdom literature. The beginnings of Greek science (especially mathematics and astronomy) and philosophy were stimulated decisively by Mesopotamian antecedents. In a much broader context, eastern influences helped shape the development of Greek religion, crafts, art and architecture, technology (both civil and military), coinage, and writing. Although more debated, such influences are visible also in social, legal, and political phenomena, such as tyranny, the enactment of written law, and the symposium.[64]

Two facts seem undeniable. One is a remarkable openness among Archaic Greeks toward the Near Eastern and Egyptian civilizations, which they admired for their age and accomplishments and from which they were eager to learn. The Greeks were aware of many differences, but their tendency to define their own identity through a negative comparison with the 'barbarians' is a later phenomenon that was fully developed only by the mid-fifth century as a consequence of their political conflicts with the Persian empire in the late sixth and fifth centuries.[65] The other fact is the coincidence, in the 'Geometric' and especially 'Orientalizing' Periods (eighth/seventh centuries), between the evolution of Greek polis society and a phase of comprehensive cultural interchange between the Greeks and their eastern and southern neighbours which made a deep and lasting impact on many facets of Greek society. What still needs to be explored and understood much better – and on both sides – is not the fact or even range of such cultural interchange and influence, but their preconditions and limits and the exact modalities of transmission and effect. One of the decisive questions is how such foreign impulses were integrated into Greek – or, for that matter, Etruscan and Roman – culture.

[63] For the latter, Bernal 1987, 1991, 1993; see Levine and Peradotto 1989, Lefkowitz 1996, Lefkowitz and Rogers 1996, Burstein 1996a.

[64] Hesiod: Walcot 1966, West 1966: 1–31, 1978: 3–30, Penglase 1994. Homer: Burkert 1991, Rollinger 1996; see also Duchemin 1995, West 1997. Science, philosophy: Neugebauer 1957, Dicks 1970, Lloyd 1991b, Pichot 1991, Zhmud 1997: 179–93, 261–70, Haider 1988, 1996, Burkert 1992. On the other issues mentioned, see the bibliography cited in Raaflaub and Müller-Luckner 1993: xviii n.40; in addition: S. Morris 1992, Matthäus 1993. Generally: Dunbabin 1957, Helck 1979, Haider 1988, 1996, Burkert 1992, Kopcke and Tokumaru 1992, Burstein 1996b.

[65] Schwabl 1962, Diller 1962, Walser 1984: ch. 1, Hall 1989, Georges 1994; see also Reverdin and Grange 1990, Dihle 1994, Bichler 1996, Weiler 1996.

(For example, so far those who postulate that the Greek polis grew out of Phoenician roots have not explained under what conditions, how exactly, and to what extent such 'roots' might have been 'transplanted' into Greek soil and flourished there.[66]) Another challenge consists of distinguishing carefully between various spheres or types of influence: the diffusion of objects of art and material culture, of myths and cults, political and social structures, and finally political concepts and ideas probably followed markedly different patterns.[67]

Nevertheless, at first sight the search for such influences in the sphere of early political thought seems promising. Egypt was the site of the earliest large-scale state formation in human history. The organization and maintenance of this state and the legitimation of power and rule of its king required forms of thinking that by the very nature of their purpose must have been 'political'. City-state systems and territorial empires soon developed in Mesopotamia and Anatolia, then in the Levant as well, succeeding each other in a constant process of rising and falling dynasties and powers, and interacting with each other through diplomacy, alliances and wars. Both within these states and in their forms of interaction we should expect to find reflections of political thinking. Unfortunately, however, this field of inquiry is complex and still insufficiently developed, due in part to the nature of the evidence, in part to the specialists' reluctance to attempt synthesis and generalization.[68] Hence a few general remarks must suffice here, focusing on one major idea that pervades all societies concerned: justice.

As H. W. F. Saggs emphasizes, 'Everywhere in the ancient Near East, the giving of justice was an essential function of the ruler, whether king or tribal leader. Social injustice was an offence against the gods.' According to Egyptian thought, human society was by nature incapable of maintaining a viable and lasting social order; left to itself, it tended to be chaotic, unequal, and unjust, divided into poor and rich, weak and strong, oppressed and oppressors. Such inequality was understood as an expression of disorder, injustice and untruth (*isfet*), as opposed to order, justice and truth (*ma'at*). *Ma'at* was not equality but an order in which oppression was avoided, the strong protected the weak, and the weak, in a system of mutual obligation, supported the strong through obedience and loyalty. Jan Assmann calls this the principle of 'vertical solidarity'. Accordingly,

[66] Drews 1979, Gschnitzer 1988: esp. 300–2, Bernal 1993; see the discussion in Raaflaub and Müller-Luckner 1993: 394–7.

[67] Raaflaub and Müller-Luckner 1993: xxi, Humphreys 1993d.

[68] Frankfort et al. 1946 is an exception. See also Voegelin 1956, Weber-Schäfer 1976, Vernant 1982, Raaflaub and Müller-Luckner 1993. On the following section also Halpern and Hobson 1993, Irani and Silver 1995.

the Egyptian ideology of kingship emphasized the pharaoh's protective function and his responsibility for justice and order. The supreme god had established the king 'to dispense justice among his people, to placate the gods, to realize *ma'at*, and to destroy *isfet*'. Hence, too, the state, rooted in divine order, was seen as indispensable for protecting humans from each other and providing a strong framework for justice and order. It was the individual's obligation to fit himself by word and deed into this system of good order.[69]

Similar concepts of divinely sanctioned justice are found in Mesopotamia and Iran.[70] In Mesopotamia, too, the human world order was supposed to reflect the order of the divine cosmos. It was the individual's duty to meet his obligations at his place in this order. The highest god was represented at the head of the state by the king who was ruler and supreme judge. As Thorkild Jacobsen puts it, 'The national kingship was the guarantee of "the ways of Sumer" (that is, the ways of civilized Mesopotamia), the orderly, lawful pattern of life. Its function in the world was to give protection against enemies external and internal, to insure the reign of justice and righteousness in human affairs.' Despite these principles, justice was long seen as a favour that could not be claimed but obtained only through the right connections on the divine and human levels. In the second millennium, however, the perspective gradually shifted and the idea of justice as a right began to prevail. This, not surprisingly, was the period of Hammurabi and his great collection and publication of laws. In the prologue, Hammurabi claims to have been appointed by the gods 'to make justice appear in the land, to destroy the evil and wicked so that the strong might not oppress the weak'.[71] Whatever their exact nature and function, collections of laws like Hammurabi's stand at the beginning of a long development in the sphere of the enactment of written law which produced the early Greek and Roman law collections, eventually resulted in the massive late antique codifications of Theodosius and Justinian, and shaped western law, legal procedure and legal thought into our own century.[72] A similarly influential tradition

[69] Saggs 1989: ch. 8 (156 for passage quoted), Assmann 1990 (201–12 on the text cited), 1993 (22 on 'vertical solidarity'); Wilson 1946, Baines 1995, Morschauser 1995, Lorton 1995. Bibliography in O'Connor and Silverman 1995: 301–38.

[70] On Old-Persian *arta*: Briant 1995: 523, 1996: 138–9 and ch. 6.

[71] Greengus 1995: 471. Similarly, in the inscription on his tomb in Naqš-i Rustam, the Persian King Darius declares: 'By the will of Ahura-Mazda, I am such that I am favourable to the just and unfavourable to the unjust: I do not want the weak to submit to the will of the strong, nor do I want the strong to experience wrong on the part of the weak!' (Briant 1996: 224; cf. 1995: 522).

[72] Jacobsen 1946 (197 for passage quoted), Wilcke 1993, Westbrook 1995, Foster 1995, Greengus 1995: 471–2, Berlin 1996. On the laws of Hammurabi: Westbrook 1989, Bottéro 1992: ch. 10. Influence on western codes: Westbrook 1988, Sealey 1994: ch. 2.

originated in thoughts about social justice among the ancient Hebrews – thoughts, furthermore, that were presented to rulers and people alike by charismatic prophets who were unique both in claiming direct inspiration by the one and only God and in denouncing 'particular cases of social evils, holding up any individual, however powerful, to public condemnation'.[73]

A general concern for justice and good order sanctioned by the supreme gods, the king as supreme leader in charge of maintaining and dispensing justice, the enactment of written law as a means to enhance justice, and a concept of social justice that protects the weaker members of society from abuse of power by the stronger (including the possibility, attested in Mesopotamia, among the Hurrians, and in Israel, of cancelling debts to offer relief to the impoverished[74]): these are phenomena that find obvious parallels in Archaic Greece. It is especially striking that Hesiod, who strongly insists on the importance of justice to the wellbeing of human society, draws broadly on Near Eastern traditions. Solon also emphasizes the need to uphold divinely supported justice and, like the Near Eastern king, steps between the rich and the poor, the strong and the weak, to protect both from each other; he urges the restoration of a traditional form of 'good order' (*eunomia*) that shows remarkable similarities to the Egyptian concept of *ma'at*, introduces measures of debt relief and thereby realizes a central concern of Near Eastern social justice, and is the author of perhaps the most comprehensive collection of laws enacted in Archaic Greece.[75] Given such correspondences, it is tempting to assume that the political thinking of these two men was also directly influenced by Near Eastern precedents.[76]

This is probably true to some extent – but things are more complex. There exist, for example, interesting similarities between Hesiod and his near-contemporary, the Hebrew prophet Amos, and recently the suggestion was made that, rather than searching for individual traces of direct influences, we should consider as the source of such analogies an intellectual *koinē* in the Eastern Mediterranean of the first part of the first millennium.[77] Moreover, the Greeks' own views of Near Eastern antecedents

[73] Saggs 1989: 15–16. See Irwin 1946, Voegelin 1956, Silver 1983, 1995, Seybold and Ungern-Sternberg 1993, Avalos 1995.

[74] Westbrook 1995; V. Haas in Raaflaub and Müller-Luckner 1993: 378.

[75] Hesiod: section 4 and n.64. Solon: section 6; Fadinger 1996. His position in the middle: fr. 36.20–7; 37; 5W.

[76] In the case of Solon, a strong ancient tradition suggests that as well; but see Szegedy-Maszak 1978, Lefkowitz 1981: 44–5.

[77] Seybold and Ungern-Sternberg 1993 with bibliography. Cf. Yamauchi 1980 for a comparison between Solon and Nehemiah.

are often naive and questionable. For example, their admiration of ancient civilizations and their obsession with the principle of the 'first discoverer' (*prōtos heuretēs*), and with analogizing similar phenomena in different cultures, induced them to assume that the later must depend on the earlier and to construct historical circumstances that explained such apparent influences; hence they often failed to perceive differences behind superficial similarities and to recognize the possibility of growth or discovery in more than one historical or cultural context.[78]

For all these reasons, we should appreciate real analogies without overlooking obvious and important differences. In Near Eastern societies, legislation and jurisdiction are the responsibility of the king and his appointees. Although he may react to, or anticipate, popular complaints, he alone decides whether and how to act, and when he acts it is usually to uphold divinely sanctioned order. For example, the measure of debt cancellation is introduced at the Mesopotamian king's assumption of power and at irregular intervals during his reign; it is designed to give temporary, not permanent relief, to demonstrate the king's care for his people, and to increase his popularity. Irregularity and unpredictability insure the measure's success; even when it is institutionalized to take place at regular intervals – as in Israel, at the initiative of priestly circles opposed to the kings – it is legitimized directly by the highest divine authority.[79] In Greece, as we have seen, the principle of upholding justice is voiced as a demand by the powerless (Hesiod) and realized programmatically, upon massive popular pressure, by an elected mediator (Solon). Protest and reform are prompted by the elite's failure to live up to their obligation. This obligation is founded not in divine law outside or above society but in communal values and norms. Jurisdiction is the responsibility of all members of the aristocracy and handled, individually or collectively, in a public setting. Written law is enacted, upon communal approval, by lawgivers whose mandate rests on a decision by the entire community. The cancellation of debt in Athens is only the prelude to much more incisive measures: the permanent abolition of debt bondage and the fixation of the free citizens' political rights and responsibilities.[80] In all these respects, we might conclude, Near Eastern influence is partial, limited to giving impulses and suggesting means and procedures (such as the cancellation of debt, the inscribing of law on stone); the scope, purpose, realization,

[78] Hence the frequent traditions about travels of Greek thinkers to Egypt where they supposedly were inspired by ancient wisdom: Lloyd 1975: 49–60, 147–9; Zhmud 1997: 57–60.

[79] Westbrook 1995; cf. Finley 1982: ch. 9, esp. 162–3. Role of the people: Dandamayev 1981; Robinson 1997: 16–22 with bibliography.

[80] Raaflaub 1985: 54–65.

and social-political significance of such measures in the Greek context are determined by the structure and needs of polis and society and, since these differ greatly from Near Eastern societies, turn out to be substantially different, too.

In fact, as two examples will illustrate, the differences are fundamental. First, the relations of the Near Eastern kings and the Archaic *basileis* to their supreme gods differ strongly. Accordingly, political and religious structures and thinking are much more intertwined in the Near East than in Greece. The early Greek poets certainly attribute to the gods (particularly Zeus) an important role as promoters and enforcers of justice, but the problems their political thinking is concerned with fit into an entirely human framework of cause and effect. The gods are thought to punish evildoers and their communities and, through seers, poets, or leaders blessed by them, to offer advice about salutary measures to be taken in a crisis, but they neither cause nor resolve such a crisis. Rather, the crisis is caused by specific human mistakes or irresponsible acts within a given society, and it must be resolved by that society itself. It is man's responsibility for the wellbeing of his community, therefore, upon which political reflection focuses from the very beginning. This is obvious already in Homer and Hesiod, and Solon makes it explicit.[81] In other words, in Greece political thinking does not originate in a setting of comprehensive and absolute divine order and justice, whose maintenance is recognized as the supreme duty of the divinely authorized and legitimized king; it does not, as in Egypt, stand in the horizon of *ma'at* or, as in Mesopotamia, in that of a comprehensive conception of the cosmos as a state, nor again, as in Israel, in that of the laws of Yahweh.

The second example concerns precisely the Mesopotamian idea of the cosmos as a hierarchically structured state that is ruled, with absolute authority, by the gods under the leadership of the sky god, Anu. The principle of authority, 'the power which produces automatic acceptance and obedience, is a basic constituent in all organized human society. Were it not for unquestioning obedience to customs, to laws, and those "in authority," society would dissolve in anarchy and chaos.' The human world structurally corresponds to the cosmos; in cosmic hierarchy, man's position corresponds to that of slaves in human society. It is the function of humans and state to serve the gods and to perpetuate the cosmic order.

[81] Esp. *Od.* 1.32–44; Solon 4W. The different concepts of the origins of evil are illustrative: in Hesiod humankind receives the evils as punishment for the wrongs committed by its champion, Prometheus (section 4); the analogy with the suffering of the polis for the injustice of 'one man' (*WD* 238–47) is evident. In Sumerian myth the evils were created at the whim of some gods who momentarily forgot their responsibility (Jacobsen 1946: 165).

The individual, whether high or low, is tied into a strict hierarchy that determines the system of values and norms. 'In a civilization which sees the whole universe as a state, obedience must necessarily stand out as a prime virtue. For a state is built on obedience, on the unquestioned acceptance of authority. It can cause no wonder, therefore, to find that in Mesopotamia the "good life" was the "obedient life".'[82] It is difficult to think of a starker contrast to Greek society.[83] Clearly, in such a system thought and action of the individual were severely restricted. Independence of mind and thought were not valued; political thinking almost by definition was restricted to the ruling circles and focused on legitimizing the existing order and distribution of power in order to secure their stability and permanence. The king's responsibility to maintain social justice equally served the primary purpose of anticipating dissatisfaction and stabilizing the system.

These conclusions are not intended to imply any kind of value judgment. Near Eastern political thinking served the needs of societies, communities and states that differed massively from their early Greek counterparts; accordingly, it was radically different in nature, function and expression. Hence its influence on early Greek political thinking, although by no means negligible, was perhaps more limited than the broad range of cultural influences noted at the beginning of this section might initially lead one to believe.

10 Conclusion: the beginnings of political thinking in Archaic Greece

Archaic thinking, as reflected in the early poets and philosophers, often focused on values and relationships, justice and good order in the polis, that is, on political problems that were of great importance for the wellbeing of the community. If we assume, as seems plausible, that such early political thinking developed together with the polis, the polis itself must be one of the factors that were decisive for its emergence (sections 1, 3). But the question of what causes and preconditions made such thinking possible or necessary requires a broader answer. More research is required here but, tentatively, the following aspects might be emphasized.[84]

Comparison helps to define some negative conditions: unlike most Near Eastern societies, Archaic Greek society was not dominated by a sacred kingship; obedience and subordination were not the principal

[82] Jacobsen 1946: 138–9, 202. [83] Vernant 1982.
[84] See also Voegelin 1957, Vernant 1982, Meier 1989, 1990: 29–52.

virtues. Authority was not unassailable; criticism and independence were not discouraged (section 9).

After the turmoils of the Dark Ages, the polis gradually became the predominant form of community in Hellas (section 3). No large and centralized territorial states emerged because, it seems, the formation of such states was necessitated neither by major external threats nor by economic needs. For centuries the Aegean world was left to itself; it developed outside the power sphere of major empires. From about the mid-seventh century, wars, mostly in the form of conflicts between neighbouring poleis, usually did not threaten the existence of the community. The leadership in these poleis was weak: the overall leader was a *primus inter pares* whose position was based on his personal resources and qualities. The members of the 'proto-aristocratic' leading class depicted in the epics of Homer and Hesiod enjoyed basic equality, despite differences in wealth, power and authority. In their intensive competition, the paramount *basileus* was vulnerable to criticism like everyone else.

Although the aristocracy that gradually emerged were ambitious, their efforts to set up barriers against the other members of the community failed because, despite their glorious self-presentation, only a relatively small gap separated them from the broad class of independent farmers. These 'masses' played an indispensable role in the communal army and assembly; hence polis society contained a strong egalitarian component. The elite therefore depended on the farmers, had to recognize and respect their sentiments and were in turn open to criticism, and the poleis as small and open communities provided fertile ground for criticism and conflict. Furthermore, because of the lack of massive external pressure and the limited role of war, there was no need for a strong, disciplined, and cohesive elite. Typically, the aristocracy sought to prove their excellence in an alternative arena, that of athletic competition, which assumed great importance in the Archaic age.[85]

All this happened in a period of rapid social change. The polis developed into a tight unit in which the communal element was strengthened at the expense of the individual *oikos*, and power and political procedures were formalized and somewhat depersonalized. Colonization, seafaring and trade offered many opportunities for success and economic gain. Social and political mobility and hence the pressure on the aristocracy increased. This complex development was compounded by social and economic crisis and often violent confrontations between the wealthy land-

[85] The comparison with Rome is useful here: Raaflaub 1984: 552–66.

owners and large parts of the smaller landholders who were tied to the former through various forms of dependence (sections 5–6). In such crises it became necessary to find new ways of resolving conflicts. Often those involved agreed upon a process of mediation and legislation by a person or group of persons who stood above the parties. Institutions and customs varied greatly among poleis: comparison was easy and must have stimulated reflection. The colonizing movement provided many opportunities for experimentation with new solutions that in turn influenced developments in Greece as well. In short, there developed in the Greek world an increasingly widespread, highly developed, and highly respected culture of political thinking which found its expression in remarkably complex, radical, and innovative solutions (sections 6–7).

These factors, some of which existed already in the late eighth century when the Homeric epics were composed, became more pronounced and significant over the next two hundred years. They explain why political reflection became possible and necessary and why it was broadly based, not limited to ruling circles. Within this framework we might identify one more factor which perhaps provided the immediate cause that provoked the earliest manifestations of political thinking and remained one of its most cogent stimuli. This is the dissatisfaction with the shortcomings of elite leadership and the discrepancy between the interests of community and individual which form the core of Homer's, Hesiod's, and Solon's political concerns. By observing, criticizing and even rejecting some of the values, norms, and attitudes of the aristocracy, the early thinkers were provoked to analyse the essential problems of the community, to conceptualize its needs, and to propagate its values.[86]

[86] On conditions favouring the development of political thought in early Greece, see Vernant 1982, Meier 1989, 1990: especially chs.2 and 3; Cartledge 1998, forthcoming. Some sections of this chapter are based on Raaflaub 1989. I thank Pierre Briant, Andrea Gnirs and the editors for helpful advice.

3

Greek drama and political theory

SIMON GOLDHILL

Tragedy compromises political theory. From the very beginnings of philosophy as a discipline, there has been an uneasy and often conflictual relation between the way that philosophy defines its theoretical project, and the questions that drama allows. Plato, the first policeman of political thought, invents – and founds – a history of struggle between poetry and philosophy and, notoriously, banned drama from his *Republic* for ethical, psychological and epistemological reasons.[1] Yet the ambivalence of his evident attraction to the poetry he dismisses at such length also leads to an anecdotal tradition that before he embarked on philosophy, even Plato wrote tragic verse. Aristotle attempted to save drama for pedagogy: he allowed theatre a role in the education of the philosophically trained man at least.[2] Yet Aristotle, for all that he set himself critically against his teacher Plato's arguments, also contributed to the devaluation and exclusion of drama both by his development of philosophy as a privileged and formal system of argumentation, and by his recognition of a peculiar pleasure in tragedy: 'tragic pleasure' has often since been utilized to impugn the seriousness of theatre's teaching.[3] Many modern philosophers have followed Plato's lead, and mention drama or other literature solely to dismiss the play of narrative and character from the rigorous field of theory. Nietzsche, from his oblique perspective on the discipline of philosophy, formulates a particularly influential and striking view of this rejection of drama when he argues that 'Socratism' destroyed tragedy: rationalist argument, embodied in the figure of Socrates, brings about the – tragic – death of the Dionysiac spirit of tragedy.[4] For Hegel, however, no less influentially engaged with the 'tragic spirit' than Nietzsche, tragedy continues to offer a particular and crucial exploration of the questions of a citizen's life – how life in the polis should be lived – in a way which shows up the deficiencies of particularly a Kantian perspective on ethics. Thus, more recently, Bernard Williams, writing within the tradition of this

[1] Ferrari 1989, Nehamas 1982, Gould 1990 (with further bibliography).
[2] Halliwell 1986, Rorty 1992 (with good further bibliography), Else 1986.
[3] Barish 1981. [4] Silk and Stern 1981.

debate and turning back towards ancient tragedy, can assert that it is a requirement of philosophy to utilize what dramatic texts can provide: 'Philosophy . . . has to make demands on literature'.[5]

This long and not yet finished tradition of contest between philosophy and tragedy, which is nothing less than the question of the boundaries and limits of political theory, finds its most telling case in the classical polis of Athens, where tragedy and philosophy have their founding moments. The history of political thought in the polis will always need to articulate its position on (or against) tragedy. Although comedy has often been construed as a threat to political order – which has resulted in some modern theoretical discussion, particularly after Bakhtin[6] – and although Plato himself also worries about comedy's effect on the citizen (*Laws* VII.816d–817a; cf. *Laws* II *passim*), it is with tragedy that political thought has been fundamentally concerned (see below, section 4). Critical disagreement is particularly fraught here. Paradigmatic of one pole of the debate is the following: 'there is a clear distinction between the tragedians' mode of engagement with political themes and the more rigorous analytic approach that developed around the middle of the fifth century. The emergence of the latter marks the beginning of Greek political theory as such.'[7] In contrast with that claim of a distinct and clear rupture between tragedy and political theory stands this, the other pole of the debate: 'tragedy was as close as one could come to a theoretical institution . . . In its form, content and context of performance, tragedy provided, by example and by precept, a critical consideration of public life . . . Drama was a theoretical act.'[8] So, if, as one well-known political scientist has declared, 'political philosophy constitutes a form of "seeing"',[9] what place in it is there for the *theatron*, the 'place for seeing'? In this chapter, the question to be faced, as the uneasy boundaries between theatre and philosophy are negotiated, is not just 'was tragic thought political?', but rather, 'at what levels and in what ways does tragedy contribute to the history of political thought and theory?' Or even: 'what does it mean when political theory tries to proceed without tragedy?'

1 The institution of the theatre

Political theory's appropriation or refusal of ancient drama will depend in part on its description of the institution of theatre as political. It is a com-

[5] Williams 1993: 13.
[6] Bakhtin 1968, Stallybrass and White 1986, Hirschkop and Shepherd 1989 (with good further bibliography). [7] Winton and Garnsey 1981: 38. [8] Euben 1986: 29.
[9] Wolin 1960: 17.

monplace that 'the political' as a translation of the Greek *ta politika*, 'things to do with the polis', includes all aspects of a citizen's life, and thus theatre is in this sense evidently 'political'. But there are more precise and compelling ways that the production of ancient Athenian drama can be called 'political'. The institution of theatre is analogous to the two other great Athenian democratic institutions for the staging of speeches, the law-court and the assembly. Each congregates a body of citizens, constituted in a privileged way as the collective of the polis, and requires the hearing and judging of arguments in a competitive context. Let us look first briefly at this constitution of an audience of citizens. For in the performance culture of democracy, with its central commitment to public debate and collective decision-making, to be in an audience is not just part of the social fabric of life. It is a fundamental and defining political act. Within the ideology of the shared duties of participatory citizenship, to be in an audience is *to play the role of the democratic citizen*.

The festival of the Great Dionysia, the major occasion for tragedy and comedy in the polis, was the largest formal collection of citizens in the calendar. The standard figures estimate a total of between 14,000 and 17,000 (compared to around 6,000 for the Assembly and up to 6,000 for the law-court – though usually considerably fewer). The vast majority of those present were citizens – adult, enfranchised males. As we will see, foreign ambassadors were required to be in the theatre, and an increasing number of foreign visitors, attracted to tragedy in particular as a cultural event, attended, as did metics (alien residents of Athens). It is unlikely – although the evidence is far from certain – that women attended (especially citizens' wives and daughters), or slaves, except for the public servants of the Council (*Boulē*). More important than the precise demography of the audience, however, is the way that the theatre seating constructed a political map of the city. There were special seats reserved for the members of the *Boulē*, the five hundred strong executive of government, together with their official slave staff of eight. There were special seats for the foreign ambassadors of the states of the empire at the front, along with certain priests and other state dignitaries. There was a special section for ephebes, young men on the point of adopting full citizen obligations. There is also some evidence that each wedge of seating (*kerkis*) was reserved for a particular tribe, the major sociopolitical division of the democratic order since Cleisthenes. Certainly tickets were issued on a tribal basis. A further *kerkis* was reserved, it is reasonably assumed, for foreigners and metics. By marking in such striking spatial terms the age-classes and socio-political categories of the polis, the theatre thus puts the city on display. The audience as collective articulates the sociopolitical organization of the polis. It constitutes – performs – what can be called 'the civic gaze' – the scene of collective, political viewing and judging which forms the public space for citizens' action.[10]

This sense of the city on display is strongly emphasized by the rituals which opened the Great Dionysia. There were four major ceremonials performed in the theatre in front of the assembled citizens before the plays began, each closely aimed at the expression of civic ideals.[11] In the first, the ten generals, the leading military and political figures of the state, poured a libation for the opening sacrifice. Only very rarely indeed in the calendar did these most important elected officials act as a group together in such a ritual fashion – and with regularity only here in the theatre. This emphasizes the power and organization of the polis under whose aegis the festival is mounted, and the political importance of the occasion itself. Second, there was an announcement by a herald of the names of citizens who had benefited the state in particular ways and been awarded a crown for their services. This expressly praised and supported the democratic tenet of an individual's duty to serve the state, and the obligation between individual and the community. Again, the political frame of the polis is clearly highlighted. Third, there was a procession which displayed all the silver paid in tribute by the states of the Athenian empire – a ceremony that glorifies Athens as a military and political power. It was for this – to watch their own tribute paraded – that the foreign ambassadors were required to attend the theatre. Fourth, there was a parade of ephebes whose fathers had been killed fighting for the state. These orphans were brought up and educated at state expense, and when they reached the age of manhood, they were presented in the theatre, in full military panoply, again provided by the state, and they took an oath promising to fight and die for the state as their fathers had before them. The military obligation of the citizen towards the state is ceremonially and graphically displayed.

Each of these ceremonials promotes and projects an idea and ideal of citizen participation in the state, and an image of the power and glory of the polis of Athens. It uses the civic occasion to glorify the polis. This elaborate ceremonial space before such a vast collection of citizens consequently could become a highly charged scene in the political life – in its most narrowly defined sense – of the citizens. Aeschines mocks

[10] For discussion, see Goldhill 1995 and 1997. Evidence is collected in Pickard-Cambridge 1968 and the texts in Csapo and Slater 1995.

[11] For discussion and the evidence, see Goldhill 1990.

Demosthenes for fawning before the most important foreign ambassadors. Demosthenes prosecutes Meidias for punching him whilst assembled in the theatre. This speech shows well how much personal honour was staked before the citizen body in the theatre. 'Those of you who were spectators at the Great Dionysia', declares the orator, 'hissed and booed him as he entered the theatre, and you did everything that showed loathing . . .' (Dem. 21. 226). Demosthenes' description of the scene is full of theatrical language, as the social drama of Meidias in the theatre becomes the subject of debate on the stage of the law-court.[12] The theatre was a space in which all the citizens were actors – as the city itself and its leading citizens were put on display.

Each aspect of this festival's organization embodied a strong sense of a specifically democratic polis ideology. The playwrights were chosen by the Eponymous Archon and funded by the state. This was termed 'to be granted a chorus'. The chorus itself (like the actors, always and only citizens) was funded by the liturgy system – a rich individual was selected by state officials to finance each production; and the competition between these elite *chorēgoi* was a contest for status and honour in the public realm.[13] The judges of the dramatic competition were chosen by lot from panels which enforced representation from each of the tribes. Ten judges were chosen, but only five votes – again chosen randomly – counted in the decision. There was also a special fund called the Theoric Fund which paid each citizen to attend the theatre. This was organized at deme level (a deme is a spatially constituted subsection of a tribe), and clearly corresponds to jury pay (and, eventually, assembly pay), each of which was seen by conservative writers as one of the most scandalous elements of democratic practice, not least because it enabled – encouraged – poorer citizens to do their civic duty. The Theoric Fund was legally protected in an extreme way (which says something of its perceived importance): it was against the law even to propose changing the law of its establishment. After the festival, in accordance with democratic accountability procedures, a special Assembly was held (in the theatre) to review the running of the festival. It is not merely that the Great Dionysia required extensive state involvement: it is rather that at each point a specifically democratic construction of financial and judgmental principles is at work in the institution of theatre.

The institution of the Great Dionysia, for which tragedy and comedy form a centrepiece, is thus in the fullest sense a *political* occasion – an occa-

[12] See Wilson 1992. [13] See Wilson (forthcoming) for discussion of *chorēgia*.

sion to say something about the polis, for the *politai* (citizens) to compete and to play the role of citizen, in a showpiece for democracy. It is a major event in (and not just commentary on) the political life of the city. Above all, it constitutes the democratic citizen as a *theatēs*, a 'spectator' performing an evaluative and participatory role within a collective. The *mot juste* for this spectating is *theōria*, which means not merely 'viewing' but also specifically 'official viewing by participation in a formal ceremonial event'.[14] What is more, there can be little doubt that ancient writers conceived of theatre as an educative experience: the poets are 'the teachers of the people'. It is in part because of poetry's, and, in particular, tragedy's privileged role in the didactic discourse of the polis that Plato bans it from his city – as he attempts to establish his own discipline of philosophy as the one true didactic medium. Tragic theatre, then, is a political institution conceived to teach the citizen. Theatre is a fundamental factor in the politicization of the Athenian citizen, in *putting political reflection in the public domain*.

2 Political themes of tragic writing

Theatre, then, is in the strongest possible sense a *political* event. So, in what ways can the texts of tragedy and comedy be said to contribute to a history of political theory or political thought? Where is theory to be located in the *theōria* of the *theatron*? To answer these questions, I will look first in general terms at how tragedy has been read by modern critics as political writing for the fifth century, and, second, I shall outline some particularly significant general thematic concerns of the genre of tragedy which bear on the political discourse of the city.

It is important to recall from the outset, however, that these modern attempts to place tragedy's contribution to political thought take place within a highly significant context of much broader and more widely shared intellectual concerns about Greece, history and the political. Indeed, it is impossible to discuss the way critics have treated tragedy's political engagement without an awareness of how an idealized image of 'the glory that was Greece' has informed particularly nineteenth- and twentieth-century thought.[15] It is Hegel who paradigmatically instantiates how for many modern writers tragedy plays a fully integral and formative role in a theory of history and politics, and many contemporary

[14] Here it is worth noting that *theōria* is the word from which English 'theory' is derived.
[15] Butler 1935, Jenkyns 1980, Detienne 1981, Silk and Stern 1981, Turner 1981, Clarke 1989.

discussions of tragedy are articulated against Hegel's massive influence.[16] His reading of Sophocles' *Antigone* (and Greek tragedy in general) perfectly exemplifies the complex and comprehensive intertwining of a view of tragedy with the broadest conceptualization of politics and history. For, although lines from the *Antigone* occur on occasion in the *Phenomenology* as mottos or literary glosses for particular points, Hegel's interpretation of the *Antigone* – as a dramatization of a clash between individual and State as a clash of Right and Right – is wholly implicated in his political and historical thinking[17] (for all that it may seem to some to have 'rather slender ties to Sophocles' drama'[18]). Indeed, it is not only as a model of political or ethical action that *Antigone* is significant for Hegel. For on the one hand, tragedy's 'higher language' has a specific force in Hegel's argument, which is developed in parallel to the writings of his friends Hölderlin and Schelling about language, and which is deeply influential in a specifically German tradition in which Nietzsche and Heidegger also have exemplary positions. Tragedy's special language constitutes a privileged expressiveness, a privileged access to things. Tragedy's sublimity changes the possibilities of understanding the world; it grants what Nietzsche calls 'metaphysical consolation . . . from another world'.[19] On the other hand, ancient Greece ('that paradise of the human spirit'[20]) and in particular the polis as a society, provides a fundamental model for Hegel's sense of history and of ethical action. An idealized Greece grounds Hegel's conceptualization of change and progress.[21] In Hegel's writing *Antigone* is thus fully part of an argument about history, about politics, about thought. Indeed, it would be hard to write a history of German political thought that did not recognize 'the tyranny of Greece' over German intellectual practice. *Antigone* is in this sense a text of nineteenth-century political thought. Tragedy is, for Hegel *et al.*, good to think (politically) with.

The twentieth century has continued this engagement. Luce Irigaray, for example, is one particularly influential figure in a series of feminist writers who have used the *Antigone* in its Hegelian guise as a way of thinking about the family and the state, and about female subjectivity and ethical action.[22] Irigaray focuses on Hegel's denial of Antigone's self-consciousness: she can act ethically, but she cannot know what she is doing or,

[16] Hegel's texts on tragedy are conveniently collected in Paolucci and Paolucci 1962. For discussion, see Steiner 1984.
[17] Steiner 1984, Silk and Stern 1981: 312–26.
[18] Pritchard 1992: 87.
[19] Nietzsche 1872: ch. 17.
[20] Hegel 1948: 325.
[21] Shklar 1971.
[22] Irigaray 1985: 214–26; further discussions in 1989: 81–100. Scattered other comments listed by Chanter 1995: 285 n.5.

better, why it is right. Irigaray stresses against Hegel how the marginality of Antigone to the categories of gender can be seen as a challenge to the polarizations of gender – an argument which exemplifies Irigaray's desire to 'question again the foundations of our symbolic order in mythology and in tragedy, because they deal with a landscape which installs itself in the imagination and then, all of a sudden, becomes law'.[23] Because *Antigone* is part of political thought, it must be re-read. So contemporary commentaries of varying lengths and sophistication, and classicists drawing on such material, continue to make *Antigone* (and Antigone) part of contemporary feminist thinking on the family and the State.[24] Although Irigaray rather startlingly claims (in a way which looks back through Kate Millett to Engels and Bachofen) that 'the work of Sophocles . . . marks the *historical* bridge between matriarchy and patriarchy'[25] (my emphasis), it is primarily as a text in the history of cultural imagination (or, in Irigaray's more technical psychoanalytic perspective, as a stay of the Symbolic) that *Antigone* enters these arguments. Re-telling – reanalysing – the *Antigone* is part of political theory's commitment to changing thinking.

Even from such brief examples, it can be seen that tragedy – its narratives and language – has been a significant element in modern political theorizing, particularly in the nineteenth and twentieth centuries, a way of exploring the political thinking of the present by a turn to the formative past. These discussions form an essential context for contemporary understanding of tragedy's political thought, and constantly influence the discussions of particular plays and themes. With that much background, let us now begin, then, to investigate how modern critics have understood drama, and in particular tragedy, as contributing to the political discourse of fifth-century Athens. For ease of exposition, I will distinguish three strategies or traditions of criticism (which in practice can – and do – combine in many different ways).

The first strategy is to locate a narrowly defined and specific political message in a play. In general, tragedy, which is located in the past, and which involves figures other than Athenian citizens, and which is normally set in cities other than Athens, avoids any direct contemporary reference, particularly reference to the cut and thrust of policy making in the city. Consequently, in the case of tragedy (unlike comedy (see below, section 4)) the pursuit of political significance in this first sense requires a

[23] Baruch and Serrano 1988: 159.

[24] A selection: Elshtain 1982, Dietz 1985, Mills 1987, Zerilli 1991, Pritchard 1992, Chanter 1995, Saxonhouse 1992, Lane and Lane 1986, Sourvinou-Inwood 1989, Foley 1996.

[25] Irigaray 1985: 217. For the tradition of Millet, Engels and Bachofen see Goldhill 1986: 51–4.

strategy of applying tragedy's examples – the drama of the other – directly to the contemporary political scene. In its least compelling guise, this has often led critics to allegorize freely – suggesting, for example, that the *Oedipus Tyrannus* of Sophocles is 'about' Pericles, or that Aeschylus' *Persians* is a defence of Themistocles (who is not even named in the play's account of the Greek victory over the Persians).[26] In a more general way, however, tragedy can be seen to be speaking to particular aspects of state policy – to have a political agenda. Euripides' plays that centre on the disasters of the Trojan War have often been seen as criticizing Athenian imperial policy and its losses – and thus criticizing the politicians who proposed or supported such military policy. It is a striking fact, at least with historical hindsight, that the *Trojan Women*, with its tortured sense of suffering and ironic reversal, was produced the year after the Athenians voted to destroy Melos and in the year that the Sicilian expedition – destined to be so crushing a disaster for the Athenians – was being debated and prepared. But the play's very generalizing, as well as suitable caution about such hindsight, makes it hard to limit its message to any particular policy or group of politicians, for all that it may seem specifically relevant to a historical circumstance.[27]

One particularly important exception to this avoidance of direct engagement with contemporary policy is Aeschylus' *Oresteia*, which I shall discuss in some detail below (section 3). The *Eumenides*, the third play of the trilogy, does end in Athens with the foundation of the Areopagus, a court whose constitution had been recently – and violently – reformed; and it also includes references to a recently concluded military treaty with the state of Argos. This has led critics, as we will see, to try to reconstruct Aeschylus' political views and the political message of the trilogy. Even with this exceptional case, however, one of the advances produced by thinking more broadly about the Great Dionysia as an event (as outlined in the second section of this chapter) has been that the complexity of the public exchange which is the production of meaning in the theatre has been articulated in a more developed and nuanced way.[28] The engagement of a multiform audience in the interpretative process; the literary, ritual and ideological framing of the plays; and the dynamics of agonistic political performance in the theatre: all make it much harder to defend the simple claim that the playwright has a direct and specific political message, which an audience receives, and which is recovered by a

[26] See e.g., Podlecki 1966, Knox 1957, Zuntz 1955.

[27] For discussion and bibliography see Croally 1995.

[28] Dodds 1960, Dover 1957; superseded by Macleod 1982, Goldhill 1986, Rose 1992, Meier 1993, Griffith 1995, Seaford 1995.

critic. Indeed, although comedy's innumerable contemporary political gibes still receive considerable attention as a constitutive part of the public discourse of the polis, there are fewer and fewer critics who find tragedy's political force in such narrowly conceived commentary either on the policies of the state or on individual political figures.

The second major tradition of political reading has concentrated on how tragedy contributes to the understanding of the political process itself. Tragedy's educative function can be located in the retelling of the myths of the past for the democratic polis. The *Oresteia* with its massive tale of the genesis of law, the social control of violence, and its conclusion in the city of Athens itself, is a particularly good example for this model of tragedy educating the citizen into citizenship. Thus Christian Meier, setting himself against the first tradition I have outlined, writes paradigmatically: 'What Aeschylus thought of [the Areopagus] reforms is not only a moot point, but one with little bearing on our interpretation of the trilogy.'[29] It is rather the condition of citizenship – what it means to live as a free adult male in the community of the polis – which is explored in tragedy; and it is in this way that tragedy contributes to a discourse of politics. So Jean-Pierre Vernant, in one of the most influential twentieth-century studies of tragedy, has attempted to define what he calls 'the tragic moment', the socio-historical conditions of possibility for the genre and its conflicts.[30] He contrasts the mythic and heroic tradition, on the one hand, embodied in Homer and distinguished by its expression of divine causation, with the civic world of law, on the other, embodied in the institutions of the democratic city and distinguished by its demand of human agency and human responsibility. Tragedy is a sign and symptom of the clash between these two systems, 'an expression of torn consciousness' – and thus what tragedy repeatedly sets at stake is precisely the notion of agency and responsibility central to any understanding of democracy and the citizen's role in the political process. In this way, tragedy's investigations of power, control, violence, authority (and so forth) constitute a public discussion of the *citizen as political subject*.

A third tradition, which is very closely related to the second, focuses more specifically on the deployment of mythic narrative, and, often, on how this intersects with issues of gender. Tragedy's plots are drawn from the great sequences of myth and epic poetry, and not only is each play a dramatic recomposition of such earlier stories, but also each play refers (particularly through its choral odes) to a host of related mythic narratives by way of framing, qualifying, commenting on the staged action. At the

[29] Meier 1993: 115. See also the works cited in n. 28.

[30] Vernant and Vidal-Naquet 1981.

same time, not only do many plays stage ritual actions, but also the language of tragedy is replete with ritual expressions which constantly articulate the action in terms of a religious understanding of transgression and order. In this way, tragedy is not just rewriting mythic and epic narrative for the new political frame of the democratic polis, but also offering and exploring interconnections between myths, projecting, promoting and developing the mythic and ritual patterns which inform civic idea(l)s of political order. Thus the *Oresteia* (also) retells a story of matriarchy overthrown, and deploys the history of the Amazons to explain the history of the Areopagus, and envisages violence as a corrupt sacrifice – as part of its normative projection of the order of the city.[31] Similarly, Euripides' *Ion*, through its tale of the early royal family of Athens, traces, displays, and questions the founding Athenian myth of autochthony – being born from the soil itself – which is central to Athenian self-representation as a polity.[32] On this reading, tragedy' s political thrust lies also in the way it constructs and scrutinizes normative mythic and ritual models that inform a sense of political order fundamental to the citizen as political subject.

So there has been and there continues to be a marked range of response to the question of how tragedy contributes to the political discourse of the polis – from seeing tragedy as offering a specific commentary on particular policies or individuals, through a more general engagement with major political issues of the day, to an education of the citizen into citizenship, both by the interrogation of the categories of participation and by the construction of the citizens' imaginary and symbolic world. The more broadly that the Great Dionysia has been viewed as a political event, the more critics have moved from focusing on localized and specific political agendas to finding in tragedy an interrogation of the categories of citizenship.

For the second and final part of this section, I wish to move on to look at how this interrogation of the categories of citizenship works. By way of introducing the political thematics of tragedy, I shall begin by considering three general thematic interests, common to many plays of the genre, which bear directly on democracy and on the political thought of democracy.

The first concerns that fundamental question of democracy, how to conceptualize and institutionalize the relationship of the individual to the collective. We have already seen how the institution of theatre itself articulates a set of dynamics between outstanding individuals and the col-

[31] See Zeitlin 1978, 1965, Bowie 1993, Vernant and Vidal-Naquet 1981: 150–74.
[32] Zeitlin 1989, Loraux 1984/1993a: 184–236.

lectivity of democracy, from the formation of the collective in an audience from whom the elite *chorēgoi* are distinguished, to the collective chorus on stage from whom the individual actors are to be distinguished. The plays themselves are fundamentally concerned with this political issue. Now, Homer's epics, the *Iliad* and the *Odyssey* (also performed before the city, in the Great Panathenaea) certainly raise the question of how a hero relates to his wider community. In the *Iliad*, Achilles, insulted, withdraws from his community, refuses all blandishments and appeals to return, and prays for his own side's destruction. Achilles is dangerous precisely because of what happens to the bonds of *philia* – mutual and reciprocal ties of duty and obligation, the very making of community – around him. Achilles, the supreme hero, in his very extremeness is transgressive as he is transcendent. The *Iliad*, in short, makes Achilles a problem of integration.[33] The *Odyssey*, in turn, is the narrative of how the trickster Odysseus can be reincorporated into the society of Ithaca, as he attempts through murder and trickery to reassert his rightful place. A tale of reintegration in which significantly Odysseus is never seen in place as king – only travelling to and from his proper place on his property. In Homeric epic, the boundaries of the group are set at stake by its heroes.

Tragedy rearticulates such concerns within the changed context of the fifth-century polis. Indeed, rewriting the stories of the past for the contemporary city is a fundamental part of tragedy's work, rediscovering the political in the inherited resource of valorized narratives. Paradigmatically, the *Oresteia*'s move from the royal family in Argos in the *Agamemnon* to the law-court in Athens in the *Eumenides* redefines the *Odyssey*'s familial solution to conflict as one which requires the institutional frame of the polis. The household cannot be a sufficient locus of order (*dikē*) any more. So, the extant corpus of Sophocles returns obsessively to the figure of the hero – Ajax, Oedipus, Philoctetes, Heracles – and, as has been much discussed by modern critics, to the dangerous and attractive commitment to self over and against community which each hero differently represents.[34] In *Philoctetes*, Philoctetes has been left on a desert island for ten years and the play revolves precisely around the question of how he can be reincorporated into the military collective at Troy. So committed is he to hating his enemies – as a self-definition – that he would rather die in agony alone than act in any way which could be seen to help his enemies. In *Ajax*, the humiliated Ajax attempts and fails to kill his commanders. He too can conceive of no act that might not benefit one

33 See Redfield 1975, Schein 1984.

34 See especially Knox 1964, Winnington-Ingram 1980, Segal 1981, Whitlock-Blundell 1989.

of his enemies, and consequently resorts to suicide. After this drama of failed community, the remainder of the play is taken up with a debate about how Ajax is to be viewed by the community and its leaders. The hero is a central figure in Sophoclean drama not just because of connections with a significant literary tradition or with religious institutions of the polis, but most importantly because this is the figure through which the basic political issue of a relation between an individual and a community can be most strikingly broached. Commitment to self, commitment to family, commitment to polis, are seen as *conflicting* obligations, as tragedy again and again depicts the tensions within the normative construction of the citizen's political role in society.

How to conceive of the collective and its obligations, and how to conceive of the individual's role within the collective, are questions central to the political scope of tragedy. This leads, however, to my second point. Tragedy also scrutinizes the construction of the autonomous judging individual as a democratic ideal. For Aristotle, the staging of the process of practical reasoning – the reasoned response to the archetypal tragic question, *oimoi, ti drāsō*: 'Alas, what should I do?' – is the essential justification for the educative role of tragedy for the citizen (a position opposed to his teacher, Plato). For Aristotle, the subject, like a good philosophically trained citizen, evaluates a situation, judges and acts. Yet tragedy critically explores the potential of such autonomy. The gods repeatedly undercut the surety and self-confidence of the strong individual. For Oedipus, to flee because of an oracle will be to fulfil the oracle. For Ajax, a decision to kill the Atreids is deflected by Athena's imposition of blind insanity. Pentheus is led to his death, dressed as a woman, by a disguised god he fails to recognize. If the legal and political institutions of the fifth-century democratic polis presuppose the possibility of a responsible, judging, autonomous individual, tragedy constantly depicts the barriers, dangers and lures of such a construction. Creon's final words to Oedipus in the *Oedipus Tyrannus* make a suitable sentence for many a tragic figure (*OT* 1522–3): 'do not seek for control in all things: for what you did have control over, did not follow you in life'. Tragedy shows humans locked into narratives over which they have no control, with partial, doubtful knowledge of events or misplaced confidence, aiding and abetting their own misfortune in violence. Tragedy's causal narratives threaten the security of the responsible democratic (or Aristotelian) subject.[35]

This is nowhere clearer – and this is my third point – than in the sphere

[35]Goldhill 1990b.

of communication. The democratic polis depends on the public exchange of language. The law-court and the assembly are routes to power for the citizen as well as the major policy making institutions of the state, the place where the ideals of the polis as well as the status of individuals are contested and promoted. In both institutions, the citizen judges opposing arguments and makes a decision. How language works in the city becomes a pressing intellectual concern of the fifth-century enlightenment – and of tragedy especially. Tragic language – integral to Hegel's political thought, it will be recalled – has become in recent years a defining element in a view of tragedy as a historical event.[36] For Vernant, there is 'a multiplicity of different levels' in tragic discourse, which 'allows the same word to belong to a number of different semantic fields'. Different characters 'employ the same words in their debates but these words take on opposed meanings depending on who utters them'. (He cites here Antigone's and Creon's uses of *nomos* and *philia*.) Thus, he concludes, 'the function of words used on stage is not so much to establish communication between the various characters as to indicate the blockages and barriers between them . . . to locate the points of conflict'. 'The tragic message . . . is precisely that there are zones of opacity and incommunicability in the words men exchange.'[37]

Tragedy indeed displays language's failures and violences. The *Oresteia*, a trilogy whose plotting turns on the activity of persuasion and deceit, fragments and contests the language of *dikē* throughout. Claims to *dikē* reverberate with puns, etymologies, and double senses, as the pattern of violent revenge (*dikē*) turns towards the order (*dikē*) of the city.[38] The reintegration of Philoctetes in Sophocles' *Philoctetes* is negotiated through scenes of verbal deception, doubt and violent cursing, which explore the relation between word and deed, authority and trust in communication.[39] Euripidean characters repeatedly turn to debate the double senses of words, as enmeshed in the ambiguities of language, they forward tragedy through silent withdrawal, violent trickery, or failed belief. As Phaedra programmatically expresses it in the *Hippolytus* (395), 'with the tongue, there is nothing to be trusted'.[40] Tragedy indeed puts language itself in the public domain to be contested, on display and at risk in the glare of democratic scrutiny.

These three thematic nexuses of tragic writing – the relation of individual and community, the autonomy of the subject, and the dangers of lan-

[36] See Vernant and Vidal-Naquet 1981: 6–28, Goldhill 1986: 1–78, Segal 1981.
[37] Vernant and Vidal-Naquet 1981: 17–18. [38] See especially Goldhill 1986: 1–56.
[39] See especially Segal 1981. [40] See Knox 1952, Segal 1972, Goldhill 1986: 107–37, Goff 1990.

guage – go to the very heart of the democratic polis. They show how tragedy finds its political force not only in issues of social obligation and moral doubt, but also in the very principles of democratic conceptualization. In the same way that the institutional structure of ancient theatre can be seen to be political in a full and compelling sense, so too its writing is fully and intricately political from the specific reference to contemporary matters, to the broadest abstractions of democratic thought. The institution of tragedy thus represents the remarkable process of the developing city putting its developing structures of thought at risk and under scrutiny in the public arena of a civic festival. It is in this that we can locate the role of tragedy in 'the politicization of the citizen'.

3 The *Oresteia*

It is time now to look at two exemplary works to see in more detail where and how political argument, political thought, and political theory can be located. There are several plays which have become mainstays of writing on political thought because of their express content. Euripides' *Suppliant Maidens* stages democratic arguments about the benefits and horrors of monarchical rule;[41] Aeschylus' *Persians* offers a range of political and theological reasons for the Greek victory over the Persians;[42] Euripides' *Phoenician Women* has its characters discuss exile and the causes for attacking one's own country.[43] Individual plays also have been subject to close reading in terms of their political vocabulary, to see how specific images, debates and representations draw on the expectations and tropes of fifth-century discourse: the *Prometheus Bound*, for example, stands as one of the most developed expositions of the discourse of tyranny from the democratic polis.[44] But in the space available here, I will look only at two of the most commonly discussed works, Aeschylus' *Oresteia* and Sophocles' *Antigone*, both of which have long held centre stage in the discussion of tragedy and political theory.

The *Oresteia* has already been mentioned several times in this chapter. It is not only the dramatic work which most influences later Greek tragedy, but also the text which has most often proved central to the debate on tragedy's political power, both because of its thematic focuses and because of its engagement with contemporary politics. It is also the work which has most polarized scholars. From one perspective, 'it would be

[41] See Croally 1995: 208–15 with further bibliography.

[42] See Hall 1989 with further bibliography.

[43] See Rawson 1970 with further bibliography.

[44] See Cerri 1975, Lanza 1977.

absurd to characterise Aeschylus' *Oresteia* trilogy . . . as a work of political theory. Aeschylus is not concerned to offer an argued analysis of the concept of justice of the kind presented in Plato's *Republic*.'[45] Even if there is clearly a focus on 'political themes', and even if there is 'reflection that reaches the most abstract level', 'the rigorous analytic approach'[46] of Plato must be distinguished sharply from 'Aeschylus' exploration of political questions and possible answers', which are 'figurative, indirect and allusive: they constitute neither an analysis nor an argument'.[47] From the counter-perspective, 'the transition to democracy in Attica was never perceived as clearly as it was by Aeschylus': the *Oresteia* was a 'turning point of the history of political thought'.[48] 'The real political content of tragedy . . . belonged to an area of political thought that transcended temporary factional groupings':[49] the 'dramatist was a political educator',[50] who 'does not so much solve problems as deepen our understanding of them'.[51] The question here is not so much whether the *Oresteia* (and by extension, Greek tragedy in general) is concerned with political matters, as the degree to which anything 'theoretical', any coherent 'political thought', should be predicated of it.

The trilogy's narrative – one of the most complex of all Greek drama – retells Homer's paradigmatic story of Orestes in a new and problematic way. Where Orestes in Homer can return in glory, kill the usurper of his father's throne, and provide the example of heroic behaviour for the young prince Telemachus, in Aeschylus Orestes is faced – centre stage, in the central scene of the central play – with the grim double bind of being forced to kill his mother to take revenge for his father and regain his rightful place. It is this turning of a lauded example into a tortured problem of competing obligations that gives the work its specifically tragic power. It is the search for the solution to the questions of this tragic crisis that structures the work's political narrative. For the trilogy's action is dominated by a series of violent killings, perpetrated in the name of rightful revenge, and the final play establishes the law-court in Athens as a means of avoiding the continuation of this reciprocal violence. The move from the household, wracked by internal strife, to the city's sense of social order redefines the conditions of possibility for closure: where for Homer the proper order of the household defines social normativity, for Aeschylus there is now the necessary frame of the polis and its institutions. Aeschylus has, precisely, *politicized* Orestes' story.

45 Winton and Garnsey 1981: 38. 46 Winton and Garnsey 1981: 38.
47 Farrar 1988: 37. 48 Meier 1990: 137. 49 Meier 1990: 89. 50 Euben 1990: 67.
51 Euben 1990: 94.

It is the foundation of the court of the Areopagus to which I wish to turn first to explore this sense of closure and order in the polis. Let us look first at the political terms in which the court is established. Orestes, pursued by the Furies after the matricide, goes first to Delphi, where he is ritually purified by Apollo, and then to Athens where he takes sanctuary at the altar of Athena. (Religious ritual is necessary but insufficient for Orestes' return to society. The political solution is required.) The goddess herself establishes a court, the Areopagus, to judge his case on the grounds first that 'the issue is too great for some one human to judge' (*Eumenides* 470–1). The city's patron deity here appeals to the democratic ideal of collective judgment, as she founds the institution central to democratic process. Law is not for a king or a judge to declare, but for the collective, instantiated in the jury, publicly to perform. So, as the jurors are about to vote on Orestes' case, Athena delivers a long speech of foundation for the court in highly significant political terms (681–710). First, it is to be a permanent institution (681–5) (and not a temporary or specific solution). Second, the name of the court is given and etymologized as the hill (*pagos*) of Ares, in remembrance of a sacrifice to Ares, made before Theseus fought the invading Amazons (685–90). By this reference, the court is placed within an ideological history of the city. Not only is Theseus the founder of the polis as a polis (and an important figure in the city's self-representation), but also the Amazons, whom he fights and destroys, stand against the polis's order at every level: as wild, Eastern women, who make war, pillage, ride, and have no male control, they embody transgression, and they are consequently often depicted on state-funded temple architecture (such as the Parthenon) in the process of being defeated by the city's founding father.[52] The court, via its very name, is thus set within the nexus of normative ideals and authoritative narratives that make up a city's history.

Third, Athena describes the court in (glowing) political terminology (690–9):

In it, citizen respect
And inborn fear will restrain
Wrongdoing, day and night alike,
If the citizens do not revolutionize the laws.
You will never discover good drinking, if you pollute
Shining water with foul influxes and mud.
I counsel the citizens to uphold and respect
Neither anarchy nor tyranny;

[52] See Merck 1978, Tyrrell 1984, du Bois 1984.

And not to cast dread from the city wholly.
For who among mortals is just who fears nothing?

The repetition of the word 'citizen' and 'city' constructs the broad (political) frame. The court is to institutionalize a political principle of 'respect' and 'fear', a principle of hierarchical obligation and ties that restrains wrongdoing, and keeps the people between the despotism of tyranny and the chaos of anarchy. Tyranny, the rule associated with the East, is the constantly deprecated Other of democracy; anarchy is the accusation levelled at democracy by oligarchic apologists. Athena's injunction to the citizens fully implicates the law-court within the political ideology of democracy.

The injunction not to revolutionize laws, and not to pollute drinking water with foul influxes and mud, is perhaps the most politically charged sentence in the speech (for all its evident generalizing). For in 462 BC, four years before the *Oresteia* was produced, the Areopagus had been extensively reformed by Ephialtes, who had engineered the transfer of most of its statutory business to the citizen courts (the Areopagus was manned by ex-archons only and hence maintained an image of exclusivity). This increased democratization of the courts had major implications for the highly agonistic political life of the elite in the polis, and was highly contentious: Ephialtes, indeed, was assassinated shortly after the reform, and Cimon, a leading conservative opponent, was exiled. It may seem at first sight, then, that Aeschylus' Athena is opposing such drastic legal reform ('do not revolutionize the laws'), and some critics have been keen to appropriate Aeschylus to a conservative agenda.[53] The reformers themselves, however, had acted under a slogan of a return to the court's original function and the removal of accretions ('foul influxes'), and first degree murder was one of the areas of jurisdiction the Areopagus retained after the reforms. Consequently, other critics have seen Aeschylus (or Athena) as a partisan supporter of the democratic reforms by having the court established to judge murder with a warning against adding new laws to this original foundation.[54] The very generalizations of Athena's speech, however, and the metaphoric, proverbial language of their expression make it hard to assume that Aeschylus' Athena is promoting an explicit, clear and partisan position of this type.[55] Rather, it seems best to conclude that while the speech alludes to a highly contentious issue (and thus is inevitably open to partisan reading), it works to frame the estab-

[53] See e.g., Sidgwick 1887: 25. This has not been much followed in the twentieth century.
[54] As far back as Drake 1853. Most critics suggest Aeschylus supports the reforms but in a moderate or qualified way: Dover 1957, Dodds 1960, Podlecki 1966, Macleod 1982.
[55] See Meier 1990, Sommerstein 1989: 215–18 (an excellent summary).

lishment of the court with a privileged vocabulary of positive political evaluation: the court is necessary for 'respect', 'fear', order and wellbeing: the court is to be (704–6) 'untouched by gain, full of reverence, sharp of spirit, a vigilant guard of the land on behalf of the sleeping citizens'. It is the fundamental contribution of the court to the city's order as part of democratic process that is emphasized – an emphasis that rehearses the central place of law and its institutions in democratic ideology. As the play will end with a procession which instantiates the collective ideal of the polis, so the court is depicted as a bulwark of the city as a whole.

The Areopagus is thus established in specifically democratic and idealized political terms. How then does this democratic institution function in the narrative as a response to the tragic crisis? At one level, the court allows not merely Orestes' acquittal, but also, more generally, an escape from the cycle of reciprocal violence that has repeatedly threatened social order. As the Furies are persuaded to accept the decision of the court (and not turn in aggressive hate against Athens itself), the exchange of language replaces the exchange of violent action, and the city's order emerges as the condition of possibility both of containing violent transgression and of the good, civilized life that such containment brings. Hence the trilogy ends with the chorus and Athena celebrating the society of the city of Athens in a procession that recalls the Panathenaic festival, a celebration of the whole city as a city. In this sense, the *Oresteia* offers a charter for the polis: it articulates an aetiological account of how the polis and its institutions can deal with the potential for violence and transgression. The solution to the tragic crisis is to be found in the institutions of the polis and is thus necessarily and fully a political solution.

At a further level, each act of reciprocal violence in the trilogy's narrative has been strongly marked as a conflict between male and female. In each case, the male has had to reject a tie of the household or blood-family in order to assert his wider social and political position: Agamemnon sacrifices his daughter for the Panhellenic expedition against Troy; Orestes kills his mother to reclaim his patrimony and social status as Argive leader. The narrative in this way displays how violence is (tragically) produced by competing and conflicting obligations. It is significant that not only does Athena vote for Orestes' acquittal for reasons specifically tied to gender roles (734–43, 'I favour the male in all things . . .'), but also her consequent argument with the Furies is the first conflict of the trilogy *not* to rehearse a stark polarization of male and female. What is at stake in the trilogy's movement towards the city as the site of legal justice is thus also the widest sense of the city's social order – male and female, city and household – and it is here that the implications of the work's ending have been most strongly debated. For one tradition of criticism – which can be broadly characterized as liberal-humanist – the conclusion of the play joins male and female, after conflict, in a balance necessary for social cohesion, and the conflicting obligations of city and household come together in the final image of the city as a collective unit escorting the Furies to their new home on the acropolis. Against this progressivist reading, another tradition of criticism – which can broadly be characterized as Marxist and feminist – sees the conclusion of the work as a founding text of patriarchy's suppression of women and the family in the interests of the state.[56] Far from linking male and female, family and state, in harmonious progress, the *Oresteia* demonstrates that 'maternal authority and rights are dead, destroyed by the audacious revolt of the male'.[57]

Now, other readings of the end of the *Oresteia* can certainly be recorded, as can criticisms of and differences within both of the traditions sketched above. The point I wish to emphasize here, however, is that by staging the scene of judgment as an issue that involves gender roles and the order of the city, the *Oresteia*'s conclusion becomes a story which requires a political reading, which can only be read from a political perspective, and be used to express a political perspective. To read the *Oresteia* is to engage with the question Socrates raises in Book II of Plato's *Republic*: what is the justice of a city? Both the repeated return to and rewriting of the *Oresteia* by dramatists from Sophocles onwards, and the history of criticism of the *Oresteia*, demonstrate tellingly how such an engagement with political thought via this trilogy has not yet been ended. The *Oresteia* politicizes its audience.

Central to the *Oresteia*'s concern with the justice of the city is the *language* of *dikē*. As I have already indicated, the *Oresteia*'s thematic concern with how language and persuasion in particular function is in part focused on the term *dikē* (and its cognates). *Dikē* has a wide range of senses from the abstract ideas of 'right', or 'justice', through 'retribution', 'revenge', to the particular legal senses of 'law-court', 'law-case'. It is a fundamental term for the expression of social order – and political theory – in that it both indicates the proper organization of society as a whole, and delineates right action for individuals, and the institutions through which such order is maintained. The *Oresteia* returns obsessively to this term: each act of killing is expressed by its perpetrator as an act of *dikē*, and explored by the chorus as such. Let me offer just two examples.[58] When Electra in the *Choephoroi* discusses with the chorus how to pray at the

56 See for further discussion and bibliography, Goldhill 1986: 33–56.

57 De Beauvoir 1972: 111 n.9.

58 Lengthier discussions in Goldhill 1986: 33–56.

grave of her father, they instruct her to summon a saviour. She asks (120) if they mean 'a juror or someone who brings retribution', a *dikastēs* or a *dikēphoros*. The chorus retort 'Say simply, someone who will kill in return.' Electra's distinction looks forward to the *Eumenides* where the Furies' pursuit of *dikē*, retribution, leads to a trial (*dikai*) before jurors (*dikastai*) who evaluate the justice (*dikē*) of the case. Her question, especially in comparison with the chorus' claim of the simplicity of 'killing in return', lays bare a disjunction, a tension, in the language of 'right': it articulates the complexity of reciprocal action within a familial and civic frame.

So, my second example, when Agamemnon returns from Troy, he enters with the following words (*Agamemnon* 810–16):

> To Argos first and the gods of the land
> It is right (*dikē*) I give due greeting; they have worked with me
> To bring me home. They have helped me with the vengeance (*dikē*)
> I have wrought on Priam's city. Not from the tongues of men
> The gods heard justice (*dik-*), but in one unhesitating cast
> They laid their votes within the urn of blood.

The triple repetition of *dikē* and *dikaios* (the adjective from *dikē*) in three consecutive lines is strongly marked. In the first instance, *dikē* seems to imply a general standard of correct behaviour for the king with regard to the gods. In the second case, it seems to imply the retribution of blood for blood. But in the third case, *dikē* (in the plural) implies 'cases', 'pleas', as indeed the gods' voting procedure suggests a legal process and looks forward to the *Eumenides*. Even the phrase for 'unhesitatingly', *ou dichorrhopos*, punningly echoes the repetition of *dik-* in the previous lines. Aristotle derives the word *dikē* precisely from this term's root (*dicha*: 'separately', 'in two parts'). Even as the returning king appropriates the claims of right to his cause, the language of *dikē* fragments and reveals its tensions and disjunctions.

In this way – and many such examples could be cited here – tragedy explores how normal, political, evaluative language is used within social conflict, and becomes a source of social conflict. Yet as tragedy dramatizes the blockages and barriers of humans trying to communicate with this evaluative language, an audience of the play is put in a remarkable position. From one perspective, an audience can see how words take on different meanings, depending on who uses them and in what circumstances. From another perspective, an audience can appreciate the widest range of meaning, even as it can see a particular character using a term in a specific way. This not only produces a particular depth and semantic richness in tragic language, but also works to uncover the tensions and ambiguities within the evaluative vocabulary of the polis. This is nowhere more strongly articulated than in the *Oresteia* where the language of *dikē* – socio-political order, right – is fragmented and split under Aeschylus' tragic scrutiny. The foundation of the court constructs the aetiology of civic order and a solution for Orestes' position, but the dissemination of the language of *dikē* (along with the trilogy's recognition of conflicting obligations) continues to raise a question for such order, continues to expose the potential for fissure in the very language and ties of social structure.

The *Oresteia*'s complexity and length make it particularly difficult to treat briefly, but three points have emerged from my discussion that are important to my overall argument. First, the narrative of the *Oresteia* redrafts a central Homeric tale as a tragic story of conflicting obligations, and relocates its normative import within the institutional structure of the democratic polis.[59] The politicized narrative becomes a resource for conceptualizing the city as locus of justice and the citizen as agent of *dikē*. Second, the play displays and articulates tensions and conflict within the language of *dikē* in which the city's order is formulated. It dramatizes both the dangers of the powers of language, and the slippage and disjunction in the language of power. It opens to scrutiny the complex interrelations of political order and the language of political order in the democratic polis. Third, the *Oresteia* requires political engagement and negotiation by its audience (as the history of its criticism shows). By ending in Athens with the foundation of a central political institution of the democratic city, and by making the order of the city itself the play's concluding celebration, the *Oresteia* more than any other tragedy makes its story of the past inform the political present of its audience. The *Oresteia* is thus both a contribution and a provocation to political thought.

4 *Antigone*

The second work I wish to look at is Sophocles' *Antigone*. I have already discussed how it is a central text in modern political philosophy's appropriation of ancient tragedy, particularly in response to the way the play dramatizes competing obligations of state and family. Here I want to discuss one particular scene which has not been adequately treated in such debates, but which will lead to a most important set of points about how

[59] For further discussion of the rewriting of Homer see Goldhill 1986: 147–54.

the 'and' of 'tragedy and political theory' is to be conceived. The scene in question is the argument between Creon and Haemon, his son, after Creon has condemned Antigone to death. Haemon is betrothed to Antigone, it will be remembered, and comes to try to persuade his father to reconsider Antigone's punishment.

Creon essays a long argument that constructs an analogy between the family and the state based on the necessity of obedience and discipline in both. 'Yes, this should be your heart's fixed law', he begins (639–40), 'in all things to obey your father's will'. This patriarchal principle is extended to a traditional picture of the propriety and happiness of the harmonious family, where the authority of the father and the obedience of the son unite the household in common duties and against common enemies. (The many tales of intergenerational conflict establish and frame this ideal.) Typically for the fifth century, however, this description of the idealized household turns to the defining arena of the polis (661–73):

> He who does his duty in his own household, will be found righteous in the city also. But if anyone transgresses and does violence to the laws, or thinks to dictate to his rulers, such a one can win no praise from me. No, whomsoever the city may appoint, that man must be obeyed, in little things and in great, in just things and unjust; and I feel sure that one who thus obeys would be a good ruler no less than a good subject, and in the storm of spears would stand his ground where he was set, loyal and dauntless at his comrade's side. But disobedience is the worst of evils. This it is that ruins cities; this makes houses desolate.

I have quoted this speech at length to emphasize the clarity of its political position, its evident theoretical stance. Creon, in a manner which can be paralleled from other genres of writing, and especially in Plato, argues for the necessity of obedience to the laws, even when a citizen disagrees, even when the law seems unjust, even in small matters.[60] (There is scarcely any tradition and no valorization of civic disobedience in the classical polis.[61]) What is more, the citizen committed to obedience will be good at ruling (*archein*) as well as being a good subject (*archesthai*) – a remark more pointed in a society where positions of authority are regularly distributed by lot, thus circulating the positions of 'ruler' and 'subject' – whereas disobedience (*anarchia* – the breakdown of authority) destroys cities as it disrupts households. In the polarized world of political argument, what is not obedience is an absence of all forms of control. The military gloss on this is an inevitable turn of democratic rhetoric. One who knows how to

[60] See Woozley 1979, Kraut 1984. [61] Daube 1972.

obey, in battle would 'stand his ground, where he was set, loyal and dauntless at his comrade's side'. The ephebe, who played such a marked role in the pre-play ceremonials, took a formal oath when he became a citizen and a soldier precisely to stand firm by his comrade wherever he was set in the line. Creon's manipulation of such a binding obligation of Athenian citizenship, together with his traditional normative picture both of the household and of the value of obedience, invests his speech with considerable force as a statement of political principle.

Haemon's reply offers a counter-image. After stressing the political awkwardness of putting Antigone to death (683–704), he argues that a man, like a tree in a winter's flood, should be prepared to bend or break. Otherwise, like a man who will not furl his sails in a storm, he will sink. The *ēthos* (705) of a ruler is what is at stake here: as Creon had put it earlier, the character of a ruler can be tested only in the practice of rule (175–7).

The dialogue which follows, however, forces both figures into different rhetorical stances. 'Is the city to prescribe to me how I am to rule?', asks Creon, 'Am I to rule by any other judgment than my own?', and 'Is not the city held to be its ruler's?' – as his assertion of the necessity of obedience to authority slips towards the asseverations of a (stage) tyrant, a figure dependent solely on his own judgment, who cannot be bound, as all democratic authority is, by the will of the people; who regards the city as his own. (Paradigmatically, it will be recalled, Athena's reason in the *Oresteia* for establishing the court is precisely that the issue is too great to be decided by a single human (*Eumenides* 471–2).) In the agonistic exchange, Creon's democratic argumentation becomes distorted to the extreme of anti-democratic political purpose. Yet Haemon, who argued for flexibility, ends up threatening his father and running from the scene to the site of Antigone's death, where he will kill himself. The appeal to flexibility of character becomes the extreme commitment of self-destruction.

There are two conclusions I wish to stress from this analysis of a family's men arguing political principle over a particular case. The first is this: the expression of political theory in tragedy is always part of a scene of persuasion. Tragedy's dialogue stages language as performative. Language in and as action. Creon's exposition of such a strongly traditional political understanding of authority is formulated to guarantee his son's obedience to a particular decision. Tragedy shows the arguments of political theory to be part of a political power play between characters. Political theory is (for Creon) an act of self-justification for (his) political action, and part of his political performance in itself. This leads to my second point, however. For Creon's self-justificatory arguments are part of a narrative, a tragic narrative leading Creon to grim collapse. The figures' arguments are not the play's argument – and it is in the relation between the two that critical reading takes place: to what degree do Creon's arguments contribute to the tragic outcome of the narrative? How is the move from the espousal of a normative democratic position on authority to a self-serving claim of personal authority to tragic destruction to be evaluated? How is the clash between Creon's self-justification and Antigone's and Haemon's arguments to be judged? Critical readings have repeatedly explored – and declared on – such questions.[62] The exposition of the theoretical position is framed by the irony, reversal and inexorable teleology endemic to tragic narrative. Tragedy's enunciation of political theory investigates how theory plays a role in citizens' tragic narratives.

The *Antigone* is in this way 'a play about practical reason and the ways in which practical reason orders and sees the world'.[63] It does not merely offer a challenge to the 'ruthless simplification of the world of values which effectively eliminates conflicting obligations',[64] but also it poses a question of the relation of theory to practice in political reasoning. Winton and Garnsey – to return to the opening statements of this chapter – distinguish tragedy's political thematics from political theory on the grounds that although there is in tragedy 'reflection that reaches the most abstract level', nonetheless 'the focus of such reflection remains the particular issues and individuals in each case'[65] (as if the relation between abstraction and exemplarity could be so easily formulated). Even if it were true that tragedy's reflection did not reach towards the most general case of the human condition itself (the concluding lines of the *Antigone* are about 'practical thought' itself and 'happiness'), their argument damagingly represses the way that theory's interface with practice must depend precisely on 'cases' or 'particular' issues – and that tragedy shows again and again how problematic that interface can be. The exemplary case of Creon indeed encapsulates the tragic misprision and misuse of theoretical positions in politics.

5 Comedy

Philosophical and pedagogical tradition from Plato onwards is preoccupied with tragedy. This is how it has come to play an integral role in the history of political thought. Comedy, which was also produced at the

[62] See Segal 1981: 152–206, Winnington-Ingram 1980: 117–49, Knox 1964: 62–117, Goldhill 1986: 88–106, each with further bibliography. [63] Nussbaum 1986: 51.
[64] Nussbaum 1986: 63. [65] Winton and Garnsey 1981: 38.

Great Dionysia and at the secondary drama festival of the Lenaia (though it was introduced as a formal competition much later than tragedy), has not enjoyed such a fate. Plato in his final work allows a citizen to watch comedy so that he can find out what *to phortikon*, 'the vulgar and base', is – but prohibits the citizen from learning comedy (*Laws* VII. 816d–817a). Plutarch, although he finds literature an excellent preparation for philosophy, when properly used, advises against having Aristophanes ever read at symposia even, since everyone would need a tutor to explain its obscurities and since it is too rude for a proper citizen's sociality (*Table Talk* VII.8.712a). From Plato to Hegel to Nussbaum, comedy finds little place in the history of political theory.[66] Consequently, so far, this chapter too has focused on tragedy.

Yet modern and ancient readers of Aristophanes have extensively debated the 'political thought' of individual plays and, indeed, of comedy as a genre. For comedy, unlike tragedy, is almost always set in the contemporary polis, involves contemporary characters or types, and has an evident political agenda. The *Acharnians*, for example, begins in the assembly of Athens, where Athenian ambassadors are denounced by the play's hero, an Athenian citizen called Dikaiopolis ('Just City'). He goes on to make speeches about the causes of the Peloponnesian War (with arguments that echo Herodotus' *History*), and to enact his desire for peace by making a private treaty with the Spartans, that leads to him and his family enjoying the benefits of peace apart from the city. Finally, he prepares a great feast as the general Lamachus (almost certainly in the audience) is depicted preparing for war. It is not hard to see how the duties of a citizen towards the community and family, the citizen's military and social obligations, the religious and political frames of action – all of which we have seen to be central to tragedy's political thematics – are also fundamental to this play's plotting. What is more, the *Acharnians*, like most old comedy, includes a *parabasis*, that is, a scene in which the chorus directly addresses the audience about a matter of contemporary political interest (in this case, the benefit for the polis to have an insulting comic poet rather than a flattering politician, and the dangers of modern rhetoric humiliating the old). In this way, comedy is clearly involved in an integral way with the political discourse of the polis.[67]

In a similar way, Aristophanes dramatizes the perils and obsessions of

[66] For a discussion of how philosophers see humour as a problem for the good citizen, however, see Goldhill 1995b: 14–20, and Halliwell 1991.

[67] On *Acharnians* and its politics, see for bibliography and discussion Goldhill 1991: 167–201, esp. 188 n.74.

the law-courts (*Wasps*), the violence and stupidity of the political process and of the behaviour of politicians (*Knights*), the fantasy of political Utopias (*Birds*, *Ecclesiazusae*), the pretensions and politics of education (*Clouds*). In short, comedy presents a carnivalized repertoire of the city's political operations. Aristophanes even – notoriously – insults members of the polis by name, depicts himself getting into political fights with major political leaders, and writes whole plays attacking particular citizens of fame or disrepute (such as Socrates in the *Clouds*, Cleon in the *Knights*).

For all this evident political engagement, modern and ancient critics have strongly disagreed about the political thrust of the performance of comedy. Some have believed the play's (self-)representation of the poet as a fearless democrat speaking out to the city against modern excesses, the foolishness of war and the corruption of politics. Such critics emphasize the consistently conservative slant of Aristophanes' attacks, his repeated invective against the deprivations of war, the vitriolic attacks on Cleon, the populist leader, and, above all, the institution of the *parabasis*, where the poet as *sophos*, authoritative figure of wisdom, speaks out to the polis on matters of concern, like an orator in the assembly.[68] In such a vein, an ancient commentator tells us that the *Frogs* was uniquely voted a second performance 'because of its parabasis', and the pertinence of its advice. Other critics, however, have pointed to the carnivalesque fantasy of comedy, which allows the hero fulfilment of any kind, outwitting even the gods; to the special licence comedy has; to the playful, outrageous and scatological humour which underlies every Aristophanic proposition – and concluded that it is precisely the humour of comedy which prevents there being a serious (political) point to it.[69] Still others – the majority – have attempted to find a middle position, often allowing a measure of 'serious comment' to the *parabasis* or the appeal for peace or the attack on Cleon – but seeing the primary aim of the playwright to be making the audience laugh and thus winning the comic competition.

Perhaps it is best to emphasize first that the striking similarity of thematic focus and range of questions between comedy, tragedy and, say, Plato's dialogues or Thucydides and Herodotus (for all the differences of treatment), indicates a significant continuity in the political discourse or civic ideology of Athens. Comedy certainly is one relevant strand in the polyphony of democratic political language, and as such will necessarily be of interest to political historians. Second, comedy, like tragedy, pre-

[68] Different versions of this in e.g., de Ste. Croix 1972, appendix xxix; Henderson 1980, Konstan 1995.

[69] Different versions of this in e.g., Dover 1972, Reckford 1987, Heath 1987.

sents a transgressive view of the polis: if tragedy approaches political questions through the depiction of other places and other times and through the violent disruptions of tragic dissolution, comedy approaches its politics through images of the city made other by parody, exaggeration, inversion, and fantasy, and through the violent upsets of comic disruption. Throughout the drama festival – a political occasion, as we have seen – political thought is approached obliquely, via detours. It is this in part which makes comedy (and tragedy) such difficult material for the political historian to handle. Third, comedy's claims to make serious political points cannot be determined – either now from such a distance or in any contemporary setting – without paying due attention to the role of the audience – severally and collectively – in negotiating its position with regard to comedy's transgressions. Political, intellectual, social differences (not to mention the fragilities of mood and comprehension) will inevitably and profoundly affect comedy's impact, how a joke is (not) taken. (The same is true for tragedy.) Who you laugh with and at, defines you; links you with and separates you from others. With comedy, even to ask the more nuanced question '*How* funny? *How* serious?' will inevitably provoke the question 'For whom? Under what circumstances?'. This is not merely to subsume the question of comedy's political force to an all-subsuming ambiguity of literature. Rather, it is to mark how comedy in the polis is a space in which citizens negotiate the boundaries of the acceptable and the proper, police the limits and licence of (political) discourse. Comedy is the formal institution where lines are drawn – and crossed – between invective and acceptable licence, between principle and utopian fantasy, between the release of joking and the humiliation of degradation. Not just 'recognizing the vulgar', as Plato puts it, but exploring – and exploding – what counts in the serious business of citizenship. 'Laughter', as Nicole Loraux writes, 'maker of its own space, producer of distances, allows a better negotiation of the real.'[70] As such, it is as telling for the cultural historian as it is an important performance within the political culture of the state.

6 Conclusion

This chapter has shown first how the festival of the Great Dionysia is a major political event in the Athenian calendar, which proclaims its roots in the democratic polis at all levels of its organization and practice.

[70] Loraux 1984/1993a: 237.

Through ritual, seating, ceremony, finances, judging, this politically charged occasion promotes and projects the ideals of the democratic polis. The plays performed at this festival also have a strong political focus. Yet tragedy's willingness to recognize and explore the violent civic dissolution created by conflicting obligations, by the misunderstandings of language, by the failure of human control, produces the remarkable image of the developing city prepared to put its own principles to public critical scrutiny. It is here that the force of tragedy as a 'politicization of the citizenry' is to be located – in the staged anatomy of the tensions within political ideology and in the problematic interface between political theory and practice.

A definition of political theory that requires of it abstract and general argumentation of a self-consciously analytic nature – a subset of the discipline of philosophy, as it were – will inevitably exclude tragedy as an institution and as texts from its field. It is an 'obvious fact' that 'these texts are not philosophy'.[71] Yet not only have the texts of tragedy repeatedly been made an integral part of political philosophy, but also tragedy's exemplary, didactic narratives of conflict and tension both reflect on central principles of democratic thought, and dramatize how political theory itself becomes part of political discourse and political practice. Tragedy provokes the question of what happens to political theory when its seclusion as theory is compromised by the narrative dramas of practice, example and conflict. It continues (thus) to prove good for thinking (politically) with.

[71] Williams 1993: 14.

4
Herodotus, Thucydides and the sophists

RICHARD WINTON

1 The sophists

Let us begin by considering three Athenian texts of the fifth and fourth centuries BC.

The first, short enough to quote in full, is a fragment of what was probably a satyr (i.e. serio-comic) play.[1] Controversy continues as to whether the author of these forty-odd lines of verse was the tragedian Euripides (c. 485–c. 406), or Critias, uncle of Plato, versifier, political pamphleteer, and leading member of the oligarchic junta that overthrew Athenian democracy in 404 following Athens' defeat by Sparta, who was killed in the course of its suppression the following year. The speaker is Sisyphus, archetype of villainy and cunning – whose never-ending punishment was and remains legendary:

> There was a time when human life had no order, but like that of animals was ruled by force; when there was no reward for the good, nor any punishment for the wicked. And then, I think, men enacted laws (*nomoi*) for punishment, so that justice (*dikē*) would be ruler (*turannos*) . . . and *hubris*[2] its slave, and whoever did wrong would be punished. Next, since the laws prevented people only from resorting to violence openly, but they continued to do so in secret, then I think for the first time some shrewd and clever (*sophos*) individual invented fear of the gods for mortals, so that the wicked would have something to fear even if their deeds or words or thoughts were secret. In this way, therefore, he introduced the idea of the divine, saying that there is a divinity, strong with eternal life, who in his mind hears, sees, thinks and attends to everything with his divine nature (*phusis*). He will hear everything mortals say and can see everything they do; and if you silently plot evil, this is not hidden from the gods, for our thoughts are known to them. With such stories as these he introduced the most pleasant of lessons, concealing the truth with a false account. And he claimed that the gods dwelt in that place which would particularly terrify men; for he knew that from there mortals have fears and also

[1] DK 88 B 25; text, translation, and commentary in Davies 1989.
[2] On this recently much debated term see Cairns 1996.

> benefits for their wretched lives – from the revolving sky above, where he saw there was lightning, the fearful din of thunder and the starry radiance of heaven, the fine embroidery of Time, the skilful (*sophos*) craftsman. Thence too comes the bright mass of a star, and damp showers are sent down to earth. With fears like these he surrounded men, and using them in his story he settled the divinity in a fitting place, and quenched lawlessness (*anomia*) by means of laws (*nomoi*) . . . Thus, I think, someone first persuaded mortals to believe (*nomizein*) there was a race of gods.

The element of this text I want to focus on here is the role of the *sophos*, which in crucial respects reverses that of the skilful orator as conventionally depicted by fifth- and fourth-century critics.[3] Sisyphus' *sophos* does indeed exercise his powers of persuasion to get his audience to accept as true an ingenious idea he knows to be false; and he does this by playing on their emotions, and giving them pleasure (contrast Thucydides, who acknowledges that his *History*, while having the merit of recording facts, may be found unpleasing because of its failure to tell stories (*to mē muthōdes*, 1.22)). Unlike the conventional orator, however, our *sophos*, far from covertly pursuing his own illegitimate self-interest, seeks to prevent the covert pursuit of illegimate self-interest by others; he achieves, not personal aggrandizement, but the common good, bringing into being a moral Utopia in which even the thought of wrongdoing is suppressed.

Our second text also comes from drama: Aristophanes' comedy *The Clouds*, produced in 423 but extant in an incompletely revised version dating from a few years later (designed, it seems, for reading rather than performance).[4] Here rhetoric goes hand-in-hand with *disbelief* in traditional divinities and *contempt* for the law: Socrates figures as the head of an ivory-tower educational establishment which, however, teaches the very down-to-earth skill of gaining victory in court even when one is in the wrong. The issue between this novel type of education (*paideusis*) and the traditional upbringing of Athenian youth is personified in the characters Right and Wrong, who argue their rival cases before a prospective pupil. Wrong, who emerges the victor, rejects observance of the *nomoi* of men in favour of indulging the compelling forces (*anankai*) of nature (*phusis*) – a policy that the rhetorical skills he imparts make it possible to pursue scot-free. Wrong offers a Utopia of unrestrained immorality: shameless, ruthless and successful pursuit of self-interest and self-indulgence.

A young man's choice between good and evil is also the theme of our final text, a summary written in the first half of the fourth century of a fifth-century prose work that has not itself survived. Xenophon's

[3] On attitudes to rhetoric see Ober 1989. [4] Dover 1968, Sommerstein 1982.

Memorabilia is the longest and most important of his Socratic writings;[5] the section that concerns us (II.1) presents Socrates in discussion with Aristippus, a hedonist who rejects the cares of political office in favour of the pursuit of personal satisfaction. In response to Aristippus Socrates deploys *inter alia* the gist of a celebrated composition concerning Heracles which its author, Prodicus 'the wise' (*sophos*), has 'declaimed before multitudes'. 'When Heracles ... was just becoming an adult – at that time when young men are becoming independent and are beginning to show whether they will direct their lives down the path of virtue (*aretē*) or that of vice (*kakia*) – he went off and sat down in a peaceful spot, uncertain which path to choose' (II.1.21). As he was sitting there, he saw two women approaching: one natural and unaffected, the other dressed so as to display charms artifice had enhanced. Eager to get in first, the latter ran up to Heracles, offering him a life of pleasure and ease. Heracles asked her name: 'My friends call me Happiness' (*Eudaimonia*), she replied; 'my detractors, Vice' (*Kakia*). At this point her rival (whose name, fittingly, goes unmentioned by any of the speakers), states what she has to offer Heracles: the arduous pursuit of honour through service to others. Vice, she goes on to argue, in fact involves not ease and pleasure but going to immense pains to procure pleasures that are unreal because unnatural ('You force yourself to have sex before you want it, with all sorts of devices, and using men as women ... *My* friends enjoy their food and drink without trouble, for they wait until they truly desire them' (II.1.30, 33)). Heracles' choice is straightforward: 'Thus', concludes Socrates, 'does Prodicus trace the education (*paideusis*) of Heracles by Virtue.'

Rhetoric; education; morality: the themes interwoven in each of the texts we have been looking at take us to the heart of what, for all the difficulties of evidence and interpretation it presents, was clearly a major new force in Greek society of the second half of the fifth century: the sophistic movement. Amid much that is controversial, there is general agreement that the sophists were professional teachers of rhetoric, study of which, they argued, best prepared young men for the challenges and opportunities of citizen-life – especially life as a citizen of democratic and imperial Athens.[6]

The sophists cannot speak for themselves: they were indeed prolific authors, but only a handful of their works survive in other than brief and

[5] On Xenophon see further Gray, in Ch. 7 below.

[6] Guthrie 1969 is basic. Texts, in the original, in DK; Sprague 1972 translates these, following their numbering, except for Antiphon; see also Gagarin and Woodruff 1995 (whose translations are used here, with slight alterations). Other recent studies: Classen 1976, Kerferd 1981a and 1981b, de Romilly 1988 (1992). Rhetoric: Kennedy 1963, Cole 1991. The term *rhētorikē*, it may be noted, is not itself found until the early fourth century BC.

fragmentary form. Not only that; our prime source of information on all aspects of the sophists, Plato – who of course figures very prominently in his own right later in this volume – is at once hostile and elusive.

Plato presents the sophists as a group of itinerant and rival individuals, mainly from poleis other than Athens, where, however, they make their greatest impact. The most notable among them are Protagoras, from Abdera on the northern coast of the Aegean, the eldest and the first to charge fees;[7] Gorgias, from Leontini in Sicily; Hippias, from Elis in the north-western Peloponnese; and Prodicus, whom we have already encountered, from the Aegean island of Ceos. For Plato, the sophists essentially belong rather to the history of publicity than to that of ideas, a judgment articulated by the antithesis between the sophists and Socrates that pervades Plato's writings. Socrates is not only not a sophist; he is an anti-sophist, a philosopher, committed not to rhetoric but argument, disinterested inquiry rather than professional rivalry, reason not emotion, the give and take of conversation as opposed to the dogmatism and unclarity of books.[8]

Plato honoured Socrates' rejection of the written word by writing, not treatises in his own name, but dialogues in which he himself never participates.[9] The sophists, by contrast, figure very prominently, and many ideas and arguments are put into their mouths or attributed to them; two passages particularly noteworthy here are the 'Great Speech' of Protagoras in the dialogue that bears his name (320c–328d), an analysis of the origins and nature of human society, of particular interest as offering one of the few systematic rationales of democracy to be found in ancient Greek texts, and Thrasymachus' account of justice in Book I of the *Republic* (338c ff.). To what extent are such passages reliable evidence for the actual views of the individuals concerned? When, as occasionally happens, Plato purports to be quoting more or less *verbatim* from published writings (which is not the case in either of the examples just cited), it is reasonable to suppose that he is indeed doing so; for the most part, however, there are grounds for scepticism. There is no question but that to some (much-debated) extent Plato attributes to *Socrates* ideas and arguments not in fact deployed by the historical Socrates; how much less reliable, then, one might think, is Plato likely to be in his handling of individuals to whom he was profoundly antipathetic?[10]

[7] Schiappa 1991.

[8] Thomas 1992 sets Plato's critique of the written word in historical context.

[9] The problems thus generated are considered by Lane, in Ch. 8 below.

[10] For a modern parallel, one might think of the writings of F. R. Leavis considered as a source of information on the Bloomsbury Group.

Most of Plato's dialogues are *prima facie* realistic reports of conversations set in Athens in the lifetime of Socrates, but attempts to establish precise 'dramatic dates' (where these are not determined by reference to Socrates' trial and execution in 399) have certainly proved inconclusive and, insofar as they suppose Plato himself to have been concerned with chronological precision and consistency in detail, seem fundamentally misconceived. It has indeed been attractively suggested that Plato's vagueness as to chronology is itself to be understood in terms of his rejection in principle of the public life of Athens: precise dates would in the ordinary way be given by naming the eponymous archon of the year in question.[11]

The debate on this issue – the accuracy and fairness of Plato's presentation of the sophists[12] – involves a number of wider questions. It is clear that the sophists both spoke and wrote on very diverse topics; how far, however, was this a matter of serious intellectual inquiry rather than of professional showmanship and exemplification of the novel techniques and forms of analysis, exposition and argument that made up the core of their teaching?[13] And, whatever the answer given to that question, to what extent were the sophists, at any rate in areas other than rhetoric, *original* thinkers? Finally, what effect did they have, at Athens and elsewhere, and how significant was it? There is little agreement as to how these questions are to be answered; nor is agreement likely, given the inadequacies of our evidence. New evidence may however be expected to continue to emerge, above all from papyri;[14] meanwhile, it must be said that in two central respects discussion has not always been altogether free from confusion. First, what sense is being given to the term 'sophist'? Are sophists to be identified by their role as professional teachers of rhetoric? By their espousal of certain doctrines, above all such as involve rejection of traditional morality and traditional religious beliefs? By their being identified as sophists by Plato, or their having identified *themselves* as sophists, as we may be sure Protagoras did – and Socrates did not? (Modern unclarity here, it should be noted, ultimately derives from contemporary controversies: the term *sophistēs* (plural *sophistai*), not found earlier than the fifth century but certainly not invented by Protagoras, had by the end of the century come to have an exclusively negative connotation.[15])

[11] Vidal-Naquet 1990: 127f. The chronological vagaries of Plato's dialogues were noted in antiquity: Athenaeus, 217c ff.

[12] A debate still dominated by Grote 1888: ch. 67; cf. Turner 1981.

[13] For the former view, see e.g., Kerferd 1981a; for the latter, Striker 1996.

[14] A scrap of papyrus has recently transformed our understanding of Antiphon (below).

[15] Guthrie 1969: 27–34.

Secondly, when an idea in, for example, a play by Euripides or a speech in Thucydides is characterized as 'sophistic', is one being told that this is an idea we can also attribute to one or other of the sophists, or sophists generally (however identified); or are we dealing with the much stronger thesis that what we find in the play or speech is there as a result of the influence of some particular sophist, or sophists generally (however identified)?

What matters for our purposes is that the period that saw the efflorescence of sophistic education also saw the emergence of systematic reflection and argument on broad political issues, conducted in purely human terms. The sophistic movement constitutes an obviously plausible matrix for this development; on the other hand, speculative and critical inquiry of the sort that had arisen in sixth-century Ionia was by the second half of the fifth century well-established in the Greek world as a whole,[16] and there seems little reason to suppose that only sophists or their pupils were capable of intellectual response to the twin revolution in Greek politics effected by Athens during the decades between the Persian and Peloponnesian Wars: radical democracy at home, imperialism abroad.[17] It is noteworthy here that in his critique of previous work in Book II of the *Politics* Aristotle has nothing to say of the sophists; he does though discuss at length (1267b–1269a) the views of their contemporary, the town-planner Hippodamus of Miletus, 'the first individual not himself engaged in politics to speak on the nature of the best constitution' (*politeia*).[18]

The considerations set out above suggest a sadly negative conclusion: a *history* of the intellectual developments we are concerned with is an impossibility. Attempts to produce general intellectual histories of the period,[19] to establish the authorship of anonymous texts such as the pseudo-Xenophontic *Athenaion Politeia* (*Constitution of the Athenians*) (below), and the *Dissoi Logoi* (*Contrary Arguments*),[20] or to identify who originated a particular type of inquiry[21] – enterprises such as these, rewarding in detail as they often are, in the last analysis cannot but fail as *historical* inquiries. At the same time it is worth observing first that this is

[16] Hussey 1972; texts, with commentary and translation: Kirk, Raven, Schofield 1983.

[17] On the Athenian empire see Meiggs 1972.

[18] On whom see Burns 1976.

[19] Such as Havelock 1957 and Ostwald 1986.

[20] DK 90: a short work dating from the very late fifth or early fourth century, of no great intellectual penetration but immense historical interest, that marshals contrary arguments on a number of for the most part moral issues; text, translation and commentary in Robinson 1984.

[21] E.g., Cole 1967.

surely a matter for regret;[22] secondly, that it is surely important not to beg the question as to what constitutes worthwhile evidence.[23]

There exist good general accounts of the sophists, and the relevant ancient material is readily accessible.[24] What it may be useful to offer here is a sketch of some central themes of political reflection and controversy to be found in that material.

The traditional polis, in one sense a community of equals, comprised in broader perspective two essentially unequal elements: citizens and gods.[25] In the fifth century the polis becomes problematic in respect both of its human and its divine dimensions.

The first two of our opening texts strikingly exemplify the fifth-century challenge to traditional religious belief. To be sure, Greek criticism of Greek religion antedates the fifth century, a century traditional religion largely survives; it does however seem to be the case that this century sees traditional beliefs contested in unprecedentedly radical ways and on an unprecedentedly wide scale. It is no longer merely a matter of scepticism as to some particular episode concerning the gods, or of criticism of divine immorality as portrayed in the classic accounts of Homer and Hesiod; the fifth century invents the category of myth, establishes a range of intellectual disciplines that marginalize or exclude supernatural factors in explaining the material they address, and – as we have already seen – expresses doubt and disbelief as to the gods' very existence.[26] 'Concerning the gods', Protagoras wrote, 'I am not able to know either that they exist or that they do not, nor can I know what they look like; much impedes our knowing, the obscurity of the matter and the brevity of human life' (DK 80 B 4). Prodicus is reported (in post-classical and in some cases fragmentary texts) to have explained the traditional gods as deified fruits of nature and human benefactors of early mankind.[27] Both,

[22] Contrast the view that the question as to whether or not Antiphon the Athenian oligarch, highly praised by Thucydides at VIII.68, and 'Antiphon the sophist' of Xenophon, *Memorabilia* II.6 are the same person 'is of minor interest for the history of philosophy' (Guthrie 1969: 286). Cf. n. 41 below.

[23] As happens in one recent discussion of our opening text, Davies 1989: 29 arguing that if (as seems likely) the fragment comes from a satyr play, this 'must entail a modification of the likelihood that we are dealing with a serious document', 'constituting an important sub-section of a chapter in the history of ideas'. Contrast Dover 1988: 150: our text is 'one of the intellectual monuments of the fifth century'.

[24] See n.6 above.

[25] Burkert 1985, Easterling and Muir 1985, Bruit Zaidman and Schmitt Pantel 1992, Bremmer 1994, Parker 1996.

[26] Nestle 1942, Guthrie 1969: ch. 9, Richardson 1975 (allegorical interpretation), Detienne 1981 (1986), Muir 1985, Lloyd 1987, 1990.

[27] DK 84 B 5; Heinrichs 1984.

together with other contemporary figures, are said to have faced prosecution at Athens on grounds of religious unorthodoxy – as Socrates indubitably did. However, the reliability of our evidence for these prosecutions remains a matter of dispute;[28] it is certainly difficult to reconcile prosecution of Protagoras with Plato's reference (*Meno* 91e) to the high reputation he enjoyed throughout his forty-year career, and more generally neither Protagoras nor Prodicus, one would suppose, could have had any interest in outraging public opinion at Athens or elsewhere. On the other hand, the impact of the 'Affair of the Mysteries' in 415 and Socrates' trial and execution in 399 suggest that by the later fifth century many Athenians believed that disrespect for, if not disbelief in, the traditional religion of the city was both widespread and dangerous.[29]

Prodicus' theory as to the origin of the gods obviously recalls our Sisyphus fragment, which is one of a number of fifth- and fourth-century texts concerned with the emergence and early development of civilization.[30] Greek myth had much to say of relevance to this theme, Hesiod offering a particularly noteworthy account of the human condition that links the origins of mankind with both the Heroic Age of the Trojan War and Theban saga and the bleak realities of his own day – the myth of the five races of men, four of metal (gold, silver, bronze and iron), the latter two separated by the race of heroes.[31] This story is preceded by an alternative explanation of the present ills of mankind, the story of Prometheus and Pandora; both present man's original state in idyllic terms. The fifth century reverses Hesiod's analysis: mankind is rescued from the brutish[32] condition in which it originally found itself by acquiring the various elements of civilization. A key term here is *technē*, 'craft' or 'art', denoting the application of mind to the mastering of some particular field of activity of practical benefit to mankind as a whole.[33] Such a view of human development was not in principle incompatible with traditional religious belief, as for example the mid-fifth-century if questionably Aeschylean *Prometheus Bound* shows; it is however clear that certain versions of this theory presented the rise of civilization in terms of purely human activity, an approach our opening text (conceivably as a *reductio ad absurdum*) takes to its ultimate extreme.

One such version is to be found in Protagoras' 'Great Speech', where, to be sure, it is first stated in *avowedly* mythical form. Mankind, we are told,

[28] Dover 1988: ch. 13. [29] Murray 1990b, Parker 1996: ch. 10.
[30] Guthrie 1957, Cole 1967, Guthrie 1969: 79–84 (texts in translation), Dodds 1973.
[31] *Works and Days*, 106–201. Commentary: West 1978. [32] O'Brien 1985.
[33] Heinimann 1961.

emerged upon the earth equipped by Prometheus with fire, stolen from Athena and Hephaestus, and thus with the technical crafts, but, lacking *politikē technē*, was unable to establish cities, and therefore incapable of fighting off hostile animals (the art of war, *polemikē technē*, forming part of *politikē technē*[34]) – until Zeus, to save mankind from the threat of extinction, sent down Hermes with the gift of *politikē technē*, comprising justice (*dikē*) and respect for others (*aidōs*),[35] to be distributed not, as are the technical crafts, to some and not to others, but to all; for the polis cannot endure unless all its members possess at least basic competence in *politikē technē*. In demythologized terms, as the latter part of the 'Great Speech' makes clear, Protagoras is offering a rationale of *nomos* viewed as a human institution: men must live in the polis, and the polis demands a certain level of morality of all its members. *Aretē*, 'virtue', identified by Protagoras with *politikē technē*, is inculcated from one's earliest years; and the law punishes wrongdoers as a lesson in *aretē* to themselves and others.[36]

Protagoras gives a positive account of *nomos*; a negative counterpart is reported in Book II of Plato's *Republic* (358e ff.). Many people, it is stated, see justice (*dikaiosunē*) as a purely human institution, designed to serve the interests of the weak mass of men, who are at once reluctant to suffer wrong themselves and unable to wrong their fellow-men with impunity. On this view, someone in a position to do wrong and get away with it (whether by virtue of superior strength, or the ability – such as that Gyges' ring gave him – to go undetected) could have no reason to obey the law. An analysis of *nomos* very much along these lines is presented in the opening section of a substantial fragment of a work by Antiphon entitled *Truth*.

> Justice (*dikaiosunē*) therefore, is not violating the rules (*nomima*) of the city in which one is a citizen. Thus a person would best observe justice to his own advantage if he paid heed to the laws (*nomoi*) when in the presence of witnesses, but to the demands of nature (*phusis*) when not in the presence of witnesses. For the demands of the law are adventitious, those of nature inescapable . . . Thus someone who violates the laws avoids shame and punishment if those who have joined in agreement do not observe him, but not if they do. But if someone tries to violate one of the inherent demands of nature, which is impossible, the harm he suffers is

[34] This remark brilliantly encapsulates the Greek understanding of the relationship between hoplite and citizen: Vernant 1968. [35] On the term *aidōs*, see Cairns 1993.

[36] On the 'Great Speech' as a whole, Farrar 1988: ch. 3. Authenticity: Cairns 1993: 355 n. 37. Greek views on punishment: Saunders 1991: Part 1. See also Penner, in Ch. 9 section 4, and Rowe, in Ch. 11 section 2, below.

> no less if he is seen by no one, and no greater if all see him. (*CPF* 1.1.192–4 (= DK 87 B 44 A))

The contrast between *nomos* and *phusis* here highlighted, a contrast to be discerned in all three of our opening texts, as in the above passages of the *Protagoras* and *Republic*, constitutes the single most fertile and most influential idea to emerge in fifth-century Greece.[37] It served to focus and articulate an array of interrelated antitheses: between nature and culture; between nature and convention; between nature and nurture; between nature and art; between the natural and the artificial; between reason and instinct; between appearance and reality; between the parochial and the universal; between the transient and the eternal; between fact and value; between choice and necessity. The commitment its adoption regularly signals, to revealing what lies concealed beneath the surface of things, links it with both theory (Presocratic and Socratic philosophy, medicine, history) and practice (the rhetorical enterprise of 'making the weaker the stronger argument';[38] political opposition unmasked as private interest, whether ambition, envy, or greed; the sycophant's public-spirited determination to expose injustice by prosecuting wrongdoers);[39] and its deployment in political discussion effectively marks the beginning of Western political theory.

As we have seen, analysis in terms of the *nomos*/*phusis* distinction often challenges received opinion. An earlier fragment of the *Truth* uses it to question Greek assumptions about non-Greeks:[40]

> ... [the laws? of nearby communities] we know and respect, but those of communities far away we neither know nor respect.[41] We have thereby become barbarous toward each other, when by nature we are at birth in all respects equally capable of being either *barbaroi* or Greeks. We can examine those attributes of nature that are necessarily present in all men

[37] Heinimann 1945, Guthrie 1969: chs.4–5, Kahn 1981.

[38] The definition is Protagoras' (DK 80 A 21); the *ne plus ultra* of such an enterprise is one of Gorgias' few extant works, the *Encomium of Helen*, 'the most notorious woman in Greek mythology' (MacDowell 1982: 12; MacDowell gives text, translation, and commentary) – avowedly tongue-in-cheek but important for rhetorical theory.

[39] Envy: Walcot 1978; greed: Harvey 1985; sycophants: Osborne 1990, Harvey 1990.

[40] Baldry 1965, Hall 1989.

[41] Prior to the publication of the papyrus referred to above, the papyrus text of this sentence was restored to mean 'those with distinguished fathers we revere and respect, while those not from a distinguished household we do not respect or revere', a *prima facie* egalitarian observation some saw as incompatible with the oligarchic principles of the Antiphon of Thucydides, VIII.68, who could thus not be the author of the *Truth*. The new fragment has removed this argument, but has not ended the debate (which is further complicated by a third Antiphon, Antiphon the poet). For a brief introduction to the problem, Guthrie 1969: 292–4; full discussion: Narcy 1989.

> and are provided to the same degree, and in these respects none of us is singled out as *barbaros* or Greek. For we all breathe the air through our mouth and through our nostrils, and we laugh when we are pleased in our mind or we weep when we are pained, and we take in sounds with our hearing, and we see by the light of our sight, and we work with our hands and we walk with our feet . . . (*CPF* 1.1.184–6 (= DK 87 B 44 B))

Elsewhere in the same work Antiphon argues that the polis, far from embodying justice, in fact institutionalizes injustice:

> . . . to testify truthfully for one another is generally thought to be just and to no lesser extent useful in human affairs. And yet one who does this will not be just if indeed it is just not to injure anyone if one is not injured oneself; for even if he tells the truth, someone who testifies must necessarily injure another somehow, and will then be injured himself, since he will be hated when the testimony he gives leads to the conviction of the person against whom he testifies, who then loses his property or his life because of this man whom he has not injured at all. In this way he wrongs the person against whom he testifies, because he injures someone who is not injuring him; and he in turn is injured by the one against whom he testified in that he is hated by him despite having told the truth . . . Now, these are clearly no small wrongs, neither those he suffers nor those he inflicts. For it is impossible that these things are just and that the rule not to injure anyone nor to be injured oneself is also just; on the contrary, it is necessary either that only one of these is just or that they are both unjust. Further, it is clear that, whatever the result, the judicial process, verdicts, and arbitration proceedings are not just, since helping some people hurts others. (*CPF* 1.1.215–17 (= DK 87 B 44.353–5))

Thrasymachus in Book I of the *Republic* (338c ff.) and Callicles in the *Gorgias* (482c ff.) pursue a similar strategy: the former arguing that justice, supposedly committed to the principle of equality, in fact represents the interest of the stronger – the *nomoi* justice enforces being determined by the controlling element of the polis; Callicles, that the democratic polis is unjust in that it enforces equality between strong and weak.[42]

To offer political insight was not necessarily to subvert the polis. Protagoras' 'Great Speech', rebutting oligarchic dismissal of democracy as government by the incompetent, explains that on a true understanding of the matter *all* members of the polis cannot but be competent practitioners of the relevant *technē* – even if for the most part they are not particularly outstanding ones; and the anonymous author of the pseudo-Xenophontic

[42] Harvey 1965, Guthrie 1969: ch. 6.

Constitution of the Athenians,[43] a pamphlet written probably in the 430s or early 420s by an oligarchically-minded Athenian (conventionally known as the 'Old Oligarch') for a non-Athenian audience of similar outlook, undertakes to demonstrate that the features of Athenian *dēmokratia* that 'the other Greeks' criticize are in fact precisely what ensure its stability and success. No democrat, he sees democratic equality in Thrasymachean terms but justifies it – at Athens – on Calliclean grounds:

> My first point is this: it is just for the poor and the *dēmos* there to have more than the well-born and wealthy because it is the common people who man the ships and confer power on the city – helmsmen, signalmen, captains, look-out men, and shipwrights – these are the ones who confer power on the city much more than the hoplites, the well-born and the better class of people. Since this is so, it seems just to allow everyone access to political office, whether assigned by lot[44] or election, and to permit any citizen who wishes to do so to speak in the assembly. (1.2)

In a later passage the Old Oligarch condemns those Athenians who are democrats by choice rather than *phusis*:

> I pardon the *dēmos* itself for its *dēmokratia*, for everyone is to be excused for pursuing his own interests; but he who though not a member of the *dēmos* chooses to live in a democratic polis rather than in an oligarchic one is a man preparing to do wrong (*adikein*), a man who has grasped that the wrongdoer (*kakos*) is more likely to escape notice in a democratic polis than in an oligarchic one. (2.20)

The Old Oligarch turns Protagoras upside down: *aretē* is an impediment to success in democratic Athens,[45] a polis where wrongdoing constitutes not the exception but the norm. He it seems lives abroad in self-imposed exile; other Athenians who share his distaste for democracy remain at Athens but retreat into private worlds of their own – an agent no longer of civilization but unreason, the polis disintegrates. In opposition to the democratic principle of political engagement – in Pericles' positive formulation, 'we alone regard the man who takes no part in politics not as someone who minds his own business but as someone who has nothing to contribute' (Thucydides, II.40) – there develops an ideology of tranquil devotion to purely private pursuits;[46] an ideology that finds classic

[43] Translation and commentary: Moore 1975: 19–61.

[44] On this central element of Athenian democracy see Headlam 1933 (a work far wider in scope than its title might suggest).

[45] This paradox provides the theme of Aristophanes' comedy the *Knights*, awarded first prize in 424.

[46] Connor 1971, Carter 1986. Several of Aristophanes' comedies engage with this theme on the level of fantasy, above all the *Acharnians*, awarded first prize in 425.

expression in the contrast between politician and philosopher in Plato's *Theaetetus* (172c–177c). In this passage Socrates reverses Prodicus' analysis in his account of the choice of Heracles: it is involvement in the public realm that corrupts, not Aristippus' commitment to minding his own business.[47] Theory and practice here go together: while the historical Socrates held aloof from politics (a position aptly symbolized by the ivory tower of Aristophanes' *Clouds*), Prodicus regularly represented his city on diplomatic missions, as did Gorgias and Hippias theirs.[48]

For the Old Oligarch, and other critics, Athens is a polis with too much politics; our period sees the beginnings of idealization of Athens' rival, Sparta, as a polis that transcends politics, a polis the perfection of whose institutions obviates the possibility of conflict and the need for change.[49] Whether or not Critias was the author of our Sisyphus fragment, he was certainly one of those who contributed to the opening chapter in the long history of Sparta as political myth.[50]

The Old Oligarch sees Athenian democracy as one of three components of a unified power-system, of which the other two are the Athenian navy and the Athenian empire. His analysis integrates themes that in the next century bifurcate into two quite distinct intellectual disciplines: fourth-century political theory focuses on political institutions abstracted from the realities of power politics, the dominant if not exclusive concern of fourth-century historiography.[51] In this respect the Old Oligarch's approach resembles that of a more or less contemporary and far greater writer: Herodotus, whose single, massive work combines historical narrative and descriptive ethnography – and, what is of particular interest here, includes the earliest set-piece presentation we have of arguments for and against the three basic types of government recognized by fifth-century and later Greeks: monarchy, oligarchy, and democracy.

2 Herodotus

Herodotus, and his successor Thucydides, the founders of Greek historiography,[52] took as their main theme the two great crises of fifth-century Greek history: the Persian War of 480–479,[53] in which a Spartan-

[47] Burnyeat 1990: 31–9. 'Minding one's own business' (*ta heautou prattein*), it may be noted, is the *Republic*'s definition of justice.

[48] Protagoras, according to a late fourth-century source cited by Diogenes Laertius (IX.50), was lawgiver at Thurii, a colony in the instep of Italy established by Athens in the late 440s.

[49] Tigerstedt 1965–78, Rawson 1969, Finley 1975c. [50] DK 88 B 6–9, 32–7.

[51] Momigliano 1966b.

[52] Both of whom go unmentioned by Plato. Context: Finley 1975b, Fornara 1983a, Momigliano 1990. [53] Boardman 1988: chs.10–11.

led coalition of Greek states repulsed the far larger forces of the invader Xerxes, testament above all, in Herodotus' view (VII.139), to Athenian valour; and the Peloponnesian War of 431–404,[54] in which Sparta eventually gained victory over Athens and her empire, but only with the help of Persia. Herodotus and Thucydides belong in a history of political thought above all because, whether as norm or problem, the polis is itself centrally at issue in their works.

How, and in what circumstances, Herodotus' *History* came into being escapes us more or less completely, and little is known of his life and career beyond what is to be found therein.[55] Born, reportedly and plausibly in the mid-480s, at Halicarnassus (modern Bodrum) on the Aegean coast of Asia Minor, he is said to have moved to Samos to escape a tyrant's rule, and later to have become a citizen of Thurii.[56] According to some not particularly impressive evidence, Herodotus was voted a very large sum of money after he had given a public reading from his work at Athens, shortly before the foundation of Thurii; a similar performance at Olympia is said to have moved a youthful Thucydides to tears of envy. It is at any rate certain that Herodotus was still working on his *History* in the early 420s, and most scholars would date its publication to c. 425, on the basis of parody of its opening section by Aristophanes in his comedy the *Acharnians* (524ff.), produced in that year.

Herodotus wrote his *History* in order, as he states in his opening sentence, to ensure that what men have wrought is not obliterated by time, and to prevent the outstanding deeds of men, both Greeks and barbarians, from losing their renown; that, and to explain why they fought one another. His work takes the form of a basically chronological narrative, comprising two main sections. Books I–IV trace the emergence of Persia, under Cyrus the Great and his successors, as the ruling power in the Near East in the course of the second half of the sixth century, a process that involved the subjection of the Greeks of Asia Minor and the Aegean islands, and brought Persia into contact with the mainland Greeks; Herodotus however devotes the greater portion of this part of his work to accounts of non-Greek peoples affected by Persian expansionism. The longest by far of these accounts is that concerning Egypt (Books II–III), conquered with little difficulty by Cyrus' son and successor Cambyses in the mid-520s; the Scythians, who successfully defied invasion by Darius some years later, are treated at very considerable length in Book IV. In Books V–IX the narrative becomes increasingly fuller and more unified;

54 Lewis 1992: chs.9–11.

55 The basic discussion remains Jacoby 1913: cols.205–47.

56 See n.48 above, and Strasburger 1982c.

Athenian involvement in the botched attempt of the eastern Greeks to free themselves from Persian control (the 'Ionian Revolt' of 499–494) leads first to the Persian expedition against Athens that met with defeat at Marathon in 490, and on to Xerxes' invasion of Greece ten years later, when Greek defeat on land at Thermopylae is retrieved by naval victory at Salamis, followed in 479 by victory in the land-battle of Plataea in central Greece and the successful uprising of the Ionian and other eastern Greeks after the Persian defeat at Mycale. Herodotus' account of the decisive battle of Salamis (VII.40ff.), focused on its Athenian architect, the wily and insubordinate Themistocles, constitutes the climax of the entire work.

This was, so far as we can tell, an entirely novel kind of inquiry: the critical investigation, on a large scale, of not the distant – the legendary – but the recent past.[57] To be sure, Herodotus' prose epic recalls the foundation-texts of Greek literature, the *Iliad* and *Odyssey* of Homer, by his combination of their respective themes of warfare and outlandish peoples and places, his pervasive and extensive use of direct speech, and his recognition of divine intervention in human affairs. But, for Herodotus, such intervention is – at any rate typically – indirect, mediated by oracles, omens, and dreams; and Herodotus bases his narrative on solely *human* authority: to some extent the evidence of his own eyes, but for the most part oral information obtained by him from others – information of very varying quality.[58] 'My duty is to report the things reported,' he writes of one episode (VII.152), 'it is not to believe them all alike – a remark that may be understood to apply throughout my work.'

A similar attitude, at once inquiring and critical, characterizes Herodotus' portrayal of different types of society. Herodotus presents the Persian War as a confrontation between two opposed political systems: on the one hand, the Greek polis, a small-scale community of in principle free and politically equal *politai*, who are subject to the rule of law, *nomos*, and who determine policy in public debate; and, on the other, the Persian empire, a vast structure subject to the despotic and arbitrary rule of a single individual, the hereditary Persian king. There can be no doubt as to where Herodotus' sympathies fundamentally lie; but Herodotus is no

[57] The most recent complete commentary remains How and Wells 1912; Legrand 1954 is an invaluable guide. Gould 1989 (itself outstanding) briefly (150–5) surveys work since Jacoby 1913, the fundamental modern discussion; fuller bibliography in Marg 1965: 759–81. Note in particular Momigliano 1966c, Immerwahr 1966, von Fritz 1967, Boedeker 1987. Herodotus is quoted in Rawlinson's translation, with some alterations (G. Rawlinson, *Herodotus*, 3rd. edn, 4 vols. (London, 1875).

[58] On the question of Herodotus' credibility see the contrasting discussions of Fehling 1989 and Pritchett 1993.

chauvinist. Commenting in Book III on Cambyses' sacrilegious conduct in Egypt, he writes as follows:

> It appears certain to me, by a great variety of proofs, that Cambyses was raving mad; otherwise he would not have set himself to make a mock of holy rites and long-established usages (*nomaia*). For if one were to invite men to choose out of all the customs (*nomoi*) in the world such as seemed to them the best, they would, after examining them all, end by preferring their own; so convinced are they that their own usages are the best. Unless, therefore, a man was mad, it is not likely that he would make a sport of such matters. That people have this feeling about their customs may be seen by very many proofs: among others, by the following. Darius, after he had got the kingdom, called into his presence certain Greeks who were at hand, and asked what he should have to pay them to eat the bodies of their dead fathers; to which they replied, that there was no sum that would tempt them to do such a thing. He then sent for certain Indians, of the race called Callatians, men who eat their fathers, and asked them, while the Greeks stood by, and understood by means of an interpreter all that was said, what he should have to give them to burn the bodies of their fathers at their decease. The Indians exclaimed aloud, and bade him forbear such language. Such is men's wont herein; and Pindar was right, in my judgment, when he said: '*Nomos* is king (*basileus*) of all.' (III.38)

Herodotus' concluding observation applies universally, and there is no suggestion that Greek custom is superior (though to be sure the story's perspective is Greek, in that it is the Greeks who hear, and are provided with a translation of, what the Indians say, and not vice versa). The *nomos/physis* antithesis is clearly implicit, but the diversity of *nomoi* is in no way taken to subvert the authority of *nomos*: it is rather, for Herodotus, a significant but unproblematic fact. Two further points to note are that the story involves not merely *differences* but *opposites*; and that Herodotus' quotation from an author of the preceding generation, the Theban poet Pindar, provides our earliest evidence for a text that, diversely interpreted, figures in many later discussions of *nomos* – its most notable subsequent appearance occurring in Plato's *Gorgias* (484b), where it is quoted by Callicles in support of his radical critique of conventional morality as an infringement of the rights of the strong over the weak (above).[59]

The theme of this passage recurs in a more complex story that Herodotus tells in Book VII. Herodotus reports that when prior to his

[59] Gigante 1993. Our opening Sisyphus fragment appears to allude to this text of Pindar's: 'men enacted laws (*nomoi*) for punishment, so that justice (*dikē*) would be ruler (*turannos*)'.

invasion Xerxes sent heralds to the Greek states demanding their surrender he ignored Athens and Sparta, these having put to death the heralds sent for that purpose by Darius a decade or so earlier. Subsequently matters did not go well for the Spartans, who eventually sought volunteers to offer themselves to Xerxes in atonement for the heralds killed at Sparta. Two Spartans came forward, and set out for the Persian capital. In the course of their journey they received hospitality from the Persian governor Hydarnes, who at dinner urged them to submit to Xerxes: 'You have only to look at me and my position to see that the king knows well how to honour merit. In like manner you yourselves, were you to make your submission to him, would receive at his hands, seeing that he will deem you men of merit, some position of authority in Greece.' 'Hydarnes', the Spartans replied, 'you are a one-sided counsellor: you have experience of half the matter, but the other half is beyond your knowledge. A slave's life you understand; but, never having tasted liberty, you cannot tell whether it be sweet or no. Did you but understand what freedom is, you would bid us fight for it, not with the spear only, but with the battle-axe.' On reaching Susa and entering the royal presence they absolutely refused to perform obeisance, protesting that prostration before men was not one of their customs, and (luckier than the Private of the Buffs) went on to announce the purpose of their journey. 'Xerxes answered with true greatness of soul that he would not act like the Lacedaemonians, who by killing the heralds had contravened the rules (*nomima*) accepted by all mankind; nor did he wish, by putting the two men to death, to free the Lacedaemonians from their guilt.' The two Spartans thus returned home safely; the sequel however is for Herodotus 'a case wherein the hand of Heaven was most plainly manifest': precisely these men's sons, sent as envoys to Persia during the Peloponnesian War, were betrayed by the Thracian king Sitalces, made prisoner on the European shore of the Hellespont, taken to Athens, and there executed (VII.133–7).

In addition to the issue of opposed *nomoi* (here too found in association with fathers and sons), this story deploys other major themes of Herodotus' *History*: the contrast between Greek freedom and Asian servitude; recognition both of human limits and of a divine dimension to human affairs; above all the notion of reciprocity or balance, the essence of Herodotus' understanding of the mutability of human life, the fragility of happiness, the folly of excess.[60] This set of ideas, fundamental throughout the *History*, emerges in the first major element of the work, the story

[60] Gould 1991; cf. North 1966.

of Croesus, king of Lydia in Asia Minor – 'the person who first within my own knowledge inflicted injury on the Greeks' (I.5) – who appreciates the validity of the ideal advocated by the visiting Athenian lawgiver Solon – the life, and the death, of the good *politēs* – only when facing an inglorious death after losing his kingdom to Cyrus in a war he had embarked on arrogantly confident that he would thereby vastly increase his power.[61] Croesus survives, himself taking on the role of Solon in relation to Cyrus and Cambyses, under both of whom Persia prospers – within her proper boundaries; the setbacks encountered by Darius on the *European* side of the Bosporus (Scythia, Marathon) do not deter his successor Xerxes from embarking on an even more ambitious campaign of aggrandizement in Europe.

Xerxes' invasion of Greece encounters defeat: Persia succumbs to the polis, the overweening ambition of a despot – Xerxes seeks to conquer the world (VII.8), to enslave the sea (VII.35) – is checked by the forces of self-disciplined freedom united in a coalition under the leadership of the archetypically well-ordered polis, Sparta. 'Though the Spartans are free men', their exiled king Demaratus explains to a Xerxes incredulous at the notion of their standing firm against him (VII.104), 'they are not altogether free: law (*nomos*) is for them a master (*despotēs*) whom they fear far more than your subjects do you' – a further allusion to Pindar's *nomos basileus*. In accounting for the Greeks' victory over Persia, as in seeking to make sense of his world more generally, Herodotus assumes the polis as a norm, an ideal of moderation opposed to the excesses of both barbarians abroad and tyrants in the Greek world. The latter are individual citizens who seek to privatize what properly belongs to the community that comprises all citizens; all *male* citizens, that is to say, for the polis establishes boundaries between the domains of men and women that other societies challenge or transgress – with consequences grimly illustrated by episodes close to the beginning and the end of the work.[62] The fundamental opposition between Greek and barbarian, chiefly embodied in the conflict between Greece and Persia, is supplemented by other contrasts, notably that between Egypt and Scythia, countries at the south and north of Herodotus' world each antithetical to the other as well as to Greece.[63] In recounting the failure of Xerxes' over-confident bid for world-empire, Herodotus establishes a cognitive dominion of his own, successfully mastering the entire span of human space and time through the independent exercise of critical inquiry alert to its own limitations.

[61] Gould 1989: 154 (bibliography). [62] Wolff 1964; cf. Pembroke 1967.
[63] Redfield 1985, Hartog 1991 (1988), Romm 1992.

It has been argued that Herodotus does not merely reveal political preconceptions and prejudices;[64] he intends his *History* to be understood in terms of the overriding political issue of his own day. For Persia read Athens and *her* empire of the second half of the fifth century; and even, on one version of this interpretation, for Xerxes' unsuccessful invasion of Greece read Athens' disastrous Sicilian Expedition of 415–413. Pro-Athenian statements at VII.139 and elsewhere constitute no insuperable objection to this reading of the work; the issue is rather how plausible one finds the obliqueness thus attributed to Herodotus – a matter on which opinion is likely to remain divided.[65]

Whether or not Herodotus' work as a whole is to be construed as a veiled critique of Athenian imperialism, it certainly contains elements that explicitly engage with more abstract political issues. Two passages stand out in this respect, both of which deploy contemporary Greek themes within the context of episodes in the earlier history of Asia.[66] The first occurs in Herodotus' account in Book I of how the peoples of Asia, having freed themselves from Assyrian rule, became once again subject to tyranny. Among the Medes, the first people to revolt, was a *sophos* individual named Deioces who lusted for tyrannical power. The Medes lived in villages, and in his village Deioces, already a man of consequence, made a practice of just dealing (*dikaiosunē*[67]) at a time when lawlessness prevailed throughout the country. As a result his fellow-villagers chose him as adjudicator of their disputes, and, his fame spreading, so too did the inhabitants of other villages. Eventually Deioces announced that because acting as judge for others was preventing him from pursuing his own interests he would do so no longer. Lawlessness thus grew worse than ever, until the Medes assembled together and, after discussion – guided, in Herodotus' opinion, by Deioces' associates – decided to establish a king who would impose law and order and allow them to devote themselves to their private concerns. As to their choice of king, they agreed upon Deioces, who required them to grant him a troop of bodyguards and to construct a large and strongly-fortified palace, to form the centre of a new urban settlement intended largely to supplant the Medes' current places of residence – though all except Deioces were required to dwell *outside* the elaborate fortifications (the outermost circuit of which was similar in extent to that of Athens). Within his citadel Deioces rigorously secreted himself from

[64] The subject of one of Plutarch's works: text, translation, and commentary in Bowen 1992. Herodotus is notably contemptuous of the Ionians, e.g., I.143, V.69: see Alty 1982.

[65] Fornara 1971, Smart 1988 (Sicily), Moles 1996. Contrast Gould 1989: 116–20.

[66] An approach classically exemplified in Xenophon's *Cyropaideia* (on which see Gray, in Ch. 7 below).

[67] On this term see Havelock 1978: ch. 17.

public view, all business being transacted through messengers; it was, moreover, prohibited either to laugh or to spit in the royal presence. Deioces, the first to establish such court ceremonial, did so in order that those who were in fact his peers should come to regard him as different in kind from themselves and so refrain from plotting against him.

Having thus established himself as tyrant by exploiting his fellow-countrymen's need for justice, Deioces imposed strict observance of justice on those who were now his subjects. To those who sought it he dispensed justice no longer face to face but on the basis of written submissions; he himself had agents who observed and listened throughout the land, and anyone guilty of an act of *hubris* was sent for to receive fitting punishment (1.96–100). Deioces recalls both the *sophos* of our Sisyphus fragment and the gods whom the *sophos* invents: Deioces invents himself, as absolute ruler of an anti-polis, a capital fortified against his subjects at the heart of which is not an *agora*, a public meeting-place, but a palace from which his subjects are excluded – physical expression of the fact that the Medes pursue only private interests and in that pursuit obey, not the law, but a monarch (the term *nomos* occurring nowhere in Herodotus' account).[68]

The assembled Medes deliberately renounce the freedom they have only recently regained; a similar choice is made, this time by Persians, in an episode in Book III, the section referred to above that presents the earliest example of comparative constitutional analysis (though the term *politeia* does not itself occur in the passage).[69] At the time of Cambyses' death the Persian throne had been usurped by two brothers, one of them pretending to be Cambyses' brother, whom, in fact, Cambyses himself had had killed; once the truth is revealed, a conspiracy is organized and the brothers are overthrown. When shortly afterwards the seven conspirators meet to discuss the situation, three of them put forward divergent views as to future political arrangements.

The first to speak, Otanes, who had initiated the conspiracy against the usurpers, argues for the abandonment of monarchy. Cambyses' reign and the usurpation that followed have shown what monarchy involves; inevitably, for no man, however virtuous, can escape the corrupting effect of absolute power. The advantages a monarch enjoys engender *hubris*, and, being human, a monarch cannot help envying the advantages others have – a combination that leads him to perpetrate evil of all kinds. He delights in the most worthless, and resents the best, of his fellow-citizens; above

68 On these themes see Lévêque and Vidal-Naquet 1964.

69 Apffel 1957, Bleicken 1979; *politeia*: Bordes 1982.

all, he subverts established usages (*nomaia . . . patria*), violates women, and executes men without trial. By contrast, rule by the majority (*plēthos*), which enjoys the fairest of names, *isonomia*, 'equality of political rights',[70] appoints its officials by lot, holds them to account, and formulates policy in public debate.

Megabyzus endorses Otanes' criticisms of monarchy, but argues that it would be intolerable to escape from the *hubris* of a tyrant only to suffer that of the unbridled *dēmos*. The tyrant, whatever he does, at least knows what he is doing; the *dēmos*, knowing nothing – inevitably, lacking as it is in both instruction and native wit – rushes into action mindlessly, like a torrent in winter spate. What Persia needs is rule by the best (*aristoi*) – who will include the present company.

The final speaker, Darius – the last to join the conspiracy – argues in favour of monarchy against both majority-rule and (as he terms it) oligarchy. There could in principle be no regime superior to rule by the single best individual; and there is in fact no alternative to monarchy. On the one hand, oligarchy involves several individuals cultivating *aretē* in the public arena, each seeking to outdo his rivals; this produces faction, faction murder, murder monarchy. Democracy, on the other hand, inevitably involves wrongdoing, and wrongdoing in the public realm involves, not enmities, but cabals; these are eventually suppressed by a champion of the *dēmos*, whom the adulation of the *dēmos* establishes as *de facto* monarch. Darius goes on to trump Otanes' appeal to Persian history: it was a single individual, not the *dēmos* or an oligarchy, who freed the Persians from subjection to the Medes (a reference to Cyrus, founder of the Persian Empire); besides which, Darius observes in conclusion, it is better not to tamper with established laws (*patrious nomous*) that are functioning well.

The four other conspirators support Darius, who himself gains the throne thus re-established – a success he owes to the opportune neighing of his horse engineered by the wiles of his *sophos* groom (who, it is to be supposed, belonged to the *dēmos*), following Darius' appeal to him in private after the conspirators have dispersed.

The two most immediately striking features of this 'Constitutional Debate' are the total absence of any appeal to religion, and its all but entirely abstract character – the only at any rate explicit Persian references occurring at the beginning and end. Herodotus insists, in introducing the

[70] Vlastos 1964; cf. Ostwald 1969. The term *dēmokratia* does not figure in Herodotus' account of the debate (though he uses the cognate verb in a later reference to the debate (VI.43, quoted n.71 below), a passage where the noun also occurs); Otanes himself avoids the term *dēmos*, as does Megabyzus the term *oligarchia* and Darius the term *turannos*. Cf. Connor 1971: Appendix 1.

debate, that notwithstanding the incredulity expressed by certain Greeks it did indeed take place, a point to which he returns in a passage of Book VI.[71] In neither passage does Herodotus indicate the grounds of his certainty on the matter; it is at any rate generally agreed that the debate is in fact far more likely to derive from political discussion in fifth-century Greece rather than sixth-century Persia. The *nomos/phusis* antithesis at once underlies and subverts the entire discussion: each speaker maintains that in reality the Persians have no choice as to their type of government. All three speakers appeal to the criterion of stability: while Otanes and Megabyzus discern instability in the character of the ruler or rulers they reject, Darius presents an institutional analysis of how monarchy is inevitably produced by oligarchy and democracy alike. Political instability was a pervasive and often pressing concern of the Archaic and Classical polis;[72] in fourth-century and later political theory it was regularly sought from and attributed to the mixing of the three types of constitution,[73] a notion foreshadowed by the restrictions upon the revived monarchy agreed by the conspirators once Darius has won his case (III.83–4). First, Otanes, critic of monarchy and enthusiast for majority-rule, announces that while the throne is certain to be obtained by one of those present, he himself will not contend for it, since he desires neither to rule nor to be ruled. His fellow-conspirators accept his terms for standing aside, undertaking that none of them should exercise authority over Otanes or his descendants; Otanes' family thus remains the only Persian house to enjoy freedom, submitting – within the law – only to such rule as it chooses. If Otanes' family represents the democratic principle of freedom in the Persian polity, the conspirators as a whole constitute its aristocratic element: they are to enjoy privileged access to the royal presence, and the king is to marry only within their families.

Attempts to identify a precise source for the 'Constitutional Debate' among Herodotus' contemporaries are unconvincing. Whatever the provenance of its ideas, the debate is embedded in a long and complex account of Darius' acquisition of the Persian throne, a development central to Herodotus' narrative as a whole.[74] Its presence highlights the fact that, presented with an opportunity to adopt an alternative form of government, the Persians choose to retain monarchy; in contrast to the

[71] Following the suppression of the Ionian Revolt, the Persian commander Mardonius replaced the Ionian tyrants with democracies, 'a very great marvel to those Greeks who cannot believe that Otanes advised the seven Persian conspirators to make Persia a democracy' (VI.43).

[72] Ryffel 1949, Gehrke 1985. [73] Nippel 1980.

[74] Two subsequent debates also mark crucial moments in Herodotus' narrative: the debate at Xerxes' court as to whether or not to invade Greece (VII.8–18), and the debate at Salamis as to where the Greeks should make their stand against the Persian fleet (VIII.49, 56–63).

Athenians, who in a similar situation some years later opt for an entirely novel system of government – democracy – under which they achieve unprecedented power within Greece and victory over Persia (v.66–78; vi.131). The theme of stability and change that dominates the debate pervades the entire work, and brings it to its conclusion. The last episode of the Persian War that Herodotus reports is the Greek siege and capture of Sestos on the Gallipoli peninsula in the winter of 479/8, and the ensuing fate of its Persian commander, a man guilty of systematic sacrilege against the shrine of Protesilaus – the first Greek to fall in the Trojan War (ix.114–20). This man's grandfather, Herodotus goes on to record in the final chapter of his work,

> suggested a proposal to the Persians which they readily embraced, and urged upon Cyrus: 'Since', they said, 'Zeus has . . . given rule to the Persians, and to you, Cyrus, especially of men, come now, let us quit this land wherein we dwell – for it is a scant land, and rugged – and choose for ourselves some better country. Many such lie around us, some nearer, some farther off; if we take one of these, men will admire us far more than they do now. Who that had the power would not so act? And when shall we have a better opportunity than now, when we are lords of so many nations, and rule all Asia?' Then Cyrus, who did not greatly esteem the idea, told them they might do so, if they liked – but he warned them not to expect in that case to continue to be rulers, but to prepare to be ruled by others; soft countries gave birth to soft men – there was no region which produced magnificent fruit and at the same time men of warlike spirit. So the Persians departed with altered minds, confessing that Cyrus was wiser than they; and chose rather to dwell in a miserable land, and exercise lordship, than to cultivate plains, and be the slaves of others. (ix.122)

3 Thucydides

There are no dreams in Thucydides;[75] nor do two other elements that figure prominently in Herodotus – gods and women – engage Thucydides' attention to any significant degree.[76] The shadow-world of

[75] Commentaries: Gomme, Andrewes and Dover 1945–81, Hornblower 1991, 1996. Luschnat 1970 provides a detailed survey; other general studies: von Fritz 1967, Connor 1984 (Book by Book treatment); Hornblower 1987 (thematic). Note also Grene 1950, de Romilly 1951 (1963), Stahl 1966, Herter 1968, Strasburger 1982b, Farrar 1988: ch. 5. On Thucydides' own political opinions see Andrewes in Gomme, Andrewes and Dover 1945–81 vol.v: 335–8. Thucydides is quoted in Jowett's translation, with slight alterations (B. Jowett, *Thucydides*, 2 vols. (Oxford, 1881)).

[76] Gods: Hornblower 1992; women: Wiedemann 1996. Thucydides attributes to Pericles in his Funeral Speech a classic statement of the Greek, or at any rate Athenian view of female propriety: 'If I am to speak of womanly virtues to those of you who will henceforth be widows, let me sum them up in one short admonition: to a woman not to show more weakness than is natural to her sex is a great glory, and not to be talked about for good or evil among men' (ii.45).

dreams, powers that transcend the human realm, a sex confined by nature to domestic activities – these can find no at any rate central place in Thucydides' world of power politics. In a contemptuous comment noted earlier, doubtless directed against Herodotus as well as others, Thucydides acknowledges that the absence of 'stories' in his work may preclude its being, in our terms, a good read; he goes on to say that he will be satisfied if his work is judged *useful* by those who wish to study *to saphes*, 'the truth': it is designed not to win the applause of the moment but as 'a possession for all time' (*ktēma es aiei*: I.22).

Thucydides bases his superb confidence in the permanent value of his work most obviously on the claim that it provides a reliable and unpartisan account of what he believes to be the greatest event in Greek history – an event in which he himself participated. But in speaking of the usefulness of his work Thucydides asserts that 'the truth' to be found therein somehow relates also to *future* events, which *kata to anthrōpinon*, 'given the human condition' or 'in the nature of human affairs', are likely to show similarities with events of the past. Whatever his exact meaning in this passage,[77] his account of the Peloponnesian War patently does transcend the limited concerns of the historian of fifth-century Greece; indeed, a recent magisterial treatment of the war opens with the remark: 'It is not an unreasonable attitude to be interested in the Peloponnesian War for what Thucydides made of it and not for its own sake.'[78] How does Thucydides' account of a particular war achieve universal significance?

First and foremost, those engaged in the war are themselves presented as understanding individual events in universal terms. The most striking example occurs in an episode structurally and thematically at the heart of the work, the account at the end of Book v of Athens' expedition in 416/5 against the Aegean island of Melos (v.84–116).[79] Melos, a Spartan colony, had so far remained neutral in the war, having successfully defied a previous Athenian expedition a decade or so earlier. On this occasion the Athenian generals try diplomacy before resorting to force. Their envoys are received within the city, but are not allowed to address the full citizen-body, being required to negotiate with the Melian authorities in private. Accepting this condition, which they see as designed to prevent the assembly being misled by their rhetorical skills, the Athenians propose that even in this narrower forum both sides dispense with full-length

[77] de Ste. Croix 1972: 28–33 sets out, with minimal use of Greek, the difficulties of translation and interpretation it presents. [78] Lewis 1992: 370.

[79] See Andrewes in Gomme, Andrewes and Dover 1945–81 vol.IV: 182–8, Macleod 1983b, Bosworth 1993.

speeches; rather, let the Melians challenge any point they wish to in the Athenian position as occasion arises; the Melians agree. The Athenians begin by excluding from the discussion the rights and wrongs of the situation; the one issue that can usefully be considered is the balance of power obtaining between the two parties, which is such that, if it is to avoid disaster, Melos has no choice but to submit.

The Melians first try to persuade the Athenians that Athens' interests would be better served by allowing Melos to remain neutral; then, when the Athenians, rejecting this argument, adduce the hopeless odds Melos will face in the event of hostilities, they suggest that Melos may not unreasonably hope that material support will be forthcoming from their mother-city, Sparta, and that fortune, which is in divine hands, will favour piety against injustice. These, the Athenians respond, are vain hopes. To rely on Sparta is to show oneself naive; as for the fortunes of war:

> So far as the favour of gods is concerned, we think we have as much right to that as you have. Our aims and actions are perfectly consistent with the beliefs men hold about the gods and with the principles which govern their own conduct. For of the gods we believe, and of men we observe, that where they can rule nature (*phusis*) constrains them to do so. This law (*nomos*) was not made by us, and we are not the first who have acted upon it; we did but inherit it, and shall bequeath it to all time, knowing that you and all other men, had you the power we have, would do as we do. (v.105)

After some further discussion, concerned in particular with the issue of honour, the Athenians withdraw, to learn, on their return, that the Melian position remains unchanged: no surrender. The Athenian generals at once commence hostilities; after a lengthy and eventually close siege, and treachery within, 'the Melians surrendered unconditionally to the Athenians, who put to death all who were of military age, and sold the children and women as slaves. They then colonized the island, sending out five hundred settlers of their own' (v.116).

The Athenians' analysis of their empire in terms of the necessities of nature, a matter of observation on the human level, of conjecture on the divine, has obvious connections with the themes considered in the opening section of this chapter; in particular, the Athenians' position recalls that of Callicles in the *Gorgias* (Callicles quotes Pindar's lines on *nomos basileus*; the Athenians seem to have them in mind, and to share his understanding of them). If the cosmic perspective of the Melian Dialogue is unique in Thucydides,[80] interpretation – explicit or implicit – of particular events

[80] As is its form, which is that of a dramatic script.

and situations in terms of universal *human* nature is a characteristic feature of the work as a whole.

This comprises two formally quite distinct elements: narrative and direct speech, the latter constituting between one-fifth and a quarter of the whole and in general making much the more powerful immediate impact. With the exception of Book I, largely concerned with the origins of the war, the narrative is rigidly annalistic, each year being numbered and divided into summer and winter. Thucydides rarely lifts his gaze from the particular episode at hand, and even more rarely offers explicit authorial comment or judgment, or indicates the source of his account or doubt as to its reliability. The effect is of systematic self-effacement on Thucydides' part: nothing seems to interpose between the reader and the events themselves.[81] The speeches, by contrast (which occur more or less evenly throughout the work, with the exception of the obviously unfinished Book VIII), present analysis and argument focused on the immediate issue but unlimited in their range of reference. Thucydides does not himself appear as a speaker (he figures, as an Athenian general, in one crucial episode of the narrative, Athens' loss in the winter of 424/3 of her strategic colony of Amphipolis in northern Greece (IV.104–7));[82] he is thus clearly not in principle committed to any statement or position advanced in any of the speeches in his *History*, and where, as happens on several occasions (e.g., III.37–48; VI.76–87), he presents two antithetical speeches, he cannot be in agreement with the main thrust of both.

Controversy persists as to precisely what Thucydides says about the historicity of the speeches in his *History* in his methodological remarks at I.22; it is however generally agreed that he does here acknowledge that, given the limitations of his own and his informants' memory, the speeches, necessarily less accurate a record of what was actually said than the narrative is of events, to some extent embody Thucydides' view of what in each case needed to be said.[83] Such an admission comes oddly from one so insistent – in this very section of his work – on the need for accuracy in historical writing; to try to understand Thucydides' willingness to compromise this principle we need to consider the function of the speeches in his work.

Thucydides' world – the world he depicts in his narrative, the world addressed by his speakers – is a world of poleis and their predicaments. In

[81] On the reality, Schneider 1974.

[82] Thucydides elsewhere (V.26) notes his ensuing exile, which lasted until the end of the war.

[83] de Ste. Croix 1972: 7–12 provides a clear statement of the issues, with minimal use of Greek; cf. also Gomme 1937, Dover 1973: ch. 6. On the speeches themselves, Stadter 1973; on speeches in Greek historians generally, Walbank 1985.

his analysis of Greek history from its earliest beginnings down to the era of the Peloponnesian War, designed to justify his thesis as to the unprecedented stature of that war (I.1–19), Thucydides sets out his understanding of how this world came into being, highlighting the factors that in his view stimulated and impeded the emergence and development of settled communities, and of relations of power and subordination within and more particularly between them.[84] The poleis that constitute Thucydides' world determine policy by means of formal debate in council and assembly. From the viewpoint of the decision-making body, it matters very much – given that its vital interests may well be at stake – that debate be as well informed, and policy as well judged, as possible; from the viewpoint of those addressing such bodies, it matters very much – given the requirement of majority consent – that they articulate and present their proposals as persuasively as possible. Political debate is thus a matter at once of enlightenment and obfuscation, of candour and humbug; in seeking to identify and (a crucial need) distinguish these, the inhabitants of Thucydides' world regularly have recourse to the notions of probability and self-interest. If one has an understanding of human nature in general, and of the characteristics of specific groups or communities, it is often possible to explain and predict men's actions and reactions with reasonable confidence; in particular, self-interest is taken to be a constant and authentic mainspring of human conduct (as opposed to such commonly *alleged* motives as concern for justice). In the dangerous arena of relations between poleis political argument and analysis must typically and above all be a matter of perplexed and apprehensive men, subject to the constraints of circumstance, ignorance, passion, and wishful thinking, striving to make sound decisions as to where their and others' interest truly lies, on the basis of usually partisan speeches by orators whose sincerity is often very much open to question. Political debate is thus at the same time indispensable and problematic; it is this predicament that Thucydides' combination of speech and narrative enables him both to instantiate and transcend.[85]

All Thucydides' speakers necessarily purport to tell the truth as they see it, and to have their audience's interests at heart – a commitment manifested, when occasion demands, by strikingly outspoken criticism, such as that addressed to the Athenian assembly by both Cleon and Diodotus in the Mytilene debate (III.36–49).[86] On that occasion the Athenians agreed to overturn the previous day's decision, instigated by Cleon, to

84 de Romilly 1956: ch. 4, Parry 1989c.
85 de Romilly 1956, Macleod 1983a.
86 Macleod 1983d.

punish Athens' ally Mytilene for its revolt (428/7) by executing all adult males and enslaving the children and women. In some cases Thucydides explicitly indicates whether in his view these pretensions to truthfulness and sincerity are justified: so, for example, he expresses (II.65) unqualified admiration for Pericles' oratory prior to and during the Peloponnesian War; endorses (IV.55; VII.28; VIII.96) the contrast drawn by the Corinthians, in a speech addressed to the Spartans, between the Spartan and Athenian characters, a contrast entirely in the latter's favour (I.70: the Spartans torpid, hesitant, and unadventurous, the Athenians hyperactive, bold to a fault, innovatory); and unmasks long in advance (VI.1) the Athenian envoy's protestations at Camarina (VI.82–7) that Athens has no intention of subjugating Sicily, as – he frankly acknowledges – she has done her allies in the Aegean. For the most part, however, Thucydides' judgment upon the speeches in his *History* remains implicit in his narrative; a narrative that realizes between author and reader an ideal relation all too rare between Thucydidean orator and audience. Thucydides' narrative is truthful; it is free of bias;[87] it is useful. Just as the Athenians were right to place their trust in Pericles' unique insight and integrity, so Thucydides invites his readers to have confidence in his narrative, embodying as this does the results of laborious and critical inquiry (I.22), and insights such as the distinction between the avowed and the 'truest' causes of the war (I.23; 88)[88] and recognition of the events of the period 431–404 as elements of a single war (V.26).

Thucydides lived to see the end of the Peloponnesian War, but not to complete his account of it: his narrative breaks off abruptly in 411.[89] Athens' ultimate defeat constitutes, however, the central focus of the work as a whole. For Thucydides, the Peloponnesian War was lost by Athens, not won by Sparta; Athens, as Pericles feared before the war began,[90] proved her own worst enemy. Moreover, Athens is destroyed by the very qualities that made her great – the qualities Pericles celebrates in the Funeral Speech he delivered in the first winter of the war (II.35–46):[91] energy; boldness; versatility – Athens failing to produce another Pericles

[87] Unlike the reports of his informants, I.22; V.26, his exile enabled him to follow events from both sides. [88] Momigliano 1966b, de Ste. Croix 1972.

[89] On when Thucydides wrote what we have, and how far tensions, if not contradictions, are discernible therein – long-standing issues on which opinion remains divided – see Gomme, Andrewes and Dover 1945–81 vol.v, Appendix 1, 'Indications of Incompleteness', and Appendix 2, 'Strata of Composition'. Andrewes comments that between 'those critics for whom Thucydides is a secure observer with fixed opinions' and 'those for whom the *History* gives an impression of tension and internal struggle, the difference is perhaps too subjective for fruitful argument' (Gomme, Andrewes and Dover 1945–81 vol.IV: 186).

[90] 'I am more afraid of our own mistakes than I am of the plans of our enemies' (I.144).

[91] Loraux 1981 (1986).

after his death in 429. Under Pericles' stewardship, Thucydides writes in a rare passage of extended analysis (II.65), Athens was 'in name a democracy, in fact it was a matter of rule by the leading man'; Pericles' successors in the Athenian political elite, all much of a muchness, vied with one another for the favour of the people,[92] and thus eventually brought ruin on the city – though even after the Sicilian catastrophe Athens held out for an astonishing length of time against a Sparta now financed by Persia, finally submitting only when undermined by faction, *stasis* – that political cancer inherent in human nature but appallingly aggravated by the 'violent teacher' war, as Thucydides expounds in a later analytic passage (III.82–3), following on from his account of its first manifestation during the Peloponnesian War (at Corcyra (Corfu)), that portrays the phenomenon in terms which subvert current notions of progress.[93] The key figure in Thucydides' account of post-Periclean Athens is the flawed genius Alcibiades, a Pericles without principle or judgment.[94] He it is who urges the Athenians to embark on the Sicilian Expedition, an enterprise utterly at odds with Pericles' policy of not seeking to expand the empire until the war was won; far from restraining the people's dangerous enthusiasm for the venture, Alcibiades stimulates it with a speech (VI.16–18)[95] on which the Sicilian narrative of Books VI and VII as a whole constitutes a devastating commentary.

The Melian episode immediately precedes the account of the Sicilian Expedition. Thucydides makes no explicit connection between the two campaigns; collocation and thematic linkage speak for themselves.[96] As with Melos, Athens had been baulked in an earlier attempt to gain control of Sicily, a failure she took the harder because it came at a time when unexpected success at Pylos (IV.65)[97] had gone to her head; in embarking upon the renewed attempt in 415 she herself signally fails to act upon the coldly prudential principles the Athenian envoys urge the Melians to follow. In the Melian Dialogue the Athenians deploy the very latest moral ideas in seeking to spare Melos the horrors of war; in Sicily the Athenian commander, addressing his men on the verge of the decisive battle, a battle the Athenians' desperate situation has forced upon them, 'spoke to them of

[92] The tensions thus generated are not only exemplified but articulated at length in the Mytilene debate (III.36–49), the first post-Periclean meeting of the assembly that Thucydides presents using direct speech.

[93] Macleod 1983e, Gehrke 1985. (III.84 is generally agreed not to be genuine.)

[94] Westlake 1968: ch. 12.

[95] Macleod 1983c.

[96] On this aspect of Thucydides' technique see de Romilly 1956, Kitto 1966: ch. 6.

[97] IV.1–41: in 425, bad weather forced an Athenian fleet bound for Sicily to shelter at Pylos on the south-western coast of the Peloponnese; the Athenians fortified the headland, and the upshot of the ensuing campaign was their capture of some 120 Spartans, who, they announced, would be executed should Sparta invade Attica again.

their wives and children and ancestral gods, as men will at such a time; for then they do not care whether their commonplace phrases seem to be out of date or not, but loudly reiterate them in the belief that they will be of some service in the dread of the moment' (VII.69). At Melos the Athenians experience diplomatic failure followed by military success; in Sicily diplomatic failure (the Athenian speaker in the debate at Camarina (VI.75–88) fails to persuade the city to support Athens against Syracuse) precedes military disaster on a scale unprecedented in Greek history.[98] Melos, a Spartan colony of seven hundred years standing (V.112), is re-settled by Athenians (V.116) – a reversal foreshadowed at Amphipolis, where the Spartan Brasidas posthumously ousts the Athenian Hagnon as founder (V.11); after their final naval defeat in the Great Harbour at Syracuse, a defeat that reverses Salamis, the Athenians, 'sailors become landsmen, depending on hoplite rather than naval power' (VII.75),[99] shunted this way and that by enemy pressure in the course of their retreat, find themselves in a situation similar to that of the vagrant inhabitants of Greece prior to the emergence of settled life in the polis. To be sure, those Athenians who survive the retreat are indeed finally settled – as captives in the Syracusan stone-quarries, which the Syracusans 'thought would be the most secure place in which to keep them' (VII.86): primitive quarters indeed for citizens of the Athens celebrated by Pericles in his Funeral Speech.

The antithesis between Melos and Sicily recalls the collocation in Book II of the idealized Athens of the Funeral Speech and the account of the Plague at Athens (II.47–54),[100] an account in which description of the disease itself, based on personal experience and revealing close acquaintance with contemporary medicine, is followed by analysis of the moral disintegration it engendered among the Athenians, the apocalyptic tone of which is matched only by the analysis of *stasis* in Book III (above) and the latter stages of the narrative in Book VII of the catastrophe suffered by the Athenians in Sicily. The Plague coincided with the second Peloponnesian invasion of Attica, and their combined effect was to reverse support for Pericles' policy of steadfast resistance to Sparta; the Athenians were now

98 'Of all the Hellenic actions which took place in this war, or indeed of all Hellenic actions which are on record, this was the greatest – the most glorious to the victors, the most ruinous to the vanquished; for they were utterly and at all points defeated, and their sufferings were prodigious. Fleet and army perished from the face of the earth; nothing was saved, and of the many who went forth few returned home. Thus ended the Sicilian Expedition' (VII.87). Cf. Cornford 1907, Stahl 1966, Macleod 1983f.

99 Cf. I.18: in the face of Xerxes' advance in 480 'the Athenians resolved to evacuate their city, broke up their homes and, taking to their ships, became sailors'.

100 Parry 1989b, Rechenauer 1991.

eager to make peace, even going so far as to seek to open negotiations with the enemy – only to be rebuffed by the Spartans (II.59). The citizen-body was united in criticism of Pericles, to which he responds in his third and last speech (II.60–4). Here, as in his two previous speeches, Pericles exercises true leadership by articulating, for the benefit of his fellow-citizens, insights that would otherwise elude them. In his speech urging rejection of the Spartan ultimatum in 432 (I.140–4), he argues that to regard the rescinding of the Megarian Decree[101] as a slight matter, not worth a war, would be a superficial view, and that Athens could reasonably hope for victory if she followed the strategy he proposed (abandonment to the enemy of Attica outside the Athens-Piraeus fortification-system; firm control of the empire, but no attempt to expand it). In the Funeral Speech, eschewing an otiose catalogue of Athenian military achievement (II.36), Pericles offers instead an analysis of the principles that underlie Athens' greatness. Now, in his final speech – which succeeds (II.65) in its aim of restoring the Athenians' morale – Pericles discloses an entirely novel perspective on Athens' empire. The empire, he explains, is not simply a matter of rule over the allies; Athens' domain extends over the entire expanse of one of the two spheres of human activity: Athens' fleets can sail unchallenged any seas they choose. If only the Athenians can grasp what this means, they will realize how parochial a matter is the loss of their properties in Attica. Pericles puts the Athenians' current difficulties into perspective: Athens

> has the greatest power of any up to this day, and the memory of her glory will always survive. Even if we should be compelled at last to abate somewhat of our greatness (for all things have their times of growth and decay), yet will the recollection live, that, of all Hellenes, we ruled over the greatest number of Hellenic subjects . . . To be hated has always been at the time the lot of those who have aspired to empire; but he judges well who accepts unpopularity in a great cause. Hatred does not last long, and, beside the immediate splendour of great deeds, the renown of them endures for ever in the memory of men. (II.64)

The Athenian empire did indeed decay; and, for Thucydides, responsibility lay with Athens herself. Her two crucial mistakes Thucydides saw as first the decision to embark on the Sicilian Expedition, and secondly the failure to make proper use of Alcibiades' military genius (II.65; VI.15). Just before the Sicilian Expedition set out there occurred the mutilation

[101] A decree excluding Megarians from all ports in the Athenian Empire and from Athens' own market (I.67), revocation of which, the final Spartan embassy to Athens stated (I.139), would secure peace. Cf. Lewis 1992: 371, 376–8.

of the Hermae (vi.27ff.),[102] an episode to Thucydides' mind of little significance in itself which, however, Alcibiades' political enemies successfully exploited by playing on the Athenians' fear of tyranny. Condemned to death, Alcibiades defected to Sparta; the vortex of suspicion and indeed panic generated less by the Hermae affair itself than by the official investigation into it threatened to destroy the Athenian political elite. The loss of Alcibiades proved disastrous to the Athenian cause in Sicily; at home, the Hermae episode 'opened up a fatal breach of mistrust in Athenian political life, between the *dēmos* and its traditional aristocratic leaders'.[103] Pericles had succeeded in restoring both confidence in himself and unity of purpose against Sparta in the wake of the profound trauma of the Plague and renewed Peloponnesian ravaging of Attica; his epigoni, at a time of at any rate formal peace with Sparta, exploit an essentially trivial matter (which, however, like the Plague, baffled all attempts to get to the bottom of it (vi.60; cf. ii.48)), and the *apprehensions* of the *dēmos*, in order to destroy a political rival – in whom lay Athens' only hope of success in Sicily.

In Thucydides' account of the Hermae affair in Book vi Alcibiades' opponents remain anonymous (as do Pericles' critics in Book ii); one of them, Androcles, a man particularly influential with the *dēmos* who 'was not least responsible for the banishment of Alcibiades', is later (viii.65) named by Thucydides as having been assassinated by the oligarchs in the course of their overthrow of Athenian democracy in 411 – an event whose roots lay in the Hermae affair and the disaster in Sicily. In Book viii Thucydides gives a detailed account of the course of this oligarchic movement, both at Athens and on the island of Samos, the Athenians' naval base in the campaign to retrieve the situation in the Aegean, where many of their subject-allies had revolted in the mistaken expectation of a rapid Athenian collapse. Thucydides recognizes the achievement of the conspirators (viii.68): 'an easy thing it certainly was not, one hundred years after the fall of the tyrants, to destroy the liberties of the Athenian *dēmos*, who not only were a free, but during more than one half of this time had been an imperial people'. This success they owed, Thucydides believed, above all to the outstanding ability of their leaders, in particular Antiphon (who may or may not have been Antiphon the sophist (above)), for whom Thucydides expresses his admiration in striking terms. His overall judgment of the oligarchic revolution is however unreservedly hostile:[104] the conspirators' motives, methods, and policies all appear in a negative light

102 Dover in Gomme, Andrewes and Dover 1945–81 vol.iv: 264–288, Murray 1990b.
103 Murray 1990b: 149. 104 Westlake 1989.

(a far more emollient account of these events is provided by the Aristotelian *Constitution of the Athenians*[105]). As always, the focus of Thucydides' interest is the war: the successful overthrow of democracy at Athens set the city against the fleet at Samos, where the oligarchs failed to establish themselves – and where Alcibiades, no longer in favour with the Spartans, succeeded in regaining the confidence of the Athenians (viii.81). It is in this situation of immense peril for Athens that Alcibiades at last does his polis, rather than merely himself, some service – a service only he could have done: he succeeds in persuading the Athenians at Samos *not* to sail against Athens, a move that would have involved the abandonment of the Aegean to the enemy, with disastrous consequences (viii.86). At Athens, by contrast, dissension rapidly emerges among the oligarchs as to whether prosecution of the war or entrenchment of oligarchy should be their first priority; with civil war on the point of breaking out between the rival factions the devastating loss of the island of Euboea leads to the non-violent removal of the extreme oligarchs and the establishment of a more broadly-based regime, the 'Constitution of the Five Thousand'. Thucydides' approval of this development (viii.97) is explicit but ambiguous: disagreement persists as to whether he is saying that the new regime was the best constitution Athens enjoyed in his lifetime, or that never in his lifetime did the Athenians conduct their political affairs better than at this juncture.[106] The basis of Thucydides' approval, at any rate, is clear: the establishment of the Five Thousand obviated the risk of civil war, *stasis* of the kind and on the scale that, as described in Book iii (above), spread throughout the Greek world in the course of the war. While extremism triumphed elsewhere, at Athens there occurred a 'moderate mixing-together (*xunkrasis*) in respect of the few and the many',[107] which 'raised the city from the parlous state of affairs into which it had fallen'. Alcibiades was formally recalled from exile; city and fleet reunited in vigorous prosecution of the war; in 410 a major naval victory led to the restoration of full democracy at Athens – events[108] that take us beyond the point where Thucydides' narrative breaks off.

[105] The relevant section of this work (chs.29–33), together with other evidence, is treated in detail by Andrewes in Gomme, Andrewes and Dover 1945–81 vol.v: 184–256.

[106] Donini 1969; Andrewes in Gomme, Andrewes and Dover 1945–81 vol.v: 331–9.

[107] Thucydides may, but need not, here have in mind the notion of a 'mixed constitution', on which see the discussion of Herodotus' 'Constitutional Debate' above. At vi.18 Alcibiades deploys the language of 'mixture' in speaking of the relationship between young and old in the body politic; on this passage see de Romilly 1976.

[108] On which see Lewis *et al.* 1992: 481ff.

5

Democritus

C. C. W. TAYLOR

Discussion of the ethical and political views of Democritus of Abdera (born c. 460 BC) cannot avoid preliminary consideration of our evidence for that area of his thought. In all other areas except ethics and epistemology we are virtually wholly dependent on doxographical evidence. When we come to ethics, by contrast, the doxography is meagre (see DK 68 A 166–70), but on the other hand we possess over two hundred purported quotations from Democritus on ethical topics. Yet far from giving us greater confidence in our judgments in this area, the problematic character of these quotations has the opposite effect. This is because the great majority of those quotations are contained in two collections, those of Stobaeus and the so-called 'Sayings of Democrates' (*sic*), where they are presented in isolation from any context and without attribution to any specific work.[1] It is therefore necessary to undertake a brief consideration of the authenticity of this material before proceeding to discuss the content of Democritus' ethical and political views.

Scepticism about the authenticity of the ethical fragments is grounded in two primary considerations, first the silence of Aristotle and Theophrastus on Democritus' ethical writings and secondly the fact that our sources for the bulk of the fragments, the collections of Stobaeus and 'Democrates', cannot plausibly be thought to have been compiled from direct access to texts of Democritus. Stobaeus' anthology is clearly based on earlier collections which included, besides excerpts from extant texts of authors such as Plato and the tragedians, anecdotes and maxims attributed to such famous figures as Pythagoras and Socrates, which cannot have had their origin in works written by their supposed authors. Since Stobaeus never cites any Democritean title, but merely ascribes citations to Democritus by name, it is virtually certain that he found his material in a collection of such maxims. This is confirmed by the fact that thirty max-

[1] The texts discussed in this chapter are printed in DK and Luria 1970. They are cited by their DK numbering. The sayings in the 'Democrates' collection appear as 68 B 35–115. The main scholarly studies of Democritus' ethics are listed below, n.12.

ims are common to the 'Democrates' collection and to Stobaeus. This is clearly an unpromising basis for claims to preserve the actual words of Democritus, and were we wholly dependent on the material preserved in these collections we should be forced to acknowledge that we could have no good grounds for confidence in the authenticity of any of the so-called fragments.

The situation is, not, however, quite as bad as that; we have *some* evidence external to the collections of maxims regarding the existence and content of the ethical works of Democritus, and some confirmation from other sources of the wording of a few of Stobaeus' quotations. The evidence of the existence of the ethical works serves to rebut the argument against the authenticity of the fragments from the silence of Aristotle and Theophrastus. Diogenes Laertius' list of works (IX.46) establishes the existence in the time of Thrasyllus (first century AD) of texts of a number of writings of Democritus on ethics, including a work *On Cheerfulness* which Seneca appears to have read (*Tranq. An.* II.3). Cicero is familiar with Democritus' doctrine of the supreme good and with the terminology in which it was expressed (*Fin.* V.23; 87) though it is unclear whether he had read the original texts. The silence of Aristotle and Theophrastus must therefore have some other explanation than that Democritus did not write on ethics. As far as Aristotle is concerned, three points should be made. First, his ethical treatises mention the views of earlier writers, except Plato, very sparsely. Second, the extant works in which he discusses the atomists at length (principally *Phys.*, *GC*, *Cael.*, *de An.*) deal with other subjects. Third, he is reported to have written two works on Democritus, both lost (with the exception of a single passage preserved by Simplicius (DK 68 A 37)). For all we know, these works may have included some discussion of Democritus' ethics. As regards Theophrastus, Plutarch preserves evidence (*Fragm. de Libid. et Aegr.* 2) of his having responded to an ethical thesis of Democritus', indicating that he did not in fact pass over the latter's ethics in total silence. How systematic his discussion was we have no means of knowing.

A few of Stobaeus' maxims are also attributed to Democritus by earlier writers. DK 68 B 170–1 occur in Stobaeus' lengthy excerpt from the history of ethics by the first-century AD writer Arius Didymus (II.7); B 33 and 188 are cited by Clement, B 3 by Plutarch and B 119 by Dionysius of Alexandria (quoted by Eusebius). We can, then, be reasonably certain that copies of ethical writings by Democritus existed in the library of Alexandria in the first century AD, and that the writers mentioned had access to his writings, either directly or via compilations of excerpts from them.

It is at the very least a reasonable conjecture that the Democritean sayings in Stobaeus and 'Democrates' derive ultimately from that source. How much of that material is from the hand of Democritus himself is much harder to determine. A number of Stobaeus' sayings contain vocabulary attested in the doxography as Democritean,[2] while the content of a few other sayings in his collection connects them fairly firmly with Democritus' native city of Abdera and its mother-city, Teos. B 260 closely echoes the wording of an oath taken thrice annually by magistrates at Teos and Abdera, while B 252, 254, 263 and 279 also show traces of legal terminology associated with both cities.[3] B 257–60 are closely connected in subject-matter, setting out in legalistic terminology a list of immunities for the killing of various kinds of anti-social persons and (apparently) animals; B 257 contains the Democritean term 'wellbeing' and B 258 'cheerfulness', thus linking this series (already linked to Teos via B 260) with the others which contain Democritean technical terms.

It does not seem to me possible to divide this material into the exclusive and exhaustive categories of 'genuine' and 'spurious' on grounds of style or content. Indeed, the hypothesis (which has considerable antecedent probability) that the ethical writings of Democritus underwent a continuous process of anthologizing and excerpting over a period of centuries puts those categories themselves into doubt. How much paraphrasing, abbreviation and so on must a passage undergo before it ceases to be 'genuine'? In this study I shall proceed on the following assumptions:

1 A substantial amount of the Democritean material in Stobaeus derives from Democritus' own writings.
2 We have grounds for greater confidence in the genuineness of a quotation from Stobaeus when that quotation is also ascribed to Democritus by a writer earlier than Stobaeus.
3 The 'Democrates' sayings, even if (as is likely) their ultimate source is the writings of Democritus, represent a stage of transmission of the tradition more distant from Democritus himself than that represented by those passages counted as genuine under clauses 1 and 2.

Our evidence indicates that Democritus was concerned with both moral and political questions, and also with the connections between

[2] *Euthumos*, *euthumia*, etc. (cheerful, cheerfulness, cf. Cic. *Fin*. v.23, 87, Stob. II.7.3i, Epiphan. *Adv. Haer*. III.2.9) occur in B 3, 174, 189, 191, 258, 279 and 286, *euestō* (wellbeing, cf. Clem. *Strom*. II.130, D.L. IX.46) in B 257, *athambia* (freedom from fear, cf. Cic. *Fin*. v.87) in B 215 and the cognate adjective *athambos* in B 216 (the latter the only recorded occurrence of this word). B 174 also contains the only recorded occurrence of the noun *aterpeiē*, distress, an alternative form of *aterpia*, attested as Democritean by Clement (*Strom*. II.130) and Stobaeus (III.1.46), while the adjective *aterpēs* occurs in B 233.

[3] For details, see Lewis 1990.

them: that is, with how the individual should live, how the political community should be organized, and how the individual should contribute to that organization. It shows that he was engaged with the wide-ranging contemporary debates on individual and social ethics of which we have evidence from Plato and other sources. On what Socrates presents as the fundamental question in ethics: 'How should one live?' (*Gorg.* 500c, *Rep.* 352d), Democritus is the earliest thinker reported as having explicitly posited a supreme good or goal, which he called 'cheerfulness' or 'wellbeing', and which he appears to have identified with the untroubled enjoyment of life (B 188: 'Joy and sorrow are the distinguishing mark of things beneficial and harmful'; see also A 166–7, 169, B 170–1).[4] It is reasonable to suppose that he shared the presumption of the primacy of self-interest which is common both to the Platonic Socrates and to his immoralist opponents. Having identified the ultimate human interest with 'cheerfulness', the evidence of the testimonia and the fragments is that he thought that it was to be achieved by moderation, including moderation in the pursuit of pleasures (B 211: 'Self-control increases joys and makes pleasure greater'; B 219: 'The courageous man is he who overcomes, not only the enemy, but pleasures also. But some are masters of cities, yet slaves to women'; see also B 191, 210, 214, 222–4, 232–5, 245, 283–4, 285–6, Democrates B 70). He also emphasized the importance of discriminating useful from harmful pleasures (B 207: 'One should choose, not every pleasure, but pleasure in what is fine'; see also A 167, B 189, Democrates B 71, 74), and of conformity to conventional morality (B 174: 'The cheerful man who undertakes right and lawful deeds rejoices sleeping and waking, and is strong and free from care; but he who takes no heed of what is right and does not do what he should is distressed by all these things, whenever he remembers any of them, and is frightened and reproaches himself'; also B 215, 217, 256). The upshot is a recommendation to a life of moderate, enlightened hedonism, which has some affinities with the life recommended by Socrates (whether in his own person or as representing ordinary enlightened views is disputed) in Plato's *Protagoras*, and, more obviously, with the Epicurean ideal of which it was the forerunner (cf. Theod. *Cur.* XI.6).

An interesting feature of the fragments is the frequent stress on individual conscience. Some fragments stress the pleasures of a good conscience and the torments of a bad one (B 174 (quoted above), 215), while others recommend that one should be motivated by one's internal sense

[4] For fuller discussion, see Gosling and Taylor 1982: ch. 2.1.

of shame rather than by concern for the opinion of others (B 244: 'Even when you are alone, neither do nor say anything bad; learn to feel shame before yourself much more than before others'; see also B 264, Democrates B 84). This theme may well reflect the interest, discernible in contemporary debates, in what has come to be known in the modern period as the question of the sanctions of morality. A recurrent theme in fifth- and fourth-century criticisms of conventional morality is that, since the enforcement of morality rests on conventions, someone who can escape conventional sanctions, for example by doing wrong in secret, has no reason to comply with moral demands. Thus Antiphon (DK 87 B 44) contrasts the ineffectiveness of moral sanctions with the inevitability of harm for one who contravenes the natural norms which prompt one to seek one's own advantage; and the author of the Sisyphus fragment (DK 88 B 25) attributes the origin of belief in the gods to the contrivance of a clever individual who aimed to deter wrongdoers by the pretence that, while they might evade human punishment, they could not escape the all-seeing gods. The most celebrated expression of this thought is Glaucon's tale of Gyges' ring in Plato's *Republic* II; someone with the gift of invisibility (like the legendary Gyges) would be a fool not to take advantage of the resulting ability to do wrong with impunity (359b–360d). An opponent of immoralism who, like Democritus and Plato, accepts the primacy of self-interest therefore faces the challenge of showing, in one way or another, that self-interest is best promoted by the observance of conventional moral precepts.[5]

The attempt, however pursued, to ground morality in self-interest involves the rejection of the antithesis between law or convention (*nomos*) and nature (*phusis*) which underlies much criticism of morality in the fifth and fourth centuries. For Antiphon, Callicles, Thrasymachus and Glaucon, nature prompts one to seek one's own interest while law and convention seek, more or less successfully, to inhibit one from doing so. But if one's long-term interest is the attainment of a pleasant life, and if the natural consequences of wrongdoing, including ill-health, insecurity and the pangs of conscience, give one an unpleasant life, while the natural consequences of right-doing give one a contrastingly pleasant life, then nature and convention point in the same direction, not in opposite directions as the critics of morality had alleged. (We have no evidence as to whether Democritus had considered the objections that conscience is a

[5] Fuller treatment of immoralism and the use of the *nomos–phusis* contrast (discussed in the following two paragraphs) in Winton, Ch. 4 section 1, above.

product of convention, and that exhorting people to develop their conscience assumes that it must be.)

Though the texts contain no express mention of the *nomos–phusis* contrast itself, several of them refer to law in such a way as to suggest rejection of the antithesis. B 248 asserts that: 'The aim of law is to benefit the life of men', thus contradicting Glaucon's claim (*Rep.* 358c3–6) that law constrains people contrary to their natural bent. B 248 is supplemented and explained by B 245: 'The laws would not prevent each person from living as he pleased, if one did not harm another; it is envy which prompts the beginning of civil strife.' So law frees people from the aggression of others, thus benefiting them by giving them the opportunity to follow the promptings of nature towards their own advantage. B 252 is the strongest expression of the integration of *nomos* and *phusis*: 'The city's being well run is the greatest good: if it is preserved everything is preserved, if it is destroyed everything is destroyed.' A stable community, that is to say, is necessary for the attainment of that wellbeing which is nature's goal for us. This quotation encapsulates the central point in the defence of *nomos* (emphasized in Protagoras' myth (*Prot.* 322a–323a) and the 'Anonymous Iamblichi' (DK 89, 6–7)) that law and civilization are not contrary to nature, but required for human nature to flourish, a point also central to the Epicurean account of the development of civilization (see especially Lucretius v).[6] The claim in B 181 that it is better to be persuaded not to do wrong than to be restrained by law is not inconsistent with this fundamental thesis; the fragment does not imply any contrast between law and nature, but between reasoned acceptance of norms and their imposition by fear of sanctions (cf. Democrates B 41: 'Abstain from wicked deeds not from fear, but because one ought not'). Persuasion will, in Democritus' view, presumably centre precisely on the message of B 245, 248 and 252, that obedience to the law is in the interest of the individual.

The evidence of the fragments of Democritus' views on specifically political questions, such as the best form of political organization, is not wholly unambiguous. In B 251: 'Poverty in a democracy is as much more desirable than so-called wellbeing under tyrants, as freedom is more

[6] Another reminiscence of the *Protagoras* occurs in B 247, whose cosmopolitan sentiment recalls Hippias' use of the *nomos–phusis* contrast to exalt the natural affinities of intellectuals over the artificial political boundaries which divide them (337c–e). I do not suggest that Plato was responding directly to Democritus (nor, as is not chronologically impossible, that Democritus was responding to Plato), but rather that they provide evidence of issues current in the later fifth and early fourth centuries. There is, of course, no inconsistency in maintaining both that law and society are necessary for the development of human nature and that some particular laws or conventions are contrary to nature.

desirable than slavery', a firm preference is stated for democracy over tyranny. The dictum associates the former with freedom and the latter with slavery, but that falls short of the claim that democracy is as such the best kind of constitution. In B 226: 'Free speech is a part of freedom, but there is risk in choice of the right time', Democritus praises the value of free speech (*parrhēsia)*, while characteristically adding a warning against exercising it at the wrong time. In B 254 'When the wicked (*hoi kakoi*) assume official positions, the more unworthy they are the more heedless they become, and the more they are filled with folly and boldness', the dangers of official positions being filled by the wrong people are stressed. While that may be merely an expression of the truism, compatible with any political system, that things go badly when unprincipled people hold power, it may have a more specific message of hostility to the allocation of offices by lot, one of the features recognized as characteristic of democracy (Arist. *Pol.* 1294b8).[7] B 267: 'Rule belongs by nature to the superior' is a paradigm oligarchic slogan, which is yet compatible with a moderate democracy in which office is elective. (On Democritus' assumption of elective magistracies, see below.)

Some fragments express an almost quietist attitude, stressing the dangers inherent in political activity: B 253 gives the depressing message that it is bad for one either to stick to one's own business without involvement in public life (for then one acquires a bad reputation), or to take part in community affairs, however honestly (for one is bound to make enemies). The dangers facing even the honest citizen in office seem to be the theme of the textually corrupt B 266. I read the ambiguous opening sentence as: 'There is no way in the present organization of society not to do wrong to rulers, even if they are altogether good.'[8] This then appears to be explained by what follows, whose central theme is that as things stand, the honest magistrate who has prosecuted wrongdoers while in office is liable to find himself under their authority once he demits office, and thus open to their vengeance.[9] Yet despite its dangers, active involvement in

[7] For the use of *kakos* ('bad', 'wicked') to refer to non-noble elements in society, see Raaflaub, in Ch. 2 sections 5 and 6, above.

[8] The sentence may also be translated: 'There is no way in the present organization of society for rulers not to act wrongly, however good they may be.' The point of that even more pessimistic dictum might be that the honest ruler would be obliged to prosecute wrongdoers who had done him no personal harm, thus violating the principle of justice that one should not harm those who have done one no harm (cf. Antiphon 87 B 44 (= CPF 1.1*215–16)). But that contradicts the concluding sentence of the fragment, in which Democritus says that we should seek for ways to ensure that the person who has *done no wrong*, even in zealously prosecuting wrongdoers, does not become subject to them when he leaves office.

[9] Cf. B 3's warning against *polupragmosunē*, behaving like a busybody, in private or in public life.

communal life is assumed to be necessary for communal and individual good. The office-holder must expect criticism if he does harm, while his doing good will be taken for granted – 'for he was not chosen in order to do harm, but to do good' (B 265; note that it is assumed that magistracies are elective). But while good conduct in office may not win popular favour, it represents the highest form of personal goodness: 'He has the greatest share of justice and goodness who administers the greatest offices worthily' (B 263). There is an obligation not to let criminals go unpunished (B 261–2), despite the dangers inherent in enforcement of the law (see B 266 above): the series of immunities (B 257–60) pronounced in favour of those who impose the death penalty on wrongdoers is presumably designed to mitigate those dangers. The greatest good is the city's being well run (B 252), which presupposes social concord (B 249–50), which will be achieved if the wealthy feel concern for the poor and seek to help them (B 255; cf. B 282 on the proper use of wealth as a public benefactor (*dēmōphelēs*)).

Overall, we may take it that Democritus held that the best form of government is a moderate democracy, in which magistracies are elective and citizens are encouraged to take an active interest in government and in the welfare of their fellow-citizens. Abdera appears to have had a democratic constitution in his lifetime,[10] and it is possible that he himself may have held office.[11] The main interest of his political fragments is not, however, in their contribution to political theory narrowly conceived (which is modest), but in their relevance to the wider questions of the relations between individual and social goods and between *nomos* and *phusis* which are central to the ethical and social thought of the fifth and fourth centuries.[12]

[10] See Lewis 1990.

[11] Some coins of Abdera dated (on the most recent dating) c. 414 BC, bear the legend *epi demokrito* 'in Democritus' term of office'. For details see Procopé 1990: 309–10. It is of course not certain that the Democritus in question was the philosopher.

[12] The most recent general study of Democritus is Salem 1996 (includes bibliography). Major studies of his social and political thought include Havelock 1957, Moulton 1974, Müller 1984, Hussey 1985, Nill 1985, Farrar 1988, Procopé 1989 and 1990. Versions of this chapter have appeared in 'Anaxagoras and the Atomists', in C. C. W. Taylor (ed.), *Routledge History of Philosophy* I: *From the Beginning to Plato*, Routledge, London and New York 1997, and in C. C. W. Taylor, *The Atomists: Leucippus and Democritus. A text and translation with a commentary*, Toronto U.P., 1999. Permission from these publishers to reprint this material is gratefully acknowledged.

6

The orators

JOSIAH OBER

1 Introduction

With the rise of persuasive public speech as a distinctive field of endeavour in Athens during the fifth and fourth centuries BC, Greek political thought becomes deeply involved with democratic Athenian political practice and with Athenian legislative and judicial institutions. Significant political ideas and a distinctive form of political/ethical reasoning were developed by Athens' practising political orators (*rhētores*); evidence for their ideas and style of reasoning survives in their preserved public speeches. Certain of the political ideas developed by practising orators challenged, and were in turn challenged by, teachers of formal rhetoric (*rhētorikoi*); this critical rhetorical tradition survives in some of the speeches of Isocrates. The political ideas and reasoning propounded by *rhētores* and the counter-arguments of the *rhētorikoi* in turn provided an important part of the intellectual context for the development of the political philosophies of Plato and Aristotle.[1]

The Athenian *rhētores* are noteworthy as the primary surviving source of ancient political writing that is genuinely sympathetic to democracy. The speeches of Athens' public orators were written to influence large public bodies, especially the citizen assembly (*ekklēsia*) and people's courts (*dikastēria*); another important venue was the (nearly) annual *epitaphios*: a public oration spoken over Athenians who had died in battle during the previous year. When addressing democratic audiences, composed primarily of ordinary citizens, the Athenian speaker necessarily paid close attention to the established social and political notions, opinions, and beliefs (i.e. the political ideology) common to most members of the Athenian citizen body (*dēmos*).[2] Assembly and courtroom speakers who ignored or too overtly contravened their audiences' deeply-entrenched

[1] Relationship between theory and practice of rhetoric: Pilz 1934, Cole 1991, Worthington 1994. Athenian democracy as the context for development of rhetorical practice: Jones 1957, Montgomery 1983, Finley 1985, Mossé 1994. Intellectual context for the work of Plato and Aristotle: Ober 1998. [2] Ober 1989, Yunis 1996: 2–18.

ideological convictions were unlikely to win many votes. Since the corpus of orations by Athenian orators is composed of speeches by highly successful speech-writers (including Lysias (d.380), Demosthenes (384–322), and the latter's contemporary, Aeschines), the corpus, read as a whole, provides an indirect guide to the political ideology of democratic Athens in the late fifth century and throughout much of the fourth. Ideology is sometimes regarded as antithetical to rational thought. But in the more ambitious Athenian orations, the raw material of popular ideology provides a basis for sophisticated arguments about the nature and substance of democratic politics. These arguments, while not rigorously logical, are often plausible. They are also strikingly different in form and content from discussions of democracy found in the canonical Greek political philosophers. In these terms, rhetoric and popular ideology seem worthy of consideration under the general rubric of 'political thought'.

2 Historical background and institutional context

The central importance to political and judicial decision-making of the persuasive speech, delivered according to well-established social protocols by an acknowledged member of the community to an audience of his peers, appears early in Greek literature. The Homeric epics portray the importance of the individual public speaker in military policy and judicial decisions and they reveal some of the conventions governing pre-classical public speaking. While high-status elders (e.g., Nestor) played especially prominent roles as speakers, skill in public address was a factor – along with prowess in battle, wealth and birthright – in determining an individual's status in the early polis. Homer's Achilles and Odysseus (for example) are great warriors and athletes, but also renowned orators.[3] The Thersites episode in *Iliad* 11, however, defines the limits of eloquence as an independent variable in Homeric society. When low-born Thersites addresses the Achaean assembly, he seems at first both rhetorically skilled and accurate in his pessimistic assessment of the military situation and the failings of Agamemnon. Yet his inferior social status precludes his speech having any positive political impact; the assembly of warriors expresses its approval when Odysseus beats Thersites into a cowed silence with the speaker's staff.[4]

[3] Homeric speech contests: Martin 1989: 65–77.
[4] For further discussion of the Thersites episode see Raaflaub, Ch.2 section 3 above.

The contexts of public speaking change dramatically with the development of Athenian democracy in the decades following the revolution of 508/7 BC. By the 450s BC, a full democratic institutional apparatus was in place, the public oration over the year's war dead had become a centrally important civic ritual, and until 322 (barring short counter-revolutionary interruptions in 411 and 404 BC) the primary Athenian decision-making bodies were the *ekklēsia* and *dikastēria*. In the *epitaphios*, the speaker, selected on the basis of personal reputation and ability, addressed the whole Athenian free society: citizens, children, women, and resident foreigners. The typical funeral oration (to judge by the few surviving examplars) emphasized traditional aristocratic conceptions of excellence as inherited through birth, manifested in a courage-centred code of behaviour; and demonstrated by noteworthy deeds. The extent to which those pre-democratic values were transformed by the context of the democratic polis is debatable. In an *epitaphios* delivered in 431 BC (as reported by Thucydides), Pericles claims that the imperial splendour of the democratic polis renders it capable of resolving apparent contradictions between worth, opportunity and desert; between privacy, civic participation and public propriety; between thought, speech and action – and he thereby justifies the sacrifice of the fallen citizen-warriors. Pericles' speech has been variously read as an unabashed celebration of the democratic polity, as an exploration of Athens' unrealized potential as an 'education to Hellas', and as a demonstration of democracy's incapacity to transcend aristocratic values.[5]

The situation, as regards both audience and discourse, was different in the decision-making bodies. While magistrates (especially the generals) were expected to address the assembly on matters within their sphere of competence, the rules of the *ekklēsia*, the body responsible for all important decisions on domestic and foreign policy, allowed any Athenian citizen to express his opinions to the several thousand citizens in attendance for as long as he could hold their attention. When the mass audience became bored or irritated by a speaker, he was summarily shouted down. Typically, the content and wording of a decree of the assembly was worked out in the course of open debate among a number of speakers representing a range of opinions and interests.[6] Once the wording of the decree was set, the assembly voted; a simple majority of those present

[5] Incapacity to transcend aristocratic values: Loraux 1986 (1981); exploration of potentiality in Athenian life for the education of Hellas: Connor 1984: 63–75; celebration of democracy: Finley 1942: 143–9.

[6] Decrees developed in open debate: Jones 1957: 99–133, Hansen 1987: 49–93, 1991: 141–50.

determined its success or failure. If the measure passed the assembly, it was written up and often inscribed on a stone stele. The name of the proposer was permanently attached to the decree, a mark both of his rhetorical success and (by the late fifth century) his legal responsibility for the policy. Likewise, in the *dikastēria*, prosecutor and defendant in both public (generally speaking, criminal) and private (civil) actions were amateurs rather than professional barristers, and they spoke *in propria persona*. Each litigant was allotted equal time (measured by a water clock; the amount of time varied with the importance of the case) to address juries typically numbering between 200 and 500 members. Judging by preserved speeches, Athenian juries construed legal relevance broadly, but speakers who strayed too far from the point, or who offended the sensibilities of their listeners, could expect vocal complaints from jurors. In both assembly and courtroom, the democratic rules pitted speakers, often members of wealth and status elites, against one another in a contest judged by ordinary citizens.[7]

The citizen-speaker in the democratic assembly or in the people's courts was protected by Athenian law and by egalitarian social mores from the punishment suffered by Thersites. But the prospective Athenian speaker faced a daunting prospect nonetheless, and the stakes were high. The fate of a polis could hang on the question of which speaker was best able to capture the assemblymen's attention and win their approval. An adverse decision of the people's court could mean a litigant's financial ruin, exile or death. Meanwhile, coincidentally with the growth of democracy in the early and mid-fifth centuries, Athens was becoming wealthy and powerful, the intellectual, artistic and political centre of the Greek world. As a result, Athenians had strong incentives to sharpen their rhetorical skills and private Athenian resources were quite capable of supporting professional teachers of eloquence.

In the mid-fifth century self-styled experts in rhetoric flocked to Athens; many of the so-called sophists became famous for teaching ambitious men how to formulate and present arguments suited to winning the acquiescence of large public audiences. As Plato (*Gorgias* 452c–454b) and Aristotle (*Rhetoric* 1395b1–1396a3) each suggest, an important element of the special skill (*technē*) taught by the rhetorician lay in making the speaker's rhetorical goals appear to be fully congruent with the audience's pre-existing beliefs and preferences. Athenians lacking rhetorical training or uncertain of their skills, who found themselves involved in

[7] Procedure in Athenian assembly and courts: Hansen 1991; status of speakers: Ober 1989.

litigation, might avail themselves of the services of a legal speech-writer (*logographos*) who would compose a suitable oration, carefully crafted to fit the known ideological predilections of the jurors, the putative character of the speaker, and the specific legal situation. The litigant would commit the speech to memory and recite it in the courtroom.

3 The corpus of orations by Athenian orators

In the late fifth and fourth centuries, *rhētorikoi* seeking students, *logographoi* hoping to impress potential clients, and *rhētores* intent on influencing a reading public circulated orations in written form. A body of these speeches was canonized during the Hellenistic period as the works of the 'Ten Attic Orators'; roughly 150 speeches and a number of fragments survive. The corpus can be divided roughly according to the Aristotelian categories of epideictic (display, including the funeral orations and surviving speeches by Isocrates), dicanic (law-court), and symbouleutic (advisory to assembly or council).[8] The fifteen surviving symbouleutic orations attributed to Demosthenes are good sources for the development of fourth-century Athenian politics and foreign policy. But the largest and, from the perspective of political thought, the most interesting rhetorical category is the dicanic. Within this category the most important speeches are those written and delivered *in propria persona* by practising *rhētores*.

In speeches delivered in major public trials, the political orator was afforded enough time and an audience suited to the development of relatively complex ideas. Surviving speeches, especially by Demosthenes, Aeschines, and their contemporary Lycurgus, suggest that Athenian jurors expected prominent politicians to spend much of their allotted time in elaborating political concepts of greater generality than was seemingly demanded by the immediate legal situation.[9] The orator's approach is typically to cast his argument in the form of a public reminder of what the jurors, represented as good citizens of the democratic polis, already knew or believed. It is impossible to determine just how much of a given oration is based on pre-existing popular assumptions about politics and justice, and how much is genuinely original to the speaker. Yet in most cases it seems safe to conjecture that the ideas being promulgated are regarded by speaker and audience as congruent with popular ideology, and that the

[8] Definitions of dicanic, symbouleutic, and epideictic rhetoric: Kennedy 1963.

[9] The issue of the relationship of published speeches to spoken originals is complex. Most students of rhetoric tend to assume a relatively close relationship, but cf. Worthington 1991.

speaker's attempt to clarify and refine the tenets undergirding democratic institutions and practices was regarded by his listeners as a valid and salutary enterprise.

4 Popular wisdom and the problem of erroneous public decisions

A fundamental idea informing public rhetoric is that democracy is a particularly good form of government because the *dēmos*, as a collective body, manifests a high degree of practical wisdom. This wisdom is attributed to several sources. First Athenians are innately more intelligent than other peoples. Next the aggregated intelligence of a collectivity (*ekklēsia* or *dikastērion*) yields superior wisdom (cf. Arist. *Pol.* 1281a40–b10). Finally, democratic institutional structure and the correct decisions made by democratic bodies help to educate the citizens and, especially, the youth. Popular wisdom consists of, first, an accurate apprehension by the *dēmos* of 'brute facts' of nature, and of 'social facts' and their consequences; next, a recognition that the good of the ordinary citizen is consistent with the good of the *dēmos*, the democracy, and the state; and finally, a willingness on the part of citizens to act accordingly in their public and private capacities. Thus demotic wisdom is (jointly and severally) at one with patriotic loyalty to Athens and widespread participation in the democratic regime. It consequently allows for the formation of excellent policy in the assembly, for just judicial decisions, and for their effective implementation. Democratic judgments, legislative and judicial, will further the common good of the democratic community and will be in the best interests of the individual citizen.[10]

The assumption that the *dēmos* was innately politically wise and capable of making correct decisions on complex matters and implementing good policy underpinned democratic ideology. Given that Athens flourished through much of the democratic period, there was considerable empirical evidence to support the doctrine.[11] But in all periods Athenian citizens were occasionally confronted by the uncomfortable fact that the *dēmos* was not always wise: some popular policies went wrong; some innocent men were convicted in the courts, and the guilty sometimes went free. The perceptible gap between the general hypothesis of popular wisdom and the observed fact of errors committed by democratic bodies demanded explanation; the attempt to close the gap led Athenian orators

10 Popular wisdom: Ober 1989: 163–5.
11 General continuity between fifth- and fourth-century democracy: Bleicken 1987.

to develop arguments about the functioning of democratic politics. The most fruitful area of explanation involved the assumption that the generally wise *dēmos* was liable to misdirection through malicious eloquence. Speakers might mislead democratic bodies by providing inaccurate or incomplete information about affairs, or stimulate in their audience an unwholesome desire for unworthy or unobtainable objects. In either case, the problem was traced to the complex relationship between the *dēmos* and the elite *rhētores*. The democracy could not function without the highly educated public speaker, but the relationship between speaker and audience was fraught with overt and potential conflicts. The nature and consequences of these conflicts were analysed in detail by orators in the context of legal conflicts with other speakers. Since only one party to a debate could be advocating the wisest, most patriotic, and best decision, each speaker attempted to explain the source of his opponent's refusal to acknowledge the superiority of his own position. The *rhētores* thereby developed ideas about the character and roles appropriate to citizens and leaders in a just democratic society. Notably, these ideas focused on the purposes and results of speech and willed collective action, rather than on the *nomos–phusis* distinction so central to other genres of Greek political thought.

Various explanations were offered for a rival speaker's recalcitrance. (1) He could be sincerely ignorant of the best policy, either because he was inherently unable to understand complex matters or because he lacked information about them; this pointed to the need for public speakers who possessed superior intelligence, excellent educations, and first-rate sources of information. (2) He might wilfully advocate an inferior policy or judicial outcome because he did not actually wish for the best for the democratic state. His lack of patriotism could be (2a) a function of his personal venality: he might be in the pay of the state's internal or external enemies; this pointed to the need for public speakers who possessed personal resources adequate to insulate them against monetary temptations. Alternatively (2b), a speaker's deepest loyalty might lie with some sociopolitical group other than the *dēmos* and the state. Since *rhētores* were typically members of elites of education and wealth (and, given points 1 and 2a, almost necessarily so), a common claim was that a rival placed the interests of his elite social class above those of the state as a whole. This pointed to the need for speakers who associated their own primary political identity with the *dēmos* and its ideals.

Demosthenes' *Against Meidias* (346 BC, possibly not delivered) demonstrates how the several elements sketched above could yield general arguments about abstract political ideas.[12] The legal case at issue seems trivial: Demosthenes, a prominent *rhētor*, charges Meidias, a fellow *rhētor*, with having struck Demosthenes in the Theatre of Dionysus when the latter was serving as chorus-producer (*chorēgos*). Demosthenes suffered no physical harm from the assault; rather he argues that Meidias' action constitutes a profound threat to the Athenian system of justice and to the freedom, the political equality, and the personal security of each Athenian citizen. Demosthenes reasons as follows: Meidias was a very rich man; he believed that his economic superiority, along with his rhetorical skills, gave him warrant to act as the superior of all poorer, less-accomplished citizens in public as well as in private life. Meidias (and other rich men of his ilk) recognized that the laws and social protocols pertaining under the democracy made the poor citizen the rich man's equal in the public realm, prevented the rule of the rich, and guaranteed the freedom of each citizen. Democratic freedom and equality allowed each citizen to participate in politics and offered him security from the threat of degrading physical and verbal abuse from social superiors – i.e., the fate of Thersites. Thus, according to Demosthenes, Meidias and the rich as a class recognized in the democracy an impediment to their selfish desire to deploy power in public, and to enjoy its fruits by dominating and abusing their social inferiors. They were therefore enemies to the democracy and wished for its overthrow. Meidias' wilful contempt for the established rules of the democracy was manifested in (*inter alia*) his arrogant public behaviour towards Demosthenes. This behaviour was intended not merely to humiliate a personal enemy and a social equal, but to undermine the democratic regime by demonstrating Meidias' ability to impose at will the hierarchical norms of private life within the public realm of the theatre.

Demosthenes argues that the threat to democracy represented by Meidias' behaviour is real; a lack of effective public response (i.e., the failure of the jury to convict Meidias) would encourage Athenian elites to act arrogantly and so would lead to the loss of the freedom, equality and personal security of each citizen. Demosthenes supports this position by discussing the nature of democratic law. The laws of Athens, he tells the jury, have no independent existence or innate strength; their force exists solely in the decisions of juries and the behaviour of citizens. Juries are composed of ordinary citizens, whose individual standing and collective authority are threatened by the desires of elites to dominate social inferiors. The only thing standing between the weak ordinary citizen and the

[12] For the political ideas developed by Demosthenes in *Against Meidias*, see Ober 1996: chapter 7, with MacDowell 1990.

rapacious elite is the system of laws. But the laws themselves have effect only through a sustained pattern of judicial decisions and subsequent actions. 'So the laws are powerful (*ischuroi*) through you and you through the laws. You must therefore stand up for them in just the same way as any individual would stand up for himself if attacked; you must take the view that offences against the law are common concerns' (*Meid.*223–5).

Demosthenes develops an argument focused on the pragmatic basis of Athenian democracy. It explains how democracy is maintained in the face of the organized hostility of powerful and highly motivated internal enemies. The benefits of democracy to the citizen are described in terms of three attributes (freedom, equality, security) familiar from modern liberal political theory. Yet Demosthenes does not predicate these attributes on a doctrine of individual rights, nor does he ground them in concepts of inherency or inalienability. Rather, Demosthenes argues in pragmatic and performative terms that democracy exists in the constant practice of public bodies and law-abiding citizens: the freedom, equality and security of the citizen were not for him properties that attached naturally to the individual, that existed in any sense independently of political behaviour, or that would be naturally manifest in the absence of governmental constraints. Instead, these attributes were understood as dynamic matrices of social relationships and behaviours, created and maintained through the ongoing participation by ordinary citizens in the activities of the *dēmos* as a collectivity. Absent that participatory activity, democracy would be merely a name; stark hierarchies familiar from private life and the virtual slavery of the weak would replace equality and freedom; justice would be defined by the will and the good of the powerful rather than that of the *dēmos*.

Demosthenes' argument suggests that the *rhētor* of the Meidias type will address the *dēmos* only to aggrandize himself or to lead the masses astray, but his argument also retains an essential place for the good *rhētor* like himself. The performative democratic system explicitly requires the initiative of an individual citizen: if the democracy is to survive, some individual must choose to indict Meidias before the people's court and someone must stand up against him in the Assembly. An important part of the intellectual apparatus developed by the Athenian orators concerned the attributes of the good *rhētor*, his rhetoric, and his role in the democracy. This constellation is particularly well spelled out in speeches by Aeschines (*On the Embassy*, 346 BC) and Demosthenes (*On the Crown*, 330 BC).

Aeschines was indicted by Demosthenes for treasonous actions allegedly committed while serving as ambassador. He defends himself in part by reference to his career and character, arguing that both are well known to the citizenry and render him incapable of treason. First, Aeschines is loyal to the ideals of the *dēmos* (*dēmotikos*). He learned demotic ideals from his citizen parents, and through the civic education he received through growing up in the democratic polis and paying attention to the decisions of public bodies. Thus, Aeschines casts himself as the Athenian Everyman – he claims to embody the common virtues of the good citizen, and thus his public orations embody the voice of the people. Next, he is moderate in his desires and middling in his social standing (*metrios*). Because he possesses enough wealth to be free from the constraints imposed by poverty, and has no use for the excessive wealth of the very rich, he is incorruptible. This, he claims, is no bald assertion: he has lived his whole life in Athens and is well known to many people; his life is an open book. A good civic education, a moderate lifestyle, and an acceptance of the legitimacy of ongoing public scrutiny of both public and private behaviour, are therefore the cornerstones of the speaker's claim to be worthy of addressing the *dēmos*. When he speaks out in public, the Athenians can assume that they are attending to an authentically demotic voice.

In *On the Crown* (which responds to another speech of Aeschines entitled *Against Ctesiphon*) Demosthenes subscribes to many of Aeschines' stated ideals: he too claims to be *dēmotikos*, *metrios*, well brought up and incorruptible. But he balances these demotic virtues with various elite attributes: Demosthenes somewhat coyly alludes to his wealthy upbringing and his superior education, which are pointedly contrasted to Aeschines' humble origins and early career as an actor and public clerk. Demosthenes advertises himself as possessing a rare ability to weigh the meaning of complex events, special and reliable sources of information, and the leisure (provided by inherited wealth) to develop policy and to prepare speeches that are genuinely valuable to the democratic state. And thus, he suggests, the good elite *rhētor* can be, especially in a time of emergency, not only the articulate voice of the unspoken will of the people, but a leader. Democracy is thus not incompatible with the leadership of an elite individual with original ideas, but that individual must demonstrate his complete loyalty to demotic ideals and he must maintain a style of life that is regarded by the *dēmos* as suitably moderate.

Athenian *rhētores* were quite capable of developing complex political ideas. But these ideas were expressed in a form foreign to philosophical discourse. Not only were general political ideas formally subordinated to the overt purpose of achieving the specific end of persuading an audience to vote in a certain way, but the ideas expressed were at times seemingly contradictory: freedom of speech (*isēgoria*, *parrhēsia*) was regarded as an admirable ideal and vigorous debate among orators proof that the democracy was working well, and yet full consensus, predicated on like-mindedness (*homonoia*) among all patriotic citizens, was proclaimed the basis of good policy. Citizens were to be free from coercion, and yet were expected to be careful monitors of one another's public and private behaviour.[13] Public speakers were to be at once ordinary citizens, voicing the will of the people, and bold leaders boasting exceptional skills and elite attributes. The *rhētor*'s position was itself highly contradictory: his skill at speaking rendered him an extraordinarily powerful figure in a regime predicated upon public speech and action, and yet he was also the creature and servant of the *dēmos*, utterly dependent upon the continued approval of the masses for his position and indeed (given the stakes in the *dikastēria*) for his life and fortune.

These contradictions and discomforts were innate to the relationship between public speech, democratic politics and demotic political ideology. The ordinary citizens dominated public institutions and their unsystematized notions of justice and propriety defined the principles of the democratic state. As a result, those who sought to elucidate political principles in the context of public institutions were constrained to make narrative sense of an unsystematic, pragmatically structured pattern of public behaviours. The accounts they offered necessarily occupied the middle ground logically excluded by a philosophical discourse that proceeded inexorably from unquestionable premise to conclusive demonstration. Democratic audiences, especially at major political trials, expected to hear and to be educated by discussions of abstract principles (including freedom, equality and justice), but they also expected each speaker to respect the sometimes contradictory tenets of popular ideology. The result is a body of political thought often unrecognized as such – in part because it was regarded as the antithesis of philosophy in the Platonic tradition.

The split between the reasoning implicit in democratic rhetoric and philosophical reasoning has as its defining moment the trial of Socrates in 399 BC. The incompatibility of philosophy and rhetoric is seemingly established by Socrates' inability to persuade a majority of Athenian jurors of his innocence through a discourse that abjured the customary acceptance of contradictions and adherence to popular ideology. The breach was not fully healed by Aristotle's attempt in the *Rhetoric* to

[13] Private life and public monitoring: Cohen 1992, Hunter 1994.

explain a form of reasoning that was less rigorous than formal logic and yet remained in fair correspondence with observed social facts. Yet the empirical success of the seemingly irrational democratic *politeia*, especially in the fourth century, in terms of its ability to maintain stability, autonomy and autarky,[14] posed a serious challenge to philosophers who were hard put to explain why the rule of the many was not, after all, the most just form of practical government, at least for a large polis.

[14] See the account of Athenian constitutional history in the *Constitution of the Athenians* (*Athēnaiōn Politeia*) produced by Aristotle or (more probably) within his school.

7

Xenophon and Isocrates

V. J. GRAY

Xenophon (c.430 to at least 356 BC) and Isocrates (436–338 BC), contemporaries of Plato, had the opportunity to learn from Socrates and other philosophers who aimed to produce political virtue. Isocrates' own 'philosophy' took the form of an 'education through speaking and writing' that prepared pupils to play their part in domestic and international politics. His speeches served as models. Xenophon spent his maturity in exile from Athens 'hunting, writing his works and entertaining his friends' in Scillus in the Peloponnese.[1] His works also offer a 'philosophic' education in political virtue and sound government.

Aristotle believed that the aim of community government was to implement the common good. For him the polis was the supreme community, and its goal the greatest good (*Pol.*1252a1–7; cf. 1278b30–1279a21, 1282b14–22). Xenophon and Isocrates addressed the government of other communities as well as the polis. Xenophon's *Cyropaedia* sought to explain Cyrus' successful government of eastern kingdoms (1.1.1–6); his *Hiero* dramatized the reform of tyrannical rule of a polis, while his *Oeconomicus* 7–21 examined Ischomachus' successful government of his household; his *Constitution of the Spartans* (*Lacedaimoniōn Politeia*) described the excellent laws of the Spartan Lycurgus.[2] These works made a lasting impression on political thought.[3] Xenophon's models seem undemocratic (a Persian prince, a tyrant, an aristocratic householder, Sparta), and he had no reason to love the Athenian democracy that had procured his exile and executed his teacher Socrates, but the principles that inform his models are consistent and have broad application.[4] Isocrates wrote speeches that also endorse various kinds of government:

[1] For his life: D.L.II.48–59, Anderson 1974.

[2] These texts are chosen because they analyse successful government, but political thought is also found in *Hellenica*, *Anabasis*, *Agesilaus* (Tuplin 1993, Dillery 1995, Hirsch 1985).

[3] Tatum 1989: 3–33 traces the influence of *Cyropaedia*. Machiavelli used *Cyropaedia* and *Hiero* for his own mirror of princes. *Lac.Pol.* became part of the legend of Sparta: Tigerstedt 1965 for classical antiquity; Rawson 1969 for the later European tradition.

[4] Luccioni 1947: 108–38 certainly reads his works as anti-democratic.

Areopagiticus (probably 354) persuades the Athenians to restore their ancestral constitution, while *Panathenaicus* (339) proves their ancestral constitution superior to the Spartan constitution; *ad Nicoclem* (c.372) shows the prince Nicocles of Cyprus how to rule his subjects, while *Nicocles* (c.368) shows his subjects how to behave toward their king; *Panegyricus* (380) and *Ad Philippum* (346) persuade first the Athenians and then Philip of Macedon to unite and lead the Greeks against Persia.[5] Isocrates adopts various political stances and models according to his audience and argument. He praises monarchy when speaking in the *persona* of Nicocles to his subjects but in his own voice champions their ancestral democracy to the Athenians. He professes that oligarchy, democracy and monarchy are all the same when he wishes to elevate the 'rule of the best' to a principle of management that can make all of them successful (*Panath.*132), but he prefers even a badly managed democracy to oligarchy when he needs to prove his democratic credentials (*Areop.*70). He calls attention to his two different versions of the story of the Seven against Thebes, which support different views of Athens (*Panath.*172).[6] Heracles benefits the Greeks when offered as a model to Philip (*ad Phil.*111–14), but not when compared with Theseus (*Helen* 23–4). Yet it is also possible to find some consistent political thought in Isocrates.

1 Democracy

Paul Cartledge says: 'What was on offer for distribution within the civic space of the polis was *timē*, status, prestige or honour, both abstractly in the form of the entitlement and encouragement to participate, and concretely in the form of political offices (*timai*).'[7] Xenophon appears to endorse a wide distribution of honours in the Athenian democracy according to the principle that he attributes to Socrates throughout *Memorabilia*:[8] that to be honoured in a community, you need to be valued, and to be valued, you need to be useful/helpful, and this requires knowledge and communication of the private and common good. Socrates believed that people in private life should honour even fathers, relatives or friends only if they were of 'use' or 'help' to them; the rule was to cast off what was useless and potentially 'harmful' too (*Mem.*1.2.51–5). The rich minority and the poor majority within the Athenian *dēmos* were subject to

[5] Mathieu 1925, Cloché 1963, Eucken 1983, Too 1995 are the main studies of Isocrates.
[6] Gray 1994. [7] Cartledge, Ch. 1 above, p. 15.
[8] This extensive literary representation of Socrates' views, largely in conversational form, gives us some agreed Socratic features.

the same rule (I.2.58–61). The poor did not have an obvious use, and some said that Socrates recommended they be dishonoured (like Thersites), but Xenophon disagreed; Socrates would have been suggesting a beating for himself if he had argued that way, since he was also poor and *dēmotikos* (I.2.60). To the contrary, he championed the usefulness of the poor and held that the insolent rich should be punished if they were not useful 'in speech, action, to the army, city, *dēmos*'. He advised the wealthy Criton, plagued by sycophants, to give shelter and support to Archedemus, who was 'capable in speaking and acting, but poor' (II.9.4). Archedemus in return used his skills to drive away the sycophants. We might think him a cheap expedient 'used' by the rich; Xenophon insists: 'He was a *friend* of Criton and was *honoured* by Criton's other friends' (II.9.8).

The *dēmos* distributed public honour and dishonour out of considerations of use. The court executed Socrates as harmful to the polis, in the strongest possible public expression of dishonour for uselessness, though Xenophon argued that he was very useful and should have been honoured greatly (I.2.61–4). The assembly honoured men with election to office, and Socrates advises a sequence of those so honoured or wishing to be honoured that they prove useful to the *dēmos* they serve (III.1–7, e.g. III.6.3). He opposed the random ballot that the Athenians used to select many of their officials because it contradicted the principle of honour for use, and gave power to men who were incompetent and might do great harm (I.2.9), but in truth exclusive recourse to the ballot found no champions in any tradition.[9] Xenophon thus made Socrates look democratic, but dramatic dialogue and the desire to prove him useful in a variety of contexts produced some *ad hominem* criticisms of democracy. Socrates expresses contempt for the assembly, as men intent on profit who have no thought of politics, when he wants to get a 'useful' political contribution to their welfare from a man who fears their scorn (*Mem.*III.7.5–7).[10] Yet he defends their election elsewhere of a man who turns a profit, on the grounds that he will look after the common wealth as well as his own (III.4.1,12).

Xenophon knows that 'honour for use' can restrict access. Theramenes restricts citizenship to those who are capable of 'helping' the polis 'with horse and shield' (*Hellenica* II.3.48). The most exclusive version of the principle was monarchy, where the most useful man took all the honour. But the Persian prince Cyrus in *Cyropaedia*, who is largely fictitious and must be taken as a free expression of Xenophon's political ideals,[11] has an

[9] Loraux 1986 (1981): 175 and 182–9; on the same grounds that competence was required.
[10] Luccioni 1947: 114–15 credited Xenophon himself with Socrates' *ad hominem* views.

inclusive tendency. He formed a new army of equals, which made rich and poor alike 'useful' with spear and shield. Here the military equivalent of Archedemus finds his useful place. The Persian commoners were excluded from the training of the elite 'equals' because they needed to make a living, but Cyrus needed more elite manpower to defeat his uncle's enemies (*Cyr.*II.1.1–11), so he armed commoners in the same way as the elite and gave them the same opportunities in his army (II.1.12–19). Both commoners and elite then voluntarily chose reward for merit over equal reward regardless of merit (merit = use, reward = honour), confident in their ability with shield and spear (II.2.18ff., II.3.1–16). Cyrus is careful to manage his equal opportunity, blending the commoners in with the elite by means of training programmes, competitions, rewards and punishment, as well as humour (II.1.20ff., II.2.1ff.). Pheraulas the *dēmotēs* is the paradigm of this new equality. He is glad of equal opportunity (II.3.7–16), but wants to produce equal outcomes through his own effort and skill in what he calls the 'democratic contest' the commoners will now take up with the elite (II.3.15). Xenophon believed that competition stimulated excellence (e.g. *Hiero* 9.4–7, *Lac.Pol.* 4.2). Pheraulas indeed becomes a man of such means that his Sacian friend cannot believe that he ever came from the village plot he describes, but he has also adopted the values of Cyrus, considering material goods a burden, and finding his true freedom in delegating management of his wealth to the Sacian (VIII.3.35–48). Cyrus likewise draws on his friends for what he needs – who give what he wants because they owe it all to him (VIII.2.15–23). Pheraulas is now a ruler in his own right and endorses men as easier to rule than other creatures because of their gratitude, the very opposite of the view expressed in the preface that stirred Xenophon to study the model of Cyrus, who has created this utopia (VIII.3.49–50, cf. I.1.1–3). Class feeling remains, but it is turned to good use in the military competition of commoners and elite, and tactfully handled when the commoner Pheraulas finds an acceptable way of making the former elite accept the orders he brings from Cyrus (VIII.3.5–8).

Xenophon explicitly makes equality at home depend here on empire, a revealing equation. The liberation of the commoners produced an army and an empire which supported commoners and elite and made domestic production no longer necessary. The question of resources is crucial. Xenophon's principle might be seen at work in the Athenian empire,

[11] Herodotus I.95–216 gives a very different account of his career. Tatum 1989, Due 1989 and Gera 1993 offer a range of views on the historicity of the work. Luccioni 1947: 201–54 believes that the work makes Xenophon a monarchist.

which provided resources for the united democracy that won it. Spartan equality (captured in the very word *homoioi* the citizen elite employed to describe themselves) also facilitated expansion, but this excluded the *perioikoi* (peasants) and helots (serfs) who provided many of the resources.[12]

Isocrates rejected contemporary Athenian democracy as a political model, because the random ballot produced an inferior kind of equality in which the most useful men were not honoured (*Areop.*21–3). He promoted instead a democratized version of the ancient constitution, crediting this with the aristocratic 'rule of the best' in which the *dēmos* chose the best men (*Areop.*16–19 and *Panath.*114,130,143).[13] Yet in a striking assertion of the power of the *dēmos* over these 'best men', much bolder in its expression than Xenophon's, he has the ancestral *dēmos* rule their elected officials as a *turannos* would his slaves, 'appointing, punishing and judging', distributing honour for use and dishonour for uselessness (*Areop.*26–7). It is the *dēmos* too who set up the Areopagus to preserve order, train the citizens to virtue and punish wrong, and put them into suitable occupations (36–45: Xenophon's Socrates admires the Areopagus for their justice, *Mem.*III.5.20). Isocrates admittedly disparages contemporary leaders of the democracy, and presents himself as one who does not participate in the democracy when he professes an inability to take part in loud and lively debate and declares a preference for written speeches.[14] Yet he commits himself even to the contemporary democracy in order to win his audience: they look godlike in comparison with the oligarchy of the Thirty (*Areop.*62–70). He also justifies the contemporary constitution in order to serve other arguments: *Panath.*114–18 says that the contemporary democracy had to be introduced to build sea power and ward off the Spartans. This serves the larger argument about the viciousness of Sparta.

2 Rulership

Xenophon and Isocrates agree that the quality of the management is more important than the type of constitution, and that democracies, oligarchies, tyrannies and kingships are all doomed if they are not properly ruled (*Cyr.*I.1; *Panath.*132–3; *Agesilaus*1.4). Xenophon's Socrates sees the division between the ruler and the ruled as something that could be

[12] See further below, pp. 152–4.

[13] This was a tendency of the times, as Josiah Ober says (Ch. 6 above), particularly in the *epitaphios*: see Loraux 1986 (1981), esp. 218–20 on Isocrates, who shares many of its *topoi*, and Thomas 1989: 213–21. Xenophon *Mem.* III.5.9–12 also uses the *topoi* of the *epitaphios* to praise the earlier military supremacy of Athens; cf. Loraux 1986 (1981): 199.

[14] Too 1995: 74–112.

proved dialectically (*Mem*.III.9.11: 'when it was agreed . . .'). Thus Aristippus failed to persuade Socrates that there was a middle way in which he would avoid ruling or being ruled (*Mem*.II.1.11–15). The secret of successful rule was knowledge. Cyrus proves that 'ruling men is easy if one does it with knowledge' (*Cyr*.I.1.3). 'Socrates said that kings and rulers were not those who held the sceptres, nor those elected by anyone at all, nor those allotted to office, nor those who forced their way or cheated, but those who knew how to rule' (*Mem*.III.9.10). The knowledge was of how to define and implement the common good. Successful rulers knew how to care for the interests of the ruled better than the ruled themselves, so that the ruled honoured them for their use and gave them willing obedience. The rulers renounced desire for the goods of the community, but their paradoxical reward was to be given the honour of free use of these goods because of their perceived usefulness to the community (*Cyr*.VIII.3.15–23).

The theory has broad application to armies, households, cities. Cyrus' conversation with his father before his first command describes the ideal military leader (*Cyr*.I.6.7ff.).[15] He is better in all ways than those he rules, but particularly in caring for their interests. He looks to their survival, providing material necessities and securing their health as far as lies within human control; he empathizes with them in joy and sorrow, trusting in the gods for the rest. Rulership looks a little like friendship. Cyrus secured friendship and loyalty through measures like these (*Cyr*.VIII.2.1–28). Criton also secured the service of Archedemus by providing him with food and shelter (*Mem*.II.9). Xenophon believed women to be as useful as men and as capable of rule and friendship. Their main contribution was to the household estate (*oikos*), but this was the basis of the military and economic wellbeing of the polis, which was a collection of *oikoi*. *Oeconomicus* 7–21 contains Socrates' account of the management of the household estate of Ischomachus and his wife, full partners in the production of their wealth.[16] *Mem*.III.9.11 had women rule men in wool production because they had greater knowledge. This woman rules the workers within the house while her husband rules the workers outside, neither sufficient without the other, the house more important than the fields in that it preserves their harvest (*Oec*.7.18–43). The source of her honour is Ischomachus in the first instance, but he invites her to make him her servant by proving herself better than he is and adding more than he does to the increase of their resources (7.42). Socrates credits her with

[15] Due 1989: 147–206 gives a recent description of ideal leadership; see also Wilms 1995.

[16] Pomeroy 1994 on the wife of Ischomachus: commentary *loc. cit.*

intellectual 'manliness' on the grounds that she looks after her own property as she does her children (9.18–19, 10.1).[17] Ischomachus has already compared her to the elected male rulers in a well-administered polis (9.14–15: guardian of law, garrison commander, council). His analogies for her household are masculine: a chorus, an ordered army, a warship, a merchant ship (8.1–17). She looks after the health of her slaves as Cyrus looked after the health of his men (*Oec.*7.37). Her woman housekeeper is to have the manly qualities of self-control, forethought and justice (*Oec.*9.11–13). Xenophon is consistently disposed to find male virtue in women: Socrates draws out a definition of friendship as a virtuous pursuit from the courtesan Theodote (*Mem.*III.11.5–18, cf. II.6.9–14); Cyrus recognizes the 'manly' contribution of Tigranes' wife to his campaign (*Cyr.*VIII.4.24); Panthea is paired with her husband in friendship to Cyrus, and she commits suicide over his body as Cyrus honours them both for their service (*Cyr.*VI.4.2–11; VII.3.8–14). Xenophon believed that slaves were also capable of recognizing the leader who looked to their interests, and of being rulers in their own right. They were technically compelled to obey, but Ischomachus wants to secure their willing obedience (*Oec.*12.3–20), and teaches the bailiff he has purchased (12.3) how to rule his workers (13.3–5).

Xenophon's *Hiero* addresses the reform of rulership toward knowledge when it dramatizes the instruction of Hiero the tyrant of Syracuse by Simonides the wise poet – producing a well constructed dialogue in the Socratic style.[18] The poet asks the tyrant to compare his happiness as private man and ruler (1.1–2). The tyrant rejects the poet's suggestions that the ruler derives happiness from (a) greater sensual pleasure, (b) greater possessions, (c) greater honour. He diagnoses instead a great *un*happiness arising from a lack of the love and security he had in private life, which he does not know how to reclaim from his people as their ruler (1.8–7.13). Hiero's ignorance of how to be happy goes hand in hand with ignorance of how to rule, which is synonymous with making others happy. Simonides teaches him that he can reclaim his private happiness by looking to the welfare of the community (8–11). The ruler's kind words mean more than the private man's. He can earn more gratitude for praise, and delegate punishment to avoid hatred. He should set up competitions and honour people for doing good for the community. His mercenaries should guard and defend the whole community. He should use his revenues to promote the polis as his *oikos* and compete with other rulers in

[17] See Cartledge, Ch. 1 above, p. 13 on 'manliness'.
[18] Luccioni 1947: 255–68 on *Hiero* as the reform of tyranny toward 'monarchy'; also Gray 1986.

bringing happiness to his city. Simonides is appealing directly to enlightened self-interest. Hiero is subject to no authority outside himself, but his own desire for true honour and affection from his community is higher than any external constraint, and he now has the knowledge to achieve it.

Isocrates substitutes for Simonides when in his own authorial voice he advises Nicocles the heir to kingship in Cyprus about the art of rule.[19] *Ad Nicoclem* begins as *Hiero* did, with the comparison of the life of the private man and the tyrant, but Isocrates claims that though people see the honours, wealth and powers of monarchs, they conclude from their fears and perils that it is better to remain in private life (4–5). He argues against them that kingship can secure happiness by identifying that happiness with the welfare of the community.[20] Nicocles should assist his polis in misfortune, preserve it in prosperity and give it increase (9). He should be 'a good demagogue' honouring the best and ensuring justice for the rest (16), spending his revenues on the polis (like Hiero) as he would his own *oikos* (19). His bodyguard should be the virtue of his friends, the loyalty of his subjects and wisdom (21). Xenophon's principle is restated, that men give willing obedience when they believe that the king looks to their affairs with greater perception and care than they do (24). The precepts that follow (24–39) cover a huge range of summarized advice, with brief rationale, without exemplification and in no particular order, as Isocrates will later say (*Ant.*67–8). No examples are given of just how Nicocles should tread the fine line between warmth, which is needed in human relations, and dignity, which fits his kingship (34; cf. Cyrus). The surrounding advice about the right moment to speak and act (33) and the right balance between study and practice (35) seems disconnected. The antithetical style seems often to generate the rather proverbial thought: 'Envy not those who have acquired greatest power over others, but those who best use what they have, and think that you will be completely happy not if you rule the whole world through fear and peril and evil, but if you are as you should be and stay as you are now, with moderate desires, failing in none of them' (26).

Isocrates then in *Nicocles* has Nicocles address his subjects in his own voice as proof of his reform. 'Nicocles' refers back to Isocrates' advice on kingship, which he says they have heard (11). He dispels their mistrust of eloquence (1–9) to justify his advice on how they should behave (10–11).

[19] Eucken 1983: 213–64, a major treatment of the Cyprian speeches.

[20] King Theseus is Isocrates' mythical model, who in the story of the Seven against Thebes gave his power to the ancestral *dēmos* and then risked his life on behalf of Greece (*Panath.*129, *Helen* 36–7). Adrastus of Argos in contrast sent his people to destruction in the private cause of his relative Polyneices (*Panath.*168–71).

He naturally defends monarchy as the best constitution and his own tenure as legitimate (12–13). He opposes the idea that the good and the bad should be worthy of the same honours, which he says oligarchy and democracy espouse (14–16); monarchy chooses the best man, concentrates experience, facilitates action, honours the best men and identifies the interests of the common wealth with his own (17–26). He bases his right to rule on lineage (27–8), but also on his merits as the 'best citizen' to look after their affairs: his just administration of state property (29–35), his self-control, his sexual fidelity (36–47). On this basis he issues precepts that he expects his people to obey (48–64).

Both Xenophon and Isocrates support enlightened monarchy and take their rulers as far along the road to community service as is possible in the circumstances. Isocrates could not tell Nicocles outright to abolish his hereditary position. Hiero's fear of his subjects is so palpable that Simonides has to proceed from the very smallest suggestions for change. Aristotle also believed that reform had to be adapted to the circumstances; the reformer must be able to discern not only what is best but what is possible, since he will have to render aid to existing constitutions as well as create new ones (*Pol.*1288b21–1289a7). Further, though Aristotle considered tyranny perverse because it looked only to the good of the tyrant, yet he believed that where one man was supremely able to define and implement the common good, that man could expect to be obeyed (*Pol.*1325b10–15). This is the model that Xenophon and Isocrates are endorsing. Plato's philosopher king was another expression of it. Isocrates perhaps ingeniously refuted the suggestion that he was a monarchist by claiming that he advised Nicocles on behalf of his *subjects* 'as a free man and one worthy of this city should' (*Ant.*40, cf.67–72). His advice indeed assists a whole state, since the reform of the leader is of benefit to all (*ad Nic.*8). He asserts his independence of fear and favour of monarchy when he warns Nicocles against receiving the advice of flatterers (3–4: to reinforce the value of his own), and urges him to listen to criticism (42–54). He repeats the performance in *ad Philippum* (14–24); *ad Nicoclem* and *Nicocles* are in fact part of a trilogy which includes *ad Demonicum* and states in turn the habits required of an aristocrat, a king and his subjects: 'what customs to pursue and what to avoid' (*ad Nic.*2.6).

The theory of ideal leadership of course had its limits. There were useless rogues whose friendship could never be courted even in private life (*Mem.*II.6.16,19,27). Proxenus wins the gentlemen with praise, but has no antidote for the rogues except silent disapproval, which makes them plot against him as a man easy to manage (*Anabasis* II.6.20). Cyrus rejects from his army those who will be useless and damaging to his cause (*Cyr.*II.2.23–7). He wins willing obedience from a range of other nations but he rules the hostile Babylonians with a bodyguard to secure his person (VII.5.58) and a standing army and garrison for the city (VII.5.66–8). The reformed Hiero also kept a bodyguard against rogues (*Hiero* 10.1–2). Xenophon recognized also that kingship had its own special demands. Cyrus asserted the dignity of kingship by denying free access to his person when he became king of the Babylonians (*Cyr.*VII.5.37–57). This event sees him retire into his palace, require attendance, and use harsh methods to secure it (VIII.1.16–20: he confiscated the estates of those who did not attend, and they soon appeared). He used cosmetics, costume and theatre for himself and his senior management to produce public reverence (VIII.1.40–1). Yet he was still capable of sharing a joke at the expense of Pheraulas with his Sacian subject (VIII.3.26–32). Isocrates tells Nicocles to cultivate the same blend of dignity and warmth (*ad Nic.*34).

3 Sparta

Plato and Aristotle followed a long tradition of considering the constitution of the Spartans a model government, even while they criticized some of their customs.[21] Herodotus had already attributed their military success to their constitution (I.65–8, VII.101–4), but Xenophon's *Constitution of the Spartans* is the first full description available to us of the customs that the Spartans adopted under the laws of Lycurgus.[22] It is often read as praise of the Spartans, but it is praise of the laws, and limited praise at that, seeking to explain only how they made the Spartans 'the strongest and most renowned' city in Greece (1.1). Xenophon's brief acknowledgment that the Spartans no longer follow the laws has been read as a recantation of praise of Sparta (14). Yet it is not inconsistent with praise of their *laws*.[23] They failed precisely because they abandoned these laws, as the Persians failed when they abandoned the laws of Cyrus (*Cyr.*VIII.8).[24] His acknowledgment should be rather read in conjunction with his challenge to other Greeks of his time to adopt the laws that the Spartans no longer follow (10.8). *Mem.*III.5.14–16 makes Socrates suggest that the Athenians

[21] Tigerstedt 1965: 228–309.

[22] Ollier 1934: xiii–xl, Luccioni 1947:139–74, Chrimes 1948, Tigerstedt 1965: 161–9.

[23] Tigerstedt 1965: 169 does not distinguish praise of Lycurgus from praise of Sparta. Luccioni 1947: 170 is more perspicacious. Lycurgus is the focus of praise: 1.4, 2.2, 2.13, 3.1, 4.7, 5.1 etc.

[24] The parallel is instructive. Luccioni 1947: 246–54, Due 1989:16–22 think that the Persian lapse reinforces the praise of the laws of Cyrus in *Cyropaedia*; cf. Hirsch 1985: 91–7, Tatum 1989: 215–39; Gera 1993: 299–300 is reluctant to decide.

should remedy their contemporary military decline by adopting the customs of their ancestors or by imitating the Spartans. *Mem.*IV.4.15–17 also offers Lycurgus as a model.

The general purpose of law in empire, household and polis was in Xenophon's view to produce good behaviour through the positive and negative stimuli of praise and blame. His Socrates maintains that the function of law is to indicate 'what to do as well as what not to do' (*Mem.*IV.4.13). The combination of coercion and persuasion in Plato's *Laws* is in this tradition. Ischomachus praises the 'king's law' that he exercises in his household by rewarding virtue as well as punishing vice, and he criticizes the written laws of the Athenians because their focus on punishment offers an incomplete stimulus to virtue (*Oec.*14.4–10). Both Cyrus and Ischomachus also define 'king's law' as 'law with eyes' (*Cyr.*VIII.1.21–2; cf. *Oec.*12.20). This living law is more flexible than written codes. Cyrus refuses to press the death penalty against the king of Armenia in order to make him a willing and valuable friend (III.1); he refuses to punish the boy with the coat too small who took from another a coat that was too big – in order to make them both well suited (I.3.16–17). The laws of Lycurgus give the ephors this flexibility (*Lac.Pol.*8.4). Their encouragement of love bonding is an instance of a positive stimulus to virtue (2.12–14).

Xenophon's argument in praise of the laws of Lycurgus is that they were the opposite of those of other Greeks, in that they regulated the customs of the citizens from the cradle to the grave to produce military strength. The laws reverse the normal behaviour of women to ensure that their children will be strong (1.3–10). Children are brought up differently for the same purpose (2). The laws endorse the virtue of obedience to authority in young men who would be released from authority in other states (3). They require the highest ranks, who would be ashamed to be seen obeying in other states, to run to the commands of ephors (8). They make virtue a matter of public rather than private interest (10.4–7). Their more technical military customs produce superior preparations for war, military dress, manoeuvres (not so hard to learn: 11.5), chains of command, encampments, and leadership (11–13). *Lac.Pol.* ends with Lycurgus' superior arrangements for the preservation of the constitution (15).[25]

In *Panathenaicus* Isocrates compares Athens and Sparta. He never disputes the excellence of the customs that produced the military strength of the Spartans, but he argues that they did not invent those of their customs

[25] The order of chapters 14 and 15 is reversed in some editions and translations.

that have a claim to excellence, that the customs they did invent were not excellent, that they used their military strength to oppress the rest of Greece and that their famed equality could not compare with true democracy.[26] He claims that others regularly contrasted the obedience of the Spartans with the contemporary indiscipline of the Athenians; but that he speaks of the ancestral Athenian constitution, which established laws that lasted a thousand years (144,148) and created a military supremacy that was used to benefit the Greeks (151–2). These laws were identical with the laws of Lycurgus, he says, but no imitation. The military achievements of the ancestral Athenians show them to have possessed military excellence at an earlier time (168–74). Lycurgus also imitated the Athenians when he created an aristocratic form of democracy (153–4). Yet the Spartans reserved their equal rights for a select group (*Panath.*177–81; cf. *Areop.*61). They disinherited the *perioikoi* (here called the *dēmos*) and made them bear the brunt of their wars. The ephors even now put *perioikoi* to death without trial. The Athenian *dēmos* was far better treated under Theseus.[27] Isocrates goes on to reinforce his criticisms of Sparta when he describes how he read through a draft of his speech with his pupils, one of whom insisted that the Spartans had still 'invented' the 'best customs' (202–14: without mention of Lycurgus). Isocrates ridiculed the idea of Spartan *invention*, because it implied that there were no clever or good people in the world before the Spartans arrived in the Peloponnese a mere 700 years ago. He added that such unlettered people could not in any case have invented the *best* customs. They did invent the custom by which they teach their boys to steal, flog those who fail and honour those who succeed, but other Greeks have not adopted this for obvious reasons. Isocrates' pupil replied that he meant the customs that produced their martial success and concord rather than their general morality (217). Isocrates admitted these customs but condemned their use in unjust wars (215–28; cf. *Busiris* 19). Yet he records that he regretted having been so rough on the Spartans, and refused to make further comment when the pupil found an ingenious way of reading his criticism as praise (229–65). This has been modernly read as recantation of his criticisms.[28] They remain published in the speech nevertheless, and a recognition of the consultation between Isocrates and his pupils as a *topos* suggests that they remain strongly held.[29] Isocrates' comparison of Athens and Sparta

[26] Tigerstedt 1965: 187–97 is the fullest account. Also Mathieu 1925: 168–71; Cloché 1963: 90–2.
[27] See n.20 above.
[28] Tigerstedt 1965: 193–6 'a complete palinode', due, he says, to the author's senility.
[29] Gray 1993.

clearly shapes his negative image of Sparta to contrast with the positive image of Athens. His arguments are sometimes ingenious. Xenophon's narrower focus on military supremacy rather than morality leads him to praise the stealing and the flogging of those who were detected because it helped the boys to steal successfully as they would have to in war (*Lac.Pol.* 2.6–9).

4 Panhellenism

Panhellenism meant concord (*homonoia*) and equality among the poleis of Greece, for conquest of the Persians and greater Greek prosperity; it seems to apply to the international arena the equation of *homonoia* with military success within the polis (*Mem.*IV.4.15–16). Xenophon's *Anabasis* expresses part of the ideal in the relatively cosmopolitan army of the Ten Thousand; his *Agesilaus* praises the Spartan king as a philhellene who led an army of Peloponnesians to liberate the Greeks in Asia and other eastern nations from Persian control;[30] but his most complete model for concord and conquest is, paradoxically, the pan-orientalist Cyrus of Persia. Cyrus created concord among his Persians, and between them and a variety of other nations, for conquest of the Assyrians. He made them all prosperous. Isocrates looked for a similarly successful Panhellenic leader. *Panegyricus* promoted the claims of the Athenians to leadership of the Greeks against the Persians, in order to persuade the Spartans to accept their hegemony and set an example of concord to the rest of Greece. This failed. *ad Philippum* encouraged the Macedonian king to reconcile Athens, Argos, Thebes and Sparta and win their goodwill for a similar crusade under his leadership (30–1, 82). Isocrates argued that he should repay them for their mythical favours to his ancestor Heracles and lead them against the East in imitation of Heracles who led the united Greeks in the first Trojan War and subjected many other non-Greeks besides (109–12).[31] Philip and his son Alexander the Great implemented a version of this theory, but left garrisons in Greece to enforce concord and obedience. Political realities regularly fall short of models.

[30] Dillery 1995: 41–98. Hirsch 1985: 39–55 argues against the opinion that Xenophon is a committed panhellenist in *Agesilaus*.

[31] Too 1995: 130–49 reads Isocrates' panhellenism in several key passages as 'subverted by a discourse biased toward Athens' and as a discourse on his own rhetorical identity.

8

Socrates and Plato: an introduction

MELISSA LANE

1 Approaches to Platonic interpretation

To introduce Socrates and Plato is to introduce the problem of the relation between them. Although other contemporaries left portraits of Socrates as well, it is Plato's writings – primarily a body of dialogues in which Plato himself never appears[1] – which stamped the figure of his teacher indelibly on the history of Western philosophy. Because Socrates is best known to us as a character in Plato's writings, there arises what has been called the 'Socratic problem'. Can a real or 'historical' Socrates, with distinctive beliefs, be identified on the basis of the testimony roughly contemporaneous[2] with his life which survives from Aristophanes, Plato, Xenophon, and (a generation later) Aristotle?[3] Or is, perhaps, the Socrates we value largely the portrayal Plato makes of him?

The 'Socratic problem' is complicated by the fact that Plato's 'Socrates' seems to argue for contradictory positions in different dialogues. For example, in *Protagoras* (352–8) Socrates argues that because no one does wrong willingly, vice results simply from ignorance, an argument which assumes that only rational beliefs determine action. But in *Republic* IV he explains vice as due to the two irrational, or less than rational, parts of a tripartite soul when not stably governed, as they should be, by the third and rational part. This apparent contradiction has often been resolved by assuming that the *Protagoras* is one of a group of dialogues written early in Plato's career (the 'early'[4] dialogues), in which the character 'Socrates' is

[1] He is, however, mentioned three times. He is listed among the young men who have associated with Socrates at *Ap.*34a1; at 38b6 he is said to be one of those ready to act as guarantors if Socrates is fined. At *Phd.*59b10 Plato is said to have been ill and so to have missed the death of Socrates, the very death he is as author about to describe.

[2] An important source from seven centuries later is Diogenes Laertius' *Lives* of Socrates and Plato. Other ancients such as Aeschines of Sphettus, Antisthenes and Aristippus are known to have written 'Socratic' conversations also, but their works do not survive except in fragments.

[3] Aristophanes *Clouds*; Xenophon *Memorabilia*; for Aristotle, see n.17 below.

[4] Most concur in placing at least *Apology*, *Crito*, *Ion*, *Hippias Minor*, *Laches*, *Charmides*, *Euthyphro*, *Lysis* and *Protagoras* as early; *Gorgias*, *Euthydemus*, and *Hippias Major* are arguably still early but with evident connections with the 'middle' period. See however the discussion of Kahn below,

meant by Plato to represent the historical Socrates' views, whereas the *Republic* is one of the 'middle period' dialogues in which Plato is using Socrates simply as a mouthpiece for his own theory.[5] The introduction of irrational parts in the soul is accompanied, on most accounts of a 'middle period' Plato, by the introduction of a metaphysics of 'Forms': objects intelligible to reason which are the ultimate source of explanation for contradictory appearances in the phenomenal world. The 'early' dialogues, in which Socrates asks various interlocutors for definitions of the things referred to by universal names, are on this view contrasted with the 'middle' dialogues in which Socrates offers arguments for the existence of Forms. And this picture of Plato's writings as moving from a 'Socratic' period without Forms, to a 'middle' period with them, has been extended by a group of twentieth-century scholars concerned with logic and language to identify a 'late' period in which Plato purportedly shows himself critical of, or at least indifferent to, the Forms.[6]

Telling some such story of Plato's 'development' is the characteristic strategy of one of the two main schools in Platonic interpretation, although each 'developmentalist' is liable to tell a somewhat different story of exactly which intellectual moves show Plato 'progressing', and which are the dialogues where such progress is made. Against the developmentalists stand the 'unitarians', again members of a very broad church. The most dogmatic unitarian position, like that of the neo-Platonists, assumes that Plato never contradicts himself or advances contradictory arguments, and interprets the dialogues in line with that assumption. The loosest unitarian position belongs, perhaps, to those who find developmental assumptions unhelpful in reading Plato, and who prefer to consider the arguments of different dialogues as answering different questions or exploring different problems rather than as straightforwardly contradictory.

We shall shortly look more closely at the arguments and evidence for the controversy between developmentalists and unitarians. But it is

Footnote 4 (*cont.*)

pp. 160–1. *Rep.* 1, in which Socrates compels Polemarchus and Thrasymachus to admit the weaknesses in their own definitions of justice, is widely but by no means universally regarded as a Socratic dialogue appended to the larger 'middle-period' work in which Glaucon and Adeimantus become the interlocutors of Socrates.

[5] Penner, Ch. 9 below, develops this and other contrasts between the early and middle dialogues.

[6] The case for a group of late dialogues 'critical' of Forms, beginning with the *Parmenides* and including above all the *Sophist*, was made most forcefully by G.E.L. Owen in (*inter alia*) 1953a (1965). His attempts (a) to treat the *Politicus* – generally agreed to be late – as renouncing the political theory of the *Republic*, while (b) relegating the *Timaeus* and *Critias* to the middle group as containing Forms, were convincingly rebutted by Cherniss 1957 (1965) and Gill 1979, but his general picture of a late and critical group remains influential (see e.g. McCabe 1994).

important to see how quickly our opening question, about whether the views of the historical Socrates can be recovered from Platonic texts, has led us to enter the lists of a debate as to how to read those texts themselves. In short, the 'Socratic problem' depends on and leads to a broader 'Platonic problem'. The former asks whether Socrates' own views can be determined; the latter, what use Plato means to make of Socrates in the various dialogues, and more generally, which if any philosophical position(s) Plato means his use of the dialogue form to convey or defend. The author and absent character Plato is as much a problem for readers of the dialogues as the virtually ubiquitous character 'Socrates'.

2 The chronology of Plato's dialogues

The urge to extract a chronology from, or impose a chronology on, the dialogues may be considered twofold. The purely logical thought is that writers have to compose their works, during their lives, in some order or other, and that it is simply bad luck that so little of Plato's own order is known to us (no dating of the dialogues from Plato's pen survives).[7] Yet such logic by itself need not lead very far. Works may be revised or in process over extended periods of time; conversely, if there is no special tension felt among the works of an author, there may be little pressure to try to establish a chronological ordering of them (this is the case with the works of Aristotle, the chronology of which is uncertain to a comparable extent). In Plato's case, however, the tensions between arguments remarked above, and the special question of Socrates, have suggested to many that if a chronological order of writing could be established, the relation between divergent Platonic arguments could be better assessed. So the logical thought that there must be an ordering is spurred on by the philosophical thought that such an ordering would help to explain the continuities and discontinuities – indeed, to establish even which arguments to count as continuous or discontinuous – among the Platonic dialogues.

The move from a neutral interest in chronology to some sort of developmentalist position hinges on making some assumption about what a chronological order would signify. One example of such an assumption, which could endow chronology with intellectual significance, would be to assume that Plato must always have tried to write down exactly what he

[7] In the third century BC the librarians of Alexandria arranged the dialogues, like tragedies, into trilogies. At or before the beginning of the Christian era they were rearranged into tetralogies in the ordering still used for their conventional publication today. See Guthrie 1975: 39.

believed to be true at any time. If his writings change in a demonstrable order over time, those changes correspond to and express changes in his thoughts and beliefs. One such view sees the dialogues as charting the course of a Plato who begins by reflecting on Socrates' ethical beliefs, goes on to develop a metaphysical foundation for them, and then becomes critical of his own metaphysics and seeks various ways to start afresh.[8]

The flaw in this kind of view, which may be labelled 'naive developmentalism', is that it risks ignoring and so flattening out the dramatic features of the dialogue form and the effect these have on the reader. If Plato's aim in writing dialogues was in part to stimulate readers to do philosophy for themselves, as has been persuasively argued,[9] it follows that the dialogues may be better interpreted as focusing more on what he believed heuristically useful as a propaedeutic to philosophy than on his own current philosophical beliefs. Dramatic awareness is still consistent with a broadly developmental picture of the dialogues, but makes it more difficult to read off a chronology from the arguments within them.

Unitarianism is vulnerable to a converse form of naiveté. In general developmentalism tends to exaggerate surface conflicts among the dialogues, unitarianism to undervalue them. If naive developmentalism assumes that Plato always put all his cards straight out on the table, naive unitarianism assumes that if Plato sometimes played opposite cards he meant himself to be seen as playing the same ones. The more sophisticated unitarians emphasize not that all the dialogues agree, but that different dialogues may make use of comparable intellectual resources in the service of pressing different problems. It may be noticed that, in giving a unitarian answer to the Platonic problem, one is likely to make the Socratic problem nugatory. If Plato is saying more or less the same thing in all his writings, then there is little point in singling out some as representing the true Socrates (unless one wants to assert complete philosophical agreement between Socrates and Plato). In contrast developmentalism leaves more scope for identifying Socrates' own arguments in some dialogues as opposed to others. However, the more sophisticated each view becomes, the more likely they are to converge on a reading of the dialogues alive both to their changing concerns and pervasive likenesses.

Despite the theoretical possibilities of convergence, the two schools of interpretation with their contrasting attitudes to chronology have been in sustained polemic since the nineteenth century; what is more, this polemic has been based on remarkably little relevant evidence. As noted

[8] This is roughly the view of Gregory Vlastos, on which see below.
[9] E.g. by Burnyeat 1990: 2–3; cf.65–8 and the argument of his 'Introduction' generally.

above, no dating of the dialogues by Plato survives (else there would be no controversy). Some dialogues are linked to others by internal references to their arguments, and others are tied to events in Socrates' life or other political or biographical events, but these stage-directions establish the dramatic context rather than anything about the order of composition.[10] External literary evidence is also scant. Aristotle remarks that the *Republic* preceded the *Laws*,[11] and a Christian-era writer adds that the *Laws* was unfinished at Plato's death,[12] while the *Apology* has long been assumed to have been Plato's first dialogue, in defence of a recently executed Socrates. With so little evidence to go on, argument about what Plato must have meant, and how his thinking seemed to have developed, may seem the only recourse for those eager to date the dialogues.

The nineteenth century, however, brought ingenious attempts to study, not the substantive claims made in the writing, but rather features of Plato's prose style suitable for statistical measurement. In so doing scholars sought to convert internal literary evidence into what might count as objective evidence for the chronological ordering of the dialogues. This method of measuring changes in an author's style claims to be able to detect objective statistical variation in features such as vocabulary, rhythm and use of vowels. Yet such statistical variation, once again, proves nothing unless one posits a hypothesis to explain it: should one assume that writers vary their style consciously or unconsciously, and what do these variations signify?

Stylometrical studies of Plato have pursued both the 'conscious' and 'unconscious' paths. Some have examined the incidence of specialized vocabulary and prose rhythms, assuming that Plato made conscious choices about these when he wrote, and assuming further that at certain points in his life he came under certain influences which determined the choices he made (e.g. the prose style of Isocrates). Other studies have looked instead at features of prose which, they assume, Plato could not or did not consciously manipulate, but which rather betray some aspects of an ageing process.

In sum, the purported objectivity of stylometry depends as much on interpretative assumptions as do the older methods of establishing the

[10] *Ap.*, *Cr.*, and *Phd.* all refer to the events of Socrates' trial and its aftermath; *Tht.* and the linked pair of *Sph.* and *Plt.*, as well as *Euthphr.*, refer to the preceding events of Socrates being indicted. This sequence has been emphasized by studies following the work of Leo Strauss (cf. e.g. Strauss 1964), such as Miller 1980: 1–2. Without further assumptions, these internal dramatic sequences neither settle the chronological question nor show that it is necessarily redundant or flawed.

[11] Arist.*Pol.*1264b26.

[12] D.L.III.37 reports that the *Laws* was still on wax tablets when Plato died, and was published posthumously by his student Philip of Opus.

order of the dialogues by philosophical arguments. Each kind of stylometric study, moreover, has a characteristic weakness. On the one hand, the studies of purportedly conscious variations in Plato's prose make the overly strong assumption that he used certain specific stylistic effects only at the same time in his career, and then moved on to others, whereas there is no reason not to suppose that in writing each dialogue he chose afresh the appropriate stylistic policies. On the other hand, the studies of unconscious variation make assumptions which are overly weak: they are – not unreasonably – too vague about the correlation between specific phenomena and their chronological significance. On balance the claims of stylometry to revolutionize Platonic studies by providing hard evidence of chronology must be judged a disappointment. Stylometric studies at best support the identification of a group[13] of 'late' dialogues (that is, clustered with the assumed-to-be-late *Laws*), but do nothing to support the division between early and middle involved in the Socratic problem.

3 The Socratic problem revisited

If dating Plato's dialogues cannot validate some of them against others as portraying the authentic Socrates, how can Plato's varying use of Socrates as a character be understood? Two recent and contrasting views will illuminate the range of possibilities. Charles Kahn has developed a version of what was characterized above as sophisticated developmentalism. His thesis hinges on a notion of prolepsis, which is the claim that versions of ideas in certain dialogues must be read as preparing the ground for, or hinting at, more developed versions in other dialogues. Unlike the extremes of naive developmentalism or unitarianism, a notion like prolepsis is designed to account for both similarities and differences among different dialogues. Kahn still advances a developmental chronological ordering, but he considers the dialogues of definition – sometimes viewed as prototypically early – rather as 'pre-middle' works in which the characteristic concerns of Socrates such as definition and virtue are proleptic of Platonic middle period concerns.[14] This reading brings 'Socrates', who for Kahn simply is Plato's Socrates, much closer to middle-period Plato

[13] Brandwood 1990: 249–51 concludes that study of prose rhythm establishes one group of six dialogues as distinct: *Timaeus*, *Critias*, *Sophist*, *Politicus*, *Philebus*, and *Laws*.

[14] Kahn 1981 (1992) orders the dialogues which he assumes to precede the second Sicilian voyage of 367–365 (see Schofield, in Ch. 13 below) as follows. 'Pre-systematic': *Ap.*, *Cr.*, *Ion*, *H.Mi.*, *Gorg.*, *Menex.*; 'pre-middle' and 'Socratic' group (his real innovation): the four 'dialogues of definition' *La.*, *Chrm.*, *Lys.*, *Euthphr.*, plus the proleptic *Prot.*, *Euthd.*, *Men.*; 'middle': *Symp.*, *Phd.*, *Crat.*, *Rep.*, *Phdr.*; 'post-middle': *Prm.*, *Tht.*

than other and perhaps more naive developmentalists had done. The flexible notion of prolepsis also offers room for interpreting Plato as keeping certain cards up his sleeve, or shaping his writing for certain purposes, rather than as laying the complete state of his soul and mind bare in every dialogue.

The latter was part of the view about Socrates and Plato defended by Gregory Vlastos,[15] a view consisting of two claims. First, Vlastos claimed that Plato identified throughout his writing career with the views he puts in Socrates' mouth. Second, he argued that for the first part of his writing career Plato put in his Socrates' mouth precisely the views of the historical Socrates, whereas after that Plato himself suffered a sea-change and began to use 'Socrates' simply as a spokesman (out of homage to the deep ethical principles he still shared with his teacher). Vlastos takes naive developmentalism to its extreme, by arguing that Plato's dialogues at each stage record his 'honest' views, even if these are sometimes no more than a 'record of honest perplexity';[16] and he also takes an extreme stance on the Socratic problem, by insisting that the 'Socratic' dialogues represent not just Plato's view of the man, but an accurate historical account. His argument is that where Plato's writings concur with the testimony of Aristotle[17] and Xenophon, there lies the historical truth about Socrates.

This is the plank of Vlastos' case which has been most questioned by critics.[18] And their criticism returns us to the heart of the Socratic problem. For Vlastos' strategy obscures the fact that Aristotle and Xenophon, too, wrote not as dispassionate recorders but as ambitious philosophically minded men themselves. No student, or student of students, of Socrates can be assumed to have recorded an accurate historical account of the man. Even their allegiance to him could well have given them reason to alter or exaggerate certain features in the aftermath of his controversial death.

The Socratic aspect of Vlastos' case is, then, doubtful; so too, for reasons offered above, is his 'naive' assumption about Plato's writing technique and the nature of its correlation with the state of his philosophical understanding. What remains, and in fact constitutes common ground

[15] Vlastos 1988 and 1991: 45–80 and 81–106.

[16] This is how Vlastos 1954 (1965) diagnosed the attacks on the theory of Forms which Plato put into Parmenides' mouth in the eponymous dialogue.

[17] Aristotle identified some theses as Socratic (that virtue is the same in everyone, *Pol.* 1260a21), and distinguished others as Socratic rather than Platonic (noting that Plato, not Socrates, 'separated' the Forms, *Metaph.* 1078b3). But on other points it is not clear whether he is ascribing a given position to Socrates, Plato, or both ('Socrates proposes [communism of women and property] in the *Republic* of Plato', *Pol.* 1261a5; 'the thesis in the *Meno*', *An.Pr.* 67a21–2).

[18] See especially Beversluis 1993.

with Kahn, is Vlastos' opening endorsement of 'the fundamental assumption that Plato's dialogues record the development not of Socrates' mind but of Plato's'.[19]

In the end, the attempt to establish a separate 'Socratic' presence in the dialogues must rest primarily on the quality of the philosophical case for identifying certain arguments as yielding a coherent moral and methodological position, a task undertaken by Penner in the chapter on Socrates to follow. Whatever one's conclusions about the Socratic problem, moreover, the Platonic problem will remain. And here we may be best served by adopting the potential convergence between unitarians and developmentalists indicated above. One example of this convergence would be to speak of 'developments' in the plural, an idiom for the constant development and redevelopment which Plato makes of his own thought as he interrogates, refracts and revises recurrent problems in the context and for the purpose which each dialogue differently unfolds.

The dialogues cannot, then, certify the chronological ins and outs of Plato's engagement with Socrates intellectually. Yet their presentation of Socrates as a uniquely charismatic philosophical talker and thinker testifies to the profound impact which the older man had on the younger. It will be useful to conclude with a reminder about the defining historical moment which decisively shaped both the literary and the philosophical cast of Plato's response to Socrates.

4 The death of Socrates

Socrates (b. 470 BC) was born a generation after Pericles. He and his contemporaries saw Athens' imperial power and democratic pride grow to unprecedented heights. The centre of Greek learning, Athens hosted both native and foreign teachers of argument among whom Socrates was classed by many, and from whom Plato appears anxious to distinguish him. According to both Plato and Xenophon, Socrates was unique as a teacher in refusing to accept payment, in refusing to put his talents to the confining service of argument in the assembly or courts, and – according to Plato – in his method of careful questioning of anyone reputed to possess either knowledge or virtue. Plato delights in contrasting Socrates' truth-focused conversation with Gorgias' bombastic rhetoric, or with Euthydemus' and Dionysodorus' dishonest trickery.

But for Plato and all Plato's readers Socrates was never so distinctive as

[19] Vlastos 1988: 102.

in his death, which followed the nadir of the city's defeat by Sparta in the Peloponnesian War and two bloody, if brief, suppressions of democracy. He was tried and executed in 399 BC on charges brought by two Athenian citizens: the charge of worshipping other gods than those of the city, and the charge of corrupting the young (which may have reflected the disturbing fact that several of Socrates' closest associates – figures who are depicted in Plato's dialogues and were, moreover, his close relatives – took part in the brutal regime of the 'Thirty'). It is in the course of Plato's depiction of Socrates' defence speech – his *Apology* – that we learn most of what we think we know about Socrates' chosen mode of life before that. Most significant is his commitment to testing claims of wisdom or knowledge, and his commitment (in life as in conversation) to the ethical question of what is the best way to live for the sake of the soul. The *Apology* celebrates Socrates' existential refusal to countenance any other approach to fulfilling that commitment than the one he has been pursuing all his life – he claims on divine authority – even if it will cost him that life at the hands of the civil power. And it is a plausible conjecture that Plato's career as a writer of dialogues at any rate began as an attempt to vindicate the memory of his teacher against the vilification and controversy engendered by the trial – by showing the true nature of his philosophical activity and the moral challenge it presented.[20]

[20] It cannot be proved that none of the dialogues was written before the death of Socrates, but the probable motive of vindication convinces the great majority of scholars that this is unlikely.

9

Socrates

TERRY PENNER

There is in Plato's early dialogues (here labelled 'Socratic') a certain 'intellectualism' that is quite foreign to the middle and later dialogues (here labelled 'mature Platonic' dialogues).[1] Indeed, that intellectualism, with its implication that *only philosophical dialogue* can improve one's fellow citizens, is decisively rejected by Plato in the parts of the soul doctrine of the *Republic*. On that doctrine, it is essential to the improvement of citizens that their appetites and spiritedness be *controlled*, either by *their* reason or by the reason of the intellectual elite. This contrast between dialogue in 'Socrates' and control of one's lower parts in 'the mature Plato' – one which even those most opposed to 'developmentalism' will be hard pressed to deny – is explored in section 1 below. But there are also striking continuities between 'Socratic' and 'mature Platonic' thought, of a sort sometimes missed by 'developmentalists'. If for 'Socrates' what is required for an individual's human goodness is that individual's full intellectual grasp on the real human good, so for 'the mature Plato', such a grasp *by those in the intellectual elite* is quite as necessary for the goodness of all the citizens. These continuities (concerning attitudes to the good, the ideal, the sciences and practical politics) are explored in sections 2 and 3 and section 5 *ad finem*. Sections 4 and 5 explore these continuities and contrasts as they show up in the three most overtly political 'Socratic' dialogues: the *Protagoras*, the *Apology* and the *Crito*.

[1] On the distinction between 'early', 'middle' and 'late' dialogues, and on the distinction between 'developmentalists', 'unitarians', and others, see Lane, Ch. 8 above. 'Intellectualism' is explained in section I. This chapter remains neutral on the delicate question of 'the historical Socrates'. Such expressions as 'Socrates', 'the mature Plato', are mere labels. Nor is the label 'mature' to be taken to suggest any kind of superiority on any psychological or political question. *Against* any such superiority, see Penner 1990, 1996.

1 The discontinuity between 'Socratic' intellectualism and 'mature Platonic' irrationalism about human behaviour

In the Socratic formulas 'Virtue is knowledge, vice ignorance' and 'No one errs willingly',[2] we find what to the modern reader must seem an almost total omission of the role of the irrational, of emotion or of moral evil in human life. 'If only we could *discuss* things for long enough, if only we could *understand* what is best,' Socrates seems to say, 'all would be well, and all conduct would be virtuous!' For Socrates, when people act badly or viciously or even just out of moral weakness, that will be merely a result of intellectual mistake. As if what moderns call the *will* were not at issue in questions of conduct – nor indeed base or irrational desires or emotions – but rather solely knowledge (science, one's intellectual understanding)!

All of this raises the question: what does Socrates have by way of a doctrine of the will – or at least of desire – or of the conative part of the human being? How can Socrates hope to treat of desire or the will solely in terms of the understanding? Enter the Socratic formula 'All desire is for the good.' It's not that desire gets omitted in Socrates' theory. It's just that everything anyone does is taken to proceed from the same basic desire. But how can this be? Don't we all do different actions – some of them good, some of them bad? The answer is that we need to consider particular actions we do as immediate means to further ends, which may themselves be means to yet further ends, and so on, till we come to a single ultimate end which we all have – the maximizing of our own happiness – which is the good.[3] So the explanation of the fact that in essentially the same situation, different people will do different things, is not that they differ in their 'character' or 'will' or desires; it's that they differ in what they believe to be the best means to the single end they all have. Mistakes in action are thus always due to mistaken beliefs as to what is a means to what, not to good or bad ends desired. Thus good people differ from bad people not in what they desire as their end, but solely in the beliefs they have as to what are the best means to that end (*Men*. 78b4). Such is 'Socratic intellectualism' concerning desire and action.

Four clarifications must now be made. First, the good in question is not

[2] *Men*. 87bff. with *Euthd*. 281b, *Prot*. 355e–7e, 360cd, 361ab; also 358c–360a, *Gorg*. 488a, 509e, *Hi. Mi*. 371e–373a with 376b, *Ap*. 25d with 37a.

[3] *Gorg*. 466a–468e, *Men*. 77a–78b, *Euthd*. 278e–282c, 288c–292e; cf. *Lys*. 219c–220b with 216d–217a, 221b–222a, as well as *Smp*. 199c–206a.

just, as most modern interpreters have simply assumed without further argument, the *apparent* good – what the agent *thinks* his or her ultimate good is – but the *real* good. It will be objected here that Callicles' end of maximizing bodily pleasures (*Gorg.* 491e–492c) is different from Socrates', and so is merely the apparent good – that Socrates and Callicles have different 'values'.[4] But this objection fails to see that Callicles may be represented as desiring pleasure simply as the best means to his own real happiness – so that later (we may hope) he will say 'I see now that the happiness I desired could not have been got from the life of maximizing bodily pleasures.' (In this scenario, he comes to admit that he was mistaken about pleasure as means to his own happiness.) But then Callicles and Socrates differ in their ends not at all – each desires the real good – but solely in their beliefs as to what is the best means to that end.[5] Callicles' actions are bad ones solely because of his beliefs about means.

Second, while the good postulated as end of all our actions is an idealized good (as just seen), it is also the case that the good which Socrates postulates as end of all our actions is our *own* good.[6] The theory of desire is one which makes self-interest the fundamental motive of all action. This makes such an end realistic enough to be considered a possible explanation of even vicious human conduct – provided that the beliefs about means to that end are sufficiently mistaken. (The hit man thinks he can be made happy on the money got from killing people. The Calliclean superman thinks he can be made happy by seeking the maximizing of bodily pleasures.[7]) Once again, this empties the ends of human action of any *differential* moral content.

[4] If matters of 'fact' are opposed to matters of 'value', then the idea of 'values' is one which neither Socrates nor Plato could have accepted. Values, so understood, are ultimate, and unquestioned, *apparent* goods: things one [ultimately] *thinks good*, where no question can be raised as to whether what is *thought good* is *in fact* good. (Cf., as an example of this, the Humean notion, discussed in section 3 below, of assigning reason to means, and will to ends, thereby in effect allowing ultimate ends to be specified – by will – *quite independently* of any questions concerning the truth about what is good. Cf. also nn. 11 and 12 below.) For Socrates and Plato, on the other hand, questions of *good* are questions not of value but of what is *in fact* good (beneficial, advantageous, happiness-maximizing). For them, Socrates and Callicles do not have different values, nor (as is suggested immediately below) do they have different ends. They have the same end, namely their own real good – whatever that might be. They differ only in their beliefs as to what the means might be to their own real good.

[5] See Penner 1991 and Penner and Rowe 1994; *contra* Santas 1979: 183–9 with nn. Cf. also n.12 below for the mature Plato as also holding that desire for the good is desire for the real good.

[6] *Gorg.* 468a–d, esp. b6, d3, *Men.* 77a–78b, esp. 77c8–d3, 77e6–78a7; cf. *Smp.* 204e6–7.

[7] The ignorance of the hit man or of the Calliclean superman (on whom see Schofield, in Ch. 10 section 2 below) is what Aristotle calls 'ignorance in the choice', *EN* III .1.1110b30–3, which is not at all for Aristotle an intellectual matter. It is what Aristotle distinguishes as *practical* rather than *theoretical* ignorance, practical ignorance representing a corruption of the rational by the irrational (by means of habituation). Socrates would not have granted any such distinction.

But if the idealized good here is purely egoistic, it needs to be emphasized, especially in the context of the Greek world in the fifth century BC, that this version of egoism is not at all the depressing form of egoism we find in the speeches of Thucydides, for example. It is central to Socrates' view that (as a matter of fact) harming others results in harm to you. So, as Plato puts it at *Ap.* 24e–26a, if Socrates is charged with corrupting the young he must be being charged – not with malice or malevolence but – with *failing to know that* harming those around one will result in harm to oneself. But then what he, the accused, needs is not punishment but instruction.[8] It may seem odd, and even offensive, to think of a good person as a person good at getting his or her own happiness. But given that, by the Socratic doctrine about harming others, you won't be good at getting your own happiness if you do harm others, it is not clear what exactly is offensive about such an account of human goodness. For the self-interest in question will never be the selfishness of being prepared to harm others as a means to one's own good.[9]

The third clarification is that the situation of mistaken *action* is represented by Socrates, *not* as a situation in which I (mistakenly) *did what I wanted*, but as a situation in which I did *not* do what I wanted at all, but merely *what seemed best.* (And Socrates is well aware of how paradoxical a claim this is: *Gorg.* 466b11–467c2.) This is sometimes wrongly interpreted either (a) as a doctrine of a 'true self' as opposed to any actual, or empirical self ('I wanted to do the bad action, but my true self didn't'), or (b) as involving a special sense of 'wants' – 'real wants' as opposed to my actual wants. ('Though I *wanted* to do the bad action, what I *really* wanted – what I *would* have wanted had my beliefs all been correct – was *not* to do it.') This sort of interpretation will be supported by considerations such as these: 'What better evidence could there be that I had an *actual* want to eat this chocolate bar, or that my *empirical* self wanted to eat this chocolate bar, than that I *did* precisely eat this chocolate bar?' (So, certainly, will a behaviourist argue, and so does Aristotle argue: *EN* III.4.1113a5–9.) It is as if only my 'true self' desired, or only my 'real desires' were for, the real good, while my actual self desired, and my actual desires were for, the apparent good.[10]

[8] Cf. Xenophon *Memorabilia* 1.2.50. On this view, punishment will never be appropriate, only dialogue. Cf. Penner 1992: 161 n.51; and on opting for instruction over culpability, *Hi.Mi.* 371e–373a with 376b; *contra* McKenzie 1981: ch. 10.

[9] Cf. *Cri.* 47a–49d, *Rep.* 1.335b–e, *Gorg.* 474b–481b. Contrast, for example, Price 1995: 16–17.

[10] On the supposed 'true self', see Cornford 1932: 50–3; Berlin 1958 (1969): 132–44, 154; Dodds 1959: 236. Cornford and Berlin both run together the two positions here being *contrasted*: the 'Socratic' position (all desire is for the good) and the 'mature Platonic' position (some desires are irrational and not for the good).

But these interpretations represent a failure to work hard enough at how Socrates in effect uses the means–end distinction to determine the identity of the object or action desired. It is not enough to say that I wanted to eat this chocolate bar *tout court* (*Gorg*. 468c1–7). Rather, we must bring out the means–end structure embedded in that object or action desired (467e–468d, esp. 468a5–b1, b4–8, b8–c1). Once that is done, we then need to consider which of the following action-descriptions describes that action of eating the chocolate bar that I *wanted* to do:

(a) the eating of this chocolate bar that is in fact the best means to maximizing my happiness, or
(b) the eating of this chocolate bar that turns out to be rather a means to making me more miserable than I would have been by abstaining?

Obviously (a). But *ex hypothesi* in this situation there *is* no such action as the one described by (a).[11] But (b), which *does* describe the actual action in the world which I *did* do, since it does not fit the description (a), cannot be the action I wanted to do. Hence the conclusion that the action done merely 'seemed best' to me.

So, then, there is no arbitrary re-definition of 'wants' here as 'real wants', and no reason to speak of a 'true self' as opposed to an 'actual' or 'empirical' self. We don't need to speak of a special sense of 'want' in order to say that I didn't want to do the actual action that I did. And it was not just some 'true self' of mine that didn't want to do that action. It was I myself.[12]

[11] It is presumably not an option to say I desire to do action (a) in a possible world other than this world. For surely we desire to act, if anywhere, in *this* world. Oedipus doesn't want to marry the Queen of Thebes in some other world where she is not his mother. Rather – unfortunately for him – it is (if anyone) the Queen of Thebes in *this* world (with all of her properties, known and unknown) that he wants to marry.

[12] On this view, I don't *know* what action I wanted to do. By contrast, Cartesians and empiricists think I can't fail to know what I want; and, as we have seen, both Aristotle and behaviourists think my actions *proof* of what I wanted. 'The mature Plato', on the other hand, where he *does* speak of desire for the good, is with 'Socrates' – the good one seeks being 'that which every soul pursues, and for the sake of which it does all things, divining it to be something, but being in perplexity and not able to grasp sufficiently what in the world it is, nor to use any such stable conviction concerning it as it has about other things . . .' (*Rep*.VI.505e–506a). Notice that to describe the action I *thought* I wanted as the action I wanted forces an *incoherence* onto the action desired. For it becomes (see preceding note) 'the action that I did in *this* world (whatever that action might be – you fill in the blanks, even, if it be so, "the action that was *not* the best means to maximizing my happiness") which *was* in fact the best means to maximizing my happiness'. Such an action being an *Unding*, it follows that there can be no such thing as a science of doing 'whatever action I want to do' (as that phrase is usually understood). Gorgias' science of rhetoric, being just such a supposed science, Socrates will deny to be a science at all. (The problem of rationally accounting for such incoherences in one's desires is not different in kind from that of accounting for the beliefs of someone who, like Frege over extensions of predicates, is unbeknownst to himself committed to an inconsistency – in Frege's case, to the Russell paradox.)

It will be obvious that the above considerations have only the most unpromising of implications for a useful notion of 'the will of the people' in political theory.

The fourth clarification goes beyond questions of belief, desire and the good to knowledge: the knowledge Socrates identifies with virtue. Consider again 'No one errs willingly' (viz., at getting their own good), and the way in which Socrates emphasizes here the subsumption of virtue under knowledge, science or expertise. (One of the most familiar moves in a Socratic dialogue is of course the insistence upon comparing a virtue with such arts or sciences as medicine, navigation, cobblery, arithmetic, horse-training, boxing, and so forth.) If the point of 'No one errs willingly', as used by Socrates, is that error in action is the product of ignorance, then if one has the relevant knowledge or science, one will not act in error. Now, it might seem (as both Aristotle and Aquinas insist, in differentiating virtues from sciences) that one *can* always err willingly – with respect to any science whatever. But, as against this, it is Socrates' view that there is one science at which no one errs willingly – the science of one's own good, that is, one's own happiness. (Compare economic man: he too can have an economic motive to err willingly at any science whatever – except for the science of his own economic good!).[13] It is to the science of one's own good, above all others, that Socrates thinks we should devote ourselves primarily.

With such attitudes to desire, the good, belief, knowledge and the means–end structure of actions (and desires to do particular actions), it should be clear that for Socratic intellectualism, the only access to a person's 'moral character' is by way of reason: that the only reliable way an agent's conduct may be changed for the better is by improving the agent's overall grasp of what is a means to what, and, in particular, of which general means will lead to the real good. But, now, the means–end structures involved in choosing well what one does over a lifetime are going to be fairly complicated[14] – there being hardly a single 'thing one believes' about what is good, anywhere in one's belief-system, that may not, at some point, become relevant to what one does. It should therefore be clear that simply *telling* someone what the best action is to do in a particular case (even if one had that knowledge oneself), or forcing on someone a recommendation as to what to do, is not going to be of much help to the agent. The only thing that will be of help is for the agent to come to a better understanding for himself or herself of all the truths involved in seeing what is a means to what – over a complete life. This is one reason why

[13] See Penner 1973, 1992.

[14] No one will think that the means–ends structures necessary for successfully building the Golden Gate Bridge will be less than enormously complicated. But surely living a good life will be far more complicated than this. No wonder that talking and arguing about these questions every day is indispensable to living a good life.

Socrates doesn't just *tell* his interlocutors what he himself thinks;[15] why he wants to examine for the most part solely the interlocutor's own views (as a whole); and why he doesn't *force* his answers on his interlocutors.[16] To the extent that people *don't* fully understand, they will constantly vacillate in their answers to questions about how to live, as they pursue, or come upon, various ill-assorted and incompletely reconciled considerations bearing on the matter before them. And this will be true whether the questions involved are theoretical or practical. This is why Socrates believes that only untrammelled, daily pursuit of questions of the nature of human goodness – only the pursuit of the examined life – gives one a chance at gaining that steadiness of judgment about the good that will enable us to do well and maximize happiness.[17]

We have here a moral psychology that is striking enough to delay us some considerable time. What needs to be singled out, however, for purposes of assessing the differences between Socrates and the mature Plato, is Socrates' apparently wilful ignoring of the need to control and even seduce the irrational desires and emotions in our lives – the base (and, in Christian thought, sinful) impulses that always threaten to let us down in acts of weakness or immorality or vice, especially when we are not deterred by fear of higher (political, social or religious) powers. For Socrates, intellectual understanding, and intellectual understanding alone, will make us better human beings.

By contrast, the mature Plato fixes on the idea that he needs to address himself to the influencing of human behaviour by means other than intellectual. There are appetites, the *Republic* holds, which bring us to act in certain ways even when the person (the rational part of a person's soul) thinks it best *not* so to act. We see from such desires of the appetitive part of the soul, Plato thinks, that, contrary to the Socratic view, desires are *not* all for the good (*Rep*. IV.438a). Hence, appetite, and in addition the *spirited part* of a person, must be brought (by the right kind of education) to *obey* reason. The education in question is *not* – as it would have to be for Socrates – purely intellectual. It is not a question of the appetitive or spirited parts coming to *understand* what things reason says it is best to do and

[15] See Penner 1992: 144 with n. 74; *contra* Vlastos 1958 (1971b): 16–17, on Socrates leaving Euthyphro nothing to hang on to. [16] See below, section 5, p. 187.

[17] For steadiness of judgement in a situation which calls for choice of action, see *Prot*. 351b–357e, esp. 352bc, 357c2–3 with 356d–357a. Knowledge of which option is best (or which most pleasant) over a complete life, is *strong* because *stable* under assault by all sorts of appearances of the good (or the pleasant) in different temporal perspectives. For steadiness of judgement in theoretical contexts, see *Euthphr*. 11b–e, *Meno* 97d–8a where knowledge of *what piety or virtue are* will be stable (cf also *Lys*. 213e, 214d, 216c, *Ion* 541e–542a, *Gorg*. 481de, 482ab, 491bc, 493a, 499bc, 527b–d). Cf. Penner 1997a, 1996.

then wishing to do them. It is a matter of those lower parts being brought, by proper training, to agree to do what reason commands – to *obey*. Accordingly, in Plato's ideal state, education is – except in its very final stages of the education of the ideal rulers (the guardians) – largely an education in *character*, not in *knowledge*. Where beliefs *are* involved – the military, who rank just below the guardians, are selected from the others by their ability to *preserve* beliefs as to what is just and lawful handed down to them by the guardians – the preservation of these beliefs is largely a matter of non-intellectual tenacity. It is not, as in Socrates, a matter of beliefs that are stable *because* the soldier will see that they are true, no matter from what perspective they are presented.[18] In fact, even when we come to the final stages of the higher education of the guardians, the *Republic* remains preoccupied with two tasks, not just one. It is preoccupied not just with coming to see the truth by way of philosophical dialectic, but also with making sure that the guardian's character is such that it cannot be turned away from the search for knowledge by emotional considerations.

2 Some continuities between 'Socratic' and 'mature Platonic' thought: (i) the centrality of the question of the teaching of virtue, and (ii) the sciences and idealization

The most striking continuity between Socratic ethical thought and mature Platonic ethical/political thought is the shared belief that the first question of ethics or of political philosophy is 'How is virtue to be acquired?' (which itself presupposes an answer to the question 'What is virtue?'). This is a direct legacy of Socratic thought, and informs Plato's utopian political investigations throughout.[19] The difference is merely what one would expect from the difference in moral psychology described

[18] It is arguable that when we come to the discussion of the military in the *Republic* we come upon a change in the notion of *what a belief is* from what it is in the Socratic dialogues – at least in the case of the beliefs of those who are not intellectuals. If so, then this change is of the very greatest importance to political philosophy. In the Socratic dialogues, Socrates tests a belief by exploring its relations to what appear to be quite distinct beliefs. For example, in the *Laches*, Nicias is *refuted* when he maintains what seems plainly to be a *Socratic* belief – that courage is the knowledge of the fearful and the hopeful. And he is refuted because he does not see the connection between this belief and what appear to be other Socratic beliefs. Similarly for Critias in the *Charmides* (if the beliefs that temperance is doing 'one's own' and that temperance is knowing oneself are Socratic). But when the mature Plato comes to thinking about the beliefs the military must preserve, he is evidently not interested at all in the military coming to *understand* how their apparently different beliefs all fit together. He is interested mainly in their continuing to assent to sentences they initially assented to. (He wants them to continue to do what they have been ordered to do, and preferably not to ask questions or raise objections.)

[19] Cf. Rowe 1984: 123.

in section 1: that for Socrates there is no substitute for *everyone*'s striving to answer such questions, whereas for the mature Plato, only the philosopher rulers need strive to discover what virtue is, virtue then being imparted mostly by persuasion, habituation, praise and blame, punishment and reward, without the need for actual understanding except in members of the ruling elite.

A second striking continuity between the Socratic dialogues and the middle or later dialogues has to do with an attitude towards the sciences which is common to Socrates and the mature Plato. In Socrates, we have already seen that the concern for the sciences is patent, virtue being knowledge or a science, and being everywhere compared to arts and sciences. It is true that, because of appetite, the mature Plato does not believe that what Socrates thinks of as the science of the good (the science of the human good, the science of happiness) is *sufficient* for the best life possible in given circumstances. *A fortiori*, he does not believe that virtue *is* the science of the human good. All the same, he does continue to think that there *is* a science of human good, which science becomes a science of ruling, and which is in turn the science of the good of the city. And this science *in the philosopher rulers* is still *necessary* to the achieving of the good for the city. Knowledge of the human good is quite as necessary for virtue as it is in Socrates.[20]

One way in which this common attitude to the sciences generally, and to the science of (human) good in particular, can be brought out is by seeing a common attitude towards the necessity for idealization when thinking about the sciences. This point is generally recognized for the mature Plato (the ideal state, the Platonic Forms), but less often seen in Socrates. Consider Socrates' claim that virtue is knowledge. Obviously, then, virtue is teachable. All one needs to do is find a teacher. But it now turns out to be Socrates' view that this knowledge with which virtue is identifiable is going to be *forever beyond our grasp*. For (a) Socrates admits the truth of what the Delphic oracle told his friend, Chaerephon (*Ap.* 20d–23c) – that no one is wiser than Socrates; and (b) Socrates acknowledges that he himself has no knowledge [of the good]. (The obvious conclusion here – that there are in fact no teachers of virtue – seems to be what lies behind the

[20] *Contra*, Irwin 1973, 1995 thinks that Plato's attitude to the sciences shifts from a morally neutral conception of science (induced by a 'craft analogy', and in the service of a conventional hedonism) to a Sidgwickian science of moral good (induced by reflection on the Form of the Good). Cf. also White 1979: 35–9, 46–9, 52–8. Irwin's idea is that the interest of the Form of the Good to Plato lies in the provision of a *non*-egoistic good: two different conceptions of good, two different conceptions of science. The present treatment takes it that it is the same conception of science, the same conception of good.

Socratic position at *Men.* 94c–95b and 95c–99b, especially 96b–d and 98d–99b, that while virtue is knowledge, it is not teachable. It *would* be teachable if only someone actually *had* the knowledge which is virtue.) So if virtue is knowledge, no one will have knowledge and no one will have virtue.[21]

Now Socrates apparently does not think that the fact that no one has knowledge does anything to damage his claim that dialectical search, every day, for such understanding, is our best and only hope for living the best life available to us (*Ap.* 37e–38a). It will be instructive to ask *why* he sees no difficulty here. If no one *has* such knowledge, and no one in the future is going to do *that* much better than Socrates (so that there is no reasonable hope that anyone ever *will* have it), what is the point of pursuing it?

The situation with virtue here is the same as it is in the mature Plato with the Platonic Forms – the Forms representing, as they do, the answers to such questions as 'What is Justice?', 'What is the Good?', 'What is the Square?', 'What is Cutting (or Burning)?', 'What are Earth, Air, Fire and Water?' The notion of Platonic Forms about which it is very difficult to arrive at the truth – on the Good, the *Republic* can offer us only an analogy with the Sun, while on Earth, Air, Fire and Water, the *Timaeus* can give us only a 'likely story' – and even the notion of Forms as ideals (not to mention the concern with ideal cities) is continuous with this idealizing Socratic approach to virtue. Indeed, the mature Plato is surely one of the inspirers of what is arguably an ideal of modern science: that there is a truth out there if only we can keep going long enough to close in on it. No one currently *knows* the laws of physics; but no one thinks it irrational to suppose there *are* such laws, nor do they suppose that pursuing such knowledge is fruitless just because no one has the knowledge. The position must be, then, that it is at best *reasonable to suppose* that we shall do better in (a) supposing there are objective answers to questions about the laws of nature, about the Forms, and about virtue, and in (b) pursuing those answers – even though there is no *knowledge* that there are such answers *or* that we shall obtain them.

That, for Socrates, there *are* objective truths out there about virtue and the good seems clear enough from an important passage at *Euthphr.* 10a–11b: If piety is loved by the gods, what makes it piety is not that the

[21] Contrast Vlastos 1994: 39–66, on Socrates' claim to ignorance as insincere; also Irwin 1973: 40–1 and Kraut 1984: 280–5 on Socrates' thinking he has true belief, or at any rate many true beliefs. The present reading is the only one which coheres with the considerations in nn. 14, 12, and 17 above; and cf. Penner 1992: section VI.

gods love it; rather the gods love it because what piety is, it is independently even of what the gods may think of it. Piety is something *there* to be discovered, not something we, or the gods, create. The attitude of the mature Plato is no different. When we wish to cut, *Crat.* 386e–387b insists, it is not the case that we wish to cut merely in accordance with our linguistic conventions for the use of the word 'cut', or even in accordance with our *beliefs* about what cutting is (387a2, b3), but solely in accordance with the real nature of cutting – presumably *whether or not* we know exactly what that real nature is. Whether with piety or with cutting, the idealizing assumption spoken of above takes it that in those circumstances, it is *reasonable* to suppose (though we do not know this, nor perhaps will we ever know it) that it is the most beneficial policy to attempt to arrive, as best one can, at that real truth about piety or cutting. So with the virtue that Socrates seeks, and so with the Platonic Forms and with laws of nature.[22]

3 A further continuity between the 'Socratic' dialogues and the middle and late dialogues: (iii) the sciences and the good

This attitude to idealization in science – we may not know the truth, but there *is* a truth, and we do well to seek to know it even if we may never come to be fully in possession of it – is thus common to Socrates and the mature Plato. Quite as important is the connection in Socrates and the mature Plato between the sciences and the good – the idealized real good (cf. *Rep.* VI.505e–506a, quoted in n. 12 above). This connection is virtually unique in Western thought. It produces in Socrates and the mature Plato either many more sciences of the good, or at least one more science of the good than there will be on any *strict* Western conception. At the same time there will be many fewer sciences of the good than there will be on any *loose* Western conception.

First, on there being *more* sciences of the good in Socrates and Plato. I begin with those *applied* sciences which all of Socrates, the mature Plato, and Aristotle view as subsumed under an architectonic of sciences aimed ultimately at the good for humans.[23] Carpentry's end is the *making* of such things as shuttles, weaving *uses* those shuttles as means to its end of

[22] If the real laws of nature can be thought of, in Humean fashion, as constant conjunctions (of real attributes), then the Platonic Forms may be thought of as the real attributes.

[23] Cf. *Crat.* 387e–391b with *Euthd.* 281a–b, 288e–292e, esp. 289b–290d, 291b–292e; also *Rep.* X.601c–602b; and compare the similar thought at Arist. *EN* I.1, where *all* the sciences, it appears, are taken to be subordinate to the human good.

making coverings; *another* science then *uses* those coverings as means to its end of *making* shelter for human beings, and so on through the hierarchy of *making* and *using* sciences till we reach that end which is the human good generally – living well, happiness (individual good in Socrates, individual and political good in Aristotle and the mature Plato).

Here, not only are all these subordinate sciences sciences of good, but there is also a single science of the human good – which is at least one more science than moderns will normally suppose there to be. But what about other applied sciences? What of the pure sciences? There seems no good reason for an interpreter of Socrates and the mature Plato not to suppose that for every pure science there are corresponding applied sciences – the latter consisting of what Kant calls 'rules of skill' derived as 'hypothetical imperatives' ('wear black if you want to get away with stealing jewels at night') from the former ('Black is the colour hardest to discern at low illumination'). The same idea is present also in the thought that the aim of science generally is explanation, prediction and *control*. On such a view, the sciences are all, in one way or another, sciences of the good, and indeed of *our* good. (And it is presumably this hierarchy of all the sciences under the sciences of the human good that explains the otherwise incomprehensible claim at *Rep*. VI.508e that the Form of the Good is the cause both of the *being* and of the *knowledge* of everything else: what a shuttle *is* depends upon what weaving is, and so on, just as knowing what a shuttle is depends upon knowing what weaving is, and so on.)

Even if we leave aside the suggestion that all sciences are sciences of the good, this seems shockingly different from modern ideas. 'Applied sciences may make the provision of optimal means scientific. But they are in themselves surely "morally neutral". Their ends, and certainly any ultimate ends, are not scientific questions, but questions of one's values. There are no sciences of ultimate good.' Hume typifies this modern attitude. On the one hand, there is *reason* employed for determining *means*; and on the other hand, there is *will* which – quite independently of reason – is always decisive for determination of *ends*; so that, in our terms, judgments about means are *factual* judgments, while judgments about ends are *normative* – *value-judgments* or *moral judgments*. There will be sciences of means *relative to a specification of an end* (the relevant good); but no science of the good. There can be sciences of means to any arbitrary end, but no sciences of ends.

The contrast with Socrates and the mature Plato could not be clearer. Throughout Plato's dialogues, it is a scientific question what the good is – and so also what the human good is and what happiness is. Not only are all sciences sciences of the good; there is also a single science of the human good – of a sort unlikely to be granted by moderns.

On the other hand, if Socrates and the mature Plato allow for more sciences, skills, and technologies of the good than will be allowed by moderns, with their fact/value dichotomy, it is also the case that there are many supposed sciences, skills, and technologies which Socrates and the mature Plato would *not* allow. In particular there will not be a science for just any arbitrary specification of an end of the sort just mentioned. For Humeans, there is no question of asking for the relation between the arbitrarily specified end willed and (what is for Socrates and the mature Plato the ultimate end) the human good. But for Socrates and the mature Plato, it is crucial that we ask just how that subordinate end is supposed to be itself a means to the human good. For moderns, the subordinate end can be *just whatever you want it to be*. But, as we have seen in n. 12 above, there is going to be an incoherence in the idea of *whatever you want*, understood as: what you want regardless of whether or not it will serve your further aims. For an action you *think* or *say* you want won't be one you really do want if you have any mistakes whatever in your beliefs as to what is a means to the end of your real happiness. This is the basis on which Socrates denies that there could be sciences (skills, techniques, technologies) of rhetoric, cosmetics, cookery, sophistic (either *à la* Gorgias or *à la* Protagoras or – implicitly – *à la* Pericles: the art for making us do well in our personal affairs and in the political life of the city) – not to mention advertising, winning elections, lobbying, publicity (contriving public popularity) and being socially popular.[24]

It might indeed be wondered how it is, if rhetoric is not a science, that such people as Gorgias are *in fact* more successful than others at persuading people. But Gorgias' supposed science will have just the kind of incoherence in the object of his desire which was pointed out above.[25] Gorgias glories in the idea that *without any knowledge of medicine*, he can persuade the patients of his brother, the doctor, that it is best for them to undergo surgery when the doctor himself cannot persuade them (*Gorg.* 455d–456c). It follows, indeed, that he can persuade such patients that it is best for them to undergo surgery *whether Gorgias himself knows whether*

[24] If Ion tells us what Homer says about medicine without knowing the truth about medicine, that will involve similar incoherence: cf. Penner 1988. It is arguably on such grounds that Socrates mocks poetry as 'divinely inspired', and Plato excludes tragic poetry from the ideal state (*Rep.* x). The apparent distortions of Simonides' meaning in Socrates' mockery of poetry at *Prot.* 338e–348a turn similarly on the question whether Simonides can be supposed to mean *anything* coherent, if we suppose he intends to speak of virtue *in this world*: see nn. 11–12 above.

[25] See n.12 (with n.11).

it is medically best or not (cf. also *Prot.* 313c–e). Now plainly Gorgias with this supposed expertise is not going to make much of an adviser on medical matters. But he still insists that if he *wants* to persuade the patient to undergo surgery, he *can*. Thus he could persuade someone to pursue the end of living happily till the age of ninety by being a lifelong heavy smoker (or he could achieve some end of his own by persuading that person to succeed in living till ninety by lifelong heavy smoking). Plainly by this means Gorgias isn't going to gain *anything* he wants[26] – unless by accident.[27]

It is this concern with the coherence of what is presumably a *very* complicated means-end structure that makes it the case that the persistent and crucial Socratic question is – since persuasion is always persuasion about *something* – persuasion about *what?*[28] (If Gorgias doesn't have the knowledge of medicine, then it can't be persuasion about the *real* medical good. At best, it will have to be persuasion about the *seeming* or *apparent* medical good – which can only result in the incoherence mentioned. The incoherence envisaged here, it is reasonable to suppose, is of a piece with the kind of incoherence we find in the ideas of Socrates' interlocutors as they try to say what courage is, or how best to educate the young (the *Laches*); what friendship is and how to become a friend (the *Lysis*); what temperance is (the *Charmides*); what piety is or whether Euthyphro acts piously in prosecuting his father (the *Euthyphro*); whether a rhapsode has knowledge of what Homer is saying (the *Ion*); whether the unwilling or the willing falsehood-teller (Achilles? Odysseus?) is the better person (the *Hippias Minor*); what rhetoric is, whether it is a science, whether the all-powerful tyrant Archelaus is happiest, or, alternatively, whether the unrestrained seeker of bodily pleasure is happiest (the *Gorgias*); what sophistic is and whether virtue is one and teachable (the *Protagoras*); what virtue is and whether it is teachable (the *Meno*); and what justice is and whether the just person is happier than the unjust in (the arguably Socratic) *Republic* I. Since Socrates thinks that nothing short of intellectually seeing one's way through all such incoherences is the only way to bring oneself to living

[26] See Penner 1988 on Thrasymachus surprisingly opting for a science of *real* advantage over the 'might is right' view. In the mature Plato, compare what is in effect ridicule, at *Plt.* 295b–296a, of the idea of a science of legislation (cf. also *Phdr.* 259e–262c, as well as 275c–277c on the shortcomings of writing in the absence of discussion).

[27] See the first of the 'Two Notes' in Penner 1997b.

[28] Cf. *Gorg.* 447d–461b, esp. 449e–450c, 451de, 452de, 453e–454b, resulting in 455a, which is assailed in the sequel. Similarly, cf. *Prot.* 312c–e, resulting in 318a–319a, which – failing a proper answer to that question in the Great Speech of 320c–328d – is arguably being assailed in the discussion of knowledge in the rest of that dialogue: section 4 below. See also n.14 above on the complexity of the means–end structure.

well, the only philosophical method must be exactly the kind of Socratic dialectic we find in those dialogues.

On such grounds, then, does Socrates deny that there can be such sciences as rhetoric *à la* Gorgias, and on such grounds, more generally, does his conception of the sciences represent a considerable contraction of the realm of the sciences from that allowed in the modern view (of objective means to arbitrarily chosen ends).[29]

Let us return now to such failed sciences (pseudo-sciences) in a more overtly political context. If Gorgias is not much of an adviser on matters of health, Socrates thinks, nor is Pericles (or Themistocles) going to be much of an adviser in matters of personal or political good – at least if we suppose that in the ironic suggestion that (a) Pericles *has* virtue but (b) cannot teach his sons, we have a *reductio ad absurdum* of the claim that Pericles *does* have virtue. But this supposition is amply confirmed by *Gorg.* 513e–522e, especially 515d–516d, and *Men.* 94ab within the wider context (92e–95a, 99d–100b) of discussion with Anytus, the spokesman for politicians (*Ap.* 23e). Unless one knows what the individual human good is, or what the good of the citizens as a whole is, there can be no science of persuading concerned with *apparent* individual human good, and no science of persuading concerned with the *apparent* good of citizens as a whole. As we might put it, Pericles is the kind of bungler in political matters – working entirely with his knack of making the alternatives (carefully tailored to the protestations of the many)[30] *appear* good to the many (without knowing whether or not these alternatives are good) – as Charles Bovary was in matters of surgically correcting a club foot. There is no Form of – and no science of – the apparently corrected club foot.

A word more on Socrates and Plato on pseudo-sciences. It is often claimed that while Plato attacks rhetoric, he himself doesn't hesitate to use rhetoric in attacking the likes of Gorgias. This claim shows a complete misunderstanding of the Socratic-Platonic charge against rhetoric. Since rhetoric *à la* Gorgias proceeds without even feeling the *need* to ascertain the truth about the subjects on which it speaks, *it cannot be a science*. Let Socrates use whatever rhetorical turns of phrase he likes. Let him even be wrong about what he says. What is not true is that he thinks he can do

29 *True* sciences of rhetoric, had by those with knowledge of the matters the persuasion concerns (*Gorg.* 517a with 508c, 503ab; cf. *Phdr.* 259e–262d, 273d–274b), are the exception that proves the rule. There is no science of the merely apparent good. Indeed, for Plato, there are no Forms, and so no sciences, of the apparently *anything*. In modern terminology, there are no phenomenological sciences. Aristotle doesn't see what Plato's problem could possibly be here: cf. *PA* I.1.639a12–15, *EN* III.4.1113a5–9 and especially *Top.* VI.146b36–147a11.

30 Cf Callicles and the *dēmos*: *Gorgias* 481d–482c with 510c–e, 512d–513d, and cf. similar passages in the mature Plato, for example, *Rep.* VI.488a–489b, 492c–493e.

what he is trying to do independently of a concern for the truth of the matter he is speaking of.[31]

Thus Socrates and the mature Plato stand together, and opposed to rhetoricians, sophists and practical politicians, on the need for genuine science if the first goal of ethics and politics – the virtue of the citizens – is to be assured. This continuity is in no way impugned by the following consequence of the considerations in section 1 above: that in his *methods* for contriving the virtue of the citizens, the mature Plato is closer to the non-intellectual methods attributed to Protagoras in the Great Speech than he is to anything in Socrates.

4 Socrates' response to the democratic political theory of the teaching of virtue which Protagoras propounds in the *Protagoras*

Socrates' opposition to Protagoras in this dialogue has three main parts: the raising of the question just exactly what Protagoras' expertise or science is, Protagoras' account of his science of politics, and the confutation of Protagoras' conception of virtue and knowledge. The dialogue can give the impression (gained by many in the audience) of being a miscellaneous series of contests between the two philosophers. Is there more of a unity to this unique way of, amongst other things, having Socrates treat of the science of politics?

The dialogue runs as follows:

(a) 309a–319a: Socrates questions a would-be student of Protagoras: What science does Protagoras teach? What is sophistic knowledge *of*? The same science as various poets and others have taught in the past (though they concealed the fact that they were sophists)? Doing well in one's affairs and in acting and speaking in political life? Such a science the Athenians (who are wise) and Pericles (who is virtuous) evidently suppose is not teachable. For (i) the Athenians allow only experts to speak on matters involving expertise; but on issues of the good order of the city they allow *anyone* to speak; and (ii) Pericles provides teachers for his sons on all matters of expertise, but none for virtue, nor can he convey his own virtue to them.

(b) 320c–328d: Protagoras' Great Speech, explaining that it only seems there are no teachers because virtually *everyone* teaches – that also being why the sons of the virtuous aren't any more likely to turn out virtuous

[31] Similar remarks apply to the equally irrelevant charge that while Plato attacks poetry, he himself writes as a poet: cf. n. 24 above.

than others. There would *be* no cities if it weren't the case that pretty well everyone had the one thing needful to life in the cities – justice, temperance, piety, that is, together, virtue. Virtue is taught ostensively, action by action, using punishment, reproof, threats, blows, the teaching of good poetry, gymnastics, and by getting the citizens to treat laws as patterns for behaviour.

(c) 328d–334c: Socrates' – apparently totally non-political – response: Does Protagoras really think that justice, temperance, and piety are one, and also wisdom and courage? Or are these virtues quite unlike each other, both in themselves and in their operation? Protagoras thinks the latter; and Socrates begins replying with arguments that temperance, wisdom and justice are one, while piety is, at the very least, 'very like' justice.

(d) 334c–338e: Socrates nearly breaks off the argument, because Protagoras will not give short answers to Socrates' questions.

(e) 338e–348a: By a compromise, Socrates offers to answer Protagoras' questions, and Protagoras questions Socrates about education by way of poetry and literary criticism. Does the poet Simonides contradict himself in certain verses concerned with the acquisition of virtue? Socrates wrests from Simonides' poem several morals: one, that it is hard to become good (which is in fact inconsistent with Protagoras' theory of near-universal virtue, and more in line with Socrates' claim that no one is wiser than he, Socrates, is, and Socrates has no knowledge of the good), and, in addition, two intellectualist morals that are apparently quite unintended by Simonides.[32] These are that the only way to become a worse person is to become less knowledgeable, and that no one errs willingly [at getting what is good for them].

(f) 348b–349b: Socrates explains why he is happy to talk with Protagoras, since he alone of virtuous people *can* teach others his virtue (and charges a fee for it!).

(g) 349b–360e: Protagoras conceding on every other point in (c), and denying only that courage is wisdom, Socrates argues finally that courage *is* identical with wisdom, by way of showing that while a person with mere belief (appearance) will vacillate 'up and down' under the effects of different perspectives on future pleasures and pains, or goods and bads, one with the 'measuring art' – the knowledge of what is pleasant and painful, good and bad, fearful and heartening – will never choose mistakenly, and so will never be 'overcome' by pleasure or fear or whatever (cf. n. 17 above). This wisdom *is* courage.

32 Supposing that Simonides had *some* coherent intention. Cf. nn. 11, 12, 24 above; also Penner 1992: section VII.

(h) 360e–362a: We have come to a laughable result: Socrates holds that virtue (all of justice, temperance, courage) *is* knowledge but that it is not teachable, while Protagoras holds that it is *not* knowledge (courage being different from wisdom or knowledge), but that it *is* teachable. We need to go back and determine what virtue is, and then decide whether or not it is teachable.

We need not worry about the last difficulty for Socrates – that he thinks virtue is knowledge but not teachable (above, section 2, p. 173). The difficulty the dialogue as a whole is raising is about Protagoras' democratic conception of virtue in (b). The difficulty is twofold. First, Protagoras seems to think that the political knowledge of adult citizens as a whole is almost entirely adequate to the teaching of virtue. A far more profound understanding of the human good is not sought even for the rulers: democracy will function quite adequately with only a little fine-tuning, for a fee, from Protagoras. We can have in the supposed science introduced in (a) only the kind of rudderless conception of individual and political goodness that we have already seen in Gorgias' conception of rhetoric. Second, there is the matter of the non-intellectualist methods Protagoras thinks adequate to conveying virtue to the citizens. We have punishment, blows, the memorizing of the laws, music, gymnastics, and case-by-case ostensive definition, but also, in (d) and (e),[33] long rhetorical speeches, poems, and laconic shafts of wisdom without the ability to answer further questions. What is needed is rather intellectual discussion of the kind produced by question and answer, that stops for no practical reason,[34] but solely when the truth is arrived at. Nor, of course, will Socrates grant the view of Protagoras that most citizens are virtuous to a very considerable degree – an idea Socrates succeeds in eliciting from Meletus at *Ap.* 24d–25c, and which he proceeds to ridicule.[35] The argument of the dialogue as a whole, though especially of (c)–(e) and (g), is that virtue is solely understanding, and as to understanding, even the great Protagoras is shown by this very dialogue to fall short by a considerable measure.

Thus Socrates' response to Protagoras' political philosophy is not only, in itself, totally non-political; it also suggests just one method for conveying virtue to citizens as a whole, and that is the non-political method of just such intellectual discussion as the *Protagoras* itself consists in (Protagoras' Great Speech excepted). It is worth noting that on the need

[33] On (e) see n.24 above. [34] Cf. n.38 below.

[35] Contrast Kraut 1984: 270–9, who takes it that Socrates *does* hold that most people in a democracy do know more or less what is good.

for ascertaining the truth by such Socratic methods, the mature Plato is at one with Socrates – even while at the level of implementation (once more because of his different moral psychology), he supposes it wise to employ just such devices as are employed by Protagoras.

5 The political philosophy of Plato's *Apology* and *Crito* and another continuity between Socrates and the mature Plato: (iv) the attitude towards practical politics

The *Apology* presents itself as Socrates' speech at his trial on a charge of (a) corrupting the young and (b) not believing in the city's gods, instead introducing new demigods of his own. The activity which is supposed to constitute the corruption of the young that Socrates is charged with is in fact Socrates' philosophical activity – the dialectical search, every day, for how best to live – which activity his accusers evidently wish to bring to a halt. Socrates slyly suggests that this philosophical activity is nothing less than a divinely imposed mission. For, as we have seen, when his friend Chaerephon went to the Delphic Oracle, and asked whether anyone was wiser than Socrates, the Oracle said No. Since Socrates thought he knew nothing on any matter of importance, it was plain, he says, that the god wished him to *examine* those (politicians, poets, even craftspeople) who appeared to have knowledge (a science) concerning virtue: and, in showing that they did not, to show his own superior wisdom – a human wisdom residing merely in his not supposing that he has that knowledge (*Ap.* 20c–23c). The enmity this was likely to incur, and did incur, can be seen from Socrates' mischievous examination of two of those accusers – Meletus at *Ap.* 23e–28a and Anytus at *Men.* 89e–95a with 100b and *Ap.* 23e. As for this talk about the gods, Socrates says (*Ap.* 37e–38a), if it be thought ironic, it is no matter. For the key point is whether or not it is the greatest good to a human being to talk every day about virtue and so on, and to examine oneself and others on these things – on the grounds that the unexamined life is not worth living. But whatever we may say of the reference to the gods, there is certainly no irony in the representation of Socrates as taking the examining and refuting of others on questions of virtue, and the inciting of anyone – richer or poorer (33b), younger or older, citizen or foreigner, but especially citizens (30a) and (as we see from his practice) the young – to put virtue ahead of all other goods, to care for *their* souls (29d–30c, 30d, 31b, 36c with 39d), as his mission in life.

As for political and more generally civic activity, the *Apology* represents

Socrates as appearing for the first time in his life in court, and as without interest in speaking in any manner other than that conversational manner in which he engaged in the *agora*. (This conversational manner we may suppose to be what we know as philosophical dialogue. We see it even in the little dialogues inserted into, or reported in, *Ap.* 20a–c, 24c–26a, 26b–28a.) The *Apology* also represents Socrates' intellectual activity as always in the capacity of a private person. Not only is this trial his first appearance in court, he has also never appeared before the assembly publicly to offer counsel; for, in opposing many unjust and illegal things, he would not have survived. The implication is plain enough: many illegal and unjust things must be let go in a higher interest – that of talking to citizens one-on-one privately and not as a political or institutional act (29d–30c, 31b–32a).[36] To survive, one must be a private person and not engage in politics. From such political action, his divine voice turns him away (31c–32a). Yet for all that, Socrates represents his private questioning – which true enough took place in public, though not before a public forum – as of the greatest service to the state. Socrates is the gadfly who keeps people's interest concentrated on questions of virtue (30e–31a).

We see little interest here in democratic (or even oligarchic) 'communal decision-making effected in public after substantive discussion by or before voters . . ., and on issues of principle as well as purely technical operational matters'[37] – where characteristically the decision is taken in an antecedently determinate time,[38] and without regard to whether or not the opposing parties have come to a common mind on the issues involved. Socrates has no interest in practical politics. The staying away from practical politics shows up in the *Apology* with the observation that Socrates never held any office, though he did once serve on the council.[39] On this one occasion of serving on the council, Socrates found himself in a position where he *had* to act, and did act – in opposition to the public. He tried, alone among those on the council, to stop a furious assembly from trying the admirals from the naval disaster at Arginusae illegally, *en bloc*. Only one other overtly political act is recorded in the *Apology*. When the

[36] Socrates is castigated for this by Vlastos 1994: 127ff.

[37] Cartledge's characterization of 'politics in the strong sense': Ch. 1, p. 11.

[38] On antecedent time limits, cf. *Ap.*24a, 37b, where it is pointed out that one on trial is only allowed a limited amount of time for a defence, regardless of the length of time it would take to bring out the truth; cf. *Gorg.* 453a–456a, esp. 455a. On the willingness of those in practical politics to proceed without agreement, merely by way of votes, the contrast with the methods of Socrates is almost too obvious to mention.

[39] Election to the council was by lot: Aristotle, *Ath.Pol.* chs.43–4. Rhodes 1981, in his commentary *ad loc.*, says one would nevertheless have had to volunteer in order to be in the lottery from which the choice was made. If so, and if Socrates volunteered out of a desire to offer public counsel, the historical Socrates will have differed from the Socrates depicted in Plato's *Apology*.

Thirty Tyrants ordered Socrates to help in the illegal arrest of the wealthy Leon of Salamis, he refused, and would probably have lost his life had the Thirty not been overturned shortly thereafter.[40]

On one point, indeed, the *Apology* shows Socrates little less than defiant of the court, and, by implication, of the democracy as a whole. For he says to the court that should the jurors wish to impose one sort of verdict in the trial – to let Socrates go if he will just stop his philosophical inquiries, though if he continue, he'll be put to death (29c–30c) – he would disobey. But this surely implies that, had the Athenian democracy passed a law against philosophical activity of the sort that Socrates engaged in – something they perfectly well might have done – *then he would disobey*. This point (as Grote saw) Socrates puts, rather in the manner of a very slightly less defiant Antigone, by saying that he embraces and loves his fellow Athenians, but he will follow the commands of the god (to philosophize) rather than the commands of the state. Either acquit me, he says, or put me to death. I won't obey the command to stop my philosophical inquiries, even if I die many times over.

Such, then, are the main lines of the political thought of the *Apology*. On the one hand, a policy of lying low politically in order to carry out his mission as a philosopher; on the other hand, a willingness to defy the state if there is interference with his mission as a philosopher, and, in addition, where lying low is impossible and he has been put on the spot, a willingness even to endanger his life rather than act unjustly or disgracefully. Should the expression 'care for the soul' turn out to cover *both* pursuit of the philosophical mission which justifies the general policy of staying out of politics, *and* acting justly when the political situation would otherwise force him to act unjustly, then the political thought of the *Apology* may be paraphrased as: Put care for the soul ahead of everything, and especially above engaging in political action; but when political action is forced on you, act justly out of care for your soul.[41]

But, now, when we turn to the *Crito*, it can suddenly appear that the *Apology*'s account of Socrates' attitude to commands from the state is

[40] The Thirty included both Plato's mother's cousin Critias (as *de facto* leader) and also his mother's brother Charmides. Leon of Salamis is said, at *Ep.* VII.325c, to have been a friend of the democrats who four years later put Socrates to death – on a charge of impiety which the author of the letter says Socrates, least of all people, deserved.

[41] Here is a possible reason why it would harm one's soul to act unjustly when politically pressured to do so: we have seen above that the only form (voluntary) action can take in Socrates is doing what one regards as the best means to what is in fact the best end. To act unjustly then, on the Socratic assumption that acting unjustly and harming others is bad for one, requires that one find a way so to re-state one's reasons for acting that one comes to believe that what is in fact worse is better. This is to find premises in one's system which will endanger the very coherence of one's belief structure – in ways that can harm one in the rest of one's life.

flatly contradicted by Socrates' insistence in the *Crito* that, even though he was unjustly convicted, he should not attempt to escape the death sentence imposed upon him by the courts, but should submit to it. In general, the *Crito* at any rate *seems* anxious to offer a theory of *political obligation* – on the citizen's *moral obligations* to the state.[42] The centrepiece of that theory is a certain 'persuade or obey' injunction which shows up in the mouth of the personified Laws. This doctrine, according to the most likely interpretation, enjoins that, in a war, or in the law-courts, or anywhere else, if the state commands you to do something, *even if in so doing it acts unjustly*, then unless you can succeed in persuading otherwise, you must obey the state's command. The reasons given for this injunction are: (1) It is the state's laws that enable the parents' marriage and their procreation of the citizen. (2) The state sees to it that the parents nurture and educate the child. (Indeed, the *Crito* notes that nurture and education, no doubt added to a more direct tie of affection and benefits, justify also an injunction to obey one's *parents* even if they treat one unjustly.) And (3) Socrates, having become familiar with the laws of Athens, and nevertheless staying in Athens when he was free to leave with all his belongings for other states he regarded as having good laws, shows he has (tacitly) agreed to abide by the laws and to abide by legal verdicts of the courts, even if those verdicts are in fact unjust.

Talk of tacit agreement in (3) may suggest, as it did to Hume ('Of the Original Contract') that we have here a social contract doctrine. But this is certainly not right. As any obligations of gratitude to parents would have to be antecedent to any social contract, so presumably would obligations of gratitude to a state and obligations to contract more generally.[43] What, then, of the *Crito* being about such *antecedent* moral obligations? This otherwise tempting account of the *Crito* is unfortunately undercut by what we have found in our case of hypothetical disobedience in the *Apology*. If the *Crito* is about our moral obligations to the state, the *Apology* will be announcing an intention to act immorally.[44] (For presumably our moral obligations are those considerations we regard as *not to be over-ridden*.)

[42] See e.g. Vlastos 1973–4, Kraut 1984: 40.

[43] The Hobbesian idea of a social contract which Hume is attacking is that of an agreement that *generates* all moral obligations. But if the obligation of gratitude to parents is prior to the existence of any state, then so is the obligation of gratitude to anything (even a state) that would provide for procreation and education of children. Why then should the obligation to keep agreements be any different? No motivation is left for a social contract generating *all* moral obligations. Platonists have always argued that the very *idea* of generating all obligations from some *declaration* of ours is incoherent: see, for example, Cudworth (d. 1688) 1731: I.i–iii with *Rep.* II.358eff., 369bff., *Euthphr.* 10a–11b (discussed briefly above).

[44] Socrates is similarly defiant and uncooperative over his sentencing (*Ap.* 36b–37a).

If one is anxious still to find in the *Crito* an account of our moral obligations to the state, there seem to be the following choices. First, one can simply grant that the *Crito* is inconsistent with the *Apology*. Second, one can think of Socrates as addressing different audiences in the two dialogues (Grote). Third, one can deny one of the halves of the inconsistency, either by denying that the *Apology* threatens *real* disobedience (de Strycker and Slings), or by denying that the Laws in the *Crito* express Socrates' real views, expressing rather what Socrates thinks necessary to convince Crito (Gary Young). Fourth, one can keep the view that the *Crito* is about our moral obligations to the state, but work some casuistry to keep the *Apology* and *Crito* consistent. One way to carry out this fourth option is (a) to say there is only one form of disobedience allowed, namely, when the state forbids one the persuasion alternative in 'persuade or obey'. This example narrows down *philosophizing when the state forbids it* to merely this (political/legal) persuasion involved in 'persuade or obey' (Woozley). Another way to carry out this fourth option is (b) to distinguish one's other-things-being-equal (*prima facie*) obligations from one's all-things-considered (actual) obligations (as in Ross and Rawls), and then say that the *Crito* does not speak of our moral obligations to the state all-things-considered, but rather only of a *prima facie* obligation, while one's all-things-considered obligation leads to one's obeying another *prima facie* obligation, to obey the commands of god (Ernest Barker, Vlastos, and, more explicitly, Santas).[45] A fifth option is to keep the *Crito* as about our all-things-considered moral obligation to the state, but so liberalize 'persuade or obey' (to '*try to* persuade, or obey') that the disobedience of which the *Apology* speaks after all *does* fall under the 'persuade or obey' rubric, since Socrates in his trial is so evidently *trying to persuade* the jury that it is well for him to philosophize, and since, in addition, it conforms to justice and the good of the state that he should.[46] These options are all ponderable and deserving of consideration, though the most persuasive is that involving the distinction (admittedly nowhere explicit in Plato) between *prima facie* and actual duties. And in fact in the solution to be proposed directly, something *like* the distinction between the 'other things being equal' and the 'all things considered' will be crucial.

All the options so far considered take the *Apology* and *Crito* to be wrestling with questions of *moral obligation to the city*. In the light of the remarks about the real (and egoistic) good above, one might wonder

[45] Scholars cited in the elaboration of options 1 to 4: Grote 1865, de Strycker and Slings 1994, Young 1973, Woozley 1971, Ross 1931, Rawls 1971, Barker 1918, Vlastos 1971a, Santas 1979.

[46] Cf. Kraut 1984, and *contra* Penner 1997b.

whether perhaps more promising than any of these options is the following: drop the (deontological) idea that the *Crito* is about any *moral obligation* to persuade or obey, and consider the possibility that the talk of justice in the *Apology* and *Crito* demands interpretation in *purely teleological* terms (roughly the hypothetical imperative, or counsel of prudence, 'Do this if you want to be happy', where by Socratic – and even Kantian – lights, everyone does want to be happy). Perhaps in the *Crito* Socrates is just saying that *in the sorts of circumstances* under consideration in the *Crito*, it won't, in fact, be *good* for you (conducive to your happiness) to harm the state. (Just as it won't be good for you to harm or act unjustly towards your parents, even if they harm or do injustice to you.) What sorts of circumstances are these? In the *Crito*, it is a matter of escape, and therefore refusal to abide by a verdict of the court (even if unjust) – without even *offering* persuasion as to why Socrates should not abide by unjust verdicts. It is a matter of 'doing violence to' (*biazesthai*: 51c) the laws of the state. On this sort of refusing to 'do violence', compare also 48e ('unwillingly'), 49c–e ('see to it that you do not agree to something you do not believe'), where Socrates says he also doesn't want Crito to go along with his decision not to escape *unless he is genuinely persuaded that that decision is best.*[47] There is an important matter here of trying to get people to see the truth *for themselves*. The same is arguably owed to the state, even though the state does not afford Socrates, or indeed anyone else, the time to accomplish such a large task.[48] What we have here is presumably the intellectualist point that the only way to get someone to change their views beneficially is to bring them to see for themselves the truths involved. Better to risk injustice from others than to worsen others by further doing violence to their understanding in harming them back – a worsening which will itself be harmful to you.

Now, Socrates' refusal to escape must surely be regarded as a pretty extreme case of beneficial obedience. So Socrates *must* think that in *most* cases, if parents or state command Socrates to do something, even if it is unjust, obedience will be best for him, if persuasion fails. Such a claim is consistent with there nevertheless being some cases where it *would* be good for Socrates to disobey – say, where a command of the state would force him to do harm to his soul. If doing harm to Socrates' soul here is stopping him from philosophizing, from that 'care of the soul' which consists in Socratic inquiry into the nature of human goodness, we would have the desired resolution of the contradiction: almost always it is best to

[47] Cf. n.41 above. [48] Cf. n.38 above.

obey even an unjust command, once persuasion has failed; but where a command would force on one something that would interfere with care for one's soul, then it is better to disobey (though of course only after persuasion has failed).

For this account to succeed, it must make plausible the obvious suggestion that lies behind this resolution: our one best hope in human life is this same care for the soul which consists in continuing Socratic inquiry, and in engaging in dialogue every day about human goodness (*Ap.* 38a). But just that is what the account of Socratic intellectualism in section 1 above ensures. For the only reliable way to make oneself or anyone else a better person – and so someone who is good at getting happiness – is by means of Socratic dialectic. This also explains the policy of lying low politically, by and large ignoring political injustices inflicted on oneself and others, and instead engaging only in private conversations. As for the state, Socrates' idea seems to be that it is best that we love it, as it is best we love our parents; and where the state's commands (or our parents' commands), even if unjust, do not substantially interfere with this care for the soul, it will be best for us to obey those commands. Even when its commands do substantially interfere with care for the soul, it is best for us, as an expression of our love for the state (or of parents), to offer persuasion to it, prior to disobeying – as Socrates' behaviour at his trial leads us to expect he would if he were to disobey the command to stop philosophizing.

Such is the rationale for Socrates' somewhat submissive-looking attitude to commands from the state, and from one's parents, even when unjust to him and others, while at the same time announcing he will disobey any command to stop philosophizing.[49]

Two further points about Socrates' attitude to the state. First, it is arguable that Socrates' belief that it is best to lie low politically is continuous with Plato's belief that the only politics it is worth thinking about is utopian politics. Second, Socrates' view that one does best to stay out of politics is not to say that he does not accord to politicians such credit as is due to traffic engineers, public health officials, generals, cobblers or navigators. Socrates' point is merely (a) that navigators don't walk about on shore giving themselves airs as if their passengers had been made better

[49] The *Euthyphro* aims to cast doubt on a case of prosecuting one's father for murder. But surely Euthyphro's case against his father is, on any standard moral view, a pretty reasonable one. Why doesn't Plato choose a less ambiguous case? The case is only unambiguous, surely, on the assumption that it is good for one to love one's parents, and not coerce them, even when they have acted unjustly. (Cf. also *Prot.* 345e–346b.)

people by their transporting them safely (*Gorg*. 511d–512d); and that (b) it is *dangerous* to counsel the state. That danger the mature Plato also knew well – if only from the end of his 'older friend' Socrates (*Ep*. VII.324c–326b).

6 Conclusion

The differences between the approaches of Socrates and the mature Plato to politics do not reside in their attitudes to whether the central question of politics is about institutional arrangements, or rather about science. The notion of a science is central to both. The difference resides rather in a different place – the alleged existence of irrational desires which the mature Plato asserted against Socrates, with the consequent playing down of the Socratic concern for intellectual dialogue in one's relations with *all* others. Most of the Western philosophical tradition since Plato has, perhaps unfortunately, followed the mature Plato rather than Socrates on this point.

10

Approaching the *Republic*

MALCOLM SCHOFIELD

1 Introduction

Plato's shortish dialogue *Charmides* ends with the following sequence, initiated by a response on the part of Charmides to the question whether he thinks he needs the Socratic 'charm' which will cure the soul (176b–d):

> I am sure, Socrates, that I do need the charm, and as far as I am concerned, there is no obstacle to my being charmed by you daily, until you say that it is enough.
> Very good, Charmides, said Critias. If you do this *I* shall take this as a proof of your moderation – that is, if you allow yourself to be charmed by Socrates, and never desert him in things great or small.
> You may depend on my following and never deserting him, he said. If you who are my guardian command me, I should do very wrong not to obey you.
> And I do command you, he said.
> Then I will do as you command, and begin this very day.
> You there, I said, what are you two making plans about?
> We are not making plans, said Charmides. We've made them.
> Then you are about to use force, I said, without giving me the chance of a scrutiny?
> Yes, I shall use force, he said, since he orders me. In the face of this you had better plan what you will do.
> No plan is left open to me, I said. When you put your hand to action of any sort and are using force, there is no human being who can oppose you.
> Don't, then, he said; don't oppose me, not even you.
> I won't oppose you, then, I said.

On the surface these are light exchanges. But beneath there is menace. Given that Socrates' avowedly erotic interest in the young Charmides was a major preoccupation of the opening scene of the dialogue, it is hard to avoid taking its last few sentences as playing with the idea of rape. And given knowledge that Critias and Charmides were to be prominent members of the bloody junta known as the Thirty Tyrants, Charmides' use of language implying contempt for consultation and constitutional process (Jowett's translation has 'conspiring' for 'making plans'), and his appropriation of the vocabulary of diktat and violent confrontation, may plausibly be taken as hinting at his political future.

This passage may serve to illustrate the unexpected potential for political resonance which may lurk in the pages of virtually any Platonic dialogue, however apparently unpolitical its main themes. But sometimes the topic of a dialogue is more political than might initially be supposed. *Charmides* is itself a case in point. It could be read as purely or narrowly ethical in its focus on *sōphrosunē* (moderation). Yet that would be to miss its engagement with aristocratic pro-Spartan ideology. *Charmides* is among other things a critique of the claims of a complex of values epitomized by *sōphrosunē* understood as *kosmiotēs* (order (in behaviour)), *hēsuchiotēs* (quietness), *aidōs* (respect), *apragmosunē* (inactivity), whose political connotations are familiar e.g. from Thucydides' presentation of the Spartans.[1]

No less menacing are the final words Plato puts in Anytus' mouth at the conclusion of his conversation with Socrates in the interlude of *Meno* (94e–95a):

> *Anytus* You seem to me, Socrates, to be too ready to run people down. My advice to you, if you will listen to it, is to be careful. I dare say that in all cities it is easier to do people harm than good, and it is certainly so here, as I expect you know yourself.
>
> *Socrates* Anytus seems disgruntled, Meno, and I am not surprised. He thinks I am slandering our statesmen, and moreover he believes himself to be one of them. He doesn't know what slander really is: if he ever finds out he will stop being disgruntled.
>
> (trans. after Guthrie)

Plato foreshadows Socrates' prosecution for impiety by Anytus and Meletus under the restored democracy. There is nothing intrusive in this introduction of a political dimension into the discussion. The whole Anytus section has been designed to explore the general political implications of the question Socrates and Meno have been debating of whether virtue can be taught, and specifically to argue that if there *are* any teachers of virtue, they are not to be found among the leading statesmen of the

[1] Cf. North 1966: 95–107.

Athenian democracy in its great period: Themistocles, Aristides, Pericles, Thucydides son of Melesias.[2] Here is a theme taken up in other Platonic writings too – for example in *Protagoras*, whose inquiry into wisdom and virtue likewise has the same kind of political thrust, clearly exhibited in the stretch of the dialogue which includes Protagoras' Great Speech and the exchanges leading up to it.[3]

Thus Plato gives Socrates as interlocutors various key figures in political or more generally public life with whom his name was associated for better or worse; his discussions of virtue allude to crucial moments in the politics of late fifth-century Athens; and he indicates their critical bearing on the moral and intellectual foundations of aristocratic and particularly democratic ideology. No dialogue exemplifies this better than *Gorgias*.

2 *Gorgias* and *Menexenus*

Gorgias is an 'extraordinary production',[4] memorable above all for the explosive confrontation it stages between Callicles and Socrates: a clash between rhetoric and philosophy, between moral integrity and the pursuit of political power. The friction generates some unforgettable images. Socrates sees himself as a doctor judged by a jury of children, with a cook for prosecutor (521e). Callicles thinks his strong man is suppressed by the weak as lion cubs are tamed by their captors (483e–484a). But to Socrates the superman in his desires resembles the condemned in Hades trying to fill a sieve from a leaky jar (493a–c).

By contrast with the dialogues mentioned in the introductory section, *Gorgias* is much more explicitly focused on questions of political theory: for example, how best to run the city (520e), what sort of service (*therapeia*) to the city is appropriate (521a), who practises true political expertise (*politikē technē*) (521d)? Perhaps this directness in its engagement with politics – most strikingly illustrated by 'its passionate and outspoken criticism of Athenian politics and politicians from the Persian Wars to the disaster of 404 and the execution of Socrates five years later'[5] – is a function of its directness as a literary and philosophical artefact in general. *Gorgias* exhibits the 'simple mime' form of dialogue: no frame conversation, no ironic narrator, no elaborate cast of characters presented in a sub-

[2] The moral to be drawn is presumably one about the nature of democracy as such, which Plato decides – doubtless for a variety of reasons – to illustrate from the fifth century.

[3] See further Winton, in Ch. 4 section 1; Penner, in Ch. 9 section 4.

[4] Guthrie 1975: 294. Edition and commentary on the Greek text: Dodds 1959; translation with notes: Irwin 1979. Some representative discussions: Kahn 1983, Vickers 1988: ch. 2, Penner 1991, Yunis 1996: chs.5 and 6, Wardy 1996: ch. 3.

[5] Guthrie 1975: ibid.

tle pattern of relationships. It has little of the urbanity found in most of the rest of Plato's writing. After the opening conversation with Gorgias Socrates comes to speak 'of himself and his isolation in Athens with a passionate bitterness which strikes us as new (471e–472b)'.[6] Perhaps in no other dialogue (and certainly no 'early' dialogue) is Socrates so assertive and persistent in what is in essence a single line of argument. And Charles Kahn sees *Gorgias* as conceivably the only one in which we can penetrate Plato's cunning as a writer and 'read off the state of his thinking [i.e. at that moment]' from the work in front of us.[7]

Some readers have gone further. For them *Gorgias* 'reflects a personal crisis'.[8] This interpretation is articulated most eloquently by E. R. Dodds, author of the great modern edition of the dialogue:[9]

> In the light of the *Seventh Letter* . . . it is fairly clear that the *Gorgias* is more than an *apologia* for Socrates; it is at the same time Plato's *apologia pro vita sua*. Behind it stands Plato's decision to forgo the political career towards which both family tradition and his own inclinations (*Ep*.VII 325 e1) had urged him, and instead to open a school of philosophy. The decision was, as he tells us,[10] the outcome of a long internal struggle, and that struggle seems to have left its mark on certain pages of the *Gorgias*: we shall hardly be wrong in hearing an echo of it in Socrates' bitter words about the cloud of false witnesses from the best Athenian families whom Polus can call to prove him mistaken (472a–c); or in the sneer of Callicles at people who turn their backs on public life 'to spend the rest of their days whispering in a corner with three or four young lads' (485d); or in Socrates' final call to a new way of living, without which there can be no true statesmanship (527d–e).

Such conjecture must remain speculation. It does however fit fairly well with such other pointers as we have to the absolute date of *Gorgias*, at any rate if we suppose that Plato's final decision for philosophy and against politics as conventionally understood was reached between (say) five and ten years after the death of Socrates (399 BC). For around 389–387 he made his first visit to Sicily and south Italy, where he probably had his first serious exposure to Pythagoreanism and according to the *Seventh Letter* reflected further on politics: *Gorgias*, as perhaps the first of his dialogues both to betray Pythagorean influence and to deal explicitly with the

[6] Dodds 1959: 16. [7] Kahn 1988: 82. [8] Guthrie 1975: 296. [9] Dodds 1959: 31.

[10] Dodds' formulation here is misleading. What Plato decided after a period of despair and confusion, according to *Ep*. VII, was that philosophy, not political involvement, is the way to get a real understanding of political justice and that 'pertaining to private persons', and that philosopher rulers are the only cure for the ills of humanity (326a–b). Nothing is *said* about 'a school of philosophy'.

nature of politics, may have been composed soon after his return to Athens. Again, the dialogue closest to *Gorgias* in its preoccupation with democratic rhetoric is *Menexenus*, securely dated to just after the King's Peace of 387/6.[11]

It is time to leave the context and look at the text of *Gorgias*. Allusion has already been made to its nagging length. In three successive Socratic conversations the dialogue weaves into its discussion of rhetoric, the stated theme, increasingly elaborate and sometimes repetitive arguments on justice, happiness and the good. It culminates in a review of Athenian democracy, and the impotence of goodness in it, which is followed by an eschatological myth of divine judgment. The argumentative structure of *Gorgias* is accordingly intricate and complex. Its object is apparently straightforward – to achieve a correct understanding of what the opposition of rhetoric and philosophy really consists in, and to bring the reader to a choice between them (500c):

> You see that our arguments are about this, something even a person of small intelligence will be concerned for as the most serious of issues: how are we to live? Is it to be the life to which you summon me: those 'manly' activities – speaking before the populace and practising rhetoric and being a politician in the present mode? Or this life of philosophy?

And the key elements of the contrast as Plato works it out are simple enough. Yet the confrontation between the two positions raises in an acute form some fundamental problems in Plato's use of the dialogue form. If rhetoric and philosophy present incommensurable modes of thought and discourse, how can the common search for truth which Socratic conversation undertakes have any hope of success with interlocutors not committed to its methods or objects? If Socrates is to obtain any agreements with dedicated exponents of rhetoric, must he not resort either to logical trickery or to rhetorical stratagems of his own, devices which undermine the philosophical status of any such agreements?[12] Moreover the sequence of binary oppositions Socrates uses to differentiate philosophy from rhetoric has struck some readers as underargued.[13]

Plato does something to mitigate our disquiet by articulating contestation of the Socratic viewpoint. What gives *Gorgias* its unusual power and

[11] These remarks on dating follow the detailed treatment by Dodds 1959: 18–30.
[12] Not surprisingly *Gorgias* has been a favourite exemplar for interpreters who stress the *ad hominem* character of Socratic dialectic, and its consequent hospitability towards what other critics would regard as just fallacies: cf. e.g. Kahn 1983, McKim 1988.
[13] Cf. e.g. Vickers 1988: ch. 2.

life as a dialogue is the vigour with which an alternative conception of how rhetoric differs from philosophy is set out and developed in the speeches of the rhetorician Gorgias himself, his pupil Polus, and the Athenian politician Callicles, and has then to be resisted in each new version by a Socrates made to argue strenuously for his views, forging as he does so the conceptual machinery needed for the task. Roughly put, the alternative conception sees rhetoric as a supremely effective instrument of political power, essentially amoral and certainly – at any rate so far as Polus and Callicles are concerned – unconstrained by conventional views of right and wrong, the noble and the shameful. Callicles in fact claims that the exercise of power by those naturally equipped to use it is a more authentic form of virtue and indeed of justice than such views can begin to envisage. Philosophy, by contrast, is at worst logic-chopping (so Polus: 461b–c) or an inferior rhetoric (so Callicles: 482c–e), at best a liberal form of education (*paideia*) for the young, but not a pursuit suitable for a grown man (Callicles again: 485a–486d).

To the Platonic Socrates this is a gross *mis*conception. He will argue that rhetoric is no *technē* or expertise, despite its pretensions, but merely a knack of pleasing the people. It conveys only the illusion of power: it promotes the real interests neither of its practitioners nor of those they seek to manipulate. What philosophy discovers is paradoxically a true rhetoric (503a–b, 504d–e, 517a) and a true politics (521d). For politics in the true sense is a real *technē* capable of a rational account of what it cares for (500e–501a) – namely, the good of the soul (464b–c, 501b). Its object, pursued by legislation and the justice of the courts (464b–c), is to make the citizens good (513d–e, 521a–e). Socrates' arguments against the alternative analysis and for his own are inextricably intertwined. One key stratagem, crucial in each of his three conversations, is the manoeuvring of the interlocutor – whether by logic or 'shaming' or a combination of the two – into an admission that power *has* to be subject to the constraints of justice if it is really to be power. A grasp of what is admirable or again advantageous, requisite for the exercise of power, is shown under pressure to have an inescapable moral dimension.[14]

But Socrates also works hard on other terms at issue. Thus an important passage of the Polus section contends that we count as having power only if we do what we *want*, not what we *think* best: for we want for ourselves what is really good, not what only seems good.[15] So understood,

[14] But note the reservations expressed by Penner, Ch. 9 pp. 184–8 above, about how far the Socratic conception of justice is properly described as a 'moral' one.

[15] For fuller discussion of the distinction see Penner, in Ch. 9, pp. 165–6 above.

power turns on knowledge of good and bad, or of what happiness (*eudaimonia*) consists in. And Socrates then argues that it is not the excess of a tyrant like Archelaus of Macedon but only justice which brings happiness (466a–474c). Similarly, once the virtue of Callicles' superman is ultimately explicated as the courage and intelligence with which he satisfies whatever desires he happens to have (491e–492a), Socrates can characterize the Calliclean theory as crude hedonism. This then leads to a demonstration that, because the good and the pleasurable are quite different things, the superman cannot be guaranteed to achieve the good. That would require a *technē*, but all that is ever needed to acquire and produce pleasure is a knack born of habit and experience. Now the good produced by a *technē* is always a matter of order (*taxis*, *kosmos*). In the human soul this principle of order is moderation (*sōphrosunē*), which involves all the other virtues and therefore ensures a person's success and happiness. The intemperate are in truth *a*political beings, incapable of community and friendship. And they do not possess the only power worth having: the power of avoiding injustice (492a–508c).

So politics properly understood requires a true *technē* capable of making people good: wealth and empire are otherwise worthless. The history of Athens, and above all Periclean Athens, has been a disaster precisely because the leading politicians of the fifth century left the citizens worse – wilder and more unjust – than when they started. They practised neither the true *technē* of rhetoric just described nor even Callicles' rhetoric of flattery. For had they pandered successfully to popular appetite they would hardly have been rejected by the populace – as eventually happened to all of them. As for the present, the only practitioner of the genuine *politikē technē* alive in Athens is Socrates himself. But he will be condemned by the court. The Athenians will inevitably prefer the blandishments of rhetorical cuisine to the moral dieting and surgery in which Socrates is expert (511a–522e).

Scholars once liked to think that *Gorgias* was conceived as a reply to a manifesto or polemic by some contemporary writer, e.g. Isocrates or Polycrates, author of an *Accusation of Socrates* published some time after 394 BC.[16] But if there was a particular occasion which prompted the writing of the dialogue it is now irrecoverable. Besides Gorgias himself the author most clearly in Plato's sights is Thucydides.[17] Thucydides had anticipated Plato in representing the Athenian people as prey to the

[16] See further Dodds 1959: 27–30.

[17] The discussion in this and the next paragraph is due to Yunis 1996: chs.3–5. See also Winton, in Ch. 4 section 3; and Ober, in Ch. 6 section 4 above.

manipulation of orators who knew how to gratify its whims. This was in fact a commonplace of criticism of Athenian democracy, as is apparent, for example, from the Theban messenger's speech in Euripides' *Supplices* or the gross comedy of Aristophanes' *Knights*.[18] But nowhere is it more brilliantly summed up than in the rebuke to the *dēmos* Thucydides puts in the mouth of the politician Cleon (III.38.4–7):

> You are responsible [i.e. for the failure of deliberation], since you have instituted a bad kind of contest, you who are habitual spectators of speeches and audiences of deeds. . . . You are the best not only at being deceived by novelty in speech but also at refusing to follow a previous decision, slaves of each new oddity and suspicious of the familiar. And each of you wishes most of all to have the ability yourself, or failing that, in competition with those who speak with ability, not to be thought to lag behind them in wit, but to applaud a smart remark before it is out of the speaker's mouth. And as you are quick to perceive in advance what is being said so you are slow to foresee what will come of it, seeking (if I may say so) a world unlike the one we live in while thinking too little about present circumstances. In a word, overcome by the pleasure of listening you are more like spectators sitting to watch sophists than persons deliberating about a polis. (trans. after Yunis)

But for Thucydides things had been different under the leadership of Pericles. While the politicians who succeeded him 'began to surrender even policy-making at the people's pleasure' (II.65.10), Pericles' proud boast, wholeheartedly endorsed by Thucydides, was that he not only understood policy but instructed the people, for love of the city – and he was above trying to make money from it (II.60.5–6). Plato rejects this view of Pericles' oratory and of what he achieved by it. Early on in *Gorgias* he argues against the claim that rhetoric instructs the people. It merely persuades: instruction is the province of sciences or proper forms of expertise, such as arithmetic (453d–455a). When he turns to Pericles in particular he charges him with making the Athenians 'idlers and cowards, chatterers and spongers, by initiating the practice of payment [i.e. for attendance on juries or in the assembly]' (515e). The implication is that Thucydides was right to think that the Athenian democracy became degenerate, but wrong to blame this on the post-Periclean generation of politicians. The seeds of corruption were sown by Pericles and his illustrious predecessors.

Plato's dissent from Thucydides' evaluation of Pericles' oratory is made

[18] Euripides *Supplices* 409–25, Aristophanes *Knights* 752–5, 904–11, 1111–20, 1207–13, 1355–7, with Yunis 1996: ch. 2.

all but explicit in *Menexenus*, best interpreted as a companion piece to *Gorgias*.[19] This short dialogue begins in sarcastic vein, as Socrates greets young Menexenus as he comes from observing a meeting of the Athenian Council (234a–b):

> Evidently you think you're at an end of education and philosophy, and having got what you need in that department have it in mind to go on to greater things, and are planning to rule over us older people – at your age: so that your household will never fail to provide an overseer for us.

Menexenus had in fact been trying to find out who had been chosen to deliver the annual speech for the war dead. Socrates' sarcasm flows on unabated (234c):

> My dear Menexenus, dying in battle has to be a fine thing many times over. The deceased gets a fine and splendid funeral, even if he was a poor man. Again, he will have had his praises sung, though he may be no good, by men of wisdom, who deliver not random words of praise but long-prepared speeches.

And so on. The audience on such occasions – including, supposedly, Socrates himself – get carried away; and because the speakers include in their eulogies the city itself and its living citizens, 'their praises make me feel very grand, and I am always carried out of myself as I listen and am bewitched by their charms, and all in a moment I think myself to have grown bigger and grander and finer than I was' (235a–b).

'Such is the dexterity of our orators' (235c) – but according to Socrates it is actually quite easy to do. And he proceeds to offer a piece he claims he has learned off by heart from his teacher Aspasia, the courtesan who was Pericles' partner. Recitation of this pastiche oration takes up most of the rest of the dialogue. It was inspired, Socrates says, partly by Pericles' funeral speech (which he alleges was really written by Aspasia, however). Another, and even more important, source is Lysias' showpiece *Epitaphios* or *Funeral Speech*. Plato outperforms Lysias by doing what he tries to do better, but also by driving the same stock themes to the point of absurdity (although in this genre it is not altogether clear when such a point is reached). The best illustration is the treatment of Athenian defeats at the hands of Sparta. According to both Lysias and Thucydides' Pericles these are to be put down simply to Athenian disunity, not to any failure of courage or skill. *Menexenus* then takes the next step, and argues that since Athens was not defeated by others, but only by itself, the city does not

[19] For *Menexenus* see e.g. Vlastos 1964, Guthrie 1975: 312–23, Loraux 1986. The present discussion is based on a draft by Christopher Rowe.

only have a reputation for invincibility – it actually is invincible.[20] W. K. C. Guthrie's verdict on Plato's purpose is or should be incontrovertible: 'as by argument in the *Gorgias*, so here by example, by faithfully following the spirit and method of the traditional *epitaphios*, he has warned of the dangers of an eloquence that poisons the soul by flattery'.[21]

3 *Republic*: a sketch

Republic's date of composition is not known with any exactness.[22] A work of such vast scale probably took several years to write. The *Seventh Letter* (327e–328c) suggests that the dialogue's key idea of philosopher rulers was already in Plato's mind by the time of his first visit to Sicily (389–387 BC), and known at least to his intimates before his second visit (c.367). A common and plausible inference is that *Republic* was composed and circulated at some time between the two visits. If a good number of the early dialogues are to be dated to the 380s, and if *Symposium* and *Phaedo* also predate *Republic*, composition in the mid to late 370s seems as good a guess as any.

Republic is a misnomer: the Latin origins of the title deriving ultimately from Cicero's attempt to emulate Plato in his *de Re Publica*, 'On the commonwealth'. The Greek name of the dialogue is *Politeia*. '*Politeia*' is the standard word for constitution or political system or ordering of the political structure. So 'political order' would give a better sense of what Plato has in mind. There is a further and deeper complication. It quickly becomes apparent that the dialogue is primarily an inquiry into justice (*dikaiosunē*), conceived as a virtue or moral excellence of individual persons: the disposition to do what is right or fair, or more broadly to act morally. The philosophical task *Republic* undertakes is the project of showing that justice so conceived is in the best interests of the just person, even if it brings nothing ordinarily recognizable as happiness or success, or indeed (as with the sentence of death passed on Socrates) quite the opposite. Thus *Republic* carries forward the thinking about justice begun in earlier writings of Plato such as *Apology*, *Crito* and *Gorgias*. Why, then, the title's suggestion that it is a work of political rather than moral philosophy (if for the present we permit ourselves the use of this contestable dichotomy)?

[20] See Loraux 1986: 140–1. The idea is especially ironic, as she points out, given that for Plato being defeated or over-mastered by oneself is the *worst* that can happen to a person.

[21] Guthrie 1975: 320.

[22] Edition and commentary on the Greek text: Adam 1963. Translations are numerous: see e.g. Bloom 1968, Cornford 1941, Grube (rev. Reeve) 1992, Lindsay 1935, Shorey 1930. Introductory studies include Annas 1981, White 1979.

The setting of the dialogue, established on the very first page, already perhaps implicates the promise of the title in ambiguity. The conversation of *Republic* takes place in a house not in Athens itself, but in Piraeus, the port and economic centre, where Socrates becomes for the time being the half-unwilling guest of Cephalus, not a citizen but a wealthy resident alien (in the arms manufacture business), and his son Polemarchus. The most vocal member of the company assembled is a visiting sophist, Thrasymachus of Chalcedon. However when Socrates turns to explicit discussion of what a city is in Book II, his partners in discussion are Plato's brothers Glaucon (with whom he travelled to Piraeus) and Adeimantus (whom they have encountered on the road in Polemarchus' company): i.e. aristocratic Athenian citizens. These circumstances invite the question: is politics to be at the centre or the periphery of the dialogue?[23]

One way of answering this question is to attend to the formal structure of *Republic*. After Book I, an inconclusive Socratic dialogue which nonetheless introduces, particularly in the conversation with Thrasymachus, many of the themes pursued in the rest of the work, the interlocutors agree to take an indirect approach to the problem of individual justice: they will consider the nature of justice and injustice in the polis, in the hope that it will provide an illuminating analogy. Books II-IV spell out the class structure required in a 'good city'. It is suggested that in such a community political justice consists in the social harmony achieved when each class (economic, military, governing) performs its own and only its own function.This model is then applied to the individual soul. Justice and happiness for an individual are secured when each of the corresponding parts of the soul (appetite, emotion, reason) performs the role it should in mutual harmony. In working out the idea of psychic harmony Plato formulates a conception of the complexity of psychological motivation, and of the structure of mental conflict, which leaves the simplicities of Socratic intellectualism far behind, and has reminded interpreters of Freudian theory, particularly in Books VIII–IX. Here he examines different forms of *un*just political order (notably oligarchy, democracy, and at greatest length tyranny) and corresponding conditions of order, or rather increasing *dis*order, in the soul.

Political theory therefore plays a large part in the main argument of the dialogue, even though the ultimate focus is the moral health of the soul, as is confirmed by the conclusion of Book IX and by the second half of Book X, which brings the dialogue as a whole to an end. In the last pages of Book

[23] So Brunschwig 1986.

IX Plato returns again to the comparison of the lives of the just and the unjust person, and has Socrates claim that on a variety of counts it is now clear that the just life is incomparably happier than the unjust. Socrates suggests that it may not matter whether we can actually establish a truly just political order, provided we use the idea of it as a paradigm for founding a just city within our own selves. In Book X he says to his interlocutor: 'Yet we haven't discussed the greatest rewards and prizes that have been proposed for virtue' (608c). And with this a proof of the immortality of the soul is launched, by way of prelude to the final eschatological myth, which is designed first to warn of divine judgment, with heavenly bliss assured for the just but gruesome punishment in hell for the unjust; and then to intimate that after that there will come a moment of choice for every soul (617d–e):

> Here is the message of Lachesis, the maiden daughter of Necessity: 'Ephemeral souls, this is the beginning of another cycle of mortal generation that will end in death. Your guardian spirit (*daimōn*) will not be assigned to you by lot: you will choose your guardian spirit. The one who draws the first lot must be the first to choose a life which will always by necessity be with him. Virtue knows no master. Depending on whether a person accords it honour or dishonour, each will possess it to a greater or lesser degree. The responsibility lies with the chooser. The god has none.' (trans. after Grube (rev. Reeve))

This account of *Republic* has left out the central Books V–VII. They explore the notion of political order (purportedly by way of digression) much further than is on the face of it necessary for the purposes of inquiry into individual justice. This is where Plato develops the notion of a communistic governing class, involving the recruitment of talented women as well as men, the abolition of the family, and institution of a centrally controlled eugenic breeding programme. And it is where, in order to meet the problem of how the idea of the just city he has been elaborating might ever be put into practice, he has Socrates introduce philosopher rulers (473c–d):

> Unless either philosophers rule in our cities or those whom we now call kings and potentates engage genuinely and adequately in philosophy, and political power and philosophy coincide, there is no end, my dear Glaucon, to troubles for our cities, nor I think for the human race.

What Plato has in mind when he makes Socrates speak of troubles is in the first instance civil war (e.g. 421c–423d, 462a–b, 545d–e), but doubtless also the corruption fuelling it. As Socrates goes on to acknowledge

(494a–497b), such corruption makes the emergence of an upright philosopher ruler an improbability – and incidentally leaves highly questionable the prospects of anyone but a Socrates developing moral order in the soul when society without is infected with moral disorder.

Here we touch on another broadly political preoccupation of *Republic*, worked out at various places in the dialogue. It offers among other things a radical critique of Greek cultural norms. This is highlighted in the censorship of Homer proposed in Books II and III, and in the onslaught on the poets, particularly the dramatists, in Book X, and their expulsion from the ideal city. But these are only the more memorable episodes in a systematic attack on Greek beliefs about gods, heroes and the departed; on contemporary music, dance and gymnastics and their ethical basis; on the morality of erotic courtship; and on medical and judicial practice. *Republic* substitutes its own austere state educational programme, initially focused on the training of the emotions, but subsequently (in Books VI and VII) on mathematics and philosophy. Plato sees no hope for society or the human race without a wholesale reorientation, fostered by an absolute political authority, of all the ideals on which we set our hearts and minds.

Interpreters otherwise as far apart from each other as Karl Popper and Leo Strauss see *Republic* as a profoundly conservative work.[24] The conception of politics it recommends is of course anti-democratic through and through; and it offers a regressive view of human society, if the idea of a rigidly controlled, hierarchically ordered community closed to social or political innovation, where the political elite do not engage in economic activity, is to be judged a forlorn attempt to return to the illusory securities of some imaginary past. But Plato's recipe cannot plausibly be represented as conservative without a huge exercise in deconstruction of his text. There is little *Republic* would preserve either of existing political structures (no Greek city was governed by a meritocratically selected intellectual elite) or of conventional moral beliefs and practices. The dialogue is itself written in such a way as to require the reader to be continually shifting and broadening perspectives on the huge range of concerns it embraces, from the banalities of its opening conversation between Socrates and the aged Cephalus to its Platonist explication of the very notion of philosophy in the epistemology and metaphysics of Books V–VII. At the apex of the whole work Plato sets his presentation of the Form of the Good, as the ultimate goal of the understanding that philoso-

[24] See Popper 1962, vol. I, Strauss 1964, Wood and Wood 1978.

phy pursues by use of the hypothetical method. *Republic* offers a metaphor of its own progress in the potent symbol of the cave. We are like prisoners chained underground, who can see only shadows of images flickering on the wall. What we need is release from our mental shackles, and a conversion which will enable us gradually to clamber out into the world above and the sunlight. For then, by a sequence of painful reorientations, we may be able to grasp the Good and understand how it explains all there is.

In sum, it is as though Plato is saying: if you want to think properly about justice, think radical thoughts about everything else first. While discussion of the city in Book II is formally introduced to illuminate the justice of the individual, it turns into a theoretical prescription for the transformation of society. Yet this project itself provokes further questions which launch the more ambitious intellectual journey of Books V–VII. The dialogue eventually returns to its starting point. But the philosopher who has fed on the vision of the Good will inevitably approach the issue of what good there is in justice with a different mindedness from someone still working with the notion of advantage to an individual which was used in setting the terms of the original problem.

The more detailed and lightly annotated account of *Republic* which now follows makes no attempt to introduce or debate all the issues of political theory raised in or by the dialogue, although some are signposted in footnotes. It focuses on the way Plato presents his fundamental problem about justice, and then makes some suggestions as to how the principal stretches of text devoted to speculation about the polis may be read as designed to unfold – gradually and circuitously – an answer to that problem.

4 The problem

The problem is first articulated in Book I, whose argumentative style is quite unlike that of the rest of *Republic*.[25] It is a 'Socratic' elenctic dialogue in which the views of a sequence of interlocutors are cross-examined and found wanting by Socrates, in the manner familiar from e.g. *Laches* and *Charmides*, to say nothing of *Protagoras* and *Gorgias*. The book does not end in formal *aporia*. But although it concludes with agreement between Socrates and Thrasymachus that the just are happy and the unjust miserable, and that there is no advantage in being miserable, only in happiness, the agreement is factitious – Thrasymachus does not mean

[25] On Book I see Lane, in Ch. 8, p. 155 n.4 above, and e.g. Annas 1981: ch. 2. For orientation on Thrasymachus' position: Chappell 1993, Algra 1996, Everson 1998.

the answers he gives. And anyway Socrates professes himself dissatisfied because they have been attempting to determine whether justice is wisdom or folly, and whether it is something profitable, making a person happy, before they know what it *is*.

Book 1's triad of interlocutors is reminiscent (no doubt designedly) of *Gorgias*. Cephalus is a senior figure released from the discussion more quickly than Gorgias, whose 'heir' Polus is matched by Cephalus' heir Polemarchus, a spokesman for the traditional 'help friends, harm enemies' conception of justice. The most striking parallel, however, is between Thrasymachus and Callicles. Like Callicles Thrasymachus makes a violent intrusion into the conversation, and like him he is sulking by the end of it, and refusing anything but token participation. As with Callicles, Thrasymachus' role is to be critic of the conventional respect for justice with which both associate Socrates. But the vantage point of the critique is different. Whereas Callicles espouses belief in a natural hierarchical justice which directs that the strong should rule the weak, Thrasymachus holds a cynical reductive view of all talk about justice. What he offers is a *commentary*, expressed in the language of *Realpolitik*, on the language of morality. With his intervention the moral argument of *Republic* accordingly takes an explicitly political turn.

Thrasymachus couches his account of justice in terms not of the personal virtue *dikaiosunē* but of *to dikaion*, the just. And when called upon to explicate his thesis that the just is nothing but the interest of the stronger, he gives a political analysis. Each kind of regime makes laws in its own interest, democracy democratic laws, tyranny tyrannical laws, and so on. So justice is the interest of the prevailing regime. For Thrasymachus there is nothing to be said for or even about morality as something constitutive of the identity of the individual – of what a person *is*. It is to be understood only as behaviour defined as according with laws imposed by the power of a political authority, and required by its interests (338c–339a).

Discussion of Thrasymachus' proposal continues the political focus. Questioned as to whether rulers can always identify their interests correctly, he insists that they do so insofar as they exercise a *technē* of rule (340d–341a). This opens the way for Socrates to probe his position on the nature of rule by asking whether *technai* in general promote the interests of others or only of their practitioners, and whether making money is an essential ingredient of the *technē* of ruling: themes that will recur as central preoccupations of later books of *Republic*. The debate reflects a fifth-century intellectual background – shared with *Gorgias* and most of Plato's early dialogues – in which it was taken for granted that any practice must count as exercise of a *technē* if it is to be regarded as a serious and effective human pursuit.[26] Socrates and Thrasymachus conduct their discussion almost wholly by means of analogies. For example, to the other-regarding focus of medicine Thrasymachus opposes the self-interest of sheep-farming (341c–347a). Although Plato gives Socrates the last word, most readers are left doubting that this is the best way to try to settle what sort of practice ruling is.

Book I ends with a sequence of swift and sometimes tricksy arguments deployed by Socrates against Thrasymachus' further claim that '*in*justice [subsequently renamed *euboulia*, good judgment] on a sufficiently large scale is stronger, more indicative of freedom, and more masterful than justice [*dikaiosunē*, construed as law-abiding behaviour]' (344c). That claim is supported by an analysis with a strong political orientation once more. In the restatement of Thrasymachus' position offered by Glaucon at the beginning of Book II, the myth of Gyges' ring makes it clear that what he has in mind in his praise of injustice is admiration for free-riders exploiting general acquiescence in the rule of law. Thrasymachus himself argues that the ultimate free-rider is the tyrant: someone who by the ambition and success of his exploitation of the system actually seizes supreme power, enslaves the citizens, and is generally admired and thought happy on account of the perfection of his injustice (344a–c).

Glaucon's version of Thrasymachus' position introduces the notion of a social contract (358e–359b).[27] This turns it into a more articulate theory than it sounded when enunciated by Thrasymachus himself. The theory presents an *a priori* account of the origins of law, and so of justice conceived of as obedience to law. It can best be presented by consideration of the matrix below, which represents the order of preference a rational agent will opt for – according to this view – in ranking various possible patterns of behaviour in his interactions with others:

	My behaviour to others	*Their behaviour to me*
1.	Wrongdoing	Non-retaliation
2.	Refraining from wrongdoing	Refraining from wrongdoing
3.	Non-retaliation	Wrongdoing

Rational persons would prefer (1) to (2) because what is good by nature is pursuit of one's own self-interest, if necessary at the expense of the inter-

[26] See e.g. Schaerer 1930, O'Brien 1967: ch. 2, Irwin 1995; ch. 5, Parry 1996; also Penner, in Ch. 9 section 3 above.
[27] The account of it offered here is due to Denyer 1983. For the fifth-century background, see Winton, in Ch. 4 section 1 above; also Taylor, in Ch. 5 above.

ests of others. But weakness and necessity dictate (2) as the pattern they will aim for in most circumstances. For opportunities to realize (1) are few and far between: ordinarily individuals are not in a strong enough position to commit wrong against others without suffering retaliation. And if (2) is not secured, there is the likelihood that sooner or later a situation will arise in which (3) is the outcome. But (3) is to be avoided at all costs, since the badness of suffering wrong far exceeds the good which is achieved by committing it. So in order to guard against (3) rational persons will strike an agreement that each will refrain from wrongdoing on the understanding that everyone else will do the same, that is, a contract to ensure (2). The proof that (1) nonetheless reflects what human nature pursues as good, as opposed to the merely conventional good of equal treatment represented by (2), is apparent if we consider how people *would* behave if they *were* strong enough to do wrong against others without suffering retaliation (359b–360d). Someone like Gyges, who had the power of making himself invisible at will, would opt for (1) simply because he knew he could consistently accomplish it. In short, he would exploit the system as a free-rider.[28]

The Gyges scenario leads Glaucon into a comparison between the lives of the just and the unjust person which will be the underlying preoccupation of the whole of the rest of *Republic*. He takes extreme cases of each. The unjust man is imagined as someone who like Gyges has all the power and resources he needs to achieve his ends, and who additionally enjoys the reputation of justice. The just person, by contrast, is supposed to have a reputation for injustice, and to be the victim of every conceivable physical outrage, culminating in crucifixion. Which is the happier?

Glaucon's arguments are supplemented by a detailed examination by Adeimantus of popular attitudes to just and unjust behaviour (362e–367e). The scrutiny is designed to show that they betray no conviction whatever that being just is intrinsically desirable. First, there is a preoccupation with the *reputation* justice or injustice brings: the consequences – in this life or the next – of being *thought* just or unjust are their principal concern. Second, ordinary people and poets alike qualify both their endorsement of justice and their criticism of injustice by stressing that the one is hard and irksome, the other sweet and easy and more profitable. The vicious are admired, if wealthy and powerful, the weak and poor dishonoured even if virtuous. Third and most strikingly, the

[28] For Thrasymachus, of course, all ruling powers of whatever complexion are successful free-riders.

gods are thought to smile on the wicked but send misfortunes to the good. And religion has invented mechanisms by which we can be absolved from any injustice we may have committed (366a):

> If we are just, our only gain is not to be punished by the gods, since we lose the profits of injustice. But if we are unjust, we get the profits of our crimes and transgressions, and afterwards persuade the gods by prayer and escape without punishment. (trans. Grube (rev. Reeve))

From all this any young person would conclude that the best strategy for life is to cultivate the illusion of being just but practice injustice.

Plato has both Glaucon and Adeimantus indicate the strategic role within the dialogue of these reformulations of Thrasymachus' case. Their interventions have been designed not to advance a thesis to which they are themselves committed, but to elicit from Socrates a much stronger statement of his opposing viewpoint than he presented in Book 1. He is requested to praise justice for itself, not for its consequences or its reputation. For he has agreed that on his view it is the sort of good which is to be pursued on its own account as well as because of what results from it, and not merely – as the contractarian analysis claims – something unwillingly practised as a necessity. More specifically, what is wanted is argument to show 'what each [i.e. both justice and injustice] is, and what power it has simply by itself if it is in the *soul*' (358b; emphasis mine), or 'what effect for good or ill each exerts on the person who has it, simply by itself' (367b). This is the challenge to which the remaining 250 pages of *Republic* are a response. Its focus is on the individual and the soul. But an adequate response to Thrasymachus' treatment of justice could hardly avoid addressing political issues too.

5 The response: (i) a first model

The challenge Glaucon and Adeimantus throw down is developed over ten pages of taut, sophisticated, lucidly organized and deadly serious philosophical argumentation. The view of justice it encapsulates goes back to the sophists, particularly Antiphon's *On Truth* and the *Sisyphus* fragment.[29] But Plato has borrowed it for his own dialectical purposes and – we may guess – brilliantly elaborated its theoretical structure and rhetorical presentation. Both the matter and the manner of the reply he puts in Socrates' mouth come as something of a shock.

29 See Winton, in Ch. 4 section 1 above.

We might have expected a resumption of the Socratic cross-examination of interlocutors which dominated Book I. Instead Socrates shifts into a speculative mode which is sustained for the whole of the rest of the dialogue. It would be hard to conceive a greater contrast either with the elenchus or with Glaucon and Adeimantus' procedure. Where they presented a disciplined and tightly focused set of arguments, Socrates – to confine ourselves for the moment just to Books I–III – embarks on a rambling, largely descriptive story of what a good city might be like, and what education and living arrangements would be appropriate for the 'guards' or military specialists who are to conduct its military operations and (as emerges subsequently) to govern it. The point and overall coherence of the story are in some respects obscure. In places it seems distinctly arbitrary. And some of its claims and proposals can hardly be meant seriously. At one point – later on, in Book VII – Socrates is given the mildly self-critical comment: 'I forgot that we were playing' (536c). Play seems an apt description for what he offers us. Plato is effectively asking us to relax our minds: to forget for the time being the fierce stringencies of proof and counter-proof, and to ask ourselves instead 'What if . . .', chasing a few hares down apparent by-ways if the mood so takes us. The rationale of this way of proceeding will presumably emerge only later.

Socrates' decision to talk first about the city is also a surprise. His mission as described in *Apology* was focused on care of the soul. And that focus is apparent both in early dialogues in general and in Plato's previous writings on political themes: notably *Crito* and *Gorgias*. Book I of *Republic* had ended with discussion of justice as what makes the soul perform its function well. So when Glaucon and Adeimantus asked for a demonstration of the power justice has in itself in the soul, they and we were expecting something quite different from what we get. Socrates offers an analogy to justify talking first about the city. If something written in small letters is hard to make out, the situation can be retrieved if one finds the same message written in larger letters on a larger surface. Armed with a grasp of the large version, readers are equipped to return to the small letters and check whether they are the same. So with justice. A city can be characterized by justice no less than an individual – but it is larger, and so perhaps there is more justice in it than in the individual, and easier to make out. This argument is not very convincing. It threatens to beg the question whether justice as predicated of a city is the same sort of thing as justice in an individual. And the idea that there might be *more* justice in the city than in an individual in some interesting and relevant sense is ill-defined, to say the least. But perhaps we should put our doubts on hold, and turn to look at the first of the models Plato invites us to play with.[30]

He certainly has Socrates begin with a fundamental question: why is it that cities come to be in the first place? Socrates gives a simple answer. Humans are not self-sufficient, but have many needs requiring satisfaction if they are to lead a civilized life (369c):

> Because people need many things, and because one person calls on a second out of one need and on a third out of a different need, many people gather in a single place to live together as partners and helpers. And to this common settlement we give the name of city. (trans. after Grube (rev. Reeve))

Socrates then imagines that he and his interlocutors are to construct a city 'in *logos*' – i.e. in speech or theory. In setting about this task the key principle he calls in aid is the notion of specialization. The *optimal* way of satisfying our many needs is to collect together specialists in (and only in) the relevant crafts and skills. This is because a specialist with a natural gift for his craft will do a better job more efficiently than a non-specialist, or than someone practising more than one craft.

It initially appears that at the limit an extremely small community indeed could meet at any rate basic needs: (1) a farmer, a builder, a weaver, and a shoemaker would perhaps suffice. But further reflection on the principle of specialization suggests that this conception of what one might call the minimal city is unstable. For production of the tools required by those producing the basic necessities of civilized life must – by that principle – be put in the hands of (2) a second wave of specialists: smiths, carpenters, herdsmen, etc. (2) in its turn similarly dictates the need for (3) exporters and importers, since the numbers in the city who will be required to practise all the specializations already generated can probably not be supported by local resources alone. But the existence of (3) exporters and importers generates a further need, for (4) many more farmers and other craftsmen to supply home and overseas consumers. And (4) will in turn create the need for coinage and the market. Hence (5) middlemen will be required to operate the market, which provides the conditions for (6) labourers offering the use of their bodies for pay. Adeimantus is invited to agree that their city is now 'complete' (*telea*: 371e).

What are we to take to be Plato's point – relative to the strategic objects

[30] The treatment of the 'economic city' which follows draws on Schofield 1993. Its role in Plato's argument has often been found puzzling: see e.g. Annas 1981, 77–9.

of the dialogue – in developing this dazzling and dazzlingly original set of ideas? They constitute the invention of something like the concept of an economy: a sort of transcendental deduction of the market. But that has been little noticed by the commentators. And in a way they are right not to notice it. Nothing in *Republic* or any other dialogue suggests that Plato thought understanding the economy was a project to be undertaken for its own sake, as something of independent importance.

A better assessment construes the passage as proleptic and provocative in a variety of ways.[31] First for consideration is its bearing on the question of justice. This point is in fact raised explicitly by Socrates as soon as Adeimantus has said 'Perhaps' to the suggestion that the city is now complete (371e–372a):

> Where are justice and injustice to be found in it? With which of the things we examined did they come in?
> I've no idea, Socrates, unless it was somewhere in some need that these people have of one another. (trans. Grube (rev. Reeve))

The reader can be more specific than Adeimantus, and pinpoint the passage which introduces the principle of specialization. This can be formulated as the rule (S) that, where people need the products others make or supply, it is best that each stick to one task or function for which his natural capacities best equip him. Rule (S) anticipates the principle which Book IV will make the essence of justice in city and soul alike. Indeed Socrates there refers back to our passage, when he suggests that the answer to the question of justice 'seems to have been rolling around at our feet from the very beginning, and we didn't see it' (432d), and then points specifically to the rule 'that everyone must practise one of the occupations in the city for which his nature is best suited' (433a). Doing one's own job – and not meddling with what isn't – turns out to be what justice consists in. Why does Plato not clinch this definition when he first proposes the rule, in his account of the economy? Doubtless because other occupations besides the economic – military and governing functions – need to be introduced before he has in place a political structure which will permit the analogy with the structure of the soul to be developed in his theory of individual justice. And as we shall see, he also has other issues he wishes to pursue before he gets to that point. For the present a hint that discussion of the economy is relevant to the problem of justice will suffice for his purposes.

[31] For the general approach cf. Vegetti 1995: 11–18.

Is the economic community Socrates has described an *ideal* city? This is a second problem raised by the passage, and pursued rather more insistently by Plato in the immediate context than the first, although again the reader is left to do much of the real work. He has Socrates give – tongue in cheek – a rosy account of the life the citizens will enjoy, in terms designed to recall myths of the golden age of Kronos (372a–d). Glaucon knows his leg is being pulled, and breaks into the discussion wondering whether there might not be a little relish in the diet, and the whole business of eating made more comfortable by the introduction of couches and tables. This suggestion is greeted by a comic explosion on Socrates' part. He construes Glaucon's remarks as a request for a city devoted to luxury, infected with the disease of injustice, and in a sort of mocking echo of the *Kulturgeschichte* invention motif found for example, in Aeschylus' *Prometheus*, he pretends this is the occasion for introducing a great range of 'superfluous' arts, no longer focused on the necessities of civilized life. He lists e.g., painters, musicians, poets, rhapsodes, actors, dancers, theatrical agents, the makers of cosmetics; wet-nurses, dry-nurses, beauticians, barbers, cooks, confectioners, doctors. After this outburst the argument settles into a less playful tone, initiated by the observation that a city which is intent on unlimited acquisition of possessions will inevitably be expansionist (372e–373e). Hence the origins of war (373e). The passage as a whole is too brief and rhetorical to furnish a deep insight into injustice. Yet we register the implication that uncontrolled appetites are the source of the fever that grips the luxurious city.

The notion that the economic city was a model of rustic simplicity and a paradigm of moral health is fantasy. What Socrates' account of it really showed – and was evidently designed to show – was that adoption of principle (S) has an inexorable dynamic. At first sight it seems to permit derivation of just a minimal community existing in order to satisfy the basic needs of civilized living. But given continued adherence to the principle, it is hard to see why the minimal community should not expand into a large urban centre dominated by international trade and a market for wage labour. The pretence that a society with a developed market economy would be the ideal community of the golden age is, as Cornford said, 'a satire on sentimental nostalgia for a supposed primitive state of nature'.[32] By suggesting that the city is 'complete' with the introduction of retailers and wage-earners 'whose minds wouldn't at all qualify them for membership in our community, but whose bodies are strong enough

[32] Cornford 1941: 59.

for labour' (371e), Socrates already signals the impossibility of any unambiguous appraisal of the society he has described.

A third issue is the theoretical status of his account. It omits mention of much that users of the word 'polis' might have regarded as essential to a city: fortifications and a military capability, religion, governmental functions, provision for participation in political and judicial decisions. Nor is there any attempt to locate the family and the reproduction of the species within its framework. Contemporary readers acquainted with earlier political theory might have experienced a sharper shock. Protagoras' account of the origins of civilization in *Protagoras* (321c–323a), which may be modelled by Plato on sophistic sources,[33] describes the fundamental industrial achievements of early man in terms echoed verbally here, but sees them like religion as *pre-existing* the foundation of cities. For Protagoras cities are impossible without military and political skills. Thus *Republic*'s economic city excludes what is plausibly regarded in *Protagoras* as indispensable to the polis, and includes what *Protagoras* treats no less plausibly as prepolitical.

The game Plato is playing here is not easy to make out. Commentators agree that the talk of the city coming into being (369a) does not indicate any *a priori* historical reconstruction or genetic analysis of the origins of civilization or the city-state. As Cornford pointed out,[34] when Plato offers a speculative historical account of the origins of laws and constitutions in Book III of *Laws* it follows a quite different sequence, and is based on an almost wholly distinct set of ideas. So we need not infer from the introduction of the guards *after* the city is complete that he believes war and the development of military arts postdated that of economic activity. If its significance is not diachronic, does Plato intend to suggest some logical or theoretical relationship between war and economy? For example that an economy devoted exclusively to the satisfaction of basic needs has no aggressive dynamic (373b–c), in contrast to one programmed for luxury and the unlimited acquisition of possessions, which will inevitably involve hostile designs on the territory of other communities (372e–373e)? This certainly corresponds better to the text. But it will not do as the full story, or even as the most important part of it. We may leave aside the implausibility of supposing that it is demand only for luxury items from abroad, not the need for foreign supplies of more basic products, which will be likely to provoke war. More important is that nothing in Plato's subsequent discussion of the guards presupposes an economy

[33] For discussion see e.g. Cole 1967, Guthrie 1969, Kerferd 1981.

[34] Cornford 1941: 59.

focused on luxury. On the contrary, at one point in his account of the puritanical regime proposed for their education he has Socrates remark that the interlocutors have been purging what they earlier described as a city of luxury (399e). This is strictly a *non sequitur*, since it was *not* the military, by Plato's argument, which conceived the appetite for high living in the first place, but those they exist to protect. The *non sequitur* simply reinforces the sense that the introduction of the warrior after the economic class does not really have much to do with a theoretical concern about the relationship between economy and war.[35]

It seems best to conclude that Plato must have been well aware that his isolation of an economic city in the particular terms he specifies was no more than a highly abstract and artificial model of one dimension of human social activity. These features of the model indicate the sort of role it will really play in his argument, that is, in helping to spell out the nature of justice. It is ill-designed to function as an ideal to which we should try to conform ourselves: it articulates a limited system of relationships, not an imitable pattern of living. But these limitations on its scope are just what make it an excellent paradigm to think with.

6 The response: (ii) a causal story

The principle of specialization requires that if the city has to be prepared for wars, there must be a specialist class trained to conduct them. These specialists are named 'guards', and indeed Plato works out a number of his key theses about them by pursuing the analogy with guard *dogs*. But while the role of the guards in fighting wars against external enemies is never forgotten in his account, it is not its dominant feature. Plato's hugely extended treatment (375–412) of how guards should be educated does not make specifically military virtues or skills its focus. And in the pages immediately following it, the notion of guarding is subjected to some deft manipulation which results in a significantly different understanding of the whole idea.[36]

The most important form of behaviour now designated 'guarding' turns out to be rule or government, apparently conceived above all as

[35] According to Clay 1988: 26, in making discussion of the good city begin with the introduction of luxury and war Plato 'suggests that an initial act of injustice lies at the foundations of Kallipolis', and so 'forces upon us' (ibid.28) the question of 'how it is that political philosophy is possible only in an unjust society'. But such alleged deconstructive implications are never touched on subsequently in *Rep.*

[36] For a full discussion of this section of *Rep.* see Nettleship 1914: ch. 5, Barker 1918: ch. 9 (who rightly stresses its Spartan affinities), Vegetti 1995: 261–356.

taking precautions against the acquisition by citizens of the power to mount an *internal* threat to the wellbeing of the city. The specialists who were originally called guards are now seen as younger people, whose military role is redefined as 'assisting and helping the decisions of the rulers' (414b). Rulers themselves are to be chosen from among the guards in general, on account of intellectual and moral qualities which make them the 'best guards of the conviction they have that they must do whatever they judge best for the city' (413c), and in this sense good guards of *themselves* and their education. For that is what makes a person 'most useful both to himself and to the city' (413a). In other words, new forms of activity are recognized as exemplifying guarding; and in the end guarding as an activity is reinterpreted as an expression of guarding construed as a reflexive psychological disposition.

This pattern of analysis, moving from external to internal, effect to cause, behaviour to disposition, is typical of Plato's treatment of the guards, inasmuch as the emphasis of the entire account falls on their qualities of soul.[37] Plato frames his discussion with two passages which both dwell on the need for guards to possess innate opposite characteristics of gentleness (reflecting a philosophical impulse) and fierceness (an emotional quality) requiring to be harmonized (375a–376d, 410a–412a). He thereby signals his intention to make the problem of harmonization, initially presented as intractable, the leading issue to be addressed by his educational proposals. And he thus foreshadows the eventual definition of individual justice as psychic harmony, although harmony embracing the appetitive as well as the rational and emotional parts of the soul. So the method of studying the city in the hopes of understanding justice in the soul turns out to be a suppler and more complex procedure than might initially have been supposed. Both the model of the economic city and the proposed educational programme for the guards contribute to that end, but in quite different ways.

The explicit suggestion at the outset of the educational section, however, is that discussion of education will help us to see how justice and injustice arise in the *city* (376c–d). *What* help it gives towards this is not immediately apparent. Perhaps we should take Plato's emphasis to be on the causal *origins* of justice and injustice in the city. He makes Socrates comment early in the discussion that 'the beginning is the most important part of every enterprise' (377a). The context of this remark is concern over the myths children are taught when they are still young and malle-

[37] Cf. Lear 1992.

able. Myths mould them. The stories they take into the soul imprint a pattern upon it. Hence the sustained efforts Socrates makes to establish what are the right kinds of myth for children to hear, by way of a memorable critique of Homer and other poets. Its political rationale quickly becomes evident.[38]

The initial subjects of the critique are the accounts in Homer and Hesiod of war in heaven: the plots of one generation of gods against their predecessors, hatreds between individual deities, or enmities between gods and heroes and their kin generally. But those who are to guard the city must be got 'to hold the belief that it is shameful in the extreme to fall easily into mutual hatred' (378e). Stories like these must not be told – even if they were true – if future guards are to be persuaded 'that no citizen has ever been at enmity with another, and that such a thing would be an impiety' (ibid.). After his treatment of the guards' education is completed, Socrates suggests that it would be advisable for all the adult citizens to be told a 'splendid fiction that would, in the best case, persuade even the rulers, but if not, then the rest of the city' (414c) – or perhaps (Glaucon thinks) only later generations, i.e. when children and so susceptible to story-telling. This 'fiction' – sometimes translated 'noble lie' – is the charter myth of the city Socrates and the other interlocutors are 'founding', and is allegedly derived from Phoenician sources. Its principal theme is the natural brotherhood of all the citizens, since the myth will teach that all of them were 'fashioned and nurtured within the earth' (414d), and are all therefore children of one mother. There is then a rider explaining that nonetheless they belong to different classes because they are made of different metals, with the warning that the city will be ruined if those made of iron or bronze, and so fitted to be farmers or artisans, ever become guards. But the main point of attempting to inculcate belief in such a story is clear. It is to make the citizens 'care more for the city and each other' (415d).

Here, then, is a further set of hints about justice. It will turn out to be something brought about by the mutual care which produces social harmony. The fact that Plato intimates this conclusion in his treatment of fiction and its uses in moulding the human soul suggests an additional complexity: mutual care in a community will not come about unless people come to hold the deeply ingrained *belief* that that is the natural order of things. Confirmation that this is his drift comes in a later passage. When Socrates raises the question of how much detailed legislation the

[38] On the critique of poetry see e.g. Ferrari 1989.

interlocutors should devise for their city, he comments that it is all insignificant provided that the one great thing is 'guarded': education and upbringing (423e). Everything else flows from that. It is as though Plato is saying: 'Exploring the political is not just a helpful way of getting clear about the soul. It is a project which necessarily leads anyone who undertakes it back to the soul, and its beliefs and dispositions – or at any rate, anyone who engages in it in the constructive way founders of cities must do, committed as they will be to achieving social harmony before all else. Without shaping souls it is impossible to build or change society.'

What Plato proposes in order to achieve an appropriate blend of virtues in the soul is a radical and thoroughgoing reform of every aspect of Greek culture. Physical training, for example, is to be focused not on the body as distinct from the soul, but is conceived as forming with music an integrated strategy for harmonizing the spirited and wisdom-loving parts of the soul. Music is treated as particularly important, because 'rhythm and harmony infiltrate the inmost part of the soul more than anything else does' and 'make a person graceful' (401d). Moreover it sharpens perceptions, so that someone properly brought up in it will acquire – in advance of rational understanding – a distaste for anything shameful and a deep attachment to what is fine and noble. Many of the reforms in music as in other spheres are directed towards the development of two virtues in particular: courage and moderation, which Plato here associates with behaviour under emotional stress and with deliberately chosen activity respectively (399a–c):

> I don't know all the musical modes. Just leave me the mode which would appropriately imitate the sounds and accents of someone who is courageous in battle and in every activity forced upon a person, or who is failing and facing wounds, death or some other misfortune, and who in all these circumstances stands up to what befalls him steadily and patiently. Leave me also another mode: appropriate for someone who is engaged in a peaceful action, not forced upon him but voluntary, such as persuading someone of something and making a request (whether it be a god in prayer or a human being by instruction and exhortation), or, by contrast, holding oneself back when someone else tries to instruct one or get one to change one's mind – and who as a result acts intelligently, and does not behave arrogantly but in all these circumstances acts moderately and in a measured way, and is content with the consequences. Leave me, then, these two modes, a forcible and a voluntary one, which will best imitate the tones of voice of the unfortunate and the fortunate, the moderate and the courageous.

But the intention is also to foster other more distinctively aristocratic virtues, as the stress on what is fine and noble already suggests: liberality of mind, largeness of style and perspective, and cognate qualities, as befits those who are to be 'craftsmen of freedom for the city' (395c).

Harmony and political independence for the city are therefore to be secured principally by the education of an elite, selected because they have the natural endowments of spirit and reflectiveness needed in guards: an education radically reconstructed to foster the requisite harmony between dispositions of the soul. This set of ideas constitutes another model for thinking about justice.[39]

7 The digression: (i) unity and the good city

It will come as no surprise that Socrates in due course puts it to the interlocutors quite explicitly that the city they have been constructing 'fits the footprint of the good' (462a) inasmuch as it avoids division and achieves unity: there is no greater good than what binds it together and makes it one. This assessment in the digression of Book v recapitulates earlier discussion and anticipates later. It looks back to the beginning of Book iv, where the happiness of the whole city is *de facto* explicated as the condition of unity it enjoys because each class performs only the functions to which it is naturally suited. It looks forward to Books vi and vii, and to the metaphysical conception of the Form of the Good as what supplies the ultimate unifying explanation of everything there is.

The beginning of Book iv is the point in *Republic* at which the totalitarianism of Plato's political thinking, found objectionable by critics from Aristotle (who of course did not speak of 'totalitarianism') to Karl Popper (who did), starts to become apparent.[40] Socrates has been confronted with an objection. Guards are to be restricted to a communal way of life, forbidden economic activity, and denied private property beyond the bare minimum. So someone might say, says Adeimantus, that they get no good from the city which in truth belongs to them, and can hardly be particularly happy. Socrates offers the counter-suggestion that living as they are to do the guards might well be very happy. But his key point is that the aim has not been to make one particular class happy, but the whole city so far as possible. The interests of the totality are to be made to predominate over those of any part of the whole. Happiness for the parts – the constituent

[39] As this section will have made clear, it is emphatically not an intellectualist model. For the contrast with Socratic ethics see Penner, in Ch. 9 section 1, pp. 170–1.
[40] See Popper 1962, vol.1; also e.g. Holmes 1979, Taylor 1986, Reeve 1988: ch. 4.

classes of the polis – is not a matter Socrates and his interlocutors should concern themselves with in the construction of the city, but something to be left to 'nature' (421c), i.e. to the course of events.

The happiness of the whole city, as conceived at the beginning of Book IV, will consist simply in the fact that it is well organized according to the principle of specialization. Socrates is in effect commandeering Adeimantus' word 'happy' to insist that good order is a more important value than the satisfactions and successes of individuals or groups which the expression usually conveys.[41] This would probably not have struck contemporary readers as a particularly novel or adventurous claim in itself. There was a long tradition of political thought in which the *eunomia*, 'law-governed order', and *homonoia*, 'unanimity', of the city were advocated as values which should override individual or factional interests.[42] In any historical Greek polis of Plato's time the relatively close-knit fabric of society, emphasized during frequent episodes of warfare, was such that the relative importance Socrates attaches to the good of the city would have been accepted as a commonplace in most quarters. Nor does his position involve postulation of any proto-Hegelian idea of the State (as distinct from civil society). So Socrates' thesis is not totalitarian if totalitarianism is construed as necessarily tied to the characteristically modern attempt at radical and coercive politicization of diverse forms of civil association, hitherto independent of the State, 'such as the unions, the press, the police, sport, science, law, art, family life, education and, of course, the economy'.[43]

But the way Socrates uses the principle of specialization to achieve good order in the city bears uncomfortable resemblances to the practices and ideologies of modern totalitarian states. It is true that *Republic* does not recognize violence or the threat of violence as a dominant or regular instrument in maintaining the structures it recommends, although the bonds of social harmony are to be maintained by 'both persuasion and necessity' (519e). Instead it employs something no less characteristic of totalitarianism: propaganda. We have already mentioned the 'splendid

[41] Sometimes it is suggested (against e.g. Popper 1962, vol.1) that Socrates conceives the happiness of the whole city as nothing more than a shorthand for the happiness (so far as can be achieved) of all the citizens: so Vlastos 1977. But see Brown 1998 for a demonstration that the city is in fact treated as a whole with its own needs and characteristics, above all a need for unity and harmony. To that extent readings of the *Republic* which find in it anticipations of the Hegelian organic conception of the state have some justification.

[42] See e.g. Raaflaub, in Ch. 2 section 6 above, and Ober, in Ch. 6 section 4 above.

[43] Holmes 1979: 116, who adds: 'The "line between state and society" did not yet exist, and thus could neither have been defended nor destroyed.'

fiction' of the brotherhood of all the citizens and the natural rightness of the class system, which builds something like false consciousness into the foundations of the political settlement. When Socrates comes to work out the communistic breeding arrangements to be imposed on the guards, he stresses again that the rulers will need to 'make frequent use of falsehood and deception' (459c), drugging those they rule into accepting the provisions to be implemented. It is assumed that in this sphere, as elsewhere, existing political and social structures have been swept aside. But sweeping them aside could scarcely be achieved without violence. Socrates conceives that the slate would be wiped clean by sending into the countryside everyone over the age of ten, so leaving the children to be brought up in the laws and customs he is recommending. Coercion on a massive scale, as in Ceaucescu's Romania or the 'cultural revolution' of Mao Tse-tung's China, is presumably what is envisaged. Moreover, while the dichotomy of state and society may find no purchase in the ancient Greek context, many of the points at which the totalitarian state threatens civil society correspond to places where *Republic* submits to the control of the city institutions or social practices which in Plato's Athens were regarded as properly belonging within the domain of the family or the inidivual. One of these is education: in Athens no concern of the city, but on Socrates' proposals to be prescribed by it down to the last detail, and to be preserved without any change whatsoever if the rulers are to ensure the survival of its wellbeing. Another – as Adeimantus noticed (419a) – is the regulation of the lives of the guards, and the consequent proposal that there be communal arrangements with regard to women and children: Socrates goes to the extreme lengths of not simply subjecting the family to control by the city, but abolishing it altogether.[44]

It is sometimes held that the political proposals of *Republic* are designed to be risible.[45] On such a view, the remedy Socrates is represented as recommending for the ills of society contains so many harshnesses, internal difficulties and downright absurdities as to deconstruct itself. Or even if it does not (or Plato does not think it does), it is taken as merely an ideal blueprint which he could never have expected or even wanted to see implemented. In particular, Book v's advocacy of women guards and communal breeding and child-rearing provisions have been construed as a

[44] Plato's modern apologists have pleaded paternalism (Taylor 1986, Reeve 1988: ch. 4), or less plausibly a concern for rights (Vlastos 1977, 1978, 1989) on his behalf. Cf. also Bambrough 1967.

[45] See e.g. Bloom 1968: 380–1, 1977: 323–8, Hyland 1995: ch. 3, following Strauss 1964.

reductio ad absurdum of what Socrates pronounces a 'perfectly good' city (427e). Attention has been drawn to the similarities between what is proposed in *Republic* and the fantasy of a communistic Athens controlled by women in Aristophanes' *Ecclesiazusae* or *Assembly of Women* (c.393–2 BC). Socrates admits that various features of the suggestions he makes about women guards may seem ridiculous.

What needs to be appreciated is that Plato himself makes the issue of the status of the proposals particularly of Book V a theme in its own right.[46] They have originally been mentioned in passing near the beginning of Book IV, which ends with a provisional answer to *Republic*'s question about what justice is, and an indication that various forms of vice – and their corresponding constitutional models in the larger letters of the city – are now to be examined. But at the start of Book V Adeimantus and Polemarchus derail the argument by insisting on hearing more about the apparently irrelevant topic of women and children. Socrates is portrayed as embarking on further discussion of it only with great hesitancy, precisely because he thinks his ideas may be dismissed as just a 'prayer' (450d; cf.540d), i.e. an idle wish, not anything feasible or really desirable, and anyway likely to stir up a 'hornets' nest of arguments' (450b). Consequently he is at pains right through Books V–VII to stress that the arrangements he is advocating there are certainly desirable and in one sense or another practicable, even if ways and opportunities of putting them into practice are extraordinarily difficult to envisage. He makes this claim not just about the case for women guards and for the breeding and rearing programme, but above all with respect to the *sine qua non* of all the other provisions: the existence of a philosopher ruler or rulers able and willing to put them into effect.

Women guards are discussed first. In addressing the thought that the idea of women performing this role is simply ridiculous, Socrates treats it at one juncture simply as a response to what is 'against custom' (452e), points out that *male* nakedness in gymnastics has ceased to amuse as once it did (452c–d), calls fear of such mockery 'childish' (451a), and regards this kind of humour as ignorantly inappropriate (457a–b). His argument *for* the idea is one of the most sustained individual stretches of reasoning in *Republic*, quite different in style from the treatment of the guards in Books II–IV, where Socrates was mostly just explaining what he thinks would be appropriate, rather than trying to demonstrate anything. It turns on a serious and careful appeal to nature, and is designed to mount a

[46] Noted (with opposite interpretations) e.g. by Strauss 1964: 116–27, Burnyeat 1992; also Halliwell 1993, an authoritative guide on all issues in Book V.

critical challenge to reliance on cultural assumptions about the sexes. Its siting at the beginning of Book v means that it constitutes the first stage of the great philosophical excursus of Books v–vii: we should not be surprised if it does some real philosophical work. Its basic premise is the claim that there is no reason to think human nature any different from animal and particularly canine nature where questions of sex and (the next argument will add) eugenics are concerned. If a bitch hunts with the dogs and takes minimal time off for childbirth, why should not women of suitable ability become guards like men of the same ability, even if their nature is in general 'weaker' (455c–456a)?[47] So since there *can* be 'sharing (*koinōnia*) in the work of guarding the other citizens' by women with men (466d), for the good of the city there *should* be – and what is more, they should share in education and training (including participation naked in public gymnastics) and in all their activities. The grounds of the 'should' are spelled out more explicitly in *Laws*, where Plato continues to insist on the desirability of training and using women as well as men for military functions, as with Herodotus' Amazonian Sauromatae: it is remarkable mindlessness to make only half of the citizens available for war at the same cost and effort as double the number (803–5).[48] This is not feminism. It is true that gender is rejected as a cultural construct. But deconstructivist feminists would be likely to press deeper doubts: about the objectivity of the notion of rationality which governs the whole argument of Books v–vii of *Republic*. And there is not a glimmer of a concern with rights.[49]

Socrates and Glaucon agree that his argument for the possibility and desirability of women guards escapes any wave of criticism which might threaten to submerge it. Indeed, Socrates has gone out of his way to articulate and rebut the contrary view that women are naturally different from men, and should therefore – in accordance with the sort of thinking sanctioned by the principle of specialization – be assigned a different function in society. A bigger wave, however, is on its way. The next proposal Socrates makes is presented as 'following' (457c) the provisions for women guards, in the sense that it continues to work out the idea that the city needs to make optimal use of its human resources. If we can achieve a better breed of bird or dog by genetic engineering, why should the same strategy not work with humans? Hence a eugenic programme involving tight

[47] Glaucon – always more preoccupied than Socrates with the feasibility and practical application of his proposals (cf. e.g. 527d) – volunteers the view that 'there are many women better than many men in many fields' (455c).

[48] On the role of women in the 'second-best' city of *Laws* see Cohen 1993, Saunders 1995a.

[49] On the much-debated question of whether Plato was a proto-feminist see the comprehensive study of Bluestone 1987; also Okin 1979, Vlastos 1989, Lovibond 1994.

control of mating by the city, and communal nursing arrangements for the offspring to minimize interference with the military functions of women guards. The core of this proposal is introduced as follows (457c–d):

> All these women are to be shared by (*koinas*) all the men, and no one woman is to live privately with any one man. And the children too are to be shared, with parents not knowing their own offspring nor children their parents.

Glaucon comments that there is much more scope for disbelief here, regarding both the possibility and the benefits of what is proposed. The challenge to show that this form of communism is desirable is not met by stressing its reproductive utility or functional efficiency. Instead Plato writes an extraordinarily eloquent passage celebrating a much more intense and radical form of unity than has been claimed for the interlocutors' city so far (462a–464b). He has Socrates suggest that without the ties of the traditional family the guards as a group – as 'the city' – will constitute a single great family. Since everyone perceives everyone else as father or sister or grandmother, any one person's success or misfortune will be shared as pleasure or pain by all. There will be an end to the privatization of these emotions, and maximal agreement in saying that this is 'my' sorrow or 'my' joy. When one individual has a good or bad experience, the sympathy felt throughout the city will be like the sensation felt throughout the body when any one of its parts is affected by pain or pleasure. The unity produced by abolition of the family, together with that of private property, is a recipe for harmony and peace; and Socrates spells out in some detail the disappearance of occasions for conflict which he represents as its consequence (464c–465d).

Plato's attachment to this vision of the social good appears to have remained undiminished. He sketches it briefly once again in *Laws*, where in terms clearly designed to recall this section of *Republic* he reiterates his allegiance to the idea that the best city is one where the old saying 'among friends things are held really in common' is observed so far as possible throughout the entire city (739a–d). His treatment of the other issue – whether such a city could actually come into being – is guarded and highly nuanced. In *Laws* the ideal is presented as a model to be emulated rather than a scheme for implementation: what is wanted is that constitution which will resemble it as closely as possible while being suitable for humans, not gods and heroes (739d–e). A similar interpretation is indicated by Socrates' discussion in *Republic* itself.

These indications are both substantive and formal in character. As to substance, Socrates makes it clear even as he is describing it that the eugenic programme would be an immensely difficult project to carry through successfully. He recognizes that it will require control over sexual drives or 'erotic necessities' (458d) which will only be enhanced by the close physical proximity, not least during gymnastic training, in which men and women are to coexist. As we have noted, he envisages the need for frequent deceptions by the rulers to persuade the guards to accede to the requirements of the programme (459c). And he writes laws to cover various kinds of breach of the rules, whether caused by 'dangerous weakness of will' or otherwise, which he appears to regard as inevitable (461a–c). When in Book VIII he imagines the degeneration of the ideal community, it is significant that he postulates as cause a miscalculation in the computations governing optimal mating seasons (546a–547a). In chapters 2 to 4 of Book II of the *Politics* Aristotle argues that the extreme degree of unity hypothesized for that community would be the ruin, not the salvation, of the city; and that even if it were not, Socrates' account of how such perfect unity is achieved will not work – he succeeds in producing at best a 'watery' kind of friendship. Modern commentators have followed Aristotle in diagnosing all manner of tensions and contradictions in Plato's efforts to reconcile the ideal of social unity with the conditions which actually govern the way humans develop emotional attachments or antipathies towards each other.[50]

As to form, Socrates is represented as strikingly evasive on the question of feasibility. Where women guards were concerned, he addressed the parallel question first and at length before turning briefly to ask whether, given that it is feasible, it would be a desirable provision. On sharing of women and children he defers the issue of practicability not once but twice (458b, 466d), and is finally made to address it only by an intervention from Glaucon (471e). When he finally does confront it he opts for the same response as is given in *Laws*. What the interlocutors have been constructing in speech or argument (*logos*) is a *model* (*paradeigma*) of a good city. Their project is to be compared with the way they have approached the problem of justice. The point of inquiring into what justice is and of considering the perfectly just man is not to prove that there could be such a person, but to have a bench-mark to use in their discussions about happiness. Whoever approximates most closely to the paradigm would then be agreed to come closest to being happy. Just so with the city: the request to show that a city such as has been described is a possibility misses the

[50] Cf. e.g. Bloom 1968: 384–6, Halliwell 1993: 19–23.

point. If Socrates is to accede to it, 'possibility' must be interpreted not as full implementation of the ideal, but as an account of 'how a city could live in a way that most closely approximates to the description' (473a) the interlocutors have given. *Laws* shows what such an approximation might be like. For example, even though there is to be apportionment of land under the 'second best' constitution, it is still to be regarded as the common property of the city (739e–740b). And although the institution of the family is retained, the city is to use a variety of means to ensure that there remain always the same number of households all of roughly equal size, for example by providing for the transfer of surplus males from one family to another, and by making the birth-rate a matter of public concern (740b–741a).

Once again, therefore, *Republic* gives the reader a model for thinking with, rather than a blueprint designed to be exactly reproduced; and this time it explicitly says that this is what it is doing. 'Thinking with' does not exclude 'acting upon'. The dialogue's theoretical discussion of justice points to the conclusion expressed on the last page of Book x that 'we should practise it with understanding in every way we can' (621c). In drafting his account of the perfect unity of the harmonious city Plato presumably means to supply a basis for guidelines which are to inform – in whatever approximations to the ideal – the work of legislators and makers of constitutions.[51]

8 The digression: (ii) philosopher rulers

The introduction of the idea of philosopher rulers is the greatest of all the revolutionary moments Plato has prepared for readers of *Republic*. It provides the context for the visionary account of philosophy itself that is offered at the heart of the dialogue, and for the approach to *Republic*'s focal point, the Form of the Good, through the successive analogies of Sun, Line and Cave. The idea of a specifically philosophical impulse in the soul was already adumbrated in the initial discussion of the education of the guards. Now it is articulated as the all-consuming passion (*erōs*) for a comprehensive rational understanding of eternal reality and truth, to be nurtured by a rigorous and extended higher education in all the mathematical sciences from arithmetic to astronomy. This philosophical perspective is something readers are being invited to reach for, not anything they are already presumed to possess. In Books v–vii it is described – notably in images and analogies – rather than practised; and the emphasis, as

[51] In other words, *Republic* already looks forward to *Laws* (cf. Laks 1990): see further Laks, in Ch. 12 section 3 below.

in the accounts of philosophy in *Phaedo* and *Symposium*, is on the desire for understanding rather than its possession. Socrates is presented as stressing the sketchy and provisional nature of what he has to say, and on his reluctance to speak about things he does not know as if he knew them.

Paradoxically this is the most supremely optimistic passage of the entire dialogue: paradoxically, because the grounds Socrates registers for doubting the prospects for either political or moral and intellectual progress are formidable. The moral and intellectual condition of humanity at large is represented by the Cave as one of utter ignorance and triviality and almost total complacency. Yet Socrates focuses on the possibility of conversion and painful ascent to virtue and clarity of understanding. As for the political sphere, Socrates anticipates a third and even bigger 'wave' of criticism when he reformulates *Gorgias*'s idea of a true politics, and proposes that rule by philosophers or philosophizing by rulers is the one single change necessary and sufficient for making the ideal city – or a close approximation to it – a reality. It threatens to deluge him with 'outright laughter and contempt' (473c). The next few pages are devoted to explanation of what 'philosopher' should be taken to mean in this context: a lover of eternal truth. But the criticism predicted duly arrives, when Adeimantus puts the objection, in terms reminiscent of Callicles' outburst in *Gorgias*, that philosophers are either weird misfits (if not thoroughly vicious) or if perfectly decent useless to cities (487b–d). Nothing daunted, Socrates replies with an indictment of the corruption of society which resonates with Plato's contempt for the Athenian democracy during the period of his lifetime. He imagines a ship controlled by ignorant and quarrelsome sailors who refuse to believe that there is any such craft as navigation, and would write off a real helmsman as a useless stargazer. Just so in cities as they are now: a true philosopher will be branded as useless, not because he really is so, but because the populace is incapable of thinking otherwise (487e–489c). In such societies most persons with philosophical potential are indeed corrupted, the more so the greater their talents (489–99). But that shows only that society needs radical transformation. And Socrates ends his reply to Adeimantus with three pages of argument in which he reiterates again and again that it *can* be transformed, provided only that cities are governed by philosopher rulers who have somehow escaped the prevailing moral degradation and are able to work with a clean slate – something he insists will be difficult but not impossible (499–502). This conclusion is restated at the very end of Book VII, when the outcome of the entire discussion of Books V–VII is summarized (540d–541a).

What is it about philosophers that makes them uniquely suitable to establish and then govern the ideal or near ideal city? In some passages Plato puts the emphasis on understanding: mere belief or opinion is unstable. Socrates says to Adeimantus (497c): 'There will always need to be an element in the city which is in possession of the same principle of political order as you the lawgiver had when you were establishing the laws.' This is what is required if guards are to be capable of guarding the laws and ways of life of cities. Now the inquiry has been seeking to discover the *good* city, and it has emerged that the political good consists in harmony and unity. It is therefore to be expected that philosopher rulers will try to grasp the nature of the Good, which – it will be suggested – is the ultimate principle of order among the Forms and cause of all that is right and noble. They must study it if they are to be capable of intelligent private or public activity, and will order (*kosmein*) the city and private individuals and themselves by using it as a model (*paradeigma*).

But more often the stress is as much on the philosopher's passionate desire for truth and its workings on and in his soul (490b):

> He does not slacken in his passion (*erōs*) until he grasps the nature of each 'what it is' in itself with the part of the soul which is the right one for grasping such a thing [viz. the one that has kinship with it]. And when he gets close to it and really has genuine intercourse with it, and begets understanding and truth, then he knows, he truly lives, he is nourished, and in that way – but not before – his birth pangs cease.

Or again, in a passage reminiscent of *Gorgias*' appeal to an order exhibiting 'geometric equality' as what holds together not only society but the cosmos at large, Socrates describes the same process in terms of assimilation. Most people look below to human affairs, and become filled with envy and hatred. But not so philosophers (500c): 'They look towards and make study of things that are ordered and always the same, that neither do injustice to each other nor have it done to them, but are all ordered rationally; and they imitate them and try to become like them so far as possible.' As in the ethics of the early dialogues, knowledge of the good implies being good. And as philosophers are themselves shaped, they will shape the lives of others when placed in positions of rule – doubtless by the educational processes described in Books II and III, not by imparting knowledge (500d):

> And if he [i.e. the philosopher] should be compelled to put what he sees there into people's characters, whether individually or with regard to the people at large, instead of just shaping himself, do you think he will be a poor craftsman of moderation, justice and popular virtue in general? Not in the least.

Thus whether Plato puts his emphasis on the intellectual or the motivational aspects of philosophical understanding, the ultimate point is the same: only philosophers can grasp the order and harmony they find in eternal reality, and only they can be guaranteed to reproduce them in their own lives and those of the citizens, both by the constitutional provisions they institute and by personal moral influence.

In the extract just quoted from Book VI Socrates assumes that philosophers will need to be *compelled* to rule. This assumption is explicitly articulated in Book VII, which propounds the paradox that the city that is best to live in and freest from *stasis* is the one where those who are going to rule are least eager to do so. The reason given for the philosophers' reluctance to descend again into the cave is that they think a life of continuous education is like being in heaven; and it has earlier been agreed that it would be impossible for someone with the largeness of outlook associated with study of all time and all being to consider the life of man to be anything of much significance. But the plan was never to make one particular class in the city do especially well, but to engineer harmony in the city by implementation of the principle of specialization. What will compel philosophers to take their turns at ruling, as something not admirable but necessary, is their sense of justice – that is the political or social justice associated with that principle. They will be persuaded that performing a role they can discharge better than anyone else is what they owe to the city which has educated them – in their own interests as well as those of the other citizens – to be rulers (519c–521b).

So for *Republic* the choice between the philosophical and the political life is not a matter of either/or, but – in the circumstances of the good city – both/and. Scholars have spilled much ink on the issue of whether Plato could show that by taking their turns at ruling philosophers *would* be happier than if they avoided them.[52] Yet it is hard to see that, given an understanding of individual happiness as psychic harmony, it should actually make a difference whether they philosophize always or rule sometimes. Presumably their psychic harmony, which is a matter of *self*-rule, will not vary, even if they take greater pleasure in philosophizing. Scholars have also wondered whether in making the same persons both rule and philosophize Socrates breaches the principle of specialization.[53] But that principle operates with regard only to constituent functions of the life of the city. The pursuit of philosophy is not such a function. It is conceived both as beyond and above the political (taking us outside the cave) and as part

[52] E.g. Kraut 1973, Cooper 1977, Annas 1981: 266–71, White 1986, Reeve 1988: 197–204.
[53] E.g. Bloom 1968: 407, Hyland 1995: 102–3.

of the rulers' education, preparing them for the function of government. There is of course a tension between philosophy and politics, but it is not a conflict between two civic roles.

Optimism such as the passionate and visionary Books v–vii communicate is designed to be infectious. The possibility of the accession to power of a philosopher ruler, even if remote, is something *Republic* wants its readers to come to believe in, even if it draws attention to the insecurities of belief. Plato has also made it clear, however, that the *point* of his account of the ideal city, whose practicability turns on the possibility of philosopher rulers, is *not* that it should be fully realizable. He seems to be trying to steer between two opposite dangers. One is that readers might take his project as mere wish-fulfilment fantasy. To fend off this criticism he takes himself to be under an obligation to show that his proposals contain nothing strictly impossible for humans to achieve. The other is that readers might think we can 'grasp truth' in action as fully as we can in speech. So he is at pains to insert reminders that he is 'story-telling' (501e) and 'playing' (536c), and to suggest that like a painter's his picture retains its validity as a model even if it cannot straightforwardly be replicated in practice. Nonetheless the weight and positioning of Socrates' insistent assertions that what he proposes is possible if difficult to accomplish indicate that Plato took the charge of fantasy to pose the greater difficulty.[54]

9 The response: (iii) justice and the city within

Book v begins with a retrospect and a prospect (449a):

> This is the sort of city and political ordering (*politeia*), then, that I call good and right, and also this sort of man. All the other political orderings I call bad and in error, given that this one is right, both as regards administration of cities and in the case of character of soul of individuals. And they come in four species of badness.[55]

The prospect of discussion of these four species is then interrupted by the further treatment of the good city and its rulers in the digression of Books v–vii. But the interlocutors need to return to the study of corruption in city and soul. For what Glaucon and Adeimantus required from Socrates was a comparison between the perfectly just and the supremely unjust person if they were to be convinced of the effect for good and bad justice

54 Cf. Annas 1981: 185–7, Laks 1990.

55 I.e. four principal species: the number is actually infinite (445c).

and injustice have in the soul. The account of corrupt orderings – both of cities and of souls – is duly resumed in Books VIII–IX. Comparison of just and unjust lives (or as they are now redescribed, the lives of persons with philosophical and tyrannical souls) occupies its main concluding section. Plato here represents the motivational pandemonium of the world as it is as a downward spiral of progressive disorder: from 'timocratic' cities and individuals, where the spirited part of the soul dominates with its desire for honour, victory and good reputation; through oligarchy, a regime whether of city or soul dedicated to satisfaction of the necessary appetites, and democracy in individuals and societies, where unnecessary appetites are in control, producing the 'freedom' to do what one likes which Plato so despises; to tyranny, portrayed as the miserable outcome of the chaos of absolutist rule over an immeasurably wretched soul by appetites that are not merely unnecessary but lawless. All of this is worked out with a wealth of brilliantly imaginative psychological and sociopathological observation.

The identification of the paradigmatically unjust life as tyranny provides a clue to the resolution of a cluster of puzzles which has much troubled the commentators. *Republic*'s central proposal, that justice for the individual is psychic harmony, is perceived by many readers as a fundamental flaw in the execution of the dialogue's basic project.[56] In the first place, the main argument presented for the proposal towards the end of Book IV is invalid. It appeals to the principle that where two things x and y are both called 'F', the basis on which 'F' is predicated of x must be the same as or analogous to the grounds for predicating 'F' of y. So if the city is called 'just' because each class does its own job and no other's, the reason why an individual is called 'just' will similarly be because each element in the soul performs its own function and no other (434d–435c). But the principle supporting this inference is false as a general principle. It assumes that words are univocal, but – as Aristotle was fond of pointing out – univocal they very often are not. It is not plausible, for example, that if individuals are to be called 'healthy' because of their robust constitution, this will be the reason why we do or should predicate 'healthy' of cities. A healthy city is rather one which provides a physical and social environment tending to promote health in individuals. Secondly, Book IV does not make much effort to show that justice as psychic harmony is characteristically associated with just behaviour, i.e. fair or moral treatment of *other* individuals. It *asserts* that someone whose soul is in this

[56] So influentially Sachs 1963; other views: e.g. Vlastos 1971a, Annas 1978.

condition will not be party to embezzlement, theft, betrayal or oath-breaking, nor adultery, disrespect towards parents or neglect of the gods (442d–443a). But it does not try to prove the point; and just action is actually explicitly redefined, not in such a way as to attempt to capture the idea of honest or dutiful behaviour towards others, but as 'what preserves this inner harmony and helps to bring it about' (443e). So Plato's Socrates faces the charge that he has made justice something which is of intrinsic benefit to the just individual only by turning it into a characteristic unrecognizable as justice.

Republic's view of justice and injustice emerges from Book IX's treatment of the tyrannical soul in an altogether more convincing light.[57] To begin with, the association of injustice with tyranny and lawless appetites is something common opinion, as represented by Glaucon and Adeimantus, already accepts. It is built into Glaucon's picture of the free-rider Gyges as the perfectly unjust man. So the proposition that unjust behaviour, in its most rampant form, is the product of lawless appetites can be treated by Socrates as uncontroversial. All he now needs to sustain his own position on injustice and to undermine Glaucon's thesis – directly the claim that injustice is intrinsically preferable to justice, but indirectly therefore the social contract account of justice – is to take three further steps. These are the suppositions that, first, rampantly unjust conduct is rampant because lawless appetites are insatiable; second, insatiable appetites are necessarily anarchic; third, since psychic anarchy is the cause of rampant injustice, it is best interpreted *as* the core of injustice itself: which will be a supremely wretched condition because of the insatiability of the desires that constitute it. If we now ask what sort of person would be *least* likely to engage in the behaviour characteristic of the perfectly unjust man, there seems much plausibility in *Republic*'s proposal that it is someone whose soul is in a condition of psychic harmony as far removed as can be conceived from the psychic anarchy which is to be equated with injustice. Socrates has given three sketches of what such a condition might be like. The education of the guards is designed to habituate contrary impulses of the soul into a harmonious pattern focused on noble and graceful behaviour. This notion of harmony is then incorporated into the fuller treatment in the account of individual justice at the end of Book IV: the rational and spirited parts of the soul work together in controlling the appetitive part, whose natural insatiability and propensity to cause havoc in a person's life are already remarked upon. But a more complete unity is envisaged in what

[57] For the interpretation which follows see Kraut 1992.

is said in Book VI about the motivations of philosophers. They have a single-minded passion for understanding; and 'when someone's desires incline strongly in one direction, they are thereby weakened in the others, as if they were a stream that has been diverted in that direction' (485d). The appetites which fuel unjust behaviour are in that case starved of energy. Now the psychic condition of someone whose motivating dispositions are so described may fairly be regarded as the *cause* of a wholly virtuous person's total aversion to such behaviour. And for that reason it would be reasonable of Socrates to identify it with justice.

In Books VIII and IX Socrates becomes increasingly fond of describing psychic harmony as the political order or polity (*politeia*) of the soul. This gives rise to some memorable images. A person with an oligarchic soul 'is not free from internal *stasis* – he is double, not one' (554e), like the city divided between rich and poor Socrates has warned against in Book IV. Within the citadel of the soul of the democratic person an elaborate drama of infiltration and counter-insurgency, expulsion and restoration is fought out. Most important of all are the exchanges between Glaucon and Socrates at the close of Book IX, which may serve as a brief commentary on the argument of *Republic* as a whole. Socrates turns once more to the education of children. We do not allow our children to be free 'until we establish a polity within them as in a city, and by fostering their best element with our own we establish within it a guard and ruler like our own to take its place – and *then* we let them be free' (590e–591a). In response to the account Socrates goes on to give of the way such a free person will live his life and care for his soul, Glaucon remarks that he will hardly want to engage in politics. Socrates reports the reply he gave (592a–b):

> Yes, by the dog, I said, he certainly will, at least in his own city. But not perhaps in his country of birth, unless some divine good luck comes his way.
>
> I understand, he said. You mean he will in the city we were just now describing as its founders, the one located in our speech – for I think it exists nowhere on earth.
>
> But perhaps, I said, it is laid up in heaven as a model for anyone who wants to look up at it and as he looks to make himself into a settlement patterned upon it. It makes no difference whether it exists or will exists anywhere, since he would engage in the activity only of this city and no other.
>
> Probably so, he said.

Readers of *Republic* need always to remember the pervasiveness of 'perhaps' and 'probably' in the dialogue, and the nuances of agreements and understandings by the interlocutors that do not quite settle the meaning. This subtle passage has sometimes been read as a renunciation by Socrates of his earlier endorsement of the possibility that the ideal city (or an approximation to it) might come into being.[58] A heavy-handed interpretation. What Socrates is saying is that in the world as it is ('his country of birth') an individual should care only for the polity of his own soul – *unless* 'some divine good luck come his way', i.e. (presumably) if his country were turned into the ideal city by the advent of a philosopher ruler. Glaucon misses the point, so Socrates clarifies what he means by 'his own city': the polity he should make of his own soul. And he makes a qualification to what he seemed to imply in his previous remark: the politics of that polity are the *only* politics he should ever engage in, whether he is citizen of an ideal city or not.

This is a distinction which both does and does not make a real difference. At every stage of the inquiry undertaken by the dialogue care of the soul has turned out to be the key to the proper conduct of everything else one might take to be the province of politics. 'This inner polity is the foundation of the foundation of Kallipolis.'[59] So in one sense there is no new turn here in the position Socrates is advocating. But from another point of view the passage represents a sad retreat into quietism from the political vision of the central books. There too Socrates imagines someone who – against massive odds – 'consorts properly with philosophy' (496a) and manages to remain free of the madness and corruption of the society about him. Such a person will in this context abstain from politics: he will 'keep quiet and mind his own business' (496d). And he will be content if he lives his life pure of injustice or impiety and leaves it with a noble hope – like the Socrates of the *Apology*. 'Not the least of achievements', says Adeimantus. 'But not the greatest either', replies Socrates, 'if he does not happen to find a suitable *politeia*. For in a suitable one his own growth will be fuller, and he will preserve the commonwealth as well as his private interests' (497a; cf. 499b).[60]

[58] So e.g. Hyland 1995: 84. [59] Clay 1988: 32.

[60] Engaging no doubt in that public activity in aid of justice, worthy of a good man, which Socrates thought too dangerous to undertake (*Ap.* 32e; cf. 31d–32a). On the *Republic* as a meditation on Socratic quietism see Ober 1998: ch. 4.

11

The *Politicus* and other dialogues

CHRISTOPHER ROWE

As a political work, the *Politicus*[1] is generally regarded as a poor relation of the *Republic* and the *Laws*: on the standard view, it reflects rather scrappily on issues arising out of the *Republic* (especially in relation to the idea of philosopher rulers), and somehow prepares the way for the *Laws*. But such an approach fails to do justice to its argument. Once its twists and turns are properly understood, it stands out as a major document of Platonic political theory in its own right; less bulky though it may be than either of the other two works, and certainly less appealing than the *Republic*, it offers real illumination of some central themes, and adds some important new elements which are not in any way superseded in the *Laws*.

The first, and perhaps chief, problem for the interpreter is to understand the structure of the argument, and its outcome or outcomes.[2] The dialogue has four main components: a long series of 'divisions' aimed at defining the *politikos*, the 'politician' or (more traditionally) the 'statesman',[3] together with his 'art' or expertise ('statesmanship'); a cosmological myth, inserted into the divisions at an early stage, which allegedly helps take them forward; a discussion of the role of law in ideal and actual societies, which similarly interrupts the process of division, though it is formally motivated by it; and, after the divisions have been completed, a description of the role of the statesman in 'weaving together' complementary character traits or kinds of temperament among the citizens. Because the results of the long search for a definition may in themselves appear relatively meagre (and parts of it, as the main speaker admits, downright tedious), there is a temptation for interpreters to privilege other individual elements in the dialogue: the myth, the discussion of law,

[1] The literature on the *Politicus* is relatively small; but see esp. Diès 1935, Skemp 1952, Kahn 1995, Rowe 1995a, 1995b, Lane 1998.

[2] There is a general sense among commentators that the structure of the *Politicus* is rather untidy, even messy (see e.g. Annas and Waterfield 1995); my own view (see Rowe 1996) is that it is, on the contrary, rather tight, if complex.

[3] 'Statesman' in this context is probably preferable, since it is what politicians ought to be that is in question, not what they (currently) are, and 'statesman' at least lacks the often pejorative connotations of 'politician'.

or the concluding section, on the statesman as weaver. It is in its latter parts that the *Politicus* perhaps makes its most distinctive contribution to Platonic political theory, by isolating statesmanship as a second-order expertise, which judges the 'right moment' (*kairos*) for the application of other kinds of expert knowledge, and of different temperaments and perspectives.[4] Here at last, we may feel, Plato leaves behind more abstract considerations, in order to acknowledge – more clearly than he does anywhere else – the obvious truth that the statesman must deal with the world as it actually is.[5] Yet the fact is that these issues emerge only relatively late in the conversation, and any overall treatment of the dialogue must acknowledge that fact. Whatever new sense of 'realism' we ultimately wish to attribute to the Plato of the *Politicus*, it appears at best as a kind of qualification to, or as corrective of, an argument of which the main preoccupations lie elsewhere.

This is the starting-point for the account of the *Politicus* that follows. Each of the four components in the dialogue is treated in turn, sometimes with reference to relevant material in other dialogues (particularly the *Protagoras* and the *Euthydemus*). Finally there is a specific discussion of connections between the *Politicus* and the *Timaeus-Critias*, and of the relationship of the *Politicus* to the *Laws*.

1 The definition of the 'statesman' in the *Politicus*

The fictional conversation supposedly recorded in the *Politicus* takes place on the same day as that of the *Sophist*, and employs – rather more systematically – the same method of division that had been used there to define the sophist and his 'art' or *technē*. The method involves taking a very broad kind or class (*eidos*, *genos*)[6] within which the definiendum is agreed – by those taking part in the argument – to be located, and then successively dividing this kind or class, with the irrelevant parts being discarded. The definition will then be constituted by the names of the undiscarded parts. In the present case, a visitor from Elea (hereafter the Visitor: traditionally the 'Stranger'), who also presided over the conversation in the *Sophist*,

[4] See section 4 below.

[5] See esp. Lane 1998. Lane rightly points to the stress that is laid on the essential *ordinariness* of weaving, as the analogue of statesmanship; and also to the extensive parallels for the role assigned to the notion of the *kairos* elsewhere in contemporary Greek political discussion.

[6] On what exactly it is that is divided in each case, see S. M.Cohen 1973, Rowe 1995: 5–8, and Lane 1998: 16–18. The *Politicus* in general makes no explicit metaphysical or ontological claims (see pp. 237–9 below).

gets a young man who shares Socrates' name to agree to begin from the kind or class labelled as 'expert knowledge' (*epistēmē*), which they then immediately divide into practical or productive and theoretical; because statesmanship has more to do with the use of the intellect than actual production, the 'practical' sorts of expertise are left to one side, while the theoretical ones are divided into the purely theoretical and those which have some kind of directive role – and so on. After some wrong turnings, and a great deal of treatment of methodological questions, a definition is reached (though it is stated only in abbreviated form):

> The expertise that controls all of these [sc. the sorts of expertise that belong respectively to the orator, the general, and the judge], and the laws, and cares for every aspect of things in the city, and weaves everything together in the most correct way – this, embracing its capacity with the appellation belonging to the whole [i.e. polis], we would, it seems, most appropriately call statesmanship [*politikē*]. (305e2–6)[7]

Among the details omitted in this summary are that the statesman will 'care for', in the sense of directing the care of, a human herd, which consists of land-animals without horns that go on two feet. These elements, along with a lengthy division of weaving (279a–283a), introduced as a model or 'paradigm' (*paradeigma*) for the final division that leads to statesmanship, plainly have at least as much to do with lessons about method as they have with political theory; and indeed even the inquiry into statesmanship is said to be '[more] for the sake of our becoming more able dialecticians in relation to all subjects' than it is for the sake of statesmanship itself (285d4–7). It is this feature of the *Politicus* – the way in which it combines methodological topics with political ones – that accounts for the somewhat plodding nature of some parts of the conversation. However the Visitor's methodological preoccupations in themselves sometimes have a direct pay-off for political theory: thus a discussion about the appropriateness of spending so much time on *weaving* leads to the identification of the sort of measurement (in accordance with *to metrion*, or 'due measure') which is fundamental to statesmanship, particularly in its twin roles of directing other arts, and of combining, producing a single 'fabric' from, different elements in society that would by themselves tend to excess and deficiency. The very persuasiveness of the metaphor of weaving, as it comes to be applied to statesmanship in the last movement of the dialogue, in itself owes much to the extended

[7] This is the final outcome of the divisions themselves; but by the end of the dialogue, it is amplified by the results of the discussion of the statesman as a weaver of souls (311b7–c6).

demonstration – originally designed, at least officially, as an illustration of method – of the similarities of structure between the activities of statesmanship and weaving.[8]

In any case, whatever other purpose it may serve, the search for the statesman is plainly also meant to be of value for its own sake. The most important single aspect of it is the initial (and familiar) identification of statesmanship as a kind of *expert knowledge*. No one has any claim at all to the title 'statesman', or *politikos*, unless he – and there is no mention of female rulers or experts in statesmanship in the *Politicus* – possesses the relevant expertise. In fact the very form of the term *politikos*, with its *-ikos* ending, implies some sort of specialization, i.e. in the relevant activity or *technē*. But the conditions Plato would set for the possession of *politikē technē* are such that no existing 'politician', and perhaps no existing human being, could meet them. The *politikoi* to whom the Socrates of the *Apology* says he went first, in his search for someone wiser than himself (*Ap*. 21b–22a), are on this account only so-called 'statesmen', not the real thing. (There is, perhaps, an ironic touch in his subsequent pairing of them, at 23e–24a, with 'the *dēmiourgoi*': the term *dēmiourgos* does duty for both 'public official' and 'craftsman', and it is the craftsmen who turn out to possess the expert knowledge, in their own sphere, which the *politikoi* lack in theirs.) The real statesman will be someone who has the capacity to provide unerring answers to all questions for which we might or should look to a legislator, or the law itself, including the most important questions about the ends of human life; but he will be wiser – or would be, if he ever existed – than any conceivable set of laws, insofar as he would be able in principle to advise and direct in every particular situation, adapting his prescriptions to the prevailing circumstances. No law, of course, can do that, being inescapably general, and necessarily laying things down 'for the majority of people, for the majority of cases, and roughly, somehow, like this' (*Plt*. 295a4–5).

The *Politicus* does not commit itself as to whether such a person could ever be found. The *Laws* comes out clearly against such a possibility (most explicitly at 875a–d); the most that the Eleatic visitor will say in the *Politicus* is that '. . . it is not the case that a king [sc. of the ideal sort described, 'kings' being synonymous with 'statesmen'] comes to be in cities as a king-bee is born in a hive, one immediately superior in body and mind . . .' (*Plt*. 301d8–e2), which seems to leave it open that one might

[8] On the general subject of the interpenetration of dialectical method and politics in the *Politicus*, see esp. Lane 1998.

conceivably come to be in a city here or a city there. But, as the older Socrates says about his ideal city in the *Republic* (592b2–3), 'it makes no difference at all whether it exists anywhere or will exist' – makes no difference, that is, to the argument. The figure of the ideal statesman, someone completely knowledgeable and competent to exercise judgment in all important spheres, is to serve as a standard, to which we must approximate as nearly as we can. The first requirement, presumably, will be to acknowledge that there is such a thing as expertise in ruling, which can be acquired – to whatever degree – by the appropriate study (as illustrated, perhaps, by the progress of the two participants in the *Politicus* itself); as things are, no city, and no 'statesman', acknowledges any such thing.

From this perspective, the wise statesman or king of the *Politicus* is the equivalent of the imaginary philosopher kings and philosopher queens of the *Republic*. They too combine theoretical knowledge with practical understanding: they have not only scaled the heights of philosophical knowledge, and come to know the Good Itself, but have also acquired the practical expertise needed for the application of that knowledge. But in place of an indefinite plurality of ideal rulers, the *Politicus* envisages a monarch, probably as a result of the way in which it uses the extraordinary elusiveness of the knowledge in question as a way of excluding the possibility that either mass-rule, or oligarchy, could be consistent with expert government. So e.g. at 297b7–c1:

> [It is not possible to contradict our earlier point] that a mass[9] of any people whatsoever would never be able to acquire this kind of expert knowledge and so govern a city with intelligence, but we must look for that one constitution, the correct one, in relation to *a small element in the population, few in number, or even one* ...

After this point, that the ideal constitution will be a monarchy is assumed.

If the *Politicus* is insistent about the need for the ideal statesman's knowledge, it is less explicit than we might have wished about what the content of his knowledge is.[10] We may infer, however, that it will centre on the 'greatest and most valuable' things (also 'finest and greatest') that are referred to in the immediate sequel to the passage at 285d4–7, cited above, about the purpose of the whole conversation:

[9] Or 'plurality', *plēthos*: cf. 300d–e.

[10] We are certainly told some of the things he will know *how to do* (direct other arts/sciences, like generalship and rhetoric; 'weave together the fabric of the state'); what we miss is any explicit account of how he would acquire the ability to do these things.

> I certainly don't suppose [says the Visitor] that anyone with any sense would want to hunt down the definition of *weaving* for the sake of weaving itself. But I think the majority of people fail to recognize that for some things, there are certain perceptible likenesses available to be easily understood, which it is not at all hard to point out when one wants to make an easy demonstration to someone who asks for an account of one of these things involving no trouble and without recourse to verbal means; conversely, for those things that are greatest and most valuable, there is no image at all which has been worked in plain view for the use of mankind, the showing of which will enable the person who wants to satisfy the mind of an inquirer to satisfy it adequately, just by fitting it to one of the senses. That is why one must practise at being able to give and receive an account of each thing; for the things that are without body, which are finest and greatest, are shown clearly only by verbal means and by nothing else, and everything that is now being said is for the sake of these things. But practice in everything is easier in smaller things, rather than in relation to the greater.

The 'some things' talked about in the second sentence comprise whatever has some analogue to it readily available to our senses (as statesmanship has not, if weaving is the best analogue or model we can find, and given the number of words it has taken to introduce it). The 'greatest things', for their part, are evidently either identical with or related to 'what is fine, just, and good', which are the things the citizens under the best constitution will have true beliefs about, guaranteed – so it seems to be suggested – by the actual knowledge of the statesman himself (309c5–8).

If so, then this will fit the comparison proposed above between this ideal figure and the philosopher rulers of the *Republic*, whose title to rule rests on their knowledge of the Good. The difference is that there are no explicit metaphysical commitments in the *Politicus*, of the sort that we find in the *Republic*. If, for example, 'the greatest things' are 'without body', that does not itself entail that they are the sorts of things the *Republic* refers to as 'forms' or *eidē*/*ideai*; the immediate context suggests rather that the point is simply that they are not perceptible, which would be equally true given any plausible account of things like goodness and justice, or none at all. What we can say without doubt, however, is that the *Politicus* is an investigation of what statesmanship *is*, and that it is not and cannot be based on what actual statesmen are like (because all without exception are non-ideal). It seems to follow that statesmanship somehow exists without being instantiated, and that its structure is accessible to us, if we look for it in the right way. But that in itself already begins to sound like a Platonic form; and much the same account would probably have to be given of 'the greatest things' themselves. What has changed, it seems, between *Republic* and *Politicus* (if we may rely on the usual view that the latter was written some time after the former) is not so much Plato's metaphysical commitments themselves as the prominence he wishes to give them.[11]

2 The myth of the *Politicus* and other political myths

The impressive cosmological myth in the *Politicus* gives a kind of pseudo-history of the universe, which is actually a way of describing different aspects of its present state.[12] Once upon a time, the Visitor tells young Socrates, there was a Golden Age of Kronos, when even the stars and planets were guided on their way by the 'greatest god', and on earth, life was maintained and preserved without effort or suffering on the part of human beings; there was no getting of wives or children (because reproduction was divinely arranged, with babies being born from seeds like plants in the earth), and there were 'no constitutions' (271e8), but each separate herd of human beings was pastured by its own guardian deity, who saw to all its needs. But then at the appointed time the god let go of the steering-oars of the universe, 'and its allotted and innate desire turned it back again in the opposite direction' (272e5–6). There were great tremors in the earth, and great destructions; and for a time everything went into reverse, including the direction of human growth. But then the universe managed to set itself in order, resuming its proper course:

> After this, when sufficient time had elapsed, it began to cease from noise and confusion and attained calm from its tremors, and set itself in order, into the accustomed course that belongs to it, itself taking charge of and mastering both the things within it and itself, because it remembered so far as it could the teaching of its craftsman and father. At the beginning it fulfilled his teaching more accurately, but in the end less keenly; the cause of this was the bodily element in its mixture, its accompaniment since its origins long in the past, because this element was marked by a great disorder before it entered into the present world-order. (273a4–b5)

[11] Cf. Kahn 1995; and, for references to different, and more radical, views of the development of Plato's metaphysical ideas, see Lane, in Ch. 8, p. 156 n.6 above.

[12] See Brisson 1995: 360–1.

So, eventually, as this 'age of Zeus' draws to an end, the supreme deity ('the greatest god') sees that he has to take control again, and the whole cycle begins once more.[13]

It is not difficult to detect here something very like the view of the world described in the *Timaeus*,[14] as the result of an uneasy combination of the work of reason and 'necessity', the latter represented especially by the limitations imposed by the shifting material with which the (fictional?) divine creator had to work. The immediate question, however, is what the role of the story is within the argument of the *Politicus*. It is introduced as a means of helping to correct mistakes that have been made in the process of division, and is duly followed by an analysis of those mistakes: most straightforwardly, the divine herdsmen in the age of Kronos represent what would actually be picked out by a definition of the statesman of the kind that had resulted, which made him the 'carer for', or even the 'rearer', of the human herd. But we may well wonder, as we are twice prompted to do by the Visitor himself (277a–b, 286b–c), whether the size of the myth is not out of all proportion to this simple function, which might easily have been achieved by other, less elaborate means. At the same time, the Visitor's final view seems to be that it was not, after all, excessive. He may thus be said to offer us an implicit invitation to discover some larger, and simultaneously less obvious, meaning in the myth.

One favoured approach has been to identify the divine herdsmen of the age of Kronos with the philosopher rulers of the *Republic*, and to see in the separation of that age from our own (that of Zeus) Plato's *rejection* of the ideal of philosophical rule.[15] This reading, however, depends on our taking the Visitor – especially in his remark about the disanalogy between human rulers and 'king-bees'[16] – to imply pessimism about the prospect for ideal statesmen. On this account, the dialogue argues the need for expert, that is, philosophical, rule, but finally decides that it is unlikely to materialize, and that we shall have to settle for second-best, the rule of law (300c). This, as I shall argue in the following part of this chapter, is nei-

[13] On the standard interpretation of the story, the age of Kronos is identical with the period of reversal. For the interpretation presupposed here, which involves a cycle of three stages (age of Kronos, reversal, age of Zeus), see Lovejoy and Boas 1935: 156–9, Brisson 1994: 478–96, 1995, Rowe 1995 (which however departs in some important matters of detail from Brisson).

[14] That is, if we take the whole account as pseudo-history, as suggested above, and as describing a synchronic state in diachronic terms. By no means all commentators accept this view (see e.g. Robinson 1995: xxv–xxvii), but it has a good pedigree (Dillon 1995), and above all it squares with the *tone* of the passage, which is explicitly marked as being – in part – 'playful' (268d8). It also avoids the problem that the *Timaeus*, with which the *Politicus* myth has close verbal and thematic links, contains no hint of heavenly reversals (though there are also problems about the precise status of the *Timaeus*' cosmological account).

[15] See e.g. Grube 1935: 279, Owen 1953a: 329–36.

[16] See p. 236 above.

ther the only nor the most natural interpretation of the tenor of the dialogue. More immediately, if the divine herdsmen are philosopher rulers, it is strange that it should explicitly be said that in that time there were 'no constitutions', no political arrangements, at all; for what the *Republic* describes is nothing if not a constitution (the very title of the work, in Greek *Politeia*, might itself in fact be better rendered as *Constitution*).[17]

If there is a single overall theme in the myth that relates to human affairs, it is about the similarity and the difference between divine and human reason. Human reason achieves only with difficulty what divine reason achieves effortlessly. Yet at the same time reason is our only weapon against chaos, destruction and disorder. There is an echo here of the argument of Book x of the *Laws*, according to which mind and its products are prior to mere mechanical causation: reason is as fundamental to the proper functioning of the human herd as it is to the functioning of the universe at large. Read in this way, the larger aspects of the myth fit neatly into the economy of the dialogue as a whole, insofar as that is occupied, first and last, with the case for rational government. True, the story does not once mention the 'art of ruling'. However it ends with a description of the acquisition of the arts in general that preserve mankind. 'We are now at the point that our account has all along been designed to reach', declares the Visitor (274b1–2): when, at the beginning of the present era, we were deprived of the god's help, most animals went wild, and we were preyed on by them, and were generally without the resources for survival.

> This is why the gifts from the gods, of which we have ancient reports, have been given to us, along with an indispensable requirement for teaching and education: fire from Prometheus, crafts from Hephaestus and his fellow-craftworker [Athena], seeds and plants from others. Everything that has helped to establish human life has come about from these things, once care from the gods, as has just been said, ceased to be available to human beings, and they had to live their lives through their own resources and take care for themselves, just like the cosmos as a whole, which we imitate and follow for all time, now living and growing in this way, now in the way we did then. (274c5–e1)

Quite who in fact 'gave' us the arts and crafts is left unsaid; presumably, since the gods had previously ceased to manage human affairs directly, we are meant at least to question the 'ancient reports' of their divine origin. The *Laws*, at least, attributes the discovery of technical skills – including, as it happens, those belonging to the statesman – to outstanding human

[17] Laks 1990: 211–12; cf. also Gill 1979.

individuals (677c–d); in the present passage, too, we may note the important rider that the 'gifts' in question come 'with an indispensable requirement for teaching and education' (they have to be worked for, and learned). In any case, 'the point that our account has all along been designed to reach' plainly centres on the necessity of expert knowledge as a whole, and that must presumably include the expert knowledge of the statesman, given that that is the subject of the whole context surrounding the myth. But the nature of political expertise, of course, has as yet not been established; in particular, it has not yet been distinguished from the pretended expertise of contemporary *politikoi*. Once that contrast has been drawn, the visitor will specifically describe the disastrous consequences for cities of the lack of true political understanding (301e–302b).

One of the main features of this 'true statesmanship' is that it is hard to acquire. The other arts require 'teaching and education'; the art of ruling is 'practically the most difficult and the most important thing to acquire' (292d4), so that – as we have seen – those who possess it will be vanishingly small in number. With this view of political expertise we may contrast a quite different one, which in other dialogues Plato alternately reports and parodies: namely the democratic view, according to which the necessary qualities are spread indiscriminately among the citizens at large. Such a view is argued for by Protagoras in the 'Great Speech' he is allowed to deliver in the *Protagoras*, though its original source seems to be the self-image of the Athenians themselves.[18]

Before this speech, Protagoras has said that he teaches men to become good, and active, citizens: that is, the 'art of politics'. Ah, responds Socrates, I thought the Athenians didn't suppose such a thing can be taught, because whereas, when other things are debated in the assembly, they call on the relevant experts for their opinions, when it comes to the government of the city they allow anyone, from any walk of life, to offer their advice, without asking them for their qualification to do so; and the 'wisest and best' men, like Pericles, also evidently fail to teach their sons the expertise they have. Protagoras could presumably have replied that the Athenians are wrong, that exceptionally able individuals can be taught this art of politics, and that he is the one to teach them. But instead he sets out to argue that Athenian practice is in fact consistent with the teachability of the expertise in question: it is a condition of the existence of cities

[18] See also the discussions of the 'Great Speech' by Winton, Ch. 4 section 2, and Penner, Ch. 9 section 4 above. An important vehicle of the Athenians' self-image was the genre of the funeral speech, of which Thucydides re-creates the most famous example; that, or the original version of Pericles' speech, is one of the sources of Plato's parody of the genre, in the *Menexenus*. See Schofield, in Ch. 10 section 2 above.

that their citizens possess it, and that is why 'people generally, and especially the Athenians' allow everyone a say when it comes to 'political excellence' (*Prot.* 322d5–323a3).

Not every city is in fact governed democratically, but – Protagoras suggests – nature declares that they *should* be, or might be, if they had the institutions that Athens has: the view there, at any rate, is that everyone who is not terminally corrupted is capable of acquiring the relevant qualities, through teaching. The teaching comes from formal schooling (325c–326c), from the laws (326c–e), and from one's fellow-citizens (326e–328a). What is in question here is clearly a shared value-system,[19] which Protagoras sums up as 'justice and moderation and scrupulous living; taking it all together, I term it the excellence of a man'. It is something 'that everyone must share in, and must accompany everything a man undertakes to learn or to do, whatever it may be' – including political 'actions' (325a1–5); the virtues or excellences in question are indispensable, if these actions are to be successful (thus, for example, the successful conduct of war will depend on the existence of an organized community: cf. 321c–d).

The basis of the whole argument is that the 'political virtues', especially 'justice and respect for others', are necessary for successful human living, and that they are in a sense natural to human beings. These ideas are put over in the myth with which Protagoras starts his speech: the arts and crafts, stolen by Prometheus, with fire, from Hephaestus and Athena, are not sufficient for survival, but have to be supplemented by the institution of cities, and the gift from Zeus of the virtues in question, or rather of the capacity for them. In making the gift, Zeus himself underlines the paradox: when Hermes, his agent, asks whether these new gifts should be distributed on the same basis as the arts and crafts, i.e. only to a few, Zeus replies:

> To all – let all have their share. Cities would never come into existence if only a few shared in them, as they do in the arts. Furthermore, lay it down as my law that anyone who is incapable of sharing in respect for others and in justice shall be put to death as a plague to the city. (322d1–5)

This alleged distinction between 'the political art' and other forms of expert knowledge is exactly what is denied by the *Politicus*: the political art, as much as – or rather even more than – the others, is a matter for individual specialists. The myth and the following sections of the *Politicus* thus

[19] Cf. Ober 1993.

constitute a kind of counter to the democratic myth, in either of its versions: the 'art of ruling' is not something that everyone can learn, as Protagoras suggests (or Plato suggests, on Protagoras' behalf),[20] nor does it come naturally, as an Aspasia[21] or a Pericles would have it. The idea of a democracy based on merit is absurd and based on mere hopeful and self-deluding assertion; what is necessary to the survival of the city is something that is actually beyond most people – if not all.

3 King or law?

At *Politicus* 291a, quite near the end of the search for the true statesman, the visitor from Elea says that he has caught sight of a mixed and strange crowd of people, whom he identifies as the 'greatest magicians of all the sophists, and the most versed in their expertise': the 'politicians', the so-called experts in ruling. What makes them magicians and sophists, on his account, is that they are illusionists on the largest scale, pretending to a knowledge that they do not possess, and about the most important matters. The long discussion that ensues is designed primarily to establish this view of them, and so justify separating them off from the genuine statesman.

In outline, the argument is as follows. People currently divide constitutions according to various different factors: the number of people in power (whether one, few, or many); whether they are rich or poor; whether they rule with or without the consent of the ruled; or whether or not they stick to established law and custom. However it was agreed at the beginning that statesmanship was a matter of expert knowledge, which is distinct from all the other proposed criteria. No actual constitution is in fact based on the requisite expertise; if it is indeed a necessary condition of statesmanship, and of running a city, then there are actually no genuine constitutions, and *a fortiori*, no genuine statesmen.

> It must then be the case, it seems, that of constitutions too the one that is correct in comparison with the rest, and alone a constitution, is the one in which the rulers would be found truly possessing expert knowledge, and not merely seeming to do so, whether they rule according to laws or without laws, over willing or unwilling subjects, and whether the rulers are poor or wealthy – there is no principle of correctness according to which any of these must be taken into any account at all. (293c5–d2)

[20] There is probably no reason to think that the real Protagoras might not have said something like what Plato puts into his mouth in the dialogue; nevertheless the speech itself is a Platonic construction.

[21] The supposed author of the speech Socrates claims to recite in the *Menexenus* (see n.18 above).

The Visitor then employs an analogy with doctors that he has introduced just before this passage:

> And whether they purge the city for its benefit by putting some people to death or else by exiling them, or whether again they make it smaller by sending out colonies somewhere like swarms of bees, or build it up by introducing people from somewhere outside and making them citizens – so long as they act to preserve it on the basis of expert knowledge and what is just, making it better than it was so far as they can, *this* is the constitution which alone we must say is correct, under these conditions and in accordance with criteria of this sort. All the others we generally say are constitutions we must say not to be genuine, and not really constitutions at all, but imitations of this one; those we say are 'law-abiding'[22] have imitated it for the better, the others for the worse. (293d4–e5)

Here young Socrates makes a crucial objection: can it really be right to say that the person with expert knowledge will be justified even in overriding the laws? Of all the criteria mentioned, the one most familiarly used for identifying good government (which is after all what is at issue), at any rate among more conservative critics, would probably have been the degree of readiness with which a city would accept change to its existing laws: the more difficult it made the process, the better. Thus there might after all be some actually existing constitutions, and some politicians, that would pass muster. It is at this point that the visitor introduces his criticism of laws as a whole, that they lack the flexibility that would be required to cater properly for the infinitely various conditions of human life. Were there to be someone who had the requisite knowledge, it would be absurd to insist that he be tied down by written prescriptions, if he saw something that would work better.

> And is it not the case that there is no mistake for wise rulers, whatever they do, provided that they watch for one great thing, that by always distributing to those in the city what is most just, as judged by the intelligent application of their expertise, they are able both to preserve them and so far as they can to bring it about that they are better than they were? (297a5–b3)

This takes us back to a previous conclusion: that other constitutions, where this sort of wisdom is lacking, are mere 'imitations' of this best one – 'some of imitating it for the better, the others for the worse' (297c3–4).

This is a puzzling notion, and young Socrates is duly puzzled (as he says, he failed to understand it the first time too). The Visitor explains by

[22] Or 'those people generally called "well-governed"', which will probably turn out for the most part to be the same ones.

means of an imaginative fiction: suppose that doctors or sailors were required to operate wholly according to the book. Would the consequences not be wholly absurd? The result, in fact, would be the destruction of the very arts of medicine and seamanship themselves. A requirement, in the sphere of politics, merely to 'stick to the law and established precedent' would ultimately have the same effect. Yet at the same time, the Visitor claims, a constitution based upon such a principle would be better than a set of arrangements under which those in power operated in their own interests, or out of favouritism, without reference to the laws. This latter sort of situation is what was meant by a 'bad imitation' ('altogether' bad, as it is now said to be: 300e1). It 'imitates', or mimics, the state of affairs under the best constitution in that the ideal statesman, too, is always ready to change the laws, and it does so 'badly' because the knowledge that justified *his* abandoning the written code is now absent.

Visitor Now we said – if we remember – that the knowledgeable person, the one who really possesses the art of statesmanship, would do many things in relation to his own activity by using his expertise, without taking any notice of the written laws, when other things appear to him better, contrary to the things that have been written down by him and given as orders to people who are not currently with him.

Young Socrates Yes, that's what we said.

Visitor Well, any individual whatever or any large collection of people whatever, for whom there are actually written laws established, whatever they undertake to do that is different, contrary to these, on the grounds that it is better, will be doing, won't they, the same thing as that true expert, so far as they can?

Young Socrates Absolutely.

Visitor Well then, if they were to do such a thing without having expert knowledge, they would be undertaking to imitate what is true, but would imitate it altogether badly; but if they did it on the basis of expertise, this is no longer imitation but that very thing that is most truly what it sets out to be? (300c9–e2)

But it was previously agreed that no large number of people – whether large enough to form a democracy or an oligarchy – is capable of acquiring any sort of expertise whatever. 'So', concludes the Visitor, with young Socrates' agreement, 'the requirement, as it seems, for all constitutions of this sort [i.e. those ruled by 'few' or many, without knowledge], if they are going to produce a good imitation of that true constitution of one man ruling with expertise, so far as they can, is that – given that they have their laws – they must never do anything contrary to what is written or to ancestral customs.' The same conclusion is extended to the case of the single ignorant ruler.

Rule by one person, few, or many may be either law-bound or law-less. This gives us six types of constitutions (so far as the Visitor and young Socrates are prepared to call them constitutions at all), or seven if we include ideal monarchy: kingship and tyranny, 'aristocracy' and oligarchy, and two types of democracy, or rule by the *dēmos*. (The *dēmos* is identified with the poor, as opposed to the rich; conversely oligarchies, and 'aristocracies', involve the rule of the rich over the poor.) Of these, kingship, 'aristocracy' and the better type of democracy will apparently be 'good', or 'better', imitations of the best, just so long as they 'never do anything contrary to what is written or to ancestral customs'. The reason why they should operate like this is plainly, once again, that the requisite knowledge which would justify their changing anything is lacking. But it is not then immediately obvious what they will have in common with the best constitution, to warrant their being called 'imitations' of it (even if it is clear why they are 'better' than the other sort). The main features of the best constitution, after all, are that it is based on knowledge, and that the laws may be changed, which are precisely the features that the 'law-bound' constitutions do not have.

The most common solution to this problem is to suppose that the constitutions in question are good imitations insofar as they have good laws, presumably bequeathed to them by knowledgeable legislators in the past. The upshot would be a policy of abiding by the 'ancestral constitution', which might be the kind of thing that young Socrates had in mind. If the ideal monarch is not available, then (the Visitor would be suggesting) the second-best thing will be a total conservatism (cf. 300c1–3: '. . . the second-best method of proceeding, for those who establish laws and written rules about anything whatever, is to allow neither individual nor mass ever to do anything contrary to these, anything whatsoever'). However there are considerable objections to this interpretation. Firstly, the Visitor will be endangering the very claim which he is supposed to be supporting, namely that *all* current politicians are impostors. The closer the laws of a given city are to those that would belong to the ideal one, the less those who run it will tend to look like 'sophists' and 'illusionists'. If the rulers in such a case did not possess knowledge themselves, the laws they observed would be greater or lesser approximations to those 'imitations of the truth' – 'the things issuing from those who know which have been written down so far as they can be' (300c5–6);[23] even if such rulers would still, strictly speaking, be usurping the role which ought to be held by a genuinely expert statesman (insofar as ruling requires the genuine article), nevertheless their actions would be guided indirectly by something resembling the truth. For such people, the Visitor's descriptions ('sophists', 'magicians', etc.) would seem at the least somewhat harsh.

A second, and probably more damaging, objection is that not only are the wise ancient legislators of non-ideal cities not mentioned, but it appears to be assumed – at any rate for the purposes of the argument – that the laws of these cities will in fact derive from ignorance. The only description of their legislative processes that we are given is the one summarized at 300b, which refers to 'the laws that have been established on the basis of much experiment, with some advisers or other having given advice on each subject in an attractive way, and having persuaded the majority to pass them'. The description, like the longer passage on which it depends (298a–299c), is admittedly a caricature, but it is not replaced by anything else. We seem to be left with an absolute contrast between the laws of the ideal city, as based on knowledge, and those of any other city, which in the absence of experts can only be based on 'much experience', the advice of 'some advisers or other' (who might in principle include experts, but without any special attention being paid to their opinions: cf. 298c), and the approval of the majority, who are certainly assumed to be ignorant. It is difficult to see how laws established in this way could turn out to be 'imitations of the truth', 'written by those who know', which would presuppose the guiding hand of an ideal statesman. But in that case there can be no guarantee that they are good laws; and if so, this surely cannot be the feature of law-bound cities which is picked out by calling them 'good imitations' of the best.

These objections to the standard interpretation of 'good imitation' seem to be decisive, and to require us to look for an alternative. One possibility[24] is to suppose that the Visitor is offering us a paradox: the best way of 'imitating' the best constitution will be not to try to imitate it at all. After all, the main distinguishing feature of the best constitution is that the king may change his instructions at any time, if he judges it necessary (and his judgment, of course, will always be correct), whereas the law-bound constitutions will change absolutely nothing, ever. But there

[23] These 'imitations of the truth' are usually interpreted as being laws in general (so most recently Annas and Waterfield 1995); but the argument would not justify such a description of all laws. Rather, they are those laws which the knowledgeable legislator would write down, as faithfully to the truth as one can ever write anything (for the qualification, see *Phaedrus* 275d ff.).

[24] Suggested to me by Malcolm Schofield.

is no indication that such a paradox is in the offing: these constitutions are consistently said to be imitating (*mimeisthai*) the best (293e, 297c, 301a). Perhaps they imitate, or mimic, it just to the extent that all existing constitutions do so (by pretending to be constitutions, in the same sense that all existing rulers pretend to the role of the ideal statesman), and are better imitations just in that they are better than the other type (the law-less). Yet there is still also one special way in which they will genuinely resemble the best constitution. If the ideal statesman is not bound by his laws, nevertheless he will certainly need to put laws in place, both because he cannot be everywhere at once, and in order to cover those occasions when he is physically absent from the city (295a–296a; cf. 300c). But then it will clearly not be up to the citizens at large to start changing his prescriptions, since they do not have the expertise to do so; and in general we may say that it is true of the best city that it will not change the laws when the expertise required for doing so is not present. In that case, in not changing its laws, the law-bound constitution will be genuinely reproducing a feature of the ideal (as the law-less constitution fails to do: that both it and the ideal constitution change their laws gives only a superficial resemblance between them, insofar as the circumstances of the change will be quite different). There is no suggestion that the law-bound constitution will stick to the legislation it has because it *recognizes* that it lacks the expertise necessary to justify any change; nevertheless it will be true of it both that it does lack it, and that it does not change its laws.[25]

In any case, whichever of these readings we adopt, the Visitor – and no doubt Plato – will be taking up a uncompromising position: that there is nothing good, except perhaps through happy accident, in any existing constitution (if we exclude the possibility of the instantiation somewhere of the ideal type). We may get things right, sometimes, but without knowledge we are more likely to get them wrong – and regularly do. This

[25] It is tempting, again, to suppose that this is because they are at least moderately good (so that any change, in the absence of expertise, might well be for the worse); and indeed a little later, when the relative desirability – or liveability – of the three law-bound and the three law-less constitutions is being discussed, law-bound monarchy, and by implication the other two law-bound types, are judged preferable on condition that they have good laws (302e). But, as we have seen, that is not and cannot be the basis of their superiority in the present context; it is rather that they *have* laws, and stick to them. Still, it must be conceded that those laws must at least not be wholly intolerable (which would put the decision between them and the lawless types at risk), and that will perhaps be guaranteed to the extent that they are founded on experience and general agreement. We need not, of course, assume Plato to be committed to the idea that anything quite like his (absolutely) law-bound type of constitution ever existed or would be likely to exist. There will be approximations to it; but in itself it will be as much a theoretical construct as the ideal statesman himself, and derived from the same thought-experiment, which pushes the single premise about the necessity for expert knowledge to its uttermost limit.

is an extreme position, but it is wholly consistent with the way in which the Visitor began, and will end, by dismissing all existing politicians, without exception (291a–c, 303b–d).[26] It is also consistent with the following, chilling, passage, which strongly recalls the pessimism of the myth:

> Do we wonder, then, Socrates, at all the evils that turn out to occur in such constitutions, and all those that will turn out for them, when a foundation of this kind underlies them, one of carrying out their functions according to written rules and customs without knowledge, which if used by another expertise would manifestly destroy everything that comes about through it? Or should we rather wonder at something else, namely at how strong a thing a city is by its nature? For in fact cities have suffered such things now for an unlimited time, but nevertheless some particular ones among them are enduring and are not overturned; yet many from time to time sink like ships, and perish, and have perished, and will perish in the future through the depravity of their steersmen and sailors, who have acquired the greatest ignorance about the greatest things – although they have no understanding at all about what belongs to the art of statesmanship, they think they have completely acquired this kind of expert knowledge, most clearly of all. (301e6–302b3)

But most importantly, the Visitor's position is consistent with his identification of statesmanship as a form of specialized *expertise*: if that is what it is, and no actual 'statesman' or constitution recognizes the fact, then all must inevitably be found lacking. The same, essentially theoretical, starting-point is also what explains the provocative rejection of all other considerations, and of any limitation whatsoever on the statesman's power, just so long as he *knows*.

However, if that is what statesmanship really *is* (see section 1 above), there is no guarantee that even the best and most accomplished of actual statesmen will fully exemplify it. Plato's awareness of the difference between the ideal and the actual is illustrated by the brief treatment with which the present part of the *Politicus* ends, of the question

> which of these 'incorrect' constitutions is least difficult to live with, given that they are all difficult, and which the heaviest to bear? Should we take a brief look at this, although a discussion of it will be a side-issue in relation to the subject now set before us? And yet, at any rate in

[26] Passages like these create serious difficulties for a common type of reading of the *Politicus*, which sees it as including a (reluctant) reconciliation to existing forms of government. Such readings must, at best, attribute 'tensions' to the argument of the dialogue, or 'complication and even confusion' (so Annas and Waterfield 1995: xxii); such verdicts, presumably, should be accepted only as a last resort.

> general, perhaps everything that all of us do is for the sake of this sort of thing. (302b5–9)

'This sort of thing' seems to be the living of a tolerable life, and 'these "incorrect" constitutions' are the six types that actually exist. Monarchy will be best of all the six, if it is 'yoked' in laws, and they are good laws, and worst if it is law-less (i.e. if it is tyranny); with democracy it will be the other way round, because

> we may suppose [the rule of the mass of people] to be weak in all respects and capable of nothing of any importance either for good or for bad as judged in relation to the others, because of the fact that under it offices are distributed in small portions among many people. (303a4–6)

That there are actually any monarchies that have good laws, or any similarly endowed democracies, is not said, and given what he has previously said we are entitled to doubt whether the Visitor means to allow that there are; but at least it is raised as a possibility. Somehow, somewhere, the importance of the role of *knowledge* in the government of cities might begin to be acknowledged; and then they might begin to do what cities are meant to do, which is to set about making the citizens 'better than they were, so far as possible' (297b3).

4 The statesman as director and weaver

In the puzzling dialogue *Euthydemus*[27] old Socrates raises the question what the 'kingly' or 'political' art *does*. It has previously been agreed that none of the things usually counted as good (health, wealth, and so on) are so unless we know how to use them, and that we can only acquire such knowledge through philosophy. Since philosophy is the acquisition of knowledge, the next step is to establish what sort of knowledge we need to acquire: not that of the expert gold-digger, businessman, doctor, orator, or general, because none of these sorts of knowledge include the crucial ingredient of knowing how to use their products. Finally, Socrates suggests that it is the expert in the kingly art who will know how to use the products of the other kinds of expertise. But then (291d–e) he asks the question about what the product of *this* art or expertise is (on the assumption that it has one, like other kinds of expertise). It must be something good; but if so, it cannot be any of the things that political knowledge is

[27] The *Euthydemus* takes the form of a report by Socrates to Crito of a conversation he had had with Euthydemus and others the day before. The report is interspersed with discussion with Crito of the subjects talked about; for simplicity's sake I shall treat the dialogue as if it were a straight conversation between two people.

usually thought to produce (wealth, freedom, stability . . .), because it has been established that these are not good in themselves. It makes people wise and good; but what kind of wisdom and goodness does it impart? The only kind of good it can impart is itself: then it will make people wise and good in this respect, and they in turn will do the same for others – but we have no specification of what it actually consists in, 'and we are just as far away, if not further, from knowing what that knowledge is that will make us happy' (292e4–5).

Here the discussion of the topic ends. Quite what we are to make of it is unclear, and it may be that we are meant to accept Socrates' formal conclusion that the argument has simply reached a dead end. However, since this part of the dialogue is plainly designed to contrast with the playful sophistic sparring which occupies most of the rest, there might easily arise a suspicion that we are being guided towards some sort of conception of the true 'art of politics'. Three points seem to emerge. Firstly, the art is not directly concerned with the production of those things that are normally supposed to be its ends; secondly, it either is, or includes, knowing how to put such things to good use; and thirdly, it imparts this knowledge to others.[28] Only one sort of knowledge seems to meet these specifications: the sort that would result from philosophizing, and from Socratic dialectic – and that, after all, is where the first movement of the argument left us.

Here the *Euthydemus* might seem to meet up neatly with the *Politicus*. We earlier saw[29] reason to suppose that the knowledge of the ideal statesman or king of the *Politicus* is itself based in philosophical understanding, that is, understanding reached by a rational, dialectical process, the nature of which the dialogue teaches us at length. To the extent that it is a work of political theory, at the core of that theory is not a demand for autocratic government by experts (though if such were to be found, they would surely have to be installed as kings), but rather an insistence on the priority of discovering the true ends of life. At the same time, it is assumed that these will include the virtues; the primary task of true political expertise – as in the *Euthydemus* – is to make people *good*.

But there is one important difference between the two dialogues. The *Euthydemus* appears to suggest that there is nothing more to what the

[28] If we extract these elements from the context, we will of course be presupposing that Socrates (or Plato) can find his way out of the nest of apparently incompatible ideas that cause the impasse, without actually abandoning any of them. But again the implied contrast with sophistic procedures strongly suggests that he should not be introducing, for merely strategic purposes, premises he is not prepared to defend.

[29] See section 1 above.

political art 'does' than imparting its knowledge, or, perhaps more realistically, the habit of looking for it; and the art itself would represent simply the ideal summation of philosophical understanding. Virtue is treated implicitly as a consequence of knowledge, as so often in the so-called 'Socratic' dialogues (whether or not the *Euthydemus* is to count as one of these). As for ordinary political ends, these are simply set to one side. The *Politicus*, however, discovers a 'product' of the statesman's art which extends beyond the practice and teaching of dialectic. This is, first, in its direction of the most important subordinate arts, those of the orator, the general, and the judge. In all of these cases,

> what is really kingship must not itself perform practical tasks, but control those with the capacity to perform them, because it knows when it is the right time to begin and set in motion the most important things in cities and when it is the wrong time; and the others must do what has been prescribed for them. (305d1–4)

Secondly, the statesman will see to the 'weaving together' (311b7) of the more 'courageous' and competitive elements among the citizens with the more 'moderate' and pacific,[30] so that both make their proper, and opportune, contribution to the life of the city.[31] In both these roles, he seems to acquire a direct involvement in practical politics of the sort that is denied to the ideal king of the *Euthydemus*.[32] Up to a point, both ideas may be seen as a restatement of the general point which is central to the *Euthydemus* discussion, that nothing is good or useful in separation from knowing how to use it (which derives from philosophy alone). But if – as the *Politicus*, and the *Republic*, recognize – the majority of people will never be philosophers, making them good will require more than a diet of dialectic. The art of statesmanship must find other methods.[33] That is why the *Politicus* finds room in the hierarchy of 'arts' for a (reformed, philosophically-directed) art of rhetoric; for it is presumably this that would be the chief means to the inculcation of right beliefs in the citizens at large (309c).[34]

[30] On this (final) section of the *Politicus*, see esp. Lane 1995, 1998, Dixsaut 1995, Bobonich 1995.

[31] There is a clear, if partial, parallel in *Republic* v, in the shape of the discussion of methods for ensuring the unity of the city.

[32] For the conception of kingship/statesmanship in the *Euthydemus*, we may compare Socrates' claim in the *Gorgias* to be the only true *politikos*, just in virtue of his telling the ungarnished truth.

[33] Cf. Penner, in Ch. 9 section 1 above.

[34] The result is a kind of *rapprochement* with the views put in Protagoras' mouth (section 2 above): all the citizens will have (a degree of) virtue, and it will be produced by methods that are superficially not unlike those Protagoras describes. Similarly in the *Republic*. But Protagoras' methods will be based in custom and convention, not in philosophy.

5 The *Politicus*, the *Timaeus-Critias*, and the *Laws*

A close relation of the ideal constitution of the *Politicus* appears in another of Plato's fictional essays in prehistory, the story of Atlantis in the *Timaeus* and *Critias*. The story, supposedly recovered by Solon from a priestly archive in Egypt, is about how, once upon a time, the originally virtuous kings of Atlantis – a vast and wealthy empire, based on a large island outside the straits of Gibraltar – went to the bad and tried to conquer the rest of the world, but were resisted and finally defeated by Athens. Atlantis itself, after violent earthquakes and floods, at last disappeared beneath the waves, and all the people of Athens too were engulfed. This early Athens, we are told, was (as it happens) very like an ideal city that those present had been discussing the day before; and the description of this ideal city makes it resemble the city of the *Republic* in so many respects that we can hardly be blamed for supposing that it is the *Republic* – or something like it – that we are meant to have in mind. (The 'guards' who constitute the fighting force are to be separated from the rest of the citizens, educated and fed at public expense, barred from having private property and families, and so on.) The main difference from the *Republic* is that there is no direct mention of philosopher rulers, and probably no room for them in any case; the city seems rather to be run on the basis of divinely-inspired laws, which provide the kinds of institutions that allow it to run well, most importantly by providing for the education in virtue of its citizens.[35] The kings of Atlantis, by contrast, are said to have 'had control of the men [in their several cities] and *of most of the laws*' (*Critias* 119c3–4), the exception being those laws which govern their relationships with each other, which had been written down for them by their ancestor Poseidon. This arrangement worked well at the beginning, because – as befits the children or descendants of a god – they were perfectly virtuous individuals, who were capable of counting everything apart from their own virtue, including their massive wealth, as of little importance. But as their distance from their divine origin increased, and the divine element in their natures grew accordingly weaker, so things began to go wrong . . .

The *Critias* is unfinished, breaking off in mid-sentence, and the precise moral of the whole fiction which it takes over from the *Timaeus* can probably not be established with any certainty. But there can be no doubt about the general tenor of the story: that Athens defeats Atlantis, that it

[35] See especially *Tim.* 24b–d.

does so because of the superiority of its institutions and its people, and that its people are of superior quality at least primarily because of the quality of its institutions, which it got directly or indirectly from the gods. Equally, we know that the Atlanteans are defeated because their rulers are corrupted, and lose the wisdom and self-mastery which kept them subject to divine law. It was presumably those same qualities that allowed them to 'be in control of the laws' in their treatment of their subjects: if they 'punished and killed whomever they wished' (119c4–5), that was because they knew, then, who should be punished and killed. In this respect, and in respect of their control of (most of) the laws, they are as like the ideal king of the *Politicus* as the 'guardians' of ancient Athens are like the soldiers and future rulers of the city of the *Republic*.

But the city, and the citizens, over which they rule are entirely different from those ruled by the paragon of the *Politicus*. There, the citizens in his care share delegated power under his control, and indeed his main concern as weaver of the fabric of the city will evidently be to ensure the combination of different types of character among the holders of public office:

> This is the single and complete task of kingly weaving-together, never to allow moderate dispositions to stand away from the courageous, but by working them closely into each other as if with a shuttle, through sharing of opinions, through honours, dishonour, esteem, and the giving of pledges to one another, drawing together a smooth and 'fine-woven' fabric out of them, as the expression is, always to entrust offices in cities to these in common. (301e7–311a2)

Similarly in the Athens of the *Timaeus-Critias* the 20,000 guards seem to share office between themselves:

> They then conducted their lives in this fashion, guards of their own citizens, and leaders of the other Greeks, who willingly accepted their leadership; and so far as possible they maintained their own number, of men and women, those within the age-range for fighting wars, permanently around the figure of twenty thousand. So, endowed with characters of this kind, and in some such way as this administering both their own city, and Greece, with justice . . . (*Critias* 112d3–e3)

By contrast, the standing army of Atlantis – which is reinforced when needed by contingents drawn from the rest of the population – appears to be constituted by the kings' bodyguards, 'the more trustworthy' of which live around the acropolis, where the royal residence is, and the most outstanding within it (as the citizen soldiers of 'primitive' Athens themselves live on the acropolis, around the temple of their patron gods, Athena and

Hephaestus). In general, Atlantis in the far west is figured as an eastern, non-Greek monarchy – like Persia, whose parallel defeat by a later Athens is celebrated in the funeral speeches parodied by the *Menexenus*. Her kings rule, in the beginning, just because of their divine origins, and their consequent superiority to the remainder of the population. But as time progresses, they become more like them, and the character of their rule turns from kingship to tyranny.

The contrast between the decline of Atlantis, and the more stable properties of prehistoric Athens, finds a more prosaic expression at *Laws* 875a–d:

> . . . no human being has in his nature the capacity both to recognize what is beneficial to mankind in regard to its political arrangements and, once he has recognized it, always to be able and wish to do what is best. . . . If in fact someone has the natural ability to acquire the relevant expert knowledge to an adequate degree, and after this rules over a city without being subject to examination, with absolute power, he would never be able to abide by his previous decisions and to live his life nurturing the common good as the guiding element in the city, and keeping the private good subordinate to the common, but his mortal nature will always impel him towards his own enrichment and private interests . . . Granted, if by divine good fortune some human being were born with a nature that gave him the capacity to acquire [the ability to resist these inevitable tendencies], he would not need laws which would rule over himself; for no law and no ordering of things is superior to knowledge . . . But as things are, since it is nowhere to be found at all, except to some small extent – for that reason we must choose the second option, the ordering of law, which looks and pays regard to what is for the most part, but is powerless to cover everything. (*Laws* 875a2–d5)

The kings of Atlantis were originally more than human, and so could do – at the beginning – what the Athenian here says no mere man could ever do. But Athens, ruled by law, turns out to be the more durable society. It is only in a city permanently inhabited, or ruled, by divine beings that power could ever be given to an individual, rather than to the law (cf. *Laws* 739d–e, 713c–714a).

It is the *Laws* itself that describes the 'second option', the rule of law. This is not the 'second-best' of *Politicus* 300c, which consisted simply in the principle of strict adherence to law. Certainly, the law in Magnesia will be very difficult to change, and in most cases – after an initial period – is envisaged as likely to be fixed for all time. But that is not, as in the case of the 'law-bound' cities of the *Politicus*, because of the absence of the expert legislator. The legislator of the *Laws* is himself an expert, directly comparable to the ideal statesman of the *Politicus* – at the least, an approximation to him: thus the main speaker, a visitor from Athens, claims the authority of 'very considerable experience and *inquiry* in such matters' (*Laws* 968b). His legislation, like that of the ideal statesman, will be an 'imitation of the truth' (so far as this is possible);[36] and it will remain fixed just insofar as, and so long as, no better alternative can be devised by reason. Imperfect though his laws may be, as all laws must be, they are the only 'monarch' to whom, in the actual world, we should submit.

[36] If much of its detail coincides with contemporary Athenian legislation (see Morrow 1993 (1960)), that is, in principle, accidental: what is included is there because rational consideration shows it to be *right*.

12

The *Laws*

ANDRÉ LAKS

1 A singular work

The *Laws* can be considered the first work of genuine political philosophy in the Western tradition. Admittedly it was conceived within an already complex tradition of philosophical legislation and speculative constructions, in which the *Republic* holds an important place. But so far as we can judge, the *Laws*' combination of an investigation into the foundations of legislation with the concrete elaboration of detailed laws is without precedent. From this point of view, the *Republic* is at best a sketch, whereas the *Laws* breaks ground for future political thought.

Part of the work's importance lies in its having created a new genre, or rather two, by combining two approaches which posterity would come to distinguish. The *Laws* is at once an exposition of political principles (comparable to Rousseau's *Social Contract* or Hegel's *Principles of the Philosophy of Right*), and a treatise of applied legislation (comparable to the *Project for the Constitution of Corsica* or the proposal for a German Constitution). Moreover, several concepts elaborated in the *Laws* have proved of lasting value to political philosophy. The so-called principle of Lord Acton, that absolute power corrupts absolutely, is already formulated in the *Laws*. More positive philosophical ideas first articulated in the *Laws* include the 'mixed constitution', the 'rule of law', and last but not least the 'legislative preamble'. Plato himself presents this last item as his greatest legislative innovation (722e1–4).

Despite its historic importance, the work has been neglected, or even treated with contempt – by philosophers in particular.[1] Part of this reac-

My special thanks to the editors of the volume and to John Palmer for helping me to improve the English in which this chapter is written.

[1] Fundamental works on the *Laws* in English include the general study of Morrow 1960, and the work of Saunders, now synthesized in Saunders 1991, which focuses on the penal aspect of the *Laws* (see also his translation of the *Laws* (1970)). The creative studies of Bobonich 1991, 1994 will be integrated into a forthcoming book. In Germany, Hentschke 1971 represents substantial progress in understanding the dialogue. Schöpsdau 1994 is the first volume of a general commentary on the *Laws*, which will replace the outdated work by England 1921. It testifies to the renewal of interest in the *Laws*.

tion may be explained by the difficulties the work poses for the reader. The length of the work seems excessive, the material arid, and the style tortuous. Most off-putting of all is its organization, a tangle which seems to defy understanding. Yet independently of such formal considerations, there are three crucial reasons for the relative neglect the *Laws* has suffered.

(1) The influence of the *Laws*, important as it may be, has been largely indirect. The central idea of the 'mixed constitution', in particular, is more familiar from its reworking at the hands of Cicero and Polybius than from the *Laws* itself. This seeming contingency of intellectual transmission in fact manifests a certain logic. In Cicero, the Platonism of the *Laws* is integrated into a Stoic perspective (the theory of natural law); in Polybius, the mixed constitution is identified with the destiny of Rome. In both cases the breadth of the resulting orientation has eclipsed the original Platonic vision set out by the improbable avatars of a small Cretan colony.

(2) The second reason has to do with the history of reception of Plato's political thought. In the cultural milieu of speculative philosophy and the Protestant tradition, the *Laws* was simultaneously not 'philosophical' enough to command attention, and too 'catholic' to be above suspicion. Indeed, one could write a history of the comparison drawn between the organization of the Platonic city and that of the Roman Catholic church, both of which were seen as repressive and anti-individualistic. Unsurprisingly this comparison was made especially by thinkers in the Anglo-Saxon liberal tradition, moulded by John Stuart Mill's and George Grote's readings of Plato. In this context the *Laws* appears to accentuate, almost to the point of caricature, the most unfortunate tendencies of the *Republic*, and more precisely to prefigure authoritarian or even totalitarian regimes. In this regard nothing is more telling than Cornford's 1935 rewriting of the Dostoyevskian tale of the Grand Inquisitor in a Platonic vein: were Socrates to return to the city of the *Laws* to promote his principle of free discussion, he would be put to death – as surely as would a returning Christ by the Church which acts in his name.[2]

(3) To these two general reasons must be added the fact that the *Laws* occupies a singular position in the Platonic corpus (so much so that its authenticity was still questioned not so very long ago).[3] On the one hand

[2] Cornford 1950 (1935). The framework of Cornford's essay is found in Mill 1978 (1866), who went so far as to compare the Nocturnal Council (on which see below, section 5) with the Torquemadian Inquisition. The parallel between the Platonic city and the medieval Roman church stems from the Protestant theologian F. C. Baur. On his reception in England, cf. Turner 1981: 436.

[3] Müller 1951.

the work's voluminous legislative codification is unique in Plato (hence its documentary importance for legal history). On the other hand, the actual philosophy in the work seems to have been reduced to a strictly subservient role ('philosophy' is referred to only twice in the whole work (857d2, 967c8), and is never discussed as such). Neither of these two features – which have wrongly been seen as complementary – sits well with the received image of 'Platonism'. Moreover, the *Seventh Letter*'s recounting of Plato's adventures in Sicily was long thought to invite a reading of the *Laws* as a document of political disappointment, a reading also thought necessary to explain why certain of its features apparently contradict the better-regarded *Republic*. A crucial question, then, is whether the *Laws* can claim any philosophical legitimacy whatsoever.

Before turning to this question, however, it will be useful to give an idea of the structure and the content of the work. Not only does the reader need guidance, but, as we shall see, the formal construction of the work is highly relevant to its political programme.[4]

2 The structure and content of the *Laws*

The *Laws* presents itself as a conversation about legislation among three old men: an anonymous Athenian, called the 'Stranger' by his interlocutors (since the conversation takes place in Crete he is indeed a stranger there); Megillus of Sparta; and Clinias, citizen of the Lacedaemonian colony of Knossos. The three old men discourse on 'constitutions and laws' – a diversion appropriate to their age (685a7ff., 769a1ff.) – while walking on the road from Knossos to the grotto of Zeus on Mount Ida (625b).

The walk is doubly linked to the theme. First, the route is the same one that Minos, the legendary lawgiver of Crete, followed every nine years to receive the teachings of Zeus (624a7–b3). Now 'the god' – the first word of the dialogue, as is often noted – will soon turn out to be the foundation of the Platonic legislation, as he is of the Doric laws.[5] Although Plato does not use the word 'theocratic', he is not far from coining it, as the following passage indicates: '[The actual constitutions] are named after the power that rules in each case. Now if that is the sort of name that must be given

[4] For a synoptic view of the whole work, see Saunders 1970: 5–14, and Schöpsdau 1994: 95–8. References to themes treated in various parts of the dialogue are usefully assembled at the beginning of each section of Stalley 1983.

[5] Crete and the Peloponnese had been invaded by the Dorians toward the end of the Mycenean period. They shared a common dialect and a culture which in important respects set them apart from other Greeks, especially the Ionians, to which Athens was felt to be historically linked by the Greeks (see Herodotus 1.56).

in our city, it should be called after the god who really does rule over men who are rational' (713a1–4).[6] Moreover, theological developments are in various ways central to Plato's political programme (see especially Books IV.713a–714b, 715c–718a, XII.966c–968a, and the whole of Book X).

Thus the walk taken by the three interlocutors represents the progression towards the first principle of legislation. But it also and more subtly symbolizes a space of leisure and liberty where the constraints of everyday life can be provisionally suspended. Taking one's time, making pauses, not being forced to do anything, are essential features of a walk through the countryside, even if a god is the destination. This formal freedom is relevant to the content of the dialogue, where it will become important to escape the urgency of actual legislating even as one speaks of legislation. That is because, for reasons to be seen, actual legislating is treated in the *Laws* mainly as the effect of a resented 'necessity' (see e.g. 857e10–858c1, cf. 859b7–c2).

The overall structure of the work can be sketched as follows. Books I–III raise two general questions about the principles of legislation: what is the purpose of the laws (I–II), and what are the conditions of their authority (III)? After the short development that places the legislative task under the guidance of the god, the rest of the first two books present a critical analysis of Doric institutions, arguing that the laws must be an instrument of complete virtue and not solely the single military virtue of courage (624a–632d, cf. 963a). The mode of exposition changes in the third book. That the division of powers and a mixed constitution can alone guarantee the authority of the laws is established by reference to the historical fate of the three Doric cities of Argos, Messene and Sparta – their story being embedded in the larger framework of the development of human civilization (677a).[7] While Sparta had been able to avoid tyranny by adopting a mixed constitution, Messene and Argos had not (682e–693d). The story of how Sparta defeated its former allies plays in the third book a role analogous to the critique of Doric institutions in the first two. This is why the third book, in contrast to the first, emphasizes the relative worth and suitability of Spartan institutions rather than their several weaknesses. This change of perspective is typical of the *Laws*, which artfully oscillates between praise and blame of Doric institutions. It should be noted from the outset, however, that despite a strongly marked Doric context, on the whole Athens is more of a paradigm for the

[6] The term 'theocracy' does not appear before Josephus *Contra Apion* II.16. On the relation between 'noocracy' and 'nomocracy', cf. below, p. 271.

[7] The assumption is that the history of man, like the history of the world, is cyclical.

Laws than Sparta (see below, section 5). Although this makes the *Laws* a delicate exercise in political balance, the will to achieve a synthesis of the two most important trends in Greek (political) culture (see above, n. 5) is as unmistakeable as it is bold.

The Spartan constitution, however 'mixed' it may have been, remained profoundly defective. Just as Sparta's laws sought to promote the virtue of the citizens while being blind to virtue's true nature, so its division of powers made no reference to the only real 'god' that counts, namely, as 713a1–4 (quoted above) implies, 'intelligence' or 'reason' (*nous*). To owe the stability of one's institutions to the foresight of a god, as the Spartans do (691d8–e1), is not quite enough to make Sparta a 'theocracy' and even less a 'noocracy' – no doubt the most adequate characterization of what the Platonic state is meant to be.

Just as the present has a past, the past points to a possible future. Because they are what they are, the Doric institutions can be reshaped by taking into account the criteria they do not meet. At the end of Book III, Clinias reveals that he will soon be called, with nine others of his fellow citizens, to write the laws for a new Cretan colony (702c2–8), which in the course of the work (but not until 848d3) is several times referred to as 'the city of Magnesia'.[8] From his point of view it is pure luck that the conversation has turned to the theme of legislation (702b4–6). Clinias' satisfaction is shared by the Athenian. The projected foundation of a Doric colony presents a natural opportunity for adapting the principles sketched in the first three books. Not only do Doric cities cultivate virtue (if not the whole of virtue) and have a tradition of mixed constitutions, the foundation of a colony under appropriate conditions provides the best possible circumstances for the adoption of a new set of laws (708a–d). Not least among the benefits of legislating for a new colony is that the legislator will have to *talk* to the new colonists upon arriving at the site of the new city. This address, although first performed without comment on its rhetorical or political status, will turn out to be one of these 'preambles' whose importance has already been stressed – indeed, the most important preamble of the *Laws*. In brief, the projected city of Magnesia does much more than simply provide a particular case by which to test a model. It gives the Athenian the unexpected chance to develop the details of a legislative project conforming to his political ideas. However concrete and detailed its description of laws and however much Magnesia remains the frame of reference (cf. e.g. 752d–e), the *Laws* is not conceived for this par-

[8] Cf. 860e6, 919d3, 946b6, 969a5f. The last passage shows that the name is chosen *exempli gratia*.

ticular case. Conversely, the Athenian's proposals are only proposals. It will fall to the Cretans responsible for the colony to adopt them for their new land. Thus, the situation also exemplifies an important principle that recurs throughout the *Laws*: the legislator's dissociation from power (702d, 739b, 746c). Books IV to XII are devoted to elaborating the institutions of a Magnesia which, however imminent its foundation may be, remains an ideal Magnesia.

The major articulations within Books IV–XII, which encompass the proper legislative work, are on the whole clear, even if the reader must face a number of obscurities. It is important to distinguish between those obscurities that are contingent and those that could be called essential. Certain features of the *Laws*, especially disorder in the two last books, suggest that Plato died before he could put the final touches to his work.[9] Some of the obscurities, however, are due to the specific way in which Plato envisages the legislative task. The overall structure of the legislative work tends to be blurred as a result of the constant and deliberate 'postponement' of legislation. There are a variety of reasons for this postponement, some purely technical, some linked with Plato's conception of the law. While the latter are the most interesting philosophically (as we shall see), it is important to realize that they are already at work behind the other, seemingly more technical factors.

Postponement of the legislative work is, in the first place, a consequence of a strict definition of legislation as a kind of expert knowledge or art (*technē*). The task of legislation is twofold: first, it must specify a 'constitution' (*politeia*), which involves the establishment of magistracies and the definition of their powers. Second (to use the technical expression) it must 'give' the laws 'to' these magistracies. Laws are thus strictly speaking the prescriptions that the magistrates must enforce (735a5f., 751a5–b2). So the 'constitution' itself, according to this terminology, is not a law although it does fall within the field of the legislator's expertise. As we shall discover, this distinction between constitution and law is extremely important for Plato's project. It implies that there are things to be discussed from a legislative point of view even before one can talk about 'laws' – or, for that matter, 'constitution'. For legislation, insofar as it is an 'art', will want to define the conditions under which it is itself best exercised (709a–e).[10]

[9] It is generally assumed that Plato's pupil Philip of Opus edited the text after his death. On this, see Tarán 1975: 128ff.

[10] The distinction between 'conditions' and 'laws' is still important in Rousseau's *Contrat Social* (see book 2, chs. 8–10).

Books IV and V are devoted to these 'preconditions'. They are fairly heterogeneous, and deal with an ensemble of practical questions relating to geography, demography and economy. They also take up a series of theoretical (or meta-legislative) questions, such as the nature of the authorities by which the new constitution and laws will be adopted, the general form of the constitution (a section containing the passage on 'theocracy'), and the form of the law (which includes the theory of the preambles). The definition of legislation as expert knowledge is itself part of this development.[11] The first piece of 'legislation' proper concerns the regulations for marriage (IV.720e10–721e3). But these are introduced simply to illustrate the difference between a law and a preamble, and the next piece of actual legislation does not appear until Book VIII.

The last precondition, that dealing with preambles, is in a sense also the most important, for it bears on the overall form of the legislation. A law, in the strict or 'simple' sense, is an order accompanied by the threat of punishment in case of transgression (721b). The legislator's expertise, however, extends beyond this narrow specification of law. In addition to the threat of punishment, there is another form of legislative speech, whose function is to 'persuade' before such a threat and punishment are needed, namely the 'preamble' (see below, section 6). The legislative task is accordingly 'double', not 'simple' (721b4f.). In fact, the preamble, because it precedes the law, will contribute to a more drastic postponement of the laws themselves than does even the discussion of the necessary preconditions, or, for that matter, of the 'constitution'.

The theoretical explanation of the nature of a preamble occupies the end of Book IV. It is preceded by the first section of the so-called 'general preamble' of the laws, a call to respect the gods (715c–718a). The second section follows at the beginning of Book V and contains an exhortation regarding one's duties towards one's parents, friends, fellow-citizens, and, most importantly, towards one's own soul. This long address to the new Cretan colonists is an impressive sermon, occupying a great part of Book V (down to 734e). It is striking that this general preamble is not followed by any particular law, at least in the sense in which 'law' has been officially defined at the end of Book IV. For the legislator at the beginning of Book VI, having dealt with some further 'preconditions' at the end of Book V, turns to the 'constitution' or the establishment of the magistra-

[11] The two series intertwine in a complex way. The order is as follows: location of the city, 704a1–705b6; origin of the population, 707e1–708d9; nature of power under the authority to be established by the new laws, 709d10–712a7; general form of the constitution, 712b1–715e1; the form of legislation (the legislative preamble), 718d2–723d4; regulations for property and the possession of goods, 737c1–747e11.

cies (*katastasis archōn*, 751a5, cf. 735a5). The constitution itself can in a certain sense be described as 'laws'. Indeed, the Stranger does talk about 'constitutional laws' for the occasion (734e5), not without signalling a certain embarrassment. Setting up a system of magistracies is legislation only in an extended sense of the term, for 'laws', strictly speaking, already presuppose the existence of the magistrates (to whom they are 'given' for enforcement). Moreover, these constitutional laws are not penal laws of the kind discussed at the end of Book IV in connection with the definition of a 'preamble'. Thus, at the heart of the work we find a preamble without a law (the general preamble of Books IV and V) preceded by a quasi-law without corresponding preamble (the constitution). The confusion, however, is only apparent. For a citizen who obeys the persuasive instructions of the general preamble would thereby *ipso facto* anticipate and respect the content of the legislation that follows the organization of the magistracies.

One can thus understand why, aside from the 'constitutional laws', the legislative work does not begin until the end of Book VI (768d7–e3). It should immediately be added, however, that Book VII, which is for the most part devoted to laws about education (and which takes up the laws for marriage and procreation mentioned at the end of Book IV), employs the specific form of *unwritten* laws. Orality and tradition, obviously, work as a functional equivalent, indeed as a possible or perhaps even desirable substitute, for the persuasive, non-coercive preamble. Thus the successive postponements of the legislation, as well as the implicit changes in the scope of the word 'law', point to a conception of legislation itself as largely negative, in as much as it primarily involves penal coercion. Punishment is the last resort when the resources of persuasion – philosophical or otherwise – have been exhausted, even though the *Laws* actually suggests that punishment itself, including the death penalty, has a certain curative purpose.[12]

Contrary to what the reader might expect, the laws in the restricted sense of the term (the legal code) are not presented in connection with the magistracies to which they are attached. In fact, no less than three principles must be taken into account to explain the fairly complex order of exposition followed in Books VII to XII: (1) the chronological principle of the cycle of human life and its nodal points – marriage and procreation, education, military service, political life, death and funerary arrangements; (2) a reality principle according to which activities linked

[12] On this point, see Saunders 1991: 182f.

to survival must be regulated (842e3–5, cf. 842d1–e1); (3) the principle of penal regulation, which rests on a classification of transgressions in order of their degree of seriousness (884a1–885a7).[13]

Discussion of the phases of the human life cycle continues from the end of Book VI until the first part of Book VIII and resumes intermittently in Books XI–XII. The corresponding regulations can be identified with the ensemble of laws which the Athenian, at the end of Book IX, had said were designed for the education of 'gentlemen' (*chrēstoi anthrōpoi*, 880d8). In strong contrast with these regulations, a second group of laws, distinguished by the importance of threat and penalties, furnishes the material for Books IX to X (and, in part, XI), which deals with the 'major' transgressions (853a5). These laws are paradigmatic, in that they are imposed by 'necessity', but this necessity is not – as with the agricultural laws – imposed by basic human needs. It signals rather a failure of education. This explains why this part of the legislative task takes place under the sign of 'shame' (853b4).

The arrangement of topics is further complicated by the presence of preambles. In some sense, preambles simply precede a law (or group of laws), in accordance with the function assigned to them in Book IV. Yet, because this amounts to suspending the law (temporarily at least), they also offer a further way to postpone it. Such is certainly the effect of the general preamble in Book V. Preambles can also metamorphose into discussions of principles (as in the case of the law against impiety in Book X), even as the future legislators of the Cretan colony replace the citizens as the natural audience of these 'introductions'. Space is thus allotted, at the very core of the legislative work, to meta-legislative reflection that calls into question the status of the legislative enterprise itself.

The *Laws* is thus knit together by digressions that vary from a few sentences to extended discussions and that possess a certain degree of autonomy in themselves.[14] This feature encourages a reading of the *Laws* as a sort of anthology. Such a reading is explicitly endorsed by the *Laws* itself, in that schoolmasters are invited to read excerpts from the dialogue with their pupils (811a). The degree of irony is difficult to assess here. There are good reasons to think that an overall interpretation of the *Laws* could proceed along similar lines. In any case, the most striking moments of the

[13] In order of decreasing gravity: offences against the public domain, homicide, aggression, *hubris* (including offences against the gods), crimes against property, thefts, misdemeanours relative to contracts and sales or to the judicial process.

[14] For example: 644d7–645c6 (the human marionette); 719e7–720e5 (medicine and legislation); 739a1–e7 (the three constitutions); 806d7–807d6 (the life of leisure); 857b3–864c11 (punishment and responsibility).

work are undeniably those when the immensity of the task undertaken is abruptly placed under the perspective of the ultimate questions about man and the meaning of his existence. Flashes of sublimity thus illuminate a work otherwise so densely textured as to have been censured as 'frigid' even in antiquity (Lucian, *Icaromenippus* 24). This is especially true of passages that underscore the contradictions and limits of the legislative enterprise, as, most famously, when the Athenian, talking about the restrictions that will be imposed on dramatic performances, assimilates his own constitution to 'the truest tragedy' (817b5). From this point of view, the *Laws* is not only without precedent but also without any later equivalent in the history of political thought. This is not the least interesting feature of the work.

3 Three models for interpreting the *Laws*: completion, revision, implementation

The interpretation of the *Laws* depends crucially on its relation to Plato's two other great political dialogues, the *Republic* and the *Politicus*. How is this relation to be understood? The *Laws* accomplishes three things in a single stroke. It completes a programme which had been sketched in the two preceding works; it revises the model of the state which they had drawn; and finally it portrays a practical realization of that model. While each of these three tasks reflects an essential purpose of the *Laws*, there is also a certain tension among them. Yet this tension does not threaten the coherence of the overall project. For the *Laws* itself aims at articulating a certain tension, one which mirrors the radical and irreducible polarity between the human and the divine.

3.1 Completion

The task of completion is in a way the most obvious of the three. The *Republic* and the *Politicus* are little more than outlines of political philosophy. They present programmes of relatively high generality with little detail about political mechanisms. Apart from the fact that the true politics in the *Republic* is in the soul, of which the city is the 'image' (cf. what is said about justice in 443c–d), there are two further reasons explaining why this work deliberately leaves aside the greater part of its particular legislation (426e4–427a7). First, the political theory of the *Republic* is almost exclusively concerned with the highest magistrates. More importantly, they are considered less as administrators of the city than as potential philosophers, that is to say, in a capacity that is precisely not that of administering the city. The *Republic* focuses less upon the city than upon a certain tension between the city and philosophy.

This tension still persists in the *Politicus*, albeit in a different guise. Instead of the conflict, so typical of the *Republic*, between the aspiration to a theoretical life and the requirements of government, in the *Politicus* we find a philosophical devaluation of politics: the search for the true statesman is a purely dialectical exercise (285c–286b). For the rest, the *Politicus* concentrates even more than the *Republic* on an ultimate source of power: the 'monarch' of the *Politicus* may well have better claim to the title of philosopher king than his counterpart in the *Republic*, since his power is subject to no principle of alternation. Although the dialogue already contains some of the conceptual resources that will be developed in the *Laws* (for example, the ideas of mixture and measure), there is only marginal treatment of the specific content of the laws.[15]

By contrast with the *Republic* and the *Politicus*, the *Laws* is political from beginning to end, resolutely and without procrastination, even though it stresses the difficulties of the legislative task and indulges in a certain degree of existential despair (803b3–5: human affairs are unworthy of great attention despite the necessity of taking an interest in them). Within these limits, one might describe the *Laws* as marking a 'politicization' of Platonic political philosophy.

One of the *Laws*' most striking features is its traversing of the entire spectrum from the specification of fundamental political principles to their most detailed instantiation: we have socio-economic classes and professions described, we know how the citizens spend their days (which are full to the point that the highest organ of government, the Nocturnal Council, must meet at dawn), we know they are concerned with participating in assemblies and religious festivals, sending their children to school, engaging in legal proceedings, providing for the water supply, drafting their wills – in brief, conducting all the business of life. One could on the basis of the *Laws* write a study on 'daily life in the Platonic city' – a project which, manifestly, neither the *Republic* nor the *Politicus* could support. In this respect also, the *Laws* is less 'frigid' than one might think.

So detailed are the institutions of the *Laws*' city that one can draw specific comparison with actual institutions. In fact one crucial task for interpretation is to understand the strange correspondence between principles of Platonic philosophy and some contemporary, even local, realities. Morrow's fundamental study has made clear how much the institutions

[15] See Rowe, in Ch. 11 section 3 above.

of the *Laws* owe to historical Athenian institutions.[16] From an Hegelian or Marxist perspective it might be said that such a construction, in which differences from and similarities to actual institutions are intertwined, testifies to the limits imposed on philosophy by given socio-historical circumstances: despite, or rather due to, its professed project of reform, the *Laws* provides one of the best philosophical images we have of the Greek city. Yet it is equally striking that this intertwining can be related (indeed demands to be related) to the basic concepts of Platonic philosophy itself. At this point the two further perspectives of revision and implementation, to some degree complementary, come into play.

3.2 *Revision*

Although the *Laws* may be seen as completing the political programmes indicated in the *Republic* and the *Politicus*, this movement towards closure is accompanied by a significant movement away from these earlier works. The *Laws* is dominated by a certain pattern of 'retreat' that Plato compares to a move on a chessboard when one player, whether under compulsion or for tactical reasons, must withdraw his pieces from a line called 'sacred' (739a1–5). Such retreats are characterized in the *Laws* by means of two contrasts. On the one hand, the city of the *Laws* is frequently said to occupy 'the second rank', in contrast with the 'best' that holds the first rank (739a4f.; 739b3; 739e4; 875d3). On the other, its institutions are specifically presented as destined for men, in contrast with others that apply to the gods (732e; 853c3–8; 874e–875d; cf. 691c–692a and 713e–714a). The two contrasts do not always appear together, but they are functionally equivalent. Thus, the 'first' or best city and the 'second-best' are not to be thought of as both located within the human sphere but as referring to two orders that are in principle radically different (though as we will see in a moment, the situation is made more involved by the complexity of the relation between 'humanity' and 'divinity').

The various retreats in the *Laws* take four main forms which together constitute the encompassing framework for the legislative work:

(1) There is to be some allowance for private property, to satisfy the distinctively human egocentric impulse (739e6–740a2; cf. 731de, 736e–737b).

(2) A rule of law rather than of individual rulers is to be established so that men do not abuse power (713e3–714a2; 874e8–875d5).[17]

[16] Morrow 1960.

[17] In this sense, the constitution of the *Laws* is a 'nomocracy'. On the relationship between this 'nomocracy' and the 'noocracy' it claims to be (see above, p. 260–1 with n.6), see below, p. 271 with n.20.

(3) There is to be a 'mixed' constitution, for much the same reason (691c–692a; at 756e8–757a5 a different argument is given).
(4) 'Human' forms of praise, involving an appeal to personal pleasure, are to be instituted in contrast to other forms of praise appealing to 'honour' and 'reputation', and thus qualifying as divine (732e7–733a4).

These four basic tenets can be ranked according to their degree of relevance to political life. At the bottom, the possession of property concerns production and so sheer survival (which, strictly speaking, falls outside the scope of 'politics'). At the top, the constitutional regime and the rule of the law define the very form of the government. Between these two levels, human praise represents the commonest form of political communication within the political body. As the *Laws* fleshes out this general framework through detailed legislation, the contrast between a first and second rank, between divine and human, is constantly at work, although most of the time it remains implicit. The treatment of laws pertaining to sex (837a–842a) is an exception – but an understandable one, since erotic desire, as an especially virulent form of *human* desire, has no direct counterpart in divine existence. This suggests the possibility of deciphering the particular legislative decrees of the 'second city' by asking, in each case, what their purported analogues would be in the 'first city'.

One special, and especially interesting, case of 'second-best' concerns the question of the new legislation's enforcement. This question is, of course, not itself institutional, but rather relates to the very possibility of institutions. The problem was already raised in the *Republic*: in order for the realization to be as close as possible to the model, the material must be of the most malleable kind possible. The *Republic* describes, at the end of Book VII, the rustication of all citizens and children older than ten years. The status of this rustication has been much discussed by commentators. One can argue that Plato is quite realistically referring to procedures that were not unknown in the Greek world.[18] In any case, it would be somewhat strange to credit such a device to a city of gods. Be that as it may, it is difficult to escape the impression that the *Laws* adopts a more 'human' procedure than the *Republic*. Instead of the ideal blank slate on which the philosopher king of the *Republic* would be able to draw the ideal city, the working hypothesis of the *Laws* is that of a new colony, certainly a less radical way of starting afresh, but one quite common in the context of Greek political culture.

As we have seen above, the *Laws* is in some way a continuation of both

[18] Myles Burnyeat once adduced (orally) the case of Mantinea, whose citizens were sent to 'villages' after being defeated by Sparta in 386/5 BC (Xenophon *Hellenica* V.2.7).

the *Republic* and the *Politicus*. As far as revision is concerned, the status of these two dialogues is different. The changes with respect to the *Republic* are obvious, for the community of goods, the possibility of a philosopher king, the necessity of a radical new beginning, from which the *Laws* 'retreat', featured prominently in that dialogue. By contrast, the *Politicus* already suggests that a human monarch might be wishful thinking (though this is not asserted: 301c–e), and for the first time emphasizes a distinction between intellect and law that paves the way for the *Laws*, even if the notion of 'second-best' at 300c is not strictly that which will be at work in the *Laws*.[19]

One should be wary, however, of treating the *Politicus* as simply heralding the revisions of the *Laws*. Alongside clear reprises of the *Politicus* in the *Laws* there is also a critique, and this on the very issue where the two would seem to stand in common contrast to the *Republic*, namely in their shared interest in the role of 'laws'. First, whereas the *Politicus* treats the law either as a useful expedient in the hands of the expert statesman or as a mindless second best that is our most hopeful option if no true statesman is available, law is in the *Laws* an embodiment of divine reason: 'we should . . . obey whatever share of immortality we have in us in running our households and our cities, giving the name of "law" (*nomos*) to the distribution of intelligence (*nous*)' (713e8–714a2).[20] This embodiment of reason in law accounts for the difficulty in determining whether the constitution of the *Laws* is more a nomocracy or a noocracy.

Second, and equally important, there is a new emphasis on the crucial element of the form of the law. While the *Politicus* is mainly interested in the 'substitutive' aspect of the law (laws stand in when the monarch is absent), the *Laws* concentrates on the implications of law's 'epitactic' dimension (the laws are orders addressed to someone). This change in perspective entails a major displacement, such that the *Laws* ends up adopting a position regarding political 'persuasion' very different from that officially defended in the *Politicus* (or for that matter the *Gorgias*).[21] The agreement of the citizens – and not just the achievement of the Good –

[19] On this, see Rowe, in Ch. 11 section 3 above.

[20] The same *Cratylus*-like 'etymology' linking *nomos* with *nous* recurs in Book XII, 957c5–7: the future judge, who more than anybody else should learn in order to become better, must study the laws, provided that they are correctly set up, 'or it is in vain that our divine and prodigious law would possess a name fitted to reason'.

[21] I say 'officially', because this is the argument developed at 296a–297b. In fact, the *Politicus* does need 'persuasion' to distinguish between monarch and tyrant (291e). It is consistent, then, that 'rhetoric' should be made one of the three main 'auxiliaries' of the true ruler at 304a–e. But this means that, as far as persuasion is concerned, there is a tension within the *Politicus* between two strains of thought, a tension from which the *Laws* tries to escape.

appears henceforth as an integral part of the political art (compare *Plt.* 293a9–c4 and *Gorg.* 521e6–522a3 with e.g. *Laws* IV.722d2–723d4).[22] It is true that criticism of the *Politicus* remains for the most part implicit in the *Laws* and is in any case less provocative than the rescissions of the *Republic*, whose formulations are in some cases echoed almost word for word (711e–712a, on the coincidence of power and wisdom; 739c, on the community of goods and families). However, the significance of the disappearance of the *Politicus*' notion of law as essentially 'substitutive' in a work entitled *Laws* can scarcely be underestimated.

The dynamic of distancing functions in the *Laws* not only in relation to the *Republic* and the *Politicus*, but also in relation to a model which is in some way internal to the *Laws* itself. For instance, what the *Laws* retreats from in the case of communal institutions is arguably something more extreme than anything we find in the *Republic*, since the *Laws*, in sketching the outlines of the 'first city', specifies that this community should extend, as much as possible, to the 'entirety of the constitution' (739c1f.), whereas the *Republic* explicitly limits communism to the guardians alone. This internal distancing becomes still more evident when one turns to the topic of 'persuasion'. According to a crucial passage in Book IX, it turns out that the 'preambles' introduced at the end of Book IV are not necessarily meant to be rhetorical pieces based on praise and blame (as one would have thought), but rather should – under ideal circumstances – take the form of quasi-philosophical discussions carried out by means of rational argument (see below, section 6). This utopia of rational discussion between the legislator and the citizens, in comparison with which rhetorical persuasion of the sort we often see at work in the *Laws* appears to be only a 'second best', has no counterpart whatsoever in either the *Republic* or the *Politicus*.

Finally, revision is in some cases milder than one would expect, or even so mild that it becomes difficult to assess. Here, the situation is different for each of the four basic political features listed above. The first revision we hear of in the *Laws*, the substitution of a regime of private property for communism, is deep and irreversible. However, as we have seen, this is less a piece of legislation than a precondition of legislation in general. At the top level, on the other hand, it is much less clear to what extent the Nocturnal Council essentially differs from the philosopher kings of the *Republic*. One might suggest that the sole difference consists in the substitution of collegiality, as a minimal form of control, for alternation in

[22] Laks 1991: 423f.

power, in circumstances where the aspiration to the theoretical life is no longer available as a guarantee against the temptations of power.[23]

Thus, if there is a critique of the *Republic* and of the *Politicus* in the Laws (as there surely is), it is tempered to the extent that the ideals of these two dialogues have been integrated into an 'ideal' city reconstructed within the *Laws* itself which may or may not coincide exactly with the earlier ideal. The 'relational' aspect of the *Laws*, so striking at first glance, is in this way somewhat complicated. Such complexity in no way precludes the claim that 'distance' must be considered a fundamental category for interpretation of the *Laws*. Quite the contrary, not only is distance the consequence of retreat from any ideal, it is also a necessary condition for the implementation of a political model.

3.3 *Implementation*

From one point of view the two perspectives so far considered, completion and revision, are not opposite but complementary. This holds good to the extent that the *Laws* is supposed to be, if not the practical implementation of a model, at least the first stage (still theoretical in nature) of such an implementation. For if implementation means embedding a model in material to which it is not necessarily suited, and which will consequently prove resistant, it will imply both completion and revision. Such a perspective recommends itself for at least two reasons. Generally speaking, it fits well with Platonic paradigmatism; more specifically, it allows one to view the *Laws* as occupying a position in the domain of politics analogous to that occupied by the *Timaeus* in the domain of cosmo-physiology.[24] Both dialogues rely on a similar pattern. The 'model' to which the craftsman-demiurge looks in the *Timaeus* (the Forms) has its analogue in the *Laws* in the political model of the 'first city'; to the *Timaeus*' material 'receptacle' (the *chōra*), out of which the elementary triangles and the four elements will emerge, corresponds the human material that the legislator must shape into a political body. Even more striking is the fact that the material *chōra* of the *Timaeus* is identified with 'necessity', for the legislator of the *Laws* must also grapple with necessity (e.g. 857e10–858a6), which marks the limit of his actions.[25]

[23] See also below, section 5.

[24] The *Timaeus* also has a political aspect since it is, as a whole, conceived as an introduction to the *Critias* (see Rowe, in Ch. 11 section 5 above). Note, however, that the emphasis in the *Critias* is not on political institutions, and that ancient Athens belongs (with Atlantis) to a remote past, which makes it closer to the first city of the *Republic* than to the *Laws*.

[25] On the parallel between the *Timaeus* and the *Laws*, see Laks 1990.

The differences between the *Laws* and the *Timaeus* are no less instructive than the analogies. Especially significant is the importance accorded in the *Laws* to the length of time past and the indeterminacy of the future, as well as to the existence of degrees of possibility. In contrast with the *Timaeus*' demiurge, the legislators of the *Laws* are human beings who do not possess the straightforward 'goodness' of the demiurge (*Tim.* 29e), and who must remain 'prudent'. As for the material they must work with, far from having the relative simplicity of 'matter' in the *Timaeus*, it consists of the complex deposit of an already lengthy history, of which Book III gives such a vivid picture. Above all, while the world itself is one, there are numerous cities on earth. It is in this context that one must understand the mention, alongside the first two cities (the best and the second-best), of a 'third city' (739e5), to which Plato never reverts and which has occasioned much puzzlement. There are good reasons to think this third city is identical with the city of Magnesia that will be established by the Cretan legislative body once the discussion in the *Laws* is completed. But at the same time, this third city stands for the open series of all cities that would be willing to engage in self-reform, whether they are colonies or not. These cities, of course, would differ greatly from one another, depending on a variety of circumstances which Plato does not spell out.

The *Laws* can thus be read, from the point of view of conditions of implementation, as reflecting the differences between nature and history. The treatment of the question of possibility is in this regard significant. Compared with the *Timaeus*, the centre of interest in the *Laws* is displaced: it is not the implementation of the model as such but rather the conditions of its realization. Whereas formally this links the *Laws* to the *Republic*, as there the philosopher king is first introduced as the condition of possibility for the realization of the just city (473c–d), it also points to the fact that only the *Laws* gives full attention to the concatenation of 'human' factors which the *Republic* had deliberately neglected.

Although the notion of implementation does take account of certain important aspects of the *Laws* and offers a consistent and elegant way of understanding the relation between the *Laws* and the *Republic*, nonetheless it does not do full justice to its complexity. After all, the *Laws* presents itself less as an implementation of a model than as a model of another kind. Its discussion remains theoretical. The real legislation will come later (702d). If strict communism must be discarded, this is because it is appropriate for gods but not for men. The distance between god and man is precisely what makes revision indispensable. This does not mean that the *Laws* gives up the paradigm of the first city: on the contrary, the second city will keep 'as close as possible' to the first one (739e2).

In some sense, then, between the *Republic* and the *Laws* there is neither 'revision' nor 'implementation', but only change from one level (the divine) to another (the human). For things to be otherwise, the city of the *Republic* would have to be taken not simply as an ideal model but as a political programme meant to be 'possible' as it is. The *Republic* is notoriously ambiguous in this regard: it can be (and has been) read both as a utopia and as a blueprint for political action. By opting for the latter interpretation – there would be no point of speaking about 'retreat' otherwise – the *Laws* itself represents the first attempt to achieve clarification on this matter. This is no mean merit. By so resolutely taking into account the human factor, the *Laws*, in its specific and still very Platonic way, opens the path to Aristotle. One might even go so far as to wonder whether there is already something truly Aristotelian in the *Laws*.

4 Man and god: the anthropology of the *Laws*

If the *Laws* elaborates the institutions of a city that is 'second-best' insofar as human beings are second-best in comparison with gods, one should conclude that these institutions are, so far as humans are concerned, the best possible. This must be emphasized. It also makes it all the more important to understand what it is, according to the *Laws*, to be a human being and in what respects humans are different from gods. Finding an adequate answer to this question is made difficult by the fact that the gods, in this context, are described as men of a certain kind, namely as men who would be capable of living in the first city (739d6–e1). Of these godlike men the *Laws* tells us little except negatively. One can nonetheless get a sense of who they are by assimilating them to the ideal citizens of the *Republic* (even though, for reasons given above in section 3, the two cannot be completely identified).

The nature of the difference between the godlike men of the *Republic* and the human men of the *Laws* is not to be found in the nature of their psychological make-up. In the *Laws* as in the *Republic*, man is a complex unity in whom rational and irrational elements coexist. Although the irrational element is itself composite, it is in the end reducible to what engages in the search for pleasure and, symmetrically, the flight from pain. The rational part, on the other hand, is directed not towards pleasure but towards the good. If there is a difference between godlike men and mere humans (as there surely is), then it is to be located in the kind of relation that obtains between these constituents, rather than in the constituents themselves.

The relation depends upon the respective force or intensity of the constituents. From the vantage point of the *Laws*, the *Republic*, in subordinating the guardians to communism and in entrusting power to the most accomplished guardians (the philosophers), has ignored the facts of human nature, and simultaneously overestimated the power of the rational part while underestimating that of the irrational part. The retreat embodied in the framework of the second city reflects a reassessment of the situation. If praise is to persuade by promising pleasures, this is because 'that which is by nature the most human are the pleasures, pains and desires, from which every mortal animal is of necessity utterly suspended, as it were, and caught up by the most intense engagements' (732e4–7). Power must be limited by the double device of the rule of law and the division of powers, because 'human nature, which impels the irrational flight from pain and search for pleasure, will always urge him [the hypothetical monarch] to strive for more and act egoistically' (875b6–8, cf. 713c6–8).

The same kind of considerations apply to the endorsement of private property, which, as it comes just before the proper legislative work begins, emblematically represents all the other changes. To the extent that pleasure and pain make up what man properly is, property is the paradigmatic source of pleasure.[26] The 'retreat from the sacred line' consists, in the most general formulation, in knowing how to deal with what is 'properly' human even at the cost of a certain compromise. At issue is understanding what, exactly, is the nature of this compromise. This is the sole criterion by which to measure the distance between the 'second-best' city of the *Laws* and its first city.

The question is complicated (and so made even more interesting) by the fact that although the man of the *Laws* is not a god, he is nevertheless not merely man. On the contrary, man is what he is because there is something divine in him – and this is true even of his pleasure. Without this divine element he would be less than a man: a wild beast (766a3f., cf. 808d4f.). But if a bestial propensity always remains inscribed in him, man's essential nature is, rather, that of a tame animal – the divine form, as one might say, of animality (765e3–766a4).

This dual nature is made clear in the 'anthropological' passage of Book 1, which comes in connection with an analysis of human motivation

[26] Plato is obviously playing with the double meaning of the word *idion*.

(644c1–645c8). Man is there compared to a 'marionette' (*thauma*, 644d7), under the joint control of the golden thread of reason, which is precious but weak, and the strong iron threads of the irrational impulses. The analogy is famous, but its meaning is often misunderstood. The 'marionette' image lends itself to a pessimistic, even tragic, interpretation, which the Athenian himself might at first sight seem to endorse when he remarks in Book VII that 'man has been devised as a toy for god' (803e4f.). The marionette, however, is a rather exceptional thing, a prodigy or object of 'astonishment' (the primary meaning of the word *thauma*). The human marionette is astonishing in its capacity for harmony in spite of its being controlled by disparate elements (reflecting precisely the conflict between the rational and the irrational elements). Gold and iron can in certain circumstances move in the same direction.

The prime example of such harmony is the pleasure of dance, present from earliest childhood, which can develop (with proper training) into the joy of participating in the choral processions of the religious festivals – one of the main activities in the Platonic city, in the time left over from agriculture and politics (803e). In the dance, the conflict between contrary influences is resolved in a peaceful way, for the pleasure in dance is a pleasure in order and hence a rational pleasure (664e–665a). Thus dance stands for all other possible mediations between the rational and the irrational elements. The irrational pleasures that escape mediation can be considered either as the properly human part of man or, from another perspective, as what remains in him of the beast, just as the god whom men honour can be identified with their own reason.

The human prodigy would not be so prodigious if he were more commonly encountered. As things are, irrational desires are so tenacious as to be in the end ineradicable. This is why a distinctively human city must be devised. There are two ways in which the 'second' city deals with the chronic conflict between rational and irrational forces: compromise and constraint. Of its four basic features, two at least – the division of land and the allowance of 'human' arguments based on pleasure – are clearly on the side of compromise, while the mixed constitution (in its principal aspects) and the subjection of magistrates to the law represent moderated forms of constraint. The degree of constraint varies (depending on the degree of irrationality involved) in the formulation of particular laws. Indeed the strict concept of law treats law as a form of violence imposed by reason on the irrationality of the desires. The violence involved in a law is measured not simply by the amount of threat it contains (719e9, 890b5), but by the degree to which orders are 'mixed' or 'unmixed' (722e7–723a4; cf. 722b4-c2). All the same, it should be stressed that the two complementary aspects of compromise and constraint are conceived by the *Laws* as residual elements. The *Laws* is most interested in the possibility of a convergence between the rational and the irrational – in most cases a cultivated rather than spontaneous convergence (dance is probably the only example of such spontaneity). In this regard, the dialogue can be seen as undertaking a systematic exploration of the possible manifestations of the human prodigy. Hence the interest displayed in phenomena like rational emotions (among which a central place is given to 'shame', *aidōs*), non-argumentative forms of discourse (in particular, praise and blame, representing the most important features of the preambles), myths and public opinion (especially regarding the existence of gods, cf. 886a and 887d), and, last but not least, the entrenched political mechanisms of Sparta and even more of Athens. In this respect, the mixed constitution of the *Laws* is just such an *institutional* prodigy.

5 Political institutions[27]

The 'constitutional laws' of Book VI are specified by reference to two symmetrical forms of political irrationality: autocratic despotism on the one hand, unchecked democracy on the other. Though opposed in form, despotism and democracy are to a great extent similar in their effects. The despotic exercise of power can only stimulate the irrational desires of the monarch and his 'striving for having more' (*pleonexia*, 875b6). These very same desires are left free to flourish in the hearts of all the citizens by a democratic regime, which is essentially characterized by licence and striving after pleasure (cf. the critique of democracy as 'theatrocracy', 700d–701b).

The relation between these two regimes is identical to that obtaining between two opposed Aristotelian vices. Both extremes are due to excess of a certain element (power in one case, freedom in the other), whose right measure is found in the 'mean'. Licence must be rationally controlled if genuine freedom is to be possible, just as power must be limited if real authority is to be exercised. This is what political mediation is all about. Book III mentions two historical paradigms of such mediation, the (good) monarchy, represented by the Persia of Cyrus, and the good democracy, represented by Athens under the ancestral constitution (693dff.). One

[27] This section is greatly indebted to Morrow 1960, which should be consulted for questions regarding institutional detail (the wonderful index to his book facilitates any such search).

could say that these two regimes are, at the historical or phylogenetic level, functionally equivalent to what dance is at the individual or ontogenetic level.

The 'mixed' – or better, 'mean' – constitution of the *Laws* is the most accomplished form of political mediation between democracy and monarchy yet to be achieved. It is, as it were, a mediation of mediations. As the mediation progresses, the terms 'democracy' and 'monarchy' acquire new senses. Genuinely 'democratic' institutions are now those which assure the effective *participation* and *representation* of citizens in political life; genuinely monarchical ones, those which guarantee the exercise of *competence* (the gulf between this and modern – as well as ancient – usage is obvious). While these two demands remain potentially opposed, they nevertheless tend to blend together – which is precisely what successful mediation is supposed to achieve.

Authority does not simply tolerate the liberty of the citizens but rather constitutes its condition of possibility. That is, true liberty depends on submission to a single legitimate power, that of the law (here we find a particularly strong prefiguration of ideas which will recur in Rousseau). The magistrate of the 'mean' constitution of the *Laws* is not a tyrant whose power must be limited but rather a ruler who incorporates the necessary limits in the very exercise of his functions. (This does not mean that he does not have to account for the way he discharges his duties, for the possibility of abuse is inscribed in human nature.) Conversely, the democratic assembly is not simply an Athenian assembly shorn of some of its prerogatives. The liberty of the *Laws*' democratic assembly is not the negative liberty of licence, but the positive liberty to strive for the good. This explains, at least in part, why 'freedom' counts as one of the three declared ends of legislation alongside 'wisdom' and 'concord' (693b4, 701d7f.).[28]

The logic of mediation demands that liberty should be no more the exclusive possession of the people than wisdom should be confined to the magistrates. In other words, a mixture is required not simply between the ingredients (external mixture) but also within them (internal mixture). There is a democratic aspect to the 'monarchical' (= competent) magistrate, who looks after the interests of the community, as the tyrant fails to do; and there is a monarchical aspect to the 'democratic' assembly, which selects most of the magistrates. In the city of the *Laws* the competence of the assembly is extensive, and liberty itself belongs to all. As a site of concord and friendship, the city of the *Laws* is justified in claiming that it is

[28] The term 'freedom' is overdetermined, in that it certainly also refers to 'political' freedom or the independence of the city.

the sole genuinely constitutional regime, in comparison with which other regimes have 'non-constitutions' (832b10–c3).

Its political institutions resemble those of a Greek (democratic) city. There are two types of governmental bodies. The first type is the assembly, of which there are three instances: the assembly itself (*ekklēsia*), the council (*boulē*), and the Nocturnal assembly (to which one may add the popular judicial courts). The second kind is the magistracy. Magistracies are defined by their functions, which are, in order of appearance: maintenance of the law (37 law-guardians), defence (military officers: 3 generals, 2 hipparchs, 10 taxiarchs and 10 phylarchs), religion (priests, indeterminate in number), economics (60 *agronomoi* – 5 per tribe – responsible for rural life, 3 *astunomoi* responsible for the city, 5 *agoranomoi*, responsible for the markets), education (one officer only, the sole case of non-collegiality), accounts and audits (the *euthunoi*, doubtless more than 12), and justice (selected judges of the high court).[29]

The complementary principles of representation and competence may guide analysis of these institutions.

(a) *Representation*. The principle of representation operates, on the one hand, in the composition and functions of the assembly, and on the other hand in the method for selecting magistrates and the council.

(1) The assembly (*ekklēsia*) is, on all counts, a democratic institution *par excellence*, because it consists in the entire body of citizens (women probably included). Its main tasks are to assign the magistracies (except for the 'superior judges' and the minister for education) and to elect the members of the council. It is thus granted the authority to select the city's authorities. Its other tasks have to do with the common good. The assembly judges public crimes in the first instance (767e–768e); involves itself in the regulation of festivals and sacrifices, which by definition concern the entire community (cf. 772c–d); decides whether to extend rights to strangers who have rendered service to the city (850b–c); and awards, in the name of the city, its supreme honours (921e, 943c). The *ekklēsia* thus serves as the legitimate expression of the constitutive citizens of the community.

(2) Three types of representation can be distinguished: administrative, economic, and political. If administrative representation (by tribes) plays only a minor role, being confined mainly to the rural magistracies, economic representation is more important. Its privileged location is within the council, which was in the corresponding Athenian institution elected by the tribes. This is because inequality of wealth, however restricted it

[29] For a useful summary of the distribution and functions of the various magistracies, see Stalley 1983: 187–91.

may be in the Platonic city, is a potential source of civil conflict. It is thus important that the different classes be reflected in the sphere of institutions. The uniquely complicated system of elections designed to ensure this shows the importance which Plato attaches to this problem.[30] But by far the greatest attention is paid to political representation, which is also philosophically the most interesting case. The care Plato takes over this issue is evident in the fact that nearly all the magistrates are chosen through elections involving the entire citizen-body.

The scheme is elaborate. It combines a phase of 'nominations' open to all citizens with a final selection by vote. The more important the officers who are to be entrusted with power, the more guarantees are installed against haste. Most remarkable are the mechanisms for choosing the guardians of the law (the 37 *nomophulakes*) and those responsible for auditing the accounts (the *euthunoi*, whom we may call the 'auditors'). In the case of the guardians of the law, each citizen writes on a tablet the name of the candidate he judges most qualified to discharge the office (he must be over the age of 50). These names are submitted to public deliberation for three days. Objections can be made and names retracted, while the 300 names most often cited in discussion are retained. These are then reduced to 100 in a second round and finally to the number of those required to serve (753b–d). The selection of the auditors is less involved. Each citizen proposes the name of one person (again, a nominee must be over 50); the 50 per cent of nominees named most often are retained; and this process is repeated until the necessary number of auditors has been selected (945e–946c).

Such institutional mechanisms make the constitution of the *Laws* look like a democracy oriented toward the selection of persons competent to hold authority. Its procedures sound somewhat more democratic than the formula used in the *Menexenus* to label the ancestral constitution of Athens ('aristocracy with the approbation of the people'), which Morrow uses to characterize the *Laws*. True, one would not want to say that, in the *Laws*, the people govern. Nor, for that matter, are they sovereign, since the only element in the *Laws*' theory that properly counts as sovereign is *nous*.[31] Still, the citizens do choose their magistrates.

(b) *Competence*. If the principle of representation is mainly expressed in

[30] The fact that voting is not obligatory for the very poor is better explained as a concern to avoid elections themselves harming economic activity, than by a secret oligarchical design to give greater weight to the richer voters. The latter was the interpretation offered by Aristotle, *Pol.* 1266a14ff.

[31] 'Noocracy' is the constitution of the *Laws*, see above, pp. 260f., 271. For the distinction between sovereignty and government, see Rousseau, *Social Contract*, Book III, ch. 1.

the procedures for selecting officials, the complementary principle of competence is guaranteed in two different ways: first, eligibility to serve as magistrates depends upon certain requirements; second, and more important, there are different levels of magistracies and assemblies. The greater the understanding of the law an office requires, the more developed must be the candidates' knowledge and education. Thus the principle of competence is epitomized in the Nocturnal assembly, whose role is precisely to preserve and deepen understanding of the law (951e–952a).

The majority of magistrates are chosen by the assembly without any conditions for eligibility other than age. In two cases, however, there is a second tier of eligibility and election. The minister of education is to be chosen for a five year term from the existing guardians of the law by a secret vote of all the magistrates (766b). The entire body of magistrates (apparently together with the members of the council) are responsible for the annual election of the members of the high court (767c–e). Such contraction of the electorate depends upon the nature and responsibilities of the posts involved. In this respect, the minister of education and the high court occupy positions that are to some extent symmetrical. The ministry of education is the most important magistracy in the city (765e1ff.), for the education of children is the foundation for everything else, including in particular obedience to law. Conversely, the function of the high court, which is the court of last resort for judging all crimes and the only court for judging crimes against the community, is to correct failures of the educational system.

All the magistrates, whether chosen by the assembly or by their peers, are subjected to a preliminary examination (*dokimasia*) conducted either by the council or by the *nomophulakes*. This procedure was characteristic of ancient Athens, and Plato gives few details about it, implying that he accepts current practice, which involved verifying compliance with formal conditions (age, citizenship, etc.), as well as the candidate's good character. Where procedural details are given, an emphasis is placed on possession of specific competences, a feature which departs somewhat from Athenian practice.

The body which in modern accounts of the *Laws* is usually called the 'Nocturnal Council' (because of 962c10), but which should really be called the 'Dawn Council' (after its time of meeting, 951d and 961b), is the most important institution in the *Laws*' city (its 'soul' and 'head', according to 961d2f.). It is also the institution farthest removed from existing institutions, Athenian or otherwise. Interpretation of the dialogue has long suffered from the belief that this dawn assembly is an 'appendix' that is badly integrated into a constitution already complete without it (it is not even mentioned until Book XII). Some even declared the Nocturnal Council an instance of human authority set 'above' the law. Morrow has already done justice to these essentially superficial interpretations.[32] That a body like the Nocturnal Council should be indispensable to the Platonic city, founded as it is on education, would seem self-evident. A few passages in the preceding books announce or presuppose such an institution.[33] That it should be fully discussed only in the final book is not only rhetorically effective (in the order of discourse, the head comes last), but also logically proper: the 'auditors' themselves do not appear until Book XII, for their magistracy presupposes all the others – they are 'magistrates of magistrates' (945c1). By the same token, those who study the law come after the law has been completed. In some sense, then, the Nocturnal Council cannot but be 'external' to the other institutions, since it is the instrument of their preservation. The problem it resolves is symmetrical to the one that related to the founding of the city, with the important difference that it is by definition impossible to institutionalize the inception of a political regime.

The construction of the Nocturnal Council corresponds to the requirement, formulated in the *Republic* (497c8–d2), that the city include within itself 'an element having the same conception of the constitution as you, the legislator, had in formulating its laws' – a circumlocution seeming to imply a philosophical institution. The Nocturnal Council is just such a quasi-philosophical institution, even if its concerns are more immediately oriented towards politics and the law than are those of the philosophers in the *Republic*. The study of the law requires extensive knowledge. The sciences useful for clarifying problems about the laws (952a) include kinetics (on which the refutation of atheism in Book X is founded) and mathematical knowledge, to which this same book makes a somewhat cryptic allusion (894a).

Since the Nocturnal Council does not govern (it exercises no magistracy), it cannot put itself 'above the law'. Its power lies in its intellectual and moral authority. If it is the head of the city, it is no more than that: the city's golden thread, as it were, which needs external 'help' to enforce its views (cf. 645a5ff.). Still, it would be a mistake to think here of separation of powers. The Nocturnal Council does include some of the key magistrates of the city: the ten eldest *nomophulakes*, a certain number of priests

[32] Morrow 1960: 512.

[33] The talk of a 'short education' (735a4) presupposes a programme of higher education, and this is announced as something yet to be developed at 818a1–3.

and 'auditors' who have achieved a high reputation, and the minister of education. The other members may be former magistrates (including all the former ministers of education) or particularly meritorious citizens who have accumulated valuable experience, especially if they have travelled outside the city (951d–e, 961a–b). Each of the senior members is matched by a junior member, aged between thirty and forty. Besides the help which the juniors render their seniors (they lend them their eyes and ears, 964e–965a), this arrangement clearly reflects the pedagogical vocation of the Nocturnal Council. While devoting themselves to the advanced study of scientific disciplines in relation to the law, the members of the council also train their successors.

(c) *Control and Compromise*. The two basic forms of political institution, the assembly and the magistracy, embody at different levels the two basic principles of representation and competence. The degree of mediation achieved by these institutions, however, should not obscure their limitations. These limits are revealed by the place granted to constraint (the mildest form of which is control) and to compromise.

The exercise of offices is subjected to a series of formal, institutionalized controls, which are, as it were, a minimal trace of the 'threat' remaining within a system largely dominated by the principles of representation and competence. Such controls aim above all to prevent corruption, the possibility of which is inherent in human nature. Tenure of magistracies, for example, is limited, and individuals are not eligible for reappointment. In the judicial realm control is assured by the existence of an appeal mechanism, for public crimes (it seems) as well as private ones, and by legal guarantees. For instance, the death penalty can be pronounced only in exceptional circumstances and by an extraordinary joint sitting of the high court and the *nomophulakes* (855c). But the most important control is the auditing of accounts, to which all magistrates (including the auditors themselves) are subjected. All magistrates, high and low, are presumed potentially liable to corruption, even though this is far from inevitable (contrast the case of absolute power) and indeed is supposed to remain exceptional.

Just as they must make room for threat, however residually, the political institutions must also acknowledge a minimal form of compromise. This is because, while the procedures regulating the selection of magistrates in effect must be accepted by the citizens (since they involve all citizens' participation), this acceptance cannot be taken for granted. This is nowhere so clear as in the famous passage in Book VI about the two kinds of 'equality'.

According to an 'ancient adage' (Pythagorean), friendship is founded on 'equality' (757a5f.). What is involved is not 'arithmetical' equality, in which each citizen is worth the same as any other, but that 'truer and better' (757b5f.) geometrical or proportional equality which Socrates had already recommended to Callicles in the *Gorgias* (508a4–8). One cannot, however, simply substitute one for the other. Because the term 'equality' is ambiguous, it requires interpretation. Now most people will take it in an arithmetical, egalitarian sense. Appeal to geometrical equality will then tend to reproduce, at a higher level, the very disagreement which it was meant to prevent. This is why some limited scope must be granted to the lesser form of equality (i.e. the arithmetical), by institutionalizing the democratic choice by lot which is its characteristic political expression.

Although the democratic choice by lot is usually presented as a concession made to human nature, it is also interpreted, more positively, as the expression of 'divine chance' (*theia tuchē*). Accordingly, it is used for assigning the annual religious offices (759b–c). It also plays a role in the composition of the courts for popular justice (768b) and in deciding between the last few surviving candidates in an election (763d, on *astunomoi*).

The introduction of an egalitarian principle at the constitutional level may be seen as the counterpart of the allowance for private property at the economic level (see above, section 3.2). Popular misunderstanding of true equality, like the impossibility of total communism, sets the limits of the human prodigy. But despite this parallel there is an important difference. No man, simply as man, can renounce personal possessions. Hence the radical step taken in Book v. By contrast, it would seem possible that a majority of citizens, if properly educated, should eventually be able to acknowledge the superiority of geometrical equality over arithmetical equality: the *Laws*' pedagogical programme insists on training in elementary mathematics (818b–e). This may well explain why selection by lot (which relies on arithmetical equality) plays only a marginal and largely symbolic role in the procedure for distributing offices.

6 The forms of political speech: what is a preamble?

The polarity between control and compromise in the field of political institutions relates to a larger question, that of the limits of education (*paideia*), taken in the restricted sense given to this term in Book I (education as 'education to virtue', 643e4, cf. 653b). Indeed, education is where the *Laws*' constitutive tension between ideal and reality features most prominently. Just as human institutions must, in order to satisfy human nature, make allowance for private property (and, for that matter, arithmetical equality) and must also include mechanisms of control to prevent abuses, so education is limited on one hand by rhetorical persuasion and on the other by legal constraint.

What is at stake here is the extent to which persuasion, in itself a non-violent procedure (in as much as its medium is speech), can also be made uncompromisingly rational. Can legislative (and more generally political) speech in principle eliminate penal violence, and can compromise be eliminated from legislative speech? These questions, although they are not explicitly treated in the dialogue but must be reconstructed on the basis of evidence scattered through the whole work, constitute much of its philosophical interest.

As we have seen, the *Laws* gives the laws a foundation that is theological or 'noetic' (intellectual).[34] Yet one of the most striking features of the work is its reserve about the promulgation of laws. Not only can the legislator not content himself with producing laws (719e7–720a2), but, in some sense, making laws is not his priority: his real task is 'to educate the citizens, not to legislate' (857e4–5). The overall composition of the work reflects this attitude. When Aristotle says that the *Laws* contains practically nothing but laws (*Pol.*1265a1f.), he has in mind the distinction between the laws and the constitution, which Plato deals with only in Book VI. In fact the approach to the laws in the *Laws* is conceptually dominated by a *critique* of the law. This would not be possible unless different senses of the word 'law' were involved when the law is being given a theological foundation and when it is being criticized. Thus the very title of the work names a problem.

What must a law be, then, if we are to make sense of the idea that the legislator goes beyond legislating and even gladly renounces it? This question concerns both the scope of the law and the definition of its form.

The task of the Platonic legislator is to state 'what one must do with regard to the beautiful, the just, and all the other great notions . . . relevant to virtue and vice' (890b7–c3; cf. *Rep.* 484d1–3 and *Plt.* 309c5–d4). This all-encompassing description implies that the whole of human life can potentially become the object of legislative attention. Because the human prodigy is so fragile, Plato has every reason to exploit this potential for broad legislative scrutiny. The attention devoted to the details of behaviour is one of the most striking features of Platonic legislation. This atten-

[34] Above, pp. 260f.

tion makes it in some ways similar to the great religious codes and to wisdom literature. In particular, everything pertaining to 'private' life is to be strictly regulated, for what we call 'private' is actually the scaffold of the entire legislative edifice (793c, cf.780a1–7).

Now the point where the Platonic legislation is broadest in scope, as far as content is concerned, is also where the form of the law becomes most problematic. There are actually two reasons why law is ill-adapted to the private sphere. The first is contingent. To regulate and regiment private life is to undertake a potentially infinite task. It would be extremely difficult (and would even provoke laughter, 789e) to conceive a code of laws covering every detail of daily life. The second reason goes deeper. A law, in the strictest sense, is more than a simple prescriptive statement; it is a coercive prescription (773c6, e4), stipulating penalties in the case of transgression (789e4, 790a1f.). But there is no way that the punishment of domestic crimes (provided that it is adapted to the relative insignificance of the deed, which Plato assumes) can prevail over the immediate interests or fancies of those concerned. The legislator who would legislate in this domain would simply expose himself to the anger of his subjects, especially that of women (cf. 773c7, 789d8–790a7).

The legislator thus confronts a dilemma. He cannot restrict his legislation to the sphere of the political community properly speaking, for the so-called 'private' sphere is not really private. On the other hand, it is impossible to have recourse to the law in this sphere: not only would this be 'neither appropriate nor decent' (788b5f.), it would also prove ineffective. To resolve the dilemma would require the legislator to produce statements that would be functionally equivalent to laws without, however, being laws. What to call statements of this kind is an open question. Plato can refer to them as 'unwritten laws' (793a9f., cf. 773e3) or as 'an intermediate between admonition and law' (822d6f.). Most often they are presented as a discourse of praise and blame (see e.g. 730b5–7; 773e2–4; 824a10f.). Clearly, these descriptions correspond to the function assigned in Book IV to the preambles to the laws, although the emphasis is more specific – at stake is the philosophical relevance of 'mores' (Hegel's *Sitte*). In this respect, it is remarkable that women's resistance to the idea of (domestic) laws, far from being an obstacle to the legislative enterprise, as it might at first seem, in fact fosters a legislative project that is essentially committed to reduce the extension of the law. This is because the law, in the *Laws*, represents a certain kind of violence (*bia*, 722b7). But the law is violent in two rather different senses.

In the case of penal laws the violence involved is clear. Such laws represent a juridical conception of the law as embodied in existing legislative codes. From this perspective a law involves two distinct elements, a command and a threat, as can be illustrated with Plato's own example: 'When somebody reaches the age of thirty, let him be married, before he reaches thirty-five. If not, he will be punished with a fine and a dishonour, a fine of such and such amount, a dishonour of such and such kind' (721b1–3). Like every other legislative code, the *Laws* regularly stipulates the penalties, or threats (890b5; cf. 719e9), to be imposed in case of transgression, such as death, blows, confiscation of goods, or exile.[35]

But this conception of the juridical threat is deepened by an analysis (which remains largely implicit) of the command itself. Taken by itself, an order is no less violent than a threat, in as much as it does not give reasons. From this perspective, coercion is only the extension of a violence already present in the 'imperative' with which Plato, in at least one passage, identifies the law (723a5). One could go so far as to suggest that the command is in some respects even more 'violent' than penal violence. The threat is only relatively violent – it is not, by definition, the execution of the punishment but rather a specific form of persuasion, namely dissuasion. A command, however, to the extent to which it is accompanied by no reason at all (even dissuasive), is naked violence: this is why Plato calls the 'unmixed law' (unmixed, that is, with the persuasive preamble) a 'tyrannical order' (722e7–723a2). Be that as it may, whether the law is considered as a simple command or as a penal law, its inherent 'violence' induces a redescription of the legislator's task as an enterprise of persuasion. The site of this persuasion is not the law itself but the 'preamble', which is the generic form of all the para-legislative statements. Although the preamble should officially precede the law (723a2–4; cf. 720d6–e2), in many cases Plato gives a looser meaning to the term 'law' such that the preamble itself becomes part of the law (cf. the expression 'unmixed law'), or the entire reasoned prescription is called 'law' (as is often the case).

This explains why the elaboration of the laws, in the *Laws*, is accompanied by an impulse to reach beyond the law. We have already seen how this is reflected, at the level of composition, in the repeated postponement of the work of legislation (see above, section 2). But this formal feature has a substantive counterpart. Part of the philosophical programme of the *Laws* is to *reduce* the law (as far as its form is concerned), so that dialogue can become the ideal form of the legislative discourse.

This move, probably one of the most puzzling features of the work, is

35 Plato's penal system, which in important respects is more progressive than the legislation of his time, is thoroughly analysed in Saunders 1991.

directly linked to the difficult question of the status of persuasion in the *Laws*. Against the tendentious but widespread interpretation which reduces the preamble to an exercise in manipulative rhetoric, some commentators have recently insisted that the persuasion at issue in the work is in principle rational.[36] Now it is true that the two passages of the *Laws* which come closest to explaining the nature of a preamble give a major role to argument. But it is important to realize how argumentation comes in. The framework is provided by an extended analogy between the legislator and a doctor (719e7–720e5 and 857c4–e6). The way Plato develops the medical analogy, which is frequent in the Platonic corpus, is entirely new. Two kinds of medical practices are distinguished. The good or 'free' doctor is one who, unlike the 'slave' doctor, is not content to simply give his patient the appropriate medicine but, in the Hippocratic tradition, involves the patient in his own cure through verbal exchange.[37] The patient's state is an object of discussion. The *Laws* even goes so far as to picture the doctor 'going back to the general nature of bodies' in his quasi-philosophical discussion with his patient (857d). The hyperbole is evident, but so is the reason for it: the Socratic model of a dialectical conversation constitutes the horizon within which the theory of legislative preamble must be situated. This is the more remarkable, of course, in that the *Laws* has been read as Plato's ultimate treason against Socrates (see above, section 1).

This is not to say, of course, that a Platonic preamble is a Socratic dialogue. On the contrary, the distance between the theoretical conception of preambles emerging from the passages of Books IV and IX under consideration and the actual preambles which one actually finds in Books V–XII is striking. Certainly, the long preamble which constitutes the major part of Book X, in which Plato gives us the final version of his kinetics, has a nicely argumentative flavour (although the argument is hardly dialectical, given the fact that, past a certain point, Clinias and Megillus are unable to follow what the Stranger is saying: cf. 893a). But this is the exception. For the most part, preambles are speeches of praise and blame. One may well ask just where these forms of address get their persuasive force (a general question which the *Laws* invites, although it does not explicitly deal with it), but it is in any case much more a matter of 'rhetoric' than of properly 'rational' procedures.[38] Indeed, if actual lying is not practised (as it is in

[36] Hentschke 1971, Bobonich 1991.

[37] *Epidemics* I.5: 'The patient must oppose himself, with the doctor, to the illness.' On the medical analogy, cf. Jouanna 1978 and Laks 1991: 422f.

[38] Cf. Stalley 1994, criticizing Bobonich 1991.

the *Republic*), its potential usefulness is explicitly invoked (663d6–664a7). Moreover, the ancestral myths of retribution, which figure in most of the preambles attached to criminal laws, strangely if interestingly blur the contrast between persuasion and threat. Even though dissuasion may well be considered a kind of 'persuasion', it also remains essentially a threat and hence a kind of violence.

The distance between theory and practice, however, should not worry us. Rather the reverse, for not only does the medical analogy, if properly construed, imply the recognition that legislative discourse will not be able to follow the medical model of free discussion,[39] but the gulf between theory and practice, ideal and reality, runs through the *Laws* as a whole. The contrast between the paradigmatic notion of a preamble and its 'approximate' realizations (often a far cry from the alleged model) not only reminds us that we are in a second city, made for humans, but also implies that humanity is not itself homogeneous. The whole gamut from beast to god can be found among the citizens of the second city. The astounding variety of preambles that the legislator must employ is only the consequence of this diversity.

One of the most paradoxical aspects of the work, in this respect, is that the famous preamble of Book x, which is closest to discursive speech and thus (one might think) to the paradigm of Socratic discussion suggested by the medical analogy, is not presented as an ideal at all. The crime which it seeks to deter is the worst of all, for atheism by definition calls into question the very possibility of theologically founded legislation. The nature of the adversary explains the reticence with which the Athenian develops his argument based upon physical theory to establish the rationality of the universe. Recourse to such argument is imposed on him, against his will, by the complicity between Presocratic physics, which makes nature the principle of everything, and the sophistic critique of human conventions (889b–890a). Conversely, common sense is praised for finding in the ordered arrangement of the heavens enough of an argument to prove the existence of the gods (887d–e). This praise of common sense, which might surprise one coming from Plato's pen, shows that the preamble of Book x is not so close to the model of rational discussion sketched in Book iv as one might have thought. It also confirms Plato's attention, in his late political work, to what one might call the spontaneous manifestations of rationality of the 'human prodigy'.

39 To show this in detail would exceed the scope of this chapter. Unfortunately, no adequate analysis of the two highly complex passages and their relationship is available.

7 Conclusion

Plato's last and longest work is an impressive document not only of Platonic political philosophy, but of Platonic philosophy in general. Posidonius the Stoic, although a great admirer of Plato, must have found the work too Platonic for even his taste, for he vigorously rejected the theory of preambles on the grounds that a law should 'be brief, so that the unskilled may grasp it more easily': its goal, he insisted, was to 'order, not argue' (*iubeat lex, non disputet*) – a formula that would eventually find its way into a sixteenth-century commentary on the Digest.[40] Plato, on the contrary (if Clinias can be taken as his mouthpiece, which seems to be the case in this context), claimed that 'refusing to facilitate explanations [concerning the law] as best as possible' amounted to an act of 'impiety' (891a5–7).

Precisely because the work is so deeply Platonic, one should not be surprised if it happens not always to square exactly with other Platonic dialogues, even the 'late' ones: for all the continuity in the corpus, most Platonic dialogues begin from scratch, and the *Laws* is no exception in this respect. Admittedly, some of the doctrinal 'changes' that feature so prominently in the *Laws* have a very special status, as I have argued (above, section 3). One may also wonder about other items that could not be analysed here, such as Plato's treatment of the Socratic principle 'nobody does wrong voluntarily' within a conceptual framework that implicitly rejects the identification of virtue with knowledge,[41] or the startling rehabilitation of the written word, put in the very language that had served to condemn it in the *Phaedrus*: 'and in some sense a legislation relying on insight (*phronēsis*) draws its strongest help from the fact that legal instructions, once put in writing, do not move at all . . .' (890e6–891a2).[42]

Most striking in the *Laws*, however, in comparison with the rest of the corpus, is the new emphasis placed on 'god' in the conduct of human affairs, and more generally on piety. Not that concerns for god and piety are not to be found in other dialogues, such as, to name only a few obvious instances, the *Euthyphro*, the *Symposium*, the *Phaedrus* and the *Republic*. But it is fair to say, I think, that only in Plato's *Laws* does god possess such a centrality. The way the task is set in Book I, the theodicy in Book X, the very idea of law as an expression of divine reason, show that the *Laws* endorses, and is meant to be a commentary on, the famous Orphic line

[40] F. Duaren (in *Digest.* 1.3). The source for Posidonius' views on the *Laws*, and for the formula, is Seneca's *Letter* 94.38 (= F178 Kidd).

[41] Cf. 859c–864b, on which see Saunders 1968, and 691a5–7.

[42] Cf. *Phaedrus* 275d.

quoted at a crucial juncture in the general preamble of Book IV: god 'has the beginning, the end and the middle of all that is' (715e7–716a1). In this respect, Plato's *Laws* is not only the first work in genuine political philosophy, as I have argued above, but also the first theologico-political treatise. This makes it all the more important, for the better and for the worse, in the history of political thought, but also explains why, in spite of its insistence on the 'human factor', the work remains so distant from Aristotle, in the very moment where it seems to pave the way for him. This is because it is, in its fundamental orientation, an anti-Protagorean treatise: god, not man, is the measure of political order.[43]

[43] 716c4–6.

13

Plato and practical politics

MALCOLM SCHOFIELD

According to W.K.C.Guthrie in his *A History of Greek Philosophy* 'the primary aim of education for statesmanship never left [Plato's] thoughts. It was certainly his intention that many of his pupils should leave the Academy for politics, not as power-seekers themselves but to legislate or advise those in power, and we have the names of a number who did so.' The distinguished historian P. A. Brunt takes a different view:

> The evidence on the political activities of Plato's pupils is too weak to sustain in itself the thesis that it was one of his chief aims to prepare them for statecraft. Some were falsely labelled his pupils, but there is no proof that the rest were impelled by his teaching to take part in public affairs, still less that they tried to implement his ideas, or succeeded. The testimony of Isocrates suggests that his disciples were primarily devoted to unworldly studies, and this is supported by Plato's own skit in the *Theaetetus* on philosophers of his own kind.

As these contradictory assessments[1] suggest, the sources on Plato and practical politics are not easy to handle, and interpretation tends to reflect the more or less self-conscious preconceptions of the interpreters about for example the Academy (how far was it yet an institution?), or the general credibility of ancient biography and epistolography, or the still more general issue of the impact on public life made by philosophy now or then. The present writer inclines to scepticism or minimalism in all these areas.

There is in fact quite a lot of evidence to consider.[2] But it is of doubtful quality. One problem is that much of what we are told reflects ancient polemic for or against Plato. Thus the late gossip-writer Athenaeus has a section which collects material, probably mostly dating back to the end of the fourth century BC, designed to show that 'many of his pupils were disposed to tyranny' (508d).[3] Plutarch, on the other hand, lists associates of

[1] Guthrie 1975: 23, Brunt 1993: 330.

[2] See the review by Brunt 1993; what follows focuses on the key items only.

[3] See *Deipn.* 504a–509d, with Brunt 1993: 289 (cf. 332–4), who notes that a main ultimate source appears to be an oration delivered around 307 BC by Demosthenes' nephew Demochares.

Plato notable for their thoroughly admirable achievements on the public stage: the Athenian generals Chabrias and Phocion 'from the Academy' (*Col.*1126c), and the liberators of Sicily (Dion) and Thrace (Python and Heraclides). And he tells readers that 'among his companions Plato sent Aristonymus to the Arcadians, Phormio to the people of Elis and Menedemus to those of Pyrrha, in each case to put their constitutions in order' (ibid.). He adds that two other associates of Plato – Eudoxus and Aristotle – drew up laws for Cnidus and Stagira respectively (their native cities). Controversialists amass their ammunition as best they can, and it is often difficult or impossible to tell how much truth there may be in their claims or implications.[4] Even where a writer is not obviously grinding an axe, what is preserved may be only an anecdote, as likely as not *ben trovato*. Thus among a list of communities said to have asked Plato himself to assist in devising a constitution for them is a story relating to the foundation of Megalopolis in 369 BC (Diogenes Laertius III.23):[5]

> Pamphile says in the twenty-fifth book of her *Memorabilia* that when they were founding Megalopolis, the Arcadians and Thebans invited Plato to be their lawgiver. But when he learned that they were opposed to equality of possessions, he would not go.

Yet the aim of settling Megalopolis was to establish a centre – with democratic institutions – for the anti-Spartan Arcadian federation: was Plato the obvious choice to devise the appropriate legislation? Probably not merely anecdotal, on the other hand, is the evidence that Aristotle, during his time in the Academy, addressed his *Protrepticus* to the Cyprian prince Themison (otherwise unknown) c. 353 BC. It seems not unlikely that this was an attempt to invade Isocrates' field of patronage in Cyprus.[6] Last but not least in this review of the nature of the evidence, seven out of the thirteen extant letters ascribed to Plato in the manuscript tradition deal with matters arising from his visits to Sicily c. 367 and c. 360 BC. The seventh in particular provides a great deal of detail about this adventure, and much that bears on questions of political theory. But its authenticity is still contested, although the chances that it really is from Plato's hand are agreed to be higher than for any of the other letters.[7]

[4] See e.g. Owen 1983.

[5] Also recorded by Aelian *Ver.Hist.* II.42. It is similarly alleged that Plato refused an invitation to legislate for the people of Cyrene: Plu. *ad Princ.* 779d, Aelian *Ver. Hist.* XII.30 (believed by Dusanič 1978, but not by Riginos 1976, 191–3).

[6] So Owen 1983: 9, on Aristotle Fr.50 Rose; cf. Düring 1961: 173–4.

[7] For bibliography on the letters see nn. 24–7 below.

It was to be expected that those attracted to study with Plato would be mostly wealthy and mostly aristocrats, some with political ambitions or subsequent political histories. What is well-nigh impossible to assess is what influence association with Plato or the Academy may have had on the political outlook of (for example) the general Phocion or – another Athenian public figure listed as a pupil – the orator Lycurgus.[8] We do not have much information about what sort of education they would have acquired in the Academy: the easy assumption that it promoted the programme of higher education advocated in *Republic* Book VII is merely an assumption.[9] So it is difficult to speculate about how Plato might have equipped pupils either to advise princes or exercise rule themselves. Glenn Morrow, one of the many scholars convinced that the Academy was a school for statesmen, thinks it 'clear' that its members were prepared there for that role 'by the study of Greek law and politics' *inter alia*.[10] Not a shred of evidence supports his claim. One might have guessed from the key role it is given in the *Republic* in the scheme for educating philosopher rulers that mathematics would have figured prominently in the studies Plato fostered. But although we hear quite a bit about his encouragement of research in mathematics, especially by formulating problems (e.g. what uniform motions will account for the apparently disorderly behaviour of the planets), there is no concrete evidence of its actually being taught in the Academy – unless Isocrates' denigration in his *Antidosis* (353 BC) of the uselessness of geometry and astronomy as a preparation for public life is taken as referring to Plato's practice as well as his theory.[11] Isocrates includes in his strictures eristical or logic-chopping 'dialogues' (*Panathenaicus* 26). This sounds like an attack primarily on Plato's literary production. Nonetheless it may also hint at the teaching methods of the Academy, if the precepts for dialectical controversy offered in Aristotle's early *Topics* may be taken as addressed to those he taught and worked with there. Interestingly none of the philosophical examples Aristotle chooses to illustrate the rules for dialectic he recommends is taken from political theory, although every other area of philosophy is well represented.[12] He himself probably taught rhetoric already in his Academic period, but it

[8] Phocion: Plu. *Col.* 1126c, *Life of Phocion* 4.2; Lycurgus: D.L. III.46. Discussion: Renehan 1970.

[9] So Cherniss 1945: ch. 3.

[10] Morrow 1960: 5; Saunders 1986 thinks we can infer from the *Laws* the sorts of policies and procedures Academic political 'advisers' would have been taught to recommend.

[11] Isoc. XV.258–69.

[12] Jacques Brunschwig, Budé editor of the *Topics*, comments (*per litteras*): 'A remarkable absence. Did the members of the Academy abstain from discussing such matters, or was Aristotle not interested in such discussions, or not willing to take part in them?'

was presumably to Isocrates' rival school that budding orators would in the first instance look for instruction.

It is time now to turn from generalities to the examination of particular instances where some form of Platonic involvement in politics is documented or suspected. An interesting example, which illustrates some of the difficulties for interpretation, is the case of Erastus and Coriscus of Skepsis in the Troad, the Rosencrantz and Guildenstern of ancient philosophy, listed as pupils of Plato by Diogenes Laertius (III.46). How did their names reach Diogenes or his source? There are two identifiable possibilities, not mutually exclusive. One is the story of Aristotle's move to the court of Hermias, tyrant of Atarneus near Skepsis, probably just after Plato's death. Different versions of the story were current, some belonging to a tradition hostile to Hermias, others (probably deriving from the life of Aristotle by the second century BC writer Hermippus) much more favourable.[13] The favourable version, which appears in two works both preserved on papyrus, has Aristotle, Erastus and Coriscus[14] accept an invitation from Hermias, who is represented as making the town of Assos available to them for their philosophical discussions. Hermias is said to have shifted from tyranny to a 'milder' form of rule. There is associated talk of 'Plato's saying', but as often in papyrus texts the fragmentary context makes any conjecture about what saying is being referred to nothing more than that.[15]

The other work on which Diogenes Laertius might have been drawing is the sixth of the letters attributed to Plato. This brief document is addressed jointly to Hermias and to Erastus and Coriscus, as neighbours who have fallen out but should now be reconciled as the friends they once were. Plato – or 'Plato' – plays upon the complementary qualities of Hermias, the man of experience and practical gifts (whom however he has never met),[16] and Erastus and Coriscus, long-time members of the Academy, naive in the ways of the world but trustworthy and possessed of 'that noble wisdom which understands the Forms' (322d). Some scholars would like to think the letter really was written by Plato, but this is

[13] Texts in Düring 1957: 272–83. Further discussion: Mulvany 1926, Wormell 1935, Owen 1983.

[14] And one other philosopher, whose name the fragmentary state of the papyrus makes it impossible to identify. On the basis of Strabo XIII.1.57 (the hostile tradition) it has usually been reconstructed, against the papyrus evidence, as Xenocrates; for a refutation of the suggestion see Owen 1983: 6–10.

[15] The two texts are: Didymus *In Dem. comm.* 5.51–63 Diels and Schubart; Philodemus *Ind.Acad.* V.1–22 Dorandi.

[16] This is contradicted by the isolated and unreliable testimony of Strabo (XIII.1.57), who says he studied at Athens with both Plato and Aristotle. The truth here is probably irrecoverable.

rendered unlikely by its combination of exiguous content and portentous conclusion, where the author seems to resort to intimations of numerology and esoteric theology to get his readers to treat his efforts as something like a sacred text. It reads more like a late rhetorical exercise composed by someone who has spotted in the favourable version of the Hermias story scope for an addition to Plato's correspondence.[17]

Guthrie suggests that Erastus and Coriscus are the best attested example of the fulfilment of those missionary intentions we saw him ascribing to Plato.[18] But nothing in the evidence supports the hypothesis that they went to Hermias' court as legislators or advisers, still less (as the normally cautious Brunt supposes)[19] that after leaving the Academy they had themselves come to power in their native Skepsis. It rather sounds as though like kings and princes throughout the succeeding Hellenistic age, Hermias extended his invitation primarily from a desire to satisfy a curiosity about philosophy and to secure some intelligent and cultivated company. The one thing clearly attested by the fragmentary evidence is that he went out of his way to provide his guests with conditions suitable for the pursuit of philosophical discussion, away from the seat of government in Atarneus itself – a point perhaps picked up by the writer of the sixth letter, which asks Hermias not to burden Erastus and Coriscus with care for 'human and necessary wisdom' more than he must (322e). Hermias' regime may indeed have become less absolute: at any rate, an inscription records a treaty between 'Hermias and his associates' with Erythraea.[20] Just at the point where readable text in the papyrus gives way to gaps, it looks as though Philodemus was suggesting that his philosophical friends believed that he had changed to monarchy (from tyranny) through the influence of philosophy (*Ind.Acad.* v. 13–16).

Similarly cautious conclusions are in order for the examples of political involvement on the part of associates of Plato cited by Plutarch (*Col.* 1126c). Of the three instances he gives where Plato 'sent' companions of his to put constitutions in order, two appear from other evidence to concern cases where the reformer allegedly despatched was a citizen of the community in question: Phormio of Elis and Menedemus of Pyrrha (nothing is known about Aristonymus, the other name mentioned in this context).[21] This fuels the suspicion that it was as leading public figures commanding the respect of their fellow-citizens that they did their

[17] Cf. Aalders 1972: 170–1, Brisson 1987: 127–32. [18] Guthrie 1975: 23.
[19] Brunt 1993: 292. [20] See Tod 1948: 105, Düring 1957: 277.
[21] Phormio: *Praec.* 805d (where he is said to have overthrown the ruling oligarchy); Menedemus: Phld. *Ind.Acad.* VI.2–3.

legislative work, not as Platonic emissaries. As for the liberation of Sicily by Dion or of Thrace by Python and Heraclides, Plutarch does not claim in so many words that these exploits were inspired by Platonic ideals (ibid.). According to Aristotle the latter pair killed the Thracian king Cotys to avenge their father (*Pol.* v.10.1311 b20–2). Plutarch's *Dion* and the *Seventh Letter* ascribed to Plato both represent Dion as motivated by commitment to political freedom, but that is hardly an exclusively or preeminently Platonic or philosophical preoccupation.[22]

The most celebrated instance of the involvement of the Academy in practical politics is Plato's own Sicilian adventure. The fullest accounts of this are given in the two works just mentioned, and indeed it has sometimes been suspected that the *Seventh Letter* is the sole source from which all other accounts of the affair derive. This may be too sceptical a view, since one of Plutarch's sources was the Sicilian historian of Sicily Timaeus, who probably drew himself on the work of Philistus, a rival of Dion at the court of Dionysius II, for his narrative of events there.[23] The *Seventh Letter* represents Plato as visiting Syracuse for the first time in the reign of Dionysius I at 'around the age of 40' (c. 388/7 BC: 324a). But its main focus is on subsequent visits: one shortly after the accession of his son, the younger Dionysius (c. 367/6), and another some years later (c. 361/0). On both these later occasions, if we believe the letter, Plato went at Dionysius II's invitation, but under strong moral pressure from Dion (the new tyrant's uncle), whom he had met back in 388/7 and had come to admire greatly. According to the letter, his object in accepting the first of the invitations was to lend assistance to Dion's plan to turn Dionysius into a philosopher ruler. While the conversion of Dionysius to true philosophy remained a goal the second time around, Plato's agreement to return to Sicily was conceived in the first instance as an attempt to reconcile Dionysius and Dion, now bitterly estranged from each other. Both ventures were humiliating failures.

The *Seventh Letter* is purportedly addressed to the friends of Dion – apparently soon after his assassination (c. 353 BC) at the instigation of an Athenian acquaintance of Plato's named Callippus – in response to a request to say whether like them he still shares Dion's political ideals. In fact it is an elaborate and ingeniously constructed defence of Plato's own conduct relating to his entanglement with Dionysius and the intrigues of court at Syracuse. It continually stresses how every step Plato took was

22 The argument of this paragraph is indebted to Brunt 1993: 289–90.

23 Cf. e.g. Brunt 1993: 314–19.

motivated by devotion to philosophy and (despite appearances) to his friendship with Dion – notwithstanding grave misgivings on his part, reinforced throughout his dealings with Dionysius, about the chances of their leading to a satisfactory outcome. It makes the philosopher speak his mind frankly to the tyrant in the classic style characteristic of encounters between the wise and the powerful, typified by Solon's encounter with Croesus or Diogenes the Cynic's with Alexander the Great.[24] And the letter is also a philosophical apologia: conveyed in a digression designed to show that Plato's philosophy is original and inimitable and something he discussed with Dionysius on one occasion only, so that the versions of it circulating under the names of others (including Dionysius' own) must be dismissed as inauthentic. This curious stretch of text has been plausibly interpreted as an attempt to counter allegations that Plato plagiarized from the Pythagoreans, since the letter clearly identifies the Pythagorean Archytas of Tarentum as the leading figure among those who made egregious claims for Dionysius' prowess as a philosopher.[25]

Is the *Seventh Letter* by Plato?[26] It is written in a Greek style which Hellenists and their computers find indistinguishable from the Greek of Plato's late group of dialogues.[27] It contains no unquestionable anachronisms or historical errors. Attempts to argue that its accounts and reminiscences of Platonic ideas or doctrines are demonstrable distortions of them have not succeeded.[28] The story it tells is admittedly rambling and at times confusing. But if Plato was the author, he was an old man by the time he composed it; the manner and design of *Laws* are similarly digressive. Readers have sometimes thought various other features of the letter's content odd if really by Plato: a consideration however which tends to cut both ways, since a forger might be expected to take more pains to stick closer to the verifiably Platonic. What is clear is that the letter is the work of an ingenious and powerful writer, steeped in Plato's writings and his habits of thinking and expression.

Many scholars have consequently availed themselves of the use of Occam's razor and concluded that the most reasonable hypothesis is that the author *is* Plato. Yet the issue of authenticity is likely to remain open. The present writer finds himself hesitantly in the sceptic camp, mainly for

[24] Cf. Hdt. I.30–3, D.L. VI.38, 60, 68.

[25] See Lloyd 1990. The philosophical digression has sometimes been viewed as a non-Platonic interpolation into an otherwise authentic document: see the discussion in Guthrie 1978: 402–17; also Tarrant 1983, Brisson 1987, 145–58.

[26] There is a huge if undistinguished bibliography on this subject. For orientation see Morrow 1962, Gulley 1972, Aalders 1972, Brisson 1987.

[27] See Brandwood 1969, Deane 1973, Ledger 1989.

[28] See e.g. Solmsen 1969 *contra* Edelstein 1966.

two reasons. First, there is no wit or humour, black or otherwise, in the letter, not even the rather lumbering playfulness characteristic of late works like the *Sophist* or the *Laws*. Second, on the evidence of the dialogues no writer has ever had a deeper aversion than Plato to self-disclosure: is it credible that he should decide at the end of the day to tear off the mask and speak for once in his own voice on matters which must have caused him much pain?

There are some questionable (but not incontrovertibly false) notes struck by that purportedly Platonic voice. A general point is that the writer explains himself at considerable length and in consistently defensive tones of pained sincerity. Plato was an aristocrat, who – to judge from the dialogues down to and including the *Laws* – retained the self-assurance of his class, and a writer to whom irony became second nature. Then there are more particular instances. For example, one might doubt whether Plato himself would have stooped to the melodrama of the following sentence (349d): 'And he [sc. the tyrant Dionysius] looked straight at me and said in a very tyrannical manner: "I never made any agreement big or little with you."' Even the most compelling passage of the whole document – the writer's account of Plato's disillusionment with politics following the rule of the Thirty Tyrants and the judicial murder of Socrates – ends with something hard to reconcile with the conventions of the Platonic dialogue (326a): 'I was forced to say, praising the true philosophy, that it is from its vantage point that it is possible to set eyes both on political justice and all the justice relating to private persons.' There follows a reprise of the proposition put forward in the central books of *Republic* that there will be no end to the evils which encompass the human race until philosophers become rulers or rulers learn to do philosophy. Adherence to this thesis is represented as tilting Plato into the decision to go to Syracuse (328c): 'By persuading one man only I would be in the position of having sufficiently engineered every good thing [i.e. as regards laws and constitution].' '*I* was forced to say . . .': but of course it was not exactly *Plato* who said any of this,[29] but his 'Socrates' – quizzically and with elaborate acknowledgment (notable here by its absence) of the counterintuitiveness of the claim and the difficulty, even assuming it realized, of achieving an approximation to the ideal polity.

It has sometimes been suggested that the political thought of the

29 When the writer later becomes explicitly preoccupied with what Plato has or has not said in writing (341b–342a), the dialogues' arguments about Forms are likewise treated as Plato's own (342a).

Seventh Letter is a confused amalgam of *Republic* and *Laws*.[30] This is principally because the passages just referred to conjure with the ideal of a philosopher ruler, whereas in other passages the writer represents his main purpose as having been to advise Dionysius on the need to introduce constitutional government and the rule of law throughout Sicily, in terms reminiscent of *Laws*.[31] I think the difficulty arises because the *Seventh Letter* has been subject to interpolation: the *Laws*-like material mostly comes in a section offering advice to the Sicilians in general and the friends of Dion in particular, which looks as though it has been pasted fairly crudely into the middle of the exculpatory narrative. The interpolator I am conjecturing must have thought that the letter in its original form failed to give the counsel it had been asked for, and so himself supplied what was lacking.[32]

It would be convenient if in pursuing the question of what Plato really hoped to achieve in Sicily one could set issues of authenticity and interpolation aside. But clearly it makes or could make a difference whether it is *Plato* who is saying that he went with the original hope of converting Dionysius to a philosophical way of life, or someone else who is putting that claim in his mouth – even if that someone were writing soon after the events in question with some good information at his disposal. On the assumption that the author is Plato himself, it is hard to resist the conclusion that he really did go because he thought there was some chance of making of Dionysius a philosopher ruler who would (as Plutarch puts it) 'cure Sicily of all her maladies' (*Dion* 11.2). For the issue of Dionysius' aptitude for philosophy and commitment to it is a central preoccupation of the letter, which shapes the whole construction of the narrative. If Plato is insincere about its importance the whole document loses much of its credibility and leaves his object in composing it a mystery. So on the hypothesis of Platonic authorship we seem to be obliged to suppose that

[30] Cf. e.g. Gulley 1972: 116–22. Ancient Platonists apparently took a different view: Alcinous (*Didaskalikos* ch. 34) uses the categories of Aristotle's *Politics* IV.1 to describe the polity Plato envisages in *Ep.*VII as (like that of *Laws*) 'on the basis of a hypothesis', i.e. given certain less than ideal assumptions; but more particularly 'as a result of correction' (*diorthōsis*). But *Republic* is dismissive of attempts to improve society by correction or 'reform' (425e, 426e).

[31] *Laws* 709d–711a proposes that the best and quickest way to bring about the 'best city' is for the lawgiver to find a tyrant (i.e. absolute monarch) who is possessed of great natural aptitudes and common or garden moderation (*not* philosophical wisdom), and persuade him to allow the lawgiver to proceed with his work. This passage has often been interpreted as Plato's articulation of the relation he wished he had had with Dionysius; *Republic*'s ideal of philosophy and power coinciding in one person is tacitly abandoned (cf. *Laws* 875a–d).

[32] Interpolated section: 330c–338a (with the coda at 352a). The request: 323e–324a (actually it does not have to be construed as soliciting advice). Advice is certainly promised: 326e; but 351a–e (cf. 326c–e) may be regarded as the passage where (before interpolation) it was primarily delivered.

in accepting Dionysius' first invitation, Plato allowed himself to suppress to a degree the sense *Republic* so palpably communicates of the immense unlikelihood of the realization of the ideal of a philosopher ruler. There is also an implication which bears on the rest of the evidence relating to political activity on the part of members of the Academy. The *Seventh Letter* treats the Sicilian adventure as Plato's one real opportunity to turn word into deed, and to put his philosophy into political practice. There is no suggestion that his teaching in Athens over the years had long been designed to do just that, by preparing young aristocrats for statesmanship. Perhaps one may also infer that if he *was* asked to provide constitutions for other cities or send them legislators, he would not have regarded such invitations as opportunities to implement his philosophy.

Suppose however that the *Seventh Letter* is not the work of Plato's own hand. In that case we can allow without much discomfort that the document *might* simply be spinning a purely speculative yarn about the motivation of the Sicilian adventure, even if many of the factual details are correct. The existence of the letter would then do nothing whatever to illuminate the question of why the adventure was undertaken. And that conclusion points to the verdict to be pronounced on the document all things considered. Given that its authenticity is at least doubtful, the positive attempt to extract from it information about Plato's views on the relation between philosophy and political practice, or on the policies he favoured in this regard, must be unsafe; but the possibility that the letter really is by Plato or by someone who knew his mind should also dictate caution as to how far we can simply bracket its evidence when we think about the issue.[33]

33 My two concluding paragraphs owe much to Brunt 1993: 325–32.

14

Cleitophon and *Minos*

CHRISTOPHER ROWE

As later chapters will show, Plato's political ideas were immediately and immensely influential. Aristotle's own political thinking largely starts where Plato left off, and much of Hellenistic constitutional theory shows an indelibly Platonic imprint. However, at least at first sight, this influence seems to owe relatively little to the post-Platonic Academy itself. The major figures who immediately succeeded Plato, Speusippus and Xenocrates, seem by and large to have been more interested, or at any rate more innovative, in ethics (and metaphysics) than in politics, though Speusippus is reported as having written an *On Legislation*, Xenocrates a *Politicus*, in one book, and – interestingly – an *Elements of Kingship for Alexander*, in four.[1] Polemon, who took over the headship from Xenocrates, and taught the Stoic Zeno, was also primarily known for his contributions in ethics.[2] After him, with Arcesilaus, the Academy takes a sceptical turn; when Antiochus of Ascalon, in the first century BC, announces a return to the positive doctrines of the 'Old Academy', his version of 'Platonic' (and Aristotelian) political ideas turns out to be a heavily Stoicized one.[3]

Yet this broad-brush picture cannot be quite right. There clearly was continuing and direct engagement with Plato's political writings on the part of the Academy: the field was not left entirely to Aristotle. Thus the second part of the famous two-day disquisition at Rome, for and against justice, by the Academic sceptic Carneades seems to have exploited Glaucon's case against, in *Republic* II;[4] and we also have fairly secure, and

[1] D. L. IV.5, 13, 14.

[2] Various fourth-century individuals, perhaps including Xenocrates himself, who were either members of the Academy or associated with it, were evidently also involved in practical politics at Athens and elsewhere (Schuhl 1946, Morrow 1960, Isnardi Parente 1988, Saunders 1986); but it is impossible to tell to what extent that involvement was rooted in or even influenced by Academic or Platonic ideas (cf. Schofield, in Ch. 13 above).

[3] Dillon 1977: 78–81, Annas 1995.

[4] Lact. *Inst.* V.14.3–5.

reasonably extended, evidence of the close reading of both the *Republic* and the *Laws* within the 'Old Academy' itself.[5]

The evidence in question is in the shape of the *Cleitophon* and the *Minos*. These two dialogues are among a number of works – at least most of the *Letters*, as well as short dialogues – which although included in the Platonic corpus are either certainly or probably not by Plato himself; on the other hand these pseudo-Platonic pieces usually show a sufficiently detailed knowledge of his methods and strategies to suggest that they originated within the ambit of the Academy (and to explain how they became attached to the corpus, though the motivation of many of the pieces remains unclear). The *Cleitophon* and the *Minos*[6] are specifically political in content, and each is quite striking in its own way. The particular interest of the *Cleitophon* is the mildly critical and ironic tone which its author uses (critical, that is, of 'Socrates' in the *Republic*, and hence of Plato). What distinguishes the *Minos*, for its part, is that it seems to imply a response, and an accommodation, to the new kind of political agenda which was dictated by the conquests of Alexander, and subsequently by the Hellenistic kingships. (The same agenda was no doubt also reflected in Xenocrates' *Elements of Kingship*.) There is no obvious way of establishing the date of either work, but from a modern perspective the *Cleitophon* may well appear closer to, and the *Minos* further from, the undoubted works of Plato.

Cleitophon is named after its main speaker, who makes a brief appearance in Book I of the *Republic* (340a–b), during Socrates' conversation with Thrasymachus. The connection with the *Republic* seems to be made immediately, by Socrates' opening remarks: he has heard that Cleitophon has complaints about time spent with him, and prefers Thrasymachus' company (in the *Republic*, he appears rather as someone trying – however unsuccessfully – to get Thrasymachus off Socrates' hook).[7] Cleitophon denies this, or rather half-denies it: the truth is that he used to be

[5] On the history of Plato's texts after his death, see Barnes 1991. They seem (unlike Aristotle's: see Rowe, in Ch.19 below) to have been in reasonably wide circulation; cf. e.g. D. L. III.66, and, for the political works, Cicero's project for a Roman *Republic* and *Laws* (see Atkins, Ch.24 below). But 'reasonably' is an important qualification, if it was noteworthy that Arcesilaus 'possessed [Plato's] books' (D. L. IV.32, Solmsen 1981: 104).

[6] Others are e.g. *Theages* and *Lovers* (also known as *Rivals*) and the considerably longer *First Alcibiades*. All of these, and indeed the *Cleitophon* and *Minos* themselves, have had their defenders: see Guthrie 1978: ch.4, Pangle 1987. It is always hard to prove a negative (in this case that the works in question are not by Plato), but the balance of the arguments would probably now seem mostly to support the rejection at any rate of the dialogues just mentioned, with the *Alcibiades* probably the most controverted case; on *Cleitophon* and *Minos* in particular, see below.

[7] At the beginning of the dialogue, too (328b), Cleitophon is perhaps implied to be a follower of Thrasymachus, by the way in which he is listed with him; but of course he also shows himself ready to follow Socrates' argument – which is essential to the point of the *Cleitophon*.

enthralled by Socrates (407a5–6), and still is – up to a point: Socrates is very good at protreptic, and his talk about the need for us to care for our souls is persuasive enough, but how exactly are we supposed to go about it? If what we require is 'the art of justice' (409a), what does that consist in? Cleitophon describes how he went and asked Socrates' friends, without being able to get any satisfactory answer from them; finally he asked Socrates himself, and *he* said 'harming one's enemies and helping one's friends', but then it turned out that the just man will in fact harm no one (410a–b: here we have a kind of summary of an earlier part of *Republic*, though actually the definition in question comes from Polemarchus, not Socrates). So now, at a loss for an answer, Cleitophon means to go off to Thrasymachus, or someone else: perhaps Lysias, another rhetorical expert (406a, 410e), though he will always praise Socrates as well as criticize him.

The real point of the piece begins with the description of the *Apology*-style search for some substantive Socratic teaching about justice: 'I went first to those you most think worth something' (408c8; cf. *Ap.* 21b9, 22a3). Just as Socrates showed everyone else not to know anything, so none of those who might have been expected to know what Socrates thought the next step should be, after the protreptic stage, including Socrates himself, turns out to have any clear idea of what it is. This resembles pure parody. But when Cleitophon asks what exactly it is that is the *ergon* ('product', 'outcome') of justice, the first set of substantive answers turns out to consist in the ones which Thrasymachus rules out at *Republic* 336c–d, and which Socrates plays at accepting; the *Cleitophon* now gives the kind of argument that Thrasymachus might have used, and thus itself becomes a kind of commentary on the *Republic*. The lines that follow this passage in the *Republic* (uttered by Thrasymachus) suggest the general theme of the *Cleitophon*: '. . . so that Socrates can do what he always does, *not answering himself* but taking hold of the answers someone else gives and testing them to destruction (*elenchein*)' (337e).[8] This perhaps is why the author, somewhat clumsily and artificially, ends the section (410a–b) with Socrates' refutation of Polemarchus' account of justice as helping friends and harming enemies: clumsily, because to fit his scheme, that account has to be attributed to Socrates himself (but at least half of Thrasymachus' accusation is illustrated: Socrates in the end gives no answers).

[8] Admittedly, not much is made of *Socrates'* testing of others in the *Cleitophon*; the boot is on the other foot. But Alcibiades' description of Socrates in the *Symposium* similarly plays down the destructive aspect of his conversations (and there is in general more than a little in common between Cleitophon's position in the *Cleitophon*, proposing to abandon Socrates, and Alcibiades' in the *Symposium*).

However there is another aspect to this apparent misattribution. By and large, the *Cleitophon* abides by the dramatic conventions of the dialogue form; the *Republic* is referred to, not as a written work by an author called Plato, but as representing actual conversations between Socrates and others. The real target, though, is Plato, not Socrates, and it is after all Plato who puts Polemarchus' proposal in Polemarchus' mouth, only to knock it down again (it is *Plato* – in the *Republic* – who has no real answers). There was someone, Cleitophon says just before, 'who seemed to say very clever things' (409d3), namely that the *ergon* of justice was 'making friendship in cities' (409d5–6): when further identified as 'like-mindedness' or 'concord' (*homonoia*, 409e), this recalls the provisional account of 'self-control' (*sōphrosunē*, as agreement between the different classes in the state about who should rule) which immediately precedes that of justice in *Republic* IV ('doing one's own'). There are in fact some difficulties in clearly distinguishing the two virtues on the basis of what is said here, but this is evidently not what is in the mind of the author of the *Cleitophon*, who raises problems of a different sort. (The argument is: 'like-mindedness' must be either *homodoxia*, a matter of sharing the same beliefs, or knowledge; but friendship is always a good, and beliefs can be harmful; so it must be knowledge – but that means we are back where we started, because what we were looking for was what *kind* of knowledge justice is.)[9] In any case, by whatever route he reaches it, he gets to a conclusion that is uncomfortably close to the truth. Even in Book IV, where the original question about justice is supposed to receive at least a working answer, little headway is actually made.

What emerges is a quite competent critique of a central aspect of the *Republic*. In principle there is nothing to prevent us from supposing Plato himself to be indulging in self-criticism, and self-parody; but on the whole it seems not quite good enough for that.[10] At the same time it looks like an inside, i.e. genuinely Academic, job, not only because of the knowledge of Plato – and especially of one particular text – that it betrays, but because of the absence of any hostility in its approach. Its tone recalls that of Aristotle's remark at the beginning of *Politics* IV (1288b35–7), that his

[9] For what seems to be a later career for the argument of the *Cleitophon* here, in the context of Stoicism, see Schofield 1991: 128–9. Schofield says that '[t]here is good reason to think that Chrysippus knew the *Cleitophon* and regarded it as by Plato', but if so, the question will be whether Chrysippus was in a better position than us to judge (Schofield suggests not).

[10] This is not quite so subjective a criterion as it may sound; see Slings 1981 for a complete account of the oddities and inconcinnities of the dialogue (to add to its alleged 'clumsiness', and the way in which it slightly misses the target: see above).

predecessors (Plato at least included), 'even if everything else they say is fine enough, fail to hit on those things that are of practical use'.

The *Minos* is in many ways an attractive and accomplished dialogue. But it is a strange mixture: while it is written in a manner which closely resembles that of the so-called Socratic dialogues, its subject-matter is more akin to that of the *Politicus* and the *Laws*; at the same time it contains important elements which are (perhaps subtly, but nonetheless genuinely) at odds with what we find in the undisputed parts of the Platonic corpus. It consists in a conversation between Socrates and an unnamed companion, on the subject of *law* (*nomos*). What is law, Socrates asks? He manoeuvres his partner into the answer that it is 'what a city decides' (*dogma tēs poleōs*, 314c2: the phrase *dogma poleōs* also appears in a fleeting definition of law at *Laws* 644d). But if so, he argues, it must comprise only those decisions or judgments which are true; in this sense it consists in a discovery of what is the case (what is actually just), and anyone who misses in his aim at this also misses what is 'lawful' (*nomimos*) (315a–316b). The anonymous respondent objects to this that 'we are always changing the laws, this way and that' (316c1–2), to which Socrates' response is that laws in the political sphere are the province of the expert ('good kings and good men', 317a8–b1), just like 'laws' in every other sphere – and the expert lawgiver will always establish the same laws about the same things. If we see people changing the laws, that is a sign of their lack of expertise; the expert will simply lay down what is correct, which will not need changing. Thus 'what is correct (*orthon*) is kingly [expert] law, and what is incorrect, what seems to be law to those without expertise, is not; for it is 'lawless' (*anomon*)', that is, because not laid down by the expert (317c5–7). But who then is it, Socrates goes on, that establishes the best laws (*nomoi*) for the souls of men, in the way (e.g.) that the herdsmen knows best how to tend (*nemein*) his cows? The king, of course – which is where we were before, but now there is a new step. There are ancient authorities, for example, Marsyas and Olympus, who laid down the 'laws' that apply in music, and whose pronouncements remain valid; are there any equivalents to Marsyas and Olympus among legislators? Not Lycurgus, at Sparta, because he was relatively recent; what about those ancient kings in Crete, Minos and Rhadamanthys? Then follows a long excursus on Minos,[11] which issues in

[11] The excursus includes an ingenious passage on two Homeric lines (*Odyssey* XIX.178–9) which are alluded to at *Laws* 624a–625a; in this respect, and perhaps in others (as e.g. when it picks up the definition of law at *Laws* 644d), the *Minos* begins itself to resemble – like the *Cleitophon* – a kind of commentary on Plato. (I owe this point, and others, to suggestions by Malcolm Schofield.)

the suggestion that the greatest indication that he was a good legislator/herdsman (*nomothetēs/nomeus*), someone good at *nemein/dianemein*) is that his laws remain unchanged (*akinētoi*), 'because he had discovered the truth of what is the case relating to the government of a city' (321b2–4). The argument seems to be: (true) laws do not change, so if we can find someone whose laws have not changed, then we will have found someone who is a truly expert legislator and king.

The author of the dialogue seems to be anxious to show that there are true laws in existence, and that there have been true kings/legislators (and so presumably could be again). This seems to go beyond anything to which Plato would – or indeed consistently could – have committed himself. The very idea of laws that are 'correct', and unchangeable because 'correct', runs directly counter to the argument of the *Politicus* (at least), one of whose main conclusions is that law is by its very nature imperfect (because of the problems of applying general laws to particular situations); nor is there any shift from this position in the *Laws* (which also has important criticisms to make of 'the laws of Minos' in Crete).[12] The chief function of the ideal king in the *Politicus* is to supply the deficiencies of law; and law will only be sovereign in those cases where he is absent.[13] In short, what the author of the *Minos* wants – an ideal king issuing 'correct' laws, valid for all time – is actually ruled out by Plato's argument: laws can be expressions of reason[14] without being in principle unchangeable,[15] and indeed reason will sometimes dictate that even the most carefully framed laws may need to be changed,[16] on the grounds suggested by the *Politicus*.

Commitment to the idea of the good king, who will issue 'correct' laws, is more typical of Hellenistic kingship theory than of Plato;[17] in this respect the *Minos* perhaps stands somewhere between the two. The work is thoroughly imbued with Platonic ideas and strategies: thus, for example, the author contrives to end the dialogue with the sort of *aporia*

[12] See e.g. *Laws* 630c–d.

[13] *Politicus* 302e10–11 might be taken as saying 'good written rules are what we call laws', but is more likely to mean 'written rules are what we call laws (sc. but these must be good [if monarchy is to be the best of the six actual types of constitution]' – where 'goodness' must be merely relative, unless the 'monarch' is to be identified with the ideal king, which he cannot be; the passage is concerned with distinguishing them). See Rowe 1995 ad loc.

[14] Law, as the *Laws* puts it, punningly, is a 'distribution of reason' (*tou nou dianomē*, 714a); the more – even tiresomely – extended punning in the *Minos* appears to combine this idea with the treatment in the *Politicus* of the expert king or statesman as a special kind of herdsman (*nomeus*).

[15] There is, perhaps, a certain slippage in the *Minos* between law as unchanged, and law as *unchangeable* (*akinētos* could mean either); though of course, according to the argument, if a good law were changed it would cease to be a law at all.

[16] See *Laws* 656d ff., 772b ff., 951a ff. (On connections with the *Laws*, Trevor Saunders gave some helpful pointers.)

[17] See Hahm, in Ch.23 below.

typical of one of Plato's 'Socratic' works ('but what are the things that the good legislator and herdsman will distribute to the soul and so make her better? That, shamefully, we don't yet know . . .': 321d). But what he ultimately gets from Plato is something which, on close reading, turns out not to be there.

15

Aristotle: an introduction

MALCOLM SCHOFIELD

1 Politics, the legislator, and the structure of the *Politics*

Aristotle's *Politics*[1] does not itself articulate any consolidated account of how the nature and scope of inquiry into politics are to be conceived. For that we need to turn to statements elsewhere in his writings, and particularly at the beginning and end of the *Nicomachean Ethics*. Adoption of this expository strategy is just one index of the fact that for Aristotle ethics and politics are not two distinct even if connected disciplines, but one and the same subject. The name for this subject is 'politics'; and the systematic, drily analytical treatises which have come down to us under the titles of *Ethics* and *Politics* deal with different aspects of it. Politics so understood is a pursuit or a form of knowledge which has as its aim the achievement of the good for human beings – both individually and collectively, in their cities or peoples.

According to Aristotle that good consists in happiness or human fulfilment, which is analysed as 'activity of soul in accordance with excellence', i.e. a life exemplifying the moral and intellectual virtues. Roughly speaking, ethics – as its name indicates – is the subdivision of politics concerned with understanding the *habits* of character which constitute the moral virtues necessary for human fulfilment. The other subdivision studies *politeiai* or constitutions, construed as different ways of organizing government in a city or nation; it is presumably viewed as the more obviously or directly political part of politics. Under these rather bare and brute descriptions ethics and politics (in this narrower sense) might seem to have little to do with each other. But on the Aristotelian conception

[1] Greek text: Ross 1957a, Dreizehnter 1970; commentaries: Newman 1887–1902, Schütrumpf 1991, 1996; English translations: Sinclair 1981, Barker 1995 (1946), and Saunders 1995b (Books I and II), Robinson 1995 (III and IV), Keyt 1999 (V and VI), Kraut 1997 (VII and VIII), Everson 1996; French translation: Pellegrin 1993. Collections: Fondation Hardt 1965, Barnes et al. 1977, Keyt and Miller 1991, Patzig 1990, Lord and O'Connor 1991. Philosophical studies: Mulgan 1977, Miller 1995. General accounts of Aristotle: Ross 1995, Düring 1966, Lloyd 1968, Guthrie 1981, Barnes 1982, Barnes 1995. Complete translation of Aristotle's works: Barnes, 1984.

humans are essentially social animals, and the way the governments of the communities in which they live out their lives are organized may make a huge difference to their prospects of acquiring virtue and achieving happiness.

The key to Aristotle's conception of politics is the figure of the legislator.[2] Referring back to the opening two chapters of the *Ethics*, he writes (*EN* I.9, 1099 b29–32):

> We stated that the chief good is the goal of political understanding; and it devotes most of its concern and effort to making the citizens be of a certain character, viz. good and capable of fine deeds.

When he turns a little later to the topic of virtue he amplifies the thesis (I.13, 1102 a7–12):

> The true politician [i.e. the person possessed of real political understanding] is thought to have put most of his effort into studying virtue. For he wants to make the citizens good and obedient to the laws. As an example of this we have the lawgivers of the Cretans and the Spartans, and any others there may have been with the same concerns.

Aristotle is of course well aware that this is not the way the word 'politician' is commonly used (VI.8, 1141 b23–9):

> Political understanding and practical wisdom are the same state of mind, but their essence is not the same.[3] Of the practical wisdom concerned with the city, the architectonic form is legislative understanding, while the form comparable to particular instances of a universal is what is known by the name common to them both, 'political': this has to do with action and deliberation, for a resolution [i.e. of a council or assembly], as the outcome of deliberation, is something requiring action. That is why people say that they [i.e. those politicians involved in deliberation and consequent action] are the only ones engaged in politics, because they are the only ones who 'do things' – in the same way that artisans 'do things' [i.e. as opposed to architects].

The identification of the true politician as the lawgiver who commands a strategic and directive understanding comparable to the architect's goes back once again to the beginning of Book I (I.2, 1094 a26–b7):

> The chief good would seem to be the object of the most authoritative form of knowledge, and the one that is most architectonic. And that seems to be the knowledge characteristic of politics. For it is this which ordains what other forms of knowledge should be studied in cities, and

[2] Bodéüs 1981. [3] Cf. Aubenque 1963, Wiggins 1980.

> which each class of citizens should learn and up to what point. And we see even the most highly esteemed of capacities subordinated to it – e.g. generalship, household administration, oratory.[4] So since politics [i.e. in this strategic sense] uses the other forms of knowledge, and since again it legislates as to what we are to do and what we are to keep away from, the goal aimed at by this form of knowledge will include that of the others. Hence it is politics which has as its goal the human good.

These quotations will have explained why for Aristotle ethics as the study of moral virtue falls under politics: if its object is to make people good, it will need a proper understanding of the virtues and of the life of happiness which exemplifies them. But not surprisingly these texts give no sense of the rationale for the study of constitutions which is the principal focus of the *Politics*. Aristotle is nowhere as explicit on this topic as might be desired. His most helpful discussion of the matter is contained in the last chapter of the *Ethics*, which is clearly designed to prepare the ground for the *Politics* – or at any rate for *a* work on constitutions.[5]

The chapter takes as its starting point the observation that 'where there are things to be done the goal is not studying and identifying each of them, but actually doing them' (x.9, 1179 a35–b2): politics (including ethics) is a form of *practical*, not (like e.g. mathematics) theoretical, knowledge, even if its practice needs to be informed by theory. Given that from our exploration of the virtues we now know what goodness is, we still need to explain how people *become* good. Aristotle accordingly turns to the question of how far training can produce goodness, and this issue leads in turn to the role of law and legislation, as shaping the characters of those who have the capacity for virtue and deterring those who have not by the fear of punishment.

In proposing a general study of legislation he indicates two distinct sorts of reason for undertaking the enterprise. First, successful lawgiving, and the ability to assess the merits of particular legislation, are largely matters of experience: just as people learn to be skilled in medicine not by reading the textbooks, but by practising as doctors.[6] Nonetheless collections of remedies and suggestions about how different sorts of patients should be treated are thought to be useful for those with the relevant experience. Similarly collections of laws and constitutions could be useful to those who have the ability to study and judge what is good or bad in them, and what provisions suit what sorts of city. Even those who lack it might perhaps come to comprehend these things better. Second, Aristotle

[4] Cf. *Rhet.* 1356 a26–8, 1359 b10.

[5] Gauthier and Jolif 1970, Bodéüs 1991a, ch. 3.

[6] Cf. Pl. *Plt.* 294–301, with the discussion by Rowe in Ch. 11, section 3 above.

complains that his predecessors have left the field of legislation uninvestigated. It is time for a proper examination. Without it philosophical inquiry into things human will be incomplete.

Anybody who has waded through Plato's *Laws* may be forgiven for feeling some surprise at this claim about previous work on the subject. Its rationale may be conjectured from other remarks Aristotle makes here and elsewhere. Commenting explicitly on the *Laws* in Book II of the *Politics*, he observes that it consists mostly of laws, i.e. proposals for legislation, but does not have much on the constitution.[7] His own view is that laws must be framed with a view to the constitution. This implies a methodological point: discussion of the constitution is the prior, more general, and theoretically more important task, the devising of particular laws a secondary matter, and one which requires constant reference to the constitution.[8] Aristotle seems to have this point in mind in our *Ethics* passage, for the proper treatment of legislation he plans will be about that 'and indeed about constitution in general'. His predecessors may have useful things to contribute – and these he will review – 'on particular topics', but not on legislation viewed in the light of general issues relating to the comparative merits of different constitutions.[9]

Implicit in Aristotle's complaint about his predecessors is another criticism. Their approach to the topic of legislation was insufficiently empirical. His will be based on 'the collected constitutions'. We know what he had in mind. The ancient catalogues of Aristotle's writings list such a collection, consisting (according to the more reliable versions) of accounts of the constitutions of 158 cities. These are generally presumed to have been the work of his school, even if he had a hand in preparing some of them. Only one of the 158 survives, the *Constitution of the Athenians*, preserved more or less intact on papyrus rolls acquired for the British Museum from an Egyptian source in 1888–9. It contains a history of the changes to which the Athenian constitution had been subject from the earliest times to the restoration of democracy in 403 BC, followed by an analysis of the constitution in the author's own day.[10] The assumption underlying the massive research project required to compile the collection was apparently that only by this means would it be possible to acquire the evidence needed for solid explanations of what makes a constitution successful or not. For Aristotle says that he will try to use the collection 'to study what

[7] *Pol.* II.6, 1265 a1–4. This seems tendentious of Aristotle.

[8] E.g. *Pol.* III.11, 1282 b6–13, IV.1, 1289 a10–15. Cf. Bodéüs 1991b.

[9] 'Constitution in general': 1181 b14; review of predecessors: 1181 b15–17.

[10] See von Fritz and Kapp 1950, Rhodes 1981.

sorts of things preserve and destroy cities, and likewise the particular kinds of constitutions, and what causes some cities to conduct their political life well, others badly' (*EN* x.9, 1181 b17–20).

The *Politics* does in fact contain material corresponding precisely to what this passage promises. Book v is a treatment of what causes the preservation and destruction of constitutions; and it makes frequent reference to practices and incidents in a wide range of Greek cities (and among non-Greek peoples too). The last chapter of the *Ethics* concludes with a statement of the ultimate destination to which such a causal account will lead (x.9, 1181 b20–2):

> When we have studied these matters we will perhaps get a better overview of the question of what sort of constitution is best, and how each should be organized and what laws and customs it must use if it is to be at its best.

The intention is thus to return in the end from study of constitutions to the architectonic project of legislation which is the prime function of the true politician.

The later books of the *Politics* do in a sense work out the prospectus Aristotle offers in the statement just quoted. This may indeed explain why they are placed as they are at the end of the treatise, after the treatment of what preserves and destroys constitutions in Book v. Book vi discusses how democracy and oligarchy can be constructed for greater stability, and Books vii and viii what conditions and provisions would be needed to achieve the ideal city and to produce for it an ideal aristocracy. The later chapters of Book vii and all of the incomplete Book viii are specifically concerned with the laws and customs necessary for educating its citizens for virtue. While Book vi may be construed as exploiting the considerations argued in Book v about the connection between political instability and perceived injustices in the distribution of public goods, links between Book v and Book vii are perhaps not so obvious.[11] But Book v warns of the difficulties caused by disproportionate increases in the population or by a territory not naturally adapted to political unity, and these are precisely the sorts of issues Book vii addresses at the outset of its discussion of the ideal city.

Aristotle's prospectus speaks of 'a better overview' of the question of the best constitution. This should not suggest that empirical study of con-

[11] Books vii and viii are often thought to represent a stratum of the *Politics* earlier than Books iv–vi, even though the developmental story in which this conjecture originally belonged (see Jaeger 1948) has been abandoned in most respects. For discussion of the compositional problems of *Pol.* see briefly Ch. 18 below, and more fully Rowe 1977 (1991).

stitutions and reflection upon them is *all* we need if we are to achieve this understanding. The point is rather that this way we will improve on the comprehension of the issues we have already got from more abstract and theoretical discussions of what a constitution is and what are good and bad, suitable and unsuitable constitutions. Theory is indispensable, but needs to be enriched and extended and applied in the light of empirical inquiry. In our *Politics* the more theoretical discussions of these matters occupy Books III and IV, and supply the conceptual framework presupposed in the later books. Book II surveys earlier theoretical attempts to delineate the ideal city, and actual constitutions which approach the ideal; and it adds a postscript on notable legislators of the past. It offers the kind of review of his predecessors' contribution to the subject that is promised at the end of the *Ethics*. Book I, on the fundamental nature of the city and its relation to the household, serves as a preface to all that follows.

Scholars have sometimes suggested that the last paragraph of the *Ethics* simply does not supply a 'recognizable synopsis' of the *Politics*.[12] Some have concluded from this that Aristotle there looks forward to a new version of the *Politics*, in the event never realized, or to a different kind of treatise altogether.[13] It seems better to suppose that the remarks he makes at the end of the *Ethics* are intended not as a synopsis, but as a characterization of the *Politics* we actually have from a particular point of view – one which explains the focus on the later rather than the earlier books. It is presented as analogous to a medical textbook: offering general but practical guidance, based on case studies, to the practitioner – the politician conceived as lawgiver.

2 *Sitz im Leben*

Aristotle's identification of the true politician with the architectonic lawgiver – responsible not for isolated pieces of legislation but for implementing a whole constitutional scheme – reflects a common Greek understanding of how their political institutions were and indeed should be created, which is reflected, for example, in popular conceptions of the work of Lycurgus and Solon, in the role actually assigned to lawgivers in the foundation of colonies, and not least (despite Aristotle's strictures) in the legislative project of Plato's *Laws*. More unusual – but again borrowed from his Platonic inheritance – is his proposal that the ultimate object of legislation is the moral education of the citizens. He notes that only at

[12] Burnet 1900 ad loc. [13] E.g. Bodéüs 1991a: ch. 3.

Sparta and one or two other places does the lawgiver 'seem to have devoted concern and effort to questions of upbringing and suitable forms of activity' (*EN* x.9, 1180 a24–6).

None of this should be surprising if one recalls the salient features of Aristotle's biography.[14] Born the son of Philip of Macedon's court physician in 384 BC, at Stagira in northern Greece, he joined Plato's Academy in 367, where he stayed until Plato's death twenty years later. Then he left for Atarneus in Asia Minor and the court of Hermeias, another former member of the Academy, whose niece he married. After moving briefly to Mytilene on Lesbos he was summoned back to Macedon by Philip in 342 to be tutor to the young Alexander, in the event for only two years. On Philip's death in 335 he returned to Athens, to teach and pursue his encyclopaedic researches, in the area of the popular gymnasium called the Lyceum. He remained until Alexander's death in 323, when apprehensive of anti-Macedonian sentiment he retired to ancestral estates at Chalcis in Euboea. There he died of an illness the following year.

Three points relevant to Aristotle's conception of politics stand out. First, Stagira was and no doubt prided itself on being a Greek polis (it was a colony of Chalcis and Andros), and much closer in size to Aristotle's ideal than the Athens he came to study in. He never seems to have doubted that being Greek and living in a small polis was the supreme form of human existence, nor that study of the polis was worth the investment of huge intellectual resources over a long period. Second, in living all his adult life away from his native town he never had even the opportunity for involvement in the daily hurly-burly of politics as ordinarily understood. He did have the chance to witness Athenian political life in action, however, and seems to have regarded it as a theatre for demagogues, exhibiting many of the features of the worst kind of democracy.[15] He compares the claims of the political or practical life and the life of study both in the *Ethics* (Book x) and the *Politics* (the beginning of Book VII), and awards the palm to study and contemplation.[16]

Third, while the Academy in the period of Aristotle's membership was a forum for philosophical controversy, not the home of doctrinal orthodoxy, his intellectual formation well into his maturity was shaped within a broadly Platonic mould.[17] Thus in metaphysics he early on rejected Plato's theory of Forms, and with it the transcendent status of the good. More important is that he continued to share the conviction that philosophy is the search for unchangeable first principles. In politics he is highly

[14] See Düring 1957, Chroust 1973: vol.I. [15] Strauss 1991. [16] See e.g. Kraut 1989.
[17] See the influential account of Jaeger 1948, challenged and modified by Ross 1957b, Owen 1965.

critical of the collectivist proposals of the *Republic*, and construes the point of political life as the creation of an environment in which individuals perform fine deeds. Yet Plato's political thought continued to provide much of the detailed problematic of Aristotle's own work in this area, as well as much of its overall intellectual framework. And he agreed with Plato in both the *Republic* and the *Laws* on the percipience of the Spartans in viewing politics as in essence legislation designed to mould the behaviour of citizens by education and regulation.

At no point is the gulf between Aristotle's political ideals and those implicit in Athenian democratic ideology wider than it is here. To judge from the fourth-century orators, the rule of law on which Athenian citizens harped continually was valued above all because it represented freedom from the intrusions characteristic of arbitrary autocratic government. And in the competitive processes of litigation and the decisions of the courts law was standardly interpreted in accordance with the perceived interests of the *dēmos*: it was in their control, not they in its.[18] Aristotle no doubt interpreted this as the lawlessness typical of extreme democracy.

It might have been thought that someone who had spent considerable time at the court of Philip of Macedon would have been more interested in the imperial ambitions of absolute monarchy, and its impact on the independence of even the most powerful Greek states, and less preoccupied with the cultivation of moral wellbeing in a small-scale community.[19] Claims to have found indirect evidence that the *Politics does* reflect such an interest have not withstood criticism. This goes for the detection, for example, of a covert reference to Alexander the Great in Aristotle's discussion of the hypothetical person qualified to exercise monarchical rule because his pre-eminence in virtue so overshadows the attainments of all other citizens. At one point he suggests that if the Greeks could become one *politeia*, then by virtue of their qualities of mind and temperament and their excellent political institutions they would be well qualified to rule over everyone else. This too has been seen as an allusion to Macedonian hopes for a Panhellenic conquest of Asia, echoed in Plutarch's anecdote (doubtless apocryphal) of how Aristotle tried unsuccessfully to persuade Alexander to behave as a leader towards Greeks, but as a master towards barbarians. But on Aristotelian principles the suggestion must be counterfactual: Greece *could* not be one *politeia*. What is

[18] Cf. Cohen 1991, 1995.

[19] Aristotle is credited with works entitled *On Monarchy* and *Alexander*, conceivably composed in the period 342–335: D.L. v.22.

much clearer is that Aristotle thinks absolute monarchy by and large a rather primitive institution, suitable for communities where virtue and intelligence are not as widely distributed as he implies they have been in Greece for some centuries.[20]

3 Aristotle's analytical models

At its most general and fundamental level Aristotle's analysis of the polis is a highly abstract exercise in rational choice theory. He envisages a community of persons who associate because of their need to make a living, but who have as their goal the good life, i.e. a life of fulfilment exemplifying the characteristically human virtues. These persons are assumed to be free and equal: naturally free, that is, capable of determining strategies for living, and so (on his view) entitled to a status enabling them to exercise that capacity; and equal, in that their capacities for strategic thinking are all roughly equal. How should such a community govern itself? The form of rule appropriate to it is what Aristotle calls political rule, in contradistinction from despotic rule (suitable for the direction of slaves or naturally slavish persons) and monarchy (the right way to run e.g. one's household).[21]

Political differs from despotic rule in that (i) rule is exercised in the interests primarily of the ruled, not the ruler, and (ii) there is ruling and being ruled by turns.[22] Aristotle says little to explain or defend (i), but its rationale is obvious: given the basic objects for which the community exists, the point of government must be to enable its members to achieve them. On (ii) he is more forthcoming. It would be better for the same persons to rule always, if that were possible – because ruling requires specific skills and virtues, and as in other spheres where this is true specialization is likely to be more efficient and produce better results. But given the hypothesis of the natural equality of all the citizens, and assuming it to be impracticable for them *all* to be in office simultaneously, justice (i.e. fairness) requires that all should rule, but taking turns – with everyone *out* of office, at any rate, in the same boat for the time being.[23] This constitution, i.e. system of allocating offices,[24] requires adoption of a norm: the princi-

[20] Pro Macedonian resonances: e.g. Kelsen 1937, Ober 1991, Bodéüs 1991a, ch. 9. Anti (devastatingly): Ehrenberg 1938, ch. 3. Pre-eminent virtue: *Pol.* III.13. One *politeia*: *Pol.* VII.7, 1327 b29–30. Plutarch's anecdote: *Alex.Fort.* I.6. Primitive institution: *Pol.* I.2; III.15, 1286 b8–10.

[21] I.7, 1255 b16–20.

[22] III.6, 1278 b30–1279 a16. Aristotle here refers to 'exoteric arguments': very likely a reference to the lost *On Justice* (cf. Moraux 1957).

[23] II.2, 1261 a34–b5.

[24] III.6, 1278 b8–10.

ple that the *law* should rule, rather than any particular individual citizen.[25]

Aristotle explores what he presents as a problem with this conception of political rule. The merit of political rule is that if government is conducted in the interest of the governed, all have the opportunity to develop and display the moral virtues – courage, moderation, and so on. The difficulty is that only a person holding office at a given time is in a position to exercise practical wisdom, or at any rate to exercise it in its most important sphere, for the good of the whole community. So it appears that the system of political rule does not after all enable citizens to achieve the good life, or at any rate not as fully as possible: the good citizen is not identical with the good human being. In Book VII Aristotle in effect offers a solution to this problem, by making *all* the mature citizens of his ideal aristocracy perpetual rulers, once they have served their apprenticeship in the subordinate positions naturally appropriate to younger men. This is an ingenious attempt to rework both democratic principles and the egalitarianism traditional in Greek aristocratic ideology into a single pattern.[26]

But things do not stay so simple. The abstract model of what Aristotle calls the 'political community' gets elaborated by a variety of complications, which have the effect of making it much more nearly a model of the historical Greek polis, and at the same time of diluting its egalitarianism. The complications come in two main varieties. First, the issues of who should be admitted to membership of the citizen body and how participation in rule should be organized are in practice much contested. This comes about for reasons Aristotle connects together in an analysis which effectively involves the introduction of what we would call classes – primarily economic classes, but as well as the rich minority and the poor masses the well born (i.e. the hereditary landed aristocracy) and the virtuous (i.e. the true moral elite) are sometimes made parties to the argument.[27]

The rich, for example, will say that they are *not* on an equality with the poor, and that their worth (*axia*) is such that they deserve more of the ruling positions or honours (*timai*) than them. The poor, for their part, will typically counter that the free (in this context the free-born) status common to all the citizens does or should make them equal in everything. And they foment unrest when they perceive an inequality between what they

25 III.16, 1287a10–23.
26 Problem set: III.4; *de facto* solution: VII.14.
27 III.9–13, IV and V.

own and what the rich do – for while honour, the traditional goal of the political life, motivates the educated elite, what the masses are interested in is gain. Aristotle himself sees merit in these and many similar conflicting contentions about what he calls 'worth' or 'merit', but which we might diagnose as arguments about status and the claims to participation in rule they are designed to advance. And he suggests that it would be prudent for oligarchies to introduce more egalitarian features into their constitutions, and for democracies to restrict eligibility for some offices to those who satisfy a certain property qualification, or to allow such positions to be filled sometimes not by lottery but by voting.

Aristotle has here enriched his model by considerations drawn from a fairly elaborate, if often schematic and stereotyped, political sociology.[28] The other main complication in his theory is introduced by a functional analysis, derived in its basic approach from Plato in the *Republic*, of what makes the polis – now interpreted as the society as a whole – a self-sufficient unit.[29] The crucial distinction Aristotle draws is between the integral parts of a political community and functions that are merely necessary for its existence, although also important is his anti-Platonic idea that the city is made up of households, a sphere – below the threshold of political discourse proper – to which women and chattel slaves are relegated. The distinction between parts and necessary conditions is a shaky one, but Aristotle's point is that political deliberation and the exercise of jurisdiction are activities intrinsic to the pursuit of the good life, namely to the basic aim of political association, and a military capacity is clearly in the public interest. But farming and labouring, marketing and the practice of artisan crafts are neither – they simply supply the economic needs of the individuals who live in the polis. In his ideal aristocracy Aristotle would accordingly bar from citizenship those involved in subsistence farming, crafts and trade. These occupations make people small-minded and give insufficient leisure for political activity and the acquisition of virtue. They have no proper place in the exclusive club of the leisured exploiters of their labour which constitutes the citizen community.[30] No wonder Aristotle's political philosophy both attracts and repels, combining as it does penetrating insight into both first principles and the dynamics of political struggle with proposals born of crude class interest.[31]

28 Cf. e.g. de Ste Croix 1981, Finley 1983, Ober 1991.

29 IV.4, VII.8–9.

30 Cf. e.g. Wood and Wood 1978.

31 The material in section 3 has appeared in an expanded version in Schofield 1999: ch. 6.

16

Naturalism

FRED D. MILLER, JR

Aristotle's *Politics* is distinguished by the place of honour it accords to the concept of nature. At the outset, the political relations of ruling and being ruled are among the things that develop naturally (cf. *Pol.* I.2, 1252a24–6). In addition, the polis or city-state exists by nature and a human being is by nature a political animal (e.g. 1253a2–3). Most of Book I is concerned to show that the household is natural because its constituent relations – master/slave, husband/wife, parent/child – are natural. Again, in Book III the inquiry into political constitutions commences with the significant remark that one must first make a hypothesis about the end of the polis and about the kinds of rule found in human communities. Aristotle recalls his earlier argument that a human being is by nature a political animal (III.6, 1278b15–19), and he observes that some forms of political rule are natural, namely, those whereby the rulers seek the advantage of the ruled (cf. 1279a8–13). These characterize constitutions which are correct or just without qualification (1279a17–21). This lays the ground for his detailed classification and evaluation of political systems. Finally, in his account of the best constitution (*Politics* VII–VIII) he states that the lawgiver must follow nature in planning the education of the citizens (VII.17, 1337a1–3).

Unfortunately, Aristotle does not offer an explicit analysis in the *Politics* of his use of the term *phusis* or 'nature' and derivative terms, so that it is difficult to interpret and evaluate his version of political naturalism.[1] However, in the *Metaphysics* and works devoted to natural science, especially *Physics* II, he analyses the concept of nature and develops distinctions which resurface in the *Politics* and the ethical treatises. This suggests

[1] Aristotle also makes reference in the *Rhetoric* to 'common' or 'natural' law which is 'eternal and never changing' (I.13, 1373b9–13; I.15, 1375a31–b2). However, he does not develop a theory of natural law as do the Stoics and Thomas Aquinas. Indeed, he seems to retreat from the *Rhetoric*'s equation of the natural with the eternal in his discussion of natural justice in the *Nicomachean Ethics.* Here he distinguishes two senses of 'by nature': for the gods the natural is immutable, but 'for us something exists by nature, but everything is changeable, and yet some things exist by nature and some do not exist by nature' (V.7, 1134b24–30; cf. I.33, 1194b37–9, 1195a3–4). On the difficulties of reconciling these different discussions, see Miller 1991.

that Aristotle's account of nature in his natural philosophy may shed light on the role of this concept in his political philosophy.

1. 'Nature' in Aristotle's natural philosophy

Aristotle uses the term *phusis*, 'nature', in different ways. Following the Presocratics, he calls the universe or cosmos as a whole 'nature' (e.g. *Metaph.* IV.3, 1005a32–3; XII.10, 1075a11). More important for him, however, is the nature *of* a particular entity. *Metaphysics* V.4 distinguishes several senses of 'nature':

(1) the coming-to-be of growing things, i.e., growth
(2) the primary internal component from which the growing thing grows
(3) more generally, the source of the primary movement which is present in each natural entity intrinsically and not accidentally
(4) the primary matter of which something consists or out of which it comes to be
(5) the form or substance which is the end of the process of becoming
(6) by extension, every substance, because the nature of a thing is a kind of substance.

The original senses are (1) and (2), for a tree grows (*phuetai*) to maturity, the tree is a growing thing (*phuomenon*), and the process is biological growth (*phusis*). The other senses of 'nature' are related to Aristotle's four causes (explained in *Metaph.* V.2): nature operates as an efficient or moving cause (cf. 3), as a material cause (cf. 4), and as a formal and final cause (cf. 5 and 6). Of these, however, sense (3) is arguably the most basic: nature as a causal principle explaining the movements of things in themselves independently of anything else.

The canonical text for this concept is *Physics* II: 'Some beings are by nature, and some are due to other causes. Those which are by nature are animals and their parts and plants and the simple bodies (i.e. earth, fire, air, water), for we say that these and such things are by nature.' The definition of nature follows: 'each of them has in itself a principle of motion and rest, some regarding place, others growth and diminution, and others qualitative alteration' (II.1, 192b8–15). The concept of nature is thus used to explain the phenomenon of self-motion, for example a stone falling downward or an acorn growing into an oak tree.

Nature is distinguished from any external force acting on a body. However, the most illuminating contrast is with artistic production (192b16–33). A product of art (*technē*) such as a bed exists because an external cause, the artisan (*technitēs*) or craftsman (*dēmiourgos*) practising the art of bed making, fashions some matter, namely wood, into the form of a bed. The bed *qua* material thing still has a nature, as is evident from the fact that it has an innate impulse to fall downward. But *qua* bed it is due to art rather than nature. Aristotle adds that the nature is an internal cause in an intrinsic rather than accidental sense. An intrinsic cause produces an effect always or for the most part: for example, a sculptor makes a statue, or a doctor heals a patient. An example of accidentally caused self-motion would be a doctor curing himself. In this case, it merely happens to be the case that the same man is both a doctor and a patient. The characteristics linked in a particular instance of accidental causation will at other times occur separately, so that they are not regularly conjoined. Nature by contrast is an intrinsic cause of self-motion: a thing moves or is at rest in a regular way (e.g. an acorn grows into an oak tree rather than an olive tree) because it possesses a distinctive nature.

Although art differs from nature as a cause, Aristotle frequently compares them, remarking in particular that 'art imitates nature' (*Phys.* II.2, 194a21–2; *Meteor.* IV.3, 381b6). The most important parallel is that a natural process, like the practice of an art, is for the sake of something:

> When things have an end (*telos*), the earlier and later stages are for the sake of this end. Therefore, things occur naturally in the same way that actions are done, and each action is done in the same way that things occur naturally, if nothing stands in the way. An action is done for the sake of something, and thus things also occur naturally for the sake of something. If a house had come to be by nature, it would have come to be in the same way as it does now by art. And if things that come to be by nature came to be not only by nature but also by art, they would come to be just as they do naturally. One thing then occurs for the sake of another. Generally sometimes art completes what nature is not able to accomplish fully, and other times it imitates nature. So if artistic processes are for the sake of something, it is clear that natural processes are too. For the early stages stand to the later in the same way in artistic and natural processes. (II.8, 199a8–20)

Aristotle's concept of nature is thus inextricably linked to his *teleology*: the theory that natural phenomena occur for an end (*telos*).[2] Natural processes also resemble human actions in that they are for the sake of a good.

[2] Aristotle tries to defend his natural teleology elsewhere, for example in *Physics* II.8 and *Parts of Animals* I.1. This theory has been widely discussed by commentators. For overviews of the literature see Gotthelf 1997 and Miller 1995: 336–46.

For example, animals sleep because this is beneficial for them (*Somn.* 2, 455b17–18).[3]

However, the analogy between natural teleology and human purposiveness is also carefully qualified. Whereas art is a human capacity involving reason (cf. *EN* VI.4, 1140a6–10), natural processes do not involve inquiry, deliberation, or intelligence (199a20–3). Although Aristotle frequently speaks of nature in personified terms – for example, it acts as a craftsman (*PA* II.9, 654b31; *GA* II.6, 743b23), like a god it 'does nothing in vain' (*Cael.* I.4, 271a33; *PA* II.13, 658a8; *GA* II.4, 739b19) – these expressions are metaphorical. In natural things the natural end is an innate form or substance which guides the process of development (*Meteor.* IV.2, 379b25–6; cf. *Phys.* II.2, 194a28–9). In the case of plants and animals their seeds contain forms which direct their development so that the offspring become the same natural kind as their parents (*PA* I.1, 641b12–30; *GA* II.4, 740b24–741a5). Thus, sense (5) of 'nature' in *Metaphysics* V.4 is related to sense (3). However, Aristotle also speaks of things as 'natural' in an extended sense if they arise as a part of a natural teleological process. For example, birds make nests and spiders spin webs in order to promote the natural ends of sexual reproduction or self-preservation. These are due to natural impulses in the birds and spiders not to deliberative choice. Hence, bird nests and spider webs, along with the birds and spiders themselves, are called 'things which come to be and exist by nature' (*Phys.* II.8, 199a6–8, 29–30).

Aristotle remarks that other philosophers identified nature with the material constituent of a thing (*Phys.* II.1, 193a9–30). Their view is that ultimately the elements out of which a thing is composed determine its affections, states, and dispositions. Aristotle's view is that 'the form rather than the matter is nature, for each thing is called [what it is] when it is actually rather than when it is potentially' (193b6–8; cf. *PA* I.1, 640b28–9). Nonetheless, he recognizes that matter as well as form has a claim to be called the nature of a thing since it also explains certain of its inherent characteristics (*Metaph.* VII.7, 1032a20–5). Thus he sometimes speaks of matter as 'necessary nature' in contrast with the form or final cause (*Phys.* II.9, 200a8–9; cf. II.8, 198b10–14). This is sense (4) in *Metaphysics* V.

Two related expressions have important uses in Aristotle's natural science as well as his political science: *kata phusin* and *para phusin*. First, *kata phusin*, 'according to nature', is associated in natural science with regular-

[3] On natural ends as goods cf. *Phys.* II.2, 194a32–3; II.7, 198b8–9; *Metaph.* I.3, 983a31–3; V.2, 1013b25–7.

ity, because it involves intrinsic rather than accidental causation. 'According to nature' implies 'always or for the most part'.[4] It is on this ground that Aristotle rejects Empedocles' view that the adaptive features of animals result from chance or spontaneity[5] – for example why teeth grow in such a way that the front teeth are suitable for biting and the back teeth useful for grinding (*Phys.* II.8, 198b16–199a8). Similarly, in generation a given seed does not give rise to any plant or animal by chance, but each organism arises from a specific parent (*PA* I.1, 641b23–30).

Second, behaviour *para phusin*, 'contrary to nature' – opposed to *kata phusin* – is typically due to some external power (*dunamis*) or force (*bia*) which contravenes the operation of nature. For example, an arrow's natural motion of falling to the earth is contrasted with its violent, unnatural upward motion when it is shot from a bow. Whereas a body has a single natural motion due to its own nature, its unnatural motions are indefinite and innumerable (*Cael.* III.2, 300a21–7; 301b17–30). This distinction between natural and unnatural motions is central to Aristotelian mechanics. The unnatural also occurs in the biological realm, whenever the formal nature is unable to control the material nature in the process of sexual reproduction (*GA* IV.4, 770b9–27). The result is a monstrosity or mutilation, for example an offspring with superfluous toes or androgynous sexual organs. In general, the unnatural is posterior to the natural, because it is a deviation from the natural during its generation (*Cael.* II.3, 286a18–20).

2 The naturalness of the polis

The *Politics* begins with two observations: First, the polis as the most authoritative and inclusive community aims at the highest good. Second, some have erroneously thought that there is only one type of rule, which is called by different names depending on the number of subjects: despotic, household, kingly, political.[6] As we shall see, Aristotle argues

[4] *Phusei*, 'by nature', also has this sense. See *GC* II.6, 333b5; *PA* III.2, 663b30; *MM* II.8, 1206b38. Both *kata phusin* and *phusei* characterize the natural upward movement of fire at *Phys.* II.1, 192b35–193a2. Two senses of 'natural' are distinguished at *GA* IV.4, 770b11–13: eternal and necessary, versus for the most part but capable of occurring otherwise. The latter applies in the sublunary region and allows for exceptions.

[5] Chance (*tuchē*) and spontaneity (*to automaton*) are, along with craft, external causes distinguished from nature (cf. *Metaph.* XII.3, 1070a6–7; VII.7, 1032a12). They are discussed in *Phys.* II.5–6. Aristotle argues in *Phys.* II.8 that a chance or spontaneous outcome may accidentally promote an end, but it does not occur for the sake of an end and thus will not be present always or for the most part.

[6] Aristotle probably has Plato in mind: cf. *Statesman* 259c1–4. He is especially concerned to refute those who identify all forms of rule with despotic rule (cf. *Pol.* I.3; III.6).

against this that different forms of rule are appropriate for different forms of natural association. But first he applies his method of analysis: 'In other matters a compound must be divided into its uncompounded constituents, for there are smallest parts belonging to the whole. So too if we look at the components out of which the polis is composed we will also see better how these types of rule differ from each other and whether something pertaining to an art belongs to each of them.' He adds that one will theorize best about such things 'if one looks at things developing naturally (*phuomena*) from the beginning' (1252a18–26). This is the context in which Aristotle undertakes his defence of his three naturalistic doctrines:

(1) The polis exists by nature.
(2) A human being is by nature a political animal.
(3) The polis is prior by nature to the individual.

Politics I.2 combines these three claims with praise for the lawgiver: 'Therefore, the impulse for the [political] community is in everyone by nature, but he who first established it is the cause of very great goods' (1253a29–31). The phrase 'he who first established it' is clearly a reference to the lawgiver, since Aristotle's subsequent argument emphasizes that humans need law and adjudication which are found only in the polis. The emphasis on law and legislation is not surprising in view of Aristotle's overriding concern with how the polis is to be ruled. However, Aristotle here implies that the existence of the polis is due *both* to nature *and* to the lawgiver or politician.[7] The interpretation of his argument is made difficult by the fact that he does not explain in *Politics* I how he is using the concept of nature.

2.1 *'The polis exists by nature'*

Aristotle argues that the polis is natural because it develops naturally out of natural communities (I.2, 1252a26–b34). The first communities are unions of male and female, which result not from deliberate choice but from a natural (*phusikon*) striving to leave behind offspring like the parents, and associations of natural ruler and subject (viz. master and slave), which are for the sake of self-preservation and mutual advantage. The household arising from these two communities is itself a community established according to nature (*kata phusin*) for everyday needs. The village in turn comes to be out of several households for non-daily (i.e.

[7] Aristotle generally uses the term *politikos*, 'politician' or 'statesman', for someone possessing political expertise in distinction from an ordinary citizen (cf. IV.1, 1289a7; V.8, 1308a34). The lawgiver or legislator (*nomothetēs*) is a politician who frames the constitution and 'lays down laws' (III.1, 1274b36–7; VII.14, 1333a37).

higher) needs as a natural extension (*apoikia*, literally 'colony') of the household.

> The community composed of several villages which is complete is a polis, and it attains the limit of total self-sufficiency, generally speaking. Although it comes to be for the sake of mere life, it exists for the sake of the good life. Therefore, every polis exists by nature (*phusei*), since the first communities are also such. For it is their end, and nature is an end: what each thing is when its coming to be is completed we call its nature, for example, of a human being, a horse, or a household. (I.2, 1252b27–34)

At first sight this argument might appear to be a direct application of sense (3) of 'nature' in *Metaphysics* V: namely, an intrinsic internal cause of self-motion. For nature first appears in the form of a natural striving or impulse for self-preservation and sexual reproduction, and the household, village, and ultimately the political community are natural extensions of this primal cause. The polis thus resembles a human being or a horse as a nature or end 'growing' out of more primitive communities. However, Aristotle never in fact says that the polis has a nature in the sense of an internal-cause of self-motion. Moreover, this interpretation seems to allow no role for the lawgiver who 'first established' the political community. For Aristotle compares the lawgiver to a craftsman practising an art (VII.4, 1325b40–1326a5). Just as a craftsman makes a bed by imposing a certain formal structure on wood, the lawgiver imposes a form, i.e. a constitution, upon materials, that is a given population and territory (cf. III.3, 1276b1–11, VII.4, 1326a35–8). The polis is, then, a sort of artefact.[8] But in the strict sense of 'nature', the same thing cannot both exist by nature and be an artefact with an external cause. Finally, it is questionable whether the argument so interpreted is valid: how is the naturalness of the first communities supposed to lead to the naturalness of the polis which arises out of them? Even if it is granted that the polis is prior to the households and villages in the sense of being more complete than they are, it does not follow that it exists by nature even if they do. A basket made out of straw is prior to the parts of which it is composed and the parts are ultimately produced by nature, but it nonetheless exists by craft rather than by nature. On this reading Aristotle's conclusion that the polis exists by nature is a *non sequitur*.[9]

However, these difficulties might be avoided if the polis is understood

[8] Cf. Keyt 1991b:119, 'a polis is an artifact of practical reason just as a ship or a cloak or a sandal is an artifact of productive reason'.

[9] These difficulties are detailed in Keyt 1991b. Favouring the strict interpretation of 'nature', Keyt concludes that 'there is a blunder at the very root of Aristotle's political philosophy'.

to exist 'by nature' in an extended sense. As noted above, the *Physics* speaks of the products of teleological impulses, for example, bird nests and spider webs, as existing 'by nature' in an extended sense (II.8, 199a6–8, 29–30). Similarly, the *Politics* may be claiming that a thing exists 'by nature' if it has as its function the promotion of an organism's natural ends and it results, in whole or in part, from the organism's natural capacities and impulses. On this interpretation nature and the lawgiver might function as joint causes of the completed polis.[10] That is, the polis could come to be when a lawgiver devises a constitution for a sufficiently large population with the innate aptitude and inclination for political life. Because humans are by nature political animals, they will have this potential for the political community unless they are in deviant or unnatural condition – as Aristotle thinks is the case with many non-Greek or 'barbarian' nations (see *Pol.* VII.7).

This also suggests a way of understanding Aristotle's argument that the polis exists by nature because it comes to be from natural forms of association. He may be reasoning that if the polis is a natural extension of naturally existing communities it also exists by 'nature' – not in the narrow sense of having an internal source of motion, but in the wider sense described in the preceding paragraph. That is, the polis fulfils the highest natural ends of human beings in that it promotes the good life, and it arises out of the natural human impulse for communal existence. Therefore, the polis exists by 'nature' not in the sense that it possesses a nature of its own like a living organism, but in the sense that it arises from and promotes the nature *of human beings*. This would help to explain why Aristotle argues next that human beings have a political nature.

2.2 *'A human being is by nature a political animal'*

The argument that a human being is a political animal more than a bee or any gregarious animal explicitly rests on natural teleology: 'nature does nothing in vain' (I.2, 1253a7–18). Only human beings have speech (*logos*), other animals have mere voice. The nature of non-human animals has developed to the extent that they perceive what is painful or pleasant and can signify these things to one another. Because nature has given a young animal the capacity to perceive pain, nature has also provided it with voice so that it can communicate this perception to its parents. Human speech exists in order to reveal what is advantageous or harmful, and hence also

[10] Barker 1946: 7 remarks, 'art co-operates with nature: the volition and action of human agents "construct" the state in co-operation with a natural immanent impulse'. Cf. Miller 1995: 40–5 for a fuller statement of this interpretation; also Saunders 1995b: 59–63.

the just and the unjust; for human beings, in distinction from other animals, perceive good and bad, just and unjust. 'A community in these things makes a household and a polis.'

The comparison of humans to other political animals resembles a passage in Aristotle's *History of Animals*: 'Political [animals] are those whose function (*ergon*) becomes some one common thing, which not all the gregarious animals do. Such are the human being, the bee, the wasp, the ant, and the crane' (I.1, 488a7–10). Aristotle evidently uses the term 'political animal' (*politikon zōion*) in a broad, biological sense to refer to any creature with the innate capacity to perform a common function with others of the same kind. Having a common function involves cooperation, and a group can cooperate in more complex and effective ways to the extent that its members can use reason and speech to coordinate their activities. Hence, human beings are political animals more than other species.[11]

This argument has been influential,[12] but it contains an apparent difficulty. For it implies that a community such as a household or polis can exist only if its members are able to perceive goodness and justice. But Aristotle holds that humans can possess moral perception (in contrast with sense perception) only if they possess to some extent ethical virtue and practical wisdom, which they acquire not by nature but through habituation.[13] Indeed, Aristotle concludes *Politics* I.2 by arguing that it is only through the laws of the polis that human beings acquire ethical virtue and justice (1253a31–9). Thus, it would appear that Aristotle's argument undercuts rather than supports his claim that the polis exists by nature.[14]

However, Aristotle understands moral capacities, like other capacities, as having different levels or degrees of actualization (cf. *de An.* II.5, 417a21–b2; *GA* II.1, 735a9–11). Before being educated or habituated, young children may have the innate capacity to perceive justice, because they are human beings and as such are able to acquire practical wisdom and ethical virtue. But this is a first-level undeveloped capacity: until they are educated, they will not yet actually be able to distinguish just from

[11] Cf. Cooper 1990. Similar interpretations are offered by Kullmann 1991 and Depew 1995. However, other commentators contend that Aristotle uses *politikon zōion* equivocally, so that it means 'polis-dwelling animal' in the *Politics* but has a different sense in the *HA*: cf. Mulgan 1977: 23–4, Keyt 1991b: 123–4, and Schütrumpf 1991: I.215–19.

[12] The argument is even echoed by Charles Darwin in the *Descent of Man*, ch. 4, although he attributes the doctrine to Marcus Aurelius and Seneca. On parallels between Darwin and Aristotle see Arnhart 1994.

[13] See *EN* II.1, 1103a18–b6; VI.9, 1141b14–22, 1142b20–30; VI.13, 1144b1–14. Aristotle's accounts of nature, habit, and reason in *EN* X.9 and *Pol.* VII.13 are discussed below.

[14] See Keyt 1991b: 133–5.

unjust deeds. After they have become fully educated, they have the developed capacity to perceive just and good actions, but they may not be exercizing it because they are asleep or focusing on other things. This is a first-level actualization of the capacity. Only when the person actually perceives something just is the capacity fully actualized. Aristotle's conclusion that humans are by nature political animals only assumes that nature gives humans moral perception in the sense of an innate first-level capacity. This is consistent with the claim that the polis exists by 'nature' in the extended sense.

2.3 *The polis is prior by nature to the individual*

This thesis has totalitarian overtones for modern readers, which are reinforced by Aristotle's comparison of citizens to bodily organs (I.2, 1253a20–7).[15] He argues that the whole is necessarily prior to the part, for if the whole is destroyed the foot or hand should not be called the same things, except in a homonymous sense, as one speaks of a stone foot or hand.[16] For the part will be corrupted. The reason is that these things are defined in terms of their function and capacity, which they cannot perform when severed from the whole. But since the individual is not self-sufficient when separated from the whole, he stands to the polis in the same way as other parts to the whole. So it is clear that the polis is prior by nature to the individual.

This suggests that the polis is prior to the individual in the same way that an animal is prior to its constituent organs. The parts cannot exist in separation from the whole, but it can exist without some of its parts. This way of reading the argument is especially tempting if the polis, like an animal, is supposed to have a nature in the sense of a self-moving principle. However, this 'social organism' interpretation of the analogy faces the difficulty that human beings obviously can exist apart from the polis. This is not merely in the trivial sense that they do not slip out of existence whenever they leave the polis, but also in that they do not become subhuman beasts when this happens. Indeed, Aristotle himself implies that a human being *can* be separated from the polis by chance.[17] An example

[15] See Barnes 1990. Popper 1962, I. ch. 11 views Aristotle's *Politics* as essentially a footnote to Plato's totalitarian political philosophy.

[16] Things are homonymous if they have the same name but different definitions (*Cat.* 1, 1a1–6). For other examples of this homonymy argument see *Meteor.* IV.12, 390a10–13; *de An.* II.1, 412b17–22.

[17] 1255a3–4: 'he who is without a polis (*apolis*) by nature and not due to chance is either a base person or better than a human being'. Two sorts are *apolis* by nature: 'he who is incapable of being in a community or who needs nothing due to self-sufficiency is no part of polis, but is either a beast or a god' (a27–9).

that would have been familiar to Aristotle was the hero Philoctetes, who bemoans the fact that he is 'without a polis' (*apolis*) in Sophocles' play about him. Although Philoctetes was obliged to live in solitude on an island, he did not cease to be a human being.[18]

There is, however, another way of understanding the argument. The thesis that the polis is prior to the individual is ambiguous, because Aristotle distinguishes different senses in which one thing can be 'prior' to another. One of these may be called 'priority in separateness': *X* can exist without *Y*, but *Y* cannot exist without *X*. For example, either Castor or Polydeuces is prior to the Dioscuri. The other sense may be called 'priority in completeness': *X* is more complete or perfect (*teleioteron*) than *Y*. For example, a plant is more complete than the seed from which it grows.[19] If the second sense of 'priority' is operative, then Aristotle's thesis is that the polis is prior in the sense of being more complete or perfect than the individual. This agrees with other statements in *Politics* I.2: that the polis is complete or perfect (*teleios*) (1252b28), and that the individual is completed or perfect (*teleōthen*) unless he is separated (*chōristhen*) from the polis (cf. 1253a31–3). The point of the organ analogy, on this reading, is that, when humans are separated from the polis, they can only exist in an imperfect or corrupt condition.[20] This suggests another view of cases like Philoctetes. Although human beings could exist apart from the polis, they could not develop their innate moral capacities if they lacked access to the laws and educational institutions of a polis. Further, even if their capacities had been previously developed, they could not fully exercise them outside of a polis. In this sense they would fail to realize their nature and would be 'less than human'.[21]

In conclusion, the arguments of *Politics* I.2 may be interpreted in different ways. If it is supposed that Aristotle uses the term 'nature' in the strict sense of *Physics* II.1, his arguments contain serious internal difficulties. However, these may be alleviated if the concept of nature in the *Politics* is viewed in the extended sense suggested above. This interpretation has the disadvantage that it assumes an analysis of 'nature' which is not made

[18] The Philoctetes example is due to Keyt 1991b, who develops an objection along these lines. Aristotle was acquainted with Sophocles' *Philoctetes* (cf. *EN* VII.2, 1146a219–20).

[19] The several senses of 'prior' (*proteros*) are distinguished in *Metaph.* V.11 and *Cat.* 12. I have introduced the expressions 'priority in separateness' and 'priority in completeness' for the sake of clarity. Aristotle himself refers to both senses of 'prior' considered here on different occasions as 'priority in substance (*ousiai*)' and 'priority in nature (*phusei*)'.

[20] Cf. Aquinas, *Commentary on the Politics*, 39 (Spiazzi 1951): 'just as a hand or foot cannot exist without a human being, so also one human being cannot live self-sufficiently by himself if he is separated from the city'.

[21] Cf. Miller 1995: 45–56, and Saunders 1995b: 70–1.

explicit by Aristotle, but it permits a more charitable reading in which Aristotle's arguments at least appear coherent and plausible (if somewhat less exciting) when they are considered in relation to his other writings. This is not, however, to assert that these arguments are impervious to attack on other grounds. Aside from the natural teleological framework presupposed by his arguments, which has frequently been criticized by modern philosophers since Francis Bacon and Thomas Hobbes, he makes other controversial assumptions. Aristotle himself regarded two of these claims as pivotal: first, that the household – the basic building block of the polis[22] – exists by nature; and second, that human nature can be perfected only if individuals are habituated and educated within the polis. The following two sections will examine his arguments for these two assumptions.

3 The naturalness of the household

Aristotle begins his discussion of the household[23] (*Politics* I.3–13) by applying his analytic method, distinguishing the first and smallest parts of the household: master, slave, husband, wife, father, and children. If these are grouped in pairs, there are three corresponding parts of household management:

Master/slave	Despotic rule
Husband/wife	Marital rule
Father/child	Paternal rule

His main object is to determine the function of these different forms of rule, in order to distinguish them from each other and to relate them to the correct form of political rule. He first treats despotic rule in chapters 4–7 (the discussion of property acquisition in chapters 8–11 being an appendix to the analysis of slavery), and then considers the two forms of familial rule (marital and paternal) in chapters 12–13.

3.1 The master/slave relation

Aristotle assumes that the household exists by nature (I.2, 1252b12–14; cf. 30–1). Depending on whether it attains its natural end of serving human everyday needs, it will be in a natural (*kata phusin*) or unnatural (*para phu-*

22 Cf. III.9, 1280b33–5: the polis is 'the community in living well of households and families for the sake of a complete and self-sufficient life'.

23 The Greek term for 'house' is *oikos*, from which derive the terms *oikia*, 'household', *oikonomos*, 'household manager', *oikonomia*, 'household management', and *oikonomikē* [*sc. epistēmē*], 'household science'.

sin) condition, and the proper role of the household manager is to keep it in a natural condition. Significantly, Aristotle begins his discussion of the master/slave relation by noting a fundamental challenge to this assumption: 'Other people think that being a master is contrary to nature (*para phusin*); for they think that one person is a slave and another free by law (*nomōi*), and that there is no difference by nature (*phusei*). Hence it is not just, for it is due to force (*bia*)' (I.3, 1253b20–4). The presuppositions are that a relation is just only if it is natural (cf. I.5, 1254a18–19), and that a relation cannot be natural if it is due to force.[24]

Aristotle tries to meet the objection within the context of a general justification for property ownership. Just as the specialized crafts need their proper instruments to fulfil their function, the householder needs the proper instruments to fulfil his function, which is the maintenance of life. A possession (*ktēma*) is an instrument for life, and property (*ktēsis*) is a number of such instruments. One cannot live or live well without property. Hence, the household manager needs property to carry out his function. A possession is spoken of in the same way as a part. Therefore, just as a part belongs wholly to another thing, a possession belongs wholly to its owner. A slave is a human being who is the possession of a household manager, who is the master. Therefore, someone who belongs not to himself but to another by nature is a slave by nature. The implication is that if slavery is natural it is also just.

The upshot of this argument is that when the household manager uses things as instruments they become assimilated to him (or to the household) as if they were its parts. The analogy between a possession and a part is problematic, since Aristotle elsewhere points out that what functions as the necessary condition of a thing may not be a part of it (cf. VII.8, 1328a21–b37). Presumably the point of the analogy is that *X* belongs to *Y* by nature when *X* serves the natural ends of *Y*. However, Aristotle himself is aware that this argument as it stands is far from conclusive. For the household might acquire things which it is against nature, and consequently unjust, for it to possess – for example, human beings who are free by nature. So the argument requires qualification.[25]

In order to argue that some human beings are slaves by nature, Aristotle invokes a doctrine which has important applications throughout his entire philosophy, which may be called 'the principle of rulership':

[24] Cf. Keyt 1993 on Aristotle's 'anticoercion principle'.

[25] There is also the problem that property, including nonhuman possessions, may be unjustly acquired by a household, for example, by taking it in the wrong way from another. Aristotle addresses this problem in his discussion of the acquisitive art in *Pol.* I.8–11.

> Whenever a thing is established out of a number of things and becomes a single common thing, there always appears in it a ruler and ruled. (This is true whether it is formed out of continuous or discrete parts.) This [relation of ruler and ruled] is present in living things, but it derives from all of nature. For even in things that do not have a soul there is a sort of rule, for example, of harmony. (I.5, 1254a28–33)

On Aristotle's view, whenever there is an orderly community, this order must be produced and maintained by a ruler (*archōn*) who is in a position of authority.[26] Throughout the *Politics* Aristotle assumes that order within the household depends on the exercise of rule by the household manager, and, similarly, that political order depends on the exercise of rule by the politician. The principle of rulership thus underlies his general theory of political rule.

Aristotle first applies the principle of rulership to the soul, which is the natural authority (*kurios kata phusin*) within a living organism (I.5, 1254a34–6; cf. *de An.* I.5, 410b10–15): 'The soul rules the body with despotic rule, but the intellect rules appetite with political and kingly rule. It is evident from this that it is natural (*kata phusin*) and advantageous for the body to be ruled by the soul and for the passionate part [of the soul] to be ruled by the part which possesses reason. And it is harmful to all of them if they are equal or the ruling relation is reversed' (I.5, 1254b4–9; cf. I.2, 1252a30–4). This passage explains the rationale for the principle of rulership within a living organism: the resulting union will be natural and mutually advantageous for the ruled part as well as the ruler. Aristotle then applies the principle to cases of human rule: to the rule of humans over other animals, to the rule of the male over the female, and to the rule of the superior over the inferior in human communities generally (I.5, 1254b10–16). On the same grounds Aristotle defends natural slavery: if someone is inferior to normal humans in the same way that the body is inferior to the soul or that a beast is inferior to a human, then this person is by nature a slave. If someone has as his function the use of his body and is incapable of anything better than this, then he is inferior to normal humans in this way. Hence, he is a natural slave. Such a person has a defective rational faculty, in that he lacks the deliberative faculty and cannot reason for himself, but he can follow reasons when they are given. If his master possesses and exercises reason in the full sense, then despotic rule is both advantageous and just for the slave as well as the master (I.5, 1254b16–26, 1255a1–2; cf. I.13, 1260a12).

[26] The assumption was easy for a Greek to make, given the link between the Greek noun, *taxis*, 'order', and the verb, *tassein*, 'to order' or 'command'. The noun *kosmos*, 'order', and verb, *kosmein*, had similar associations.

Aristotle palliates his doctrine of slavery in certain ways. In addition to holding that despotic rule should be advantageous for the slave as well as the master, he recommends humane treatment: indeed, masters ought to inculcate virtue in their slaves (i.e., the sort of virtue slaves are capable of). This is because slaves are tools for (virtuous) action rather than mere production (I.4, 1254a1–8) and they share in their masters' lives (I.13, 1260a39–40). He also disagrees with those who claim that slaves are devoid of reason and that they should just be given orders without explanations. They should be admonished even more than children (I.13, 12660b3–7). Aristotle also importantly accepts a fundamental point made by the critics of slavery:

> Being enslaved and a slave are said in two ways. For someone can be a slave or be enslaved according to law (*kata nomon*). For the law is a kind of agreement by which those who are vanquished in war are said to belong to the vanquishers. This just claim (right) is indicted by many legal experts, just as they indict an orator for unlawfulness, on the grounds that it is terrible if that which is forced will be a slave and ruled by that which is able to use force and is superior in power. (I.6, 1255a4–11)

Aristotle maintains it is unjust and contrary to nature to use coercion to enslave a person who is free by nature. He thus implies that the common practice of Greeks enslaving other conquered Greeks was unjust (see *Pol.* I.6), and that those who were enslaved in his day were for the most part unjustly so. Even so, his theory of natural slavery is manifestly flawed. He provides no empirical basis for his claims about the defective psychology of large numbers of human beings, and he seems to reason that if certain people act slavishly this is as a result of their innate inferiority rather than of coercion and habituation (I.13, 1260a9–14). Critics have also pointed out inconsistencies in his arguments. For example, his defence of slavery hinges on the claim that despotic rule is mutually advantageous for master and slave (I.2, 1252a34; I.5, 1254b4–9; I.6, 1255b4–15). But in *Politics* III he remarks that despotic rule is advantageous to the master primarily and to the slave only accidentally, because the continued existence of the slave is necessary for that of the master (1278b32–7). This implies that slaves can be sacrificed whenever their existence is no longer necessary. Thus this qualification seems to undermine the argument of *Politics* I that despotism is just and even 'friendly' because it is mutually advantageous (I.6, 1255b13).[27]

[27] Cf. *EN* VIII.12, 1161b2–8, which denies that there can be justice or friendship between master and slave because they have nothing in common. This passage does allow that the master can have friendship and justice with the slave, but only *qua* human not *qua* slave. Aristotle's psychological argument for slavery is also criticized convincingly by Smith 1991, who provides further references to the critical literature, for which see also Garnsey 1996.

Aristotle's theory of natural slavery cast a long historical shadow extending to the antebellum American South in the nineteenth century, when apologists for slavery sought, rather implausibly, to enlist Aristotle as an ally. One historian has remarked, 'In the bitter slavery controversy, defenders of the peculiar institution found next to the Bible itself a deep source of inspiration in Aristotle, whose heavily qualified and contradictory statements on the justice of slavery were taken as a flat endorsement.'[28] Earlier Juan Ginés de Sepúlveda (1490–1573) defended Spanish colonization of the New World and the enslavement of native Americans, making appeal to Aristotle's *Politics*. However, other Aristotelian philosophers such as Francisco de Vitoria (c. 1483–1546) and Bartolome de Las Casas (1474–1566) criticized the conquest and enslavement of the Indians as a violation of natural law on the grounds that these peoples were naturally free.[29]

3.2 Property ownership and acquisition

Aristotle's discussion of property ownership and acquisition in *Politics* I.8–11 is essentially an appendix to his account of slavery, since a slave is a part of property (I.8, 1256a1–3). It involves further applications of the naturalistic theory discussed above. For example, he distinguishes natural from unnatural forms of the art of acquiring possessions (*chrēmatistikē*). Aristotle claims that the natural, defensible form of the acquisitive art is a part of household management or at any rate a subordinate art serving household management (I.8, 1256a10–16, b26–7; I.10, 1258a34). In support of this he deploys familiar doctrines. For example, food and other goods are provided to human beings by nature, which 'makes nothing incomplete and does nothing in vain' (I.8, 1256b20–1). He also argues that the acquisitive art is natural and just only if it provides the necessary means for the natural ends of the household and polis. Thus, 'true' or natural wealth is not unlimited, but is limited to the amount of property sufficient for the good life (I.8, 1256b30–9). This provides the main basis for Aristotle's distinction in *Politics* I.9–11 between natural and unnatural forms of acquisition. For example, barter involving useful things, such as the exchange of wine for grain, for the sake of natural self-

[28] Wish 1949 cites authors of the American South who invoked Aristotle in defence of slavery.

[29] Cf. Skinner 1978: vol. II, ch. 5 and *The Cambridge History of Political Thought 1450–1700*: ch. 5 for detailed discussion of scholastic natural-law theorists during the Reformation and Counter-Reformation. Vitoria, an influential teacher at the University of Salamanca, also developed a theory of just war out of texts of Aristotle and Aquinas. Through his influence on later thinkers such as Francisco Suárez (1548–1627) and Hugo Grotius (1583–1645), Vitoria is credited with helping to found the modern theory of international law.

sufficiency is not against nature (*para phusin*). The innovation of money as a means of exchange makes possible the art of commerce (*kapēlikē*), which involves exchanging things for money in order to make a profit. In contrast to the natural acquisitive art, commerce has for its end the unlimited accumulation of wealth and is thus inherently unnatural (I.9, 1257b23–31).

A defender of commerce might object that it is no more unnatural than other arts such as medicine, which can also serve the ends of the household or polis. Aristotle, however, adds the argument that commerce is peculiarly pernicious because it engenders a false view of the good life: as consisting of the unlimited gratification of desires, which requires unlimited wealth. This leads one to use one's faculties in an unnatural way (I.9, 1257b32–1258a14). Aristotle also suggests that commercial exchange 'is not according to nature but from one another' (I.10, 1258b1–2), which suggests that if one party makes a profit the other party must be a loser. Aristotle finds usury (*obolostatikē*) even more objectionable, because the creditors use money to produce wealth. Their gain comes from money itself and not from the purpose for which money was introduced, namely to facilitate exchange. The Greek word for interest, *tokos*, means 'child', indicating that it is money generated from money. Hence, this is the 'most unnatural' form of acquisition (I.10, 1258b2–8).

Aristotle's arguments that commerce and usury are unnatural were very influential in the ancient and medieval eras, but they have been largely rejected by modern philosophers and economists.[30] For example, he in effect views all commercial exchange as a 'zero-sum game', failing to recognize the mutual gains from trade. Further, he fails to grasp that economic gains in the form of profits and interest may perform valuable economical functions, which modern economists have endeavoured to explain. His psychological critique of commerce is also questionable. From the definition of commerce as the art of exchanging things in order to make a profit (I.9, 1257b4–5), it does not follow that a merchant's sole aim in life is to maximize his profits.

3.3 *Familial relations*

Aristotle applies the principle of rulership to the male/female and father/child relations in a familiar but somewhat sketchier fashion. He contends that wives like children should be ruled as free persons, but

[30] For critical overviews see Susemihl and Hicks 1894: 23–31 and Finley 1977. A more sympathetic treatment of Aristotle's economic arguments is offered by Meikle 1995, who provides additional references to the secondary literature.

wives should be subject to political rule and children to kingly rule. For 'the male is by nature more capable of leadership than the female, unless he is constituted in some way contrary to nature, and the elder and perfect [is by nature more capable of leadership] than the younger imperfect'. In political rule individuals generally take turns in ruling and being ruled because they are inclined to be equal by nature, 'but the male is always related in this manner to the female' (I.12, 1259a39–b10). He remarks further that the female (unlike the natural slave) has a deliberative faculty but it is without authority (*akuron*) (I.13, 1260a13). By this he seems to mean that a woman's rational faculty does not have authority over the woman herself, because she cannot control her passions fully and is thus unable to act in accord with practical wisdom unless she is under male governance.[31] He does maintain that women should be educated to be virtuous because they comprise half of the free citizens in the polis (I.13, 1260b13–20), but he also thinks that women have a subordinate form of virtue and that their proper role is in the household rather than in the political sphere (cf. I.13, 1260a20–31; II.5, 1264a40–b6; III.4, 1277b21–5). However, Aristotle offers no evidence for his thesis that women are not psychologically equipped to rule, apart from the fact that males are generally observed to rule over women (I.13, 1260a9–10). It did not occur to him that the dominance of men over women in ancient Greece might instead be the result of deeply ingrained traditions and the absence of technologies favourable to greater freedom for women.[32]

Aristotle's arguments that slavery and female subservience are natural and that usury and commerce are unnatural contain serious difficulties. Moreover, such doctrines point to a general problem for political naturalism: the difficulty of disentangling the strands of nature and convention in the social fabric. There is an understandable temptation to deem what is normal in one's own culture to be 'natural', and what is abnormal to be 'unnatural'. But even if a practice or institution is ubiquitous, it does not follow that it must be explained in terms of innate psychological facts.

4 Nature and education

Aristotle's defence of political naturalism in *Politics* I.2 concludes with the following argument:

31 This is the traditional interpretation, defended by Fortenbaugh 1977 and Smith 1983. Another interpretation is that the deliberations of women do not have authority *over men* because men will not follow them: cf. Saxonhouse 1982: 208. However, this interpretation seems to make Aristotle's argument that male dominance is *natural*, rather than merely conventional, fallacious.

32 See Miller 1995: 240–4.

> The impulse for this sort of community is in everyone by nature, but the one who first established it was the cause of the greatest goods. For just as a human being is the best of animals if he is perfected, he is the worst of all if he is separated from law and the administration of justice. For injustice is cruellest when it possesses arms. But when a man is born he possesses arms to be used for practical wisdom and virtue, although they can be used for the opposite ends. Therefore he is the most unholy and savage when he lacks virtue and he is the worst concerning sex and food. And justice is political; for the administration of justice is the order of the political community, and justice [as a virtue] is judgment about what is just. (I.2, 1253a31–9)

This argument assumes Aristotle's philosophy of education: that is, human nature can be perfected only through the acquisition of virtue and practical wisdom, which requires education and habituation in the legal system of a polis. This passage also supports Aristotle's thesis that it is the task of the lawgiver and politician to make the citizens good.[33]

The assumption that human nature can be perfected only through the acquisition of virtue and practical wisdom agrees with central doctrines of Aristotle's ethical works: for example that a human being is excellent (*spoudaios*) by nature, and that a wicked person is in an unnatural condition (*para phusin*) (*EE* VII.2, 1237a16; VII.6, 1240b20–1); and happiness is analysed by reference to the distinctive function of a human being or his soul (*EN* I.7, 1097b24–5; *EE* II.1, 1218b38–1219a1). Nature serves as a standard of value: 'what is proper to each thing by nature is best and pleasantest for it' (*EN* X.7, 1178a5–6; cf. I.9, 1099b21–2; IX.9, 1170a13–16; 1170b1–2, 15).

However, the claim that virtue is a 'natural' condition for human beings presents a difficulty of interpretation, because Aristotle himself argues that ethical virtue does not exist 'by nature':

> Ethical (*ēthikē*) virtue comes about as a result of habit. Hence, its name involves a slight variation from that of habit (*ethos*). From this it is also clear that none of the ethical virtues arises in us by nature. For none of the things that exist by nature can become other [than its nature] by habituation. For example, a stone which moves downward by nature could not be habituated to move upward, not even if you threw it up ten thousand times in order to habituate it, nor could fire be habituated to go downward nor could anything else that naturally [does a specific kind of thing] be habituated to act otherwise. Therefore, the virtues do not

[33] *Pol.* VII.13–14; *EN* I.9, I.13 and II.1. Aristotle also emphasizes the educative role of the laws especially in *EN* X.9. He is following Plato, who discusses public education at length in the *Republic* and *Laws*.

> arise either by nature or against nature, but we are naturally able to acquire them and we are perfected [or completed] through habit. (*EN* II.1, 1103a17–26; cf. *EE* II.2, 1220a39–b5)

If Aristotle is consistent, he must evidently be using 'nature' in different senses when he claims that virtue is a 'natural' condition of human beings but denies that virtue comes to be 'by nature'. This closely parallels the problem discussed above concerning his doctrine that the polis exists by nature: a consistent interpretation requires that we impute to him a distinction between different senses of 'nature' not made explicitly in his extant writings. According to such an interpretation, when Aristotle claims that virtue arises by habit rather than 'by nature', he understands 'nature' in the sense of a person's *mere* nature, namely the person's innate constitution, apart from habituation or any other intervention. When Aristotle speaks of virtue or happiness as a 'natural' condition, he is thinking of the *natural end* of human beings. When he equates 'natural' with 'good', he evidently has the natural end in view. He is talking about the condition people are in when they have properly developed. By 'natural virtue' Aristotle has in mind the aptitudes and tendencies inherent in persons to acquire full moral virtue if they are properly trained and educated.[34]

What, then, are the respective roles of habit and nature in the process of education? Aristotle in fact states that *three* different factors are involved in human development: nature, habit, and reason. This triad is discussed somewhat differently in two separate passages: *Nicomachean Ethics* X.9, 1179b20–1180a24 and *Politics* VII.13, 1332a38–b11. The aim of the former passage is to argue that the laws are necessary for the acquisition of virtue. Here nature is perfunctorily dismissed as a source of virtue: the goodness belonging to nature is not under our control but is due to 'some divine causes' and is found only in the truly fortunate. Thus, he seems to have mere nature in view. Regarding reason, he notes that arguments and teaching do not have strength with all persons, 'but the soul of the student must have been moulded beforehand with habits for enjoying and hating in a noble way, just like earth that is to nourish seed'. Habituation is necessary for moral education, because a person who is governed by his passions will not respond to argument: 'His character must first have an affinity with

[34] On these two senses of 'nature' in Aristotle's ethics and politics, see Annas 1993: 142–58, who refers to them as 'mere nature' and 'nature proper'. Similar distinctions are made by Irwin 1985: 416–17 and Nichols 1992:18. Of the different senses in *Metaph*. V.4, 'mere nature' seems to correspond most closely to sense (4), i.e. nature understood as a material cause, and to be opposed to nature in sense (5), i.e. nature as a formal or final cause.

virtue, loving the noble and hating the base.' Young persons should be taught to enjoy or disdain the appropriate sorts of activities. Otherwise, they will enjoy the wrong things and be resistant to moral reasoning. The household alone is not sufficient, because parents and private individuals generally lack the influence and compelling power of the laws. Further, individuals are more likely to abide by rules than other individuals. Hence, coercively enforced laws are necessary to produce virtuous citizens.[35]

Politics VII.13 takes a somewhat different view on the triad of nature, habit, and reason, with each of them having a necessary role in the educational process. Nature is a precondition: 'one must first grow as a human being and not as another animal, and thus have a certain sort of body and soul'. But growth alone does not suffice, because some natural attributes can develop for better or worse, depending on how one is habituated. 'The other animals live mostly by nature, although in some slight ways by habits as well, but a human being also lives by reason, for he only has reason.' In human beings these factors should be in harmony. 'For people do many things contrary to their habituation and nature as a result of reason if they are persuaded that another condition is better' (1332b3–5). Aristotle does not, however, explain this 'harmony' (*sumphōnia*). Is his point that reason should adapt itself to the dictates of nature and habit, or that the latter pair should conform to reason?[36] Unless this issue can be clarified, there is a serious ambiguity in Aristotle's naturalistic philosophy of education.

Aristotle's account of the best system of education in *Politics* VII and VIII conforms to this natural hierarchy. He distinguishes between two parts of the soul, the rational faculty and the desiring faculty, and notes that the former is better.[37] The rational faculty is also divided into better and

[35] Similarly, *Politics* VIII.1 advocates a public system of education. Appealing to the above mentioned doctrine that the polis is prior by nature to the individual, Aristotle argues, 'one should think not that any of the citizens belongs to himself, but that all belong to the polis; for each citizen is a part of the polis; and the care of each part naturally (*pephuken*) looks to the care of the whole' (1337a27–30). However, in contrast to *Politics* VIII.1, *Nicomachean Ethics* X.9 makes an important qualification at 1180a24–b13: where there is no public system of education, then, *faute de mieux*, private individuals should try to educate their children and friends, although they should acquire the legislative science which guides the lawgiver in framing a system of laws favourable to education. Further, a father's statements and habits have an influence like the laws and habits of the cities, because his children are 'predisposed to love and obey him by nature (*tēi phusei*)'. Aristotle even adds that individual education may have an advantage over common education in that it can be adapted to individual needs. Nonetheless, like a gymnastics teacher or a doctor, the educator will be most effective if he knows the universal principles for producing morally virtuous citizens.

[36] Newman 1887–1902: ad loc. understands the passage in the former way, Annas 1993: 143, in the latter.

[37] This is explained elsewhere as due to the principle of rulership: cf. *Pol.* I.2, 1252a31–4; I.5, 1254b6–9.

worse parts: contemplative and practical reason. The activities associated with these parts also form a hierarchy, because the activities belonging to the part which is better by nature (*phusei*) are more choiceworthy (1333a27–8). The educator is thus to be guided by the maxim that 'what is most choiceworthy for each individual is always the highest it is possible for him to attain' (1333a29–30). Aristotle recalls the triad of nature, habit, and reason in *Politics* VII.15, and reiterates that they should be in harmony. He asserts that the three form a normative hierarchy: 'reason and intellect are the end of our nature, so that birth and care for habits should be provided for the sake of these things' (1334b14–16). This corresponds to the natural order of generation: 'just as the body is prior to the soul in generation, so also is the irrational [part of the soul] to the rational part. And this is evident: for children have spirit and wishing, and also desire, directly when they are born, but reasoning and intellect naturally (*pephuken*) arise as they develop' (1334b22–5). This defines the main stages of education: 'Therefore first it is necessary to care for the body before the soul, and next the appetite; but the care of appetite is for the sake of the intellect, and care of the body is for the sake of the soul' (1334b28). In general, then, education should follow the natural development of the individual: 'one ought to follow the distinction of nature, for all art and education wish to fill what is left out of nature' (1337a1–3). In making this injunction, however, Aristotle does not explain how education can 'follow' nature if it supplies what has been 'left out of nature'. For example, if moral virtue is not itself the result of nature, how can we say that the morally educated person is 'naturally' superior to the uneducated? It would seem that Aristotle is again using 'nature' in two senses: education should follow nature (i.e. the natural end) and supply what is left out of nature (i.e. mere nature).[38]

Aristotle's political naturalism thus presupposes his philosophy of nature. Even if it is agreed that in the *Politics* and ethical treatises he often uses 'nature' in an extended sense rather than in the strict sense of the *Physics* and other natural scientific treatises, it is still true that the naturalism of Aristotle's politics and ethics depends upon the naturalism of his physics and biology. Moreover, even if a polis is not to be thought of as a living organism, it resembles an organism in an important respect. An organism has within it an organizing and guiding formal principle: its soul. The polis also has a similar internal principle: its constitution (cf. *Pol.*

[38] Cf. Annas 1993: 147–8, who points out that the problem recurs in Peripatetic philosophers including Alexander of Aphrodisias, *de Fato* 27, 197.25–198.26.

III.3, 1276b7–8; IV.4, 1291a24–8). An organism can function well and be healthy, or function badly and be sick; hence it can live in a natural condition (*kata phusin*) or unnatural condition (*para phusin*). Similarly, a polis can be in a natural or unnatural condition; that is, it can be in a just or unjust condition, or have a correct or deviant constitution. Accordingly, political justice and the analysis of constitutions are two central components of Aristotle's political theory, which are to be discussed in the following two chapters.[39]

[39] I am grateful to David Depew for valuable suggestions.

17

Justice and the polis

JEAN ROBERTS

The aim of all of Aristotle's practical philosophy is to provide a description of the best life for a human being, along with an understanding of how that life is to be achieved or at least approached. The discussion of individual happiness (*eudaimonia*) in the ethical writings and the discussion of political arrangements in the *Politics* are complementary and equally necessary parts of that inquiry. The happiness of an individual is that of a naturally political animal whose life and happiness are essentially interwoven with that of his[1] fellow citizens. The happiness of a city is nothing other than the happiness of the individuals who constitute it. The best or happy life is the life of virtue. Justice, in one of its forms, is complete virtue in an individual. The best life is thus the just life, and the best city the one populated by just citizens. This much said, much remains to be explained, in particular, what Aristotle thought justice was.

Aristotle's writings about justice, found chiefly in the fifth book of the *Nicomachean Ethics* and the third book of the *Politics*, are notoriously difficult. If there is any explanation for this apart from the combination of the complexity of the issues being dealt with, the state of our texts, and the identity of the author, it has to do with Aristotle's characteristic method of answering philosophical questions. He approaches all topics through the views of his predecessors, often quite explicitly. This is not simply for purposes of showing that all of them were at least partly wrong and only Aristotle wholly right. It is the effect of Aristotle's considered views about how human beings come to have knowledge.

> The investigation of the truth is in one way hard, in another easy. Evidence of this is that while no one is able to attain the truth adequately, no one fails entirely either, but rather each says something about the nature of things, and although individually they contribute little or nothing to the truth, something sizeable comes from all of them taken together. (*Metaph.* II.1, 993a30–b4)

[1] I use the masculine here (and throughout) advisedly; in describing Aristotle's views it seems misleading to disguise the fact that the virtue and happiness he is mainly concerned with is that of free males.

Aristotle's own thoughts about justice will be shaped by his canvassing of the available alternatives for whatever bits of the truth they might contain. This dialectical and synthesizing method gives rise to direct engagement with what was, as the previous chapters of this volume attest, a substantial tradition of political thought.

1 Natural and conventional justice

Aristotle's dialectical method is well illustrated by his contribution to the by then traditional nature–convention (*nomos–phusis*) debate.[2] He claims that there is some truth on both sides, that is, that justice is both natural and conventional. While allowing that some justice is conventional, Aristotle, not surprisingly, stands mainly on the side of natural justice. As with any Aristotelian virtue, the character of justice is to be determined by looking to the nature or functioning of the creature whose virtue it is. Justice and injustice are peculiarly human, and will then be defined by looking to human nature. There is, for Aristotle, a fact of the matter about what human beings are and about what constitutes virtue or excellence in something with such a nature.[3]

The two alternatives, nature and convention, had been taken as exclusive. To claim that justice was natural was to claim that there was an objective fact of the matter about what constituted justice in a person or in a political system. Particular persons or systems might then either meet that standard, which was taken as universal, or not. To claim that justice was conventional was to deny that there was any universal objective standard and to insist that justice was entirely constituted by the beliefs and practices of particular communities. Democracy, on this view, would be just for the Athenians because it was embodied in Athenian law and seemed just to the Athenians, but would not be just in Persia. The differences in conceptions of justice could be explained by pointing to differences in the power relations which would explain either the imposition of, or the agreement to, some particular picture of justice in terms of the imagined advantage of some or all involved.[4] In any case, to hold that all justice was conventional was to hold that there were no claims of justice apart from local practices; any common claims were only accidentally common and there was no external stance from which to criticize the standards of any community.

When Aristotle says that political justice, which characterizes relations

[2] See Winton, in Ch. 4 section 1 above. [3] See Miller, in Ch. 16 above.

[4] Thus this view of the origins of justice gave rise naturally to worries about whether or not being just was to the advantage of the just. See Striker 1987.

between citizens of a polis, is both conventional[5] and natural (*EN* v.7, 1134b18–19), he is carving out a new position on the traditional question. There is, of course, a sense in which anyone who thinks that there is more to justice than local conventions will be willing to talk about conventional justice. Conventional justice will be whatever is thought to be just, and may be opposed to what is really or naturally just. There are certainly passages in Aristotle's writings in which this seems to be all that he has in mind in speaking of the conventionally just.[6] Here in the *Nicomachean Ethics*, however, he is not simply asserting that there is natural justice, on the one hand, and various conventional beliefs about justice which may well differ from it, on the other. Here he is arguing for the naturalness of justice (or at least arguing against an argument against it), and at the same time admitting that some of what is just is genuinely conventional in the sense that it is made just by seeming to be just or being agreed to be just.

Again, that Aristotle should say that part of political justice is just by nature is hardly surprising. Human nature is the same everywhere and so then also is human virtue.[7] Practical wisdom (*phronēsis*), looking to the human good, will discern what is just. On this particular topic Aristotle may have thought that what he saw as very widespread agreement that there was natural justice constituted a reason for believing in it.[8] In addition, those who thought there was no natural justice had illicitly inferred the conventionality of all justice from variations in beliefs about justice.

> It seems to some that everything is of this sort [just only by convention] because what is by nature is supposed to be unchanging and have the same force everywhere, like fire which burns both here and in Persia, and they see what is just changing. In a way this is right, but in a way it is not. Perhaps among the gods what is by nature does not change, but among us it is possible for something both to be by nature and also to be entirely changeable; there is nevertheless a difference between what is by nature and what is not by nature. It is clear, among the things which can be otherwise, which are by nature and which are not but are conventional and by agreement, despite the fact that both are similarly changeable. The distinction is the same as in other cases. The right hand is by nature

[5] This translates *nomikos*. I use this rather than 'legal' to highlight the connection to the traditional nature–convention debate.

[6] *Rhet.* I.10, 1368b7–9; I.13, 1373b4–9; I.15, 1375a31–3. See also *MM* I.33, 1195a4–5.

[7] Strictly speaking, Aristotle may believe this only of Greek free males. Women and slaves, being somewhat defective in nature relative to free males, will have different virtues. There are also passages in which he seems to suggest that non-Greeks similarly are defective in ways that would seem to prevent the full development of Aristotelian virtue, for example, *Pol.* III.14, 1285a19–22 and VII.7, 1327b23–9.

[8] *Rhet.* I.13, 1373b6–9.

> stronger, although everyone could become ambidextrous. Things which are just by agreement and in accordance with advantage are like measures; measures for wine and corn are not the same everywhere but are larger in wholesale markets and smaller in retail. Similarly, just things which are not natural but of human devising are not the same everywhere, otherwise constitutions would be the same and they are not. Nevertheless, only one is the best everywhere in accordance with nature. (*EN* v.7, 1134b24–1135a5)

The point of the comparison with ambidexterity is the following. Those who thought that all justice was simply a matter of convention were led to this view by noticing the variation in political arrangements. This is, however, to fail to realize or consider that what is natural can be distorted or changed by human practice. Although we are by nature right-handed (there is, Aristotle thinks, a good biological explanation for this and the normal and usual process of human development reflects this)[9] we can distort or hide this fact by learning to do things with our left hands. The just by nature can be determined by looking at what always or for the most part contributes to the common good. Certain types of action, honouring parents, standing one's ground on the battlefield, paying debts, are always or almost always just. Nevertheless, as in the case of ambidexterity, the naturally just may be hidden by human practice. So one cannot infer from different beliefs about justice to the conventionality of justice. The variability may well be due to moral error, that is, to distortions of nature.[10]

It is more difficult to determine what Aristotle means in conceding that some of what is just really is just only by convention. The conventionally just is described not only as like measures for corn and wine which differ in size according to use and by agreement (*EN* v.7, 1134b35–1135a3), but more abstractly as that about which it 'initially makes no difference one way or the other, but when it has been established, it does matter' (v.7, 1134b20–1). Examples of things just by convention are paying one mina in ransom, sacrificing a goat rather than two sheep, any legislation dealing only with a particular case, like making a sacrifice to Brasidas, and decrees (v.7, 1134b21–4). A few pages earlier he describes money as existing only by convention, and in explanation of its conventionality mentions that it plays the economic role it does only by agreement and that it is in our

[9] On this see Miller 1991: 289–92.

[10] The proper reading of this example has long been subject to dispute. The interpretation given above is roughly that of Jackson 1879: 107, and of the ancient Greek Aristotelian commentator Heliodorus *in EN* 182.8–18 (Heylbut 1889). An alternative was offered by Aquinas *in Ethic.*v.xii.1028–9 (Spiazzi 1964, Litzinger 1964) and, more recently, by Miller 1991: 287.

power to strip it of its conventional function and make it useless (v.5, 1133a28–31).

This suggests that at a certain specific level there may be nothing in the nature of the human good which determines one way or the other which of various available means to an end are the best, 'initially it makes no difference one way or the other'. Justice may require that a sacrifice be made, as the needs of the marketplace require that there be some standard measure of commodities, but what exactly that sacrifice, or the size of the measures, is to be is not fully determined by the end to be served. While it may not matter which way it is, it may very well matter that it be one way or the other, and thus there is need for a practice or law to settle which of the reasonable alternatives is to be adopted. What is just only by convention is genuinely arbitrary in the sense that some other alternative could have been agreed to or stipulated that would have served the purposes at hand as well as the option chosen. At some point the sacrificing of a goat is made just, but prior to that it is neither just nor unjust. It is important to note here, however, that since Aristotle thinks that there is also natural justice, which will provide a standard which any actual law should not violate, the range of matters appropriately settled simply by convention will be restricted by the naturally just. It is also important to note here that the conventionally just is subjective only at the level of the final details. There may be no objective fact of the matter about whether it is better to sacrifice a goat or two sheep, and thus no ground for criticizing the initial stipulation of one or the other. There may very well, however, be an objective fact of the matter about whether or not it is better to offer a sacrifice, or about whether or not it is better to do something to honour whoever is being honoured by the sacrifice. Convention comes in only where the matter at hand becomes morally neutral.

It may not be so obvious why things like decrees intended to cover only a single situation should fall into the category of the conventionally just, since this may suggest that it is the narrowness or the particularity of the decision rather than the moral neutrality of the matter which is critical. Now it is an important piece of Aristotelian dogma that a type of action which is not always just may be just in a particular case because of unusual factors in the situation. In other words, some variability in the just is due to the real complexities and complications of human life. It is usually just to return what one owes, but not if one owes a knife to a madman.[11] At a certain level of description of action, there will be no type of action which

[11] The point was stated explicitly by Plato in the *Politicus* 294a10–b6, but is implicit in even the earliest Socratic dialogues. The knife example is from the *Republic* 331c1–9.

is always just. Natural justice cannot be fully captured by any set of rules. Discretion and wisdom and judgment are thus an intrinsic part of virtue, and law, which by its very nature speaks in general terms, will always fail to cover every actual case neatly. There will then be a sort of decision, calling for what Aristotle calls equity (*epieikeia*) (*EN* v.10, 1137b11–25), that has to be made about a particular case. This will not, however, be a decision which in principle can hold for only a single case; it ought to hold for any exactly similar situation.[12] The ability to accommodate one's judgments to particular situations in this way is part of practical wisdom (*EN* vi.7, 1141b14–16; vi.11, 1143a25–32). There is then presumably nothing arbitrary or subjective in decisions of this sort. It is important to see that this is a matter of the complexity of natural justice and not a claim about the conventionality or subjectivity of decisions about particular cases.

When Aristotle says then that legislation for particular cases is only conventionally just, he is presumably not thinking here of cases in which one might, due to something about the situation, be inclined to make an exception to a general law in the interests of justice, or to find just a type of action which is not usually just. He must be assuming that the very fact that the decision is conceived of as holding only for a single case shows that there is some genuinely arbitrary element. The thought, again, is that sometimes in deliberating about the possible means to one's ends, which may themselves be required by natural justice, one gets to a point where reasons for one option rather than another have given out. If this is so, then the distinction between the natural and the conventional here may after all be as obvious as Aristotle claims. What is just merely by convention will be that for or against which there is no argument appealing to the human good. Natural justice may require that a city honour its heroes, or it may require that a city honour some of its heroes, or it may require that a city honour all of its heroes except those who fall into some very particular sort of category; it may not require that this be done by offering sacrifices.

Aristotle's concession to those who thought all of justice conventional is thus quite minimal, as indeed it would have to be given his belief in natural justice. Most of the variation in beliefs about justice, or between the laws of particular cities, will be due to moral error. Many beliefs and practices will simply be aberrations of natural justice. Those beliefs and practices will be just merely by convention in the sense that they are the conventions or laws of a particular city, but justice conventional in this

[12] This is presumably the point of the claim at *Rhet.* i.15, 1375a31–2 that the equitable is stable and unchanging.

sense is to be held up to the standard of natural justice and may very well turn out to be contrary to natural justice and hence, strictly speaking, unjust. On the other hand, some things can only be just by convention, the genuinely neutral about which natural justice has nothing to say. Finally, it may well be a matter of natural justice that one obey even those laws which are just only by convention, in either sense.[13]

2 Justice as a virtue of individuals

What now is naturally just? The most explicit description of justice appears in the early chapters of the fifth book of the *Nicomachean Ethics*. Justice is commonly opposed, Aristotle says, both to what is contrary to law and to the unfair or grasping. This is taken as warrant for dividing it into two distinct virtues. 'The just is therefore the lawful and the equal, and the unjust is the unlawful and the unequal' (*EN* v.1, 1129a34–1129b1). This initial description is broad and loose enough to cover even what may not turn out to be in accord with natural justice at all. Aristotle is abstracting here from the difficult substantive issues about what the law ought to say and about who or what ought to be taken as equal.

Law always, Aristotle says, aims at some sort of common advantage (v.1, 1129b14–17). The lawful is what 'produces and guards happiness and its parts for the political community' (v.1, 1129b17–19). Law requires virtuous action and forbids vicious action (v.1, 1129b19–24). Since law in so doing is aiming at the happiness (however that is conceived) of the political community (however that is conceived), 'this kind of justice is complete virtue, not without qualification, but in relation to others' (v.1, 1129b25–7). 'Justice alone of the virtues seems to be another's good, because it is (exercised) in relation to another' (v.1, 1130a3–4).

The narrower kind of justice that has to do with equity and fairness, 'particular' justice, is part of the broader kind identified with complete virtue, 'universal' justice. It is also distinct from each of the other individual virtues which make up the parts of universal justice.[14] Particular justice has mainly to do with the appropriate handling of shareable goods, chiefly money, safety and honour (v.2, 1130b2). Like universal justice, it is a virtue of a person as related to others (v.2, 1130b1–2). There are other Aristotelian virtues constituted by the correct beliefs and feelings about

[13] On this point see MacIntyre 1988: 120–1.

[14] There are well-known difficulties involved in distinguishing particular justice from each of the other individual virtues of character, most connected in one way or another with the emotional component that Aristotle sees as part of any virtue. On this see Williams 1980, Young 1988, and Irwin 1988: 427.

money, safety and honour, but not as sharable goods. The unjust are not simply mistaken in their beliefs and feelings about these goods; they are unfair. They will not simply misuse these goods, they will mishandle these goods to the detriment of others. They suffer from *pleonexia* or graspingness (v.1, 1129b4–11).

Particular justice, equality, is further divided into the distributive (*nemētikon*) and the corrective (*diorthōtikon*) (v.2, 1130b30–1131a1). The former is a matter of distributing goods in proportion with merit or worth. In the same way as the lawful will be described as just, whatever the content of the law, so everyone will describe as just the distribution of equal goods to those of equal worth, while differing about what the relevant standard of worth should be. 'All agree that the just in distribution has to be in accordance with some standard of merit or worth, they do not, however, all pick the same standard: supporters of democracy choose freedom, oligarchs choose wealth or good birth, and supporters of aristocracy choose virtue' (v.3, 1131a25–9). Aristotle, perhaps not entirely helpfully, further describes this kind of equality as a kind of geometric proportion.[15] 'In geometrical proportion it follows that the parts stand to each other as the wholes do' (v.3, 1131b13–15). If the common funds of a partnership are to be distributed on the basis of financial contribution to the partnership, then if A contributed twice as much as B, A should get twice as much as B, thus maintaining the ratio of the original contribution in the distribution.

The corrective form of equality also in a way has to do with the distribution of goods, but in situations of exchange. Here justice is having 'an equal amount both before and after' (v.4, 1132b19–20). This, again perhaps not helpfully, is described as a matter of arithmetic proportion. The point though is that there are kinds of dispersal which do not reasonably look to any merit or worth in the persons involved, as distributive justice does, but only to the value of the goods in question. This is the sort of justice required in the determination of penalties, which Aristotle thinks of as restoring balance by compensating the victim for the harm done.[16]

[15] Helpful or not, thinking of justice in mathematical terms was not original to Aristotle (see Harvey 1965). Democracy was not always, even by Aristotle (*Pol.* vi.2, 1317b2–4), thought of as distributing in accordance with geometric rather than arithmetic proportion. It will look arithmetic if it is seen as distributing equally without looking to any standard.

[16] There is no need to take this as his entire theory about punishment, which, as Hardie 1980: 194 and Irwin 1988: 625 note, would make it a very sorry one. Aristotle's very subtle account of voluntary and involuntary action (*EN* iii.1–5) as well as his description of punishment as cure (*EN* ii.3, 1104b16–18), make it clear that he thinks of public response to wrongdoing as far more than a making of restitution for the injury done. There is no reason to assume that he didn't, like Plato (*Laws* 862b1–c4), distinguish between the compensatory and curative functions of punishment.

This is not a matter of straightforward reciprocity, if that is taken to mean that one should suffer exactly the injury done, since, despite the Pythagorean claim to the contrary, that may not in fact properly compensate and so equalize the situation (v.5, 1132b21–31). Aristotle does, however, speak approvingly of 'reciprocity in accordance with proportion', which is introduced as the principle covering fair trade and exchange (*EN* v.5, 1132b31–3).[17]

Justice is thus exercised by persons playing their proper role in a community. Justice as complete virtue insures the proper regard and concern for the happiness of the other members of the community. Justice as equality ensures that divisible goods are properly apportioned. Humans are members of various communities and there is room for justice of a kind in any of them, but the most important is the polis. The justice that holds between those who share in the self-sufficient life of the polis, that is, between fellow citizens, is opposed to the secondary and derivative sorts which might exist between those who share in a different sort of community, for example, the family, and is called political justice (v.6, 1134a26–30). It is this with which Aristotle is mainly concerned.

Both universal justice and particular justice in all of its guises shape Aristotle's conception of the good polis. Universal justice is what should be demanded by perfectly framed law, and as complete virtue describes the perfect man and also the perfect citizen in a city with perfectly framed law. Particular justice in its distributive form will determine the proper distribution of offices and power in the polis, as well as of any other shareable good that is appropriately distributed in accordance with some standard of merit or worth. And although Aristotle has much less to say about the rest of particular justice in the *Politics*, he does say that 'reciprocal equality preserves the polis' (*Pol.* II.1, 1261a30–1; *EN* v.5, 1132b34–5), and means by this to insist on the importance of fairness in the exchange of goods and services, taken in the broadest possible sense so that it includes even the sharing of political office when the deserving are too numerous to hold it simultaneously. Finally, the sort of corrective justice which determines fair compensation for victims of injury will be particularly required in judges and juries.

Aristotle does not, in offering this rather elaborate taxonomy of kinds of justice, directly confront any of his predecessors except the

[17] It is not clear whether this is supposed to be a third kind of particular justice, along with distributive and corrective justice, or whether it is a part or aspect of corrective justice. See Ritchie 1894, Hardie 1980: 191–201, and Irwin 1988: 428–30 for the outlines of the long-standing scholarly debate on the question.

Pythagoreans, perhaps because here there was no standing debate about kinds of justice for him to negotiate. On the other hand, while not calling just anything which would not have been recognized as such, he has implicitly criticized all who failed to see that more than one state of character had been labelled 'just' and that different sorts of deliberation are required in determining what is just in different types of situation calling for the allotment of shareable goods.

3 Individuals as citizens

Before thinking about the application of Aristotle's conception of justice to political arrangements, it is worth pausing to consider the import of his identification of (one kind of) justice as complete virtue and as obedience to correctly framed law. Aristotle takes happiness (*eudaimonia*) as the end of all human action, and identifies the happy or best life as the life of virtue. So the best life for an individual human being, insofar as that is a matter of character, will be constituted by being just, where justice is understood as complete virtue with respect to others. Moreover, it is the business of law to attempt to instil this character in citizens, or, at the least, to make them behave as though they had that character. This broad and far-reaching conception of justice is an indication of the vast distance between Aristotle's conception of the relation between the individual and the polis and modern liberalism's view of the relation between a citizen and his or her 'State'.[18]

One can go at this from either end. There is, in Aristotle, both a different conception of the individual and a different conception of the political community. Aristotle thinks of individuals as essentially social or political in a sense which ties the good of any individual to the good of his fellow citizens (*EN* I.7, 1097b8–11). Being human means that one can only live a self-sufficient life as part of a community in which certain functions necessary for the self-sufficiency of the community are performed. It is a fact about human beings that they can only live a distinctively human life in a city, not because they need the cooperation of others in attaining individually defined ends, but because living a distinctively human life requires that one be part of what is essentially a joint function.[19]

The fact that the individual Aristotelian virtues (courage, temperance, generosity, and so on) turn out to constitute as a whole the same state of

[18] See Cartledge, in Ch. 1 above.

[19] Aristotle provides lists of the necessary parts or functions of the polis at *Pol.* IV.4, 1290b38–1291b2 and VII.8, 1328b5–23.

character as justice understood as another's good is neither an accident nor an arbitrary stipulation on Aristotle's part. Since the virtues he describes are from the beginning thought of as those of a social or political being, the recommended states of character, even when being viewed as constitutive of an individual's good, are in fact states which promote the good of others. Courage will do to illustrate the point. The courageous man is one who neither exceeds nor falls short in feelings of fear and confidence and who chooses courageous action for its own sake. Courage in its primary form is a virtue of the battlefield. Courage can thus be defined as a characteristic of an individual. It is nevertheless obvious that such behaviour could constitute good functioning only for someone who had an essential interest in the preservation of his city. Aristotle's entire list of individual virtues can in a similar fashion be easily seen as a list of states enabling the possessor to have the proper emotional and cognitive stance toward various objects important to human beings who live together in a group and need so to live.[20]

Correlatively, 'the polis is a certain number of citizens' (*Pol.* III.1, 1274b41), that number being whatever is required for a self-sufficient life (III.1, 1275b20–1). It is distinguished from other sorts of human communities by the citizens' common concern with justice and the common good, and with each other's virtue (III.9, 1280a31–b12). It is also a community of those who are dissimilar, since what makes the city, as opposed to the individual, or other groupings of individuals, self-sufficient is the collective performance of disparate functions. The life which the citizens of a city live jointly has to be well lived by them all, or at least by many, in order to be truly well lived by any. Thus, Aristotle says, even in the *Nicomachean Ethics* where he is focusing on the happiness of individuals, that it is the end of political science, happiness for the city, that is the highest and most complete end of human action to which all other ends, including the happiness of individuals, are subordinated (*EN* I.1, 1094a26–b10). Aristotle does not mean that the happiness of the polis is more important than that of its individual citizens in any sense which suggests that the happiness of an individual might conflict with that of the whole.

> It is impossible for the city to be happy as a whole unless all, or most, or some, of the parts are happy. Happiness is not like evenness, which can belong to the whole without belonging to either of the parts; this is impossible in the case of happiness. (*Pol.* II.5, 1264b17–22)

[20] See Miller, in Ch. 16 above, and Roberts 1989.

The happiness of the city is constituted by the happiness of the citizens. This explains why Aristotle is able to endorse the identification of the just with the lawful. It is the laws and practices of the city which ought to embody the proper conception of the final end. Laws ought to aim at the happiness of the city, which is to say the happiness of the citizens, which is to say the virtue of the citizens. The law then ought to demand justice, understood as complete virtue.

This deeply social conception of the person explains why Aristotle feels no need to justify the existence of the state, and why no individual rights, operating as a moral fence between the individual and the authority of the state, form any part of his theory of justice.[21] The proper end of the polis is the happiness of the citizens, not their mutual protection from harm. If the happiness of the citizens can only be truly attained if attained jointly, that is, if there is no such thing as genuinely individual happiness, then each necessarily has an interest in the good of the others. So each citizen has an essential interest in the virtue of the others. Aristotle seems to have thought that the only way to achieve, or try to achieve, this widespread virtue is by having the law demand it, and in general by having the polis educate its citizens. In any case, given the sort of interest any individual has in the virtue of others, as well as in his own, there would be no reason to object to moral education by the polis except on grounds of effectiveness. One needs also to add here that Aristotle includes in human virtue everything which contributes to a well-lived human life, in other words, every distinctively human activity can be performed virtuously or not. Thus can it seem obvious that law needs to speak to every facet of the citizens' lives.

4 Just individuals and just citizens

Given that Aristotle's virtues are the virtues of an essentially political creature, in other words, of one who is naturally a citizen of a polis, and that the law of a perfectly run city will demand complete virtue of its citizens, it is clear that in the absolutely ideal case the virtue of a man and that of a citizen will coincide. And indeed in the ideal case described in the final books of the *Politics* this is so. Nevertheless, in normal, non-ideal cases the connection is more complicated.

> Just as a sailor is one member of a community, so too do we say is the citizen. Insofar as sailors differ in capacity (for one is a rower, one a pilot,

[21] See Barnes 1990 and Sorabji 1990. For the claim that Aristotle had a conception of citizen, if not natural, rights, see Miller 1995.

> one a lookout, and another has yet another name of this kind), it is clear that the most accurate account of the virtue of each will be peculiar to each. Yet there is also a common account which fits all. For the preservation of the ship is the function of all of them; each of the sailors aims at this. The same holds for citizens. Although they are dissimilar, the preservation of the community is their function, and the constitution is the community. For this reason the virtue of a citizen is necessarily relative to the constitution. Since there are many forms of constitution, it is clear that there cannot be a single and complete virtue of the excellent citizen, but we do say that a man is good by having one virtue, which is complete. It is clear then that it is possible for someone to be an excellent citizen without possessing the virtue in accordance with which he would be an excellent man. (*Pol.* III.4, 1276b20–35)

The logic of the argument may be clear, but Aristotle never explains what he means in claiming that the virtue of a citizen is relative to the constitution. 'The constitution[22] (*politeia*) is the arrangement of those who inhabit the city' (III.1, 1274b38) or, more precisely, the 'arrangement concerned with the distribution of offices in cities, and with which element is to be authoritative, and with the nature of the end of each community' (IV.1, 1289a15–18). 'It is clear then that those constitutions which look to the common advantage are correct by the standard of the unqualifiedly just, any which look only to the advantage of the rulers err and are deviations from the correct constitutions' (III.6, 1279a17–20). The 'deviant' constitutions are later more bluntly dismissed as 'contrary to nature' (III.17, 1287b39–41). Constitutions are further divided into those ruled by one (kingship if correct, tyranny if deviant), by a few (aristocracy if correct, oligarchy if deviant), or by many (polity if correct, democracy if deviant) (III.7, 1279a32–b10).[23] Oligarchy and democracy are almost immediately redescribed as rule by the wealthy and the poor, rather than the few and the many (III.8, 1279b39–1280a3).

It is the political structure or constitution that defines any given polis. This is reflected in Aristotle's definition of a citizen as not merely one of the number who are required for self-sufficient living but as 'one who is entitled to participate in deliberative and judicial office' (III.1, 1275b18–19). Although Aristotle often uses the word 'citizen' in a broader

[22] 'Constitution' is the standard translation of *politeia*, but may have connotations absent in the Greek. A *politeia* is not a document, but the legal, and therefore social, structure or form of a polis.

[23] This classification in terms of the number of rulers is the first and the simplest classification of constitutions in the *Politics*. Further classifications and descriptions abound as Aristotle proceeds. See Rowe, in Ch. 18 below.

sense so that it includes all free native males,[24] by the strict definition a far greater part of the population will count as citizens in a polity or democracy than do in a kingship or tyranny, which on this account will have only a single citizen. Nevertheless, insofar as the polis is identified as the polis by the arrangement of offices and the end for which they are employed, that is, by its constitution, it is clear that it is those who hold those offices who determine the nature of the polis. That is, the citizens, in the narrower and stricter sense, are that segment of the population which determines the actual character of a given city.

What then makes someone a good citizen in a particular constitution? Being a good citizen is said to be a matter of preserving the constitution (III.4, 1276b28–9), so what is the difference between acting so as to preserve an oligarchy and acting so as to preserve an aristocracy? One might naturally think that one preserves an oligarchy, if one is wealthy and so exercises power, by exercising that power in one's own interest and that of one's wealthy peers, and if one is poor and without power by obeying the wealthy and powerful. That is, one does what one can to preserve the constitutional form of the city. In an aristocracy this would mean exercising power, if one is virtuous, for the common good, or obeying the virtuous if one is not virtuous oneself.

The good man, as described in the *Nicomachean Ethics*, will be a person of firmly established virtuous character, who will have all of the individual virtues, and who will therefore reliably choose good action for its own sake due to his possession of practical wisdom (*phronēsis*), which is the capacity to correctly discern the good both for oneself and for men in general (*EN*.VI.5, 1140b7–11). This is not, by Aristotle's own admission, a state of character easily attained, even under the best of political conditions. In the ideal city, which aims successfully at instilling virtue in all the citizens, who then take turns performing political tasks, it is clear that being a good citizen will be the same as being a good man. The virtue of all the citizens is what makes this the ideal city.

In the 'correct' or just constitutions, kingship, aristocracy, and polity, complete virtue will not be needed in all the citizens, since some will need only to obey and not need the virtue required for ruling. In a polity, even those who rule, although they do it justly (for the common good), are not

[24] See Newman 1887–1902: I, 570, and Cooper 1990: 228. Both the description of the polis as the number of citizens required for a self-sufficient life, and the distinction between correct and deviant constitutions, which assumes that someone other than the ruler or rulers have interests to be served, suggest that Aristotle did not consistently think of citizens as he narrowly defines them.

persons of full Aristotelian virtue. So it is clear that even in the just forms of constitution being a good citizen does not require being a good man. In the deviant forms of constitution it looks quite different, since it appears that not only does one not need to be fully virtuous to be a good citizen, but that being a good citizen requires that one act contrary to virtue. If the virtue of an oligarch is ruling in his own interest and mistreating the poor, then clearly an oligarch must be unjust in order to be a good citizen of his polis.

The matter may, however, be more complicated than this, for there is a question about whether, for example, the virtue of an oligarch, the state of character or kind of behaviour which preserves that form of constitution, really is simply a matter of ruling in one's own interest to the detriment of the ruled. Aristotle's lengthy later discussion of how to preserve various types of political structure certainly suggests otherwise. While insisting that citizens need to be educated relative to the constitution, he also notes that educating someone in a way which will contribute to the preservation of an oligarchy will be educating them not to wallow in luxury but to treat the poor justly and decently (v.9, 1310a22–5; v.8, 1308a3–11). In other words, deviant constitutions are preserved only by moving them toward justice. The extreme case is tyranny, the worst of the deviant constitutions. The tyrant who follows Aristotle's advice for preserving his power, and who would then have the virtue appropriate to that sort of constitution, is barely recognizable by the end.

> As a result of these things he will necessarily not only have a finer and more enviable reign in virtue of ruling over better people, who will not be beaten down, and will accomplish this without being feared and hated, but his reign will be longer, and moreover, with respect to his own character he will either be virtuous or half virtuous, not wicked but only half wicked. (v.11, 1315b4–10)

All of this suggests that in an unjust constitution the virtue of a citizen may not lie in aping the injustice of the constitution, but in at least behaving in a manner consistent with genuine justice. This will, of course, not amount to genuine justice, as long as it is just behaviour engaged in purely in an attempt to maintain a position of power.[25]

If this is right, then it is not so obvious as has sometimes been thought[26] that genuine virtue is incompatible with good citizenship in a deviant constitution. Was Socrates prevented by his virtue from being a

[25] For two different views about Aristotle's intentions in discussing the preservation of deviant regimes, and of the substance of his recommendations to their rulers, see Rowe 1977 (1991) and Irwin 1988: 457–60. [26] Newman 1887–1902: III, 155.

good citizen of Athens? This certainly does not follow from the fact that it is possible to be a good citizen without being a good man, since that may be explained by the weaker requirements for good citizenship in less than perfect constitutions. It would only follow if being a good citizen in a less than perfect city required states of character inconsistent with real virtue. Aristotle does suggest that stability requires that those who hold office be friendly toward the established system (v.3, 1303a14–20; v.9, 1309a33–5). If this means that the citizens need to believe that the constitution of their city is genuinely just, then this would be impossible for the perfectly virtuous who would see any deviant arrangement as deviant and unjust. Nevertheless, they might well believe, as presumably Aristotle thought the wise would, since it seems to be his own view, that change or revolution is not the answer and that political stability has its own worth. Thus they might have a sort of limited affection for the present arrangement however defective it might be in some absolute sense. Indeed it is part of the practice of practical and political wisdom to do the best that can be done under the circumstances with which one is presented (iv.1, 1288b21–1289a25).

If, however, the virtue of a citizen in a deviant constitution, properly understood, is really an aping of genuine justice, and so compatible with genuine justice, this gives rise to yet another question, which Aristotle does not answer.[27] For now it looks as though the virtue of a citizen could conflict, at least prima facie, with the laws of a particular city, since actual law will not always be aimed correctly at the preservation of the constitution. The issue may not arise for Aristotle simply because he is, in speaking of the virtue of a citizen, thinking mainly of citizens as those who rule, rather than as those who are ruled and must obey. It is also possible that he says nothing about it because there is nothing to be said of a general nature.

In any case, the main point of the discussion of the relation between the virtue of a man and that of a citizen is surely to emphasize again the importance of the common good to individual good. Only in a city which aims at the common good, ruled by men of practical wisdom, will genuine virtue and therefore genuine happiness be cultivated. There is something lacking in any city in which one can be a good citizen without being a good man. Plato had assumed that even in the best of political arrangements not all the citizens would be fully virtuous, even if all were perfect as citizens. Aristotle allows that constitutions can be correct or just even if full moral virtue is not required of all, since the rulers' aiming at the

[27] Mulgan 1977: 57 and Robinson 1962 (1995): 14.

common good ensures that the city as a whole is aiming at the proper end of cities, and those who rule do not treat the non-ruling citizens unfairly. But not all constitutions which are just are perfect, because not every citizen will be living a life of full virtue.

5 Justice and the distribution of power in the city

Having divided constitutions broadly into the just and unjust on the basis of whether or not those in power aim at the common good or only their own, Aristotle goes on to discuss the other defining feature of a constitution, who holds power and office. This is for him a question of distributive justice. The difficult question about distribution always has to do with the correct standard of worth to be employed in distributing goods in proportion to worth. It is easy enough to say that those of equal worth should get equal amounts of whatever good is being distributed, the arguments, as Aristotle notes, are about what constitutes equal worth.

Deviant constitutions do this incorrectly, and Aristotle goes to some pains to explain how the most common of these, democracies, which grant power to the poor majority, and oligarchies, which grant power to the wealthy minority, go wrong.

> Democracy arose from those who are equal in a certain respect thinking themselves equal simply or without qualification (for because all are similarly free they take themselves to be equal without qualification), and oligarchy from assuming that being unequal with respect to one thing they are unequal simply or without qualification (for being unequal in wealth they assume themselves to be unequal generally). (v.1, 1301a28–33)

The error here is also described as one of speaking of justice only of a kind, or up to a certain point, while taking oneself to be speaking of justice without qualification (III.9, 1280a9–11; 21–2). The error is not in the belief that there is real equality or inequality where the respective parties believe there is. The error lies in thinking that this kind of equality or inequality is what should count for purposes of distribution of political office, or in other words, in taking these as the only respects of equality or inequality that might be relevant to that question. Moreover, Aristotle suggests, neither party has offered any justification for the implicit claim that freedom or wealth is all that counts for these purposes.

> They say nothing about what is most important here. If they formed a community and joined together for the sake of possessions, then they

> would share in the city to the exact extent that they share in wealth. If this were so, then the argument of the oligarchs would seem to have some weight, for it would not be just if someone contributing one mina were to share equally in a hundred with one who had contributed all the rest. (III.9, 1280a25–30)

They fail, in proposing their particular claims, to look to the nature and end of the community to be ruled in determining who should rule.

Aristotle later repeats the point by insisting that not every kind of equality or inequality can constitute a reasonable claim to political power. If anything at all could count then we would have the ridiculous situation of height or good complexion counting as grounds for political power. Two important points follow. One, there cannot be different kinds of pre-eminence appealed to because one needs something commensurable if one is to weigh different claims. Two, the characteristic appealed to must be relevant to the dispute. Flutes are only reasonably given to those who will play them well, and not to the handsome or the well born, even if the handsome or well born are more handsome or well born than the flute players are talented. 'For it is necessary that pre-eminence in wealth or birth contribute to the task or function (*ergon*), but they contribute nothing' (III.12, 1283a1–3). The flute example establishes only that the sort of characteristic to be used as the standard of worth for the distribution of a good must be one which is somehow relevant to the nature of that good. It is in some ways too simplistic an example for the case at hand, since flutes are not honours distributed by the community. Thus Aristotle does not infer from it, as one might expect and as he has often been taken as doing,[28] that political office should go to those who have talent for ruling, that is, those of political virtue, because they have talent for ruling. He claims at this point only that any reasonable sort of claim to political rule must centre on features which are part of the polis.

> In these matters a claim has to be made by reference to the constituents of the polis. Thus the well born and the free and the wealthy have a reasonable claim to honour. For there have to be freemen and those paying assessments (for there could not be a polis entirely constituted by the poor, just as there could not be a polis of slaves). But if these are necessary, clearly justice and military[29] virtue are as well. For a city cannot be administered without them. Whereas without the former there can be no polis, without the latter it cannot be administered well. (III.12, 1283a14–22)

28 Newman 1887–1902: I, 250, Keyt 1991a: 248, Irwin 1988: 428.

29 This is what most of the manuscripts have, a few have 'political' instead.

The point here is not that the free, wealthy and virtuous all have equal claims to honour, which would be ruled out on grounds of incommensurability in any case. They are, nevertheless, all able to make the right sort of appeal, since each can claim to make an essential contribution to the functioning of the polis. This is a very different sort of claim on behalf of the wealthy and the free than the simple-minded and often criticized claim that merely being equal in freedom, or being unequal in substance, gives one a legitimate claim to political office. The principle here is that those characteristics which make one a necessary part of the city, in virtue of which one contributes to the overall functioning of the city, give one a claim on political honour or authority.[30] To the extent that the end of the city is living well the virtuous have the strongest claim, to the extent that the end of the city is simply to live or to preserve itself, the wealthy and the free have claims as well (III.13, 1283a23–6). Of course, since the true end of the polis is not simply living, the claims of the virtuous will trump those of the merely wealthy or free.

> The city is a community of families and villages for the sake of a complete and self-sufficient life. And this is, as we claim, living happily and well. Therefore one ought to say that the political community is for the sake of good actions rather than for living together. For this reason those who contribute most to such a community have a greater part in the city than those equal or greater in freedom or birth but unequal in political virtue and also than those who, while exceeding in wealth, are exceeded in virtue. (III.9, 1280b40–1281a8)

Thus it is virtue which constitutes the standard of worth or merit according to which political functions or tasks in the city are to be distributed. The discussion about appropriate sorts of claims also suggests, however, that were there to be a city without any virtuous persons or without enough to fill political offices, in which case living well would not be a viable aim, the wealthy and the free would then have reasonable claims on the basis of their contribution to the lesser end of simply living.

One might well think that this settles the matter and indeed this is, in outline, Aristotle's answer to the question about what the appropriate criterion of worth ought to be. There is, however, a puzzle (*aporia*) which

30 In terms of self-sufficiency there could not be a city without slaves either, or some people to perform the tasks like farming that Aristotle thinks are, in the ideal city, to be performed by slaves (VII.9, 1328b33–1329a2). This is because he thinks that certain kinds of work exclude the full development of virtue, and therefore happiness, and does not want to allow, in the ideal case, that not all the citizens can be perfectly happy (VII.9, 1329a19–24). The problem is neatly, if speciously, avoided by refusing to count all who are necessary to the existence of the city as part of the city (VII.8, 1328a21–37).

he thinks needs to be resolved (III.10, 1281a11). It is possible, he thinks, to make any claim look suspicious. In a democracy, the many poor have authority and use it for their own advantage and to the disadvantage of the wealthy minority. This will be just in the narrow sense of being lawful, but it can hardly be real justice, or virtue of any kind, since it is bound to destroy the city, and virtue cannot be destructive of what it is the virtue of (III.10, 1281a19–20). Moreover, the principle implicit here, that the stronger may compel the weaker, would justify tyranny. Nor would things be any different if the original scenario is reversed and the wealthy minority has power over the poor majority. All of this is simply another mode of attack on regimes or constitutions already and fairly easily established as incorrect and unjust; what it emphasizes is that any just distribution must be one which tends to the preservation of the city and not to its destruction. The further difficulty introduced here is that there seems to be a similar problem for rule by the good or decent (*epieikeis*) or by a single person who is the best. If the same minority of persons, or worse, the same person, has authority over everything all the time the others will be left without office and therefore without honour (*atimoi*). Aristotle insists in a number of places that those who have no authority at all will be enemies of the constitution, and presumably then insofar as this suggests instability in the arrangement it also points to injustice.[31] Instability is only a symptom of injustice; it is not said to constitute or explain injustice. So the question is what could be wrong with these cases of distributing honour in accordance with virtue, which was supposed to be the proper criterion of worth for just distribution of political office.

The resolution of the puzzle comes in the form of an ingenious argument, but one which perhaps came naturally to someone with Aristotle's dialectical methodology.

> The many, none of whom is individually an excellent man, may nevertheless when joined together be better than those who are virtuous, not as individuals but as a group, just as dinners to which many contribute can be better than those provided by a single expenditure. For, being many, each may have a part of virtue and practical wisdom, and when they are joined together the multitude becomes like a single man, having many feet and many hands and many senses, and so too in connection with

[31] The destabilizing effect of leaving many without honour is mentioned in a number of places. The point is attributed to Solon at II.12, 1274a15–18, and explicitly endorsed by Aristotle at III.11, 1281b28–30. Book V, which discusses civil conflict (*stasis*), identifies the perception of injustice which inevitably accompanies leaving many without office as a prime cause. See Rowe, in Ch. 18 below.

> character and thought. This is why the many are better judges of musical works and the works of the poets, for different ones understand different parts, and all together understand the whole. (III.11, 1281a42–1281b10)

If the partial virtue of many individuals may, when added to that of all the others, outweigh that of a virtuous individual, this will justify, not allowing any of them as individuals to hold office, but allowing the group, as a group, to share in deliberating and judging (III.11, 1281b31). If then virtue is to be taken as the characteristic which grounds a reasonable claim to political honour, certain groups may have at least as strong a claim as virtuous individuals. Thus, although virtue is the standard by which claims to office are to be judged, that fact in and of itself may do rather little to settle questions of just distribution in particular cities with particular populations. The virtue of a small group of virtuous men, who as such would be deserving of rule in an aristocracy, might be outweighed by either that of the multitude or that of a particularly outstanding individual (III.13, 1283b14–35).

That, of course, still leaves things somewhat unclear. Virtue has the strongest claim, since the end of living well to which it contributes is a higher end than that of simply living to which wealth and freedom contribute. In the ideal polis all citizens will be virtuous (and free and wealthy enough). In actual cities virtue tends to be rare and does not necessarily overlap with wealth, and thus just distribution of office in real life will be far more difficult to determine. The virtuous, whether as individuals or groups, may get the first claim, but what happens after that remains mysterious at this point. What Aristotle has done is suggest the sort of claim which is reasonable, but there is no way to establish in advance how the just distribution will go in particular cases, without looking at particular cities and their particular citizens. Just such an inquiry occupies the following books of the *Politics*.

Complications and difficulties in the application of Aristotle's principle aside, it should be clear by now that Aristotle had a coherent and original conception of political justice. Although his just polis resembles Plato's in putting the virtuous in positions of power, Aristotle's reasons for doing this are importantly different. Having criticized Plato for looking to the happiness of the city as a whole instead of the happiness of individual citizens, Aristotle was not inclined to make the justice of assignments of political tasks hang directly on the smooth functioning of the city as a whole. It is not the undeniable fact that the virtuous will do the best job of performing an important civic function, and thereby play a useful role in a well-run city, that makes Aristotle argue for their having political power. In making the assignment of political tasks a matter of distributive justice, Aristotle is admitting that these roles are more than component parts of the joint function which constitutes the life of any city. Political office, as anyone from as far back as Homeric times could have attested, was an honour (*timē*), a naturally desirable social good. Aristotle's important addition to the picture comes with his insistence that that honour be given to those who deserve it and in his providing a reasoned criterion for determining desert. The justice of a political structure has become, in Aristotle, a matter of fairness to individual citizens.

18

Aristotelian constitutions

CHRISTOPHER ROWE

1 Introduction: the nature of the *Politics*

One of the chief problems about discussing any aspect of Aristotle's political thought, but especially his thinking about constitutions, is the apparent disorder of the *Politics*.[1] The relatively loose and dialectical nature of the argument is certainly responsible for some of its unevenness: the repetitions, the omissions of promised discussions of particular topics, and the sudden turns, perhaps as the focus changes between two opposing series of reflections. But even when all of this is taken into account, it is hard not to conclude that at least some of the larger pieces do not quite fit together. This fact is reflected in the old fashion, begun in the nineteenth century, for placing Books VII and VIII after the end of Book III.[2] Books VII and VIII contain a treatment of the 'best constitution'; since the end of Book III, as it stands, promises one, there seem to be good grounds for allowing that promise to be fulfilled. Yet this easy solution turns out to cause as many problems as it resolves, since not only do Books IV–VI turn out to contain more backward references to III than VII and VIII, but IV–VI are a considerably more inappropriate sequel to VII–VIII than they are to III. In that case, the most that can be said is that VII and VIII might once, in some different *Politics*, have followed Book III.

A second solution, sometimes combined with the first, is to explain the anomalies of the text by introducing the hypothesis of an evolution in Aristotle's thinking about politics. According to one version of this hypothesis,[3] Books II–III and VII–VIII represent an early, utopian stratum in the *Politics*, IV–VI a later 'empirical' one; what we call the *Politics* would in this case represent an uneasy combination of elements from different phases of Aristotle's philosophical career. According to this view, he moves away from a Platonic preoccupation with ideal constitutions, and becomes more interested in the kinds of issues that relate directly to the

[1] This chapter is intended as a fresh approach to the issues; in the event, its outcome turns out to be encouragingly close in many respects to the conclusions reached in Kahn 1990 and Fortenbaugh 1991. [2] So e.g. Newman 1887–1902. [3] Jaeger 1948.

realities of political life. When he complains that 'most of those who write about constitutions, even if everything else they say is fine enough, fail to hit on those things that are of practical use' (*Pol.* IV.1, 1288b35–7), he is allegedly also marking out his attitude to his own earlier practice.

However Aristotle himself, in the same context, clearly says that writing about the 'best absolutely' and saying what is 'of practical use' are not only compatible, but are actually both to be properly regarded as parts of the business of political philosophy. There is no sign of his supposing that the second somehow replaces the first. Indeed, they are for Aristotle in practice as well as in theory *complementary*, insofar as the ideal serves as a standard for judging the actual. Although – as we shall see – there are some problems about exactly how it can fulfil this role, these problems are not resolved by the hypothesis that the construction of the best state came first, since it is hard to see what the point is of thinking about what the best political arrangements would be unless this is supposed to have some consequences or other for our thinking about how things actually are.

Of course, the consequence might just be to suggest the necessity of abandoning all existing arrangements, and substituting others. This usually seems to be the view taken by Plato, whose descriptions of 'best constitutions' – whether first-best, as in the *Republic*, or second-best, as in the *Laws* (the 'second city') – are accompanied by the explicit suggestion that any other sort of arrangement (unless perhaps it is some kind of approximation to the best) will be no constitution at all. In that case, unless the best constitutes a set of immediately practicable proposals, as it evidently does not (and is not intended to do, even in the case of the 'second-best'), we might seem to be left with no way forward. Here Plato perhaps gives grounds enough for Aristotle's generalized complaint about others who write about constitutions, that they say nothing 'of practical use'; though a more generous, and probably more accurate, reading would be that the cities of the *Republic* and the *Laws* are meant to provide models, to which societies would approximate by selecting, modifying and adapting the 'ideal' institutions and laws in accordance with the prevailing conditions. (Nevertheless, insofar as that would evidently require rethinking from the ground up, it would probably still count, from Aristotle's point of view, as 'lacking in practical use'.) Aristotle's own recommendations, as we shall see, may be seen in part as an explicit working out of this process, except that in his case what would be involved would be the *reform* of existing institutions.[4] If so, the relationship between the 'empirical' parts

[4] In this sense, Aristotle advocates *starting from where we are now*, in a way that Plato does not; and this is an important difference.

of the *Politics* and 'utopian' thinking of some sort (even if not of the sort that is actually reflected in Books VII–VIII) should be rather close. Chronological and biographical hypotheses about the work will be irrelevant, except perhaps to explain how its still somewhat ill-fitting parts came to be sewn, or tacked, together.

2 Aristotle and Plato

Even a cursory comparison of the *Politics* with Plato's *Republic*, *Politicus* and *Laws* is sufficient to demonstrate the very close connections between Aristotle's political thinking and Plato's. It is not just that Aristotle frequently criticizes Plato (more often than not, without mentioning him by name), nor that his larger programme in the *Politics* seems in part determined by his predecessor's (see section 1 above); the very development of individual arguments, and of treatment of particular topics, often resembles a conversation with Plato as a silent partner. This is nowhere more true than in the case of the topic of constitutions.

In Plato's most systematic treatment of constitutions, in the *Politicus*, they are divided into three broad types, each with two sub-types. Cities could be governed by one person, by a few people, or by many; and in each case the sovereign body could either adhere to established law, or they could operate on the basis of what they happened to think best from day to day. In the absence not only of the ideal, knowledgeable statesman, but also of any procedure for arriving at a set of consistently good laws (insofar as any such procedure must depend upon knowledge), even a city which took the option of governing itself according to law would rest on the most insecure of foundations; but this would be better – or at least less bad – than the alternative, of saying goodbye to law and operating according to the preferences and whims of those in power.

It is part of this (highly dialectical) context in the *Politicus* that Aristotle seems to have in mind in the following passage from Book IV of the *Politics*. He has previously said that there are three 'correct' forms of constitution, namely kingship, aristocracy, and a form he calls, and says others call, *politeia*, which is also, puzzlingly and often confusingly, the word in Greek usually translated as 'constitution'. (For the time being, I shall refer to this third form by simply transliterating it, in fairly traditional fashion, as 'polity', reserving specific discussion of its name for later, when the main features of the type have been described.) Each of these three 'right' forms of constitution has its own corresponding 'deviant' form (*parekbasis*), and Aristotle is now arranging the latter in order:

> Of these deviant forms, it is evident which is the worst, and which of them is the second worst. The deviant form of the first and the most divine must necessarily be the worst, and kingship must either have only the name without the substance, or exist by reason of the great superiority of the person occupying the kingship. Thus tyranny must be the worst, and at the furthest remove of all the deviant forms from being a [true] constitution [or, alternatively, 'from a polity'[5]], oligarchy the next worst (for oligarchy is a very different thing from aristocracy), and democracy the most moderate. In fact one of our predecessors has also expressed the same view, but as a result of looking to a different criterion. His judgment was that if all of them were of a moderate and reasonable sort (*epieikēs*), I mean if there were a good oligarchy, or a good example of the other types, democracy was worst, and if they were all bad, democracy was best. But our view is that these constitutions [by which Aristotle seems to mean primarily oligarchy and democracy] are wholly mistaken, and that it is not appropriate to say that one oligarchy is better than another, but only that it is less bad. (IV.2, 1289a38–b11)

Not for the first or the last time, Aristotle's account of Plato (who is surely the 'predecessor' in question) is less than wholly accurate, since although Plato does use the term 'best' as well as 'worst' in his comparison between constitutions, his position on what Aristotle calls the 'deviant forms' is substantially the same as Aristotle's own: they are all 'faction-states' rather than constitutions.[6] However Aristotle's identification of three 'right' constitutions is a new departure.

For the Plato of the *Politicus*, the only constitution worthy of the name is the one ruled by knowledge in the shape of the ideal king or statesman. This would have the same name as, but would be quite distinct from, ordinary, law-bound, kingship – itself, of course, to be distinguished from tyranny, which is supposed to operate without laws. Rule by a few people which is strictly according to established law is called 'aristocracy', while if it pays no attention to law, it is simply 'oligarchy' (though in fact both are clearly treated as cases of rule by the few *rich*); between the two types of 'rule by many', i.e. the type under which law rules and the type under which it does not, there is no distinction of name, both being called 'democracy'. Since under all six of these constitutions apart from ideal

[5] So Sinclair 1962 (1981), and Saunders in his revision of Sinclair, though it is not clear that the argument will have justified *this* conclusion.

[6] For a less ambiguous division of monarchy, oligarchy and democracy into good and bad forms, see Isocrates, *Panathenaicus* 130–3: a 'good' constitution, of whatever type, is one in which the best people rule, with a view to the advantage of the city rather than to their own private gain (cf. *On the Peace* 91).

monarchy rule is exercised in the interests of the rulers (which is what Plato means by calling them 'faction-states', or *stasiōteiai*), Aristotle proceeds in effect to lump each pair together, and contrast them with his three 'correct' constitutions, which are 'correct' precisely in that they do what constitutions are supposed to do. 'If a city is a kind of community [a *koinōnia*, a group with something in common or shared, *koinon*, between its members], and if it is a sharing in common [*koinōnia* again] by citizens in a constitution . . .' (III.3, 1276b1–2): Aristotle is plainly committed to both premises, and they provide the basis of his notion of 'deviant forms'.

> It is therefore evident that all those constitutions which consider what is to the common advantage are correct constitutions, as judged in terms of what is just absolutely [i.e. as opposed to what is merely just according to some partisan notion of justice]; whereas those that consider only what is to the personal advantage of those in power are all mistaken, and deviant forms of the correct constitutions. For such deviant forms are despotic, and the city is a community of the free. (III.6, 1279a17–21)[7]

The preceding discussion has just ended on the subject of offices, and of how some people like to hold on to them because of the profit they bring: since a 'constitution' is, or is expressed particularly in, an 'arrangement of offices' (e.g. IV.2, 1289a15–16), a 'deviant' constitution will be one in which 'offices' (including assembly and courts) are arranged and used for purposes other than the good of the whole. Under (Aristotelian) kingship and aristocracy, and the special constitutional form called 'polity', by contrast, they will be put to proper use.

Aristotle is by and large content to work with this new scheme of six constitutions, and Books III–VI are mainly built around it. But as soon becomes clear, it is a fairly rough and ready division. There turn out to be many different varieties of oligarchy, and of democracy, some of which border on ('so-called') aristocracy and polity. Again, polity is frequently described as a mixture of democracy and oligarchy. There is also the question of where, if anywhere, the (absolutely) best constitution fits in: sometimes it seems to be identified with kingship and aristocracy (see III.18, 1288a32–b2; IV.2, 1289a31–3; IV.3, 1290a24–8), yet the constitution described in Books VII and VIII cannot immediately be identified with either of these, since it is a case neither of rule by one individual nor of rule

[7] A 'correct' constitution, then, will be a just one; but it will be just insofar as it does not treat those who are free and equal (1279b8–13), and so deserve a share in the constitution, as slaves, ruled for the benefit of their masters (1278a32–7). But the question then is: who is to count as a full member of the community? Aristotle's own answer to this question, in the context of the ideal constitution of Books VII–VIII, itself turns out to reintroduce a kind of despotism (see esp. VII.8, and section 7 below).

by a few. Nor can *this* 'best constitution' be meant to be the same as polity, in that it, like kingship and aristocracy, distributes office on the basis of individual excellence, which polity does not. But that in itself means that there will be a radical difference between the first two and the third of the 'right' constitutions. Aristotle seems to recognize this:

> It remains for us to discuss what is called 'polity' and tyranny. We have located our treatment of 'polity' here [i.e. alongside tyranny] even though neither it nor the sorts of aristocracy we have just discussed [and associated with it] are deviant forms of constitution, because strictly speaking all these constitutions fall short of the most correct constitution, and so too they come to be counted with these [sc. deviant forms proper], and [at the same time] these [deviant forms] are deviant forms of them [sc. insofar as they are 'correct'] . . . (IV.8, 1293b22–6)

So polity, from another point of view, can actually be classed as 'deviant'. The immediate task is to understand how the same thing can apparently receive both of two contrary descriptions.[8]

3 Kingship, aristocracy and polity

The starting point is that polity, broadly defined as 'rule by the many which considers what is to the common advantage', is both like and unlike the other two 'correct' constitutions. It is like them just insofar as they too, of course, are concerned with the common good (and actually realize it), but unlike them insofar as it does not distribute office primarily according to merit or 'virtue'. So, for example, Aristotle associates the polity with a 'hoplite' constitution, i.e. one in which citizenship is restricted to those with the resources to equip themselves with heavy arms (II.6, 1265b26–9; III.7, 1279a37–b4; III.17, 1288a12–15). This criterion has to do with wealth rather than any sort of virtue (cf. IV.7, 1293b7–12), even if soldiers, hoplites, are supposed to have one particular sort of 'virtue', namely the military sort. (The passage in III.17 – with which we may compare e.g. IV.7, 1293b20–1 – does in fact refer to 'distribut[ion of] offices among the wealthy according to merit [virtue, *aretē*]', but even here property, and not virtue, is the primary consideration, insofar as it determines citizenship itself.) The same conclusion follows even more directly if polity is to be regarded – as Aristotle repeatedly suggests elsewhere – as a 'mixture' of oligarchy and democracy, since as such its essential feature will be just that it balances the claims and interests of the rich and the poor.

[8] For the question, and for the answer to be offered, cf. Fortenbaugh 1991: 235–7.

Now this is an absolutely crucial difference between polity and the other two so-called 'correct constitutions', because virtue or excellence enters into Aristotle's account of the city, the fundamental political unit, itself. As he says almost at the very beginning of the *Politics* (I.2, 1252b29–30), 'while [the city] comes into existence for the sake of life [i.e. to enable its citizens to survive], it exists for the sake of a good life', and the good life (as we are reminded by IV.11) is the life of Aristotelian virtue, as described in the *Ethics*. The absolutely best constitution will be the one – like that of Books VII and VIII – which not merely distributes power according to degree of virtue, but actually has the production of virtue in its citizens as its chief purpose. As we shall see, kingship and aristocracy, as they appear in the list of 'correct' constitutions, are probably ultimately to be treated merely as species of the absolutely best constitution, insofar as they possess both relevant features (distribution of power according to merit, and systematic concern for the quality of the citizens and their life); polity, by contrast – usually, if (as we have seen) not quite always – has neither, and so will 'fall short' of the best. It is on these grounds that IV.8 declared it to be a 'deviant' form ('strictly speaking all these constitutions fall short of the most correct constitution, and so too they come to be counted with [the deviant forms] . . .').

Yet at the same time, and from a different perspective, a polity is a 'correct' constitution, just insofar as it 'considers the common advantage'. The goal or *telos* of the political community is the life of virtue; and according to one well-known Aristotelian principle, it is the *telos* of a thing which defines what it essentially is. In that polity falls short of this, it will fail to be a true political community (or will be 'deviant', in the literal sense of the Greek word *parekbasis*: it sets out, as it were, for the appropriate destination, but goes off the road). But Aristotle is unwilling to say this (it is not a deviant form, he firmly asserted in IV.8, even if there is a way in which, 'strictly speaking', or 'in truth', it is), just as he does not say, in the *Ethics*, that most human beings are not really human beings because they do not achieve the human 'end', even to the degree to which they are capable of it. For one thing, political science would then be in danger of becoming purely theoretical, and, as he declared at the beginning of Book IV, it is part of its business to say something which is practical and useful. But in any case, if it is true of a polity that it 'considers', aims at, the common advantage (III.6, 1279a17–18), then it will genuinely overlap with the 'most correct' constitution; it can even in a sense be said to have the same aim as the best constitution ('the common advantage'), which it has simply misidentified. (Similarly, on the individual level, all human beings desire what is genuinely good, though most of us are satisfied with what merely appears so.) In this way, the identification of the city – and therefore of its constitution, as its mode of organization – with the achievement of 'a good life' becomes a kind of limiting case, and the true 'deviants' will be just those constitutions that fail to live up to the idea of a community at all.

A constitution can, then, be 'correct' while also 'falling short'. Kingship and aristocracy, for their part, do not fall short at all. But they arise, or are appropriately instituted, only in the most exceptional circumstances:

> We must first determine to what [sets of circumstances] a kingship, an aristocracy and a polity are appropriate. The sort of people [the Greek has the term *plēthos*, which at bottom indicates an indeterminate plurality; here 'a population'] that is suited for kingship is one that is naturally such as to produce (*pherein*)[9] a family outstanding in virtue in relation to political leadership;[10] the sort (*plēthos*) that is suited for aristocratic rule is one which is naturally such as to produce (*pherein*) a collection of people (*plēthos*) capable of being ruled, in the mode that belongs to free men, by those qualified by virtue to lead in relation to political rule; and the sort (*plēthos*) that is suited for polity (*politikon*) is one in which there naturally exists a collection (*plēthos*) of citizens [or, with a different manuscript reading, 'a people of warlike ability'] capable of ruling and being ruled according to a law which distributes the offices to the well-to-do on the basis of merit. So when there turns out to be a whole family, or else some individual among the rest, that possesses such outstanding virtue that it surpasses the virtue of everyone else [i.e. taken together[11]], then it is just that this family should be vested with kingship and be sove-

[9] For the translation of the verb adopted here, see Newman 1887–1902: I.290. There are serious problems about the passage as a whole, which induce despair in some commentators (e.g. Schütrumpf 1991), but it seems just about possible to make sense of it.

[10] I.e. possessing the outstanding virtue which would qualify them for (monarchic) rule: see e.g. III.13, 1284b25–34, IV.2, 1289b1. 'Political' leadership, or rule, is presumably that which treats the subjects as free rather than slaves (see n.7 above); there is clearly no reference in this case to 'ruling and being ruled by turn' (see Schofield, Ch. 15, pp. 318–19 above). The 'sort of people' that 'naturally produces' a kingly family is perhaps one in which there is a permanently unequal distribution of the capacity for virtue (cf. III.18, 1288a39–b2); similarly in the case of an 'aristocratic' sort of people. But both sorts must apparently also be virtuous: see below.

[11] The possibility of *adding together* the individual excellences of a large body of people has been introduced in III.11, and must be what is in Aristotle's mind here, since it has just been said (1287b41–1288a5) that monarchy will be 'neither just nor expedient' if the monarch is merely *better* than his subjects ('excels them in virtue': see below). This interpretation seems to be confirmed by 1288a26–8, which rejects the possibility that the outstanding individual in question should merely share in ruling on the grounds that 'it is not of the nature of the part to exceed the whole, and this is what will have turned out for someone who exceeds to such a degree' (sc. if he is ruled by anyone else).

reign over all, and that this one individual should be king . . .' (III.17, 1288a6–15)

This passage constitutes a kind of rider to a long discussion of the question whether it is ever justified for a single outstanding individual to rule in place of laws. While the whole context strongly recalls a similar discussion in Plato's *Politicus*, and probably in large part starts from it, the tone, and outcome, of Aristotle's argument are rather different.

It is a highly dialectical argument, which now puts the case on one side, now the one on the other. Two important points, however, clearly emerge from it. The first is that Aristotle generally approaches the notion of ideal kingship from his perspective on the city as a community of *equals*.[12] From such a perspective, the outstanding individual may even be seen as problematic, even for 'correct' constitutions, namely those that 'consider the common good' (III.13, 1284b3–7).[13] This is a far cry indeed from Plato's presentation of the ideal king or statesman as *the* solution (if only on a theoretical level) to all political problems. Thus Aristotle's main conclusion to the whole discussion of kingship, which he announces just before the long passage last quoted above (from III.17), is that

> it is clear, at any rate from what has been said, that among those who are like and equal (whatever we may say of anyone else) it is neither expedient nor just that one individual should be sovereign over all, either when there are no laws, on the basis that he is himself [a kind of incarnate] law, or when there are laws, and whether he is a good man ruling over other good men, or whether neither he nor they are good, and not even if he excels them in virtue – except in a certain way. (III.17, 1287b41–1288a5)

That is, in normal circumstances monarchy will not be a good thing; and those normal circumstances involve especially a population which can be described as 'like and equal', whatever their level of moral attainment ('whether he is a good man ruling over other good men, or whether neither he nor they are good'). 1288a6–15 then explains the 'in a certain way' ('and not even if he excels them in virtue – except in a certain way'; though

[12] This typically Aristotelian perspective, in combination with the apparent validation of non-expert views in III.11 (see preceding note), gives sense to 'looking to Aristotle for a philosophy that recognizes communal "discourse" rather than "technical expertise" as constituting our political essence' (Newell 1991: 191, citing Beiner 1983, with Gadamer 1975); the case of kingship will turn out to be less damaging to this project than Newell suggests.

[13] It is not clear how it could be a problem for kingship, or for aristocracy, since these are actually ways of handling exceptional individuals. What Aristotle means is presumably just that such individuals are generally problematic even for those constitutions that actually do 'consider the common good'; but I shall suggest that in any case kingship and aristocracy, as described in Book III, are ultimately types of only marginal importance in Aristotle's scheme.

as Aristotle says at 1288a6, he has already explained it, 'in a way', before). There will be (exceptional) populations suited to kingship, and aristocracy, and in such cases virtue should be given its head – provided that it is so outstanding as to excel that of everyone else. The subjects will themselves be virtuous, or inclined towards 'the most choiceworthy life', i.e. the life of virtue (1288a36–7);[14] and that is perhaps what makes them 'capable of being ruled' by others, of the right kind.[15] That the subjects are of this sort means that kingship and aristocracy are 'expedient' in their case, and is also essential for Aristotle's treatment of kingship and aristocracy as forms of the best constitution, since the best constitution must be that which promotes the best life (see e.g. VII.1). But the primary condition of the appropriateness of kingship and aristocracy is the presence of quite exceptional virtue in one or more persons; otherwise it will not be just. (Merely to be better than others is not enough, because there are other competing criteria for the distribution of power. A godlike virtue, however, could have no competitors.)

Here we come to the second important point about the whole context of the latter part of Book III, which is a kind of corollary of the first point.[16] Aristotle's description of the conditions of ideal kingship seems to be necessitated by a continuing acceptance – at least from III.13 on – that it is appropriate for someone with (absolutely) outstanding virtue to rule, not to be subject to those inferior to himself (a point repeated in III.17 itself: 1288a19–28), even though his main argument tends towards the conclusion that perpetual monarchy, under most conditions, is not the right answer. As we have seen, he does not approach kingship, as Plato does, as something desirable in itself; nor in fact is it clear why he should *prefer* a situation in which one person was outstandingly better than everyone else. Rather, we should expect him to prefer, as an ideal, that everyone should be as good as possible (an idea, of course, which underlies the last part of the description of kingship and aristocracy in III.18).[17] The reason why Plato opts for ideal monarchy is that he insists on the need for *expertise*, which, he holds, is likely to be very rarely found (so that we shall be lucky to find any single person who has it, let alone a number of such

[14] I refer here to a part of another problematical sentence; but at least the part itself is reasonably clear.

[15] This specification is only explicitly made in the case of an 'aristocratic' people (1288a11–12), but it presumably also applies to one that is 'kingly'. The whole context suggests that aristocracy is a kind of variant of monarchy, with the rule of one person merely replaced by the rule of more than one (a few).

[16] See preceding page.

[17] 1288a36–7: 'with some capable of being ruled and others capable of ruling with a view to the most choiceworthy life'.

people). For Aristotle, by contrast, if there is such a thing as expertise in ruling, it will in the ideal case derive from virtue itself (thus e.g. in IV.13 outstanding virtue is paired with the possession of an equally outstanding 'political capacity': 1284a6–7, 9–10).[18] Since virtue is, at least in principle, a goal for all, the emergence of a single individual towering over all the rest might even count as a sign of the others' failure. But in any case, the final outcome of Aristotle's discussion is not in doubt: if such a person does arise, then he should be given sovereign power; otherwise monarchy is neither appropriate nor desirable.[19]

Evidently no actual examples of kingship or aristocracy (as described in III.17–18) do exist, although there are plenty of 'aristocracies so-called':

> But there are some further [forms of constitution] that show differences both in relation to those ruled oligarchically, and in relation to what is called 'polity', and are called aristocracies. Where office-holders are chosen with reference not only to wealth but also to virtue, this form of constitution is different from both the others and is called aristocratic. For in those [cities] which do not make the procurement of virtue [among the citizens] a matter or public concern, there is nevertheless a group of individuals who are those of good reputation, and who are counted as moderate and reasonable (*epieikeis*) . . . [Aristotle gives examples: Carthage, which 'pays regard to' virtue as well as wealth and the consent of the people, and Sparta, which takes into account the first and the third.] There are thus these two kinds of aristocracy alongside the first, [which is] the best constitution [presumably together with kingship]; and there is also a third kind, consisting of all those varieties of what is called polity which incline more towards oligarchy. (IV.7, 1293b6–21)

The form of polity which appears in III.17 – the 'hoplite' constitution,[20] which in many ways resembles, if it is not identical with, the so-called 'middle' constitution introduced in IV.11 – is probably also an idealized version of the general type. But that there are supposed to be close approximations to this idealized version in existence is surely not in

[18] Cf. *EN* VI.8, 1141b23–6, quoted by Schofield, Ch. 15, p. 311 above, and *Pol.* III.4–5. What is envisaged is very different from the kind of 'art of ruling' that Plato proposes, even apparently at the time of the writing of the *Politicus*, i.e. one based on philosophical knowledge: Aristotelian virtue is grounded in precept, habituation, and the growth of insight. The political expert may also be a theoretician like Aristotle himself, offering advice to those in the practical business of governing; his understanding – if Aristotle is to be consistent – presumably ought to mimic part of that possessed by the ideal politician. On the issues here see further Hutchinson 1988: 40–9, Newell 1991: 199–200; and, for the most extended treatment, Leszl 1989.

[19] On the implications of the conclusions reached here about Aristotelian kingship and aristocracy for the treatment of the 'best constitution' in Books VII–VIII, see section 6 below.

[20] See p. 371 above.

doubt (the last passage cited confirms, at least, that there are real 'varieties' of such a form of polity). The list of 'correct' constitutions thus combines one realizable type with two that are more remote, if not actually beyond the bounds of possibility. But the virtuous state, whether with one, or few, in control (or even many, as in the constitution of Books VII and VIII), remains as a model to remind Aristotle's readers of what a city *might* be, and in a better world would be. Moreover, the boundaries between types are sufficiently permeable, as the case of the 'so-called aristocracies' shows, to make that reminder useful, even despite the fact that the conditions needed for realization of the absolutely best are beyond human control. It is, after all, within the power of ordinary cities and legislators to introduce 'aristocratic' elements into existing systems, and so to recognize, to however limited an extent, what Aristotle regards as the (nearly) absolute claims of virtue.

That this is the kind of way his mind is working is confirmed, in a small way, by a passage in Book II, where he is discussing Plato's *Laws*:

> The whole arrangement tends to be neither a democracy nor an oligarchy, but a constitution intermediate between these, what they call a 'polity'; for it is made up from those who serve as hoplites. If his [sc. Plato's] notion in constructing this constitution is that it represents the one, of all constitutions, which is most accessible to cities, he may perhaps be right; but he is not right if he thinks of it as the best after the first [i.e. the 'first city', which is identified with the ideal city of the *Republic*]. For one might assign more praise to the constitution of the Spartans, or else some other more aristocratic constitution. (II.6, 1265b26–33)

This amounts to an even more cavalier treatment of Plato than usual, since the *Laws* for the most part describes precisely the sort of constitution which Aristotle himself wants to call aristocratic, that is, one founded on, and training its citizens in, virtue (as he must have known, since the similarities between *Politics* VII and VIII and the *Laws* are far too close to be accidental); what is more, Plato specifically compares the constitution of the *Laws* to the Spartan constitution, and finds it superior. However the point Aristotle is making is unambiguous: the 'polity' should not necessarily be the limit of legislators' ambitions. Given such an approach, and a readiness to embark on the dialectical discussion of *possibilities*, the peculiar mix in the *Politics* – especially in the earlier books – of the empirical and the utopian or ideal becomes wholly intelligible. So it is, for example, that a discussion of claims to political power brings up the special case of the presence of a single, god-like individual; that leads into what looks like an empirical treatment of types of kingship, but actually includes the hypothetical case of the ideal king alongside historically existing types (III.9–18).

4 Mixed and 'deviant' constitutions

Polity is 'correct' because it is true to the idea of a community. But as we have seen, a correct constitution is also a just one: '[i]t is therefore evident that all those constitutions which consider what is to the common advantage are correct constitutions, as judged in terms of what is just absolutely . . .' (III.6, 1279a17–19). 'Absolute' justice is here contrasted with the specific, and mistaken, conceptions of justice which are found in the 'deviant' forms of constitution; it is the same sort of justice which in III.17–18 dictated that if an individual or family of absolutely outstanding merit should be found, in a certain sort of community, they should be given kingship in that community.

> As we have said before, this is not only so [i.e. just] according to the kind of justice which is usually put forward by those who establish constitutions, whether aristocratic, or oligarchic, or again democratic (all of them make their claims on the basis of superiority, but not the same kind of superiority) . . . (III.18, 1288a19–24)

The backward reference is to a passage like that at III.13, 1283a23–9:

> In terms, then, of contribution to the city's existence, it would seem that all of the things mentioned [wealth, birth, virtue, the quality of judgment that may derive from numbers of people working together], or at any rate some of them, might correctly press their claims [to honours and office]; but in terms of contribution to a good life, the claims of education and virtue, as we have said before, would possess the greatest justice. But since it is not the case either that those who are equal in only one respect should have an equal share of everything, or that those who are unequal in one respect should have an unequal share of everything, all such constitutions [i.e. those that depend wholly on claims of equality and inequality in this way] must be deviant forms.

This brings us especially to democracy and oligarchy: it is especially the democrats who think that they are equal in all respects because they are equal in one (that they are born free like everyone else), and the oligarchs who think that they are unequal – that is superior – in all respects because they are unequal in one (wealth). So the democrats claim an equal right to office and honours, the oligarchs an 'unequal' one; and, says Aristotle, both are in a way right and in a way wrong: justice *is* equality – but only for those who deserve an equal share, and it *is* inequality – but only for those who deserve an unequal share, because they are themselves superior in some relevant respect (III.9).

Democrats and oligarchs thus have irreconcilable conceptions of justice. Aristotle, like Plato before him, treats the two forms of constitution as polar opposites. But in that case the difference between them cannot be merely – as their names suggest – that the one involves rule by the many, the other by the few; and indeed Aristotle goes so far as to suggest that ultimately number has nothing to do with it, except in so far as 'oligarchy' is usually associated with rule by a minority, 'democracy' with rule by the majority. If we are looking for the real essence of oligarchy, he concludes in III.8 (and the point is repeated in IV.4), it is that the rich have the power, and the real essence of democracy is that the poor have it. This position is fundamental for his analysis of actual constitutions, because most of these are oligarchies or democracies of one type or another (IV.11, 1296a22–3) – so that people begin to class all constitutions under one or the other head, treating aristocracy as a sort of oligarchy and polity as a sort of democracy, 'just as, in the case of the winds, they treat westerlies under the head of northerly, and easterlies under that of southerly' (IV.3, 1290a18–19). The rich, as well as the poor, will always be with us, and the distinction between them is ineradicable (one cannot be both rich and poor); there is therefore a natural tendency to see it as fundamental everywhere (IV.4, 1291b2–13). Aristotle rejects this tendency:

> It will be truer and better to put it in terms of our own distinctions, and say that there are two constitutions that are well put together, or one,[21] and that the others will be deviant forms of these, some of the well-mixed harmony [i.e., apparently, of polity] and others of the best constitution; and these [deviant forms] will be oligarchical when they are too severe and despotic, and democratic when they are relaxed and soft. (IV.3, 1290a24–8)

This loose and difficult sentence introduces one of Aristotle's central ideas, that of *mixture* as a solution to political problems.[22] The 'well-mixed harmony' is either the polity itself, or the related 'so-called aristocracies' which, as we have seen, are elsewhere treated as mixtures *par excellence*, and possibly superior to polities. Contrasted with this sort of

[21] One, perhaps, in the case that 'polity' is treated as itself a 'deviation' (section 2 above); kingship and aristocracy are, not for the first time, treated together (section 3).

[22] This idea dominates much of the argument of Books IV–VI, which deal with the classification of actual constitutions, the causes of constitutional change, and possible methods for preventing such change; see below.

'harmony' are the two deviant forms, oligarchy and democracy, which are both essentially one-sided: the one, in terms of the image, resulting from over-tightening of the strings of the instrument, the other from under-tightening (the image itself is evidently somewhat loose, but serves its purpose). Oligarchic rule tends to be 'despotic' or repressive, presumably for the remainder of the population, while democratic rule is looser, which suggests one interpretation of the democratic idea of 'freedom', in terms of 'living as one pleases' (VI.2, 1317b11–17). Aristotle suggests that both alternatives are intolerable, because contrary to that 'absolute' or unqualified justice which is essential to human society.[23] Given that constitutional alternatives, in any given case, must inevitably be limited by the quality of population available, there will always be oligarchies and, especially, democracies (in the light of increases in population: III.15, 1286b20–2), but these may be made more moderate, less unmixed, versions of themselves.

The way in which this is to be done is by combining democratic with oligarchic institutions, and vice versa. So for example, under a democracy the function of deliberation and decision-making about political issues is given to all citizens, under an oligarchy only to some; but

> when some of the citizens are in control of some things [but not all], for example, when all the citizens are in control in regard to war and peace and the examination of office-holders, but specific office-holders are in control of everything else, and these are elected or chosen by lot [one editor changes the text to read 'elected *and not* chosen by lot, which makes slightly better sense], then the constitution is an aristocracy [or, with an alternative manuscript reading, 'then it is an aristocracy or polity']. If those in control of some things are elected, and those in control of some other things are chosen by lot, and chosen by lot either on its own or from candidates selected in advance, or if decisions are given to a joint body, some of whom are elected and some chosen by lot, some of these features belong to an aristocratic constitution [especially that of election, on the assumption that election is on the basis of merit], others [sc. those involving mixing of different arrangements] to polity itself. (IV.14, 1298b5–11)

Proper mixing in this way will produce closer and closer approximations to the 'well-mixed harmony' which is polity or (so-called) aristocracy.

This whole discussion belongs to that part of the *Politics* (Books IV–VI,

[23] See especially I.2, 1253a29–39.

often called the 'empirical' part[24]) in which Aristotle turns from predominantly theoretical questions to questions of a more practical sort. The programme is laid out at the end of IV.2:

> We must first distinguish how many different varieties of constitution there are, given that there are more than one type both of democracy and of oligarchy; then [we must consider] which is most common [or 'accessible': *koinotatē*] and which most choiceworthy after the best constitution; and again, if some other constitution has turned out to be aristocratic and well put together, and at the same time fits the case of most cities, which it is; then also which of the others is choiceworthy for which [peoples] (for perhaps for one people democracy is more a necessity than oligarchy, while for another it is the other way round); and after this in what way the person who wishes to set up these constitutions, i.e. each kind of democracy and also of oligarchy, should set about it; and finally . . . we must embark on the question in what ways the constitutions are destroyed and in what ways they are preserved, both in general and in respect to each individual type, and through what causes these things most tend to come about. (IV.2, 1289b12–26)

The most 'common' or 'accessible' type will presumably be polity; it is under this second question ('which is most common . . .') that the discussion of the 'mixing' of democratic and oligarchic elements seems to belong. The list as a whole introduces Aristotle's attempt to say something 'of practical use', instead of merely talking about the best conceivable (IV.1, 1288b35–9, partially quoted in section 1 above).

I propose to end the present part of the chapter by asking about the precise relationship that is supposed to exist between the discussion of the 'absolutely best', as illustrated most obviously by Books VII and VIII, and Aristotle's allegedly new and more practical questions; especially the question about the most 'accessible' type of constitution.[25] First,

[24] Cf. pp. 366–8 and Schofield, Ch. 15, pp. 312–15 above. The label, as I have suggested, is misleading, if it is taken as implying an absolute contrast with other ('utopian') parts; there is also a serious question about the extent to which the contents of IV–VI are in fact based on empirical research, rather than on further applications of theory (see following paragraph).

[25] If this is interpreted as meaning 'the *best* that is accessible to most cities', it may be identified with the 'middle' constitution which is abruptly introduced in IV.11. The 'middle' sort of people on whom this constitution is based (i.e. those who are 'in the middle', *mesoi*, between the very rich and the very poor: IV.11, 1295b2–3) are admittedly said to be in short supply (1296a22–4); however the middle constitution is probably to be seen as an ideal form of 'polity' (cf. IV.11, 1295a25–34), in that, if the latter is seen as a way of avoiding the damaging polarization of rich and poor, that will ideally be achieved by a constitution based on those who are 'in the middle'. The middle constitution also resembles the 'hoplite' version of polity, insofar as being a hoplite entails only moderate ('middling') wealth.

however, it will be useful to say a little more, and more directly, about Books IV–VI themselves. Book IV essentially deals with the detailed classification of constitutions, but itself already strays into the question about their destruction and preservation. Book V then takes up the question directly, both in general terms and with reference to particular types: democracies, oligarchies, and – surprisingly – tyrannies;[26] Book VI essentially picks up and develops points from the previous two books, especially with relation to democracy and oligarchy. Aristotle's programme at the beginning of IV might lead us to expect V and VI to supply a pathology of real, live states, perhaps of the sort we find in Thucydides. If so, we are likely to be disappointed. Although the two books do frequently refer to actual cases, they use these not as raw data for investigation, but rather for purposes of illustration, and then only fitfully.[27] What they offer is for the most part highly general, resting on exhaustive surveys of theoretical possibilities (especially in relation to the methods of distributing offices), and on the extended development of two basic ideas: that extreme versions of the three types of 'deviant' constitutions, to which most actual constitutions belong, are less likely to survive than moderate ones, and – in the case of democracy and oligarchy – that moderate versions will be those that move towards the middle ground, and/or the kind of mixture of democracy and oligarchy that is now firmly associated with 'polity' (IV.8). Tyranny, for its part, should either actually change in the direction of kingship, or appear to do so.

How, then, do such practical, even pragmatic, issues relate to the treatment of the 'absolutely best'[28] constitution in Books VII and VIII?[29] It seems fair to assume two things: first, that the 'absolutely best' should, in principle, provide the standard by which other constitutions are judged (if it is best, after all, then it is better than the others, and the others are presumably worse by the same criteria by which it is judged to be best); and second, that the 'mixing' recommended in Books IV–VI, of oligarchic and democratic elements, will improve those cities to which it is applied. It ought then follow that these cities will have become better by

[26] See below, p. 384. On Aristotle's analysis of political change, see esp. Wheeler 1951, Polansky 1991.

[27] So, e.g., in V.7: 'Changes in aristocracies [i.e. 'so-called' aristocracies] are especially likely to go unobserved because the dissolution happens gradually; this is something we said before in a general way about all constitutions . . . This is what happened in the case of the constitution of Thurii . . .' (1307a40–b7).

[28] The 'absolutely' best contrasts with what may be best under given conditions: thus the 'middle' constitution in IV.11 is introduced as 'best for most cities and most men' (1295a25–6).

[29] For the general issues here, see Schofield, Ch. 15, pp. 310–15 above, Roberts, Ch. 17, pp. 360–5 above, Rowe 1977 (1991), Irwin 1985, and Rowe 1989 (but the following discussion modifies the views expressed in both Rowe 1977 (1991) and 1989).

the standard of the best. But it is not clear that this is so. According to Aristotle's argument, they will certainly have become more just. However justice is not exclusive to the best constitution; while it is certainly just, in virtue of the way it distributes power (i.e. to those who merit it), other constitutions will apparently be equally just, including polity itself, which falls short of the best. (The people to whom it gives power may be inferior to those who would hold it under the best constitution; but among the people actually living under a polity, those who most deserve power will have it – which is surely what is meant by justice in this context.) It will also be the case, largely if not exclusively as a consequence of the greater justice of the new arrangements resulting from the mixing, that the cities in question will be more stable. This consequence is obviously of some importance, given that Aristotle assigns the major part of two whole books to a discussion of the causes of and cures for instability; but again, stability is surely not itself what defines the best. Although it would presumably be the most stable, or as stable as any constitution could be, insofar as it involves a citizen-body united in a single aim, the best constitution is best because of that aim (and its achievement), and not because of the stability that flows from it.

But in that case improving an inferior or 'deviant' constitution ought to mean ensuring that it somehow paid more attention to virtue; and since virtue has no role whatever in either democracy or oligarchy, no amount of mixing them, in the way that Aristotle proposes, is likely to help improve them in that direction.[30] If so, then we might be justified in beginning to doubt whether this part of the programme of Books IV–VI really coheres with the remainder of the *Politics*; and it may be added that the tone of that programme in general, both as laid out in IV.1–2 and as actually executed, sometimes suggests that what 'political science' (*politikē*) has now become is a neutral set of techniques for organizing political communities, independently of any external standard. An example is the last question in the list at the end of IV.2, 'in what way the person who wishes to set up these constitutions, i.e. each kind of democracy and also of oligarchy, should set about it'; for this appears to include even the most

[30] That might look like an overstatement, in the light of what is said about the 'middle' kind of people in IV.11 (if the middle constitution is indeed a kind of polity: see n.25 above), since Aristotle lays some stress on their lack of the vices that tend to go with extremes of wealth and poverty (1295b3–21: the wealthy tend e.g. to get above themselves and commit large crimes, while the poor are not to be trusted and are too liable to petty crime . . .). The difficulty is that one could hardly turn a democracy or an oligarchy into this kind of middle constitution without some kind of equalization of property, an idea which Aristotle criticizes severely in II.7; practical reform is then going to have to rely on other measures, which would not either produce a 'middle' class, or promote virtue in any other direct way.

extreme type of democracy described towards the end of IV.4 (1292a4–30), in which the people become like a composite tyrant. Then too there is the essay at the end of Book V on 'how tyrannies are preserved'.

Yet Aristotle is plainly more against extreme democracies than moderate ones, and even more plainly against tyrannies; if, as he holds, they are not an appropriate solution for any community (any *Greek* one), it would be at least ungenerous to insist that he would include his observations about some of the less palatable ways in which tyrannies are in fact preserved in the category of the 'useful'. As for the proposals for mixing democracies and oligarchies, the outlines of a justification of these are perhaps suggested by the argument in section 3 above: that insofar as polity borders on 'so-called aristocracies', which do have something genuinely in common with true aristocracy, i.e. rule by the best, to make cities approximate more closely to polities will in a genuine – if still accidental – way bring them closer to the best. Or, to put it in another way, the closer they are to being 'correct' constitutions, i.e. real ones, the more chance they might have (given people of quality, and a following wind) of becoming genuinely comparable with the best.[31]

5 'Polity'

The form of constitution called *politeia* ('polity') is clearly central to Aristotle's scheme. It is probably best described as an attainable ideal (of sorts), which has close connections with something people call, not wholly misleadingly, 'aristocracy'. It is introduced in a number of different guises, but between these there is a detectable family resemblance: if it is a mixture between democracy and oligarchy, or somehow in the middle between them (II.6, 1266a26–8), or equally capable of being called both, or neither (IV.9, 1294b13–16, 34–6), then it will not be wholly inappropriate to think of it also as a kind of restricted (hoplite) democracy. All such descriptions are probably of the notional type, 'polity'; as with the other types (kingship, aristocracy, democracy, and so on), actual varieties are probably best treated as species, or variant forms.

In any case, as we have seen, it stands for the 'correct' form of rule by many, where 'many' means at least considerably more than a few. For Aristotle, the natural state of affairs will be for the citizens to 'rule and be ruled', that is, for each to take his turn at ruling: a city implies a collection of citizens, who barring exceptional circumstances (i.e. the ones that call

[31] And if so, of course, people living under them will have become more like those living under the best constitution, at least to the extent of having the kind of virtue attributed to the *mesoi* in IV.11.

for ideal kingship or aristocracy, or else where people of insufficient quality happen to have acquired membership of the city) will be free and equal. 'A city aims at being, as far as possible, composed of people who are equal and alike . . .' (IV.11, 1295b25–6). It is this idea that is probably captured by the name 'polity': in other words, it stands for 'citizen constitution'. The usual way of taking the name is to associate it with the idea of 'constitution' itself,[32] for which Aristotle himself gives some encouragement, in that he notices the fact that the two things share the same name: 'when the mass of the people govern with a view to the common advantage, the form of government in question is called by the name common to all the constitutions – *politeia*' (III.7, 1279a37–9). On the face of it, 'constitutional government', or something similar, seems appropriate enough as the name of the thing in question. This is, after all, supposed to be a '*correct*' form of constitution, by comparison with the deviant forms, which as deviant are hardly 'constitutions' at all.[33] However, this is an Aristotelian idea, whereas the name itself is introduced as one in wider circulation: when it makes its first appearance in the *Politics*, it is that form of constitution which '*people call "politeia*"' (II.6, 1265b28; similarly on numerous occasions). What some people call *politeia*, outside Aristotle (especially the orators), is something like 'free government', which is opposed to tyranny,[34] and this looks close enough to his idea, if we remember that democracy – which is usually the kind of thing the orators themselves have in mind – is for him, as a type, anything but free.[35] 'Polity', then, will stand for that form of government which operates when men are genuinely free, because, in virtue of their (genuine) equality, they rule and are ruled in turn.[36]

This conjecture seems, in fact, to be confirmed by Aristotle himself. In III.7, after he has made the point about the name 'polity', he goes on:

> This [i.e. that people should call it by the name *politeia*] is reasonable enough: it is possible for one individual, or a few people, to be outstanding in virtue; but when there is a larger number, it is hard to expect perfection in relation to all kinds of virtue, but we could most expect it in the virtue required for war; for this does occur in large numbers of people. This is why in this form of constitution the most sovereign group is the group that fights for it, and those who share in it are those who possess heavy arms. (1279a39–b4)

[32] E.g. Robinson 1962: 24, Lévy 1993: 85–6. [33] Lévy 1993.

[34] E.g. Isocrates *Panegyricus* 125 (cf. *Letter* 6.11).

[35] Isocrates certainly means democracies, at least in the first instance; given his preference for election to, and high property qualifications for, office (*Areopagiticus* 20–7), an Isocratean 'polity' might not be so far removed from an Aristotelian one – with the difference that Isocrates will still be happy to classify it as a democracy. [36] Cf. Meier 1990: 20.

It is not easy to see what exactly 'constitutional rule' has to do with this explanation of why 'polity' is called what it is. However we can fairly readily reconstruct some sort of argument based on the meaning '*citizen-rule*': 'the name is apt for this kind of "mass-rule" in the common interest, because ruling in the common interest implies a certain quality, and the only kind of virtue which we can expect of large numbers is military virtue (courage); but those to whom the constitution belongs – the citizens – in this case are the hoplites'. In the Greek, it will help that the words for 'city' (*polis*), 'citizen' (*politēs*), and 'constitution' (*politeia*) are close together in derivation and sound, as only the first two are in English.

6 The absolutely best constitution

Given the view just mentioned, that the idea of citizens 'ruling and being ruled' is somehow inbuilt into the notion of a city, it is appropriate that the (absolutely) best constitution in Books VII and VIII should turn out not, after all, to be either a kingship or an aristocracy, but a kind of virtuous form of polity (i.e., a constitution that fits the general description of a polity, but is systematically concerned with virtue in a way that polities are not). But the unsatisfactory nature of the treatment of kingship and aristocracy at the end of Book III has in any case half-prepared us for such an outcome.[37] As we saw, these two forms became identified with the 'absolutely best' on the tails of the dialectical discussion of absolute kingship; they then slotted in, reasonably neatly but also slightly curiously, alongside polity or 'citizen-rule' on the 'correct' side of the six-fold classification of constitutions. But then in Book VII,[38] the very kind of situa-

[37] See section 3 above.

[38] Questions about the unity of the *Politics* arise again here. So e.g. in IV.2 (1289a30–3), Aristotle speaks in a way that might suggest that the best constitution is to be seen exclusively in terms of kingship and aristocracy as described in Book III: 'we have spoken about aristocracy and kingship (for to consider the best constitution is the same as to talk about these names; each of these is essentially composed on the basis of a virtue provided with resources', i.e., apparently, the resources required for virtue. (I assume here both that the 'best' of VII–VIII is neither a kingship nor an aristocracy as described in III, and that the backward reference is to III as we have it.) However the passage *can* also be taken in a way that allows in the constitution of VII–VIII. The point would be this: in talking about aristocracy and kingship, we have *de facto* talked about the best constitution, because understanding what these two forms are enables us to understand the essential features of the best, namely . . . On this reading, there would be room for the constitution of VII–VIII just insofar as it too possesses those features. There is no final way of deciding between these two readings of the passage; but that also means that it is by itself no bar against our discovering a real continuity between III and VII–VIII, as I hope to have done – though the promise at the end of III of an immediate treatment of the subject of the best constitution remains a problem: see p. 366 above. IV.3, 1290a24–8 may also be less tractable; see p. 379 above.

tion as envisaged at the end of III seems to be set to one side as too unlikely (in a Greek context) to need to be taken into account:

> If then the one group were to differ from the rest by the same degree that we suppose the gods and the heroes to differ from human beings, having immediately, first, a great superiority in physical terms, and then also in terms of their minds, so that the superiority of the rulers were indisputably evident to those ruled, it is clear that it would be better for the same people to be ruled and to rule, once and for all; but since this is not easy to conceive, and we do not find anything like the difference Scylax reports among the Indians between the kings and those they rule, it is evidently necessary for many reasons that all should share on the same basis in ruling and being ruled in turn. (VII.14, 1332b16–27)

It is this kind of society – one in which 'all share on the same basis in ruling and being ruled in turn' – which is described in Books VII and VIII. As we should expect, it is a society which devotes itself, communally and individually, to a life of virtue (probably involving a mixture of practical and theoretical activity);[39] political power is also distributed on the basis of merit, but of course, since all the citizens are trained in virtue, all may expect, at a certain age, to have to take their turn in office. As I said earlier,[40] what is described is remarkably like the city of Magnesia in the *Laws*. But Aristotle begins again at the beginning. He first embarks on a discussion about the best kind of life, which any constitution claiming to be best would have to aim at, for both city and individual. Having reached the expected conclusion, that it is a life of virtue (though there are also some new points, which are not wholly predictable either from the earlier books of the *Politics* or from the *Ethics*), he then asks what kinds of conditions would need to be assumed in order to make such a life consistently possible. Finally, he starts on, but does not finish, a description (largely unremarkable, and largely familiar to readers of Plato) of the kind of education system which would be required by the virtuous city.

7 The ideal and the actual

This virtuous city, we must remember, represents what might occur if the world were as – to use an Aristotelian phrase – it 'wishes to be', and if human nature were 'completed' to the fullest possible extent. He is, however, perfectly well aware that the world is not like that, and that it will in fact go on being full of democracies and oligarchies, though evidently

[39] Rowe 1990: 221–5. [40] See p. 377.

with more of the former. There is no commitment on his part to the *realizability* of the 'absolutely best': it is a purely theoretical construction, which reflects above all his view of the best human life. Such constructions, as the programme at the beginning of Book IV suggests, form part of the business of the political scientist, its purpose being – so it seems – to provide him with a rational standard for judging, and maybe somehow for improving, actual political arrangements. The fitfulness with which that standard of the best constitution seems to be applied in the 'empirical' books (IV–VI), and the sheer distance that separates Aristotle's vision of the ideal from the realities of political life, as he himself describes them, may ultimately seem to leave Books VII and VIII as little integrated in content as in form into the remainder of the *Politics*. But there should be no temptation to see the description of the ideal state as a kind of Platonic appendix; for it is still a constitution on this model – foreshadowed from the very beginning of the work – which defines what a constitution properly is.

If so, however, it is in at least one important respect an unfortunate and unacceptable model. As one recent commentator writes,

> As it stands, the so-called ideal *polis* [sc. understood as co-extensive with its citizens] is not a political community at all, since it is not self-sufficient for life, much less for the good life (1252b27–30). Rather, it is an exploiting elite, a community of free-riders whose ability to pursue the good life is made possible by the willingness of others to forgo that pursuit. Even leaving aside the question of slavery, the 'ideal' *polis* is thus characterized by systematic injustice.[41]

Aristotle holds, like Plato, that only certain sorts of occupation are compatible with a life of virtue: soldiering, ruling (holding office, sitting in court, etc.), and philosophizing.[42] This means that his good man is inevitably parasitic on others, and the *Politics* accordingly assigns all other necessary occupations to non-citizens: slaves, resident aliens, and serfs of foreign origin (VII.4, 1326a18–21; 9, 1329a25–6; 10, 1330a25–31). Even by Aristotle's lights this must be unjust, unless the slaves are all so-called 'natural' slaves, and the others selected for commercial and manual tasks because they are incapable of anything more; but there is no indication that this is the case (rather the reverse).[43] There is nothing for it but to suppose that it is all a matter of aristocratic prejudice – and a borrowed one at that, since Aristotle was himself a resident alien at Athens. If he was capable of seeing (as he probably was), in the context of the virtuous life,

[41] Taylor 1995: 250. [42] E.g. VI.4, 1319a26–32. [43] Annas 1996.

that even the most desirable activity – 'theoretical' – could be combined with less desirable, that is political, ones,[44] why should he not also accept that the good man and citizen might also be a farmer, or a shoemaker (and farmers and shoemakers good men and citizens)?[45] He is at least consistent, for the same attitudes repeatedly surface elsewhere in the *Politics* (e.g. in the classification of the varieties of democracy in Book VI, and Book IV). Yet the very fact that it is so easy to skirt them, and construct an alternative, and more inclusive, model of an 'Aristotelian' political community, perhaps limits the damage that they do to the *Politics* as a work of political philosophy.

[44] Cf. p. 387 above. [45] Cf. Taylor 1995: 249–50.

19

The Peripatos after Aristotle

CHRISTOPHER ROWE

1 The fate of Aristotle's writings

Aristotle evidently intended only some of his works for wider circulation, or 'publication'; these were the so-called 'exoteric' works, mainly dialogues, which are now lost apart from some fragments. The genuinely Aristotelian parts of our corpus Aristotelicum represent an assemblage of collections of notes on particular topics, or more finished treatises, which evidently would only have been available for consultation by individuals, especially (we might suppose) members of his school; if in principle they might have been more widely available, it is hard to imagine a large demand for such a large body of relatively intractable material. It is thus possible to argue[1] that other schools might not have had the direct access to Aristotle's work that, living in a different age, we might incautiously presume; nor indeed are the fragmentary remains of the later Peripatetics sufficient to prove that in later periods of the school, after Theophrastus, even they had a complete collection in Athens. The first systematic edition was evidently that of Andronicus of Rhodes, at Rome, in the first century BC. Aristotle left his library, which also included a large collection of other books, to Theophrastus, and Theophrastus left it to another Peripatetic, Neleus; and reports in Strabo (XIII.1, 54, 608–9) and in Plutarch (*Life of Sulla* 26) suggest that at some point between then and Andronicus' editorial activity at least a proportion of the corpus was sufficiently 'lost', or inaccessible, to need to be 'rediscovered' – or to be capable of being described in such terms – when Sulla brought Aristotelian manuscripts back with him to Rome from Asia Minor.

Whatever the sources, veracity, and implications of these reports as a whole, some version of them might as well have been true of the *Politics*: while there may have been close reading of Aristotle's writings on the subject (in whatever form) within the Peripatos itself, his wider influence on

[1] As has in fact been argued for the Stoics: Sandbach 1985.

political thinking in the two centuries or so after his death is likely to have been not so much through that as through the circulation of certain key ideas – like that of the mixing of constitutions – and of classificatory schemes. Stripped of their original argumentative contexts, these were all the more easily assimilated to and combined with ideas from other, and especially Platonic, sources. But such assimilation or combination will of course have been easier in some cases than in others. It has been suggested, on the basis of rather scrappy evidence, that some later Peripatetics attempted to square Aristotle's polis-centred ethical and political outlook with the larger Stoic vision of human beings as citizens of the world.[2] If so, the attempt was surely doomed from the start, to the extent that Aristotle sees belonging to a polis and sharing its specific goals as partly constitutive of humanity itself.

2 Aristotle's successors in the Peripatos

Even apart from such issues, Aristotle's polis-based perspective is likely to appear narrow and backward-looking, given the loss of autonomy apparently implied by the absorption of a large part of the Greek world – a process which began a decade and a half before his death – into the empires instituted by Alexander and his successors. However it is at best an oversimplification to assume that the idea of the polis, as a 'center of allegiance and a source of pride', and involving the active participation of its citizens in legislative and judicial processes, no longer existed in the Hellenistic age.[3] The degree of independence which individual *poleis*, or groups of *poleis*, enjoyed in the new age of empires and kingships appears to have varied widely. While it is striking that Aristotle seems to have paid so little attention to the newly emerging political realities (the shape and consequences of which may in any case not have been so obvious to a contemporary observer as they are to us),[4] the old issues about the organization and administration of the polis still remained very much alive.

Our knowledge of writing on political theory in the later Peripatos is extremely thin. But the signs are that the later Peripatetics, while looking back to Aristotle himself, also saw the need to adapt to current political conditions. Theophrastus, Aristotle's immediate successor as head of the

[2] Annas 1995. [3] Gruen 1993: 354.

[4] The absence of any clear reference to Alexander's achievements in the genuine parts of the corpus might itself suggest that Aristotle's political writing and research predated them; it is nevertheless striking, if he once served as the young Alexander's tutor (e.g. Plu. *Life of Alexander* 7–8).

school, is paired with him by Cicero[5] as having taught 'what kind of person should be a leader in the state', and having written at greater length 'about the best condition of the state' (i.e. the best constitution); Cicero adds that Theophrastus gave fuller treatment to the subject 'what are the changes in the circumstances of a state and the critical moments in time that must be dealt with as the situation demands', which appears to resemble the sort of subject handled in Books IV–VI of Aristotle's *Politics*. The surviving evidence about the nature of Theophrastus' *Laws* (in twenty-four books, compared with one *On the Best Constitution*, although the latter subject might well have been treated elsewhere in Theophrastus' voluminous output), may reflect a general preference on his part for detailed research and for particular questions over broader theoretical constructions – a preference which is in line with the kind of programme for research into constitutions that Aristotle himself instituted. On the other hand Diogenes Laertius (V.42–9) attributes to Theophrastus a work on kingship addressed to Cassander, one of Alexander's successors, along with three others on the same subject, and one on tyranny.[6] Kingship was evidently – and understandably – a topic of greater interest for Theophrastus than it was for Aristotle;[7] whether or not he judged this 'the best condition of the state' we have no way of knowing.

Diogenes also reports Strato of Lampsacus, Theophrastus' successor, as writing *On the Philosopher-King* (V.59), and as teaching Ptolemy II Philadelphus in Egypt. He makes no connection between these two reports, nor should we supply one; however the emergence of Hellenistic monarchies clearly allowed room for the practical realization of the idea – itself at least as old as Herodotus[8] – of the wise man as adviser to princes.[9] (Theophrastus' *On Kingship to Cassander* points in a similar direction.) Another Peripatetic, Demetrius of Phaleron, became governor of Athens for ten years under Macedonian rule; Cicero acclaims him as an outstanding example of a statesman who also excelled in political theory (*Leg.* III.14).

The pseudo-Aristotelian *Economics* (in three disparate books, probably of separate authorship), itself marks the integration of the structure of the polis into the wider world of the Hellenistic kingship, identifying four forms of administration (*oikonomia*): those belonging respectively to the

[5] *Fin.* V.11, tr. Sharples. [6] Cf. Hahm, Ch.23 below, p. 457 n.3.
[7] See Rowe, Ch.18 above, pp. 386–7.
[8] See e.g. Herodotus I.29–32, on Solon at the court of Croesus.
[9] On philosophy and politics in the context of Plato and the Academy, see Schofield, Ch.13 above.

king, the satrapy or province, the polis and the individual household (1345b11–14). So too, in a more complex and messier way, does another pseudo-Aristotelian work, the *Rhetorica ad Alexandrum*. This has been attributed to Anaximenes of Lampsacus (a historian and rhetorician roughly contemporary with Aristotle), mainly on the basis of the relatively flimsy evidence of a passage in Quintilian (III.4.9); it is almost certainly of later origin. Prefaced by a curious letter purporting to be by Aristotle to Alexander,[10] it includes a classification of types of rhetoric and advice about the sorts of things to be said by speakers in different contexts; one of its sections advises on the sorts of laws that are appropriate for democracies and oligarchies. This section, and the classification of rhetoric, are recognizably Aristotelian in origin (unless, of course, Aristotle himself was borrowing from the author of the *Rhetorica ad Alexandrum*, or both – even less probably – from a third source), though there are some innovations. The most un-Aristotelian aspect of the whole piece is probably its definition of law as 'a common agreement of the city, laying down in written form how we must act in each sort of situation'.[11] By itself, this definition suggests a kind of sophistic relativism.[12] However it follows another definition, this time of 'the just', in terms of the unwritten custom expressed in the habitual behaviour of 'all or most people' (1421b36), which makes the whole passage look more familiarly Aristotelian;[13] and it is wholly reasonable that a work on rhetoric should describe law in terms of an agreement, insofar as the orator's task will be to persuade the citizens meeting in legislative assembly to agree to the right laws. The author lays down clear criteria for legislative advice, which include not only whether a proposed law is consistent with others, and whether it promotes agreement (*homonoia*) among the citizens, but also – a thoroughly Aristotelian (and Platonic) notion – whether it conduces to their moral improvement (*kalokagathia*). The author is no relativist; and whoever wrote the introductory letter certainly did not take him as such, because the letter modifies the definition of law to read 'law is *reason defined in accordance with common agreement of the city* . . .' (1420a25–7). Law here is compared and contrasted with the reason of the king (Alexander): 'just as their shared law usually guides those of the cities that govern

[10] On this letter, see Hahm, Ch.23 below, pp. 458–61. Another curiosity in the same genre, and of equally uncertain date, is preserved in the Arabic tradition; this letter-writer urges Alexander to settle prominent Persians in Europe (as the Persians have historically removed many Greeks from their home cities, but also for more strategic reasons), and looks forward to a day when the world will become one single kingdom providing peace, and the leisure for philosophy, for its people (see Stern 1968).

[11] 1422a2–4, more or less repeated at 1424a10–12.

[12] Cf. Arist. *Pol.* III.9, 1280b10–11.

[13] Cf. e.g. *EN*. VIII.15, 1162b21–3.

themselves towards the best, so your reason (*logos*) might lead those subject to your rule to what is beneficial to them' (1420a22–5).

This analogy provides a justification of a sort for the curious notion (or fiction) of offering a handbook of advice for the orator and politician, operating within the context of the polis, to an autocrat with imperial ambitions. Alexander is to imitate the greatest Greek politicians, and their non-Greek counterparts, by prefacing actions with reasoning about what is beneficial (1420b27–1421a2); he is to do this by embracing 'the study of reasoned speech' (*tēs tōn logōn . . . philosophias*, 1421a16), an Isocratean phrase[14] which identifies the ability to reason with the ability to speak. If the author of the letter has any claim at all to Peripatetic credentials, it hardly extends further than his appropriation of the (essentially) Peripatetic document on to which he has tacked it.

A further illustration of the mix of continuity and innovation in later Peripatetic political theory is the handling of two characteristically Aristotelian topics by Dicaearchus of Messene: 'a pupil of Aristotle's' listed by Cicero in the *de Legibus* along with Demetrius as among those who, after Plato and Aristotle, 'illuminated the whole subject of politics in their discussions'. The first of the topics in question, which seems to have been a favourite in the Peripatos, and which is of special importance to Cicero himself, is that of the choice between the philosophical and the practical life. Cicero contrasts Dicaearchus with Theophrastus as arguing for the priority of the life of practical activity (*Att.* 2.16.3). Aristotle himself, who thought of the human intellect as divine, had argued for the Theophrastean ordering;[15] Dicaearchus' argument may have been based on his outright denial of the immortality of the soul (*Tusc.* 1.77), though since Aristotle also rejected personal immortality, there must have been more to it than that. We are even less well-informed about Dicaearchus' views on the second topic, that of the best constitution, but they seem to have been genuinely novel. Material apparently deriving from Dicaearchus' *Tripoliticus*, preserved for us by the Byzantine scholar Photius (fr. 71 Wehrli), marks him as the first to have recognized the 'mixed constitution' as itself a separate form of constitution – an idea which is fundamental to later political thinking. The mixture is of kingship, aristocracy and democracy; the best arrangement would combine the essentials of each. The appearance of democracy in the list rather than

[14] See esp. *Against the Sophists* 18.

[15] Antiochus of Ascalon – a Platonist in name, but at least as much a Peripatetic (and a Stoic) in ethics, and himself an important philosophical influence on Cicero – seems to attempt a compromise position by blurring the distinction between *theōria* and *praxis*: Cic. *Fin.* v.58.

Aristotle's 'polity' or 'citizen constitution' (an idea which by and large seems to have died with Aristotle) suggests a greater affinity with Plato's *Laws* than with the *Politics*, though Dicaearchus' identification of the mixed constitution with the Sparta of Lycurgus has its precedent in both. What is unclear is whether this idea of Dicaearchus' was meant to have any sort of practical application, and if so, how (though of course even the most theoretical construction, like Plato's ideal city in the *Republic* or Aristotle's ideal constitution in *Politics* VII and VIII, may serve as a model and goal). Later Polybius (and Cicero) would be able to identify republican Rome as the mixed constitution *par excellence*; and it may be that Dicaearchus' inclusion in the mix of real kingship (rather than the 'kingship' of reason and law which is envisaged in Plato's *Laws*) is itself a nod in the direction of Hellenistic kingship. But equally this mixed form might just be a theoretical construction applying Platonic and Aristotelian thoughts about mixing to a basically Aristotelian list of three 'correct' constitutions. Arius Didymus' first-century BC epitome of Peripatetic ethics referred to a 'form of rule which is mixed from the correct forms':[16] either this is Dicaearchus' mixed constitution, or else a similar idea played a wider role in post-Aristotelian Peripatetic political theory than is apparent from the slight remaining evidence.

[16] Stob. II.151.1.

PART II

THE HELLENISTIC AND ROMAN WORLDS

*

Map 2. The Roman empire, 45 BC–AD 69.

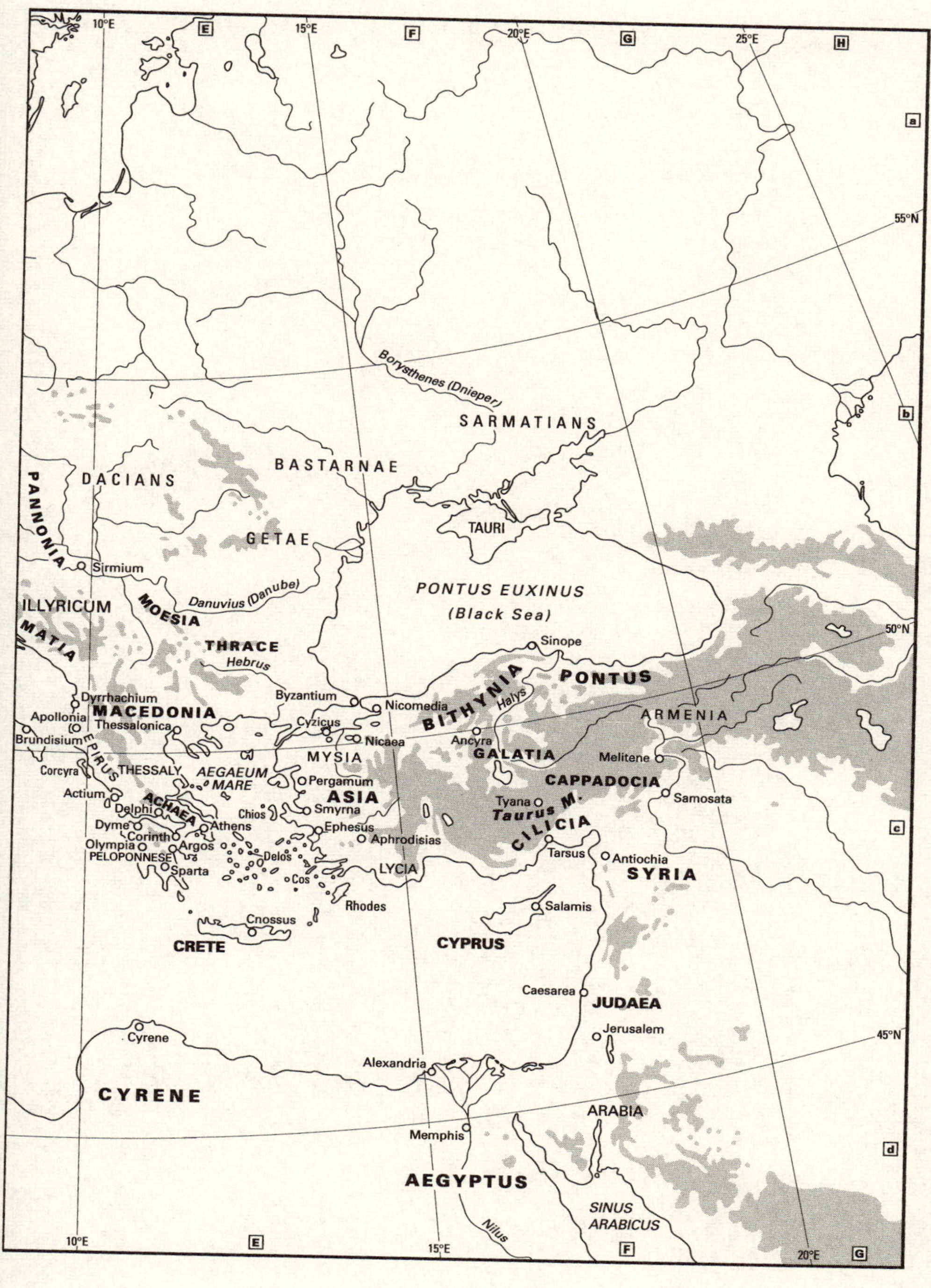

10°E
15°E
20°E
25°E
E
F
G
H
a
b
c
d
55°N
50°N
45°N
Borysthenes (Dnieper)
SARMATIANS
BASTARNAE
DACIANS
PANNONIA
TAURI
GETAE
Sirmium
PONTUS EUXINUS
(Black Sea)
ILLYRICUM
MOESIA
Danuvius (Danube)
MATIA
THRACE
Hebrus
Sinope
BITHYNIA
PONTUS
Halys
Byzantium
Nicomedia
Dyrrhachium
MACEDONIA
Apollonia
Thessalonica
Cyzicus
ARMENIA
Brundisium
EPIRUS
Nicaea
Ancyra
MYSIA
GALATIA
Melitene
Corcyra
THESSALY
AEGAEUM
MARE
Pergamum
CAPPADOCIA
Actium
ASIA
Samosata
ACHAEA
Delphi
Chios
Smyrna
Tyana
Taurus M.
Dyme
Athens
Ephesus
CILICIA
Corinth
Aphrodisias
Olympia
Argos
Tarsus
PELOPONNESE
Delos
Antiochia
Sparta
LYCIA
SYRIA
Cos
Rhodes
Salamis
Cnossus
CRETE
CYPRUS
Caesarea
JUDAEA
Cyrene
Jerusalem
Alexandria
CYRENE
ARABIA
Memphis
AEGYPTUS
SINUS
ARABICUS
Nilus

Introduction: the Hellenistic and Roman periods

PETER GARNSEY

The transition from Classical to Hellenistic philosophy coincided with the passage from a Greek world in which the polis was the dominant political formation to one presided over by large central states. The first of these was the kingdom of Macedon. The advance of Macedon was swift. In no more than four decades, beginning with the rise to power of Philip II in 359BC, Greece was subdued, the massive Persian empire conquered (334–327), and democracy in Athens crushed (in 319). In this last act Macedon was all but finishing off not only democracy (only Rhodes remained democratic, for a time), but also the independent polis. In fact, freedom and independence had been enjoyed in their fullness in the fifth and fourth centuries only by a few hegemonic poleis (principally Athens, Sparta and Thebes), which dominated the mass of smaller Greek poleis through their leagues, or polities (such as Caria under Mausolus in 377/6–353, and Thessaly under Jason in the 370s). Athens was the last of the hegemonic poleis. After the death of Alexander in 323, the unified Macedonian empire quickly gave way to the Successor Kingdoms of the Hellenistic age based on Macedon, Syria and Egypt, which in turn were absorbed, finally and conclusively, by Rome. After establishing itself, at the expense of Carthage, as the leading power in the Western Mediterranean, Rome in the course of the second century BC became dominant also in the Eastern Mediterranean.[1]

These states, with the notable exception of Rome before the late first century BC, were ruled by monarchs, who controlled, to be sure, an extensive web of city-states. Cities actually increased in both size and number in the Hellenistic period. Alexander had founded Greek poleis throughout

[1] For general histories of the period treated below see e.g. Walbank 1981, Errington 1990, volumes VII.1 & VIII–X of *The Cambridge Ancient History*, Wells 1992, Cameron 1993. For politics specifically, see Finley 1983. Specialist bibliography for the main thinkers and schools of thought in political theory is provided in the various chapters. General studies and useful collections include Aalders 1975, Laks and Schofield 1995, Powell 1995, and Part I of *The Cambridge History of Medieval Political Thought, c. 350–c. 1450*.

his empire, many of them bearing his name, and we find new cities called after the Seleucid monarchs, bearing names like Seleuceia and Antioch, throughout their sprawling empire. The Ptolemies in Egypt adopted a different policy with regard to city foundation, having less need than the Seleucids of garrison cities. The functions served by their principal city, Alexandria, were not so much protective as administrative and cultural, in the latter case involving the promotion of the exclusive Greek *paideia*. In referring to the city as Alexandria near Egypt rather than Alexandria in Egypt, the Greeks were asserting the superiority of their culture and declaring their interest in keeping their distance from the native Egyptians.

In the Hellenistic cities there was still the appearance of continuous political activity: there was competition for offices and faction-fighting. But the top offices lost much of their power and appeal, in consequence of the removal of foreign and military affairs from the control of the cities. There was a corresponding rise in the prestige of certain liturgies, or public services, at the expense of the regular magistracies, particularly those liturgies connected with cult, games, and social and cultural life (centred on the gymnasium). As a result, the boundary between magistracies and liturgies became blurred, reinforcing the oligarchic tendency. Meanwhile the poleis enjoyed only as much autonomy as the king and his ministers allowed.

The king was an absolute not a constitutional monarch. He ruled through a limited circle of functionaries, drawn largely from a wider group of 'friends' or courtiers, who were his intimates and his representatives among the cities that fell within his kingdom. They collected taxes, commanded garrisons, and generally interfered in the internal affairs of the cities; they were also capable of exploiting their special relationship with the king to plead a city's cause. Their reward for loyal and efficient service to the king took the form of gifts of land and cash, revenues from subject cities, symbols of status (special clothing, attendants, titles), privileged access to the king, and the prospect of further profitable tasks and assignments. The Greeks made them the butt of their jokes. This story circulated about one Bithys:

> When Lysimachus thrust a wooden scorpion into his cloak, he jumped up in utter fright, and realizing then what the thing was, he said: 'I will now give *you* a shock, your Majesty – give me a talent'. (Athenaeus, *Deipn.* VI.246e)

Bithys was one of the powerful friends of Lysimachus, king of Macedon, but here he is introduced as a parasite. Parasites, flatterers, slaves – in 'republican' Greek circles these were standard names for the king's friends. The hostility of Greeks to the royal courtiers was grounded in their inherited value system, according to which service to another was *ipso facto* servile. The fact that such service was not in this context associated with humble material circumstances and social and political marginalization, as it was in traditional Greek society, but was the avenue to enrichment and power, only added to the disgrace.

Political philosophy in its heyday was a precipitate of active politics and was unlikely to thrive once the open discussion of political issues had ceased. It did not however disappear: from the early part of the period there is evidence of the persistence of traditional constitutional theory in the Peripatos (Theophrastus, Dicaearchus, Demetrius), and of writings by Peripatetics and Stoics on laws and on the Spartan constitution (Theophrastus, Cleanthes, Persaeus; Dicaearchus, Persaeus, Sphaerus, respectively) . Nor is a cessation of activity in this area between these writers and Polybius in the mid-second century at all likely. But the Hellenistic age was a creative period in moral, not political, philosophy. In Classical thought, moral and political philosophy were virtually inseparable: good man *was* good citizen. In the Hellenistic period moral philosophy threatened to break free. Both Epicureans and Stoics placed their emphasis on the individual, his conduct and his goals. Those goals, pleasure for the Epicurean and goodness for the Stoic, were no longer to be sought within the framework of the poleis, but in the setting of the universe. The necessity and responsibility of each individual, the Stoics argued, were to align himself with the divine laws of nature that governed this wider world. 'The Stoics', recalled Clement of Alexandria, writing in the early third century AD, 'say that the heavens are in the proper sense a city, but that those here on earth are not – they are called cities, but are not really. For a city or a people is something morally good (*spoudaion*)'.[2] Conventional political concepts such as citizenship, freedom and slavery, were not ignored, but they were redefined as moral terms and set in the context of the 'cosmic community'.[3]

These doctrines were appropriate to the Hellenistic era, but they were not born in that age. They were a creation of the same society that produced the great works of Classical political philosophy. A spirit of disenchantment with existing political institutions was widespread in mid-to-late fourth-century Greece (and already abroad as early as the age of Socrates). It reached its height in the Cynics, who turned their backs on

[2] *Strom*. IV.26 [= *SVF* III 327]. It is not clear how extensively the idea of the cosmic city was used in Stoic moral philosophy before the Christian era.

[3] See Diogenes Laertius VII.32–3.

society and politics altogether. Less radical thinkers of other persuasions agonized over the 'choice of life' question, whether one should become involved with the ruler, or more broadly, with the political system – so that *On Lives* was a characteristic genre of the period. The early Stoics contributed to this debate, as did Peripatetics, such as Strato, a pupil of Theophrastus. Though profoundly influenced by Cynicism, the Stoics did not, as did Diogenes and his followers, preach or practice withdrawal from political life altogether. However, when Stoic philosophers (some, not all) did engage in politics, the recorded sphere of their operations was the royal court, not the city *agora*. Some Stoics, for example Persaeus and Sphaerus, respectively pupils of Zeno the founding father and Cleanthes, Zeno's successor, served as advisers of kings. (Persaeus was also a man of action, holding Acrocorinth for Antigonus Gonatas, king of Macedon from 276 BC.) Others, such as Zeno, Cleanthes and Chrysippus, declined to do so, but not apparently on principle. Chrysippus recommended that the wise man should become king or advise a king, while Cleanthes (though not, it would seem, Chrysippus) was one of several leading Stoics who wrote a treatise on kingship. There is a continuing dialectic: the issue of engagement in politics becomes a matter of lively interest in Roman political philosophy – conspicuously so in Cicero, Seneca and Epictetus – and in Roman political life, as witnessed in the lives and deaths of the younger Cato, Seneca, Thrasea Paetus and Helvidius Priscus. All of these except Cicero were professed Stoics, all except Epictetus Roman senators.[4]

Strato the Peripatetic is said to have written two treatises on politics: *On Lives* and *On Kingship*. The second of these was one of many composed on this subject in the Hellenistic age. For the treatise on kingship was the standard work of political philosophy of the period. This was predictable and appropriate, but here too there was an earlier tradition on which to draw. The works of Xenophon and Isocrates included prototype kingship treatises.[5] The Classical philosophers had ranked monarchy high, Plato in the *Politicus* designating it the best form of government, provided only a king could be found who was wise, while Aristotle concedes that the 'one best man' should be sovereign in some circumstances. Half a century later the Stoic paradox was circulating that only the wise man was good, free and king (although here, at least in the first instance, moral rather than political leadership was in view).

[4] See Brunt 1975.

[5] See Isocrates, *Euagoras*, *Nicocles*, *ad Nicoclem*; Xenophon, *Agesilaus*, *Cyropedia*, *Hiero*. For discussion see Gray, Ch.7 section 2 above.

For information as to the style and content of the Hellenistic kingship treatises we are largely dependent on the symposium of pseudo-Aristeas' *Letter to Philocrates* (probably mid-second century BC) and complete works from the Roman period beginning with Seneca's *de Clementia* (*c.* AD 55–6) which is usually taken as true to type.[6] The evidential value of such works apart, their existence attests the continuity of the genre throughout our period, and together with the similar phenomenon of imperial panegyric and the so-called pseudo-Pythagorean tracts on kingship (see below), confirm the dominance of kingship as the focal point of political discussion and debate.

The kingship that was the subject of these treatises was not the traditional Greek kingship, but absolute kingship. Similarly, the treatises were not works of analysis in the style of Aristotle. There was no classification of kinds of kingship, nor was kingship weighed against its rivals for the palm of best constitution: it was taken for granted that it was. Much attention was given to the qualities of the ideal, virtuous king. He was a man of noble spirit, who kept before him the welfare of his subjects, and in return was hailed as their chief benefactor and saviour.

Hellenistic kings received worship. Following the example of Alexander, they were ready to exploit, for the extra authority that they bestowed, the connotations of divinity and absolutism. (Among Oriental rulers, the Egyptian pharaoh but not the Persian king was traditionally worshipped as a god in his lifetime.) Did Hellenistic writers represent kings as divine? Perhaps not, but the ideas of the king as emulator of god, his representative on earth and the incarnation of the divine *logos*, are widespread in late Hellenistic and early imperial Roman thought, Stoic as well as Platonic.[7] The airing of such ideas was not confined to kingship treatises, but they are echoed in certain works of this genre which belong to the Platonic tradition, though commonly assigned to Neopythagoreans (substantial fragments are extant). Their date of composition is uncertain, but probably falls in the last century BC or the first century AD. For Ecphantus, the king is 'a human being of a higher order than ordinary men . . . he is produced from the same substance as men, but has been moulded by a better craftsman, on the model of god himself as archetype'. For Diotogenes, the king verges on godhead: 'In nature god is the highest of the high, on earth and among men the king holds this station . . . The king, his rule unaccountable, himself the embodiment of law, is as god among

[6] In extant Roman literature, Cicero's *pro Marcello* (46 BC) addressed to Julius Caesar is in some sense an ancestor of Seneca's treatise.

[7] This and related subjects are covered by Centrone, Ch. 27 below.

men.'[8] If it *were* legitimate to read such texts as reflecting contemporary political ideology – a risky procedure – then the Roman Principate provides as appropriate a setting as the late Hellenistic world. It is true that the official Roman view of the emperor's status was that he was first citizen rather than divine. Augustus, in order to swing the Roman nobility behind his rule, had withheld from himself the title of king and the status of a god.[9] Nevertheless, his Roman subjects deified him after his death, having prepared the way in his lifetime with sundry honours carrying clear or veiled religious connotations – not least the title *divi filius*, 'son of the god', which he assumed soon after the assassination (and deification) of Julius Caesar. The Greek world meanwhile had anticipated the establishment of the official state cult of the emperor, viewing the Roman emperor as a successor of the Hellenistic kings.

The ambiguity of the position of the first emperor lay in the fact that he was a monarch who professed to have restored the Republic, whose political ideology had been resolutely anti-monarchical. Early Rome was a city-state under the rule of the few. In this respect it was comparable to the Greek city-states of the Hellenistic period, which were also in the hands of oligarchies. In Roman historical mythology, however, liberty had been won for the citizenry through the expulsion of Tarquin the Proud, the last of the Etruscan kings. This was a myth which never died. Julius Caesar was murdered because he showed every sign of progressing from perpetual dictator (which was bad enough) to Hellenistic-style king. It was a descendant of the expeller of Tarquin and founder of the Republic, M. Junius Brutus, who struck the first blow. The rejection of the kings and their replacement by two consuls and an advisory group of elders ('fathers') constituted the kernel of the myth of Rome as the virtuous ancient state, the possession of its citizens, who had won liberty and preserved it by devoted service to the fatherland. The Roman Republic evoked a quite different kind of reflection from the Hellenistic kingdoms or the Principate, as can be seen above all in Cicero, but also in his second-century precursors in the realm of constitutional and ethical theory, respectively, Polybius from Megalopolis in Achaea in the sixth book of his *Histories*, and the Stoic Panaetius of Rhodes (insofar as his thought can be reconstructed).

The Republic as the possession of its citizens: it would be more accu-

[8] See Thesleff 1965. Ecphantus: Stob. IV.272.10–14 (= Thesleff p. 80); Diotogenes: Stob. IV.265.4–12 (= Thesleff p. 72).

[9] Not all emperors abided by the Augustan tradition, for example, Domitian (AD 81–96), a notoriously 'bad' emperor. Contrast Trajan (AD 98–117), whose sobriquet was *optimus princeps*, not *dominus et deus*.

rate to say that the Republic was the possession of a select few of its citizens, and that political liberty was their preserve. As the Republic progressed, the pool of citizens became ever larger and more dispersed, and only a minority were physically able to take part in politics at Rome. The Roman political system gave ordinary citizens very little chance to participate in political decisions, let alone to hold office.[10] We have to wait for Cicero, writing at the very end of the Republic, to provide a full account of the rationale and ideology of the system. In his vision, full involvement in political life, the privilege and the duty of ruling and being ruled, should be reserved for those judged to be equal in terms of dignity or merit.

A basic requirement for membership of this elite group was leisure. Only those who did not have to work for a living were free to devote themselves to the main business of the state, that is to say, politics and warfare. In both Greece and Rome it was above all the existence of slavery which made possible the full participation of the citizen class, or as in Rome a privileged section of that class.[11] Romans had no interest in justifying or explaining this fact. For example, no Roman counterpart to Aristotle arose to provide a rationale for slavery in terms of the innate irrationality of a whole section of humanity, the 'natural slaves'. Cicero had almost nothing to say about slavery in the three key theoretical works, *de Re Publica*, *de Legibus* (both incompletely extant) and *de Officiis*.[12] Romans saw slavery as a structural feature of their society, an economic and political necessity, and that was that. Some masters found it expedient to extend favoured treatment culminating in manumission to selected slaves who served them well, or with whom they had developed affective relationships. In so doing, they were not undermining the slave system but ensuring its survival. Those who had achieved freedman status moved effortlessly into the class of masters and patrons, if they had not already 'owned' slaves when still themselves of slave status (a common enough practice). The only risk to the existing order lay in maltreatment of slaves by masters sufficiently extreme to provoke assassination or mass revolt. Some writers report such occurrences with impartiality bordering on

[10] For Rome as the 'possession' of the people (and for other meanings of *res publica*), see Schofield 1995a. For the recent argument of F. Millar that Republican Rome was 'quasi-democratic', or more democratic than has been thought, and for some reactions to it, see Millar 1984 and 1986, North 1990, and the articles of Rosenstein, Williamson, North and Harris in *Classical Philology* 85 (1990).

[11] For a classic statement, see Finley 1981: ch. 6, and also Finley 1980.

[12] On attitudes to slavery see Garnsey 1996. The section that follows draws on this work. For a problematic passage in Cicero *Rep.*III see Atkins, in Ch. 24 section 5.2 (p. 495 below). The best treatment of the practice of slavery in Rome is Bradley 1994.

sympathy for the slaves – as does Diodorus (a Greek from Sicily), in connection with the Sicilian slave revolts of the late second century BC, drawing on an earlier *History* by the Stoic philosopher Posidonius (from Apamea in Syria). But we may suspect that ultimately prudential rather than humanitarian considerations underlie their treatments. Seneca's uplifting doctrine of the common kinship of all rational humans whether slave or free raises the discussion to a higher level. Even so, the doctrine is not used as a springboard for an attack on slavery as an institution, but simply to discourage masters from dealing harshly with their slaves, again, we may suspect, in the interests of the personal security of the master-class and of domestic and civil peace. In general, the relationship between master and slave was regarded as a private matter in which the state had no interest. Some Roman emperors issued edicts prohibiting certain specific acts of cruelty, but more in hope than expectation.[13] Few courts would have taken the side of a slave against his master.

The rulers of Rome, then, were free to engage in politics by courtesy of their slaves. Moreover (as already indicated), their conduct as masters remained largely ungoverned, insofar as it belonged to the domestic sphere, traditionally the domain of the *paterfamilias*. It was otherwise with their behaviour in the public sphere, and in aspects of their private lives thought to impinge thereon (the boundary between public and private was not clearly demarcated in the case of the Roman elite). The leadership class was, according to the ideal, uncorrupted and incorruptible, avoiding wealth and luxury, and staying out of commerce. These standards could not continue to be upheld (if they ever had been) as the riches of empire fell into their laps. It is nonetheless important that the ideology was not declared redundant. A succession of sumptuary laws from the early second century BC reminded the aristocracy of the stern moral code of their ancestors. It was a function of a special magistracy, the censorship, to uphold traditional standards of conduct among the governing class, and censors sometimes exercised the authority of their office to expel flagrant offenders from the Senate. The rule that senators should not involve themselves in commerce was encased in law in 218 (in the *lex Claudia*) – and again in 59 (in the *lex Iulia de repetundis*), a mere decade from the beginning of the civil war that brought down the Republic. The distrust of commerce features in the preface of the *de Agri Cultura* of the elder Cato, composed towards the middle of the second century BC, and around a century later, in Cicero's *de Officiis* (1.150–1). Romans of Cicero's day

[13] See e.g. Buckland 1908: 36–8.

were brought up on morally improving stories of the piety, patriotism and self-denying *poverty* of Rome's heroes. In *de Re Publica* and *de Officiis* Cicero dwells on the virtues of the statesman that were disastrously absent in the avaricious and self-seeking politicians of his own day. His model statesmen, for example those introduced in the early chapters of *de Re Publica* Book I, include Scipio Africanus, hero of the epic war against Hannibal (and ancestor of Scipio Aemilianus, who will shortly enter and dominate the dialogue), and the elder Cato, another notorious enemy of Carthage. Both were renowned for their frugality.[14]

The Romans were obsessed with morality.[15] Why? The explanation in my view is to be sought in the nature of Rome as a conquest-state, the most successful of its kind that the Mediterranean world had thus far seen. The enormous and sustained effort of empire-building imposed extraordinary demands on every section of Roman society. We are inclined, with reason, to think first in this connection of rank-and-file citizens and allies, the small farmers of Rome and Italy who fought for Rome year after year. But total commitment was required from Rome's leaders too, who were expected to put patriotic interests first. The virtues that are the subject of Cicero's *de Officiis* are all ultimately public virtues, oriented towards service to the state, which was held to be the highest calling for a Roman.[16] The Republic (according to Cicero) had lost its way precisely because it was dominated by self-seeking men hungry for power and wealth.

The regime that replaced it after civil war was, probably inevitably, a monarchy, but an idiosyncratic one. The first emperor, Augustus, was officially a magistrate receiving his powers from the traditional organs of government, the Senate and the popular assembly. The title he chose for himself, *princeps*, first citizen, had good Republican overtones, recalling the statesman of pre-eminent moral authority (*auctoritas*) of Cicero's *de Re Publica* and *de Legibus*. In practice, the enthronement of Augustus spelt the end of politics in the sense of the active participation of the traditional governing class in decision-making; this was already suspended from the beginning of the civil war in 49 BC, if not before.[17] The Senate had lost for ever its control of the deliberative and legislative spheres, and the ambition of individual members of the upper classes had to be channelled into the service of the emperor if it was not to be branded a threat to the new

[14] The two men are mentioned in the same breath in Seneca *Ep.* 87. See, for Scipio, *Ep.* 86. The Roman hero who gets most space in this section of *de Re Publica* is Cicero himself.

[15] See, recently, Edwards 1993, Toner 1995.

[16] See the account of Atkins, Ch. 24 section 7.2 below.

[17] See Finley 1983 and n.10 above.

order. All that remained was for the real powers of the emperor to be openly accepted and acknowledged in law, and for the ideology of the *civilis princeps* who ruled in cooperation with the traditional governing class, themselves exemplars of a traditional morality, to give way. Change in these directions was inevitable, but surprisingly slow. It was facilitated by the gradual transfusion of personnel and transformation of attitudes that overcame the upper classes themselves. For men whose ideal was obedience rather than liberty were advanced into the Roman aristocracy through the favour and patronage of the emperor and his friends.

Under the Principate, political theory once more revolved around the theme of kingship, Seneca leading the way in a work dealing with an unambiguously regal virtue. In the *de Clementia* (of *c.* AD 55) he reminded the young Nero of the need for a *princeps* or *rex* to rule with justice, beneficence and mercy if he was to deserve the respect and veneration of his subjects. Epictetus' *Discourses* (early second century AD) offers a useful antidote to this unrealistically hopeful work. Looking back on the reigns of certain first-century emperors, in particular, Nero and Domitian (whose edict of AD 89 drove philosophers such as Epictetus out of Rome), he returns repeatedly to the themes of despotism, punishment, fear, and slavery.[18] The following exchange with a twice-consul is typical (*Diss.*IV.1.12–14):

> 'Who is able to compel me', you say, 'except the lord of all, Caesar?' Then even you yourself have admitted that you have one master. But that he is the common master of all, as you say, let not this console you at all: but know that you are a slave in a great family. So also the people of Nicopolis are used to exclaim, 'By the fortune of Caesar, we are free'.

The 'good king' in Epictetus is no earthly king as in *de Clementia*, but God (*Diss.* I.6.40). Slavery was still under the emperors a distinctive feature of Roman society, but now slaves freed their masters for political slavery, not, as under the Republic, for political liberty.

An elevation of the status of the emperor and a change of his image were notable developments of the third century, although accelerating rather than beginning in that period. This was a consequence of the endemic insecurity of the times, which were marked by continual warfare and a rapid turnover of emperors. The men who rose to the top were no longer members of the leisured and propertied aristocracy, but professional soldiers,

[18] Writing soon after, and in reaction to, Domitian's reign, Dio Chrysostom from Prusa in N.W. Asia Minor celebrated the reign of 'the best of emperors', his friend Trajan, with optimistic treatises on kingship in the Hellenistic tradition.

who placed a higher valuation on strength, discipline, authority and security, than on traditional practices and ideology. The novelty of their power, usurped rather than inherited, the circumstances in which it was won, and their authoritarian temper led them to widen the gap between themselves and the rest of humanity, including the aristocracy, and to surround themselves with a mystique with religious overtones. In portraiture, an anti-Classical style was favoured, showing emperors in a rigid, frontal stance, towering over all others. In court ceremonial, *adoratio*, or prostration, and the kissing of the edge of the imperial robe, replaced *salutatio*, the traditional greeting of patrons by their favoured friends and clients at the greater man's house. The emperor gave up his civilian dress, and took on the purple military cloak, while the wearing or display of purple became an imperial monopoly. In titulature emperors starting with Aurelian (AD 270–5), so long as they were pagan, were 'master and god' (*dominus et deus*). Diocletian (AD 284–305) took the title Jovius Augustus after Jupiter, and Maximian his colleague Herculius Augustus after Hercules. This practice could not survive the conversion of emperors to Christianity. A Christian emperor could not be a god. He could, however, be represented as divinely chosen, the viceregent, companion and 'heavenly messenger' of God, and his court portrayed as a model of heaven. Eusebius of Caesarea (AD *c.* 262–339), who theorized such notions with the cooperation and approval of Constantine, was drawing from the well of (pagan) kingship theory.[19]

Christianity from the first was viewed with distrust by the secular authorities.[20] Jesus died a criminal's death, executed by the state. The claim that he was King of the Jews, seen against the background of Judaic messianism, carried a political message, raising the spectre of a revolt against Rome. The movement that he inspired had parallels with forces of disorder and rebellion in Palestine. Christianity gradually established a separate identity apart from Judaism, but this did not at once raise its standing in the eyes of the Roman authorities. It was illegal and always vulnerable to attack, though not actually targeted for general persecution before the mid-third century and early fourth. Christians were regarded as atheists because they denied the gods of Rome. Their refusal to take an oath by the emperor's guardian spirit or sacrifice to the traditional Roman deities raised doubts about their acceptance of his authority.

The precarious position of the Church stimulated the tendency toward millenarianism that was a characteristic feature of the earliest Christian

[19] See, recently, Cameron 1991: e.g. 53–6.
[20] See Young, Ch. 31 below, for a much fuller account of the historical process which I summarize here.

following, and offered at least potentially a vigorous form of intellectual challenge to the supreme authority of the state. Insofar as Christian millenarianism entailed a rejection of political activity in the here-and-now, there are parallels with Cynicism and other Hellenistic movements which, in confronting 'choice of lives' issues, opted for rejection of rather than engagement in politics.[21] The difference is that in the minds of Christian millenarians the here-and-now would quickly pass away. The kingdom of God was expected imminently. Moreover, as in the Judaic tradition, that kingdom was normally thought of as temporal and historical. In a standard reconstruction, Christ would come again in glory, and, surrounded by the nations, establish an earthly kingdom based in Jerusalem (the Montanists preferred Phrygia); he would rule for 1,000 years until the coming of the New Heaven and the New Earth.[22]

Millenarianism is connected in early Christian communities with social radicalism. It seems that some Christians believed that their lives were already an anticipation of the millennium, that the egalitarian vision of the eschatological church (which appears canonically in the Pauline epistles)[23] should be reflected in actual social relationships between Christians and in the structures of their communities. Paul sought to manage and control these disruptive tendencies, standing firm by the conventional hierarchies of a patriarchal and slave society.

Paul's espousal of conventional social values is carried over into the political arena. For Paul and other New Testament writers the powers that be are ordained by God.[24] In contrast, millenarianism is associated with hostility to the state. This is vividly and famously exemplified in the portrayal of the Roman empire in Revelations 17 ff. (from the second half of the first century), as the Beast to whom the dragon had entrusted his world-wide dominion, as the harlot arrayed in purple and scarlet, drunk with the blood of saints and martyrs of Jesus. Hippolytus (around AD 204) in Book III of his *Commentary on Daniel* identified the empire with the last of the four beasts of the seventh chapter of the prophecy of Daniel, 'exceedingly terrible, with its teeth of iron and claws of bronze; and which devoured and broke in pieces and stamped the residue with its feet' (Daniel 7:19). The empire was the kingdom of the devil, the very opposite of the kingdom of Christ, and the appearance of Christ under the first emperor Augustus is treated by Hippolytus as a huge paradox.

21 See Downing 1992; also Crossan 1991: e.g. 72–88. Possible parallels with the Jewish Qumran community are considered briefly by Downing and in more detail by Vermes 1981: 211–21.

22 On millenarianism, see Cohn 1957, Rowland 1988, Daley 1991.

23 See e.g. Galatians 3:28, 1 Corinthians 12:13, Colossians 3:11. All three are by Paul – I follow Kummel 1975 – and are datable to the mid-first century AD.

24 Romans 13:1–7, Titus 3:1; cf. 1 Peter 2:13–17.

A more conciliatory line, grounded as we saw in the New Testament, was developed by Justin Martyr in his *Apology* (*c.* 155), by Melito bishop of Sardis (*c.* 160–70), and by Origen in his tract against Celsus (early third century). As Melito wrote to Marcus Aurelius:

> Our philosophy first grew up among the barbarians, but its full flower came among your nation in the great reign of your ancestor Augustus, and became an omen of good in your empire, for from that time the power of the Romans became great and splendid. You are now his happy successor, and shall be so along with your son, if you protect the philosophy which grew up with the empire and began with Augustus. Your ancestors nourished it along with other cults, and the greatest proof that our doctrine flourished for good along with the empire in its noble beginning, is the fact that it met no evil in the reign of Augustus, but on the contrary everything splendid and glorious according to the wishes of all men.[25]

It is in this tradition that Eusebius, the source of this citation, stands, with the difference that he in effect hijacked millenarianism and brought it into service of the new order. For in 312 Constantine became emperor having defeated Maxentius in war, and on the eve of the decisive battle was converted to Christianity. The message of Eusebius was that the history of the Church and temporal history, specifically the history of Rome, had come together in the reign of Constantine. His rule could be seen as a foretaste or replica of the Kingdom of God on earth.[26] Eusebius' enthusiasm was an understandable response to the dramatic change, following the conversion of Constantine, in the fortunes of the Church from a persecuted to a tolerated and then, quickly, to a favoured institution.

The state's embracing of Christianity afforded the Church obvious opportunities to expand and flourish, but carried equally conspicuous risks. The Church of the fourth century was both richly endowed and caught up in affairs of state. The fourth-century expansion of monasticism, a movement that had arisen in the previous century, was in part a reaction to the increased 'secularization' of the Church. Monasticism may be read as a form of millenarianism. The communities set up from the 320s in Egypt by Pachomius (*c.* AD 292–346), for example, were seen as an ideal utopian society over against the earthly world, as a present embodiment of the future Kingdom of God.[27]

In the early fifth century, Augustine offered a theoretical reinterpretation of the millenarial tradition. In his account, the *City of God*, history

[25] Eusebius *Hist.Eccl.* IV.26.7–8. [26] See Wallace-Hadrill 1960, Barnes 1981, Cameron 1991.
[27] Rousseau 1985.

and eschatology are related but in a complex way. Both Babylon, the Earthly City, and Jerusalem, the City of God, are on earth, but neither is to be identified with existing, earthly institutions, whether Roman empire or Christian Church. Both empire and Church are human institutions corrupted by sin, but both have a part to play in the unfolding of the divine plan, the Empire to promote civic peace, the Church to provide the sacraments, and more broadly, a religious culture. Both have within them elements of the two Cities. Only on the day of judgment will the true membership of each City be revealed.[28]

Early Christian thinkers stood in an ambiguous relationship with Classical philosophy. As products of a Classical education, all were to some extent in contact with it, some were thoroughly versed in it. Though dedicated to subverting it, they could not escape its influence. Frequently they took over and employed Classical idioms and models as a springboard for their own rival patterns of thought. Eusebius' ideas on kingship, and Gregory of Nyssa's on freedom,[29] for example, owe a heavy debt to the Platonic intellectual tradition. Lactantius used Ciceronian ideas of equity in order to attack inequality and injustice in the societies of (pagan) Greece and Rome. Augustine, in his more thoroughgoing demolition of Classical theory and Classical models of moral and political conduct, was unable to avoid employing the methods and concepts of Classical philosophy, not to mention the techniques of Classical rhetoric. And although the nature and goals of his intellectual inquiries could not have been anticipated by the founders of Stoicism and the other Hellenistic philosophies, it would be wrong to imagine that their interests did not overlap. In particular, Augustine was as preoccupied as they had been with 'choice of life' questions, more especially in *City of God* with the duties and obligations of Christian citizens in the world, a world whose end was no longer thought to be imminent.

[28] The bibliography for Augustine, whose work lies outside the scope of this volume, is extensive. For an introduction to Augustine and some predecessors, see Markus 1988b.

[29] See Gaïth 1953.

21

The Cynics

JOHN MOLES

> Diogenes was a Greek philosopher who lived in a tub; one day he was sunning himself when Alexander the Great, smitten by desire to see the great philosopher, approached and asked if there was anything he could do for him, to which Diogenes responded: 'Get out of my light'.
>
> (Cic. *Tusc.*v.92; D.L. vi.38)

The Cynics[1] had no ideals of their own and assumed the worst of everybody else; hence the modern usages 'cynic' and 'cynical'.

Among non-classicists today these are perhaps the two dominant, although contradictory, images of Cynicism. The first projects Diogenes' behaviour, which some might regard as merely loutish, as illustrating a truly admirable independence of spirit; indeed, some versions add that Alexander delightedly exclaimed: 'Had I not been Alexander, I would have wished to be Diogenes' (Plu. *Alex.* 14.5; D.L. vi.32). The second projects the Cynics as, if not positively immoral, at least unpleasantly amoral. Neither seems to encourage claims that the Cynics made an important contribution to ancient political thought, and the contradiction between the two is but a pale reflection of the many difficulties involved in the attempt to uncover a true picture of Cynicism. Any assessment, therefore, of the Cynic contribution must begin by resolving these difficulties.

1 The problem of evidence

Virtually all the writings of the Cynics themselves are lost, but a disparate mass of evidence survives: quantities of sayings and anecdotes; numerous

[1] Texts/fragments/testimonia: Paquet 1988, Giannantoni 1990: ii.5.b–n; critical discussions: Giannantoni 1990: 195–583; general books: Lovejoy and Boas 1935, Dudley 1937, Höistad 1948, Kindstrand 1976, Goulet-Cazé 1986; collections of papers: Billerbeck 1991, Goulet-Cazé & Goulet 1993, Branham and Goulet-Cazé 1996; my own views (which have fluctuated in detail): Moles 1983a, 1993, 1995a, with fuller documentation than is desirable here; potted accounts in my entries on the Cynics in *The Oxford Classical Dictionary* (Oxford 1996, 3rd edn) and in Zeyl 1997.

Cynic prose and poetic fragments, of greatly varying size; letters (Cynic in content but not written by the putative writers); the Diogenic discourses of Dio Chrysostom (*c.* AD 45–120), sophist and (mostly Stoic) philosopher; more or less systematic accounts of Cynicism by the Epicurean Philodemus (first century BC), the Stoic Epictetus ('On Cynicism';[2] early second century AD), and the biographer Diogenes Laertius (probably third century AD), Book VI of whose *Lives of the Philosophers* treats the Cynics and remains the most important single source;[3] numerous allusions, with some discussion, in the Stoic philosopher Seneca (writing *c.* AD 55–65); several works of the rhetorician and satirist Lucian (second century AD); two speeches of the Roman emperor and intellectual Julian (fourth century AD); numerous Christian allusions to Cynicism; and a great quantity of Cynic-influenced literature, particularly that of the satiric tradition.

Within this mass, numerous different tendencies can be observed: the invention of sayings and anecdotes, a general phenomenon of ancient biography accentuated by the flamboyant and self-dramatizing behaviour of leading Cynics; idealization and bowdlerization of Cynicism (Epictetus); making Diogenes look like Socrates; making the Cynics look like Stoics (Epictetus, elements of Diogenes Laertius), sometimes in order to legitimate a formal philosophical 'succession' (Socrates–Antisthenes–Diogenes–Crates–Zeno); projecting the Cynics as exemplars of primitive or simple virtue; projecting the Cynics as stern, but just, critics of the vices of human society; polemical misrepresentation (Philodemus); representing Cynics as frauds and hypocrites, hence suitable butts for comic ridicule (Lucian); portraying Cynics as threats to social and political stability (Roman imperial texts); appropriating a Cynic persona for self-portrayal (Dio; sometimes Lucian); contrasting early Cynics and their allegedly debased descendants; comparing, and contrasting, Cynics and Christian ascetics.

Of these tendencies, some are clearly distortions (many of Philodemus' claims are merely silly), although distortions help to define truths; some are not clearly distortions but conflict with others; some seem *a priori* reasonable but require the support of hard evidence. Thus any picture of Cynicism must be a synthesis of widely different types of material and of thousands of different items, each of which should, ideally, have been subject to exact scrutiny (by conventional criteria such as the attempt to distinguish between primary/early and secondary/late material). The

[2] Billerbeck 1978. [3] Goulet-Cazé 1992.

synthesis must also allow for the possibility of difference between different Cynics and different periods of Cynicism. And it will always be vulnerable to the accusation of circular argument. Nor is it merely a matter of establishing facts: Cynic behaviour, sayings and writings themselves pose interpretative problems.

Unsurprisingly, therefore, the genesis, status, significance, value and influence of Cynicism were all controversial in the ancient world and remain so. Nevertheless, the source problem can be exaggerated. The loss of nearly all Cynic writings does not matter as much as one would anticipate, and in any case we can get close to the most important written work in all Cynicism (Diogenes' *Politeia*). Even the volume and diversity of the surviving evidence has a positive aspect, as indicating the interest, importance and vitality of the Cynic tradition.

2 Reconstructing Cynicism

The term 'Cynic' ('doggish') was certainly used from the fourth century BC of Diogenes, nicknamed 'the dog', and of his followers, hence the English 'Cynicism' ('Cynism' in ancient Greek and many modern languages) as the name of the general movement. There has, however, been controversy from ancient times as to whether Diogenes or Antisthenes (*c*. 445–365 BC), one of Socrates' closest followers, was the first Cynic.[4]

The case for Antisthenes depends on Cynic-looking elements in his thought and in the attested titles of some of his works; on his having taught philosophy in Cynosarges, a gymnasium for non-Athenians whose name can be interpreted as including 'dog'; and on the ancient tradition that Diogenes was one of his pupils. But the whole ancient tradition agrees in calling Diogenes, not Antisthenes, 'the dog'; some elements of Antisthenes' philosophy (notably his study of language and logic) are emphatically un-Cynic; and direct association between Diogenes and Antisthenes is chronologically problematic (below). The case for Antisthenes should thus be attributed to the general ancient desire to construct traditions based on master–pupil relationships, to the specific project of tracing Stoicism back in unbroken succession to Socrates, and to Antisthenes' undoubted influence on Diogenes, transmitted not through direct association but through Antisthenes' writings.

In the reconstruction of Diogenes' life[5] and activity, the general distortions in the ancient traditions about Cynicism are exacerbated by the fact

[4] Giannantoni 1990: IV.223–33, 1993, Döring 1995.

[5] Goulet-Cazé 1994.

that Diogenes was himself a flamboyant self-dramatist, who provoked extremes of admiration, hostility and imaginative invention, thus inspiring a rich and varied Diogenes-legend. Ancient and modern reactions to Diogenes range from appreciation of his undoubted wit to admiration (often tinged with exasperation) for his supposed integrity, denial of his philosophical significance, revulsion at his cult of shamelessness, dislike of the threat he was thought to pose to conventional social and political values and misguided attempts to make him respectable. All accounts, ancient and modern, are, therefore, necessarily controversial. But the picture is less obscure than one might fear.

Diogenes (*c.* 412/403–*c.* 324/321 BC) was a native of the Black Sea port of Sinope, where his father, Hecesias, was in charge of the mint; he was exiled; and he spent the rest of his life in Athens and Corinth. The date of his arrival in mainland Greece and the question of his relationship with Antisthenes remain disputed. On the most reasonable reconstruction, Diogenes and his father were accused, rightly or wrongly, of 'defacing the currency' – thus one of Diogenes' great slogans (D.L. VI.20) originated as an apologetic and metaphorical reinterpretation of a literal act; the literal 'defacement of the currency' caused Diogenes' exile; and both events occurred after Antisthenes' death. Hence Diogenes' exile was the catalyst for a dramatic change of life, and his pupilship under Antisthenes should be regarded as fictitious. In a similar spirit of rationalizing minimalism, the stories of Diogenes' consultation of the Delphic oracle (clearly modelled upon Socrates') and of his capture by pirates (D.L. VI.21, 29–31, 74–5) should be rejected; on the other hand, the encounter with Alexander seems authentic (though it would have occurred before Alexander became 'the Great').[6]

The main outlines of Diogenes' activities in Athens and Corinth are clear. Over time he evolved a way of life which entailed the barest minimum of material possessions: coarse cloak, folded double for warmth in the cold (no under-tunic); staff for physical support and protection; knapsack for food; wine-jar for 'house' (the 'tub' of later tradition); no shoes. It also entailed the barest minimum of food: cold water from springs and fountains, not wine; vegetables, especially greens and lupins (though Diogenes was not committed to vegetarianism). These items were variously obtained by living off the land, begging and stealing. Diogenes' lifestyle also involved the performance in public of all natural functions (eating, drinking, urinating, defecating, masturbating and fornicating),

[6] Hammond 1993: 28, 282.

characteristically in the *agora*, a sacred area off-limits to such earthy activities. The main point of the appellation 'dog' is shamelessness, for which dogs were renowned.

Diogenes was highly vocal, launching verbal attacks upon a whole range of targets: all forms of convention, marriage, family, politics, the city, all social, sexual and racial distinctions, worldly reputation, wealth, power and authority, literature, music, and all forms of intellectual speculation; and upon their various human representatives. Many of these attacks exemplify the slogan 'deface the currency', 'currency' being a metaphor for law, custom and convention. Diogenes' aggressiveness is another implication of his nickname. The attacks were generally witty, the wit often savage, often vulgar, often paradoxical, sometimes utilizing literary parody and allusion. Diogenes' oral performances also included justifications of his peculiar way of life, a way of life which was adopted by countless Cynics over the centuries, down to the sixth century AD.

Fundamental questions arise. Was Diogenes a mere buffoon, a mere exhibitionist, as many ancient and modern critics claim? Is there anything here which is serious and implies thought? Can Cynicism be described in any useful sense as a philosophy?

That Diogenes was well educated might be inferred from his social background, and is confirmed by his knowledge of Homer and tragedy, his use of literary allusion and parody, and his own writings (below). He also shows familiarity with the life and thought of philosophers both earlier (the Presocratics, Socrates, Antisthenes and the elder Aristippus) and contemporary (Plato). When he wants, he can indulge in technical philosophy, so much so that (as we shall see) one of his syllogisms defied solution until 1991. This last example indicates intelligence, as do many of his sayings and actions. Diogenes, then, illustrates a phenomenon that is always unsettling for clever intellectuals: that of the clever intellectual who rejects intellectualism in favour of some very simple creed or mode of life, in whose articulation, however, he continues to deploy cleverness. Any one (in the ancient or modern world) who dismisses Diogenes with patronizing contempt is a fool, as many of his contemporaries learned to their cost. In the series of verbal skirmishes between Diogenes and the great Plato recorded by ancient tradition Diogenes typically comes off better (e.g. D.L. VI.25–6, 40, 58, 67).

What, then, of Diogenes' exhibitionism? Of course, if one holds that there is no shame in performing natural functions in public, some degree of what others will decry as mere exhibitionism is inevitable. But Diogenes' performance in public of natural functions often took the form of full public performance, and masturbation was one of his star turns (D.L. vi.69). Later, Diogenes' closest follower, Crates, achieved notoriety by having intercourse with his 'wife' Hipparchia in the *agora* (D.L. vi.96). How can such seemingly outrageous behaviour be justified?

And what of Diogenes' characteristic humour? Here the ancient tradition provides an immediate, though partial, answer: the Cynics specialized in the serio-comic (*spoudaiogeloion*), the exposition of serious thought through humorous means.[7] But what was the thought?

It is obvious that Cynicism was first and foremost how Cynics actually lived and behaved (even Diogenes Laertius, who presents Cynicism as a philosophy, attests ancient debate whether Cynicism was a philosophy or a way of life (vi. 103)). It was never a formal philosophical school: it never had, and obviously could never have, a physical school-building; equally, it never had, and could never have, any philosophical doctrine. Yet established philosophers of the time thought that Cynicism embodied some sort of philosophical project. Plato famously dubbed Diogenes a 'mad Socrates' (D.L. vi.54), Aristotle seems to allude to Diogenes in a serious ethical context (*Pol.* 1253a26–9), and Theophrastus certainly does so (D.L. vi.22). Diogenes and later Cynics do to some extent engage in philosophical debate with other philosophers. That debate mostly takes the form of verbal skirmishing but sometimes extends into written works, such as Diogenes' *Politeia* or the polemics between Cynics and Epicureans.[8] Diogenes himself claimed that his goal (*telos*) was virtue (D.L. vi.70, 72, 104), and this claim was taken seriously by reputable philosophers of different schools in succeeding generations. In popular philosophy, Diogenes often appears as the philosopher *par excellence*. Diogenes also claimed 'wisdom' (D.L. vi.72), had many personal followers (described in the ancient tradition as 'pupils') and wrote numerous works,[9] some of which bear what look like conventional philosophical titles, and which evoked responses from established philosophers. (Denial of Diogenes' writing reflects the bowdlerizing tendency, anxious to detach the great Diogenes from the disgusting propositions circulating under his name.)

Cynicism, then, is a way of life, but one which makes philosophical claims, and in this sense the polarity between 'way of life' and 'philosophy' is false (just as, conversely, one's philosophy should affect one's way of life). These philosophical claims are grounded in a criterion accepted by

[7] Kindstrand 1976: 47–8, López Cruces 1995: 77–84.
[8] Gigante 1993: 198–203 (Menippus, Colotes and Menedemus), 211–23 (Philodemus).
[9] Goulet-Cazé 1994: 817–20.

practically all ancient philosophies: 'life according to nature' (D.L. VI.71). The crucial question is how this criterion is to be understood. It is certain that Diogenes gave it a 'hard primitivist' interpretation: hence his constant appeals to animals, primitive man, uncivilized barbarians (all uncontaminated by civilization) and the gods as moral standards, and his representation of the Cynic way of life in Golden Age terms (D.L. VI.44). This hard primitivism underpins all the characteristic Cynic modes of behaviour and attitudes. It is important to appreciate the extreme radicalism of the Cynic stance. When Diogenes says, 'I do not need material possessions (or whatever)', he is not saying, 'I do not *need* them but it is all right for me to have them', nor 'I do not need them, but it's all right for *you* to have them (because you have a legitimately different perspective)'. He is saying, 'these things are bad and prevent the attainment of virtue'.

As hard primitives, Cynics claim 'self-sufficiency' (D.L. VI.105), 'freedom' (D.L. VI.71), and 'passionlessness' (D.L. VI.2, 15), and they describe their way of life alike as 'simple', because natural in the most extreme sense, 'easy', because wholly anti-intellectual, and 'difficult', because of its enormous physical demands. Hence Diogenes' (highly selective) admiration of Sparta (D.L. VI.27, 59). Toil and suffering naturally acquire positive moral value in Cynicism, an idea expressed in the paradox *ponos agathon*: 'suffering is a good'. Overcoming these difficulties requires constant practice *(askēsis)*.[10]

Of course, the core claim that virtue consists in living in accordance with primitivist nature is not self-evidently true, though it belongs to a long tradition of thought which reflects an understandable human desire that the world be a fundamentally good place and the problems of life merely a distortion of the natural order. Another obvious objection to the Cynic programme is that it is impossible. To both these difficulties the Cynic way of life itself provides some answer. That way of life *is* virtue in action, and it shows that the programme can be implemented. Like the appeal to 'living according to nature', this answer may be regarded as philosophically unsatisfactory, on the ground that Cynicism does not argue its position 'properly'. But that objection carried and could in principle carry little weight with Diogenes.

If the Cynic way of life shows that the programme *can* be done, Cynic exhibitionism immediately finds a creditable explanation: it is partly for the benefit of other people. This raises the question of the Cynic's relations with others.[11]

[10] D.L. VI.71, Goulet-Cazé 1986. [11] Moles 1983a: 109–16, 1993: 269–77.

It is clear that the Cynics recognized the kinship or community of the wise: they used the tag 'the wise man is the friend of his like' (D.L. VI.105), one of Diogenes' syllogisms appealed to 'wise men's being friends of the gods' and 'their having possessions in common' (D.L. VI.72 (below)), Diogenes himself had followers and Crates claimed to be 'a citizen of Diogenes' (D.L. VI.93). This kinship transcends the conventional barriers between men and women (as we shall see) and between races (hence Cynic appeals to the right behaviour of barbarian peoples).

More problematic is their relationship with mankind at large. Contrary, perhaps, to first impressions, Cynicism is a missionary philosophy. Cynic exhibitionism provides other human beings with a model to imitate or a demonstration of the falsity of their own values. By example and exhortation the Cynic energetically tries to convert others to the Cynic life of virtue. He claims a large range of titles ('scout', 'overseer', 'benefactor', 'teacher', 'ruler', 'doctor', 'reconciler', 'good spirit', 'helper', 'saviour', etc.) which imply a didactic and proselytizing role towards others and indeed a profound concern for other human beings (*philanthrōpia*). These apparently altruistic elements of the Cynic's behaviour cannot be dismissed as later embroideries inspired by the more humane character of Crates. They are all, or almost all, documented for Diogenes himself and some for his predecessor Antisthenes.[12]

How, then, to explain the criticisms and insults which the Cynic directs at humanity in general, or the apparently disdainful fashion in which he divides humanity into an elite of sages and the mass of the foolish or insane? The explanation is simple enough. As a matter of fact there is a great gulf between the sage and the ignorant majority and only the former is a human being in the truest sense. Yet Cynic virtue is 'easy' and represents man's natural state. Consequently, even the imbecile masses can be regarded as *potential* human beings, and the gulf between the Cynic and ordinary human beings is not insuperable. Hence the common modern assumption that Cynicism is completely negative is misconceived: of course Cynic teaching is largely negative, because it aims to expose the falsity of conventional values, but the point is to isolate the only thing that matters, the Cynic way of life 'according to nature', which itself is positive – and to commend it to others. Epictetus (III.24.64) is thus right to describe Diogenes as 'loving all mankind'.

Thus far we have tried to reconstruct Cynicism as it were in a vacuum and without prejudice. Another approach is to plot Cynicism against

[12] Documentation in Moles 1983a: 112 n. 73.

existing traditions. While Diogenes' way of life was original and distinctive, it can be seen to be constructed from many diverse, and mostly Greek, elements: the belief (espoused by certain types of holy men and wise men) that wisdom was a matter of action rather than thought; the principle (advanced by various sophists, fifth-century primitivists and Antisthenes) of living in accordance with nature rather than law/convention; the tradition, perhaps sharpened by contemporary disillusionment with the polis, of promulgating ideal societies or constitutions, often with Golden Age associations; a tradition of 'shamelessness' (reflected by the symbol of the dog in literature and by the supposed customs of certain foreign peoples); Socratic rejection of all elements of philosophy except practical ethics; Socrates' pursuit of philosophy in the *agora* rather than in a school; an anti-intellectual tradition; the tradition (variously represented by Odysseus, Heracles, the Spartans, and to some extent by Socrates) of physical toughness as a requirement of virtue; the image of the suffering hero and the wanderer (Odysseus, Heracles, various tragic figures); the tradition of mendicancy (represented both in literature and in life); the life of asceticism and poverty (as represented by various wise men and holy men and labourers); the tradition of the wise or holy man who promises converts happiness or salvation; and various humorous traditions (the jester's practical and verbal humour; Old Comedy's outspokenness and crudity; Socrates' serio-comic wit).

Bizarre, perhaps repulsive, insufficiently grounded in philosophical theory, Cynicism nevertheless exhibits a coherence which in its own terms is quite powerful.

3 The Cynics and politics

What room does this picture of Cynicism leave for conventional politics? Seemingly, none. But before we can accept this conclusion, we must consider the evidence regarding Diogenes' celebrated 'cosmopolitanism'.[13] That evidence may: (a) force us to modify our conclusion; (b) reveal an incoherence in Diogenes' position; (c) validate our conclusion but open up further perspectives.

The two key texts are in Diogenes Laertius. VI.63 records a saying: 'Asked where he was from, he said: "[I am] a citizen of the universe."' Although this saying comes in a literary form, the *chreia* (a brief anecdote including an apophthegm), which is much used in the 'Diogenes-legend',

[13] This whole section reworks Moles 1993 and 1995a with some modifications and changes of emphasis.

the question was as common in life as in literature and had particular point for the stateless Diogenes. Nor does the extreme rarity of the word *kosmopolitēs* or its first being attested in Philo (*Opif.* 3, *Mos.* I.157 [first century AD]) count against authenticity: Philo or his Stoic sources must have got the word from somewhere and the Cynics were renowned for their verbal resourcefulness, including coinages. Numerous ancient sources link Diogenes with 'cosmopolitan' sentiment. The false attribution of that sentiment to Socrates is naturally explained as retrojection of Diogenic material upon the 'father' of the whole Cynic-Stoic 'succession'. There is much evidence from Cynics and non-Cynics that 'cosmopolitanism' was a big Cynic claim, which presumably starts with the first Cynic.

The other text comes in Diogenes' 'doxography' in VI.72, which requires full quotation:[14]

> (a) He said that all things belong to the wise, using the sort of arguments we have stated above (VI.37):
>
> All things belong to the gods.
The gods are friends of the wise.
The possessions of friends are held in common.
Therefore all things belong to the wise.
>
> (b) With regard to the law (*nomos*), he held that it was impossible for there to be political government (*politeuesthai*) without it. For he says:
>
> Without a city there is no profit in something civilized;
and the city is civilized.
Without law there is no profit in a city.
Therefore law is something civilized.
>
> (c) He would ridicule good birth and reputations and all those sorts of things, saying that they were the ornaments of vice (*prokosmēmata kakias*).
>
> (d) And he said that the only correct citizen-state (*politeia*)[15] was the one in the universe (*kosmos*).

[14] This section follows the translation and arrangement of Schofield 1991: 141–2, with modifications as in Moles 1995a: 130.

[15] Translation of *politeia* is difficult. 'State' *tout court* misleads, but some reference to 'state' is desirable, because: (a) *politeia* alludes to the workings of the institution traditionally known as the 'city-state'; (b) 'state' can be used both of the political institution and of the individual, hence allowing a paradoxical transference of reference. The 'citizen' prefix attempts to give the term 'state' concrete political reference and also emphasizes the closeness of the formulations of VI.72 and VI.63. The translation of the title of Diogenes' work as 'Ideal State' has disadvantages, but fewer than those of such translations as 'Republic' or 'Constitution', and makes the point that such a philosophical work aims to describe what ought to be rather than what is – though, as we shall see, the Cynic 'state' is not utopian.

(e) And he said that women should be held in common, recognizing no marriage, but saying that the man who persuades should go with the woman who persuades.[16] And because of this he thought that sons too should be held in common.

A preliminary problem is posed by the difficult syllogism in (b), which has occasioned considerable debate. Its authenticity is supported by two factors: its position in the doxography and its relationship to a syllogism of Cleanthes the Stoic (Stob. II.103.14–17 [= SVF I.587 = Long and Sedley 1987: § 67.I]), which reads approximately as follows: 'If a city is a habitable construction to which people may have recourse for the dispensation of justice, then a city is surely civilized. But a city is that sort of habitation. So a city is civilized.' While text and interpretation are controversial, this latter syllogism, which defends the city and 'civilization', clearly aims to refute (b). Diogenes, then, is giving 'the civilized' a pejorative meaning (as it must have in Cynicism) and attacking law, the city and 'the civilized' as interconnected: 'Diogenes' argument is – as one would expect – *antinomian*, directed against those who sympathize with his aversion to the city and its manners, but who hold to the view rejected by him that the rule of law is indispensable'.[17]

Many scholars have supposed that the whole of VI.72 derives from Diogenes' lost *Politeia* ('Ideal State'). The content fits: a general 'political' focus, two syllogisms (a formal mode alien to Diogenes' oral philosophizing), a specific allusion to 'the correct state' (a fourth-century term), and in (e) a radical proposal for sexual relations and the rearing of children suitable to a *Politeia* of radical cast. The arrangement also has a logic. The first syllogism, indubitably Diogenic, concerns legitimate possessions or needs. The second syllogism, also Diogenic, concerns something that is conventionally regarded as necessary for civilized life but which the Cynic rejects, along with the city and civilized life itself. The rejection of 'the civilized' etc. is followed by a rejection of similar things within the city ('good birth and reputations and all those sorts of things'), expressed by a characteristic Cynic attitude, 'ridicule'. These similar things are designated 'ornaments of vice'. Then comes the cosmopolitan sentiment, introduced by an 'and', which seems to imply a precise logical connection.

The links with the preceding material are marked. After the false political and social values of the second syllogism and of the 'good-birth' section comes the correct political system. After the plurality of false values comes the single correct value (a typical Cynic contrast). There is also an

[16] On text and interpretation see Schofield 1991: 12 n. 21.

[17] Schofield 1991: 134.

implicit contrast between 'law' (and custom etc.), as in the false things of (b) and (c), and the *natural* order of the *kosmos* in (d). The use of the term 'correct state' illustrates the Cynic technique of appropriating and reinterpreting the rhetoric of his opponents and values that he rejects (thereby 'defacing the currency' verbally). Nor does the Cynic merely unite theory and practice (itself no mean feat): he unites exterior and interior, in contrast to those who pursue the 'ornaments of vice'. And whereas 'good birth' etc. are the *prokosmēmata* of vice, the Cynic state is in the *kosmos*: false *kosmos* yields to true *kosmos*. The final item, on wives and sons 'in common', links by ring-structure to the first item, on possessions held 'in common'. This ring-structure seems to emphasize 'communism' as the alpha and omega of Diogenes' *politeia*, in implicit contrast with the exclusiveness of worldly possessions and of gradations of birth and reputation and so on, and in implicit parallel to the doctrine of 'cosmopolitanism', the *kosmos* naturally being the 'common' home of everyone, as the Cynic writer of [Heraclit.] *Ep*. 9.2 describes it.

VI.72, therefore, represents a coherent and close summary of Diogenes' *Politeia*. But what is this 'cosmopolitanism'? It seems to combine a negative and a positive.

The negative is the rejection of the city and *ta politika* ('politics'): cf. (b) and (d). This rejection coheres with the slogan 'deface the currency', with numerous fragments and *testimonia*, with the tragic verses applied by Diogenes to himself: 'cityless [*apolis*], homeless, deprived of country [*patris*], a beggar, a wanderer, living life from day to day' (D.L. VI.38, where Diogenes is not lamenting his condition, but boasting of it), and with our general picture of Cynicism: the Diogenic Cynic must reject the city as 'contrary to nature'.

The positive consists in the primacy of the 'state in the *kosmos*'. Once we have jettisoned the assumption that Cynicism is completely negative, interpretation becomes relatively easy. First, Diogenes' sentiment must be seen against the background of a general tradition, variously represented by proverbial wisdom, philosophers and sophists, in which the polis or *patris* or some similar concept is rejected, or revalued, in favour of an internationalist or cosmopolitan ideal; some of these formulations are very similar to Diogenes'.[18] Second, since rejection of the city promotes Cynic freedom and virtue, by another re-evaluation of conventional terms, Cynics use the words *patris*, polis, *politeia* and so on as metaphors for the Cynic way of life itself (D.L. VI.93; Epict. *Diss*. III.22.84–5). This

[18] Documentation in Moles 1993: 264 n.18. For the specific interaction with Aristippus' claims in Xenophon *Memorabilia* II.1.12–13 see Moles 1993: 265.

idea is implicit in VI.72: items (c) and (d) contrast – (c) concerns things that produce vice, (d) concerns the thing that produces virtue. Consequently, the Cynic *politeia*, the Cynic 'state', is nothing other than the 'state' of being a Cynic,[19] which is at once a material or social state and a moral state (Cynic moral virtue being dependent on rejection of conventional social and political values). The point is clear in Crates' *Pera*, a Homeric poetic parody, whose blend of wit, literary sophistication and earthiness and elevation of sentiment perfectly illustrates the appeal of Cynic *spoudaiogeloion* (D.L. VI.85; Demetr. *de Eloc.* 259; Clem. *Strom.* II.20.121):[20]

> There is a city, Knapsack, in the midst of the winey sea of illusion,
> Fair and rich, surrounded by dirt, owning nothing,
> Into which sails neither foolish parasite,
> Nor glutton delighting in a prostitute's buttocks,
> But it bears thyme and garlic and figs and loaves,
> As a result of which they do not make war against one another for these things,
> Nor take arms for money, nor for glory . . .
> Free from the slavery and torture of servile pleasure,
> They love immortal kingship and freedom . . .

Diogenes' Cynic 'state' is viewed as being coextensive with the *kosmos* and in some sort of positive relationship with it and its constituent elements.[21] As a child of nature or noble savage, the Cynic regards the natural world as bountiful, and feels a sense of kinship with the animal world, which provides him with models for his way of life. He feels a sense of kinship also with other wise men, wherever they may be. He can live his natural life anywhere on earth. He even feels potential kinship with mankind at large. What of the gods? The evidence about Cynic attitudes to the gods raises problems.[22] Nevertheless, Diogenes and other Cynics can describe the gods as man's benefactors, because they have created a naturally good world (D.L. VI.44), and project them as a paradigm for Cynic self-sufficiency (D.L. VI.51, 104). Consequently, they can describe themselves as 'god-like' (D.L. VI.51, 104, 105), as 'friends of the gods' (D.L. VI.37, 72) and as their messengers and agents (Strabo XV.1.63–4 (= Onesicritus fr. 17a); Plu. *Alex.* 65.2; D.L. VI.102; Epict. *Diss.* III.22.2, 23, 53, 69). In VI.72 item (a) attests Diogenes' inclusion of the gods in his *kosmopolis*.

[19] There are earlier parallels for this kind of move, both implicit as in the general tradition already mentioned and explicit (notably Pl. *Rep.* IX.592b3): Diogenes' version remains extremely arresting and radical.

[20] Dudley 1937: 44, 56–7, Höistad 1948: 129–31.

[21] For the following arguments see Moles 1993: 268–9.

[22] Goulet-Cazé 1996, Moles 1995a: 138 n.27.

It will be useful to pose a series of specific questions about Diogenes' *Politeia*.[23]

First, what is its status? The Cynics rejected literature *tout court* (not merely 'bad' literature), but wrote more voluminously and variously than any ancient philosophical school:[24] relatively formal philosophical treatises, dialogues, tragedies, historiography, letters, 'diatribes' (moral homilies in lecture form), various kinds of poetry and of literary parody, prose-poetry hybrids. This paradox reflects a familiar philosophical compromise: while written philosophy is a poor substitute for real philosophizing, it may be a necessary vehicle for increasing one's audience. (The other customary motive, philosophical exploration, means little to Cynics, who in their own estimation have solved all philosophical problems.) With its syllogisms and universalizing propositions, Diogenes' *Politeia* looks like a formal philosophical work and it is essentially serious. Yet there is also an element of spoof: Diogenes can play the conventional philosophical game yet deconstruct the political philosophy of conventional philosophers such as Plato and Aristotle. Furthermore, when Diogenes and other Cynics use written works to convey moral lessons, they prefer 'entertainment' genres to formal works, and their projected readership only includes fellow-philosophers at the margins. In short, within Cynic writings 'formal' works of philosophy take second place to 'entertainment' genres, and the whole business of writing takes second place to practical philosophizing on the streets. Diogenes' *Politeia*, then, is important because it crystallizes Cynic philosophy in a text to which subsequent philosophers could respond and which can serve as a bench-mark for our general reconstruction of Cynicism. But it cannot *add* much to Cynic philosophy, except insofar as it may have to cover events that have not yet occurred (such as babies).

Hence the second question, applicable to all 'ideal states': is Diogenes' 'state' intended to be practicable? Since Diogenes' 'state' is in the first instance the 'state' of being a virtuous Cynic, the answer must basically be 'yes', though with a few qualifications. Even Cynics sometimes admitted that they had not quite attained the pinnacle of virtue. Cynic 'free sex' might produce children, who would have to be reared, as in item (e). Cynics might consort, both sexually and otherwise, with other Cynics, so that the Cynic 'state' might acquire a plural dimension, which would obviously increase, the more converts the Cynics made, and potentially include all humankind.

[23] For some of the following arguments see Moles 1995a: 138–58.

[24] Branham 1993.

Third, what implications does the Cynic 'state' have for existing civic institutions? Diogenes' claim that there was nothing out of place in taking something from a temple (D.L. VI.73) and his advocacy of gymnastics, including nude gymnastics by women (D.L. VI.70; Phld. *Stoic.* col.19.17), entail the continuing existence of these institutions. But the saying about taking something from a temple is double-edged: while it allows the continued existence of 'temples', it denies their *raison d'être*. If there is nothing 'out of place' in taking things from a temple, the whole notion of 'sacred space' is subverted (as it is by Diogenes' 'using any place for any purpose' (D.L. VI.22)). A Cynic must reject a social institution such as marriage, because it is an institution of *nomos* and an infringement of individual freedom. He will not advocate the dismantling of buildings such as temples, even though they did not exist in the primitive era when man was uncorrupted, because they have a practical Cynic usefulness, but he will not use them in the conventional way. Of course if a universal Cynic state were ever to come to pass, many areas would lack such amenities, because they would never be built in the first place.

Hence the fourth question: is there a fundamental inconsistency, or even, as many, ancients and moderns, have claimed, a fundamental hypocrisy, in Cynicism? On the one hand, there is an absolute theoretical rejection of the conventional ('incorrect') polis; on the other hand, although we hear of occasional Cynics in the country,[25] the great majority, like Diogenes, lived and begged in poleis and slept in baths and temples and so on. In fact, there are several good answers to this question. (i) The Cynic's missionary role commits him to living among the foolish and immoral masses. (ii) He must demonstrate the immediate practicability of his way of life. The principle 'use the things that are present'[26] allows *ad hoc* use of certain existing civic institutions, coupled with denial of their status as civic institutions (above). (iii) Item (a) (p. 424 above) bears directly on the question of begging and exploiting already-existing material amenities. Fundamentally, the Cynic does not recognize private ownership or property at all: everything is 'his' because he has a stake in the *kosmos*. Thus to beg (or steal) something from someone or some place is to take something to which *qua* Cynic one has a right.

There is, then, a legitimate distinction between those who live in the city but do not accept the city *qua* city and those who live in the city and do accept the city *qua* city, although this distinction may become blurred in practice, thereby allowing the greater degree of accommodation with

[25] Downing 1993: 287. [26] Bion frr. 16–17 with Kindstrand 1976: 218–19.

existing political and social realities that we find in certain later developments of, or departures from, Diogenic Cynicism (developments which we may characterize alternatively as 'not truly Cynic' or as 'soft-Cynic').[27]

Fifth, does the Cynic state have social consequences? As far as the Cynics themselves are concerned, certainly. Marriage and the family are dead; sexual relations depend on reciprocal free choice; incest is permissible (as sanctioned by the 'natural' behaviour of animals). However unappealing some aspects of this package, it entails full sexual equality, an ideal realized in the celebrated 'dog marriage' of Crates and Hipparchia (D.L. VI.96–7). In the long and dismal litany of ancient philosophers' thoughts on the relations between the sexes the Cynic position is cause for celebration. As for other people, Diogenes does not attempt to enforce his social package: he employs a mixture of criticism and persuasion; on the other hand, the more converts he makes, the greater the social consequences. Otherwise, and quite understandably, Cynics were generally regarded as social nuisances.

Sixth, does the Cynic state have economic consequences? Item (a) (p. 424 above) has been interpreted by some as entailing the abolition of private property; Cynicism was famously described by Goettling as 'the philosophy of the proletariat',[28] and people described as Cynics later involve themselves in redistributionist schemes. So Cercidas of Megalopolis (end of the third century BC) invoked the (invented) god 'Sharing' in proposals for land redistribution (fr. 4 Powell (= fr. 1 Livrea)), perhaps with direct allusion to item (a).[29] In the light of everything argued hitherto, it is obvious that for the Cynics themselves there are serious economic consequences. Diogenes advocated the abolition of money (the suggested substitution of knuckle-bones is a characteristically derisive joke (Athen. IV 159c; Phld. *Stoic.* col.16.6–9)). Cynic virtue/self-sufficiency/freedom entails the renunciation of all but the most basic material possessions, as Crates famously demonstrated (D.L. VI.87–8). Cynic converts must act likewise, and the more numerous they are, the greater the economic upheaval. The description of Cynicism as 'the philosophy of the proletariat' would not be unreasonable, if taken to mean that Cynicism *champions* poverty, but not that it seeks to *alleviate* poverty. In this the Diogenic Cynic has no interest, since for him poverty is a blessed state, provided only that it suffices to sustain life.

Seventh, does the Cynic state have political consequences? Certainly, though they require careful definition. Since the Diogenic Cynic rejects the polis and all other political institutions (kingship, tyranny, etc.) as

[27] Moles 1995a: 144–5. [28] Goettling 1851: 251. [29] López Cruces 1995: 123–30.

contrary to nature, he is *committed* to anarchy. To the Cynic, worldly 'power', 'rule', etc. is not merely indifferent: it is positively bad. He does not simply ignore it: he attacks it. He attacks it with words, but in so doing, he is not thereby eschewing action. For he wants to persuade others (both rulers and ruled) to reject worldly power in just the same way as he himself does. Consequently, when worldly power sees Cynicism as a threat (as did the agents of Roman emperors), it is right to do so. Could a Diogenic Cynic justify violence in the pursuit of anarchy, as did Russian anarchists of the nineteenth century? The answer is surely no, even though we do hear later of self-styled Cynics involved in armed insurrection. For the Diogenic Cynic is deeply opposed to arms, civil strife and warfare, which he attributes to the 'unnatural' greed for riches (D.L. VI.50, 85 (Crates' *Pera*)). He should convert others by example and persuasion, not coercion. His strength is moral, not military. His 'virility' comes from personal toughness, not from the false *machismo* of armed might. He will resist the attacks of kings and tyrants on his personal freedom, but not to the point of violence. In the last analysis, he will claim to be free even when enslaved, as Diogenes did in the fictitious story of his enslavement (D.L. VI.74), even though this ultimate inner moral freedom is something much more restricted than normal Cynic freedom.

Is there any way in which a Diogenic Cynic could support political freedom? We do hear of later Cynics doing this; it is true that Diogenic Cynics attack monarchs and tyrants with particular virulence (D.L. VI.43, 50; D.Chr. *Or.* VI.35–62; Plu. *An Seni* 783c–d). But a Diogenic Cynic has no interest in freedom as a political institution, since such 'freedom' gives him rights which he does not want and imposes obligations which he must reject. Indeed, there is adequate evidence that Diogenes and Cynics like him criticized democracy (e.g. D.L. VI.24, 34, 41). It is readily comprehensible that Cynics should attack 'monarchs' or 'tyrants': if all political systems and all politicians are deluded, tyrannies and tyrants are particularly so, because their devotion to false values is so extreme; in certain cases (times of philosophical repression for example) their activities will directly infringe the freedom of Cynics; and in general they will harm other people, for whom Cynics have philanthropic concern. In short, advocacy of political freedom is a distortion of Diogenic Cynicism.

What of kingship? Cynics described themselves as 'kings', 'rulers', and so on (D.L. VI.29; Clem. *Strom.* II.20.121), and some scholars have argued for a more or less unified tradition of 'Cynic kingship theory' from Antisthenes down to Dio Chrysostom.[30] Onesicritus, follower of

[30] Notably Höistad 1948.

Diogenes, wrote a history of Alexander which attested the encounter with Diogenes and represented Alexander as a 'philosopher in arms' and as the divine saviour and world-king of the Cynic *kosmopolis*. Bion of Borysthenes, whose philosophical orientation is largely Cynic, ended his days as one of the court-philosophers of the Macedonian king Antigonus Gonatas. Two of Dio Chrysostom's kingship orations addressed to the Roman emperor Trajan (*Or.* 1 and 4) show clear Cynic influence, and for a time Dio, like Bion, played the role of court-philosopher.[31]

But for two reasons 'Cynic kingship theory', in the sense implied, is a mirage. (a) Although Antisthenes wrote about kingship and certainly influenced Diogenes, later Cynics and Dio Chrysostom, he himself, as we have seen, was not a Cynic, and his general political stance, fairly represented by his comparison of the *politeia* to fire (go too close and you burn, go too far away and you freeze (Stob. IV.192.7–9)), is distinctly less radical than that of the Diogenic Cynic. (b) For the Diogenic Cynic the worldly king is defective in three respects (all deriving from Cynic exaltation of 'nature'): (i) he is rich; (ii) his 'kingship' is a false 'external' state rather than an inner moral state; (iii) his kingship is a form of *nomos*. The Cynic 'king', then, is the absolute antithesis of the worldly king, and it is therefore self-contradictory for a self-professed Cynic to recognize, still less praise, a worldly king. Diogenes' response to Alexander is the correct Cynic response. Cynic terminology can only be applied to a worldly king by the negation of an essential part of the Diogenic Cynic message. The works of Onesicritus and Dio accordingly represent an uneasy compromise between Cynic philosophy and worldly power. It is perfectly true that Cynic moral values such as personal integrity, superiority to luxury, devotion to toil, and so on can overlap with, and be pressed into the service of, certain elements of conventional rulership ideology. Cynics, Greek and Hellenistic kings and Roman emperors can all agree upon the value of Heracles as a moral exemplar; Cynic emphasis upon toil and suffering finds some echoes in traditional Roman attitudes.[32] None of this, however, controverts the fact that 'Cynic kingship theory' in the Diogenic sense entails an absolute rejection of worldly kingship.

4 Significance and influence

Since the Cynic 'state' is the 'state' of being a Cynic, there is a sense in which the influence of Cynic political thought means the influence of Cynicism generally. This was immense and wide-ranging, affecting Greek

[31] Moles 1995a: 145–50, 155–6. On Dio see further Gill, in Ch.29 section 3 below.
[32] Griffin 1993: 252–8.

and Roman philosophy, rulership ideology, literature and (later) religion. The topic is unmanageably vast. But even within philosophy it is virtually impossible to isolate political thought from ethics in general. The very extremeness of Cynic positions on material possessions, individual ethics and politics in the narrow sense catalysed the definition of other philosophies' positions. Stoic ethics are greatly influenced by Cynic: the link in the first instance being the master–'pupil' relationship of Crates and Zeno, founder of Stoicism. The legitimacy of Cynicism was debated within Stoicism, reactions ranging from nearly total acceptance (Aristo of Chios) to partial acceptance (Zeno, Chrysippus), to outright rejection (Panaetius), to a fluctuating mixture (Seneca), to bowdlerizing and idealizing redefinition (Epictetus).[33] Even Epicureanism was not untouched:[34] Epicurus' injunction that 'the wise man should not cynicize' (D.L. x.119) conveys reluctant acknowledgment of the fact that key Epicurean values look embarrassingly like (and no doubt partly in origin were) diluted Cynicism.

The ancient tradition makes much of Diogenes' 'cosmopolitanism', and, while that cosmopolitanism was not itself a new concept, it became strongly associated with Diogenes and the Cynics, partly no doubt because of Diogenes' verbal inventiveness; partly perhaps because on a superficial view it seemed incongruous that Cynics should expound so elevated a conception; partly also because of the absoluteness of Diogenes' rejection of the polis, which far exceeded the partial withdrawal from politics of his predecessors Socrates and Antisthenes and thus gave his cosmopolitanism added force; and partly because of the concomitant boldness of his move in making his own way of life the instantiation of citizenship of the *kosmopolis*.

Thus the Cynics set the agenda for philosophical discussion of cosmopolitanism. In particular, Cynic cosmopolitanism influenced Stoic cosmopolitanism far more than current scholarly opinion[35] allows. The Cynics did not bequeath to the Stoics a purely negative concept ('we reject the city') to which the latter added positive value: rather, Cynic cosmopolitanism already contained all the essential positive qualities which the Stoics endowed with a fuller exposition, and which they integrated into a fully-developed physical system. The 'Golden-Age' cosmopolitanism of the later Epicurean Diogenes of Oenoanda (second century AD) also seems to show Cynic influence.[36] Diogenes' prescriptions for every-day life and his rejection of the conventional polis also greatly influenced the Stoics:

[33] Dudley 1937: 96–103, 127, 190–8, Billerbeck 1978, 1979: 3–18, Goulet-Cazé 1986: 159–91.
[34] Gigante 1993. [35] E.g. Goulet-Cazé 1982, Schofield 1991: Appendix H.
[36] Moles 1995a:142–3.

Zeno's *Politeia* has some clearly Cynic elements;[37] Cleanthes, as we have seen, was impelled to confute Diogenes' syllogism against law and the city; Chrysippus' *Politeia* retained some 'outrageous' Cynic prescriptions.[38] The sheer starkness of the Cynic political, or anti-political, statement demanded a response, whether positive or negative. More generally, in asserting a 'cosmopolitanism' which rejected the city and transmuted the very notion of citizenship into a metaphor for the Cynic life according to universal nature, the Cynics provided the impetus for a crucial move in ancient political thought: that between theories based on the polis and those based on natural law.

Nor should we ignore the important 'soft-Cynic' tradition represented by Onesicritus and Dio Chrysostom, whereby Cynic values were harnessed to conventional rulership ideology. If it is difficult to attribute moral value to Onesicritus' encomium of Alexander, it nevertheless has importance in being the first work to fuse Cynic philosophy with the ideology of world conquest, thereby creating a potent version of the Alexander myth, and influencing both subsequent interpretations of Alexander (notably Plutarch's two essays *On the Fortune of Alexander*) and Roman imperialist ideology (which had to accommodate, and outdo, the achievements of the greatest 'world-conqueror' of the past). By contrast, Dio Chrysostom's deployment of Cynic thought in his speeches to Trajan is subtle and nuanced, and yet, in the Fourth Oration at any rate, retains much of the elemental moral force of Diogenic Cynicism. In the end that is the significance of the Cynics: simultaneously magnificent and absurd, they set a standard of moral integrity which could not be ignored, whether by the general public, by other philosophers, or by the political powers to which they were so resolutely opposed.

[37] Baldry 1959: 14, Schofield 1991: Ch.1. [38] Erskine 1990: 14.

22

Epicurean and Stoic political thought

MALCOLM SCHOFIELD

1 Introduction

'If Aristotle could have returned to Athens in 272 BC, on the fiftieth anniversary of his death', speculate Long and Sedley, 'he would hardly have recognised it as the intellectual milieu in which he had taught and researched for much of his life.'[1] It had been eclipsed as a cultural centre by Alexandria, thanks to the patronage extended by the Ptolemies to a galaxy of scientists and literary men. In philosophy Athens remained the magnet. But the leading thinkers in the Academy and the Lyceum had in the interval been challenged by a host of rivals, some still active or influential: as well as the Cynics we may instance the younger Aristippus and his followers (known to later writers at least as Cyrenaics), various dialecticians such as Stilpo, Philo and Diodorus, and above all the Stoics and Epicureans. These philosophers did not pretend to the encyclopaedic range of scientific and cultural interests characteristic of the Academy and the Lyceum. Philosophy as practised by Stoics and Epicureans started to resemble the specialist discipline of modern times.[2] And their systems of thought have often been perceived as constituting the deracinated philosophies of life one might expect in an age when political power was ebbing away from the city-state to the cosmopolitan courts of the Hellenistic kings. On this view the individual and his happiness become the new exclusive focus of moral reflection, displacing obsolescent questions about the best political order for the city.

But quietism, far from constituting a shared philosophical perspective, was a key issue explicitly addressed by both schools, and given diametrically opposite answers by them. Should the sage, that is, the wise man or

[1] Long and Sedley 1987: I.1.

[2] No attempt to give a general account of the Epicurean and Stoic systems is made here. Introductions: Long 1986a, Sharples 1996; a generous selection of texts with translation and commentary: Long and Sedley 1987.

perfectly rational person, engage in politics? The Epicureans said: no – unless some emergency forces him into it. The Stoics said: yes – unless something prevents it (Sen. *de Otio* 3.1). Neither reply, however, was worked out in terms which support the diagnosis of deracination. The debate was conducted largely within the well-established intellectual framework of the polis that Greek thinkers had always, with few exceptions, taken for granted.

The question was by no means the only issue relating to politics which was discussed by these schools. As we shall see, the Epicureans developed a sophisticated account of the origins of society and of law in terms of the optimalization of a mutual interest in security, and they were insistent on the need for government. Politics is viewed as a serious business, concerned with matters of life and death; and the claims of sophists to have an expertise in politics, as evidenced in their command of epideictic rhetoric, are strenuously rebutted.[3] There still survive among the *Key Doctrines* of Epicurus (341–271 BC) maxims on justice conceived as a contract for mutual non-aggression, and deriving the validity of laws from their efficacy in securing common advantages. In a few tantalizing fragments we can glimpse the Epicurean conception of what an ideal community of friends would be like. As for the Stoics, Plutarch tells us that 'Zeno happens to have written a lot (given his conciseness), Cleanthes too a lot, and Chrysippus a very great deal on the political order, being ruled and ruling, judicial decisions, and oratory' – even if none of them took up the responsibilities of political life (*Stoic Contradictions* 1033b–c). Although we have only a few extracts and scraps of other testimony about most of these writings, rather more information is available about the ideal community of the wise described by Zeno (334–262 BC), founder of Stoicism, in his work *Politeia*, conventionally translated *Republic*, but less misleadingly as *Political Order*. Like Diogenes the Cynic before him, Zeno described a community of the virtuous and free in which all the political and religious institutions of the city-state were swept away, and women and children were possessed in common. Love and friendship were to be the bonds generating the common purpose that holds the city together.

For evaluating the theoretical stance of Epicureanism and Stoicism towards politics and the life of the polis as they actually were, however, the crucial evidence is supplied by their answers to the question whether the wise person is engagé. The two leading treatments of that issue – by

[3] Evidence: principally Philodemus' *Rhetoric*, which appeals to Epicurus himself on the subject: e.g. II.256.7–259.5 Sudhaus. Discussion: Müller 1987.

Epicurus and by Chrysippus (*c.* 280–206), third head of the Stoa – were offered in each case in works entitled *On Modes of Life*, in which the authors evidently debated alternative views of the right choice of life for a rational person. These treatises stood in a long tradition:[4] we have seen it develop from Plato in the *Gorgias* and *Republic* through Aristotle into the Hellenistic Lyceum, where Theophrastus and Dicaearchus debated the problem. We shall make its treatment in Stoicism and Epicureanism the focus of our study of the political thought of the two schools.[5]

2 Epicureanism[6]

Epicurus' work *On Modes of Life* ran to four books, and was clearly one of his most important ethical writings (D.L. x.28). No actual quotations from it survive, but we know some of the major theses it propounded. Book 1 condemned participation in politics, Book 2 the Cynic way of life (*ibid.* 119). Although the sources attribute no major positive prescription to the treatise, there can be little doubt that it will have recommended the quiet life of 'withdrawal from the many' (*Key Doctrines* 14) in company with friends (*ibid.* 27–8). 'Live unnoticed' (*lathe biōsas*) was one of the Epicureans' most notorious slogans, summing up in two words the way the key decision should go. For the Epicureans' advice on more specific practical choices we have to rely on a hotch-potch of evidence, and notably on a disorganized scissors-and-paste compilation reproduced by Diogenes Laertius (*Lives of the Philosophers* X.117–21). This includes the barest summaries of their stances *inter alia* on sexual relations and marriage (negative), behaviour at a symposium (restrained), music and poetry (the wise person will discuss but not write it), and making money (he will do so only from imparting his wisdom, when hard up).

What was the rationale of the thesis that the truly rational person will keep out of politics? This has to be reconstructed principally from the sayings collected in the *Key Doctrines*. Here we find the clue to the motivation of all Epicurus' social and political thinking: *security* (*asphaleia*), together with its verb equivalent *being confident* (*tharrein*).[7]

To get a first sense of the way reference to security works in the relevant texts we may begin with three remarks which between them cover the basic range of Epicurean concern with society. The first is quoted by

[4] General treatment: Joly 1956. [5] Useful overview: Aalders 1975.

[6] Major studies: Philippson 1910, Müller 1972, Goldschmidt 1977, Long 1986b, Mitsis 1988, Alberti 1995.

[7] A study specifically devoted to Epicurus' concept of social security is Barigazzi 1983.

Plutarch from the end of a book by Colotes, one of Epicurus' associates (*Col.* 1124d):

> Those who put in order laws and customs and established kingship and government in cities brought life into a state of much security and tranquillity and banished turmoil. If anyone gets rid of these things, we shall live the life of the beasts, and one man on meeting another will practically devour him.

But social security is not enough, as Epicurus himself insists at *KD* 13:

> There is no benefit in creating security with respect to men if things up above and things beneath the earth and generally things in the infinite cause apprehension.

Freeing men's minds from fear of death and the gods is of much greater importance than the achievement of security *vis-à-vis* other humans, as is to be inferred from the prominence accorded to the need for a proper view of the gods and the afterlife at the beginning of the *Letter to Menoeceus* and again the *Key Doctrines*. Nonetheless personal fears and social security are closely connected subjects; the sort of thinking appropriate to the one is also apposite to the other (*KD* 28):

> The same judgment that makes us confident on account of there being nothing terrible that lasts for ever, or even for long, also makes us perceive how security within these very determinations is especially perfected by friendship.[8]

'Security with respect to men' (*KD* 13) is an expression which in one variant or another recurs a number of times in the *Key Doctrines*. Thus *KD* 6 talks of the goal of 'being confident from men', which must be a derivative of 'security from men' (*KD* 7, 14: 'from' is plainly defensive), and is to be compared with 'being very confident from neighbours' (*KD* 40). It is 'security from men' that Colotes probably has chiefly in mind when he praises the work of the original lawgivers. And the same idea takes centre stage in the longest early text setting out the bases of Epicurean social and political thought that we possess. This is an extract from a work entitled *Against Empedocles* by Hermarchus, Epicurus' successor.[9]

What Hermarchus presents is a genetic account of the origin of law, which is itself part of a story about the development of life in communities. A number of stages are identified. First came a period when people

[8] Reading φιλίαι (von der Muehll) for φιλίας (MSS) and κατειδέναι (Bollack) for κατεῖναι (MSS).

[9] Preserved in Porph. *Abst.* 1.7–12; cf. Longo Auricchio 1988, Obbink 1988, Vander Waerdt 1988.

banded together in communities, because all perceived that that was the best way each could best ensure their own security against the threats posed by wild animals and hostile human neighbours. Members of such communities refrained from killing each other because that would weaken the effectiveness of the group in achieving this object. Other evidence suggests that this conduct was probably represented by Epicureans as a *natural* although rational response by primitive man to his surroundings[10] – or as we might put it, not a calculated but a spontaneous pattern of behaviour.

Then comes a time when 'forgetfulness of the past' sets in. The reasons for this are briefly and indeed cryptically expressed. They are apparently three in number: (a) interbreeding – presumably with members of other communities, diminishing the fear of other men beyond the limits of one's own community; (b) wild animals have been extruded – wolves, lions, and so on no longer dare to live near human settlements, attacks by them upon members of the community are infrequent, and so doubtless they are not so greatly feared either; (c) the pattern of scattered settlements which preceded the formation of communities is so distant in time as to recede from the memory. The consequence is a slackening of the commitment to the mutual interests of the community and in particular greater readiness to kill other members of it, so weakening its defensive capacity.

Finally, the intelligentsia, perceiving the dangers of this situation, make a rational (i.e. calculated) appraisal of the advantages of community, reinforcing and sharpening through reasoning a natural impulse dulled by the causes listed above. They succeed in getting most other members of the community to require a keener sense of these advantages, even though immediate fear of external attack is no less diminished. But the focus of Hermarchus' account is their invention of law, and with it a system of punishment for those unable to perceive the mutual benefits of community, or unwilling to accept the constraints on behaviour which such a perception dictates. What is achieved by the introduction of laws, and above all by the law against homicide, is a formalized substitute for perception of mutual advantage and consequential self-restraint. Fear of the penalties attached to non-compliance likewise represents an efficacious alternative to the fear of the loss of common advantage which would be the outcome of rational appraisal. For Hermarchus the first legislators are

[10] Thus we may extrapolate from the general theory of human development and discovery sketched in Epicurus' *Letter to Herodotus* (D.L. x.75) and there applied to the example of language (*ibid.* 75–6; cf. Lucr. v.1028–90).

evidently cultural heroes comparable with Epicurus himself, since law and its observance constitute a system of social security analogous to the prophylactic against fear of death and the gods provided by Epicurus' philosophy for the individual.

Hermarchus says nothing about justice in the passage we have been discussing. From the *Key Doctrines* 31–8 it becomes clear that Epicurus himself envisaged an intimate relation between law and justice. For justice is focused on mutual advantage, particularly that to be gained from an agreement to refrain from harm to others in the community provided they in their turn refrain from harming oneself:

> Nature's justice is a token[11] of advantage relating to not harming one another and not being harmed. (*KD* 31)

The predicate *just* appears to be applied primarily to laws, conceived as devised for mutual advantage. A law which achieves this purpose 'has the nature of the just' (*KD* 38) and 'fits the preconception' of the just (*KD* 38). It may achieve it at one time or place without doing so at others. Where and when it does not the law ceases to count as just. The reference to agreement indicates a contractual basis to both justice (conceived now as a characteristic of persons) and law. A little later in the extract from Hermarchus we learn that it is impossible to make contracts with other animals because they lack the rationality requisite for law-governed association: even if the *invention* of law is the work of intellectuals, its acceptance and observance depend on the mutual agreement of those who accept and observe it. And that agreement is what justice or fair conduct (*dikaiosunē*), as Epicurus explicates it, consists in (*KD* 33).

Epicurus strikes a palpably deflationary tone in his maxims on justice. Not merely is their focus mutual advantage. Justice is presented as nothing but a function of advantage. The implication is that philosophers like Plato who discuss justice as though it were an eternally valid independent ideal are pursuing a phantom. Epicurus' remarks about injustice have the same flavour:

> Injustice is not *per se* bad, but in the fear that arises from the suspicion that one will not escape the attention of those who have been given the authority to punish such things. (*KD* 34)

[11] The Greek expression translated as 'token' is σύμβολον. It is sometimes taken to be equivalent to συνθήκη (*KD* 32 and 33), and translated 'pledge' etc. accordingly. But what Epicurus means is that when we *call* some outcome or arrangement 'just' (he uses the adjective δίκαιον) we simply have in mind the advantage that is secured when people refrain from mutual harm (cf. e.g. *KD* 36): which is something that really accords with and satisfies human nature.

> No one who secretly infringes any of the terms of a contract people have made with one another relating to not harming and not being harmed can have the assurance that he will escape detection, even if he does so thousands and thousands of times. Right up to his death it is unclear whether he will in fact escape. (*KD* 35)

The free-rider's problem is not infringement of an absolute standard nor even the likelihood of punishment, but the same affliction which Epicureanism constantly addresses: fear (*KD* 34), lack of assurance (*KD* 35), disturbance of mind (*KD* 17).

How close is Epicurus' conception of a contract not to harm others, provided they do not harm oneself, to the sort of sophistic theory of Hobbeist character developed in Glaucon's speech in Plato *Rep.* 358e–360e? It is sometimes represented that whereas Glaucon's theory makes man naturally aggressive, accepting the contract *faute de mieux*, Epicureanism makes him naturally oriented towards security, and so welcoming the contract as a means to his true goal. The wise man will certainly so orient himself (Stob. IV.90.7–8; Porph. *Marc.*27). But others will not, whether from a desire to make a pre-emptive strike or out of false conceptions of the good, as is indicated for example, by Colotes' reference to the bestial life men would be reduced to if law and government were abolished (Plu. *Col.* 1124d, quoted above).[12]

Membership of a law-governed community provides protection against some basic threats to life and happiness. Epicurus suggests two further social strategies designed to reinforce the consequent sense of confidence. The first is that withdrawal from 'the many' (*KD* 14) referred to at the beginning of this section. Its rationale is now apparent. We are to 'live unnoticed' (Plu. *An Recte* 1128a–1129b) and take no part in political life because politics is a dangerous business founded on a false view of how security is to be attained. This theme is frequently heard in the surviving evidence, as at *KD* 7:

> Some have wanted to become famous and respected, thinking that this way they would achieve security from men. If, then, the life of such persons is secure, they attain nature's good. But if it is not secure, they do not possess what, in line with what is natural, they desired in the first place.[13]

[12] Further discussion e.g. by Long and Sedley 1987: I.134–5, Mitsis 1988: 79–97; *contra* e.g. Denyer 1983. For other questions relating to the justice of the wise man see Vander Waerdt 1987, Annas 1993: 293–302.

[13] There are a number of texts where Epicureans allow or appear to allow participation in politics in various circumstances: e.g. Plu. *Tranq. An.* 465f, Cic. *Rep.* I.10, Sen. *de Otio* 3.2, D.L. X.121. A discussion: Fowler 1989: 126–30.

The second policy recommended by Epicurus complements the first. A private life, avoiding public notice, is not to be a life of solitude. We need friends: for the benefits friends perform, but much more for 'the assurance of their help' (*Sent. Vat.* 34). Whereas life would otherwise be 'full of dangers and fear', the formation of friendship 'strengthens the mind' (Cic. *Fin.* 1.66). Without friendship we are unable 'to hold on to a joy in life which is steady and lasting' (*ibid.* 67). But although the prospect of security is what makes it rational to acquire friends, friendship would not be friendship unless we loved our friends as much as we love ourselves (*ibid.* 67–8): which may mean taking risks (*Sent. Vat.* 28) and suffering pain (Plu. *Col.* 1111b) and even dying (D.L.x.121) on their behalf. Utilitarianism requires us to be non-utilitarian.[14] The *Key Doctrines* end with a remark which is generally taken to sum up Epicurus' view of friendship – and which will serve as a summary of his social philosophy (*KD* 40):

> As many as had the power of acquiring being very confident from neighbours, these also lived in this way most pleasurably with each other, having the firmest of pledges; and after having the fullest sense of identity with each other, they did not grieve over someone's untimely death as if it called for commiseration.[15]

The main objection to the general Epicurean position is put succinctly by Plutarch: the Epicurean wise man shares in the advantages of a life in a city-state but makes no contribution to them (*Against Colotes* 1127a). The Epicureans claim to attach high value to the security which law, political order, magistracies and kingship promote (*ibid.* 1124d), but put them in jeopardy by 'withdrawing themselves and their associates from the political order, saying that great commands bear no comparison with the crown of an undisturbed mind, and declaring that to be a king is just a mistake' (*ibid.* 1125c). Against the charge of parasitism, the best defence of their advocacy of the quiet life is perhaps to stress the realism about politics which it presupposes. There will always be plenty of people who want fame and power at whatever the cost, as Epicurus seems to have conceded.[16] So

14 So interpreted Epicurus will intuitively have hit upon a paradoxical insight now associated with rational choice theory: see e.g. J. Elster, *Sour Grapes* (Cambridge 1983), *Ulysses and the Sirens* (Cambridge 1984). If so, his thinking was too sophisticated for his successors, who developed associationist (*Fin.* III.69) and contractarian (*ibid.* 70) explanations of why we love our friends for their own sake. More on the Epicurean theory of friendship in: Bollack 1969, Mitsis 1988: ch.3, Annas 1993: 236–44; on its practice in Epicurean communities see e.g. Festugière 1955: ch.3, Frischer 1982: ch. 1 and 2, Clay 1983.

15 The much later Epicurean Diogenes of Oenoanda (second century AD) developed a radically utopian (Fr. 56) and cosmopolitan (Fr. 30) vision of the ideal community: cf. Smith 1993 ad loc.

16 Cf. Plu. *Tranq. An.* 465f, Lact. *Inst.* III.17.6, with Fowler 1989: 126–7, 132–3.

unless there is a general collapse of public order or a threat to the body politic, there is as a matter of fact no *need* for the rational person, intent on his own security, to enter the political arena.

3 Zeno's *Republic*

The Stoics disagreed.[17] But their disagreement might not have been readily apparent from the foundation document of Stoic political thought, Zeno's *Republic*, which shared many themes in common with Cynic repudiation of the city, and especially with Diogenes' work of the same name. Diogenes Laertius records the witticism that the book was written on the dog's tail. Chrysippus in his *On Republic* – evidently written as a defence or reaffirmation of Zeno's *Republic* – seems to have emphasized its Cynic features: e.g. permissibility of incest, uselessness of weapons (a doctrine not explicitly attested for Zeno, but attributed by Chrysippus himself to Diogenes' *Republic*). And the polemic *On the Stoics* by Cicero's Epicurean contemporary Philodemus takes as its focus attempts by other Stoics (some of them at least of his own time) to explain away the indecencies or apparent indecencies of Zeno's treatise.[18]

Our principal source of information about the contents of Zeno's book, admittedly deriving from a hostile witness, confirms its Cynic flavour (D.L. VII.32–3):

> But there are some, including Cassius the Sceptic and his followers, who attack Zeno on many points. They say first (1), that at the beginning of the *Republic* he proves general education useless; second (2), that he says that all who are not good men are personal and public enemies, slaves, estranged from each other, parents from children, brothers from brothers, kin from kin, when – in the *Republic*, once again – he makes the good alone citizens and friends and kin and free (the result is that, on Stoic premises, parents and children are at enmity: for they are not wise); (3) that he lays down the doctrine, likewise in the *Republic*, that women should be held in common, and (4) (in the 200s)[19] that neither temples nor law-courts nor gymnasia should be built in cities; (5) that on coinage he writes as follows, that 'it must not be thought that coinage should be introduced for purposes of exchange or for travelling abroad'. And he

[17] General accounts: Erskine 1990, Schofield 1991. On Zeno's *Republic* also: Baldry 1959, Dawson 1992: ch.4. Griffin 1976 (1992) contains much pertinent to Hellenistic Stoicism.

[18] Dog's tail: D.L. VII.4; Cynic features in Chrysippus: D.L. VII.131, 188, S.E. *M* XI.192 (= *PH* III.246), Plu. *Stoic. Rep.* 1044b–e, Phld. *Stoic.* col. 15.31–16.1; Stoic embarrassment: Phld. *Stoic.* col. 9.2–15.20 (see further Dorandi 1982b), D.L. VII.34.

[19] I.e. somewhere between lines 200 and 300: Schofield 1991: 6 and nn.9 and 11.

requires (6) that both men and women should wear the same dress and that no part of the body should be hidden away.[20]

There are echoes here not only of Cynic teaching, but of Plato's *Republic* – as the title of Zeno's work was doubtless meant to draw to the reader's attention. All of the specific provisions (1) to (6) correspond to something in Plato's *Republic*, sometimes by way of endorsement, as with (3) and (6), sometimes more critically, as with (1), (2) and (5).

(1) and (2) are the items of greatest interest. Education and the redefinition of kinship and family relations are central Platonic preoccupations. Zeno's position on both is more radical than Plato's, and presumably for similar reasons in each case. Plato's *Republic* transforms the family by making it coextensive with the community of guards, and offers this as the recipe for harmony in the city. Zeno likewise recognizes no family but the community as a whole, but for him this provision merely removes an obstacle to harmony. The key to friendship and true kinship is moral virtue and its precondition wisdom: only the morally virtuous are capable of proper social relationships. Of course, Plato had posited virtue and in particular wisdom among his guards, and certainly in his claims about their social cohesion assumes that their moral and intellectual education has been efficacious (cf. *Rep.*416bc). So virtue as well as proper institutions figures indispensably in his account also. The difference in emphasis, however, is unmistakable. Plato makes a heavy strategic investment in social stratification in the city as a whole and a regulated communism for the guards in order to achieve his objective of concord. Zeno relies much more on the moral perfection of the individual. This difference is presumably reflected also in their provisions on education. Plato advocates a thorough overhaul of the ordinary education system, with censorship of poetry, reforms of music and gymnastics, and the introduction of higher as well as elementary mathematics. Zeno thinks that the only education we need is an education for moral simplicity, and no doubt rejects studies such as music and geometry as the Cynics did (D.L. VI.104).

Nowhere is the contrast between his position and Plato's more striking than on questions of sexual relations, not least because Zeno apparently made his proposals on love and sex central to his whole theory.[21] The principal doctrine of the *Republic* on this issue was in stark contradiction to Plato's social regimentation: there should be no rules governing sexual

[20] On problems of text and translation see Schofield 1991: 3–8.

[21] See further Schofield 1991: ch.2. Evidence: women, D.L. VII.131 (cf. VI.72); Heracles: D.L. VI.2, 11, 10–15; teenagers: Sextus *M* XI.190, *PH* III.245; indifferent point: Sextus *PH* I.160, III.200, Orig. *Cels.* IV.5; virtue and happiness: D.L. VII.87, Stob. II.75.11–76.1, 77.16–21.

relations – mate with any woman at all, as the Cynics advise. In other works he went further: do not avoid incest; have sex with any teenager you like, male or female, whether you have an established attachment to the person or not. This is pure Cynicism. And just as the Cynic assault on convention complements an ideal of natural self-sufficiency, which other texts tell us is to be achieved by laborious effort (*ponos*) as exemplified by the Cynic hero Heracles, so Zeno's rejection of rules governing sexual intercourse seems to have been complemented by a conviction that the only real good, and the only thing relevant to happiness, is virtue. Sexual taboos can be abandoned because at the end of the day it is quite *indifferent* who has sex with whom – indifferent, that is, to happiness: the virtuous can do what they like without its affecting their virtue, understood as rational consistency producing a 'good flow of life'. Thus in his abandonment of Plato's trust in laws and institutions controlling the key matter of sexual relations, Zeno's recipe for the good life has to rely much more than does even Plato on moral education, i.e. an education which will produce moral virtue.

Where Zeno appears to have diverged from the Cynics is in the attention which he like Plato gives to the promotion of the political ideals of friendship and concord. This is closely bound up with education for moral virtue, as the following texts suggest:

> The wise man will love those young persons who by their appearance manifest a natural endowment for virtue, as Zeno says in the *Republic* and Chrysippus in the first book of *On Lives* and Apollodorus in his *Ethics*. (D.L. VII. 129)

> Pontianus [one of Athenaeus' *dramatis personae*] said that Zeno of Citium took love to be a god who brings about friendship and freedom, and again concord, but nothing else. That is why in the *Republic* he said that Love is god, there as a helper in furthering the safety of the city. (Athenaeus 561c)

Love here is, of course, not sex, although in keeping intimate personal relationships at the centre of his account Zeno sustains the focus characteristic of the communist tradition in general and of Cynicism in particular. What he has in mind is the sublimated passion of a mature person for the young resulting in concern for their moral wellbeing, to which Plato gives canonical expression in the *Symposium* and the *Phaedrus*. Plato was thinking of homosexual attachments between males, and so very likely was Zeno. It is unclear whether he managed to reconcile this element in his proposals with the principle of the community of women and the thesis that the same virtue belongs to a man and a woman. Zeno's own distinctive contribution is to find in love so conceived the dynamic not just of the moral education of individual citizens but of friendship and concord in the community at large. Presumably his idea is that if the wise man's concern for his beloved's wellbeing is reciprocated and bears moral fruit, the other too will attain wisdom and virtue, and love will be consummated as friendship.[22] Another Stoic text makes the *knowledge* possessed only by the wise – and the concord this establishes – into a key condition of friendship:

> They leave friendship something found among only the wise. For only among these is concord about the affairs of life to be found. Concord is knowledge of common goods. (Stob.II.108.15–18)[23]

Philodemus (*Stoic.* col.12.1–11) tells us that right at the start of the *Republic* Zeno promised that the book set forth something suitable to the time and place he was living in, evidently in contrast to Plato's dialogue. No doubt the point was a Cynic one: you don't need an elaborate philosophical education; the remedy for human ills is in your own hands – practise virtue.

4 Later Hellenistic Stoicism

The main themes of subsequent Stoic social and political philosophy were rather different, to judge from the surviving evidence. As we have noted, Chrysippus' *On Republic* reiterated many of Zeno's Cynic themes; and his advocacy elsewhere of the doctrine of the cosmic city represented an influential development of Zeno's basic conception of a community of the good and wise. But *On Modes of Life*[24] had a very different emphasis, with its notably anti-Cynic stress on the variety of roles it is appropriate for the wise person to play on the public stage (the theatrical metaphor itself, pervasive in Epictetus, seems to go back to figures like Bion of Borysthenes and the maverick Stoic Aristo).[25] Chrysippus goes out of his way to emphasize the depths of his immersion in the world immediately about him: whether he opts for the court or politics or teaching, he will be making money; and he will 'practise oratory and engage in politics as though

[22] Community of women: D.L. VII.131; virtue unisex: D.L. VII.175, Phld. *Piet.* col.5.8–11; friendship the *telos*: D.L. VII.130.

[23] On the Stoic conception of friendship see Fraisse 1974: 348–73.

[24] Evidence: Plu. *Stoic.Rep.* 1043a–e, D.L. VII.188–9, Stob. II.109.10–110.8; cf. 94.8–20. Further discussion in Schofield 1991: 18–20, 119–27.

[25] Bion: e.g. fr.16A Kindstrand; Aristo: e.g. D.L.VII.160. Cf. e.g. Ioppolo 1980: 188–92.

wealth were a real good, and reputation and health too' (Plutarch, *Stoic Contradictions* 1034b). This sounds like a reproof to Plato for promoting too idealistic a conception of political and indeed philosophical activity. Chrysippus' interest in life at court, and his assumption that conventional city-state politics involves using the good offices of one's friends to line one's pockets, indicate a reponse to the changed political circumstances of Hellenistic times. Otherwise what is most striking about his account of the political life is just how thoroughly traditional it is.

Only the wise are kings, according to a famous Stoic paradox probably first propounded by Zeno. Chrysippus explained that by kingship here was meant supreme rule by someone not required under the law to give an account of his conduct as ruler.[26] The paradox was defended by the argument that a ruler must know what is good and evil: on Stoic premises only the wise person can command that knowledge, so only he is *qualified* for rule in general and kingship in particular (D.L. VII.122). Next best to being king oneself is acting as adviser to a king at court or on campaign. This was particularly recommended where the king in question showed a disposition to virtue and an eagerness to learn, but Chrysippus is quoted as allowing it even in cases where there was no evidence of that. In line with this doctrine leading members of the school did indeed take up positions at court. Zeno's favourite pupil Persaeus became adviser to Antigonus Gonatas of Macedon, and eventually one of his generals. And we hear tell of Sphaerus (mid to late third century BC) at the court of Ptolemy Philadelphus in Alexandria, as well as by the side of Cleomenes III of Sparta, where he is said to have assisted the king in the reintroduction and reform of the traditional Spartan scheme for habituating and indoctrinating boys into the military ethos.[27] It has sometimes been suggested that the early Stoics had a theoretical commitment to democracy which Zeno at Athens and Sphaerus in Sparta will have endeavoured to promote in practice, but the evidence does not sustain this hypothesis.[28]

Chrysippus seems to have painted life at court in rather exotic colours. By contrast, it was in the context of a traditional conception of the participatory activity in the polis expected of citizens in general and politicians in particular that he gave his most general account of the behaviour

[26] Thus exploiting a notion of kingship much canvassed in previous philosophy: see e.g. Rowe, in Ch.11 section 3 (p. 244 above), on Plato.

[27] Persaeus: e.g. D.L. VII.6, Phld. *Ind.Stoic.* 12.3–15.11, Plu. *Aratus* 18–23; Sphaerus: e.g. D.L. VII.177, 185, Athen. 354e, Plu. *Cleomenes* 2, 11.

[28] Sanguine view: e.g. Erskine 1990; sceptical: e.g. Tigerstedt 1974, Vander Waerdt 1991.

appropriate to humans as social animals. 'It is in agreement with human nature', says Cicero of the Stoic view (*Fin.* III.68) 'that men should want to undertake and carry out public duties of state, and in order to live in accordance with nature, take a wife and want children by her.' 'Descent into marriage', as it is elsewhere described (Stob. II.94.14), and the production of children are seen as social or political obligations: i.e. obligations incumbent on men as naturally social, and therefore willingly undertaken by them. Provided his country has a moderate government, the wise person will be prepared to endure hardships and death on its behalf. As for politics proper, he will play his part, especially when the political order shows signs of progress towards the perfect forms of constitution. There will be circumstances when 'something prevents' him: probably usually corruption in society, making it difficult or impossible for him to benefit his country, or 'to encourage virtue and restrain vice' – which is said to be the point of politics. In line with this his special province is said to be education, the drafting of legislation, and the writing of improving books.

Where did the philosophical life fit into Chrysippus' scheme of things? This too was conceived as a practical and social form of existence. Chrysippus refused to equate it with the quiet life of leisured retirement: that he criticized – in a thinly veiled reference to the Peripatetics and Epicureans respectively – as nothing but a thinly veiled or frankly acknowledged hedonism. He seems to have preferred to describe the third way of life he endorsed as 'being a sophist': that is, setting up and practising as a professional teacher of philosophy. The reason for this provocative and apparently bizarre choice of nomenclature is not far to seek. Plato had insisted in the *Republic* that government and making money were two utterly different and indeed properly speaking incompatible practices. Again, one of his principal indictments of the sophists who throng the pages of his dialogues is that their fundamental motivation is mercenary, despite their professed concerns for virtue and knowledge. He implies that a true philosopher will not seek or accept payment. Chrysippus seems to have thought these attitudes unrealistic, and at odds with the proper evaluation of money: not a true good, to be sure, but something 'preferred', even if ultimately indifferent from the point of view of achieving happiness. For him a mode of life implies (as it evidently need not for Epicurus) making a living, which in turn implies making money. He stresses this not only with respect to the philosophical life, even going so far as to discuss the details of the etiquette governing the charging procedures. He also insists that the wise person will make money from life at court, if he chooses that mode of life, or from politics and his friends in high places.

The most important idea underlying Chrysippus' treatment of these issues is the notion that humans are by nature social animals. The Stoics articulated this notion with the aid of their distinctive concept of *oikeiōsis*.[29] Although the word *oikeiōsis* is difficult to translate adequately, it is not hard to formulate the core thesis of the Stoic theory. They held that man is not motivated solely by self-interest, but has a natural impulse to *identify with* other humans, perceiving them as related to himself, and being concerned for them on that account. Cicero (*Fin.* III.62–3) gives some indication of how they argued for this thesis. All social animals – such as ants, bees and storks – exhibit altruistic behaviour. Hence conduct of this kind on the part of humans, who are the most variously and ambitiously sociable of all animals, must be natural to them. Its causal origin lies in parental identification with offspring. This phenomenon might have been regarded as self-evidently natural, but the Stoics made an argument from probability: nature would not have equipped animals for reproduction, but then left them without concern for the wellbeing and nurture of their offspring (*Fin.*III.62). The Stoics must then be assuming that if this one form of altruism is natural to us, there is reason to suppose that other forms of it, too, are expressions of human nature.

If humans are naturally altruistic, why do not more of us promote each other's interests more often and more consistently than we actually do? The Stoics found no difficulty in attributing this failure to the corruption of human nature by the social environment (D.L. VII.89). So their conception of human nature has a strongly normative cast; and their accounts of the impulse to identify with others are expressed in terms of what we *should* do. Nonetheless the appeal to nature is intended as an explanation of the most salient *fact* about humans, that they are social animals – *politika zōia*, as the Stoics put it (e.g. D. I.3.2, from Marcian), exploiting the Aristotelian expression – and as such given to altruistic behaviour.

Fin. III.62–3 does not make it clear exactly how the particular form of sociability constituted by *oikeiōsis*, namely a natural disposition to identify with others and their interests, is to be conceived as the origin of *justice*.[30] In other texts reflecting Hellenistic Stoicism the connection

[29] The social form of *oikeiōsis* is discussed in the classic study of Pembroke 1971, and e.g. by Blundell 1990, Engberg-Pedersen 1990, Striker 1991: 35–61, Annas 1993: 262–76, Schofield 1995b.
[30] Cf. Plu. *Stoic. Rep.* 1038b; Porph. *Abst.* III.19.4.

appears to be worked out differently in different places. This suggests that certainly Zeno and perhaps Chrysippus too had been somewhat inexplicit on the issue. Stoics of the second century BC seem to have tried to tell a more determinate story. Thus it was probably Antipater who interpreted the principle that no man ought to commit injustice against any other as the idea that no one should commit violence against another, and who derived this idea from natural *oikeiōsis*: if nature tells every man that he ought to treat the interests of any other man, just because he is a man, as not alien from himself, that precludes violating those interests (*Off.* III.28; cf. *Fin.* III.63, *Leg.* I.33). Panaetius apparently took a rather different tack. For him the virtue associated with *oikeiōsis* and natural sociability is focused on the preservation of human association and bonding as such, and justice conceived as 'assigning to each his own due' (as in the official Stoic definition), or as refraining from harming anyone, is treated simply as a particular application of the more fundamental and more general obligation to maintain human society (*Off.* I.11–20).[31]

But what *is* my due? What *are* my interests? One pertinent issue which debate threw up was the legitimacy of private property. Antipater apparently sought to make individual interest coincide with common interest. Cicero represents Diogenes of Babylon, Stoic representative on the Athenian embassy to Rome in 155 BC, as suggesting what the logical consequence of this assimilation is: there will be nothing which is properly speaking a person's own due.[32] Should we therefore not buy and sell, but simply give things away (*Off.* III.53)? *Fin.* III.68 seems to offer a response to this line of attack. It exploits an analogy. The theatre is in common ownership, but the seat a person occupies is quite properly called his seat. So the fact that we inhabit a common city or universe does not preclude its being just that each of us have his own. *Off.* I.21, presumably due to Panaetius, defends the same doctrine in different terms. Things are not private but common by nature. But something may legitimately become someone's own by virtue of long occupation, force of conquest, a contract, a lottery, and so on; and anyone else trying to appropriate it will be violating 'the justice of human association'.[33]

[31] On Antipater and Panaetius see further Striker 1991: 35–50, 58–9, Schofield 1995b: 195–205.

[32] But if nothing is anyone's due, justice as conceived in the standard Stoic definition is an empty concept (although Cicero does not point this out).

[33] See further Annas 1989, Erskine 1990: ch.5, Schofield 1999c. Disputes such as these have sometimes been seen as bearing on or even influenced by contemporaneous issues in Roman public life and intellectual debate: see e.g. Behrends 1977, Erskine 1990: chs. 7 and 8 (sanguine), Strasburger 1965 and 1966, Jocelyn 1976/7, Rawson 1985: ch.4 (sceptical).

When the Stoics talked of justice as something natural, it was not only human nature that they had in mind. Plutarch (*Stoic. Rep.* 1035c) quotes Chrysippus as writing in his *On the Gods*:

> It is not possible to discover any other source of justice nor any other origin than from Zeus and from universal nature. For from here everything of this sort must have its source, if we are going to have anything to say about good and evil.

This thesis underpins Chrysippus' further claim (D.L. VII.128) that justice exists by nature not by posit; i.e. that what counts as just and unjust is something to which there is an objectively correct answer irrespective of the positive law of particular states or communities. The mediating idea which connects the objectivity of justice (and its naturalness in that sense) with universal nature is *reason*. Chrysippus holds that the just and the unjust are determined by law, and law he understands not as any human convention, but as right reason applied to the practical end of moral injunction and prohibition. Right reason in an individual is in harmony with universal nature, insofar as universal nature simply *is* reason at work, prescribing the proper order of the universe. It is therefore only to be expected that our reason should be directive: divine reason is directive; and we can only have been equipped with reason so that it may direct us. It is equally to be expected that when our reason has acquired proper understanding we will be in a position to know what under its direction we should and should not do. This is presumably one ground for calling it 'law': the role it plays in our lives is an internalized version of the function which in any particular state is usually performed by the external positive law.[34]

Oikeiōsis theory shows how the impulse to justice is a function of a general human and indeed animal motivation. But appeal to universal nature supplies what is in the end more fundamental: explanation of the role of moral imperatives in the entire scheme of things. This explanation belongs to the Stoic theory of providence, according to which the universe is designed as the common home and city of gods and men, who form a just community as the only beings partaking in reason, which is natural law (cf. e.g. Cic. *ND* II.154). Some of the crucial moves are set out in a syllogistic chain of reasoning (Cic. *Leg.* I.23):

[34] Right reason and law: Plu. *Stoic.Rep.* 1037f, Stob. II.96.10–12, 102.4–6, D.L. VII.88. Although *kathēkonta* ('appropriate actions') seem to form a system of moral rules, the fact that they do is not connected in the sources with natural law (*pace* Striker 1987).

> Since nothing is better than reason, and this exists in both man and god, man's first association with god is in reason. But those who have reason in common also have right reason in common. Since that is law, we men must also be reckoned to be associated with the gods in law. But further, those who have law in common have justice in common. But those who have these things in common must be held to belong to the same state.

Here we re-establish contact with Zeno's city of the virtuous and wise. If Zeno assumes mutual knowledge and physical proximity among his citizens, the assumption is now tacitly dropped, as is his preoccupation with love and sex. Otherwise there is a striking resemblance with the community specified in Cicero's text. The cosmic city, too, as the reference to *right* reason indicates, is a community whose only criterion of membership is virtue and wisdom. It is indeed the *only* true city. The Stoics define a city as a morally admirable group or organization of humans which is administered by law (Clem. *Strom.* IV.26; D. Chr. *Or.* 36.20). But the only group of persons that is governed by law properly understood, that is, interpreted not as positive law but as right reason at work, are those who consistently heed right reason, i.e. the virtuous and wise. Nor is Zeno's conception of concord and friendship as the bonds uniting his city forgotten. As Plutarch puts it (*Comm. Not.* 1086f):

> If a single sage anywhere at all extends his finger prudently, all the sages throughout the inhabited world are benefited. This is the job they assign to friendship; this is how, by the beneficial acts common to the sages, the virtues are brought to fulfilment.[35]

It has sometimes been supposed that what Stoicism advocated was a world state: a political system in which the unity of all mankind would find expression. In a notorious passage (*Alex. Virt.* 329a–f) Plutarch connected the ideas of Zeno's *Republic* with the exploits of Alexander the Great. Alexander's success in bringing under his own supreme authority Greeks and barbarians scattered over a vast extent of territory, and his attempts to obliterate cultural differences between them, were represented as Stoic philosophy put into practice. It will be clear from our discussion why Plutarch's story must be rejected as an account of Stoicism, quite apart from doubts historians may entertain about its reliability with regard to Alexander.[36] As developed by Chrysippus, the ideal city of Zeno's *Republic* is indeed in a sense a universal community, whose citizens

[35] On justice, the cosmic city and universal nature see further Long 1983, Schofield 1991: chs. 3 and 4, Schofield 1995b.

[36] See further Tarn 1933, Badian 1958, Baldry 1965: ch. 4, Schofield 1991: App. A.

are (as Diogenes the Cynic claimed of himself: D.L. VI.63) *kosmopolitai*. However it is universal not in that it includes all mankind, but because it is made up of gods and sages wherever they may be: not a wider community, but a wholly different sort of 'community'.

When Chrysippus used words like 'city' and 'law' in such a context he intended a radical transformation of their meaning, robbing them of anything ordinarily recognizable as political content. As we have seen, his allegiance to this viewpoint did not prevent him from making the sage engagé. But in the discussions of the leading Stoics of the early Roman empire – Seneca, Epictetus, Marcus Aurelius – the claims of citizenship of the universe come to dwarf those of the existing societies in which we find ourselves: the cosmic perspective increasingly overshadows the vantage point of ordinary life, without ever entirely displacing it.[37] It is important for understanding the political thought of the Hellenistic age that this *is* a later development.

5 Roman epilogue

Plutarch includes the following story[38] in his account of how Brutus went about assembling the conspirators who would do Julius Caesar to death (*Brutus* 12.3–4):

> Of his other friends, too, Brutus excluded Statilius the Epicurean and Favonius the devotee of Cato. This was because, when in the course of joint philosophical dialectic he indirectly, in a roundabout way, put them to the test along the following lines, Favonius replied that civil war was worse than a law-flouting monarchy, while Statilius said that it was not appropriate conduct for someone who was wise and intelligent to take on risks and worries on account of people who were bad and foolish.

The replies given by Favonius and especially Statilius will not surprise us, given the accounts in sections 4 and 2 above of Stoic and Epicurean political thought respectively. The chief interest of Plutarch's account is what it tells us about the depth of the Greek philosophical culture absorbed by Roman aristocrats of the late Republic. From it they had acquired a language for debating critical issues of contemporary politics and for formulating the choices which as public actors they could not avoid making. Plutarch's evidence is abundantly confirmed by Cicero's correspondence for the years 50–43 BC, which reveals him and a host of friends and

[37] See further Gill, in Ch.29 below.

[38] For discussion see Sedley 1997, which defends the authenticity of the story.

acquaintances engaging in just such debates and formulations, whether in light banter or deadly earnest. Use of the language of philosophy sometimes reflected deep commitments: defeat in the civil war at Caesar's hands led Cato to Stoic suicide and converted Cassius (as Cicero interpreted it) to Epicureanism and – for the time being – political quietism.[39]

Mostly lost, however, are works of Stoic or Epicurean political theory dating from the main Hellenizing period in the culture of the Roman Republic. For example, Cicero suggests that the Stoic Panaetius, confidant of the statesman Scipio Africanus, shared Polybius' interest in constitutional theory and its application to the Roman system of government (*Rep.* I.34). But not a word survives about Panaetius' views on the subject, although the doctrine Diogenes Laertius ascribes to the Stoics in general that a mixed Dicaearchan constitution is best (VII.131) should almost certainly be attributed to him, not to Zeno or Chrysippus. Where Epicureanism is concerned we are somewhat better placed. Two works survive from the 50s BC: Lucretius' poem *de Rerum Natura*, dedicated to the Roman senator C. Memmius; and a treatise by the Greek Philodemus of Gadara, fragmentarily preserved in the library of his Epicurean circle at Herculaneum, which was entitled *On the Good King according to Homer*. Philodemus dedicated it to his patron, the leading Caesarian politician L. Calpurnius Piso, perhaps on the occasion of his accession to the consulship in 59.

The bulk of Lucretius' poem is devoted to exposition of the Epicurean physical system.[40] But for Epicureans the ultimate point of the study of physics was to relieve the human mind of fear of death and the gods. And by a variety of means, from exhortations to Memmius to savage satire on the false values of Roman society (most notably the delusions of religion), Lucretius invests *de Rerum Natura* with ethical and existential purpose. In particular, in the prefaces to the first three books there are attacks on the hollow idea that security can be achieved by wealth and the Sisyphean labour of political power; 'in this time of adversity for our country' Lucretius laments the miseries of civil war waged against kin. This theme becomes an explicit topic in Book V, where in his discussion of the origins and development of life on earth he gives a much more elaborate version than Hermarchus of the initial formation of communities and the subsequent creation of law. Lucretius' account (V.925–1157) is plainly designed to reflect the history of Rome from the reign of the early kings, but still

39 Further discussion: Momigliano 1941, Brunt 1986, Griffin 1986, 1989, 1995.

40 See Bailey 1947; and on Book V e.g. Furley 1978, Manuwald 1980, Fowler 1989.

more to comment on present discontents. The first communities were transformed by leaders of 'outstanding intellect and strength of mind' into fortified citadels. There these paragons governed as kings, rewarding looks, strength and intellect.[41] But then private property was invented and gold discovered. The desire to amass these and enjoy them in peace – a perversion of true wealth, which is to live sparingly with a tranquil mind – prompted men to ambition for fame and power, which led to regicide and ultimately to the rule of the mob. This was when, exhausted by violence, men were taught to settle for laws and magistrates.[42] Lucretius' narrative of the struggle for hegemony has evident contemporary resonances, and indeed he makes the reference all but explicit (v.1131–5):

> Let them sweat out their life-blood, worn away to no purpose, battling their way along the narrow path of ambition. Their wisdom is second-hand: what they are after is something they value from hearsay rather than their own senses, and that is no more use now or in future than it was in the past.

Similar morals lie close to the surface of *On the Good King*.[43] This work is in effect a contribution to the 'mirror of princes' literature to which Epicurus' own *On Kingship* (D.L. x.28) very likely also belonged. By presenting his material in the original guise of a learned essay on Homer Philodemus cleverly avoids any direct suggestion that Piso has regal, not magisterial, powers. The treatise contains nothing distinctively Epicurean in doctrine, but probably this is due principally to the conventions of the genre, which seems to have dealt in variations of stock themes inherited from Isocrates' *To Nicocles* and similar writings rather than in argument from philosophical first principles.

The surviving portions of Philodemus' work are largely preoccupied with the role of the king in promoting peace. He must exhibit such qualities as forbearance (*epieikeia*) and gentleness (*prāotēs*, *hēmerotēs*), widely attested elsewhere as key ingredients in the ideology of Hellenistic rulers fostered by both them and their subjects. His models should be Odysseus, who nipped public disorder in the bud at the great assembly in *Iliad* II, and Nestor, who bent his efforts to resolving the quarrel between Achilles and Agamemnon. Both are paradigms of wisdom free from passions. Cities

[41] This treatment of kingship perhaps owes something e.g. to Polybius (VI.5.4–6.12) and the Stoic Posidonius (Sen. *Ep*.90.5–7). Cf. Cole 1967.

[42] Lucretius probably adumbrates a version of the 'cycle of constitutions' otherwise attested in Cicero and Polybius: see Schrijvers 1996.

[43] See Murray 1965, Dorandi 1982a, Gigante 1995: ch. 4.

prosper more when guided by good counsel than under arms, as witness the polity of the Phaeacians. And Homer makes it clear that he values deliberation and education in it as much as he hates those who love war and strife.[44]

[44] This chapter reuses material from Schofield 1996 and Schofield 1999d.

23

Kings and constitutions: Hellenistic theories

DAVID E. HAHM

In the Hellenistic age changing political conditions set the stage for refinement and adaptation of the classical analysis and evaluation of forms of government.[1] The most significant development was the rise of powerful autocratic monarchies on the model of the Persian and Egyptian kingships. By the second century BC even the traditional kingships of mainland Greece, such as the Macedonian elected kingship and the limited dual kingship of Sparta, had been transformed into the autocratic Hellenistic type. Greek city-states continued to exist, but had to work out a new relationship with the monarchs, whose imperial ambitions encompassed the entire eastern Mediterranean. Most either settled for reduced autonomy under the authority of one of the monarchies, or banded together into an independent regional league. The development of regional leagues, chiefly on the Greek mainland, was another development that affected Hellenistic thought.

A third was the disappearance of the distinction between democracy and aristocracy or oligarchy. In the wake of intervening political and economic developments, the typical free city-state remained a democracy, but with a strong executive component, dominated by a narrow group of old wealthy families.[2] Since such cities regarded themselves as democracies despite their aristocratic orientation, the classical distinction disappeared. The significant difference was now between a city with a high degree of self-rule and one administered by an agent of one of the Hellenistic kings, often in the shadow of a military garrison.

Throughout the period kingship and constitutional theory continued to occupy the attention of philosophers of all four major schools, though none of their works has survived.[3] The literature on kingship, directed

[1] Sinclair 1951: 242–4, Tarn and Griffith 1952: 47–78, Walbank 1981: esp. 60–122, 141–58, 1984: 62–74. [2] O'Neil 1995: 103–33.

[3] Sinclair 1951: 248–53, Aalders 1975: 5–16. The titles are preserved in Diogenes Laertius' bibliographies. See further Rowe, in chs. 14 and 19 above, and Garnsey, ch. 20, pp. 403–5

mainly to the kings of Macedonia, presumably discussed the character of a desirable monarch.[4] It gave shape and substance to a tradition that continued throughout antiquity into the Middle Ages.[5] Constitutional literature continued to treat classification and change, at least partly on the basis of the writings of Plato and Aristotle (Polybius VI.3.5, 5.1; Stob. II.147.26–152. 25).[6] In the changed political circumstances internal political organization and its improvement received special attention. Peripatetics in the late fourth and early third centuries, and then Stoics in the second century, discussed the optimal organization of magistracies and the importance of a balance of powers to prevent oppressive monarchies (Cic. *Leg.* III.12–16). The Peripatetic Dicaearchus advocated a mixed constitution, combining kingship, aristocracy, and democracy, and admired the Spartan constitution of Lycurgus as an example (Phot. *Bibl.* 37).[7]

More specific evidence for the thought of the period comes from two pseudonymous texts that contain advice for a king ('Aristotle' *To Alexander* and 'Aristeas' *To Philocrates*), and two historical texts that use contemporary theories to describe and interpret political history (Polybius and Diodorus Siculus). These date from, or reflect the thought of, the second century BC, and each addresses the political realities of one or more of four of the major powers of the time: the Macedonian monarchy, the Egyptian monarchy, the Achaean democracy, and the Roman Republic.

1 Kingship theories

The two pseudonymous texts, addressed to the Macedonian and Egyptian monarchies respectively, contain advice on ruling a kingdom. In each case the advice is ostensibly given to some earlier historical king on the basis of contemporary political conditions and a current concept of human nature and psychology. In each case the king's education (*paideia*) is identified as the key to effective rule, and the pseudonymous text ostensibly makes a contribution to that education. Though they have much in common in their conception of the character of the ideal king, they differ in their political and psychological assumptions and in their form of presentation.

The Macedonian example is a fictional letter purportedly written by Aristotle to Alexander the Great and preserved in the Aristotelian corpus

[4] Fraser 1972: I.485, Walbank 1984: 65, 76–7; cf. Goodenough 1928.

[5] Hadot 1972, Walbank 1984: 75–84; cf. Schubart 1937a, 1937b. On the Medieval 'Mirror of Princes' (*Fürstenspiegel*) see *The Cambridge History of Medieval Political Thought c. 350–1450*: 218–21, 326–8, 483–5.

[6] Aalders 1968: 72–81, 1975: 7–9, Moraux 1973: I.423–34, Annas 1995.

[7] Wehrli 1944: 28–9, 64–9, Sinclair 1951: 250–2. Some Stoics concurred (D.L. VII.131).

as an introduction to a rhetorical treatise, the *Rhetorica ad Alexandrum*.[8] The letter, an attempt to persuade the king to study rhetoric and reasoning, is written in the tradition of the kingship advice of Xenophon and Isocrates; but it is based on a more systematically articulated theory of the function and authority of the king, which must have been developed in the Hellenistic Greek political climate. Kingship is presented in explicit contrast to democracy:

> Whereas among democratically governed people actions are referred to the law, among those subject to the rule of a king, actions are referred to rational discourse (*logos*).[9] So just as autonomous cities are normally guided to the most noble condition (*kalliston*) by the common law, those subject to your royal rule can be guided to an advantageous state (*sumpheron*) by your rational discourse. For, in fact, law is simply rational discourse defined by a city's common agreement (*koinē homologia*), detailing how people ought to act in specific situations. (1420a19–27)

The comparison with democratic institutions, which runs through the argument, presupposes a theory in which monarchy and democracy are the only viable alternatives.[10] That point of view is characteristic of the Hellenistic age, and, in particular, of mainland Greece, where the tension between democratic autonomy and Macedonian hegemony had been shaping public life and debate since the fourth century BC.

The conception of the king serving the same function as the law in a democratic city-state evokes a specific link with Macedonia. It is reminiscent of the connection drawn by the philosopher Anaxarchus of Abdera, who told Alexander in India that he was 'the law and the definition of justice' for his subjects (Arrian IV.9.7–8; Plu. *Alex.* 52.3–7; cf. *Max. cum Princ.* 781a–b). In this he was following the precedent of Plato and Aristotle in elevating the ideal ruler, where one exists, above the law.[11] When one of Alexander's successors, Antigonus the One-Eyed, took the title king in 306 BC (the first of the successors to do so), he established a personal form of kingship, not linked to a specific geographical region, thereby setting the precedent for the Antigonid dynasty of monarchy unrestricted by law or tradition.[12]

[8] The most recent text is Fuhrmann 1966; English translation in Forster 1924 and Hett and Rackham 1937: 267–75. For date and discussion see Wendland 1904: 499–509, Sinclair 1951: 254–5. See also Rowe, in ch. 19 section 2 above.

[9] *Logos*, here translated 'rational discourse', refers to reasoning, to edicts and announcements based on reasoning, or to both together.

[10] The comparison occurs also at 1420b12–14 and 1420b27–1421a2. The final argument (1421a23–4) contains a political, though not necessarily democratic, analogy of the general as saviour of the army.

[11] Bosworth 1996: ch. 4.

[12] Billows 1990: 155–60, 323–5, Walbank 1981: 55–7, 1984: 62–7.

The equation of a king's edicts and actions with constitutional law presupposes a wise and virtuous king. In appealing to the king to develop his reasoning capacity and virtues, the author of the letter uses vaguely Platonic psychological assumptions. Human beings differ from animals in possessing reason (*logos*) in addition to appetite (*epithumia*) and passion (*thumos*). Reason is a 'divine endowment' that enables human beings to achieve virtue, wellbeing, and happiness (1420a27–b12, 1421a6–15). The implicit hierarchic structure of this conception of human nature grounds a series of arguments that link the moral and utilitarian value of reason in each of four kingly concerns: political status (1420a11–27), moral worth (1420a27–b19), effective government (1420b19–1421a3), and personal wellbeing and satisfaction (1421a4–24). For the first, the author argues:

> It is nobler (*kallion*) and more kingly to have a soul endowed with good judgment than to have one's bodily form well clothed. It would be strange if the one who is foremost in action were seen to be inferior to ordinary people in rational discourse (*logōi*, 1420a15–17).

In subsequent arguments he claims that rational discourse is the criterion of moral worth and the basis of praise and blame (1420a27–b8), the divinest of human capacities (1420b19–20), and the greatest honour bestowed by god on living creatures (1421a8–10).

Each of these moral arguments is linked with a utilitarian argument, beginning with the passage quoted above, where it is argued that the king will use rational discourse (*logos*) to guide his subjects to an advantageous condition (*sumpheron*) (1420a23–5). The author goes on to point out that rational discourse is essential as the means of justice and benevolence, the two essential constituents of kingship (1420b5–11), and as the basis for national security (1420b19–1421a3) and for personal security and happiness (1421a12–24).[13]

To heighten these utilitarian appeals the author couches them in military metaphors, evoking in the king fears for his own security: 'Rational examination of what is advantageous is the very citadel of security' (*akropolis sotērias*, 1421a1–2). To develop the reasoning ability, 'education is established as the protector of the soul (1421a17–18). . . . As the general is saviour of the army, reason (*logos*) with education is the leader (*hegemōn*) of life' (1421a23–4). Since reasoned discourse and action based on it are the means of achieving a king's primary objectives, training in rational

[13] Cf. 1420b12–19, where the king's life and rational discourse parallel democratic law in providing exemplars (*paradeigmata*) of behaviour, hence serving as instruments of governance.

discourse (*logos*) is paramount, whence the author's commendation of the subsequent rhetorical handbook.

Different political assumptions, psychology, and rhetorical strategy may be found in the so-called letter of *Aristeas to Philocrates.*[14] This text is actually a fictional report of the circumstances surrounding the translation of the Hebrew Old Testament into Greek, the so-called Septuagint. As part of an account of this endeavour the author describes a series of seven banquets, over the course of which Ptolemy II Philadelphus allegedly asked each of the seventy-two translators a question pertaining to life or ruling a kingdom (*Arist.* 187–292).[15] Each responded with a precept formulated to indicate that the principle in some way originates from God. The king approved each answer and then thanked the Jewish wise men for the 'education in kingship' (*Arist.* 294).

The text is generally believed to have been written in Alexandria in the last half of the second century BC.[16] The audience and purpose of the letter and of the so-called symposium on kingship in it are still disputed. Nevertheless, it is safe to say that the extent and detail of its fictionalized political documents and discussions point to political aims. Moreover, the author's intimate knowledge of second-century Ptolemaic administrative language and practices suggests that he was close to the court, if not a high-ranking official, and in a position to comment on, or even contribute to, Egyptian policy and governance.[17] In this context the symposium takes on significance as a Jewish contribution to Hellenistic Greco-Egyptian political policy and administration.

The precise nature of that contribution, however, is not obvious. The seventy-two questions and answers show no systematic organization other than to begin with the essential constituent virtues of kingship: justice (*dikaion*) tempered by clemency (*epieikes, makrothumia*), and benevolent concern for the welfare of subjects (*pronoia, euergetein*, *Arist.* 188–90).[18] The interrogation then meanders through a wide range of practical matters from diet and family relations to public policy, public relations, and a host of administrative details, sometimes, but not always, linking the recommendations to the constituent virtues.

[14] The standard texts are Wendland 1900, Thackeray 1902 (reprinted with English translation by Hadas 1951), and Pelletier 1962. Cf. Sinclair 1951: 289–93, Hadas 1951, Tcherikover 1958, Zuntz 1959, Jellicoe 1966, Fraser 1972: I. 696–703, Murray 1967, 1987, Schmidt 1986, and Troiani 1987 for interpretations.

[15] The banquet is presumably modelled on those attested for the Ptolemaic and Jewish courts (Zuntz 1959: 31–6, Murray 1967: 346–8, Fraser 1972: I. 702–3).

[16] Proposed dates vary from *c.* 160 to *c.* 100 BC (Fraser 1972: I.696; II.970, n. 121, Hadas 1951: 3–54, Schmidt 1986: 116–43, Murray 1967: 338–40, 1987: 16).

[17] Fraser 1972: I.698–9.

[18] Murray 1967: 353–9, Zuntz 1959: 25–31.

Though the proffered advice is eminently practical, there is virtually no argumentation or attempt to persuade the king of the utility of the recommendations. Instead, they are justified as bestowed or sanctioned by God. Even the kingly qualities of justice, clemency, and benevolence, which were traditionally advocated for their utility in securing popular favour, are formally recommended on the grounds that God is just, forgiving, and benevolent to human beings (*Arist.* 187–8, 205). Sometimes, too, the author construes the king's virtuous action or the people's subsequent favour as the result of divine intervention (*Arist.* 230, 265, 273), an object of prayer rather than of rational choice. Though the derivations from God may look like superficial additions, they thoroughly transform the argumentative basis of the advice. Aristeas' kingship advice, in essence, integrates a Greek theory of kingship with Jewish theological justifications.[19]

Moreover, the Greek theory itself is tailored to Egyptian political conditions. There is no comparison to democracy, a political form with which neither Egyptians nor Jews would have had any experience. Many of the specific recommended administrative practices are modelled on actual Ptolemaic practice.[20] The questions and answers are then placed in a recognizable Egyptian social setting, a Ptolemaic banquet capped by philosophical discussion.[21]

The Greco-Egyptian theory behind Aristeas is further illuminated by the first-century Greek historian Diodorus Siculus, whose idealized description of the way of life of the early Egyptian kings embodies the same conception of kingship (1.70–1).[22] Diodorus describes and analyses the function of Egyptian cultural institutions and practices and does so without Jewish modifications. The theory underlying these two accounts differs from the Macedonian in its low regard for human reason and its compensatory legalistic basis for kingship. Human beings by nature seek pleasure and competitive advantage (*pleonexia*), a fact that inevitably predisposes them to self-indulgence, aggression, and injustice (D.S. 1.71.3; *Arist.* 222–3, 277–8; cf. 108). People also possess a capacity for reasoning (*dianoia*, *nous*, *Arist.* 222, 276), but most use it to advance their pleasure and selfish interests (*Arist.* 222–3, cf. 277–8). Given the overwhelming

[19] Zuntz 1959: 22–4, Murray 1967: 344, 353–61. Zuntz's attempt (1959:24–31) to reconstruct a Hellenistic kingship treatise that might have served as source is not convincing (Murray 1967: 350–3).

[20] Cf. Murray 1970: 157–61, 168–9. The problem of achieving justice and equity in an ethnically diverse nation (*Arist.* 267) is one problem that would hardly have affected Macedonia.

[21] Zuntz 1959: 31–6, Murray 1967: 346–8.

[22] Hadas 1951: 43–5, Murray 1970: 168–9. Diodorus' account was almost certainly drawn from Hecataeus of Abdera (late 4th cent. BC), who was probably responsible for first interpreting Egyptian kingship in Greek terms (Murray 1970: esp. 157–61, Fraser 1972: 1.496–505).

impulses to pleasure, greed, and glory, self-control is the necessary condition for correct reasoning and hence claimed as the most potent form of rulership (*archē kratistē*, *Arist.* 221–2) and the essence (*horos*) of kingship (*Arist.* 211). Only after a person has brought the passions under control can reasoning help in controlling them, in avoiding deception, and in fulfilling one's obligations and intentions (*Arist.* 255–6, 276; D.S. I.70.6, 71.3).[23]

The self-control that is the necessary condition for kingship and civil society is brought about by training. The theory stipulates that the king must always be subject to the laws (*Arist.* 240, 279; D.S. 1.70.1–71.1). Egyptian laws and customs regulate every aspect of the king's life, his upbringing, daily schedule, diet, associates, religious rituals, and administrative procedures. From his earliest youth the future king is trained not to fall victim to the attractions of glory and wealth, but to practice self-control and moderation (*Arist.* 211, 248, 279). When he is grown, the priests recite daily prayers in which they rehearse the kings's virtues, enumerating all the qualities and actions of an ideal king. Diodorus explains that this is to accustom the king to the proper mode of life and by the implicit threat of divine punishment to motivate him to live accordingly (D.S. 1.70.5–8).[24] The king is also obliged to listen to 'beneficial counsels and deeds of the most eminent men' read aloud from 'sacred books'.[25] This is to ensure that the king has the best moral and administrative principles in mind when he makes decisions (D.S. 1.70.2–9; cf. *Arist.* 239, 284). Moreover, he is strictly bound by the law in rendering decisions and meting out punishments (D.S. 1.71.1). On the Greco-Egyptian theory the king's life and administrative actions are not based primarily on rational personal choice, but on customs and laws, sanctioned by god and handed down by priests and wise men from generation to generation (*Arist.* 240, 279; D.S. 1.70.1–2, 71.1–3).

The *Letter to Alexander* viewed a king with an educated capacity to reason as the sufficient basis of the social order, equivalent to the law in a democratic society, and accordingly advocated an education in logic and

[23] Having a sharp mind (*noun oxun*) and being able to make acute judgments is a gift of god (*Arist.* 276, cf. 236).

[24] According to Diodorus curses for wrongdoing by the king were called down on his servants and advisors (1.70.7), so the king was never obligated to receive admonition or correction from an inferior. Plutarch reports that Demetrius of Phalerum in the late fourth century shared this concern and urged Ptolemy to read books dealing with kingship, because they contained the things that the king's friends were not bold enough to recommend (*Reg. et Imp. Apopth.* 189d).

[25] The Greek Diodorus attributes the laws to 'the wisest men' (D.S. 1.71.3), but implies that they are sanctioned by the gods (D.S. 1.70.5–8). The Jewish author claims that the laws were originally implanted in the minds of the lawgivers by God (*Arist.* 240).

rhetoric to train the king for independent judgment and action. The Greco-Egyptian theory forgoes training the king's reasoning capacity for a different kind of training, namely, disciplining the king's passions under the guidance of an ancient, divinely ordained law that totally controls the king's behaviour. An outside observer, Diodorus Siculus, credits these ancient institutions for the nearly five millennia of extraordinary prosperity that Egypt experienced under autocratic rule (D.S. I.69.6, 71.5). The author of *Aristeas to Philocrates*, an insider and member of the second-century court, seems more interested in reinforcing the ancient tradition with a new work, modelled on the Egyptian literature that transmitted the ancient tradition. Bringing Greek kingship theory and Jewish theology together in an Egyptian framework, the anonymous author created a work that justified Jewish involvement in Ptolemaic government and might even have had the potential to enhance its moral tone.

2 Constitutional theory

Among the cities of mainland Greece, where democracy had flourished, Classical constitutional theory was adapted to contemporary democratic practices and disseminated among the leaders of the democratic Achaean League and later among the leaders of the Roman Republic. In the mid-second century BC the Achaean statesman-historian Polybius recorded and applied one such theory to the history of Greek cities and kingdoms and then extrapolated from it to create a theory applicable to the emerging powers of the west, Carthage and Rome.[26] The constitution, in his view, defined a nation's character and thus accounted for its decisions and the success or failure of its endeavours (VI.2.9–10).[27] By showing how constitutions changed and affected events he hoped to explain the past and allow more accurate prediction of a state's future development and history.

The phenomenon that most interested him was how Rome managed to bring 'nearly the whole of the inhabited world under a single rule in less than 53 years' (I.1.5; III.1.4, 2.6; VIII.2.3; XXXIX.8.7). He found the explanation in her superior constitution and devoted an entire book (VI) to the task of explaining its origin, nature, and the basis of its strength. He

[26] The standard text is Weil and Nicolet 1977. For Polybius' life see Walbank 1972: 1–31, Eckstein 1995: 1–16; for his political theory Ryfell 1949: 180–232, von Fritz 1954, Cole 1964, Petzold 1977, Trompf 1979: 4–115, Podes 1991a, 1991b, Hahm 1995, and Eckstein 1995.

[27] Pédech 1964: 303–17.

hoped to supply information for statesmen to use to improve their own constitutions (III.118.11–12) and make intelligent, informed political decisions (VI.2.8–10).

The theory that Polybius chose as a foundation for this project was one that he attributed to 'Plato and other philosophers' (VI.5.1). The theory is not really Platonic, though its major elements have parallels or analogues in Plato.[28] Its precise source is unknown; the best guess is that it originated in the shadow of the Academy and was created in, or at least transmitted to, Polybius' political circle in Achaea, by two fellow-Achaeans, Ecdemus and Demophanes.[29] Both studied with the Academic philosopher Arcesilaus in Athens and later played a role in the creation of the democratically organized Achaean League.

Polybius harmonizes this theory of constitutional change with a classification and evaluation of constitutional types resembling those of Plato (*Plt.* 291d–292a, 302c–303b) and Aristotle (*Pol.* III.7, 1279a22–b10). Three generic types, differentiated by the proportion of rulers (one, few, or many), are each subdivided into an improved and an unimproved or deviant variety (VI.3.5–4.6). All are unstable; the most stable and therefore best constitution is one that combines the virtues of the three improved varieties (VI.3.7–8; 10.1–11). Polybius' classification differs from that of his predecessors in construing a good government as one based on the consent of the governed, a consent that is earned by intelligent and virtuous governance.[30] He elaborates on this in his account of the origin of kingship:

> When the leading and most powerful person always applies his strength in support of the aforesaid [moral notions] held by the people, and his subjects become aware that he is one who apportions to each as he deserves, they submit to him, no longer because they fear his force, but rather because they approve of his judgment and they join in preserving his rule. (VI.6.10–11)

Unimproved or deviant constitutions, in contrast, are those in which rulers either rule by force and fear (VI.4.2, 6.10–12, 8.4–5) or, in the case of a deviant democracy, by bribery and corruption (VI.9.5–7). Thus Polybius' theory sets itself apart from the Classical theories by conforming to the basic assumption of Hellenistic democracy, such as was exemplified in his Achaean homeland, namely, formal popular sovereignty with executive power in the hands of civic-minded magistrates.[31]

[28] Von Fritz 1954: 44–95, Trompf 1979: 6–45. [29] Cole 1967: 163–6.
[30] This mark is implicit in the definitions (VI.4.2–5) and description of origin (VI.6.10–12, 8.1–3, 9.3–4). [31] O'Neil 1995: 103–33.

As a historian and statesman who saw constitutional stability as the basis for a nation's strength and success, Polybius was vitally concerned with constitutional change and needed a theory capable of explaining past changes and predicting them in the future. Neither Plato's schematic, logical decline in *Republic* VIII, nor Aristotle's comprehensive compilation of motives for change (*Politics* V), permitted reliable predictions. The theory Polybius adopted consists of a set of rigorous laws of constitutional change, which he calls a 'generalized conception' (*koinē epinoia*) or a 'generic pattern' (*katholikē emphasis*, VI.5.2–3), presumably denoting a universal description covering all or most cases of actual constitutional change.[32]

It is easy to misunderstand Polybius' universal description. In a brief outline of the theory he enumerates six changes, each leading to the emergence of one of the six constitutional types (VI.4.6–11). The sequence begins with (generic) monarchy, from which kingship arises by improvement through human initiative. It degenerates into tyranny. From tyranny aristocracy emerges and declines into oligarchy. Then democracy appears and declines to mob rule, only to set the stage for the re-emergence of monarchy.[33] Polybius concludes by saying one can best appreciate the profound difference between good and bad versions of the three basic types by examining their origins and changes, adding that 'one who has an overall view of how each naturally develops may be able to see when and how and where the growth, flowering (*akmē*), change for the worse (*metabolē*) and end will occur again' (VI.4.12). Though Polybius makes no claim to be able to predict the precise timing of every such change, he is confident that one can predict which type will arise next (VI.9.10–11). He calls the process as a whole 'the cycle (*anakuklōsis*) of constitutions, nature's pattern of administration (*phuseōs oikonomia*), according to which the constitutional structure develops and changes and returns again to its original state'.

The biological metaphor of birth, growth, flowering, and decline, together with the description of the process as a cycle, might suggest that Polybius believed society was programmed by nature to follow a predetermined sequence of changes, one that includes in three places an inevitable decline from a good constitution to its respective deviant form. Prediction, then, might be thought to be based on the cyclical sequence *per se*: one identifies the position of a constitution in the cycle and simply

[32] Hahm 1995: 8–37, esp. 8 n.5, 12–13; cf. Podes 1991b.

[33] If one counts the original generic monarchy as a separate constitution, there are seven in the sequence. For difficulties of interpretation see Hahm 1995: 14–16 and n. 22; 27–30.

reads off future developments from the pattern. The obvious incompatibility of a rigid cycle of constitutions with real history, combined with Polybius' obscurity on the correspondence of the biological model of growth, flowering, and decline with the sequence of constitutions has opened his theory to criticism and suggests, rather, another interpretation.[34] It suggests that the biological terminology may more plausibly be regarded as a vivid metaphor for the fact that constitutional change follows regular patterns, ultimately rooted in human nature and hence as natural and predictable as human behaviour.

When Polybius gives a complete, formal explanation for the constitutional changes that he outlined in seven stages (including the origin of the primordial state of monarchy), he does not use any biological metaphors, but rather explains everything in terms of human psychology (VI.5.4–9.9).[35] Polybius as a historian followed Thucydides in seeking psychological explanations for the individual and communal decisions that determined history.[36] He believed that the way relationships among individuals are configured determines how the psychology of the various individuals will shape the communal decisions and the execution of those decisions. The configuration of relationships among individuals is what Polybius takes to be a constitution.

Human nature has two aspects: an animal nature moved by instinct, and a mind or reasoning faculty (*nous*, *logismos*, VI.6.4). It follows from this that human relationships and interactions, including constitutions and their changes, will be governed by two distinct processes, a non-rational competition for power and self-aggrandizement, and a rational attempt to rise above this competition to construct a better, cooperative social order. Polybius explains in detail how he understands these two processes to combine to produce one sequence of constitutional changes, namely, the rise and decline of kingship (VI.5.4–7.8).

To allow the essential features of the process to stand out, Polybius pictures the origins of society as a simple natural gathering together under the leadership of the strongest and most aggressive member of the group. Since this development is paralleled among irrational animals, moved only by instinctive impulse, Polybius calls it a 'most authentic function of nature' (*phuseōs ergon alēthinōtaton*), adding that 'herding together' by species for defence against natural enemies was due to 'natural weakness' (VI.5.5–8, cf. 6.8). His explanation recognizes an instinctive aggressive-

[34] For criticism see, e.g., Ryfell 1949:186–232, Aalders 1975:109–10, von Fritz 1954: 89–95; with the attempted resolution of Trompf 1979: 15–45.

[35] Petzold 1977, Podes 1991a, 1991b, Hahm 1995.

[36] Walbank 1972: 40–3, 58–9, 157–9.

ness and also presupposes an instinctive drive to compensate for weakness by cooperation. When the instinctive tendency toward aggression leads to internal competition, we see the societal consequences of the first natural process: the strongest and most aggressive individual ends up in control, thereby constituting a 'monarchy'.

The second factor affecting human behaviour and social relations is reason, which brings about the improvement of monarchy to kingship. It results from a gradual change in the psychological relationship between the ruler and the ruled. As the monarch begins to use rational judgment to make decisions in conformity with generally held conceptions of what is just (*dikaion*) and admirable (*kalon*), his subjects, who had been obeying out of fear, begin to recognize the rationality of his judgment and submit to his rule voluntarily. Their commitment leads them to defend the king against all challenges and to preserve his rule even when he is old and too weak to hang on to it by his own physical strength (VI.6.10–12).

Kingship thus arises under two conditions: (1) that a monarch govern by reasoned decision in accord with universally held moral concepts; and (2) that the people recognize the rational basis of his rule and submit to it voluntarily (VI.6.10–12, 7.3–4; cf. VI.4.2). Since the monarchic constitution itself arose from the instinctive competitive tendency of the inhabitants, Polybius must explain how they came to subordinate their natural instinct for self-aggrandizement in favour of mutual benefaction. The key is the development of shared moral conceptions by the use of reasoning. Thus Polybius' theory of constitutional improvement is built on a moral theory, which is itself rooted in human rationality.[37]

The citizens of a community discover moral notions by reasoning out the utility of certain types of actions, such as respect and care for parents, and risking one's life to defend the community. From reflection on the utility of public benefaction and returning favour for favour, the community develops a shared conception of what is admirable and just and is then prepared to become a kingship, as soon as it finds a strong leader who acts in accord with the shared values. Polybius assumes other shared moral values, such as freedom and equality, will emerge under other social circumstances (VI.9.2–4; cf. 8.4).

Polybius, in effect, subscribes to a utilitarian ethic of enlightened self-interest with the particular moral values evolving over time from changing circumstances. Such a concept of morality has affinities with Epicurean ethics, but it differs in that moral obligation is not based on a

[37] Cole 1967: 80–96.

compact of individuals, agreeing out of self-interest not to harm each other. It is based, rather, on the family, a product of the instinctive natural impulse to sexual intercourse, and on a desire to reinforce the instinctive reciprocity of benefaction that characterizes the relationship of parents and children within the family (VI.6.1–5).[38]

It is worth noticing that the kind of kingship explained by Polybius' theory is not very different from the ideal kingship reflected in contemporary kingship theories. Polybius' king wins the approval and favour of his subjects by paying attention to their needs and feelings. He defends the city against attacks, renders fair judicial decisions, and leads a moderate life. The result is a strong, united city, characterized by military strength and economic prosperity (VI.7.4–5). Such kings, like their counterparts in the Egyptian and Macedonian kingship theories, are alleged to have lived only in the past, when according to Polybius' democratically oriented theory, kings were elected, or at least ratified, by the people (VI.7.2–4).

Polybius' theory traces the subsequent changes. When kings 'began to receive their position by hereditary succession and began to have their security and more than enough provisions for living simply handed to them, they began to follow their desires', and to lead a life of luxury, self-indulgence, and rapacity. The result was a degeneration of kingship into tyranny (VI.7.6–8). The cause of this degeneration is the feeling of security that accompanies hereditary rule. On Polybius' psychological assumptions the commitment to reciprocal benefaction and the moral notions of justice and honour that form the basis of kingship arise out of a utilitarian calculation of advantage and can only arise among people who feel a sense of vulnerability. The only dependency or vulnerability for a king in a secure, prosperous kingdom presumably comes from the necessity of being elected or ratified by the people. Even this last vestige of vulnerability is removed by hereditary rule. Apparently Polybius believed that virtue cannot be taught, but must be learned by relevant personal experience. Despite the fact that many kingship theories, including that of the *Letter to Alexander*, looked to education to improve kings, Polybius was committed to the opinion that secure hereditary monarchs are doomed to become tyrants, with or without moral training, and all can look forward to jealousy, hatred, and eventually revolution (VI.7.6–8.1).

Polybius' account of the other constitutional changes, those leading to aristocracy, oligarchy, democracy, and mob-rule, are treated briefly with little in the way of explanation, except to indicate how they differ from

[38] For Platonic and Aristotelian precedents see Trompf 1979: 16–22, Lord 1991: 61–8. Cole 1967: 80–130 speculates that the theory derives ultimately from Democritus.

the fully explained monarchic constitutions (VI.8.1–9.9). The natural process of competition for power, which accounts for the proportion of rulers (one, few, or many), is almost ignored in a desire to show how every type of simple constitution is bound to decline to its deviant form. Degeneration was of paramount concern because it held the key to constitutional stability and national strength. Since degeneration results from a ruling power's unqualified security, the only way to prevent decline is to limit the ruling power's security. Because such limitation is difficult to maintain indefinitely in a simple constitution, none can be deemed ideal. The best constitution has to be a mixed constitution, which creates conditions that preclude unqualified security for the rulers (VI.3.7–8; VI.10.1–11).

In the theory adopted by Polybius, the traditional constitution of Sparta served as an example of a stable, mixed constitution. The Spartan lawgiver Lycurgus was portrayed as a wise king, who understood the principles of constitutional degeneration and

> brought together all the virtues and distinctive features of the best [simple] constitutions, so that none might grow beyond its proper point and change into its corresponding evil, but rather, with the force of each being counteracted by [that of] another, none would tilt [the scale] and outweigh the others for any length of time, but the constitution would over time be balanced in equilibrium and would last indefinitely in accord with the principle of counteracting forces. (VI.10.6–7)

Polybius here introduces the influential metaphor of 'checks and balances', but he identifies the operative mechanism as a psychological state in which fear blocks any permanent manifestation of self-aggrandizement:

> The kingship is prevented from turning arrogant on account of its fear of the people . . . and the people in turn do not dare to scorn the kings on account of fear of the elders, who . . . will always assign themselves to the just [cause], so that the part . . . diminished by adherence to tradition [viz. the kings] will always become greater and weightier by the added force of the elders. (VI.10.8–10)

The stability of the Spartan mixed constitution depends on the condition that no constituent get absolute control and with it the unqualified security that triggers oppressive, self-interested rule. As the longest-lived of any Greek constitution it qualified for the title of best constitution (VI.10.11–14, cf. 3.7–8).

As we noted above, Polybius' primary interest in political theory arose from its utility as a tool to help explain history and to assist statesmen in anticipating or controlling political developments. As a historian he applied it to illuminate constitutional changes that came within the purview of his history. He viewed the ruthless conduct of the Macedonian king Philip V as the consequence (and hence empirical evidence) of the degeneration of Macedonian kingship to tyranny. Philip II, Alexander the Great, and Antigonus Doson, all kings who reigned before Polybius' birth, were cited as examples of kingship at its acme (V.9.8–10.8). Antigonus' successor, Philip V, though he came to the throne in 221 BC with the requisite natural attributes and was accepted by his subjects (IV.77.1–4; VII. 11.4–9), had tendencies in opposite directions, namely, both toward benevolence and toward self-aggrandizement, and had advisors that encouraged him in these two opposite directions. Eventually, under pressure from the unprincipled advisors, he yielded to his baser instincts and became a cruel tyrant (IV.82–6; V.9–12; VII.11–14).[39] Though this explanation for degeneration deviates from the theoretical prototype of Book VI in admitting a change in mid-reign, Polybius motivates the change in accord with his theory by emphasizing the unquestioned security in which Philip began his reign, an experience similar to that of a hereditary king (VII.11.1–9).

The Achaean nation, Polybius' own people, followed two segments of the paradigm of constitutional change. It began as a kingship for several generations and then degenerated into a tyranny. When the tyrants were overthrown, the Achaean cities became democracies (II.41; IV.1.5–6). Polybius finds the manifestation of democracy not only in the relation of individuals in their local cities (*poleis*), but in the relation of the cities to each other in what he calls the Achaean 'nation' (*ethnos*), a league uniting the entire Peloponnesus into one city in every way except for a single wall (II.37–8).[40] By 181 BC, however, the masses (*polloi*, *ochlos*) were in control under the leadership of Callicrates (XXIV.8–10). This, Polybius claims, 'was the beginning of the change for the worse' (XXIV.10.10). In the end, in conformity with the paradigmatic description of the demise of the ochlocratic constitution (VI.9.7–9), the Achaeans elected Critolaus and Diaeus (XXXVIII.10.8, 13), who pandered to the masses and obtained illegal absolute power, evoking Polybius' sardonical comment, 'In this way he [Critolaus] obtained a kind of monarchic power' (XXXVIII.11.9–11;

[39] Pédech 1964: 231–2, Walbank 1972: 93. Modern assessments of Philip's reign are more nuanced, e.g. Walbank 1940: esp. 261–5.

[40] The democratic nature is recognizable from its values of freedom (*eleutheria*), equality (*isēgoria*, *isotēs*), and free speech (*parrhēsia*, II.37.9, 38.6–8, 42.6); compare VI.9.4–5.

13.6–7). Thus Polybius portrays Achaea as reflecting first a decline from kingship to tyranny, and then a decline from democracy to mob-rule to monarchy.

Polybius also applied his theory to changes in the Spartan constitution in the third century BC. The revolution of Cleomenes, with the consequent transformation of Sparta into a typical Hellenistic autocratic monarchy, is not only characterized as the creation of a tyranny, but is described in such a way that it is compatible with the origin and nature of Sparta's mixed constitution. That mixed constitution had come into existence by a planned action of a single Spartan king, Lycurgus (VI.10.1–11). Kingship, on Polybius' theory, was already an improved constitution. Polybius construed Lycurgus' action as a second, further improvement, incorporating a balancing mechanism to prevent degeneration. When he describes the end of the mixed constitution, he does not call it a 'degeneration' or 'change for the worse' within a given generic type, but a 'dissolution of the ancestral constitution' and a 'transformation' (*metastēsantos*) into tyranny (II.47.3; IV.81.14). He makes it clear that this was accomplished by a single intentional action of a single individual, just as the mixed constitution was created.

The theoretical principles that were applied to interpret historical patterns in the past were also used by Polybius to anticipate future changes. The basis for prediction was the conception of human behaviour that he used to ground his theory of constitutional change and his explanation of historical events.[41] His account of constitutional changes is, in fact, carefully constructed to allow it to serve as a basis for making predictions: it is grammatically formulated to describe each constitutional change in a result clause following one or more temporal clauses, stipulating the conditions that trigger that change. For example, 'When [kings], receiving their position by hereditary succession, began to have their security and a superabundance of means provided for them . . . tyranny came to be from kingship' (VI.7.6–8). 'Whenever the people [alienated by the exploitative tyrant] got leaders [angry enough to rebel against him] . . . kingship and monarchy were totally destroyed and aristocracy got its start' (VI.8.1).

These are, in effect, natural laws of sociopolitical change. Some, like degeneration within a generic type, are fully necessitated so that even the timing is predictable.[42] Others, such as changes from one generic type to another (e.g., the appearance of aristocracy or democracy), while psycho-

[41] Hahm 1995: 32–7.
[42] One generation for hereditary kingship or aristocracy (VI.7.6–7), two generations for democracy (VI.9.4–5); see Hahm 1995: 24–32.

logically explainable, depend on contingent factors and indeterminate temporal conditions and hence are predictable only in certain respects. Thus Polybius' cycle of constitutional change is not presented as a rigidly necessitated sequence of events, but as a logically organized series of discrete laws of societal change, chosen, as he himself implies, for brevity and pedagogical clarity (VI.5.1–2).

Polybius' most extensive and challenging application of the theory was to the Roman constitution. It was here that he departed from the existing theory, presumably circulating in his Achaean homeland, to create his own variant, capable of explaining the unique nature and history of the Roman constitution. The bulk of Book VI was, in fact, devoted to the Roman constitution. In compiling the history of the Roman constitution Polybius was a pioneer, accomplishing for Rome what Aristotle and his students had done for Athens and the Greek city-states.[43] Though this portion of the book is lost, we know that he interpreted its development as an incremental process of natural evolution, in explicit contrast to the artificial, instantaneous creation of the Spartan mixed constitution by the deliberate action of a single individual. The Roman constitution, he states, arose by 'many struggles and actions, in which the Romans repeatedly chose the better course, on the basis of new understanding acquired in disasters' (VI.10.14). In so doing Polybius identified a second type of mixed constitution, one that develops naturally.

Of Polybius' analysis of the nature and working of the Roman constitution we are better informed than of its origin (VI.11–18, cf. 19–42).[44] We learn that Rome's mixed constitution differed from Sparta's in the basis of its stability. Whereas the Spartan constitution was stabilized by the ability of one group (the 'aristocratic' elders) to switch sides and thus maintain equilibrium between the other two, the Roman constitution is stabilized by the fact that none of the three elements can function without the consent of the other two. The consul, for example, the monarchic element, is responsible for leading the army and conducting wars. The Senate, the aristocratic element, appropriates funding for the army and reappoints the consul annually to continue conducting the war as proconsul, while the people, the democratic element, ratify or annul the consul's treaties and other actions (VI.12, 15). Without the cooperation of the Senate and people the consul is unable to carry out his monarchic function of conducting war and ruling subject nations. Comparable cooperation is required for the other parts to perform their functions (VI.13–14, 16–17).

[43] For attempts to reconstruct this lost portion see von Fritz 1954: 123–54, Walbank 1957–79: I.663–73, Trompf 1979: 49–54.

[44] Von Fritz 1954: 155–252.

This constitutionally established cooperation is the key to Rome's stability, strength, and success:

> The power of each of the parts either to harm another or to cooperate is such that their union is adequate for all situations. Thus it is impossible to find a better form of constitution. (VI.18.1)

Its effectiveness is due to two features: it can unite the entire community and consolidate the effort and strength of every member, so that it is irresistible in its chosen projects; and it is self-correcting, if ever any part begins to grow beyond its proper level of strength and attempts to dominate the others (VI.18).

As in all of Polybius' political analyses the operative factor is psychological, namely, fear. When there is a threat from without, there is a

> common fear [that] compels [all of] them to come to agreement (*sumphronein*) and cooperate with each other . . . in public and in private for the complete achievement of the chosen project. (VI.18.2–3)

When peace and prosperity bring affluence and ease of living, which turns the Romans 'to hybris and arrogance', the constitution comes to the rescue, preventing one part from becoming dominant by providing another part that blocks its movement, so that 'all remain in the established state, blocked from fulfilling an [aggressive] impulse and fearing from the very beginning deterrence by the others' (VI.18.5–8). Thus the real basis of Roman stability is the interdependence of the parts and the will to cooperate, engendered by the recognition of that interdependence.

The practical consequence of the resulting unity is that 'nothing that ought to be done fails to be done, because everyone competes in devising plans to meet the challenge; and once a decision is made, the opportunity to carry it out is never missed, because everyone works together . . . to complete the project' (VI.18.2–3). This, in essence, is the reason that Rome was able to conquer 'nearly the whole of the inhabited world in 53 years' (I.1.5).

A naturally evolved mixed constitution, such as Rome had, is the most stable of constitutions, but still subject to decline. Polybius compares Rome's constitution to that of Carthage, which was also a naturally developed mixed constitution. The comparison constitutes an essential element in his principal historiographical project, explaining Rome's conquest of the Mediterranean world. This conquest had begun with the defeat of Carthage, Rome's competitor for world dominion. Carthage's mixed constitution, in his judgment, was not as perfectly evolved as Rome's (VI.51–6). In addition, it had reached its acme earlier, so that, when Rome confronted Carthage in the Second Punic War, Carthage's constitution had already begun to decline (vi.51). Polybius invokes this decline to help explain Rome's victory, and, in so doing, he raises the spectre of potential decline for Rome as well.

Polybius complements his innovative analysis of the origin and flowering of the Roman constitution by extrapolating to the next stage, using the same Greek theory he had adapted to explain its history to the present.[45] He had the evidence of Carthage to support his venture, but the pattern of decline that he envisions is formulated in conformity with the paradigm of simple constitutional change. In contrast to the Spartan pattern of deliberate instantaneous creation, followed by deliberate, instantaneous reconstitution into tyranny, Polybius envisions a gradual natural transformation corresponding to its gradual natural origin. Though his specific analysis of the origin is lost, we may conjecture that in developing into a mixed constitution each of the parts was portrayed as following the paradigmatic pattern of its own type. When each part reached its acme simultaneously, in the late third century BC, Rome achieved her notable internal stability and military invincibility. Polybius expects that the three parts will simultaneously begin to decline.

To describe the outcome of the interconnected declines, he formulates two new 'laws' of societal change on the model of the original paradigm:[46]

> (1) Whenever a state achieves absolute security and permanent prosperity, the standard of living becomes increasingly lavish and the citizens become increasingly competitive for offices and other objects of desire.
> (2) Whenever the people think they have been injured by some (the few) because of greed and are flattered by others (the many) because of love of office, they withdraw from the practice of sharing rule with the other elements in the mixed constitution and thereby reconstitute the state as an ochlocracy.

The outcome depends on the interaction of the many and the few. As the paradigm stipulated, prosperity turns people (specifically the aristocratic few) to (oligarchic) greed and competitive display of wealth (cf. vi.8.4–5). At the same time it turns the democratic many to the excessive love of political office, a characteristic of mob-rule (cf. vi.9.5–6). This combination is fatal to the mixed constitution. The greed of the few naturally alienates the people, preparing them for revolution as soon as they find a leader (cf. vi.8.4–9.1). The people, having become a deviant democracy,

[45] Hahm 1995: 41–5. [46] Paraphrased from vi.57.6–9.

with individuals craving office and flattering the masses to get it, have an abundance of aspiring leaders; but neither they nor the leaders any longer partake of the shared moral values that conduce to a good constitution. When these people (the masses) revolt against the leadership of the (now oligarchic) few and refuse to obey them, they *de facto* destroy the mixed constitution. Since they themselves have already degenerated from democracy, the reconstituted state is *de facto* an ochlocracy or mob rule.

Polybius has been praised for what seems to be an uncanny anticipation of the Roman Revolution; but that was only part of his achievement. His significance lies in discovering and preserving a Hellenistic Greek theory that had been formulated as a set of quasi-scientific laws of human behaviour, compatible with his own conception of historical causation, and in applying it creatively to Hellenistic Greek and Roman history. His application to Greek history was relatively straightforward, since it had been developed on the basis of Greek constitutions; but his application to Rome required him first to compile the history of the Roman constitution and then to adapt the theory to analyse a constitution of a new and unfamiliar type. Though his analysis may have missed many aspects of Roman Republican political institutions, it succeeded in recognizing the importance of a balance of political power among different socio-economic groups. In acknowledging that Rome had learned the importance of such balance by painful experience it also highlighted Rome's genius for compromise and efficient management (VI.10.13–14).[47]

[47] Walbank 1972: 155–6. For detailed evaluation see von Fritz 1954: esp. 306–52.

24

Cicero

E.M. ATKINS

1 Introduction

Cicero could read in his well thumbed text of Plato's *Republic* that political constitutions did not endure forever. Experience reinforced the message of philosophy that the Roman Republic was unlikely to withstand the recurrent civil wars that marked the years of his adult life. Cicero, along with his contemporaries, preferred to analyse historical change in moral terms. Thus, he argued that the traditional constitution of the Republic was intrinsically the most stable available, and the only reason for its weakness was the corruption of the ruling classes. To the modern historian, his conservatism may seem nostalgic or impractical; yet his *de Re Publica* was received with immediate enthusiasm, while *de Officiis* proved one of the most influential of all Classical works. Cicero's strength as a political philosopher lay in the creative and enduring expression that he gave to a remarkably fertile set of aristocratic ideals.

I have described Cicero's political philosophy as creative. However, much scholarship since the late nineteenth century has been devoted to discovering the precise ways in which his thought is derivative. Cicero the philosopher has been supposed habitually to have imitated a lost Greek 'source'; and his texts have been mentally translated back into Greek in order to learn more about their alleged author. Unsurprisingly, Cicero's arguments have seemed both unoriginal and anachronistic. However, the presuppositions, the methods and the results of the source-hunters have not stood up to close scrutiny. In particular, we can no longer ignore the wealth of evidence for Cicero's wide reading in Greek philosophy and history, and his easy familiarity with philosophical concepts (shown, for example, by jokes in his letters) as well as his outstanding ability to organize ideas and arguments. Cicero exploited Greek philosophy intensively; but whatever he borrowed, he thoroughly appropriated and transformed for his own purposes. Consequently, his political philosophy needs to be illuminated by the concrete circumstances of his own age.[1]

[1] Boyancé 1936, Douglas 1968, Bringmann 1971.

2 The historical background[2]

Rome had been founded by Romulus, so tradition related, and ruled by six subsequent kings. The last of these, Tarquinius Superbus ('the arrogant') was expelled by Junius Brutus in 510 BC. Kings were replaced by a pair of magistrates called consuls, whose term of office was limited to one year. The council which had advised the king became the Senate. Gradually, the body of citizens (consisting of free adult males) was organized into a variety of popular assemblies and also acquired a limited political role.

The fully developed system included four types of senior magistrate. The two consuls possessed *imperium* or executive power. They were the supreme military commanders; they also initiated debate in the Senate and proposed legislation. They were assisted by praetors, whose responsibilities included the dispensation of justice at Rome and the governing of provinces. Beneath them were the aediles, who oversaw the administration of the city, and the quaestors, financial officers. During the second century these magistracies were organized into a tightly structured career ladder known as the *cursus honorum*, 'course of honours'. New regulations preserved the competitive element of the system while preventing talented individuals from attaining pre-eminence too suddenly or too permanently. In this way the collective influence of the Senate was preserved.

The major role in governing Rome fell to the aristocratic elite who formed the Senate. Their role was to discuss policy and advise the executive magistrates; in practice, their decisions were normally authoritative. By the end of the fourth century the Senate was composed of ex-magistrates. The Senate's core was a small group of noble families whose names dominated the lists of magistrates over the years. However, it was not a closed body, and there was a steady influx of newcomers, to the Senate and even to the consulship.[3] These were often men like Cicero himself from the leading families of towns outside Rome. Wealthy members of non-senatorial families came to be known as *equites* ('horsemen'; singular *eques*). Equal to the senators in social standing, they concerned themselves with property and finance and not political careers.[4] The Roman system cannot therefore be divided neatly into groups either of rulers and ruled, or of rich and poor. *Equites* were wealthy, but had almost no political privileges or duties. On the other hand, an individual *eques* might by election enter the governing class.

[2] Standard accounts: Brunt 1988: ch. 1, Crawford 1992, *The Cambridge Ancient History* vol. IX.
[3] Wiseman 1971, Hopkins 1983: ch. 2. [4] Brunt 1988: ch. 3.

The duties of the popular assemblies included the passing of legislation proposed by the magistrates, the declaration of war and the hearing of criminal trials, as well as the election of magistrates. In theory, therefore, the democratic element of the constitution was not inconsiderable. However, the system of voting was such that the wealthy wielded disproportionate influence; while in practice only those from the upper ranks of society stood for office. Moreover, the occasions on which the people defied the united advice of the Senate were rare. On the other hand, disagreements or competition among senators could sometimes offer them an opportunity to decide important issues.[5] The plebeian assembly [6] also elected ten tribunes who were charged with defending the interests of the common people.

Finally, religion was an integral part of Roman political life. Political procedures were subject to religious control, since unfavourable auspices could be used to nullify decisions or postpone debates. The Romans believed that the flourishing of the city depended upon the goodwill of the gods, and therefore that the disregard of cultic obligations or solemn oaths, for example, was politically damaging. It is unsurprising therefore that the major priesthoods tended to be held by men who were or had been leading magistrates, and that election to them was considered socially prestigious.

So much for the structures of the constitution. How did the politics of Republican Rome actually work? Cicero himself considered as true patriots those who supported the collective authority of the Senate, and he often described such men as *boni*, 'good', a term with social, moral and political undertones. Other politicians tended to favour measures that had popular appeal, and preferred to legislate directly through the people's assembly. Cicero characterized such men as 'popular', and distrusted them.[7] It would be a mistake to think of two parties with organized long-term programmes. Most senatorial decisions were pragmatic responses to the needs of the moment. It was also extremely rare for an individual magistrate consistently and coherently to propose popular reforms. Personal factors weighed heavily in the scale of political decisions. Senators were influenced not only by the content of a proposal, but also by the reputation of its proposer, and by considerations of kinship, political friendship and personal obligation.

[5] Millar 1984, 1986.

[6] Consisting of the *plebs*, that is, those citizens who were not members of the original noble families.

[7] The terminology is, however, slippery; see Hellegouarc'h 1963:484–505, 518–25, Seager 1972.

If such factors affected even senatorial debate, they were more significant still when it came to elections: to win votes one needed a public name. This was an open-air society where success depended upon being visible. Victorious generals were honoured with triumphal marches through the streets, in which their conquered victims were displayed in chains. Noble families paraded lavish funerals. Important court-cases took place in public, so that a powerful orator could readily win the people's favour. Politicians gave speeches before the assembled populace to defend their actions in the Senate-house. Candidates won office on the strength less of manifestos than of their capacity to impress with their existing record and reputation.

There was scope, therefore, for brilliant individual careers within a basically oligarchic government. From the late second century, there were signs of the friction between individuals and Senate that would become intolerable in Cicero's day. Scipio,[8] ironically one of Cicero's heroes, more than once exploited his popularity to force the Senate's hand. But to later historians, the supreme examples of popular politicians were the two Gracchi. Tiberius Gracchus, as tribune in 133 BC, introduced a law to limit the holding of public land by wealthy individuals, thus freeing it for the use of poorer farmers. A decade later, his brother Gaius used the popular assembly to pass a range of measures including a further agrarian law. The Gracchi strained the tolerance of their peers in the Senate, and each of them died a violent death. Gaius' murder led to the setting of a significant precedent: the consul who executed some of his followers without trial claimed the authority of an emergency decree passed by the Senate (*senatus consultum ultimum*). This declared that the *res publica* was in extreme danger, so that normal constitutional procedure might be suspended.[9]

The Gracchi were seen in retrospect as the personal heralds of popular revolutionary change. However, gradual and impersonal causes also underlay the military and constitutional upheavals of the first century. The empire grew enormously from the mid-second century. It was necessary in order to govern it that individuals should control efficient armies for long periods far from Rome itself. The troops, therefore, came to wield enormous collective power, to make or destroy leaders, and to demand land on which to settle after their retirement. Relationships with conquered allies, who were gradually being assimilated into the empire, provided another source of tension. It is unsurprising that the empire

[8] There were several Scipios. I refer, except where indicated, to Scipio Aemilianus Africanus (185/4–129), adopted grandson of Scipio Africanus Major (236–184/3).

[9] Stockton 1971: 92–6.

could no longer be effectively governed by the debates of a relatively harmonious aristocratic council situated in its metropolis.

The first century saw the steady increase in the power of and the rivalry between individual military commanders. Gaius Marius, consul for the first time in 107, created a precedent by encouraging the enrolment into the army of those without property. Poor soldiers were more dependent upon their generals, and armies became more closely bound to individual leaders. At any rate, it was not long before the generals were to turn their power against one another. The troops' inhibitions about killing their fellow-citizens were perhaps weakened by the Social War of 91–88 in which Rome defeated her Italian allies, and then offered them citizenship in the subsequent settlement. There followed a decade of intermittent civil war, which ended when Sulla revived the dictatorship in 81, and treated his defeated enemies without mercy. From then on, any exceptionally gifted individual caused anxiety to the advocate of cooperative senatorial government. The rise of Cicero's contemporary Pompey was particularly spectacular, as his precocious military success won him both a series of special commands over a period of several years and the consulship of 70 BC, before he was technically qualified to stand as a candidate. The career of such a man provided him with a loyal and experienced army, and the potential power to override constitutional precedents with the threat of force. Aristocratic competition was becoming dangerous.

3 The aristocratic code[10]

The ethics, or at least the moral rhetoric, of Roman society showed a remarkable degree of continuity from the late third to the mid-first century. Our evidence comes mainly from the literature and inscriptions of the elite. (Cicero's own extensive writings, by their very survival, inevitably wield a disproportionate influence.) The vocabulary of such men is shaped by their aristocratic preoccupation with war and politics. They interpreted political success and failure in uncompromisingly moral terms. Conversely, their moral language is of its essence social and political.

The aristocrats represented their ideal as inherited; they made frequent appeal to an amalgam of moral and constitutional precedents which they described as *mos maiorum*, 'the custom of the ancestors'. History and tradition mattered, and that for three reasons. First, these men learnt their ethics from their predecessors, especially from exemplary stories of heroism.

[10] See further Knoche 1934, Balsdon 1960, Hellegouarc'h 1963, Earl 1967, Hölkeskamp 1987.

Secondly, the pre-eminent position of the elite had remarkably little protection in law; it relied upon a powerful respect for precedent. Thirdly, the family rather than the individual was the primary location of reputation and of pride. The older noble families emphasized this last point. Those 'new men' who rose to prominence by their own efforts in the second and third centuries insisted that personal virtue rather than lineage alone merited glory.

Virtus was the quality of a *vir*, that is 'manliness'. It was revealed especially in warfare. The plural *virtutes* could refer to specific acts of heroic courage. But *virtus* also entailed justice and honesty, both in personal and in international matters. Trickery and the breaking of promises were condemned; *fides*, i.e. faithfulness and trustworthiness, was a pre-eminent virtue. Avarice, corruption and luxury were also the targets of high-minded critics who painted a nostalgic picture of antique frugality. This stern streak in Roman morality had an institutional counterpart in the office of censor, responsible for examining the *mores* of the citizens, and in particular of senators. Wisdom, too, was required of the aristocrat, whose business was as much with politics as with war. By winning a reputation for offering sound practical advice in the Senate or before the people, he would acquire *auctoritas*, the influence that guaranteed a respectful hearing.[11]

Public service was intended for the public eye. Military and political success contributed to one's *dignitas* or public standing, intrinsically linked to one's sense of self-worth. Great achievements won *gloria*, which consisted both of the acclaim of one's peers and of widespread popularity.[12] One reason for the importance of glory was, of course, eminently practical, as office and therefore entry to the Senate was secured by popular election. Reputation thus constituted both an end and a means within this code. Popularity was secured also by building networks of clients and political friends, whether through a judicious use of benefaction, or through services in kind, in particular legal advocacy. To command influence, *gratia*, was to be owed gratitude, and correspondingly political loyalty was a standard method, particularly for poorer dependants, to discharge obligations. The aristocratic ethos was thoroughly competitive; however, the virtues of courage, wisdom and piety were all to be exercised in the service of the *res publica*. All sides, even in the late Republic, consistently represented their own actions as patriotic: in theory, individual and familial ambitions were channelled to benefit the greater whole. There

[11] Balsdon 1960. [12] Knoche 1934, Sullivan 1941, Long 1995.

was thus an inherent tension in the system between competitive and socially directed values, a fact that would become sharply apparent as the crises of the first century exerted their pressures on moral language.

Finally, another watchword of the tradition, and a slippery one, was liberty. For the aristocrats themselves it consisted primarily in preventing the individual dominance of one of their number: Junius Brutus, who had expelled the last king, was the first Republican hero. The Roman people valued their own freedoms: their equality before the law, their right of appeal against serious penalties, their powers of suffrage. Even a man like Cicero, who instinctively distrusted popular power, frequently appealed to 'the liberty of the Roman people' (see e.g. Cic. *Agr.* II *passim*; *Planc.* 15; *Phil.* VI.19).[13]

The widespread use of such propaganda reminds us how pervasive were the inherited ideals of the Republic's elite. It was not only the nostalgic conservatives who appealed to the *mos maiorum*. When Augustus looked back on his career and claimed to have restored the *res publica*, he too was constrained by the limits of moral vocabulary. The language of *virtus*, *prudentia*, *dignitas*, *beneficia* and *libertas* could be reshaped, but it could not be rejected. It was forged, of course, by the ideals of the aristocrats, at once competitive and patriotic, and survives largely within their own texts. However, some of these texts are designed to appeal to a popular audience. The code of the elite moulded that of wider society, and indeed influenced many a later generation.

4 Cicero's early career[14]

Marcus Tullius Cicero was born on 3 January 106 BC in Arpinum, a town seventy miles south-east of Rome. His family were local landowners, cultured, but with no previous experience of public office in Rome. His father ensured that Marcus and his brother, Quintus, would not be disadvantaged by lack of education. They studied in Rome under the supervision of L. Licinius Crassus (consul 95 BC), one of the finest orators of his day. Later, Marcus learnt civil law from Q. Mucius Scaevola 'the Augur' (consul 117 BC) and then from his cousin Q. Mucius Scaevola 'the Pontifex' (consul 95 BC). These men and their friends encouraged in Cicero a lifelong admiration for moderate conservatism in politics.[15]

The philosophical interests that Cicero maintained throughout his life

[13] See further Wirszubski 1950, Brunt 1988: ch. 6.

[14] Standard accounts of Cicero's life: Shackleton Bailey 1971, Stockton 1971, Rawson 1975, Mitchell 1979, 1991.

[15] Mitchell 1979: ch. 1.

originated in his youth. When first in Rome, he met the blind Stoic teacher Diodotus, who would later live in Cicero's house, and Philo of Larissa, the head of the Platonic Academy. From 79 to 77 he visited Greece for further study in rhetoric and philosophy, and heard the lectures of the famous Stoic Posidonius in Rhodes, and of the Academic Antiochus of Ascalon in Athens. (In his old age he will recall the latter evocatively in the preface to a dialogue set in the grounds of the Academy (*Fin.* v.1–5).)

At this point, it would be helpful to clarify the choices of philosophical allegiance available to the young man.[16] The Academy, founded by Plato, had in the third century taken a sceptical turn under Arcesilaus. The legacy of this remained in the form of a quarrel between Cicero's own two teachers: Philo wished to maintain a modified scepticism, while Antiochus wished to return to the 'Old Academy', as he called it. In fact his philosophy was a fusion of the views of Platonists, Aristotelians and Stoics, which he quite deliberately assimilated. In ethics he believed that there was only a verbal difference between the Stoic view that virtue was the only good, and the Peripatetic view that it was the supreme good. Both the Stoa and the Academy had prominent adherents in Rome. In particular, the younger Cato became known as a model of unbending political Stoicism (and would provide inspiration to a later generation of critics of the early emperors). The Stoa, sceptical Platonism or the 'Old Academy' were possibilities; not quite yet a repristinated Aristotelianism, for Aristotle's works were only now being rediscovered in Athens for eventual introduction to Rome. There was one final option: to follow Epicurus, with his denouncing of religious superstition and his advocacy of empiricism and a restrained hedonism. Cicero's closest friend Atticus, and eventually a surprising number of reputable contemporaries, chose that course.

Cicero himself was loyal throughout his life to Plato and his Academy. In his early writings, and in the philosophical corpus he produced in his last years, he certainly followed Philo's moderately sceptical interpretation of Platonism: one should listen to both sides of a case, and prefer the more plausible, but without rash assertion or claims to certainty. It has been argued, although not conclusively, that Cicero turned to a more dogmatic Platonism in his middle years.[17] At any rate, he showed sympathy both for Stoicism, with its high-minded ethical principles and support for engagement in politics, and for the Peripatetic tradition whose adherents

[16] On Cicero: Douglas 1965, Powell 1995. On the philosophical schools: Long 1986a, Long and Sedley 1987.

[17] For: Glucker 1988; against: Görler 1995.

included Demetrius of Phaleron (born *c.* 350 BC), a rare example of philosopher and statesman combined. For Epicureanism alone, despite Atticus, Cicero had little respect or sympathy. Its hedonism he interpreted harshly; while he saw its preference for withdrawal from political life as untimely and unRoman.

Cicero sustained his philosophical interests throughout his life, supported by his own fine libraries and his conversation and correspondence with like-minded friends. His letters testify to this; and as he himself tells us, even his speeches were 'packed with' philosophical maxims (*ND* 1.6).[18] Yet it must also be significant that his actual philosophical writing was undertaken in periods when he was withdrawn from, or at least disillusioned with, political life. Philosophy thus tended to provide a remedy for the failings of the *res publica* rather than an immediate programme for action.

It was advocacy that originally offered a route for this young man, who possessed more talent than wealth or lineage, to make a name and influential friends. He began his career under Sulla, showing some courage in defending Sextus Roscius of Ameria against a powerful henchman of the dictator. (Legal cases, as so many of Cicero's own speeches testify, were rarely without political implications.) In 75, he climbed the first rung of the 'course of honours', being elected quaestor and serving in Sicily. Six years later he was to renew his ties with the Sicilians, and make a stand against extortion of Rome's subjects by officials in the provinces, by prosecuting Verres on account of his corrupt governorship of the island.

Cicero progressed steadily up the ladder of honours, eventually being elected consul in the earliest legitimate year. This was an outstanding feat for someone from an undistinguished family. His first action was to lead the defeat of proposals for the redistribution of land. Although he skilfully presented himself as acting in the interests of the people, he was signalling clearly his opposition to reform in the tradition of the Gracchi. Cicero himself was to look back on his consulate with unrestrained pride in the moment when he foiled a conspiracy led by Catiline, one of his defeated rivals for office.[19] He acted decisively to defeat the conspirators; and when senators and *equites* alike rallied to the cause, he saw incarnated, albeit briefly, his political ideal of cooperation between the orders.[20] However, he inspired lasting hostility in some quarters by executing several conspirators on the pretext of a *senatus consultum ultimum*.[21]

[18] Boyancé 1936. [19] Stockton 1971: ch. 4–6. [20] Strasburger 1956.
[21] See above, p. 480.

Cicero hoped that he would spend the years following his consulship enjoying the prestige and authority appropriate to his position, and playing a leading role in guiding the government of Rome. He miscalculated badly. The next decade was dominated by an uneasy alliance between Pompey, Marcus Crassus and Julius Caesar. Another significant figure, personally hostile to Cicero, was Publius Clodius; a patrician by birth and a populist by method, he could exert influence across the political spectrum. The enmity between the two men was confirmed irrevocably when Clodius drove Cicero into exile under the threat of punishment for unlawfully executing the conspirators of 63. Cicero's exile, in 58, and his restoration in the following year left a permanent mark on his political affiliations: implacable hostility to Clodius, resentment against those aristocrats who had failed to give him their support, and lasting gratitude to Pompey, whom he saw as the instigator of his recall.

There were many signs in these years that government by senatorial consensus was doomed. Populist legislation such as that on land reform continued to divide conservatives from reformers; Caesar as consul in 59 simply lost patience, and by-passed the customary consultation with the Senate to legislate directly through the people. Clodius and Pompey vied to court the popular assemblies, whose affiliations were vulnerable to dramatic vacillation. Both Pompey and Caesar were suspected of harbouring regal ambitions, and the threat of the army that the latter controlled during his extended provincial command was always in the background. There were times when the trio of allies seemed on the point of a breach; and Cicero took advantage of one such moment in spring 56 to outline his own brand of patriotic conservatism, and to plan opposition to a law supporting Caesar's land reforms. Before he could do so, however, the alliance had recemented itself. Cicero was forced to recant, and worse still was put under orders to use his advocacy to defend personal enemies of his own. It seemed that the essence of a free *res publica*, free senatorial debate and freedom in the law-courts, had disappeared (e.g. *Q.Fr.* III.5.4). Moreover, elections by the people were under threat: Pompey, Cicero surmised, had been planning the consulships and provincial commands for the next few years (*Att.* IV.8a.2, November 56). The organized influx of troops and the threat of violence jeopardized free voting; while bribery threw Rome into chaos by preventing the consular elections of both 54 and 53 (cf. e.g. *Q.Fr.* II.15.4; *Att.* IV.15.7–8).

Cicero's shifting political attitudes during this period were shaped by fear and ambition as much as by principle. He bitterly lamented the loss of the *res publica*; yet he was prepared for pragmatic reasons to support, and at times to cultivate, Caesar as well as Pompey. In theory, he was more in agreement with the senatorial aristocrats; however, he was also resentful and distrustful of them. He veered from periods of despair to moments of rash over-confidence. It was during one of the latter that he delivered the speech *pro Sestio*, and it is here, if anywhere, that we can see the political ideal that he would have promoted if he had felt himself consistently secure: loyal men of all classes, rich and poor, political and commercial, should unite in support of the *res publica* and in rejection of sedition and revolution. Typically, he emphasizes the harmonious cooperation of members of all the political orders.[22] The whole people should elect, and be eligible to enter, the Senate. The Senate's counsel should guard and guide the city; and the magistrates should act on their authority as their ministers. The Senate's task should include the preservation of the liberty and welfare of the people (*Sest.* 137).

5 The writings of the fifties

5.1 The best orator[23]

During these years of political frustration, Cicero took time from practical politics in order to write. His first choice of topic is instructive. His three volumes *de Oratore*, composed in the years 55–54 (*Att.* IV.13.2; *Fam.* I.9.23) are largely devoted to discussing the techniques of rhetoric. However, the explicit subject is not oratorical science, but rather the best orator. He, of course, will turn out to be a statesman: his fields of action are the law-courts, the assemblies and the Senate. The complete orator, it is claimed at the beginning of the dialogue, upholds the safety of the *res publica*. Indeed, even the first civic societies were gathered and organized by the power of eloquence (I.30–4; cf. *Inv.* I.2–3; *Sest.* 91). *De Oratore*, therefore, prepares the ground for the developed political philosophy of *de Re Publica* and *de Legibus*.

This work provides the first example of Cicero's careful dramatization of his philosophical dialogues. The setting is the Tusculan villa of Antonius, one of the great orators of the preceding generation. The second leading character, L. Licinius Crassus, had been Cicero's own rhetorical mentor. The date was 91 BC, during the tribunate of Drusus, whose attempt to introduce wide-ranging reforms had led to a political crisis. He was supported by Crassus, and opposed by the consul Philippus. The

[22] Strasburger 1956. Lepore 1954 argues for a significant development in Cicero's view.
[23] *De Oratore*: text: Kumaniecki 1969; text and commentary: Wilkins 1879–92; text and translation: Rackham and Sutton 1942. See also Michel 1960.

dialogue represents Philippus as flouting the due authority of the Senate, and as responsible for the decade of external and civil war that followed. Cicero uses such details to construct a political and philosophical tradition that stretches from Scipio to Cicero himself. (At III.13 the comparison between Cicero and Crassus is made explicit.) This tradition, which lays dubious claim to historical accuracy,[24] represents a moderate aristocratic conservatism, devoted to the welfare of the people, combining the best of Greek theory and Roman practice. Oratory is its tool for public service.

De Oratore is shaped by a debate on the question: need the orator be widely learned? Crassus argues that the best orator must be not only eloquent, but also thoroughly familiar with law, political philosophy, ethics and psychology. For he must be able to grasp the details of a case, to offer wise public counsel and to understand how to sway his listeners. Oratory must not be limited to technical competence in rhetoric. Antonius, by contrast, reports the views he had once heard from certain Athenian philosophers. The Stoic had rejected rhetoric altogether. The Academic had held that rhetoricians taught nothing of the necessary subject matter: what was needed was natural ability informed by philosophy. Antonius himself argues that Crassus' ideal of all-round education is scarcely attainable. A skilful orator could win cases by relying on eloquence without deep expertise in law or philosophy.

Underlying this debate is a theme that Cicero will repeatedly revisit: the contrast, or complementarity, between Greece and Rome. Greece had provided the philosophers, Rome (recently at least) the orators. But, Crassus argued, the educational division between the two, which stemmed from Socrates' own eloquent denunciation of eloquence in the *Gorgias*, had been disastrous. The ideal orator would unite wisdom and persuasion, content and form. In doing so, he would also reunite theory and experience. Indeed, Rome herself had already provided examples of such a union, for instance in the law code of the Twelve Tables, a complete source for political philosophy (I.193), and in men like Scipio, who combined Greek learning with distinguished political and military careers.

The function of the orator is threefold: to win goodwill, to instruct the mind, and to move the emotions. It is the third of these that leads philosophy and rhetoric, ideals and practical politics, to disagree. Persuasion, according to the philosopher, should appeal only to the intellect, not to the emotions; a man who knew his subject would be eloquent enough, as

24 Astin 1967: appendix.

Socrates argued (1.63). The Stoics were more explicit still. Emotion was in itself a sign of foolishness. The wise man must aim only to instruct. The ideal was put into practice by Rutilius Rufus, who refused to use rhetorical ploys to defend himself and was exiled (1.227–30). Such behaviour, Antonius commented, was more suited to Plato's fictional city than to real life (1.230, cf. 1.224; *Att.* 11.1.8 for a similar comment on the behaviour of Cato). For the leaders of a real city have to govern citizens who are not wise. The orator's job is not simply to frame policy, but also to make it effective. Therefore, in a constitution with a democratic element he must persuade the ordinary citizen, whether in the assembly or in the law-courts. Indeed, the ability to sway the wills of others (presumably for good purposes) is the mark of a free man, and its flourishing the mark of a free people (1.30–2).

Oratory is the means by which the multitude allow themselves to be led by the Senate, to entrust their freedom to its care (cf. 1.226). The more flamboyant techniques of rhetoric, aimed primarily at arousing emotion, are more suited to popular speeches. The orator must, though, also know how to stir even the wise members of the Senate. He does so here by understanding his subject rather than his audience's psychology. He must also respect the right of other senators to a fair hearing (11.333–40). In *de Re Publica* these two uses of oratory will find their constitutional location in the twofold counsel exercised by the aristocrats, as leaders of the people and as fellow-senators.

5.2 *Cicero's* Republic[25]

The titles of Cicero's twin volumes *de Re Publica* and *de Legibus* betray his ambitions: to do for Roman political theory what his master Plato had done for Greek. Cicero's appropriation of Plato is self-consciously critical.[26] On the one hand, his *de Re Publica* broadly follows Plato's *Republic*, providing parallel discussions of the definition of justice, the origins of the best city, underlying philosophical principles, education, and finally the afterlife. Furthermore, he adopts from Plato two fundamental principles: that stability is the primary criterion for the success of a *res publica*; and that its flourishing depends upon the education of its leaders. On the other hand, Cicero treats similar themes empirically and concretely, with the focus always on Rome, in sharp and deliberate contrast to the timeless

[25] *De Re Publica*: full text and testimony: Ziegler 1955, Powell forthcoming; selected text and commentary: Zetzel 1995; text and translation: Keyes 1928; text, French translation and commentary: Bréguet 1980; translation with notes, Sabine and Smith 1929, Rudd 1998. References use the numbering in Keyes' text.

[26] See further Zetzel 1995: 3–16.

idealism of Plato (see e.g. II.21–2, II.52, II.66). The greatest statesmen, such as Scipio, Laelius and Philus, the heroes of this dialogue, 'added the foreign learning that stems from Socrates to the homespun custom of our ancestors' (III.5). It is Rome's distinctive virtue that she can supplement Greek theory with practical wisdom (II.29–30; cf. III.4–5).

The text of *de Re Publica* has a complex history. The dialogue was published soon after completion in 51 BC (*Att.* V.12.2; *Fam.* VIII.1.4). One episode from the sixth book, the 'Dream of Scipio', has been well known throughout its history; indeed thanks to the very popular commentary by the Platonist Macrobius (fl. late fourth or early fifth century), it became one of the most familiar Classical texts of the Middle Ages.[27] But the rest of the work was long known to scholars only from references in later writers, until in 1819 a fragmentary text of up to a third of the total was discovered. This contained substantial sections of the first two books and parts of the third, though very little of the remainder of the work. Interpreters must still rely heavily on later references, in particular quotations and summaries given by Lactantius and Augustine. However, the structure and the order of the contents of the work can be safely identified.[28]

The subject of *de Re Publica*, Cicero told his brother, was 'the best condition of the city, and the best citizen' (*Q.Fr.* III.5.1). Broadly speaking, the first three books treat the first of these, and the final three the second. Cicero also divided the debate into three; each pair of books was provided with a separate preface and covered the discussion of a single day. The first day analyses the 'best condition of the *res publica*'. Book I discusses the strengths and weaknesses of the three simple constitutions: democracy, aristocracy and monarchy. Scipio concludes that stability will best be ensured by a 'moderated' mixture of the three types (I.45, I.69). Book II describes the history of the growth of Rome to the point where it exemplified the mixed constitution. Rome provides a visual aid, as it were, to complement theoretical reason (II.52). The second day establishes the foundations for a flourishing *res publica* and its leaders, discussing justice and human nature. The third day completes the account of the best citizen, covering topics that include the education of a statesman and his proper conduct in a crisis. It is likely that the 'Dream of Scipio' brought the volume to a close.

The central subject of the first day, the mixed constitution, has a prehistory in Greek thought. The Athenian in Plato's *Laws* had argued that a balance of liberty and wisdom was needed in order for a city to survive (*Leg.*

[27] Lewis 1964. [28] Zetzel 1995:16–17, Ferrary 1995:48–51.

III.690d–701e). Aristotle recommended incorporating features of more than one type of constitution, for example the absence of a property-qualification associated with democracy together with the elections of an oligarchy (*Pol.* IV.9). Nearer to Cicero in time and in place was the Greek historian Polybius, a close friend of the historical Scipio. His *Histories*, written in the mid-second century, included an analysis of the Roman form of government, which had proved its capacity to endure. He attributed this to a distinction of powers: for example, the consuls have supreme control in war; the Senate control the treasury; while the powers of the people include the conferring of honours and the bestowing of punishments. In this way, the three parts of the *res publica* co-operated with each other. Opposition from the other two parts could prevent any one part from growing too powerful and too arrogant; for each part needed the consent of the other two in order to function (VI.11–18).[29]

Cicero can on occasion use the language of checks and balances (II.57, *compensatio*; II.59, 'ut . . . potestas minueretur'; cf. *Leg.* III.16). However, his favoured metaphor is that of 'mixing' or 'tempering', comparable to musical harmony: 'What the musicians call harmony in a song, is concord in a city, and it is the tightest and best bond of security in any *res publica*' (II.69; cf. II.42, II.65). Cicero's primary emphasis is on the way that the mixed constitution remains stable by preserving the element of value in each of the three simple constitutions. Thus the consuls provided Rome with a regal element, exercising executive power (*imperium*), and also inspiring the affection of the multitude. The Senate provided a wise aristocratic council to offer advice on policy (*consilium*). The people, who elected magistrates and passed laws, possessed genuine freedom (*libertas*) (cf. I.55, I.69, II.57). At the same time, the weaknesses revealed in the arguments against each simple type are remedied. Monarchy limited *consilium* to too few; aristocracy deprived the majority of liberty; while democracy lacks the 'grades of dignity' that even democrats in practice wish to bestow (I.43, I.53).

Consilium, *libertas* and *imperium* are thus the key elements of the Roman *res publica*. A constitution is characterized particularly by the location of *consilium*; and it is also *consilium* that preserves it: 'every *res publica* . . . must be ruled by some type of *consilium* so that it will be permanent' (I.41). Not power, but authority, is for Cicero the most important element of political life.[30] Scipio argues that an aristocratic council will be better able to form policy than a single individual, and wiser than the people as a whole

[29] Von Fritz 1954: ch. 8; see further Hahm, in ch. 23 section 2.

[30] Cf. Balsdon 1960: 43–4.

(I.52, II.15, II.56–8). Such a council should be elected, and the proper criteria for selection are virtue and wisdom, not wealth or birth (cf. I.51–3). A deep-seated trust in accumulated experience underlies the belief that policy is best formulated by a group of the elite. Book II illustrates the point historically: Scipio puts into the mouth of Cato the Elder the claim that each generation adds its own improvements; no one man alone could foresee every necessity (II.1–2, II.37). (The dramatic device itself symbolizes the resources of tradition.) So, for example, Romulus realized the value of a wise geographical location and of a Senate, while Numa fostered peace and religion. Within a single generation also, the best men should learn from each other; wise policy will be formed only by allowing and listening to genuine and cooperative debate. The view is more congruent with Cicero's brand of Academic philosophy than with Plato's own epistemology. Relatedly, Cicero is clearly aware that giving *consilium* effectively requires expertise in the rhetoric that Plato explicitly rejected (cf. *de Orat.* I.225–6, III.129, 139).

The statesman must be able to persuade the people. The arguments on behalf of democracy emphasize that liberty should have real substance: access to office and to judicial service, for example, should not be limited by wealth or family (I.47). The mixed constitution is seen as tempering the excesses of extreme democracy (cf. I.44, I.66–9); but it is arguable that significant democratic elements remain. For example, Cicero seems to assume that any citizen may stand for political office (II.59: Senate distinguished by honour, but not wealth; cf *Sest.* 137). In the Greek tradition, elections were seen as aristocratic; the democratic method of selection was the lot. In Rome, Cicero implies, it is elections that constitute the people's exercise of choice. *De Legibus* will decree that the Senate consist of ex-magistrates, rather than be selected by the censors, and will describe this as a popular measure: 'for no one shall enter the highest place except through the people' (*Leg.* III.27). *De Re Publica* takes popular liberty seriously; for Cicero well recognizes the dangers of instability from depriving the people of freedom, and he highlights the role of the tribunate in protecting their liberty and channelling their potentially subversive power (II.57–9; cf. *Leg.* III.19–26). It is important, however, to remember that many of the wealthy and well born were not senators; the interests of the people were therefore neither uniform, nor identical with the interests of the under-privileged.

Elections provide the mechanism for integrating the freedom of the people with the guidance of the few. Right at the beginning of the discussion Scipio defined the words *res publica* (literally 'public thing') as *res pop-*

uli, 'thing' or 'property of the people' (I.39). A true constitution is the property of the people. (In Book III he will argue that corrupted forms of government are not true *res publicae* because they fail to live up to this definition (III.43–5).) However, in an extreme democracy, the masses do not necessarily serve the true good of the whole. Scipio solves this problem by exploiting the metaphor of *res* as property. Government is like a trust, which is offered freely by the people to the magistrates to be used for the good of the former (I.51–2, II.56, cf. III.45; *Off.* I.85, I.124). Book II draws attention to the fact that even the kings of Rome were chosen by popular election (II.25, 31, 33, 35, 37–8, cf. 23, 43). The democratic element in the mixed constitution is genuine: for election legitimates the authoritative deliberation of the Senate and the executive power of the magistrates.[31] At the same time, elections remove the possibility of direct misgovernment by the people.

The magistrates, in particular the consuls, provide the monarchical elements in the constitution. Book I ends with Scipio explaining why, if he had to choose between the three types of constitution, he would choose monarchy. As well as winning the affection of the ruled (cf. I.55, II.23), monarchy also allows power to be exercised more effectively, particularly in a crisis such as war (I.63). On the other hand, monarchy is very easily corrupted into tyranny, the worst sort of government (I.65, II.43). Why does Scipio, apparently the spokesman for Rome's 'traditional' constitution, offer qualified support for the monarchy? A Platonist's respect for the rule of the wise may lurk in the background here, combined with the recognition that the period of the kings was an authentic part of Rome's political past. Cicero may also have wanted to emphasize the necessity of the sort of strong and popular leadership that he believed he had provided as consul. On the other hand, Scipio noted that consulships, because they last only a year, do not carry the same threat as monarchy of degenerating into tyranny (cf. II.43). Thus Rome can exploit the advantages of rule by philosopher statesmen, while limiting its risks.[32]

At the end of Book II, Scipio emphasizes that a harmonious mixed constitution cannot exist without justice; indeed, he insists that without it the *res publica* cannot be run at all (II.70). Philus requests a fuller discussion of the topic of justice. At the end of the fragmentary Book III, the interlocutors return to the topic of distributive justice within a *res publica*, and Scipio concludes that corrupted forms of the three simple constitutions are not in fact *res publicae* (III.43–8). However, the bulk of the extant

[31] Schofield 1995a; cf. Millar 1984, 1986. [32] Powell 1994:26–7.

discussion of Book III deals with the question of external justice: how should Rome treat other nations? The text as it exists does not anywhere clarify the connection between the two types of justice.

The discussion of the second day begins, then, with the speakers replaying the arguments that Carneades gave on successive days on the occasion of a famous Athenian embassy to Rome in 155 BC. Philus, playing devil's advocate, reported his attack on justice; Laelius replied on justice's behalf. The most illuminating account is preserved by Lactantius (*Inst.* V.14.3–5, V.16.2–13). Philus established that justice was either 'natural' (the Stoic view) or 'civil' (the Epicurean view). Then he proved that natural justice was indeed just, but not sensible (*prudens*, interpreted as 'in one's interest'). The Stoic claim that justice was single, unchanging and innate in human beings was met by examples of the variety of legal systems across cultures and over time. 'Natural law' was supposed to be independent of these; but in fact all living creatures naturally act for their own interests. On the other hand, 'civil justice' was sensible, but not just. The Epicureans accepted that there were a variety of culture-specific justices; for their justice consisted of an agreement not to harm or be harmed. But their openly acknowledged motive is self-interest; and justice exists for the sake of others. Moreover, the Epicurean will act unjustly in cases where he has no fear of subsequent punishment. Philus then produced a series of examples intended to force the choice between justice and good sense: if you are selling an insanitary house, will you openly declare its defects to a prospective purchaser?

Plato had compared just and unjust souls and cities. Philus' arguments and Laelius' reply treat of both personal and political justice. Plato's Glaucon had proposed a choice between two lives, one of just suffering and the other of unjust flourishing (*Rep.* II. 360e–362c); Philus offered a choice also between two parallel cities (III.27–8). The main challenge to Laelius is to prove that Roman imperialism is just as well as sensible. The original context of Carneades' arguments is highly significant: Carneades was a member of an Athenian embassy sent to Rome in 155 BC to appeal against a fine imposed upon Athens for attempting to seize the small town of Oropus. Could it be just for Athens to expand her territory? If not, how could Rome justify her own imperialism? Carneades' virtuoso display had a serious intention: either both Rome and Athens could be called just; or else neither could, but self-interest should take precedence over justice.

The dramatic context of *de Re Publica* is also important. Scipio was in the process of attacking Tiberius Gracchus precisely with the claim that his agrarian reforms were depriving Italian allies of their rights (cf. Cic. *Agr.* II.45–6). In Book VI, the story of Scipio's dream will recall the struggle between the loyal ally of Rome, Masinissa, and the rebellious Carthage. The evidence for Laelius' argument comes from summaries by St Augustine. Some scholars, relying on one passage, perhaps freely reported by Augustine (August. *CD* XIX.21), have interpreted it thus: Rome's subjects are naturally liable to act unjustly, and will therefore be saved from themselves by wise Roman rule.[33] However, two other passages of Augustine distinguish clearly between two types of rule, one compared to the mastership of slaves, the other to paternal rule. The rule of generals and of magistrates over citizens and allies alike should be paternal and protective (*C. Iul.* IV.12.61 [=III.37]; *CD* XIV.23 [=III.37]; cf. *Off.* II.27). The justification for Rome's imperial expansion was to defend her allies (Nonius, p. 498 M [=III.35]). Unless Rome's allies obeyed her from free will rather than fear, the *res publica* would not be secure (*Rep.* III.41). The allies need to be governed not because they are wicked or slavish, but because they are weak (rebellious allies are an exception, not the norm). Rome's empire is thus implicitly distinguished from the non-Greek empires that Aristotle had characterized as the rule of a master over slaves (*Pol.* III.14). It is Rome's beneficence towards her allies that justifies her continued rule (cf. also *Off.* II.75, III.49, 87–8).

The subject of the second half of *de Re Publica* was 'the best citizen'. The loss of most of the relevant discussion has meant that commentators have concentrated on the discussion of constitutions; we need to remember that political ethics mattered as much to Cicero as political systems. Indeed, the preservation of the latter depended upon the former: the statesman preserves the city through both wise decisions and moral example.[34] Cicero's book was itself written to influence those very aristocrats upon whose *mores* and *consilium* Rome's stability depended: *moribus antiquis res stat Romana virisque* (*Rep.* V.1 (August. *CD* II.21), quoting Ennius' *Annales*).[35] Unfortunately we can only glimpse the characterization of the best citizen in Book V. His aim will be the happiness of the citizens, which will consist in wealth, glory and virtue, and he will achieve this by inculcating a sense of shame by educating public opinion. Concern for praise, and even glory, will nourish his own ambitions. He must be thoroughly familiar with the highest principles of justice (those, presumably, to be discovered in *de Legibus*). A possible reconstruction makes Manilius, the legal expert, argue that a statesman requires a complete knowledge of civil law, Scipio that a practical acquaintance with it is sufficient.[36]

The administration of the law is described as 'regal'. Some scholars have

[33] Büchner 1984: 323–4; cf. Sabine and Smith 1929: 218 n. 75, Ferrary 1988: 370–1.
[34] Ferrary 1995. [35] 'Rome's foundations are her ancient customs and her heroes.'
[36] See further Sabine and Smith 1929: 244 n. 2, Büchner 1984: 398, 401, 404–5.

argued that the 'ruler' (*rector*) or moderator of the *res publica* mentioned here is not simply a model statesman, but the holder of a specific quasi-legal office: perhaps Cicero was envisaging a role for a man like Pompey, or even himself. In fact, *rector rei publicae* means nothing more than 'statesman' (cf. *de Orat.* I.211; *Rep.* VI.13 (a mention of several *rectores*)). (It is clear from Book II that Scipio was arguing not for a new constitution but for the renewal of the traditional one.) Cicero's object (following Plato) is to discuss not the constitution of the city, but the education and ethics of its leading men.[37]

The little that remains of the early part of Book VI suggests that Cicero's characters discussed civic discord and the corresponding internal disharmony of an individual. The only substantial extant section of the book is the 'Dream of Scipio'. Scipio reports a dream in which he met his dead grandfather, the great general Scipio Africanus the elder, who gave him a tour of the heavens. There is a well-known Platonic precedent: at the end of the *Republic*, Socrates tells the story of Er, who died and came back to life having seen the rewards and punishments in store for the souls of the dead. Cicero's atmosphere of realism is worth noting. The story of Er was a legend; Scipio's account of the afterlife claims only the status of a dream in which he encounters an historical personage (Macrobius *Somn.* I.1.2–3; Pl. *Rep.* X.614b–621b). The thorough politicizing of the afterlife is also striking. The dream occurred after a discussion with a Roman ally at a crucial point during the struggle between Rome and Carthage. Scipio discussed politics both with him, and then in the dream with his grandfather, who predicted Scipio's future military and political career. The celestial perspective puts earthly ambition firmly in its place: true glory cannot come from so small and so ephemeral a home (VI.21–5, cf. I.26). Yet the reward for loyal statesmen is heaven. For politics is a sacred duty, laid upon men by God. As Scipio declares to his grandfather:

> Since, Africanus, a path to the entrance of heaven lies open to those who have deserved well of their country, although since boyhood I have followed in my father's footsteps and yours, and not fallen short of your renown, now as this great reward has been revealed, I will strive more keenly still. (VI.26; cf. VI.13, 16)

Thus Cicero exploits Plato's doctrine of the immortality of the soul to reinforce his ideal of patriotic service.[38]

In a letter to his brother, Quintus, Cicero explains that he had toyed

[37] The *locus classicus* for the debate is Reitzenstein 1917 *versus* Heinze 1924. Recently, and conclusively, see Powell 1994.

[38] Cf. *Sest.* 47–8, *Rab. Perd.* 29–30.

with the idea of casting himself, instead of Scipio, in the leading role. This possibility was attractive because it would have enabled him to touch directly on political disturbances (*Q.Fr.* III.5.1–2, October or November 54). In the end, he retained his original cast, and the dramatic date of 129 BC. However, his constitutional analysis addresses the concerns of contemporary Rome: how far should the Senate be in control of policy? How much influence should be granted to the people? Might monarchy be the solution to Rome's problems? And, above all, how can stability be restored to the turbulent and violent city?

Cicero's answers to questions of this sort cohere closely with the aristocratic programme of *pro Sestio*, and with the hints in his contemporary letters. Free senatorial debate and leadership, summed up as *consilium*, is essential to the life of the *res publica*. On the other hand, Cicero was also concerned to protect a degree of popular liberty and to defend against force and corruption the proper mechanism of the expression of the people's will, that is, free elections. However, as far as the evidence shows, he allows no space for practical policies to alleviate the hardships of the poorer classes. In this again he is consistent with his political practice. The proposals of populist politicians such as the Gracchi are rejected because their policies favour one group of society rather than another. Cicero does not seem to consider the possibility that such proposals might genuinely benefit the people as a whole.

De Re Publica gives philosophical expression to the instinctive Roman appeal to ancestral practice. Cicero's method is, as far as one can tell, original; but he uses it to argue for a constitutional balance that he claims as thoroughly traditional. However, his traditionalism has its own distinctive emphases. One of the catch phrases of his speeches was *otium cum dignitate* or 'peace with honourable standing'. The peace belongs to the people as a whole, the honour to the senators.[39] Cicero selects from Roman moral tradition not, for example, the glorification of military success, but rather the respect for wise political counsel. The few are to govern with honour not because they are warriors, or noble, or even rich; they are 'good' primarily in the philosophical sense of wise and virtuous. *De Re Publica* implicitly blames the failure of the traditional constitution on the corruption of the ruling class. Cicero's basic remedy, in good Platonic tradition, is not constitutional, but ethical: to restore the patriotic and aristocratic ideals that the Roman ruling class supposedly possessed in the Republic's prime.

39 Wirszubski 1954, for a survey of interpretations; Balsdon 1960.

In 51, Cicero's friend Caelius reports that *de Re Publica* is being widely read and approved (*Fam.* VIII.1.4). Its popularity is perhaps not surprising: Cicero had exploited his philosophical learning to identify and explain the importance of the very elements of the *res publica* most threatened by contemporary events.

5.3 *The laws of the best republic*[40]

De Legibus is intended to complement *de Re Publica*, following Plato's example, as Cicero saw it: it reveals the laws appropriate to Scipio's 'best condition of the city' (*Leg.* I.15, II.23, III.12). The setting is Cicero's own family home at Arpinum, and the cast, Cicero himself, his closest friend, Atticus, and his brother, reinforce the implicit assimilation of his and Scipio's circles of acquaintance. The text of *de Legibus* is incomplete. The first book describes the 'source' of justice; the second the religious laws of the best city; and the third its provisions for magistracies. At least five books existed (Macrobius *Sat.* VI.4.8); later books probably included the topics of the law-courts and of education (cf. III.47, III.29–30).

Scholarship has emphasized the Stoic origins of Cicero's 'theory of natural law', and indeed used *de Legibus* I as a primary source for Stoic ideas on the subject. It is worth remembering that Cicero sees himself as an Academic, and assumes that his basic principles are common to Stoics, Aristotelians and Platonists alike.[41] The application of these principles is unlike that of other extant texts influenced by or witnessing to Stoicism. Cicero is not concerned with Zeno's 'city of the wise' or Chrysippus' 'cosmic community', but with the actual laws applicable to a real city or empire. Just as in *de Re Publica*, he sees the combination of reason and concrete realism as the mark of Roman philosophy. On the one hand, the law of nature (*ius naturae*) is discovered by one's use of independent reason, unlike Roman law which we learn from tradition (III.49). On the other hand, generations of Roman statesmen have, through the intelligent assimilation of cumulative experience, developed a code of laws largely identifiable with the *ius naturae* itself (II.23, III.12). As such, these laws ought to be irrevocable (II.14).

Book I aims to establish the existence of the *ius naturae*, the origin of the virtue of justice, which is identified also with reason. The argument falls into two parts; at I.33 Cicero marks the end of a preamble intended to

40 *De Legibus*: text and translation: Keyes 1928; text, French translation and commentary: De Plinval 1959; commentary on Book I: Kenter 1972. See also Rawson 1973, Girardet 1983.

41 Ferrary 1995: 67–8.

make it 'easier to understand that justice is located in nature'. Two slightly different resumés of this are given, by Cicero himself in advance at 1.16, and by Atticus retrospectively at 1.35. It is possible to reconcile them by interpreting them as summarizing three points:

(i) that certain *munera* (gifts and duties) are distributed by the gods to men;
(ii) that there is a single shared principle by which men lived together (*coniunctio hominum* (1.16); 'unam . . . vivendi . . . rationem' (1.35));
(iii) that a natural affection and consequent fellowship (*societas*) of justice is shared by them.

In fact, the intervening discussion lacks clear structure, and though it includes these three elements, they are not covered in that order. Cicero begins by defining true law as right reason, that is the full development of the reason that exists instinctively in all human beings at birth. Because this reason is shared by gods and men, they also share a single community (1.18–23). Human beings have further been equipped by the gods with a variety of other benefits, psychological, physical and external (1.25–7). They are thus contrasted with other animals; but compared with each other they could scarcely be more alike, in their virtues, and even in their vices! This similarity is taken to prove the 'fellowship and union' between them, and the fact that they are 'born for justice' (1.28–32). If they develop uncorrupted, that is, they will become just. Wise men love one another as much as they love themselves (1.33–4).

The logical sequence of thought in this passage is frequently obscure. However, the main elements of his position are clear. To say that justice exists by nature is to say both that all human beings if they develop uncorrupted will become just; and that the nature of their justice (that is, their right reason) will be identical. It is this identity that grounds their shared way of life and their community (which includes the gods also).

The second section of Book 1 (unfortunately incomplete) contains a series of arguments directed primarily against a contractual account of justice (despite the fact that Cicero has claimed at 1.39 that he is not debating with the Epicureans). It is nature and not the threat of punishment that inspires true justice. The latter cannot be identified with written laws; mere legislation could sanction robbery or adultery. Nor can considerations of utility ground true virtue, which must be sought for its own sake. A good man, like a good tree, does not depend upon mere opinion: there are objective, and uniform, grounds for justice.

The relation between the two sections is not easy to interpret. The second is intended to examine the claim that justice exists by nature in the more systematic manner of the Hellenistic schools (1.36). In fact, the first part seems to describe the basis of natural justice; that is, the nature of human beings. The second proposes objections to the view that justice exists by agreement rather than nature. Hence the importance of insisting on the uniformity of reason. The imaginary opponents do not deny that justice exists; rather they hold that there are many justices as there are communities that agree on an enforceable code of behaviour. Cicero's reply is that only one justice, the *ius naturae*, in fact exists.

Lactantius has preserved an extended description of 'true law' from *de Re Publica*, which emphasizes its universality and unchanging nature, as well as its independence of written law codes (*Inst.* VI.8.6–9 = *Rep.* III.33). It is tempting to identify this with a code of natural moral law to which actual laws ought to conform (a sense of 'natural law' familiar from later political theory). However, in *de Legibus* it is human and divine reason, not a code of behaviour, that is called law: 'for [law] is a power of nature, it is the mind and reason of a wise man, it is the measure of justice and injustice' (I.19). Actual laws are the precepts of the wise. The role of the wise leader, as described in *de Re Publica*, is to teach and to legislate. The laws that he frames are identical, we may suppose, with those of *de Legibus* II and III; the concrete legislation of these books, therefore, must be identified with the precepts of the *ius naturae*.[42]

However, this interpretation of the relationship between the *ius naturae* and the specific laws of Books II and III is not without difficulty (in a later work, he will suggest a different relationship between natural and civil law: see *Off.* III.69). Cicero himself was born outside Rome, as he emphasizes in the very prefaces of *de Legibus*. He had served as an administrator in Sicily and governed the province of Cilicia. He was well read in Greek literature and history. He recognized the force of the sceptical insistence on the cultural variety of laws and customs. Furthermore, he would later argue that civil conventions themselves deserved respect: to flout that was to lack a sense of shame (*Off.* I.148). Could he really insist that, with one or two minor adjustments, the traditional laws of Rome should apply universally and permanently? It seems that he did; we cannot underestimate the theoretical power of his patriotism, underpinned by the epistemological assumption that reason and accumulated experience ought to deliver the same conclusions.

A related problem concerns change over time. True law, like the best

[42] Girardet 1983: 97–105, Ferrary 1995: 68–70.

city, should be everlasting. However, there is a role, albeit limited, for new legislation (the veto is to be used to encourage caution here (III.42–3)). Cicero seems to assume that legislation develops healthily not when it adapts to changing circumstances, but rather when it approximates even more closely to the complete *ius naturae*. However, he also, apparently, allows a magistrate to override explicit laws in a crisis: 'The safety of the people is their supreme law' (III.8). Ultimately, the purpose of the law is the survival of the *res publica*, which should be immortal. The wise statesman's actions conform to right reason, that is, true justice. Can they conflict with the just determinations of the law normally in force? Cicero's justification of his own unconstitutional measures against Catiline, and his later support for extra-legal moves against Antony (see below p. 513), suggest that he thinks so. But if the specific measures of the *ius naturae* can be suspended in an emergency, why can they not also be adapted to the less dramatic circumstances of history? To claim universal appropriateness for the laws of Classical Rome ultimately fails to convince even on Cicero's own terms.

Finally, what of the actual laws of Books II and III?[43] The religious provisions of book II confirm the integral and pragmatic place of religion in the political life of Rome; it grounds oaths, treatises and good behaviour (II.16). In particular, Cicero defends the authenticity of augury, which was used both to annul laws and to postpone the business of assemblies. The discussion of the tribunate in Book III deserves particular attention. Quintus argues that it has been the cause of repeated disorders in Rome. Marcus replies that the tribune moderates the potential violence of the people, and satisfies their pretensions to liberty in a relatively harmless way. Quintus remains unconvinced (III.16–17, 19–27). It is also worth noting the role envisioned for the Senate as a model of virtue for the rest of the citizens, which recalls the concerns of *de Re Publica* V. The detailed provision for the office of censor, the discussion of which is lost, would probably have supported this. Ultimately morals, like religion, are for the preservation of the *res publica*.

In April 46, Cicero wrote to Varro that even if one could not serve the *res publica* in the forum and Senate house, one could at least do so by writing about *mores* and laws (*Fam.* IX.2.5). Perhaps he was intending to return to complete *de Legibus* at this point. However, the work is not mentioned in the retrospective catalogue of his philosophical writings in the preface to *de Divinatione* II, written in 44. Cicero may have been conscious of those

[43] See further Keyes 1921, Rawson 1973: 342–54.

shortcomings in the book's conception and execution that trouble modern commentators; perhaps he was dissatisfied with it for other reasons. At any rate, it is likely that the work was not published in Cicero's lifetime.

6 The civil war and its aftermath

'Caesar could no longer endure a superior, nor Pompey an equal' wrote the poet Lucan, with the advantage of a century's hindsight (*Bellum Civile* I.125–6). The alliance between the two could not long survive the death of Crassus in battle in 53. It was only a matter of time before they confronted one another directly. In the event, the crisis came at the beginning of 49; the immediate question was whether Caesar would lay down his command of the armies, with which he had been lawfully governing Gaul until then, and upon which his safety depended. The Senate, backing Pompey, insisted on this. Caesar crossed the Rubicon and marched on Rome. Civil war had begun.

Cicero saw the folly of war, and did what he could to mediate. He eventually joined the Pompeian camp, but took no active responsibility. After the defeat and death of Pompey in 48, he returned to Italy and became one of the many recipients of Caesar's magnanimous pardon. Cato fought on with his customary determination, and then fell on his sword after defeat at Utica, rather than yield to Caesar's clemency.

Cicero's letters of this period, in particular those to Atticus, provide us with an opportunity to observe his use of moral argument for the purposes of urgent practical decision. Cicero clearly saw himself as making philosophically informed choices; for he set out formal arguments for himself, and in Greek as well as Latin: 'Should someone strive by any means to overthrow a tyranny, even if his city will be completely endangered thereby?' 'Ought a statesman to live quietly in retirement while his country is under a tyranny, or ought he to take every risk for the sake of freedom?' (*Att.* IX.4.2).

Cicero vacillated at length over actual choices, yet he used remarkably consistent moral language to describe the possibilities.[44] Peace was better than even a just civil war (*Att.* VII.14.3). But when peace was not possible, then he must consider his duty to country, to family and to friends. If he could put family first, he would remain neutral; but he could not. Nor, finally, could he persuade himself that neutrality would best serve the *res*

[44] Brunt 1986.

publica; even though it could be argued that neither side had the country's true interests at heart. The obligations of friendship (*amicitia*) pointed to Pompey, to whom he recognized a strong debt of loyalty; for Cicero saw him as the agent of his recall from exile. Moreover, it was possible at least to hope that Pompey, who was supported by the *boni*, aimed to restore the *res publica* rather than establish his own tyranny. A further consideration was the standard he had set in his own career, which made one role more fitting for him than another (*Att.* IX.11a.1–2: the idea would be fully theorized in *De Officiis* (see below p. 513)).

Even after his pardon, Cicero's retrospective views of his and others' behaviour were inconstant. Sulpicius' retirement to Samos was at least secure; but Cato's resistance more glorious (*Att.* XI.7.4). If the Pompeians did win in Africa it would put him at risk, but it would benefit 'everyone' (*Att.* XI.21.3). Yet it was better that conceding defeat had enabled some at least of the *res publica* to survive (*Fam.* XV.15.1). The middle course he himself had taken was 'more sensitive to shame' than those who stayed behind, yet 'more sensible' than those who failed to return (*Fam.*IX.5.2): the continuing self-justification reveals Cicero's sense of unease.

Officium, *res publica*, *dignitas*, *amicitia*, *gloria*: the concepts with which Cicero debated with himself and his friends were the building blocks of a moral and political philosophy. Before very long, he would incorporate them into structures more systematic and more consistent.

Peace was re-established, but not (in the eyes of the conservatives) the free *res publica*. Julius Caesar had become dictator; and in 46 the office was extended for ten years. Cicero's only forays into public life were in three speeches pleading for clemency for former opponents of Caesar; and clemency was a virtue proper to a monarch rather than one leading senator among equals. There was no opportunity for a free and serious contribution to political debate. Once again Cicero turned to study as a profitable way of spending his time and consoling himself for the loss of the *res publica*. (Further consolation would soon be necessary: in February 45 his beloved daughter Tullia died soon after giving birth to a son.)

7 Philosophy for Romans

7.1 *The philosophical encyclopaedia*

Cicero's main project was to provide a philosophical encyclopaedia in Latin for his Roman audience. He wrote dialogues to allow himself to argue the case of the various schools whose views he wanted to represent. (His philosophical inspiration was Plato, and more particularly the

Academic practice of arguing 'for and against' a case; but the genre is also a natural one for an orator and lawyer to employ.) Cicero did not see philosophy simply as an escape from public service (indeed, he was sensitive to criticism on the point). He repeatedly insisted in the prefaces to his works that his writing constituted a different way of assisting the *res publica*. His earlier philosophical writings had had an obvious political import. Cicero had suggested that he would return to writing political philosophy (*Fam.* IX.2.5, to Varro). He did not do so immediately; it was not a safe venture. Instead, he presents his philosophical works as serving Rome by ornamenting her with a Latin literature to rival that of Greece (e.g. *ND* I.7–8; *Fin.* I.10), and with educated citizens (*Acad.* I.11).

Between April 46 and March 44, Cicero wrote successively on oratory, the importance of philosophy, epistemology, ethics and theology, touching on political themes only in passing. Soon after the Ides of March, we find him using the preface to the second book of *de Divinatione* to provide an account of his recent philosophical corpus, which he presents as almost complete. The recent assassination of Caesar has held things up; it has also initiated a shift in Cicero's attitude to his writing. Now that he is being consulted once again about the affairs of state, philosophy must take second place. Furthermore, his justification for writing has become subtly more political: Latin philosophy not only adorns Rome; it might also educate the youth of a society undone by the collapse of *mores* (*Div.* II.4). From now on, the content also of Cicero's philosophical writings will become more political. Caesar's death has liberated his pen.[45]

De Amicitia (*On Friendship*) deals with a topic of major political importance.[46] Senatorial careers were forged by political friendships; and when civil war loomed ties of the dictator's friendship carried weighty implications. After Caesar's death his supporters' loyalty to his aims was sustained by their memory of his friendship (for a moving instance of this, see Matius' reply to a letter from Cicero, *Fam.* XI.27 and 28). *De Amicitia* is dedicated to Cicero's friend Atticus, who was well known for his refusal to engage in public life. However, its chief spokesman, Laelius, and its dramatic date soon after the suspicious death of his friend Scipio, links the book to the *de Re Publica*. An important section (*Amic.* 35–44) argues that one must not be led by friendship into violence against the *res publica*. Criticism in this context of Tiberius Gracchus (accused here of aiming at monarchy) and of his loyal brother, Gaius, provide a thinly veiled attack on Caesar and his effective successor, Mark Antony (*Amic.* 41). It is worth

[45] Bringmann 1971: 182–95. [46] Brunt 1965.

noting, however, that Cicero's Laelius values loyalty even to friends who fail in virtue (*Amic.* 61).

In the summer of 44, Cicero wrote a book *de Gloria*, which is now lost. We can only guess at the content, with the help of the full discussion of glory in *de Officiis* (see below). But the message was undoubtedly political; and Cicero had some hesitation about publicizing the book (*Att.* XVI.2.6; *Att.* XVI.3.1).[47] The implicit target was presumably the supporters of Caesar whose posthumous reputation Cicero would undoubtedly have described as 'false glory'. During this period Cicero was also planning a dialogue on the murder of Caesar, which he mentioned only guardedly to close friends (*Fam.* XII.16.4; *Att.* XV.3.2; *Att.* XV.4.3; *Att.* XV.27.2). The last reference to this (*Att.* XV.13.3, 25 October) suggests that secrecy is no longer needed. By now Cicero was beginning a return to open political combat; and meanwhile he had already begun writing his *de Officiis*.

7.2 *The duties of a statesman*[48]

De Officiis was the final, and the most obviously political, work of Cicero's philosophical cycle. It was completed by early December 44; and composed while he was beginning to engage again in public life (*Att.* XV.13a.2; *Att.* XVI.11.4; *Att.* XVI.14.3). He had already crossed Mark Antony by delivering the *First Philippic* on the 1 September; he was privately circulating the *Second Philippic*, in which he attacks Antony without mercy; in January he would return to the Senate-house and forum to arouse the opposition to Antony with a series of speeches that would constitute the remaining *Philippics*.

De Officiis addresses many of his concerns during this period of personal and political crisis: the danger to society of personally ambitious and powerful individuals; the duty of public service compared with the attraction of philosophical retirement; the proper use of public benefactions. In short the book argues that a flourishing *res publica* depends upon the virtues of its leading citizens and, conversely, defines those virtues in a thoroughly political manner.

Why the title: *de Officiis*? Cicero was following a Greek Stoic tradition of writing about *to kathēkon* ('the appropriate action' is perhaps the best English translation). However by using the word *officium* (and self consciously using the plural (*Att.* XVI.11.4)) he gave his discussion a thoroughly Roman nuance. Unlike *kathēkon*, *officium* is intrinsically linked to a

[47] Bringmann 1971: 199.

[48] *De Officiis*: text: Winterbottom 1994; text and commentary: Holden 1854; text and translation: Miller 1913; translation and commentary: Atkins and Griffin 1991.

role or relationship: one might talk of the *officium* of a consul, or of a friend. Moreover, an *officium* requires a beneficiary ('obligation' is often the most useful translation). The word is given its moral life by the complete web of personal and institutional relationships that structured Roman society. Cicero extends the common usage by talking of the *officia* of a specific virtue; and he gives concrete content to this idea by treating the duties of the virtues as owed to society, in particular to the society of the *res publica*.

Unlike the other philosophical works of the years 46–44, *de Officiis* is not a dialogue. Formally, it is a letter of advice addressed to his son Marcus, at the time a student in Athens. It is in three books. In the first Cicero asks the question: in what does *honestas* (honourableness) consist? He answers by describing in detail the four cardinal virtues. In the second book he adds: what is *utile* (useful)? The third book discusses and resolves a series of individual cases in which the honourable and useful courses appear at first sight to conflict.

The broad structure of the book follows that of the work on *kathēkon* by Panaetius, a leading Stoic of the second century. Pliny the Elder (*Nat.* preface, 22) compared the relation between the two works to that between Cicero's *de Re Publica* and Plato's *Republic*. Many scholars have defended (or assumed) a much closer dependence by Cicero on Panaetius' lost work;[49] however, it is arguable that a close examination of the specific passages where he declares his debt to Panaetius does not support such an interpretation. Cicero is not intending to expound Panaetius (*non interpretatus*, II.60, cf. I.6); indeed, he specifically criticizes and modifies even the structure of his work, as well as the details (e.g. I.10, III.7).[50] It is worth noting that Cicero, as a loyal Academic, refers to Plato roughly as often as he does to Panaetius. At the same time, Cicero's brand of sceptical Academic philosophy gives him the freedom to adopt a fundamentally Stoic line throughout *de Officiis*.

In particular, Stoicism underpins the work in one very important way. At I.6 Cicero tells us that advice on duty can only be offered by those who believe that honourableness is to be sought for its own sake. The Stoic view is uncompromising: nothing is good except the honourable. Academic and Peripatetic opinion was a little more accommodating: honourableness is the supreme good, but other goods can contribute in a small way to happiness. Cicero assimilates the second view to the first, effectively interpreting the position of the Old Academy in Stoic vein

[49] The classic account is Pohlenz 1934. [50] Atkins 1989: ch. 1, pp. 20–6.

(III.11). Thus, he concludes that nothing can be honourable unless it is beneficial, nor beneficial unless it is honourable. This conclusion is basic to the argument of the entire work, and frequent reference is made to it.

Because honourable actions are always beneficial, and therefore always useful, and vice versa, there must be a close link between the content of Books I and II. The two questions, 'Is this action x honourable?' and, 'Is this action x useful?' ought always to receive the same answer. Yet Cicero needs to reach the answer by different routes. Take the example of generosity. Beneficence which exceeds one's means is not truly virtuous for two reasons: that it is unjust to one's family and close descendants who ought to be one's first concern; and that it often makes the 'generous' giver greedy for other goods so that his beneficence may continue (I.44). But cannot excessive beneficence be (politically) useful? No, Cicero argues, because the resultant greed leads to robbery which destroys the goodwill that is needed to acquire the benefit of glory (II.54).

But if all and only honourable actions are useful, what is the purpose of Book III? How can the honourable and the useful courses of action conflict? Cicero's answer is that they cannot in fact conflict; but they often appear to do so. Book III offers a series of cases in which the theory is thus difficult to apply. This may be because it is genuinely unclear whether a proposed course of action is honourable; so for example, Cicero stages a debate between the Stoics Diogenes and Antipater on whether a corn-merchant must reveal the true state of the market during a famine (III.50–3).[51] Alternatively, an obviously dishonourable course of action may appear, misleadingly, to be useful. Lulled into forgetfulness by the apparent advantages of, for example, wealth, one may be tempted to overlook the basic truth that 'nothing is good unless it is honourable'. In such cases, Cicero's response is to repeat the premise again (e.g. III.81); the function of working through such examples is therapeutic.

The content of what is honourable is thoroughly shaped by our social duties. Justice, which Cicero describes as 'the mistress and queen of the virtues' (III.28), develops from our natural desire for company, in particular that of our children, spouse and friends (I.11–12). We are also heavily dependent on our fellow human beings for both practical sustenance and for the higher pleasures of law and civilization (II.12–17). At III.21, Cicero lays down a 'rule of procedure' to be followed in deciding cases of apparent conflict:

[51] Annas 1989, Schofield 1999a: ch. 9

> for one man to take something from another and to increase his own advantage at the cost of another's disadvantage is more contrary to nature than death, than poverty, than pain and than anything else that may happen to his body or external possessions.

This is because theft and violence destroy the natural fellowship of the human race. In fact every case in Book III is decided by referring to some aspect of justice, interpreted as the duty to preserve society.

The 'rule of procedure' applies to our dealings with all other human beings. In theory, 'nature prescribes that one man should want to consider the interests of another, whoever he may be, for the very reason that he is a man' (*Off.* III.27). However, our duties are graded with our relationships: we owe more to family than to strangers. The primary focus of the ethics of *de Officiis* is the society of the *res publica*: 'parents are dear, and children, relations and acquaintances are dear, but our country alone has embraced all the affections of us all' (I.57). *De Officiis* rarely mentions duties to strangers, and when it does so, they are minimal (e.g. I.51, the duty to show someone the way) or negative (e.g. extreme cruelty towards enemies and rivals, and the banishment of foreigners from a city, are forbidden (*Off.* III.46–7)). By contrast, a detailed description of the ethics of public service, that is duties to the *res publica*, constitute the bulk of the work.

The flourishing of the *res publica* is the primary moral goal of *de Officiis*, and the analysis of the virtues is structured around it. This enables Cicero to provide an answer to the most topical political question of all: was the assassination of Julius Caesar justified? The 'rule of procedure' forbids violence or theft against fellow-members of a society, who are compared to the limbs of one body (III.22). However, 'there can be no fellowship (*societas*) between us and tyrants' (III.32). For tyrants are like lifeless limbs that damage the rest of the body and need to be amputated. It is not simply acceptable, but honourable and even necessary to destroy them; and this for the very same consideration that normally forbids harming a fellow-citizen: the health of the society as a whole.

Justice is the virtue that is derived directly from sociability. However, the other virtues also are shaped indirectly by it. At the end of Book I, Cicero compares the virtues with one another. He concludes that the duties of justice conform more closely to nature than those of wisdom: no one would choose an entirely solitary life of scholarship (I.158). Thus the virtue of justice ought to modify the impulses of the philosopher. (This evaluation is confirmed by the number of paragraphs devoted to the respective virtues: two to wisdom and twenty-one to the social virtues of justice and liberality.) Again, greatness of spirit that lacks justice is not a true virtue; in fact it leads to socially destructive violence (I.157).

The general idea of justice is subdivided into justice proper and liberality, something for which there is no Greek philosophical precedent.[52] At first sight this is surprising: what does the impartial virtue of justice have to do with the highly partial one of liberality and beneficence? The answer lies in the social and functional nature of Cicero's analysis. The two virtues are described as 'the reasoning by which the fellowship (*societas*) of men with one another and the communal life (*communitas*) are held together' (I.20). Justice and liberality together forge the bonds of society. For Cicero they form two sides of a single coin.

Cicero's detailed analysis of justice is also illuminated by its social function. At I.23 he distinguishes between two types of injustice: that of actively harming others and that of failing to prevent harm to others. At I.31 he describes two 'foundations' of justice, not harming another and serving the common good. Injustice, then, can take a passive as well as an active form: neglecting to defend others or deserting one's duty (I.28). The motives that Cicero lists for such injustice include laziness, the distractions of business, absorption in philosophy and a reluctance to make enemies. This is no abstract theorizing: Cicero lived in a society in which political life depended upon wealthy volunteers driven by varying mixtures of ambition, inherited pride and public spirit.

Similarly the virtue of *fides*, trustworthiness or faithfulness, is described as a foundation of justice. Mutual trust is the cement of civil society, a necessary condition of the bonds formed by the exchange of favours and obligations (I.22, cf. II.84); *fides* is also the virtue required of those in public office by the citizens who need to rely on their fair and efficient administration. It had long had an important place on the Roman moral map: Numa had dedicated a temple to the goddess Fides. The idealist's standard was set by the example of Regulus, who had kept his oath to the enemy at the price of being tortured to death. Cicero examines various claims that he should have broken his oath either for the sake of his own benefit, or because the oath could be claimed invalid. 'Regulus' appeals to a trio of virtues to corroborate his insistence upon *fides*: patriotism, courage and justice in warfare. The lengthy discussion (III.99–111) both raises the moral stakes and integrates several ethical themes of *de Officiis* as a whole.[53]

A final function of Cicero's account of justice is to provide an uncompromising defence of private property, consistent with his long-standing

[52] Atkins 1990: 263–7. [53] Gill 1988.

opposition to populist political measures. At I.20 he argues that 'one should treat common goods as common and private as one's own' and goes on to list the types of origins of private ownership of land. At II.84 he argues against the cancellation of debt in language drawn from his wider analysis of justice: 'for there is nothing that holds a *res publica* together more powerfully than *fides*; and that cannot exist unless the paying of debts is enforced'. Here he exploits the double sense of *fides*: both mutual trust and financial credit are necessary to preserve the bonds of society. II.73 advances a similarly strong claim: the redistribution of land is to be condemned because cities were created for the purpose of safeguarding property.

De Officiis provides a full and formal account of justice outside the *res publica* in one area, that of war.[54] Legal procedure must be followed in declaring war and in authorizing soldiers to fight (I.36–7). The purpose of war should be a just peace. The technical justification of redress must be present (I.36); the legitimacy of defensive wars is assumed. However, the glory of empire is an acceptable motive (I.38). Fair play must be preserved in the conduct of war; in particular oaths must be kept to an enemy (I.39–40, III.99–115: the example of Regulus). The defeated must be treated with generosity; indeed many of Rome's former victims are now her citizens (I.35). Rome's treatment of her allies is idealized here, as also, for example, in *de Republica* Book III. Her 'kindness' has made her a haven for other peoples and won her great praise (II.26). Occasionally Cicero slips into a more realistic acknowledgment of the economic motivations of imperial rule (II.85). The Roman idealization of military glory is not entirely suppressed; but Cicero does at least require some ethical limits to its prosecution.

Liberality is discussed first as a part of social virtue in Book I, and secondly as one of the means to the 'useful' end of power and influence in Book II. (It is so important a means, indeed, that the discussion takes up a third of the book.) Once again, Cicero's social and political concerns shape his discussion. The virtuous benefactor must first avoid any actual or potential injustice. Cicero refers to the redistribution of their victims' land by Sulla and Julius Caesar, as an example of contemporary rapacity driven by the desire for political popularity. (At II.78–9 he explains why such behaviour is in fact counter-productive.) Secondly, one should give in accordance with the recipient's 'worth' (*dignitas*). Here Cicero articu-

[54] See further Barnes 1986.

lates the ethics of reciprocal service: not only a man's general character, but in particular his attitude and previous service to oneself should be considered.

The same criteria are given a pragmatic justification in Book II. There the political reference becomes even clearer. Extravagant expenditure for the sake of political prestige is criticized (II.56–60); while agrarian legislation and the cancellation of debts are treated as examples of unjust and inexpedient liberality. Cicero firmly recommends personal service above financial gifts as a method. The reference to his own case is explicit: born in a relatively obscure family, he won his name and his friends through the talent he used on others' behalf in the law-courts (cf. II.67).

The virtue of courage or greatness of spirit (*fortitudo*, *magnitudo animi*) posed a delicate problem for Cicero. The man of great spirit performs great deeds (I. 66). Thus military bravery provided a customary path to glory; and glory was greatly prized in the moral tradition of the Roman elite. Yet Greek philosophers from Plato onwards warned that *doxa* (the Greek word means both 'glory' and 'opinion') was treacherous and valueless. Furthermore, Cicero had learned from the experience of a lifetime that able and ambitious individuals, backed by personal armies, could exploit their courage to destroy political peace and stability. Cicero's analysis must accommodate an ambiguous inheritance.

A great spirit is revealed in two things: in

> disdain for things external, in the conviction that a man should admire, should choose, should pursue nothing except what is honourable and seemly, and should yield to no man, nor to agitation of the spirit, nor to fortune;

and in the performance of great and beneficial deeds (I. 66–7). Cicero underpins the popular view of courage as revealed in action (especially military and patriotic) with a philosophical account of psychology. The man whose spirit will not be swayed by emotions such as fear, greed or the desire for glory will face adversity or temptation bravely. The only goal for him is what is honourable. Accordingly, Cicero is able to argue that great statesmen (including himself) have often displayed greater spirit than the heroes of war: for the latter may have been activated by glory rather than the good of the *res publica*. Once again, we see how individual virtues are shaped by the needs of society: 'if loftiness of spirit . . . is empty of justice, if it fights not for the common safety, but for its own advantages, it is a vice' (I. 62). The observation that the greatest spirits are those most vulnerable to the passion for glory (I.26, cf. I.65) develops a hint in Plato (*Rep.* VI.491e). However, this is no armchair philosophy: the reference to Caesar is both explicit, and acutely appropriate.

Caesar is presented as an example of injustice motivated by the desire for glory and power. Could Cicero not simply have followed his Greek philosophical mentor by insisting that glory has no value at all? He preferred to take seriously the powerful role that glory played in the Romans' public imagination.[55] After all, the most selfless of statesmen needed enough ambition to overcome difficulty and defeat (cf. I.71). He acknowledged that glory really was *utile*, a genuinely valuable means of acquiring the personal support one needed in life (II.12–17, II.31). He then attempted to neutralize the threat of untrammelled ambition by arguing, in familiar style, that glory-seeking must be limited by justice. Thus the three elements of glory – being loved, being trusted and being admired – could only be won (or so Cicero argues) by just behaviour. The intention is clear: to persuade the powerful that ambition must aim at patriotic rather than selfish ends.

There are traces in *de Officiis* and elsewhere in Cicero's writings of a distinction, which would become a commonplace, between true glory (sometimes called *laus*, 'praise') and false glory.[56] The latter was vitiated either by the injustice of the agent, or by the unreliability of the judgment of the masses. The glory won by the younger Gracchi was false (II.43): it was not granted by good men; and it did not last. 'Those who seek a good reputation among good men, which alone can truly be called "glory", ought to seek leisure and pleasures for others, and not for themselves' (*Sest.* 139; cf. *Rep.* I.26, VI.21–5; *Tusc.* III.3–4; *Phil.* V.49–50; *ad Brut.* I.3.2–3).

Cicero's fourth virtue brings together a loose group of moral qualities, including moderation, modesty, fittingness, calm emotions and external lifestyle. The lynch-pin of the group is shame: 'the part of justice is not to harm a man, that of shame not to outrage him' (I.99). The concern with the visible nature of ethics is thoroughly appropriate to the Roman elite, being in the public eye in a society shaped by public speaking and life out of doors. What you wear and the style of your house may cause offence as easily as whether you lose your temper. What is *decorum*, fitting or seemly, is judged so by the public who can see you. It is also, however, dependent on context: time, place and agent may all help to determine appropriate behaviour. Here Cicero adds a further refinement

[55] Knoche 1934, Sullivan 1941, Long 1995.

[56] Knoche 1934: 112–23, Atkins 1989: 102–9.

(borrowed, most scholars believe, from Panaetius[57]). Each individual wears four 'masks' (*personae*): not only that of humanity in general, but also of his specific character, of circumstances given by fortune, and of one's career. Once again the discussion is fitted to Cicero's own context; for example, his advice about choosing a career (I. 115–21) could hardly be more relevant to the addressee of the book, his student son. It is also politically significant; in particular, his argument that individual character may alter duty comes to a climax with the example of Cato. Constancy, that is consistency with his own previous life, required his suicide at Utica; others might be excused a less heroic response (I.112; cf. *Fam.* IX.5.2, and p. 503 above).[58]

In *de Officiis*, in short, we can see Cicero using the resources of his philosophical education to articulate a conservative moral response to the revolution through which he was living. The *mos maiorum* is given its most intelligent restatement; and in the process, the language of *honestas*, *dignitas*, *officium*, *beneficia* and *gloria* is reshaped to meet present needs. The four virtues of *de Officiis* are borrowed from Greek philosophy; but they are analysed in sharply contemporary terms. Wisdom was not wisdom without justice: thus it was incumbent upon statesmen like Cicero himself to return to the political fray. *Magnitudo animi* without justice was mere savagery: the reference not only to Caesar but also to Mark Antony could hardly be missed. *De Officiis* was the philosophical counterpart to the *Philippics*.

Cicero's final, sustained onslaught against Antony in early 43 served only to sharpen the tragic irony that had marked his career. Much of that had been spent in indecision, vacillation and disillusionment. Yet in the two crises in which he had acted with unquestioned energy and purpose his poor judgment compromised his reputation and even his own theory. Faced with Catiline twenty years before he had argued that the over-riding needs of the *res publica* justified extra-constitutional action. Once again with Mark Antony; so, for example, in the eleventh *Philippic* he appealed dramatically to the divine law to authorize Cassius' extra-legal use of force against one of Antony's associates (*Phil.* XI. 28). Meanwhile, his imprudent encouragement of war, and of the young Octavian as its instrument, was helping ensure that the demise of the *res publica* would be permanent. In the long run the heated rhetoric of the *Philippics* merely sealed the temporary alliance of Antony and the future Augustus. Cicero

[57] See Gill 1988; an alternative approach in Atkins 1989: ch. 3.
[58] But see Gill 1988 on the contrasting treatment of Regulus.

met his death on 7 December 43, the only consular victim of their proscriptions. Tradition at least relates that he died heroically (Plut. *Cic.* 48; Livy *apud* Sen. *Suas.* VI.17).

8 Conclusion

The content of Cicero's political thought was shaped in precise ways by his experience, most profoundly by his experience of repeated civil war. In the days of the Senate's primacy, as he saw it, aristocratic debate had decided both external policy and internal disputes; military glory was the reward for fighting the enemies of Rome. Now, the city's leaders had begun to turn their personal armies against one another, and therefore against Rome. Cicero's intellectual response was to analyse those elements of the traditional constitution that had given it peace and stability, and to diagnose its failure.

The resulting moral and political theory is rooted in its context in society in at least four specific ways:

(i) The analysis of political change
Cicero inherited from Greek theory a horror of political upheaval, which was confirmed by the events of his life. He learnt from Aristotle (perhaps indirectly) that stability requires the complementary balancing of different groups of interest. He shared with Plato (and with Roman historiography) a moral analysis of decline. But his moral diagnosis of the failure of the aristocratic elite is distinctive. The duty of this class is public service, and above all wise counsel; but their temptation is to seek personal glory through warmongering. Cicero's task, therefore, is to reintegrate ambition into a system of patriotic virtues.

(ii) The centrality of the *res publica*
The fundamental role of patriotism within Cicero's theory constitutes an original development in political thought. The function of justice is to preserve society, in particular that of the *res publica*. The other virtues are shaped by this. The virtues of the individual find their point in the good of society (a conclusion that would stand, I believe, even if the psychological discussion of *de Re Publica* had survived). Appeals to the overriding value of the *res publica* were commonplace in Roman legal and political oratory. The *senatus consultum ultimum* even provided a constitutional mechanism to corroborate them. Cicero appropriates this conventional sentiment and makes it central to his ethical system.

(iii) The nature of the *res publica*

The *res publica* is the foundation; but what exactly does *res publica* mean to Cicero? Stable government that respected law and precedent at least; but that would be widely shared. Cicero's preoccupation with the role of the Senate gave his republicanism a specific nuance. The *res publica* flourished when government was arranged by free aristocratic debate. When force or bribery controlled honours and policy, the *res publica* was lost.

Hence Cicero's interest in the thoroughly Roman concepts of *dignitas*, *auctoritas* and *consilium*, as well as his concern with oratory. At the same time, Cicero did not neglect the role of the people. They, too, had proper claims to liberty; and to ignore these was to court disaster. However, they should be integrated into the system of predominantly aristocratic government through elections to offices (and consequent entry to the Senate).

(iv) Rome as the best *res publica*

Plato's ideal city was imaginary; Aristotle's collected constitutions were less than perfect. Cicero Romanizes the Platonic tradition from within by presenting republican Rome at her peak as an incarnation of the best possible constitution. Here was the city and statesmen that theory could describe, but only experience produce. Cicero's exaggerated patriotism encouraged him to a strikingly un-Platonic trust in historical and empirical evidence for the political enquiry.

In short, Cicero's extended reflection upon social and political matters was thoroughly conditioned by contemporary events. Civil war teaches Cicero that he can no more embrace unqualifiedly the Roman nobility's passion for glory than he can endorse the Greek philosopher's disdain for it. Again, popular discontent reveals the importance of the tribunate for constitutional stability. Just as his personal letters and public speeches betray the grip of philosophy on his imagination, so his theoretical writings reveal his continuous intellectual engagement with the realities of political life. In consequence, his writing of political philosophy was a thoroughly political act (which is why it was dangerous at times to publicize). Greek philosophy equipped him with tools for his theorizing, but Rome provided the raw material.

To say this much is not to claim that Cicero's practice was consistent with his theory. His political judgment was continuously inconsistent, and his final display of constancy served only to hasten the end of the *res publica*. Nor is it to argue that his theory was timely in the sense that it could have provided a practical remedy for the ills of his age. The empire had long outgrown government by a quarrelsomely competitive group of aristocrats, and moral education, however high-minded, would not turn back the clock. However, the eventual imposition of monarchy was at the cost of brutal warfare and the ruthless extermination of opponents. It may have been naive, but it was not, surely, valueless, to suggest an alternative strategy for restoring and maintaining peace.

The ethos of the Roman Republic, to which Cicero gave personal philosophical expression, was to possess a lasting appeal, particularly through the influence of *de Officiis*. Men who knew little of the specific targets of Cicero's theory would recognize the enduring themes of patriotism and public service, of courage and ambition, of benefaction and of friendship, the ethical themes, in short, of aristocratic politics and of war. The ruling elite of the Roman Republic were thoroughly versed in such matters. Under the pressure of contemporary crises, Cicero modified and articulated their insights for posterity to reappropriate.

25

Reflections of Roman political thought in Latin historical writing

THOMAS WIEDEMANN

Isolating 'political thought' in Latin historical narratives is more difficult than in the works of historians who wrote in Greek. Explicit theorizing was not a Roman characteristic. But that does not mean that what Roman historical writers[1] wrote did not reflect their conceptions of political institutions and structures and of how they changed over time. The further that a particular statement about historical events deviates from 'real' history (as in the analyses which we find in Plato or Aristotle, or in the Greek elements in Cicero), the easier it is to identify – and isolate – such a statement as 'political thought'; but statements that *correspond* to the collective morality of a culture represent 'political thought' too.

Rome was a society used to accepting authority, whether that of the head of the household (*paterfamilias*) at home (*domi*) or the commander (*imperator*) in war (*bello*, *militiae*). From the fourth century BC on, warfare became the most important element in the Roman value-system. In war, obedience to the commander could not afford to be challenged;[2] but the language in which domestic political issues were discussed was equally based on authority – that provided by the speaker's *virtus* (proved by his own great deeds or those of his ancestors) or by ancestral tradition, *mos maiorum*, from which the speaker selected those precedents (*exempla*) which supported his argument. When the consul Cornelius Scipio Nasica at a *contio* (formal public gathering) in 138 BC heard views with which he disagreed, he did not try to persuade, but told his assembled fellow-citizens: 'Please be silent. I know better than you what is best for the state.'[3] Theoretical speculation of the kind which had developed in the fifth cen-

[1] General studies include Dorey 1966, 1969, 1971, Luce and Woodman 1993, Mellor 1993, Walsh 1974, Woodman 1988.

[2] Liv.XLIV.36.12–14. Three classic texts on the primacy of warfare at Rome: Brunt 1971, Hopkins 1978, Harris 1979. Cf. also Rich and Shipley 1993, Wiedemann 1996.

[3] 'Tacete, quaeso, Quirites, plus ego quam vos quid rei publicae expediat intellego': V.Max. 3.7.3.

tury BC, when the democracies of Syracuse and Athens had practised forms of decision-making which required mass-approval, were frowned upon, and even explicitly rejected as Greek. A notorious instance of the rejection of Greek theory is the criticism of the educated elite put into the mouth of Marius (a non-aristocratic general who won the consulship seven times between 107 and 86 BC) by the historian Sallust (Gaius Sallustius Crispus, mid-first century BC): 'What they know from hearing and reading, I have partly seen, and partly actually done; what they have learnt from books, I have learnt from service in the field: you must consider for yourselves whether words or deeds have more weight.' Sallust's Marius has just mentioned two categories of such books – Roman history, and Greek military textbooks.[4] The contrast between Roman practice, learning by example, and Greek theory, learnt from books, runs through much Roman writing.[5] But that contrast, in a set speech which itself was unthinkable without the *exemplum* of Thucydides, reveals a paradox about the treatment of political thought by Roman historians: history performs a specifically Roman function – preserving the deeds of the ancestors, *acta maiorum* – but like other Latin literature from at least the early second century BC on, it includes Greek writings among the precedents it draws upon. (One of the earliest known Roman historical texts, a history of the war against Hannibal (218–202 BC) by the senator Fabius Pictor, was in fact written in Greek as propaganda to counter the accounts by Hannibal's supporters Sosylus the Spartan and Silenus of Agrigentum.) This paradox is not specific to historical literature; it is implicit in any Roman political speech structured according to the precepts of Greek rhetoric. When Cicero in 66 BC speaks in support of a law granting extraordinary command in the war against Mithridates of Pontus to Pompey, his speech may take the form of a Hellenistic encomium, but he knows that if it is to persuade the Roman listener he must end by appealing to the *auctoritas* of the proposal's supporters (*Man.* 51–68).

Like oratory, historical writing – described by Cicero as 'the most rhetorical type of writing' (*Leg.* I.5) – reflects Roman political ideas and presuppositions, but presents them in forms which draw heavily on the

[4] Sal. *Jug.* 85.13f. Cf. 85.12: 'acta maiorum et Graecorum militaria praecepta'. Sallust's *Jugurtha* describes a war against the Numidians in North Africa between 112 and 105 BC, and his *Catiline* is an account of an attempted coup at Rome in 63 BC. The surviving fragments of the *Histories* (covering the period 78–67 BC) have been translated with a commentary by McGushin (2 vols.: 1992 and 1994).

[5] Cf. Quint.*Inst.* XII.2.30; Sen. *Ep.* I.6.5: 'The route by way of teaching is a long one; through *exempla*, it is short and effectual'.

arsenal provided by Greek rhetoric. This leaves the modern scholar analysing a speech in a Latin history with the problem of assessing just how much of the rhetorical packaging and the political theory would have been discounted as such by a Roman audience, even if we assume that there was any relationship at all between the historian's text and historical reality. Thus historians who believed that the emperors who ruled Rome in the second century AD were something similar to a President for Life selected by their predecessor misunderstood Tacitus' account of Galba's speech on adopting Piso (*Histories* I.15f.) as a programmatic statement in support of this so-called 'adoptive principate'.[6] In fact the speech is one of a pair, the other being that made by Mucianus in urging Vespasian to seize the purple at *Histories* II.77; in the first speech the desperate Galba makes unsubstantiated rhetorical claims in the hope of staving off rebellion, in the second the canny Mucianus reveals all the real advantages of an imperial candidate able to promise the certainty of dynastic succession. The two speeches reflect the realities of power-politics in AD 69, not two different theories of government.

That is not to say that Greek political theory had no place in Roman politics. The idea that political conflict could be analysed in terms of 'democrats' versus 'aristocrats' may have entered the Roman political agenda in the 130s BC primarily because that was what the Gracchi brothers learnt from their Greek tutor, the Stoic Blossius of Cumae, but it resulted in a conflict between the Senate and the equestrian *ordo* whose results were as real over the next seventy years as its origin was artificial. If Sallust found that distinction between 'democrats' (*populares*) and 'aristocrats' a useful way of explaining conflict, it left nineteenth- and twentieth-century historians convinced that a conflict between aristocratic senatorial (agrarian, conservative) and 'middle class' equestrian (commercial, progressive) interests was applicable to the political struggles that brought about the end of the Republic.

While the theoretical schemata drawn up by Greek speculation may be exploited by Roman writers – the tripartite categorization of constitutions as monarchy/ aristocracy/ democracy, the idea that there was a

[6] E.g. Garzetti 1974: 310f., Shotter 1991: 73. The twelve books of Cornelius Tacitus' *Histories* covered the period AD 69–96; the first four and part of Book V survive (up to AD 70). Of the eighteen books of the *Annals* (AD 14 – 68), I–V, 5 (AD 14–29), VI (31 – 37) and XI–XVI (47 – 66) survive. A panegyrical life of Tacitus' father-in-law Agricola (governor of Britain between AD 78 and 84), a description of Germany, and a discussion of rhetoric (the *Dialogus de Oratoribus*) also survive. The *Histories* were written during the reign of Trajan, and the *Annals* that of Hadrian, and appear to reflect the political issues raised by the careers and styles of these two monarchs. Syme 1958 remains authoritative.

natural tendency to slip from one into another[7] – they make little use of such theories in explaining or ordering the political development of Rome. Even in texts which do make use of Greek rhetoric and theory, exemplification is crucial. Tacitus' version of Nero's accession speech – which Tacitus explicitly says was drawn up by Seneca[8] – bases Nero's claim that he will be a better ruler than his predecessor Claudius on his intention of following both advice and precedents to achieve good government, 'consilia sibi et exempla capessendi egregie imperii' (*Annals* XIII, 4). This Roman attitude to *exempla* has implications for the way in which political development is perceived: if *exempla* from the fifth century BC are to be relevant in political arguments of the first century BC,[9] then differences and changes in political structures have to be played down. Political history was perceived as a series of *exempla* of individual leaders who had a greater or lesser share of power (if so great a share that they could be represented as *reges*, kings like the Tarquins, then they provided an *exemplum* to be avoided) and who exercised that power in different ways. It was not that they were sceptical of (for instance) the fable of the expulsion of the Tarquins in 509 BC (a fable clearly borrowed, probably by Fabius Pictor, in order to parallel the account of the overthrow of the Peisistratid tyranny at Athens in the same year: Herodotus v.62–5), but rather that it was realized that constitutional change was a minor issue compared with the question of how political power was distributed between leaders. It was the way in which political supremacy was exercised that interested historical writers, not so much the form it took – hence modern uncertainty as to exactly when Sulla laid down the 'Dictatorship for the Restoration of the Republic' to which he had had himself appointed after he seized power in 81 BC: his resignation made no difference to the fact that he continued to be Rome's leading political figure until he died in 78. This has resulted in much misplaced speculation

[7] E.g. Tacitus *Annals* IV.33: 'All nations and cities are governed either by the people, or by an elite, or by individuals; a constitution put together from selected elements mixed together is easier to praise than to bring about – and when it is brought about, it cannot last long.' Tacitus is explaining to the reader why his apparently unexciting material illustrates a major constitutional change towards despotism. On the origins of the theory of the three constitutions, first appearing in Herodotus III.79–83, see Winton in ch. 4 section 2 above; on its application to Rome, Lintott 1997; and on its reception in modern Europe, Nippel 1980.

[8] See Griffin, in ch. 26 section 1, p. 542 below.

[9] The classic account of the history of the Roman republic was that of Livy (Titus Livius), writing in the time of Augustus. Books I–X and XXI–XLV survive, covering the periods down to 292 and from 219 to 168 BC. We also have summaries of the lost books. One of Livy's major sources, the lost histories of Licinius Macer, represented the struggle of the patrician and plebeian 'orders' in the fifth and fourth centuries BC as analogous to that between the Optimates and *populares* of his own time.

by modern historians about the various 'constitutions' through which Augustus exercised control over Rome: such speculation is really relevant only to modern-day concerns about constitutionality.[10]

Since the Romans themselves thought in terms of *exempla*, and constitutional analysis was of little interest to them, one view of the development of their constitutional history was that the shift from monarchy to republic was a minor one – there were simply two magistrates with *imperium* instead of one, but the institutions of magistracy, Senate and assemblies continued to function in much the same way. But at the same time as asserting continuity, thought in terms of *exempla* also gave political structures enormous flexibility: if innovation worked, then it too could later count as exemplary – a point made by Julius Caesar in the speech Sallust gives him warning against setting aside the law against executing Roman citizens without trial – but also explicitly stated in Augustus' formal account of his achievements, the *Res Gestae*: 'By proposing new laws I restored many ancestral *exempla* which were no longer being followed in our own age, and I myself left many *exempla* for later generations to follow.'[11] Insofar as there are any public traces of political thought about the nature of the Principate, they are not so much about the ideal 'constitution' as about the exemplary *princeps*: and the *exemplum* is always necessarily provided by Augustus. The political system was judged not with reference to a constitution or constitutional ideal, but with reference to the *exempla* provided by its greatest player.

Of course, that does not imply that Roman historians thought that there was no difference at all between the Republic and the Principate; one difference that was obvious to them was that between a political system in which decision-making was a public process, and one where decisions were taken 'privately', within the imperial household (Tac.*Hist.* 1.1). But they thought primarily in terms of changes in the distribution of power between individuals, not constitutional changes. Romans did not have 'revolutions': what Sallust's Catiline promises his followers is not a new constitution, but the redistribution of wealth (including the income from the empire), magistracies, priesthoods, and plunder currently controlled by the political elite (*Cat.*21.2; cf.20.7).

When Roman writers deploy the theme that the history they are writing is useful, what is meant is not that it provides a framework for understanding human nature or the possible ways in which commun-

10 Grziwotz 1986; reviewed in *JRS* 78 (1988) 267.

11 Sal. *Cat.* 51.27; Augustus *Res Gestae* 8.5; and see on Tacitus *Annals* III pp. 529–30 below.

ities can be controlled politically, but that they are providing a storehouse of further *exempla* to assist decision-making.[12] One consequence was that political behaviour could not be divorced from moral judgment: if the principal function of a precedent is to legitimate proposals for current action (and their proposers), then *exempla* have no value unless they are either good or bad.[13] Livy's history is not the only text to be liberally sprinkled with *exempla* of individuals' bravery in war on the one hand, and of celebrated morality or immorality on the other.[14] Even the bravery or loyalty of those Romans fighting on the *wrong* side is recorded – witness Catiline's heroic death (*Cat.* 60.7, 61.4), or the *fides* of Gaius Gracchus' otherwise unknown supporter Pomponius (Vell. II.6.6). In the quite different genre of the *commentarius*, which takes its rhetorical power from pretending to be in the tradition of purely objective reporting of events, we also find such *exempla*: in the accounts of the Gallic and Civil Wars written by Caesar and some of his officers, for instance, examples of exceptional bravery, especially by centurions, are held up to be emulated (and in order for Caesar to win the political support of their municipalities).[15] Historical material is seen as a series of *exempla*: not just in historians like Livy, but in Valerius Maximus' collection of *Famous Deeds and Words* or in Frontinus' collection of military tricks, the *Stratēgēmata*. Indeed, the collecting and preserving of such precedents was seen by Romans as the origin of the 'annalistic tradition' of historiography: lists of omens and details of the ceremonies performed to expiate them published on whiteboards each year by the president of the board of experts in religious law, the *Pontifex Maximus* (hence called the *Annales Maximi*).[16] Cicero comments on how badly they compared with Greek historiography, seen as literature: 'nothing can be more dry' (Cic. *Leg.* I.6).

Livy's history achieved such success as the Roman national epic that it eclipsed all earlier annals not just because it represented the Romans as heroes, but because it provided a wonderful series of *exempla*: 'no other state has ever been more powerful or more venerable or richer in good examples'.[17] But the Greek packaging around these *exempla* is clear in both content – the florid descriptions of battles and of the sack of cities, digressions and speeches – and form: the extent of Livy's rhetorical *amplificatio* is striking where it can be checked directly against his annalistic sources

[12] Sal. *Jug.* 4.1 and 6 (on ancestral masks); Liv. *Preface* 10; Tac. *Hist.* I.3 and *Ann.* IV.33.
[13] Cf. Earl 1967. [14] Fries 1985, Moore 1989, Oakley 1985. [15] E.g. *Civ.* III.53, 91, 99.
[16] Frier 1979.
[17] 'Nulla umquam res publica nec maior nec sanctior nec bonis exemplis ditior fuit', *Preface* 11.

(Claudius Quadrigarius, Valerius Antias).[18] There are also stories taken from Greek writers, for example, how in 494 BC Menenius Agrippa used the comparison between the limbs of the body and the different sections of society to persuade the plebeians to abandon their secession – a comparison first found in Xenophon, and common enough in Greek social thought to be exploited by St Paul.[19] Livy developed other stories with a Greek background which he found in his sources. Anti-tyrant fables include not just that of Lucretia but also the overthrow of the Decemvirs in 449 BC because of Appius Claudius' attempt to rape Verginia, and the abolition of debt-bondage in 325 BC because of L. Papirius' attempt to rape C. Publilius.[20] One of the most important elements of Greek thought in Livy (as throughout Latin literature) was the concept of the barbarian.

If political theory is absent from the surviving thirty-five books of Livy's history (and there is no reason to believe that Livy's handling of internal conflict in the years from 133 BC was any more analytical of constitutional forms than that of the patrician/ plebeian conflict in Books II to IV), it was because creating a coherent narrative structure for his material was more important to Livy than political analysis. It has even been argued recently that the polarity between patricians and plebeians could have been invented by Livy himself (or by one of his annalistic sources) as a structure for providing internal coherence to the disparate fables and *exempla* which make up the material of the first five books (pentad).[21] But for a study of Roman political thought, Livy is disappointing not so much because explicit theoretical analysis is lacking (or that his analytical categories are unsophisticated), or that literary intentions take priority, as that he is a Roman writing for Romans, and therefore takes it for granted that political and social institutions need not be explicitly described. Herodotus, Thucydides and their successors had to describe Spartan or Athenian institutions to an audience which included non-Spartans and non-Athenians; there was no need for Livy to explain the powers of Roman magistrates, assemblies or law-courts in similar fashion. Hence the confusion among historians, even today, about what (for instance) exactly the *equester ordo* (conventionally translated 'knights'; wealthy landowners who were not senators) was. The extent to which Livy's history is integrated into the common culture of Rome is shown by

[18] Richter 1983, comparing Liv. VII.9.7–10.14 with Aulus Gellius IX.13.7–19 and Liv. VII.4.1–5 and 9 with Cic. *Off.* III.112.

[19] Liv. II.32.9ff.; see below pp. 524–5 for its use by Florus; Xen. *Mem.* II.3.18; 1 Cor. 12.12.

[20] Liv. I.57.6ff.; III.44ff.; VIII.28. On the reliability of Livy's account of early Roman history, cf. Cornell 1995; Miles 1995.

[21] Mitchell 1990.

the largely fruitless arguments as to whether he himself supported the traditional Republic or the Augustan monarchy – a particularly burning issue during and after the regimes of Mussolini and Hitler.[22] Whatever Augustus' quip that Livy was a 'Pompeian' may have meant, it does not mean that in his history he treated Republic and Principate as two different political systems between which Romans had to choose, if unwillingly. When he spoke of 'the present age, in which we can endure neither our vices nor their cure' (*Preface* 9), he was not talking of the Republic and the Principate as constitutional systems, but about political (im)morality and the need for control.

In terms of Roman political thought, one moral quality that plays a particularly important role in Livy's history is *fides*, good faith. Since so much historiography deals with warfare, it is *fides* as a relationship between Rome and its allies, or enemies, that occurs most frequently as an explanation for why the Romans intervened militarily in distant places; and the need to present the Romans as acting in pursuance of their treaty-obligations (*foedera*) even leads him into self-contradictions, as in the chronology of the siege of Saguntum, where he cannot believe that Rome failed to act immediately to protect its allies (XXI.15.3–6, contradicting 6.3). That account illustrates another fundamental principle of Roman political behaviour in inter-state relations, that of the 'just war', *bellum iustum*, which via the writings of St Augustine was to become a major element in mediaeval political thought.[23] Livy's insistence that the Romans never waged war without first having established that it was the enemy, not they, who were wrong and had refused to pay compensation (*res repetitae*) reflects Augustus' interest in the college of fetials (the experts in inter-state ritual), and his exploitation or invention of a 'fetial rite' for declaring war against Cleopatra in 32 BC, shortly before the publication of Book I.[24]

Livy's account of Roman history is too large scale – and too little of it survives[25] – to make it easy to trace his view of the development and functioning of political institutions. This can more easily be done with the shorter accounts written in the annalistic tradition. Florus, in the mid-second century AD, divided his history into two books, with the Gracchi

22 'The Emperor and his historian understood each other', Syme 1939: 317; the history as 'an attempt to sell' the Augustan system, Cochrane 1940: 103.

23 Russell 1975. See also Atkins, in ch. 24 section 7.2, p. 510 above

24 The legendary *exempla* are provided in Book I.24 (*foedus* between Rome and Alba) and 32.6–14 (restitution); for what actually happened in the mid-Republic, cf. Rich 1976; for Augustus, Wiedemann 1986; for an unhistorical analysis by a Roman law specialist, see Watson 1993.

25 Of the original 142 books, only I–X (down to 292 BC) and XXI–XLV (219–168 BC) survive.

as the dividing line. Again, moral criteria, and the idea of a moral decline, predominate: from the time of the Numantine War on (in Spain, 143–133 BC: I.34.19), an iron age replaces a golden one. The internal conflicts of the late Republic are explained largely in the terms of increasing wealth leading to a lust for power and thus ultimately to civil war (I.47.7, 11). At the same time, Florus is well aware of the importance of political issues such as land redistribution, or the desire of Italian allies for citizenship; but he prefers to analyse them in moral terms – the Social War was a crime against the city that was mother and parent (II.6.2, 6). Words like *nefas* and *furor* are used liberally, as is the image of the Roman community as a single body. Elsewhere the Gracchi are said to have given Rome two heads. Civil discord is the result of the lust for power and the envy it provokes. Pompey, Crassus and Caesar were simply individuals seeking to achieve, increase, or retain power, not the representatives of interest-groups. Florus' emphasis on the so-called first triumvirate as controlling Rome for a decade well illustrates how Romans saw formal political institutions as less important than alliance between individuals (*fides*).[26]

One other interesting feature was Florus' use of the idea that Rome had gone through four historical stages analagous to the age-grades of the human life-span (an idea probably borrowed from the Elder Seneca). Thus the *discordia* of the plebeian secessions is ascribed to the 'youth, as it were' of Rome (I.17). The idea that youth implies inexperience and is an explanation for political instability is a commonplace in Roman historiography (see p. 531 below).

The two-book summary of Roman history written by Velleius Paterculus during Tiberius' reign also relies heavily on competition, *aemulatio*, as an explanatory factor both for heroism and for strife; his widening of the theme to provide an explanation for the cultural flowering of fifth-century Athens and Augustan Rome is remarkable.[27] That emphasis on rivalry and on the envy it provokes had always corresponded to the reality of ancient political life,[28] and was as relevant to Rome as to any Greek polis. Here we may refer to a Greek text which gives us a real insight into political behaviour in a Roman province at the beginning of the second century AD: Plutarch's brilliant analysis of 'How to rule a

[26] Single body: 'Corpus fecit ex membris et ex omnibus unus est', II.6.1; Gracchi, II.5.3; *invidia* of Pompey's power, II.13.8; 'Caesare dignitatem comparare, Crasso augere, Pompeio retinere cupientibus, omnibusque pariter potentiae cupidis', II.13.11; 'rupta primum coniurationis fides', II.13.15.

[27] I.17.6: 'alit aemulatio ingenia, et nunc invidia, nunc admiratio imitationem accendit'. On Velleius, Woodman 1975.

[28] Cf. the role of envy, *phthonos*, in Pindar (Bulman 1992), or Herodotus (Gould 1989).

community' (*Praec.* 798ff.).[29] It is to Greek writers that we must turn for systematic political analysis of Rome, often wildly wrong. The best-known instance is Polybius' attempt in Book VI to force Roman politics onto the Procrustean bed of the theory of the mixed constitution,[30] resulting (for example) in failure to understand the place of the equestrian *ordo*. Other analyses by Greek writers are valuable in drawing our attention to aspects of Roman politics which surprised them – for example, the *patria potestas* or the Roman willingness to grant manumitted slaves citizenship[31] – but their works are examples of Greek, not Roman, political thought. That even applies to the political ideas which we find in the history of Cassius Dio, twice Roman consul (on the second occasion, in AD 229, as the emperor's colleague). Historians have long been concerned about the extent to which the pair of speeches in which Agrippa and Maecenas try to persuade Octavian of the advantages of a restored Republic and a monarchy respectively (Book LII) expresses his own personal views of reforms that he felt were needed in the Severan period: 'He put some of these reforms into practice immediately and some later, leaving others to be done by those who would rule after him . . .' (LII.41.2). Just how much of this can be isolated as the Roman political thought of his time, rather than speculation by himself or others, is controversial. It is interesting that while Dio is Greek enough to be entirely clear that the essential characteristic of the principate is that it was a monarchy, he does not see Roman constitutional history in terms of a simple monarchy/ republic/ monarchy sequence. His use of the word *dunasteia* at LII.1.15 for the period between Sulla and Augustus is more helpful for an understanding of Roman politics than much theorizing about constitutional forms.[32]

It is also to Greek accounts of Roman history that we must look for traces of Stoic ideas of political justice. The account of the Roman empire in the universal history of Diodorus Siculus is heavily coloured by the Stoic ideology of Posidonius, whose lost history of the late Republic (culminating in the conquests of Pompey) was one of Diodorus' major sources.[33] Posidonius is thought to have originated the idea that the decline in Roman public morality began when the destruction of Carthage in 146 BC removed the fear of competition from another state; from that date on Romans could afford to abandon justice in favour of the unrestrained exploitation of their subjects (resulting in discontent and

[29] See Centrone, in ch. 27 section 3 below. [30] See Hahm, in ch. 23 section 2 above.
[31] Dionysius of Halicarnassus, *Ancient History of Rome* II.26 and IV.24 respectively. Cf. Gabba 1991.
[32] Rich 1989, Reinhold 1988: 165f.; generally Millar 1964. [33] Sacks 1990: ch. 5, esp. 142 ff.

rebellion, of which the Sicilian slave wars were a prime example), and political violence at home in a struggle for power and for the wealth of the empire that went with power.

Sallust[34] borrowed from Posidonius the idea that the fall of Carthage was a decisive factor in the collapse of Roman political morality (*Jug.* 41.2), but he uses several other explanatory factors too, such as the luxury to which Sulla's soldiers had become accustomed while stationed in Asia (*Cat.* 11.5), or the natural propensity of 'the young' (as a category) to foment instability.[35] If Posidonius' influence on Sallust is not clear, Thucydides' certainly is – even on the grammatical structure of some of Sallust's sentences.[36] Many of the elements for which there are Greek parallels have been ascribed to Sallust's reading of Thucydides: for example, the link between success and envy and the slippage from monarchy to despotism (*Cat.* 6, on the regal state and the shift to the Republic), or the theoretical statements about human nature and the superiority of the intellect over mere physical courage in both prefaces, which develop Aristotelian themes. The political rhetoric of the attack on the *pauci potentes* (powerful few) in Catiline's speech to his potential supporters (*Cat.* 20) or of the tribune Memmius' attack on the *superbia paucorum* (pride of a few) at *Jug.* 31 is presented in terms of Greek political ideology (even if that language was being used by Roman politicians in his own time). Like Thucydides' Melian dialogue, the *Catiline* has a pair of speeches, here featuring Caesar and Cato the Younger, in which the most suitable form of punishment for the manifestly guilty rebels is discussed. Caesar in particular uses arguments about the history of punishment which are reminiscent of those used by Thucydides' Diodotus. Such arguments will hardly have persuaded a historical Roman audience.[37] Indeed, when we look more closely, we find that for all its Thucydidean tone, Caesar's speech relies on the support of Roman authorities: he refers to the ancestral *exemplum* of the treatment of the Rhodians, he criticizes Silanus' proposal as non-Roman, he attacks scourging and execution on the grounds that they are, of all things, a Greek import, and warns of the dangers of setting a precedent. Cato's speech, too, for all its reference to Thucydides' analysis (III.79f.) of the way the meanings of words change in time of civil conflict, ends with traditionally Roman arguments: the

[34] Earl 1961 is still well worth reading. Cf. also Drummond 1995.

[35] *Cat.* 17.6; 37.7; 43.2 (*iuventus, filiifamiliarum*). 'Youth and Politics', Eyben 1993: 52ff.

[36] Scanlon 1980.

[37] It is worth noting that Cicero explicitly criticized those who think that Thucydides should be an *exemplum* for Roman oratory: *Orat.* 30–2.

exemplum of Torquatus' execution of his son for disobedience and the claim that executing a criminal caught *in flagrante* was entirely in accordance with *mos maiorum*.[38]

The introduction to the *Jugurtha* makes it clear that Sallust's theme there is not just to preserve the memory of a great war, but to analyse the conditions which later led to the 'devastation of Italy', *vastitas Italiae*, in a series of civil wars of which that between Marius and Sulla, the co-heroes of the Jugurthine war, was just the first. That theme of civil war is repeatedly drawn to the reader's attention by means of Thucydidean speeches and Herodotean digressions. Early on in the text, the dying king Micipsa lectures his sons on the essential requirement of a successful state: 'Small states grow through concord, great ones collapse through conflict.'[39] The speech of Memmius (31) and a digression on the reasons why factions disturbed the functioning of Roman public life (41–2) explicitly continue that theme. But perhaps more interesting are the two other digressions in the *Jugurtha*, because their relevance to Sallust's theme is not immediately apparent. The first examines the diverse ethnic origins of the North African population, emphasizing the fable of the collapse of unity among the followers of Hercules (the symbolic founder of political order) after his death (*Jug.*17–19); the second recounts the myth of how a pair of Carthaginian brothers, the Philaeni, competed with a pair from Cyrene in a competition to fix the boundary between their two cities (*Jug.*79–80). The implication is that cooperation within the community will bring success abroad; and indeed the following section of the *Jugurtha* describes exactly that: success in war comes as a result of cooperation between Marius and Sulla.[40]

Augustus had suppressed civil conflict. He had also removed from the agenda of public politics most of its traditional components – 'war and peace, income and legislation, and the other things that constitute Roman affairs', as the consciously Sallustian Tacitus has Thrasea Paetus complain in the Senate (*Ann.* XIII.49.2). What was now central to Roman political thought was the personal behaviour of the emperor, in particular the way he exercised his power toward the Senate. Those with power had to behave *as though* it was the Senate that had the authority to select, or at least approve, an emperor (*Hist.* II.37). Many of the issues handled by Tacitus clearly reflect the politics of the reign of Hadrian – not just the

38 *Cat.* 51.5, 51.17: 'aliena a republica nostra'; 51.39, 51.27: 'omnia mala exempla ex rebus bonis orta sunt'; 52.11, 52.30ff., 52.36 fin: 'more maiorum supplicium sumundum'.

39 *Jug.* 10.6: 'concordia parvae res crescunt, discordia maxumae dilabuntur'.

40 Wiedemann 1993: 48–56; Kraus 1999. Romans could not help but be conscious of the symbolism of the Romulus and Remus story for their own civil conflict.

way power was transferred to him at the death of Trajan (cf. the accession of Tiberius in AD 14 in *Annals* I), or whether an emperor should stay at Rome or go to the provinces, as Hadrian did (cf. *Ann.* III.47 on the rebellion of Sacrovir in Gaul in AD 21), but also the relationship between emperor and his chief minister, the Praetorian Prefect (Hadrian had problems with more than one of his Praetorian Prefects), and more generally how the deep suspicion between the Senate and an emperor like Hadrian could be resolved. Tacitus' characterization of Tiberius (reigned AD 14–37) wrestles as much with the problem of Hadrian as with that of Domitian (AD 81–96), whose *damnatio memoriae* (formal condemnation) after his overthrow in AD 96 made him unproblematic by the time the *Annals* were written. The *Histories* were written earlier, and reflect the concerns of Trajan's reign – for instance the 'secret of power', *arcanum imperii*, notoriously referred to in *Hist.* I.4, that an emperor could be made in one of the provinces, which was actually relevant to the events of 97 (when the legions' discontent at the removal of their beloved Domitian forced Nerva to select Trajan, one of the provincial army commanders, as his successor) rather than those in the spring of 69. There are some significant omissions among the political issues handled by Tacitus: the role of client kings in the political framework (which we would expect to be mentioned at *Hist.* II.82); or the importance of an emperor's taking on the identity of a 'Caesar' (e.g. in Vitellius' initial rejection, and ultimate acceptance, of the title in AD 69: *Hist.* II.90).

For Tacitus too, explicit theorizing about the nature of the Principate hardly goes beyond comparing an emperor with the *exempla* provided by his predecessors.[41] The theme of how each emperor fits into the continuing sequence of *exempla* provided by Roman history is pursued throughout Tacitus' narratives, but perhaps especially interesting in *Annals* III, where the historian (having described Tiberius' accession in Book I and built up Germanicus in Books I and II as a potential, but lost, alternative) prepares the reader for revealing the full tyranny of Tiberius in Books IV–VI (the primacy of the Praetorian Prefect Sejanus and his subsequent sudden removal and execution in AD 31). Central to the book is a Sallustian digression on the origins of law which points out that most laws (at any rate since the codification of the Twelve Tables *c.* 450 BC) were passed as a result of discord between Senate and equestrians, or to grant someone unconstitutional powers or to drive opponents into exile (III.27.1). It was Augustus who imposed order on the legal system (after

[41] Cf. *Ann.* XIII.3.2, where the accession of Nero prompts a list of comparisons (beginning, interestingly enough, with Julius Caesar rather than Augustus).

an earlier unsuccessful attempt by Pompey). The digression functions to reveal the reality of the principate: the authority of the *exemplum* provided by Augustus is more powerful in Roman political thought than the force of law. Tacitus reports constant appeals to the precedent of Augustus: it is Augustus' habit of travelling with Livia which permits governors to take their wives with them (III.34.12); Tiberius reads out an Augustan precedent for prosecuting a governor of Asia (III.68.1). When it is suggested that the emperor should judge who is fit to be a provincial governor, Tiberius warns against making the emperor replace the law: 'Emperors have enough responsibilities, and even enough power. Each time power spreads wider, the scope of the laws is restricted. Magisterial power should not be used when there are laws in place.'[42] Yet a few chapters earlier Tacitus had pointed out how deference to the emperors was far more successful than any law in curbing luxury – and then had directly added a note on the significance of Augustus' using *tribunicia potestas* to symbolize his autocracy (III.55.5, 56.2). Episode after episode unmasks the contrast between the reality of Tiberius' imperial power and the constitutional forms he tries to maintain. A soldier called Helvius Rufus wins the *corona civica* for bravery while fighting in Africa. Constitutionally, it ought to be awarded by the proconsul; actually it has to be granted by Tiberius, who then complains that the proconsul has failed in his duty (III.21.3). History deals with the facts of political power, not constitutional theory.

Even the imperial lives of Suetonius contain no explicit theorizing about imperial power. Certainly the four cardinal virtues of Hellenistic thought constitute one of the structural frameworks for Suetonius' descriptions of the lives of emperors.[43] When that occurs in discussion of (for example) self-control as exercised (or not) by Caligula, Nero or Domitian, then the issue of the relations between emperor and elite, how the limits of an emperor's power were negotiated through Caligula's sexual control over senators' wives, is there; but for all his grounding in the intellectual tradition of Hellenistic grammar, Suetonius shows virtually no interest in analysing these imperial virtues.[44]

Suetonius wrote biography, recognized in antiquity as quite a different

[42] III.69.6: 'satis onera principibus, satis etiam potentiae. minui iura, quotiens gliscat potestas, nec utendum imperio, ubi legibus agi possit'.

[43] The structure of Suetonius' *Lives*, as of much other Greek and Roman biography, can usefully be seen in terms of the rules of panegyric as described (for instance) by Menander the Rhetor's treatise *On Kingship*: Russell 1981. Cf. Barton 1994.

[44] Wallace-Hadrill 1982, 1983; for Seneca and Pliny on imperial virtues, see Griffin in ch. 26 below.

genre from history.[45] We should not expect to find a discussion of policies, let alone analysis of political institutions. Even wars are minimized, in stark contrast to what is found in the genre of historical narrative. Narratives are eschewed (death scenes, most conspicuously that of Nero, are an exception, and of course political motives may, but need not, enter into the deaths of princes). Explanations for such events are described in terms of personal, not political factors: for example, the plot by Silius and Messalina to replace Claudius (*Claudius* 26.2). Historical incidents are not narrated, let alone analysed, but referred to in order to illustrate character. All of which makes the modern historian's task of (for instance) restoring dynastic politics very difficult. The same applies to later imperial biographers; Marius Maximus, who wrote in the early third century AD, is lost but thought to be the surprisingly reliable source for the first part of the late fourth-century *Augustan History* where again major questions about political institutions constantly impinge – indeed, have been thought to be the central propaganda purpose of the whole work. Once again the relation between emperor and Senate is central, and associated with it the extent to which military emperors should be expected to share the education of the cultural elite.[46] And of course the author raises the celebrated question of whether a child should become emperor: 'The gods protect us from emperors who are children.'[47] That issue had already been a problem when the seventeen-year-old Nero succeeded Claudius (Tac. *Ann.* XIII.6): but we may note that there it had been answered in accordance with Roman political thinking – by appealing to the *exempla* of Pompey (aged seventeen) and Augustus (eighteen). It was largely the rhetorical exploitation of *exempla*, and the vivid narration of both good and bad *exempla* selected from the early Republic such as Lucretia, Horatius on the Tiber bridge, or the wicked Decemvir Appius Claudius, or from the line of emperors, that was to inspire those in later centuries who had read their Latin historians to look to Rome for their ideals of good kingship, or of republicanism.

[45] Momigliano 1971: 99. On the difference between writing a 'life' and writing history, cf. Plu. *Alex.* 1.

[46] The treatment of emperors by Ammianus Marcellinus equally lacks systematic analysis, though it deals with the same kinds of issues in the same personal, moral terms. Cf. Matthews 1989. Literature on the *Augustan History* is massive: a good starting-point is Syme 1971.

[47] 'Di avertant principes pueros': *SHA Tacitus* 6.5.

26

Seneca and Pliny

MIRIAM GRIFFIN

A century after Cicero's death, another Roman senator, also a gifted orator, again demonstrated the power of philosophical writing in Latin,[1] but in a different vein and a different style.[2] Like Cicero Seneca regarded the *moralis pars philosophiae*, which traditionally included political theory, as the most important branch of philosophy,[3] but unlike Cicero, who used a leisured periodic style suited to the balanced tone of a sceptical Academic, Seneca expounded ethics in a nervous epigrammatic style suited to the passionate tone of a committed Stoic. And whereas Cicero had been inspired by the example of Plato and the Peripatetics to compose a *de Re Publica* and to embark on a *de Legibus*, Seneca did not write about the relative merits of different constitutions and showed little confidence in what could be achieved by legislation.[4] Indeed it is often said that Seneca showed no interest in political theory and restricted the *moralis pars philosophiae* to individual ethics.[5]

Similar points have been made about Hellenistic philosophy itself, including Stoicism, and Seneca's *de Clementia*, his most explicit work of political theory, is clearly indebted to lost Hellenistic works on kingship, of which there were many Stoic examples.[6] Moreover, between Cicero's time and Seneca's there had been important political developments with the advent of the Principate. Cicero had placed his faith in the Roman Republican constitution which, he believed, had once realized the Greek ideal of the mixed constitution, equitable and durable. The divisive trends he perceived, however, led to protracted civil wars and Caesar's dictatorship, which shattered the dream of constitutional

[1] Quint. *Inst.* x.1.123–4 could find few other philosophical writers worthy of mention. Seneca's contemporaries Musonius Rufus and Epictetus discoursed in Greek.

[2] For recent bibliography and survey articles on Seneca see *Aufstieg und Niedergang der Römischen Welt* II.36.3 (1989): 1545–2012.

[3] *Ep.* 89.18. Even in his *Natural Questions* moral concerns are paramount.

[4] *Clem.* I.23, *Ben.* III.16.1; cf. Tac. *Ann.* XIII.27.

[5] E.g. Momigliano 1950b (1969): 239ff., Hadot 1969: 80–1, Cooper and Procopé 1995: xxv–xxvi.

[6] Persaeus (D.L. VII.36); Cleanthes (D.L. VII.175); Sphaerus (D.L. VII.178).

stability.[7] The new political system designed by Augustus, while claiming constitutional continuity with the old, was actually an unavowed autocracy with a royal family and an imperial court.

The career of Seneca himself illustrates how things had changed. Born in Corduba in Spain of Italian immigrant stock, Seneca had his senatorial career interrupted by an eight year period of exile because of a liaison with one of the emperor's sisters and was recalled in AD 49 through the intervention of another of Caligula's sisters, now married to the emperor Claudius. Agrippina wanted him to tutor her son Nero in rhetoric.[8] However much his attainment of the consulship from non-senatorial beginnings might seem to parallel the career of Cicero, in the pages of Tacitus Seneca ascribes his rise to power to Nero: 'You have heaped on me enormous influence and immeasurable wealth so that I often think to myself, "Am I, sprung from equestrian and provincial origin, counted among the leaders of state?"' (*Ann.* XIV.53). Indeed Seneca could exercise far more political influence as adviser to Nero than as a senior senator. The new system, relying, as it did, on a disjunction between constitutional forms and the practical workings of government, did not suggest that analysis of the constitutional forms was the key to understanding and reforming government and society.

That does not mean that Seneca's writings are only concerned with individual ethics. Indeed, no reader of Seneca can fail to see how much his practical interest in public life and political events was reflected in what he wrote. Not only does he explicitly claim in *de Clementia* that Stoic doctrine was an appropriate source of advice for *principes* (*Clem.* II.5.2), but he elsewhere speaks candidly of the difficulties faced by imperial *amici* in trying to tell the Princeps the truth (*Ben.* VI.32). The numerous examples he draws from recent Roman history reveal a clear conception of how a Princeps should treat senators and *equites*, conspirators and sycophants. Moreover, his works, like Cicero's, are largely addressed to men engaged in public affairs, to senators and equestrian officials.[9] In fact, Seneca frequently subjects to ethical scrutiny areas of conduct that are more social than individual, more public than private: the exercise of free speech at the imperial court; the spirit in which to exercise jurisdiction; the need

[7] Note the sour remark of Tacitus in *Ann.* IV.33.1 (quoted by Wiedemann, in ch. 25 p. 520 n.7 above) in comparison to the belief of Polybius in the relative durability of the mixed constitution (VI.10.11–14, 18) and the even greater optimism of Cicero (*Rep.* I.69).

[8] Dio Cassius LX. 8.5, Tac. *Ann.* XII.8.2, XIV.55.3. For his attempt to secure recall earlier by writing the *Consolatio ad Polybium*, see p. 544 below.

[9] See below, p. 545. The *ad Polybium* is addressed to a freedman serving the emperor in an official capacity.

for discrimination in supporting candidates for office or in receiving, when in office, financial contributions towards official games; the political circumstances in which it is right to enter or withdraw from public life, or indeed from life altogether.

Only if political thought and, indeed, political theory are not conceived in too narrow a sense, can Seneca's contribution be understood. For it is a substantial contribution and continuous with Cicero's, but its affinities are less with Cicero's earlier works of formal political philosophy and more with the *pro Marcello* and with *de Officiis*. In *de Clementia*, addressed to Nero as Princeps, Seneca went further than the *pro Marcello*, addressed to Caesar the Dictator, in exploiting the potential of political eulogy for theoretical exposition,[10] and in *de Beneficiis*, as doubtless in his lost *de Officiis*, Seneca provided a code of social morality for the members of the Roman governing class like Cicero's but added to it, through paradox and hyperbole, a certain hortatory thrust.[11]

Seneca's political thinking also resembles Cicero's in being heavily indebted to Roman political concepts and ideals. It is well to remember that even in *de Re Publica* Cicero had rated abstract Platonic conceptions below the traditional Roman distrust of institutionalized education and the traditional Roman faith in the historical evolution of their political institutions,[12] while in *de Legibus* he was trying to adjust existing Roman institutions to meet an ideal standard of natural law. Similarly, Seneca's *de Beneficiis*, though ultimately based on Stoic ideas about universal nature and human nature, also raises to the level of theory the concepts and standards of Roman society. To such an extent is this the case that the scale and depth of Seneca's achievement can only be appreciated when set alongside less theoretical Roman thinkers of the period. Of these the Roman historians and jurists receive separate treatment in this volume, but the younger Pliny will be treated here. His *Panegyricus* exhibits interesting points of comparison with *de Clementia*, while his *Letters* make contact with Seneca's treatment, in *de Beneficiis* and elsewhere, of upper class social morality.

The allusions throughout Seneca's works to the basic tenets of Stoic philosophy leave no room for doubt about his grasp of the whole Stoic system of interlocking doctrines. Of these the logical branch is not represented in his surviving works and fragments, but he wrote a number of works on physics (and metaphysics) and his output in ethics is

10 Griffin 1976 (1992): 149–50.

11 For paradox in *de Beneficiis*, see Inwood 1995.

12 *Rep*. IV.3; I.70; II.2–3, 21–22.

voluminous. The rhetorical teacher and writer Quintilian, a younger contemporary from a different part of Spain, although severely critical of his style, had to admit that Seneca knew a lot and worked hard. When Quintilian adds, 'in philosophy he did not take enough trouble, but he was nonetheless an outstanding castigator of vice' (*Inst.* x.1.129),[13] he probably means that Seneca, unlike his hero Cicero, never composed a systematic account of the three branches of philosophy. Instead he either treated selected topics in great detail, exploring all their ramifications, or he moved from one topic to another in a leisurely fashion, as in the *Natural Questions*, or with great rapidity, as in the *Moral Letters*. Thus it is not surprising that the area of ethics that dealt with law and the organization of human society is touched on piecemeal in the letters and in various other works as part of a discussion on anger, or on peace of mind, or on benefits, or on the apolitical life.[14] The nearest Seneca came to devoting a complete work to a central political topic is *de Clementia*, and even this work, although it starts by describing the obligations and duties of a virtuous ruler, is concerned for over half its length with the analysis and inculcation of the one virtue from which it takes its title.

1 *De Clementia*

Seneca never explicitly describes how the particular topics he treats relate to the fundamental doctrines of Stoicism, nor does he clearly locate them within that logically structured system. Nonetheless, the basic tenets which underpin them often emerge. In *de Clementia* and *de Beneficiis* the two fundamental and interrelated ideas are divine providence and the social nature of man – inter-related because, as Seneca makes clear, providence provides security for its favourite creation, the human animal, by encouraging him to live with others in an organized and harmonious society.[15]

Book I of *de Clementia* treats many themes that had featured in the

[13] Quint. *Inst.* x.1.125–31: 'plurimum studii, multa rerum cognitio'(128); 'in philosophia parum diligens, egregius tamen vitiorum insectator fuit (129)'. Aulus Gellius (xii.2.1) writing half a century later, says that some thought his learning common and plebeian, others that he was not without learning and a knowledge of his subject.

[14] The works involved are *de Ira*, *de Tranquillitate Animi*, *de Otio*, *de Beneficiis*, and the *Epistulae Morales*. The authors of the volume on Seneca in the series Cambridge Texts in the History of Political Thought chose to include *de Ira*, *de Otio*, selections from *de Beneficiis*, and *de Clementia* (Cooper and Procopé 1995: xxv).

[15] *Ben.* iv.18.2–4, iv.17.1–4, vi.23.3–4, cf. *Clem.* ii.5.2. The link is perhaps implied in Cic. *Fin.* iii. 68. On the two ultimately linked Stoic approaches to justice via metaphysics and via human nature, see Schofield 1995b: 191–212.

Hellenistic works *On Kingship* about the virtuous ruler. 'Have I of all mortals found favour and been chosen to serve on earth in place of the gods?', Nero is made to say (I.1.2). Even if this vague expression is meant to indicate selection by the gods,[16] there is no question of unrestricted rule by divine right. Though the ruler has power comparable to the gods over individuals and nations (I.1.2, 5.7), his position also imposes obligations. He must imitate their justice, beneficence and clemency in using it (I.5.7, 7, 26.5); he must be to his citizens as he would wish the gods to be to him (I.7.1). In addition, he must suffer constraints on his conduct and his speech so as to behave in a way appropriate to his position. This is the 'noble servitude' of supreme rule, a traditional formula attributed to one of the Macedonian kings.[17] If he rules well the ruler is entitled, not only to the support and protection of his subjects, but to veneration and worship like the gods (I.19.8). He is not, however, a god: he takes second place to them in this veneration (I.19.9) and is a 'man set over men' (I.7.2). The ruler is not himself divine, and there is therefore no real connection between this idea and the imperial cult, though the idea of earning veneration by meritorious conduct is also implicit in the Roman custom of deifying a worthy emperor after his death. Rather, Seneca's ideas have their roots in the Stoic paradox 'Only the wise man is king', for the wise man through his virtue is on a par with the gods except for his more limited time and means for the exercise of virtue. It is for his virtue, and on condition of that virtue, that Seneca's ruler deserves veneration even while alive.[18]

What of the terrestrial means by which god's deputy is chosen? In *de Clementia*, as elsewhere, Seneca views hereditary succession with equanimity,[19] but he is in fact indifferent to the way in which the ideal ruler achieves power: 'No one could imagine anything more becoming to a ruler than mercy', he says, 'whatever the manner and whatever the legal basis of his accession to power over other men' (I.19.1). Nor is legitimacy a concern for the ruler once in power, for there are no legal restraints on what he can do. The gods have given him their own power to give and to

[16] The vagueness of the expression is deliberate according to Adam 1970: 49–50. Griffin 1976 (1992): 148 n.2 supports the idea that selection by the gods is implied, comparing Plin. *Pan.* 80.4, which is, however, more explicit. *Clem.* I.21.2 'the great gift of granting and taking away life, which the gods have given him' supports the idea.

[17] *Clem.* I.8.1; Aelian *Ver. Hist.* II.20.

[18] A practice Seneca refers to in *de Clementia* itself (I.10.3). For further discussion, Griffin 1976 (1992): 219–21.

[19] I.11.4, cf. *Ben.* IV.31–2. Pliny was to combine the idea of selection by the gods (*Pan.* 52.6, 80.4–5) with the methods of adoption and hereditary succession in his *Panegyricus* 5, 8, 94.

take away life (I.21.2). Nero is made to boast, 'I watch over myself *as though* the laws, which I have summoned from decay and darkness into the light, will call me to account' (I.1.4). It is his own choice to observe them, and he can, and should, use his power to save lives in defiance of the law (I.5.4). His power is compared not only to that of the gods, but to that of a father (and the Roman *patria potestas* legally conferred the power of life and death over children (I.15.1)) and to that of a slave-owner.[20] This is clearly the 'irresponsible rule which none but the wise man can sustain', as Chrysippus characterized kingship (D.L. VII.122).

The metaphor of the mind and the body, which the Stoics applied to the relation between divine reason (*logos*) or providence and the world, Seneca applies to the relation of ruler to the commonwealth (*res publica*).[21] It clearly rules out any idea that the ruler might share power or even exercise the same type of power as any of his subjects.[22] The metaphor, however, carried no presumption that the form of government should be monarchy. Indeed Cicero had said that 'kings, military commanders, magistrates, senators and popular assemblies govern citizens and foreign subjects as the mind governs the body' (*Rep.* III.38). Seneca, it is true, in a problematic passage of *de Beneficiis* criticized Brutus for killing Julius Caesar 'contrary to Stoic teaching, because he feared the name of king, when the best form of government is under a just king' (II.20), but there is little evidence elsewhere for such a clear Stoic preference.[23] In *de Clementia*, Seneca merely says that natural law lays down that a king should, like the 'king' of the bees, have no sting.[24] The point being made is not that kingship is the form of government decreed by nature, but that nature decrees what the correct character and behaviour of the king (once he exists) should be. Indeed Seneca shows a deliberate indifference to the title of his ruler. Not only is Nero offered advice suitable to '*principes* or kings' (II.5.2), not only does Seneca alternate the words *rex* and *princeps* in

[20] Cf. *Ben.* III.18.3 where the power of kings, generals and slave-owners is described as equivalent, and absolute over their subordinates.

[21] *Clem.* I.5.4; cf. Cic. *Rep.* III.38 vs. Arist. *Pol.* 1254b5. Note that the analogy had also been applied in the Republic by Cicero to the relations between the laws and the state (*Clu.* 146) which suggests that, when applied to the ruler, it approximates to the strong sense of the ruler as the incarnation of law (νόμος ἔμψυχος): see Griffin 1976 (1992): 138 n.5.

[22] Cf. Tac. *Ann.* I.12.3: 'he had not asked the question so that there should be a division of what could not be separated, but so that he [the Princeps] should admit that the *res publica* has one body and must be ruled by one mind'.

[23] Moreover, Brutus was in fact not a Stoic but a follower of Antiochus of Ascalon's Old Academy. For an attempted explanation of the passage, Griffin 1976 (1992): 203–6. Cf. also Sedley 1997.

[24] Arist. *HA.* V.553b denies this feature and Plin. *Nat.* XI.52 says it is controversial. D.Chr. *Or.* IV.62–3 has Seneca's comparison, and at III.50 he infers from the organization of cattle and bees that the rule of one strong man over his inferiors is natural for man.

the course of his discussion (I.7.1, 13, 16.1), but he uses the formula '*principes* and kings and whatever other title guardians of the public order may bear' (I.4.3).

Constitutional form is also irrelevant to another idea central to Seneca's conception of the ideal ruler. That is the traditional contrast between the king and the tyrant (I.11.4–13). Seneca does not draw the contrast along Platonic lines of rule according to law or not according to law (*Politicus* 301–2), but of virtuous or vicious behaviour, and clemency versus cruelty in particular. Seneca in fact states explicitly that a tyrant and a king (the good ruler) are the same in power, but the king exercises control over himself for the public good (I.11.4). Thus Sulla, whatever his respect for the constitution, could be called a tyrant, while the tyrant Dionysius I of Syracuse was better than most kings (I.12.1–3).

Though there is no external constraint of law or constitution on the ideal ruler, his position imposes specific duties (I.14.1), as do all the roles that individuals assume in society.[25] Among them is that of encouraging virtue in his subjects by example (II.1.3–4): 'from the head comes the health of the body' (II.2.1). The ruler must try to cure vice and to restore the health of his citizens by gentle treatment, giving an example of kindness even when chastisement proves necessary (I.16.1–17, 22). The virtue which the ruler inculcates was traditionally thought of as virtue in general, and Seneca contains a hint of that idea (II.1.4), but his theme demands that he emphasize clemency in particular.

Seneca's decision to stress the virtue of clemency stems in large measure, as will appear, from the contemporary political situation, for this quality was bound to assume prominence in the mind of an adviser to Nero. But he makes plain its relevance to the function of human society in general, as the Stoics saw it: 'no school is kinder, more lenient, more philanthropic, or more concerned for the common good, so that it is its avowed object to be of use and help and to regard not merely self-interest, but the interest of each and all' (II.5.2). The concept of *clementia* has no exact equivalent in Greek, but one aspect of it is covered by the Greek term *philanthrōpia* (love of humanity). The ruler by encouraging this virtue then works with divine providence to strengthen the bonds of human society, for man is a social creature born for the common good (I.3.2). Indeed even on Epicurean premises, Seneca argues, clemency is the virtue most appropriate to man (I.3.2). But it is the man in power who has the

[25] Sen. *Ep.* 94.1, 3, 11, 14–15; cf. Marcus Aurelius III.5. Seneca likens the imperial role via the Princeps' title *pater patriae* to that of a father (I.14.2) and distinguishes it from that of a slave-owner, however kind (I.18.1).

most opportunities to employ it – in overlooking injuries to himself, in sparing the enemy in foreign or civil war (I.20–1) and in punishing wrongs done to others (I.22–4).[26]

Seneca had already touched on these themes in the three books *On Anger* addressed to his brother Annaeus Novatus, a senator like himself who later, under his adoptive name of L. Junius Gallio Annaeanus, was to encounter St Paul while governor of the province of Achaea. Seneca stressed how this vice, deplorable in a private individual, became in an absolute ruler destructive to others and dangerous to himself (III.16.2).[27] He had shown how the habit of anger drives out clemency and leads to cruelty (II.5), and presented his reader with grisly examples of foreign kings, Roman generals and governors, and the emperor Caligula (I.18.3–6; I.19.3; III.16.3–19). Seneca's skill in exploring tyranny in general is demonstrated by his tragedies, but in the treatise he could, more particularly, stress how cruelty could damage the loyalty of Rome's foreign subjects (II.34.4) and lead to imperial assassination (I.20.8–9). Starting from the natural basis of human society in *philanthrōpia*, he had argued that anger should not accompany even deserved and necessary punishment, which a ruler should use to reform offenders, deter wrong-doers and protect society (I.5–6; I.19.2, 19.7).

The very overlapping of themes with a treatise devoted to one vice brings out the originality of *de Clementia*. For the work combines the study of a particular virtue with themes traditional in writings on kingship. The fact that the virtue, though akin to the social virtue of justice, is not identical with it, underlines the message that the most important things in securing good government are not the form of constitution and the provision of legal restraints, but the right education to ensure good character in the ruler and the right advice to encourage him in the best use of his power. Seneca had been personally committed for some time to providing both of these for the young ruler, and one of the purposes of *de Clementia* was to give a practical demonstration of the way in which he was using praise combined with admonishment to keep Nero on course. Seneca had prepared himself well for his task. *On Anger* had specifically addressed the education of children of the privileged class. 'We must work neither to encourage anger in them nor to blunt their native gifts . . . It [the spirit] rises when praised and given confidence in itself; but these

[26] Cf. the connections made by Cicero, in his exposition of Stoicism doctrine, between φιλανθρωπία, the protection of the weak, and the duties of men who have the resources to protect others (*Fin.* III.66).

[27] *Acts* 18.11–17. Cicero had made the point in writing to his brother Quintus when he was governing Asia (*Q.Fr.* I.1.37).

very factors engender arrogance and irritability. We must guide the child between the two extremes, using now the curb, now the spur . . . At any victory or praiseworthy action, we should allow him to hold himself high but not to swagger, for joy leads to exultation, and exultation to conceit and an exaggerated opinion of oneself' (II.21.1–5).[28]

The relevance of *de Clementia* to its contemporary Roman context explains other original features: the paramount importance which Seneca attributes to the role of clemency in criminal jurisdiction, and the precision with which he defines its relation to the determination of penalties in particular. The explanation is to be sought in the political circumstances of Nero's early years of rule when the work was composed. *Clementia* is a virtue exercised towards those inferior in power (I.5.6, II.3.1). In Republican Rome it was a recognized virtue of members of the governing class, displayed mainly towards foreign enemies,[29] but it sprang into prominence with the propaganda efforts of Julius Caesar to win over his Roman opponents during the civil war. Under the dictatorship Cicero instinctively saw the appropriateness of Hellenistic works on kingship and used them in speeches like the *pro Marcello* and the *pro Ligario* to celebrate the Greek virtues that approximate to the Roman *clementia*: *epieikeia* (forbearance), *praotēs* (mildness), and *philanthrōpia*.[30] Despite Caesar's end, *clementia* found a place among the four virtues attributed to Augustus on an honorific shield, and it featured in honours to later emperors. Claudius included it in his accession promises,[31] but became in fact notorious for his cruelty and contempt for proper judicial procedure. His judicial abuses were conspicuously ridiculed in Seneca's *Apocolocyntosis*, a satire on Claudius' death in AD 54, in which the dead emperor is held up as a counter-example of the qualities heralded in the new ruler. They were among the abuses specifically renounced by Nero shortly after the accession speech written for him by Seneca.[32] On the traditional dating, *de Clementia* appeared at the end of 55 or in 56.[33]

The incomplete second book, unlike the first, is characterized by a concern with definition and terminological exactitude. It carefully distinguishes clemency from related concepts like pity (*misericordia*), forgive-

[28] Tacitus may well have had this passage in mind when he described how Burrus with his severity and Seneca with his dignified tactfulness controlled the perilous adolescence of the Princeps by directing his deviations from virtue into licensed indulgence (*Ann.* XIII.2).

[29] E.g. Cic. *Off.* I.88. Wirszubski 1950: 150–3 shows its application in the conduct of *principes viri* to other citizens, notably in jurisdiction.

[30] *Marc.* 9, 12, 18; *Lig.* 29–30.

[31] *Res Gestae divi Augusti* 34.2; Josephus *Antiquitates* XIX.246 (ἐπιείκεια).

[32] *Apoc.* 7.5, 12.3.19ff., 10.4, 14.2; Tac. *Ann.* XIII.4.2; Dio Cass. LXI.3.1.

[33] The only real evidence is *Clem.* I.9 where Nero, who was born 15 December 37, is said to have completed his eighteenth year.

ness (*ignoscere*) and pardon (*venia*): *clementia* differs from the first in being an exercise of reason, not an emotional response; from the second and third in that it does not fail to punish what it judges should be punished and does not remit the penalty it believes to be due. Seneca's final definition of clemency is 'moderation which stops short of what could deservedly be imposed' (II.3.2), that is, it involves the choice of the mildest of a range of penalties that could justly be imposed. This definition seems designed to suit the flexible system of *cognitio* which was the procedure used in trials before the Princeps as well as in trials before the Senate, provincial governors and the Prefects in Rome, all of whom would have ample opportunity to follow the emperor's example should he decide to act on Seneca's advice.[34] These courts were not bound to impose penalties laid down by statute, as were the jury courts which dominated the judicial scene in the late Republic, but could take into consideration mitigating factors such as the age of the defendant, as well as the issues of deterrence, reform and security, each case being examined in the light of the basic principles of punishment.

The political context of *de Clementia* is then the key to its original features, the particular combination of themes chosen and the particular aspects of clement behaviour which are emphasized. It is therefore tempting to see some political message to his reading public in the picture Seneca gives of the blessings acknowledged by Nero's citizens: 'a security deep and abundant, law dominating every type of violation . . . the happiest form of commonwealth which lacks no element of supreme liberty except the licence to ruin itself' (I.1.8). His allusions to the possibility of self-destruction, should the governed lose or refuse the discipline of rule (I.1.1; I.3.5; I.4.2), have historical overtones, for the Principate was designed to avert a repetition of the civil wars in which the Republic had perished. Seneca's development of the metaphor of the ruler as the soul of the commonwealth has in fact a particular relevance to Rome, for he moves from a general metaphysical justification of the ruler's indispensability within a monarchical system to a specific historical justification for the Principate:

> if the great mind of the empire should be withdrawn, such a disaster would be the end of the Roman peace, bringing the fortunes of our great people to ruin. That people will only escape the danger for so long as it can endure the reins. Should it ever snap them or not allow them to be

[34] The newly published *senatus consultum de Cn. Pisone patre* singles out on ll. 90 ff. the virtues of *clementia* and *magnitudo animi* along with *iustitia* in the context of the penalties imposed in a criminal trial (Griffin 1997: 256).

> replaced when shaken loose accidentally, the unit and structure of this mightiest of empires will shatter into many parts, and this city's dominance will come to an end with its obedience . . . For long ago Caesar so imbedded himself in the commonwealth that neither could be withdrawn without the destruction of both. For he needs strength and the commonwealth needs a head. (I.4.1–3)

Neither the organic view of the position of the Princeps in the *res publica* nor the prudential acceptance of the Principate on historical grounds would have shocked his readers.[35] Indeed one of Seneca's aims was to reassure the Roman upper classes that the beneficent character of the new government would be maintained, despite the rumour that Nero had murdered Claudius' son Britannicus and despite the popular notion that the advice of a Stoic adviser would be unrealistically high-minded (II.5.2). Nonetheless, some further aim is suggested by the difference between the message of *de Clementia* and the 'form of the future Principate' sketched before the Senate by Nero in the accession speech which Seneca had composed. There the new regime was said to be based on the authority of the Senate and the consent of the soldiers, with power shared between the Princeps and the Senate which would recover its ancient functions.[36] Though this formula was no more constitutionally precise than the organic metaphor of *de Clementia* and both were ideological statements, they were entirely opposite in spirit.

A clue to this further aim is to be found in the terminological peculiarity of *de Clementia*, whereby Seneca combines the titles *rex* with others including *princeps* in giving his advice (above, pp. 537–8). Though Nero is never explicitly called *rex*, he is called that by implication: 'You think it hard for freedom of speech to be taken from kings' (I.8.1). Yet, after the tyranny of their last king, the Romans hated the title of king (Cic. *Rep*.II.52), and Augustus is said to have taken the name Augustus when he realized that to take the name of Romulus would suggest monarchical ambitions (Dio Cassius LIII.16.7). Seneca must be deliberately urging his reading public – a wider educated group, presumably, than the senatorial audience of the accession speech – to concentrate on the reality of the Principate, not the euphemistic title. He tries to combine frank acceptance of the Principate on historical grounds with advocacy of a new ideology: instead of pretending that an approximation of the old Republic

[35] Cf. Tac. *Ann*. I.12.2 (quoted at p. 537 n.22 above) for a senator using the organic metaphor of mind and body.

[36] Tac. *Ann*. XIII.4. The stress on abuses of jurisdiction is, however, common to both works.

still survived and trying to hold the Princeps to that model of conduct, let us accept that we have a monarch and set before the Princeps the qualities of ideal kingship. *De Clementia* itself is a contribution towards that end, teaching the Princeps that if he exercises his absolute power virtuously, he will be rewarded with praise, support and safety. Not surprisingly, his enemies explicitly held Seneca responsible when, in the event, Nero seemed to grasp what his mentor said about his merits and about the absolute extent of his power, but not what Seneca taught about the need for self-discipline: they labelled him a 'tyrant-trainer' (*turannodidaskalos*).

2 Seneca's eulogies and Pliny's *Panegyricus*

A more conventional eulogy of the Princeps is to be found half a century later in Pliny's panegyric on the emperor Trajan.[37] After Nero had been declared a public enemy by the Senate and driven to commit suicide, Rome again suffered the horrors of civil war until Vespasian won a conclusive victory in AD 69, thereby establishing the Flavian dynasty. Pliny pursued a successful senatorial career under Vespasian's sons and, after Domitian's murder, under Nerva and Trajan. The published speech is an expanded version of Pliny's actual speech of thanks to the Princeps for his consulship, delivered before the Senate in AD 100. The fact that such a custom was already established under Augustus,[38] and by a decree of the Senate (*Pan.* 1.2, 4.1–2), shows the political realities, for formally Pliny had been elected by the Senate and People. Moreover, in urging on Trajan, often through the counter-example of the tyrant Domitian, the senatorial ideal of a Princeps, Pliny advocates the voluntary adoption of a style of rule that masks the reality of his power: this is *civilitas*, behaving like a citizen among other citizens or, as a later Greek writer put it, '*as if* under a Republic'.[39] Whereas Seneca was moved by the counter-example of Claudius to concentrate on jurisdiction, Pliny was inspired by detestation of Domitian to preach accessibility and appreciation of talent, discouragement of flattery, refusal of excessive honours.

Like Seneca Pliny instructs through praise: 'I must obey the decree of the Senate which has declared that, under the form of a vote of thanks delivered by the voice of the consul, good rulers should recognize their own deeds and bad ones learn what theirs should be' (4.1). Trajan is praised for his simple style of life, for showing respect for the Senate and

[37] For its character, see Radice 1968 and Fedeli 1989. [38] Ovid *Ex Ponto* IV.4.35 (AD 8).
[39] Dio Cassius LVII.11.3. On *civilitas*, see Wallace-Hadrill 1982: 32–48.

senators, for going through the lengthy formal procedures of election to the consulship. The content of the praise is more personal and concrete than Seneca's. Trajan's actual career is briefly traversed (9). Pliny is more explicit than Seneca in saying that Trajan was selected by the gods (1.3–5), and he applauds the particular procedure by which the divine will took effect, namely adoption by his immediate predecessor Nerva (94.4) – which does not prevent him from praying at the end that Trajan should be succeeded by a son of his own, with adoption under Jupiter's guidance as a second best (94). Like Seneca Pliny invokes the title of *pater patriae* in describing the Princeps' benevolent style of rule. Pliny's emperor too is said to be pre-eminent in virtue, but Pliny emphasizes that Trajan is regarded and regards himself as one among equals (21.4). His moral example is expressly contrasted with the oppressive moral legislation of Domitian (45.6), and the contrast between tyranny and kingship appears as the replacement of *dominatio* by *principatus* (45.3). Most indicative of the difference between the two works, however, is Pliny's comparison of Trajan to those who expelled the Tarquins: as they rid Rome of *reges*, so Trajan rid her of *regnum* (55.7).

Pliny's speech is therefore less theoretical and less original than Seneca's treatise. There is no grounding in conceptions of nature and no novelty in ideology. Though Pliny probably used *de Clementia*, his speech is closer in spirit to Cicero's *pro Marcello*. In fact, Seneca himself had written a piece more in this vein over a decade before *de Clementia*. His *Consolatio ad Polybium*, addressed to one of Claudius' powerful freedmen secretaries, contains indirect eulogy of the emperor (7, 13) who, Seneca hoped, would show him clemency and restore him from exile.[40] It anticipates many of the themes of the later treatise – the absoluteness of Caesar's rule, his enslavement to duty, his moral example, his clemency – but the theoretical underpinnings are missing, and there is more concrete detail: about Claudius' odious predecessor Caligula, about Claudius' conquests, about his scholarship, and about his son and heir.

After the *ad Polybium* and *de Clementia*, Seneca never again wrote so specifically about government, and his incidental allusions to it are neither as positive nor as constructive. He dwells on the way hereditary succession elevates a bloodthirsty Caligula or a ludicrous Claudius.[41] He harps on the loss of freedom that accompanied the end of the Republic, the precise

40 13.2 fixes its composition to shortly before Claudius' British triumph of AD 44 (Dio Cass. LX.23.1).

41 *Ben.* IV.31.2, 32.3: the point is to illustrate the way providence shows gratitude towards the ancestors and descendants of the virtuous.

moment being marked by the death of Cato, who now becomes more of a hero to him than Augustus was in the *Apocolocyntosis* and *de Clementia*.[42] The Principate is now as irredeemable as it was inevitable, and he blames Brutus for killing Caesar in the vain hope 'that liberty could exist where the rewards both of supreme power and of servitude were so great, or that the state could be restored to its former constitution when its ancient ways had been abandoned, and that equality of civic rights and the supremacy of the law could be maintained when he had seen thousands of men at war to decide not whether but to which of two masters they would be slaves' (*Ben*.II.20.2). These views are the conventional ones of the Roman governing class for which the Principate was a necessary evil, all too prone to turn into tyranny on the despised Oriental model.[43]

3 *De Beneficiis*

Seneca's most creative thinking went into working out principles of conduct for individuals of the higher social classes. His addressees were either senators like himself,[44] or more often *equites*, the class from which Seneca originally came and in which his younger brother Annaeus Mela elected to stay. But most of these too had public careers, for one of the important developments of the imperial system was to employ *equites* in public positions, as financial agents of the Princeps like Lucilius, procurator of Sicily,[45] as administrators like Seneca's father-in-law Pompeius Paulinus, Prefect of the Corn Supply,[46] or as commanders of troops in Rome like Annaeus Serenus, Prefect of the Fire Brigade.[47]

Among Seneca's extant works, the one that is closest in spirit to Cicero's *de Officiis* is *de Beneficiis*, composed between 56 and 64.[48] The metaphysical foundations of this work are similar to Cicero's and to those of *de Clementia*: divine providence and the social nature of man. However, Cicero and Seneca exhibit differences of emphasis. Both speak sometimes in terms of nature and sometimes in terms of god or gods in treating the origins of man's innate social instincts. But whereas Cicero speaks more

[42] *Ep*. 95.70, *Prov*.II.10, *Const. Sap*. 2.3, *Tranq. An*. 16.1, *Ep*.24.7, *Ben*. VI.32.4, III.27. *De Providentia* is undatable, see Griffin 1976: 400–1. For the dates of the others, see below pp. 545, 558.

[43] At all periods, however, Seneca described Caligula's tendency to Oriental despotism (*Brev. Vit*. 18.5, *Ben*. II.12.1–2), and at *Clem*.I.10.2 he already describes the advent of the Principate in terms of subjection.

[44] His older brother (above, p. 539) was the addressee of *de Ira* and *de Vita Beata*.

[45] To him *de Providentia*, *Quaestiones Naturales* and the *Epistulae Morales* are addressed.

[46] Addressee of *de Brevitate Vitae*.

[47] To him *de Constantia Sapientis*, *de Tranquillitate Animi*, and *De Otio* are addressed.

[48] For the date, see Griffin 1976 (1992): 399.

often in terms of the laws of nature or of natural law, Seneca prefers to speak in terms of god or gods.[49] Seneca's divine providence is thus more personalized, and he can make more of the injunction to imitate the gods. Whereas Cicero alludes to the benefits of the gods (*Off.* II.11) and to our duty to maintain the social fellowship they have ordained (II.11, III.28), for Seneca their beneficence is a model from which correct human conduct can be inferred (*Ben.* I.1.9–11, IV.25). Their example teaches us to give without thought of repayment, to include even the ungrateful when excluding them would mean depriving the good as well (IV.28); to benefit the unworthy in order to honour their ancestors (IV.30–3);[50] to feel grateful for a share in communal benefits provided they are not given self-interestedly (VI.20–3).

Another difference concerns the old debate as to whether natural sociability or practical necessity directed man to live in communities. Cicero makes it clear that the social instinct of *oikeiōsis*, a manifestation of the natural law implanted as reason in man, directs us to form communities in which we learn to receive help from our fellow-men (*Off.* I.12, II.14), moving on to form cities in order to protect our possessions (II.73). The result is that we meet all our needs by exchanging benefits (II.15). He denies that man embarked upon communal life *in order* to provide for life's necessities (I.158).[51] That is to reverse cause and effect. Seneca agrees with Cicero that the social instinct and the conviction that we should behave virtuously towards our fellow-men are not devised by man to cope with his weakness, but are innate, and that the good effects in terms of help and security result from them. But for Seneca divine providence gave man reason and the instinct to fellowship *in order* that he could live in security through an exchange of services (IV.18). Therefore Seneca can reconcile the two approaches to the origins of society by attributing to the divine the motive of helping man cope with his weakness, while making social virtue an end in itself for man (IV.17–18; VI.23.3–4). Some of the most stirring passages in Seneca convey his vision of divine concern for man, but the glimpse of a personalized deity is not just a rhetorical device deployed for greater pedagogic effect or a 'mere metaphor', as has been said of Cleanthes and the Old Stoa.[52] If the argument above is sound, it seems to have issued in a new conception of the origins of society.

Seneca also wrote a *de Officiis*, but it is lost.[53] It might have helped to

[49] Cicero does speak of the gods in *Off.* III.28, I.160, II.11. Seneca speaks of nature in e.g. *Ben.* IV.17.

[50] See p. 544, n.41 above.

[51] As Plato (*Rep.* II 369b) and the Epicureans held. The view is attributed to Carneades in the speech against natural justice in Cicero's *de Re Publica* III.23.

[52] Edelstein 1966: 34.

[53] A phrase is quoted by the grammarian Diomedes (*Gramm.Lat.* I.366.13).

explain why he thought the subject of giving and receiving benefits worth a treatise of seven books to itself, when Cicero made it a subordinate topic.[54] Cicero saw beneficence and liberality as closely linked to justice: together they made up the fourth cardinal virtue, thought of as justice in the broader sense (I.152) or as the composite virtue of sociability.[55] It is true that as this social virtue is 'the mistress and queen of all the virtues' (III.28), the exchange of benefits does bulk large in *de Officiis* as that aspect of the social virtue which holds together the fellowship of men and the communal life (I.20, 22). But for Seneca, who similarly says, 'Our task is to talk about benefits and to regulate a practice which more than anything else holds human society together' (*Ben*. I.4.2), the relation of beneficence to justice does not seem to be closer than its relation to the other virtues (e.g. III.18.4, II.31) or to virtue as a whole (I.1.12, 15.2, IV.1.3, 10, 21.3, III.18.4).[56] Whereas for Cicero liberality and beneficence must be exercised in accordance with the norms of justice (I.42, II.71),[57] for Seneca conferring a benefit is an act of virtue which exhibits, like other virtuous acts, the characteristics of rationality and appropriateness to the giver, the recipient, the time, the place and the circumstances (II.16.1, IV.10), and derives its value from the intention of the giver (IV.21.3).

Why Seneca regards the giving, receiving and returning of benefits as so fundamental to human society is made clear by what he indicates of the relationship between *beneficia* and *officia*. Though conferring benefits is a duty of man as a man (IV.12.5) and the characteristics of rationality and fulfilment through intention alone (I.1.8) are those of *officium* in general, there is a distinction between a benefit and a duty, though it is an elusive one. The network of *gratia* is set off by an act of beneficence which the giver is under no obligation to perform, but the return of that *beneficium* is a matter of *officium*, that is, the fulfilment of an obligation (III.18.1).[58] Receiving a benefit creates a relationship of friendship which is then con-

[54] Inwood 1995: 243–5 argues that Seneca only seems to be unusual in devoting seven books to the topic because of the accidental loss of other works by Stoics and other philosophers. But he points out that the topic was usually discussed in works περὶ καθήκοντος (rendered *de officiis* by Cicero) or περὶ χάριτος (*de gratia*). Hecato is cited frequently by Seneca but it is uncertain if the work he used was the attested περὶ καθήκοντος or a hypothetical περὶ χάριτος.

[55] See Atkins, in ch. 24 section 7.2 above; also Atkins 1990: 260–6.

[56] *Ben*.VI.41.2 does say 'quanto melius ac iustius' and *Ep*. 81.19–21 compares gratitude to justice as something which is vulgarly thought only to affect others, but then adds, 'quod virtutum omnium in ipsis pretium est'.

[57] Atkins 1990: 261.

[58] Though Seneca gives this as the view of others, his terminology elsewhere appears to endorse it (*Ben*. VI.18.1–19.1). Yet there are exceptions, e.g. *Ep*. 81.7 ('officii meminisse'); *Ben*. II.18 (the exchange of benefits is an 'ex duobus officium' like the obligations of parent and child, husband and wife). The distinction of III.18.1 is accepted by Hellegouarc'h 1963: 164–5. The warning of Saller 1982: 17–21 is salutary. Cic. *Off*. I.48 might suggest that the same act could be a *beneficium* from the point of view of the receiver and an *officium* from the point of view of the giver. For a similar asymmetry, see below, p. 548.

solidated by further interchanges of benefit (II.18.5, 21.2, cf. *Clem.* I.9.11). So whereas family connections determine our duties to each other, the prime way of bringing into relationship with each other those not related by birth or marriage is through the exchange of benefits. The maintenance of this network is crucial for Seneca, as for Cicero (*Off.* II.63), but Seneca attaches far less importance to the utility of beneficence to the giver in terms of glory, influence and power.[59] For him it is the maintenance of the 'game', that is, the social process, that is valuable for human society, and the moral gain of conferring benefits that is valuable for the individual. The 'player' can help to make the game a success by giving his benefit to the right person, but ultimately the material return is unimportant to him. The recipient, however, regards himself as bound to repay, regardless of the benefactor's attitude (I.10.4, VII.16, 22). This asymmetry in the moral code imposed on donor and recipient facilitates the maintenance of the social practice, for donors are not discouraged from giving by the ingratitude of recipients, while recipients are not afraid to receive because they lack the means for material repayment (II.35.2–5, VII.16). The process is therefore not vulnerable to fortune on the mental level, where intention is what counts, and although it is vulnerable on the material level, where a physical repayment is made by the recipient in addition to the gratitude which already fulfils his obligation (II.33–4), the attitudes here advocated maximize its chance of survival. For donors continue to hand over tangible benefits and recipients do their utmost to reciprocate tangibly.[60]

Seneca's advice is sometimes criticized as unrealistic. Exchange of favours, it is said, was a central mechanism of Roman society and, though there was an elaborate etiquette governing it, most Romans could not be expected to be more altruistic than other people.[61] In part the objection misconstrues the style of discourse and the pedagogic technique of hyperbole.[62] Seneca himself warns us against this in a discussion of the precept to forget the benefits we have conferred while remembering those we have received: 'Certain things we teach in an exaggerated form so that they result in due measure. When we say "He [the donor] must not remember [giving a benefit]", we really mean "He must not trumpet it, nor boast, nor be heavy-handed about it"' (VII.22.1–2). Cicero has

[59] Cic. *Off.* II.32, 65, 69–70, 71fin. For Seneca a benefit should not be given 'utilitatis causa' (for the sake of expediency): *Ben.* IV.12.2, cf. IV.20.2, 18.4; *Ep.* 81.19.

[60] The instrumental importance of the code shows in IV.18.4. See Inwood 1995: 259.

[61] Macmullen 1986: 522. This article treats the role of *beneficia* as 'instruments of control'.

[62] Diogenes the Cynic used the image of the chorus leader who deliberately sets the note a bit high in hopes of getting it just right (D.L.VI.35).

similarly been accused of giving unrealistic advice in *de Officiis* because, in exhorting his son and, through him, youth in general, he deliberately chose the more uncompromising Stoic morality rather than the perfectly respectable Academic and Peripatetic perspective (III.20). In fact, the negative examples in both writers show their awareness of the more sordid realities of life.[63] Though Seneca seems more abstract, more universal and less specifically Roman than Cicero, because he frequently raises the level of his discourse to that of the Wise Man and is concerned to emphasize the unimportance of material repayment next to intention, *de Beneficiis* too is revealing about the social *mores* of the Roman elite. Indeed, when compared, the two works indicate that there was substantial continuity in this respect between the Republic and the Principate.[64]

We still hear about members of the Roman governing class rescuing friends from the pirates (*Off.* II.55; *Ben.* I.5.4, VII.15.1); defending men on capital charges (*Off.* II.66; *Ben.* III.9.2, IV.12); helping their peers with the expenses of advancement (*Off.* II.62; *Ben.* II.21.5) or helping to pay debts (*Off.* II.55; *Ben.* III.8.2); exercising patronage with regard to magistracies, priesthoods and provinces (*Off.* II.67; *Ben.* I.5.1, IV.3). What is noticeably missing in Seneca is the emphasis that Cicero gives to public liberality – euergetism – as opposed to generosity to individuals: whereas Cicero's peers were motivated by political ambition to adorn Rome with buildings, only Agrippa is mentioned by Seneca as having contributed public buildings in the city (*Off.* II.60; *Ben.* III.32.4). For communal benefits in Rome were now dominated, directed and largely provided by the Princeps.

This is just one sign of the fact that the existence of a Princeps introduced new elements to be included in the code covering beneficence. Seneca writes with two distinct types of men in mind, the ruler and the ruled. 'He has given me this [office], but gave more to him, and gave sooner to that man' (*Ben.* II.28.1). Most of the Roman examples of generosity concern the Emperors, who are shown giving money to individual senators (I.15, II.8.1, II.27.1–2) or conferring magistracies (I.5.6) or pardoning individuals (III.27, II.12.1), but also making grants of citizenship and immunity to whole peoples (VI.19). Problems of reciprocity arise

[63] Chaumartin 1985 even finds specific criticisms largely aimed at the emperor and his circle.

[64] Saller 1982: 120–43 shows that economic, social and even political patronage by the senatorial aristocracy survived the Republic: the Princeps could not absorb it all and the upper classes often functioned as intermediaries in dispensing patronage. Similar resemblances to Cicero in Quintilian's description of the orator's place in politics are noted by Morgan 1998, who thinks Quintilian means to imply that the form of government is unimportant, provided properly educated men are running it.

here: not only the general question of what gratitude we owe for benefits received as part of a group (VI.19), but the more difficult one of how we can repay at all. Seneca speaks of '*principes* or *reges* whom fortune has placed in positions where they can give many gifts but can receive very few and those very unequal to what has been given'. These men of preeminent power can, however, be repaid in loyalty and services (*Ben.* V.4.2–3). Seneca's own position had made him acutely conscious of the importance of that task.

> I will show you what those at the summit of power are in need of, what the man who possesses everything lacks – someone, in fact, who will tell him the truth, who will deliver him from the constant cant and falsehood that so bewilder him with lies that the very habit of listening to flatteries instead of facts has brought him to the point of not knowing what the truth really is. (*Ben.*VI.30.3)

He also knew the difficulties confronting 'friends of the Princeps'. He says of the respectable Augustus who claimed to regret the loss of his advisers Agrippa and Maecenas, 'It is characteristic of the kingly attitude to attribute the virtue of speaking the truth to those from whom they no longer are in danger of hearing it' (VI.32.4). When Cicero had treated the theme of honest friendship compared to sycophancy, the emphasis was on men like himself being advised and flattered (*Off.* I.91), except when they chose to play the demagogue and flatter the people (*Amic.* 95–9).

Seneca touches on some of the themes of *de Clementia* in delineating the proper demeanour of the Princeps as benefactor: the gifts that please are those that are bestowed unostentatiously and with a look of human kindness by one who, although my superior, puts himself on terms of equality with me (II.13.2–3). The requirement that a *beneficium* be not only properly motivated but done in accordance with reason is specifically applied to the Princeps. Though only the Wise Man can judge correctly when, where, why, how, and to whom benefits should be given (II.16.1, *Ep.* 81.10), others should use their reason to the best of their ability. Augustus and Claudius are juxtaposed as good and bad examples. One senator remarks, 'From the deified Augustus I would rather have the judgment, from Claudius the benefit': that is, to receive from Augustus meant to be rationally judged as deserving; while Claudius gave 'by chance and thoughtless impulse' like a gift of Fortune (I.15.3–6). Tiberius erred in the other direction, for he required impoverished senators to prove their desert as before a judge (II.8.2) and turned a favour into a moral assessment accompanied by rebuke (II.7–8). The anecdote provokes Seneca: 'It is not appropriate even for a Princeps to give in order to humiliate.'[65] In putting so much stress on good judgment in the exercise of liberality and patronage, Seneca is in line with other imperial authors.[66]

Modern scholars, impressed by the lack of institutionalized systems of promotion in Rome, are often tempted to conclude that the Princeps dispensed patronage in return for loyalty and gratitude, not on 'universalistic and rational criteria of seniority and merit (in the modern sense)', and that gifts were 'not deserved', 'not due but magnanimously bestowed'.[67] It would be more accurate to say that patronage was given on the basis of qualities according to which men can be rationally assessed and compared, but the merits considered were not specific skills or experience, but literacy, industry, honesty and good character. For Seneca, it is a source of complaint when the Princeps does not give in accordance with virtue and dutifulness (II.28.2).

Seneca is often vague in his description of benefits, so that it is not clear whether the donor is the Princeps or another (e.g. I.5.1, II.28.1–2). Nor does he envisage 'kings and rulers' as the only persons of power needing frank advice (*Ep.* 123.9). Moreover, to the Princeps himself, as to kings, more ordinary gifts can be given in reciprocation (VII.4.2, III.18.3). Not only did the republican social patterns of upper-class life remain in place, but the etiquette of benefactions between members of that class was applied to relations between them and the Princeps, for, in theory, the Princeps was one among equals, and it was in the interests of all parties concerned that the theory be respected. The utterances of Pliny, a senator entangled in a web of real favours, give us a detailed glimpse of the social ambiguity that Seneca's teaching implies.

4 Pliny's correspondence

Pliny's letters have been described as 'a handbook for the perfect Roman senator. They are not only autobiographical testimony, but are also intended to be didactic, exemplary'.[68] Many of the letters he published (Books I–IX) are letters of recommendation or recount his gifts and favours. They are intended to exhibit the high standards he observed in

[65] Tiberius' practice is regarded with more sympathy by Tacitus (*Ann.* 1.75.3–4), who found Nero's too undiscriminating in his generosity to impoverished senators (*Ann.* XIII.34).

[66] For Tacitus, see n.65 above and *Hist.* 1.52 where Vitellius' generosity is criticized as 'sine modo, sine iudicio'; Fronto *ad M.Caes.* V.37; Dio Cassius LXXII.19 (cf. LII.15.3, 19.1–2); *SHA Hadr.* 10.3–6; Plin. *Pan.* 44.7; *Ep.* X.13.

[67] Quotations from Saller 1982: 110, Cotton 1984: 265.

[68] Veyne 1976 (1990): 9. One may be less disposed to agree with the end of the sentence, 'which falsely makes their author seem highly pleased with himself'. See also Parker 1988.

discharging the 'duties to friends' which he mentions as a special area of obligation, between official duties and those of private life (*Ep.* III.5.19,VII.15.1, IX.37.1). Book X, comprising his correspondence with Trajan, which he probably did not intend to publish,[69] contains letters requesting favours on behalf of himself and others and letters of gratitude, all clearly following the prevailing etiquette punctiliously in order to win imperial approval. These letters then show us the social code, even if we may doubt whether it was as consistently observed as Pliny represents it, even in his own case.

Pliny's description of the code conforms very closely to the exhortations of Cicero and Seneca, but also shows that a generally educated man, even if he was not formally trained in philosophy, could be aware of what philosophers said.[70] Letter V.1 conveys his pleasure in receiving, in recognition of past generosity in the matter of a legacy, a reward 'in reputation' as well as 'good conscience', for the beneficiary has now left him a legacy: 'I am not enough of a Wise Man to be indifferent as to whether recognition and a kind of reward accrues to what I believe to have been a virtuous act' (10–13). The language here is reminiscent of *de Beneficiis* II.33.3 where Seneca explains, 'The first fruit of a benefaction is that of conscience . . . while both one's reputation and the things which might be owed in return are a secondary reward.' Pliny also illustrates qualities which Seneca attributes to the recipient of *de Beneficiis*, whom he uses as an example (V.1.3–5): Pliny himself confirms his benefits by giving more (*Ep.* II.13.9), and he praises the philosopher Artemidorus for being of such a 'generous nature' that he exaggerates the service of his friends (III.11.1).

Pliny knew that his Roman readers would sympathize with his weakness for glory.[71] In Letter I.8 he tackles the problem directly, depicting his own hesitation about publishing a speech he had delivered to a select audience when he dedicated a library built for his native city of Comum. The speech gave the rationale for his generosity, showing that it sprang, not from impulse, but from the rational application of moral principles,

[69] The main reasons for thinking that Pliny did not publish Book X are that the letters finish abruptly during the term of his governorship, that *Ep.* I.1 suggests that he only intended to publish letters by himself, a practice observed except in Book X, and that *Ep.* I.10.9 shows that he regarded letters written as part of professional duties as 'inlitteratissimas'.

[70] Pliny may only have acquired what philosophy he knew through studying rhetoric with Quintilian (Plin. *Ep.* II.14, VI.6), who recommended the reading of philosophers (XII.2.8, X.1.35, 1.123) and believed like Cicero that the deployment of philosophical themes was the province of the orator (I.proem.10–17). But, for political reasons, Pliny was keen to stress his friendship with the Stoic philosophers who had been prosecuted by Domitian and cultivated by Nerva and Trajan (*Ep.* I.5, 10, II.18, III.11, IX.13.1–3).

[71] Tac. *Hist.* IV.6.1: 'the passion for glory is the last from which even philosophers divest themselves'. And on Cicero, see Atkins, in ch. 24 section 7.2 above; also Long 1995: 213–16.

and Pliny says that working over the speech helped him to avoid the regret that can follow impulsive generosity, as Seneca had pointed out (*Ben.* IV.10.2–3). Moreover it reinforced the freedom from avarice that goes with the love of generosity (cf. *Ben.* IV.14.4). Finally, he stresses the excellence of his next generous project, financial help for the rearing of children in Comum: unlike games and gladiatorial contests, this is something popular yet genuinely in the public interest. Here too he is at one with the moralists.[72] The letter incidentally reminds us where the euergetism of the upper classes was channelled under the empire: if Rome was the preserve of the Princeps and the imperial house, others could supply amenities to their native towns.

That Pliny expresses ideals which he expected his readers to share is apparent, not only from his obvious desire for approval, but from the fact that he even published letters which failed to secure the requests made on behalf of his friends. His purpose here was clearly to celebrate his intentions and efforts, not his material benefactions.[73] Moreover, in requesting promotion for his friends, whether from provincial governors or from the Princeps, Pliny often casts his requests in such vague terms that we have to guess what precisely is being requested (e.g. *Ep.* II.13, III.2, X.26, 87). Pliny means to stress that the judgment implicit in a benefaction is more valuable than the benefit: 'for though you grant him the highest office in our power, you could give him nothing better than our friendship' (II.13.10).

Pliny also confirms Seneca's idea that the Princeps is also expected to exercise *iudicium* (*Ep.* IV.8.1, X.13, II.9.2–3). He had praised Trajan in the *Panegyricus* for encouraging industry, integrity, thrift and virtue in giving good men priesthoods and provinces and showing that they enjoyed his friendship and his favourable judgment (44.7–8). He shows that the Princeps is supposed to respect the possibility of reciprocity and the necessity for gratitude, as Seneca had suggested: Trajan, in contrast to his predecessor, acknowledges obligations and confers benefits, not as a 'mighty Princeps', but as a 'not ungrateful friend'.[74] The word 'friend' here points to the way in which the established etiquette of the Republic could be used to mask the realities of power and reinforce the requirements of imperial *civilitas*, for *amicus* had always been used as a euphemism for *cliens*, and Pliny also uses it of his own inferiors in rank or age when recommending them (II.13, III.2, 8, X.87, VI.6). At the other extreme, the

[72] Cic. *Off.* II.56; Sen. *Ben.* I.11–12.1.

[73] Syme 1960 (1979): 477–95.

[74] *Pan.* 60.5–7, cf. *Ep.* X.51 where Pliny writes fulsomely to Trajan of his 'not venturing to respond with equivalent gratitude, however much it may be in my power to do so'.

word *indulgentia*, used frequently of and to the Princeps, might be held to make explicit a relationship of inequality.[75] But a pretence of deference had always been part of upper-class politeness. In fact, Pliny uses similar language to his peers of their generosity,[76] while Trajan speaks of himself and Pliny together 'indulging' the people of Prusa in Bithynia (x.24).

Pliny thus suggests that Seneca's picture of the Roman scene is not unrealistic. He teaches by example an ideal of social relationships that closely resembles Seneca's. What Seneca supplies, and what is totally lacking in Pliny, is the systematic analysis of the code and its grounding in a general theory about the nature of the universe and the nature of man.

The same is true of their remarks about the lowest level of society. For Pliny in *Letter* VIII.16 takes issue with those 'fine men and philosophers' who say that one should not grieve at the death of a slave but treat it as a mere financial loss. He goes on to claim exceptional *humanitas* in allowing his slaves to make wills as part of his conception of the household as a miniature *res publica* where slaves have the kind of privileges that citizens have in the real *res publica*, being allowed to make wills. Though the harsh attitude which Pliny criticizes, and which apparently combines the Stoic prohibition on grief (as a passion) with the non-philosophical idea that a slave was only a possession, has left some traces in Seneca (*Tranq. An.* 11.3; *Ben.* VI.2.3), he normally drew from the Stoic notion that all men were equal by nature (*Cons. Marc.* 20.2; *Clem.* I.18.2) humanitarian conclusions like those of Pliny. In fact, the idea of the *domus* as a miniature *res publica* had already been treated in Seneca's *Letter* 47, one of the most humane statements on slavery preserved from antiquity. Though earlier Stoic philosophers seem to have deduced from the natural equality of man only the most minimal principles of humane treatment, Seneca gave expression to the most advanced views and practices of his own time.[77] Seneca regarded the slave as entitled to everything covered by man's duty to man and as capable of putting even his master under obligation for virtuous acts towards him (*Ben.* III.18, 21, 22). But, as with other social distinctions imposed by fortune not virtue, slavery as an institution is accepted (*Tranq. An.* 8.8–9).

Seneca also advances reasons of expediency for treating slaves well. The size of some slave households made masters feel threatened and, to protect them, the law had made punishment for the murder of the master

[75] E.g. *Ep.* II.13.8, X.4, 5, 10, 12, 13, 26, 51, 87, 94, 106. The view expressed is that of Cotton 1984: 245–266.

[76] *Ep.* IV.15.11, 15.13 (the Senate), cf. *CIL* VIII.20684 where a fellow-citizen of Saldae in Mauretania makes a dedication to an imperial procurator of Hadrian as 'amico indulgentissimo ob beneficia quae in se contulit'.

[77] Griffin 1976 (1992): 257–8, 259, 261, 265–6, 274.

more and more severe. However, the law had also tried, by discouraging excessive cruelty, to diminish the danger to society from slaves driven to desperation. Seneca alludes to the ability of ill-treated slaves to obtain relief, though not redress, from an official (probably the Prefect of the City) by seeking asylum at shrines or the emperor's statue (*Ben.* III.22.3). His own advice to masters is not to make enemies of their slaves by cruelty but to earn their loyalty by kindness (*de Ira* III.5.4; *Ep.* 47.2–9). While the two opposite tendencies in the law are best explained as different approaches to preventing danger to individuals and to society, Seneca's own utterances need not be read as mere cynical advice to his own class on how to reinforce the institution of slavery by encouraging servile acquiescence.[78] The argument from expediency is after all explicitly made; that from humanity is fuelled by a moral concern at least for the moral wellbeing of the master.

5 Seneca on public versus private life

Seneca conveys more strongly than either Pliny or Cicero the moral conflicts that autocracy creates. He reverts time and time again to the question of whether or not one should abstain from public life in certain circumstances, after a number of years, or altogether. It is true that the factors considered include those already canvassed by Cicero and Sallust under the Republic – the evil means needed to fulfil political ambition in a morally corrupt commonwealth,[79] unsuitability through inadequate rank, fortune, talent or health, or outstanding talent for intellectual activity.[80] But the new political conditions also make their appearance, notably in *de Tranquillitate Animi*: danger may prevent freedom of action or speech (4.3, 5.4), so that silent obstinacy may be the only way to serve one's fellow citizens (4.6); the commonwealth may be in such a condition that the good man cannot help (5); a man may be unsuited to public life because he is prone to freedom of speech that may harm him, or because he is prone to arrogant defiance unsuited to court life (6.2).

Though Seneca alludes often to the Stoic expectation that men should serve their fellow-men by entering public life unless there is an impediment, only once in his extant works does he give a systematic treatment of the Stoic theory and its implications. That is in the incomplete essay *de Otio* where, challenged by his addressee Annaeus Serenus (above, p. 545),

78 The view taken by Finley 1980: 121; 178 n. 108 and Bradley 1986: 161–72.
79 Cic. *Off.* 1.69, 71, Sall. *Cat.* 3.3–5, *Jug.* 3–4; cf. Nepos *Att.* 6.2; Sen. *Tranq. An.* 3.2; *Ep.* 118.3.
80 Cic. *Off.* 1.71, 121; Sen. *Tranq. An.* 6.2, 7.2, *de Otio* 6.

Seneca promises to defend his recommendation of a life of private leisure devoted to philosophy and to show that Stoic principles permit total devotion from youth to such study or the passing on of one's duties to others after years of public service (2). Only a lengthy but incomplete discussion of the first topic remains. Here Seneca points out that precepts of the Stoa and the example of its founders allow for a life of contemplation, for the impediments that justify initial abstention or later withdrawal offer considerable scope (3.3), and he adduces the particular causes already mentioned.

Seneca next proceeds to argue that a life of philosophical study, even in the absence of such impediments, fulfils the demand of Stoicism that a man benefit his fellow-men and serve the general interest, for the man who cultivates virtue as his way of life prepares himself morally to benefit others (3.5). He then has recourse to the doctrine of the cosmopolis: there are two *res publicae*, the lesser (one's own commonwealth) and the greater (the whole world) in which we are fellow-citizens with all men and gods. Some serve both, some only one or the other, and we can serve the greater better in leisure by providing god, through our study of moral and natural philosophy, with a witness to his works (4). Moreover, the *summum bonum* advocated by the Stoics is life according to nature, but nature has given man a thirst for knowledge, a position in the centre of the universe from which he surveys it, a body which allows him to bend his head to contemplate the heavens, and a mind that can move on from the sensible world to the truths beyond. It is therefore in accordance with nature for man to spend the short span of life nature has given him in contemplating her. Finally, the Stoa lays down that nature intended us for action and contemplation (cf. *Ep.* 94.45), but to employ the fruits of one's contemplation in the service of humanity by writing and teaching satisfies the requirement (5.8–6).

Seneca's preference for drawing inferences from Stoic first principles, rather than exploring the qualifications attached to their recommendation to participate, is underlined by the last surviving section of the essay (8). Though the section is itself incomplete, Seneca seems to be suggesting that the teaching of Chrysippus, that the Wise Man should not enter politics if the condition of the *res publica* is not suitable, effectively rules out his participation in any terrestrial *res publica* because none of them will tolerate the Wise Man or be tolerable to him. Chrysippus' advice is thus self-contradictory, like saying that the best course is to set sail but not on a sea where shipwrecks commonly occur or there are frequent storms – which is tantamount to praising sailing while forbidding one to weigh anchor.

Nonetheless, it would be wrong to conclude that Seneca rules out political participation – he was about to discuss retirement after active service – or that he dismissed altogether the qualified approach of the Stoics. Rather he particularly disliked the argument from the political circumstances of the state, as is clear from his remark, 'No *res publica* will ever be available to those who search for it *fastidiose* ('arrogantly' or 'fussily)' (8.1), and from the lengthy treatment of this particular impediment in *de Tranquillitate Animi*. There Seneca, giving advice to ordinary imperfect men (not the Wise), and specifically to those already embarked on political life (2.9, 3.1), combats the view of the Stoic philosopher Athenodorus of Tarsus that actual political life is so corrupt that it is always right to withdraw from it (3.1). His own recommendation is to mix leisure with public affairs whenever totally active life is prevented by the activities of fortune or the condition of the state. There are other countries in which to perform the duty of a man, if not a citizen (4.4). However, the emphasis is on one's own commonwealth, and it emerges that pressure of circumstances may reduce one's usefulness to mankind to what Athenodorus had recommended, the mere exemplification of virtue (4.6–7, cf. 3.6) or giving advice to friends (4.3, cf. 3.3, 3.6). The real difference is that Seneca insists that no state is so bad that all honourable action is precluded (4.8–5.3) and therefore objects to the speed and completeness of the withdrawal advocated by Athenodorus: one must show constancy and fulfil one's choice of public life by limiting that life to what is possible. The cosmopolis here is thought of in terms of all men (not gods) and is more like the negative Cynic conception of it, a way of denying that one's own city is the only possible focus of existence.

In the letters to Lucilius retirement from public life to a life devoted to philosophy again emerges, as in *de Otio*, as preferable to the life of civic duty rather than as an impoverishment of that life, as it is in *de Tranquillitate Animi*. This is true for the Wise Man and the imperfect man, but the concern with the right pace and manner of withdrawal is even more to the fore. One must not immediately give in to circumstances (*Ep.* 22.8). One must retire without ostentation, even offering excuses of ill health and laziness rather than admitting to a preference for philosophy and peace (68.1, 3–4). It is dangerous to practise philosophy contumaciously and to use one's virtue as a reproach to the vices of others (103.5, 19.2, 4). The resentment of those in power is mentioned (14.10–11, 14). Seneca's worries emerge clearly from the fact that he devotes a whole letter to arguing 'that it is an error to believe that those who have loyally dedicated themselves to philosophy are stubborn and rebellious, scornful of magistrates, or kings, or of those through whom public affairs are managed' (73.1). The argument is that those who have retired from affairs of state are grateful for the security and peace provided by the ruler who thus enables them to follow their chosen pursuit.

Seneca's preoccupation with the justification and manner of political abstention and withdrawal has its origin in Nero's regime, not in the Stoic system. He himself in AD 62 requested permission from the emperor to withdraw on grounds of ill health and old age, and, when he finally withdrew in 64, he lived like an invalid.[81] His writings on the subject, however, cannot be securely related to his own situation at the time of writing, for that cannot be independently established. *De Tranquillitate Animi* and *de Otio* can at best be fixed between AD 47 and 64, while the letters belong later in 64–5.[82] Moreover, Seneca's concerns seem to be more general than autobiographical. By the time of his retirement in 64, one Stoic senator had been killed in exile after Nero had been persuaded of the seditious tendencies of the sect, and the prominent Stoic senator Thrasea Paetus had absented himself from the Senate.[83] *Letter* 73 suggests that the argument from the bad condition of the state had actually been adduced by Stoic dissidents. In any case, Seneca's fears that defiance would bring philosophy into disrepute were well founded, for just after his death in 65 Stoic senators and philosophers were punished on charges of political opposition.[84]

6 Conclusion

Seneca's writings show that Stoicism did not offer definite directives on the best form of government, or on political conduct, though it provided vocabulary and concepts for analysing possible courses of action and doctrines, as well as precepts and examples from which inferences could be drawn. They show how the fundamental dogmas about divine providence, the social nature of man, the cosmopolis, could be used to illuminate the use of political power, the relationship between ruler and ruled, the obligations of members of the governing class. Seneca's political thought is thus both abstract and concrete, of its time, but universal.

81 Tac. *Ann.* XIV.54, XV.45.3.
82 Griffin 1976 (1992): 316–17; 396; 399.
83 Tac. *Ann.* XVI.22.1.
84 Tac. *Ann.* XV.71, XVI.22: Thrasea's abstention was particularly remarked.

27

Platonism and Pythagoreanism in the early empire

BRUNO CENTRONE

1 Preliminary considerations

The Platonism of the first centuries of the empire does not constitute a single current of thought, still less the work of a school. To refer to Platonist authors from the time of Eudorus (active *c.* 25 BC) until the rise of Neoplatonism the term 'Middle Platonism' is often employed: a historiographical category which poses considerable problems. There is not in fact any single Middle Platonist philosophy, but rather a group of writers who may be described as Platonist by virtue of their allegiance to a nucleus of 'orthodox' positions, contaminated in many instances by Aristotelian and Stoic doctrines, and not the same nucleus in all cases. That is true for political thought too. The authors of most interest from this point of view, Philo of Alexandria (20/15 BC–AD 45/50) and Plutarch of Chaeronea (AD 45–100), despite sharing features in common, stand far apart from each other. For the political thought of other Platonists of the period we do not have sufficient evidence, but there is nothing to suggest political theories of any great originality or with significant contemporary impact.[1] The consolidation of Rome's supremacy on the world stage in the first centuries of the empire certainly did not provide favourable conditions for theoretical political thought to flourish: the apparent inevitability of Roman domination limited the scope for political reflection. It tended to oscillate between wary pragmatism and purely theoretical idealism.

This is exactly the situation reflected in the work of Philo and of Plutarch alike. Both played an active role in the political affairs of their cities, with the principal aim of safeguarding good relations with their

[1] For example Alcinous' *Didaskalikos* (1st or 2nd century AD) contains a single brief chapter on politics (ch. 34), summarizing Plato. See Whittaker 1990, Dillon 1993. For Middle Platonism in general see Dillon 1977.

Roman masters. In neither of the two, however, does theoretical reflection on politics play a big part in their thinking or take on a systematic form. The programmatic and utopian strain in Plato's political thought was certainly unable to exercise any influence in the different circumstances of their time. But what Platonic philosophy continued to offer was a general theoretical framework for political reflection. And both for Philo and for Plutarch a look at their oeuvre as a whole will permit us to reconstruct the general lineaments of a political theory. Their common Platonic inheritance is the fundamental distinction between two orders of reality: the divine realm of immutable Forms constitutes the model for the world of becoming, which is implicated in continual change and dominated by the passions. The ultimate object of political action is reproduction of the ideal order in the world of contingency, so far as that is possible. Hence – in harmony with Plato – a strong ethical inspiration for politics.

In the historical documents of the time, above all in the Roman imperial ideology and also in non-Platonic thinkers such as Seneca, we find widely attested the idea of the king as representative of God on earth and as incarnation of the divine *logos*.[2] This notion had already been developed in Hellenistic theory; and in Philo and Plutarch, too, there are many allusions to a theory of kingship. The king is charged with the mission of realizing divine order in the world: he is like God on earth, introducing order and concord through the medium of law, of which he is a living incarnation. The ideal of assimilation to God, going back to Plato and widely diffused in Platonism, was here applied to the realm of politics, and imitation of divine virtue was not confined to the private sphere of the sage. This development constituted the reception of the key idea of philosophers in power. It is the main way in which the Platonic conception of kingship and the ideal of a philosopher ruler sketched in the *Politicus* were to exercise their influence.

These basic themes are also found in a group of treatises which go under the names of ancient Pythagoreans, but probably date to the imperial period (first centuries BC and AD) and may properly be considered as belonging to the Platonic tradition. Despite their scholastic and derivative character, they develop a highly systematic treatment of their subject matter, and this makes it possible to entertain the hypothesis that they exerted influence on later political thought, right down to medieval political theology and the absolutist theories of the sixteenth century.[3]

[2] See Chestnut 1978.

[3] Kantorowicz 1952a: 267–71 (= 1965: 131–5), 1952b: 170–4 (= 1965: 264–70), 1957 *passim*.

2 Philo of Alexandria

Philo came from an influential and wealthy Jewish family. The cultural formation to which he was subject was eminently Greek. He wrote in Greek and had scant knowledge of Hebrew. But he was devout in the practice of his religion, as he himself testifies when he speaks of his pilgrimages to Jerusalem (*On Providence* II.107). He was influenced by the principal philosophical currents of the time, but the decisive impact is that exercised by the philosophy of Plato, whose works he knew well, and particularly by Alexandrian Platonism. The frame of reference which is most important for understanding him, however, is constituted by holy scripture. Besides apologetic writings and philosophical and theological treatises, a considerable part of his oeuvre, and perhaps the most interesting, is made up of commentaries – whether organized by themes or sections of text – on the Bible (particularly the Pentateuch) in the version of the Septuagint, which was in circulation by this time. Characteristic features of his exegesis are the use of conceptual categories whose original home is Greek philosophy, and of an allegorical method borrowed from Greek tradition but already in use in Judaism too. The governing idea is that biblical personages and incidents symbolize reality and truth belonging to the realm of the intelligible, and that scripture in general represents the journey of the soul towards the transcendent, conceived as the ultimate goal of life.[4]

These elements situate Philo at a point of intersection between Judaism and Hellenism. And it is much debated whether he should be considered basically a Greek philosopher who nonetheless remained rooted in his religion, or a Hebrew mystic who from the outset deployed the armoury of Greek thought in the service of revelation.[5] Philo's influence cannot be documented with any certainty in pagan authors, by whom he is never mentioned directly. On the other hand it is evident in the Fathers of the Church, who as well as harbouring an interest in his theology and his apologetics appreciated his contribution to scriptural exegesis, and used the allegorical method in order to reconcile biblical revelation and rational truth. It was they who originated the legend of a Christian Philo, or at least a fellow traveller,[6] thus guaranteeing the transmission of his works.

[4] The lives of Moses and Abraham sum up the journey of the soul; other figures symbolize virtues or faculties of the soul, e.g. Adam *nous* (intellect), Eve sensation, Cain and Abel the soul as it inclines to evil or to good.

[5] The major representatives of these opposite readings are Wolfson 1947 and Nikiprowetsky 1977. The debate is reviewed by Runia 1986: pt. I; see also Runia 1990.

[6] A bishop, according to some testimonies; they also make him meet Peter. On the reception of Philo among the Fathers see Runia 1993.

For Philo's politics[7] and the history of his time two apologetic writings are of great interest: *Legatio ad Gaium* and *in Flaccum*. In these he recounts some episodes which saw his active engagement in politics in a role of the first importance. It is likely that his involvement in civic business, despite his reluctance, was by no means restricted to occasions such as these, although as a Jew he took no part in the actual government of Alexandria. Of his remaining writings none can be considered strictly speaking a political treatise. Of great interest for his conception of ruling and kingship, however, are *On Joseph* and *Life of Moses*. Joseph embodies the ideal statesman, Moses the philosopher king, the paradigmatic lawgiver whose activity is more important than practical politics. But Philo does not mean to elaborate a theory or an organized programme. Although necessary, politics is something of secondary importance, an 'adjunct' to human life. The object of life itself is to follow reason and worship God.

From its foundation Alexandria in Egypt had a large resident Jewish community. The Jews' relations with the other groups in the population, Greeks and Egyptians, were difficult, whether for economic and religious reasons or because of the particular privileges they were accorded by the Romans.[8] The *in Flaccum* provides evidence of these tensions and of the precarious condition of the good relations between Jews and Romans. The story of Flaccus, Roman Prefect in Alexandria, functions as a warning of their inherent difficulties. After ruling well for a period he took up an anti-Jewish posture, and was complicit in a pogrom carried out by the local population. In consequence of this he was arrested by order of the emperor Gaius (Caligula), exiled, and executed. The *Legatio*, written after Claudius' election as emperor, continues the story. Philo recounts his participation in an embassy to Gaius in AD 39, probably sent with the aim of winning back the rights abolished by Flaccus. Gaius now appears in a very different light. Philo is sharply critical of his policy of persecution against the Jews and his insane project of self-deification, especially his announcement during the course of the embassy that a statue of himself, complete with the inscription 'Zeus', was to be erected in the Jewish temple. The work comes to an abrupt end as it is narrating a second meeting of the ambassadors with Gaius, which he breaks off in the face of their refusal to recognize his divine nature. In a palinode which has not survived Philo perhaps told the story of the fall of Gaius, in the light of a conception of providence as God's constant protection of his chosen people.

7 On which see above all Goodenough 1938, Barraclough 1984.

8 On the political situation at Alexandria see Barraclough 1984: 421–36.

The purpose and intended readership of these writings have been the subject of discussion.[9] Philo is probably intending to issue a warning to the persecutors of the Jewish people that an inauspicious fate awaits them, and to supply reassurance to waverers among his coreligionists. In any case, the two works attest Philo's personal engagement in politics, and his aim of maintaining good relations with the Romans in order to safeguard the religious freedom and the traditional privileges of the Jews.

When we turn to his exegetical works, we find Philo employing political categories in describing the universe and its relationship to its creator. The universe is for him the most perfect of the works of the Father, the supreme deity. It can be defined in Stoic fashion as a great city founded upon law and administered justly by a 'great king'.[10] So to deal with Philo's conception of the political we must begin with the origin and constitution of the world. The highest of divine powers are those associated with creation and kingly rule (*basilikē*) – hence the title 'Lord', since in virtue of the capacity to exercise such rule God governs with justice all that has come into existence. He alone is able to govern the world justly because he is its maker: he brings order out of disorder. The third of his powers, uniting the first two, is the *logos*, which is all-pervasive, and is the principle of moral action.[11] The maker and ruler of the world is also its lawgiver, and his law is the *logos* of nature, which prescribes what has to be done and forbids what must not be done. The world therefore has a single polity and a single law. Following the law of nature is essentially the same as contemplating the order of nature and the constitution of the cosmic city.[12]

Man is in the first place a citizen of the world, which God, who himself is in need of nothing, has entrusted to him in its entirety. Humans are only secondarily citizens of other states. The wise man has no country other than his own virtues.[13] More generally, the political life is only something supplementary to the life of the person who is living in accordance with nature, and particular constitutions are similarly supplementary to the single law and polity of nature (*Jos.* 29). In contrasting particular cities with the ideal of a single cosmic city, Philo conceives of the divine *logos* as providing for a restoration of equality (*Immut.* 176):

[9] On the *Legatio* see Kraus Reggiani 1984.

[10] *Quaest.Ex.* II.42, *Jos.* 29, *Mos.* I.166, *Abr.* 74.

[11] *Cher.* II.27–9, *Poster.* 127.

[12] *Mos.* II.48, *Abr.* 6.1. On the Stoic inspiration of this theory see Schofield, in ch. 22 section 4 above.

[13] *Jos.* 69, *Mos.* I.157, *Abr.* 31. Here there are perhaps echoes of Cynicism; see Moles, in ch. 21 section 3 above.

> The divine *logos* . . . forever moving through cities, peoples and countries, distributes to one the goods of the others, and to all the goods of all, but changing the ownership from time to time so that the whole world may be inhabited as a single city, and the best form of constitution introduced – democracy.

However there are in fact many cities, with different constitutions, laws and customs. The political life takes many varied forms, and is involved in constant change. The statesman, therefore, should be a versatile person, capable of adapting to different circumstances.

Implicated as it is in the sphere of what comes to be and passes away, the political life is a second-class activity in comparison with the practice of things divine. Philo is a convinced advocate of the superiority of the contemplative over the practical life. Nonetheless the best form of life is attained (by what is called 'transmigration') only after a person has developed a good grasp first of household economy, then of politics.[14] Politics, however, can be practised on a higher plane, involving the imitation of God's kingly rule. In view of the analogy between universe and city, good government means reproducing within the city God's government of the world. The ideal form of government is therefore monarchy, although Philo constantly asserts that democracy is the best constitution. But by democracy he does not mean rule by the people, something he views with disapproval. The term signifies rather alternation in the exercise of power, such that each obtains in turn what is his due.[15] There is a close connection here with the notion of equality (*isotēs*), regarded as what generates justice and conceived in terms of geometrical proportion.[16] So conceived democracy, as the principle according to which God has ordered the universe, does not contrast with monarchic rule.[17]

Philo's paradigms of kingship are to be found in two important figures from the Bible, Joseph and Moses, while Roman emperors such as Gaius represent by contrast negative archetypes. Other Romans are judged very favourably by Philo: Augustus, for example, displays some features of the ideal king (*Legat.* 143). But none bears comparison with the Jewish lawgivers of the past. The king as lawgiver is superior to the statesman, who is a figure intermediate between the private citizen and the king. The statesman does not have absolute power, because he serves another king, the

[14] *Migr.* 89, *Spec.* II.64, *Fug.* 36.
[15] *Spec.* IV.231. Cf. Goodenough 1938: 86–7, Barraclough 1984: 512 and 521.
[16] For the idea of proportionate equality see Pl. *Gorg.* 508a, *Laws* VI.757b–c; Arist. *EN* 1131a2–b18.
[17] Cf. Plato *Menex.* 238c.

people, and he is not a free person, directed in his behaviour as he is by a host of masters. True kingship, on the other hand, is not required to give an account of itself to anyone.[18] While Joseph embodies the perfect statesman, Moses is the incarnation of the ideal king. The king surpasses all other humans, but remains after all a mortal creature (II.6); Philo speaks not so much of assimilation to God as of emulating divine virtues. With other men the king shares in material being (*ousia*),[19] and like other men he is made of dust. But insofar as he holds the rank of king he is an image of the deity.[20] Man enjoys kinship with God because he shares reason with him, but the Lord is the only true king.[21]

Following Plato, Philo contends that cities can approximate to the good only if philosophers are kings or kings philosophers (*Mos.* II.2). Human kingship is something bestowed by God with the concurrence of his subjects, and the office of king is conferred in consideration of his natural gifts and his virtues, not 'by means of arms or the arts of war'.[22] Moses was brought up as a prince (I.8), and as a boy he was called the 'young king' (I.32). In him the capacities for kingship and philosophy are combined, and also those for lawgiving, prophecy and priesthood. Although not formally speaking a king, Moses was in fact the best of kings, lawgivers and priests (II.187). As God is the shepherd of his people, so – in line with a widespread Greek tradition of thought which goes back to Homer – should the ideal king be shepherd of his. The tending of sheep is held in high regard as a preparatory exercise for kingship, and Moses, who was marked out for the job of leading humankind as a civilized flock, was trained in this art following his marriage to the daughter of the priest.[23] As shepherd Philo's king exhibits another feature which is often found in kingship theories of the Hellenistic and imperial periods: humanity (*philanthrōpia*), which goes together with love of justice, love of goodness, hatred of evil (II.9). As the shepherd takes care of his flock, so the essential aim of the king is to benefit his subjects by taking care of their interests and providing for the common good (I.150–1). Closely connected is the idea of imitation of the king on the part of his subjects. The king is the only one who can attain the perfection of virtue and carry its imprint in his soul, and who can achieve happiness by possessing

[18] *Jos.* 35, 148: *anhupeuthunos*. Cf. among ps.-Pythagorean texts Diotog.72.22 (discussed below, p. 572); also Plu. *de Unius* 826e. [19] Cf. Ecphantus 80.2–4, below p. 572.
[20] Antonius Monachus, *Melissa* II Sermo CIV (= Migne *PG* vol. 136, pp. 1011–12).
[21] *Abr.* 41, *Somn.* II.99. [22] *Mos.* I.148; cf. *Abr.* 261, *Quaest. Gen.* IV.76.
[23] Gaius, on the other hand, abused the concept of shepherd. He took himself to be of divine origin, contending that someone whose job it is to lead other animals is their natural superior (*Legat.* 76).

something close to divine power (*Abr.* 26). Other humans can only aspire to copy that model by imprinting an *image* of virtue in their souls. Because subjects tend to emulate those who govern them, bad rulers will corrupt the entire community, while good ones will be able to convert even the most vicious to self-control.[24]

The legislative function of the king is another feature deeply rooted in the tradition of Greek thought, and its notion of the king as living law.[25] Philo's lawgiver is a living law inasmuch as he performs the main function of the law: which is to prescribe what is just and to forbid what is wrong (*Mos.* II.4, *Deter.* 141). Moses was living and rational law long before he actually became a legislator. For Philo he is the best lawgiver in history; his written laws are copies of the models imprinted in the soul (*Mos.* II.11), that is, of the divine *logos* implanted there, which is the model for the creation of man. For this reason Moses' laws are stable and unchangeable, and will endure so long as the world continues in being. And this is why Jewish institutions are praised and honoured all over the inhabited world, while the laws of other countries keep being altered all the time (II.12–13, 17–19). Philo is probably criticizing Plato when he claims (II.49–51):

> Among lawgivers some straightaway set out what should and should not be done, and determined penalties for transgressors, others – considering themselves superior – did not begin with that, but founded a city in *logos*, and then fitted the constitution they considered most appropriate to the city so founded, by means of the imposition of laws. Moses, on the other hand . . . considering it beneath the dignity of the laws to begin his own writing by founding a city made with human hands . . . introduced an account of the creation of the great city, taking the laws to be the most faithful image of the constitution of the universe.

The faculty of prophecy, in which Moses again excelled, is an addition to the usual kingly attributes which is special to Philo. The gift of prophecy is rendered necessary because man cannot attain to the full understanding of things, whether human or divine, by the use of reason alone (II.2–6). Joseph, the statesman *par excellence*, is an interpreter of dreams, and in particular of that dream which is human life, where all is subject to change and nothing can be grasped securely (*Jos.* 125–47). If the statesman can interpret dreams, he will be able to distinguish between just and unjust, good and evil, goods that are authentic from deceptive ones, identified by Philo as bodily and external goods. Because whatever happens does so in

[24] *Mos.* I.160–1, *Virt.* 70. Cf. the story of Joseph and his brothers: *Jos.* 87ff. This idea recurs in the ps.-Pythagorean literature and in Plutarch (p. 572 n.49 below).

[25] See Hahm, in ch. 23 section 2 above.

accordance with God's will, and nothing can go right without his providential care, the king must attend to things divine by means of rites and prayers in order to gain God's favour (*Mos.* II.5).[26] The office of high-priest can even be regarded as more important than that of king (*Legat.* 278).

The duality of Philo's cultural formation is confirmed by this brief survey of his political thought. As in Stoicism politics is grounded in the law of nature. But that law finds its incarnation in Mosaic law. The principal themes of Philo's teaching – rule and kingship – are rooted in Greek tradition. But for the realization of his ideal he looks to Judaism. And he constantly refers to the scriptures as the source of human wisdom.

3 Pseudo-Pythagorean literature

The ancient Pythagorean school, which exercised a significant influence on the politics of the Greek cities of South Italy in the fifth century BC, suffered almost total extinction in the fourth. From then on Pythagoreanism survived only sporadically, mostly as a philosophy inspiring individual personalities who continued to lead a Pythagorean 'way of life'. The figure of Pythagoras and the philosophy of the Pythagoreans were, however, the subject of a great deal of attention in Plato's Academy. Developing the affinities which really did exist between Plato's philosophy and Pythagoreanism, the Academics did not hesitate to attribute doctrines they themselves had worked out to ancient Pythagoreanism, with the aim of giving them dignity and securing for them the *imprimatur* of authority.[27] In this way they had a strong influence on the image of Pythagorean philosophy constructed in later doxography, and assured its survival in a form profoundly transfigured by Platonizing interpretation. In consequence the philosophical links between Platonism and what subsequently represented itself as Pythagoreanism were always very strong, but at the same time confusion between the two was also nurtured.

Between the fourth and first centuries BC the existence of Pythagorean groups cannot be clearly documented, although an interest in Pythagoreanism of a literary or antiquarian nature is well attested. This explains the production of apocryphal writings attributed to Pythagoras or ancient Pythagoreans, some of which probably go back to the third and second centuries BC.[28] Beginning with the first century BC, however,

[26] Compare in ps.-Pythagorean literature Diotogenes' king, whose duties include worshipping God (Diotog. 71.23–72.3). [27] Burkert 1972: 53–96. [28] Burkert 1961.

there is evidence of a real renaissance of Pythagoreanism, although how widespread it was is uncertain. At Rome in particular figures such as Nigidius Figulus attempted to revive the ancient *disciplina* (Cic. *Tim.*1), and in the cultural ambience of Alexandria there are visible signs of renewed philosophical interest in Pythagorean doctrines. Between the first century BC and the second century AD there appear on the scene authors who explicitly define themselves, or come to be defined (not always on clear grounds), as Pythagoreans. Some of these, such as Moderatus of Gades and Numenius of Apamea, seem to claim a Pythagorean identity while professing doctrines that are substantially Platonic. There was no officially established Pythagorean school nor any body of doctrine which represented orthodoxy. Even in the imperial period the existence of actual groups or circles of Pythagoreans – such as might try to revive the Pythagorean way of life without being tied to profession of a philosophy – is highly conjectural.

From authors whose names are known no significant doctrines on political topics have been transmitted. More important for the history of political thought are the apocryphal writings, which constitute a heterogeneous corpus of imposing dimensions. Many of these treatises, which bear the names of ancient Pythagoreans, sometimes unknown, are written in Doric, the dialect spoken by Greeks in South Italy and Sicily in Pythagoras' time. But here it is an artificial language, which only reproduces the commonest features of Doric, and is employed with the aim of authenticating the attribution of the writings to ancient Pythagoreans. Some of these works have their own independent manuscript tradition, but others have survived thanks above all to the learned Byzantine scholar John Stobaeus (fifth century AD), who in his *Florilegium* has transmitted various fragments. Here we are concerned mostly with brief compilations, scholastic in character, but worked up and ornamented with archaisms and poetic expressions. The conceptual level is not high, and the authors rarely try to present arguments for their theses, whose credibility is presumably guaranteed simply by the mask of ancient Pythagorean authorship: a name like Archytas represented unquestionable authority. In the later Platonic tradition, too, we find constant reference to Pythagoras, considered as source of all revelation.[29] It is perhaps for this reason that some of these writings continued to be used and taken as important in antiquity, despite the mediocrity of their contents. Their date and place of origin remain controversial. Candidates are Rome,

[29] O'Meara 1989 *passim*.

where Pythagoreanism exercised several different kinds of influence; Alexandria, a vibrant cultural centre where an interest in Pythagoreanism is attested in authors like Eudorus; and Southern Italy, the area where one might most expect the Pythagorean tradition to have been maintained. Chronologies proposed have swung wildly between the fourth century BC and the second AD, but many scholars are now inclined to narrow the limits of the composition of these treatises to between the first century BC and the first century AD, situating them within the framework of Middle Platonism.[30]

The symbiosis of Platonic and Pythagorean ideas in the philosophies of the early Academy make it difficult to separate out elements in these texts that might ultimately be of Pythagorean origin. Distinctively Platonist doctrines come to be presented as Pythagorean, and it is difficult to establish whether the authors of the treatises considered themselves Platonists rather than Pythagoreans. The doctrinal content seems however to be indebted essentially to Platonism, and despite internal inconsistencies those written in Doric seem to rely on a single schematic and scholastic system. All the principal themes are worked through in relation to it, including political theory, which occupies a prominent position, even in the amount of space allotted to it. Here too it is difficult to isolate distinctively Pythagorean elements. Certainly there never existed in ancient Pythagoreanism a systematic political or constitutional theory that writers of the imperial period could have remoulded.[31] And the involvement of Pythagoras and his followers in the political life of South Italy in the late sixth and early fifth centuries BC is hard to evaluate. Members of the sect took part in the aristocratic government of Croton, but it is not clear that Pythagoreanism in its original form should be described primarily as a political movement. It is more probable that the Pythagorean community was focused on practice of a particular way of life, and that some of its adherents attained important political positions.[32] The role actually played by Pythagoras himself in political affairs is quite uncertain. Much later he came to be treated as the founder of a politically oriented educational programme and as the author of legislation,[33] but this supposed activity of his has left no concrete traces. Equally incredible is the tradition that mythical legislators such as Zaleucus and Charondas were

[30] Thesleff 1965 is a collection of the writings, which are cited according to the page and line numbers in his edition. On ps.-Pythagorean literature in general see Burkert 1961, 1971, Thesleff 1961, 1971, Moraux 1984: 605–83, Centrone 1990: 13–44.

[31] For the characterization of Pythagoreanism as a political tendency a decisive role was played by the Peripatetics Aristoxenus and Dicaearchus, who championed the ideal of the practical life.

[32] Von Fritz 1940: 95 and *passim*.

[33] E.g. Iambl. *VPyth.* 129–30.

connected with Pythagoreanism. Nor was there any particular political tendency to which Pythagoreanism was indissolubly attached. When it was transplanted to Tarentum after its adherents had suffered persecution it took on a form close to democracy. Other Pythagoreans followed the tradition of a way of life totally isolated from any political involvement.

The most celebrated among the political treatises are those *On Kingship* attributed to Diotogenes, Ecphantus and Sthenidas. Dating is particularly controversial: proposals range from the third century BC to the second AD;[34] the Hellenistic monarchies or the Roman empire appear to be the most likely contexts for writings which celebrate monarchy as the best form of government. Other treatises with a political content are the *On Law* of ps.-Archytas, which many scholars incline to date to the Hellenistic period,[35] and the *Republic* of ps.-Hippodamus.[36] Discrepancies between individual works are immediately evident. While in the treatises on kingship monarchy is extolled, ps.-Archytas champions a mixed constitution which tempers democracy, oligarchy and aristocracy; ps.-Hippodamus, who takes Plato's polity in the *Republic* as his model, seems to have a preference for aristocracy. Notwithstanding these differences, the overall impression given by the pseudo-Pythagorean writings is of a single systematic theory, in the political sphere as elsewhere.

That system is based on an idea – the doctrine of two fundamental principles – which goes back to the Platonism of the early Academy. All reality is the outcome of the interaction of these principles, called variously form and matter or limit and unlimited. But the supreme principle governing the universe is God, who in some versions is accorded a position higher than the pair of principles just described.[37] The universe is a system articulated in different sub-systems: world, city, family, individual and individual soul. All these systems display an analogous structure, and microcosm and macrocosm are strictly parallel.[38] A *sustama*[39] consists in the harmonization of dissimilar and contrary parts with a view to unity

[34] Hellenistic period (3rd century BC): Goodenough 1928, Thesleff 1961, and (with reservations) Aalders 1975: 28 and n.96. first–second century AD: Delatte 1942. For Ecphantus the period of the Severi (Burkert 1971) or of Domitian (Squilloni 1991) has been suggested. See below, p. 575 n. 53.

[35] Delatte 1922: 71–124, Thesleff 1961, Aalders 1975: 27–38, Isnardi Parente 1979: 222–3. Moraux 1984: 605–7, 667–77 includes it among writings to be dated between the first century BC and the first AD.

[36] The other treatises which fall under consideration are Aresas, *de Natura Hominis*; Damippus, *de Prudentia et Beatitudine*; Eccelus, *de Iustitia*; Euryphamus, *de Vita*; Hippodamus, *de Felicitate*; Callicratidas, *de Domi Felicitate*; Metopus, *de Virtute*; Onatas, *de Deo*. What makes these writings 'Pythagorean' is not their doctrinal content, but their false paternity.

[37] Arch. 19.4–20.17, Damipp. 68.11–18, Onat. 139.1–140.19.

[38] Damipp. 68.20–69.4.

[39] Callicr. 103.21–3.

and goodness, and for the advantage of those parts. Such is the polis too: 'the polis, which is the outcome of the harmonization of different and varied elements, imitates the ordering and harmony of the cosmos' (Diotog. 72.21–2).

Every system is characterized by binary opposition. The better ought to rule and direct, the worse should obey;[40] and in this the harmonization of a system, its virtue, consists. On the cosmic scale the celestial region, which is in perpetual motion, governs the constantly changing sublunar realm.[41] As the work of divine intelligence, cosmic harmonization is not subject to chance and can never come to an end, although in the sublunar region it is possible for the worst part to prevail – hence the origin of vice in the individual and of political disorder. Thus the political community ought to reproduce within itself the harmonization of the cosmos. The form of government best adapted for this purpose is that defined as 'political' – which reproduces God's rule over the world, and is aimed at the common advantage of ruler and subjects; the 'despotic' form of rule and the 'protective' (characteristic e.g. of trainers and doctors) aim only at the interest of the ruler or the subject respectively.[42]

> Man . . . imitated the ordering of the whole, harmonizing the community of the city by means of judgments and laws. Indeed nothing accomplished by man was so expressive of that order and so worthy of the gods as the harmonization of a well-governed city and the ordering of the laws and the constitution. (Euryphamus *de Vita* 86.8–11)

Civilization comes into being because men are not self-sufficient. Unlike God they are under the necessity of associating with each other in order to live, becoming parts of a community. To be happy humans should live in a city with a well-ordered system of government and equitable laws.[43] The harmony which results from such a system is given different names: justice, concord, unanimity, and – with reference to the city – peace, harmony, *eunomia*.[44]

The differences between the various treatises are most evident over the issue of the best form of constitution. If we begin with the kingship treatises, we find in them a coherent development of the doctrine that God is

[40] A 'law of nature', according to Pl. *Laws* III.690b; cf. *Rep.* IV.431a.

[41] Damipp. 68.22–3; Metop. 119.14–15; Occel. 125.4–5.

[42] Callicr. 105.10–27. Despite the affinities between the forms described by Callicratidas and those familiar from Aristotle (Arist. *Pol.* 1278b30–1279a16), the idea that the same form of government is appropriate to the political community as to that of the family derives from Plato: *Plt.* 259b–c; *Laws* III.690a.

[43] Euryph. 86.11–14, Hippod. 96.16–18.

[44] Eccel. 78.8, Hippod. 96.8; cf. Ares. 50.8.

the supreme principle and that there is an analogy between different levels of reality. In his unique position, the king has the responsibility of imitating the work of God. By geometric ratio, since the king stands to the city as God does to the universe, it follows that the king will be related to God as the city is to the universe. As God is the best of the things which naturally deserve honour, so the king is the best of the things on earth which deserve honour. Both have a power which is *anhupeuthunos*, not liable to render an account of itself.[45] Ecphantus gives particular prominence to the divine nature of the monarch. Although like other men in the material constitution of his body, he has been fashioned by God in his own image. His virtues are the work of God himself, for man, oppressed by his earthly matter, becomes capable of contemplating God only through an inspiration that partakes of the divine nature (79.1–7, 80.1–7). In other pseudo-Pythagorean texts this doctrine, restricted by Ecphantus to the king, is applied to humans in general: as a being of high intelligence he must be a copy of the divine nature; his ability to give form to the *logos* and to direct his eyes away from the earth to contemplate the divine reality of the heavens is possible only thanks to divine assistance.[46] Although there are doubtless reminiscences here of the *Timaeus*, the closest parallels are with Philo;[47] and notions like the creation of man in the image of God or the idea that man is an exile on earth lead one to suppose influence from Judaic tradition and the Old Testament.[48]

For all that his nature is divine, the king remains a human being, and shares the desire for emulation which God has instilled in all men. What enables humans to become assimilated – to the degree that that is possible – to God's self-sufficiency is the practice of virtue and the search for wisdom. That renders the king dear to God and at the same time to his subjects, who aspire in their turn to emulate him. The king accordingly performs the role of intermediary between God and the rest of humanity, by making it possible even for natures far from the divine to achieve a mediated assimilation to God. They contemplate divinity in him as in a mirror.[49]

> Because it is divine, kingship is difficult to look upon in its dazzling splendour, except for those who are legitimate . . . It is something pure, incorruptible and difficult to approach . . . For all others, if they sin, there

[45] Diotog. 72.19–23; cf. p. 565 n.18 above. [46] Euryph. 85.20–5.
[47] Pl. *Tim*. 90a; Ph. *Opif*. 20, 24–5, 69; *Deter*. 83–6; *Leg*. 1.38.
[48] Burkert 1971: 48–53.
[49] Ecph. 80.18–21, 82.20–83.10. A close parallel in Plu. *ad Princ*. 781f–782a, below; cf. also Philo, above p. 566 and n.24.

> is the possibility of a most holy purification if they become assimilated to what rules them: law or king. (Ecphantus *On Kingship* 80.8–10, 13–14, 22–3)

Diotogenes gives further indications about the appropriate outward bearing of the king. One form of behaviour which brings the monarch very close to God is the practice of the same benevolence and friendship towards his subjects as God shows towards the world, the shepherd to his flock, and a father to his sons.[50]

It being his duty to govern others, the king's first duty is to govern himself, by ruling his passions. The virtues ascribed to the king reflect the Platonic tripartition of the soul into reason, spirit and appetite, which is found all over pseudo-Pythagorean literature. He will be temperate in his pleasures, liberal with wealth, and prudent in his exercise of power. The corresponding vices are greed for riches and power (*pleonexia*), desire for honour (*philotimia*), and love of pleasure (*philhēdonia*), failings of the rational, spirited and appetitive soul respectively. Injustice, the supreme vice, is a condition of the soul as a whole and the political community as a whole (Diotog. 73.6–15).

Closely connected to the analogy of king and God is the description of the sovereign as living law (*nomos empsuchos*). Despite his apparent distancing of himself from the monarchical ideal, we find the same identification in Archytas also (33.8–10), who treats the written letter as life*less* law. What has primacy here is law: it gives the king his legitimacy (*nomimos*), his subjects their freedom, the community its happiness. According to Diotogenes (71.18–23) the king is living law or legal ruler: a king has to be supremely just, and that requires the strictest observance of law. The king seems to be made subject to constitutional legality at precisely the moment when his absolute sovereignty is proclaimed. One might wonder whether the notion of *nomos empsuchos* implies that the king is the source of law, or simply that he is an incarnation of the law as it exists, inasmuch as he is guarantor of its efficacy. In fact his observance of law cannot simply be a matter of his conforming to already existing law: for that law must itself conform with divine law, or else there would be no justice. The law Archytas speaks of is the law of nature, which consists in distributing to each according to his merits, and is thereby the origin of justice (33.23–5). Law so conceived 'is a possibility if there is harmony with those to whom legislation is directed – for many are unable to receive what is by nature

[50] Diotog. 73.23–74.17, Ecph. 82.1–2, Sthen. 188.3–4. For humanity (*philanthrōpia*) see also Arch. 36.4–5, and Plutarch (below, p. 579).

the primary good . . . Law is something useful to the political community, provided that it is not monarchical and designed for private advantage' (33.25–31). Laws must be inscribed not 'on houses and doors', but in the souls of the citizens;[51] and the Spartan constitution, which is here extolled, shrinks from a plethora of written ordinances. So it cannot be excluded that sometimes the king is the source of the law, sometimes he conforms to existing law (if it is just). Similarly, Ecphantus considers the possibility that government may be exercised either by the law or by the king. In any event, law is what receives the greater part of Archytas' attention. This accords with his less idealistic attitude to questions of government. He holds that the best constitution will be a mixture of democracy, oligarchy and aristocracy on the Spartan model, involving alternation of office and equilibrium between forces.

A possible explanation of these different views on the best form of government is to be found in Hippodamus' *Republic* (97.16–102.20). Here – following the Platonic model – the polis is divided into three classes: counsellors, auxiliaries, artisans. The counsellors govern the other two, the auxiliaries in their turn issue commands to the artisans in matters relating to war. Although this system is based on the domination of an aristocracy, Hippodamus also expresses a preference for a mixed form of constitution which tempers kingship, aristocracy and democracy (102.7–20). Aristocracy comes only second, after kingship, since kingship, being an imitation of the divine, is ideally the supreme form; but because it can easily degenerate into arrogance, it should be introduced only where it can be advantageous to the city. The irresponsibility of the mob similarly discourages excessive use of democracy, which ideally is a just form of polity inasmuch as the citizen is part of the community. What is generally preferable is that aristocracy be the form of constitution employed, since this permits alternation of office.

It is possible, therefore, to track down a single fundamental orientation in these writings. All recognize the superiority of kingship, but also the difficulties in realizing the ideal. In the treatises on kingship an idealizing perspective prevails, in the others a more realistic outlook which leads their authors to put the emphasis on law. Archytas favours the mixed constitution because the mutual control of political forces, with the same magistracy both exercising and subject to command, can prevent possible abuses. This safeguard, however, would appear superfluous given the presence of a virtuous monarch – an ideal Archytas too recognizes, as witness

[51] Arch. 34.30–2, Diotog. 76.2–3, cf. Plu.*Ad Princ.* 780c.

his definition of the king as 'living law'. One is reminded of Plato's *Politicus* (301a–e, 302e; cf. *Laws* IX.875c–d): if by divine chance it came about that there was a wise king, he would be the source of law and monarchy would be the best constitution; otherwise monarchy degenerates into tyranny, and it is then preferable that the laws have full authority. The predilection for monarchy in the pseudo-Pythagorean literature seems to derive from abstract theoretical reflection rather than to reflect a historical situation: since God is the supreme principle of the universe, the best form of government, which is to imitate God's rule, cannot but be monarchy.[52]

Notwithstanding the presence of a variety of influences, the pseudo-Pythagorean texts belong in substance to the Platonist tradition. There are numerous parallels with authors such as Philo and Plutarch or with the characteristic doctrines of Middle Platonism such as *homoiōsis theōi* ('assimilation to God'), an idea which assumes a paramount political importance as the basis for advocacy of monarchy. Theses paralleled in Stoicism, such as the analogy between world and city, God and king, or doctrines of Aristotelian provenance are fitted into an overall Platonic scheme. The substantial homogeneity of the material, confirmed – despite appearances – for political theory too, speaks against extending too much the time within which composition of the treatises may be supposed to have occurred. As suggested above, it is reasonable to think of a period spanning the first century BC and the first AD. The most striking analogies are with Philo, and point to an Alexandrian milieu, where a renewed interest in Pythagoreanism is well attested and an influence from Judaic tradition easy to explain.[53]

4 Plutarch

In Plutarch's work political theory and pragmatic advice for rulers are closely connected. Although not a politician by profession, Plutarch held public offices, albeit not at the highest level. In AD 68 he led an embassy to

[52] The substitution of aristocracy for monarchy in some texts also has an antecedent in Plato, for provided that the philosophers rule, it does not matter whether they be one or more: Pl.*Rep.* IV.445d–e, VII.540d; *Plt.* 293a.

[53] Delatte's argument (1942: 285), that these authors seem to know only one earthly kingdom, which has to be the Roman empire, does not take account of the abstract and idealized character of the doctrines of kingship and of cosmopolitanism (held as an ideal by Philo too, independently of the historical situation: *Immut.* 176). A particular problem arises in the case of Ecphantus, whose treatise exhibits some features which point to a relatively late date of composition: the exaggerated style; the idea that the king is not inferior to God in any of the virtues; an adulation which strikes readers as grotesque, hardly intelligible except as directed to a particular monarch (see Burkert 1971: 54, who conjectures the circle of Julia Domna, d. AD 217).

the proconsul of Achaea (*Praec.* 816d); he was eponymous *archōn* in his native city, Chaeronea, and also took on humbler offices.[54] On the other hand, the extent of his surviving writings, which represent only a part of his monumental oeuvre, attests his enthusiasm for intellectual activity. Although he is not a thinker of the first rank, his philosophical interests are considerable and his reflections on politics form a coherent part of his philosophy. Plutarch is a convinced Platonist, but his writings on politics – unlike Plato's – are not of paramount importance in his work. The extant treatises – *Advice on politics*, *Should the elderly engage in politics?*, *Why the philosopher should especially converse with rulers*, *To an uneducated ruler*[55] – are mainly practical advice for politicians, and relate largely to the historical situation of the time. In some of them, however, one can find purely theoretical reflections on politics, together with advice of wider application. Lamprias' catalogue lists several writings that have not survived, among these a *Politics*, which was perhaps wholly theoretical in character. A conspicuous interest in politics on Plutarch's part is shown by the fact that his *Lives* mainly deal with famous statesmen.[56]

The framework of Plutarch's political thought is the Greek polis of his time, and its symbiosis with the Roman empire. Plutarch himself often describes the relationship as one of quiet submission, which ensures a partial freedom and a relative autonomy for the Greek cities. In order to safeguard this situation politicians need to maintain good relations with the Romans, by ruling well and avoiding anything which might cause annoyance. Plutarch was in a position to exert an effective influence on political life at this level, and most of his political advice belongs to this context. The Greek city, not world empire, is in the foreground, and he does not seem to differentiate between politics on the larger and the smaller stage.[57]

Convinced Platonist though he is, Plutarch exhibits none of the tension characteristic of Plato between political engagement on the part of the philosopher and the superiority of the contemplative life. He does not conceive of political engagement as something 'necessary, but not noble' (Pl. *Rep.* VII.540b), nor does he advocate withdrawal, even temporarily, from political life. Political quietism and the inactive life of those who

[54] *Quaest. Conv.* 642f, 693f, *Praec.* 811a–b: *telmarchos* (? *telearchos*). He speaks of removing dung from the streets and providing for drainage.

[55] Abbreviations: *Praec.*, *an Seni*, *Max. cum Princ.*, *ad Princ.*

[56] A general study of Plutarch: Russell 1972. A thorough survey of Plutarch's work on politics in Aalders 1982a, 1992; see further Scott 1929, Jones 1971: 110–21, Wardman 1974: 197–220, Aalders 1977, Barigazzi 1981, 1982, 1984, Aalders 1982b, Desideri 1986. For reflections of theory in the *Lives* see e.g. Garcia Moreno 1992, Pelling 1995.

[57] Aalders 1982a: 27.

pride themselves on their own unconcern are deeply reprehensible (*Praec.* 824a–b). As one of the noblest of activities politics plays a fundamental role in human life, and indeed has something divine about it, a 'sacred precinct', sometimes described in terms of initiation: 'the perfect statesman engages in public affairs first by becoming an initiate, but in the end as someone who teaches and initiates others' (*an Seni* 795e). Political activity is a service to one's native country, which can claim rights superior to a parent's (792e). The statesman or good citizen should not refuse or despise any public office, however modest (*Praec.* 813c): every such office is a sacred good (816a).[58]

In agreement with Plato and the tradition of Greek political thought in general, Plutarch treats politics as inextricably connected with ethics. The object of political activity is what is morally fine and nothing else (*Praec.* 799a). Political virtue is the most perfect, and none of the goods God has bestowed upon man can be enjoyed apart from law, justice and the ruler.[59] Politics is not

> a form of service (*leitourgia*) which reaches its limit when the need it addresses is met, but a way of life for an animal that is gentle and made for the polis and for association, and naturally constituted to live the political life, aspiring to what is morally fine and treating others with humanity, for whatever time is allotted. (*Should the elderly engage in politics?* 791c)

Political activity is consequently the source of the noblest forms of pleasure, which the gods themselves are supposed to enjoy, namely those that arise from fine actions and from deeds performed for the good of the community and of humanity (786b). Politics, however, is a difficult discipline, which is exhausting to acquire and can be mastered only by those whose nature is capable of enduring hard work and setbacks (784b–c). Practising politics is at bottom the same as doing philosophy, and entering upon the political life must be a conscious choice founded on judgment and reason (796d, 798c).

Since Plato's political utopianism seems to be alien to Plutarch's pragmatism, one would have expected that the doctrine of philosophers in power would have no relevance in his work. However he states explicitly that the philosopher should rule,[60] or at least that he should advise statesmen – as Plutarch did in his own writings. Statesmen rather than private individuals: that way his teachings get widely diffused, and benefit many

[58] Here Plutarch's personal experience is clearly in the background.
[59] *Cat.Mai.* 30.3, *ad Princ.* 780e. [60] *Num.* 20.9, *Cic.* 52.4.

though taking a single route. The philosopher should waken the virtue which often lies sleeping in the ruler's soul.[61]

> He removes evil from the ruler's character or helps to direct his mind towards what is right, and thereby in a way philosophizes for the public good and corrects the common system by which all are governed . . . Philosophers who associate with rulers make them more just, more moderate, and more eager to do good . . . The discourses of the philosophers, if they are securely inscribed in the souls of leaders and statesmen, acquire the force of laws. (*Why the philosopher should especially converse with rulers* 778e–f, 779b).

A close connection between philosophy, ethics and politics emerges in the notion of assimilation to God, which for Plutarch is the goal of human life and philosophical activity. As in the pseudo-Pythagorean literature, this notion has a specific application in politics. Of particular interest in this connection is the little work entitled *To an uneducated ruler*, where various points of a theoretical character are made; in the *Lives* there are scattered hints. *Homoiōsis* or assimilation can be achieved above all by the ruler, who becomes an image of God by imitating his virtues. Plutarch lists three sorts of feelings humans have towards the divine: envy, fear and respect, which relate to three divine attributes: incorruptibility, power and virtue. Human nature is precluded from the first, and the second is in the hands of fortune, but virtue, which is the most divine attribute, can be achieved by men.[62]

Although he imitates God just by ruling, the ruler is subject to a master, the law, written not on 'wooden tablets' but in 'living reason' (780c) – which is equivalent to saying that the ruler is living law.[63] Justice is the supreme political virtue, and the aim of government is to implant divine justice in the city. Even the deity is subject to the law of justice, and without justice not even Zeus can rule well (781b). The mark of the ruler's divine nature is the *logos* within him, not outward attributes of any sort, which sometimes provoke divine anger. God grants a share of his own equity, justice and benevolence to those who seek to emulate his virtue (781a).

At the same time Plutarch deplores the outward deification of rulers, common practice with the monarchs of the Hellenistic age and the Roman emperors alike, who were frequently adorned with titles of divinity:

[61] *Max. cum Princ.* 777a, *Num.* 6.1–2.

[62] *Arist.* 6.3–4. Power without justice makes men more like beasts.

[63] Aalders 1982a: 34, notes that the idea of the king as living law, despite various hints, is not put forward explicitly by Plutarch.

> Just as God has placed in the heavens the sun and the moon as splendid images of himself, imitation and splendour of that kind in cities are exemplified by the ruler who 'in devotion to God upholds justice' – that is, he has the *logos* of God, not the sceptre, the thunderbolt and the trident . . . God is angered by those who imitate his thunders, lightnings and sunbeams, but is pleased with those who seek to emulate his virtue. (*To an uneducated ruler* 780f)

Assimilation to God requires that the soul obtains its release from the body, passing through different stages – man to hero to demi-god to god – as in a rite of initiation. That is why Plutarch criticizes the legend of the apotheosis of Romulus, who was supposed to have been taken up into heaven without warning, and is offended by the arrogant bestowal of divine honours upon Demetrius Poliorcetes.[64]

By imitating God through his virtue, the ruler becomes a model or 'rule' of behaviour to which others should conform (780b), an image of God who may thus be contemplated as in a mirror:

> As the sun, his most beautiful likeness in the heaven, appears as his mirrored likeness to those who are able to contemplate him in it, so God has set in cities as his likeness the light of justice and of his own *logos*, which the blessed and the wise copy thanks to philosophy, modelling themselves on the most beautiful of all things. (*To an uneducated ruler* 781f–782a)[65]

The statesman's difficult task is to form the character of the citizens, to implant in them obedience, leading them towards the good.[66] The ruler accounts to God for his subjects, having as 'leader in the hive' received from him the care of the 'rational and political swarm' (*Praec.* 813c). Ruling is in fact service rendered to the divine (*Num.* 6.1–2), and by accomplishing this task the ruler will be loved by God. In Plutarch as in Hellenistic kingship ideology the ruler distinguishes himself by his humane attitude (*philanthrōpia*) towards his subjects. He should before all else be afraid in case his subjects suffer evil without his knowing it, and he should prefer to suffer injustice rather than commit it. Tyrants fear their subjects, kings fear *for* their subjects.[67] Loved by the ruler, his subjects will in their turn love him for his virtue, striving to emulate him. This kind of love is the strongest and most divine (*Praec.* 821e), for it is a fine thing to be ruled by virtue.

[64] *Rom.* 28.6–8, *Demetr.* 10.2–4, 11.1, 12.1, 13.1–2, 27.6–8, 28.6, *de Is.et Os.* 360c–d, *ad Princ.* 780f.
[65] Cf. Ecph. 80.18–21, 82.20–83.10.
[66] *Praec.* 799b, 800a–b, *Lyc.* 30.4.
[67] *Ad Princ.* 781e, *an Seni* 792d.

It is in the realm of political activity, therefore, that assimilation to God is fully accomplished, since only by ruling and bringing harmony to the city is it possible to imitate the divine government of the world (*Phoc.* 2.9). Hence Plutarch's explicit predilection for the monarchical form of government, although he often speaks simply of 'ruler' (*archōn*) rather than of king. Kingship together with virtue is the supreme human good, the best constitution, and by it man can emulate God.[68] Kings, according to ancient lore, are 'pupils of the gods'; 'all would receive benefit from contact with them, once they met with their wisdom, justice, goodness and magnanimity' (*Max. cum Princ.* 776e–f). By his virtue a king can inculcate a life of friendship, concord and justice in his subjects.[69]

According to a widely-held theory which goes back to Plato, should a ruler be unjust, then monarchy becomes the worst form of constitution, degenerating into tyranny[70] – although sometimes the tyrant can be an instrument of the divine will.[71] Plutarch claimed that tyranny had occurred rarely in his time (*an Seni* 784f). But he took a not dissimilar view about the monarchical ideal: he mentions no contemporary exemplar; and although he desires good relations with the Romans, he does not stoop to flattery. On some emperors he pronounces a favourable judgment, but none of them truly achieves the heights scaled by an ideal ruler. Only in the remote past are true kings to be found, such as the mythical figure of Numa. On the other hand, some statesmen have ruled in a kingly manner even in non-monarchical systems. An example is Lycurgus, whose polity Plutarch represents as the best constitution in his *Life* (*Lyc.* 31.3 *et passim*).

In the absence of rulers who can properly claim to incarnate his ideal of kingship, Plutarch is well disposed to aristocratic government (*Dion* 10.2, 12.2). He supports the aristocratic ideal of geometrical equality, which distributes rights and offices according to merit, and is characteristic of a moderate oligarchy or a law-governed monarchy, while arithmetic proportion is characteristic of democracy.[72] Relative to property geometric equality is contrasted with greed (*pleonexia*), and consists in a well balanced distribution of wealth, which assures moderation and durability in

[68] *Amat.* 759d, *an Seni* 790a, cf. also *de Virt.Mor.* 450b, *de Frat.Amor.* 479a.

[69] *Num.* 20.12. Cf. *Praec.* 802c: Pericles' 'democracy' was in fact the rule of the first citizen.

[70] Plutarch references in Aalders 1982a: 34 n.118.

[71] *De Sera* 551f–553b. In the *de Unius* (not to be ascribed to Plutarch) monarchy is held to be the form of government to be preferred, for it is 'the only one able to sustain completely the top note of virtue' (827b). In other forms of government the statesman, although he rules, is controlled and conditioned by others. All the same, a good politician will adapt himself to oligarchy and democracy as well.

[72] *Quaest.Conv.* 719a–c.

cities. In Lycurgus' polity this principle was realized admirably.[73] There is an apparent conflict here with Plutarch's preference for a monarchical regime. However his most cherished political ideals are consistent with either a monarchical or a republican form of government: in line with the subordination of politics to ethics, what really matters if good government is to be realized is the moral quality of the rulers rather than political institutions. Anyone called to govern others must first exercise control over himself, and only those who have learnt to obey can command.[74] Besides the traditional list of cardinal virtues, together with humanity and benevolence, the ruler must have a mind fit for directing affairs, resolution and experience, and the ability to choose the right moment and the appropriate words.[75] Power of persuasion is essential for winning one's subjects' confidence, so rhetoric is for the politician an indispensable tool. His speeches should be marked by frankness, concern, charm and grandeur. Great kings of the past were 'speakers of words' (*Praec.* 801c–d, 802f–803b).

Some of the qualities essential in a ruler, such as prudence, wisdom, and foresight, are typical of old age. This is a compelling reason for the elderly to engage in politics, as is argued in *Should the elderly engage in politics?* Advanced age has never been an impediment for great politicians. What is appropriate for youth is obedience: old age is suited to command (789d). In this phase of life those youthful defects which stand in the way of right political action become less pronounced:

> The political activity of the elderly is free from ostentation and longing for popularity, not just in their speech but in their actions too . . . So they should engage in public life for the sake of the young . . . The discretion of old age, when mixed with youth boiling in the assembly, may remove what is wild and dangerous taken neat. (*Should the elderly engage in politics?* 791b–c)

The principle governing the assignment of functions is competence, not youth (791d). It is in fact timely for the elderly to engage in politics so that they can educate and instruct the young (790e).

In Plutarch's writings on politics, in particular *Advice on politics*, precepts of general validity sit alongside pieces of advice designed for the situation of the moment. Some of the latter are suggestions on tactics, sometimes

[73] But the ideal of a mixed constitution, to which Plutarch alludes only a few times, is treated as purely theoretical: Aalders 1968: 124–6.

[74] *Ad Princ.* 780b, *Praec.* 806f.

[75] *Ad Princ.* 780e, *an Seni* 792d, 796e, *Praec.* 801f, *Lyc.* 30.4, *Num.* 20.12.

Machiavellian tricks, concerning the outward appearance of the politician. They are represented as opportune for achieving agreements. The fact is that the politician lives under the gaze of an audience, having to account for his public behaviour and his private life alike, in an arena where every small fault becomes the subject of comment and gets exaggerated (*Praec.* 800d–e). He should therefore avoid the most conspicuous and reprehensible errors (800b). He should not reveal himself to be ambitious, for an excessive love of office is not noble. He should shrink from honours, except for those which represent an expression of gratitude and goodwill, and not just repayment for favours received.[76] Taking care over these exteriors is necessary because only the support of the people guarantees the politician freedom of action.[77]

The basically ethical orientation of Plutarch's political thought seems compromised by his encouragement of tricks like the following: feigning disagreement in the assembly, but then retracting it after pretending to reconsider – so that it will appear that one is acting for the common good; feigning disagreement with one's friends on matters of small importance, so that agreement with them on major issues will not appear prearranged; distributing wealth equally to soothe the common citizens, while guaranteeing concessions to the wealthy; pardoning small misdemeanours in order to pre-empt intransigent opposition (813b, 815a, 818a).

Some of the advice given reflects Plutarch's concern for good relations between the Greek cities and the Roman empire. Those who rule must remember that they in turn are ruled, their cities being controlled by proconsuls. They should not only be punctilious in their dealings with the Romans, but also make friends with those of them who are influential (813e, 814c). That does not mean excessive subservience, nor submitting every tiny problem to those in authority, making slaves of themselves against the wishes of their masters. Plutarch's ambition is that the Greek cities should retain a dignified autonomy, permitting them the enjoyment of the limited freedom the Romans concede; but too much freedom would be damaging (814e, 824c). It is the job of those in government to convince the people of Greece's political weakness, and get them to appreciate the present situation of peace and concord, and the disappearance of wars and tyrannies.[78] In recommending expedients of these kinds Plutarch is motivated by a sincere love of his country, which needs continual care and assistance from the statesman (*an Seni* 792e–f).

[76] *An Seni* 786e, *Praec.* 820b–e. [77] *Praec.* 821d, *Max.cum Princ.* 777e.
[78] *An Seni* 784f, *Praec.* 824e.

There is a fundamental tension in Plutarch's political thought between the high importance he attaches to politics and the limited scope for political action a Greek statesman actually had in the imperial period. His theoretical approach and its strong ethical inspiration – his Platonic inheritance – are in collision with the fact that there could be no alternative to Roman domination, which he did not, however, consider the worst of all possible worlds. This is why there are times when pragmatism prevails over theory, although his basic ethical outlook never weakens. One might even argue that his ethical conception of politics is in fact reinforced, because his primary objective is not the development of an intellectual project of vast proportions, but the good government of the city. In his extant writings, at least, there are only a few hints of an idealistic theory of kingship, which mostly rely on commonplace notions. Plutarch looks instead to the past in his attempt to find morally sound examples of good government which might guide the politicians of his time.

5 Conclusions

The authors we have been considering shared a preference for kingship which it is tempting to connect with the historical situation of the period. In all of them, however, this predilection seems rather theoretical. Its roots can be found in Plato's *Politicus*. The best form of government will become a reality if by divine chance power is concentrated in the hands of a single divine human, a philosopher king. It could always be said that the actual presence of a monarch of the world had removed its utopian character from the doctrine of kingship, making it more plausible. But like Plato, the thinkers we have studied recognized the extreme difficulty of finding the divine nature which would be worthy of the title of king. Philo and Plutarch both look for the realization of this ideal not in the present, but in the remote past, each of them within his own cultural tradition. Far from adopting a posture of adulation, they show themselves to be pretty critical of the practice of divinization of rulers so far as concerns externals, and pseudo-Ecphantus too alludes to the wholesale usurpation of the title of king by those who are not worthy of it. Signs of a possible inclination towards the idea of citizenship of the world, far from being based on the existence of world dominion by the Romans, are rather a consequence of the analogy between God and king, world and city.

Philo's and Plutarch's very different attitudes to politics reflect the different cultures which they inhabit. Plutarch's high evaluation of the political life is rooted in old Greek ideals focused on the city-state, while

Jewish tradition exercised a strong influence on Philo's conviction that politics is an adjunct of the one law of nature laid down by Moses. The pseudo-Pythagorean texts offer the most systematic treatment, but that seems to owe more to their authors' penchant for conceptual schematism than to a particular interest in politics. Their divergent treatments of the best form of constitution are apparently purely academic, and in line with a marked archaizing tendency. This may offer confirmation of the hypothesis that this literature is to be dated to a period in which there was no room for politics as a real enterprise.

28

Josephus

TESSA RAJAK

1 The place of political thought in Josephus' writings

The historian Josephus succeeds Philo as the exponent of a political theory centred on Judaism and expressed in Greek. The two writers are intellectually far apart, and Josephus had little penchant for philosophical speculation. Nonetheless, their backgrounds and experience are comparable. From a base within the small Jewish social elite of the Roman east, each acted for a period as political leader, defender of the Jews and delegate to the emperor; in Josephus' case, the mission marked the beginning of his career. Josephus' literary output, almost as much as Philo's, belongs to the diaspora: transferring from Jerusalem to Rome, he addressed readers in the Greek world. Admittedly, unlike Philo, who probably knew no Hebrew, Josephus, of priestly and royal stock and brought up in an Aramaic/Hebrew milieu, had to labour, he informs us, to perfect his grasp of the language in which he wrote.[1] But this he successfully did, and, for all his Roman patronage, the framework and the intellectual agenda of his writings are primarily Greek.[2]

It is commonly thought that Josephus knew and exploited Philo. Thus, part of the discussion of Jewish practices in the *Against Apion* reveals a close dependence on Philo's now fragmentary *Hypothetica*.[3] At the same time, the bulk of Josephus' extensive output is historical; there theory emerges, as we would expect, as analysis in the context of the narration of events – whether distant, recent or contemporary. Josephus is absorbed by politics and it was natural that Thucydides should be a model, influencing not only the language and the narrative, but, most relevant here, the Jewish historian's general conceptions of the attributes of leadership and of the destructive power of civil dissension (*stasis*).

[1] On all these points, Rajak 1983. [2] For Roman elements, Goodman 1994.

[3] Fragments in Eusebius, *Praep. Ev.* 8.15. Indicative parallels include the prohibition on destroying a fleeing animal or killing an animal with its young or a bird in its nest: see Terian 1985: 142–6. On Philo's *Hypothetica* in Josephus: Troiani 1978, and, rejecting direct dependence, Carras 1993. Schwartz 1990: 40–3 and 52–4, minimizes Josephus' knowledge of Philo.

Josephus joined the Jewish revolt against Rome of AD 66–73/4, but deserted at an early stage from the revolutionary side. He then witnessed and lamented the fall of Jerusalem, and was behind the scenes during the rise of the Flavian dynasty to power at Rome. The emotive charge behind his writing, an element in it of personal *apologia*, and a tendency to inconsistency, warn us not to attempt to systematize his ideas.

Nonetheless, his works may reasonably be considered for this purpose as a unified corpus. It is true that their composition extended over a long period, with the *Jewish War* written in the AD 70s, the *Antiquities* and *Life* appearing in the 90s, and the *Against Apion* after that. Their subject matter also diverges, from a rewriting of the Bible in the first half of the *Antiquities*, to a day-by-day account of the historian's personal conduct as a regional commander in the *Life*. Yet, on the relevant issues, it can be plausibly maintained that Josephus' views did not manifestly change.[4] His core readership, too, which will have consisted of both Jewish and non-Jewish readers in the Greek cities of the Roman empire, is likely to have remained fairly constant.

2 Greek-Jewish thought

Josephus drew on an extensive corpus of political ideas and concepts. The books of the Bible offered a range of doctrines and exempla concerned with government and decision-making. It appears that Josephus was familiar with the Bible in Greek as well as in Hebrew. The Greek translation, especially that of some of the later books, offered above all a ready vocabulary for describing the power of God, notably *dunasteia*, *basileia*, *archē*, *exousia*, *dunamis*; correspondingly, in the Septuagint, the people of Israel was God's slave, *doulos*; this formulation was also adopted, but more rarely, by our cautious historian.[5]

Greek-Jewish literature was created under the impact of the changing national fortunes of the Jews: exile, Persian suzerainty, the rise of the high priesthood as a political force, the revolt of the Maccabees against the Seleucids, a state under Seleucid rule, the independent Hasmonean monarchy, the declining authority of that monarchy, *stasis*, the Roman conquest, the hardening of sectarianism, revolt and the loss of Temple and capital city. One consequence of this experience was a growing capacity to

[4] Some scholars prefer, however, to emphasize evidence of development. See especially Cohen's version of the widely-accepted theory that Josephus' much-vaunted early affiliation with the Pharisees is retrojected from the 90s: Cohen 1979. But for a denial that Josephus ever meant to identify himself with Pharisaism, see Mason 1991.

[5] Gibbs and Feldman 1986: 289–90.

describe and analyse political change, and above all, in the literature which was written in Greek.[6]

The lasting importance of this Jewish-Greek tradition, to which Josephus firmly belongs, is often seen as lying in the transmission of material directly from this world into Christian literature, a process visible already in the New Testament. But Jewish-Greek political thought is valuable also in its own right, as a creative fusion of a non-Greek literary culture with Greek ideas. Interpreters have debated the proportions of the Greek and Jewish ingredients in the mix; the truth is that they are inseparable.[7]

3 Leading ideas in Josephus

Josephus accepted the regular Jewish-Greek interpretation of Judaism as a *politeia*, or, occasionally, *politeuma*, a constitutional system. Although the Jews were a dispersed race (*genos*) of whom the majority no longer resided in their homeland of Judaea, the appropriateness of the definition came from the central role in Jewish life of the Torah, that is to say the Pentateuchal texts and the code of law set out in them. The *politeia* is indeed sometimes said to be enshrined in a book.[8] The definition also served to evoke the desired moral and social cohesion of Jewish communities within the non-Jewish civic structures surrounding them.[9] The Jewish *politeia* of the writers, however, is often in large measure theoretical, virtually a city of God.

Among Josephus' works, the *Against Apion* is the only one to offer political theory *in extenso*. The work as a whole defends Judaism against a number of named detractors from previous generations, first and foremost the Alexandrian intellectual, Apion. While the first book demonstrates the superiority of the Jewish nation by proving its antiquity, the second book is devoted specifically to the refutation of slanders, and in the process it concerns itself precisely with defining, interpreting and defending the Jewish constitution. Here, Josephus' political thought is distilled and systematically set out without the need to engage with reality which

[6] Bickerman 1988, with attention to both Greek and Aramaic milieux; Mendels 1992, Rajak 1996.

[7] See especially Attridge 1976 for an analysis of the Jewish dimension in the biblical *Antiquities*.

[8] *Antiquitates Judaicae* IV.194; 302 ff.; *Contra Apionem* II.295 etc. Lebram 1974 stresses instead antecedents from Hellenistic utopias. But the parallels in Strabo and Diodorus account for only a small part of Josephus' conception.

[9] However, the term *politeuma*, sometimes taken to have been the formal definition of the Jewish entity within a Greek city, is never used by Josephus in this sense: Lüderitz 1994: 222. He uses *politeuma* for *politeia* at *Contra Apionem* II.145, 164, 165, 184, 250, 257.

makes itself apparent in his other writings.[10] It is implicit in the discussion that Jewish types are to be judged in terms of the aims and attributes of Greek constitutions. The system is held out for inspection as a realized utopia, available for emulation by the rest of humanity; it is already widely admired by philosophers, copied by legislators, and sought after by ordinary people (*Contra Apionem* II.279ff.). Plato, in excluding unedifying representations of deities, is also its imitator (II.257).

The Jewish *politeia* is also described in the *Antiquities*, in what is formally a digression within the Deuteronomic account of the death of Moses (*Antiquitates Judaicae* IV.196–301). Public and domestic regulations from Deuteronomy are combined with material from Leviticus. Other thoughts by the author on the subject are dispersed through the biblical part of the work and especially the Mosaic sections.

3.1 Theocracy and monotheism

To Josephus falls the distinction of adding a new concept to political thought. This he presents as an innovation, within the accepted framework of the three basic types of rule. Josephus speaks, indeed, of 'twisting the language' (*CA* II.165). His concept, which has endured, is *theokratia*, the sovereign rule of God. On one occasion, the lawgiver is said to have placed in divine hands 'all sovereignty [*archē*] and power' (II.167). Generally, however, supremacy rests with the Deity, and the Mosaic constitution is described as one framed in accordance with God's will (184), or as deriving from knowledge of God's true nature (250), or even just as emanating from God, much as divine origins are ascribed to Greek constitutions as a preliminary to the discussion in Plato's *Laws*. It does not seem that theocracy is necessarily incompatible with a human monarchy for Josephus, although his formulation has been taken to imply this.

The sole rulership of God is embodied in the first commandment (190). This in turn generates a governing principle, that of unity. The unity of the godhead is pictured as replicated in the structure of the world and in human institutions, the one and only Temple (II.193). In the *Antiquities*, a link is made also with the special status of the Jewish people, and the centrality of Jerusalem (*AJ* IV.199–201). Also deriving from this principle are *homonoia*, social unity, and *sumphōnia*, unanimity of opinion (*CA* II.179–80), which can be understood as guarantees against civil dissension.[11]

[10] On the whole *Against Apion* discussion, see especially Vermes 1982. Amir 1985–8: 84–5 regards the *Antiquities* material as an earlier stage in Josephus's development.

[11] On unity: *CA* II.193. Vermes 1982: 295. On *stasis*, see below, p. 594.

3.2 *The Jewish* politeia

In Josephus' eyes, a constitution fixes the framework of life, its *kataskeuē* (*CA* II.156) or *diataxis* (*AJ* IV.198) or *kosmos* (*AJ* III.84). The *politeia*, thus broadly defined, sometimes includes the entire Jewish code of life. It is therefore easy for him to follow the standard Platonic-Aristotelian line, that a *politeia* promotes the virtues through education. By contrast, he recalls that the anti-Semites Apollonius Molon and Lysimachus had alleged Jewish laws to be instructors in vice, *kakia*: *CA* II.145. In the *Antiquities* (IV.179), Moses before his death bequeaths the laws to the people, not only as an eternal possession, but also, again echoing philosophical sources, as a producer of happiness.

At the opening of his defence (*CA* II.145), Josephus lists the cardinal virtues recognized in Jewish philosophy as follows: piety (*eusebeia*), fellowship (*koinōnia*), universal goodwill (*tēn katholou philanthropian*), and, by way of additions, justice, supreme perseverance and a contempt for death. Several points are noteworthy in this hierarchy: the primary position of piety, the relegation of justice to the secondary list,[12] the emphasis on communitarian values, and the expectation of persecution. The analysis is clearly influenced by the charges requiring refutation,[13] and it is evidently appropriate to an embattled group.

That there is an *ad hoc* quality about Josephus' formulation – and that he is no philosopher – is revealed by his disconcerting readiness to alter the proposition materially only a little later in the discourse. Piety, *eusebeia*, is further accentuated, and is said to replace *aretē*, which it subsumes as the overarching category; the elements of piety are the Platonic virtues in their Jewish adaptation: justice, temperance (*sōphrosunē*), perseverance, and, lastly, harmony (*sumphōnia*, in place of the expected *phronēsis*: 171).

What the two versions have in common, then, is the prominence of the value of communal harmony as a good. Even women fall into line (181). But such group loyalty is not incompatible with openness to outsiders: the Spartan expulsions of foreigners are undesirable, and Jews are never misanthropic (261). This interesting comparison with Sparta recurs when Jewish perseverance is said to outdo Spartan; their much-vaunted tenacity thus confers upon the constitution of the Jews another attribute highly valued in Greek political thought, and exemplified by Sparta, that of stability. And Josephus observes that even the Spartan system had succumbed to its own defects in the end (222ff.; 272 ff.). Finally, he lends an

[12] In his biblical narrative, Josephus does emphasize justice as a commendable attribute in certain monarchs, though still not as a pre-eminent quality. See, e.g. on Josiah, Feldman 1993b: 123–4.
[13] See *CA* II.147–8.

extra dimension to the discussion, by repeatedly stressing his people's distinctive readiness to undergo martyrdom for the sake of the law; this is the ultimate guarantor of its preservation.[14] A law which is promised as eternal must outdo all others.

3.3 *The law and the legislator*

Nomos or its plural is the term used to refer to the Jewish law, and these words are often used synonymously with *politeia*, as in the recurring phrase 'the laws and the constitution' (e.g. *AJ* IV.194). At another moment, Josephus adopts a spurious precision, announcing that he will discuss those Mosaic laws which are specifically constitutional. In fact, the laws then discussed turn out to be nothing of the kind, but rather to include all the basic prescriptions for private life, as well as various public arrangements which are less matters of social organization than of cult: especially the festivals and the mechanics of tithing.[15]

In *Against Apion*, laws are deemed the mark of civilization, by contrast with rule by edict and custom; and since the Jewish code is an ancient one, even perhaps the most ancient, the Jews emerge as highly civilized. Josephus, as is well known, noticed the absence of the word *nomos* from the Homeric poems (*CA* II.155). The exact reference of *nomoi*, in the Jewish context, is no clearer in Josephus than in any other Greek-Jewish text. In broad terms, the laws must be equated with Torah; but it is impossible to discern whether Josephus, where he speaks of a written source (for example at *AJ* IV.194), has in mind the ten commandments, the Pentateuchal law codes, the entire Pentateuch, or even the Pentateuch together with all that already existed by way of oral law, which was understood as integral to the written Torah.

Moses, as legislator, is the sole human architect of the Jewish way of life, a system written and promulgated by him as a body of legislation, a *nomothesia* (*AJ* IV.319 ff). Moses is set firmly in a comparative context when he is pitted against Lycurgus, Solon and Zaleucus of Locri; once, too, Minos is introduced (II.161). The lawgiver is, we learn again, the educator of the nation, and Moses' institution of weekly readings ensured complete familiarity with the provisions on the part of the (male) population (175–8).[16] Moses understood, as many did not, that education had to be

[14] *CA* II.232, 272, 277–8; Gafni 1989: 124–5. See also Rajak 1997. The word used is *athanatos*; cf. *AJ* IV.179: *aidion*. [15] *AJ* IV.199–291. For this point, see Troiani 1994.

[16] The comparison with other lawgivers echoes the opening of Plato's *Laws*. While the emphasis on education is also Platonic, Josephus is more specifically concerned with instruction in the system of law. See Feldman 1993b: 118–20, on this idea in relation to Josephus' presentation in the *Antiquities* of King Josiah as teacher. See also Schroder 1996, on Josephus' version of Jewish law.

both theoretical and practical, with the dietary laws, in particular, offering the desirable element of *askēsis*. The law is also said to educate as a father and mother educate (174), and especially through the medium of Sabbath reading (175).

3.4 *Priestly rule*

That the Jewish polity is a hierocracy, a system of priestly rule, is another central principle for Josephus, deriving from his understanding of *theokratia* (*CA* II.185–7; *AJ* XI.111). This is the system he regularly endorses, even though, rather than using the term, he subsumes the dominance of the high-priestly families under the technical heading of aristocracy.

Sometimes, he assigns a non-technical spokesmanship or representative leadership (*prostasia*, or *hēgēmonia*) to the officiating high priests, but in a manner which is not irreconcilable with the aristocratic model.[17] It is worth mentioning that this predilection for the priesthood emerges as at least partly personal in origin: Josephus' priestly descent was a major source of pride, which he made more of even than he did of his royal origins. However, a remarkably similar interpretation of the Jewish system is earlier enunciated in supposed citations from a Greek writer of the fourth century BC, Hecataeus of Abdera.[18]

Hierocracy came about because God as the supreme ruler of the universe delegated power to the priesthood. The original priestly title had been allocated according to the skills and aptitudes of those selected, thus generating an aristocracy in the true sense. In a notionally inalterable system, centred on holiness, the priesthood, and above all the high priesthood, is entrusted with the permanent protection of the legal status quo, as well as with civil and criminal jurisdiction (*CA* II.187). The omission here of any mention of a lay judiciary has been noted.[19] An Aaronite high priesthood had existed for 2,000 years, with Aaron as the first in the line (*AJ* XX.224; 261). The interpretative activities of a rabbinic or proto-rabbinic class are not allowed for in this Greek version of an ideal Jewish polity.

It follows that Josephus approves of an autonomous state with a high priest at its head, such as existed in Jewish history through much of the

[17] On hierocracy in Judaean theory and practice, see Goodblatt 1994: 30–56, arguing for pre-Hasmonean origins. In relation to Josephus' theory: Amir 1985–8. On *prostasia*: Schwartz 1983/4: 33–8.

[18] On Josephus' personal relationship with the priesthood: *Vita* 1–2; Rajak 1983: 14–20. On Josephus' hierocracy generally, Vermes 1982: 294–6, Amir 1985–8: 88–92, Cancik 1987: 67–74, Thoma 1989. On Hecataeus, as cited in Diodorus XL.3.3–5, Goodblatt 1994: 31–5.

[19] Vermes 1982: 295.

Hasmonean period, and also earlier, as he believed, under Moses and Joshua (VI.84; XX.229) and probably also under the judges.[20] There is less to be commended in the kingly rule of Saul, many of the Davidic dynasty or, especially, Herod, who had devalued the high priesthood (XX. 247). On the whole, the ideal is conceived schematically: discussion in the *Against Apion* is conducted on a plane where questions such as the manner of appointment of the high priest in charge, the preferred succession, or the precise role of the high-priestly aristocracy simply do not arise.[21] Even from the long *Antiquities* excursus on the high-priestly succession (XX.224–51), we learn only that an office held for life gave way to limited tenure (XX.229). Josephus writes, indeed, as though the Temple still stood.

3.5 *Secular power*

Embedded in Josephus' narrative, and particularly in his biblical history with its strong moralizing and apologetic tendencies, appear thumbnail sketches of political skill in action and of the correct or faulty exercise of power.[22] It is once again Moses who stands out unchallenged as the perfect model. His supreme *aretē* incorporates all the virtues, and above all sagacity and wisdom.[23] The encomium on his death emphasizes his control of the passions, the power of his oratory, his generalship; but also, as the climax, the prophetic identity of the man through whom God spoke (*AJ* IV.328–9). Even the *Against Apion* offers an opportunity to delineate Moses' political achievements (II.157 ff.): he is a brave general, a shrewd counsellor, and a selfless protector; although he is effectively in sole control, and often lonely in power, his behaviour stands out as the opposite of tyrannical. But we remain in no doubt that his subjection to the divine will is what permits superhuman perfection to Moses.

However, Israel was subject at periods to less acceptable rulers, and often to outside rule. Josephus, of course, recognized such historical realities: theocracy was an ideal. This was also a long way from the uncompromising theocratic doctrine ascribed by Josephus to the revolutionary groups of 66–73/4, who refused to recognize any other master than God.[24] The originators of this doctrine, the followers of the so-called fourth philosophy (the coinage is probably Josephus' own), are said to

[20] VI.84, XX.261; however, the judges seem to be defined as monarchs at XI.112 and XX.230. See Schwartz 1983/4: 39.

[21] Cf. Thoma 1989: 201: 'Josephus evades the question how much political power might be given to the high priest.'

[22] For the terms in which leaders and prominent personalities are praised, see Villalba I Varneda 1986: 200–3.

[23] See especially Feldman 1992 and 1998a: 374–442.

[24] *Bellum Judaicum* II.117–19; VII.323, 410, 418; *AJ* XVIII.23, Hengel 1989/1961: 76 and 90ff.

diverge from the Pharisees precisely on that point. Josephus abhors their extremism and he blames the destruction of his nation on the heirs of the fourth philosophy.[25]

3.6 *Rulers, emperors, and the rise and fall of nations*

Josephus understands temporal events as part of a world-historical process. In essentially biblical terms, the destinies of nations are seen as ordained by God, and as triggered by the moral conduct of human beings. At this level, instability enters even the durable Jewish *politeia*. In the *Jewish War*, the notion of the shift of divine favour from the Jews to Rome, and, specifically, to the Flavian dynasty, is a key explanatory tool, going far beyond the historian's personal need to exculpate himself from charges of betraying the anti-Roman movement.[26] In the *Antiquities*, the doctrine finds expression in the historian's rendering of Daniel's prophecy of the succession of kingdoms, where he appears to imply, but avoids mentioning, the predestined ultimate supersession of Roman power as well.[27]

Vespasian, in the *Jewish War*, is one such ruler ordained by God for the world, and for the Jews: he may even be intended to emerge as a Messianic figure of the type of Cyrus, who had redeemed Israel from the first exile. At the same time, the Roman general and future emperor is equipped with the attributes of the good commander and of a leader of men, basking in what is a faint reflection of the panegyric lavished by Josephus on the younger Titus. It is the latter who is endowed by his protégé with the full repertoire of imperial virtues, notably courage, compassion, and clemency.[28]

World rulers may be put in position by God, but the distinction between that idea and any claim to divinity on behalf of God's ordained is carefully preserved in Josephus. So too is the distinction between sacrificing to the emperors and offering sacrifices for their welfare (*CA* II.73–7). Josephus again distances himself from emperor worship by his willingness to criticize actions such as Herod's importation of Roman military standards into Jerusalem and the erection of Caligula's cult statue in the city.[29] The rejection of idolatry, important already in the later books of the Bible, is a central theme in post-exilic writing, and such material is

[25] Josephus also seems to imply, however, that later, during the rebellion, the revolutionary leader Menahem was hailed as a would-be Messianic king. See Mendels 1992: 222 and 352n.

[26] *Bellum Judaicum* II.261, IV.353, V.19, V.367; *AJ* XX.166 etc. Linder 1972: 42–8, Rajak 1983: 99.

[27] *AJ*. X.210. Investigated anew by Mason 1994: 172–6.

[28] On readings of Vespasian as Messiah: Rajak 1983: 192. On Titus: Yavetz 1975 (showing also that Titus' ruthlessness is not wholly concealed by Josephus); Rajak 1983: 205–6.

[29] Although it has been noted that the earlier erection of the altar at Jamnia (Ph. *Leg*. 200–3) is omitted by Josephus.

highly visible in both Aramaic and Greek texts of the period. Autocratic rulers, especially oriental despots, are regularly associated with idols: these figures, often grotesque or intimidating, represent either the rulers themselves as gods or else their favoured deities. Here, then, is a distinctly Jewish reflection on monarchy, but one expressed in graphic form rather than as theory. Josephus, in his adaptation of the book of Daniel, gives full coverage to the golden image, sixty cubits by six, set up by Nebuchadnezzar in the great plain of Babylon, to which all but the Jews bowed down at the sound of the trumpet (*AJ* x.213–4).

3.7 *The masses and the idea of freedom*

Despots were anathema. But the people were no better. In the *Jewish War*, the rebel ideology of the zealots (in the narrow sense) and the *sicarii* (knifemen) is presented as the polar opposite to the stance of respectable elements in society, exemplified, not surprisingly, by the historian himself. Josephus' unrestrained disgust for all the dissidents is rooted in personal experience and in events; but the standard formulae derived from Greek political thought on mob behaviour are useful explanatory devices. It is worth remembering that the irresponsibility and capriciousness of the mob was a regular preoccupation of the Greek world under Rome. Certainly, a blanket contempt for the masses (*plēthos* or *dēmos*) runs through Josephus' thinking. A statement of Plato (*Timaeus* 28c) is paraphrased as asserting that it is not safe to expose the truth about God to the ignorance of the masses (*CA* II.224). Josephus does, however, allow that there exists one virtue, recognized by Jews and Greeks alike, which is open to the people – subservience, both to the law (*CA* II.153), and to their masters (*AJ* IV.187).

For Josephus, civil discord, *stasis*, was the prime cause of the Jewish revolt. This is the agent which undermines consensus, breeding violence, sacrilege and other forms of madness, and, in the *Jewish War*, the conflict is for the most part fought out between the rich and the poor. The damage done by discord is a theme taken up again in the *Antiquities*, especially in Book IV, in which Korah's rebellion and other protests against Moses are recounted. The influence of Thucydides on Josephus is here unmistakeable; however, unlike Thucydides, Josephus offers no more than passing reflections of a general nature on the topic.[30]

Freedom, *eleutheria*, is the stated political aim of rebel groups. Perhaps on account of the resonances of this abstraction for both Greek and

[30] Cf. also *AJ* I.117 (the tower of Babel); VIII.205 ff. (Jeroboam). On *stasis* in the *Jewish War*, Brunt 1977a, Rajak 1983: 91–4; in the *Antiquities*, Feldman 1993a: 43–51 and 1998b: 237–9.

Roman readers, Josephus, in the *Jewish War*, does not wholly disguise the admirable aspect of this revolutionary ideal. On the rock of Masada, before the mass suicide of the last of the Jewish resistance, the rebel leader Eleazar ben Yair is allowed two speeches in which to laud death over political subjection, defining the latter simply as slavery. The ideals are depicted in distinctly Hellenizing terms, and it is indisputable that they stand out starkly, and unchallenged, even if modern historians continue to differ about Josephus' underlying attitude to the episode.[31]

It is interesting that speaking in his own voice too, Josephus was ready to label foreign rule enslavement, and to take for granted the positive value of national liberation.[32] In one sense, he was doing no more than following the book of Exodus. It has been shown that in his version of I Maccabees, his minor changes serve to endorse the Hasmonean war of liberation as a meritorious human act.[33] When he argues with Apion, he uses the word *douleuein* of the condition of subjection to Rome (*CA* II.125), just as he had in Agrippa's and his own orations in the *Jewish War* (II.355–6; V.364). It is fair to say that throughout the latter work, the Roman empire is an acceptable necessity, but never a positive good.[34]

Political freedom also figures in Josephus in a wholly different context. It is a fact no less remarkable for being well known that the Jewish historian made the deliberate choice of incorporating a long narrative (the only one to survive) of the assassination at Rome of the emperor Caligula into Book XIX of his *Antiquities*. The episode is presented as an act of liberation from tyranny of the highest order: Josephus takes care to stress that 'freedom' was the conscious goal, as well as the achievement, of the conspirators, and he highlights the role of Cassius Chaerea, 'who planned for our liberty in the time of tyranny', and whose password was *eleutheria*.[35]

But Josephus was acutely aware of the dangers of liberty and a careful distinction is drawn, in Moses' parting words to the people (*AJ* IV.187–9), with insubordination, offensive arrogance (*hubrizein*) and licence, *parrhēsia*. Here, again, Josephus exploits a familiar Greek distinction. Ultimately, however, we remain in no doubt that for him liberty was more than a political value. In his mind was a religio-political ideal, intrinsic to Judaism as he presented it, and naturally therefore attainable only through the law.[36] Freedom is God's reward to those who abide by his

[31] Ladouceur 1987 stresses Josephus' reservations about the ideals behind the suicide of Masada, seeking to connect the historian's attitude with Stoic and Cynic discussions in Flavian Rome.
[32] See e.g. *AJ* III.20, 44, 64, 300; IV.42. On this, Feldman 1993d: 316 and 1998a: 435.
[33] Gafni 1989. [34] Stern 1987, Rajak 1991: 129–34.
[35] *AJ* XIX.11–273; see especially Sentius Saturninus' senatorial oration on tyranny: 167–84, culminating in the proposal of honours for Chaerea, 182–4.
[36] Feldman 1993d: 317. and 1998a: 435

precepts, enslavement his punishment. Liberty must thus be recognized as the product of discipline and submission. Once again, Josephus crystallizes and enunciates a fundamental Jewish-Greek concept, and in doing so foreshadows Christian philosophy.

29

Stoic writers of the imperial era

CHRISTOPHER GILL

1 Introduction

This chapter discusses four leading intellectuals in the first and second centuries AD. Their surviving or reported work (together with that of Seneca) provides points of access to the form that political thought took in a period in which there is no extant text that deals, in an obvious and systematic way, with political philosophy. These figures are interconnected in various ways. Musonius Rufus (*c.* 30–*c.* 101, these and all subsequent dates AD) taught both Dio Chrysostom (*c.* 40–*c.* 112) and Epictetus (*c.* 55–*c.* 135). The Stoic notebook (*Meditations*) of the emperor Marcus Aurelius (121–80) is avowedly influenced by Epictetus' *Discourses*; and his version of Stoic theory is broadly similar to that of Epictetus and Musonius. Dio Chrysostom differs from the others in combining the roles of philosopher and 'sophist' (public speech-maker), and in his philosophical eclecticism. But a significant element in the thought of his speeches is Stoic (of a type comparable with that of the other three thinkers); he also sometimes deploys the Stoicized Cynicism that appears in Epictetus.

The lives and thought of these individuals illustrate certain more general features of the period. Dio Chrysostom was a leading figure in the so-called 'Second Sophistic' movement; and his career displays how sophists, as public performers, functioned as intellectual communicators and as vehicles of Greco-Roman culture throughout the (Greek-speaking) Eastern part of the Roman empire.[1] More broadly, the careers of all four men exhibit the interlinking of Greek and Roman intellectual (and political) life, and the interplay between philosophy and politics in the period. Musonius and Marcus, though Romans, taught or wrote philosophy in Greek. Epictetus, a Greek-speaking ex-slave, taught important Romans in his school in Greece. Dio's intellectual fame from his (Greek) speech-making earned him the friendship of the emperor Trajan in a way that was

[1] See Russell 1992: 1; also Bowersock 1969.

materially helpful to Dio's political position in his own city-state (Prusa in Bithynia).

Philosophy, especially Stoicism, was also sometimes politically controversial in this period. Musonius, Dio and Epictetus were all affected, in different ways, by the expulsion of philosophers that occurred under Nero, Vespasian and Domitian.[2] Although it is inappropriate to talk of a 'Stoic opposition' (if this term is taken to mean that Stoicism is doctrinally opposed to imperial or monarchic rule as such), Stoicism provided a theoretical basis for those who wanted to signal their opposition, on ethical grounds, to the conduct of specific emperors.[3] On the other hand, the *Meditations* show Marcus Aurelius as a single-minded adherent to Stoicism, which raises the question of the relationship between his Stoic convictions and his practice as emperor.

This interplay between contemporary political life and Stoic philosophy underlies what is the most substantive issue of political thought that arises from the writings of these figures: how to locate the type of Stoic thinking that we find in all four figures (including, to some extent, Dio) within the spectrum of Stoic political theory. We can identify two main strands in the writings of these thinkers, which sometimes coexist as alternatives and are sometimes synthesized. In one strand, the dominant thought is that the guiding ideals of personal and political life should be those whose truth is established by philosophy, whether or not these ideals correspond with the ones current in any given conventional society at any one time. These ideals include those of the brotherhood of humankind, of rational or 'natural' law, of 'the city of gods and humans', and of 'cosmopolitanism' (seeing oneself as a citizen of the universe). These ideals are linked, sometimes explicitly, with the adoption of the Stoic sage or wise person (or some aspect of the sage-like perspective) as the guiding norm. Especially when there is recognition of actual or potential conflict with conventional practices, these norms may be combined with a Stoicized version of Cynicism, especially the idea of the Cynic as itinerant teacher. In the other strand, the emphasis falls rather on the thought that the Stoic goal of 'the life according to virtue' is one that is properly pursued by engagement with the practices, roles, and (to some extent) the rules of one's own, specific community. Conventional society does not only provide the context in which we can 'make progress' towards virtue

[2] Nero's expulsion of philosophers in 62 and 65–7, was selective, Vespasian's in 71, and Domitian's in 89 and 95 were general; see also pp. 601, 604, 607 below.

[3] See Brunt 1975: 7–10, 26–32, Griffin 1976 (1992): 363–6.

by learning to perform 'appropriate acts' (*kathēkonta*).[4] It can also constitute the prime context for our most ethically advanced, sage-like, actions and states, in which we realize most fully the ideals which figure in the other strand.

How does this combination of different strands of social and political philosophy relate to (broadly) 'political' thought in earlier Stoicism? They represent, in a more moderate form, two lines of thought which form part of Stoicism from its beginnings. On the one hand, we find the seemingly radical Cynic rejection of conventional ethics (in connection with the ideal 'city of the wise') in Zeno's, and possibly Chrysippus', *Republic*. On the other hand, we also find, as early as Chrysippus, and perhaps Zeno, the idea of a natural process of ethical development (*oikeiōsis*), from instinctive self-preservation to (in principle) sagehood, a process which is conceived as underlying, and occurring within, conventional social forms such as family and city-state. We also find, from at least Chrysippus onwards, an apparent attempt to negotiate between the key ideals of Stoic thought, such as the wise person and rational or natural law, and conventional social institutions, such as private property.[5] These two lines of thought can be explained by reference to different phases within Stoicism, on the assumption that Zeno's radical quasi-Cynicism was replaced, increasingly (though not uniformly) with a tendency to accommodate core Stoic ideals with at least qualified validation of conventional social structures.[6] Alternatively, we can see these two lines of thought as coordinate aspects of what is conceived from the beginning as a two-level theory. Zeno's 'city of the wise', 'the city of gods and humans', 'natural law', function, on this view, as objective norms or regulative ideals. The realization of these ideals belongs, in principle, within the social structures (e.g. family, city-state) which are the normal vehicles for personal and social *oikeiōsis*, that is, the natural impulse to identify with oneself and also with other humans. But life within these structures must be informed not only by their localized rules but also by regulative ideals; and this can give rise to interpersonal and political conflict or to 'Cynic' detachment from conventional structures.[7]

On either view, we can locate within Stoic thought the combination of strands noted above in the four thinkers treated in this chapter; indeed, in

[4] On *kathēkonta*, see Long and Sedley 1987: § 59, esp. B, D–G; also Kidd 1971.
[5] See Moles, in ch. 21 section 3 above, and Schofield, in ch. 22 sections 3 and 4 above; on *oikeiōsis*, see p. 608 below. [6] See e.g. Schofield 1991: esp. chs. 1, 4.
[7] See e.g. Annas 1993: 305–11, Vander Waerdt 1994.

the writings deriving from these thinkers, we find sustained treatment of ideas (and of the combination of ideas) for which our evidence from the early Stoics is indirect and fragmentary. A further respect in which these later thinkers continue the style of earlier Stoic theory is that their political thought does not generally take the form of constitutional theory. With the exception of Zeno's and Chrysippus' *Republic*s, we rarely find in Stoicism the ideal political theorizing of Plato's *Republic* or the (less radically idealized) constitutional revisionism of Plato's *Laws* and Aristotle's *Politics*.[8] The Stoic view is that political structures (like other social and interpersonal structures) can, in principle, function as vehicles for the attempt to make progress towards the life of virtue and sagehood. But there is no systematic advocacy (or systematic criticism) of any given constitutional form, for instance, kingship or imperial rule, considered as a vehicle of this type.

One other general point bears on the understanding of the work of all four thinkers. Insofar as politics can be given a determinate place in the Stoic three-part philosophical curriculum (normally given as logic–ethics–physics),[9] it forms part of ethics. However, we need also to distinguish between the theoretical analysis and defence of ethical principles and their practical application. In this period, 'practical ethics', both Stoic and non-Stoic, tends to be subdivided into a system of types or genres. These include 'therapy' (typically, 'curing' listeners by removing false ethical beliefs), 'protreptic' (encouraging listeners, typically to engage in serious philosophical activity), and 'advice' (based on, or helping people to grasp, key ethical principles).[10] All the texts discussed in this chapter fall under 'practical ethics' in this sense; with the partial exception of Dio, these writers presume the validity of Stoic theory, without offering an analytic account of it. Some of the differences between them derive from differences in the genre of practical ethics emphasized. Musonius' teachings, as preserved, mostly fall into the category of advice; Epictetus places more stress on the therapeutic function, which takes a more internalized, self-addressed form in Marcus' *Meditations*. In Dio's case, these functions are integrated, in turn, with the rhetorical aim of any given oration; Stoic

[8] For exceptions, see e.g. Cic. *Rep.* and *Leg.* (though these are only partly Stoic), discussed by Atkins in ch. 24 section 5 above; also, in the thinkers discussed in this chapter, Dio III.43–9 (n. 27 below). For alternative ways of understanding the relationship between the *Republic*s of Zeno and Plato, see Schofield 1991: ch. 2, esp. 22–6, Vander Waerdt 1994: 294–308.

[9] Long and Sedley 1987: § 26.

[10] See e.g. Stob. II.39.20–45.6 (Philo and Eudorus), Sen. *Ep.* 89.14, 94, esp. 1–4. See further (on Stoic practical ethics) Kidd 1971: 160–2, Brunt 1973: 19–26, Griffin 1976 (1992): 341 n.6; (on therapy) Nussbaum 1994.

philosophy forms part of the presumed intellectual background of the speeches.

2 Musonius Rufus

What is striking about the life of Musonius Rufus, as it is reported to us, is the consistency between his actions and teachings, given the interpretation of what Stoic principles require sketched in section (1). Together with other Stoic adherents, he signalled his disapproval, on ethical grounds, of Nero as person and emperor, following Rubellius Plautus into exile (62), before being exiled himself (65).[11] During his exile in Gyara, in line with his own advice in discourse IX, he used his situation as a context for virtuous action (continuing his work as a philosophical teacher). His other securely attested political acts include appealing to the armies invading Rome in 69 to make a truce and avoid violence; prosecuting P. Egnatius Celer, the accuser of the Stoic critic of Nero, Barea Soranus; and urging the Athenians not to hold gladiatorial games in the theatre of Dionysus. His principled political involvement may have played a significant role in making him a widely influential Stoic teacher.[12]

Musonius, like Epictetus (and Socrates, their shared model), wrote nothing. What are preserved are twenty-one summaries of his oral discourses by an unknown pupil Lucius and a number of fragments, presumably from similar records of his teaching, in Epictetus and other authors.[13] Although the Socratic dialogues are, in a general way, a model for such discourses, Musonius' discourses are expository rather than interrogatory. They offer advice grounded on Stoic principles, rather than the challenging 'therapy' offered by Epictetus.[14] From a modern perspective, the most striking feature of his views is his presentation of women as

[11] He returned to Rome after Nero's death, presumably recalled by Galba in 69. When Vespasian banished philosophers in general in 71, Musonius was specifically exempted, but seems to have been exiled subsequently. He was recalled by Titus.

[12] On his life, see Lutz 1947: 14–17, Geytenbeek 1963: 3–4. His pupils included (as well as Rubellius and Barea) Thrasea Paetus, Dio and Epictetus; on his influence and reputation in antiquity, see Lutz 1947: 18–24, Geytenbeek 1963: 14–15.

[13] Lucius' summaries (each between one and three pages long) are transmitted by Stobaeus, who also preserves many of the fragments; for a full list, see Lutz 1947: 146–7, whose ordering and pagination are followed here. The only modern edition is Hense 1905; Lutz 1947 contains text, translation and full introduction. Jagu 1979 contains introduction, translation and commentary in French.

[14] The fragments, both those preserved by Epictetus and by other authors, are more paradoxical and pungent than the discourses. Lutz 1947: 25–6 suggests that Lucius chose to present Musonius in the same (positive and straightforward) way that Xenophon presented Socrates.

being just as capable of virtue (and of practising philosophy) as men; and of the function of marriage as that of 'shared life' (*sumbiōsis*) and mutual concern as well as child-rearing.[15] Of related interest is his criticism of double standards regarding male and female sexual indulgence (XII); his assertion that marriage and child-rearing are compatible with philosophy (XIV); and his argument that people should have large families rather than dispose of unwanted heirs in infancy (XV). These views on gender- and sexual relationships form part of a larger body of advice on practical living, including his views on the way of life most appropriate for a philosopher (he recommends 'hands on' farming, XI),[16] and on appropriate styles of hair and beard (XXI).

Though striking, and seemingly novel, especially on gender-relationships, this advice can be seen as deriving from standard Stoic ethical thinking. In essence, Musonius is advising people how to live their lives in a way that is informed by the Stoic idea of *oikeiōsis*, especially in its social dimension. The central Stoic ideas that all human beings have 'the seeds [or starting-points] of virtue', and that the parent–child relationship is fundamental to the development of (natural) human association, underlie much of Musonius' advice.[17] These ideas are sometimes taken by other Stoic thinkers to carry implications for gender- and family-relationships similar to those drawn by Musonius, though not so explicitly stated.[18] However, to define more exactly Musonius' approach, we need to correlate it with the kinds of political thought outlined earlier. Although Musonius seems to be reformist or revisionist in advocating that women study philosophy, we should also note that 'philosophy' means for him 'practical ethics' focused on developing the virtues, and that the context in which women are to practise the virtues so developed is the conventional one of female domestic work and child-rearing. As he puts it in discourse III, 'I should not expect the women who study philosophy to shirk their accustomed tasks [including "sitting at home spinning"] for mere talk any more than men, but I maintain that their discussions should be

[15] See discourses III-IV, XIIIA–B. Musonius thus attaches to marriage the status as a context for interpersonal concern more commonly attached to male–male friendship in antiquity; see e.g. Arist. *EN* VIII.3–5, IX.4, 8, 9. For a contemporary response, see Foucault 1988: 151–2, 168–70.

[16] The preference for farming over (e.g.) crafts, as an occupation compatible with philosophy (and virtue) is common among ancient philosophers; but Musonius is unusual in recommending the physical labour of actual farming, rather than gentleman-farming, conceived as a source of status and leisure; see Brunt 1973: 10–13, and also n. 33 below.

[17] See e.g. Stob. II.65.8–9 (cf. Muson. II), Cic. *Fin.* III.62–8; also Blundell 1990.

[18] See e.g. D.L. VII.175 (Cleanthes' book-title, 'On the fact that the virtue of man and woman is the same'); Sen. *Cons.Marc.* 16.1; Stob. IV.503.18–512.7 (Hierocles and Antipater on marriage as context for fully shared life). The idea that 'the wise person should marry and have children' is a well-established Stoic theme, e.g. D.L. VII.121. See further Geytenbeek 1963: 56–8, 64–5, 67.

conducted for the sake of their practical application.'[19] In other words, what we have here is the use of Stoic ideals as regulative norms to inform lives lived within conventional social forms and practices (cf. p. 599 above). There is a stark contrast with the style of theory in Plato's *Republic*, for instance, where the same claim (that men and women have essentially the same natural capacities, including that for doing philosophy) is taken to lead to a radical revision of gender- and political relationships.[20]

The same general point applies to discourse VIII, 'That kings also should philosophize'. In Plato's *Republic* the argument centres on the claim that, in an ideal state, philosophers should be kings (or queens), and that political life should be reshaped to enable this.[21] Musonius' point is, by contrast, that kings – that is, kings in the world as it is – should practise philosophy, a point further qualified by the fact that 'philosophy' signifies mainly practical ethics, designed to develop virtues which are expressed through the conventional functions of kingship. In this respect, Musonius' discourse resembles what seems to have been the typical form of the Hellenistic 'kingship oration', in which the institution of kingship is accepted as valid, and emphasis falls on advice to use this role as a means of exercising the virtues (such as justice and self-control). However, discourse VIII is given rather more Stoic edge by the addition of the paradox that only the wise person can properly count as a king, and that he does so even if he is only 'king' over his family or himself. However, since the 'wise person' is here characterized as the one who has gained the virtues by philosophy, the link between the Stoic ideal and conventional political reality is still implicit.[22]

3 Dio

Dio Cocceianus of Prusa (later called 'Chrysostom', the 'golden tongue') is the most elusive, intellectually and personally, of the four men discussed in this chapter. Throughout his life, apart from his exile, he was a wealthy

[19] Muson. 42.16–19; trans. Lutz.

[20] See Pl. *Rep*. V.451c–461e; contrast Muson. 46.13–15 (discourse IV): women not to abandon spinning or do gymnastics with men.

[21] Pl. *Rep*. V considers two possibilities: that philosophers become rulers and that (actual) rulers become philosophers (473c11–d3), but only explores fully the first option. Cf. also Pl. *Ep*. VII (326b1–4), on which see Schofield, in ch. 13 above.

[22] See further Geytenbeek 1963: 124–9, also 33–40 (Musonius, like Seneca and Epictetus, presupposes the validity of the classic three-stage Stoic philosophical curriculum, but stresses the overall practical ethical outcome). For kingship orations, see Sen. *Clem*., with Griffin's discussion in ch. 26 section 1 above, and on Dio section 2 below.

and politically important figure in his city in Bithynia and, to some extent, at Rome. In the 60s he studied Stoic philosophy with Musonius; subsequently (perhaps coinciding with Vespasian's banishment of philosophers in 71), he repudiated philosophy and wrote in criticism of Musonius. He was himself banished by Domitian (*c.* 82) from Rome and Bithynia. He presents his exile, perhaps disingenuously, as bringing about a decisive 'conversion' to philosophy; he spent the period travelling around the Eastern Roman empire in the role of a Cynic-Stoic teacher.[23] After Domitian's death (96), Dio acquired status at Rome as an intellectual adviser to Nerva and Trajan, and resumed his economic and political role in Prusa until his death after 112.

His intellectual activities, both before and after his exile, span the categories of 'sophist' or public speechmaker, and philosopher.[24] His eighty surviving speeches fill five volumes of the Loeb Classical Library.[25] The present discussion focuses on certain speeches which exemplify his approach to political thought. This displays two overlapping tendencies, which are broadly comparable to those in Stoic thought outlined above (section 1); Dio himself eclectically combines Stoic with Cynic or Platonic themes. On the one hand, he sometimes assumes the validity of conventional social and political roles and structures (such as monarchy), and advocates the pursuit of virtue within these roles. On the other, he sometimes questions the validity of conventional thinking about social institutions or categories (such as slavery), or urges that social and political life should be lived by reference to universal regulative principles. In Dio's case, as in that of other thinkers of this period, potential conflict between these tendencies is mitigated by the fact that social questioning is not used as the basis for advocacy of institutional change.

Of the four 'kingship orations' delivered to Trajan, probably in the early 100s, the first three exhibit the first tendency, the fourth exhibits the second. The first three take what seems to be the typical form of such orations, when given by philosophers: that is, charting the virtues of a good king, and suggesting that the king addressed has (or potentially has) those virtues, as a way of trying to shape the monarch's goals. Dio avoids outright flattery by implying that he has the authority to define certain norms by which monarchic power should be guided. He uses the

[23] On his exile as ' conversion', see Dio XIII; Moles 1978 suggests that this self-presentation was designed to excuse his earlier attacks on philosophers, including his own teacher, Musonius. See also, less critical of Dio's motives, Jones 1978: ch. 6, Russell 1992: 4–6.

[24] On these categories, see Bowersock 1969: ch. 1, Jones 1978: ch. 2. Major studies of his life and work: von Arnim 1898, Desideri 1978.

[25] For a helpful edition of VII, XII and XXXVI, with introduction and commentary, see Russell 1992.

Stoic ideas of natural (rational) law to suggest that successful kings are those who subject themselves to this law, and thus create a community of reason (I.42–6). He also deploys (and advocates) Stoic or quasi-Stoic paradigms of active, other-benefiting (though also monarchic) virtue, such as Heracles, the bull, and the sun.[26] Another recurrent theme is the contrast, given added weight by mythic colour or allusions to philosophical theory, between the (virtuous) king and the (non-virtuous) tyrant.[27] The authority of Dio's advice is underlined by the more or less coded reminder that, unless Trajan adopts these ideals, and avoids tyranny, his reign, or indeed life, might not continue, a reminder given added edge by the (unmentioned) murder of the archetypical recent tyrant, Domitian, in 96.[28]

The fourth kingship oration, though belonging to the same period, exhibits the second, more interrogatory, tendency noted earlier. This speech is couched as a dialogue between Diogenes the Cynic (standing, broadly, for Dio) and Alexander the Great (standing for Trajan). Diogenes articulates the Cynic-Stoic view (with Platonic background) that kingship is conferred not merely by status but rather by the possession of the relevant kingly qualities, above all mastery over self- and other-benefiting virtue (IV.44–75).[29] The same tendency is evident in the two speeches on slavery. One (XIV, couched as a dialogue between Diogenes and an interlocutor) argues for the Platonic-Cynic-Stoic thesis that real 'freedom' is only conferred by virtue or wisdom, and that, by this criterion, even great kings are not necessarily 'free' to act as they wish.[30] The other, XV, is also couched as a dialogue, between one who upholds and one who questions the conventional Greek criteria of freedom and slavery, in which the second (quasi-Cynic) speaker effectively demonstrates the arbitrary character of conventional criteria.[31]

The three speeches just discussed, while challenging conventional

[26] See e.g. I.59–63, II.66–78, III.73–85: for Heracles and the bull as Stoic paradigms of other-benefiting virtue, see e.g. Cic. *Fin.* III.66. Another theme is the Platonic idea that humans should be subordinate to the rule of something divine, as cattle are to human shepherds: compare II.72 with e.g. Pl. *Laws* 713c–714a.

[27] See e.g. I.69–83, III.36–50. III.43–9 draws on the distinction between good (or less bad) and defective versions of constitutions (i.e. rule by one, few, many) in e.g. Pl. *Plt.* 302c–303b, Arist. *Pol.* IV.2, 1289a39–b11.

[28] See e.g. I.44–6, 84; see further Moles 1990: esp. 332–7, 346–7, 358–9; also Swain 1996: 192–6; and on kingship orations, Cairns 1989: ch. 1, esp. 19–21.

[29] Moles 1983b: esp. 272–8 also finds implied criticism of Trajan's aggressive and expansionist policies.

[30] See XIV.17–24; also e.g. Pl. *Gorg.* 467a–471e, *Rep.* IX.571a–579e, esp. 579b–e; on Epict. *Diss.* IV.1, see p. 611 below.

[31] The conclusion implied in XV.29–32 may be similar to that stated in XIV.17–18: that real 'freedom' is only that conferred by virtue.

thinking about social roles, stop short of arguing for large-scale institutional change. A further speech of Dio's (VII, the 'Euboean'), which has much intrigued modern scholars, does make recommendations about social forms, but framed as practical advice directed to individuals, rather than as revisionist social planning.[32] Through a fictional depiction of a small hunting community, the first half displays the way rural poverty does not prevent (and can positively promote) the development of virtue (103). In his commendation of actual (as distinct from gentleman-) farming, Dio recalls the teaching of his former mentor, Musonius.[33] More innovative is his claim that (for the poor as well as the rich) work which is compatible with virtue can also be found in cities. Although he rules out a very wide range of occupations on ethical grounds, and comes up with no positive examples, he suggests, against the weight of most earlier philosophical opinion, that work as a craftsman does not in principle disable the development of virtue.[34] He also argues, on the basis of (partly Stoic) ethical principles, that prostitution is wrong because it involves the maltreatment of those prostituted, and not on the more common Stoic ground that maltreatment of others involves the active party in wrongdoing.[35]

The 'Borysthenic' speech (XXXVI) also challenges conventional thinking, though in a more oblique way. Its subject is a fictionalized visit by Dio to Olbia (formerly Borysthenes), a city at the very limits of Greco-Roman civilization, threatened by the Scythians and damaged in recent wars (4–6, 15). Despite its tenuous grip on political existence and Hellenic culture, its citizens are passionately enthusiastic to hear Dio speaking about the best form of city (13–20, 24–6). Dio defines two forms of ideal city. The first recalls Plato's *Republic*, in which the rulers alone are wise.[36] The second is the Stoic idea that all rational beings (gods and humans) are co-members of a cosmic city. This is presented in a monarchic version: the city must be 'governed by a king according to law in complete friendship and harmony' (31). The monarchic colour seems to derive from a fusion of the Platonic ideal of the wise monarch with the Stoic idea of the universe as unified by divine reason, identified with Zeus as 'king of gods and humans' (35–6). A similar idea is conveyed by the succeeding myth

[32] I.e. it belongs to the genre of practical ethics, specifically, advice 'on lives' (*peri biōn*); see p. 601 above, and on Stoic versions of this advice, Brunt 1973: 19–34.

[33] See Muson. XI; cf. n. 16 above.

[34] See VII.104–8, 114–16, 124–6. Contrast e.g. Pl. *Rep*. IX.590C, Arist. *Pol*. VI.4, 1319a25–8; his views may follow those of the early Stoics: see Brunt 1973: 13–19, 25–6 (but note Zeno's disparagement of the work of builders and other manual workers: Plu. *Stoic.Rep*.1034b).

[35] See VII.138 and Brunt 1973: 18–19.

[36] See XXXVI.21: it is marked as inferior to a city in which all the members are rational (22–3); cf. Schofield 1991: 62–3.

(ascribed to 'the Magi' but strongly Platonic and Stoic in content). Its core point is that the universe functions best when most fully informed by the divine rationality of Zeus.[37] The overall message of the speech is apparently that, whatever the location (even at the margin of civilization), the really significant political norm is universal rather than culture-specific. Despite the monarchic colour given to the Stoic norm, the speech does not seem to endorse the idea that the Roman empire constitutes the earthly embodiment of the cosmic city. It implies a more thoroughgoing cosmopolitanism, though without any attempt to pursue the potential implications for revisionist political structures or contemporary political life.[38]

4 Epictetus

Little is known about the life of Epictetus (*c.* 55–*c.* 135). Born a slave in Hierapolis in Phrygia, he came to Rome as the slave of Epaphroditus, Nero's powerful freedman, who eventually gave Epictetus his freedom. He studied Stoicism with Musonius and became a Stoic teacher at Rome. When Domitian banished all philosophers in 89, Epictetus set up a 'school' at Nicopolis in Greece, on the main route between Rome and Athens, where he was visited by many distinguished Greeks and Romans, including the emperor Hadrian. The four books of *Discourses* and the *Encheiridion* (*Handbook*), a summary of his teachings, were based on the semi-formal dialogues on practical ethics which supplemented (or prepared for) more formal instruction in the Stoic curriculum. They were written by the historian Arrian; their striking style (everyday Greek, jagged and urgent in tone) suggest that Arrian has captured Epictetus' own voice.[39]

As indicated earlier, Epictetus' discourses are more challenging and interrogatory than Musonius', and are 'therapeutic' in aiming to remove false ethical beliefs and so 'cure' the personality of the interlocutor. Their function, and the character of their political thought, can be approached by examining the three-part programme of practical ethics, which is a

[37] See esp. XXXVI.52–3, 55, 58. See Schofield 1991: 84–92, Russell 1992: 21–2.

[38] Rome, as a cultural paradigm, is implicitly rejected in XXXVI.17; despite the strong pro-Hellenic colour of the speech (e.g. 18, 24–6), the generality of the political norms, and the reference to Magi (42), suggest universal categories. See Moles 1995b: 184–92, esp. 190–1; Russell 1992: 23 attaches more significance to Hellenic and Roman values.

[39] See Gill 1995, including complete translation of Epictetus, introduction and notes. On Arrian and Epictetus, see Stadter 1980: ch. 2. The fundamental studies of Epictetus' thought remain Bonhöffer 1890, 1894, both reprinted in 1968. On his educational methods, see Hijmans 1959; on the style of the discourses, Long 1982: 990–3.

recurrent, and distinctive, feature of Epictetus' teachings. The first stage is that of examining your desires and aversions, to ensure that you pursue only the ethically good (virtue) and avoid only the ethically bad. The second is that of scrutinizing the way you conduct your family and social relationships. The aim is to ensure that you act not only in a way that is 'appropriate' to these relationships, but also in a way that reflects the emphasis on the absolute priority of virtue in the first stage. The third stage is that of examining the logical relationship between the ethical beliefs applied in the first two stages, to ensure their consistency with each other and with your developing understanding of their truth. This three-stage programme in practical ethics is not designed to replace the Stoic three-stage curriculum (usually logic-ethics-physics), but to complement and prepare for it.[40]

On the face of it, it is only the second stage of this programme that bears on social and political relationships; but this stage needs to be taken in the context of the whole programme. Also, the programme as a whole, like Musonius' advice on social relationships, makes better sense if related to Stoic thinking about human ethical development, which is conceived by Epictetus as by other Stoics as 'familiarization' or 'appropriation' (*oikeiōsis*). *Oikeiōsis* consists in two interconnected aspects, personal and social. The key feature of personal *oikeiōsis* is the movement from wanting to obtain the 'preferable' natural goods, such as health and wealth, to seeing that such things are 'matters of indifference' in comparison with virtue, the only real good and the only thing that really benefits the self. The key feature of social *oikeiōsis* is recognizing the fundamentally associative character of human nature and wanting to benefit others as well as ourselves. Each aspect of *oikeiōsis* also contains the idea of movement from conventional understanding towards the sage's complete and fully coherent wisdom. In the personal aspect, this consists in making progress from a conventional idea of what 'virtue' involves towards the sage's (more 'cosmic' and reflectively based) understanding. In the social aspect, the movement is from benevolence based solely on conventional bonds, especially parental love, towards a benevolence which also embraces human beings as such, as fellow rational animals with ourselves.[41]

Epictetus' three-stage programme in practical ethics fits readily within

[40] Epict. *Diss.* III.2.1–5; see also I.4.11, II.17.14–18, III.12.12–15, *Ench.* 52.

[41] For personal *oikeiōsis*, see esp. Cic. *Fin.* III. 16–17, 20–2; for social III.62–8, discussed by Schofield, in ch. 22 section 4 above. See further Annas 1993: 262–76, also 159–76, with references to recent work; also Wright 1995, Inwood 1996 (on Epictetus and *oikeiōsis*). On Greek models of other-benefiting motivation, centred on the shared life and reciprocity, contrasted with modern notions of altruism, see Gill 1998: esp. section V.

this structure of ideas. His application of the programme in the discourses can also help to explain the connections between the personal and social aspects of *oikeiōsis* and between the conventional and the sage's understanding of what is involved. The first stage relates to the key feature of personal *oikeiōsis* (recognizing the absolute priority of virtue). The second stage – focused on roles and relationships – relates to the key feature (human associativeness) of social *oikeiōsis*. In stressing the essential link between these two, Epictetus highlights the way interpersonal and social relationships, such as the parent–child bond, constitute an important means whereby humans come to understand what it means to recognize that virtue is the only good. He also underlines the point that such relationships play this ethically significant role if and only if they are informed by a developing understanding of the priority of virtue (and of what 'virtue' means). The third stage marks the connection between Epictetus' programme of practical ethics and the Stoic three-stage philosophical curriculum, beginning with logic. Epictetus stresses that the goal of that curriculum is not just theoretical wisdom but also a (personal and social) life informed by this. He also stresses that the way we conduct our social relationships should reflect our taking the sage's understanding and way of life as our goal, for which a life that has not yet attained wisdom is a rehearsal.

This educational programme can be illustrated by Epictetus' treatment of the ethical content of social roles and of (justified) social or political conflict. Discourses I.11 and II.22 emphasize that, although family affection (*philostorgia*) and friendship (*philia*) are natural inclinations, this does not mean that all human beings are equally capable of expressing these properly. Only if people recognize that 'preferables' are matters of ethical indifference are such relationships compatible with proper human ethical development ('preferables' include the health or continued life of the other person or oneself or the material advantages of the relationship).[42] III.3.5–9 also stresses that conventional family relationships and pursuit of 'the good' (virtue) are compatible with each other if and only if this pursuit (and the related attitude towards 'preferables' and 'dispreferables') permeates the way both partners conduct the relationship:

> . . . the good is thus preferred above every form of relationship [*oikeiotēs*]. My father is nothing to me, only the good. – Are you so hard-hearted? – Such is my nature, and such is the coin which God has given me. If,

[42] On the ethical categories, see Long and Sedley 1987: §§ 58, 63, also Kidd 1971. This point underlies the apparent emotional ruthlessness of Epictetus' advice to whisper to one's child (or friend) 'tomorrow you (or I) will die'; see *Diss*. III.24.84–8, *Ench*. 3.

therefore, the good is different from the noble and just, off go father and brother and country, and everything else of that kind. (*Diss.* III.3.5–6, trans. Hard in Gill 1995)

III.10 both generalizes this theme and brings out the link between conducting social roles properly and making progress towards a sage-like understanding. Performing 'appropriate acts' (*kathēkonta*) involves both acting in a way that suits conventional roles (brother, councillor) and doing so in a way that suits one's (developing) conception of what it means to be 'human' (that is, a rational animal capable of the virtues, who also sees himself as part of a providentially shaped cosmos). The implication (one also drawn by Marcus Aurelius) is that the aspiration towards this more 'cosmic' understanding plays an important part in helping people to act virtuously and humanely within conventional relationships.[43]

A similar line of thought underlies Epictetus' treatment of political conflict. Epictetus sometimes uses as ethical exemplars members of the 'Stoic opposition', such as Thrasea Paetus, Helvidius Priscus and Agrippinus. For Epictetus, as for these figures themselves, the opposition is not to imperial rule as such.[44] Epictetus distinguishes between ethically acceptable and unacceptable emperors (IV.5.17–18); he also idealizes Socrates, for his reaction to unjust prosecution under the Athenian democracy, in the same way (e.g. II.5.18–23). These figures are exemplars because they are prepared to die or kill themselves, if the alternative is to stop using their social role (as senators or philosophers) as a vehicle for expressing virtue. They thus indicate their awareness that continued life, though 'preferable', is a 'matter of indifference' (or an 'external') in comparison with maintaining virtue. They exemplify a sage-like attitude in accepting, without unreasonable emotion (or 'passion'), the dispreferable outcome of their decision.[45]

Helvidius Priscus saw this too, and acted accordingly: for when Vespasian had sent word to him not to attend the Senate, he answered, 'It is in your power not to allow me to be a senator; but as long as I am one, I must attend.' – 'Well, then, if you do attend, at least be silent.' – 'Do not ask for my opinion, and I will be silent.' – 'But I must ask it.' – 'And I must say what seems right to me.' – 'But if you do, I will put you to death.' – 'Did I ever tell you that I was immortal? You will do your part, and I mine: It is yours to kill, and mine to die without trembling; yours

[43] See esp. II.10.10–21, also I.2.1–11. Cf. the four-*personae* theory of Cic. *Off.* I.107–25, discussed in Gill 1988: 187–92 (see also Atkins, in ch. 24 section 7, pp. 512–13 above).

[44] See e.g. *Diss.* I.1.18–30, I.2.12–24, IV.1.123, frs. 21–2. On the 'Stoic opposition', see p. 598 above. On Epictetus' relations with members of the Imperial Court, see Millar 1965.

[45] See *Diss.* I.1.19–22, I.2.21, IV.1.161–6. On the Stoic conception of 'passions' and the sage's freedom from these, see Long and Sedley 1987: § 65, esp. passages F and W; on suicide: Griffin 1986.

to banish me, mine to depart without grieving.' (*Diss*. I.2.19–21, trans. Hard in Gill 1995)

These figures are also presented as sage-like in exemplifying freedom in a specifically Stoic sense. This consists in 'freedom' from the 'constraint' of taking preferables as goods, and in recognizing that – whatever the external pressures – a virtuous response is always open to us. Stoic 'freedom' also accepts as inevitable (and as providentially shaped) the dispreferable consequences of such 'free' exercises of choice, and in so doing brings our wishes in line with the divine rationality in the cosmos.[46] 'If you wish it, you are free. If you wish it, you will have no one to blame, no one to accuse. Everything will be in accordance with your own mind, and equally, with the mind of god' (*Diss*. I.17.28). In recommending that we take such figures as models, Epictetus also raises the question whether such sage-like reactions are open to everyone (for instance, *Diss*. I.2.30–7), and through what form of life we can most effectively 'rehearse' for sagehood. On the one hand, the role of the itinerant Cynic teacher is repeatedly presented as one in which we can benefit human beings in general: social *oikeiōsis* in practice. Epictetus underlines that playing this role entails being a 'cosmopolitan' in a form that is incompatible with recognizing conventional political authority or with marriage (except in a community of Cynic sages).[47] On the other hand, he explicitly states that he takes as equally exemplary, and sage-like, figures such as Helvidius and Socrates whose exercise of 'freedom' derives from the principled way in which they play a determinate social role. In so doing, such figures exemplify the idea of 'dual citizenship' that figures elsewhere as a Stoic ideal. They take to the limit the combination of virtuous participation in one's own community and of membership in the community of human beings as rational animals ('the city of gods and humans'). Epictetus thus exemplifies the two strands in Stoic thought outlined earlier; as he brings out with special clarity, engaged social participation can serve as a vehicle of sage-like actions and attitudes.[48]

5 Marcus Aurelius

Marcus' *Meditations* present in an extreme form a paradox also raised, though less acutely, by Seneca's philosophical writings: that what seem to be the deepest reflections of a practising politician have so little overt

[46] On this kind of 'freedom' (*eleutheria*), see esp. *Diss*. IV.1; also I.17.14–28. See further Hahm 1992:40–3, Bobzien 1997; and on the sage's cosmic perspective White 1990: 49–55.

[47] See e.g. *Diss*. III.22, esp. 47–50, 55–7, 67–85; III.24.64–8; IV.1.114–16, 156–8.

[48] See *Diss*. IV.1.159–69, esp. 159–60. For 'dual citizenship' and 'the city of gods and humans', see *Diss*. II.5.26 (cf. Sen. *de Otio* 4, with Griffin, in ch. 26 section 5 above).

reference to his own political life.[49] They were written, apparently, during the last twelve years of Marcus' life, most of which were taken up with military campaigns against the German tribes threatening the northern border of the Roman empire.[50] They reflect the attachment to Stoic philosophy which had been an important part of his life since his youth, and which had, presumably, remained significant during his long period (138–61) as designated successor to his adoptive father, Antoninus Pius.[51] The work we call *Meditations* seems to have been a purely private notebook. Apart from the first book (which records, in a relatively structured way, Marcus' ethical debts to his teachers, parents, and so on), this twelve-book work consists of about five hundred short reflections, with no clear principle of organization. They are best understood as an internalized, self-addressed version of the types of practical ethics on offer in Musonius, Epictetus and others, combining therapy and advice.[52]

Marcus (unlike Musonius and Epictetus) is not a Stoic teacher; and there is room for argument about the orthodoxy of his Stoicism. In comparison with Epictetus, there is much greater stress on death and human transience; also a more pronounced 'cosmic' perspective.[53] However, the framework of thinking explored in connection with Epictetus may help us to make sense of these features of Marcus' thought, and to define the character of his political thinking. As noted earlier, Epictetus idealizes the sage-like, 'cosmic' perspective in which (in accepting 'dispreferable' events as providentially shaped) one brings one's state of mind into line with the rationality in the universe and so achieves peace of mind. This strand of Epictetus' thought seems also to be well-embedded in earlier Stoic thinking;[54] Marcus can, therefore, be seen simply as giving

[49] On the relationship between Seneca's philosophy and politics, see Griffin 1976 (1992); also Griffin in ch. 26 above.

[50] Marcus, emperor 161–80, campaigned in northern Italy and Germany in 168, 170–5 and 177–80; the headings to Books II and III of the *Meditations* note that they were written on these campaigns. See further on the dating of *Med.* Brunt 1974: 18–19.

[51] After rhetorical training by Fronto, he was directed towards Stoic philosophy by Junius Rusticus in 146–7 (who introduced Marcus to Epictetus' writings), following earlier Stoic instruction by Apollonius (*Med.* 1.7–8). See Birley 1987: chs. 2–5, esp. 44–5, 62–3, 92–103; Marcus' surviving correspondence with Fronto is an important source.

[52] The work was probably untitled; the first extant title, *To Himself*, is found on a sixteenth century MS. Edition with translation (reissued separately in 1989) and commentary: Farquharson 1944. Recent general studies: Brunt 1974, Rutherford 1989, Hadot 1998. For internalization of Stoic practical ethics, see e.g. Sen. *de Ira* III.36.3–4; also Rutherford 1989: 16–21.

[53] See further Rutherford 1989: 155–67, 225–55; Annas 1993: 175–6; on the question of Marcus' Stoic orthodoxy, see Rist 1982, Asmis 1989.

[54] See p. 611 above. See also e.g. Cleanthes' *Hymn to Zeus* (= Long and Sedley 1989: §54 I); D.L. VII.88; Epict. *Diss.* II.6.9–10 (Chrysippus); I.1.26–7 (Musonius). On the issue of the status of the idea of 'nature' in Stoic ethical philosophy, see Annas 1993: 159–79, with references to alternative views.

added emphasis and elaboration to a distinctively Stoic pattern of ideas.[55]

A related emphasis in the *Meditations* is on the shaping of one's life in the light of general regulative ideas, such as citizenship of the universe, natural (rational) law, and the brotherhood of humankind.[56] However, these ideas need to be taken in conjunction with (self-given) advice couched in more localized terms: acting 'as suits a Roman' (II.5), as 'a statesman, a Roman, and a ruler' (III.5); and a self-reminder not to become 'Caesarified' or 'dipped in the purple' (VI.30).[57] Also relevant is his unqualified tribute to the influence on him of his (non-Stoic) predecessor Antoninus (I.16) and of his family (I.17). The implication is that the combined outcome of Marcus' nature and upbringing, especially that of his Stoic teachers and adoptive father, has been to teach him how to live the life of an emperor in a way that is both compatible with the best standards of Roman constitutional government and with the Stoic ideal of 'the life according to nature' (or 'virtue').[58] This is summed up in Marcus' use of the Stoic idea of 'dual citizenship':

> What benefits each thing is living in consistency with its own constitution and nature; my nature is rational and political. As Antoninus, my city and native land is Rome, as a human being it is the universe. The only thing that is good for me is what benefits both these cities.[59]

Implied in such passages is the same framework of thinking about the (interrelated) outcome of personal and social ethical development (*oikeiōsis*) that we find in Epictetus (and the theory of *oikeiōsis* is especially relevant to understanding the programme of *Med.* I, where Marcus

[55] The elaboration includes quasi-Cynic 'bluntness' (*parrhēsia*) about bodily functions and quasi-Cynic use of the image of the 'theatre' of life (e.g. *Med.* VI.13, IX.29); see Rutherford 1989: 143–7, 172–7.

[56] See e.g. *Med.* II.16, III.4, 11, IV.3, 4, 29, XII.26, 36. See also Stanton 1968, referring also to this strand in Epictetus. Schofield 1991: 68 n. 13 finds it significant that Marcus in IV.4 refers only to a (cosmic) city of humans, not 'gods and humans' (as we find elsewhere). But since 'god(s)' are sometimes cited in this connection (e.g. II.4, 11; cf. also 'the god (reason) within us', e.g. III.5, XII.26), the variation in the formula may not be important.

[57] See also allusions to emperors who behaved in a tyrannical ('Caesarified') way: e.g. III.16 (also Rutherford 1989: 108–9). Note also the perhaps surprising inclusion, among the forces which shaped him, of members of the 'Stoic opposition' (and their goal of 'a constitution with equal laws, administered with equality (or 'fairness', *isotēs*), and a monarchy respecting above all the freedom of all those ruled'): I.14. See also Brunt 1975: 21–4, Birley 1987: 95–6, Rutherford 1989: 64–6.

[58] See esp. I.17.3 (Antoninus taught him how to strip down the pomp of imperial life while being able to do what is needed 'in a leaderly way' (*hēgēmonikōs*) 'for the public good' (*ta koina*)), and I.17.4 ('living a life according to nature'; on the latter as the Stoic goal or *telos*, see Long and Sedley 1987: § 63, esp. passage A).

[59] VI.44; cf. also III.5, IV.3.4. On dual citizenship see also p. 611 above.

enumerates his moral debts). The outcome of such development (towards which Marcus urges himself) is both a deepened recognition of the priority of virtue (expressed, for Marcus, especially in his realization of the role of emperor), and the capacity to see that expression of virtue from a sage-like, 'cosmic', perspective. One comes to see it as 'citizenship of the cosmos', or as 'brotherhood of humankind', or (in the strand of thought emphasized earlier) as bringing the 'god within' (rationality) in line with the rationality in the cosmos. Marcus sometimes stresses that doing so is not simply an exercise in reflective thought but that it can also help one to live a more humane, rational life within one's localized commitments:

> Say to yourself in the morning: 'I shall meet someone who is interfering, or ungrateful, insolent, deceitful, malicious, uncooperative' . . . But I have seen that the nature of the person who does wrong is that of my brother, not because he shares the same blood or seed but rather the same mind and element of divinity . . . I cannot be angry with my brother or hate him. We were born to work together, like a pair of hands, feet, or eyelids, like the rows of upper and lower teeth.

> The god within you should be in charge of a living creature who is a man, of mature years, a statesman, a Roman, and a ruler; one who has stood his ground, like someone waiting for the signal to leave the battleground of life and ready for this release, who needs to be bound by neither oath nor human witness.[60]

This way of understanding Marcus' view of his political role may help to place in perspective the question raised already in antiquity whether Marcus' actual practice as emperor matched his philosophical ideals.[61] In modern scholarship, this debate has sometimes taken the form of asking whether Marcus introduced legislation, or conducted policy, in a way that reflected the enlargement of conventional categories (and thus of ethical standards) that is implied in Stoic ethical theory.[62] The present discussion may suggest a rather different way of framing this issue. As Musonius especially shows, Stoic thinking may, indeed, lead to modification of conventional ideals regarding – for instance – women. But (in a way that is

[60] II.1, III.5. See also e.g. III.4–6, IV.3, XI.1; also pp. 610, 612 above, and Rutherford 1989: 169–72 on *Med.* III.4.

[61] See *SHA Marc.* 27.7 (also 19.12), quoting Pl. *Rep.* 473c–d. In fact, in *Med.* IX.29 Marcus explicitly rules out the objective of realizing Plato's *Republic*, urging himself to 'be content if the smallest thing goes forward'.

[62] See e.g. Noyen 1955, who argues that the legislation of Marcus' reign reflects enlightened (Stoic-inspired) thinking about women, children, slaves; and, on the other side, Stanton 1969, who maintains that (for instance) Marcus' emphatic preference for Commodus as successor reflects traditional Roman attitudes (indeed, *Realpolitik*) rather than Stoic political ideals.

linked with the absence of revisionist constitutional theory) this tends not to issue in programmes of social or political reform. The characteristic Stoic move is rather, to advocate the realization of Stoic ideas about the brotherhood of humankind, 'freedom', or 'natural law', within conventional social and political structures.[63] This tendency is reinforced by Stoic thinking about social and political roles as a medium through which a deepening ethical understanding (developed through *oikeiōsis*) can be expressed. What the *Meditations* lead us to expect is that Marcus will try to inform his execution of the role of emperor (conceived in the light of the best Roman political traditions) with a conception of that role as the concrete expression of 'cosmic' rationality. Our incomplete evidence for his embattled period as emperor and the preceding years as imperial successor may not make it very easy to assess Marcus' effectiveness in achieving this less revisionist objective. But the discussion of this chapter suggests that this would be the relevant criterion to apply to Marcus as a Stoic emperor.[64]

[63] The countervailing tendency is quasi-Cynic rejection of conventional structures (this may, however, be linked with the definition of ideals rather than practical action). In these later thinkers, quasi-Cynicism appears in a form which does not conflict directly with the informing of conventional roles with Stoic ideals.

[64] See also Brunt 1975: 22–3; and, for a fairly neutral account of Marcus' political career, Birley 1987: chs. 5–9.

30

The jurists

DAVID JOHNSTON

1 Introduction

In Rome, quite unlike Athens, there grew up a professional class of lawyers. These 'jurists' were originally priests, but in the course of the third century BC they came to profess a secular jurisprudence. Their role in the Roman legal system was pivotal: neither the magistrates responsible for granting legal remedies nor the judges who decided cases were lawyers; all looked to the jurists for legal advice. Although the jurists did not in the modern sense practise law,[1] this contact with practice shaped their distinctly pragmatic approach to it. But in debate and in their writing, they also developed a sophisticated analytical jurisprudence; and particularly during the 'classical' period of Roman law – from the late Republic until the early third century AD – they produced a substantial legal literature. Typical of their works were large-scale commentaries on civil law and the remedies contained in the magistrate's edict, and books of collected legal opinions. While some of their works played their part in argument of interest only to the jurists themselves, others were suited to, and written to satisfy, the diverse demands of practice or even teaching.[2]

In the surviving writings of the Roman jurists there is no extended discussion of the nature of political society, the legitimacy of its rulers, or the laws which govern or ought to govern it. Nor is there any such discussion about justice, the sources of law, or the conflict between positive and natural law. The writings which survive indicate that, although such questions were not entirely neglected, little attention was lavished on them.

Insufficient material survives in this area for any satisfactory evolution of juristic thought to be traced. It is clear that in roughly the last century of the Republic the jurists were particularly receptive to Greek influence, philosophical and rhetorical.[3] Equally, from the late Republic there was

[1] Cicero's 'agere cavere respondere' (*de Orat.* I.212) as a description of the jurist's role is true only of the earliest period; later on *respondere* came to the fore.
[2] Schulz 1946, Jolowicz and Nicholas 1972: 88–97, 374–94, Wieacker 1988: 519–675.
[3] Wieacker 1988: 618–62.

also mediation of Greek thought through the philosophical and rhetorical works of Cicero. Characteristic of this influence was a new (if short-lived) concern for system: Cicero is known to have contemplated writing (or written) a work reducing the civil law to an art (*de iure civili in artem redigendo*);[4] while the influence of dialectic is evident in the work of some late Republican jurists, notably Q. Mucius Scaevola and Cicero's friend, Ser. Sulpicius Rufus.[5] Many ideas found in the jurists which might loosely be described as 'political thought' can be traced back to Greek influence. This is the more striking since, from the beginning of the Principate, Greek discussions of legal or political institutions which were founded on the premise of a non-autocratic society were increasingly irrelevant; decidedly so by the second and third centuries AD, from which most of our sources come. These political realities matter in the case of the jurists, for they do not purport to write philosophy, and rarely allow themselves the luxury of reflection on purely abstract questions. Nonetheless, pragmatic considerations do not appear to have inspired much adjustment of received doctrine.

The juristic sources are transmitted almost entirely in Justinian's *Digest* (AD 533), a fifty-book compilation of excerpts from the works of jurists of the 'classical' period.[6] The excerpts are compiled into chapters or 'titles' with various themes; most of the material of interest for present purposes appears in the titles of the first book. Because the excerpts are filtered through the medium of this compilation, their original context is often uncertain; and what now seem sweeping statements of broad constitutional significance may have started from more humble origins and had more modest intentions.[7] A clear example is Ulpian's famous pronouncement that 'the emperor is not bound by statutes' ('princeps legibus solutus est', *D.* I.3.31): it originally concerned only his exemption from the terms of the *lex Iulia et Papia*, a pair of statutes dealing with the rights of unmarried and childless people to inherit property. It is important therefore not to take the jurists' remarks at face value for their own age; by transposition to a new context they may have taken on new meanings.

Section 2 of this chapter discusses the jurists' views on the various types of law (*ius*), natural and positive, on justice, statutes, and the powers of the

[4] Gellius I.22.7; cf. Quint. *Inst.* XII.3.10.

[5] Schulz 1946: 62–9, Stein 1966, 1978; Cic. *Brut.* 152, *D.* I.2.2.41; XLI.2.3.23; Gaius *Inst.* I.88; III.183.

[6] *D.* stands for the *Digest* and *C.* for Justinian's *Code* of AD 534. These are respectively volumes I (edd. Th. Mommsen and P. Krueger) and II (ed. P. Krueger) of the standard stereotype text of the *Corpus iuris civilis* (Weidmann, Berlin, many editions). For an outline of the compilation of the *Digest* and *Code*, see Jolowicz and Nicholas 1972: 480–96.

[7] See Johnston 1989.

emperor; section 3 deals with public and private law, the powers of magistrates, and corporations. The sources dictate that the chapter focuses mainly on the second and third centuries AD. It does the jurists no injustice to say that their original contribution to the topics dealt with in section 2 was slight; and that the real significance of their thought lay in the adumbration of the concept of the constitutional office exercisable only within legally defined limits; and of the notion of the corporation as an entity capable of enjoying and exercising legal rights. While questions such as these are quite suitable for abstract reflection, the concerns of the jurists tend towards the practical. The focus of this chapter is therefore necessarily different from that of other more purely philosophical chapters.

2 General theory of law

In the writings of the Roman jurists there are few traces of any general theory about justice, or about law and its place within the state.[8] Such statements as there are survive mainly in two introductory titles to the *Digest*, 'On justice and law' and 'On statutes, decrees of the Senate and long-established custom';[9] excised from their original contexts, these statements are not easy to interpret.

2.1 *Ius*

The jurists expended little time on abstract questions such as the relations between positive and natural law. The little they said owed much to the influence of one philosophical school or another. During the Republic there is no doubt that some jurists were acquainted with philosophical doctrines about law and the state, and some with leading philosophers in person.[10] Equally, the administration of provinces provided a motive for reflection about a law not purely for the citizens (*cives*) of Rome, and about a legal order going beyond that designed purely for those citizens (*ius civile*). Yet there is little sign that such considerations impinged much on the jurists' practice of law: such theorizing as we do find appears only from the second century AD, and is typically to be found in textbooks rather than practical works. It is by being placed by Justinian's compilers in the introductory title to the *Digest*, *de iustitia et iure*, that some state-

[8] Schulz 1946: 135–7; on Gaius, see Wagner 1978.

[9] *D.* 1.1 *de iustitia et iure*; *D.* 1.3. *de legibus senatusque consultis et longa consuetudine*.

[10] Tubero and Q. Mucius Scaevola augur were acquainted with Panaetius; Rutilius Rufus and Q. Mucius Scaevola pontifex with Posidonius: see Wieacker 1988: 641–3.

ments made by the jurists have acquired great prominence. Pre-eminent among these are the opening passage of Gaius' *Institutiones*, and the passage with which the *Digest* begins, which comes from Book I of Ulpian's *Institutiones*. First, Gaius.

> Every people which is governed by statutes and customs uses partly its own law and partly the common law of mankind. The law which each people has established for itself is peculiar to it and is called civil law (*ius civile*) as the law peculiar to that state (*civitas*). But the law which natural reason has established among all mankind is observed by all peoples and is called the law of nations (*ius gentium*), as the law all nations use. The Roman people therefore uses partly its own peculiar law and partly the common law of mankind. (Gaius, *Inst.* I.3)[11]

Gaius, who wrote in the mid-second century AD, is concerned to explain to his students that Roman law consists not merely of the positive law of Rome but also of a law which applies beyond the borders of the Roman empire. This is not a philosophical statement but one about the laws which the Romans and other peoples observe.[12] It recognizes the reality that some rules of Roman law were open only to citizens of Rome, while others, owing for example to commercial pressures, were open to non-citizens too. That is the practical purport of the dichotomy between *ius civile* and *ius gentium*. To judge from Gaius' account, any given rule of law can be said to be part of *ius civile* or of *ius gentium* but not both; these are two types of law, each for different people; and they do not overlap.[13] This is what distinguishes Gaius' taxonomy from one – superficially similar – set out by Cicero:[14] the same dichotomy appears, and *ius gentium*, the law for all peoples, is said to be founded on nature; but for Cicero *ius gentium* is a higher law which binds citizens, just as does their own *ius civile*. The same people are therefore bound by two different types of law, while for Gaius the two notions are mutually exclusive. The conception which underlies these two accounts of *ius gentium* is therefore entirely different. It is not unreasonable to suppose that here – as often – the jurist's philosophy is tempered by pragmatic considerations. So long as jurisdiction was exercised over both Roman citizens and non-citizens, there was some practical purpose in distinguishing between two categories of law,[15] one applicable and available only to citizens, and the other not restricted in that way.

Nothing is said in this passage of natural law, but Gaius hints at an

[11] Also in *D.* I.1.9. [12] Discussion: Schmidlin 1970: 174–8, Kaser 1994: 20–2.
[13] Kaser 1994: 64–6. [14] Cic. *Off.* III.69.
[15] *Contra*, Schulz 1946: 137: this was 'purely scholastic'.

issue going beyond the purely pragmatic: the law which all peoples use (*ius gentium*) is said to be the product of natural reason. The train of thought appears to be that because a rule of law is universally observed, it is natural; and because it is natural, it is valid. Lurking behind Gaius' matter-of-fact categorization of 'positive' law is the notion that *ius gentium* is motivated by, and legitimated by, its consonance with natural reason.[16]

In the passage with which the *Digest* begins, Gaius' dichotomy is no longer to be found.

> Private law is made up of three parts, for it is composed of principles of nature, nations and the state. Natural law (*ius naturale*) is what nature has taught all animals: for this law is not peculiar to mankind but common to all animals of earth, sea and air. From it comes the union of male and female which we call marriage, and the procreation and rearing of children. We see that other animals, including wild beasts, are familiar with this law. The law of nations (*ius gentium*) is what all human nations use. It is easy to appreciate that it is different from natural law, since that is common to all animals, while this is common only to men . . . Civil law (*ius civile*) neither departs from the law of nature or nations entirely nor follows them in every respect: when therefore we add something to, or subtract something from, common law we create a law peculiar to ourselves (*ius proprium*), that is, civil law. (D. 1.1.1.3–4 and 1.1.6. pr.)

Here dichotomy has given way to trichotomy.[17] The principal distinction between *ius naturale* and *ius gentium* is said to be that the former is common (*commune*) to all animals, whereas the latter is common only to men. In turn, *ius civile* is defined essentially by its difference from the other types of *ius:* elements are added to or subtracted from the *ius commune*, making a particular law or *ius proprium*.[18] The text is attributed to Ulpian (d. AD 223). Its authenticity has been questioned;[19] and, since a somewhat different version appears in Justinian's *Institutes*, its faithfulness to Ulpian is far from assured.[20] Yet there is nothing in its content which could not have been said in Ulpian's day: notions of *ius naturale* similar to this can be found among the philosophers. The real basis of the doubts about authenticity seems to be that this trichotomy has no evident practical value. In an

[16] Cf. also Gaius *Inst.*1 and 89. Gaius does not observe the dichotomy throughout his work: references to *ius naturale* creep in in *Inst.* 1.156 and 158; II.65 and 73; *D.* II.14.7 pr.; see Schmidlin 1970: 178, Jolowicz and Nicholas 1972: 104–6, Wieacker 1988: 444.

[17] Justinian's *Institutes* employs parts both of this text and the text of Gaius in 1.1.4, 1.2.pr., 1 and 11, so arriving at a confusion between dichotomy and trichotomy.

[18] *D.* 1.1.6; cf. Isid. *Etym.* v.2 'Divine laws are founded in nature, human laws in custom. The reason they differ is that different nations approve different laws.'

[19] Discussion: Schmidlin 1970: 179–82, Kaser 1994: 66–70.

[20] Just. *Inst.* 1.2 pr.

elementary work such as this, however, Ulpian may have been trying to do little more than introduce some basic concepts of *ius*. The practical value of the dichotomy between *ius civile* and *ius gentium* must have been much diminished by the extension of citizenship to all inhabitants of the Roman empire by the *constitutio Antoniniana* of AD 212. This may have freed the jurist to indulge in more purely philosophical remarks about the various types of law.

The source of these accounts of *ius naturale* and *ius gentium* has been disputed. It is generally accepted that the definition of *ius gentium*, with its reference to what men have in common, is of Stoic origin.[21] Yet the drawing of a distinction between *ius gentium* and *ius naturale* is fundamentally un-Stoic, and so too is a definition of *ius naturale* as governing all living things, since for the Stoics *ius* is confined to rational beings. The source of this part of the passage may be Peripatetic or Neoplatonic.[22] It seems necessary therefore to convict Ulpian of eclecticism. Yet in the works of the Roman jurists nothing could be less surprising. The legal enterprise, and legal argument, demand no rigid adherence to a particular philosophical position, but rather the adoption of the most convincing argument, regardless of origin. The once-popular notion that some jurists could be firmly assigned to one philosophical persuasion and others to another has now been generally abandoned.[23]

The question what weight the jurists placed on considerations of natural law deserves brief mention, since terms such as *ius naturale* and *naturalis ratio* appear not infrequently in their writings.[24] They rarely seem to be essential to the argument: where *ius naturale* conflicts with positive law, it does not prevail: most obviously so in the case of slaves since, under natural law, all men are equal[25] but, under Roman *ius civile*, slaves are not persons. 'The Roman jurists to whom theory meant little and practical results meant everything cannot have looked upon natural law as an order of higher or even equal status. They did not deny its existence and credited it with the absence of slavery in prehistoric times. But within the framework of their actual system they must have thought of natural law as inferior rather than superior to the law in force.'[26] It is here that later thought took a fundamentally different line: about AD 1140 Gratian, while adopting a definition of natural law not unlike the Roman, asserted that it 'prevails in antiquity and dignity over all laws', and that 'whatever has

21 Winkel 1988, 1993a.
22 Peripatetic: Winkel 1988, Norr 1974: 80 n. 150; Neoplatonic: Frezza 1969: 369.
23 Wieacker 1988: 640–2, with lit.
24 *Vocabularium* IV 22 s.h.v.; for post-classical developments, see Waldstein 1994.
25 *D.* L.17.132. 26 Levy 1949 (1963): 15.

been recognized by custom or set down in writing must be held null and void if it conflicts with natural law'.[27] The matter-of-fact approach of the Roman jurists to natural law attracted few followers.

The very notion of *ius gentium* (as opposed to *ius civile*) reveals a consciousness of the idea of the state itself; and of the notion of a state as an entity governed by a *ius proprium* to itself. But neither this nor occasional references to natural law and reason seem to have led the jurists to engage in any profound reflection on the nature of law and the basis of its validity in time or space. If one asks in what the distinctive approach of the Roman jurists to thinking about *ius* consists, the answer can only be that they (especially Gaius) shaped the philosophers' conceptions into a form more fruitful for the practical demands of law. And there they let it rest.

2.2 *Justice*

The most celebrated definition of justice (*iustitia*) to be found in juristic writings is this: 'Justice is a constant and enduring will to attribute to everyone his own right. The precepts of law are these: to live honourably, not to harm another, to attribute to each his own' (*D.* 1.1.10 pr.-1).

This passage, accorded prominence by its appearance early in the *Digest*, as well as in the very first paragraph of Justinian's *Institutes* (1.1.1 pr. and 1.1.3) is attributed to Ulpian. Its authenticity is seriously doubtful.[28] The content, however, is quite unexceptionable, since most of it can be traced back to Cicero or beyond. None of the propositions put forward as principles of law (*iuris praecepta*) shows much sign of originality. In Book 1 of his *de Officiis*, Cicero gives an account of the Stoic conception of justice: it is one source of what is honourable; it consists among other things in attributing to each his own; and its primary *officium* is not to harm others.[29] The *Digest* passage is therefore a basic statement of the Stoic conception of justice.

But it cannot be said that these were guiding principles which shaped the making of Roman law. Indeed, had they operated as general tests of the validity of legal rules or institutions, Roman law would have had a rather different appearance. As it is, it is all too easy to find contrary assertions elsewhere in the *Digest*: 'nobody who exercises his own right is regarded as acting fraudulently'; 'not everything which is permitted is honourable' (*honestum*).[30] The jurists' remarks about justice remain on a

27 *Decretum D.* 5.1; 8.2. 28 Honoré 1982: 111, Liebs 1982.
29 Cic. *Off.* 1.15, 20; cf. also *Leg.* 1.18–19; *Fin.* 11.34, 111.29, 70; *Inv.* 11.160.
30 *D.* L.17.55 and 144 pr.; Levy 1949 (1963): 17.

plane of abstraction quite separate from the considerations which they marshall in determining questions about law. They necessarily do distinguish between legal and moral rectitude; and flourishes in the direction of moral philosophy are simply that: flourishes.

2.3 *Statute*

'A statute is a common precept, a resolution of wise men, a restraint of wrongs committed voluntarily or in ignorance, a common covenant of the state' (*D.* 1.3.1). This paratactic definition of statute (*lex*) opens the *Digest* title on statutes and other sources of law.[31] It comes from the first book of *Definitiones* of the leading Severan jurist Papinian (d. AD 212). It emphasizes the role of statute in restraining the commission of wrongs, which is certainly true of some statutes; and it stresses the involvement of the community, the making of a common covenant. But the definition does not reflect the reality of Papinian's day: by then the popular assemblies had long since given up passing *leges*, and such legislation as there was was the work neither of assembly nor of 'wise men' but of the *princeps* and his advisers alone. This is a definition of *lex* of a distinctly Republican, and therefore anachronistic, flavour.[32]

The last clause of the definition with its common *sponsio* (promise) of the *res publica* has attracted attention. Promises in Roman private law depended on question and answer; their correspondence generated promissory obligation. Without too much procrustean effort, a *lex* can be regarded as the answer of the people to a question (*rogatio*) from the magistrate. Even so, it is not possible to treat this definition as Roman in inspiration or origin: Papinian's words pick up a definition which is in origin Greek. It can be found in a speech attributed to Demosthenes, the relevant passage of which is reproduced in Greek in the very next text in the *Digest*, from the *Institutiones* of Marcian (early third century AD):

> Law is what all men ought to obey for many reasons, and chiefly because all law is a discovery and gift of god, and at the same time a resolution of wise men, a correction of misdeeds both voluntary and involuntary, and the common agreement of the polis according to whose terms all who live in the polis ought to live. (*D.* 1.3.2)[33]

[31] It is important to distinguish between *ius* (law in the general sense) and *lex* (law in the sense of a measure passed by one of the Roman voting assemblies). The term *lex* is here translated throughout as 'statute'. For general discussion see Stein 1966: 9–25.

[32] Mommsen 1887–8: III, 301–2.

[33] See Dem. xxv.16; cf. Ducos 1984: 123–5, Wieacker 1988: 280 n. 58.

Some have seen in this a reference to the Epicurean notion of a social contract.[34] However that may be, Marcian's text continues immediately with a Stoic reference, in the shape of a quotation from Chrysippus' *On law*: here we have another instance of the jurists' eclecticism in matters philosophical.

Less decorative and more typical definitions of *lex* were given by other jurists: Gaius states that 'a statute is what the people orders and decides' (Gaius *Inst.* 1.3); the earlier jurist C. Ateius Capito (d. AD 22) had stated: 'statute is a general order of the people or plebs on a proposal from a magistrate' (Gellius x.20.2); while the later jurist Modestinus said in the early third century AD that 'the effect of a statute is to order, to prohibit, to permit, to punish' (*D.* 1.3.7). The question what makes a statute valid appears to be raised only by Julian (consul AD 148). In a discussion of the role of custom as a source of law, he observes that 'statutes themselves bind us for no other reason than that they have been accepted by the judgment of the people' and that the concept of a statute is that 'by voting the people declares its will'.[35] This again is a Republican notion about the legitimacy of statute, and hardly one which can have had any relevance in Julian's day. Indeed, with the exception of Modestinus' abstract definition of *lex*, in all these remarks about statute the Republican theme is to the fore. Here we have not coherent thinking about the binding force of statute under the principate, but merely the vestiges of a Republican myth of popular sovereignty. The lacuna is the more regrettable since newer ways of making law – by imperial *constitutio* or decree of the Senate – are said to have the force of *lex*; but the underlying basis of that force is never satisfactorily explored.[36]

2.4 *The powers of the emperor*

> An imperial constitution is what the emperor ordains by decree or edict or letter. It has never been doubted that this has the force of statute, since the emperor himself receives his power (*imperium*) by statute. (Gaius *Inst.* 1.5)

> What the *princeps* decides has the force of statute: as the people, by the royal statute (*lex regia*) which was passed regarding his power, confers on him all its own power and authority. (*D.* 1.4.1 pr.)

[34] Gaudemet 1967: 383 n. 3. Triantaphyllopoulos 1985: 9–10 discusses the various possible influences (Platonic, sophistic, Peripatetic) on this definition; and at 83 n. 63 the authenticity of the speech to which it is attributed.

[35] *D.* 1.3.32.1.

[36] Gaius *Inst.* 1.4, 5 and 7; *D.* 1.2.2.12; *D.* 1.3.32.1.

These statements appear in the works of Gaius and Ulpian respectively. They come as close as the jurists ever do to explaining the sovereignty and legitimacy of the emperor (*princeps*). They may perhaps be taken to build on Cicero's proposition that 'all powers, authorities and offices derive from the Roman people as a whole' (*Agr.* II.17). What lies behind the jurists' words is a democratic legitimation of the emperor by the people: the people conferred on him, by *lex*, its own power and authority (*imperium* and *potestas*). In the narrow sense in which the word is commonly used by the jurists, however, the people did not have *imperium*: that is the term for the power invested in the higher Roman magistrates. Here Ulpian is using *imperium* loosely; the people's transfer of all *imperium* and *potestas* can reasonably be interpreted as a transfer of their sovereignty. This may be no more than *ex post facto* rationalization of the emperor's powers, undoubted in the jurists' day. But a strong case has been made that their remarks are precise and refer to an actual *lex de imperio* passed at his accession.[37] As we have seen, while the jurists are not above flourishes of legal theory, much more characteristic of them is argument precisely founded on rules of positive law.

3 Public law and private law

3.1 Public law

Cicero, in discussing what knowledge an orator must have, places particularly heavy demands on the public-law orator, whose knowledge must encompass the experience of the past, the authority of public law, and the method and science of governing the state.[38] The jurists might have been expected to take the opportunity to supply this demand and, in studies on *ius publicum*, to consider questions such as the proper governance of the state. But there is little sign that they did.

The distinction between public and private law is brought to prominence by featuring in the very first text in the *Digest*:[39]

> There are two branches of the study of law, public and private. Public law is concerned with the Roman state (*status rei Romanae*), while private law is concerned with the interests of individuals, for some matters are of public and others of private interest. Public law comprises religion, priesthoods, and magistracies. (*D.* I.1.1.2)

[37] Brunt 1977b: 110–13. Reference to a *lex imperii* is also made in *C.* VI.23.3 (AD 232): it is said to have dispensed the emperor from the 'solemnities of law' (*sollemnia iuris*); cf. dispensation from statute in *D.* I.3.32.

[38] Cic. *de Orat.* I.201.

[39] Repeated in Just. *Inst.* I.1.4 as far as 'individuals'.

Ulpian's text was to have great influence: it was taken over by Isidore and from there it arrived in Gratian's *Decretum*.[40] But the text does not reflect the real concerns of the Roman jurists. They rarely use the expression *ius publicum* and betray little interest in public law. These points must be considered in turn. First, the term *ius publicum*.[41] It is striking that *ius privatum* and *ius publicum* are mentioned together in just one other text, and that is simply to the effect that the jurist Tubero was a great expert in both.[42] Only five other texts in the *Digest* mention *ius privatum* at all. More use the expression *ius publicum*, but they do so in varying senses: sometimes as a term for the whole legal order of Rome, sometimes to refer to mandatory rules of law. Rarely do they suggest that *ius publicum* is conceived as a separate branch of the law of the state or constitution. From the reign of Hadrian there does emerge a connection between *ius publicum* and the common good or public interest, *utilitas publica*:[43] that is cited as the motive for adopting a particular institution or rule, the institution or rule itself sometimes being described as *ius publicum*; it is in this sense that institutions such as marriage can be described as public law.[44] For the jurists, therefore, *ius publicum* sometimes means the law of Rome as a whole, and sometimes institutions of private law which serve a particularly important purpose in the maintenance of civil society.

Second, the jurists show little interest in public law in the sense of the law of the state or constitution; in Cicero's day they made a point of disregarding it in favour of private law.[45] In summarizing the period from the end of the second Punic war to the accession of Augustus, Schulz can write: 'Of the science of *ius publicum* there is little to be said.'[46] Nonetheless, a few jurists are reported to have taken an interest in public law, notably Tubero (retired 46 BC);[47] Ateius Capito (d. AD 22);[48] and Aristo (late first to early second century AD).[49] According to Aulus Gellius, Varro also wrote a book on constitutional questions, especially the Senate. This was done at the request of Pompey, when embarking on his first consulship: having experience of war but little of peace, he had little idea what to do in the Senate.[50] The book was lost.

The tradition of neglect did not last, and under the principate 'the stir-

[40] Isid. *Etym.* v.8; Gratian, *Decretum D.* 1.11.

[41] See Kaser 1986, Arico Anselmo 1983.

[42] *D.* 1.2.2.46.

[43] The general statement attributed to Julian is well known among lawyers: *D.* IX.2.51.2: 'it can be shown by innumerable examples that many things have been accepted in private law contrary to logic, on account of the common good'.

[44] Kaser 1986: 33–48; on the few 'public law' cases 53–4.

[45] Cic. *Balb.* 45; *Leg.* 1.14.

[46] Schulz 1946: 81; cf. Wieacker 1988: 492–4.

[47] Pomp. *D.* 1.2.2.46.

[48] Gel. X.20.2; XIV.7.12–13.

[49] Plin. *Ep.* 1.22.2; VIII.14.1.

[50] Gel. XIV.7.

rings of a new life are discernible'.[51] Most notable among these is the emergence during the Antonine period of a new genre of juristic works dealing with the duties (*officia*) of various magistrates. Many survive only in the most fragmentary form,[52] and the only one extant to any appreciable extent is Ulpian's ten books *de Officio Proconsulis*. By the end of the Classical period there was a substantial literature *de officio* of one magistrate or another. In the past it was generally assumed, with little justification other than the words *de officio* in the title of these works, that they were treatises of constitutional and administrative law; that they set out the powers and duties of magistrates and the limits on the exercise of their *imperium*; and that their intended readership was the magistrates themselves. But a study of the surviving material has clearly demonstrated that such questions of high constitutional law were not their concern.[53] Instead they appear to be miscellanies devoted to jurisdiction and administration which have in common only the fact that they do not fit within the more traditional genres of Roman legal literature. While this means that the most obvious quarry for the extraction of Roman constitutional theory is largely barren, vestiges of constitutional theory may still be found.

3.2 *Constitution and powers*

Although no systematic juristic account of magisterial power (*imperium*) or jurisdiction (*iurisdictio*) survives, it is possible from disjointed fragments to build up a picture of their legal regime. The fragments come overwhelmingly from the works of the jurists Papinian, Paul and Ulpian. What follows is therefore a sketch of early third century practice; sporadic earlier evidence suggests that the position in the early principate would have been similar.[54] *Imperium* and *iurisdictio*, the terms for the powers of magistrates, did not cease to matter when principate replaced Republic.[55] Although the jurists do not discuss any limits on the exercise of these powers by the emperor, they do elaborate such rules in connection with ordinary magistrates.

The main points made in our sources are these. *Imperium* was a power held only by the higher magistrates and pro-magistrates.[56] Pro-magistrates could exercise this power only within the bounds of the province assigned to them, and for the period for which it was assigned to them.

[51] Schulz 1946: 138. [52] Schulz 1946: 242. [53] Dell'Oro 1960: esp. 275 ff.
[54] E.g. Labeo – Paul *D.* II.1.6, Jul. *D.* II.1.5, Cels. *D.* I.18.17, Pomp. *D.* L.16.239.8.
[55] The relations between them are, however, somewhat problematic: see Jolowicz and Nicholas 1972: 47. [56] In general see Mommsen 1887–8: vol. I.

There were degrees of *imperium* in two senses. First, one magistrate might have *imperium* greater than another: a consul had *imperium* greater than a praetor, and within his province a proconsul or governor had the next greatest *imperium* after the emperor. Second, *imperium* could be 'undiluted' (*merum*): that included *iurisdictio* and also capital jurisdiction in criminal matters (*ius gladii* or *potestas*); or it could be 'mixed' (*mixtum*) and include *iurisdictio* only.[57]

Iurisdictio was fundamentally different, although magistrates with *imperium* enjoyed this power too. Since certain powers fell within the sphere of *imperium* rather than *iurisdictio*, they could not be exercised by lower magistrates.[58] Initially 'jurisdiction' meant only the magistrate's power to grant a civil-law remedy, but it came also to be applied to the magistrate's role in the new system of civil procedure which evolved during the principate; and, owing to the resemblance between the magistrate's acts in that system and his other official or administrative acts, the term came to be used more widely:[59] in short, as a term denoting not merely certain civil-law functions but the legal authority of a magistrate tout court. A magistrate had *iurisdictio* only over those domiciled within his province, and the jurisdiction of municipal magistrates was subject not only to territorial but also to financial limits.[60] A magistrate did not have jurisdiction over a magistrate having greater *imperium*.[61] An order pronounced by a magistrate who lacked jurisdiction was null; so too perhaps if the magistrate was invalidly appointed.[62] Jurisdiction could be exercised by the magistrate only in person, unless it was allowed by statute or convention to be delegated.[63]

The question of delegation of powers is worth closer attention. It is developed in some detail by the jurists and was to be a fertile source for mediaeval jurists. Papinian discusses what powers a magistrate is able to delegate to others. A basic distinction is drawn between powers which are attributed to him by statute, resolution of the Senate or by the emperor, and those which arise by right of office (*iure magistratus*). The former cannot be delegated, while the latter can.[64] The jurist Julian also speaks of a customary rule that only a magistrate who has jurisdiction in his own right, rather than by grant of another (*alieno beneficio*), can mandate it.[65]

[57] See Paul *D.* I.18.3, Ulp. *D.* I.17.1, Cels. *D.* I.18.17, Ulp. *D.* I.16.8 = *D.* I.18.4, Ulp. *D.* II.1.3.

[58] Ulp. *D.* II.1.4 and Paul *D.* L.1.26; the distinction mattered for the lower magistrates, who had no *imperium*.

[59] See Lauria 1930.

[60] *C.* VIII.1.2 (260); Ulp. *D.* V.1.2.6 and 5, Paul *D.* II.5.2 pr., Paul *D.* II.1.20, Pomp. *D.* L.16.239.8.

[61] Paul *D.* V.1.58; Ulp. *D.* XXXVI.1.13.4.

[62] Pap. *D.* XLIX.1.23.1, Ulp. *D.* II.2.1.2, *C.* III.3.1 (242), III.4.1 (440), Ulp. *D.* I.14.3.

[63] Pap. *D.* I.21.1.

[64] *D.* I.21.1.

[65] *D.* II.1.5.

From this several points follow. First, the distinction founded on the source of the powers indicates that there was an established concept of an office and the normal powers inherent in it. Plainly that is a prerequisite for any attempt to deal with the question whether or not a magistrate has exceeded his powers. Second, where delegation of powers is concerned, there are two restrictions: powers specially conferred, rather than inherent in an office, cannot be delegated; neither can powers which have themselves been delegated. Third, it is notable that the delegation or mandating of powers was treated much in line with the private-law rules of mandate: Labeo (d. *c.* AD 10–22) suggests that the death of a magistrate before his delegate has begun to exercise delegated powers terminates the authority to act, just as it does in cases of mandate in private law.[66] Fourth, while the sources are not extensive, it is at least arguable that the analogy of the private-law mandate, in which one person is authorized to perform a task for another, was present to the jurists more generally in considering magistrates and their powers. In any event, there is a similarity between the two so far as excess and revocation of powers are concerned.[67]

Some general conclusions can now be drawn. The most important point is that in these passages we find the jurists adumbrating the concept of an office which must be exercised according to law, and which confers on its holder powers which are defined and delimited by law. Some of those powers are taken to be inherent in the nature of the office; others are conferred expressly by legislation of one sort or another. But the magistrate must act within his powers, and acts which exceed them are void: for example, a magistrate who purports to act officially outside his province acts to no effect: as Paul notes, he is treated as a private individual.[68] It is important too to note that there is a hierarchy of *imperium*: the acts of those lower in the pyramid can be controlled by those above. As Ulpian says, 'a praetor has no *imperium* over a praetor nor has a consul over a consul' (*D.* XXXVI.1.13.4), and the solution where there is an impasse, owing to equality of powers, is to seek assistance from the emperor. These ideas about the validity of the magistrate's acts are developed particularly in connection with *iurisdictio*.[69] This is no more than we might expect: that concept provided the very foundation of private-law (and other) procedure in the courts and therefore fell within the sphere the jurists regarded as their own.

[66] *D.* II.1.6; cf. *D.* I.16.6.1, Winkel 1993b: 60.

[67] Paul *D.* XVII.1.3.2 and 5.1–4; Gaius *D.* XVII.1.4 and *Inst.* III.159–60.

[68] Paul *D.* I.18.3.

[69] Later on similar points are made about judges in *cognitio* who exceed their authority: see C. VII.48, with imperial rulings dating from AD 223 to AD 379.

Here there is a recognizable idea of the constitutional state, in which limited powers are conferred on magistrates and must be exercised within their limits. There is a sharp contrast with the stateless political community of the polis,[70] and the emergence here, perhaps for the first time, of a recognizably modern conception of the state. The scheme contains an obvious lacuna: no mention is made of the apex of the pyramid, the emperor. Paradoxically, therefore, the apparatus of a legal state where powers are conferred and controlled is created within a system of the most unrestrained absolutism. But to assert that the jurists developed a unitary theory about the nature of powers and legitimacy would anyway be to exaggerate. Papinian, for example, contemplates the attribution of powers to magistrates by decree of the emperor; while Ulpian indicates that the power of the emperor derives from the people, who conferred their *imperium* upon him. These two views do not sit well together: given the customary rule that delegated powers could not be delegated further, the emperor should have been unable to grant *imperium* to magistrates. That argument had its adherents in early modern discussion of sovereignty and powers.[71] In general, the jurists' treatment of *imperium* and *iurisdictio* was to be a fertile source for arguments about political powers and legitimacy in early modern times. It was only then that apparent inconsistencies between their views had to be smoothed into a unitary theory of sovereignty.

3.3 *Corporations*

The bias of the Roman jurists towards private law and procedure means that it is necessary to look in unexpected places to find the glimmerings of what we would now recognize as political thought. And there too are to be found many of the texts most significant in the later history of political thought.

This is true of the notion of the corporation: that is, an entity having an existence separate from that of its members and accordingly having rights and duties separate from theirs.[72] The development of the concept of a state or municipality as an entity existing apart from its members is of fundamental importance. But the difficulties in the way of developing the concept were equally fundamental. It is probable that the jurists made use of the writings of philosophers in developing their ideas.[73] For example, Pomponius (late second century AD), writing about acquisition of property, refers to the Stoic classification of bodies (*corpora*).[74] He gives exam-

[70] See Cartledge, ch. 1 section 3 above. [71] See e.g. gloss *alieno beneficio* on *D.* II.1.5.
[72] Mitteis 1908: 339–416. [73] Olivecrona 1949: 5–42. [74] *D.* XLI.3.30 pr.

ples of a body composed of separate elements (*corpus quod ex distantibus constat*): a people, a legion and a herd. The much earlier jurist P. Alfenus Varus (consul 39 BC), under reference to the stock example of the ship of Theseus, also referred to the notion of a body whose members change yet which retains its identity. Here again the examples of a legion and a people appear. The notion that a body could retain its identity in spite of changes of membership was the essential background for the jurists' development of a theory of corporations.[75]

By one philosophical route or another, the jurists appear to have satisfied themselves that there could be such a thing as a body of constant identity yet changing parts.[76] Yet philosophical doctrine did not answer the question what legal acts that body should be able to perform, or who should perform those acts for it; this was the work of the jurists. From time to time they encountered difficulty. There are clear statements recognizing the existence of a corporation: money owed to a collectivity (*universitas*) is not owed to the individuals who comprise it (and vice versa); such things as theatres and stadia belong to the *universitas* and not to the individuals who comprise it.[77] The jurists also developed notions about representation of the *universitas* by its 'organs'. Although it is disputed which corporate bodies were regarded as having capacity to be represented in this way, it is quite clear that this was true of municipalities.[78] The praetor's edict itself provided remedies to be used in actions for and against *municipes*.[79] The municipality could be represented both by its magistrates and by agents specially appointed to represent it (*actores*); their election or appointment was a matter of public law, but they could represent the municipality in private-law transactions.[80] This is the basis of a theory of representation.

On the other hand, some confusion seems to have remained in the case of legal relations which required intention (such as acquisition of possession of an object). Even some late jurists seem to have perceived it as problematic that not all the individual members of a corporation could consent to an acquisition.[81] But Ulpian tells us that in practice it was accepted in his day that municipalities could possess; and the way he puts it suggests that the solution was arrived at on pragmatic rather than technical legal grounds.[82] What lies behind this problem is an ambivalence

75 D. V.1.76, Sedley 1982. 76 Cf. Ulp. *D.* III.4.7.2.

77 Ulp. *D.* III.4.7.1, Marcian *D.* I.8.6.1. 78 Duff 1938: 37–50, 62–94.

79 Lenel 1927: 99–100. It is disputed whether the edict referred to municipalities alone or also to collectivities (*universitates*).

80 Paul *D.* III.4.10, Ulp. *D.* XIII.5.5.7–9, Paul *D.* XLIV.7.35.1; details of these developments are controversial: see Kaser 1971: 261, 304–7, Mitteis 1908: 376–90, Duff 1938: 62.

81 Paul *D.* XLI.2.1.22. 82 Ulp. *D.* XLI.2.2 and *D.* X.4.7.3.

about whose intention is relevant for the completion of certain legal acts.

Against this background, it is not possible to say that any fully-formed or coherent theory of representation of the legal person can be uncovered in the *Digest*. But the essentials of those notions are present. The catalyst for their development was provided by the fact that there were private-law interests at stake, and there was an edict relating to municipalities which demanded interpretation. Corporations and municipalities occupy only the fringes of Roman private law, but it is there rather than in public law that they belong.[83] Had the jurists regarded such matters as belonging centrally within the sphere of private law, this area of the law might have been better developed.[84] Nonetheless, the private-law dimension and the presence of an edict meant that the jurists played a much more active role in discussing and developing this area than, for example, in the question of the representation of the Roman state by its magistrates. That fell squarely within the area of public law, and was not dealt with by the jurists to any significant degree.

This example allows us to conclude that the Roman jurists did develop concepts and arguments which would now be recognized as belonging to the realm of political thought: the notion of a political entity or state as the bearer of rights and duties. Some of their reasoning fell on deaf ears; for example, Accursius in the Gloss on the *Digest* (*c.* AD 1230) expresses the view that 'a corporation is nothing other than the men who are there',[85] leaving it to the Commentators to revive the notion of a corporation as an entity. The Roman jurists developed their thoughts not in relation to the institutions of the state but in relation to the polis or *civitas*. The reason for this was that polis and *civitas* were capable of generating problems which were regarded as belonging to the sphere of private law, and were accordingly regarded by the jurists as being within their purview.

4 Conclusions

The jurists' discussions of *ius*, statute and justice do little more than attest what could hardly have been doubted: that they were educated in a tradition which instilled in them familiarity with the political thought of the main philosophical schools. Two general features of their discussions are quite striking: first, their statements of general theory are often taken not only from works of an elementary or educational rather than practical nature (*Institutiones*, *Definitiones* or *Regulae*), but also from the first book of

[83] Ulp. *D.* L.16.15, Gai. *D.* L.16.16. [84] Schulz 1951: 88. [85] Gloss on *D.* III.4.7.

such a work. They may therefore be little more than flourishes of learning intended to provide a suitably stately prooemium to those works. Second, they usually display little originality but can be connected with well-known philosophical positions, mostly of a Stoic orientation.[86] What these two observations amount to is this: that so far as we do find any general theory in Roman juristic writings, it is mostly not integrated into any kind of reasoned philosophical position on law or political thought, and it plays no observable part in the approach taken by the jurists to questions of legal interpretation. In short, it appears to be little more than recital of educated commonplaces of the day.

The jurists' treatment of the position of the emperor is not analytically profound, but does have the merit of founding his authority and power on a statute which transferred the sovereignty of the people to him. The difficulty is that, without any account of popular sovereignty, the nature of the statute or the use of the term *imperium*, which is ambiguous in that context, the remarks made by the jurists (at least in their surviving form) do not go below the surface. Whether they originally did is necessarily uncertain, but it remains clear that classic questions of political thought were not those in which the jurists either felt comfortable or made a decisive mark.

Instead the jurists' significance for political thought is to be found in private law or on its fringes. *Iurisdictio* was a term which in origin concerned the magistrate's authority to grant civil-law remedies: it was therefore very much within the field which the jurists saw as their own. For them it was important to know which magistrate had jurisdiction, where, and over whom; and, since *imperium* involved *iurisdictio*, those same questions were of significance in discussing the powers of magistrates in general. This is the background against which we find the development, admittedly piecemeal, of a theory of magistrates' powers and their exercise within the limits of the law. That theory, to some (perhaps a large) extent relied on concepts already developed for use in private law. Its development is the more remarkable within a state composed on the absolutist model. Similarly, in their concern with the corporation, the jurists were seeking to do no more than establish a basis for the private-law rights particularly of municipalities. That necessarily involved them in developing ideas about the corporation as an entity capable of having its own rights and duties, and about the representation at least in legal questions of that corporation. Private law, therefore, is the key to understanding the

[86] Nörr 1974: 134–6, Schmidlin 1970: 173–85.

nature and extent of the jurists' contributions to political thought. General theories about law and justice could safely be left to philosophers; for the jurists, questions of political theory had to be resolved only as a means to an end, and that end was the administration and application of private law.

31

Christianity

FRANCES YOUNG

1 A political movement?

In Acts 11.26 we are told that it was in Antioch that the disciples were first called *Christianoi*. It appears to have been a nickname given by others rather than the name chosen by those thus designated. The term occurs only three times in the New Testament. The form of this nickname, with its *-anos* ending, is Latinate, and words in Latin with this ending normally refer to members of a political faction, followers of a leader seeking power. So Acts implies that while the early Christians saw themselves as the pupils of a teacher (*mathētai*), they were perceived by outsiders as politically motivated.

This coheres with the Gospel evidence that Jesus was put to death on the ground that he claimed to be king of the Jews, and with indications in later material that the family of Jesus was caught up in endeavours to eliminate potential Messianic claimants. The fact that the Roman government faced two Jewish revolts in the first and early second centuries makes it likely that people claiming descent from King David would be suspect. It would appear that Jewish Christians made exactly this claim for Jesus and his family.[1] Eusebius (*Hist.Eccl.* III.12)[2] reports Hegesippus as recording that 'after the capture of Jerusalem Vespasian issued an order that, to ensure that no member of the royal house should be left among the Jews, all descendants of David should be ferreted out'. At a subsequent date, when Domitian ordered the execution of all who were of David's line, Eusebius (*Hist.Eccl.* III.19–20) speaks of 'an old and firm tradition' that 'the descendants of Jude – the brother, humanly speaking, of the Saviour' were informed against as being descendants of David. Again relying on Hegesippus, he tells how Jude's grandsons were brought before the emperor and admitted they were of Davidic lineage, but Domitian found

[1] For discussion of the Davidites, see Bauckham 1990.

[2] The text of Eusebius' *Ecclesiastical History* is found in *GCS*; translation quoted: Williamson 1989.

no fault with them, partly because of their poor economic circumstances, but also because under questioning they explained that Christ's kingdom was not of this world.

Political movements usually have a programme. Proclamation about the kingdom of God would seem to have been at the heart of Jesus' activity, and there are many hints that the Jesus-movement was linked with other Jewish groups such as the zealots[3] who sought to oust the Romans and establish a theocracy, or a restored Davidic empire, in Judaea and the surrounding regions. However, the weight to be given to these hints is uncertain. They are embedded in texts which present overall a rather different picture, that of a leader who offered no resistance, who made a demonstration by arriving in the capital on a donkey rather than a war-horse, who said, 'Love your enemies' and 'Those who take the sword will perish by the sword'. In the Gospel attributed to John, Jesus even confesses at his trial:

> My kingdom is not from this world. If my kingdom were from this world, my followers would be fighting to keep me from being handed over to the Jews. But as it is, my kingdom is not from here. (John 18.36)[4]

What evidence we have concerning Jewish Christian groups during the period of the Jewish revolts against Rome suggests that they refused to participate. Furthermore, the standard Christian apology in the second century was that given by the grandsons of Jude. Justin (*c.* AD 100–65),[5] for example, wrote:

> When you hear that we look forward to a kingdom, you rashly assume that we speak of a human kingdom, whereas we mean a kingdom which is from God . . . If we expected a human kingdom, we would deny that we are Christians, so that we might not be put to death. (Justin, *1 Apol.* 11)

The account of Paul's martyrdom in circulation by the end of the second century indicates that Nero supposed Christians to be 'dangerous armed rebels in the service of an earthly king'.[6] Paul, condemned to death, explains to two Roman officials:

> We fight not, as you suppose, for a king who is from the earth but for one who is from heaven: he is the living God who comes as judge because of the lawless deeds which take place in this world. (*Martyrdom of Paul* 4)

[3] On Jesus and the zealots, see Brandon 1968; cf. his 1967.

[4] Biblical quotations are given in the New Revised Standard Version.

[5] The text of Justin Martyr's *I Apology* can be found in Migne, *Patrologia Graeca* 6; translation (slightly altered here) in Falls 1948.

[6] Bauckham's phrase. *The Martyrdom of Paul* is quoted from Elliot 1993.

Whatever one makes of the historical origins of Christianity, these texts suggest that in the late first and early second centuries Christians were perceived as political subversives, but did not accept the description. The fact that by then the movement included large numbers of Gentiles is inexplicable if the movement's essential character reflected the aspirations of Jewish nationalism.

2 Political attitudes in the New Testament

The New Testament material suggests that earliest Christianity is most plausibly described in terms of an apocalyptic sect.[7] This certainly implied some measure of anti-Roman ideology. Some would reserve the term 'apocalyptic' for a genre of literature, but it is not implausible that literary texts generate both ideologies and social groups whose world is shaped by those ideas. The notion that God will intervene precisely to bring judgment on the powers that be is deeply engrained in early Christian literature.

The Book of Revelation[8] is clearly apocalyptic in its genre. Here we find the enigmatic references to worldly powers typical of the apocalyptic tradition, Rome being clearly the target when we read 'Alas! alas! the great city, Babylon, the mighty city! For in one hour your judgment has come' (Rev. 18.10). The ancient enemy of Israel is the cipher for the oppressive power of the day, the dwelling-place of demons. All nations have 'drunk of the wine of the wrath of her fornication' and 'the kings of the earth have committed fornication with her', thus enriching the merchants of the earth. Great will be her recompense! The whole work is a patchwork of allusions to previous texts, biblical prophecies in particular.

The attack on Rome begins in the previous chapter. There is a vision of a woman sitting on a scarlet beast, full of blasphemous names, with seven heads and ten horns (17.3). The reference is usually understood to be to the famous seven hills of Rome, and the ten emperors up to the date of the composition of this passage. This woman is not only arrayed in purple and scarlet, bedecked with gold and jewels and pearls, but she is drunk with the blood of the saints and the blood of the martyrs of Jesus. The perspective of the visions is that the Lion of the tribe of Judah, the Root of David, has conquered (5.5) – no wonder that the authorities regarded Davidic claims as subversive. Yet the focus of this text is on the Final Judgment: the Lamb, God's agent of salvation and judgment, is to bring about the

[7] On apocalyptic, two standard and contrasting works may be cited: Russell 1964, Rowland 1982. [8] On the Book of Revelation, see e.g. Bauckham 1993a, 1993b.

climax of all human history. If this text is anything to go by, the protestations by early Christians that they were not a political faction attempting to seize power, but people expecting a heavenly kingdom, would seem to be fair enough.

At the same time it is clear that those who produced this text felt alien and oppressed within the Roman world. There are a number of other hints in the New Testament that the earliest Christians adopted the mentality of exiles. The descendants of Abraham are described in Hebrews 11 as strangers and exiles on earth, looking for a heavenly homeland, and it is clear that this chapter is providing models for the Christian. 'For here we have no lasting city, but we are looking for the city that is to come' (Heb. 13.14). In 1 Peter 1.17, the readers are charged to 'live in reverent fear during the time of your exile', and they are exhorted in 2.11, as 'aliens and exiles', to maintain good conduct among the Gentiles. This text makes it clear that the Christian community believes that it has become the 'people of God' and inherits the election and promises: they are the chosen race, the royal priesthood, the holy nation, God's own people. They expect God's kingdom, but are exiles meanwhile, scattered among the nations as Jews had been for centuries. Quite casually the epistle says at the end, 'Your sister church in Babylon, chosen together with you, sends you greetings.' This presumably uses the symbolic idiom of apocalyptic to imply that the letter was written from Rome.

Yet intriguingly, this very epistle, 1 Peter, also bears witness to another attitude towards earthly authorities. Far from embodying the powers of evil, the Roman emperor and his representatives were seen as appointed by God to maintain law and order until such time as the heavenly kingdom comes. So, despite the reference to Rome as Babylon, with all its negative associations, for this author good conduct among the Gentiles included being subject 'for the Lord's sake' to every human institution, whether to the emperor as supreme, or to governors sent by him to punish wrongdoers and encourage those who do right (1 Peter 2.13–14). God is to be feared, and the emperor honoured (2.17). By implication that exhortation makes the essential issue clear: worship may be offered only to the one true God. As long as the emperor refrains from demanding divine honours, appropriate respect is perfectly in order. Certainly this author is adamant that Christians must never be caught in any kind of immoral or criminal activity. They are only to be liable to the courts 'for the name of Christ'. As he suffered, so they must. But 'it is better to suffer for doing good, if suffering should be God's will, than for doing evil' (3.17). The ultimate judgment of God is on the horizon. Meanwhile, however, the Roman empire is in some sense divinely ordained as a restraint on wrongdoing.

The authorship and date of 1 Peter are contested, but the fact that this attitude already belongs to the earliest phases of the Christian movement is clear from the Pauline epistles (those that are authentic being the first extant Christian documents). Notoriously (since the passage was used in twentieth-century Germany to justify Christian collaboration with Nazis), Romans 13 explicitly endorses the view that God appointed the established authorities, and therefore obedience is due to them:

> Let every person be subject to the governing authorities; for there is no authority except from God, and those authorities that exist have been instituted by God. Therefore whoever resists authority resists what God has appointed, and those who resist will incur judgment.

The text goes on to say that rulers have authority so as to maintain law and order, that taxes should be paid since the authorities are God's ministers, and that respect and honour should be given to those to whom they are due.

The Pauline endorsement of current social norms, such as slavery and patriarchy, parallels this acceptance, and theological justification, of the political *status quo*. On the one hand, it was a fairly standard Jewish response, allowing a *modus vivendi* with the empire, while reserving their own position: Jews would pray for the emperor, but not worship him. On the other hand, Paul certainly expected it to be a merely temporary expedient – the appointed time, he felt, had grown very short (1 Cor. 7.29).

The Pauline tradition remained shaped by these ideas. It is now regarded as unlikely that Paul himself wrote 2 Thessalonians, or the so-called Pastoral Epistles (1 and 2 Timothy and Titus), but these texts not only reflect the emerging stance of the Gentile Christian churches but were also demonstrably influential in the late second and early third centuries. 2 Thessalonians, though not itself an apocalypse, is full of apocalyptic motifs and expectations. It presupposes an oppressed community, awaiting the righteous judgment of God which will make them worthy of the kingdom of God and bring vengeance on those who do not know God or obey the gospel of Christ. Unlike Paul, who in 1 Thessalonians refuses any attempt to date the End, this document gives details of the sequence of events before the Coming of the Lord Jesus. First there is to be a great rebellion, led by a lawless usurper of God's position; but at present there is the 'restrainer' (*ho katechōn*; 2 Thess. 2.7). Whatever the original meaning of this, some of the Church Fathers[9] interpreted it as the Roman empire, which by keeping law and order delayed the coming of the End.

[9] E.g. Tertullian (*de Resurrectione* 24) and John Chrysostom (*Homily IV* on 2 Thessalonians).

Thus within the potentially anti-Roman apocalyptic tradition, the state could be regarded not as demonic but as divinely ordained.

Conversely in the case of the Pastorals we find a conformist ethic on the surface of the text alongside an implied parody of the imperial cult in its Christology.[10] The explicit advice is to offer 'supplications, prayers, intercessions and thanksgivings' for all, 'for kings and all who are in high positions' (1 Tim. 2.1–2), and to live in such a way as to ensure that Christians, whether bishop, deacon or slave, have a good reputation with outsiders. So keen are the epistles on respectability that they have often been dubbed 'bourgeois'. The motive for the prayers is 'that we may lead a quiet and peaceable life in all godliness and dignity'. These Christians are not to draw attention to themselves, not to appear radical or puritan, but law-abiding and disciplined, with orderly households, fruitful marriages and sensible diets. It looks as if this generation is settling down in the world. However, a closer look reveals that this Christian life is to be lived under God's eye and in expectation of divine judgment – for the return of Christ is still expected. Furthermore the language of the ruler-cult in the Eastern empire, as evidenced in inscriptions, ostraca and papyri, is used of Christ, who is 'Lord', 'son of God', 'King of kings and Lord of Lords', 'Saviour' and 'Saviour of the world', who 'oversees' everything, the 'good news' of whose 'epiphany' is expected, who sends ambassadors such as Paul, who has slaves and servants in his household like Caesar, and expects his soldiers to be prepared to suffer on his behalf. Christ is the divinely appointed king to whom Christians owe allegiance, rather than the Roman emperor; they have a loyalty that could and did bring them into conflict with the empire – otherwise the appeal not to be ashamed of people like Paul who suffer in prison (2 Tim. 1.8 ff.) makes no sense.

3 Developments under persecution

The texts we have considered so far not only include the earliest Christian writings, but also became scripture and so authoritative for later Christian thought. The ambivalences we have noticed both reflected the ambiguity of Jesus' teaching – 'Render to Caesar the things that are Caesar's and to God the things that are God's' (Mark 12.17 and parallels in other gospels) – and shaped divergent responses as the relationship between Church and State developed. Marta Sordi[11] has suggested that it

[10] For further discussion, see Young 1994 and references cited there.

[11] Sordi 1988.

was only extreme groups like the Montanists (see below) which maintained a negative attitude towards the empire, and that attitudes in the Great Church anticipate the features which enabled the eventual congruence of Christianity and empire. There is something to be said for that position, but it does not do justice to the complexity of the evidence. It is far from clear that early Christian texts present us with any kind of coherent theoretical position, let alone practical stance. Nor can one separate out political ideas from a complex of other views and attitudes which were in fact contested within the early Christian movement, especially in the second century.

Any attempt to give an analytical description or critical appraisal of the material is further complicated by the fact that Christianity emerged from a Jewish matrix, and that it was liable to be treated as alien in the body politic for most of the period with which we are concerned. Where once historians assumed they could identify the emerging Christian Church as opposed to both Judaism and paganism, it is now recognized that this terminology is anachronistic, that margins were blurred, and that none of the three were themselves internally homogeneous. What is clear is that the second century saw Christian groups engaged in defining their identity over against others, and these others included not only Jews and Gentiles but other Christians as well. For our purposes I shall use the labels 'apocalyptic', 'gnostic' and 'apologetic' not to identify orthodox or heretical groups, or to claim reconstruction of distinct social or community networks, but to distinguish schematically three stances that we find in second-century texts.

The apocalyptic type clearly includes the Millenarians. The Book of Revelation (20.1–6) suggested the idea of the Millennium: the serpent, who is the Devil and Satan, would be bound for 1,000 years while the martyrs would come to life and reign with Christ. This was not the final resurrection, but the establishment of Christ's kingdom on earth. Describing the Millenarians of the second century, Eusebius (*Hist. Eccl.* III.39) comments as follows:

> [Papias] . . . says that after the resurrection of the dead there will be a period of a thousand years, when Christ's kingdom will be set up on this earth in material form. I suppose he got these notions by misinterpreting the apostolic accounts and failing to grasp what they said in mystic and symbolic language. For he seems to have been a man of very small intelligence, to judge from his books. But it is partly due to him that the great majority of churchmen after him took the same view, relying on his early date; e.g. Irenaeus and several others, who clearly held the same opinion.

Whether Eusebius is right to attribute to Papias the word translated 'in material form' (*sōmatikōs*) cannot now be determined, but it would certainly reflect one emerging issue in the second century: was the kingdom of God a purely transcendent, heavenly kingdom – a spiritual reality – or was it kingly rule on this earth, a kind of political reality though eschatological? It was increasingly accepted among many Christians that at his first coming Christ had fulfilled the prophecies of suffering and humiliation, and on his return he would fulfil those that speak of triumph and glory. They expected Christ's reign as God's vice-gerent on earth, earthly powers having been dethroned.

But the gnostic position[12] tended to be anti-materialistic. The person in the know already had eternal life and belonged to the heavenly kingdom. The material world was regarded as alien, the gnostics understanding their true being, origin and destiny as belonging to the transcendent, spiritual world. This had a profound effect on their ethics. Radical asceticism, withdrawal from society and its conventions, and denial of fleshly concerns, was one logical outcome, the other was to regard all such things as irrelevant – some gnostics apparently challenged the need for believers to face martyrdom. All that mattered was the knowledge that one belonged to the spiritual elite, so conformity to this world was neither here nor there. Consequently the gnostic approach precluded serious political thought, and the postwar discoveries at Nag Hammadi,[13] insofar as they may be regarded as constituting a library of gnostic texts, confirm their lack of interest in the political situation, political theory or political change. The outlook was individualistic and cosmic, not political or social.

Thus two quite different motives for asceticism seem to emerge from the second-century material. On the one hand, gnostic otherworldliness despised the flesh and wished to be freed from it; on the other hand, apocalyptic hopes, as expressed in some of the apocryphal Gospels and Acts, clearly envisaged the perfecting of the created order, and so the need to purify the flesh for its eventual resurrection. The latter took the need for loyalty to Christ, if necessary through the path of suffering and death, with the utmost seriousness. It would seem that the Montanist movement (late second century)[14] may have been a reclamation of the older apocalyptic outlook in the face of gnostic spiritualizing. The prophet Montanus, and his daughters, Priscilla and Maximilla, seem to have predicted the Return of Christ to Pepuza in Asia Minor, where he would

[12] For recent contrasting works on Gnosticism, see Rudolph 1983, Filoramo 1990, Pétrement 1991. [13] See Robinson 1977. [14] See Heine 1989, Trevett 1996.

establish the kingdom of God. Martyrdom was highly prized, and a puritanical ethic preached.

The reasons why the so-called New Prophecy was eventually resisted by leaders of the church in the late second and early third centuries are complex. There are accusations concerning claims that Montanus incarnated the Holy Spirit, and charges that the Montanists' prophecy was false, since it was ecstatic and irrational like pagan Sibyls, not like the rational prophets of the scriptures. But a generation after its outbreak, there was considerable sympathy for the New Prophecy in the West. Its rigorist ethic and its radical stance struck chords with other Christians who were unhappy about increasing conformity with the world. There was a confrontational edge to it, which made it politically dangerous. Maybe that was sufficient reason for the church authorities to be cautious.

For meanwhile the apologetic stance seems to have become dominant – at least, it is the clearest position in the texts that the church preserved. This highlighted the tradition that Christians affirmed the Roman empire as established by God, and prayed for it, on this ground arguing that they should not be regarded as subversives. However, it also affirmed the refusal to offer a loyalty incompatible with loyalty to Christ. They were prepared to die for Christ, if a 'bad' emperor overreached himself and demanded the worship they were prepared to give only through Christ to God.

The ambivalent position of Christians is well illustrated by Polycarp, bishop of Smyrna (*c.* AD 69–155). He lived to a great old age, well respected among Christians since he was believed to have known the apostles, and presumably not an object of hostility or suspicion, given his long life, until suddenly there arose an outcry against the Christians that led to his death. The *Martyrdom of Polycarp*[15] is the earliest authentic account of a martyrdom extant, and it shows clearly how Polycarp was pressed to offer incense and say, 'Caesar is Lord', to swear 'By the luck of Caesar', and to revile Christ. Polycarp's reply was:

> Eighty and six years have I served him, and he has done me no wrong. How then can I blaspheme my King and my Saviour? (*Mart. Pol.* 9)

The conflict of loyalty is clear. However, Polycarp also tells the Governor that

> we have been taught to pay all proper respect to powers and authorities of God's appointment, so long as it does not compromise us. (*Mart. Pol.* 10)

[15] Text in Lightfoot 1885; translation quoted from Staniforth 1987.

The letter which Polycarp wrote to the Philippians[16] considerably earlier in the second century encourages the same aim as the Pastoral Epistles, to be well respected by outsiders:

> Let everyone respect his neighbour's rights, so that the heathen may have no occasion to find fault with your way of life. By so doing you will not only earn approval for the good you do, but you will avoid bringing the Lord into any disrepute. (Pol. *ad Phil.* 10)

The recipients are to pray for all God's people, and to pray too 'for our sovereign lords, and for all governors and rulers'. But the context of the letter is the time when Ignatius was journeying via Smyrna and Philippi to Rome to face martyrdom, and they are also told to pray for any who 'ill-use you or dislike you', and for the enemies of the Cross (Pol. *ad Phil.* 12).

The underlying rationale, that the God of the Christians is the Creator, therefore the universal God, and that this being God's world, the way people act and behave in it is of ultimate significance, is expressed in *I Clement*, a work included with the letters of Ignatius and Polycarp among the so-called Apostolic Fathers,[17] texts which hovered on the fringes of the canon. That all except the Christians were misguided, yet ultimately everything is under God's providential eye, would become the principal argument of the Apologists. These writers specifically set out to explain Christianity to the Roman world, usually addressing their Apologies to the emperor of the time at which they wrote. Many of them clearly owe much to popular philosophy, and endeavour to give a rational account of the awkward political stance they had inherited. To that extent they may be regarded as the first Christians to whom self-conscious political thought may be attributed.

Political philosophy had for long debated the relative merits of monarchy, oligarchy and democracy, but that theoretical argument leaves little trace in Christian writings. Monarchy is assumed as the appropriate way of ensuring justice, law and order. What Christians argue is that monarchy ultimately belongs only to God. The chief charge they combat is that of atheism, a charge attributable to the fact that they had abandoned their ancestral traditions and would not conform to the religious practices of everyone around them. Their claim is that, so far from being atheists, they worship the one true God. This means that they are doing more for political order by praying to that God for the emperor than those who are deceived by demons into worshipping the false gods and idols of the nations. The political issue, for the Apologists, is primarily religious.

[16] Text and translation as in n.15.

[17] Texts and translation as in n.15.

'Monarchy' is often used in early Christian texts where we might expect 'monotheism'. There is one source (*archē*) of all things, who alone has sovereign rule (*archē*). The providential oversight of that One God undergirds human justice, just as the *logos* of that One God is present in all human rationality – implicitly, Justin[18] claims the right of a philosopher to debate with other philosophers about the truth, recognizing that there is much in common between the philosophy of the Christians and that of Platonists and Stoics. Before Christianity religion, whether Jewish or pagan, was more a matter of following traditional practices than believing particular doctrines. Doctrine was associated with the teachings of philosophers. Indeed, philosophers might rationalize into a theoretical unity the objects of the extraordinary welter of religious practices deriving from the customs of all the different peoples within the empire, but it would be the late third century before that empire would attempt to sacralize itself by adopting a monotheistic outlook rather than appealing to the traditional gods to whom Rome owed its greatness. By contrast, the audacious claims of Christians about the One God implied, already in the second century, a challenge to religious pluralism and something like the eventual Christian take-over. Perhaps we should not be surprised that, responding to monarchian heretics who sought to affirm the monarchy of God by speaking of Father, Son and Holy Spirit as successive modes of the one deity, Tertullian (*adv. Praxeam* 3)[19] could argue by analogy with the Roman state: even if the emperor shares power with his sons, there remains only one monarchy. Monotheism and monarchy were already perceived to relate to one another.

For the time being the Roman authorities seem to have been primarily interested in the conservation of ancestral custom, for they recognized that *religio* embraced a whole set of obligations to others, family, city, state, and gods, and these obligations cemented social order. This explains why apologetic texts are so anxious to demonstrate the non-subversive and law-abiding character of Christians and their loyalty to the emperor, while resisting the charge that Christians had abandoned ancestral customs – indeed seeking to prove the antiquity of Christianity by claiming that it went back to Abraham and that Moses was earlier than any of the Greeks. Some of the Apologists contented themselves with simply asking for the same justice as everybody else – Athenagoras (*Legatio* 1–3),[20] for

[18] Justin Martyr taught as a philosopher in Rome, having been convinced of the truth of Christianity. His works (two apologies and the *Dialogue with Trypho*) head the list of significant Christian apologetic writings. For texts and translations, see n.5.

[19] Tertullian, *Adversus Praxeam*; text and translation: Evans 1948.

[20] Text and translation: Schoedel 1972.

example, asks why Christians cannot be allowed the same rights as others to worship according to their differing ancestral traditions, as long as their behaviour is not criminal.

By the third century, such arguments were becoming sophisticated. Tertullian (*c.* AD 160–240), probably an ex-lawyer, could appeal to Roman justice:[21] Why should Christians be treated in ways which were the complete opposite of everybody else (*Apologeticum* 1–4)? No homage that is not offered freely is worth anything, and everybody else is free to pay respects to whatever deities they choose (*Apol.* 28.1). The Christian case is not properly heard, judges are ignorant, they are condemned for the mere confession of the name and not for any crimes. The contrast between Christians and criminals was pressed:

> Why, evil-doers are eager to escape notice . . . ; they deny when accused; even under torture they do not easily or always confess; at all events when condemned they lament . . . But look at the Christians! There you have quite another story; not a man of them is ashamed of it . . . If he is denounced, he glories in it; if he is accused, he does not defend himself; when he is questioned, he confesses without any pressure; when he is condemned he renders thanks. (*Apol.* 1.11–13)

Indeed, Tertullian delights in the kind of rhetorical *tour de force* which exposes Roman inconsistency. If Christians were to be treated as treasonous because they challenged the traditional customs, the morals that secured society against crime and wickedness and the gods that had made Rome great, Tertullian would turn these arguments around. Romans have betrayed their ancestral customs more than Christians – what became of the laws repressing expensive and ostentatious living, and putting down theatres which corrupt the people's morals (*Apol.* 6.2)? Roman history reveals those who really were traitors – Christians have never taken up arms against the state or anyone else, since they are taught to love their enemies. The real traitors were deceivers, Romans who did pay homage to the emperor and the gods and then conspired against them (*Apol.* 35–7).

Far from flattering the emperor like most people, Christians offer prayers to the only God that is real and able therefore to be effective:

> . . . [we] invoke the eternal God, the true God, the living God, whom the Emperors themselves prefer to have propitious to them beyond all other gods. They know who has given them the empire; they know, as men, who has given them life; they feel that He is God alone, in whose power

[21] Text of Tertullian's *Apology* in *CCSL* 1.1. Translation quoted: Glover 1931.

> and no other's they are, second to whom they stand, after whom they come first, before all gods and above all gods . . . (*Apol.* 30.1)

Christians pray for the emperor because they particularly care about the emperor's welfare. It is not just that in their sacred books they are promised blessings if they pray for their enemies, but also that the continued existence of the Roman empire alone retards the dreadful woes which will accompany the End of the world (*Apol.* 32.1). So,

> . . . why need I say more of the religious awe, the piety, of Christians, where the emperor is concerned? We must needs respect him as the chosen of our Lord. So I have a right to say, Caesar is more ours than yours, appointed as he is by our God. (*Apol.* 33.1)

It is in the emperor's interest to give God the higher place and to remember he is only a man; Tertullian has no objection to calling him Lord, as long as he is not forced 'to call him Lord in the sense of God' (*Apol.* 34.1). The universalist outlook of Christians, and their lack of interest in factions and politics, should recommend them rather than cause offence, according to Tertullian. He is pleading a mutual interest between church and empire which provides interesting precedents for the turn which history took with Constantine.

Meanwhile, however, Christians were treated as scapegoats:

> If the Tiber reaches the walls, if the Nile does not rise to the fields, if the sky doesn't move or the earth does, if there is famine, if there is plague, the cry is at once: 'The Christians to the lion!' (*Apol.* 40.2)

Tertullian misses no opportunity to mock: 'What, all of them to one lion?' he asks. But the point concerns the scapegoating. Doubtless this was the result of their perceived difference, their failure to fit normal categories. Elsewhere Tertullian reveals that they were known as the 'third race' (*ad Nationes* 8 ff.).[22] Although Tertullian scorns and contests the term, this had been implicit in Christian self-understanding since the New Testament. As Greeks had seen all others as barbarians, so Jews saw all others as Gentiles; in the Greco-Roman world cultural syncretism made more plausible the contrast between Jew and Greek – the term embracing all those Hellenized peoples under Roman rule. Religious customs were part of culture, and the refusal of Jews to compromise their exclusivity in religious customs marked them out. Christians identified themselves with the Jews in adopting their literature as authoritative and refusing to

[22] *Tertium genus*: Tertullian, *ad Nationes*, text in *CCSL* 1.1. For discussion see Harnack 1908: ch. 7, especially the excursus, pp. 266–78.

compromise with idolatry; but increasingly differentiated themselves from the Jewish community, claiming to inherit the promises, to be the new people of God. The sense of being resident aliens (explored earlier) suggests the same self-consciousness of being different, a new 'race'.

Tertullian presents Christians as a 'body' knit together by their religion, discipline and future hope (*Apol.* 39.1). He explains how they meet together for prayer, for the reading of their sacred literature, for the fostering of their good habits and customs, for mutual support, especially for the weak and poor through their charitable collections and for burying the dead, and he reveals that they treat each other as kith and kin – brothers and sisters with a common Father who have all things (except wives) in common, and have a family meal or love-feast, presided over by 'elders'. At first sight this might seem to be the description of a household or a *collegium*, but there are features which, taken with other evidence, suggest an alternative society.

The terminology of the body, though no doubt for Tertullian consciously drawn from Paul (I Cor. 12 and Rom. 12), was a political commonplace, especially among the Stoics, as was the analogy between state and household. The Pastoral Epistles had depicted the church as God's household and *1 Clement* had developed further the analogies with Caesar's household, noting with approval the discipline of 'our generals' and other army officers who carried out the orders of the emperor and ensured the *pax Romana*. Indeed, the peace and order of the whole cosmos Tertullian saw as a magnificent gift of God, ensured by the empire and to be reflected in the church, where each is to win God's approval in his own rank. If at one level acceptance of the *status quo* seems implicit here,[23] we also find the sense of being exiles and belonging to another kingdom. The language of the body appears here too, as well as the political terms 'assembly' and 'congregation' (*ekklēsia* and *sunagōgē*) which Christians had used for their gatherings from the beginning. But it is in Origen (*c.* AD 184/5–254/5) that we see most clearly how easy it was to view the church as a state within a state:

> God . . . caused churches (*ekklēsiai*) to exist in opposition to the assemblies (*ekklēsiai*) of superstitious, licentious, and unrighteous men. For such is the character of the crowds who everywhere constitute the assemblies of cities. And the Churches of God which have been taught by Christ, when compared with the assemblies of the people where they live, are 'as lights in the world' . . . And so also, if you compare the council of the Church of God with the council in each city, you will find that some councillors of the Church are worthy to hold office in a city which

23 Wengst 1987.

> is God's, if there is such a city anywhere in the universe. But the councillors in every city do not show in their moral character anything worthy of the pre-eminent authority by which they appear to be superior to the citizens. (*Cels.* III.29–30)[24]

It has been suggested[25] that the church was an invisible empire, its internal organization modelled on that of the Roman State: the *ordo* (clergy) and *plebs* (laity) corresponded to the *curia* and *populus* of the muncipality, and the officers or overseers (*episkopoi*) were likewise similar to those of the *municipium*. The officials of this apparent state within a state, I would argue, had their origin in the church's perception of itself as the household of God, but given the ethical commonplace that drew analogies between state and household, the increasing convergence of civic and ecclesiastical forms is perhaps not altogether surprising. Church buildings would begin as converted houses and later adopt the secular basilica – for Christian places of worship were meeting-places where people gathered as a community, not, like temples, dwelling-places for divine beings from which all but priests and attendants were excluded. By the fourth century, dioceses followed the pattern of the empire, and episcopal arbitration, a longstanding practice based on Christians' reluctance to go to law with one another (I Cor. 6), corresponded to law-court procedures. '. . . [T]he *ekklēsia* had emerged as an antitype to the *civitas*'.[26]

'What has Athens to do with Jerusalem?' (*de Praescriptionibus Haereticorum* 7). Tertullian's famous question, together with much of his anti-world rhetoric in treatises intended for internal Christian consumption, highlights the potential opposition of type and antitype, but in his passionate and rhetorical language, as we have seen, lay also the potential for *rapprochement*.[27] Tertullian may have implied that the idea of a Christian Caesar was impossible (*Apol.* 21.24),[28] and asserted that 'all secular powers and dignities are not merely alien to but hostile to God', so

> there can be no reconciliation between the oath of allegiance taken to God and that taken to man, between the standard of Christ and that of the devil, between the camp of light and the camp of darkness. (*de Idolatria* 18–19, cf. *de Corona* 11)

[24] Text of Origen's *Contra Celsum* in *GCS*. Translation: Chadwick 1965.

[25] Cochrane 1940.

[26] Cochrane 1940: 220.

[27] Isichei 1964 entitles her chapter on Tertullian 'The Politics of Isolation'. She uses his other writings to relativize the positive statements in the *Apology*, thus arriving at a rather different overall picture from that presented here.

[28] Tertullian, *Apol.* 21.24: 'This whole story [i.e. of Christ] was reported to Caesar (at that time it was Tiberius) by Pilate, himself in his secret heart already a Christian. Yes, and the Caesars also would have believed on Christ, if Caesars had not been necessary for the world, or if the Caesars, too, could have been Christians.'

But he paved the way for those who would herald the Christianizing Emperor, Constantine, apologists such as Lactantius. Eusebius and Lactantius represent respectively the reactions of East and West to the Constantinian revolution.

4 The response to Constantine

Eusebius (*c.* AD 260–339) was already an old man when Constantine came to the throne in the East.[29] He had composed, then repeatedly revised and added to, his pioneering history of the church, embarking on his work before the Great Persecution of Diocletian and continuing as the persecution rumbled on through the time of Licinius. Since around 312 he had been working on the massive *Praeparatio Evangelica*, an apologetic assembly of quotations from the philosophers and wise men of Greco-Roman culture with links and comments. This would be followed by the *Demonstratio Evangelica* which showed how Jewish prophecies were fulfilled in Christ. The undergirding idea of all Eusebius' scholarship was the providence of the one true God. Jesus Christ was born just as Augustus created the *pax Romana*: his *Chronological Tables*, which antedate the *Church History*, already enshrine the notion that world history comes together with that coincidence. Constantine was the fulfilment of Eusebius' convictions.

Constantine's significance for his life's work puts into perspective Eusebius' depiction of the emperor. There is some evidence in the *Church History* that Eusebius bent or suppressed truths which sat uncomfortably with his views. How much more with Constantine! Eusebius glossed the less salutary aspects of Constantine's reign, notably his dirty dealings within the family, and he made it seem as though the succession was providentially satisfactory. Constantine had to play a key role in Eusebius' understanding of the divine plan for the world. For Eusebius the Christian empire was the goal of history, not the Millennium. The Christian empire he would celebrate, adopting and adapting the conventions of imperial panegyric for that purpose without embarrassment.

Imperial panegyric had always had a religious dimension, particularly in the Eastern empire where Augustus had stepped into the 'king-ideology' of earlier regimes – the Hellenistic king of Syria, Antiochus, for example, had claimed the title 'Epiphanes', god manifest. Emperors were

[29] Texts of Eusebius' works may be found in *GCS*. Translation of *Vita Constantini* in *NPNF*. For general introduction and bibliography, see my chapter in Young 1983. For relations with Constantine, see Barnes 1981.

expected to be 'godlike', answering the prayers of their subjects and bringing salvation from enemies, pirates and the lawless, ensuring peace, health and harmony by their presence. If some early Christian writings parodied the tendency to divinize the emperor, attributing salvation instead to King Jesus (see above), Eusebius christianized the theory of kingship found in Middle Platonist philosophy. Parallels have been found with Plutarch and Diotogenes, as well as the Jewish Platonist, Philo.[30]

Eusebius tells us he was privileged to deliver orations in the presence of Constantine on two occasions, of which the most notable was the celebration of the emperor's Tricennalia (335/6). The Oration for the latter occasion (*Laus Constantini*)[31] is appended to the work known as the *Vita Constantini*, a work which is itself essentially an encomium devoted to celebrating the achievements of the recently deceased emperor. Eusebius explicitly says that he will present

> those royal and noble actions which are pleasing to God, the Sovereign of all. For would it not be disgraceful that the memory of Nero, and other impious and godless tyrants far worse than he, should meet with diligent writers to embellish the relation of their worthless deeds with elegant language, and record them in voluminous histories, and that I should be silent, to whom God himself has vouchsafed such an emperor as all history records not, and has permitted me to come into his presence, and enjoy his acquaintance and society? (*VC* 1.10)

His stated intention was to write only of circumstances which have reference to Constantine's religious character.

Scholarly controversy has surrounded these crucial sources for Constantine's life and policy: is the material cited by Eusebius authentic? what exactly was Eusebius' relationship with the emperor? how Christian was Constantine? For our purposes it is only necessary to focus on the political thought inherent in these recognizably selective and panegyrical writings.

The coherence between monarchy and monotheism is now explicit:

> Monarchy excels all other kinds of constitution and government. For rather do anarchy and civil war result from the alternative, a polyarchy based on equality. For which reason there is One God, not two or three or even more. For strictly speaking belief in gods is godless. There is one Sovereign, and his Logos and royal law is one, not expressed in words and syllables nor eroded by time in books or tables, but the living and

[30] See Baynes 1934: 13–18, Setton 1941. Drake 1976 draws attention also to the precedent of Philo.
[31] For discussion and translation of *Laus Constantini* quoted here (occasionally altered), see Drake 1976.

> actual God the Logos, who directs His Father's Kingdom for all those under and beneath him. (*LC* 3.6)

In the previous sentences Eusebius has described the 'God-beloved ruler', who has been designated victor over all rivals and foreign enemies, not only as a model of piety and truth for all the earth, but as driving the imperial chariot drawn by four Caesars in the same way as the sun, 'traversing all lands, himself present everywhere and watching over everything':

> Thus fitted out in the likeness of the kingdom of heaven, he pilots affairs below with an upward gaze, to steer by the archetypal form. He grows strong in his model of monarchic rule, which the Ruler of all has given to the race of man alone of those on earth. For this is the law of royal authority, the law which decrees one rule over everybody. (*LC* 3.5)

The motif of heavenly archetype modelled on earth runs through the *Laus Constantini.* Eusebius' prologue spoke of Constantine's palace as if it were a holy sanctuary hard to penetrate, containing ineffable mysteries, and the opening of the body of the speech describes heaven in terms of the imperial court – the earth may be the footstool of the Supreme Sovereign, but 'celestial armies encircle [him] and supernatural powers attend'; a vast company gazes on his gleaming presence, and the emperor, in whose bosom resides spiritual as well as human concerns, himself praises 'to us' this One, the Supreme Sovereign, the cause of his empire (*LC* 1.2–3). If the *logos* is priest in heaven, co-ruler and all-pervasive Governor of the entire cosmos, the emperor is the *logos*' friend, appointed to rule on earth. The *logos* keeps away the powers of evil, like a shepherd protecting the flock from wild beasts; his friend, armed against his enemies, subdues the opponents of truth. The *logos*, being the Pre-existent and Universal Saviour, sows 'rational and redeeming seeds', making people fit for his Father's kingdom; his friend, the *logos*' interpreter, summons the human race to knowledge of the Higher Power, proclaiming the laws of genuine piety (*LC* 1.6–2.4).

Some claim to have looked in vain in this panegyric for distinctively Christian features. The turning point in history seems not to be the incarnation of the *logos* in Jesus Christ, but the reign of the *logos*' friend, Constantine, whose sovereignty on earth mirrors the heavenly monarchy. But Constantine embodies all the virtues because he has received in his soul emanations from heaven – reason from the *logos*, wisdom from Wisdom, goodness from the Good, justness from Justice (*LC* 5.1). Behind Constantine is the *logos*, and whatever some of his audience may have thought, Eusebius undoubtedly meant the *logos* incarnate in Jesus Christ.

The only true philosopher king is one who knows himself and recognizes his dependence upon the showers of every blessing which descend on him. He does not offer irrational and bloody sacrifices, but day and night petitions the Heavenly Father in his prayers, aware of his mortal state (*LC* 5.4; cf. 2.5). Eusebius' insistence on the mortality of the emperor enables Constantine to become a teacher and a model, one who has triumphed over his passions by modelling himself 'after the archetypal form of the Supreme Sovereign'. He is not a bit excited by all his retainers, or swollen-headed by his power; he laughs at his cloth of gold, seeing himself within as sharing 'the nature common to all'. His clothing is temperance and justice, piety and all the virtues. He is an example to all, the teacher of the 'holy knowledge of the Supreme Sovereign' (*LC* 5.4–8). Even here classical motifs predominate; for the philosopher's prayer is the model for Constantine's rational piety.

Similar themes recur in the *Vita Constantini* (left unfinished at the author's death). Now Eusebius draws on the rhetorical convention of *suncrisis* – of using classic examples comparatively in order to highlight the qualities of the figure being eulogized. He likens Constantine to Cyrus (the Persian king hailed as Messiah in Isaiah 45 because he brought to an end the exile of the Jews in Babylon), to Alexander the Great and, persistently, to Moses (*VC* I.12, 20, 40, II.12). Both were brought up in the palace of oppressors, flight and accession were features of their youth, both were appointed by God, and the drowning of Maxentius' troops in the Tiber parallels the crossing of the Red Sea. Constantine's subsequent singing of praises to God, Ruler of all and Author of victory was anticipated by Moses, as also his tabernacle set a little apart from the camp where he was in constant contact with God. Later (*VC* III.21) the philosopher king lectures bishops on peace and humility, a task he can no doubt validly undertake because he embodies all virtues in himself and his rule reflects that of God in heaven. Allegiance to God and allegiance to Constantine are virtually identified.

Church-State relations in the later Byzantine world are often characterized by the term 'Caesaro-papism'. That acceptance of the emperor as having supreme control over the Church, even in matters of doctrine, is rooted in Eusebius' reaction to the political developments of the early fourth century. Eusebius was not alone in identifying Constantine's patronage of the church as the effect of providence and God's oversight of human history. That response may in any case be regarded as the natural outworking of some strands in earlier Christian thought (see above).

Lactantius (*c.* AD 240–320) may be seen as the Western Eusebius. He too lived through the period of persecution and the arrival of Constantine. He wrote an account of the deaths of the persecutors which is as important, and as problematic, a source for historians as Eusebius' material. His major work, the *Divine Institutes*,[32] is dedicated to Constantine and contains, in some manuscripts (at VII.27), a panegyrical address to the emperor, which celebrates his raising up by the great God to restore the house of justice and protect the human race.

Often treated as an apology, the *Divine Institutes* is an exposition of the truth as Lactantius sees it. He was apparently a convert, and therefore speaks out of a sense of discovery. For Lactantius true worship is the heart of the matter. His first book argues that there must be One God, challenging the pluralism of religion in the culture around him. His principal argument is monarchical (I.3). Divided rule means chaos. The universe is the creation of one God who is also the one ruler, king of the whole earth with providential oversight of everything. To anyone who suggests that such a task is beyond a single governor, he replies that he does not 'understand how great is the force and power of the divine majesty, if he believes that the single God who could make the world, could not rule the same world which he made'. To suggest that many are involved in fashioning and governing the world is tantamount to saying that an army has as many generals as there are legions, cohorts and divisions, or that there are many minds in one body.

Clearly Lactantius' theology works with one leading analogy: the imperial monarchy is projected onto the heavens and enhanced by drawing on the standard *topoi* of the body politic and the macrocosm-microcosm. God is the great all-seeing, all-knowing ruler, served by a court of angels and ministers whose duty is obedience (II.17) – and as in a royal court on earth, some of the attendants are not trustworthy; they deceive human beings into thinking they are gods, provide the odd prodigy and receive bribes in the form of sacrifices. Following the traditions of earlier apologists, Lactantius exploits poets, philosophers and Sibyls to confirm the truth of his monarchical theology.

Constantine has been raised up by this universal Monarch to establish justice, end wickedness and demonstrate in what true majesty consists (VII.27) – in other words as God's vice-gerent on earth. He excels in virtue and prosperity and enjoys immortal glories because he defends and loves the name of God. God protects Constantine, giving him a quiet and tranquil reign. He was chosen by God in preference to others as the one to

32 Texts of Lactantius' works can be found in *CSEL* and *Sources Chrétiennes*. Translation used here (altered) McDonald 1964.

renew holy religion. Anyone ignorant of God, the Ruler of the universe, is incapable of attaining true righteousness, but Constantine, by his innate sanctity of character and his acknowledgment of the truth, performs works of righteousness. So Christians pray for the emperor as the guardian of the world. Unlike Eusebius, Lactantius accepted the traditional apocalyptic expectations. Book VII spells out prophecies of doom, destruction and judgment, followed by the planting of the holy city on earth. Yet, although the fall and ruin of the world is shortly to take place, it appears that the End is not to be feared while Rome remains (VII.25). Presumably Constantine is the guardian of the world because as 'restrainer' he ensures that the eternal city is not yet endangered. So we find the older traditions of Christianity reminted in a new situation.

Justifying the Constantinian revolution is not, however, Lactantius' primary concern in the *Divine Institutes*, nor is his work overtly concerned with political thought. Beginning with three books exposing and diagnosing the origins of false religion and false philosophy, he presents the true wisdom and true religion, arguing that they are the basis of justice, and that true worship alone produces the good and happy life. Thus he engages with the standard questions of philosophy. Political thinking is embraced in a comprehensive survey of ethics, physics and metaphysics. Fundamentally his views are theocratic.

Lactantius' principal dialogue partner is Cicero, whose works he plunders as source for information, arguments and quotations, while frequently offering a critique. He draws from across Cicero's output, though the use of the *de Natura Deorum* is particularly noticeable in the early books, the *de Legibus* and *de Officiis* in the later books. Cicero's scepticism was useful in arguing against the pagan tradition; yet his career was the 'measure of the good pagan's failure' – 'Lactantius thought that Christianity was the *sapientia* that philosophers had failed to find.'[33]

The nub of the matter for Lactantius is that true worship undergirds behaviour, and so creates a just society. Traditional religion cannot be judged true because it does not instruct and improve people with precepts of virtue and justice. Nor can philosophy be regarded as true wisdom since it does not take piety seriously. Lactantius insists:

> If the divinity which governs the world sustains the human race with unbelievable beneficence, and cherishes it with, one might say, paternal favours, surely it wants thanks to be rendered and honour given to itself . . . Where then is wisdom joined with religion? There, namely, where

33 Stevenson 1961.

> one God is adored . . . To be wise is nothing else except to honour the true God with just and holy worship. (IV.3)

The monarchical metaphors, noted already and reinforced by the language of kingship in the scriptures, oscillate with other images. The provincial governor who keeps a close eye on everything and exercises judgment (II.16; V.8) is found alongside the head of the household. For, following the commonplace that running state or household is much the same, Lactantius sees the one God as the provident *paterfamilias* of the universe, both Father and Lord, with the power of reward and punishment. It is this which undergirds his discussion of justice, the subject of Book V.

Poets and philosophers had recognized the absence of justice in the world, suggesting that it had departed from the earth when Jupiter usurped Saturn's rule. Lactantius suggests that Jesus was sent to re-establish the golden age of justice before false worship of the gods had begun. He thinks that justice and true worship are integrally related, and continuing evils on earth are explained by the fact that there is not yet by common consent a general observance of God's law:

> How blessed and how golden would be the condition of human affairs if, throughout the whole world, meekness and devotion and peace and innocence and fairness and temperance and faith should tarry! (V.8)

There would be no need for 'so many and such various laws for ruling men, when the one law of God would suffice unto perfect innocence'. Nor would prisons and punishments be required. Lactantius looks for a time when the hearts of men will be instructed in the works of justice by a health-giving infusion of divine precepts. He accepts the traditional view that 'virtue is knowledge' and believes that ignorance is the cause of wickedness.

What is particularly striking, however, is the way in which equality before God becomes a principle of justice. For Lactantius, piety and equity are the fountains of justice, and in these two fountains the whole of justice is contained. God provides breath to all, all are equal, receiving light, food, sleep, wisdom and immortality. In God's sight no one is a slave, no one a master; we have the same Father and we are all children. No one is poor, apart from the one who lacks justice; no one is rich, apart from the one full of virtues. Neither the Romans, nor the Greeks, could possess justice because their societies had people differing in degree, rich and poor, humble and powerful. Lactantius claims that Christians believe themselves to be equal (V.14).

This might seem to have political implications, but it turns out that Christians measure human things 'not by the body, but by the spirit' – in lowliness of mind, in humility, Christians are on an equality (v.15). Is equity merely spiritual then? It would seem not, since later in Book VI, Lactantius contrasts the characteristic virtues of Christians, such as almsgiving, hospitality, protection of widows and orphans, with the more utilitarian views of philosophers, claiming that Christian justice is the perfect justice. Civil law varies from one country to another and is devised by utility (VI.8); it cannot therefore be embraced as true justice and must be contrasted with the law of God (VI.9). Justice consists in being generous to the blind, lame and destitute, who may be useless in human terms, but must be serviceable to God since he keeps them alive (VI.11).

The tension between Lactantius' claims about the transformation of human society and his failure to envisage social revolution may be taken to reflect a perennial tension in Christian political thought: spiritually all may be equal, but what effect is this to have on earthly society? In a fallen world, how is the notion of equality to be cashed in practice? In the end Lactantius accepts the need for Constantine to exercise divine authority so as to ensure social order, and retains a lively Millenarian hope.

Like Eusebius, then, Lactantius welcomes and celebrates the new order. Others, however, such as the growing multitude of ascetics withdrawing into the deserts and inheriting the mantle of the martyrs, felt that the church's purity would be inevitably compromised with the world. Subsequent events would justify that suspicion.

5 The separation of spheres

Already during the reign of Constantine (AD 312–37), the church found itself engaged in protracted internal struggles over doctrine and discipline, struggles whch intensified under Constantius (emperor AD 337–61). The emperors, often in the interests of imposing unity, took sides in these disputes, using imperial power to summon and direct councils, and to impose or exile bishops. Yet both sides in the Arian and Donatist struggles were prepared to appeal to the emperor while asserting independence when the emperor's judgment went against them.

Athanasius (*c.* AD 295–373) is regarded as the chief defender of orthodoxy against the Arians. Under Constantius his view shifted away from a position close to that of Eusebius to an increasingly sharp differentiation between the powers of state and of the church. We owe it to his *Historia Arianorum* that a number of earlier documents have survived which reflect the 'growing demand for ecclesiastical autonomy'.[34] These include a letter from the now aged Hosius of Cordova, once Constantine's ecclesiastical adviser, refusing the emperor's demand that he excommunicate Athanasius:

> Cease these proceedings, I beseech you, and remember that you are a mortal man . . . Intrude not yourself into ecclesiastical matters, neither give commands unto us concerning them; but learn from us. God has put into your hands the kingdom; to us he has entrusted the affairs of his church . . . It is written, 'Render unto Caesar the things that are Caesar's, and unto God the things that are God's.'

In this work concerning the Arians, Athanasius himself asks:

> When did a judgment of the church receive its validity from the emperor, or when was his decree ever recognized by the church? There have been many councils and many judgments passed by the church [i.e. prior to the time of Constantine]; but the fathers never sought the consent of the emperor thereto . . . ? Where is there now a church which enjoys the privilege of worshipping Christ freely?

Events thus shifted political thought. This is particularly evident in the case of Ambrose (*c.* AD 340–97), whose position is largely enshrined in *ad hoc* letters and sermons.[35] Ambrose, who was to have a key role in the conversion of Augustine, was bishop of Milan, where the Western imperial court was now based.

In the first of three key incidents (AD 386), Ambrose persisted in resisting attempts by the court to requisition church property for an Arian, Auxentius. He defied troops and imperial orders with a sermon that asserted such things as: 'I fear the Lord, master of the universe, more than I do the emperor, master of this earth'; 'Christ is not a guilty defendant, but a judge'; and 'the emperor is within the church, not above the church'. Ambrose is clear that

> we render to Caesar what is Caesar's and to God what is God's. The tribute is Caesar's; we do not refuse to pay it. The church is God's; therefore in no way ought it to be awarded to Caesar, for the rights of Caesar do not extend over the church of God. (*Sermon against Auxentius*)

In the second case (AD 388) Ambrose refused communion to Theodosius until he had rescinded an order that a synagogue be rebuilt which had been burnt down by rioting monks. In a letter to the emperor

[34] Greenslade 1954. Translations of Hosius' letter and of Athanasius are taken from this volume.
[35] Texts of Ambrose's works in *CSEL*. Translation of sermon and letters is quoted from Cunningham 1982.

(*Ep.* 40), he asserted his right of freedom of speech, appealing to biblical texts and precedents: Ezekiel suggested that one is accountable for failing to warn a just man who turns away from his own justice. In a subsequent letter to his sister (*Ep.* 41), Ambrose reproduced the sermon he had preached in the emperor's presence and told of his subsequent confrontation with him. Gospel stories, and incidents such as Nathan's challenge to David, give him the authority to stand up to the emperor.

In the third case (AD 390) Ambrose forced Theodosius to do penance for the massacre at Thessalonica, again appealing to the story of David and Nathan. Ambrose claims he dare not offer the sacrifice with one present who has shed so much innocent blood; he puts God above the emperor (*Ep.* 51).

This would seem to be the fundamental basis of Ambrose's actions. As for Lactantius, so for Ambrose, piety is the foundation of all virtues, especially justice and generosity, but there is a hierarchy of pieties: to God, first, then country, then parents, then all (*de Officiis* I.27.127). But we should not underestimate Ambrose's appeal to the scriptures: it is characteristic of his *de Officiis* to marry Cicero's method and questions with scriptural solutions, precepts and examples. A bad king like Rehoboam demonstrates the truth that 'equity strengthens empires and injustice destroys them'. Benevolence is needed so that individual rights are preserved as well as the government of affairs in general (*de Officiis* II.19.95). While good kings like David and Solomon may exemplify justice and wisdom for everybody, scripture does not hesitate to present kings as also sinners called to account by men of God. That God and Caesar might be in conflict is implied by the saying of Christ appealed to by both Hosius and Ambrose.

Thus began a process whereby in the West a separation of spheres began to be articulated. Augustine's thought concerning two cities, coexisting, overlapping, intermingled throughout human history, but separate, belongs to this political context, though he was too great a thinker to identify the two cities simplistically with church and state.

In the East we find some parallel history of resistance – Athanasius' stormy career was followed by a series of incidents in which Basil (bishop of Caesarea AD 370–9) stood up to the Arian emperor Valens, refusing to be cowed by threats of exile or worse. When Valens arrived in Cappadocia and entered the church, it was Valens not Basil who half-fainted.[36] However, such stories, adorned with miraculous elements, were more to

[36] Gregory Nazianzen, *Orat.* 43 on Basil. Cf. the church historians, Socrates, Sozomen and Theodoret.

do with the sanctification of a defender of orthodoxy than a serious challenge to the accepted political theology. Likewise, the accounts of John Chrysostom's prophetic word comparing the empress to Jezebel are less to do with political theory than his championing of the poor.[37] In the East the separation of spheres was never articulated in the same way. There continued to be internal disputes, such as the monophysite and iconoclastic controversies, but they were internal to a unitive system of governance whose ideology developed the kind of ideas we have seen in Eusebius. Christ Pantocrator ruled on earth through the Byzantine emperor.

There are those who would judge that Christendom betrayed Christianity. The notions that all are equal under God and that God favours the poor and humble repeatedly surface in early Christian texts, and from time to time have inspired political theories. But there were elements in Christian thought from the beginning which encouraged the sacralizing of hierarchical social orders, and in particular the alliance of monotheism and monarchy. Neither the authoritative texts nor the earliest traditions can be regarded as homogeneous. Monarchist or Marxist? The marriage of Christianity with left- or right-wing views is now equally arguable, and debate still flourishes among Christian believers as to whether the kingdom of God is to be realized on earth through political means, or is to remain a hope for the future, in heaven or at the end of time.

[37] Ancient sources include the church historians, Socrates, Sozomen and Theodoret, as well as Palladius' *Dialogue* in defence of Chrysostom. Cf. Setton 1941.

Epilogue

MALCOLM SCHOFIELD

1 Julian and Themistius

In November AD 355 the emperor Constantius II elevated his twenty-four-year-old cousin Julian to the rank of Caesar, or number two in the hierarchy.[1] On hearing the news one of Julian's old teachers, the philosopher Themistius – author of surviving paraphrases of various Aristotelian treatises – wrote from Constantinople a letter to the new Caesar congratulating him and celebrating the advent of a Platonic philosopher king,[2] comparable with a Dionysus or a Heracles.[3] The letter does not survive, but we can infer quite a lot of what Themistius must have said in it from the successive extant panegyrics he addressed to emperors from Constantius on, and above all from Julian's reply in his *Letter to Themistius* (probably AD 356), which is also extant.[4] Themistius seems to have appealed both to history and to theory: Julian is to emulate and indeed surpass Solon, Lycurgus and Pittacus; and in switching from 'indoors' to 'outdoors' philosophy (*Ep.Them.* 262e–263a) he is not only following in the steps of philosophers like Thrasyllus and Musonius Rufus, who took up positions at court, but he is also living up to Aristotle's ideal in the *Politics*, where in a discussion of the rival claims of the active and the leisured life statesmen are praised as 'the architects of external actions' (263d; cf. *Pol.*VII.3, 1325 b21–3).

Julian's reply is not exactly uncivil, but it is lacking in grace, and it is highly critical. Consider the question of the comparative merits of the philosophical and the political life, or – as Themistius sometimes puts his

[1] On the life of Julian see e.g. Browning 1975, Bowersock 1978, Athanassiadi-Fowden 1981, Bouffartigue 1992, Smith 1995. His writings (Greek text and English translation): Wright 1913–23.

[2] A 'craftsman at being a king', as Libanius, another of Julian's teachers, and a more devoted admirer of him, puts it on one occasion (*Or.* 13.36). Libanius, too, was fond of the Heracles comparison (for which see above all Dio Chrysostom *Or.* 1): e.g. *Or.* 12.28, 44; 18.32, 39, 87, 186. On Libanius and Julian see Norman 1969.

[3] Cf. Julian *Ep.Them.* 253c. On Themistius see Vanderspoel 1995; the Greek text of his political orations is edited by Downey and Norman 1965–74, but no English translation is available.

[4] For controversy over the date see Bradbury 1987.

contrast between 'indoors' and 'outdoors' philosophy elsewhere (e.g. *Or.*8.104a–b, 31.352b–c) – the choice between two paths of philosophy: the more divine and the human, more beneficial to the community. Themistius is fond of stressing the practical orientation of philosophy as conceived, for example, by Plato and Aristotle. To take just one striking example, in a composition preoccupied with this issue one sustained sequence of argument culminates in the claim that for Aristotle even 'the god who leads this universe [i.e. the sun] and those who circle with him [the stars] engage in a form of philosophy that is both practical and political, since they draw in their train the whole of nature unswerving and uncontaminated for the whole of time' (*Or.*34.6).[5]

Julian professes himself bewildered by Themistius' preference for practice over theory (263c–266c). He sets him straight on the passage from Book VII of the *Politics* Themistius had cited in his support. He disputes Themistius' claims about Thrasyllus and Musonius. He argues that Socrates' commitment to practice rather than theory had nothing to do with power or politics, but was directed to bringing people salvation through philosophy: this way he did vastly more good than Alexander accomplished by all his victories. 'It is in your power', he tells Themistius (266a–b), 'by producing many philosophers, or even three or four, to confer more benefit on the life of humans than many kings put together.'

Julian begins his letter as he ends it with modest professions of his unworthiness for the position that has been thrust upon him. These are predicated upon a disquisition about the dominance of chance in practical affairs, which starts off in conventional rhetorical style, but then modulates into quotation of a passage in Plato's *Laws* and commentary upon it. We know from his other writings that Themistius was fond of quoting the Athenian Stranger's thesis (as he summarizes it) that 'life will be in its best and happiest condition when there comes to power a king who is young, temperate, with a good memory, brave, noble in bearing, quick to learn' (*Or.* 3.46a, 4.62a; cf. *Laws* IV.710a–b),[6] and applying it to whichever emperor was currently on the throne.[7] Julian had evidently studied with Themistius (257d) the entire passage in which this account of the 'orderly tyrant' occurs (*Laws* IV.709a–15d). He points out first that the passage begins with a reflection on the interplay of chance, opportunity (*kairos*) and expertise (*technē*) in the human domain. But then – much more interestingly – he writes out nearly in full the section which proposes that

[5] Themistius' standpoint is usefully discussed by Downey 1957, Dagron 1968, Daly 1980.

[6] This list of requirements duplicates those the *Republic* had stipulated for potential philosopher kings: e.g. VI.490c, 494b. [7] Cf. n.9 below.

human nature is unable to cope with exercising absolute power without being filled with hybris and injustice, and that this is why Kronos 'set over our cities as kings and governors not men but beings of a more divine and better race – *daimones*, "spirits"' (258b; *Laws* IV.713c–d). A main conclusion of Plato's text is that 'insofar as the principle of immortality is in us we ought to be guided by it in our management of public and private affairs, of our houses and cities, calling the dispensation (*dianomē*) of reason (*nous*)[8] "law" (*nomos*)' (258d; *Laws* IV.713e–714a).

These remarks about the corrupting effect of political power on human nature do indeed problematize the notion of what Themistius calls the 'young king' and Plato's interlocutor Cleinias the 'orderly tyrant'.[9] Julian is presumably implying – no doubt accurately – that Themistius has failed to engage with this dimension of Plato's theorizing about monarchy. His perception of Themistius' superficiality should not be unexpected in someone who had already become enthralled by the Neoplatonist teaching of Maximus of Ephesus, and subsequently of Priscus, like Maximus a pupil of Aedesius, pupil in turn of 'the divine Iamblichus'. Neoplatonist readings of Plato find in his text an elaborate esoteric metaphysics which may exist only in the eye of the beholder. But they did require of readers a more profound response to Plato than was presupposed in the rhetoric of Themistius.[10]

A little later in his *Letter* Julian quotes some passages from the chapters on kingship in Book III of Aristotle's *Politics*, to reinforce the point that the exercise of rule over other humans is something human nature cannot handle, since it gets twisted by desires and passions (260d–261c).[11] In these passages Aristotle talks *inter alia* about the relationship between kingship and the rule of law, or rule in accordance with law. And in his comments on them Julian has often been read as in effect rejecting an absolutist conception of imperial rule, and returning to something more like the constitutionalism associated with Roman republican tradition. It has been further suggested that he is more specifically rejecting Themistius' conception of the king as 'animated law' (*nomos empsuchos*),

[8] Presumably to be identified with 'the principle of immortality in us'.

[9] Themistius invariably substitutes *basileus*, 'king', for Plato's *turannos*, 'tyrant': in *Or.* 3 and 4 (addressed to Constantius), in *Or.* 8.105b–c, 119d (addressed to Valens), and *Or.* 17.215b–c and 34.16 (where the formula is applied to Theodosius). For discussion of the *Laws* passage see Schofield 1999b.

[10] For general introductions to Neoplatonism see Armstrong 1967, Wallis 1972.

[11] This is one of a number of points at which comparisons and contrasts with the thought of Augustine come to mind: on the theme of the domination of what Sallust (*Cat.*2.2) had called *libido dominandi* (lust for power) in Augustine's earthly city (e.g. *Retract.* II.49; *CD* XIV.28), see Rist 1994: 216–25.

or 'a divine law coming from above', and as such 'above the written law'.[12]

Some of the supporting reasons offered for construing Julian in this way are more compelling than others. For example, when in one of his formal panegyrics of Constantius Julian praises the emperor (we have reason to think insincerely) as someone who always behaves towards the people and the magistrates 'like a citizen who obeys the laws, not a king who rules the laws' (*Or.*1.45d), it is hard to judge how far this is an expression of Julian's own political philosophy: the formality of the genre and the brevity of the remark conspire against us. We might compare Libanius' statement in a similar context: 'What is greater than that they [sc. Constantius and Constans], though masters of the law, make the laws their masters?' (*Or.*59.162; cf. Pl. *Laws* IV.715d). This makes it look as though late antique political rhetoric was well capable of negotiating reconciliation between the principle of the rule of law and the principle that the king is above the law, so that statements of the one cannot automatically be taken as excluding recognition of the other. More weight should no doubt be attached to evidence of practice. Thus when Julian himself became emperor, he went out of his way to signal his regard for the institutions of the Republic. In his legislation and his correspondence respect for old Roman laws is emphasized. Ceremonial at court was made simpler and more austere, and the court itself much reduced in numbers. He secured the approval of the Senate for his accession to power, restored the privileges of senators, sat with them in the *curia*, and participated in their debates.[13] Yet none of this proves that Julian did not also accept a theocratic view of kingship.

In fact the *Letter* shows that a rationalist version of the theocratic idea of kingship was precisely what he did espouse. The moral Julian derives explicitly from his reading of Plato's *Laws* is that even if a king is 'in his nature a human, he must be divine and a spirit (*daimōn*) in his character, expelling categorically everything that is mortal and bestial in his soul, except what must remain to safeguard the needs of the body' (259a–b; cf.260c). And his quotations from Aristotle culminate in an extract in which Plato's position in the *Laws* is rearticulated: 'It seems, therefore, that a thinker who proposes that reason should rule is proposing that god

[12] Them. *Or.* 5.64b, 16.212e; cf. 8.118d, 17.228a. These formulae appear to derive ultimately from pseudo-Pythagorean kingship literature: see Centrone, in ch. 27 section 3 above. Discussion in e.g. Dvornik 1955 and 1966, Downey 1957, Dagron 1968, Daly 1980, Brauch 1993.

[13] Legislation: *Cod.Theod.* II.5.2, 12.1, 29.1, III.1.3, IV.12.5. Correspondence: *Frag.Ep.* 288d, *Ep. Theodor.* 453b; cf. also *Or.* 2.88b–89a. Court: Ammianus *Res Gestae* XXII.4, Socrates *Hist. Eccles.* III.1. Senate: Ammianus *Res Gestae* XXII.2.4, 7.3, Socrates *Hist.Eccles.* III.1, *Cod.Theod.* IX.2.1, 23.2. See further Dvornik 1955 and 1966.

and the laws should rule. . . . Law is reason without desire' (261b–c; *Pol.* III.16, 1287a28–32). Julian goes on to work out the consequences of this radical redefinition of law. Not unexpectedly it turns out to require respect not for any and every positive law, but only observation of those enactments, devised by someone purified in intellect and soul, which embody impartiality and the nature of justice, and which will suit posterity, not just the contingencies of the present (262a–d).

In the *Letter* Julian avows his fears that he will be unequal to the demands of the political life. But the theory of kingship he articulates there implies that *only* an ascetic Platonist philosopher such as he himself aspired to become *could* achieve reason without desire and become a true legislator. The inference we must apparently draw (Julian does not spell it out in so many words) is that such a person would no longer properly speaking be a mere man but a divine spirit, with that natural superiority over humans that a 'ruler ought to have over the ruled' (262a). Despite the initial impression he gives of problematizing or even deconstructing the very idea of kingship, Julian's theory has in the end implications no less theocratic than Themistius'. But whereas Themistius draws on some well-worn themes of rhetorical and philosophical tradition in presenting his view, Julian seems to have read more deeply and independently in the texts of Plato and Aristotle in order to work out his ideas on the subject.[14] What is distinctive in his treatment of it is the way he grafts the Platonic conception of law as the dispensation of reason (construed as the divine element within us) on to the notion of kingship – a step not taken by Plato himself in the *Laws*.[15] Julian's assumption that a real king is not human (or not just human) but a divine spirit seems to have remained an element in his thinking, to judge from the autobiographical myth of *Against Heraclius* (from his imperial period), in which he represents himself as an adopted child of Helios and Athena (229c–234c). Perhaps we should not be surprised that he ended his brief reign as emperor a fanatical autocrat.[16]

2 Augustine

The exchange between Themistius and Julian we have been examining is a debate conducted in Greek and within an entirely Greek cultural

[14] How much he owed here to Maximus and Priscus we cannot say. There are no obvious anticipations of his ideas in what little survives of Iamblichus' writings on politics, on which see O'Meara 1993.

[15] Plato implies a clear distinction (seemingly blurred by Julian) between the age of Kronos, when humans were ruled by *daimones* as their kings, and the present age, when law must rule them.

[16] Two adulatory but revealing passages in Libanius testify to his reliance as emperor on advice from his Platonist teachers (*Or.* 12.83) and on divine inspiration (*Or.* 18.172–3).

tradition, between pagan thinkers of the eastern empire whose principal philosophical authorities are Plato and Aristotle. Augustine of Hippo's *City of God*, by contrast, begun nearly sixty years later, is the work of a Christian bishop who writes in Latin and is the product of the Latin rhetorical culture of the western empire.[17] He came to be able to read Greek (with some difficulty), but the biblical and Platonist texts which ate so deeply into his mind and heart were experienced by him in Latin. And in Book XIX of the *City of God*, his most direct and sustained engagement with Classical ethical and political philosophy, the books he uses as his *points d'appui* are Varro's *de Philosophia* and Cicero's *de Re Publica*.

The polymath M. Terentius Varro (116–27 BC) is no longer a name to conjure with, even if those parts of his voluminous writings which survive – notably treatises on grammar and agriculture – are still of the first importance for scholars of antiquity working in these fields.[18] But one of his publications was already spoken of by his contemporary Cicero in terms which suggest a classic (*Acad.* I.9): the massive survey of Roman religion entitled *Antiquitates Rerum Divinarum*, in forty-one books, known to us principally from the *City of God*, where Augustine makes it the target of his critique of pagan theology in Books VI and VII. For Augustine, it is clear, Varro was one of the great authoritative voices of pagan Rome.[19] And this must have been one of the reasons why in Book XIX, when he wanted to relate Christian teaching to the views on the supreme good advanced by Classical philosophy, Augustine turned again to Varro for an analytical survey.

The other main thing Varro's *de Philosophia* supplied (which Cicero's dialogue on the same subject – *de Finibus* – does not) was an exhaustive account of all *possible* positions in ethics, developed by Varro according to his own system of classification from the scheme of Carneades taken over by his teacher Antiochus of Ascalon (cf. Cic. *Fin.* V.15–23). This feature of Varro's book will have suited Augustine's purposes perfectly. His aim in Book XIX is to demonstrate that only the Christian answer to the question of the supreme good is viable. Showing that none of Varro's 288 alternatives works must have seemed as decisive a way of preparing the ground

[17] Biography of Augustine: Brown 1967. Treatments of his political thought: Figgis 1921, Arquillière 1934, Baynes 1962, Markus 1988a, Rist 1994. Latin rhetorical culture: Marrou 1958. Edition of *City of God*: Dombart and Kalb 1955; translation: Bettenson 1984; commentary: Barrow 1950.

[18] On Varro see e.g. Dahlmann 1935, Momigliano 1950a, Rawson 1985, Tarver 1997 (with special reference to *de Philosophia*).

[19] He describes him as 'the most learned of the Romans' (*CD* XIX.22; cf. VI.2). For a survey of Augustine's use of Varro see Hagendahl 1967, vol. II ch. 6. How far the late antique curriculum in general was indebted to Varro is disputed: see Hadot 1984, 156–90.

for the demonstration as could be conceived.[20] It enabled Augustine to move – here as elsewhere in the *City of God* – 'with massive and ostentatious deliberation'[21] from the Classical into his own Christian world.

Varro had himself done much of Augustine's work for him by reducing the 288 options in the end to just three (XIX.2): we seek the primary objects of natural desire (e.g. pleasure or tranquillity) for the sake of virtue; or virtue for the sake of them; or both for their own sake (Varro's own preferred solution: XIX.3). Once Augustine has this set of formulae in his sights he can move into the attack (from XIX.4 on). He rightly takes happiness to be the focus of the Classical conception of the supreme good: as in Aristotle, so in Varro the arguments between the different options are arguments about what does or does not bring a human being happiness. What Augustine undertakes to show in XIX.4–9 is that none of the options Varro identifies succeeds in making us happy – because happiness is not to be found in *this* life at all. The chapters in which Augustine works through this argument make grim reading. It is not difficult to marshall evidence that most human lives for much of the time are miserable; and Augustine's treatment of the ills of society, where he runs through in turn the household, the city, and the relations between nations, is particularly effective.[22] He ends with demonstrations that the friendship of good people and our relationships with the angels, however much joy they bring, are so beset by dangers of loss and deceit that they prove no exception to the general rule.

The anxieties such dangers induce bring the faithful to long for something else: 'that secure condition in which peace is utterly complete and assured' (XIX.10) – an eternal peace, which can be enjoyed only in the life eternal. With the introduction of the notion of peace we reach the pivotal moment in the entire argument of Book XIX. The focus of the argument is the proposition that what satisfies the criterion of supreme good is nothing other than peace, as something such that 'nothing is desired with greater longing, nothing better can be found' (XIX.11). And in the central chapters of the book Augustine devotes considerable time and energy to defending and explicating this proposition. The key elements in the explanation are assembled in XIX.12–13. Augustine's main point is that even war or the anti-social behaviour of the extreme egoist is pursued in

[20] *CD* XIX.1 explains how Varro arrived at the figure of 288.

[21] Brown 1967: 306. But one may be forgiven for wondering just how seriously Augustine took Varro's extraordinary exercise in computation in the *de Philosophia*.

[22] XIX.6 constitutes a powerful critique of the ancient practice of torturing witnesses to extract true testimony from them. Augustine makes some acute comments on the moral binds judges find themselves in as a consequence.

order to achieve peace: peace on the protagonists' own terms – but peace for all that. He buttresses it with supplementary considerations, notably the metaphysical proposition that throughout nature even what is perverted can continue in existence only because its parts are at peace with the system it consists in or belongs to. This leads him to formulate the general thesis that peace in every sphere is what he calls *ordinata concordia*: 'systematic agreement'.

Augustine is now ready to reintroduce the major theme of the whole *City of God*: the distinction between the earthly and the heavenly cities: the earthly city preoccupied with the enjoyment of earthly peace of various sorts, the heavenly city – the community of the redeemed – with eternal peace, 'the only peace deserving the name, at any rate so far as rational creatures are concerned, consisting as it does in a society perfectly ordered and concordant in enjoyment of God and of each other in God' (XIX.17). In XIX.14–16 he discusses the hierarchical principles of order prerequisite for peace in human society, and above all in the household, with particular attention to the institution of slavery (which he explains as a punishment for sin). Then he turns to the heavenly city. The earthly city, aiming at only an earthly peace, 'puts in place concord between citizens in the matter of giving and obeying orders, so as to establish a kind of settlement (*compositio*) between human wills with regard to things relevant to mortal life' (XIX.17). It is a crucial point for Augustine that the need for civic concord is not cancelled or overridden once we adopt the perspective of the heavenly city:

> The heavenly city – or rather that part of it which is on pilgrimage in this condition of mortality, and which lives on the basis of faith – must make use of this peace also [i.e. civic concord], until this mortal state for which this kind of peace is a necessity passes away. Therefore while it leads what we may call a life of captivity in the earthly city, as in a foreign land (although it has already received the promise of redemption, and the gift of the spirit as a sort of pledge of it), it does not hesitate to obey those laws of the earthly city by which those things that are designed to sustain mortal life are regulated. Since mortality itself is common to the two cities, a concord between the two of them can this way be preserved in things that are relevant to the mortal condition. (XIX.17; trans. after H. Bettenson)

There is just one proviso: that such laws do not impede the religion which teaches the worship of the one supreme and true God. The upshot is that the earthly city is neither (as in Eusebius) modelled on a heavenly archetype nor (as with the Manichees) the realm of the forces of evil.

The argument of the passage just quoted provides the essential background for Augustine's decision to resume debate about Cicero's definition of the *res publica* or commonwealth in the concluding chapters of Book XIX, and to call for its replacement by something more plausible.[23] Cicero had proposed that the *res publica* is the *res populi*, the affairs and interests of the people as a whole. And he had offered a supplementary definition of *populus*: 'a large number gathered together, forming a society by virtue of agreement with respect to *ius* [law, i.e. a just social and political order] and of shared advantage' (*Rep.* I.39). This supplement, as Augustine correctly points out (II.21, XIX.21), is what gives the primary definition its cutting edge. Cicero can rule that where there is no *iustitia*, the virtue which must underpin all fair dealing in society, there can be no *ius*; where there is no *ius*, there is no people; where there is no people, no common interest; and where there is no common interest, no real commonwealth. In Book III of *de Re Publica* tyranny, for example, is rejected as an illegitimate form of government precisely because the tyrant is a paradigm of the vice of *in*justice. Under a tyrant a just social and political order is impossible, and the very existence of the community itself is abnegated (III.43).[24]

The anti-Ciceronian tactic Augustine employs in XIX.21 is structurally not unlike his main anti-Varronian manoeuvre. He turns Cicero's definitions against Cicero himself. For Cicero had thought that there *was* once a community which met the criterion of agreement on *ius* and mutual advantage stipulated in the definition of *populus*: Scipio's Rome. The *City of God* is designed to prove him wrong. Already at II.21 Augustine suggested that when Cicero praised Rome in the time of 'the men of old and the old morality' (*Rep.* V.1), he ought to have stopped to consider whether *true* justice flourished then, or only a fancy picture of the real thing. And he promised to demonstrate that in fact there was *no* justice at Rome, and so no community as Cicero conceived of community. The intervening books have supplied the material for the demonstration. Rome's whole history and the ambiguous status of 'virtue' in that history have been examined and found wanting. Rival claims to religious truth have been thoroughly explored – an inquiry also with direct bearing on the question of the virtue of justice, since Augustine will argue that it depends on obedience: obedience to the will of the true God (XIX.21). So now he is in a position to conclude his refutation of Cicero. The basic premiss is theological: Rome worshipped false gods. There was therefore no justice at

[23] He had first introduced discussion of Cicero's definition in II.21, where he promises to return to the issues later.

[24] See Atkins, in ch. 24 section 5.2 above; also Schofield 1995a.

Rome, and therefore – by Cicero's own argument – no *ius* and no community genuinely and consistently agreed on *ius*. Only the heavenly city counts as a Ciceronian *populus*, for only in the heavenly city is there the obedience which underpins justice (XIX.23).

But Augustine does not want the argument to rest at this point. Cicero's conviction that in Scipionic and pre-Scipionic Rome the state of society was healthier than in his own more troubled times had *some* plausibility. And as well as explaining what that plausibility consists in, Augustine needs more importantly to connect his critique of Cicero with his own theory of the two cities, and particularly with the idea that a precondition of the life of the heavenly city in its present captive phase is order in the earthly city, and the 'settlement between human wills' upon which that order is contingent. So he proposes an alternative definition of *populus*: 'A people is a large number of rational beings gathered together, forming a society by virtue of sharing in concord those things that it loves' (XIX.24).

Augustine's definition differs from Cicero's in two critical dimensions. First, by virtue of its moral neutrality his formulation is inclusive, as Cicero's was not. Provided that a city or a nation is united over whatever it is that it desires, it counts as a genuine community or society. What the earthly city loves hardly compares with the eternal peace desired and ultimately enjoyed by the heavenly city – but both loves qualify under his formula.[25] So while that makes the heavenly city a *better* community, the earthly city may nonetheless be a community. To return to the case of Rome in particular, Augustine follows Cicero himself[26] in seeing the pursuit of glory as its great unifying passion (V.13–19). It was better governed in earlier than in later times (II.21) – but Augustine seems reluctant to suggest that the Romans ceased to be a people even when with their civil wars they 'disrupted and corrupted' the concord on which their salvation depended (XIX.24). Second, Cicero's definition makes the identity of a community turn essentially on social behaviour: the consensus he speaks of is as much a matter of agreement in action as in belief. Augustine's is preoccupied with human motivation, and with the way societies are differentiated by the passions and desires which drive the behaviour characteristic of their members – although in the final analysis what dominates Rome and all merely human communities is the same thing:

[25] For more on this topic see Burnaby 1938, O'Donovan 1980, Rist 1994: 148–202.

[26] At V.13 he quotes an otherwise unattested passage from what editors print as *Rep.* V.9. But glory and its place in Roman ideology was the subject of the lost *de Gloria*, and is a major theme of *de Officiis*: see Long 1995 and Atkins, in ch. 24 section 7.2 above.

self-love, as the heavenly city is created by the love of God (XIV.28). Here the Augustine of the *City of God* is palpably the same writer and thinker as the author of the *Confessions*. And if Cicero's approach to political philosophy is roughly speaking Aristotelian, Augustine's fascination with sociopathology recalls Plato's in the *Republic*.

3 Conclusion

This epilogue has been designed to offer a glimpse of the political thinking of two intriguing figures whose lives were lived at the very end of Classical antiquity. The point is not to suggest that they were either isolated or typical in their appetite for more or less sophisticated dialectic with the great classics of Greek and Roman political philosophy.[27] Nor has much attempt been made to indicate the role of their engagement with the ideas of Plato, Aristotle and Cicero (not forgetting Varro) within the cultural context or religious and political history of their times, nor to suggest how they might look from the perspective of the medieval period their writings – not to mention their performances on the public stage – help to usher in.[28] The aim has been a more modest one: to end with a reminder that important intellectual work (in Augustine's case a monumental edifice of massive proportions) would go on being produced after the arbitrary chronological limits imposed by any periodization of history, in modes which retain recognizable continuities with the various Greek and Roman traditions we have been examining, even if they differ from one another as hugely as Julian's does from Augustine's. For some at least of the declining number of authors who were aware of it, whether in the West, the East, or the Arab world, Classical Greek and Roman political theory would remain good to think with or against for some time to come.[29]

[27] See e.g. Dvornik 1966 for a survey of the intellectual terrain from this point of view.

[28] Succinct introductory accounts of the *Sitz im Leben* of late antique political thought are available in *The Cambridge History of Medieval Political Thought*, where a fuller treatment of Augustine (covering other writings than the *City of God*) is also to be found.

[29] For the West see *The Cambridge History of Medieval Political Thought*, for the East Dvornik 1966, and for the Arabic tradition e.g. Rosenthal 1958, Walzer 1985.

Bibliographies

Note: The bibliographies are arranged in three sections: Part I.1: Archaic and Classical Greece – the Beginnings (corresponding to the Introduction and chapters 1–7); Part I.2: Archaic and Classical Greece – Socrates, Plato and Aristotle (corresponding to chapters 8–19); and Part II: The Hellenistic and Roman Worlds (corresponding to chapters 20–31 and the Epilogue). They are intended to give details only of books and articles mentioned in footnotes, mostly according to the author/date convention. In many of the more historically oriented chapters the writers of the *History* have planned their references in such a way that the reader can use them as a select guide to further reading on a topic. Writers of some of the more philosophically focused chapters have preferred to confine their references – besides mention of major editions and accessible general treatments – to items particularly relevant to the argument or interpretation being pursued in the main body of their text.

The bibliographies contain a good deal of information (best first accessed at the appropriate point in the relevant chapter of the *History*) about texts and translations of Greek and Latin authors, particularly the major figures discussed in the volume. Otherwise note the following series:

Bibliotheca Scriptorum Graecorum et Latinorum Teubneriana, B.G. Teubner: Leipzig and Stuttgart (critical editions of Greek and Latin texts) [abbreviation: Teubner]

Scriptorum Classicorum Bibliotheca Oxoniensis [= Oxford Classical Texts], Clarendon Press: Oxford (critical editions of Greek and Latin texts) [abbreviation: OCT]

Collection des Universités de France, publiée sous le patronage de l'Association de Guillaume Budé, Les Belles Lettres: Paris (Greek or Latin text with facing French translation) [abbreviation: Budé]

The Loeb Classical Library, Harvard University Press and W.Heinemann: Cambridge MA and London (Greek or Latin text with facing English translation) [abbreviation: Loeb]

I. Archaic and Classical Greece

1. The beginnings (Introduction and chapters 1–7)

Adkins, A. W. H. (1971) 'Homeric values and Homeric society', *Journal of Hellenic Studies* 91: 1–14.

Alty, J. H. M. (1982) 'Dorians and Ionians', *Journal of Hellenic Studies* 102: 1–14.

Ampolo, C. (1981) *La Politica in Grecia* (Rome and Bari).
Anderson, J. K. (1974) *Xenophon* (London).
Andrewes, A. (1938) 'Eunomia', *Classical Quarterly* 32: 89–102.
Andrewes, A. (1982a) 'The growth of the Athenian state', *Cambridge Ancient History* III.3: 360–91 (Cambridge, 2nd edn).
Andrewes, A. (1982b) 'The tyranny of Pisistratus', *Cambridge Ancient History* III.3: 392–416 (Cambridge, 2nd edn).
Apffel, H. (1957) *Die Verfassungsdebatte bei Herodot (3, 80–82)* (diss. Erlangen, repr. New York 1979).
Arendt, H. (1958) *The Human Condition* (Chicago).
Arnheim, M. T. W. (1977) *Aristocracy in Greek Society* (London).
Assmann, J. (1990) *Ma'at. Gerechtigkeit und Unsterblichkeit im Alten Ägypten* (Munich).
Assmann, J. (1993) 'Politisierung durch Polarisierung. Zur impliziten Axiomatik altägyptischer Politik', in Raaflaub and Müller-Luckner edd. 1993: 13–28.
Athanassakis, A. (1983) *Hesiod, Theogony, Works and Days, Shield: Translation, Introduction, and Notes* (Baltimore).
Avalos, H. (1995) 'Legal and social institutions in Canaan and ancient Israel', in Sasson ed. 1995: 615–32.
Baines, J. (1995) 'Kingship, definition of culture, and legitimation', in O'Connor and Silverman edd.1995: 3–47.
Bakhtin, M. (1968) *Rabelais and his World*, trans. Iswolsky, H. (Cambridge MA).
Baldry, H. C. (1965) *The Unity of Mankind in Greek Thought* (Cambridge).
Ball, T., Farr, J., and Hanson, R. L. edd. (1989) *Political Innovation and Conceptual Change* (Cambridge).
Barish, J. (1981) *The Antitheatrical Prejudice* (Berkeley).
Barker, E. (1918) *Greek Political Theory: Plato and His Predecessors* (London; repr. 1960).
Barnes, J. (1979) *The Presocratic Philosophers*, vol. I (London).
Baruch, E., and Serrano, L. edd. (1988) *Women Analyze Women* (New York).
Beard, M. (1994) 'Religion', *Cambridge Ancient History* IX:729–68 (Cambridge, 2nd edn).
Beauvoir, S. de (1972) *The Second Sex*, trans. Parshley, H. (Harmondsworth).
Beitz, C. (1991) *Political Equality: an Essay in Democratic Theory* (Princeton).
Berent, M. (1994) 'The Stateless Polis. Towards a Re-evaluation of the Classical Greek Political Community' (unpublished Cambridge Ph.D. dissertation).
Berger, S. (1992) *Revolution and Society in Greek Sicily and Southern Italy* (Stuttgart).
Berlin, A. ed. (1996) *Religion and Politics in the Ancient Near East* (Potomac MD).
Bernal, M. (1987) *Black Athena: The Afro-Asiatic Roots of Classical Civilization*, vol. I: *The Fabrication of Ancient Greece 1785–1985* (London and New Brunswick NJ).
Bernal, M. (1991) *Black Athena: The Afro-Asiatic Roots of Classical Civilization*, vol. II: *The Archaeological and Documentary Evidence* (London and New Brunswick NJ).
Bernal, M. (1993) 'Phoenician politics and Egyptian justice in ancient Greece', in Raaflaub and Müller-Luckner edd. 1993: 241–61.
Bers, V. (1985) 'Dikastic thorubos', in Cartledge, P., and Harvey, F.D., edd. *Crux: Essays in Greek History Presented to G.E.M. de Ste. Croix on his 75th birthday* (Exeter and London), 1–15.
Berve, H. (1967) *Die Tyrannis bei den Griechen*, 2 vols. (Munich).

Bichler, R. (1996) 'Wahrnehmung und Vorstellung fremder Kultur. Griechen und Orient in archaischer und frühklassischer Zeit', in Schuster, M., ed. *Die Begegnung mit dem Fremden. Wertungen und Wirkungen in Hochkulturen vom Altertum bis zur Gegenwart* (Stuttgart), 51–74.

Bleicken, J. (1979) 'Zur Entstehung der Verfassungstypologie im 5. Jahrhundert v.Chr. (Monarchie, Aristokratie, Demokratie)', *Historia* 28: 148–72.

Bleicken, J. (1987) 'Die Einheit der athenischen Demokratie in klassischen Zeit', *Hermes* 115: 257–83.

Bleicken, J. ed. (1993) *Colloquium aus Anlass des 80. Geburtstages von Alfred Heuss*. Frankfurter Althistorische Studien 13 (Kallmünz Opf.).

Blythe, J. (1992) *Ideal Government and Mixed Constitution in the Middle Ages* (Princeton).

Boardman, J. *et al.* edd. (1988) *The Cambridge Ancient History* IV: *Persia, Greece and the Western Mediterranean c. 525 to 479 BC.* (Cambridge, 2nd edn).

Boedeker, D. ed. (1987), *Herodotus and the Invention of History* (Buffalo).

Bonner, R. J., and Smith, G. (1930) *The Administration of Justice from Homer to Aristotle*, vol. I (Chicago).

Bordes, J. (1982) *Politeia dans la pensée grecque jusqu'à Aristote* (Paris).

Bosworth, A. B. (1993) 'The humanitarian aspect of the Melian Dialogue', *Journal of Hellenic Studies* 113: 30–44.

Bottéro, J. (1992) *Mesopotamia: Writing, Reasoning, and the Gods*, trans. Bahrani, Z., and van de Mieroop, M. (Chicago).

Bowen, A. J. (1992) *Plutarch: The Malice of Herodotus* (Warminster).

Bowie, A. (1993) 'Religion and politics in Aeschylus' *Oresteia*', *Classical Quarterly* 43: 10–31.

Bowie, E. L. (1986) 'Early Greek elegy, symposium and public festival', *Journal of Hellenic Studies* 106: 1–21.

Bowie, E. L. (1990) 'Miles ludens? The problem of martial exhortation in early Greek elegy', in Murray ed. 1990: 221–9.

Bowra, C. M. (1938) *Early Greek Elegists* (Cambridge MA; repr. Cambridge 1960).

Bowra, C. M. (1964) *Pindar* (Oxford).

Bremmer, J. N. (1994) *Greek Religion*. Greece and Rome New Surveys in the Classics 24 (Oxford).

Briant, P. (1995) 'Social and legal institutions in Achaemenid Iran', in Sasson ed. 1995: 517–28.

Briant, P. (1996) *Histoire de l'Empire Perse de Cyrus à Alexandre* (Paris).

Brock, R. (1991) 'The emergence of democratic ideology', *Historia* 40: 160–9.

Brown, N. O. (1953) *Hesiod: Theogony* (Indianapolis).

Bruit, L. (1992) 'Pandora's daughters and rituals in Grecian cities', in Schmitt Pantel, P., ed. *A History of Women in the West* I. *From Ancient Goddesses to Christian Saints* (Cambridge MA), 338–76.

Bruit Zaidman, L., and Schmitt Pantel, P. (1992) *Religion in the Ancient Greek City*, ed. and trans. Cartledge, P. A. (Cambridge).

Brunt, P. A. (1993) *Studies in Greek History and Thought* (Oxford).

Burkert, W. (1962) *Weisheit und Wissenschaft: Studien zu Pythagoras, Philolaos and Platon* (Nuremberg).

Burkert, W. (1985) *Greek Religion Archaic and Classical*, trans. Raffan, J. (Oxford).

Burkert, W. (1991) 'Homerstudien und Orient', in Latacz ed. 1991: 155–81.

Burkert, W. (1992) *The Orientalizing Revolution: Near Eastern Influence on Greek Culture in the Early Archaic Age* (Cambridge MA).

Burnett, A. P. (1983) *Three Archaic Poets: Archilochus, Alcaeus, Sappho* (Cambridge MA).

Burns, A. (1976) 'Hippodamus and the planned city', *Historia* 25: 414–28.

Burnyeat, M. (1990) *The Theaetetus of Plato* (Indianapolis).

Burstein, S. (1996a) 'The debate about *Black Athena*', *Scholia* 5: 3–16.

Burstein, S. (1996b) 'Greek contact with Egypt and the Levant: *c.* 1600–500 BC', *Ancient World* 27: 20–8.

Butler, E. (1935) *The Tyranny of Greece over Germany* (Cambridge).

Cairns, D. L. (1993) *AIDOS: The Psychology and Ethics of Honour and Shame in Ancient Greek Literature* (Oxford).

Cairns, D. L. (1996) 'Hybris, dishonour, and thinking big', *Journal of Hellenic Studies* 116: 1–32.

Calhoun, G. M. (1913) *Athenian Clubs in Politics and Litigation* (Austin TX).

Camassa, G. (1988) 'Aux origines de la codification écrite des lois en Grèce', in Detienne ed. 1988: 130–55.

Camassa, G. (1996) 'Legge orali e legge scritte. I legislatori', in Settis ed. 1996: 561–76.

Carter, L. B. (1986) *The Quiet Athenian* (Oxford).

Cartledge, P. A. (1977) 'Hoplites and heroes. Sparta's contribution to the technique of ancient warfare' *Journal of Hellenic Studies* 97: 11–27, repr. with addenda in Christ ed. 1986: 387–425, 470.

Cartledge, P. A. (1979) *Sparta and Lakonia: A Regional History 1300–362 BC* (London).

Cartledge, P. A. (1980) 'The peculiar position of Sparta in the development of the Greek city-state', *Proceedings of the Royal Irish Academy* 80: 91–108.

Cartledge, P.A. (1990) 'Fowl play: a curious lawsuit in classical Athens (Antiphon XVI, frr. 57–9 Thalheim)', in Cartledge, Millett and Todd edd. 1990: 41–61.

Cartledge, P. A. (1993a) *The Greeks. A Portrait of Self and Others* (Oxford). Rev. edn 1997.

Cartledge, P. A. (1993b) '"Like a worm i' the bud"? A heterology of Greek slavery', *Greece and Rome* 40: 163–80.

Cartledge, P. A. (1996a) 'Comparatively equal', in Ober and Hedrick edd. 1996: 175–85.

Cartledge, P. A. (1996b) 'La politica', in Settis ed. 1996: 39–72.

Cartledge, P. A. (1996c) 'La nascita degli opliti e l'organizzazione militare', in Settis ed. 1996: 681–714.

Cartledge, P. A. (1998) 'Writing the history of Archaic Greek political thought', in Fisher and van Wees edd. 1998: 379–99.

Cartledge, P. A. (forthcoming) *Political Thought in Ancient Greece: Elite and Mass from Homer to Plutarch* (Cambridge).

Cartledge, P. A., Millett, P. C., and Todd, S. edd. (1990) *NOMOS. Essays in Athenian Law, Politics and Society* (Cambridge).

Cartledge, P. A., Millett, P. C., and von Reden, S. edd. (1998) *KOSMOS. Essays in Order, Conflict and Community in Classical Athens* (Cambridge).

Cerri, G. (1975) *Il linguaggio politico nel Prometeo di Eschilo* (Rome).

Chadwick, J. (1976) *The Mycenaean World* (Cambridge).

Chambers, M. (1990) *Aristoteles, Staat der Athener*, übersetzt und erläutert (Berlin).

Chanter, T. (1995) *Ethics of Eros: Irigaray's Rewriting of the Philosophers* (London).
Chrimes, K. (1948) *The Respublica Lacedaemoniorum ascribed to Xenophon: its manuscript tradition and general significance* (Manchester).
Christ, K. ed. (1986) *Sparta*. Wege der Forschung 622 (Darmstadt).
Clarke, G. W. ed. (1989) *Rediscovering Hellenism* (Cambridge).
Classen, C. J. ed. (1976) *Sophistik*. Wege der Forschung 187 (Darmstadt).
Cloché, P. (1963) *Isocrate et son temps* (Paris).
Cohen, D. (1991) *Law, Sexuality, and Society: The Enforcement of Morals in Classical Athens* (Cambridge).
Cohen, D. (1995) *Law, Violence and Community in Classical Athens* (Cambridge).
Coldstream J. N. (1977) *Geometric Greece* (New York).
Cole, T. (1967) *Democritus and the Sources of Greek Anthropology* (Cleveland OH).
Cole, T. (1991) *The Origins of Rhetoric in Ancient Greece* (Baltimore).
Connor, W. R. (1971) *The New Politicians of Fifth-Century Athens* (Princeton).
Connor, W. R. (1984) *Thucydides* (Princeton).
Constant, B. (1819) 'De la Liberté des Anciens comparée à celle des Modernes', trans. in Fontana, B., ed. *Constant. Political Writings* (Cambridge 1988), 307–28.
Cornford, F. M. (1907) *Thucydides Mythistoricus* (London).
Corpus dei Papiri Filosofici Greci e Latini, Part I: Autori Noti, vol. I (Florence 1989).
Crick, B. (1992) *In Defence of Politics* (London, 4th edn).
Croally, N. (1995) *Euripidean Polemic* (Cambridge).
Csapo, E., and Slater, W. (1995) *The Context of Ancient Drama* (Ann Arbor MI).
Dandamayev, M. A. (1981) 'The neo-Babylonian citizens', *Klio* 63: 45–9.
Daube, D. (1972) *Civic Disobedience in Antiquity* (Edinburgh).
Davies, J. K. (1997) 'The "origins of the Greek polis": where should we be looking?', in Mitchell and Rhodes edd. 1997: 24–38.
Davies, M. (1989) 'Sisyphus and the invention of religion ('Critias' *TrGF* 1 (43) F 19 = B 25 DK)', *Bulletin of the Institute of Classical Studies* 36: 16–32.
Davis, R.W. ed. (1995), *The Origins of Freedom in the West* (Stanford and Cambridge).
Deger-Jalkotzy, S. (1991) 'Die Erforschung des Zusammenbruchs der sogenannten mykenischen Kultur und der sogenannten dunklen Jahrhunderte', in Latacz ed. 1991: 127–54.
Desborough, V. R. d'A. (1975) 'The end of the Mycenaean civilization and the Dark Age', *Cambridge Ancient History* III.1: 658–77 (Cambridge, 2nd edn).
Detienne, M. (1981) *L'Invention de la mythologie* (Paris) [= *The Creation of Mythology*, trans. Cook, M. (Chicago 1986)].
Detienne, M. ed. (1988) *Les Savoirs de l'écriture en Grèce ancienne* (Lille).
Dickinson, O. (1994) *The Aegean Bronze Age* (Cambridge).
Dicks, D. R. (1970) *Early Greek Astronomy to Aristotle* (London).
Diels, H., and Kranz, W. (1951–2) *Die Fragmente der Vorsokratiker* (Berlin, 6th edn).
Dietz, M. (1985) 'Citizenship with a feminine face: the problem with maternal thinking', *Political Theory* 13: 19–37.
Dihle, A. (1994) *Die Griechen und die Fremden* (Munich).
Diller, H. (1962) 'Die Hellenen-Barbaren-Antithese im Zeitalter der Perserkriege', in Reverdin ed. 1962: 37–68.
Dillery, J. (1995) *Xenophon and the History of his Times* (London).

Dimakis, P. ed. (1983) *Symposion 1979: Beiträge zur griechischen und hellenistischen Rechtsgeschichte* (Cologne).

Dodds, E. R. (1960) 'Morals and politics in the *Oresteia*', *Proceedings of the Cambridge Philological Society* 6: 19–31.

Dodds, E. R. (1973) 'The ancient concept of progress', in Dodds, *The Ancient Concept of Progress, and other Essays on Greek Literature and Belief* (Oxford), 1–25.

Donini, G. (1969) *La Posizione di Tucidide verso il Governo dei Cinquemila* (Turin).

Donlan, W. (1973) 'The tradition of anti-aristocratic thought in early Greece', *Historia* 22: 145–54.

Donlan, W. (1980) *The Aristocratic Ideal in Ancient Greece* (Lawrence KA).

Donlan, W. (1981–2) 'Reciprocities in Homer', *Classical World* 75: 137–75.

Donlan, W. (1985) 'The social groups of Dark Age Greece', *Classical Philology* 80: 293–308.

Donlan, W. (1989) 'The pre-state community in Greece', *Symbolae Osloenses* 64: 5–29.

Dougherty, C., and Kurke, L. edd. (1993) *Cultural Poetics in Archaic Greece* (Cambridge).

Dover, K. J. (1957) 'The political aspect of Aeschylus' *Eumenides*', *Journal of Hellenic Studies* 77: 230–7.

Dover, K. J. (1968) *Aristophanes: Clouds* (Oxford).

Dover, K. J. (1972) *Aristophanic Comedy* (Berkeley and Los Angeles).

Dover, K. J. (1973) *Thucydides*. Greece and Rome New Surveys in the Classics 7 (Oxford).

Dover, K. J. (1978) *Greek Homosexuality* (London).

Dover, K.J. (1988) 'The freedom of the intellectual in Greek society', in Dover, *The Greeks and their Legacy* [= *Collected Papers*, vol. II: *Prose Literature, History, Society, Transmission, Influence*] (Oxford), 135–58.

Drake, B. (1853) *Aeschyli, Eumenides, the Greek Text with English Notes etc.* (Cambridge).

Drews, R. (1979) 'Phoenicians, Carthage and the Spartan Eunomia', *American Journal of Philology* 100: 45–58.

Drews, R. (1993) *The End of the Bronze Age: Changes in Warfare and the Catastrophe c. 1200 BC* (Princeton).

DuBois, P. (1984) *Amazons and Centaurs: Women and the Prehistory of the Great Chain of Being* (Ann Arbor MI).

Duchemin, J. (1995) *Mythes grecs et sources orientales* (Paris).

Due, B. (1989) *The Cyropaedia* (Aarhus).

Dunbabin, T. J. (1957) *The Greeks and their Eastern Neighbours: Studies in the Relations between Greece and the Countries of the Near East in the Eighth and Seventh Centuries BC* (London).

Dunn, J. (1993) *Western Political Theory in the Face of the Future* (Cambridge, 2nd edn).

Dunn, J. (1996) *The History of Political Thought* (Cambridge).

Dunn, J. ed. (1992) *Democracy. The Unfinished Journey 508 BC to AD 1993* (Oxford).

Easterling, P. E., and Muir, J. V. edd. (1985) *Greek Religion and Society* (Cambridge).

Eder, W. (1986) 'The political significance of the codification of law in Archaic societies', in Raaflaub ed. 1986: 262–300.

Eder, W. (1991) 'Who rules? Power and participation in Athens and Rome', in Molho, Raaflaub and Emlen edd. 1991: 169–98.

Eder, W. (1992) 'Polis und Politai. Die Auflösung des Adelsstaates und die Entwicklung des Polisbürgers', in Wehgartner ed. 1992: 24–38.

Eder, W., and Hölkeskamp, K.-J. edd. (1997) *Volk und Verfassung in vorhellenistischen Griechenland* (Stuttgart).

Edwards, M. W. (1991) *The Iliad: A Commentary*, vol. v: *Books 17–20* (Cambridge).

Effenterre, H. van, and Ruzé, F. (1994) *Nomima: Recueil d'inscriptions politiques et juridiques de l'archaïsme grec*. Coll. Ec. Fr. de Rome 188 (Rome).

Ehrenberg, V. (1937) 'When did the polis rise?', *Journal of Hellenic Studies* 57: 147–59, repr. in Ehrenberg 1965: 83–97.

Ehrenberg, V. (1943) 'An early source of polis-constitution', *Classical Quarterly* 37: 14–18, repr. in Ehrenberg 1965: 98–104.

Ehrenberg, V. (1965) *Polis und Imperium: Beiträge zur Alten Geschichte* (Zurich).

Ehrenberg, V. (1969) *The Greek State* (London, 2nd edn).

Else, G. (1986) *Plato and Aristotle on Poetry* (Chapel Hill and London).

Elshtain, J. (1982) 'Antigone's daughters', *Democracy* 2: 46–59.

Emlyn-Jones, C. J. (1980) 'Myth and reason: the Ionian origin of Greek philosophy', in Emlyn-Jones, *The Ionians and Hellenism: A Study of the Cultural Achievement of the Early Greek Inhabitants of Asia Minor* (London), 97–132.

Erler, M. (1987) 'Das Recht (*Dike*) als Segensbringerin für die Polis', *Studi Italiani di Filologia Classica* 3rd ser. 5: 5–36.

Euben, J. P. (1986) 'The battle of Salamis and the origins of political theory', *Political Theory* 14: 359–90.

Euben, J. P. (1990) *The Tragedy of Political Theory* (Princeton).

Euben, J. P. ed. (1986) *Greek Tragedy and Political Theory* (Berkeley).

Euben, J. P., Wallach, J. R., and Ober, J. edd. (1994) *Athenian Political Thought and the Reconstruction of American Democracy* (Princeton).

Eucken, C. (1983) *Isokrates. Seine Positionen in der Auseinandersetzung mit den zeitgenössischen Philosophen* (Berlin).

Fadinger, V. (1996) 'Solons Eunomia-Lehre und die Gerechtigkeitsidee der altorientalischen Schöpfungsherrschaft', in Gehrke and Möller edd. 1996: 179–218.

Fagles, R. (1990) *Homer, The Iliad, Translated* (New York).

Farrar, C. (1988) *The Origins of Democratic Thinking: The Invention of Politics in Classical Athens* (Cambridge).

Fehling, D. (1985) *Die sieben Weisen und die frühgriechische Chronologie: eine traditionsgeschichtliche Studie* (Bern).

Fehling, D. (1989) *Herodotus and his 'Sources': Citation, Invention and Narrative Art* (Leeds).

Ferrari, G. R. F. (1989) 'Plato and poetry', in Kennedy, G. ed. *The Cambridge History of Literary Criticism*, vol. I (Cambridge), 92–148.

Fetscher, I., and Münkler, H. edd. (1988) *Pipers Handbuch der Politischen Ideen*, vol. I: *Frühe Hochkulturen und europäische Antike* (Munich).

Figueira, T. J., and Nagy, G. edd. (1985) *Theognis and Megara: Poetry and the Polis* (Baltimore).

Finley, J. (1942) *Thucydides* (Harvard).

Finley, M. I. (1975a) *The Use and Abuse of History* (London).

Finley, M. I. (1975b) 'Myth, memory and history', in Finley 1975a: 11–33.

Finley, M. I. (1975c) 'Sparta', in Finley 1975a: 161–77.
Finley, M. I. (1977) *The World of Odysseus* (Harmondsworth, 2nd edn).
Finley, M. I. (1982a) *Economy and Society in Ancient Greece* (New York).
Finley, M. I. (1982b) *Authority and Legitimacy in the Classical City-State* (Copenhagen).
Finley, M. I. (1983) *Politics in the Ancient World* (Cambridge).
Finley, M. I. (1985) *Democracy Ancient and Modern* (London, 2nd edn).
Finley, M. I. (1986) *The Use and Abuse of History* (London, 2nd edn).
Fisher, N. (1990) 'The law of hubris in Athens', in Cartledge, Millett and Todd edd. (1990): 123–38.
Fisher, N. (1992) *HYBRIS. A Study in the Values of Honour and Shame in Ancient Greece* (Warminster).
Fisher, N., and van Wees, H. edd. (1998) *Archaic Greece: New Approaches and New Evidence* (Cardiff and London).
Foley, H. (1996) 'Antigone as moral agent', in Silk, M. S. ed. *Tragedy and the Tragic* (Oxford).
Fornara, C. W. (1971) *Herodotus: An Interpretative Essay* (Oxford).
Fornara, C. W. (1983a) *The Nature of History in Ancient Greece and Rome* (Berkeley).
Fornara, C. W. (1983b) *Archaic Times to the End of the Peloponnesian War*. Translated Documents of Greece and Rome, vol. 1 (Cambridge, 2nd edn).
Forrest, W. G. (1957) 'Colonisation and the rise of Delphi', *Historia* 6: 160–75.
Foster, B. R. (1995) 'Social reform in ancient Mesopotamia', in Irani and Silver edd. 1995: 165–78.
Fränkel, H. (1973) *Early Greek Poetry and Philosophy*, trans. Hadas, M., and Willis, J. (New York).
Frankfort, H., Frankfort, H. A., Wilson, J. A., Jacobsen, T., and Irwin, W. A. (1946) *The Intellectual Adventure of Ancient Man: An Essay on Speculative Thought in the Ancient Near East* (Chicago).
Freeman, K. (1948) *Ancilla to the Pre-Socratic Philosophers* (Cambridge MA).
Fritz, K. von (1940) *Pythagorean Politics in Southern Italy: An Analysis of the Sources* (New York).
Fritz, K. von (1954) *The Theory of the Mixed Constitution in Antiquity. A critical analysis of Polybius' Political Ideas* (New York).
Fritz, K. von (1967) *Die griechische Geschichtsschreibung, Band I: Von den Anfängen bis Thukydides*, 2 vols. (Berlin).
Fuks, A. (1984) *Social Conflict in Ancient Greece* (Jerusalem and Leiden).
Funke, P. R. (1993) 'Stamm und Polis: Überlegungen zur Entstehung der griechischen Staatenwelt in den "Dunkeln Jahrhunderten"', in Bleicken ed. 1993: 29–48.
Fustel de Coulanges, N. D. (1864) *La Cité antique* (Paris).
Gagarin, M. (1974) 'Hesiod's dispute with Perses', *Transactions of the American Philological Association* 104: 103–11.
Gagarin, M. (1981) *Drakon and Early Athenian Homicide Law* (New Haven).
Gagarin, M. (1986) *Early Greek Law* (Berkeley).
Gagarin, M. ed. (1991) *Symposion 1990: Papers on Greek and Hellenistic Legal History* (Cologne).
Gagarin, M., and Woodruff, P. edd. (1995) *Early Greek Political Thought from Homer to the Sophists* (Cambridge).
Garlan, Y. (1988) *Slavery in Ancient Greece* (Ithaca NY).

Garland, R. (1992) *Introducing New Gods: the Politics of Athenian Religion* (London).

Gärtner, H. (1975) 'Die Sieben Weisen', in *Der kleine Pauly*, vol. v: 177–8 (Munich).

Gawantka, W. (1985) *Die sogenannte Polis* (Stuttgart).

Gehrke, H.-J. (1985) *Stasis: Untersuchungen zu den inneren Kriegen in den griechischen Staaten des 5. und 4. Jahrhunderts v.Chr.* Vestigia 35 (Munich).

Gehrke, H.-J. (1993) 'Gesetz und Konflikt. Überlegungen zur frühen Polis', in Bleicken ed. 1993: 49–67.

Gehrke, H.-J., and Möller, A. edd. (1996) *Vergangenheit und Lebenswelt: Soziale Kommunikation, Traditionsbildung und historisches Bewusstsein* (Tübingen).

Gentili, B., and Prato, C. (1988) *Poetarum elegiacorum testimonia et fragmenta*, vol. I (Leipzig).

Georges, P. (1994) *Barbarian Asia and the Greek Experience* (Baltimore).

Gera, D. (1993) *Xenophon's Cyropaedia. Style, Genre and Literary Technique* (Oxford).

Gigante, M. (1993) *NOMOS BASILEUS*. Con un' appendice (Naples).

Gill, C. (1995) *Greek Thought*. Greece and Rome New Surveys in the Classics, 25 (Oxford).

Godelier, M. (1986) *The Mental and the Material. Thought Economy and Society* (London).

Goff, B. (1990) *The Noose of Words* (Cambridge).

Goldhill, S. (1986) *Reading Greek Tragedy* (Cambridge).

Goldhill, S. (1990a) 'The Great Dionysia and civic ideology', in Winkler, J., and Zeitlin, F. edd. *Nothing to Do with Dionysus?* (Princeton).

Goldhill, S. (1990b) 'Character and action, representation and reading: Greek tragedy and its critics', in Pelling, C. ed. *Characterization and Individuality in Greek Literature* (Oxford).

Goldhill, S. (1991) *The Poet's Voice* (Cambridge).

Goldhill, S. (1995) 'Representing democracy: women and the Great Dionysia', in Osborne, R., and Hornblower, S. edd. *Ritual, Finance, Politics: Essays Presented to David Lewis* (Oxford).

Goldhill, S. (1995b) *Foucault's Virginity* (Cambridge).

Goldhill, S. (1997) 'The audience of Greek tragedy', in Easterling, P. ed. *The Cambridge Companion to Greek Tragedy* (Cambridge).

Gomme, A. W. (1937) 'The speeches in Thucydides', in Gomme, *Essays in Greek History and Literature* (Oxford), 156–89.

Gomme, A. W., Andrewes, A., and Dover, K. J. (1945–81) *A Historical Commentary on Thucydides*, 5 vols. (Oxford).

Goodin, R. E., and Pettit, P. edd. (1993) *A Companion to Contemporary Political Philosophy* (Oxford).

Görgemanns, H., and Schmidt, E. A. edd. (1976) *Studien zum antiken Epos*. Beiträge zur klassischen Philologie 72 (Meisenheim am Glan).

Gosling, J. C. B., and Taylor, C. C. W. (1982) *The Greeks on Pleasure* (Oxford).

Gould, J. (1989) *Herodotus* (London).

Gould, J. (1991) *Give and Take in Herodotus*. The Fifteenth J. L. Myres Memorial Lecture (Oxford).

Gould, T. (1990) *The Ancient Quarrel Between Poetry and Philosophy* (Princeton).

Gouldner, A. W. (1965) *Enter Plato. Classical Greece and the Origins of Social Theory* (London).

Gray, V. J. (1986) 'Xenophon's Hiero and the meeting between the wise man and tyrant in Greek literature', *Classical Quarterly* 36: 115–23.

Gray, V. J. (1989) *The Character of Xenophon's Hellenica* (London).

Gray, V. J. (1993) 'The image of Sparta: writer and audience in Isocrates' *Panathenaicus*', in Powell, A., and Hodkinson, S. edd. *The Shadow of Sparta* (London), 223–71.

Gray, V. J. (1994) 'Isocrates' manipulation of myth and the image of Athens, *Panegyricus* 54ff. *Panathenaicus* 168ff.', in Gray ed. *Nile, Ilissos and Tiber. Essays in honour of W.K. Lacey* (Auckland), 83–104.

Greengus, S. (1995) 'Legal and social institutions of ancient Mesopotamia', in Sasson ed. 1995: 469–84.

Greenhalgh, P. A. L. (1972) 'Aristocracy and its advocates in Archaic Greece', *Greece and Rome* 19: 190–207.

Grene, D. (1950) *Man in his Pride: A Study in the Political Philosophy of Thucydides and Plato* (Chicago) [= *Greek Political Theory: The Image of Man in Thucydides and Plato* (Chicago, 1965)].

Griffin, M. T. (1996). 'When is thought political?' (critical notice of Laks, A., and Schofield, M. edd. *Justice and Generosity* [Cambridge 1995]), *Apeiron* 29: 269–82.

Griffith, M. (1995) 'Brilliant Dynasts: power and politics in the *Oresteia*', *Classical Antiquity* 14: 62–129.

Grote, G. (1888) *A History of Greece*, vol. VII (London).

Gschnitzer, F. (1976) 'Politische Leidenschaft im homerischen Epos', in Görgemanns and Schmidt edd. 1976: 1–21.

Gschnitzer, F. (1988) 'Die Stellung der Polis in der politischen Entwicklung des Altertums', *Oriens Antiquus* 27: 287–302.

Gschnitzer, F. (1991) 'Zur homerischen Staats- und Gesellschaftsordnung: Grundcharakter und geschichtliche Stellung', in Latacz ed. 1991: 182–204.

Guthrie, W. K. C. (1957) *In the Beginning: Some Greek Views on the Origins of Life and the Early State of Man* (London).

Guthrie, W. K. C. (1962) *A History of Greek Philosophy*, vol. I: *The Earlier Presocratics and the Pythagoreans* (Cambridge).

Guthrie, W. K. C. (1969) *A History of Greek Philosophy*, vol. III: *The Fifth-Century Enlightenment* (Cambridge) [Part I of vol. III = *The Sophists* (Cambridge 1971)].

Haider, P. W. (1988) *Griechenland-Nordafrika: Ihre Beziehungen zwischen 1500 und 600 v. Chr.* (Darmstadt).

Haider, P. W. (1996) 'Griechen im Vorderen Orient und in Ägypten bis ca.590 v.Chr.', in Ulf ed. 1996: 59–115.

Hall, E. (1989) *Inventing the Barbarian: Greek Self-Definition through Tragedy* (Oxford).

Hall, J. ed. (1986) *States in History* (Oxford).

Halliwell, S. (1986) *Aristotle's Poetics* (London).

Halliwell, S. (1991) 'The uses of laughter in Greek culture', *Classical Quarterly* 41 279–96.

Halpern, B., and Hobson, D. W. edd. (1993) *Law, Politics and Society in the Ancient Mediterranean World* (Sheffield).

Hammer, D. (1998) 'The politics of the *Iliad*', *Classical Journal* 94: 1–30

Hammer, D. (forthcoming) *The Epics as Political Thought: Politics in Performance* (Norman, Oklahoma).

Hansen, M. H. (1983) *Initiative und Entscheidung. Überlegungen über die Gewaltenteilung im Athen des 4.Jhs* (Konstanz).

Hansen, M. H. (1987) *The Athenian Assembly in the Age of Demosthenes* (Oxford).

Hansen, M. H. (1989) *Was Athens a Democracy? Popular Rule, Liberty and Equality in Ancient and Modern Political Thought* (Copenhagen).

Hansen, M. H. (1991) *The Athenian Democracy in the Age of Demosthenes: Structure, Principles and Ideology* (Oxford).

Hansen, M. H. (1993a) 'The *polis* as a citizen-state', in Hansen ed. 1993: 7–29.

Hansen, M. H. (1998) *Polis and City-State: An Ancient Concept and Its Modern Equivalent* (Copenhagen).

Hansen, M. H. ed. (1993b) *The Ancient Greek City-State* (Copenhagen).

Hanson, V. D. (1995) *The Other Greeks. The Family Farm and the Agrarian Roots of Western Civilization* (New York).

Harrison, A. R. W. (1968) *The Law of Athens*, vol. I: The Family and Property (Oxford).

Hartog, F. (1991) *Le Miroir d'Hérodote: essai sur la représentation de l'autre* (Paris, 2nd edn) [= *The Mirror of Herodotus: The Representation of the other in the Writing of History*, trans. Lloyd, J. (Berkeley 1988)].

Harvey, F. D. (1965) 'Two kinds of equality', *Classica et Medievalia* 26: 101–46.

Harvey, F. D. (1985) 'Dona ferentes: some aspects of bribery in Greek politics', in Cartledge, P. A., and Harvey, F. D. edd., *Crux: Essays in Greek History presented to G. E. M. de Ste.Croix on his 75th birthday* (Exeter and London), 76–117.

Harvey, F. D. (1990) 'The sykophant and sykophancy: vexatious redefinition?', in Cartledge, Millett and Todd edd.1990: 103–21.

Havelock, E. A. (1957) *The Liberal Temper in Greek Politics* (London).

Havelock, E. A. (1972) 'War as a way of life in Classical culture', in Gareau, E. ed. *Classical Values and the Modern World* (Toronto), 19–78 .

Havelock, E. A. (1978) *The Greek Concept of Justice: From its Shadow in Homer to its Substance in Plato* (Cambridge MA).

Headlam, J. W. (1933) *Election by Lot at Athens* (Cambridge, 2nd edn).

Heath, M. (1985) 'Hesiod's didactic poetry', *Classical Quarterly* 35: 245–63.

Heath, M. (1987) *Aristophanes' Political Comedy* (Göttingen).

Hegel, G. W. F. (1948) 'On classical studies', in Knox, T., and Kroner, R. edd. *Early Theological Writings* (Chicago).

Heinimann, F. (1945) *Nomos und Physis: Herkunft und Bedeutung einer Antithese im griechischen Denken des 5. Jahrhunderts* (Basle).

Heinimann, F. (1961) 'Eine vorplatonische Theorie der *technē*', *Museum Helveticum* 18: 105–30.

Henrichs, A. (1984) 'The sophists and Hellenistic religion: Prodicus as the spiritual father of the Isis aretalogies', *Harvard Studies in Classical Philology* 88: 139–58.

Helck, W. (1979) *Die Beziehungen Ägyptens und Vorderasiens zur Ägäis bis ins 7. Jahrhundert v. Chr.* (Darmstadt).

Held, D. ed. (1991) *Political Theory Today* (Oxford).

Heller, A. (1991) ' The concept of the political revisited', in Held ed. 1991: 330–43.

Henderson, J. (1980) '*Lysistrate*: the play and its themes', *Yale Classical Studies* 26: 153–218.

Herington, J. (1985) *Poetry into Drama: Early Tragedy and the Greek Poetic Tradition* (Berkeley).

Herman, G. (1987) *Ritualised Friendship and the Greek City* (Cambridge).

Herman, G. (1993) 'Tribal and civic codes of behaviour in Lysias 1', *Classical Quarterly* 43:406–19.

Herodotus, *The History*, trans. Grene, D. (Chicago 1987).

Herter, H. ed. (1968) *Thukydides*. Wege der Forschung 98 (Darmstadt).

Higgins, W.E. (1977) *Xenophon the Athenian. The Problem of the Individual and the Society of the Polis* (New York).

Hirsch, S. (1985) *The Friendship of the Barbarians. Xenophon and the Persian Empire* (Hanover and London).

Hirschkop, K., and Shepherd, D. edd. (1989) *Bakhtin and Cultural Theory* (Manchester).

Hodkinson, S. (1983) 'Social order and the conflict of values in Classical Sparta', *Chiron* 13: 239–81.

Hodkinson, S. (1997) 'The development of Spartan society and institutions in the Archaic period', in Mitchell and Rhodes edd. 1997: 83–102.

Hölkeskamp, K.-J. (1992a) 'Written law in archaic Greece', *Proceedings of the Cambridge Philological Society* 38: 87–117.

Hölkeskamp, K.-J. (1992b [pub.1995]) 'Arbitrators, lawgivers and the "codification of law" in Archaic Greece', *Metis* 7: 49–81.

Hölkeskamp, K.-J. (1997) 'Agorai bei Homer', in Eder and Hölkeskamp edd. 1997: 1–19.

Hölkeskamp, K.-J. (1999) *Schiedsrichter, Gesetzgeber und Gesetzgebung im archaischen Griechenland*. Historia Einzelschrift 131 (Stuttgart).

Hornblower, S. (1987) *Thucydides* (London).

Hornblower, S. (1991) *A Commentary on Thucydides*, vol. I: Books 1–3 (Oxford).

Hornblower, S. (1992) 'The religious dimension to the Peloponnesian War, or, what Thucydides does not tell us', *Harvard Studies in Classical Philology* 94: 169–97.

Hornblower, S. (1996) *A Commentary on Thucydides*, vol. II: Books 4–5.24 (Oxford).

How, W.W., and Wells, J. (1912) *A Commentary on Herodotus*, 2 vols. (Oxford).

Humphreys, S. C. (1985) 'Law as discourse', *History and Anthropology* 1:241-64.

Humphreys, S. C. (1991) 'A historical approach to Drakon's law on homicide', in Gagarin ed. 1991: 17–45.

Humphreys, S. C. (1993a) *The Family, Women and Death* (Ann Arbor MI, 2nd edn).

Humphreys, S. C. (1993b) 'Oikos and polis', in Humphreys 1993a: ch. 1.

Humphreys, S. C. (1993c) 'Public and private interests in classical Athens', in Humphreys 1993a: ch. 2.

Humphreys, S. C. (1993d) 'Diffusion, comparison, criticism', in Raaflaub and Müller-Luckner edd. 1993: 1–11.

Hunter, V. J. (1994) *Policing Athens. Social Control in the Attic Lawsuits, 420–320 BC* (Princeton).

Hussey, E. (1972) *The Presocratics* (London).

Hussey, E. (1985) 'Thucydidean history and Democritean theory', in Cartledge, P., and Harvey, F. edd. *Crux: Essays in Greek History presented to G. E. M. de Ste. Croix on his 75th birthday* (Exeter and London), 118–38.

Hussey, E. (1995) 'Ionian inquiries: on understanding the Presocratic beginnings of science', in Powell, A. ed. *The Greek World* (London), 530–49.

Huxley, G. L. (1979) *On Aristotle and Greek Society* (Belfast).

Immerwahr, H. R. (1966) *Form and Thought in Herodotus* (Cleveland).

Irani, K. D., and Silver, M. edd. (1995) *Social Justice in the Ancient World* (Westport CT).

Irigaray, L. (1985) *Speculum of the Other Woman*, trans. Gill, G. (London).

Irigaray, L. (1989) *Le Temps de la différence* (Paris).

Irwin, W. A. (1946) 'The Hebrews', in Frankfort *et al.* 1946: 223–360.

Jacobsen, T. (1946) 'Mesopotamia', in Frankfort *et al.* 1946: 125–219.

Jacoby, F. (1913) 'Herodotos', in Pauly-Wissowa, *Real-Encyclopädie der classischen Altertumswissenschaft*, Supplement 2 (Stuttgart) cols.205–520 [= id., *Griechische Historiker* (Stuttgart 1956) 7–164].

Jaeger, W. (1960) *Scripta Minora*, vol. 1 (Rome).

Jaeger, W. (1966) *Five Essays* (Montreal).

Janko, R. (1982) *Homer, Hesiod and the Hymns: Diachronic Development in Epic Diction* (Cambridge).

Jenkyns, R. (1980) *The Victorians and Ancient Greece* (London).

Jones, A. H. M. (1957) *Athenian Democracy* (Oxford).

Just, R. (1989) *Women in Athenian Law and Life* (London).

Kahn, C. H. (1979) *The Art and Thought of Heraclitus: An Edition of the Fragments with Translation and Commentary* (Cambridge).

Kahn, C. H. (1981) 'The origins of social contract theory', in Kerferd ed. 1981: 92–108.

Kallet-Marx, L. (1994) 'Institutions, ideology and political consciousness in ancient Greece: some recent books on Athenian democracy', *Journal of the History of Ideas* 55.2:307–35.

Kennedy, G. (1963) *The Art of Persuasion in Greece* (London).

Kennell, N. M. (1995) *The Gymnasium of Virtue: Education and Culture in Ancient Sparta* (Chapel Hill NC).

Kerferd, G. B. (1981a) *The Sophistic Movement* (Cambridge).

Kerferd, G. B. ed. (1981b) *The Sophists and their Legacy*. Hermes Einzelschriften 44 (Wiesbaden).

Kiechle, F. (1958) 'Zur Humanität in der Kriegführung der griechischen Staaten', *Historia* 7: 129–56.

Kinzl, K. H. ed. (1979) *Die ältere Tyrannis bis zu den Perserkriegen*. Wege der Forschung 510 (Darmstadt).

Kinzl, K. H. ed. (1995) *Demokratia: Der Weg zur Demokratie bei den Griechen*. Wege der Forschung 657 (Darmstadt).

Kirk, G. S. (1975) 'The Homeric poems as history', *Cambridge Ancient History* II.2: 820–50 (Cambridge, 2nd edn).

Kirk, G. S. (1985) *The Iliad: A Commentary*, vol. I: *Books 1–4* (Cambridge).

Kirk, G. S., Raven, J. E., and Schofield, M. (1983) *The Presocratic Philosophers* (Cambridge, 2nd edn).

Kitto, H. D. F. (1966) *POIESIS: Structure and Thought* (Berkeley).

Knox, B. (1952) 'The *Hippolytus* of Euripides', *Yale Classical Studies* 13: 3–21.

Knox, B. (1957) *Oedipus at Thebes* (London).

Knox, B. (1964) *The Heroic Temper* (Berkeley).

Koerner, R. (1993) *Inschriftliche Gesetzestexte der frühen griechischen Polis* (Cologne).

Konstan, D. (1995) *Greek Comedy and Ideology* (Oxford).

Konstan, D. (1997) *Friendship in the Classical World* (Cambridge).

Kopcke, G., and Tokumaru, I. edd. (1992) *Greece between East and West: 10th to 8th Centuries BC* (Mainz).

Kraut, R. (1984) *Socrates and the State* (Princeton).

Kurke, L. (1991) *The Traffic in Praise: Pindar and the Poetics of Social Economy* (Ithaca NY).

Lane, W., and Lane, A. (1986) 'The Politics of *Antigone*', in Euben ed. 1986: 162–82.

Lang, M. (1967) 'Kylonian conspiracy', *Classical Philology* 62: 243–9.

Lanza, D. (1977) *Il Tiranno e il suo Pubblico* (Turin).

Latacz, J. (1996) *Homer: His Art and His World* (Ann Arbor MI).

Latacz, J. ed. (1991) *Zweihundert Jahre Homer-Forschung: Rückblick und Ausblick* (Stuttgart).

Lattimore, R. (1951) *The Iliad of Homer, Translated with an Introduction* (Chicago).

Lattimore, R. (1960) *Greek Lyrics*, trans. (Chicago).

Lattimore, R. (1965) *The Odyssey of Homer, Translated with an Introduction* (New York).

Lefkowitz, M. R. (1981) *The Lives of the Greek Poets* (Baltimore).

Lefkowitz, M. R. (1996) *Not Out of Africa: How Afrocentrism Became an Excuse to Teach Myth as History* (New York).

Lefkowitz, M. R., and Rogers, G. M. edd. (1996) *Black Athena Revisited* (Chapel Hill NC).

Legon, R. P. (1981) *Megara: The Political History of a Greek City-State to 336 BC* (Ithaca NY).

Legrand, Ph.-E. (1954) *Hérodote: Index Analytique* (Paris).

Lesher, J. H. (1992) *Xenophanes of Colophon, Fragments: A Text and Translation with a Commentary* (Toronto).

Lévêque, P., and Vidal-Naquet, P. (1964) *Clisthène l'Athénien* (Paris) [augmented English trans. Atlantic Highlands NJ, 1996].

Levine, M. M., and Peradotto, J. edd. (1989) *The Challenge of 'Black Athena'. Arethusa*, Special Issue.

Lewis, D. M. (1988) 'The Tyranny of the Pisistratidae' *Cambridge Ancient History* IV: 287–302 (Cambridge, 2nd edn).

Lewis, D. M. (1990) 'The political background of Democritus', in Craik, E. M. ed. *'Owls to Athens': Essays on Classical Subjects for Sir Kenneth Dover* (Oxford), 151–4.

Lewis, D. M. *et al.* edd. (1992) *The Cambridge Ancient History*, vol. v: *The Fifth Century BC* (Cambridge).

Lintott, A. W. (1982) *Violence, Civil Strife and Revolution in the Classical City 700–330 BC* (London and Sydney).

Lloyd, A. B. (1975) *Herodotus Book II*, vol. I: *Introduction* (Leiden). Repr. 1994.

Lloyd, G. E. R. (1979) *Magic, Reason and Experience* (Cambridge).

Lloyd, G. E. R. (1987) *The Revolutions of Wisdom. Studies in the Claims and Practice of Ancient Greek Science* (Berkeley).

Lloyd, G. E. R. (1990) *Demystifying Mentalities* (Cambridge).

Lloyd, G. E. R. (1991a) *Methods and Problems in Greek Science* (Cambridge).

Lloyd, G. E. R. (1991b) 'The debt of Greek philosophy and science to the Near East', in Lloyd 1991a: 278–98.

Loizou, A., and Lesser, H. edd. (1990) *'Polis' and Politics: Essays in Greek Moral and Political Philosophy* (Aldershot).

Long, A. A. (1970) 'Morals and values in Homer', *Journal of Hellenic Studies* 90: 121–39.

Loraux, N. (1981) *L'Invention d'Athènes: histoire de l'oraison funèbre dans la "cité classique"* (Paris) [= *The Invention of Athens: The Funeral Oration in the Classical City*, tr. A. Sheridan (Cambridge MA, 1986)].

Loraux, N. (1984/1993a) *Children of Athena. Athenian Ideas about Citizenship and the Division between the Sexes* (Princeton).

Loraux, N. (1987) 'Le lien de la division', *Le Cahier du Collège International de Philosophie* 4: 101–24.

Loraux, N. (1991) 'Reflections of the Greek city on unity and division', in Molho, Raaflaub and Emlen edd. 1991: 33–51.

Loraux, N. (1993b) 'Les femmes d'Athènes et le théâtre', in *Aristophane* Entretiens sur l'Antiquité Classique 38, Fondation Hardt (Geneva).

Loraux, N. (1996) 'Clistene e i nuovi caratteri della lotta politica', in Settis ed. 1996: 1083–110.

Lorton, D. (1995) 'Legal and social institutions of Pharaonic Egypt', in Sasson ed. 1995: 345–62.

Luccioni, J. (1947) *Hiéron* (Paris).

Luccioni, J. (1948) *Les Idées politiques et sociales de Xénophon* (Paris).

Luce, T. J. ed. (1982) *Ancient Writers: Greece and Rome*, vol. 1 (New York).

Luria, S. (1970) *Democritea* (Leningrad).

Luschnat, O. (1970) 'Thukydides der Historiker', in Pauly-Wissowa, *Realencyclopädie der classischen Altertumswissenschaft*, Supplementband 12 (Stuttgart) cols. 1085–354.

MacDowell, D. M. (1982) *Gorgias: Encomium of Helen* (Bristol).

MacDowell, D. M. (1990) *Demosthenes: Against Meidias (Oration 21)* (Oxford).

MacIntyre, A. (1973–4) 'Ancient politics and modern issues', *Arion* n.s.1: 425–30.

Macleod, C. (1982) 'Politics and the *Oresteia*', *Journal of Hellenic Studies* 102: 124–44.

Macleod, C. (1983a) *Collected Essays* (Oxford).

Macleod, C. (1983b) 'Form and meaning in the Melian Dialogue', in Macleod 1983a: 52–67.

Macleod, C. (1983c) 'Rhetoric and history (Thucydides 6.16–18)', in Macleod 1983a: 68–87.

Macleod, C. (1983d) 'Reason and necessity: Thucydides 3.9–14, 37–48', in Macleod 1983a: 88–102.

Macleod, C. (1983e) 'Thucydides on faction (3.82–3)', in Macleod 1983a: 123–39.

Macleod, C. (1983f) 'Thucydides and tragedy', in Macleod 1983a: 140–58.

Malkin, I. (1987) *Religion and Colonization in Ancient Greece* (Leiden).

Malkin, I. (1989) 'Delphoi and the founding of social order in Archaic Greece', *Metis* 4: 129–53.

Manfredini, M., and Piccirilli, L. (1977) *Plutarco, La vita di Solone* (Florence).

Manville, P. B. (1990) *The Origins of Citizenship in Ancient Athens* (Princeton).

Marg, W. ed. (1965) *Herodot: Eine Auswahl aus der neueren Forschung*. Wege der Forschung 26 (Darmstadt, 2nd edn).

Martin, R. P. (1984) 'Hesiod, Odysseus, and the Instruction of Princes', *Transactions of the American Philological Association* 114: 29–48.

Martin, R. P. (1989) *The Language of Heroes: Speech and Performance in the Iliad* (Cornell).

Masaracchia, A. (1995) *Isocrate: retorica e politica* (Roma).

Mathieu, G. (1925) *Les Idées politiques et sociales d'Isocrate* (Paris).

Matthäus, H. (1993) 'Zur Rezeption orientalischer Kunst-, Kultur- und Lebensformen in Griechenland', in Raaflaub and Müller-Luckner edd. 1993: 165–86.

Mau, J., and Schmidt, E. G. edd. (1964) *Isonomia: Studien zur Gleichheitsvorstellung im griechischen Denken* (Berlin, repr. 1971).

McGlew, J. F. (1993) *Tyranny and Political Culture in Ancient Greece* (Ithaca NY).
Meier, C. (1970) *Die Entstehung des Begriffs 'Demokratie'* (Frankfurt a.M.).
Meier, C. (1989) 'Die Entstehung einer autonomen Intelligenz bei den Griechen', in Meier, *Die Welt der Geschichte und die Provinz des Historikers* (Berlin), 70–100.
Meier, C. (1980/1990) *The Greek Discovery of Politics*, trans. McLintock, D. (Cambridge MA).
Meier, C. (1993) *The Political Art of Greek Tragedy*, trans. Webber, A. (Cambridge).
Meiggs, R. (1972) *The Athenian Empire* (Oxford).
Meiggs, R., and Lewis, D. (1988) *A Selection of Greek Historical Inscriptions to the End of the Fifth Century* BC (Oxford, rev. edn).
Merck, M. (1978) 'The city's achievement: the patriotic Amazonomachy and ancient Athens', in Lipshitz, S. ed. *Tearing the Veil* (London).
Millett, P. (1984) 'Hesiod and his world', *Proceedings of the Cambridge Philological Society* 30: 84–115.
Mills, P. (1987) *Women, Nature and Psyche* (New Haven).
Mitchell, L., and Rhodes, P. J. edd. (1997) *The Development of the Polis in Archaic Greece* (London).
Moles, J. (1996) 'Herodotus warns the Athenians', *Papers of the Leeds International Latin Seminar* 9: 259–84.
Molho, A., Raaflaub, K. A., and Emlen, J. edd. (1991) *Athens and Rome, Florence and Venice: City-States in Classical Antiquity and Medieval Italy* (Stuttgart).
Molyneux, J. H. ed. (1993) *Literary Responses to Civil Discord* (Nottingham).
Momigliano, A. (1966a) *Studies in Historiography* (London).
Momigliano, A. (1966b) 'Some observations on causes of war in ancient historiography', in Momigliano 1966a: 112–26.
Momigliano, A. (1966c) 'The place of Herodotus in the history of historiography', in Momigliano 1966a: 127–42.
Momigliano, A. (1990) *The Classical Foundations of Modern Historiography* (Berkeley).
Montgomery, H. (1983) *The Way to Chaeronea: Foreign Policy, Decision-making and Political Influence in Demosthenes' Speeches* (Bergen).
Moore, J. M. (1975) *Aristotle and Xenophon on Democracy and Oligarchy* (London).
Morgan, C. (1991) 'Ethnicity and early Greek states: historical and material perspectives', *Proceedings of the Cambridge Philological Society* 37: 131–63.
Morris, I. (1986) 'The use and abuse of Homer', *Classical Antiquity* 5: 81–138.
Morris, I. (1987) *Burial and Ancient Society: The Rise of the Greek City-State* (Cambridge).
Morris, I. (1996) 'The strong principle of equality and the Archaic origins of Greek democracy', in Ober and Hedrick edd. 1996: 19–48.
Morris, I. (1997) 'Homer and the Iron Age', in Morris and Powell edd. 1987: 535–59.
Morris, I. (1998) 'Archaeology and Archaic Greek history', in Fisher and van Wees edd. 1998: 1–91.
Morris, I. (forthcoming) *Archaeology as Cultural History*.
Morris, I., and Raaflaub, K. edd. (1997) *Democracy 2500? Questions and Challenges*. Archaeological Institute of America, Colloquia and Conference Papers 2 (Dubuque, Iowa).
Morris, I., and Powell, B. edd. (1997) *A New Companion to Homer* (Leiden).
Morris, S. P. (1992) *Daidalos and the Origins of Greek Art* (Princeton).

Morschauser, S. N. (1995) 'The ideological basis for social justice/responsibility in ancient Egypt', in Irani and Silver edd. 1995: 101–14.

Mossé, C. (1983) 'Sparte archaïque', *Parola del Passato* 28: 7–20.

Mossé, C. (1994) *Démosthène ou les ambiguïtés de la politique* (Paris).

Moulton, C. (1974) 'Antiphon the Sophist and Democritus', *Museum Helveticum* 31: 129–39.

Muir, J. V. (1985) 'Religion and the new education: the challenge of the Sophists', in Easterling and Muir edd. 1985: 191–218, 228–30.

Müller, R. (1984) 'Die Stellung Demokrits in der antiken Sozialphilosophie', in Benakis, L. ed. *Proceedings of the First International Conference on Democritus*, Xanthi, vol. 1, 423–33.

Müller, R. ed. (1987) *Polis und Res Publica. Studien zum antiken Gesellschafts- und Geschichtsdenken* (Weimar).

Mulroy, D. (1992) *Early Greek Lyric Poetry, Translated with an Introduction and Commentary* (Ann Arbor MI).

Murray, O. (1990a) 'Cities of reason', in Murray and Price edd. 1990: 1–25.

Murray, O. (1990b) 'The affair of the mysteries: democracy and the drinking group', in Murray 1990c: 149–61.

Murray, O. (1991a) 'History and reason in the ancient city', *Papers of the British School at Rome* 59: 1–13.

Murray, O. (1991b) 'War and the symposium', in Slater ed. 1991: 83–103.

Murray, O. (1993) *Early Greece* (London and Cambridge MA, 2nd edn).

Murray, O. ed. (1990c) *Sympotica: A Symposium on the Symposion* (Oxford).

Murray, O., and Price, S. edd. (1990) *The Greek City. From Homer to Alexander* (Oxford).

Musti, D. (1985) 'Pubblico e privato nella democrazia periclea', *Quaderni Urbinati di Cultura Classica* n.s. 20.2 [= 49]: 7–17.

Musti, D. ed. (1991) *La transizione dal Miceneo all'Alto Arcaismo: Dal palazzo alla città* (Rome).

Nagy, G. (1976) 'Iambos: typologies of invective and praise', *Arethusa* 9: 191–205.

Nagy, G. (1979) *The Best of the Achaeans: Concepts of the Hero in Archaic Greek Poetry* (Baltimore).

Nagy, G. (1982) 'Hesiod', in Luce ed. 1982: 43–73; rewritten as part of Nagy 1990a: ch. 3.

Nagy, G. (1985) 'Theognis and Megara: a poet's vision of his city', in Figueira and Nagy edd. 1985: 22–81.

Nagy, G. (1990a) *Greek Mythology and Poetics* (Ithaca NY).

Nagy, G. (1990b) *Pindar's Homer: The Lyric Possession of an Epic Past* (Baltimore).

Nagy, G. (1996) 'Aristocrazia: caratteri e stili di vita', in Settis ed. 1996: 577–98.

Narcy, M. (1989) 'Antiphon d' Athènes', in Goulet, R. ed., *Dictionnaire des Philosophes Antiques*, vol. 1 (Paris), 225–44.

Nehamas, A. (1982) 'Plato on imitation and poetry', in Moravscik, J., and Temko, P. edd. *Plato on Beauty, Wisdom and the Arts* (Totowa NJ).

Nenci, G. (1979) *La Grecia nell'età di Pericle* (Milan).

Nestle, W. (1942) *Vom Mythos zum Logos: Die Selbstentfaltung des griechischen Denkens von Homer bis auf die Sophistik und Sokrates* (Stuttgart, 2nd edn).

Neugebauer, O. (1957) *The Exact Sciences in Antiquity* (Providence RI, 2nd edn).

Nickel, R. (1979) *Xenophon* (Darmstadt).

Nicolai, W. (1993) 'Gefolgschaftsverweigerung als politisches Druckmittel in der Ilias', in Raaflaub and Müller-Luckner edd. 1993: 317–41.

Nicolet, C. ed. (1975) *Demokratia et Aristokratia. A Propos de Caius Gracchus: mots grecs et réalités romaines* (Paris).

Nietzsche, F. (1872) *Die Geburt der Tragödie* (Leipzig).

Nill, M. (1985) *Morality and Self-Interest in Protagoras, Antiphon and Democritus* (Leiden).

Nippel, W. (1980) *Mischverfassungstheorie und Verfassungsrealität in Antike und früher Neuzeit* (Stuttgart).

Nippel, W. (1988) 'Bürgerideal und Oligarchie. "Klassischer Republikanismus" aus althistorischer Sicht', in Koenigsberger ed. 1988: 1–18.

Nippel, W. (1993) 'Macht, Machtkontrolle und Machtentgrenzung. Zu einigen Konzeptionen und ihrer Rezeption in der frühen Neuzeit', in Gebhardt, J., and Münkler, H. edd. *Bürgerschaft und Herrschaft. Zum Verhältnis von Macht und Demokratie im antiken und neuzeitlichen politischen Denken* (Baden-Baden), 58–78.

Nippel, W. (1994) 'Ancient and modern republicanism', in Fontana, B. ed. *The Invention of the Modern Republic* (Cambridge), 6–26.

Nippel, W. (1995) *Public Order in Ancient Rome* (Cambridge).

Nixon, L., and Price, S. (1990) 'The size and resources of Greek cities', in Murray and Price edd. (1990): 137–70.

North, H. (1966) *Sophrosyne: Self-Knowledge and Self-Restraint in Greek Literature* (Ithaca).

Nouhaud, Michel (1982) *L'Utilisation de l'histoire par les orateurs attiques* (Paris).

Nussbaum, M. C. (1986) *The Fragility of Goodness* (Cambridge).

O'Brien, M. (1985) 'Xenophanes, Aeschylus, and the doctrine of primeval brutishness', *Classical Quarterly* 35: 264–77.

O'Connor, D., and Silverman, D. P. edd. (1995) *Ancient Egyptian Kingship* (Leiden).

Oakley, J. H., and Sinos, R. (1993) *The Wedding in Ancient Athens* (Madison).

Ober, J. (1989) *Mass and Elite in Democratic Athens. Rhetoric, Ideology and the Power of the People* (Princeton).

Ober, J. (1993) 'The Athenian revolution of 508/7 B.C.E.: violence, authority, and the origins of democracy', in Dougherty and Kurke edd. 1993: 215–32.

Ober, J. (1996) *The Athenian Revolution: Essays on Ancient Greek Democracy and Political Theory* (Princeton).

Ober, J. (1998) *Political Dissent in Democratic Athens: Intellectual Critics of Popular Rule* (Princeton).

Ober, J., and Hedrick, C. edd. (1996) *Demokratia. A Conversation on Democracies, Ancient and Modern* (Princeton).

Okin, S. M. (1991) 'Gender, the public and the private', in Held ed. 1991: 67–90.

Oliva, P. (1971) *Sparta and her Social Problems* (Prague).

Ollier, Fr. (1934) *La République des Lacédémoniens* (Lyons).

Oost, S. (1973) 'The Megara of Theagenes and Theognis', *Classical Philology* 68: 188–96.

Osborne, R. (1990) 'Vexatious litigation in classical Athens: sykophancy and the sykophant', in Cartledge, Millett and Todd edd. 1990: 83–102.

Ostwald, M. (1969) *Nomos and the Beginnings of the Athenian Democracy* (Oxford).

Ostwald, M. (1986) *From Popular Sovereignty to the Sovereignty of Law: Law, Society, and Politics in Fifth-Century Athens* (Berkeley).

Ostwald, M. (1988) 'The reform of the Athenian state by Cleisthenes', *Cambridge Ancient History* IV: 303–46 (Cambridge, 2nd edn).

Page, D. L. (1962) *Poetae Melici Graeci* (Oxford).

Paolucci, A., and Paolucci, H. edd. (1962) *Hegel on Tragedy* (New York).

Parker, R. (1996) *Athenian Religion: A History* (Oxford).

Parry, A. M. (1989a) *The Language of Achilles and Other Papers* (Oxford).

Parry, A. M. (1989b) 'The language of Thucydides' description of the plague', in Parry 1989a: 156–76.

Parry, A. M. (1989c) 'Thucydides' historical perspective', in Parry 1989a: 286–300.

Patterson, O. (1982) *Slavery and Social Death* (Cambridge MA).

Patterson, O. (1991) *Freedom in the Making of Western Culture* (Cambridge MA).

Patzek, B. (1992) *Homer und Mykene* (Munich).

Pembroke, S. (1967) 'Women in charge: the function of alternatives in early Greek tradition and the ancient idea of matriarchy', *Journal of the Warburg and Courtauld Institutes* 30: 1–35.

Penglase, C. (1994) *Greek Myths and Mesopotamia: Parallels and Influence in the Homeric Hymns and Hesiod* (London).

Pichot, A. (1991) *La naissance de la science* (Paris).

Pickard-Cambridge, A. (1968) *The Dramatic Festivals of Athens*, revised Gould, J., and Lewis, D. (Oxford). Repr. with corr. and add. 1988.

Pilz, W. (1934) *Der Rhetor im Attischen Staat* (Leipzig).

Pleket, H. W. (1969) 'The Archaic tyrannis', *Talanta* 1: 19–61.

Pleket, H. W. (1972) 'Isonomia and Cleisthenes: a note', *Talanta* 4: 63–81.

Podlecki, A. J. (1966) *The Political Background of Aeschylean Tragedy* (Michigan).

Podlecki, A. J. (1984) *The Early Greek Poets and Their Times* (Vancouver).

Polignac, F. de (1995) *Cults, Territory, and the Origins of the Greek City-State*, trans. Lloyd, J. (Chicago).

Pomeroy, S. B. (1994) *Xenophon Oeconomicus. A social and historical commentary* (Oxford).

Pritchard, A. (1992) 'Antigone's mirrors: reflections on moral madness', *Hypatia* 7:377–93.

Pritchett, W. K. (1993) *The Liar School of Herodotus* (Amsterdam).

Procopé, J. (1989 and 1990) 'Democritus on politics and the care of the soul', *Classical Quarterly* 39: 307–31 and 40: 21–45.

Pye, L. (1993) 'Political culture', in Krieger, J. ed. *The Oxford Companion to Politics of the World* (Oxford).

Qviller, B. (1981) 'The dynamics of the Homeric society', *Symbolae Osloenses* 56: 109–55.

Raaflaub, K. A. (1983) 'Democracy, oligarchy, and the concept of the "free citizen" in late fifth-century Athens', *Political Theory* 11.4: 517–44.

Raaflaub, K. A. (1984) 'Freiheit in Athen und Rom: Ein Beispiel divergierender politischer Begriffsentwicklung in der Antike', *Historische Zeitschrift* 238: 529–67.

Raaflaub, K. A. (1985) *Die Entdeckung der Freiheit*. Vestigia 37 (Munich).

Raaflaub, K. A. (1988) 'Die Anfänge des politischen Denkens bei den Griechen', in Fetscher and Münkler edd. 1988: 189–271.

Raaflaub, K. A. (1989) 'Die Anfänge des politischen Denkens bei den Griechen', *Historische Zeitschrift* 248: 1–32.

Raaflaub, K. A. (1990–1) 'I Greci scoprono la liberta', *OPVS* 9–10: 7–28.

Raaflaub, K. A. (1991) 'Homer und die Geschichte des 8.Jh.s v.Chr.', in Latacz ed. 1991: 205–56.

Raaflaub, K. A. (1992) *Politisches Denken und Krise der Polis. Athen im Verfassungskonflikt des späten 5. Jahrhunderts v. Chr.* (Munich).

Raaflaub, K. A. (1993) 'Homer to Solon: the rise of the polis (the written evidence)', in Hansen ed. 1993b: 41–105.

Raaflaub, K. A. (1995) 'Kleisthenes, Ephialtes und die Begründung der Demokratie', in Kinzl ed. 1995: 1–54.

Raaflaub, K. A. (1996a) 'Equalities and inequalities in Athenian democracy', in Ober and Hedrick edd. 1996: 139–74.

Raaflaub, K. A. (1996b) 'Solone, la nuova Atene e l'emergere della politica', in Settis ed. 1996: 1035–81.

Raaflaub, K. A. (1997a) 'Citizens, soldiers, and the evolution of the early Greek polis', in Mitchell and Rhodes edd. 1997: 49–59.

Raaflaub, K. A. (1997b) 'Homeric society', in Morris and Powell edd. 1997: 624–48.

Raaflaub, K. A. (1997c) 'Politics and interstate relations in the world of early Greek poleis: Homer and beyond', *Antichthon* 31: 1–27.

Raaflaub, K. A. (1998) 'A historian's headache: how to read "Homeric society"?', in Fisher and van Wees edd. 1998: 169–93.

Raaflaub, K. A. ed. (1986) *Social Struggles in Archaic Rome: New Perspectives on the Conflict of the Orders* (Berkeley).

Raaflaub, K. A., and Müller-Luckner, E. edd. (1993) *Die Anfänge politischen Denkens in der Antike: Die nahöstlichen Kulturen und die Griechen* (Munich).

Rahe, P. A. (1992) *Republics Ancient and Modern* (Chapel Hill NC).

Rankin, H. D. (1977) *Archilochus of Paros* (Park Ridge NJ).

Rawls, J. (1992) *Political Liberalism* (New York).

Rawson, E. (1969) *The Spartan Tradition in European Thought* (Oxford).

Rawson, E. (1970) 'Family and fatherland in Euripides' *Phoenissae*', *Greek, Roman, and Byzantine Studies* 11: 109–27.

Rechenauer, G. (1991) *Thukydides und die hippokratische Medizin* (Hildesheim).

Reckford, K. (1987) *Aristophanes' Old-and-New Comedy* (Chapel Hill).

Redfield, J. M. (1975) *Nature and Culture in the Iliad: The Tragedy of Hector* (Chicago).

Redfield, J. M. (1985) 'Herodotus the tourist', *Classical Philology* 80: 97–118.

Reverdin, O. ed. (1962) *Grecs et Barbares*. Entretiens sur l'antiquité classique 8 (Vandoeuvres-Geneva).

Reverdin, O., and Grange, B. edd. (1990) *Hérodote et les peuples non grecs*. Entretiens sur l'antiquité classique 35 (Vandoeuvres-Geneva).

Rhodes, P. J. (1981) *A Commentary on the Aristotelian Athenaion Politeia* (Oxford).

Rhodes, P. J. (1995) 'The "acephalous" polis?', *Historia* 44: 153–67.

Richardson, N. J. (1975) 'Homeric professors in the age of the Sophists', *Proceedings of the Cambridge Philological Society* 2: 65–81.

Richter, M. ed. (1980) *Political Theory and Political Education* (Guildford).

Robinson, E. W. (1997) *The First Democracies: Early Popular Government Outside Athens*. Historia Einzelschrift 107 (Stuttgart).

Robinson, T. M. (1984) *Contrasting Arguments: An Edition of the Dissoi Logoi* (Salem NH).

Rollinger, R. (1996) 'Altorientalische Motivik in der frühgriechischen Literatur am Beispiel der homerischen Epen', in Ulf ed. 1996: 156–210.

Romilly, J. de (1951) *Thucydide et l'Impérialisme Athénien* (Paris, 2nd edn) [= *Thucydides and Athenian Imperialism*, trans. Thody, P. (London 1963)].

Romilly, J. de (1956) *Histoire et Raison chez Thucydide* (Paris).

Romilly, J. de (1958) 'Eunoia in Isocrates, or the political importance of winning goodwill', *Journal of Hellenic Studies* 78: 92–101.

Romilly, J. de (1976) 'Alcibiade et le mélange entre jeunes et vieux: politique et médicine', *Wiener Studien* Neue Folge 10: 93–105.

Romilly, J. de (1988) *Les Grands Sophistes dans l'Athènes de Périclès* (Paris) [= *The Great Sophists in Periclean Athens*, trans. Lloyd, J. (Oxford 1992)].

Romm, J. S. (1992) *The Edges of the Earth in Ancient Thought* (Princeton).

Rorty, A. ed. (1992) *Essays on Aristotle's Poetics* (Princeton).

Rose, P. W. (1988) 'Thersites and the plural voices of Homer', *Arethusa* 21: 5–25.

Rose, P. W. (1992) *Sons of the Gods, Children of Earth* (Ithaca).

Rösler, W. (1980) *Dichter und Gruppe: Eine Untersuchung zu den Bedingungen und zur historischen Funktion früher griechischer Lyrik am Beispiel Alkaios* (Munich).

Rubinstein, L. (1998) 'The Athenian political perception of the *idiōtēs*', in Cartledge, Millett and von Reden edd. 1998: 125–43.

Runciman, W. G. (1982) 'The origins of states: the case of Archaic Greece', *Comparative Studies in Society and History* 24: 351–77.

Runciman, W. G. (1990) 'Doomed to extinction: the *polis* as an evolutionary dead-end', in Murray and Price edd. 1990: 347–67.

Ruschenbusch, E. (1960) 'Phonos: Zum Recht Drakons und seiner Bedeutung für das Werden des athenischen Staates', *Historia* 9: 129–54.

Ruschenbusch, E. (1966) *Solonos Nomoi: Die Fragmente des solonischen Gesetzeswerkes mit einer Text- und Überlieferungsgeschichte*. Historia Einzelschrift 9 (Wiesbaden).

Ruschenbusch, E. (1983) 'Die Polis und das Recht', in Dimakis ed. 1983: 305–26.

Ruzé, F. (1991) 'Le conseil et l'assemblée dans la Grande Rhètra de Sparte', *Revue des Etudes Grecques* 104: 15–30.

Ruzé, F. (1997) *Délibération et pouvoir dans la cité grecque de Nestor à Socrate* (Paris).

Ryffel, H. (1949) *METABOLE POLITEION: Der Wandel der Staatsverfassungen* (Berne).

Saggs, H. W. F. (1989) *Civilizations before Greece and Rome* (New Haven CT).

Ste. Croix, G. E. M. de (1972) *The Origins of the Peloponnesian War* (London).

Ste. Croix, G. E. M. de (1981) *The Class Struggle in the Ancient Greek World* (London and Ithaca NY).

Sakellariou, M.B. (1989) *The Polis-State: Definition and Origin* (Athens and Paris).

Salem, J. (1996) *Démocrite: grains de poussière dans un rayon de soleil* (Paris).

Sartori, F. (1957) *Le eterie nella vita politica Ateniese del VI e V secolo a.C.* (Rome).

Sasson, J. M. ed. (1995) *Civilizations of the Ancient Near East*, vol. 1 (New York).

Saunders, T. J. (1991) *Plato's Penal Code: Tradition, Controversy, and Reform in Greek Penology* (Oxford).

Saxonhouse, A. (1992) *Fear of Diversity* (Chicago).

Schäfer, C. (1996) *Xenophanes von Kolophon: Ein Vorsokratiker zwischen Mythos und Philosophie* (Stuttgart).

Scharr, E. (1919) *Xenophons Staats- und Gesellschaftsideal und seine Zeit* (Halle).

Schein, S. (1984) *The Mortal Hero* (Berkeley).

Schiappa, E. (1991) *Protagoras and Logos: A Study in Greek Philosophy and Rhetoric* (Columbia SC).

Schmitt Pantel, P. (1992) *La Cité au banquet. Histoire des repas publics dans les cités grecques* (Rome).

Schmitt Pantel, P. (1990) 'Collective activities and the political in the Greek city', in Murray and Price, edd. 1990: 199–213.

Schneider, C. (1974) *Information und Absicht bei Thukydides: Untersuchung zur Motivation des Handelns* (Göttingen).

Schofield, M. (1995–6) 'Sharing in the constitution', *Review of Metaphysics* 49: 831–58.

Schwabl, H. (1962) 'Das Bild der fremden Welt bei den frühen Griechen', in Reverdin ed. 1962: 1–23.

Schwertfeger, T. (1982) 'Der Schild des Archilochos', *Chiron* 12: 253–80.

Scott, J. W. (1986) 'Gender: a useful category of historical analysis', *American Historical Review* 91: 1053–75.

Scott, J. W. (1991) 'Women's history', in Burke, P. ed. *New Perspectives on Historical Writing* (Cambridge), 42–66.

Scully, S. (1981) 'The polis in Homer: a definition and interpretation', *Ramus* 10: 1–34.

Scully, S. (1990) *Homer and the Sacred City* (Ithaca NY).

Seaford, R. (1995) *Reciprocity and Ritual* (Oxford).

Sealey, R. (1994) *The Justice of the Greeks* (Ann Arbor MI).

Segal, C. (1972) 'Curse and oath in Euripides' *Hippolytus*', *Ramus* 1: 165–80.

Segal, C. (1981) *Tragedy and Civilization* (Cambridge MA).

Settis, S. ed. (1996) *I Greci*, vol. I (Turin).

Seybold, K., and Ungern-Sternberg, J. (1993) 'Amos und Hesiod. Aspekte eines Vergleichs', in Raaflaub and Müller-Luckner edd. 1993: 215–40.

Shklar, J. (1971) 'Hegel's *Phenomenology*: an elegy for Hellas', in Pelczynski, Z. ed. *Hegel's Political Thought* (Cambridge).

Sidgwick, A. (1887) *Aeschylus. Eumenides* (Oxford).

Silk, M., and Stern, J. (1981) *Nietzsche on Tragedy* (Cambridge).

Silver, M. (1983) *Prophets and Markets: The Political Economy of Ancient Israel* (Norwell MA).

Silver, M. (1995) 'Prophets and markets revisited', in Irani and Silver edd. 1995: 179–98.

Skinner, Q. R. D. (1969) 'Meaning and understanding in the history of ideas', *History and Theory* 8: 3–53.

Skinner, Q. R. D. (1989) 'The State' in Ball, Farr and Hanson edd. 1989: 90–131.

Slater, W. J. ed. (1991) *Dining in a Classical Context* (Ann Arbor MI).

Smart, J. D. (1988) 'Herodotus', in Cannon, J. ed. *The Blackwell Dictionary of Historians* (Oxford), 185–7.

Snell, B. (1938) *Leben und Meinungen der Sieben Weisen* (Munich).

Snodgrass, A. M. (1971) *The Dark Age of Greece: An Archaeological Survey of the 11th to the 8th Centuries BC* (Edinburgh).

Snodgrass, A. M. (1974) 'An historical Homeric society?', *Journal of Hellenic Studies* 94: 114–25.

Snodgrass, A. M. (1980) *Archaic Greece: The Age of Experiment* (Berkeley).

Snodgrass, A. M. (1987) *An Archaeology of Greece: The Present State and Future Scope of a Discipline* (Berkeley).

Snodgrass, A. M. (1993a) 'The rise of the *polis*: the archaeological evidence', in Hansen ed. 1993: 30–40.

Snodgrass, A. M. (1993b) 'The "hoplite reform" revisited', *Dialogues d'Histoire Ancienne* 19: 47–61.

Solmsen, F. (1949) *Hesiod and Aeschylus* (New York).

Sommerstein, A. H. (1982) *Aristophanes: The Clouds* (Warminster).

Sommerstein, A. H. (1989) *Aeschylus. Eumenides* (Cambridge).

Sourvinou-Inwood, C. (1989) 'Assumptions and the creation of meaning: reading Sophocles' *Antigone*', *Journal of Hellenic Studies* 109:134–48.

Sourvinou-Inwood, C. (1995) 'Male and female, public and private, ancient and modern', in Reeder, E. ed. *Pandora. Women in Classical Greece* (Baltimore), 111–20.

Spahn, P. (1980) 'Oikos und Polis. Beobachtungen zum Prozess der Polisbildung bei Hesiod, Solon und Aischylos', *Historische Zeitschrift* 231: 529–64.

Spahn, P. (1993) 'Individualisierung und politisches Bewusstsein im archaischen Griechenland', in Raaflaub and Müller-Luckner edd. 1993: 343–63.

Sprague, R. K. (1972) *The Older Sophists* (Columbia SC).

Springborg, P. (1990) 'The primacy of the political: Rahe and the myth of the *Polis*', *Political Studies* 38: 83–104.

Stadter, P. A. ed. (1973) *The Speeches in Thucydides: A Collection of Original Papers with a Bibliography* (Chapel Hill).

Stahl, H.-P. (1966) *Thukydides: Die Stellung des Menschen im geschichtlichen Prozess* (Munich).

Stahl, M. (1987) *Aristokraten und Tyrannen im archaischen Athen* (Stuttgart).

Stahl, M. (1992) 'Solon F 3D. Die Geburtsstunde des demokratischen Gedankens', *Gymnasium* 99: 385–408.

Stallybrass, P., and White, A. (1986) *The Politics and Poetics of Transgression* (London).

Starr, C. G. (1977) *The Economic and Social Growth of Early Greece 800–500 BC* (New York).

Starr, C. G. (1986) *Individual and Community: The Rise of the Polis, 800–500 BC* (New York).

Stein-Hölkeskamp, E. (1989) *Adelskultur und Polisgesellschaft* (Stuttgart).

Stein-Hölkeskamp, E. (1996) 'Tirannidi e ricerca dell'eunomia', in Settis ed. 1996: 653–79.

Steiner, G. (1984) *Antigones* (Oxford).

Steinmetz, P. ed. (1969) *Politeia und Res Publica* (Wiesbaden).

Strasburger, H. (1954) 'Der Einzelne und die Gemeinschaft im Denken der Griechen', *Historische Zeitschrift* 177: 227–48, repr. in Gschnitzer, F. ed. *Griechische Staatskunde* (Darmstadt, 1976), 97–122.

Strasburger, H. (1982a) *Studien zur Alten Geschichte*, vol. II (Hildesheim).

Strasburger, H. (1982b) 'Die Entdeckung der politischen Geschichte durch Thukydides', in Strasburger 1982a: 528–91 [= Herter 1968: 412–76].

Strasburger, H. (1982c) 'Herodot und das Perikleische Athen', in Strasburger 1982a: 592–626 [= Marg 1965: 574–608].
Strauss, L. (1963) *On Tyranny* (New York).
Striker, G. (1996) 'Methods of sophistry', in Striker, *Essays in Hellenistic Epistemology and Ethics* (Cambridge), 3–21.
Stroud, R. S. (1968) *Drakon's Law of Homicide* (Berkeley).
Swanson, J. A. (1992) *The Public and the Private in Aristotle's Political Philosophy* (Ithaca NY and London).
Szegedy-Maszak, A. (1978) 'Legends of the Greek lawgivers', *Greek, Roman, and Byzantine Studies* 19: 199–209.
Tatum, J. (1989) *Xenophon's Imperial Fiction: on 'The Education of Cyrus'* (Princeton).
Thom, M. (1995) *Republics, Nations and Tribes* (London and New York).
Thomas, R. (1989) *Oral Tradition and Written Record in Classical Athens* (Cambridge).
Thomas, R. (1992) *Literacy and Orality in Ancient Greece* (Cambridge).
Thommen, L. (1996) *Lakedaimonion politeia: Die Entstehung der spartanischen Verfassung*. Historia Einzelschrift 103 (Stuttgart).
Thucydides, *The Peloponnesian War*, trans. Warner, R. [Penguin Classics] (Harmondsworth 1972).
Tigerstedt, E. N. (1965–78) *The Legend of Sparta in Classical Antiquity*, 3 vols. (Stockholm).
Todd, S. C. *The Shape of Athenian Law* (Oxford).
Too, Y.-L. (1995) *The Rhetoric of Identity in Isocrates. Text, power, pedagogy* (Cambridge).
Triebel-Schubert, C. (1984) 'Der Begriff der Isonomie bei Alkmaion', *Klio* 66: 40–50.
Tully, J. ed. (1988) *Meaning and Context: Quentin Skinner and his critics* (Cambridge).
Tuplin, C. J. (1993) *The Failings of Empire: a reading of Xenophon Hellenica* (Stuttgart).
Turner, F. M. (1981) *The Greek Heritage in Victorian Britain* (New Haven).
Tyrrell, W. B. (1984) *Amazons: A Study in Athenian Mythmaking* (Baltimore).
Ulf, C. (1990) *Die homerische Gesellschaft*. Vestigia 43 (Munich).
Ulf, C. ed. (1996) *Wege zur Genese griechischer Identität: Die Bedeutung der früharchaischen Zeit* (Berlin).
Vermeule, E. (1964) *Greece in the Bronze Age* (Chicago).
Vernant, J.-P. (1965) *Mythe et pensée chez les Grecs*, vol. I (Paris).
Vernant, J.-P. (1974–80) *Myth and Society in Ancient Greece* (London).
Vernant, J.-P. (1982) *The Origins of Greek Thought* (Ithaca NY).
Vernant, J.-P. (1985) 'Espace et organisation politique en Grèce ancienne', in *Mythe et pensée chez les Grecs* (Paris, 3rd edn), 238–60.
Vernant, J.-P., ed. (1968) *Problèmes de la guerre en Grèce ancienne* (Paris).
Vernant, J.-P., and Vidal-Naquet, P. (1981) *Tragedy and Myth in Ancient Greece*, trans. Lloyd, J. (Brighton).
Vidal-Naquet, P. (1990) *La Démocratie Grecque vue d'ailleurs* (Paris).
Vlastos, G. (1946) 'Solonian justice', *Classical Philology* 41: 65–83, repr. in Vlastos 1995: 32–56.
Vlastos, G. (1947) 'Equality and justice in early Greek cosmologies', *Classical Philology* 42: 156–78, repr. in Vlastos 1995: 57–88.
Vlastos, G. (1953) '*Isonomia*', *American Journal of Philology* 74: 337–66, repr. in Vlastos 1995: 89–111.

Vlastos, G. (1964) '*Isonomia politikē*', in Mau and Schmidt edd. 1964: 1–35, repr. in Vlastos, *Platonic Studies* (Princeton 1981, 2nd edn), 164–203.

Vlastos, G. (1994) 'The historical Socrates and Athenian democracy', in Vlastos, *Socratic Studies* (Cambridge), 87–108.

Vlastos, G. (1995) *Studies in Greek Philosophy*, vol. I: *The Presocratics* (Princeton).

Voegelin, E. (1956) *Order and History*, vol. I: *Israel and Revelation* (Baton Rouge LA).

Voegelin, E. (1957) *Order and History*, vol. II: *The World of the Polis* (Baton Rouge LA).

Walbank, F. W. (1985) 'Speeches in Greek historians', in Walbank, *Selected Papers: Studies in Greek and Roman history and historiography* (Cambridge), 242–61.

Walcot, P. (1966) *Hesiod and the Near East* (Cardiff).

Walcot, P. (1978) *Envy and the Greeks* (Warminster).

Waldron, J. (1989) 'Political philosophy', in Urmson, J., and Ree, J. edd. *The Concise Encyclopaedia of Western Philosophy and Philosophers* (London).

Wallace, R. W. (1989) *The Areopagus Council to 307 BC* (Baltimore).

Wallace, R. W. (1997) 'Solonian democracy', in Morris and Raaflaub edd. 1997: 11–29.

Walser, G. (1984) *Hellas und Iran* (Darmstadt).

Walter, U. (1993) *An der Polis teilhaben: Bürgerstaat und Zugehörigkeit im Archaischen Griechenland*. Historia Einzelschrift 82 (Stuttgart).

Ward, W. A., and Joukowsky, M. S. edd. (1992) *The Crisis Years: The 12th Century BC from beyond the Danube to the Tigris* (Dubuque IA).

Weber-Schäfer P. (1976) *Einführung in die antike politische Theorie*, vol. I: *Die Frühzeit* (Darmstadt).

Wees, H. van (1992) *Status Warriors: War, Violence, and Society in Homer and History* (Amsterdam).

Wees, H. van (1994) 'The Homeric way of war: the *Iliad* and the hoplite phalanx', *Greece and Rome* 41: 1–18, 131–55.

Wees, H. van (1999) 'Tyrtaeus' Eunomia: nothing to do with the Great Rhetra', in Powell, A. and Hodkinson, S. edd. *Sparta: new perspectives* (London): 1–41.

Wehgartner, I. ed. (1992) *Euphronios und seine Zeit* (Berlin).

Weiler, I. (1996) 'Soziogenese und soziale Mobilität im archaischen Griechenland. Gedanken zur Begegnung mit den Völkern des Alten Orients', in Ulf ed. 1996: 211–39.

Welwei, K.-W. (1992) *Athen: vom neolithischen Siedlungsplatz zur archaischen Grosspolis* (Darmstadt).

West, M. L. (1966) *Hesiod, Theogony. Edited with Prolegomena and Commentary* (Oxford).

West, M. L. (1974) *Studies in Greek Elegy and Iambus* (Berlin).

West, M. L. (1978) *Hesiod, Works and Days. Edited with Prolegomena and Commentary* (Oxford).

West, M. L. (1989–92) *Iambi et elegi Graeci ante Alexandrum cantati*, 2 vols. (Oxford, 2nd edn).

West, M. L. (1995) 'The date of the *Iliad*', *Museum Helveticum* 52: 203–19.

West, M. L. (1997) *The East Face of Helicon: West Asiatic Elements in Greek Poetry and Myth* (Oxford).

Westbrook, R. (1988) 'The nature and origin of the XII Tables', *Zeitschrift für Rechtsgeschichte, röm. Abt.* 105: 74–121.

Westbrook, R. (1989) 'Cuneiform law codes and the origins of legislation', *Zeitschrift für Assyriologie und Vorderasiatische Archäologie* 79: 201–22.

Westbrook, R. (1992) 'The trial scene in the *Iliad*', *Harvard Studies in Classical Philology* 94: 53–76.

Westbrook, R. (1995) 'Social justice in the ancient Near East', in Irani and Silver edd. 1995: 149–63.

Westlake, H. D. (1968) *Individuals in Thucydides* (Cambridge).

Westlake, H. D. (1989) 'The subjectivity of Thucydides: his treatment of the Four Hundred at Athens', in Westlake, *Studies in Thucydides and Greek History* (Bristol), 181–200.

Whitley, J. M. (1991) *Style and Society in Dark Age Greece: the changing face of a pre-literate society 1100–700 BC* (Cambridge).

Whitlock-Blundell, M. (1989) *Helping Friends and Harming Enemies* (Cambridge).

Wiedemann, T. E. J. (1996) "ἐλάχιστον . . . ἐν τοῖς ἄρσεσι κλέος": Thucydides, women, and the limits of rational analysis', in McAuslan, I., and Walcot, P. edd., *Women in Antiquity*. Greece and Rome Studies 3 (Oxford), 83–90.

Wilcke, C. (1993) 'Politik im Spiegel der Literatur, Literatur als Mittel der Politik im älteren Babylonien', in Raaflaub and Müller-Luckner edd. 1993: 29–75.

Williams, B. (1993) *Shame and Necessity* (Berkeley).

Wilms, H. (1995) *Techne und Paideia bei Xenophon und Isokrates* (Stuttgart and Leipzig).

Wilson, J. A. (1946) 'Egypt', in Frankfort *et al.* 1946: 31–122.

Wilson, P. (1992) 'Demosthenes 21 (*Against Meidias*): democratic abuse', *Proceedings of the Cambridge Philological Society* 37: 164–95.

Wilson, P. (forthcoming) *The Athenian Institution of the Khoregia* (Cambridge).

Winnington-Ingram, R. (1980) *Sophocles: an Interpretation* (Cambridge).

Winton, R., and Garnsey, P. (1981) 'Political theory', in Finley, M. I. ed. *The Legacy of Greece* (Oxford).

Wolff, E. (1964) 'Das Weib des Masistes', *Hermes* 92: 51–8 [= Marg 1965: 668–78].

Wolin, S. (1960) *Politics and Vision* (Boston).

Woozley, A. D. (1979) *Law and Obedience: the Arguments of Plato's Crito* (London).

Worthington, I. (1991) 'Greek oratory, revision of speeches and the problem of historical reliability,' *Classica et Mediaevalia* 42: 55–74.

Worthington, I. ed. (1994) *Persuasion: Greek Rhetoric in Action* (London).

Yamauchi, E. M. (1980) 'Two reformers compared: Solon of Athens and Nehemiah of Jerusalem', in *The Bible World: Essays in Honor of C. H. Gordon*, 269–92 (New York).

Yunis, H. (1996) *Taming Democracy: Models of Political Rhetoric in Classical Athens* (Cornell).

Zeitlin, F. (1965) 'The motif of the corrupted sacrifice in Aeschylus' *Oresteia*', *Transactions of the American Philological Association* 96: 463–505.

Zeitlin, F. (1978) 'Dynamics of misogyny in the *Oresteia*', *Arethusa* 11: 149–84.

Zeitlin, F. (1989) 'Mysteries of identity and designs of the self in Euripides' *Ion*', *Proceedings of the Cambridge Philological Society* 35: 144–97.

Zerilli, L. (1991) 'Machiavelli's sisters: women and the "conversation" of political theory', *Political Theory* 19: 252–75.

Zhmud, L. (1997) *Wissenschaft, Philosophie und Religion im frühen Pythagoreismus* (Berlin).

Zuntz, G. (1955) *The Political Plays of Euripides* (Manchester).

2. Socrates, Plato and Aristotle (chapters 8–19)

AA.VV. (1983) *SUZETESIS: Studi sull' epicureismo greco e romano offerti a Marcello Gigante* (Naples).

Aalders, G. J. D. (1968) *Die Theorie der gemischten Verfassung im Altertum* (Amsterdam).

Aalders, G. J. D. (1972) 'Political thought and political programs in the Platonic *Epistles*', in *Pseudepigrapha* 1, *Entretiens sur l'Antiquité classique* 18, Fondation Hardt (Geneva), 145–87.

Aalders, G. J. D. (1975) *Political Thought in Hellenistic Times* (Amsterdam).

Adam, J. (1963) *The Republic of Plato*: 2 vols., edited with critical notes, commentary and appendices, by Rees, D. A. (Cambridge, 2nd edn).

Algra, K. A. (1996) 'Observations on Plato's Thrasymachus: the case for *pleonexia*', in Algra, K. A., Van der Horst, P. W., and Runia, D. T. edd. *Polyhistor: Studies in the History and Historiography of Ancient Philosophy* (Leiden), 41–60.

Annas, J. (1978) 'Plato and common morality', *Classical Quarterly* 28: 437–51.

Annas, J. (1981) *An Introduction to Plato's Republic* (Oxford).

Annas, J. (1993) *The Morality of Happiness* (New York).

Annas, J. (1995) 'Aristotelian political theory in the Hellenistic period', in Laks, A., and Schofield, M. edd. *Justice and Generosity: Studies in Hellenistic Social and Political Philosophy* (Cambridge), 74–94.

Annas, J. (1996) 'Aristotle on human nature and political virtue', *The Review of Metaphysics* 49: 731–53.

Annas, J., and Waterfield, R. (1995) *Plato: Statesman*, translation with introduction (Cambridge).

Arnhart, L. (1994) 'The Darwinian biology of Aristotle's political animals', *American Journal of Political Science* 38: 464–85.

Aubenque, P. (1963) *La Prudence chez Aristote* (Paris).

Bambrough, R. ed. (1967) *Plato, Popper and Politics* (Cambridge).

Barker, A. (1977) 'Why did Socrates refuse to escape?', *Phronesis* 22: 13–28.

Barker, E. (1918) *Greek Political Theory* (London).

Barker, E. (1946) *The Politics of Aristotle*, translation with introduction, notes and appendices (Oxford); revised with new introduction and notes by Stalley, R. F. (Oxford 1995).

Barnes, J. (1982) *Aristotle* (Oxford).

Barnes, J. (1990) 'Aristotle and political liberty', in Patzig ed. 1990: 250–63.

Barnes, J. (1991) 'The Hellenistic Platos', *Apeiron* 23: 115–28.

Barnes, J. ed. (1984) *The Complete Works of Aristotle: The Revised Oxford Translation*, 2 vols. (Princeton).

Barnes, J. ed. (1995) *The Cambridge Companion to Aristotle* (Cambridge).

Barnes, J., Schofield, M., and Sorabji, R. edd. (1977) *Articles on Aristotle*, vol.II: *Ethics and Politics* (London).

Beiner, R. (1983) *Political Judgement* (Chicago).

Berlin, I. (1958) *Two Concepts of Liberty* (Oxford); reprinted in his *Four Essays on Liberty* (Oxford 1969).

Beversluis, J. (1993) 'Vlastos' quest for the historical Socrates', *Ancient Philosophy* 13: 293–312.

Bloom, A. (1968) *The Republic of Plato*: translated with notes and interpretive essay (New York).

Bloom, A. (1977) 'Response to Hall', *Political Theory* 5: 315–30.
Bluestone, N. H. (1987) *Women and the Ideal Society: Plato's Republic and Modern Myths of Gender* (Oxford/Hamburg/New York).
Bobonich, C. (1991) 'Persuasion, freedom and compulsion in Plato's *Laws*', *Classical Quarterly* 41: 365–88.
Bobonich, C. (1994) 'Akrasia and agency in Plato's *Laws* and *Republic*', *Archiv für Geschichte der Philosophie* 76: 3–36.
Bobonich, C. (1995) 'The virtues of ordinary people in Plato's *Statesman*', in Rowe ed. 1995b: 313–29.
Bodéüs, R. (1981) *Le Philosophe et la cité* (Paris).
Bodéüs, R. (1991a) *Philosophie et politique chez Aristote* (Namur).
Bodéüs, R. (1991b) 'Law and the regime in Aristotle', in Lord and O'Connor edd. 1991: 234–48.
Bodéüs, R. (1993) *The Political Dimensions of Aristotle's Ethics* (New York).
Brandwood, L. (1969) 'Plato's seventh letter', *Revue de l'Organisation Internationale pour l'Etude des Langues anciennes par Ordinateur* 4: 1–25.
Brandwood, L. (1990) *The Chronology of Plato's Dialogues* (Cambridge).
Brisson, L. (1987) *Platon: Lettres*: Traduction inédite, introduction, notices et notes (Paris).
Brisson, L. (1994) *Le Même et l'autre dans la structure ontologique du Timée de Platon* (Sankt Augustin, 2nd edn).
Brisson, L. (1995) 'Interpretation du mythe du *Politique*', in Rowe 1995b: 349–63.
Brown, L. (1998) 'How totalitarian is Plato's *Republic?*', in Ostenfeld, E. ed. *Essays on Plato's Republic* (Aarhus).
Brunschwig, J. (1986) 'Platon: La République', in Chatelet, F., Duhamel, O. and Pisier, E. edd. *Dictionnaire des oeuvres politiques* (Paris), 638–52.
Brunt, P. A. (1993) *Studies in Greek History and Thought* (Oxford).
Burnet, J. (1900) *The Ethics of Aristotle* (London).
Burnyeat, M. (1990) *The Theaetetus of Plato*, with translation by Levett, M. J. (Indianapolis and Cambridge).
Burnyeat, M. F. (1992) 'Utopia and fantasy: the practicability of Plato's ideally just city', in Hopkins, J., and Savile, A. edd. *Psychoanalysis, Mind and Art: Perspectives on Richard Wollheim* (Oxford), 175–87.
Chappell, T. D. J. (1993) 'The virtues of Thrasymachus', *Phronesis* 38: 1–17.
Charles, D. (1990) 'Comments on M. Nussbaum', in Patzig ed. 1990: 187–201.
Cherniss, H. F. (1945) *The Riddle of the Early Academy* (Berkeley CA).
Cherniss, H. F. (1957) 'The relation of the *Timaeus* to Plato's later dialogues', *American Journal of Philology* 78: 225–66 (repr. in Allen, R.E. ed. *Studies in Plato's Metaphysics*, London 1965, 339–78).
Chroust, A. H. (1973) *Aristotle: New Light on his Life and some of his Lost Works*, 2 vols. (London).
Clay, D. (1988) 'Reading the *Republic*', in Griswold, C. L. ed. *Platonic Writings, Platonic Readings* (London/New York), 19–33.
Cohen, D. (1991) *Law, Sexuality, and Society: The Enforcement of Morals in Classical Athens* (Cambridge).
Cohen, D. (1993) 'Law, autonomy, and political community in Plato's *Laws*', *Classical Philology* 88: 301–18.

Cohen, D. (1995) *Law, Violence and Community in Classical Athens* (Cambridge).
Cohen, S. M. (1973) Commentary on J. M. E. Moravcsik, 'Plato's method of division', in Moravcsik ed., *Patterns in Plato's Thought* (Dordrecht), 181–91.
Cole, T. (1967) *Democritus and the Sources of Greek Anthropology* (Cleveland, OH).
Cooper, J. M. (1977) 'The psychology of justice in Plato', *American Philosophical Quarterly* 14: 151–7.
Cooper, J. M. (1990) 'Political animals and civic friendship', in Patzig ed. 1990: 220–41.
Cornford, F. M. (1932) *Before and After Socrates* (Cambridge).
Cornford, F. M. (1941) *The Republic of Plato*: translated with introduction and notes (Oxford).
Cornford, F. M. (1950 [1935]) 'Plato's commonwealth', in his *The Unwritten Philosophy* (Cambridge), 46–67.
Cudworth, R. (1996 (1731)) *Eternal and Immutable Morality*, ed. Hutton, S. (London).
De Strycker, E., and Slings, S. (1994) *Plato's Apology of Socrates* (Leiden).
Deane, P. (1973) 'Stylometrics do not exclude the seventh letter', *Mind* 82: 113–17.
Denyer, N. C. (1983) 'The origins of justice', in AA.VV. 1983: 133–52.
Depew, D. J. (1995) 'Humans and other political animals in Aristotle's *History of Animals*', *Phronesis* 40: 156–81.
Diès, A. (1935) *Platon. Oeuvres complètes*, 9.1: *Le politique*, translation with introduction (Paris).
Dillon, J. (1977) *The Middle Platonists* (London).
Dillon, J. (1995) 'The Neoplatonic exegesis of the *Statesman* myth', in Rowe 1995b: 364–74.
Dixsaut, M. (1995) 'Une politique vraiment conforme à la nature', in Rowe 1995b: 253–73.
Dodds, E. R. (1959) *Plato Gorgias*: a revised text with introduction and commentary (Oxford).
Dreizehnter, A. (1970) *Aristoteles Politik*: critical edition with introduction and indices (Munich).
Düring, I. (1957) *Aristotle in the Ancient Biographical Tradition* (Gothenburg).
Düring, I. (1961) *Aristotle's Protrepticus* (Gothenburg).
Düring, I. (1966) *Aristoteles* (Heidelberg).
Dusanič, S. (1978) 'The ὅρκιον τῶν οἰκιστήρων and fourth-century Cyrene', *Chiron* 8: 55–76.
Dusanič, S. (1990) 'The *Theages* and the liberation of Thebes in 379 BC', in Schachter, A. ed., *Essays in the Topography, History and Culture of Boiotia* (*Teiresias* Supplement 3: Montreal): 65–70.
Edelstein, L. (1966) *Plato's Seventh Letter* (Leiden).
Ehrenberg, V. (1938) *Alexander and the Greeks* (Oxford).
England, E. B. (1921) *The Laws of Plato*, text edited with introduction and notes, 2 vols. (Manchester).
Everson, S. (1996) *Aristotle: The Politics and The Constitution of Athens*, translation by Jowett, B., rev. Barnes, J. (1984): edited with an introduction (Cambridge, 2nd edn).
Everson, S. (1998) 'The incoherence of Thrasymachus', in *Oxford Studies in Ancient Philosophy* 16: 99–131.

Ferrari, G. R. F. (1989) 'Plato and poetry', in Kennedy, G. A. ed. *The Cambridge History of Literary Criticism*, vol. I: *Classical Criticism* (Cambridge), 92–148.

Finley, M. I. (1977) 'Aristotle and economic analysis', in Barnes, Schofield, and Sorabji edd. 1977: 140–58.

Finley, M. I. (1983) *Politics in the Ancient World* (Cambridge).

Fondation Hardt (1965) *La Politique d'Aristote*. Entretiens sur l'antiquité classique 11 (Vandoeuvres-Geneva).

Fortenbaugh, W. W. (1977) 'Aristotle on slaves and women', in Barnes, Schofield, and Sorabji edd. 1977: 135–9.

Fortenbaugh, W. W. (1991) 'Aristotle on prior and posterior, correct and mistaken constitutions', in Keyt and Miller edd. 1991: 226–37.

Fortenbaugh, W. W. (1993) 'Theophrastus on law, virtue, and the particular situation', in Rosen, R. M., and Farrell, J. edd., *Nomodeiktes. Greek Studies in Honor of Martin Ostwald* (Ann Arbor MI), 447–55.

Fortenbaugh, W. W., *et al.* edd. (1992) *Theophrastus of Eresus: Sources for his Life, Writings, Thought and Influence*, Part II (Leiden/New York).

Fritz, K. von, and Kapp, E. (1950) *Aristotle's Constitution of Athens and Related Texts* (New York).

Gadamer, H.-G. (1975) *Truth and Method* (New York).

Garnsey, P. (1996) *Ideas of Slavery from Aristotle to Augustine* (Cambridge).

Gauthier, R. A., and Jolif, J. Y. (1970) *Aristote: l'Ethique à Nicomaque* (Louvain).

Gill, C. (1979) 'Plato and politics: the *Critias* and the *Politicus*', *Phronesis* 24: 148–67.

Gotthelf, A. (1997) 'Understanding Aristotle's teleology', in Hassing, R. F. ed. *Final Causality in Nature and Human Affairs* (Washington DC).

Grote, G. (1865) *Plato and Other Companions of Socrates*, 3 vols. (London).

Grube, G. M. A. (1935). *Plato's Thought* (London).

Grube, G. M. A. (1992) *Plato: Republic*, translation revised by Reeve, C. D. C. (Indianapolis).

Gruen, E. S. (1993) 'The polis in the Hellenistic world', in Rosen, R. M., and Farrell, J. edd. *Nomodeiktes. Greek Studies in Honor of Martin Ostwald* (Ann Arbor MI), 339–54.

Gulley, N. (1972) 'The authenticity of the Platonic *Epistles*', in *Pseudepigrapha* I, *Entretiens sur l'Antiquité classique* 18, Fondation Hardt (Geneva), 103–43.

Guthrie, W. K. C. (1969) *A History of Greek Philosophy*, vol. III: *The Fifth-Century Enlightenment* (Cambridge).

Guthrie, W. K. C. (1975) *A History of Greek Philosophy*, vol. IV: *Plato, the Man and his Dialogues: Earlier Period* (Cambridge).

Guthrie, W. K. C. (1978) *A History of Greek Philosophy*, vol. V: *The Later Plato and the Academy* (Cambridge).

Guthrie, W. K. C. (1981). *A History of Greek Philosophy*, vol. VI: *Aristotle, An Encounter* (Cambridge).

Halliwell, S. (1993) *Plato: Republic* 5: with a translation and commentary (Warminster).

Hardie, W. F. R. (1980) *Aristotle's Ethical Theory* (Oxford, 2nd edn).

Harvey, F. D. (1965) 'Two kinds of equality', *Classica et Mediaevalia* 26: 101–46.

Hentschke, A. B. (1971) *Politik und Philosophie bei Plato und Aristoteles. Die Stellung der 'Nomoi' im platonischen Gesamtwerk und die politische Theorie des Aristoteles* (Frankfurt).

Heylbut, G. ed. (1889) *Heliodorus: In Ethica Nicomachea Paraphrasis* (Berlin).

Holmes, S. T. (1979) 'Aristippus in and out of Athens', *American Political Science Review* 73: 113–28.

Hutchinson, D. S. (1988) 'Doctrines of the mean and the debate concerning skills in fourth century medicine, rhetoric and ethics', *Apeiron* 21: 17–52.

Hyland, D. A. (1995) *Finitude and Transcendence in the Platonic Dialogues* (Albany NY).

Irwin, T. H. (1973) *Plato's Moral Theory* (Oxford).

Irwin, T. H. (1979) *Plato Gorgias:* translated with notes (Oxford).

Irwin, T. H. (1985) 'Moral science and political theory in Aristotle', in Cartledge, P. A., and Harvey, F. D. edd. *Crux: Essays Presented to G. E. M. de Ste Croix on his 75th birthday* (Exeter and London) [= *History of Political Thought* 6], 150–68.

Irwin, T. H. (1988) *Aristotle's First Principles* (Oxford).

Irwin, T. H. (1995) *Plato's Ethics* (Oxford).

Isnardi Parente, M. (1988) 'L'Accademia antica e la politica del primo Ellenismo', in Casertano, G. ed. *I filosofi e il potere nella societa e nella cultura antiche* (Naples), 89–117.

Jackson, H. (1879) *The Fifth Book of the Nicomachean Ethics of Aristotle* (Cambridge).

Jaeger, W. (1948) *Aristotle: Fundamentals of his Development*, trans. Robinson, R. (Oxford, 2nd edn).

Jouanna, J. (1978) 'Le médecin modele du legislateur dans les Lois de Platon', *Ktema* 3: 77–91.

Kahn, C. H. (1981) 'Did Plato write Socratic dialogues?', *Classical Quarterly* 31: 305–20 (repr. in Benson, H. H. ed. *Essays on the Philosophy of Socrates*, New York and Oxford 1992, 35–52).

Kahn, C. H. (1983) 'Drama and dialectic in Plato's *Gorgias*', *Oxford Studies in Ancient Philosophy* 1: 75–121.

Kahn, C. H. (1988) 'On the relative date of the *Gorgias* and the *Protagoras*', *Oxford Studies in Ancient Philosophy* 6: 69–102.

Kahn, C. H. (1990) 'The normative structure of Aristotle's "Politics"', in Patzig ed. 1990: 369–84.

Kahn, C. H. (1995) 'The place of the *Statesman* in Plato's later work', in Rowe 1995b: 49–60.

Kelsen, H. (1937) 'The philosophy of Aristotle and the Hellenic Macedonian policy', *Ethics* 48, 1–64; reprinted (in part) in Barnes, Schofield and Sorabji edd. (1977): 170–94.

Kennedy, G. A. (1994) *A New History of Classical Rhetoric* (Princeton).

Kerferd, G. B. (1981) *The Sophistic Movement* (Cambridge).

Keyt, D. (1988) 'Injustice and pleonexia in Aristotle: a reply to Charles Young', *The Southern Journal of Philosophy* 27, supp.: 251–7.

Keyt, D. (1991a) 'Aristotle's theory of distributive justice', in Keyt and Miller edd. 1991: 238–78.

Keyt, D. (1991b) Three basic theorems in Aristotle's *Politics*', in Keyt and Miller edd. (1991): 118–41 [revised version of 'Three fundamental theorems in Aristotle's *Politics*', *Phronesis* 32 (1987): 54–79].

Keyt, D. (1993) 'Aristotle and anarchism', *Reason Papers* 18: 133–52.

Keyt, D. (1999) *Aristotle: Politics, Books* V *and* VI: translated with a commentary (Oxford).

Keyt, D., and Miller, F. D. edd. (1991) *A Companion to Aristotle's Politics* (Oxford).
Kraut, R. (1973) 'Egoism, love and political office in Plato', *Philosophical Review* 82: 330–44.
Kraut, R. (1984) *Socrates and the State* (Princeton).
Kraut, R. (1989) *Aristotle on the Human Good* (Princeton).
Kraut, R. (1992) 'The defense of justice in Plato's *Republic*', in Kraut, R. ed. *The Cambridge Companion to Plato* (Cambridge), 311–37.
Kraut, R. (1997) *Aristotle: Politics, Books VII and VIII*: translated with a commentary (Oxford).
Kullman, W. (1991) 'Man as a political animal in Aristotle', in Keyt and Miller edd. 1991: 94–117.
Laks, A. (1990) 'Legislation and demiurgy: on the relationship between Plato's *Republic* and *Laws*', *Classical Antiquity* 9: 209–29.
Laks, A. (1991) 'L'utopie législative de Platon', *Revue philosophique*, 417–28.
Lane, M. S. (1995) 'A new angle on Utopia: the political theory of the *Statesman*', in Rowe 1995b: 276–91.
Lane, M. S. (1998) *Method and Politics in Plato's Statesman* (Cambridge).
Lear, J. (1992) 'Inside and outside the *Republic*', *Phronesis* 37: 184–215.
Ledger, G. R. (1989) *Re-counting Plato* (Oxford).
Leszl, W. (1989) 'La politica è una "techne"? E richiede un' "episteme"? Uno studio sull'epistemologia della "Politica" di Aristotele', in Berti, E., and Napolitano, M. edd. *Etica, Politica, Retorica. Studi su Aristotele e la sua presenza nell'età moderna*, (L'Aquila), 75–134.
Lévy, E. (1993) '*Politeia* et *politeuma* chez Aristote', in Piérart, M. ed. *Aristote et Athènes* (Paris), 65–90.
Leyden, W. von (1985) *Aristotle on Equality and Justice: his Political Argument* (London).
Lindsay, A. D. (1935) *Plato: The Republic*, trans. (London); new edn by Irwin, T. (1993).
Litzinger, C. I.(1964). *Thomas Aquinas: Commentary on the Nicomachean Ethics*, 2 vols., trans. (Chicago).
Lloyd, G. E. R. (1968) *Aristotle, the Growth and Structure of his Thought* (Cambridge).
Lloyd, G. E. R. (1990) 'Plato and Archytas in the Seventh Letter', *Phronesis* 35: 159–74.
Loraux, N. (1986) *The Invention of Athens: the Funeral Oration in the Classical City* (Cambridge MA).
Lord, C., and O'Connor, D. K. edd. (1991) *Essays on the Foundations of Aristotelian Political Science* (Berkeley/Los Angeles/Oxford).
Lovejoy, A. O., and Boas, G. (1935) *Primitivism and Related Ideas in Antiquity* (Baltimore).
Lovibond, S. (1994) 'An ancient theory of gender: Plato and the Pythagorean table', in Archer, L. J., Fischler, S., and Wyke, M. edd. *Women in Ancient Societies* (London), 88–101.
MacIntyre, A. (1988) *Whose Justice? Which Rationality?* (London).
McCabe, M. M. (1994) *Plato's Individuals* (Princeton).
McKenzie, M. M. (1981) *Plato on Punishment* (London).
McKim, R. (1988) 'Shame and truth in Plato's *Gorgias*', in Griswold, C. L. ed. *Platonic Writings, Platonic Readings* (London and New York), 34–48.
Meier, C. (1990) *The Greek Discovery of Politics* (Cambridge MA).
Meikle, S. (1995) *Aristotle's Economic Thought* (Oxford).

Mill, J. S. (1972), *Collected Works*, vol. xvi: *The Later Letters of J. S. Mill*, 1849–1873, vol. iii (Toronto and London).

Mill, J. S. (1978), *Collected Works*, vol. xi: *Essays on Philosophy and the Classics*, intr. by F. Sparshott (Toronto and London).

Miller, F. D., Jr (1991) 'Aristotle on natural law and justice', in Keyt and Miller edd. 1991: 279–306.

Miller, F. D., Jr (1995) *Nature, Justice, and Rights in Aristotle's Politics* (Oxford).

Miller, M. H., Jr (1980) *The Philosopher in Plato's Statesman* (The Hague).

Moraux, P. (1957) *A la recherche de l'Aristote perdu: le dialogue 'Sur la justice'* (Louvain).

Moraux, P. (1973) *Der Aristotelismus bei den Griechen*, vol. i (Berlin and New York).

Moreau, J. (1962) *Aristote et son école* (Paris).

Morrow, G. R. (1960) *Plato's Cretan City. A Historical Interpretation of the Laws* (Princeton; 2nd edn 1993).

Morrow, G. R. (1962) *Plato's Epistles* (Indianapolis).

Mulgan, R. G. (1977) *Aristotle's Political Theory: An Introduction for Students of Political Theory* (Oxford).

Müller, G. (1951) *Studien zu den platonischen Nomoi* (Munich).

Mulvany, C. M. (1926) 'Notes on the legend of Aristotle', *Classical Quarterly* 20: 155–67.

Nettleship, R. L. (1914) *Lectures on the Republic of Plato* (London).

Newell, W. R. (1991) 'Superlative virtue: the problem of monarchy in Aristotle's *Politics*', in Lord and O'Connor edd. 1991: 191–211.

Newman, W. L. (1887–1902) *The Politics of Aristotle*: with an introduction, two prefatory essays, and notes critical and explanatory, 4 vols. (Oxford).

Nichols, M. P. (1992) *Citizens and Statesmen: A Study of Aristotle's Politics* (Lanham MD).

North, H. (1966) *Sophrosyne: Self-Knowledge and Self-Restraint in Greek Literature* (Ithaca NY).

Nussbaum, M. C. (1990) 'Nature, function, and capability: Aristotle on political distribution', in Patzig ed. 1990: 152–86.

O'Brien, M. J. (1967) *The Socratic Paradoxes and the Greek Mind* (Chapel Hill NC).

Ober, J. (1991) 'Aristotle's political sociology: class, status, and order in the *Politics*', in Lord and O'Connor edd. 1991: 112–35.

Ober, J. (1993) 'Thucydides' criticism of democratic knowledge', in Rosen, R. M. and Farrell, J. edd. *Nomodeiktes: Greek Studies in Honor of Martin Ostwald* (Ann Arbor MI), 81–98.

Ober, J. (1998) *Political Dissent in Democratic Athens: Intellectual Critics of Popular Rule* (Princeton).

Okin, S. M. (1979) *Women in Western Political Thought* (Princeton).

Owen, G. E. L. (1953a) 'The Place of the *Timaeus* in Plato's Dialogues', *Classical Quarterly* 3: 79–95 (repr. in Allen, R. E., ed. *Studies in Plato's Metaphysics*, London 1965, 313–38).

Owen, G. E. L. (1953b) Review of Skemp 1952, *Mind* 62: 271–3.

Owen, G. E. L. (1965) 'The Platonism of Aristotle', *Proceedings of the British Academy* 50: 125–50; reprinted in Owen, *Logic, Science and Dialectic* (London 1986), 200–20.

Owen, G. E. L. (1973) 'Plato on the undepictable', in Lee, E. N. *et al.* edd. *Exegesis and Argument: Studies in Greek Philosophy Presented to Gregory Vlastos, Phronesis* Suppl. Vol. i: Assen, 349–61; reprinted in Owen, *Logic, Science and Dialectic* (London 1986), 138–47.

Owen, G. E. L. (1983) 'Philosophical invective', *Oxford Studies in Ancient Philosophy* I: 1–25; reprinted in Owen, *Logic, Science and Dialectic* (London 1986), 347–64.

Pangle, T. L. (1987) *The Roots of Political Philosophy. Ten Forgotten Socratic Dialogues* (Ithaca NY).

Parry, R. D. (1996) *Plato's Craft of Justice* (Albany NY).

Patzig, G. ed. (1990) *Aristoteles' 'Politik': Akten des XI. Symposium Aristotelicum* (Göttingen).

Pellegrin, P. (1993) *Aristote: Les Politiques*: traduction inédite, introduction, bibliographie, notes et index (Paris).

Penner, T. (1973) 'Socrates on virtue and motivation', in Lee, E. N. *et al.* edd. *Exegesis and Argument: Studies in Greek Philosophy Presented to Gregory Vlastos*, *Phronesis* Suppl. Vol. I: 133–51.

Penner, T. (1988) 'Socrates on the impossibility of belief-relative sciences', *Proceedings of the Boston Area Colloquium in Ancient Philosophy*, Vol. III (Lanham MD), 263-325.

Penner, T. (1990) 'Plato and Davidson: parts of the soul and weakness of will', in Copp, D. ed. *Canadian Philosophers*, Suppl. Vol. XVI, *Canadian Journal of Philosophy*, 35–74.

Penner, T. (1991) 'Desire and power in Socrates: the argument of *Gorgias* 466a–468e that orators and tyrants have no power in the city', *Apeiron* 24: 147–202.

Penner, T. (1992) 'Socrates and the early dialogues', in Kraut, R. ed. *The Cambridge Companion to Plato* (Cambridge), 121–69.

Penner, T. (1996) 'Knowledge vs true belief in the Socratic psychology of action', *Apeiron* 29: 199–230.

Penner, T. (1997a) 'Socrates on the strength of knowledge: *Protagoras* 351B–357E', *Archiv für Geschichte der Philosophie* 79: 117–49.

Penner, T. (1997b) 'Two Notes on the *Crito*: the impotence of the many, and "Persuade or obey"', *Classical Quarterly*, 47: 133–46.

Penner, T., and Rowe, C. J. (1994) 'The desire for good: is the *Meno* consistent with the *Gorgias*?', *Phronesis* 39: 1–25.

Podlecki, A. J. (1985) 'Theophrastus on history and politics', in Fortenbaugh, W.W. ed. *Theophrastus of Eresus: On his Life and Work*, vol. II (New Brunswick and Oxford), 231–49.

Polansky, R. (1991) 'Aristotle on political change', in Keyt and Miller edd. 1991: 323–45.

Popper, K. R. (1962) *The Open Society and its Enemies*, 2 vols. (London, 4th rev. edn).

Price, A. W. (1995) *Mental Conflict* (London).

Rawls, J. (1971) *A Theory of Justice* (Cambridge MA).

Reeve, C. D. C. (1988) *Philosopher-Kings* (Princeton).

Renehan, R. F. (1970) 'The Platonism of Lycurgus', *Greek, Roman and Byzantine Studies* 11: 219–31.

Rhodes, P. J. (1981) *A Commentary on the Aristotelian Athenaion Politeia* (Oxford).

Riginos, A. S. (1976) *Platonica: the Anecdotes concerning the Life and Writings of Plato* (Leiden).

Ritchie, D. G. (1894) 'Aristotle's subdivisions of "particular justice"', *Classical Review* 8: 185–92.

Roberts, J. (1989) 'Political animals in the *Nicomachean Ethics*', *Phronesis* 32: 185–204.

Robinson, R. (1962) *Aristotle: Politics, Books III and IV*: translated with introduction and comments, with supplementary essay (1995) by Keyt, D. (Oxford).

Robinson, T. M. (1995) *Plato's Psychology* (Toronto, 2nd edn).

Rorty, A. O. ed. (1980) *Essays on Aristotle's Ethics* (Berkeley).

Ross, W. D. (1931) *The Right and the Good* (Oxford).

Ross, W. D. (1957a) *Aristotelis Politica*: critical edition, Oxford Classical Texts series (Oxford).

Ross, W. D. (1957b) 'The development of Aristotle's thought', *Proceedings of the British Academy* 43: 63–78.

Ross, W. D. (1995 [1923]) *Aristotle*, with introduction and new material by J. L. Ackrill (London, 6th edn).

Rowe, C. J. (1977 [1991]) 'Aims and methods in Aristotle's Politics', *Classical Quarterly* 27 (1977): 159–72; reprinted in slightly revised form in Keyt and Miller edd. 1991: 57–74.

Rowe, C. J. (1984) *Plato* (Brighton).

Rowe, C. J. (1989) 'Reality and utopia', *Elenchos* 10: 317–36.

Rowe, C. J. (1990) 'The good for man in Aristotle's *Ethics* and *Politics*', in Alberti, A. ed. *Studi sull'etica di Aristotele* (Rome), 193–225.

Rowe, C. J. (1995a) *Plato: Statesman* (Warminster).

Rowe, C. J. ed. (1995b) *Reading the Statesman: Proceedings of the Third Symposium Platonicum* (Sankt Augustin).

Rowe, C. J. (1996) 'The *Politicus*: structure and form', in Gill, C., and McCabe, M. M. edd. *Form and Argument in Late Plato* (Oxford), 153–78.

Sachs, D. (1963) 'A fallacy in Plato's *Republic*', *Philosophical Review* 72: 141–58.

Ste. Croix, G. E. M. de (1981) *The Class Struggle in the Ancient Greek World* (London).

Sandbach, F. H. (1985) *Aristotle and the Stoics* (Cambridge Philological Society Supplementary Volume 10).

Santas, G. (1979) *Socrates* (London).

Saunders, T. J. (1968) 'The Socratic paradoxes in Plato's *Laws*: a commentary on 859c–864b', *Hermes* 96: 421–34.

Saunders, T. J. (1970) *Plato, the Laws*, Penguin translation (Harmondsworth).

Saunders, T. J. (1986) '"The RAND Corporation of antiquity?" Plato's Academy and Greek politics', in Betts, J. H., Hooker, J. T., and Green, J. R. edd. *Studies in Honour of T.B.L. Webster*, Vol. 1 (Bristol), 200–10.

Saunders, T. J. (1991) *Plato's Penal Code* (Oxford).

Saunders, T. J. (1995a) 'Plato on women in the *Laws*', in Powell, A. ed. *The Greek World* (London).

Saunders, T. J. (1995b) *Aristotle: Politics, Books I and II*: translated with a commentary (Oxford).

Saxonhouse, A. (1982) 'Family, polity, and unity: Aristotle on Socrates' community of wives', *Polity* 15: 202–19.

Schaerer, R. (1930) *Epistēmē et technē: études sur les notions de connaissance et d'art d'Homère à Platon* (Macon).

Schofield, M. (1991) *The Stoic Idea of the City* (Cambridge; repr. Chicago 1999).

Schofield, M. (1993) 'Plato on the economy', in Hansen, M. H. ed. *The Ancient Greek City-State* (Copenhagen), 183–96.

Schofield, M. (1999) *Saving the City* (London).

Schöpsdau, K. (1986) 'Tapferkeit, Aidos und Sophrosune im ersten Buch der platonischen Nomoi', *Rheinisches Museum* 129: 97–123.

Schöpsdau, K. (1994) *Platon. Nomoi (Gesetze)*, Buch I–III (Göttingen).

Schuhl, P.-M. (1946) 'Platon et l'activité politique de l'Académie', *Revue des études grecques* 59: 46–53.

Schütrumpf, E. (1991, 1996) *Aristoteles: Politik*: Buch I (Teil 1, 1991); Bücher II und III (Teil 2, 1991); Bücher IV–VI (Teil 3, 1996), trans. and commentary (Darmstadt).

Shorey, P. (1930) *Plato Republic*: with an English Translation, 2 vols. (London and Cambridge MA).

Sinclair, T. A. (1981 [1962]) *Aristotle: The Politics*. Translation revised by Saunders, T. J. (Harmondsworth).

Skemp, J. B. (1952) *Plato: The Statesman*, translation with introduction (London).

Skemp, J. B. (1980) 'How political is Plato's *Republic?*', *History of Political Thought* 1: 1–7.

Skinner, Q. (1978) *The Foundations of Modern Political Thought*, 2 vols. (Cambridge).

Slings, S. R. (1981) *A Commentary on the Platonic Clitophon* (Amsterdam).

Smith, N. D. (1983) 'Plato and Aristotle on the nature of women', *Journal of the History of Philosophy* 21: 467–78.

Smith, N. D. (1991) 'Aristotle's theory of natural slavery', in Keyt and Miller edd. 1991: 142–55.

Solmsen, F. (1969) Review of Edelstein 1966, *Gnomon* 41: 29–34.

Solmsen, F. (1981) 'The Academic and the Alexandrian editions of Plato's works', *Illinois Classical Studies* 61: 102–11.

Sorabji, R. (1990) 'Comments on J. Barnes: state power: Aristotle and fourth century philosophy', in Patzig ed. 1990: 265–76.

Spiazzi, R. M. ed. (1951) *Sancti Thomae Aquinatis: In octo libros Politicorum Expositio* (Turin).

Spiazzi, R. M. ed. (1964) *Sancti Thomae Aquinatis: In Decem Libros Ethicorum Aristotelis ad Nicomachum Expositio* (Turin, 3rd edn).

Stalley, R. F. (1983) *An Introduction to Plato's Laws* (Oxford).

Stalley, R. F. (1994) 'Persuasion in Plato's *Laws*', *History of Political Thought* 15: 157–77.

Stern, S. M. (1968) *Aristotle on the World-State* (Oxford).

Strauss, B. S. (1991) 'On Aristotle's critique of Athenian democracy', in Lord and O'Connor edd. 1991: 212–33.

Strauss, L. (1964) *The City and Man* (Chicago and London).

Striker, G. (1987) 'Origins of the concept of natural law', in *Proceedings of the Boston Area Colloquium in Ancient Philosophy*, vol. II, ed. Cleary, J. J. (Lanham MD), 79–94.

Susemihl, F., and Hicks, R. D. (1894) *The Politics of Aristotle* (London).

Szegedy-Maszak, A. (1981) *The Nomoi of Theophrastus* (New York).

Taifacos, I. G. (1979) 'Il De republica di Cicerone e il modello Dicaearcheo della costituzione mista', *Platon* 31: 128–34.

Tarán, L. (1975) *Academica: Plato, Philip of Opus, and the pseudo-Platonic Epinomis* (Philadelphia).

Tarrant, H. (1983) 'Middle Platonism and the *Seventh Epistle*', *Phronesis* 28: 75–103.

Tarrant, H. (1993) *Thrasyllan Platonism* (Ithaca NY).
Taylor, C. C. W. (1986) 'Plato's totalitarianism', *Polis* 5.2: 4–29.
Taylor, C. C. W. (1995) 'Politics', in Barnes ed. 1995: 233–58.
Tod, M. N. (1948) *A Selection of Greek Historical Inscriptions*, vol. II: *from 403–323 BC* (Oxford).
Turner, F. M. (1981) *The Greek Heritage in Victorian Britain* (New Haven and London).
Vander Waerdt, P. (1985) 'Kingship and philosophy in Aristotle's best regime', *Phronesis* 30: 249–73.
Vegetti, M. (1994) *La Repubblica Libro I*: Traduzione e commento a cura di M.V. (Pavia).
Vegetti, M. (1995) *La Repubblica: Libri II-III*: Traduzione e commento a cura di M.V. (Pavia).
Vickers, B. (1988) *In Defence of Rhetoric* (Oxford).
Vlastos, G. (1954) 'The Third Man argument in the *Parmenides*,' *Philosophical Review* 63: 319–49 (repr. in Allen, R. E., ed. *Studies in Plato's Metaphysics*, London 1965, 231–64).
Vlastos, G. (1958) 'The paradox of Socrates', *Queen's Quarterly*:46: 496–516; reprinted in Vlastos 1971b: 1–21.
Vlastos, G. (1964) *'Isonomia politikē'*, in Mau, J., and Schmidt, E. G. edd. *Isonomia: Studien zur Gleichheitsvorstellung im griechischen Denken* (Berlin), 1–35; reprinted in Vlastos 1973: 164–203.
Vlastos, G. (1971a) 'Justice and happiness in the *Republic*', in Vlastos, G. ed. *Plato* vol. II (Garden City NJ), 66–95; reprinted in Vlastos 1973: 111–39.
Vlastos, G. (1973) *Platonic Studies* (Princeton).
Vlastos, G. (1973–4) 'Socrates on political obedience and disobedience', *The Yale Review* 63: 517–34.
Vlastos, G. (1977) 'The theory of social justice in the *Polis* in Plato's *Republic*', in North, H. ed. *Interpretations of Plato* (Leiden), 1–40; reprinted in Vlastos 1995: II.69–103.
Vlastos, G. (1978) 'The rights of persons in Plato's conception of the foundation of justice', in Englehardt, H. T., and Callahan, D. edd. *Morals, Science and Society* (Hastings-on-Hudson), 172–201; reprinted in Vlastos 1995: II.104–25.
Vlastos, G. (1988) 'Socrates', *Proceedings of the British Academy* 74: 89–111.
Vlastos, G. (1989) 'Was Plato a feminist?', *Times Literary Supplement*, 17 March 1989: 276, 288–9; reprinted in Vlastos 1995: II.133–43.
Vlastos, G. (1991) *Socrates: Ironist and Moral Philosopher* (Cambridge).
Vlastos, G. (1994) *Socratic Studies*, ed. M. Burnyeat (Cambridge).
Vlastos, G. (1995) *Studies in Greek Philosophy*, 2 vols., ed. Graham, D.W. (Princeton).
Vlastos, G. ed. (1971b) *Socrates* (New York).
Vlastos, G. ed. (1971c) *Plato: a collection of critical essays*, I: *Metaphysics and Epistemology* (Garden City NY).
Wardy, R. B. B. (1996) *The Birth of Rhetoric* (London).
Wheeler, M. (1951) 'Aristotle's analysis of the nature of political struggle', *American Journal of Philology* 72: 145–61; reprinted in Barnes, Schofield, and Sorabji edd. 1977: 159–69.
White, N. P. (1979) *A Companion to Plato's Republic* (Indianapolis).
White, N. P. (1986) 'The rulers' choice', *Archiv für Geschichte der Philosophie* 68: 22–46.
Wiggins, D. R. P. (1980) 'Deliberation and practical reason', in Rorty ed. 1980: 221–40.
Williams, B. (1980) 'Justice as a virtue', in Rorty ed. 1980: 189–99.

Wish, H. (1949) 'Aristotle, Plato, and the Mason-Dixon Line', *Journal of the History of Ideas* 10: 254–66.

Wood, E. M., and Wood, N. (1978) *Class Ideology and Ancient Political Theory* (Oxford).

Woozley, A. (1971) 'Socrates on disobeying the law', in Vlastos ed. 1971b: 299–318.

Wormell, D. E. W. (1935) 'The literary tradition concerning Hermias of Atarneus', *Yale Classical Studies* 5: 57–92.

Young, C. (1988) 'Aristotle on justice', *The Southern Journal of Philosophy* 27, supp.: 233–49.

Young, G. (1973) 'Socrates and obedience', *Phronesis* 18: 1–29.

Yunis, H. (1996) *Taming Democracy: Models of Political Rhetoric in Classical Athens* (Ithaca NY).

II. The Hellenistic and Roman Worlds

(Chapters 20–31 and Epilogue)

AA.VV. (1983) *SUZETESIS: Studi sull' epicureismo greco e romano offerti a Marcello Gigante* (Naples).

Aalders, G. J. D. (1968) *Die Theorie der gemischten Verfassung im Altertum* (Amsterdam).

Aalders, G. J. D. (1975) *Political thought in Hellenistic Times* (Amsterdam).

Aalders, G. J. D. (1977) 'Political thought in Plutarch's "Convivium Septem Sapientium"', *Mnemosyne* 30: 28–39.

Aalders, G. J. D. (1982a) *Plutarch's Political Thought* (Amsterdam, Oxford and New York).

Aalders, G. J. D. (1982b) 'Plutarch or pseudo-Plutarch? The authorship of *De unius in re publica dominatione*', *Mnemosyne* 35: 72–83.

Aalders, G. J. D. (1992) 'Plutarch und die politische Philosophie der Griechen', in *Aufstieg und Niedergang der römischen Welt*, Band 36.5 (Berlin and New York), 3384–404.

Adam, T. (1970) *Clementia Principis* (Stuttgart).

Alberti, A. (1995) 'The Epicurean theory of law and justice', in Laks and Schofield edd. 1995: 161–90.

Amir, Y. (1985–8) '*Theokratia* as a concept of political philosophy: Josephus' presentation of Moses' *Politeia*', *Scripta Classica Israelica* 8–9: 83–105.

Annas, J. E. (1989) 'Cicero on Stoic moral philosophy and private property', in Griffin and Barnes edd. 1989: 151–73.

Annas, J. E. (1993) *The Morality of Happiness* (New York and Oxford).

Annas, J. E. (1995) 'Aristotelian political theory', in Laks and Schofield edd. 1995: 74–94.

Arico Anselmo, G. (1983) '*Ius publicum – ius privatum* in Ulpiano, Gaio e Cicerone', *Annali Palermo* 37: 445–787.

Armstrong, A.H. ed. (1967) *The Cambridge History of Later Greek and Early Medieval Philosophy* (Cambridge).

Arnim, H. von (1898) *Dio von Prusa* (Berlin).

Arquillière, H. X. (1934) *L'Augustinisme politique* (Paris).

Arrighetti. G. (1973) *Epicuro: Opere*. Biblioteca di cultura filosofica 41 (Turin, 2nd edn).

Asmis, E. (1989) 'The Stoicism of Marcus Aurelius', *Aufsteig und Neidergang der römischen Welt*, Band 36.3 (Berlin and New York), 2228–52.

Astin, A. E. (1967) *Scipio Aemilianus* (Oxford).

Athanassiadi-Fowden, P. (1981) *Julian and Hellenism* (Oxford); repr. 1992 as *Julian: An Intellectual Biography* (London).

Atkins, E. M. (1989) 'The virtues of Cicero's *De Officiis*' (unpublished Cambridge Ph.D. thesis).

Atkins, E. M. (1990) '"Domina et regina virtutum": justice and *societas* in *De Officiis*', *Phronesis* 35: 258–89.

Atkins, E. M., and Griffin M. T. (1991) *Cicero: On Duties* (Cambridge).

Attridge, H. W. (1976) *The Interpretation of Biblical History in the Antiquitates Judaicae of Flavius Josephus* (Missoula, Montana).

Badian, E. (1958) 'Alexander the Great and the unity of mankind', *Historia* 7: 425–44.

Bailey, C. (1947) *T. Lucreti Cari De Rerum Natura: Libri Sex*, edition with translation and commentary, 3 vols. (Oxford).

Baldry, H. C. (1959) 'Zeno's ideal state', *Journal of Hellenic Studies* 79: 3–15.

Baldry, H. C. (1965) *The Unity of Mankind in Greek Thought* (Cambridge).

Balsdon, J. P. V. D. (1960) '*Auctoritas*, *dignitas*, *otium*', *Classical Quarterly* 10: 43–50.

Barigazzi, A. (1981) 'Note critiche ed esegetiche agli scritti politici di Plutarco', *Prometheus* 7: 193–214.

Barigazzi, A. (1982) 'Note critiche ed esegetiche agli scritti politici di Plutarco II', *Prometheus* 8: 61–79.

Barigazzi, A. (1983) 'Sul concetto epicureo della sicurezza esterna', in AA.VV. (1983): 73–92.

Barigazzi, A. (1984) 'Note critiche ed esegetiche agli scritti politici di Plutarco III–IV', *Prometheus* 10: 37–64; 161–85.

Barnes, J. (1986) 'Cicéron et la guerre juste', *Bulletin de la Société Française de Philosophie* 80: 37–80.

Barnes, T. D. (1981) *Constantine and Eusebius* (Cambridge MA and London).

Barraclough, R. (1984) 'Philo's Politics. Roman rule and Hellenistic judaism', in *Aufstieg und Niedergang der römischen Welt*, Band 21.1 (Berlin and New York), 417–553.

Barrow, R. H. (1950) *Introduction to St Augustine: the City of God* (London).

Barton, T. (1994) 'The *inventio* of Nero: Suetonius', in Elsner, J., and Masters, J. edd. *Reflections of Nero* (London).

Bauckham, R. (1990) *Jude and the Relatives of Jesus* (Edinburgh).

Bauckham, R.(1993a) *The Climax of Prophecy. Studies on the Book of Revelation* (Edinburgh).

Bauckham, R. (1993b) *The Theology of Revelation* (Cambridge).

Baynes, N. H. (1934) 'Eusebius and the Christian Empire', in *Mélanges Bidez. Annuaire de l'Institut de Philologie et d'Histoire Orientales et Slaves 2* (Brussels), 13–18; reprinted in his *Byzantine Studies* (London 1955), 168–172.

Baynes, N. H. (1962) *The Political Ideas of St Augustine* (London).

Behrends, O. (1977) 'Les 'veteres' et la nouvelle jurisprudence à la fin de la République', *Revue historique de droit français et étranger* 55: 7–33.

Bettenson, H. (1984) *Augustine: Concerning the City of God against the Pagans*, (Harmondsworth, 2nd edn).

Bickerman, E. J. (1988) *The Jews in the Greek Age* (Cambridge MA and London).

Billerbeck, M. (1978) *Epiktet: Vom Kynismus* (Leiden).

Billerbeck, M. (1979) *Der Kyniker Demetrius* (Leiden).

Billerbeck, M. ed. (1991) *Die Kyniker in der modernen Forschung* (Amsterdam).
Billows, R. A. (1990) *Antigonos the One-Eyed and the Creation of the Hellenistic State*. Hellenistic Culture and Society 4 (Berkeley).
Birley, A. (1987) *Marcus Aurelius: A Biography* (London, 2nd edn).
Blundell, M. W. (1990) 'Parental nature and Stoic *oikeiōsis*', *Ancient Philosophy* 10: 221–42.
Bobzien, S. (1997) 'Stoic conceptions of freedom and their relation to ethics', in Sorabji, R. ed. *Aristotle and After*. Bulletin of the Institute of Classical Studies, Supplement 68 (London), 71–89.
Bollack, J. (1969) 'Les maximes de l'amitié', *Association Guillaume Budé*, Actes du VIIIe Congres (Paris), 221–36.
Bonhöffer, A. (1890) *Epiktet und die Stoa* (Stuttgart, repr. 1968).
Bonhöffer, A. (1894) *Die Ethik des Stoikers Epiktet* (Stuttgart, repr. 1968).
Bosworth, B. (1996) *Alexander and the East: The Tragedy of Triumph* (Oxford).
Bouffartigue, J. (1992) *L'Empereur Julien et la culture de son temps* (Paris).
Bowersock, G. W. (1969) *Greek Sophists in the Roman Empire* (Oxford).
Bowersock, G. W. (1978) *Julian the Apostate* (London).
Boyancé, P. (1936) 'Les méthodes de l'histoire littéraire, Cicéron et son oeuvre philosophique', *Revue des Etudes Latines* 14: 288–309.
Bradbury, S. A. (1987) 'The date of Julian's *Letter to Themistius*', *Greek, Roman, and Byzantine Studies* 28: 235–51.
Bradley, K. R. (1986) 'Seneca and slavery', *Classica et Mediaevalia* 37: 161–72.
Bradley, K. R. (1994) *Slavery and Society at Rome* (Cambridge).
Brandon, S. G. F. (1967) *Jesus and the Zealots* (Manchester).
Brandon, S. G. F. (1968) *The Trial of Jesus of Nazareth* (London).
Branham, R. B. (1993) 'Diogenes' rhetoric and the invention of Cynicism', in Goulet-Cazé and Goulet edd. 1993.
Branham, R. B., and Goulet-Cazé, M.-O. edd. (1996) *The Cynics: the Cynic Movement in Antiquity and its Legacy for Europe* (Berkeley).
Brauch, T. (1993) 'Themistius and the Emperor Julian', *Byzantion* 63: 79–115.
Bréguet, E. (1980) *Cicéron: la république*, 2 vols. (Paris).
Bringmann, K. (1971) *Untersuchungen zum späten Cicero* (Göttingen).
Brink, C. O., and Walbank, F. W. (1954) 'The construction of the sixth book of Polybius', *Classical Quarterly* 4: 97–122.
Brown, P. (1967) *Augustine of Hippo* (London).
Browning, R. (1975) *The Emperor Julian* (London).
Brunt, P. A. (1965) '"Amicitia" in the late Roman republic', *Proceedings of the Cambridge Philological Society* 11: 1–20; revised as chapter 7 of Brunt 1988.
Brunt, P. A. (1971) *Italian Manpower 225 BC–AD 14* (Oxford).
Brunt, P. A. (1973) 'Aspects of the social thought of Dio Chrysostom and of the Stoics', *Proceedings of the Cambridge Philological Society* 19: 9–34.
Brunt, P. A. (1974) 'Marcus Aurelius in his *Meditations*', *Journal of Roman Studies* 64: 1–20.
Brunt, P. A. (1975) 'Stoicism and the Principate', *Papers of the British School at Rome* 43: 7–35.
Brunt, P. A. (1977a) 'Josephus on social conflicts in Roman Judaea', *Klio* 59: 149–53.
Brunt, P. A. (1977b) 'Lex de imperio Vespasiani', *Journal of Roman Studies* 67: 95–116.

Brunt, P. A. (1986) 'Cicero's *officium* in the civil war', *Journal of Roman Studies* 76: 12–32.
Brunt, P. A. (1988) *The Fall of the Roman Republic and Related Essays* (Oxford).
Brunt, P. A., and Moore, J. M. edd. (1967) *Res Gestae divi Augusti: the Achievements of the Divine Augustus* (London).
Büchner, K. (1984). *M. Tullius Cicero, De re publica* (Heidelberg).
Buckland, W. W. (1908) *The Roman Law of Slavery* (Cambridge).
Bulman, P. (1992) *Phthonos in Pindar* (Berkeley).
Burkert, W. (1961) 'Hellenistische pseudopythagorica', *Philologus* 105: 16–43; 226–46.
Burkert, W. (1965) 'Cicero als Platoniker und Skeptiker', *Gymnasium* 72: 175–200.
Burkert, W. (1971) 'Zur geistesgeschichtlichen Einordnung einiger Pseudopythagorica', in *Pseudepigrapha I, Pseudopythagorica-Lettres de Platon-Littératur pseudépigraphique juive.* Entretiens Fondation Hardt (Vandoeuvres-Geneva), 25–55.
Burkert, W. (1972) *Lore and Science in Ancient Pythagoreanism* (Cambridge MA).
Burnaby, J. (1938) *Amor Dei: A Study of the Religion of St Augustine* (London).
Cairns, F. (1989) *Virgil's Augustan Epic* (Cambridge).
Cameron, A. (1991) *Christianity and the Rhetoric of Empire: the Development of Christian Discourse* (Berkeley).
Cameron, A. (1993) *The Later Roman Empire: AD 284–430* (London).
Cancik, H. (1987) 'Theokratie und Priesterherrschaft. Die mosaische Verfassung bei Flavius Josephus contra Apionem 2. 157–98', in Taubes, J. ed. *Theokratie. Religionstheorie und politische Theologie* 2: 65–77.
Carras, G. P. (1993) 'Dependence or common tradition in Philo *Hypothetica* 8.6.10–7.20 and Josephus *Contra Apionem* 2.190–219', *Studia Philonica Annual* 5: 24–57.
Centrone, B. (1990) *Pseudopythagorica ethica. I trattati morali di Archita, Metopo, Teage, Eurifamo*. Introduzione, edizione, traduzione e commento (Naples).
Chadwick, H. (1965) *Origen: Contra Celsum* (Cambridge).
Chaumartin, F.-R. (1985) *Le De Beneficiis de Sénèque, sa signification philosophique, politique et morale* (Paris).
Chesnut, G. F. (1978) 'The ruler and the logos in Neopythagorean, Middle Platonic, and late Stoic political philosophy', in *Aufstieg und Niedergang der römischen Welt*, Band 16.2 (Berlin and New York), 1310–31.
Clay, D. (1983) 'Individual and community in the first generation of the Epicurean school', in AA.VV. 1983: 255–79.
Cochrane, C. N. (1940) *Christianity and Classical Culture* (Oxford).
Cohen, S. J. D. (1979) *Josephus in Galilee and Rome. His Vita and Development as a Historian*. Columbia Studies in the Classical Tradition 8 (Leiden).
Cohn, N. (1957) *The Pursuit of the Millennium* (London).
Cole, T. (1964) 'The sources and composition of Polybius VI', *Historia* 13: 440–86.
Cole, T. (1967) *Democritus and the Sources of Greek Anthropology* (Cleveland).
Cooper, J. M., and Procopé, J. F. (1995) *Seneca, Moral and Political Essays* (Cambridge).
Cornell, T. J. (1995) *The Beginnings of Rome* (London).
Cotton, H. (1984) 'The concept of *indulgentia* under Trajan', *Chiron* 14: 245–66.
Crawford, M. (1992) *The Roman Republic* (London, 2nd edn).
Crook, J. A., Lintott, A., and Rawson, E. edd. (1994) *Cambridge Ancient History*, vol. IX (Cambridge, 2nd edn).

Crossan, J. D. (1991) *The Historical Jesus: the Life of a Mediterranean Jewish Peasant* (Edinburgh).

Cunningham, A. (1982) *The Early Church and the State*. Sources of Early Christian Thought (Philadelphia).

Dagron, G. (1968) 'L'empire romain d'Orient au IVème siècle et les institutions politiques de l'hellénisme: le témoinage de Thémistios', *Travaux et Mémoirs*, Centre de Recherche d'Histoire et Civilisation Byzantines 3: 1–242.

Dahlmann, H. (1935) 'Marcus Terentius Varro', *Paulys Realencyclopädie der classischen Altertumswissenschaft*, suppl. 6 (Stuttgart), cols. 1172–1277.

Daley, B. E. (1991) *The Hope of the Early Church* (Cambridge).

Daly, L. (1980) '"In a borderland": Themistius' ambivalence toward Julian', *Byzanteinische Zeitschrift* 73: 1–11.

Dawson, D. (1992) *Cities of the Gods* (New York and Oxford).

De Plinval, G. (1959) *Cicéron traité des lois* (Paris).

Delatte, A. (1922) *Essai sur la politique pythagoricienne* (Liège and Paris).

Delatte, L. (1942) *Les Traités de la Royauté d'Ecphante, Diotogène et Sthénidas* (Liège).

Dell'Oro, A. (1960) *I libri de officio nella giurisprudenza romana* (Milan).

Denyer, N. C. (1983) 'The origins of justice', in AA.VV. 1983: 133–52.

Desideri, P. (1978) *Dione de Prusa: un' intellettuale greco nell' impero romano* (Messina).

Desideri, P. (1986) 'La vita politica cittadina dell'Impero: lettura dei Praecepta gerendae reipublicae e dell' An seni res publica gerenda sit', *Athenaeum* 64: 371–81.

Dillon, J. M. (1977) *The Middle Platonists* (London).

Dillon, J. (1993) *Alcinous: The Handbook of Platonism* (Oxford).

Döring, K. (1995) 'Diogenes und Antisthenes', in Giannantoni, G., *et al.* edd. *La tradizione Socratica* (Naples), 125–50.

Dombart, B., and Kalb, A. (1955) *S.Aurelii Augustini De Civitate Dei*, 2 vols. Corpus Christianorum Scriptorum Latinorum 47 and 48 (Turnholt).

Dorandi, T. (1982a) *Filodemo: il buon re secondo Omero* (Naples).

Dorandi, T. (1982b) 'Filodemo, Gli Stoici (PHerc 155 e 339)', *CronErc* 12: 91–133.

Dorey, T. A. ed. (1966) *Latin Historians* (London).

Dorey, T. A. ed. (1969) *Tacitus* (London).

Dorey, T. A. ed. (1971) *Livy* (London).

Douglas, A. E. (1965) 'Cicero the philosopher', in Dorey, T. A. ed. *Cicero* (London).

Douglas, A. E. (1968) *Cicero. Greece and Rome*, New Surveys in the Classics no. 2 (Oxford, repr. with addenda 1978).

Downey, G. (1957) 'Themistius and the defence of Hellenism', *Harvard Theological Review* 50: 259–74.

Downey, G., and Norman, A. F. edd. (1965–74) *Themistii Orationes*, 3 vols. Bibliotheca Teubneriana (Leipzig).

Downing, F. G. (1992) *Cynics and Christian Origins* (Edinburgh).

Downing, F. G. (1993) 'Cynics and early Christianity', in Goulet-Cazé and Goulet edd. 1993.

Drake, H. A. (1976) *In Praise of Constantine: a Historical Study and New Translation of Eusebius' Tricennial Orations* (Berkeley, Los Angeles and London).

Drummond, A. (1995) *Law, Politics and Power. Sallust and the Execution of the Catilinarian Conspirators* (Stuttgart).

Ducos, M. (1984) *Les Romains et la loi* (Paris).

Dudley, D. R. (1937) *A History of Cynicism* (London, repr. Hildesheim 1967).

Duff, P. W. (1938) *Personality in Roman Private Law* (Cambridge).

Dvornik, F. (1955) 'The Emperor Julian's "reactionary" ideas on kingship', in Weitzmann, K. ed. *Late Classical and Mediaeval Studies in Honor of A. M. Friend* (Princeton), 71–81.

Dvornik, F. (1966) *Early Christian and Byzantine Political Philosophy: Origin and Background*, 2 vols. (Washington).

Earl, D. C. (1961) *The Political Thought of Sallust* (Cambridge).

Earl, D. C. (1967) *The Moral and Political Tradition of Rome* (London).

Eckstein, A. M. (1995) *Moral Vision in the Histories of Polybius* (Berkeley and Los Angeles).

Edelstein, L. (1966) *The Meaning of Stoicism* (Cambridge MA).

Edwards, C. (1993) *The Politics of Immorality in Ancient Rome* (Cambridge).

Eisen, K. F. (1966) *Polybiosinterpretationen: Beobachtungen zu Prinzipien griechischer und römische Historiographie bei Polybios* (Heidelberg).

Eisenberger, H. (1982) 'Die Natur und die römische Politeia im 6. Buche des Polybios', *Philologus* 126: 44–58.

Elliot, J. K. (1993) *The Apocryphal New Testament. A Collection of Apocryphal Christian Literature in an English Translation* (Oxford).

Engberg-Pedersen, T. (1990) *The Stoic Theory of Oikeiosis* (Aarhus).

Errington, R. M. (1990) *A History of Macedonia* (Berkeley).

Erskine, A. W. (1990) *The Hellenistic Stoa* (London).

Evans, E. (1948) *Tertullian's Treatise against Praxeas* (London).

Eyben, E. (1993) *Restless Youth in Ancient Rome* (London).

Falls, T. B. (1948) *Writings of Saint Justin Martyr*. Fathers of the Church series, vol.6 (Washington).

Farquharson, A. S. L. (1944) *The Meditations of the Emperor Marcus Antoninus*, ed. with trans. and comm., 2 vols. (Oxford); trans. reissued with introduction and notes by Rutherford, R. B. (Oxford 1989).

Fedeli, P. (1989) 'Il panegirico di Plinio nella critica moderna', *Aufsteig und Niedergang der römischen Welt*, Band 33.1: 387ff.

Feldman, L. H. (1992) 'Josephus' portrait of Moses (part 1)', *Jewish Quarterly Review* 82: 285–328.

Feldman, L. H. (1993a) 'Josephus' portrait of Jeroboam', *Andrews University Seminary Studies* 31: 29–51 (also in Feldman 1998b: 424–35).

Feldman, L. H. (1993b) 'Josephus' portrait of Josiah', *Louvain Studies* 18: 110–30 (also in Feldman 1998b: 424–35).

Feldman, L. H. (1993c) 'Josephus' portrait of Moses (part 2)', *Jewish Quarterly Review* 83: 7–50.

Feldman, L. H. (1993d) 'Josephus' Portrait of Moses (part 3)', *Jewish Quarterly Review* 83: 301–30.

Feldman, L. H. (1998a) *Josephus' Interpretation of the Bible* (Berkeley, Los Angeles, London).

Feldman, L. H. (1998b) *Studies in Josephus' Rewritten Bible*. Supplements for the Study of Judaism (Leiden, Boston, Cologne).

Feldman, L. H., and Hata, G. edd. (1987) *Josephus, Judaism and Christianity* (Detroit).

Feldman, L. H. and Hata, G. edd. (1989) *Josephus, the Bible and History* (Detroit).

Ferrary, J.-L. (1988) *Philhellénisme et impérialisme* (Rome).
Ferrary, J.-L. (1995) 'The statesman and the law in the political philosophy of Cicero', in Laks and Schofield edd. 1995: 48–73.
Festugière, A.-J. (1955) *Epicurus and his Gods* (Oxford).
Figgis, J. N. (1921) *The Political Aspects of St. Augustine's 'City of God'* (London).
Filoramo, G. (1990) *A History of Gnosticism* (Oxford).
Finley, M. I. (1980) *Ancient Slavery and Modern Ideology* (London).
Finley, M. I. (1981) *Economy and Society in Ancient Greece*, edited by Shaw, B. D., and Saller, R. P. (London).
Finley, M. I. (1983) *Politics in the Ancient World* (Cambridge).
Forster, E. S. (1924) *[Aristotle]: Rhetorica ad Alexandrum*, translated in Ross, W. D. ed. *The Works of Aristotle translated into English*, vol IX (Oxford).
Foucault, M. (1988) *The History of Sexuality. Vol. 3: The Care of the Self*, trans. Hurley, R. (London).
Fowler, D. P. (1989) 'Lucretius and Politics', in Griffin and Barnes edd. 1989: 120–50.
Fraisse, J.-C. (1974) *Philia: La notion d'amitié dans la philosophie antique* (Paris).
Fraser, P. M. (1972) *Ptolemaic Alexandria*, 3 vols. (Oxford).
Frezza, P. (1969) 'La cultura di Ulpiano', *Studia et documenta historiae et iuris* 34: 363–75.
Frier, B. W. (1979) *Libri annales pontificum maximorum: the Origins of the Annalistic Tradition* (Rome).
Fries, J. (1985) *Der Zweikampf in Titus Livius* (Meisenheim am Glan).
Frischer, B. (1982) *The Sculpted Word* (Berkeley, Los Angeles and London).
Fritz, K. von (1940) *Pythagorean Politics in Southern Italy: An Analysis of the Sources* (New York).
Fritz, K. von (1954) *The Theory of the Mixed Constitution in Antiquity: a Critical Analysis of Polybius' Political Ideas* (New York).
Fuhrmann, M. (1966) *Anaximenis Ars Rhetorica* (Leipzig).
Furley, D. J. (1978) 'Lucretius the Epicurean: on the history of man', in *Lucrèce*. Fondation Hardt 24 (Vandoeuvres-Geneva), 1–37.
Gabba, E. (1991) *Dionysius and the History of Archaic Rome* (Berkeley and Oxford).
Gafni, I. M. (1989) 'Josephus and I Maccabees', in Feldman and Hata edd. 1989: 116–31.
Gaïth, J. (1953) *La Conception de la liberté chez Grégoire de Nysse* (Paris).
Garcia Moreno, L. A. (1992) 'Paradoxography and political ideals in Plutarch's *Life of Sertorius*', in Stadter, P. A. ed. *Plutarch and the Historical Tradition* (London).
Garnsey, P. (1996) *Ideas of Slavery from Aristotle to Augustine* (Cambridge).
Garzetti, A. (1974) *From Tiberius to the Antonines* (London).
Gaudemet, J. (1967) *Institutions de l'antiquité* (Paris).
Geytenbeek, A. C. van (1963) *Musonius Rufus and Greek Diatribe* (Assen).
Giannantoni, G. (1990) *Socratis et Socraticorum Reliquiae*, 4 vols. (Naples).
Giannantoni, G. (1993) 'Antistene fondatore della scuola cinica?', in Goulet-Cazé and Goulet edd. 1993.
Gibbs, J. H., and Feldman, L. H. (1986) 'Josephus' vocabulary for slavery', *Jewish Quarterly Review* 76: 281–310.
Gigante, M. (1993) 'Cinismo e Epicureismo', in Goulet-Cazé and Goulet edd. 1993.
Gigante, M. (1995) *Philodemus in Italy: the Books from Herculaneum* (Ann Arbor MI).

Gill, C. (1988) 'Personhood and personality: the four-*personae* theory in Cicero, *De Officiis* I', *Oxford Studies in Ancient Philosophy* 6: 169–99.

Gill, C. (1995) *Epictetus: The Discourses, Handbook, Fragments*. Trans. Hard, R., ed. Gill, C. (London).

Gill, C. (1998) 'Reciprocity or altruism in Greek ethical philosophy?', in Gill, C., Postlethwaite, N., and Seaford, R. edd. *Reciprocity in Ancient Greece* (Oxford).

Girardet, K. M. (1983) *Die Ordnung der Welt* (Wiesbaden).

Glover, T. R. (1931) *Tertullian: Apology and De Spectaculis* (with *Minucius Felix*: *Octavius*, trans. G. H. Rendall). Loeb Classical Library (Cambridge MA and London).

Glucker, J. (1988) 'Cicero's philosophical affiliations', in Dillon, J. M., and Long, A. A. edd. *The Question of 'Eclecticism'* (Berkeley, Los Angeles and London).

Goettling, C. W. (1851) 'Diogenes der Kyniker oder die Philosophie des griechischen Proletariats', *Gesammelte Abhandlungen aus dem classichen Alterthum* 1: 251–77.

Goldschmidt, V. (1977) *La Doctrine d'Epicure et le droit* (Paris).

Görler, W. (1995) 'Silencing the troublemaker: *De Legibus* 1.39 and the continuity of Cicero's scepticism', in Powell ed. 1995.

Goodblatt, D. (1994) *The Monarchic Principle. Studies in Jewish Self-Government in Antiquity*. Texte und Studien zum Antiken Judentum 38 (Tübingen).

Goodenough, E. R. (1928) 'The political philosophy of Hellenistic kingship', *Yale Classical Studies* 1: 55–102.

Goodenough, E. R. (1938) *The Politics of Philo Judaeus. Practice and Theory* (New Haven, repr. Hildesheim 1967).

Goodman, M. (1994) 'Josephus as Roman citizen', in Parente and Sievers edd. 1994: 329–38.

Gould, J. (1989) *Herodotus* (London).

Goulet, R. ed. (1994) *Dictionnaire des philosophes antiques*, vol. II (Paris).

Goulet-Cazé, M.-O. (1982) 'Un syllogisme stoïcien sur la loi dans la doxographie de Diogène le cynique à propos de Diogène Laërce VI 72', *Rheinisches Museum* 125 (1982): 214–45.

Goulet-Cazé, M.-O. (1986) *L'Ascèse cynique* (Paris).

Goulet-Cazé, M.-O. (1992) 'Le livre VI de Diogène Laerce: analyse de sa structure et reflexions methodologiques', in *Aufstieg und Niedergang der römischen Welt*, Band 36.6 (Berlin and New York).

Goulet-Cazé, M.-O.(1994) 'Diogène de Sinope', in Goulet (1994).

Goulet-Cazé, M.-O.(1996) 'Religion and the early Cynics', in Branham and Goulet-Cazé edd. 1996: 47–80.

Goulet-Cazé, M.-O., and Goulet, R. edd. (1993) *Le Cynisme Ancien et ses Prolongements* (Paris).

Greenslade, S. L. (1954) *Church and State from Constantine to Theodosius* (London).

Griffin, M. T. (1976) *Seneca, a Philosopher in Politics* (Oxford, reissued with a postscript 1992).

Griffin, M. T. (1986) 'Philosophy, Cato and Roman suicide', *Greece and Rome* 33: 64–77, 192–202.

Griffin, M. T. (1989) 'Philosophy, politics, and politicians at Rome', in Griffin and Barnes edd. 1989: 1–37.

Griffin, M. T. (1993) 'Le mouvement cynique et les Romains: attraction et répulsion', in Goulet-Cazé and Goulet edd. 1993.

Griffin, M. T. (1995) 'Philosophical badinage in Cicero's letters to his friends', in Powell ed. 1995: 325–46.

Griffin, M. T. (1996) 'Cynicism and the Romans: attraction and repulsion', in Branham and Goulet-Cazé edd. 1996: 190–204.

Griffin, M. T. (1997) 'The Senate's version', *Journal of Roman Studies* 87: 249–63.

Griffin, M. T., and Barnes, J. edd. (1989) *Philosophia Togata: Essays on Philosophy and Roman Society* (Oxford).

Grziwotz, H. (1986) *Der moderne Verfassungsbegriff und die römische Verfassung in der deutschen Forschung des 19. und 20. Jahrhunderts* (Frankfurt).

Hadas, M. (1951) *Aristeas to Philocrates (Letter of Aristeas)* (New York).

Hadot, I. (1969) *Seneca und die griechisch-römische Tradition der Seelenleitung* (Berlin).

Hadot, I. (1984) *Arts liberaux et philosophie dans la pensée antique* (Paris).

Hadot, P. (1972) 'Fürstenspiegel', *Reallexikon für Antike und Christentum*, vol VIII (Stuttgart), 555–632.

Hadot, P. (1998) *The Inner Citadel. The Meditations of Marcus Aurelius* (Cambridge MA).

Hagendahl, H. (1967) *Augustine and the Latin Classics*, 2 vols. (Gothenburg).

Hahm, D. E. (1992) 'A neglected Stoic argument for human responsibility', *Illinois Classical Studies* 17: 23–48.

Hahm, D. E. (1995) 'Polybius' applied political theory', in Laks and Schofield edd. 1995: 7–47.

Hammond, N. G. L. (1993) *Sources for Alexander the Great* (Cambridge).

Harnack, A. (1908) *The Mission and Expansion of Christianity*, trans. by Moffat, J. (London).

Harris, W. V. (1979) *War and Imperialism in Republican Rome 327–70 BC* (Oxford).

Heine, R. E. (1989) *The Montanist Oracles and Testimonia*. Patristic Monograph Series 14 (Macon GA).

Heinze, R. (1924) 'Ciceros "Staat" als politische Tendenzschrift', *Hermes* 59: 73–94, reprinted in Heinze, *Vom Geist des Römertums* (Stuttgart, 3rd edn 1960).

Hellegouarc'h, J. (1963) *Le Vocabulaire latin des relations des parties politiques sous la république* (Paris).

Hengel, M. (1989/1961) *The Zealots. Investigations into the Jewish Freedom Movement in the Period from Herod I until 70 AD*, trans. Smith, D. (Edinburgh).

Hense, O. (1905) *C. Musonii Rufi Reliquiae* (Leipzig).

Hett, W. S., and Rackham, H. (1937) *Aristotle: Problems II: Books XXII–XXXVIII* and *Rhetorica ad Alexandrum* (Cambridge MA and London).

Hijmans, B. L., Jr. (1959) *Askēsis: Notes on Epictetus' Educational System* (Assen).

Höistad, R. (1948) *Cynic Hero and Cynic King* (Uppsala).

Holden, H. (1854) *M. Tullii Ciceronis De Officiis Libri Tres* (Cambridge).

Hölkeskamp, K.-J. (1987) *Die Entstehung der Nobilität* (Stuttgart).

Honoré, T. (1982) *Ulpian* (Oxford).

Hopkins, K. (1978) *Conquerors and Slaves* (Cambridge).

Hopkins, K. (1983) *Death and Renewal* (Cambridge).

How, W. W. (1930) 'Cicero's ideal in his *De re publica*', *Journal of Roman Studies* 20: 24–42.

Innes, D., Hine, H. M., and Pelling, C. B. R. edd. (1995) *Ethics and Rhetoric: Classical Essays for Donald Russell* (Oxford).

Inwood, B. (1995) 'Politics and paradox in Seneca's *De beneficiis*', in Laks and Schofield edd. 1995: 241–65.

Inwood, B. (1996) '*L'oikeiōsis* sociale chez Epictète', in Algra, K., van der Horst, P., and Runia, D. edd. *Polyhistor: Studies in the History and Historiography of Ancient Philosophy* (Leiden), 243–64.

Ioppolo, A. M. (1980) *Aristone di Chio e lo stoicismo antico* (Naples).

Isichei, E. A. (1964) *Political Thinking and Social Experience. Some Christian Interpretations of the Roman Empire from Tertullian to Salvian* (Christchurch, New Zealand).

Isnardi Parente, M. (1979) *Città e regimi politici nel pensiero greco* (Turin).

Jagu, A. (1979) *Musonius Rufus: entretiens et fragments. Introduction, traduction et commentaire* (Hildesheim).

Jellicoe, S. (1966) 'The occasion and purpose of the Letter of Aristeas: a reexamination', *New Testament Studies* 12: 144–50.

Jocelyn, H. D. (1976–7) 'The ruling class of the Roman republic and Greek philosophers', *Bulletin of the John Rylands Library* 59: 323–66.

Johnston, D. (1989) 'Justinian's Digest: the interpretation of interpolation', *Oxford Journal of Legal Studies* 9: 149–66.

Jolowicz, H. F., and Nicholas, B. (1972) *Historical Introduction to the Study of Roman Law* (Cambridge, 3rd edn).

Joly, R. (1956) *Le Thème philosophique des genres de vie dans l'antiquité* (Brussels).

Jones, C. P. (1971) *Plutarch and Rome* (Oxford).

Jones, C. P. (1978) *The Roman World of Dio Chrysostom* (Cambridge MA).

Kantorowicz, E. H. (1952a) 'Deus per naturam. Deus per gratiam. A note on mediaeval political theology', *Harvard Theological Review* 45: 253–77 (also in Kantorowicz 1965: 121–37).

Kantorowicz, E. H. (1952b) 'Kaiser Friedrich II und das Königbild des Hellenismus', in *Varia Variorum. Festgabe K. Reinhardt* (Münster-Köln), 169–93 (also in Kantorowicz 1965: 264–83).

Kantorowicz, E. H. (1957) *The King's Two Bodies. A Study in Mediaeval Political Theology* (Princeton).

Kantorowicz, E. H. (1965) *Selected Studies* (Locust Valley NY).

Kaser, M. (1971) *Das römische Privatrecht* 1 (Munich, 2nd edn).

Kaser, M. (1986) 'Ius publicum und ius privatum', *Zeitschrift der Savigny-Stiftung für Rechtsgeschichte (Romanistische Abteilung)* 103: 1–101.

Kaser, M. (1994) *Ius gentium* (Cologne, Weimar and Vienna).

Kenter, L. P. (1972) *Cicero De Legibus: a commentary on book I* (Amsterdam).

Keyes, C. W. (1921) 'Original elements in Cicero's ideal constitution', *American Journal of Philology* 13: 309–23.

Keyes, C. W. (1928) *Cicero: De Re Publica; De Legibus* (Cambridge MA and London).

Kidd, I. G. (1971) 'Stoic intermediates and the end for man', in Long ed. 1971: 150–72.

Kilb, G. (1971) 'Ethische Grundbegriffe der alten Stoa und ihre Übertragung durch Cicero', in Büchner, K. ed. *Das neue Cicerobild* (Darmstadt).

Kindstrand, J. F. (1976) *Bion of Borysthenes* (Uppsala).

Knoche, U. (1934) 'Der römische Ruhmesgedanke', *Philologus* 89: 102–24.

Krarup, P. (1956) *Rector rei publicae* (Copenhagen).

Kraus, C. S. (1999) "Jugurthine disorder', in Kraus, C. S. ed. *The Limits of Historiography* (Leiden, Boston and Cologne).

Kraus Reggiani, C. (1984) 'I rapporti tra l'impero romano e il mondo ebraico al tempo di Caligola secondo la 'Legatio ad Gaium' di Filone Alessandrino', in *Aufstieg und Niedergang der römischen Welt*, Band 21.1 (Berlin and New York), 554–86.

Kumaniecki, K. F. (1969) *M.Tulli Ciceronis De Oratore* (Leipzig).

Kummel, W. G. (1975) *Introduction to the New Testament* (London, rev. edn).

Ladouceur, D. J. (1987) 'Josephus and Masada', in Feldman and Hata edd. 1987: 95–114.

Laks, A., and Schofield, M. edd. (1995) *Justice and Generosity: Studies in Hellenistic Social and Political Philosophy* (Cambridge).

Lauria, M. (1930) 'Iurisdictio', *Studi Bonfante*, vol. II (Milan), 481–538.

Lebram, J. C. H. (1974) 'Der Idealstaat der Juden', in Betz. O., Haacker, K., and Hengel, M. edd. *Josephus-Studien. Untersuchungen zu Josephus, dem antiken Judentum und den neuen Testament, Otto Michel zum 70 Geburtstag gewidmet* (Göttingen), 233–53.

Lenel, O. (1927) *Das Edictum perpetuum* (Leipzig, 3rd edn).

Lepore, E. (1954) *Il princeps ciceroniano e gli ideali politici della tarda repubblica* (Naples).

Levy, E. (1949) 'Natural law in Roman thought', *Studia et documenta historiae et iuris* 15: 1–23 (repr. in Levy, E. *Gesammelte Schriften*, Cologne and Graz 1963, I: 1–19).

Lewis, C. S. (1964) *The Discarded Image* (Cambridge).

Liebs, D. (1982) 'Ulpiani regulae: zwei Pseudepigrafa', in Wirth, G. ed., *Romanitas-Christianitas* (Berlin), 282–92.

Lightfoot, J. B. (1885) *The Apostolic Fathers* (London).

Linder, H. (1972) *Die Geschichtsauffassung des Flavius Josephus im Bellum Judaicum. Gleichzeitig ein Beitrag zur Quellenfrage*. Arbeiten zur Geschichte des antiken Judentum und des Urchristentums 12 (Leiden).

Lintott, A. (1997) 'The theory of the mixed constitution at Rome', in Barnes, J., and Griffin, M.T. edd. *Philosophia Togata* II (Oxford).

Long, A. A. (1982) 'Epictetus and Marcus Aurelius', in Luce, J. ed. *Ancient Writers: Greece and Rome* (New York), 985–1002.

Long, A. A. (1983) 'Greek ethics after Macintyre and the Stoic community of reason', *Ancient Philosophy* 3: 184–99.

Long, A. A. (1986a) *Hellenistic Philosophy* (Berkeley, Los Angeles and London, 2nd edn).

Long, A. A. (1986b) 'Pleasure and social utility: the virtues of being Epicurean', in *Aspects de la philosophie Hellénistique*, Fondation Hardt 32 (Vandoeuvres-Geneva), 283–324.

Long, A. A. (1995) 'Cicero's politics in *De Officiis*', in Laks and Schofield edd. 1995: 213–40.

Long, A. A. (1996) *Stoic Studies* (Cambridge).

Long, A. A. ed. (1971) *Problems in Stoicism* (London).

Long, A. A., and Sedley, D. N. (1987) *The Hellenistic Philosophers*, 2 vols. (Cambridge).

Longo Auricchio, F. (1988) *Ermarco: Frammenti*, La scuola di Epicuro 6 (Naples).

López Cruces, J. L. (1995) *Les Méliambes de Cercidas de Mégalopolis* (Amsterdam).

Lord, C. (1991) 'Aristotle's anthropology', in Lord, C., and O'Connor, D. K. edd. *Essays on the Foundations of Aristotelian Political Science* (Berkeley, Los Angeles and Oxford), 49–73.

Lovejoy, A. O., and Boas, G. (1935) *Primitivism and Related Ideas in Antiquity* (Baltimore, repr. New York 1973).

Luce, T. J., and Woodman, A. J. edd. (1993) *Tacitus and the Tacitean Tradition* (Princeton).

Lüderitz, G. (1994) 'What is the Politeuma?', in van Henten, J. W., and van der Horst, P. W. edd. *Studies in Early Jewish Epigraphy*. Arbeiten zur Geschichte des Antiken Judentums und des Urchristentums 21 (Leiden), 183–225.

Lutz, C. E. (1947) 'Musonius Rufus: "The Roman Socrates"', *Yale Classical Studies* 10: 3–147.

McDonald, M. F. (1964) *Lactantius: The Divine Institutes*. Fathers of the Church series vol. 49 (Washington).

McGushin, P. (1992 and 1994) *Sallust, The Histories*. Text, translation and commentary, 2 vols (Oxford).

MacMullen, R. (1986) 'Personal power in the Roman Empire', *American Journal of Philology* 107: 512–24.

Manuwald, B. (1980) *Der Aufbau der Lukrezischen Kulturentstehungslehre* (Mainz and Wiesbaden).

Markus, R. A. (1988a) *Saeculum: History and Society in the Theology of Saint Augustine* (Cambridge, 2nd edn).

Markus, R. A. (1988b) 'The Latin Fathers', in *The Cambridge History of Medieval Political Thought*, 92–122.

Marrou, H. I. (1958) *Saint Augustin et la fin de la culture antique* (Paris, 4th edn).

Mason, S. (1991) *Flavius Josephus on the Pharisees* (Leiden).

Mason, S. (1994) 'Josephus, Daniel and the Flavian house', in Parente and Sievers edd. 1994: 161–91.

Matthews, J. (1989) *The Roman Empire of Ammianus Marcellinus* (London).

Meissner, B. (1986) 'ΠΡΑΓΜΑΤΙΚΗ ΙΣΤΟΡΙΑ: Polybios über den Zweck pragmatischer Geschichtsschreibung', *Saeculum* 37: 313–51.

Mellor, R. (1993) *Tacitus* (London).

Mendels, D. (1992) *The Rise and Fall of Jewish Nationalism. Jewish and Christian Ethnicity in Ancient Palestine* (New York).

Michel, A. (1960) *Rhétorique et philosophie chez Cicéron* (Paris).

Miles, G. B. (1995). *Livy: Reconstructing Early Rome* (Ithaca NY and London).

Millar, F. G. B. (1964) *A Study of Cassius Dio* (Oxford).

Millar, F. G. B. (1965) 'Epictetus and the Imperial Court', *Journal of Roman Studies* 55: 141–8.

Millar, F. G. B. (1984) 'The political character of the classical Roman republic', *Journal of Roman Studies* 74: 1–19.

Millar, F. G. B. (1986) 'Politics, persuasion and the People before the Social War', *Journal of Roman Studies* 76: 1–11.

Miller, W. (1913) *Cicero De Officiis* (Cambridge MA and London).

Mitchell, R. (1990) *Patricians and Plebeians. The Origin of the Roman State* (Ithaca NY and London).

Mitchell, T. N. (1979) *Cicero, the Ascending Years* (New Haven and London).

Mitchell, T. N. (1991) *Cicero, the Senior Statesman* (New Haven and London).

Mitsis, P. (1988) *Epicurus' Ethical Theory* (Ithaca NY and London).

Mitteis, L. (1908) *Römisches Privatrecht bis auf die Zeit Diokletians* (Leipzig).

Moles, J. L. (1978) 'The career and conversion of Dio Chrysostom', *Journal of Hellenic Studies* 98: 79–100.

Moles, J. L. (1983a) '"Honestius quam ambitiosius?": an exploration of the Cynic's attitude to moral corruption in his fellow men', *Journal of Hellenic Studies* 103: 103–23.

Moles, J. L. (1983b) 'The date and purpose of the fourth kingship oration of Dio Chrysostom', *Classical Antiquity* 2: 251–78.

Moles, J. L. (1988) *Plutarch: Life of Cicero* (Warminster).

Moles, J. L. (1990) 'The kingship orations of Dio Chrysostom', *Papers of the Leeds International Latin Seminar* 6: 297–375.

Moles, J. L. (1993) 'Le cosmopolitisme cynique', in Goulet-Cazé and Goulet edd. 1993.

Moles, J. L. (1995a) 'The Cynics and politics', in Laks and Schofield edd. 1995: 129–58.

Moles, J. L. (1995b) 'Dio Chrysostom, Greece, and Rome', in Innes, Hine and Pelling edd. 1995: 177–92.

Momigliano, A. (1941) 'Epicureans in revolt', *Journal of Roman Studies* 31: 151–7.

Momigliano, A. (1950a) 'Ancient history and the antiquarian', *Journal of the Warburg and Courtauld Institutes* 13: 285–315.

Momigliano, A. (1969 [1950b]) 'Seneca', *Quarto contributo alla storia degli studi classici e del mondo antico* (Rome), 239–56.

Momigliano, A. (1971) *The Development of Greek Biography* (Cambridge MA and London).

Mommsen, Th. (1887–8) *Römisches Staatsrecht*, 3 vols. (Leipzig).

Moore, T. J. (1989) *Artistry and Ideology. Livy's Vocabulary of Virtue* (Frankfurt).

Moraux, P. (1973) *Der Aristotelismus bei den Griechen von Andronikos bis Alexander von Aphrodisias*, I. Band: *Die Renaissance des Aristotelismus im I. Jh. v. Chr.* (Berlin).

Moraux, P. (1984) *Der Aristotelismus bei den Griechen von Andronikos bis Alexander von Aphrodisias*, II. Band: *Der Aristotelismus im I. und II. Jh. n. Chr.* (Berlin).

Morgan, T. (1998) 'A good man skilled in politics: Quintilian on power and pedagogy', in Too, Y. L., and Livingstone, N. edd. *Pedagogy and Power* (Cambridge).

Müller, R. (1972) *Die epikureische Gesellschaftstheorie* (Berlin).

Müller, R. (1987) 'Rhetorik und Politik in Philodems "Rhetorica"', in Müller, *Polis und Res publica* (Weimar).

Murray, O. (1965) 'Philodemus on the good king according to Homer', *Journal of Roman Studies* 55: 161–82.

Murray, O. (1967) 'Aristeas and Ptolemaic kingship', *Journal of Theological Studies* 18: 337–71.

Murray, O. (1970) 'Hecataeus of Abdera and Pharaonic kingship', *Journal of Egyptian Archaeology* 56: 141–71.

Murray, O. (1987) 'The letter of Aristeas', *Studi Ellenistici II* (Pisa), 15–29 (revised English version of 'Aristeasbrief', *Reallexikon für Antike und Christentum*, Suppl. 4 [Stuttgart, 1986], 573–87).

Nikiprowetsky, V. (1977) *Le Commentaire de l'Ecriture chez Philon d'Alexandrie* (Leiden).

Nippel, W. (1980) *Mischverfassungstheorie und Verfassungsrealität in Antike und früher Neuzeit*, Geschichte und Gesellschaft 21 (Stuttgart).

Norman, A. F. (1969) *Libanius: Selected Works*, vol. I. Loeb Classical Library (Cambridge MA & London).

Nörr, D. (1974) *Rechtskritik in der römischen Antike* (Munich).

North, J. (1990) 'Democratic politics in Republican Rome', *Past and Present* 126: 3–21.

Noyen, P. (1955) 'Marcus Aurelius, the greatest practician of Stoicism', *L'Antiquité classique* 24: 372–83.

Nussbaum, M. C. (1994) *The Therapy of Desire: Theory and Practice in Hellenistic Ethics* (Princeton).

O'Donovan, O. (1980) *The Problem of Self-Love in Augustine* (New Haven and London).

O'Meara, D. J. (1989) *Pythagoras Revived. Mathematics and Philosophy in Late Antiquity* (Oxford).

O'Meara, D. J. (1993) 'Aspects of political philosophy in Iamblichus', in Blumenthal, H. J., and Clark, E. G. edd. *The Divine Iamblichus* (Bristol), 65–73.

O'Neil, J. L. (1995) *The Origins and Development of Ancient Greek Democracy* (Lanham MD and London).

Oakley, S. (1985) 'Single combat in the Roman Republic', *Classical Quarterly* 35: 392–410.

Obbink, D. (1988) 'Hermarchus, Against Empedocles', *Classical Quarterly* 38: 428–35.

Olivecrona, K. (1949) *Three Essays in Roman law* (Lund).

Paquet, L. ed. (1988) *Les Cyniques grecs. Fragments et témoignages* (Ottawa, 2nd edn).

Parente, F., and Sievers, J. edd. (1994) *Josephus and the History of the Greco-Roman Period. Essays in Memory of Morton Smith*. Studia Post-Biblica 41 (Leiden).

Parker, R. (1988) 'The values of Pliny', *Omnibus* 15: 6–8.

Pédech, P. (1964) *La Méthode historique de Polybe* (Paris).

Pelletier, A. (1962) *La Lettre d'Aristée à Philocrate*, Sources Chrétiennes 89 (Paris).

Pelling, C. B. R. (1995) 'The Moralism of Plutarch's *Lives*', in Innes, Hine and Pelling edd. 1995.

Pembroke, S. (1971) 'Oikeiōsis', in Long ed. 1971: 114–49.

Pétrement, S. (1991) *A Separate God?* (London).

Petzold, K.-E. (1977) 'Kyklos und Telos im Geschichtsdenken des Polybios', *Saeculum* 28: 253–90.

Philippson, R. (1910) 'Die Rechtsphilosophie der Epikureer', *Archiv für Geschichte der Philosophie* 23: 289–337 and 433–46.

Podes, S. (1991a) 'Polybios' Anakyklosis-Lehre, diskrete Zustandssysteme und das Problem der Mischverfassung,' *Klio* 73: 382–90.

Podes, S. (1991b) 'Polybius and his theory of anacyclosis: problems of not just ancient political theory', *History of Political Thought* 12: 577–87.

Pohlenz, M. (1934) *Antikes Führertum* (Leipzig).

Powell, J. G. F. (1990) *Cicero: On Friendship and The Dream of Scipio* (Warminster).

Powell, J. G. F. (1994) 'The *rector rei publicae* of Cicero's *De Republica*', in *Scripta Classica Israelica* 13: 19–29.

Powell, J. G. F. ed. (1995) *Cicero the Philosopher: Twelve Papers* (Oxford).

Powell, J. G. F. (forthcoming) *Cicero De Republica* (Oxford).

Rackham, H., and Sutton, E. W. (1942) *Cicero, De Oratore*, 2 vols. (Cambridge MA and London).

Radice, B. (1968) 'Pliny and the *Panegyricus*', *Greece and Rome* 15: 166–72.

Rajak, T. (1983) *Josephus. The Historian and his Society* (London).

Rajak, T. (1991) 'Friends, Romans, subjects: Agrippa II's speech in Josephus' *Jewish War*', in Alexander, L. ed. *Images of Empire*, Journal for the Study of the Old Testament Supplement Series 12 (Sheffield), 122–34.

Rajak, T. (1996) 'Hasmonean kingship and the invention of tradition', in Bilde, P. *et al.*

edd. *Aspects of Hellenistic Kingship*, Studies in Hellenistic Civilization 7 (Aarhus), 99–115.

Rajak, T. (1997) 'The martyr's portrait in Greek-Jewish literature', in Edwards, M., and Swain, S. edd. *Portraits. Biographical Representation in the Greek and Latin Literature of the Roman Empire* (Oxford), 39–67.

Rawson, E. D. (1973) 'The interpretation of Cicero's *De Legibus*', in *Aufstieg und Niedergang der römischen Welt* Band 1.4: 334–56.

Rawson, E. D. (1975) *Cicero: a Portrait* (London).

Rawson, E. D. (1985) *Intellectual Life in the Late Roman Republic* (London).

Reinhold, M. (1988) *From Republic to Principate: an historical commentary on Cassius Dio's Roman History, Books 49–52 (36 – 29 BC)* (Atlanta).

Reitzenstein, R. (1917) 'Die Idee des Principats bei Cicero und Augustus', in *Nachrichten von der königlichen Gesellschaft der Wissenschaften zu Göttingen*, phil.-hist. Klasse 1917: 399–436.

Rich, J. W. (1976) *Declaring War in the Roman Republic* (Brussels).

Rich, J. W. (1989) 'Dio on Augustus', in Cameron, A. ed. *History as Text. The Writing of Ancient History* (London), 86–110.

Rich, J. W., and Shipley, G. edd. (1993) *War and Society in the Roman World* (London).

Richter, W. (1983) 'Charakterzeichnung und Regie bei Livius', in Lefèvre, E., and Olshausen, E. edd. *Livius, Werk und Rezeption: Festschrift für Erich Burck*, (Munich), 60–80.

Rist, J. M. (1982) 'Are you a Stoic? The case of Marcus Aurelius', in Meyer, B. F., and Sanders, E. P. edd. *Jewish and Christian Self-Definition* (Philadelphia), 23–45, 190–2.

Rist, J. M. (1994) *Augustine* (Cambridge).

Robinson, J. ed. (1977) *The Nag Hammadi Library in English* (Leiden).

Rosenthal, E. I. J. (1958) *Political Thought in Mediaeval Islam: an Introductory Outline* (Cambridge).

Rousseau, P. (1985) *Pachomius: The Making of a Community in Fourth Century Egypt* (Berkeley).

Rowland, C. (1982) *The Open Heaven: a Study of Apocalyptic in Judaism and Early Christianity* (London).

Rowland, C. (1988) *Radical Christianity* (Cambridge).

Rudd, N. (1998) *Cicero, the Republic and the Laws*, trans. Rudd, N., with notes by Powell, J. (Oxford).

Rudolph, K. (1983) *Gnosis*. (Edinburgh).

Runia, D. T. (1986) *Philo of Alexandria and the Timaeus of Plato* (Leiden).

Runia, D. T. (1990) *Exegesis and Philosophy: Studies on Philo of Alexandria* (Aldershot).

Runia, D. T. (1993) *Philo in Early Christian Literature. A Survey* (Assen and Minneapolis).

Russell, D. A. (1972) *Plutarch* (London).

Russell, D. A. (1981) *Menander Rhetor* (Oxford).

Russell, D. A. (1992) *Dio Chrysostom: Orations VII, XII, XXXVI* (Cambridge).

Russell, D. S. (1964) *The Method and Message of Jewish Apocalyptic. 200 BC–AD 100* (London).

Russell, F. H. (1975) *The Just War in the Middle Ages* (Cambridge).

Rutherford, R. B. (1989) *The Meditations of Marcus Aurelius: A Study* (Oxford).

Ryfell, H. (1949) ΜΕΤΑΒΟΛΗ ΠΟΛΙΤΕΙΩΝ: *Der Wandel der Staatsverfassungen*, Noctes Romanae 2 (Bern; repr. New York 1973).

Sabine, G. H., and Smith, S. B. (1929) *Marcus Tullius Cicero: On the Commonwealth* (Columbus OH, repr. Indianapolis 1950).

Sacks, K. S. (1990) *Diodorus Siculus and the First Century* (Princeton).

Saller, R. P. (1982) *Personal Patronage under the Early Empire* (Cambridge).

Scanlon, T. F. (1980) *The Influence of Thucydides on Sallust* (Heidelberg).

Schmidlin, B. (1970) *Die römische Rechtsregeln* (Cologne and Vienna).

Schmidt, W. (1986) *Untersuchungen zur Fälschung historischer Dokumente bei Pseudo-Aristaios*, Habelts Dissertationsdrucke, Reihe Klassische Philologie 37 (Bonn).

Schoedel, W. R. (1972) *Athenagoras: Legatio and De Resurrectione*, Oxford Early Christian Texts (Oxford).

Schofield, M. (1991) *The Stoic Idea of the City* (Cambridge; repr. Chicago 1999).

Schofield, M. (1995a) 'Cicero's definition of *res publica*', in Powell ed. 1995: 63–83.

Schofield, M. (1995b) 'Two Stoic approaches to justice', in Laks and Schofield edd. 1995: 191–212.

Schofield, M. (1996) 'Le Sage et la politique à l'époque Hellénistique', in Brunschwig, J., and Lloyd, G. E. R. edd. *Le Savoir Grec* (Paris), 218–26.

Schofield, M. (1999a) *Saving the City* (London).

Schofield, M. (1999b) 'The disappearing philosopher king', in Schofield 1999a.

Schofield, M. (1999c) 'Morality and the law: the case of Diogenes of Babylon', in Schofield 1999a.

Schofield, M. (1999d) 'Social and political thought', in *The Cambridge History of Hellenistic Philosophy* (Cambridge).

Schrijvers, P. H. (1996) 'Lucretius on the origin and development of political life', in Algra, K. A., van der Horst, P. W., and Runia, D. T. edd. *Polyhistor: Studies in the History and Historiography of Ancient Philosophy* (Leiden), 220–30.

Schroder, B. (1996) *Die "väterlichen Gesetze": Flavius Josephus als Vermittler von Halachah an Griecher und Römer* (Tübingen).

Schubart, W. (1937a) 'Das hellenistische Königsideal nach Inschriften und Papyri', *Archiv für Papyrusforschung und verwandte Gebiete* 12: 1–26.

Schubart, W. (1937b) 'Das Königsbild des Hellenismus', *Die Antike* 13: 272–88.

Schulz, F. (1946) *History of Roman Legal Science* (Oxford).

Schulz, F. (1951) *Classical Roman Law* (Oxford).

Schwartz, D. R. (1983/4) 'Josephus on the Jewish Constitution and Community', *Scripta Classica Israelica* 7: 30–52.

Schwartz, S. (1990) *Josephus and Judaean Politics*. Columbia Studies in the Classical Tradition 18 (Leiden).

Scott, K. (1929) 'Plutarch and the ruler cult', *Transactions and Proceedings of the American Philological Association* 60: 117–35.

Seager, R. (1972) 'Cicero and the word *popularis*', *Classical Quarterly* 22: 328–38.

Sedley, D. N. (1982) 'The Stoic criterion of identity', *Phronesis* 27: 255–75.

Sedley, D. N. (1997) 'The ethics of Brutus and Cassius', *Journal of Roman Studies* 87: 41–53.

Setton, K. M. (1941) *The Christian Attitude towards the Emperor in the Fourth Century* (New York and London).

Shackleton Bailey, D. R. (1971) *Cicero* (London).

Shackleton Bailey, D. R. (1965–1970) *Cicero: Letters to Atticus*, 7 vols. (Cambridge).

Shackleton Bailey, D. R. (1977) *Cicero: Epistulae ad Familiares*, 2 vols. (Cambridge).
Shackleton Bailey, D. R. (1980) *Cicero: Epistulae ad Quintum fratrem et M.Brutum* (Cambridge).
Sharples, R. W. (1996) *Stoics, Epicureans and Sceptics* (London).
Shotter, D. (1991) *Augustus Caesar* (London).
Sinclair, T. A. (1951) *A History of Greek Political Thought* (London).
Smith, M. F. (1993) *Diogenes of Oenoanda: The Epicurean Inscription* (Naples).
Smith, R. (1995) *Julian's Gods: Religion and Philosophy in the Thought and Action of Julian the Apostate* (London).
Sordi, M. (1988) *The Christians and the Roman Empire* (London).
Squilloni, A. (1991) *Il concetto di 'regno' nel pensiero dello pseudo Ecfanto. Le fonti e i trattati peri basileias* (Florence).
Stadter, P. A. (1980) *Arrian of Nicomedia* (Chapel Hill NC).
Staniforth, M. (1987) *Early Christian Writings*, translation revised with introd. and notes by Louth, A. (Harmondsworth).
Stanton, G.R. (1968) 'The cosmopolitan ideas of Epictetus and Marcus Aurelius', *Phronesis* 13: 183–95.
Stanton, G. R. (1969) 'Marcus Aurelius, emperor and philosopher', *Historia* 18: 570–87.
Stein, P. (1966) *Regulae Iuris* (Edinburgh).
Stein, P. (1978) 'The place of Servius Sulpicius Rufus in the development of Roman legal science', in Behrends, O. *et al.* edd. *Festschrift für Franz Wieacker* (Göttingen), 175–84.
Stevenson, J. (1961) 'Aspects of the relations between Lactantius and the Classics', *Studia Patristica* 4: 497–503.
Stern, M. (1987) 'Josephus and the Roman Empire as reflected in the *Jewish War*', in Feldman and Hata edd. 1987: 71–80.
Stockton, D. L. (1971) *Cicero, a Political Biography* (Oxford).
Strasburger, H. (1956) *Concordia Ordinum* (Amsterdam).
Strasburger, H. (1965) 'Posidonius and problems of empire', *Journal of Roman Studies* 55: 40–53.
Strasburger, H. (1966) 'Der Scipionenkreis', *Hermes* 94: 60–72.
Striker, G. (1987) 'Origins of the concept of natural law', *Proceedings of the Boston Area Colloquium in Ancient Philosophy* 2: 79–102.
Striker, G. (1991) 'Following nature', *Oxford Studies in Ancient Philosophy* 10: 1–73.
Sullivan, F. A. (1941) 'Cicero and gloria', *Transactions of the American Philological Association* 72: 382–91.
Swain, S. (1996) *Hellenism and Empire: Language, Classicism, and Power in the Greek World AD 50–250* (Oxford).
Syme, R. (1939) *The Roman Revolution* (Oxford).
Syme, R. (1958) *Tacitus* (Oxford).
Syme, R. (1960) 'Pliny's less successful friends', *Historia* 9: 362–79 (repr. in Badian, E. ed. *Ronald Syme: Roman Papers* II [Oxford 1979], 477–95).
Syme, R. (1971) *Emperors and Biography* (Oxford).
Tarn, W. W. (1933) 'Alexander and the unity of mankind', *Proceedings of the British Academy* 19: 123–66.

Tarn, W. W., and Griffith, G. T. (1952) *Hellenistic Civilization* (London, 3rd edn).

Tarver, T. (1997) 'Varro and the antiquarianism of philosophy', in Barnes, J., and Griffin, M. T. edd. *Philosophia Togata II: Plato and Aristotle at Rome* (Oxford), 130–64.

Tcherikover, V. (1958) 'The ideology of the Letter of Aristeas', *Harvard Theological Review* 51: 59–85.

Terian, A. (1985) 'Some stock arguments for the magnanimity of the law in Hellenistic Jewish apologetics', in Jackson, B. ed. *Jewish Law Association Studies* 1 (Chico CA), 141–50.

Testard, M. (1965) *Cicéron Les Devoirs*, 2 vols. (Paris).

Thackeray, H. St J. (1902) 'The Letter of Aristeas', appendix to Swete, H.B., *Introduction to the Old Testament in Greek* (Cambridge).

Thesleff, H. (1961) *An Introduction to the Pythagorean Writings of the Hellenistic Period* (Turcu).

Thesleff, H. (1965) *The Pythagorean Texts of the Hellenistic Period* (Turku).

Thesleff, H. (1971) 'On the problem of the Doric Pseudopythagorica. An alternative theory of date and purpose', in *Pseudepigrapha I, Pseudopythagorica-Lettres de Platon-Littératur pseudépigraphique juive*. Fondation Hardt (Vandoeuvres-Geneva), 59–87.

Thoma, C. (1989) 'The high priesthood in the judgment of Josephus', in Feldman and Hata edd. 1989: 196–215.

Tigerstedt, E. N. (1974) *The Legend of Sparta in Classical Antiquity*, vol. II (Uppsala).

Toner, J. (1995) *Leisure in Ancient Rome* (Cambridge).

Trevett, C. (1996) *Montanism. Gender, Authority and the New Prophecy* (Cambridge).

Triantaphyllopoulos, J. (1985) *Das Rechtsdenken der Griechen* (Munich).

Troiani, L. (1978) 'Osservazioni sopra l'Apologia di Filone: gli Hypothetica', *Athenaeum* 56: 304–14.

Troiani, L. (1987) 'Il libro di Aristea ed il giudaismo ellenistico (premesse per un' interpretazione)', in Virgilio, B. ed. *Studi ellenistici* 2: 31–61.

Troiani, L. (1994) 'The Politeia of Israel in the Greco-Roman Age', in Parente and Sievers edd. 1994: 11–22.

Trompf, G. W. (1979) *The Idea of Historical Recurrence in Western Thought* (Berkeley and Los Angeles).

Tyrell, R.Y., and Purser, L.C. (1901–18) *The Correspondence of Cicero*, 7 vols. (Dublin and London).

Usener, H. (1887) *Epicurea* (Leipzig).

Vander Waerdt, P. A. (1987) 'The justice of the Epicurean wise man', *Classical Quarterly* 37: 402–22.

Vander Waerdt, P. A. (1988) 'Hermarchus and the Epicurean genealogy of morals', *Transactions of the American Philological Association* 118: 87–106.

Vander Waerdt, P. A. (1991) 'Politics and philosophy in Stoicism', *Oxford Studies in Ancient Philosophy* 9: 185–211.

Vander Waerdt, P. A. (1994) 'Zeno's Republic and the origins of natural law', in Vander Waerdt, P. A. ed. *The Socratic Movement* (Ithaca), 272–308.

Vanderspoel, J. (1995) *Themistius and the Imperial Court* (Ann Arbor MI).

Vermes, G. (1981) *The Dead Sea Scrolls: Qumran in Perspective* (Philadelphia, rev. edn).

Vermes, G. (1982) 'A summary of the Law by Flavius Josephus', *Novum Testamentum* 24.4: 289–303.

Veyne, P. (1976) *Le Pain et le cirque* (Paris); abridged and translated into English as *Bread and Circuses* (London 1990).

Villalba I Varneda, P. (1986) *The Historical Method of Flavius Josephus* (Leiden).

Vocabularium iurisprudentiae romanae (1894–1985), 5 vols (Berlin).

Wagner, H. (1978) *Studien zur allgemeinen Rechtslehre des Gaius* (Zutphen).

Walbank, F. W. (1940) *Philip V of Macedon* (Cambridge; repr. Hamden CT, 1967).

Walbank, F. W. (1957–79) *A Historical Commentary on Polybius*, 3 vols. (Oxford).

Walbank, F. W. (1972) *Polybius* (Berkeley and Los Angeles).

Walbank, F. W. (1981) *The Hellenistic World* (London).

Walbank, F. W. (1984) 'Monarchies and monarchic ideas', *Cambridge Ancient History*, vol. VII.1: 62–100 (Cambridge, 2nd edn).

Waldstein, W. (1994) 'Ius naturale im nachklassischen römischen Recht und bei Justinian', *Zeitschrift der Savigny-Stiftung für Rechtsgeschichte (Romanistische Abteilung)* 111: 1–65.

Wallace-Hadrill, A. (1982). 'Civilis Princeps: between citizen and king', *Journal of Roman Studies* 72: 32–48.

Wallace-Hadrill, A. W. (1983) *Suetonius. The Scholar and his Caesars* (London).

Wallace-Hadrill, D. S. (1960) *Eusebius of Caesarea* (London).

Wallis, R. T. (1972) *Neoplatonism* (London).

Walsh, P. G. (1974) *Livy* (Oxford).

Walzer, R. (1985) *Al-Farabi on the Perfect State* (Oxford).

Wardman, A. E. (1974) *Plutarch's Lives* (London).

Watson, A. (1993) *International Law in Archaic Rome* (Baltimore and London).

Wehrli, F. (1944) *Die Schule des Aristoteles: Texte und Kommentar*, vol I: *Dikaiarchos* (Basle).

Weil, R., and Nicolet, C. (1977) *Polybe: Histoire, livre VI* (Paris).

Wells, C. (1992) *The Roman Empire* (London, 2nd edn).

Wendland, P. (1900) *Aristeae ad Philocratem epistula* (Leipzig).

Wendland, P. (1904) 'Die Schriftstellerie des Anaximenes von Lampsakos: III. Anaximenes' Rhetorik', *Hermes* 39: 499–542.

Wengst, K. (1987) *Pax Romana and the Peace of Jesus Christ* (London).

White, N. (1990) 'Stoic values', *Monist* 73: 42–58.

Whittaker, J. (1990) *Alcinoos: Enseignement des Doctrines de Platon* (Paris).

Wieacker, F. (1988) *Römische Rechtsgeschichte* I (Munich).

Wiedemann, T. E. J. (1986) 'The *Fetiales*: a reconsideration', *Classical Quarterly* 36: 478–90.

Wiedemann, T. E. J. (1993) 'Sallust's *Jugurtha*: concord, discord, and the digressions', *Greece and Rome* 40: 48–56.

Wiedemann, T. E. J. (1996) 'Single combat and being Roman', *Ancient Society* 27: 91–103.

Wilkins, A. S. (1879–92) *M.Tulli Ciceronis De Oratore Libri Tres*, 3 vols. (Oxford, reprinted Amsterdam, 1962).

Williamson, G. A. (1989) *Eusebius: The History of the Church*, revised with introd. and notes by Louth, A. (Harmondsworth).

Winkel, L. (1988) 'Die stoische oikeiōsis-Lehre und Ulpians Definition der Gerechtigkeit', *Zeitschrift der Savigny-Stiftung für Rechtsgeschichte (Romanistische Abteilung)* 105: 669–79.

Winkel, L. (1993a) 'Einige Bemerkungen über ius naturale und ius gentium', in Schermaier, M. J., and Vegh, Z. edd. *Ars boni et aequi* (Stuttgart), 443–9.

Winkel, L. (1993b) 'Mandatum im römischen öffentlichen Recht?', in Nörr, D., and Nishimura, S. edd. *Mandatum und Verwandtes* (Berlin and Heidelberg), 53–66.

Winterbottom, M. (1994) *Cicero De Officiis* (Oxford).

Wirszubski, C. (1950) *Libertas as a Political Idea at Rome during the Late Republic and Early Principate* (Cambridge).

Wirszubski, C. (1954) 'Cicero's *cum dignitate otium*: a reconsideration', *Journal of Roman Studies* 44: 1–13.

Wiseman, T. P. (1971) *New Men in the Roman Senate, 139 BC–AD 14* (Oxford).

Wolfson, H. A. (1947) *Philo*, 2 vols. (Cambridge MA).

Wood, N. (1988) *Cicero's Social and Political Thought* (Berkeley and London).

Woodman, A. J. (1975) 'Velleius Paterculus', in Dorey, T.A. ed. *Empire and Aftermath* (London), 1–25.

Woodman, A. J. (1988) *Rhetoric in Classical Historiography: Four Studies* (London).

Wright, M. R. (1995) 'Cicero on self-love and love of humanity in *De Finibus* 3', in Powell ed. 1995: 171–95.

Wright, W. C. (1913–23) *The Works of the Emperor Julian*, 3 vols., Loeb Classical Library (Cambridge MA and London).

Yavetz, Z. (1975) 'Reflections on Titus and Josephus', *Greek, Roman, and Byzantine Studies* 16: 411–32.

Young, F. M. (1983) *From Nicaea to Chalcedon* (London).

Young, F. M. (1994) *The Theology of the Pastoral Letters* (Cambridge).

Zetzel, J. E. G. (1995) *Cicero, De Re Publica: selections* (Cambridge).

Zetzel, J. E. G. (1999) *Cicero: On the Commonwealth and On the Laws* (Cambridge).

Zeyl, D. J. (1997) *The Encyclopedia of Classical Philosophy* (London and Chicago).

Ziegler, K. (1952) 'Polybios', in Paully-Wissowa, *Real-Encyclopädie der classischen Altertumswissenschaft*, vol. 21, 2 (Stuttgart) cols. 1440–578.

Ziegler, K. (1955) *Cicero: De Re Publica* (Leipzig and Berlin, 3rd edn).

Zuntz, G. (1959) 'Aristeas I: "The seven banquets"', *Journal of Semitic Studies* 4: 21–36.

Index

Academy (Plato's) 293–302 *passim*, 303–4, 306, 316, 435, 465, 484, 492, 498, 503–4, 506, 532, 549, 567, 570
Achaean League 458, 464, 465, 471–2
acropolis 14
Acton, Lord 258
'actuality' / 'potentiality' (in Aristotle) 324, 329–30
aediles 478
aemulatio ('competition': cf. competitiveness) 525
Aeschines (Attic orator) 138–9
Aeschines of Sphettus 155n.2
agathos / *kakos* ('noble', 'good' / 'non-noble', 'bad': cf. *aretē*, aristocracy) 39, 128, 131
agora ('place of gathering') 14, 33, 108, 183, 404, 419, 420
aidōs ('respect for others'; shame) 97, 191, 243, 278
Alcibiades (Athenian general and politician) 117, 119–21
Alcinous (Platonist, ? 2nd century AD) 559n.1
Alexander of Aphrodisias 342n.38
Alexander 'the Great' 1, 299, 303, 304, 316, 317, 391, 392, 393–4, 401, 415, 418, 432, 434, 452, 458, 459, 471, 605, 653, 662
Alexandria 402, 435, 461, 562, 568, 569
altruism 422, 449, 548, 608
Amazons 76
Ambrose, St (d. AD 397) 658–9
amicitia ('friendship') 503, 504–5
amicus ('friend', as euphemism for 'client') 553
Ammianus Marcellinus (Roman historian; d. AD 395) 531
Amos 54
anarchy, *anarchia* ('breakdown of authority') 77, 82, 431
Anaxarchus of Abdera (4th century BC Democritean philosopher) 459
Anaximander (of Miletus: 'Presocratic' philosopher) 48, 49
Anaximenes of Lampsacus (historian and rhetorician; c. 380–320 BC) 393
'ancient/ancestral constitution' 146, 153, 247, 278, 281, 472
'ancient' period ('Greek and Roman') 1, 2
andreia ('manliness', cf. *virtus*; 'courage') 13, 216–17, 253, 261, 354
Andronicus' edition of Aristotle 390
Annaeus Novatus = L. Junius Gallio Annaeanus 539
'annalistic tradition' (of historiography) 522
'anthropology' (*see also* gods, god / man, divine / human) 275–8
Antigone (Sophocles') 81–4
Antigonus Doson (regent and king of Macedon, 229–221 BC) 471
Antigonus Gonatas (king of Macedon, c. 277–239 BC) 432, 447
Antigonus the One-Eyed (c. 382–301 BC, Macedonian general) 459
'antinomianism' 425
Antiochus of Ascalon 303, 394n.15, 484, 666
Antipater of Tarsus (2nd century BC Stoic philosopher) 450
Antiphon (5th century BC 'sophist'; thought by some to be identical with Antiphon, Attic orator) 95, 97–8, 98–9, 120, 126, 207
Antisthenes 155n.2, 415–34 *passim*
Antoninus Pius (Roman emperor, AD 138–161) 612, 613
Antonius, Marcus (i.e. Mark Antony) 504, 505, 513
apeiron ('unlimited') 49
'apocalyptic' (Christian position: cf. 'apologetic', 'gnostic') 641–2
'apologetic' (Christian position: cf. 'apocalyptic', 'gnostic') 643–50

justice (*cont.*)
approaches to justice, 535n.15; justice in secondary list of virtues, in Josephus, 589; definition of justice (*iustitia*) in juristic writings, 622–3; Lactantius on, 655–7; in Augustine, on Cicero, 669–70
Justin Martyr (c. AD 100–165; Christian apologist) 413, 645
Justinian (eastern Roman emperor AD 527–65) 617

kairos ('right moment') 234
kakos: *see agathos / kakos*
Kallipolis (the 'beautiful city' of Plato's *Republic*) 232
kalon / aischron ('noble', 'admirable' / 'shameful') 195
Kant, Immanuel 60, 175, 187
kathēkon, to ('the appropriate action') 505, 506, 547n.54, 599, 610
king as 'living law' 560, 566, 573, 574, 578, 663–4
kingship (*see also* Gk. *basileus*, Lat. *rex*: 'king'; kingship, absolute; kingship/rulership theory) 146–51, 236, 244–51, 254–7, 308, 325, 334, 356, 357, 368–71, 371–8, 392, 402–3, 404, 405–6, 431–2, 531, 600
kingship, absolute (esp. Hellenistic) 402–3, 405, 406, 457–76 *passim*, 537n.20
kingship/rulership theory (*see also* kingship) 431–2, 447, 457–76 *passim*, 532, 535–43, 543–5, 549–51, 560, 564–7, 570, 572–5, 577–81, 583, 603, 604–5, 651–3, 661–5
koinon, to ('the commonwealth') 13
koinōnia ('sharing', 'community': cf. Lat. *communitas*) 221, 318–20, 325–38, 352, 370, 374, 425
kosmiotēs ('orderliness in behaviour') 191
kosmos ('government' (Doric); cosmos; order) 50n.61, 196, 334n.26
kosmoi (chief magistrates) 44
Kronos, age of 211, 239, 240

Labeo (1st century AD Roman jurist) 627n.54, 629
labour (attitudes to) 606
labourers, wage 209, 211–12, 320
Lactantius (c. AD 240–c. 320; Christian apologist) 414, 650, 653–7, 659
land-ownership 22
language (communication) 73, 79–81, 83, 483, 527
Las Casas, Bartoleme de 336
laus ('praise', 'true glory') 512
law (*see also nomos, ius*)
codification of 43, 51, 53–4, 259–60, 498; international (theory of), 336n.29; natural, theory of, 259, 321n.1, 336n.29, 345–50, 434, 451, 452, 494, 498–501, 534, 537, 545–6, 563, 573–4, 598, 599, 605, 613, 615, 616, 620–2; (other) notions/concepts of, 236, 244–51, 254–7, 264, 264–5, 271, 271–2, 277–8, 286–90, 291, 307–8, 313, 436, 439–40, 453, 459–60, 498, 537, 566, 588; Roman, 498, 500, 616–34; unwritten / written, 15, 43–4, 152, 265, 287, 308, 500, 566
law-courts (*see also* Areopagus) 62, 64, 73, 130, 132, 133, 197, 280
legitimation of power 536, 616
leisure / work 19
lex ('statute': dist. from *ius*, 'law' in a general sense) 623n.31
Libanius (4th century AD Greek rhetorician) 661n.2
liberalism 20, 259, 353
liberality 509, 510–11, 549
liberty, *libertas*: *see* freedom
'liturgies' (public services) 402, 577
Livy 520n.9, 522–4
lot (selection of officials by) 100, 128, 129, 144, 146, 183n.39, 320, 285, 492
Lucan (the poet, AD 39–65) 502
Lucian of Samosata (2nd century AD writer) 416
Lucretius 454–5
'Lyceum': *see* Peripatos
Lycurgus (Spartan lawgiver) 45, 151, 153, 307, 315, 395, 458, 470, 472, 581, 590, 661
Lycurgus (4th century BC Athenian statesman and orator) 295
lying 289–90
Lysias (5th–4th century Attic orator) 198–9, 305

Macedon 401, 457, 458, 459, 462n.20, 471
Macrobius (4th–5th century Neoplatonist) 490
Magnesia (the imaginary city of Plato, *Laws*) 256, 262, 263 (and 258–92 *passim*)
magnitudo animi ('greatness of spirit', 'courage') 511, 513
Manichaeism 668
Marcian (3rd century AD jurist) 623
Marcus Aurelius (Roman emperor AD 161–80) 329n.12, 413, 453, 597–601, 611–15